Encyclopedia of LAW and HIGHER EDUCATION

Encyclopedia of
LAW *and*
HIGHER
EDUCATION

CHARLES J. RUSSO EDITOR
University of Dayton

Los Angeles | London | New Delhi
Singapore | Washington DC

A SAGE Reference Publication

For information:

SAGE Publications, Inc.
2455 Teller Road
Thousand Oaks, California 91320
E-mail: order@sagepub.com

SAGE Publications Ltd.
1 Oliver's Yard
55 City Road
London EC1Y 1SP
United Kingdom

SAGE Publications India Pvt. Ltd.
B 1/I 1 Mohan Cooperative Industrial Area
Mathura Road, New Delhi 110 044
India

SAGE Publications Asia-Pacific Pte. Ltd.
33 Pekin Street #02-01
Far East Square
Singapore 048763

Printed in the United States of America

Library of Congress Cataloging-in-Publication Data

Encyclopedia of law and higher education / edited by Charles J. Russo.
    p. cm.
Includes bibliographical references and index.
ISBN 978-1-4129-8111-8 (cloth)
   1. Universities and colleges—Law and legislation—United States—Encyclopedias. 2. Universities and colleges—Law and legislation—United States—Cases. 3. Education, Higher—Law and legislation—United States—Encyclopedias. I. Russo, Charles J.

KF4225.A68E53 2010
344.73′07403—dc22   2009032705

This book is printed on acid-free paper.

09   10   11   12   13   10   9   8   7   6   5   4   3   2   1

Publisher:	Rolf A. Janke
Assistant to the Publisher:	Michele Thompson
Acquisitions Editor:	Jim Brace-Thompson
Developmental Editor:	Diana E. Axelsen
Reference Systems Manager:	Leticia Gutierrez
Reference Systems Coordinator:	Laura Notton
Production Editor:	Tracy Buyan
Copy Editor:	Cate Huisman
Typesetter:	C&M Digitals (P) Ltd.
Proofreaders:	Jenifer Kooiman, Sandy Zilka Livingston
Indexer:	Kathy Paparchontis
Marketing Manager:	Amberlyn McKay
Cover Designer:	Glenn Vogel

Contents

List of Entries

Reader's Guide

The Reader's Guide is provided to help readers find entries on related topics. It classifies entries in 11 categories: Cases in Higher Education Law; Concepts, Theories, and Legal Principles; Constitutional Rights and Issues; Faculty Rights; Governance and Finance; Organizations and Institutions; Primary Sources: Excerpts From Landmark U.S. Supreme Court Cases; Religion and Freedom of Speech; Statutes; Student Rights and Welfare; and Technology. Some entries appear in more than one category.

The entry "U.S. Supreme Court Cases on Higher Education" provides an overview of key legal rulings affecting higher education. In addition, there are 42 entries on specific cases, 30 of which are followed by excerpts from the opinions of the Supreme Court. The case excerpts are listed in the Reader's Guide under the heading "Primary Sources: Excerpts from Landmark U.S. Supreme Court Cases."

Cases in Higher Education Law

Affirmative Action and Race-Based Admissions

Berea College v. Kentucky
DeFunis v. Odegaard
Gratz v. Bollinger
Grutter v. Bollinger
McLaurin v. Oklahoma State Regents for Higher Education
Regents of the University of California v. Bakke
Sweatt v. Painter

Disability

Southeastern Community College v. Davis
Witters v. Washington Department of Services for the Blind

Faculty Issues

Board of Curators of the University of Missouri v. Horowitz
Board of Regents of State Colleges v. Roth
Keyishian v. Board of Regents of the University of the State of New York
Kimel v. Florida Board of Regents
Knight v. Board of Regents of the University of the State of New York
Lehnert v. Ferris Faculty Association
National Labor Relations Board v. Yeshiva University

Perry v. Sindermann
Regents of the University of Michigan v. Ewing
Slochower v. Board of Higher Education of New York City
Sweezy v. New Hampshire
Urofsky v. Gilmore

Finance and Governance

Central Virginia Community College v. Katz
College Savings Bank v. Florida Prepaid
Florida Prepaid v. College Savings Bank
Grove City College v. Bell
National Collegiate Athletic Association v. Tarkanian
Rumsfeld v. Forum for Academic and Institutional Rights
Trustees of Dartmouth College v. Woodward

Gender Equity

Cannon v. University of Chicago
Mississippi University for Women v. Hogan
United States v. Virginia
University of Pennsylvania v. Equal Employment Opportunity Commission

Religion and Freedom of Speech

Board of Regents of the University of Wisconsin System v. Southworth

Student Rights and Welfare

Technology

About the Editor

Charles J. Russo, JD, EdD, is the Joseph Panzer Chair in Education in the School of Education and Allied Professions and adjunct professor in the school of law at the University of Dayton, Ohio. The 1998–1999 president of the Education Law Association and 2002 winner of its McGhehey (Lifetime Achievement) Award, he is the author of more than 200 articles in peer-reviewed journals and the author, coauthor, editor, or coeditor of 37 books, including the *Encyclopedia of Education Law* (2008) for Sage Publications. He has been the editor of the *Yearbook of Education Law* for the Education Law Association since 1995 and has written or coauthored in excess of 700 publications; he is also the editor of two academic journals and serves as a member of more than a dozen editorial boards. He has spoken and taught extensively on issues in education law in the United States and in 22 other nations on all six inhabited continents. In recognition of his work in education law in other countries, he received an honorary PhD from Potchefstroom University, now the Potchefstroom Campus of North-West University, in Potchefstroom, South Africa, in May 2004.

Contributors

Jon E. Anderson
Godfrey and Kahn S.C.

Robert A. Boland
New York University

Kevin P. Brady
North Carolina State University

Frank Brown
University of North Carolina at Chapel Hill

Darlene Y. Bruner
University of South Florida

Carolyn L. Carlson
Washburn University

Robert Clark
Texas A&M University

Robert C. Cloud
Baylor University

Aaron Cooley
University of North Carolina at Chapel Hill

Amanda Harmon Cooley
North Carolina A&T State University

David L. Dagley
University of Alabama

Philip T. K. Daniel
Ohio State University

Marilyn Denison
Spring Independent School District

Saran Donahoo
Southern Illinois University

Suzanne E. Eckes
Indiana University

Raúl Fernández-Calienes
St. Thomas University School of Law

Richard Fossey
University of North Texas

Aimee Vergon Gibbs
Dickinson Wright, PLLC

Vivian Hopp Gordon
Loyola University Chicago

Lee H. Igel
New York University

Michael J. Jernigan
University of Dayton

Zorka Karanxha
University of South Florida

Terrence Leas
Riverland Community College

Mark Littleton
Tarleton State University

Catherine L. Matthews
Indiana University

James Mawdsley
Cleveland State University; Stark State University

Ralph D. Mawdsley
Cleveland State University

Kerry Brian Melear
University of Mississippi

Timothy E. Morse
University of Southern Mississippi Gulf Coast

Allan G. Osborne, Jr.
Snug Harbor Community School (retired)

Robert T. Palmer
Binghamton University, State University of New York

Patrick D. Pauken
Bowling Green State University

Megan L. Rehberg
University of Dayton

Janet R. Rumple
Indiana University

Charles J. Russo
University of Dayton

Robert J. Safransky
Nova Southeastern University

Steve Sanders
Mayer Brown LLP

Nanette Schmitt
East Central University

Ralph Sharp
East Central University

Clayton H. Slaughter
Indiana University

Jeffrey C. Sun
University of North Dakota

William E. Thro
Christopher Newport University

Mario Torres
Texas A&M University

James J. Van Patten
Florida Atlantic University

D. Frank Vinik
United Educators

Michele M. Welkener
University of Dayton

Tamara Yakaboski
Southern Illinois University

Michael Yates
Missouri Southern State University

Perry A. Zirkel
Lehigh University

Introduction

Brown v. Board of Education, Topeka (1954), wherein the U.S. Supreme Court initiated an era of equal educational opportunities by striking down racial segregation in public schools, certainly is the Court's most significant case on schooling. Even so, it is interesting to note that the Court's first case involving schooling emerged in the world of higher education. In 1817, the Court held in *Trustees of Dartmouth College v. Woodward* that because the charter that had been granted to the private college was contractual in nature, the state legislature could not modify its terms without the consent of the college's board of trustees. In later years the Court went on to distinguish the rights of faculty, students, and staff in public and private institutions. In this regard, the Court recognized that individuals in public colleges and universities had greater constitutional protections that their counterparts in private institutions whose rights were primarily contractual in nature.

Over the years, the amount of litigation involving colleges and universities has not been as voluminous as that from the world of K–12 education. Still, a steady stream of cases has helped to reshape the landscape of American higher education in such important areas as desegregation, race-conscious admissions plans, gender equity, and the free speech rights of faculty members. Consequently, the *Encyclopedia of Law and Higher Education* is intended to serve as a comprehensive source on the law of higher education for undergraduate and graduate students, educators, legal practitioners, and general readers concerned with this central area of public life.

Overview of the Content

In light of the importance of its subject matter for graduate and undergraduate students, educators, attorneys, and other readers interested in legal issues at the postsecondary level, the *Encyclopedia of Law and Higher Education* is a compendium of information that tells the story of law and higher education from a variety of perspectives. While the entries are arranged alphabetically, a Reader's Guide immediately follows the List of Entries in the front of the volume. To help readers find entries on related topics, this guide organizes the headwords into the eleven subject areas listed below, with each entry listed in at least one category:

Cases in Higher Education Law
Concepts, Theories, and Legal Principles
Constitutional Rights and Issues
Faculty Rights
Governance and Finance
Organizations and Institutions
Primary Sources: Excerpts From Landmark
    U.S. Supreme Court Cases
Religion and Freedom of Speech
Statutes
Student Rights and Welfare
Technology

Court Cases on Education Law

In addition, excerpts from 30 key cases are included in boxes beside the entries on the cases themselves. These cases can serve as primary sources for research on public policy aspects of education law. In addition, the Reader's Guide includes a listing of the cases by topic.

These case excerpts are preceded by brief summaries and have been edited to allow readers to focus on the key issue or issues addressed in the rulings. In keeping with the standard practice in law texts, all of the cases have been edited to remove the Supreme Court's internal citations. Most have been edited also for length; the presence of ellipses, either within the body of texts or on a separate line, indicates that material has been deleted. These edited excerpts, which are preceded by one- or two-sentence summaries, enable the reader to identify basic information on the cases. The case excerpts appear in alphabetical order among the other entries. The case titles are reproduced here as they appear in the *United States Reports,* which are the official records of the Supreme Court.

The Study of the Law of Higher Education

When one first grapples with the relationship between education and law, whether in elementary and secondary education or in higher education, it is worth keeping in mind that systematic inquiry in the law is a form of historical-legal research that is neither qualitative nor quantitative. In other words, the study of law and higher education is a systematic investigation involving the interpretation and explanation of the law in educational contexts. Moreover, legal disputes, which often have lengthy histories, can have far-reaching implications.

Perhaps the best example of a legal controversy with massive social implications for the wider American society is the debate over the right to equal educational opportunities. While the Supreme Court's 1954 decision in *Brown v. Board of Education, Topeka* stands out because it struck down segregation in American public schools, it was not decided in a vacuum. Put another way, the reality is that by the time *Brown* reached the Supreme Court, proponents of equal educational opportunities in the world of higher education, led by Thurgood Marshall and the NAACP Legal Defense Fund, had already begun to make judicial headway in the fight against racial segregation.

In *Sweatt v. Painter* (1950) and *McLaurin v. Oklahoma State Regents for Higher Education* (1950), the Supreme Court repudiated inter- and intra-institutional segregation, respectively, in higher education. In both of these cases, the Court emphasized the importance of "intangible factors," later applied in *Brown,* in connection with equal educational opportunities. Earlier, the Court was critical of racial segregation in higher education in *State of Missouri ex rel. Gaines v. Canada* (1938, 1939a, 1939b) and *Sipuel v. Board of Regents of University of Oklahoma* (1948a, 1948b).

The importance of *Brown's* predecessors notwithstanding, it still stands out as the impetus for systemic social changes in American society in a way that the parties may have been unable to anticipate. Along with federal legislation, *Brown* and other Supreme Court cases played an important role in increasing access to higher education for racial and ethnic minorities. According to the National Center for Education Statistics, 31% of U.S. college and university students were members of racial or ethnic minorities in 2005, compared to only 15% in 1976 (U.S. Department of Education, 2008, table 216). Rising numbers of Hispanic and Asian or Pacific Islander students account for much of this change. Increased minority enrollment has occurred at both the undergraduate and graduate levels. For example, in 1971 there were 1,715 African American first-year law students in the United States, compared to 2,212 in 1985. By 2007, the number of African American students attending law school had reached a high of 9,529 (Law School Admission Council, 2009).

One of the most notable changes that *Brown* engendered in helping to ensure equity in higher education was the adoption of Title IX of the Educational Amendments of 1972. Title IX not only led to equal opportunities for males and females in the arena of sports but also required equal opportunities in other areas of education. The courts initially interpreted Title IX as protecting students from harassment based on gender and later expanded its scope to forbid harassment based on sexual orientation or preference. In part as a result of Title IX, increasing numbers of women play leadership roles in higher education and, as reflected in the authorship of entries in this volume, contribute to scholarship about education generally and education law in particular. Further, the composition of student bodies in degree-granting institutions of higher education has changed dramatically over the past 40 years. For example, in 1970, men accounted for 5,044,000 students, and there were 3,357,000 female students. However, a decade later, in 1985, the numbers had changed, as women accounted for 6,223,000 students at degree-granting institutions, and 5,874,000 students were men. The most recent data reveal that as of 2005, women account for 10,032,000 students, while 7,456,000 men were enrolled (Institute of Education Sciences, n.d.).

In attempting to make sense of the evolving reality of the law, students of the law must learn to employ a time line that looks to the past, present, and future for a variety of purposes. As many of the entries in this encyclopedia reflect, the editor and contributors have sought to place legal issues in perspective, so that students of higher education and the law can not only inform policy makers and practitioners about the meaning and status of the law but also raise questions for future research as they seek to improve the quality of learning for all. The task of students differs from that of attorneys, who typically engage in legal research so that they can better understand the issues relevant to the interests of their clients. In contrast, educators qua students often must serve as advocates for their own students, faculty, and staff. Nevertheless, there is a common bond between all of those who employ education law for the betterment of the educational process.

Rooted in the historical nature of the law and its reliance on precedent, the study of education law requires students to look to the past to locate the authority governing the disposition of questions under investigation, such as equal educational opportunities, gender equity, or faculty free speech rights. This is so because the Anglo American legal system is grounded in the principle of precedent or stare decisis, the notion that an authoritative ruling of the highest court in a given jurisdiction is binding on lower courts within its purview. The law, by its very nature, tends to be a reactive rather than proactive force, one that is shaped by past events that can help lead to stability in its application in present circumstances. Therefore, students of education law need to learn to think outside the box in applying the law to emerging issues such as the impact of technology on the educational process. For example, virtual learning has expanded student access to education, and much information is now gathered via the Internet and through powerful electronic data analyses of databases. At the same time, technology has shaped the campus experience through such technologies as campus security monitoring intended to increase student safety in the face of tragedies such as the 2007 shootings at Virginia Tech.

In light of the more or less reactive nature of law, when attorneys challenge adverse rulings or when researchers study emerging questions, they each look to see how past authoritative decisions have dealt with the same issue. If there are cases supportive of their respective points of view, then regardless of the role that individuals find themselves in—whether academicians, attorneys, or students—they can argue that previous rulings should be followed. However, if precedent is contrary to their positions, then attorneys acting on behalf of their clients seek to distinguish their cases by attempting to show that they are sufficiently different and inapplicable to the facts at hand, particularly when developing policies for new and evolving issues that impact the world of higher education.

To this end, all students of the law—whether undergraduates, graduate students, administrators, faculty members, attorneys, or other interested parties—must learn that because the law is an ever-changing reality, they must constantly be prepared to engage in research on new and emerging topics that will undoubtedly reshape schooling in ways that we cannot yet conceive.

Education Law and Sound Educational Policy

Insofar as the law is an applied rather than a purely theoretical discipline, it is an essential tool not only for educators and policy makers but also for others interested in the law as it applies to education. To this end, those who are engaged in the study of the relationship between higher education and the law must help clarify the meaning of the law so that it remains a valuable tool. In particular, faculty members who teach courses involving the relationship between higher education and the law can help by instructing students to focus on such basic concepts as due process and equity, which are essential elements in the development of sound policies. Put another way, as important as abstract legal principles or theories are, faculty members who specialize in the relationship between higher education and the law must concentrate on ways to help students and practitioners to apply these concepts broadly rather than simply memorizing case holdings apart from their applications in day-to-day, real-life situations. At the same time, students need to understand the law as a practical discipline that has genuine significance in their daily professional activities as educational practitioners.

The significance of the law in higher education presents a unique intellectual challenge for educators who seek to become more proactive in policy development. Those who work in higher education need to move beyond the reactive nature of the law and to use it proactively, as a tool to help ensure that colleges and universities meet the needs of all of their constituents, ranging from students and parents to faculty, staff, and the local community. Yet the goal of making the law proactive is complicated, because most changes generated by education law typically occur only after a real case or controversy has been litigated or a legislative body has responded to a need that had yet to be addressed or resolved.

Along with balancing the tension between the proactive and reactive dimensions of education law, law classes for educators should not become "Law School 101." Rather than trying to turn educators into lawyers equipped to deal with such technical questions as jurisdiction and the service of process, courses in education law should teach educators how to rely upon their substantive knowledge of the law and how to update their sources of information, so they can develop sound policies to enhance the day-to-day operations of schools.

Classes in education law should also provide educators with enough awareness of the legal dimensions of given situations to enable them to better frame questions for their attorneys to answer. To this end, educators must recognize the great value in making their attorneys equal partners not only in problem solving after the fact but also in developing responsive policies before difficulties can arise. Such a proactive approach is consistent with the notion of preventative law, wherein knowledgeable educators can identify potential problems in advance and, in concert with an attorney, can work to ensure they do not develop into crises. Further, when officials at universities select attorneys, they would be wise to hire individuals who have specialized practices in education law, thus avoiding potential lapses in critical knowledge and ensuring their advice has the most up-to-date perspectives on legal matters.

Education Law in the Future

In applying Heraclitus's notion that "one cannot step into the same river twice" to the field of education law, we will see that it is a dynamic, invigorating, and intellectually stimulating discipline that is constantly evolving to meet the needs of today's institutions of higher learning, although it is but one part of the larger fields of both education and law. Emerging technologies such as webcams, Facebook, Twitter, and YouTube create challenges both for

legislators and the judiciary, and one can only wonder what the Supreme Court will say about issues such as student free speech in cyberspace.

Given the legal and educational concerns that these issues will raise, all those interested in the relationship between law and higher education are charged with the task of developing and implementing policies to enhance the educational environment for students, faculty, and staff. In sum, as noted above, perhaps the only constant in the relationship between higher education and the law is that as it evolves to meet the demands of a constantly changing world, it is likely to remain of utmost importance for all of those who are interested in schooling. In fact, the seemingly endless supply of new statutes, regulations, and cases speaks of the need to be ever vigilant with respect to how legal developments impact the law. Insofar as the challenge for all educators is to harness their knowledge of this evergrowing field so that they can make the schools better places for all students, the contributors to the *Encyclopedia of Law and Higher Education* hope it will be of service not only in the ongoing quest for educational equity but also in addressing new and evolving issues as they emerge in coming years.

References

Brown v. Board of Education, Topeka, 347 U.S. 483 (1954).

Institute of Education Sciences, National Center for Education Statistics. (n.d.). *Fast facts. Total fall enrollment in degree-granting institutions, by sex of student and attendance status: Selected years, 1970 through 2005.* Retrieved June 10, 2009, from http://nces.ed.gov/fastfacts/display.asp?id=98

Law School Admission Council. (2009). *Statistics on minority enrollment.* Retrieved June 12, 2009, from http://www.lsac.org/SpecialInterests/minorities-in-legal-education-min-enroll.asp

McLaurin v. Oklahoma State Regents for Higher Education, 339 U.S. 637 (1950).

Sipuel v. Board of Regents of University of Oklahoma, 332 U.S. 631 (U.S. 1948a), *mandate denied sub nom. Fisher v. Hurst,* 333 U.S. 147 (1948b).

State of Missouri ex rel. Gaines v. Canada, 305 U.S. 337 (1938), *reh'g denied,* 305 U.S. 676 (1939a), *mandate conformed to,* 131 S.W.2d 217 (Mo. 1939b).

Sweatt v. Painter, 339 U.S. 629 (1950).

Trustees of Dartmouth College v. Woodward, 17 U.S. 518 (1819).

U.S. Department of Education, National Center for Education Statistics. (2008). *Digest of education statistics, 2007* (NCES 2008-022).

Acknowledgments

As with any work of this magnitude, because many people played a hand in its development, they all need to be thanked for the part that they played in helping make the *Encyclopedia of Law and Higher Education* a reality. I would thus like to thank people in four different groupings.

Starting with all of the wonderful professionals at Sage Publications, I must begin by thanking my acquisitions editor, Jim Brace-Thompson, and Rolf Janke, vice president and publisher of Sage Reference, for having the faith in me and the encyclopedia to shepherd it through the review and acceptance process. Next, I must express my deep debt of immense gratitude to my developmental editor, Diana E. Axelsen, whose friendship and meticulous attention to detail during our often multiple daily conversations made my job of conceptualizing the final form of entries and editing them so much easier. During this phase of development there were two other professionals who also played a major role in helping get entries accepted and moving forward, SRT coordinators Laura Notton and Leticia Gutierrez. Thanks, too, to production editor Tracy Buyan, to copy editor Cate Huisman, and to proofreaders Jenifer Kooiman and Sandy Zilka Livingston. It has been a pleasure working with all of these wonderful professionals. Needless to say, I look forward to continuing to work together on future projects.

Second, I would like to express my gratitude to those who served on the editorial and advisory boards. The members of these boards evaluated the list of entries and suggested topics for inclusion, thus helping the encyclopedia to take shape. In addition, they helped me to identify authors for various topics. The members of the advisory board are Dr. Frank Brown, Carey Boshamer Professor of Education, University of North Carolina at Chapel Hill; Dr. Nelda Cambron-McCabe, Miami University of Ohio; Dr. Philip T. K. Daniel, William and Marie Flesher Professor of Educational Administration and adjunct professor of law at Ohio State University in Columbus, Ohio; Dr. Richard Fossey, professor in the Higher Education Program at the University of North Texas and a senior policy researcher at the Center for the Study of Education Reform; Mr. John Hart, general counsel at the University of Dayton; Dr. Terrence Leas, president of Riverland Community College in Albert Lea, Austin, and Owatonna, Minnesota; Dr. Ralph D. Mawdsley, Roslyn Z. Wolf Endowed Chair in Urban School Leadership in the College of Education and Human Services at Cleveland State University; Dr. Martha M. McCarthy, Chancellor's Professor, Indiana University; Dr. Ralph Sharp of the College of Education Psychology at East Central University in Ada, Oklahoma; and Mr. William E. Thro, general counsel at Christopher Newport University in Newport News, Virginia.

It would not have been possible to identify the encyclopedia as the peer-reviewed project that it is without the gracious assistance of the members of the review board: Dr. Kevin Brady, North Carolina State University; Dr. Suzanne Eckes, Indiana University; and Dr. Allan G. Osborne, retired principal, Snug Harbor Community School in Snug Harbor, Massachusetts.

These dedicated professionals spent untold hours editing entries, corresponding with authors to address weaknesses or omissions in submissions, and providing stringent peer review for all of the entries. I greatly appreciate the assistance that these editors provided in making useful suggestions and comments on the entries that they reviewed. Moreover, these editors did their work even before I had the opportunity to make final decisions on entries, and once the reviewers and I subjected the entries to peer review, they were then read and commented on by editors at Sage, who added many more useful comments and suggestions.

I would be remiss if I did not thank all of the authors who gave their expertise, time, and talent in contributing to the encyclopedia. At the outset, I solicited authors, especially for the longer anchor essays, based on their reputations and expertise. Then as part of a general call for authors, I consulted with several of my editors to ensure that I had the best possible authors for each entry. Insofar as the encyclopedia could not have been written without the assistance of these many professionals, I offer my sincere appreciation.

At the University of Dayton, I would like to thank Dr. Thomas J. Lasley, dean, and Dr. Dan Raisch, associate dean, of the School of Education and Allied Professions for their ongoing support. I would be remiss if I did not offer special thanks to Rev. Joseph D. Massucci, my chair in the Department of Educational Leadership. The friendship and support that these individuals offer on a daily basis helped make the editing and writing process easier. A special thanks is in order for my managing editor and assistant, Ms. Elizabeth Pearn at the University of Dayton, for her help getting entries in, working with authors, and generally proofreading and preparing the manuscript for publication.

Finally, keeping in mind the often-cited maxim of Supreme Court Justice Joseph Story—that the law "is a jealous mistress and requires a long and constant courtship"—I would like to take this opportunity to express my undying love and devotion to my wife, Debbie, and our children, Emily Rebecca and David Peter, and David's wife Li Hong. The two bright and inquisitive children that my wife Debbie and I raised have grown to be wonderful young adults who provide me with a constant source of inspiration, love, and joy. Last, and by no means least, as she is first, I offer my enduring gratitude to Debbie, because without her unconditional love and support I could have accomplished nothing, especially at those times when I have had to take time away from our family life to work on the encyclopedia and other professional responsibilities. Insofar as I am truly blessed to have such a wonderful, loving family, I dedicate this encyclopedia in their honor.

Charles J. Russo

Working With Legal Materials

Many of the cases and statutes discussed in the *Encyclopedia of Law and Higher Education* are available online, and excerpts from a number of U.S. Supreme Court decisions appear following the entries on those cases. Once readers become accustomed to their varying appearances, legal citations are fairly easy to read. This section provides an overview of the format of these citations and the main sources in which they are published.

Elements of a Legal Citation

- In the title of the case, the first name refers to the party filing the suit, known as the *plaintiff.*
- The second name in a case title refers to the responding party. In the initial filing, the responding party is the *defendant.*
- As a case makes its way through the legal system, the names often change places. In other words, when a party loses at trial and seeks further review, that party's name is listed first and is usually known as the *appellant* as the dispute makes its way up the judicial ladder. The responding party in this case is known as the *appellee* or *respondent* and appears second in case listings, regardless of whether that party was the plaintiff or defendant at trial.
- The first number in a citation indicates the volume number where the case, statute, or regulation can be located.
- The abbreviation that follows refers to the book or series in which the material may be found.
- The second number refers to the page on which a case begins or the section number of a statute or regulation.
- The last part of a citation typically includes the name of the court and the year in which a dispute was resolved.

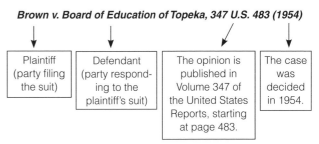

Brown v. Board of Education of Topeka, 347 U.S. 483 (1954)

| Plaintiff (party filing the suit) | Defendant (party responding to the plaintiff's suit) | The opinion is published in Volume 347 of the United States Reports, starting at page 483. | The case was decided in 1954. |

Sources for U.S. Supreme Court Cases

U.S. Supreme Court cases occupy a central place in the encyclopedia and can be located in a variety of sources.

- Official version of Supreme Court cases: United States Reports (U.S.)
- Unofficial versions of Supreme Court cases: West's Supreme Court Reporter (S. Ct.) Lawyer's Edition, now in its second series (L. Ed.2d)

The advantage of the unofficial versions of cases is that, in addition to including the entire text of the Court's opinions, publishers provide valuable research tools and assistance. In order to avoid unnecessary confusion, the encyclopedia refers to unofficial versions only when U.S. Reports citations are unavailable.

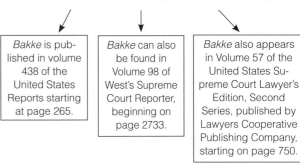

Regents of University of California v. Bakke,
438 U.S. 265, 98 S. Ct. 2733, 57 L.Ed.2d 750 (1978)

| *Bakke* is published in volume 438 of the United States Reports starting at page 265. | *Bakke* can also be found in Volume 98 of West's Supreme Court Reporter, beginning on page 2733. | *Bakke* also appears in Volume 57 of the United States Supreme Court Lawyer's Edition, Second Series, published by Lawyers Cooperative Publishing Company, starting on page 750. |

Before they appear in bound volumes, most cases are available as slip opinions, from a variety of loose-leaf services and electronic sources. Statutes and regulations are available in similar formats. State laws and regulations are generally available online from each state.

Abbreviations of Case Names

Because case names can be lengthy, they are often abbreviated. For example, *Rosenberger v. Rector and Visitors of the University of Virginia* is often listed as *Rosenberger v. University of Virginia* and further shortened to *Rosenberger* for convenience after the full title has appeared in a text. Locations (such as Virginia) and articles (the, an) are often omitted to shorten names.

Sources for Other Judicial Rulings

- Cases from intermediate federal appellate courts, also known as circuit courts of appeal, are published in the *Federal Reporter*, now in its third series (F.3d).
- Cases that are not chosen for publication in F.3d are printed in the Federal Appendix (Fed. Appx); these cases are of limited precedential value.
- Federal trial court rulings are in the Federal Supplement, now in its second series (F.Supp.2d).
- State cases are published in a variety of publications, most notably in West's National Reporter system. An abbreviated version of the court name appears with the date in parentheses for all but U.S. Supreme Court cases.

Sources for Federal and State Statutes

The official version of federal statutes is the United States Code (U.S.C.). As with Supreme Court cases, West publishes an unofficial, annotated version of federal statutes, the United States Code Annotated (U.S.C.A.).

5 U.S.C. 551 = Title 5 of the United States Code, Chapter 551 of Title 5 (the Administrative Procedure Act of 1946)

The final version of federal regulations can be found in the Code of Federal Regulations.

The Family and Medical Leave Act (FMLA) 29 U.S.C. §§ 2601 *et seq.* = Title 29 of the United States Code, beginning at Section 2601

FMLA's regulations are located at

29 C.F.R. §§ 825.001 *et seq.* = Title 29 of the Code of Federal Regulations, starting at section 825.001

State statutes and regulations follow a similar pattern. As with cases, state statutes and regulations are published in a variety of sources.

Online Legal Resources

Legal materials are available online from a variety of sources, including the following:

Legal Search Engines

http://washlaw.edu
http://www.findlaw.com

U.S. Supreme Court, Federal Courts, and Federal Government Materials

http://supct.law.cornell.edu/supct (decisions of the U.S. Supreme Court)
http://www.supremecourtus.gov (official Web site of the U.S. Supreme Court)
http://www.uscourts.gov (U.S. Federal Judiciary)
http://www.whitehouse.gov (the White House)
http://www.senate.gov (U.S. Senate)
http://www.ed.gov (U.S. Department of Education)
http://thomas.loc.gov/home/bills_res.html (Library of Congress, Bills and Resolutions)

Subscription Databases

WestLaw
LexisNexis

ACADEMIC ABSTENTION

The term *academic abstention* appears to be the creation of Harry T. Edwards and Virginia D. Nordin, because it first appeared in the literature in their 1979 book, *Higher Education and the Law*. As it applies to higher education, academic abstention reflects the ideological basis of academic autonomy and freedom that was established at the formation of universities in medieval times. The courts have traditionally exercised caution when asked to intervene in the internal affairs of institutions of higher education. This practice of academic deference evolved from a circumspection by a judiciary that hesitated to substitute its judgment for that of academicians. In light of the history and significance of this practice, this entry examines the growth and development of the important concept of academic abstention in the world of American higher education.

Historically, the American judiciary has respected the autonomy of higher education. The U.S. Supreme Court, in *Trustees of Dartmouth College v. Woodward* (1819), its first-ever case set in an educational context, articulated a traditional legal view that private colleges could best serve society when they were free from outside, namely, governmental, interference. This independence has included virtually all institutional employment, admission, teaching, and research practices in higher education. Moreover, academicians frequently invoked "academic freedom" to prevent outside forces from interfering with the internal management of colleges and universities based on

the notion that the delicate and complex nature of academic institutions demanded autonomy. The academicians maintained that lawyers, judges, and other outsiders lacked knowledge of the unique qualities and nature of the academic milieu. In buttressing their position, the academicians were of the view that only unfettered autonomy and respect for the traditional means of governance and collegiality would permit higher education institutions to achieve their lofty goals.

Such deferential treatment for higher education reflected society's early perception that academic institutions were private, complex, and fragile. If outsiders, including the courts, interfered with the internal operation of universities, then many believed that a delicate balance might be so disturbed that the institutions would flounder. According to supporters of academic abstention, then, only with the respect of other institutions for its traditional means of governance by consensus and collegiality could American higher education thrive and prosper.

Not only was the educational environment special, faculty and administrators were perceived as possessing unique qualities of virtue and ability, because their educational background and training were vastly superior to those of the general population. Additionally, faculty and administrators in higher education were charged with preserving knowledge and educating future leaders. This combination of exclusive or "special" expertise and special mission introduced the idea that outside monitoring of academe was unnecessary, even dangerous, to society's interests. These judicial impressions and perceptions are entangled with the concepts of academic freedom and institutional autonomy, concepts that have special meaning in a country with America's democratic tradition.

Judicial deference under the doctrine of special expertise has been applied in a variety of legal settings. It was employed in response to early student attempts to challenge the authority of academicians by an unsuccessful attempt to force the award of a degree where a student failed to meet the proscribed standards (e.g., *Mahavongsanan v. Hall,* 1976). Judges reasoned that the determination of student academic qualifications was of a quasi-judicial nature, requiring discretionary judgment over which legal powers such as mandamus had no authority (e.g., *Steinhauer v. Arkins,* 1902). However, judges invoked the doctrine of special expertise only when they were convinced that academic officials acted in good faith, such as when refusing to grant relief when a student unsuccessfully applied for admission to law school (*Timmerman v. University of Toledo,* 1976) and in affirming the refusal to grant a student's request for an order directing officials to reinstate and promote a medical student who had failed a third-year course in medicine and surgery (*Mustell v. Rose,* 1968).

Judges relied on the doctrine of special expertise to distinguish due process requirements for student academic and disciplinary dismissals (e.g., *Gaspar v. Bruton,* 1975). In acknowledging the subjective nature of academic decision making, courts refused to require the more extensive due process procedures associated with disciplinary dismissals. Provided that educators acted reasonably, in good faith, and without constitutionally impermissible intent, judges invoked the doctrine in deference to those better equipped to direct the academic decision-making process in higher education (e.g., *Board of Curators of University of Missouri v. Horowitz,* 1978; *Regents of University of Michigan v. Ewing,* 1985). Despite the Supreme Court's application of the doctrine, institutional officials began to administer academic dismissals with greater procedural and substantive precision (e.g., *Haberle v. University of Alabama in Birmingham,* 1986; *Mauriello v. University of Medicine & Dentistry of New Jersey,* 1986; *Nash v. Auburn University,* 1987).

Similarly, judges also deferred to the special expertise of academicians vis-à-vis faculty qualifications when institutional decisions were the result of legitimate academic decision making (e.g., *Faro v.*

New York University, 1974; *Powell v. Syracuse University,* 1978). However, the courts demonstrated a willingness to intervene in those academic areas that traditionally received judicial deference when compelling evidence of abuse of discretion (e.g., *State ex rel. Bartlett v. Pantzer,* 1971) or arbitrary action (e.g., *Wong v. Regents of University of California,* 1971) by institutional authorities was present. This pattern of judicial intervention reflected early common-law concepts regarding the exercise of authority within academic institutions (e.g., *Jones v. New York Homeopathic Medical College & Hospital,* 1892; *State ex rel. Niles v. Orange Training School for Nurses,* 1899).

Contemporary statutory enactments resulted in judges struggling with the possibility that the traditional abstention doctrine might undermine civil rights and antidiscrimination policies behind the legislation (e.g., *Powell v. Syracuse University,* 1978). Judges have made no secret that they believe themselves inadequate to substitute their judgment in purely academic matters; however, to enforce the statutory mandate for social justice, jurists have repeatedly emphasized that academic freedom does not include the freedom to engage in invidious discrimination (e.g., *In re Dinnan,* 1981; *Powell v. Syracuse University,* 1978). In this specific context, jurists find themselves torn between their constitutional and statutory obligations to ensure fair educational practices and their traditional deference to the authority of academicians (e.g., *Clark v. Whiting,* 1979; *Southeastern Community College v. Davis,* 1979).

In resolving this dynamic dilemma, judges justify intervention as a way that affords them opportunities to evaluate whether professed legitimate academic reasons are pretextual. Absent impermissible constitutional or statutory violations, judicial abstention is ensured (e.g., *Gray v. Board of Higher Education, City of New York,* 1982; *Kunda v. Muhlenberg College,* 1980; *Regents of University of Michigan v. Ewing,* 1985; *University of Pennsylvania v. EEOC,* 1990). Even so, when educational officials enforce their rules and regulations inconsistently, the likelihood of subterfuge may override any judicial predilection for deference (e.g., *Holliman v. Martin,* 1971), thereby leading to possible litigation.

Terrence Leas

See also Academic Freedom; *Board of Curators of University of Missouri v. Horowitz; Regents of the University of Michigan v. Ewing; Trustees of Dartmouth College v. Woodward; University of Pennsylvania v. Equal Employment Opportunity Commission*

Further Readings

Edwards, H. T. (1980). *Higher education and the unholy crusade against governmental regulation.* Cambridge, MA: Harvard University Institute for Educational Management.

Edwards, H. T., & Nordin, V. D. (1979). *Higher education and the law.* Cambridge, MA: Harvard University Institute for Educational Management.

Kaplin, W. A., & Lee, B. A. *The law of higher education,* 4th ed. (2006). San Francisco: Jossey-Bass.

LaNear, J. (2005). *Academic freedom in public higher education: For the faculty or institution?* Madison: University of Wisconsin–Madison.

Leas, T. (1989). *Evolution of the doctrine of academic abstention in American jurisprudence* (1989). Tallahassee: Florida State University.

Legal Citations

Board of Curators of University of Missouri v. Horowitz, 435 U.S. 78 (1978).

Clark v. Whiting, 607 F.2d 634 (4th Cir. 1979).

In re Dinnan, 661 F.2d 426 (5th Cir. 1981).

Faro v. New York University, 502 F.2d 1229 (2d Cir. 1974).

Gaspar v. Bruton, 513 F.2d 843 (10th Cir. 1975).

Gray v. Board of Higher Education, City of New York, 692 F.2d 901 (2d Cir. 1982).

Haberle v. University of Alabama in Birmingham, 803 F.2d 1539 (11th Cir. 1986).

Holliman v. Martin, 330 F. Supp. 1 (W.D. Va. 1971).

Jones v. New York Homeopathic Medical College & Hospital, 20 N.Y.S. 379 (N.Y. City Super. Ct. 1892).

Kunda v. Muhlenberg College, 612 F.2d 532 (3d Cir. 1980).

Mahavongsanan v. Hall, 529 F.2d 448 (5th Cir. 1976).

Mauriello v. University of Medicine & Dentistry of New Jersey, 781 F.2d (3d Cir. 1986).

Mustell v. Rose, 211 So. 2d 489 (Ala. 1968).

Nash v. Auburn University, 812 F.2d 655 (11th Cir. 1987).

Powell v. Syracuse University, 580 F.2d 1150 (2d Cir. 1978), *cert. denied,* 439 U.S. 984 (1978).

Regents of University of Michigan v. Ewing, 474 U.S. 214 (1985).

Southeastern Community College v. Davis, 442 U.S. 397 (1979).

State ex rel. Bartlett v. Pantzer, 489 P.2d 375 (Mont. 1971).

State ex rel. Niles v. Orange Training School for Nurses, 42 A. 846 (N.J. 1899).

Steinhauer v. Arkins, 69 P. 1075 (Colo. Ct. App. 1902).

Timmerman v. University of Toledo, 421 F. Supp. 464 (N.D. Ohio 1976).

Trustees of Dartmouth College v. Woodward, 17 U.S. 518 (1819).

University of Pennsylvania v. EEOC, 493 U.S. 182 (1990).

Wong v. Regents of University of California, 93 Cal. Rptr. 502 (Cal. Ct. App. 1971).

ACADEMIC DISHONESTY

Broadly stated, academic dishonesty involves the use by individuals in academia of unethical means such as fraud or plagiarism to achieve success in educational and job performance. Academic dishonesty by students, the primary focus of this entry, includes their copying or stealing examinations, cheating on examinations, plagiarizing reports and term papers, buying term papers, using a variety of strategies for crib notes, and, more recently, using cell phones or Internet connections in order to pass exams. Student infringement on copyright and intellectual property rights is especially prevalent when individuals plagiarize term papers.

Examples of faculty dishonesty include falsifying data to gain research grants, plagiarizing materials in their published works, failing to reveal criminal records in employment interviews, exaggerating academic or work credentials, taking credit for articles that are ghostwritten by others, and fabricating or manipulating data to reach conclusions that are threatening to ethical research. Further, excessive absences by faculty members from assigned duties may be considered as dishonest.

Administrators in higher education may engage in academic dishonesty when they use their positions to award contracts in return for financial or other rewards, falsify academic records, and, in rare cases, allow students of prominent business or government officials or athletic prowess to acquire degrees without attending classes or completing degree requirements.

Historical Background

Academic dishonesty has been prevalent in varying degrees since the founding of higher institutions. Although institutions identify unethical behavior for faculty, student, and staff in policy handbooks, they also typically have different disciplinary and honor codes for students. Such codes have a long history in the Western tradition. Aristotle's works on politics and ethics influenced academic integrity in the Western tradition. In fact, Aristotle wrote that ethical codes had to be embodied in a code of law interconnected with the whole framework of social and political systems. Aristotle also explained that young citizens had to learn these laws in order to live the life of citizens and of individuals following accepted standards of right and wrong.

"Do no harm," the crux of the Hippocratic oath, has been a model for medical and educational ethical codes. The oath includes a commitment to serve others selflessly and to avoid intentional misdeeds. Colonial schools and colleges adhered to policies requiring moral and ethical conduct. Although there were instances of deviations, accountability for responsible conduct, honesty, and service were highly prized. Punishment for immorality was harsh and swift. Schoolbooks such as McGuffey's Readers emphasized duty, honor, respect for authority, and hard work. Truth, accuracy, and industry were expected and rewarded. Schools and colleges had assessment measures for comportment in the 19th and 20th centuries.

From public schools to universities, there has been a growing culture of academic dishonesty. The larger society has been challenged by fraudulent unethical behavior in governmental, religious, economic, and business organizations. As a result, there is renewed attention throughout American society, institutions, and organizations to maintaining the highest performance modes of integrity, honesty, and responsibilities.

Academic dishonesty undermines the central values of higher education. The integrity of research by faculty and students depends on the ability to replicate findings. Responsibility for ethical behavior individually, or as a member of group, may be built from organizational expectations.

Undergraduate and graduate students are governed by academic integrity policies that identify specific behaviors of deceit or dishonesty. Student and faculty responsibilities are identified by university policies that define a variety of sanctions against students who have shown such behaviors, including being required to take courses over again, being given failing grades in courses in which they have been deceitful or dishonest, or being assigned additional class reports or work.

Responses to Academic Dishonesty

In today's complex, speed-centered, and information-oriented society, cutting corners, taking shortcuts, and operating on the fringes of ethical conduct to gain market advantage have become more common in the highly competitive business environment. The failures of Enron, WorldCom, Tyco, and other major businesses resulted from fraudulent management behavior due to pressures for profit. Regulatory action by the federal government, such as the enactment of the 2002 Sarbanes-Oxley Act, is a common approach to ethical business lapses. Interestingly, many of the major corporate executives caught in fraudulent scandals were educated in top-ranked business schools. At the same time, applicants for business and other professional schools such as schools of law or medicine have been known to try to hire high-scoring imposters to take their graduate admission tests or other appropriate standardized measures. John Hechinger (2008) notes the use of digital fingerprinting and palm scanning to validate the identity of test takers, for business school applicants in particular. To combat dishonesty, business school applicants also are photographed and videotaped while they are taking their exams.

In response to dishonesty, the law has made it clear that final disciplinary decisions need to be objective and grounded in fact. Although *Board of Curators of the University of Missouri v. Horowitz* (1987) dealt with dismissal due to a student's poor academic performance rather than academic dishonesty, it is worth noting. This is because in it, the U.S. Supreme Court illustrated the requirement that even though it was willing to defer to their expertise in matters of academic decision making, officials in higher education must base their judgments on objective, defensible criteria. Although Charlene Horowitz had excellent grades on written exams and in her clinical performance, concerns about peer relations and hygiene prompted faculty members to recommend that she be dismissed from the medical school. The Court held that it would not interfere with university and faculty decisions in their area of expertise, thus reversing an order of the Eighth Circuit that had entered a judgment in favor of the use of procedural due process in academic decisions.

In disciplining a student for unethical or unacceptable behavior, officials in higher education institutions must provide notice of infractions with opportunities for those charged to present defenses. *McMillan v. Hunt* (1992) highlights the importance of evidence in dismissing students from universities. After comparing Jacqueline McMillan's research paper with that of her roommate and talking with two students, McMillan's instructor was convinced that McMillan had plagiarized the work of her roommate. The record revealed that the roommate had finished her paper several hours earlier than McMillan and that the papers were strikingly similar. The Student Disciplinary Committee found that McMillan had violated the student honor code and recommended permanent expulsion from the university's law school. McMillan, a first-year student, unsuccessfully filed suit, claiming violations of her rights to procedural and constitutional due process. She argued that officials at the University of Akron School of Law acted arbitrarily and capriciously in dismissing her in violation of her rights. The court noted that in light of the evidence presented that the student copied her roommate's paper, combined with the fact that law school officials had a rational basis for dismissing her, it had no choice but to uphold the adjudication of the law school's Student Disciplinary Committee.

When it comes to plagiarism, students who are required to complete reports and projects may change titles and a few other items in copying each other's work. Students operate on the expectation that faculty will not have the time or inclination to ferret out their dishonesty. Charges can be brought by faculty, administrators, librarians, staff, or students for alleged violations of codes of academic integrity or for other dishonesty.

Once charged with dishonesty, students must be afforded hearings with opportunities for the accused to provide their sides of the stories. Careful adherence to legal protections for both the accused and the institution is essential. Students or accused faculty may bring charges of defamation of character. Excessive and consistent violations of ethical codes may have a demoralizing effect on classmates who do not cheat. Moreover, as Kenneth H. Ryesky (2007) points out, repeated violations can lower morale while creating cynical attitudes and disrespect for faculty members.

Insofar as students have ready access to widely advertised companies that sell term papers covering all subjects, addressing issues of academic dishonesty requires a total commitment from all institutional components of higher education. Faculty members need administrative support for their student disciplinary actions. Penalties for academic dishonesty depend on individual institutions, the seriousness of the offenses, the character and accomplishments of individuals, penalties assigned others with the same or similar offenses, and the purpose of the disciplinary actions. Sanctions may include warnings, grade reductions, course failures, additional student assignments, or other disciplinary measures as deemed appropriate.

The Family Educational Rights and Privacy Act (1974), which governs student records, protects student privacy while allowing leeway for situations when a need for information may outweigh privacy interests. It should be followed when academic dishonesty issues arise with regard to students, faculty, or administrators. Students' personal identifiable information must be kept confidential and should not be released by officials without written consent unless there are legitimate extenuating circumstances.

According to Ryesky, an emerging issue is that academic dishonesty may be viewed differently in other cultures. In our increasingly diverse society, where there are many different ethnicities and language skills, academic counselors and faculty should review college and university codes of conduct to help those from other cultures become familiar with ethical expectations.

Technology and Academic Dishonesty

Rapidly expanding technology makes it difficult to keep up with needed academic integrity codes. Educational institutions are developing new instructional delivery models. Distance learning in a digital age through online computer courses and programs creates a need for faculty surveillance of student responsibility for adhering to academic ethical principles.

Students and Internet users have developed a culture that often does not view utilizing information from the vast resources of the Internet without attribution as academic dishonesty. Plagiarism involving material readily available on the Internet is a growing problem. The software company iParadigm developed a computer program, Turnitin, that identifies matches between digital content on the Internet or in the company's databases and text in student term papers, take-home examinations, and other research assignments. This system can also be used to evaluate work by faculty members who have submitted their manuscripts for publication. Public exposure of administrative and faculty malfeasance can end careers. Clearly, it is often difficult for educational policy makers to keep up with the rapidly exploding growth of our information age.

Bernadette H. Schell and Clemens Martin (2004) identify some of the most common cybercrimes impacting academic dishonesty. Identity theft—the malicious theft and subsequent misuse of someone else's identity in order to commit crimes—is increasing. Computer hackers may destroy, manipulate, or use personal information of students, faculty, or staff. Colleges and university personnel must thus strive to protect e-mail and account information while providing or encouraging the use of antivirus software. University data banks may be compromised, necessitating that administrators take expensive corrective action.

In *United States v. Diekman* (2001), Justice Department investigators discovered that an individual had hacked into a number of government and university computers, including ones at Stanford University. The hacker also gained access to usernames and passwords from Harvard University, Cornell University, California State University at Fullerton, Oregon State University, and the Los Angeles and San Diego campuses of the University of California. In an unreported case, the 20-year-old culprit was sentenced to federal prison on a variety of claims, including unauthorized access to computers and damaging protected computers. Computer crime is so prevalent that a growing number of colleges and universities award degrees in computer crime as an area of specialization within the field of information technology. In addition, Congress has enacted legislation dealing with the growing problem.

Donald L. McCabe (2005) surveyed more than 40,000 undergraduates on 68 campuses. His survey revealed that 21% of respondents acknowledged at least one form of serious exam cheating, while 51% admitted at least one incident of cheating on written work. Faculty members often overlook or ignore suspicious behavior or do not conduct proper surveillance during examination periods. Reporting such behavior often involves much work, and for untenured faculty there may be some hesitancy to report academic dishonesty.

Individual and Institutional Responsibilities

Faculty members need to be aware of the need for clear evidence of cheating before reporting students. All institutions of higher education have their own disciplinary procedures and culture. It is essential to have total commitment to individual and institutional ethics. Faculty, administrators, staff, and students can work toward mutual enforcement of codes of conduct, creating a self-regulatory environment dedicated to academic integrity, morality, and ethics. Most higher education institutions have these policies in course syllabi that faculty members highlight during first class meetings periods and as needed throughout semesters.

Affirmative action to ensure ethical conduct requires guidance from educational, governmental, legal, religious, business, and corporate institutions. Additionally, legal counsel in institutions of higher education should engage in risk avoidance strategies to prevent defamation of character suits. In sum, to the extent that academic dishonesty threatens mutual trust and the free exchange of ideas essential in all educational institutions, educational leaders must act in concert to seek to alleviate academic dishonesty.

James J. Van Patten

See also Cheating and Academic Discipline; Disciplinary
    Sanctions and Due Process Rights; Educational

Malpractice; Family Educational Rights and
Privacy Act

Further Readings

Hechinger, J. (2008, July 22). Business schools try palm
scans to finger cheats. *The Wall Street Journal*, p. D1.

McCabe, D. L. (2005). It takes a village: Academic
dishonesty and educational opportunity. *Liberal
Education, 91*(3), 26–31.

Ryesky, K. H. (2007). Part time soldiers deploying
adjunct faculty: A war against student plagiarism.
*Brigham Young University Education and Law
Journal, 1*, 119–152.

Schell, B., & Martin, C. (2004). *Cybercrime*. Santa
Barbara, CA: ABC-CLIO.

Sinclair, J. A. (1962). *Aristotle: The politics*.
Baltimore: Penguin Books.

Legal Citations

*Board of Curators of the University of Missouri v.
Horowitz*, 435 U.S. 78 (1987).

Family Educational Rights and Privacy Act,
Pub. L. No. 93-380 (1974).

McMillan v. Hunt, 968 F.2d 1215 (6th Cir. 1992).

United States v. Diekman, docket numbers
2:00-CR-01073, 2:01-CR-00654, 5:01-CR-20115,
2:01-CR-00878 (C.D. Cal. 2001).

ACADEMIC FREEDOM

The concept of *academic freedom*, although not
enumerated in the First Amendment, is based on
freedom of speech and applies generally to all
levels of education. In its broadest sense, academic freedom is the right to teach or speak freely
without reprisal. Disputes over classroom content
and methodology typically pit the more commonly recognized faculty academic freedom to
teach what and how educators deem appropriate
against the institutional academic freedom of colleges and universities to determine the curriculum
and programs on their campuses. Educators presume that academic freedom provides greater
protection of their campus actions than case
law supports. Based on the notion that academic
freedom applies to institutions rather than

individuals, courts generally side with colleges
and universities when faculty members refuse to
follow curricular policies and administrative
directives, use or allow objectionable language in
the classroom, or criticize their colleagues and
institutions in ways not protected by the First
Amendment.

External Attempts to Regulate Faculty

The initial stage of academic freedom litigation
occurred during the 1950s and 1960s and arose
from McCarthyist concerns of subversion and disloyalty. A series of U.S. Supreme Court cases
reviewed governmental attempts to impose loyalty
requirements in education, often at the university
level. The Court issued mixed rulings on academic
freedom in the 1950s, with some judgments upholding loyalty oaths and governmental restrictions.
However, by the end of the 1960s, the Court clearly
recognized the constitutional status of academic
freedom, largely based on First Amendment freedom of speech and association, and generally
rejected external attempts to limit faculty members'
freedom of expression.

In *Keyishian v. Board of Regents of University
of State of New York* (1967), educators refused to
sign a Feinberg Certificate affirming that they were
not Communists and that if they had ever been
Communists, they had so informed the SUNY
president. In ruling for the faculty members, the
Court built on its defense of educators' freedom of
thought in *Shelton v. Tucker* (1960), acknowledging that academic freedom is a "special concern of
the First Amendment" (p. 603).

Attempts at external control of expression on
college campuses have resurfaced in the past decade,
as interest groups use educational institutions as
forums to promote their ideological viewpoints and
agendas. Challenges brought by community members and students against the content of first-year
student orientation reading assignments and student plays performed as course assignments have
generally failed. Further issues concerning academic
freedom were raised in *Urofsky v. Gilmore* (2000).
In this case, the Fourth Circuit upheld statutory
restrictions on the rights of faculty members and
other public employees to visit sites containing
sexually explicit material on publicly owned or
leased computers. Thus, this case raises questions

about the boundaries of academic freedom in the cyber age and the rights of academicians to choose for themselves, without state interference, the topics of their research and teaching.

Internal Conflicts Over Faculty Actions

After *Keyishian,* the primary focus of academic freedom litigation shifted from external attempts at control to internal conflicts. The Supreme Court has recognized that academic freedom, at times, involves a somewhat inconsistent and fundamental tension between educators who desire uninhibited, independent freedom in teaching and institutions that want autonomous decision making over their educational programs and campus activities. Over four decades, higher education has witnessed numerous legal disputes between institutional and faculty academic freedom over who has the authority to control activities within a course, language used within a classroom, and grading.

Course Content

Courts consistently uphold the authority of colleges and university officials, absent unconstitutional intent, to regulate curriculum, including the content of courses. In the 1970s, institutions prevailed when officials chose not to renew the contracts of two faculty members who failed to meet their expectations for course workload, rigor, and coverage of topics. Another court found no violation of academic freedom when officials at an institution refused to assign an additional class to a part-time lecturer after she was unwilling to explain to her students precisely what was required to receive a final grade in a writing class in which 13 of 17 students had incomplete grades.

Courts generally support colleges and universities when faculty members unilaterally change approved curriculum or practices. Illustrative of this pattern is a case from the Tenth Circuit in which the court found that a faculty member had no right of academic freedom to reject the institution's standardized student evaluation policy because she did not believe that teaching and learning could be evaluated by a standardized process. However, a university's authority to control classroom activities is not absolute. Courts ruled for faculty members in

two cases where administrators reacted to classroom content (one involved a controversial play, the other use of profane and offensive language in a pedagogical manner and related to course content) when community opposition created what one court described as administrators' unsubstantiated fear of disturbance. In other litigation, a federal appellate court remanded a faculty member's claim to a federal trial court in New York; the claim alleged that he was denied tenure as a result of community pressure in a controversy over the identification in his course, The Politics of Race, of Zionism along with Nazism and apartheid as the main forms of racism. As such decisions are increasingly politicized, it will be interesting to observe how institutions of higher learning, and undoubtedly the courts, balance the conflicting values of the free exchange of ideas in academic settings and the free speech rights of faculty members.

Courts have also agreed that officials at educational institutions have the authority to discipline faculty members who interject their religious beliefs into courses unrelated to religious topics. Two decisions upheld university restrictions (on lecture content, course materials, and optional class meetings) placed on faculty members who included religious beliefs in their lectures, and in one instance changed a departmental course syllabus to include religion as a topic in educational media and exercise physiology courses. Moreover, other courts rejected claims that officials violated individuals' rights to freedom of speech, in one case by terminating the employment of a member of a mathematics department who began each class by reading from the Bible, and in another case by choosing not to reemploy a part-time cosmetology instructor who gave two religious pamphlets on the sinfulness of homosexuality to a gay student.

Faculty Language

Courts generally hold that there is no general faculty right of academic freedom to use or permit derogatory, offensive, or profane language in classrooms. Cases from the Sixth Circuit illustrate the basic support that courts show for higher education institutions that discipline educators who, without pedagogical justification, use such language in teaching their classes. The court agreed with university officials that discharged a basketball coach for using a racial epithet for Black players in a locker room session (although he alleged it was used in a positive, reinforcing manner) and that suspended a member of an English department for using profane terms for sexual intercourse and derogatory terms for female reproductive organs (despite his claim that he used these terms in class to demonstrate an academic point).

In contrast to these two decisions, the Sixth Circuit ruled in favor of an instructor at a community college whose contract was not renewed after he used crude and offensive language in his teaching. The court determined that the First Amendment protected the faculty member's use of offensive terms for Blacks and females within an academic and philosophic discussion, not gratuitously in an abusive manner, in a class devoted in part to interpersonal communication. Other courts also blocked the punishment of educators whose use of vulgar and sexual descriptions in classroom discussions led students to file sexual harassment charges of a hostile academic environment, when the courts found the harassment policies vague and their application subjective.

Course Grading

A third category in which institutions generally prevail over faculty claims of academic freedom includes grades, grading standards, and grading policies. Courts typically reject the argument that educators' grading policies are constitutionally protected. Courts have decided that because officials at colleges and universities have basic authority over grading standards and policies, they can discipline faculty members who refuse to adhere to them, including educators guilty of unprofessional conduct in their grading. For example, the Seventh Circuit, in 2001, upheld the reassignment to nonteaching duties, along with loss of research funds, of an engineering faculty member who refused to comply with policies requiring instructors teaching courses with multiple sections to grade on a prescribed curve and to submit their grading materials to administrators. Another court accepted as one of the reasons for denial of tenure the fact that a faculty member assigned inappropriately high grades (249 of 257 students received A's or B's in a course).

A related issue is whether university officials violate academic freedom when they order faculty members to change students' grades. While the Sixth Circuit, in *Parate v. Isibor* (1989), noted that university officials infringed on a faculty member's First Amendment rights in ordering him to change a student's grade, it also pointed out that the faculty member lacked a constitutional right to determine the ultimate grade the student received and that superiors could administratively change the grade. However, the Third Circuit later split from *Parate* in asserting that a faculty member lacked a First Amendment right of expression in grade assignment where the university president ordered him to change a grade.

Faculty Criticism of Employers

Claims of academic freedom and freedom of speech often arise when educators criticize their colleagues, administrators, or institutions and later find themselves facing discipline. Under the *Mt. Healthy City School District Board of Education v. Doyle* (1977) test, courts first consider whether an employee's expression was constitutionally protected, a finding requiring that the speech dealt with a matter of public concern and was not issued pursuant to official duties. Courts have reasoned that because critical views on university spending (for example, rising administrative salaries and reduction-in-force plans), campus priorities, presidents' managerial styles, outside community influences on departmental curriculum and education, and governance issues (such as forming faculty bargaining units and campaigning for candidates for the board of regents) are matters of public concern, they are entitled to protection as such. However, faculty members have failed to meet *Mt. Healthy*'s first step when their published speech deals with internal or personal matters such as membership on committees, teaching assignment of summer and overload classes, and requests for review of faculty disputes and committee operations.

The second step of the *Mt. Healthy* test balances a faculty member's right of freedom of expression with an institution's need for efficient, harmonious operation of its programs. Educators have prevailed when officials failed to present evidence of disruption to their services or undermining of the working relationships within departments or programs, or when the institution's evidence consisted merely of administrators' undocumented fear of disruption.

However, courts have entered judgments in favor of colleges and universities that established that the faculty member's expression disrupted the efficient operation of the school. For example, the Eleventh Circuit upheld the reassignment of faculty members in mechanical engineering to other engineering departments in *Maples v. Martin* (1988) when their published criticisms of the program (among other things, on the eve of the program's accreditation visit, they called the department head dictatorial and inflexible) created an atmosphere of tension within the department. In other words, while the faculty members addressed matters that were arguably of public concern, the court believed that the expression of these views was not entitled to protection, because it disrupted the efficient operations of their original department.

At the third step of the *Mt. Healthy* test, plaintiffs must establish that their protected expression was a substantial or motivating factor in the decision subjecting them to punishment. Some institutions prevail at this stage, because faculty members present no evidence tying the discipline to their comments dealing with a matter of public concern. In other claims, courts review the institution's explanation for its negative employment decision and determine which party's evidence is persuasive. One university prevailed when officials demonstrated that they chose not to renew the contract of a confrontational writing instructor because of the disruption his style brought to the department, not because he championed diversity in his class and in faculty meetings. Yet, in another case, a history instructor established that officials at a junior college elected not to renew her contract because she participated in efforts to form a faculty chapter of the National Education Association and worked on her husband's campaign to win a seat on the institution's governing board, not because of the school's proffered reasons of poor evaluation of her teaching and the need to reduce staff due to declining enrollment.

Colleges and universities then have the burden of showing at the final *Mt. Healthy* step that they would have disciplined the employees had the protected expression not occurred. Higher education plaintiffs have not progressed to this final stage in published case law thus far.

Ralph Sharp

See also Keyishian v. Board of Regents of the University of the State of New York; Loyalty Oaths; Political Activities and Speech of Faculty Members; *Sweezy v. New Hampshire*; *Urofsky v. Gilmore*

Further Readings

Bonnell v. Lorenzo, 241 F.3d 800 (6th Cir. 2001).

Dambrot v. Central Michigan University, 55 F.3d 1177 (6th Cir. 1995).

Fossey, R., & Beckham, J. C. (2008). University authority over teaching activities: Institutional regulation may override a faculty member's academic freedom. *West's Education Law Reporter, 228*, 1–22.

Hardy v. Jefferson Community College, 260 F.3d 671 (6th Cir. 2001).

Hiers, R. H. (2002). Institutional academic freedom vs. faculty academic freedom in public colleges and universities: A dubious dichotomy. *Journal of College & University Law, 29*, 35–110.

Legal Citations

Keyishian v. Board of Regents of University of State of New York, 385 U.S. 589 (1967).

Maples v. Martin, 858 F.2d 1546 (11th Cir. 1988).

Mt. Healthy City School District Board of Education v. Doyle, 429 U.S. 274 (1977).

Parate v. Isibor, 868 F.2d 821 (6th Cir. 1989).

Shelton v. Tucker, 364 U.S. 479 (1960).

Urofsky v. Gilmore, 216 F.3d 401 (4th Cir. 2000), *cert. denied*, 531 U.S. 1070 (2001).

ACCEPTABLE USE POLICIES

Acceptable use policies (AUPs) are sets of behavioral expectations or rules adopted by college and university officials that are designed to regulate the conduct of those who use institutionally provided computer resources. At the same time, many businesses and K–12 school systems have developed such rules and policies to regulate usage, to protect the integrity of their networks, and to avoid legal problems. In educational institutions, faculty, staff members, and students are often asked to acknowledge AUPs and to agree, in writing, to comply with their terms as a condition of access to computer resources. Well-drafted AUPs can serve a useful purpose by helping to alleviate disagreements when improper uses are discovered, so that the consequences for such inappropriate uses can be more readily justified and evenly applied.

Acceptable use policies typically contain a statement of purpose along with an acknowledgment that computer resources and access provided by the institution are provided primarily for educational or administrative purposes. Those policies make users primarily responsible for compliance but also warn that computer users are subject to monitoring for compliance. Making individuals aware of such provisions in policies is designed to have the effect of deterring unacceptable conduct while providing warnings that individuals are primarily responsible for their conduct that fails to comply with the policies.

A common function of AUPs is to advise users that their use of computer resources is subject to monitoring. Users must be told that the system will be monitored for misuse and that they should not expect that their computer use, the sites they visit, or the e-mail or instant messages they send using school computer resources will be private. In addition, educational officials should condition access to computer systems to those users who expressly agree to the AUPs, including the monitoring provisions. Users who agree to comply with the provisions in AUPs, in essence, consent to monitoring as a condition of access. Including such an explicit statement in AUPs should help institutions to avoid liability under the Electronic Communications Privacy Act (1986), which makes it unlawful to intercept electronic messages. Put another way, reducing the expectation of privacy that users may otherwise think they have in using such technology should help institutions avoid legal issues when monitoring is required.

Most AUPs also contain what is tantamount to a code of conduct for users. Codes may include rules pertaining to use of appropriate language; rules to help users avoid illegal activity; and rules regulating the downloading of copyrighted materials, including music and movies; as well as rules that are designed to protect the integrity of the system (bandwidth). The challenge for administrators in higher education is to develop policies that are broad enough to address and guide conduct that may not have even been conceived of, yet narrow enough to address specific behavior in a practical

and unambiguous way. Conduct rules may also be designed to regulate harassment or disruptive conduct directed to other users. Moreover, rules designed to protect users are common, such as rules regarding the release of personally identifiable information or the sharing of access passwords.

Unacceptable uses of computer resources are frequently detailed as part of AUPs. For example, the creation, storage, display, or transmission of offensive, obscene, sexually explicit, or otherwise inappropriate documents or images are frequently prohibited. AUPs often cross-reference other policies of the institution (such as antiharassment, plagiarism, and discipline policies as well as student codes of conduct).

AUPs commonly provide notice to students that insofar as their access to computing resources is a privilege, not a right, violations of AUPs can result in having their privileges withdrawn. Another common feature of AUPs is that they often detail the consequences of violations of their terms. In addition to denial of access and/or referrals to law enforcement agencies, policies may note that violations will be subject to institutional disciplinary policies. Warnings, suspensions, and terminations or withdrawal of privileges are common consequences detailed in such policies. Furthermore, AUPs may be an important medium to inform staff of the applicability of a state's public records laws to their electronic communications, including any responsibility the staff member may have to preserve such records. Staff should also be reminded that communications may also be protected by the Family Educational Rights and Privacy Act (1974).

AUPs are designed to encourage responsible use of computer resources. As a guide to conduct, they are designed primarily so users can self-regulate their behavior. AUPs also serve as notices of rules and consequences in the event that users fail to live up to their own responsibilities for compliance.

AUPs present legal issues similar to issues arising under other college and university codes of conduct: First Amendment freedom of expression, Fourteenth Amendment due process, Fourth Amendment privacy, common-law, or statutory privacy claims, and copyright issues in addition to a variety of harassment issues, such as sexual harassment and cyberbullying.

Educational officials retain regulatory authority over computer resources that the school provides for students and staff. However, officials must make sure that policy enforcement is consistent with the terms of their institutional AUPs. In this regard, due process will require that students, faculty, and staff members be provided with clear notice of what is acceptable and what is not permitted. In addition, when taking disciplinary actions, officials must ensure that an apparent nexus to their institutions is identified before acting pursuant to AUPs.

If officials must take disciplinary actions or other consequences flow as a result of students' failure to comply with AUPs, sanctions must be taken in accord with an institution's general disciplinary procedures and applicable code of conduct provisions. Disciplinary actions or other consequences taken against faculty and staff must be taken in concert with requirements of applicable personnel policies, employment handbooks, and labor contracts.

Jon E. Anderson

See also Cyberbullying; Digital Millennium Copyright Act

Further Readings

Fossey, R., & Horner, J. (2003). Student misconduct involving the misuse of technology. *Education Law Reporter, 179*(1), 1.

McClure, P. A. (Ed.). (2003). *Organizing and managing information resources on your campus.* San Francisco: Jossey-Bass.

Legal Citations

Electronic Communications Privacy Act, Pub. L. No. 99-508 (1986).

Family Educational Rights and Privacy Act, Pub. L. No. 93-380 (1974).

AFFIRMATIVE ACTION

Affirmative action is defined as specific actions taken to eliminate the present effects of past discrimination or to prevent discrimination. As such, affirmative action plans have historically allowed policies to consider gender, race, ethnicity, or disability. Generally, affirmative action refers to hiring practices as well as to higher education recruitment and admissions practices. Typically, affirmative action policies involve granting some sort of preference in hiring or admissions to members of a minority group based on sex or race. This entry focuses on affirmative action relating to students in higher education.

Affirmative action in higher education has been extremely controversial. Critics believe that affirmative action is, in effect, reverse discrimination—so that by giving admissions preferences to members of the minority group, universities are discriminating against Caucasians. Other opponents contend that affirmative action programs benefit only students of color from middle- to upper-class backgrounds. Supporters argue that affirmative action prevents new discrimination and/or eliminates the negative effects of past or ongoing discrimination. In so doing, affirmative action programs in higher education address the education and economic gap between Caucasians and historically disadvantaged groups.

One of the most common arguments against affirmative action, or race-conscious admissions programs, is that they violate Title VI of the Civil Rights Act of 1964 and the Equal Protection Clause of the Fourteenth Amendment. According to Title VI, citizens should not be subject to discrimination on the grounds of race, color, or national origin in any program receiving federal financial assistance. The Equal Protection Clause ensures that the government provides equal protection of the laws to all and has been interpreted as meaning that the government should treat similar individuals in a similar manner. Thus, affirmative action admissions programs have typically been challenged by White plaintiffs who claim that such admissions programs violate the Equal Protection Clause, because minority applicants (similar individuals) are given a preference based upon race (dissimilar treatment).

Under equal protection analysis, when a court considers the constitutionality of a government action such as affirmative action in higher education, it must apply one of three standards: rational basis, mid-level review, and strict scrutiny. In higher education admissions cases, strict scrutiny, the highest standard of review used by the courts, is used.

Under strict scrutiny, government officials (whether federal or state) must first show that their decisions to treat people differently are justified not merely by a legitimate or important interest but by a compelling state interest. For example, in affirmative action admissions cases, courts first examine whether promoting diversity in higher education is a compelling governmental interest. If a court finds a governmental interest to be compelling, then it must explore whether the means chosen to obtain a diverse student body, through a race-conscious admissions program, are "narrowly tailored." In order to be narrowly tailored, a race-conscious admissions plan may use race as a "plus-factor"—meaning that students can gain some additional credit based on their race but that it cannot be the deciding factor—but may not utilize a quota. For example, an admissions program must be flexible in considering several elements of diversity for each applicant rather than admitting an applicant based only on race or sex strictly to meet a quota. To be constitutional, a racial classification must satisfy both the compelling interest and narrowly tailored parts of strict scrutiny.

Affirmative Action Cases in Higher Education

DeFunis v. Odegaard (1974) was the first affirmative action in higher education case to reach the U.S. Supreme Court. In this case, a law school applicant argued that he was denied admission in favor of minority applicant who was less qualified. Unfortunately, the Court never resolved the merits of the case, because DeFunis was eventually admitted to the law school, thereby rendering the case moot, at least at the federal level. As a result, the first Supreme Court case to address affirmative action in higher education admissions was *Regents of the University of California v. Bakke* in 1978. In addition to *Bakke,* four federal appellate court cases have addressed similar issues within the context of higher education. These cases set the stage for the landmark 2003 *Gratz v. Bollinger* and *Grutter v. Bollinger* Supreme Court decisions ("the Michigan decisions") that provided additional guidance on the constitutionality of race-conscious affirmative action programs in higher education.

The Supreme Court's 1978 decision in *Bakke* addressed a university's consideration of race as

part of its admissions program. Allan Bakke was a White male who was denied admission by the University of California, Davis, School of Medicine. Bakke alleged that the medical school's admissions program had violated the Equal Protection Clause by using a quota: The school had reserved 16 out of 100 places for disadvantaged minority students, thus accepting less-qualified minority applicants, according to Bakke. He claimed that the students who filled these 16 spots had lower grade point averages and test scores than White students who were rejected. Bakke alleged that his rights under the Equal Protection Clause of the Fourteenth Amendment (and under Article I of the California Constitution) had been violated, because the medical school's program treated him differently than the successful minority applicants and excluded him because of his race.

A highly divided Supreme Court held that the medical school's policy of setting aside 16 seats to be filled only by minorities was unconstitutional, thus establishing the unconstitutionality of using quotas. However, the Court reversed an earlier ruling that race could never be considered a factor in education. After *Bakke,* universities were left to wonder whether or to what extent race could be used in admissions, because there was a lack of a clear standard of whether race could be considered in admissions. Subsequent to *Bakke,* federal appellate courts in the Fifth, Eleventh, Ninth, and Sixth Circuits decided affirmative action cases in higher education. The Fifth and Eleventh Circuits did not uphold university affirmative action programs, while the Ninth and Sixth Circuits sustained the constitutionality of such policies.

In the case from the Fifth Circuit, *Hopwood v. Texas* (1996), four White students challenged their being denied admission to the University of Texas Law School in 1992. Cheryl Hopwood and the other plaintiffs filed suit, claiming that the admissions policy violated the Equal Protection Clause of the Fourteenth Amendment and Title VI of the Civil Rights Act of 1964. The plaintiff's complaint alleged that the law school had different admissions criteria for White and minority students, resulting in the admission of less-qualified minority applicants. The Fifth Circuit found in favor of the plaintiffs, holding that it was unconstitutional to consider race or ethnicity to achieve a diverse student body at the law school.

The Ninth Circuit was the first federal appellate court to address the issue after *Hopwood* in *Smith v. University of Washington Law School* (2000). The court ruled that in this instance diversity was a constitutionally permissible goal. In *Smith*, White students who were denied admission to the University of Washington Law School filed suit, alleging that law school officials practiced racially discriminatory admissions policies. Disagreeing with the plaintiffs, the court was of the opinion that student body diversity was a compelling state interest and that the university's admissions plan was constitutional in this instance.

In 2001, the Eleventh Circuit joined the Fifth Circuit in hinting that diversity in academic settings was not a compelling interest in *Johnson v. Board of Regents*. Here three White female students disputed their being denied admission to the University of Georgia. The plaintiffs claimed that minority applicants were unfairly given extra "points" during the admissions process due to their races. Agreeing with the plaintiffs, the court noted that the university's affirmative action program was unconstitutional, because it mechanically awarded diversity bonuses to its non-White applicants. The court did not definitively resolve whether diversity was a compelling state interest, instead pointing out that the disputed policy was unconstitutional, because it was insufficiently narrowly tailored.

In addition to the affirmative action cases in the Fifth, Ninth, and Eleventh Circuits, the same issue arose in the Sixth Circuit in *Gratz v. Bollinger* and *Grutter v. Bollinger*. Interestingly, the same federal trial court determined that one program was constitutional, while another similar program at the same university was unconstitutional. Subsequently, the Sixth Circuit, interpreting diversity as a compelling state interest, upheld the constitutionality of race-conscious admissions programs as long as the programs were narrowly tailored. When circuits are split on an issue, as the Fifth, Ninth, Eleventh, and Sixth circuits were on affirmative action in higher education admissions programs, the Supreme Court may intervene. In 2003 the Supreme Court addressed whether race could be considered in university admissions.

Gratz v. Bollinger involved undergraduate admissions policies. The plaintiffs, who applied to the College of Literature, Science, and the Arts at the University of Michigan, were wait-listed and

later rejected. Gratz had a 3.8 GPA, an ACT score of 25, and an impressive list of high school extracurricular activities. The other plaintiff had equally impressive credentials.

Insofar as the University of Michigan awarded extra points to minority candidates solely on the basis of their races, the plaintiffs filed a class action suit in 1997 against its Board of Regents and various school administrators in a federal trial court, alleging that its admissions program was discriminatory. Specifically, the undergraduate admissions policy at issue awarded a maximum of 150 points to any given application. Race was considered along with several other factors such as test scores, alumni relationships, and leadership skills when determining each applicant's point total. Members of underrepresented minority groups and applicants from socioeconomically disadvantaged backgrounds received an automatic 20 points under the system. The plaintiffs charged that the university's consideration of race in admissions from 1995 to 2003 violated Title VI of the Civil Rights Act of 1964 as well as the Equal Protection Clause of the Fourteenth Amendment. Ultimately, the Supreme Court, in 2003, struck down the university's undergraduate admissions program. Although it was of the view that student body diversity was a compelling state interest, the Court did not think that the undergraduate admissions program was sufficiently narrowly tailored.

Grutter v. Bollinger involved law school admissions at the University of Michigan. The plaintiff had a 3.8 undergraduate GPA and a law school admissions test (LSAT) score in the 86th percentile. Like the plaintiffs in *Gratz*, she was wait-listed and later denied admission. Grutter and other rejected applicants filed suit in December 1997 challenging the law school's use of race in its admissions program. In her class action suit, Grutter complained that the law school's affirmative action policy favored certain minority applicants and that it amounted to racial or ethnic discrimination under the Equal Protection Clause of the Fourteenth Amendment and Title VI of the Civil Rights Act of 1964.

Unlike the undergraduate program's use of points, law school officials used race as one of many unquantified factors that could enhance an applicant's chances of admission. In order to demonstrate a commitment to diversity, law school officials sought to enroll a "critical mass" of minority applicants, or a minimum number of minority students necessary to withstand compartmentalization. The law school, in arguing that diversity is a compelling interest, stressed that the presence of more than a few minority students in a classroom encourages all students to think less stereotypically while allowing the minority students to feel less isolated. In *Grutter v. Bollinger*, the Supreme Court agreed with the University of Michigan Law School that student body diversity is a compelling interest.

Having held that diversity was a compelling governmental interest, the Supreme Court addressed whether the law school's program was narrowly tailored. The Court upheld the admissions policy, because it was convinced that unlike the undergraduate admissions program in *Gratz v. Bollinger*, the law school's admissions program was sufficiently narrowly tailored. The Court explained that the policy was acceptable, because the law school's affirmative action program adequately ensured that all factors that may contribute to student body diversity were meaningfully considered alongside race in admissions decisions.

From the *Grutter v. Bollinger* example, it is evident that universities should make clear that there are many possible bases for diversity in admissions. In *Grutter* the Supreme Court noted that the law school's policy required admissions officers to consider "soft variables," or other criteria beyond grades and test scores. In other words, in order to ensure that polices can pass constitutional muster, university officials should take into account and give substantial weight to a wide variety of diversity factors besides race and ethnicity.

Gratz and *Grutter* certainly have implications for university admissions teams. Although diversity is now viewed as a compelling state interest, *Grutter* is not a license for admissions teams to implement any type of race-conscious affirmative action plan they choose. Instead, university officials may use race only when the admissions policy is narrowly tailored. In fact, a careful analysis of the Supreme Court's rationale in *Gratz* and *Grutter* provides guidance for universities that choose to implement a race-conscious admissions program.

The debate over affirmative action continues in the wake of *Gratz* and *Grutter*. Most recently, the California Board of Regents voted to eliminate requiring students to submit two SAT subject exams when applying to the University of California System. Now the university will require only that students submit scores from the main SAT or ACT exams, have taken certain college prep courses, and have a 3.0 GPA. Critics of affirmative action claim that this policy was an attempt to avoid the state ban on affirmative action. Indeed, affirmative action policies in higher education admissions will remain controversial.

Suzanne E. Eckes

See also *DeFunis v. Odegaard*; Equal Protection Analysis; Fourteenth Amendment; *Gratz v. Bollinger*; *Grutter v. Bollinger*; *Regents of the University of California v. Bakke*

Further Readings

Ball, H. (2000). *The Bakke case: Race, education, & affirmative action*. Lawrence: University Press of Kansas.

Eckes, S. (2007). Affirmative action. In G. L. Anderson & K. G. Herr (Eds.), *Encyclopedia of activism and social justice* (Vol. 1, pp. 138–141). Thousand Oaks, CA: Sage.

Eckes, S. (2008). *Grutter v. Bollinger*. In C. J. Russo (Ed.), *Encyclopedia of education law* (Vol. 1, pp. 412–414). Thousand Oaks, CA: Sage.

Office of Affirmative Action, Equal Opportunity and Diversity. (n.d.). *Glossary of affirmative actions terms*. Retrieved April 21, 2009, from http://www.uri.edu/affirmative_action/definitions.html

Tribe, L. H. (1979). Perspectives on Bakke: Equal protection, procedural fairness, or structural justice? *Harvard Law Review, 92*, 864–877.

Legal Citations

DeFunis v. Odegaard, 416 U.S. 312 (1974).

Gratz v. Bollinger, 539 U.S. 244 (2003).

Grutter v. Bollinger, 539 U.S. 306 (2003).

Hopwood v. Texas, 78 F.3d 932 (5th Cir. 1996).

Johnson v. Board of Regents, 263 F.3d 1234 (11th Cir. 2001).

Regents of the University of California v. Bakke, 438 U.S. 265 (1978).

Smith v. University of Washington Law School, 233 F.3d 1188 (9th Cir. 2000).

Title VI of the Civil Rights Act of 1964, 42 U.S.C. § 2000d (1964).

AGE DISCRIMINATION

American society is aging as health care improves, the baby boom generation approaches retirement age, and the age for eligibility to draw full Social Security benefits rises. According to the U.S. Census Bureau, the median age of the population rose five years from 1980 to 2005. The percentage of the U.S. population in the age range of 40 to 74 increased from 31.6% in 1980 to 38.6% in 2005. With the graying of the American population and the resulting greater awareness of the pervasiveness of age discrimination in society have come concerted efforts on the part of federal and state government to eliminate age discrimination in employment and higher education.

Older Americans have many avenues through which to contest age-based discrimination legally. At the federal level, both constitutional and statutory provisions provide legal protections for older students and workers who think they have been discriminated against because of their age. The Equal Protection Clause of the Fourteenth Amendment in the U.S. Constitution affords a general constitutional remedy for plaintiffs of all ages who raise claims of age-based discrimination. Further, Congress, through the Age Discrimination in Employment Act (1967), which affords protection for workers who are 40 years of age or older, and the Age Discrimination Act (1975), which covers educational institutions that receive federal financial assistance, has provided more specific defenses for students and workers. At the same time, many states have enacted constitutional and statutory measures offering protection against age bias, sometimes even exceeding the federal provisions. This entry reviews these options and education-related cases dealing with age discrimination in education and employment.

Equal Protection Clause

The Equal Protection Clause of the Fourteenth Amendment guarantees equal treatment under the law to all persons. For individuals and settings not covered by the Age Discrimination in Employment Act and the Age Discrimination Act, the general applicability of the Equal Protection Clause provides a federal basis for challenging age-based discrimination. As the Supreme Court explained in *Massachusetts Board of Retirement v. Murgia* (1976), courts apply the rational basis test in age claims brought under the Equal Protection Clause, because age is not a suspect classification, and there is no fundamental interest in governmental employment or federal fundamental right of participation in educational programs. Applying *Murgia* a year later, a federal trial court upheld Pennsylvania State University's policy of mandatory retirement at 65 for faculty and staff under the rational basis standard, as it allowed the institution to plan, change, and employ new personnel with newer skills.

Under the rational basis test, officials at colleges and universities must show only that their actions reasonably further legitimate state objectives or interests. However, as a federal trial court reminded a rejected 65-year-old applicant to the University of Maine School of Law, the judiciary will not engage in rational basis review unless the a plaintiff first establishes evidence of discriminatory intent on the part of a defendant university.

The Fifth Circuit reviewed a public university's housing policy against an equal protection claim against age discrimination. The institution required student on-campus residence but exempted all undergraduates who were 23 years of age or older. The court found that there was no rational basis for the arbitrary distinction in treatment between students ages 21 and 22 and those 23 and above; the case did not involve a claim on behalf of anyone under the age of 21. Accordingly, the court struck the housing policy down as unconstitutional. Earlier, female students at the same public university in Louisiana successfully challenged the housing policy requiring unmarried female students who were under the age of 21 and not living with close relatives to live in campus residence halls. A federal trial court determined that the policy, which was grounded solely on the reason of seeking to meet financial obligations in connection with the construction of dormitories, violated the equal protection clause.

Age Discrimination in Employment Act

The Age Discrimination in Employment Act (ADEA) of 1967 provides a federal statutory remedy for older Americans who experience age-based discrimination in the workplace. According to this law,

> It shall be unlawful for an employer—
> (1) to fail or refuse to hire or to discharge any individual or otherwise discriminate against any individual with respect to his compensation, terms, conditions, or privileges of employment, because of such individual's age;
> (2) to limit, segregate, or classify his employees in any way which would deprive or tend to deprive any individual of employment opportunities or otherwise adversely affect his status as an employee, because of such individual's age; or
> (3) to reduce the wage rate of any employee in order to comply with this chapter. (29 U.S.C. 623(a))

The ADEA protects employees and prospective employees or applicants aged 40 and above from a wide range of discriminatory actions based on age: hiring, dismissal, promotion, demotion, and transfer; conditions of employment, including compensation and early retirement incentive programs; and retaliation for exercising ADEA rights. However, if two or more applicants are 40 years of age or older, the ADEA does not afford protection to the disappointed applicant where the job went to a member of the class that the statute was designed to protect. Plaintiffs must file suit within 90 days of receiving right-to-sue letters from the Equal Employment Opportunity Commission (EEOC).

There are two types of ADEA claims. First, employees can file *disparate treatment* charges, in which they accuse their employers of taking negative or less favorable action against them on account of their ages. For example, when a former dean claimed that university officials demoted him because of his age, the institution established that he was demoted not due to age but rather to deficiencies in his performance as dean, thereby establishing that it relied on a bona fide occupational qualification in rebutting his claim.

The other type, *disparate impact* claims, involve facially neutral employer policies or practices that impact disproportionately and substantively an ADEA-protected group. In breaking with another circuit, the Seventh Circuit found no ADEA violation in a school policy that hired less experienced, and therefore generally younger, applicants because they are more affordable. Another two appellate courts upheld university policies that paid professors based on market value, even if this resulted in younger faculty being paid more than older colleagues. Courts have divided over early retirement incentive plans that offer benefits only to those educators who accept the option by a certain age.

Age Discrimination Act of 1975

The Age Discrimination Act of 1975 is a federal statute that shields both employees and, unlike the ADEA, students, from age-based discrimination in educational settings. Patterned after Title VI of the Civil Rights Act of 1964, Title IX of the Education Amendments of 1972, and Section 504 of the Rehabilitation Act of 1973, the Age Discrimination Act states that "no person in the United States shall, on the basis of age, be excluded from participation in, be denied the benefits of, or be subjected to discrimination under, any program or activity receiving Federal financial assistance" (42 U.S.C. § 6102 (1975)).

Statutory provisions in the Age Discrimination Act exempt age-based actions that are necessary for a program's operation or achievement of its statutory objective. The law also incorporates a statute of limitations for bringing claims that requires plaintiffs to exhaust administrative remedies before filing suit. Under the Civil Rights Restoration Act of 1987, the Age Discrimination Act applies to all aspects of an educational institution if any part of its operations receives federal funds. While used by plaintiffs infrequently, the Age Discrimination Act provides a statutory basis for students or employees under age 40 to bring age-based discrimination claims against colleges and universities.

State Laws

States provide additional protection against age discrimination in their constitutions and statutes. While some states, such as Delaware in the Delaware Discrimination in Employment Act, model their protections closely upon the ADEA, others, including Florida, have enacted statutes that prohibit age discrimination generally and do not limit coverage to those 40 and above. Still other states, such as Iowa and Oregon, explicitly exceed ADEA coverage by protecting all persons 18 years of age and older from differential treatment based on age.

Some plaintiffs base their challenges to alleged age discrimination primarily upon state, rather than federal, provisions. For example, in 1978 the Supreme Court of Utah reviewed the rejection of a 51-year-old applicant for admission into a graduate educational psychology program at the University of Utah. The plaintiff's admission materials exceeded the department's normal requirements in all areas, and the department and admission committee rejected her solely based upon her age. The court, while remanding the case to give the state university an opportunity to show a rational basis between the admission policy and legitimate state purposes, found that denying admission solely on the basis of age violated equal protection under both the state and federal constitutions.

Conclusion

As the American population grows older, one can expect increasing challenges to age-based discrimination in the education setting over the coming decades. Financial considerations in tight economic times may lead educational institutions to more frequent hiring and promotion of younger candidates, who are normally less experienced and therefore may draw lesser salaries. In order to avoid legal challenges of this sort, college and university officials should adhere to three key principles. First, institutional policies should formally prohibit consideration of a person's age in the process of reaching decisions regarding students and employees. Second, administrators in higher education must take steps to prevent subordinates and committees from informally considering the age of applicants and employees when making admission, hiring, promotion, and tenure decisions. Third, if needed, college and university officials should increase in-service training to make all employees, particularly those with decision-making responsibility, aware of the legal prohibitions against age discrimination.

Ralph Sharp

See also Age Discrimination in Employment Act; Disparate Impact; Equal Pay Act; Equal Protection Analysis

Further Readings

Del. Code Ann. tit. 19, § 710 (2008).
Fla. Stat. § 112.043–.044 (2008).
Iowa Code §§ 161-8.15, 216.6 (2008).
Or. Rev. Stat. § 659A.030 (2008).

Legal Citations

Age Discrimination Act, 42 U.S.C. §§ 6101 *et seq.* (1975).
Age Discrimination in Employment Act, 29 U.S.C. §§ 621 *et seq.* (1967).
Civil Rights Restoration Act, 20 U.S.C. § 1681 (1987).
Massachusetts Board of Retirement v. Murgia, 427 U.S. 307 (1976).
Rehabilitation Act of 1973, Section 504, 29 U.S.C. §§ 794 *et seq.*
Title VI of the Civil Rights Act of 1964, 42 U.S.C. § 2000d.
Title IX of the Education Amendments of 1972, 20 U.S.C. § 1681.

Age Discrimination in Employment Act

The Age Discrimination in Employment Act (ADEA) of 1967 was passed by Congress as part of its broad legislative attack on employment discrimination in the 1960s and 1970s. Concerned with incidents of age bias in the workplace, Congress enacted the ADEA as an amendment to the Fair Labor Standards Act of 1938 that substantially parallels Title VII of the Civil Rights Act of 1964. The ADEA's provisions prohibit age-based discrimination in employment decisions, benefit programs, and retirement plans. Since the statute's enactment, courts have dealt with many ADEA issues in the context of higher education, ranging from dismissal and denial of tenure to salaries and early retirement incentive plans. This entry reviews the scope and application of the ADEA in higher education.

General Provisions

The ADEA is the primary federal statutory remedy for victims of age discrimination in the workplace. The ADEA prohibits employers with 20 or more employees from discriminating against employees and prospective employees or applicants because of their age in hiring, transfer, promotion, demotion, and dismissal as well as in conditions of employment, including compensation and benefit plans. The ADEA also makes it illegal for employers to retaliate against employees or prospective employees who oppose practices made unlawful under the statute by filing ADEA complaints or suits or by participating in investigations, proceedings, or litigation under its far-reaching provisions.

Some of the statutory exceptions to the ADEA's antidiscrimination provisions are relevant to colleges and universities. Employers may take otherwise prohibited actions if age is a bona fide occupational qualification for institutions' normal operations. Moreover, except for nonhiring decisions such as transfers based on age where it may be a relevant consideration due to the nature of the work involved and involuntary retirements, the ADEA exempts bona fide seniority systems and employee benefit plans such as voluntary early retirement incentive plans if they meet specified guidelines.

The federal Equal Employment Opportunity Commission (EEOC) administratively enforces the provisions of the ADEA. Individuals must first file charges with the EEOC, which notifies prospective defendants and must attempt to eliminate alleged unlawful actions through informal negotiations before it may file civil judicial actions. The ADEA authorizes courts to award equitable relief to prevailing plaintiffs, such as reinstatement, back pay, damages, and attorney's fees.

Originally, the ADEA covered workers aged 40 to 65 but did not apply to states and their agencies. Congressional amendments extended the ADEA's coverage to state governments and their political subdivisions, including public colleges and universities; the Supreme Court upheld the constitutionality of this extension in the face of a Tenth Amendment immunity challenge in *EEOC v. Wyoming* (1983). Congress also removed the upper age limit for all but a few employment categories that are rarely an issue in higher education settings; for example, the ADEA allows compulsory retirement for firefighters, law enforcement officers, and in some circumstances bona fide executives or those in high policy-making positions.

Application of the Law

ADEA plaintiffs have two routes through which they can attempt to make their cases of unlawful discrimination. Plaintiffs can present direct evidence of discrimination, or they can proceed based on indirect evidence by meeting the steps set forth in the Supreme Court's application of Title VII in *McDonnell Douglas v. Green* (1973) and *Texas Department of Community Affairs v. Burdine* (1981), cases that were resolved under Title VII but which offer protections similar to those under the ADEA. Insofar as the protections afforded by Title VII and the ADEA are very much alike, judicial analyses often rely on analogous reasoning such that in order to be actionable, qualified employees must be over the age of 40, must have been treated less favorably than others not in the protected class, must have suffered an adverse employment action, and must file suit within 90 days of receiving right-to-sue letters from the EEOC. Once employees present prima facie cases, employers can seek to rebut them by providing legitimate nondiscriminatory reasons for acting.

Plaintiffs must first establish that they have prima facie cases of age discrimination by establishing that they were members of the protected class by being at least 40 years of age; were either qualified for the jobs for which they were not hired or met employers' reasonable job expectations in cases of dismissals, transfers, or demotions; suffered adverse employment actions; and were replaced by, or treated less favorably than, someone substantially younger than themselves. While there is no rigid standard for how significant the age difference must be to establish this last element of prima facie cases, courts generally define substantially younger as approximately 10 or more years younger than the plaintiffs. In addition, the Supreme Court in *O'Connor v. Consolidated Coin Caterers Corporation* (1996) recognized that in establishing a prima facie case, it is irrelevant if a plaintiff lost out to another person in the protected ADEA class (who was at least 40 years of age), in part because the key remains that the challenged action was taken *because of* the complainant's age.

As noted, once plaintiffs present prima facie cases of discrimination based on age, the burden shifts back to employers to produce legitimate, nondiscriminatory reasons for their adverse employment actions. At the final stage, plaintiffs have the opportunity to prove that their employers' reasons were not true and were rather pretexts for unlawful age-based discrimination.

Two appellate court rulings illustrate the application of the *McDonnell Douglas–Burdine* test in higher education ADEA claims. In *Lewis v. St. Cloud State University* (2006), the Eighth Circuit upheld the removal of the plaintiff as dean of the college of social sciences because he failed to establish a prima face case, because his permanent replacement was less than three years younger than he was. The court noted that even if the plaintiff had met his initial burden, university officials articulated three legitimate, nondiscriminatory reasons for his removal, all of which were related to deficiencies in his performance as dean. Consequently, the court found that the plaintiff was unable to show that the university's stated reasons were pretextual or that his removal from the administrative position resulted from age discrimination.

Another federal appellate court upheld the demotion and transfer of the chief operating engineer in a university's heating plan where he was unable to establish that explanations provided by university officials were pretextual. While the engineer alleged that his supervisor asked him when he was going to retire and told him he was too old to continue working in his job assignment, the court was of the opinion that the university's action was based on the recommendation of an independent investigator, and a merit board ruled the university's action adequately supported.

There are two basic types of claims under the ADEA. Disparate impact cases challenge employment policies or practices that on the surface appear nondiscriminatory but adversely and significantly affect employees or applicants who are protected by the ADEA. For instance, the Seventh Circuit upheld a private K–12 school's policy of hiring less experienced, and therefore generally younger, teachers, because they were more affordable on its salary schedule linking wages to years of teaching experience. Despite the EEOC's claim that the low minimum salary limit excluded from employment consideration a disproportionate percentage of applicants over the age of 40, the court ruled that the policy was economically defensible and reasonable. At the higher education level, two federal appellate courts upheld university compensation plans that adversely impacted older faculty. In *Davidson v. Board of Governors of State Colleges and Universities for Western Illinois University* (1990) and *MacPherson v. University of Montevallo* (1991), the courts upheld university compensation plans that based salaries for newly hired faculty and pay raises for current faculty on market value, thereby causing some older faculty to earn less than their younger colleagues.

More common in the higher education setting are disparate treatment claims in which protected or prospective employees allege that educational institutions treated them differently on account of their ages. ADEA claims in higher education frequently challenge negative institutional actions involving hiring, tenure, academic promotion, and the nonrenewal of employment contracts. Particularly in the area of tenure and academic determinations such as promotion in rank, courts are reluctant to review the merits of academic decisions absent clear evidence of unlawful age-based decisions. In this regard, courts typically readily defer to institutional decision makers insofar as they recognize that academicians are better suited to make subjective judgments involving the review of scholarship, university service, and teaching.

A good illustration of an ADEA challenge to an employee's dismissal can be found in *Wichmann v. Board of Trustees of Southern Illinois University* (1999). The Seventh Circuit upheld a jury verdict that university officials willfully violated the ADEA in dismissing a 48-year-old managerial employee who had glowing evaluations as part of a reduction-in-force plan for a program that ultimately was not eliminated. The program's accountant testified that the accounting was unreliable, because the accounting methods were allegedly changed to make apparent surpluses disappear; the deciding administrator stated in a meeting less than a month after the dismissal decision that "in a forest you have to cut down the old, big trees so the little trees underneath can grow" (p. 796); and the dismissed employee's duties were dispersed among other employees, most of whom were considerably younger than he was at the time he was released from his job.

Early Retirement Incentive Programs

The ADEA, amended in 1990 by the Older Workers Benefit Protection Act, provides a safe harbor for universities to offer early retirement incentive plans (ERIPs) to employees with tenure. ERIPs must be voluntary, made available to eligible employees for a reasonable period of time, and consistent with the ADEA's purpose of prohibiting arbitrary age discrimination in employment. Judicial determinations hinge on the specific details of incentive plans, as courts have divided over plans that require employees to retire by a certain age or either lose the incentive benefits or receive reduced benefits.

Two cases from K–12 settings should be instructive for higher education. In the first, a federal appellate court ruled that a public school board's incentive plan was a valid ERIP under the ADEA; it required teachers to retire after the school year in which they turned 55 if they were eligible with at least 20 years of service or lose a fixed sum payment and accumulated sick leave payment. In contrast, a Second Circuit court rejected a board's retirement incentive plan that offered incentives to teachers and administrators who retired between the ages of 58 and 61, but no additional early retirement benefits to educators at age 62 and beyond. The court found that this plan violated the ADEA, because the ERIP explicitly defined eligibility for the incentives in terms of age.

In sum, the ADEA protects employees and prospective employees who are 40 years or age or older from age-based employment discrimination. The ADEA applies to a wide range of basic employment decisions, including hiring, transfer, demotion, dismissal, tenure and academic promotion, benefit and retirement plans, and employer attempts to retaliate against employees for opposing practices unlawful under the statute. Courts overturn employment decisions in hiring, dismissal, and demotion when plaintiffs establish that the actions were age based. Still, appellate courts have split over the legality of early retirement plans that cut off incentives if educators refuse to retire by a specified age. Charges filed with the EEOC under all federal employment discrimination statutes (in addition to the ADEA, the Equal Pay Act, the Americans with Disabilities Act, and Title VII of the Civil Rights Act of 1964) increased 20% from 1997 to 2007 (EEOC, 2009). As the American population ages, one can anticipate that older workers on college and university campuses will continue to

rely increasingly on the ADEA to press claims of age-based discrimination.

Ralph Sharp

See also Age Discrimination; Disparate Impact; Equal Employment Opportunity Commission; Title VII

Further Readings

Equal Employment Opportunity Commission. (2009). *Harassment charges EEOC & FEPAs combined: FY 1997–FY 2008*. Retrieved June 20, 2009, from http://www.eeoc.gov/stats/harassment.html
Title VI of the Civil Rights Act of 1964, 42 U.S.C. § 2000d (1964).

Legal Citations

Age Discrimination in Employment Act, 29 U.S.C. §§ 621 *et seq.* (1967).
Americans with Disabilities Act, Pub. L. No. 101-336 (1990).
Davidson v. Board of Governors of State Colleges and Universities for Western Illinois University, 920 F.2d 441 (7th Cir. 1990).
EEOC v. Wyoming, 460 U.S. 226 (1983).
Equal Pay Act, 29 U.S.C. § 206(d) (1963).
Fair Labor Standards Act, 29 U.S.C. ch. 8 (1938).
Lewis v. St. Cloud State University, 467 F.3d 1133 (8th Cir. 2006).
MacPherson v. University of Montevallo, 922 F.2d 766 (11th Cir. 1991).
McDonnell Douglas v. Green, 411 U.S. 792 (1973).
O'Connor v. Consolidated Coin Caterers Corp., 517 U.S. 308 (1996).
Older Workers Benefit Protection Act, 29 U.S.C. § 623(f)(2) (1990).
Texas Department of Community Affairs v. Burdine, 450 U.S. 248 (1981).
Title VII of the Civil Rights Act of 1964, 42 U.S.C. § 2000e (1964).
Wichmann v. Board of Trustees of S. Ill. Univ., 180 F.3d 791 (7th Cir. 1999).

AMERICAN ASSOCIATION OF UNIVERSITY PROFESSORS

The American Association of University Professors (AAUP) was formed in 1915 following a protest over the firing of a faculty member at Stanford University. Noted economist Edward Ross lost his job at Stanford in 1900 because the founder's wife did not agree with his position on economic reform. Arthur O. Lovejoy and six other faculty members resigned in protest over the dismissal of Ross. In 1913, Lovejoy, who by this time had standing in the profession and was working at Johns Hopkins, convinced 17 other full professors to join him in sending a letter of invitation to other professors of equal rank in nine leading universities to discuss an association of professors from all fields of study. John Dewey became the first president at the founding meeting in 1915 to lead an organization that would ensure academic freedom for faculty members. Thus, the AAUP, which has significant legal implications for the professional lives of faculty members and institutions of higher learning, particularly with regard to tenure, promotion, and academic freedom, was formed. Early members of the organization were primarily interested in developing a code of ethics, protecting academic freedom, and developing standards for promotion. Today, the AAUP represents the vast interest, needs, and issues of faculty in higher education. Its purposes are to promote, protect, and advance academic freedom and shared governance, and to define and promote essential standards to ensure quality higher education.

Structure of AAUP

The AAUP is an organization of college and university faculty members with four classes of membership: active, graduate students, retired, and associate members. The association is organized and operated as a nonprofit, charitable educational organization. As stated in the organization's constitution, no part of its assets or profits may benefit an individual except in services rendered (AAUP, 2006).

The governance structure of the AAUP consists of a president, a first vice president, a second vice president, a secretary-treasurer, and a council. The council, as stated in the AAUP's constitution, consists of the president, the vice presidents, the secretary-treasurer, the chair and immediate past-chair of the AAUP's Assembly of State Conferences, the chair and immediate past-chair of the AAUP's Collective Bargaining Congress, former presidents, and 30 council members elected by AAUP members.

Former presidents continue to serve on the council for a period of three years immediately following their terms as president.

The council, which meets at least twice each year, is the elected body charged with executing the AAUP's functions and acts on its behalf as defined in its constitution. From the council membership comes the executive committee, which exercises powers delegated to it and acts on behalf of the association between meetings of the council. The executive committee also meets at least two times per year.

The AAUP has a strong committee structure that reflects its purposes and the issues facing its membership. The standing committees listed on the AAUP Web site are those on academic freedom and tenure; academic professionals; accreditation; college and university governance; economic status of the profession; government relations; graduate and professional students; historically Black institutions and scholars of color; professional ethics; retirement; sexual diversity and gender identity; teaching, research, and publication; and women in the academic profession. Three committees govern special funds, namely, those addressing academic freedom, contingent faculty, and legal defenses, that provide financial support, counseling assistance, and other services to support the AAUP's purposes and policies.

There are two advisory committees in the AAUP. The *Academe* committee advises on matters of the association's magazine, while the litigation committee offers advice on the merits of AAUP *amicus curiae*, or "friend of the court," briefs that are submitted incident to litigation. In addition, AAUP business committees help to guide the organization's business in areas involving investments, audits, nominations, elections, grievances, conferences, sanctions, and interorganizational relationships.

In 2008, the AAUP approved restructuring the organization into three entities to be known as the AAUP, the AAUP Collective Bargaining Congress (AAUP-CBC), and the AAUP Foundation (AAUP, 2008c). According to the AAUP Web site, this changes AAUP's legal existence from a simple 501(C)(3) charitable organization to three conjoined legal entities: a Section 501(C)(3) public charity, a Section 501(C)(6) professional organization, and a Section 501(C)(5) union. In essence, this restructuring allows the AAUP to engage in more intensive fund-raising, lobbying at all levels, program development, and union-related activities.

In its restructuring, the AAUP Collective Bargaining Congress became a separate entity with the purposes of developing and disseminating information and resources in support of collective bargaining (AAUP, 2008b). The AAUP-CBC promotes faculty governance, fair grievance procedures, and economic status of faculty and advances the standards that ensure the quality of American higher education.

As part of the restructuring, the AAUP established a nonprofit foundation for the purpose of accepting donations of money, property, or any other thing of value. Foundation monies are to be spent for educational and charitable purposes including, but not limited to, establishing and supporting principles of academic freedom and quality higher education (AAUP, 2008a).

Activities and Impact of the AAUP

From the beginning, the AAUP focused on the protection of academic freedom and tenure rights. In 1915, the year of its founding, Dewey appointed a committee of 15 to report on academic tenure and freedom. This was the first of 16 committees, with each given an alphabetical designation. Committee A was the committee on academic freedom and tenure. During its first year, five investigations of alleged violations of unjust dismissals were conducted under the purview of Committee A. The first investigations took place at the University of Utah, the University of Colorado, Wesleyan University, the University of Pennsylvania, and the University of Montana. The policy report of Committee A included a general declaration of principles and a set of practical proposals. These investigations brought forth the issues of academic freedom, due process, tenure to protect freedom of inquiry and teaching, and the rights of professors to speak as citizens and as experts in the field, thus setting the future agenda for the fledging organization (Pollitt & Kurland, 1998).

The AAUP publishes *Policy Documents and Reports* (known as the Redbook), which contains the major policy statements of the association. The policy statements support the purposes of the organization and the issues confronting higher education, and they are highly regarded as respected

sources on academic practice. The Redbook includes sections on academic freedom, tenure, and due process; college and university government; professional ethics; research and teaching; distance education and intellectual property; work and family; discrimination; retirement and leaves of absence; collective bargaining; college and university accreditation; and student rights and freedoms. These policy documents have been shown to have influence on college and university rules and procedures. An example is the language developed in the AAUP's *1940 Statement of Principles on Academic Freedom and Tenure*. Trower (2005) reviewed 217 institutions' employment policies in comparison to the recommended institutional regulations of the AAUP, which include the *1940 Statement of Principles on Academic Freedom and Tenure* (AAUP, 2008e).This study found that 92% of the institutions have statements regarding academic freedom, and 48% of the institutions explicitly cite or quote the *1940 Statement* (p. 34).

On the legislative front, the AAUP's government relations office is active in monitoring legislation that challenges the academic freedom of faculty and the intrusion of government control of higher education. One particular issue criticized by the AAUP is the Academic Bill of Rights (ABOR) proposed in nearly two dozen states since 2004. The AAUP's position, as stated on the government relations portion of the association's Web site, is that the ABOR is unnecessary, will compromise rather than enhance academic freedom, and at its core places academic content and faculty appointments with political officials. Currently, advocates of the ABOR are advancing intellectual diversity bills that are similar in context. Other areas of legislative priority for the AAUP are access and affordability of higher education, employee rights and employment conditions, international scholarship and national security, and funding for research.

Turning to the AAUP's legal program, the organization monitors legal developments nationwide pertaining to higher education, presents workshops, and provides resources on areas such as affirmative action, faculty workload, defamation, intellectual property, tenure, educational malpractice, and grading, to name a few. Although the AAUP does not represent individual members, the organization does submit amicus briefs in key appellate court cases. The cases for which the AAUP submits briefs generally involve issues of academic freedom, teaching, collective bargaining, faculty speech, institutional matters, publications, affirmative action, discrimination, and Internet and computer use. The AAUP has submitted amicus briefs in many notable cases, including *University of Pennsylvania v. EEOC* (1990), *Board of Regents of State Colleges v. Roth* (1972), *Perry v. Sindermann* (1972), *Gratz v. Bollinger* (2003), and *Grutter v. Bollinger* (2003).

Annually, individuals make more than 1,000 inquiries to the AAUP (2008d). Many of these grievances are resolved without the necessity of formal complaints. In extreme cases, the members of the AAUP's professional staff may recommend the institutional officials conduct a formal investigation. Investigations are carried out by appointed members of faculties. Investigative reports from 1999 onward can be found on the AAUP's Web site. If the AAUP's membership is convinced that violations are flagrant and that an administration is not open to resolving the issues, they may vote at the annual meeting to censure an institution's administration, not the institution as a whole. Censured administrations are listed by the AAUP on their Web site, and the list is published annually in *Academe*. Institutions may be removed from the censured list only by vote of the membership at the annual meeting. Members of the AAUP are encouraged to seek information on the conditions of academic freedom and tenure prior to accepting appointments at institutions with censured administrations.

The AAUP is recognized as the voice of higher education faculty and has a long history of advocacy. The association relies on its professional staff and the dedication and capacity of volunteer members to promote, protect, and advance academic freedom and shared governance and to define and promote essential standards to ensure quality higher education.

Darlene Y. Bruner

See also Academic Freedom; *Board of Regents of State Colleges v. Roth*; Collective Bargaining; *Gratz v. Bollinger*; *Grutter v. Bollinger*; *Perry v. Sindermann*; Tenure; Unions on Campus; *University of Pennsylvania v. Equal Employment Opportunity Commission*

Further Readings

AAUP. (2006). *Constitution of the association.* Retrieved November 13, 2008, from http://www.aaup.org/AAUP/about/bus/constitution.htm

AAUP. (2008a). Constitution of the AAUP Foundation. *Academe, 94*(2), 126–129.

AAUP. (2008b). Constitution of the Collective Bargaining Congress. *Academe, 94*(2), 120–125.

AAUP. (2008c). *Information on restructuring.* Retrieved November 14, 2008, from http://www.aaup.org/AAUP/about/Restruct

AAUP. (2008d). *Protecting your rights.* Retrieved November 3, 2008, from http://www.aaup.org/AAUP/protect

AAUP. (2008e). *1940 statement of principles on academic freedom and tenure.* Retrieved December 1, 2008, from http://www.aaup.org/NR/rdonlyres/EBB1B330-33D3-4A51-B534-CEE0C7A90DAB/0/1940StatementofPrinciplesonAcademicFreedomandTenure.pdf

Pollitt, D. H., & Kurland, J. E. (1998). The AAUP's first year. *Academe, 84*(4), 45–52.

Trower, C. A. (2005). What is current policy? In R. P. Chait (Ed.), *The questions of tenure* (pp. 33–68). Cambridge, MA: Harvard University Press.

Legal Citations

Board of Regents of State Colleges v. Roth, 408 U.S. 564 (1972).

Gratz v. Bollinger, 539 U.S. 244 (2003).

Grutter v. Bollinger, 539 U.S. 306 (2003).

Perry v. Sindermann, 408 U.S. 593 (1972).

University of Pennsylvania v. EEOC, 493 U.S. 182 (1990).

AMERICAN ASSOCIATION OF UNIVERSITY WOMEN

The American Association of University Women (AAUW) provides support and leadership in equity and equality issues within higher education as well as the larger society. Members of the association include women, men, and institutions that share an interest in removing discrimination and inequality as barriers to the educational, employment, and social opportunities open to women and girls. In advancing its efforts, the AAUW publishes reports, offers professional development, supports research and educational activities, advocates for community and political activities, and works to pass legislation. Following a description of the association's history, this entry provides more details on the AAUW's activities.

History and Structure

The origins of AAUW date back to 1881, when 15 alumnae from eight colleges joined together to create an organization called the Association of Collegiate Alumnae (ACA). As initially formed, the AAUW's mission was to open the doors of higher education to more women and to improve their career choices. As the national organization grew through the establishment of branch chapters, the members of the ACA began researching and writing reports on school conditions and career options, which they published in the *ACA Journal*. By its 25th anniversary, the ACA boasted 3,639 members, 36 branches, and partnerships with 24 colleges and universities. By the ACA's 75th anniversary in 1957, membership had grown to 140,000 members with 1,365 branches and 377 colleges and universities. Today, the AAUW has more than 100,000 members, 1,000 branches, and 500 college and university partners. While the organization has expanded over the years, the mission remains to "advance equity for women and girls through advocacy, education, and research."

Under the original organizational structure, the ACA established an international agenda in 1914 by creating a project to assist women in coming to the United States from other countries. The members of ACA were revolutionary women by the standards of the early 1900s, because all women experienced large-scale social limitations worldwide. By 1919, the ACA had developed additional international exchange and growth opportunities, including the Committee on Vocational Opportunities, Latin America Fellowship, and Committee on International Relations as well as a teacher exchange program with Oxford University. Focusing on domestic issues, members of the ACA argued for equal pay for civil servant jobs and the establishment of a U.S. Department of Education.

In 1921, the ACA merged with the Southern Association of College Women to form what is now the American Association of University Women and established its headquarters just two blocks away from the White House in Washington, D.C. Under the new configuration, the AAUW continued to grow throughout the nation, establish more committees, and expand its range of activities to improve the education and lives of women. The AAUW also continued its international efforts with a Refugee Aid Fund and international grants and obtained permanent observer status in the United Nations.

The AAUW remains actively committed to helping improve the educational, employment, political, and social opportunities open to women. In 1990, the AAUW adopted its current logo of the "W," which helps symbolize and reinforce the organization's focus on education and equality for women. Similarly, in 2004, the organization embraced a new slogan, "Because Equity Is Still an Issue."

Under its current structure, a board of directors governs and oversees the operations of the AAUW. Three officers and seven directors make up the board of directors; the officers include the association president, the Educational Foundation president, and the executive director. The AAUW membership elects the other seven board members at its biennial convention.

The AAUW offers two types of memberships: individual and college/university partner. Prospective individual members must hold at least an associate of arts degree. It is noteworthy that the AAUW began to extend its membership to men holding a college degree in 1987. Enrolled college students are eligible to apply for student affiliate memberships. Moreover, the institutional partnerships add organizational activities via AAUW's Campus Action Project and the National Conference for College Women Student Leaders.

Advocacy and Legislative Involvement

The advocacy initiatives of the AAUW primarily focus on achieving gender equity. To this end, the AAUW promotes the attainment of equal pay for female employees, champions the right of pregnant women both to work and to pursue an education, routinely gathers and produces materials to foster leadership development for women, and actively encourages women to vote and participate in the political process.

As an extension of its advocacy efforts, the AAUW has also played a consistent and crucial role in getting legislation passed to formally support equitable treatment for women. In the early years of the organization, these activists were among the first to picket the White House. In 1917, members of the AAUW held a vigil to draw President Woodrow Wilson's attention to the fact that women still did not have the right to vote. In this instance, the actions of the AAUW helped to promote the drafting and ratification of the Nineteenth Amendment, which finally gave voting rights to women across the United States.

During the 1960s, the AAUW continued to protest and participate in political life by lending its support to both the Civil Rights Act (1964) and the Voting Rights Act (1965). At the same time, the AAUW published documents such as "Action for a Unified Society," "Community Action Bag," and "Congress and You" to educate and urge community involvement and unification. The AAUW continued its legislative involvement in the 1970s with support of the Equal Rights Amendment, Title IX of the Education Amendments of 1972, and the Pregnancy Discrimination Act of 1978. In addition, the organization established a legislative hotline and a Capitol Hill lobby corps to monitor and inform members about gender equity issues receiving legislative attention. In 1977, the AAUW joined over 70 other organizations in the Women's March for Equality. Later, in 1981, the AAUW established a legal advocacy fund to support women filing sex discrimination cases against higher education institutions.

Following the successful passage of legislation of the 1970s, the AAUW continues to promote legislation designed to support gender equity. After years of support, the AAUW saw the Family and Medical Leave Act passed in 1993. During the 1990s, the AAUW also lent its support to various elements of the reauthorization of the Elementary and Secondary Education Act of 1965 (2002) meant to help improve the educational opportunities open to girls and the preparation of teachers.

Campus Support and Activities

Through relationships with its various college and university partners, the AAUW offers numerous additional programs and resources to college students, staff, and faculty. Each summer, the AAUW joins with the National Association of Student Personnel Administrators (NASPA) to offer the National Conference for College Women Student Leaders. With more than 500 college women attending this two-and-a-half day conference, the AAUW and NASPA provide research and presentation sessions that focus on helping women employed in higher education to develop their leadership skills. Moreover, the AAUW's Legal Advocacy Fund Campus Outreach Program seeks to address sexual discrimination or harassment on college campuses.

Nevertheless, AAUW's main campus program is the Campus Action Project, where campus teams of students and faculty design proposals to address a topic chosen by AAUW. For example, the 2008–2009 topic was "Where the Girls Are: Promoting Equity for all Women and Girls," which built upon research released by the association in 2008. As part of the Campus Action Project, the AAUW funded 10 teams to develop and implement their proposals as well as attend the National Conference to present their projects and discuss the impact of their efforts.

Research and Publications

Since its inception, the AAUW has routinely supported and promoted groundbreaking research and publications that impact women in higher education and the workplace as well as publications that more generally address issues related to equality, fair treatment, legislation, and community action. In 1885, still functioning as the ACA, the organization conducted a survey of 1,290 members that produced data that contradicted the contemporary belief that higher education was detrimental to the health of women. In 1978, the association renamed the *AAUW Journal* to *Graduate Woman*, and in 1981, the AAUW created a quarterly magazine called *Leader in Action* to address internal business.

The AAUW has also published self-focused historical works such as *The History of the American*

Association of University Women 1881–1931 (1931) and *AAUW Historic Principles: 1881–2007* (2007), the latter being part of its 125th anniversary celebration. In other publications, the association has focused on sex discrimination specifically in academia with works such as *The Living Wage for College Women* (1938), *Gaining a Foothold: Women's Transitions Through Work and College* (1999), and *Tenure Denied: Cases of Sex Discrimination in Academia* (2004). In the 1990s, the AAUW highlighted its research on girls with landmark reports and books including *Shortchanging Girls, Shortchanging America* (1991), *Schoolgirls: Young Women, Self-Esteem, and the Confidence Gap* (1994), and *Gender Gaps: Where Schools Still Fail Our Children* (1998). Today, the AAUW continues to focus on gender equity with research and reports on pay gaps, sexual harassment on campuses, and gender gaps in K–12 education.

In addition to conducting and publishing its own research, the AAUW also supports research projects on gender and other issues conducted by women. This support is governed through the AAUW Educational Foundation, and the association has a distinguished history of providing scholarships and fellowships to women. In 1888, Ida Street of the University of Michigan received the first fellowship from the Western Association of Collegiate Alumnae just prior to its 1889 merger with the ACA. In 1917, the association awarded its first international fellowship to Virginia P. Alvarez Hussey to support her studies at the Women's Medical College of Pennsylvania. Prominently, members of the AAUW also provided $156,413 to Marie Curie to purchase one gram of radium, which she used to do the research for which she won a Nobel Prize. Presently, the AAUW offers a variety of scholarships, fellowships, and grants to support women seeking to complete research, degrees, and other educational activities.

Notable Women

The AAUW has honored, supported, and benefited from the work and contributions of numerous women both in and outside of higher education. At its biennial convention, the association chooses women to acknowledge for their social, educational, political, and scientific contributions with the AAUW's Achievement Award. Some previous recipients include Florence Siebert, who won the inaugural AAUW Achievement Award for her invention of the first reliable tuberculosis test (1943); Jeannette Rankin, first woman elected to a congressional office, in 1916, in Montana (1976); Margaret Mead, anthropologist (1978); Eudora Welty, Pulitzer Prize–winning writer (1985); Marian Wright Edelman, founder of the Children's Defense Fund (1987); Sandra Day O'Connor, first woman appointed to the U.S. Supreme Court (1988); and Gloria Steinem, feminist leader and cofounder of *Ms.* magazine (2003).

Saran Donahoo and Tamara Yakaboski

See also Civil Rights Movement; Equal Protection Analysis; Title VI; Title VII

Further Readings

Corbett, C., Hill, C., & St. Rose, A. (2008). *Where the girls are: The facts about gender equity in education.* Washington, DC: AAUW Educational Foundation.

Costain, A. N. (1980). The struggle for a national women's lobby: Organizing a diffuse interest. *The Western Political Quarterly, 33*(4), 476–491.

Dey, J. G., & Hill, C. (2007). *Behind the pay gap.* Washington, DC: AAUW Educational Foundation.

Kohlstedt, S. G. (2004). Sustaining gains: Reflections on women in science and technology in 20th century United States. *NWSA Journal, 16*(1), 1–26.

Snider, C. J. (2005). Patriots and pacifists: The rhetorical debate about peace, patriotism, and internationalism, 1914–1930. *Rhetoric & Public Affairs, 8*(1), 59–83.

Wright, S. (2007). Education for liberation: Race, class, gender, and the history of education. *Journal of Women's History, 19*(2), 202–209.

Legal Citations

Civil Rights Act of 1964, Pub. L. No. 88-352.

Elementary and Secondary Education Act of 1965, Pub. L. No. 107-110 (2002).

Family and Medical Leave Act of 1993, Pub. L. No. 103-3 (1993).

Pregnancy Discrimination Act of 1978, Pub. L. No. 95-555.

Title IX of the Education Amendments of 1972, 20 U.S.C. § 1681 (2008).

Voting Rights Act of 1965, Pub. L. No. 89-110.

AMERICANS WITH DISABILITIES ACT

The Americans with Disabilities Act (ADA), which was signed into law by President George H. W. Bush in 1990, protects an array of individuals with disabilities at colleges and universities from discrimination by imposing comprehensive obligations on private sector employers, public services and accommodations, and transportation. In this respect, the ADA effectively extends the reach of Section 504 of the Rehabilitation Act of 1973 to the private sector and programs that do not received federal financial assistance.

The purpose of the ADA, as stated in its preamble, is "to provide a clear and comprehensive national mandate for the elimination of discrimination against individuals with disabilities" (42 U.S.C. § 12101). The ADA provides protections similar to those of the Civil Rights Act of 1964, which prohibits discrimination on the basis of race, color, religion, sex, and national origin. The ADA was recently amended by the Americans with Disabilities Act Amendments Act of 2008 (ADAAA). The ADAAA expanded the ADA's definition of disability as it had been interpreted by the courts.

Definition of Disability

The ADA provides a comprehensive federal directive for covered entities to eliminate discrimination against individuals with disabilities and to provide "clear, strong, consistent and enforceable standards" (42 U.S.C. § 12101(b)(2)) to help achieve this goal. The ADA defines an individual with a disability as one who has "(a) a physical or mental impairment that substantially limits one or more of the major life activities; (b) a record of such an impairment; or (c) being regarded as having such an impairment" (42 U.S.C. § 12102(2)). The ADAAA makes it clear that this definition covers persons who suffer from epilepsy, diabetes, cancer, multiple sclerosis, and other ailments even though measures may be taken to mitigate the effects of their conditions. On the other hand, the amendments specifically provide an exception so that employers can consider the mitigating effects of ordinary eyeglasses or contact lenses in determining whether visual impairments substantially limit major life activities. The ADA defines major life

activities as caring for oneself, hearing, walking, speaking, seeing, breathing, and learning. The ADA does not require individuals to have certificates from doctors or psychologists in order to be covered by its provisions.

The ADA specifically excludes a variety of individuals from its protections. In particular, those who use illegal drugs (42 U.S.C. § 12210); are transvestites (42 U.S.C. § 12208); are homosexuals and bisexuals (42 U.S.C. § 12211(a)); are transsexuals, pedophiles, exhibitionists, voyeurs, and those with sexual behavior disorders (42 U.S.C. § 12211(b)); and those with conditions such as psychoactive substance use disorders stemming from current illegal use of drugs (42 U.S.C. § 12211(c)) are not protected by the ADA.

The ADA's Five Titles

The ADA has five major sections or titles, as they are known. Title I, which protects individuals with disabilities with regard to employment in the private sector, is directly applicable to private postsecondary institutions. It is specifically applicable to the hiring process as well as the promotion and discharge of employees. This title requires employers to make reasonable accommodations for otherwise qualified individuals once they are aware of the individuals' conditions. This means that in order to be covered by the ADA, employees need to inform appropriate authorities within the institutions of their conditions and provide specific suggestions on how their needs can be met.

Title II applies to the public services of state and local governments for both employers and providers, including transportation, and especially education, because part of this title applies to public educational institutions. Under this title, state and local agencies are required to comply with regulations that are similar to those found in Section 504 of the Rehabilitation Act that cover access to all programs offered by a recipient of federal funds. Title II requires covered entities to provide accessible transportation.

Title III covers public accommodations. To the extent that this section applies to both the private and public sectors, it expands the scope of Section 504. Title III includes private businesses and a wide array of community services, including buildings on or off college and university campuses, transportation systems, parks, recreational facilities, hotels, and theaters. Insofar as the definition of public accommodations includes places of lodging, it applies to educational facilities that have dormitories or other residential facilities such as on-campus hotels. Title III also applies to recreation and dining facilities. Accordingly, Title III is particularly relevant to institutions of higher education that provide residence and dining services for students, faculty, staff, and visitors.

Title IV addresses telecommunications, specifically voice and nonvoice systems. As such, Title IV applies to any educational institution of higher learning that offers common communication systems to its students. Further, Title IV may require officials on campuses to install systems to allow individuals with disabilities to communicate to the same extent as others who are not disabled.

Title V contains the ADA's miscellaneous provisions. Pursuant to Title V, the ADA cannot be construed to apply a lesser standard than that under Section 504 and its regulations, and qualified individuals are not required to accept services that fall short of meeting their needs. Title V also contains an antiretaliation provision.

Students

In order to bring successful discrimination claims under the ADA, students bear the burden of proving that they suffered from adverse actions due to their disabilities. In the past, students with disabilities generally have been unsuccessful where officials in educational institutions can show that they had legitimate, nondiscriminatory reasons for taking adverse actions. Even so, when students claim to have disabilities that require accommodations, officials in institutions of higher education must conduct individualized inquiries into the students' situations before making any decisions.

In order to be protected by the ADA, students must substantiate that they have disabilities as defined by the statute, are otherwise qualified, and require reasonable accommodations. As indicated above, the determination of whether students have disabilities is an individualized inquiry that ordinarily depends on specific factual situations. To the extent that a great deal depends on the degree to which impairments affect individuals' abilities to participate in major life activities, whether a student

with disabilities is covered by the ADA can vary according to the particular circumstances. An impairment that may qualify as a disability for one person in a given situation may not for another under different circumstances. For example, whether a student who has learning disabilities requires accommodations may depend on the extent to which those disabilities affect the student's functioning in a given activity. Such a student may require assistance with note taking in a lecture course but not require any accommodations in a hands-on course. Ironically, prior academic success may show that a student's learning impairment does not affect the major life activity of learning, rather than necessarily showing that a student has succeeded in spite of the disability.

Courts do not uphold discrimination claims filed on behalf of students with disabilities who do not meet minimum requirements for admission or maintenance in educational programs. Postsecondary institutions do not have to lower their admission standards or provide more than reasonable accommodations to admit students with disabilities. Once accepted, students with disabilities may be required to meet the usual standards for progression. Thus, institutions of higher education may dismiss students with disabilities for failing to meet the usual academic requirements. Although officials in institutions must provide reasonable accommodations so that students with disabilities can achieve, they are not required to alter their fundamental entrance or programmatic requirements on the behalf of such students. Courts usually defer to the expertise of educational officials when evaluating whether requirements are essential to the nature of their programs. Still, the burden of proof rests on officials to demonstrate the existence of a relationship between an institutional requirement and what is expected by the professions that the programs are preparing students to enter.

A fair body of litigation has developed over the denial of requests for testing accommodations for students with disabilities. Institutions of higher learning must provide accommodations in how tests are administered but are not required to modify the contents of the tests themselves for qualified students. The purpose of testing accommodations is to allow students to be tested effectively on their knowledge and not be at an unfair disadvantage due to their disabilities. Thus, accommodations should not provide students with disabilities with an advantage over other students who are not disabled. Even so, students may be required to demonstrate that the requested modifications are actually related to their disabilities.

Employees

Employees must be able to demonstrate that they have covered impairments, that they have been treated differently from staff members who do not have disabilities, and that they have been the victims of adverse decisions based on their impairments in order to maintain successful discrimination suits under the ADA. As an initial matter, courts usually reject outright discrimination claims when employees' impairments are not covered by the ADA. Furthermore, employees with disabilities cannot succeed with discrimination claims if they lack the essential skills needed to perform jobs even with reasonable accommodations. In such situations, courts, by and large, rule in favor of employers as long as they can demonstrate that they made adverse employment decisions for essentially nondiscriminatory reasons.

Employees with disabilities are otherwise qualified if they can perform all essential requirements of their positions in spite of their impairments. When employees cannot perform essential job functions, even with reasonable accommodations, courts generally do not consider them to be otherwise qualified under the ADA. One of the essential job requirements in educational systems, particularly for instructors, is regular attendance. In this respect, employees who are unable to be present physically in campus workplaces in a reliable and predictable way are not otherwise qualified for their jobs. (Of course, institutions might be able to accommodate faculty members by allowing them to teach online, because their physical presence is unnecessary in such arrangements.) Not only are instructors expected to be present physically in classrooms, but they must also interact appropriately with students. Instructional personnel whose disabilities render them unable to interact with students are not otherwise qualified for positions that involve sustained contact with large groups of students. Consequently, since teaching is generally considered to be an essential function of an instructor's job, the inability to teach in classrooms in most situations means that individuals cannot meet all of the requirements of being instructors in spite of their impairments.

The ADA does not protect incompetent employees or those who exhibit poor performance, and employees with disabilities may be dismissed for incompetence in the same manner as other employees. Moreover, the ADA also does not protect employees who commit acts of misconduct, even when their behavior can be attributed to their disabilities. Employers are allowed to take appropriate disciplinary action against employees who commit acts of misconduct, regardless of whether they have disabilities.

Under the ADA, employers must provide reasonable accommodations so that otherwise qualified employees with disabilities can work and compete with their colleagues who do not have disabilities. Accommodations may involve such things as renovations to the physical environment, adjustments to work schedules, or minor modifications to job responsibilities. Employers are neither required to make accommodations that would essentially change the nature of the jobs nor obligated to reassign employees with disabilities to other positions. Even so, employers may have to reassign individuals who are unable to perform essential job functions with reasonable accommodations if there exists, or soon will exist, vacant positions with duties that these individuals are able to perform. Although employers are not required to make accommodations if doing so would place undue burdens on their operations, the burden of proof that requested accommodations would create undue financial or administrative burdens generally rests on employers. Thus, employers must prove that employees or applicants are unfit rather than having individuals demonstrate that they are eligible to perform job duties with reasonable accommodations.

Allan G. Osborne, Jr.

See also Civil Rights Act of 1964; Rehabilitation Act, Section 504

Further Readings

Russo, C. J., & Osborne, A. G. (2009). *Section 504 and the ADA.* Thousand Oaks, CA: Corwin.

Legal Citations

Americans with Disabilities Act, 42 U.S.C. §§ 12101 *et seq.*

Americans with Disabilities Act Amendments Act of 2008, Pub. L. No. 110-325.

Rehabilitation Act of 1973, Section 504, 29 U.S.C. §§ 794 *et seq.*

ASSISTIVE TECHNOLOGY

Assistive technology refers to the use of technological devices and situational modifications by or for individuals with disabilities to enable them to improve or maintain their functional capabilities. Because students with disabilities at institutions of higher education may use assistive technology in demonstrating their ability to meet the requirements of the programs in which they are enrolled, college and university personnel need to be cognizant of relevant legal issues. This entry provides an overview of federal legislation related to assistive technology and examines the ways in which assistive technology can enable students with disabilities to use such devices to meet the requirements of the programs for which they are qualified.

Assistive Technology Defined

While the impact of technology on the lives of persons both with and without disabilities has become pervasive, the use of certain types of technologies, known as assistive technology, has enabled individuals with disabilities to expand their functional repertoires and access environments and activities that, historically, have been inaccessible to them. Broadly speaking, the term *assistive technology* refers to two elements: devices and services.

Assistive technology devices are technological devices that enable individuals to maintain or improve their functional capabilities. An example of an assistive technology device that is common in institutions of higher learning is a desktop computer with voice recognition software. This assistive technology enables individuals with physical disabilities that prevent them from writing using pens or keyboards to produce legible texts by talking to their computers. Assistive technology services

enable individuals with disabilities to select appropriate devices to use, be taught how to use them, and to maintain the equipment in good working order. Hence the term *assistive technology* refers both to the devices and services that comprise the technological solutions that enable individuals with disabilities to maintain or improve on their functional capabilities.

Legislation on Assistive Technology in Higher Education

One subset of the population of persons with disabilities who can benefit from the use of assistive technology consists of students, both those enrolled in K–12 public schools and those enrolled in institutions of higher education, including community colleges, colleges, and universities. Although federal (and state) laws work in concert to direct the use of assistive technologies by qualified students, this entry focuses on relevant federal statutes, because they are so pervasive in scope.

The key statute at the K–12 level is the Individuals with Disabilities Education Act (IDEA, 2004). The IDEA mandates the provision of special education services, which may include the use of assistive technology, for all qualified students with disabilities between the ages of 3 and 21, inclusive. The IDEA has played a key role in promoting the use of assistive technology. This act states that because disabilities are a natural part of the human experience, their presence does not diminish the rights of individuals with disabilities to benefit from receiving an education.

There are two key elements of the IDEA with regard to assistive technology. First, all qualified students with disabilities are entitled to receive appropriate special education and related services, including assistive technology. Second, assistive technology can be provided in the form of special education, a related service, or a supplementary aid, service, or support. Further, assistive technology has been designated as one of five "special factors," which means that the need for its use by every student who is eligible for special education services under the law must be addressed annually in evaluating student progress.

To the extent that K–12 public schools are placing students ages 18 or older with moderate or more significant disabilities in specially designed programs that are located on campuses at institutions of higher education so that they can be in age-appropriate settings, the aforementioned elements of the IDEA are relevant. Consequently, although the IDEA does not generally apply in higher education, personnel at colleges and universities need to be cognizant of the circumstances under which it can come into play for specifically identified students with disabilities.

Two other federal statutes that prohibit discrimination based on disability by institutions of higher education govern the use of assistive technology by persons with disabilities who are officially enrolled in their programs. Section 504 of the Rehabilitation Act of 1973 prohibits institutions that receive federal financial assistance from discriminating on the basis of disability. On the other hand, the Americans with Disabilities Act (ADA, 1990) extends the prohibitions of discrimination based on disability to most public and private institutions of higher education regardless of whether they receive federal funds. While the nuances of which institutions of higher education are excluded from the provisions of Section 504 and the ADA is beyond the scope of this entry, the remainder of this discussion focuses on students and circumstances under which both laws apply.

Section 504 and the ADA protect students who have disabilities, who are "otherwise qualified" for the educational program or higher education activities in which they wish to participate, and who can do so by means of reasonable accommodations. Students are considered to "have disabilities" if they have physical or mental impairments that substantially limit one or more major life activities (such as learning, seeing, hearing, speaking, performing manual tasks, or caring for themselves), if they have a record of such impairments, or if they are regarded as having such impairments.

In addition to this legislation, the Assistive Technology Act of 2004 focuses on delivering assistive technology directly to persons with disabilities. Whereas its predecessor, the Technology-Related Assistance for Individuals with Disabilities Act of 1988, enabled states to develop infrastructures for the purpose of getting assistive technology to persons with disabilities, the Assistive Technology Act of 2004 shifted the focus to direct-aid programs, such as assistive technology reutilization programs and device loan programs.

Assistive Technology in Practice

Students are "qualified" for programs or activities in higher education if they meet the academic and technical standards required for admission or participation by means of reasonable accommodation; of course, students can qualify and not need such accommodations. Examples of such higher education programs, services, and activities for which students with disabilities can ask to use an assistive technology include, but are not limited to, academics, admissions, research, counseling, athletics, recreation, and transportation.

The primary reason students with disabilities seek to use assistive technology is so that they can participate in programs, services, and activities for the purpose of obtaining the same benefits as their peers who are not disabled. Once students with disabilities have proven that they are qualified for programs, services, or activities, they must be provided with the means to overcome any limitations that may result from their impairments so that they can benefit from the programs.

The process that students with disabilities must follow in procuring assistive technology varies from one institution to the next. At many colleges and universities, the process is handled by a Section 504 or ADA coordinator, typically operating out of the institution's office for student services. Regardless of the exact process that is followed, public institutions must give primary consideration to students' requests, meaning that officials must honor these preferences unless they can demonstrate that equally effective alternative accommodations exist. Private institutions may decide unilaterally what a student needs as long as it results in effective accommodation. Institutions may not charge students for the cost of assistive technology devices that the institutions are required to provide by law.

Either type of institution may be relieved of the requirement to provide accommodation for a student with disabilities using one of three defenses under these laws: Institutions need not provide accommodation if it would be excessively costly; if it would require significant alterations in the nature of a program, such as in a case where a blind student was denied admission to medical school; or if the presence of the student with a disability would result in health or safety risks to the student or others.

As for the types of assistive technologies students might request, it must be noted that neither Section 504 nor the ADA uses the term *assistive technology*. Rather, both laws refer to services and modifications need by qualified individuals with disabilities. Yet many of the services and modifications that can meet the needs of these students are considered to be assistive technology in accordance with the information about assistive technology as described here. Such assistive technologies might include speech-generating devices, assistive listening devices, voice recognition software, talking calculators, Braille printers and typewriters, large keyboards, and books on tape, as well as humans providing assistance by interpreting speech or taking notes.

As noted, students with disabilities seek to use assistive technology so that they can obtain the same benefits from a program, service, or activity as their equally qualified, nondisabled peers. However, in order to obtain these benefits, it is reasonable to recognize that students' uses of assistive technology must occur within circumstances that are meant to be all-inclusive. To this end, the provisions of Section 504 and the ADA direct officials in institutions of higher education to avoid engaging in discriminatory actions that would hinder the educational experiences of all students with disabilities, including those who use assistive technology. Appropriate actions institutions may engage in for the purpose of complying with applicable laws and creating an atmosphere of inclusivity that supports the use of assistive technology include administering programs in the most integrated setting appropriate to student needs, allowing students opportunities to participate in programs or activities that are not separate or different even if colleges or universities have permissibly separate or different programs, and selecting sites and locating facilities that can readily enable students with disabilities to use these facilities or services.

Timothy E. Morse

See also Americans with Disabilities Act; Distance Learning; Rehabilitation Act, Section 504

Legal Citations

Americans with Disabilities Act, 42 U.S.C. §§ 12101 *et seq.* (1990).
Assistive Technology Act, 29 U.S.C. §§ 3001 *et seq.* (2004).
Individuals with Disabilities Education Act, 20 U.S.C. §§ 1400 *et seq.* (2004).
Rehabilitation Act of 1973, Section 504, 29 U.S.C. §§ 794 *et seq.*
Technology-Related Assistance for Individuals with Disabilities Act, 29 U.S.C. § 2201 *et seq.* (1988).

ASSOCIATION FOR THE STUDY OF HIGHER EDUCATION

The mission of the Association for the Study of Higher Education (ASHE) is to encourage scholarly inquiry to increase knowledge and understanding of higher education in all of its multifaceted dimensions. ASHE promotes collaboration between and among its members and others who are engaged in the study of higher education through encouraging its members to engage in research, attend its conferences, and publish their findings. ASHE has been an important organization in providing networking and academic resources for the rapidly growing field of higher education degree and research programs. It currently has about 2,000 members.

Following its formation in 1976, ASHE members expanded research in graduate programs and continued to serve as a forum for discussion of graduate study in higher education. Sessions at ASHE's annual meeting typically consider course content, curriculum, and syllabi with recommendations for doctoral programs in the field of higher education through analysis of future employment needs. Currently, ASHE's headquarters is at the College of Education at the University of Nevada, Las Vegas.

Advocacy and Research on Doctoral Programs

Doctoral programs in higher education have been started and expanded as the need of universities to obtain specialized education for administrators at various levels has grown. In fact, a doctorate in higher education has become a route to positions in both administration and student personnel services. As university governance grew more complex with increased demands for research on state administrative and legislative needs, graduate higher education departments expanded their offerings and expertise into areas of finance, governance, law, college teaching, history and philosophy of higher education, research courses, faculty, students, and student personnel services. ASHE members contributed to making the study of higher education in colleges of education an academic discipline, taking its place with other academic programs. The history of higher education provides a background for the formation of ASHE in addressing challenges and opportunities facing the field, issues that its members continue to address in their research and publications.

Teaming up with other major organizations, ASHE members undertook research studies dealing with issues facing students, administrators, staff, and legislative funding issues. Due to the growing complexity of institutions of higher education, various components of doctoral programs were established, modified, and updated. Often, members of ASHE worked with their college of education deans and deans of other colleges to expand the role and function of higher education graduate programs. Doctoral programs in the field are often multidisciplinary, using the expertise of faculty of colleges of business, law, and liberal arts.

Research on Educational Equity and Access

ASHE members have consistently engaged in critical policy and equity research through quantitative and qualitative research methods, addressing issues of race, sex, diversity, and ethnicity in their research and publications. Expanding equity and access to higher education for minorities and low-income students continues to be a major focus for their research. ASHE devotes special attention to underrepresented groups in order to increase their involvement and research activities among its ranks. At the same time, student activism in higher education has resulted in increased attention to certain issues, leading ASHE to expand its focus to a range of issues including sex and race discrimination, adequate

facilities for women's athletic programs, and the needs of a growing nontraditional student population. Other topics that have also come to the fore for ASHE and institutions of higher learning recently focused on adult and lifelong learning programs for fulfilling institutional missions, the development of active learning strategies in instruction, student retention, dropouts, and mental health issues.

ASHE established an Institute on Equity Research Methods and Critical Policy Analysis. Like ASHE's other targeted programs, this institute is a collaborative effort with the University of California at Los Angeles, the Center for Urban Education at the University of Southern California, and the Institute for Higher Education Law and Governance at the University of Houston Law Center. The institute addresses minority student and population issues, targeting inequalities that exist for African Americans, Latinos, Native Americans, and Native Hawaiians. The institute's focus is to support more inclusion with the development of a core group of minority scholars with knowledge and research skills to study these issues. Finding ways to give greater visibility to the needs and interests of minority communities as well as to have more emphasis on recognizing minority scholars for their work in the field is an ongoing process. The University of Houston Law Center, for example, has been active in these outreach efforts. The institute seeks to address the historical and current inequalities that exist for minorities. As the U.S. Supreme Court grapples with the use of race and reverse discrimination in university admissions processes, universities are developing a wide range of strategies to ensure diversity among faculty and students. Affirmative action initiatives continue to be a focus of higher education.

From *Regents of the University of California v. Bakke* (1978) to *Parents Involved in Community Schools v. Seattle School District No. 1* (2007), the Supreme Court has continued to address issues of equity, access, and reverse discrimination in higher education and beyond. At the same time, ASHE members have analyzed state and federal court rulings as they affect higher education institutions.

The 1947, the Truman administration issued the *Higher Education for a Democracy* report, which called for expansion of higher education through two-year junior colleges and community colleges, institutions that were designed to use low tuition to provide easy access to a postsecondary education. Originally, many faculty members in these colleges were public school teachers with master's degrees who worked part-time in higher education. Over the ensuing years, though, community colleges expanded their offerings while growing in size and complexity. In recent years, many community colleges have become four-year colleges offering professional courses not given or with limited offerings in larger colleges and universities. Community colleges enroll the largest number of postsecondary students.

The U.S. Department of Education, under the direction of Secretary of Education Margaret Spellings, issued a report called *A Test of Leadership: Charting the Future of U.S. Higher Education* in 2006. Like the Truman report, the Spellings report called for increased student access to higher education at reasonable cost. Stressing increased quality of learning, transparency, and accountability as well as innovation, the report called for measurable and meaningful student learning outcomes. In addition, the report stressed the need to ensure that college and university costs are affordable. The Spellings report also contained recommendations for strengthening levels of retention and student achievement in colleges and universities.

Publications

ASHE sponsors, in whole or part, the *Review of Higher Education,* the *ASHE Higher Education Report Series,* and the *ASHE Reader Series* serving the academic community. In the *Reader Series,* previously published articles and book chapters are organized and edited into volumes on topics of interest to teachers and students in higher education graduate programs. The series is designed to help prepare higher education administrators, faculty, researchers, and policy makers for work in the field. With Amaury Nora as the editor of the *Review* since 2003, it serves as a model of excellence in design, format, and content. As with other journals, researchers have access to full *Review* articles through the Internet.

Recent articles in the *Review* reflect current issues in higher education. One of these is the nationwide concern of providing safe campus learning environments for students and faculty; to this end, many colleges and universities are instituting campuswide alert systems. Another issue is finding ways to maintain essential individual privacy while seeking information about possible aggressive and threatening student mental health problems. Academic dishonesty due to the ease of plagiarizing from articles and materials on the Internet is another topic that the *Review* examines. Moreover, the *Review* addresses the role of faculty in supervising student work as well as the social dimensions of student discipline, reflecting efforts to encourage student honesty and integrity. Other topics that the *Review* has covered are underrepresented minorities and faculty pay inequities along with peer review of faculty productivity and teaching effectiveness.

Academic Networking

University administrators increasingly rely on organizations such as ASHE to keep abreast of developments in the field. ASHE provides a place where faculty, administrators, and staff in higher education graduate programs can engage in networking. Often, doctoral candidates in colleges of education serve in internships in colleges and universities. They work in a variety of positions including financial aid, admissions, student unions, recruiting, and other student personnel services. Higher education degree graduates fill positions in these and other university administrative and services departments. Here, they are able to apply educational theories to practice. Top-level administrators, including university and college presidents, with a few notable exceptions, have doctoral degrees in academic disciplines. Higher education degree graduates often fill middle management positions. ASHE's annual meetings provide opportunities for higher education graduate students and junior faculty to report on their research efforts.

Membership in the Association for the Study of Higher Education includes a subscription to the aforementioned *Review of Higher Education,* through which ASHE provides a Web site with a job and career center, a searchable directory of higher education degree programs in the United States, and a special "what's new" section. ASHE remains an important organization due to its ongoing contributions to the ever-expanding field of higher education research and study.

ASHE members have supported efforts to strengthen requirements for advanced degrees in higher education, adding in-depth research components, thereby making higher education degrees much sought after for many administrators and staff who already have positions at universities and colleges but seek to strengthen and update their administrative skills to receive higher financial rewards. ASHE also has a global outreach through its members and contacts throughout the world. It has always had a strong international component, with members from other countries contributing to annual meetings. Internationalism is also evident in the diversity of student, faculty, and staff populations in higher education degree programs. ASHE also offers preconference forums in public policy and international higher education at its annual conferences.

Ethical Standards and Accreditation

ASHE has incorporated principles of ethical conduct in its commitment to maintaining high standards of conduct, research, and professional responsibility. Ensuring proper attribution for contributors to research and publication as well as taking responsibility for individual and group work is an important ethical principle for ASHE. Members of ASHE are cautioned and encouraged to maintain professional respect and civility in their relationships and interactions with others.

Issues such as distance learning and the growing number of part-time, contingency, and adjunct faculty members with limited support services and job security have also been subjects of research for ASHE members. As institutions such as the University of Phoenix represent a trend in new instructional strategies with growing enrollment of distance learning students, accreditation, faculty preparation, assessment, and accountability have been a challenge to this growing educational delivery system. Concerns about educational quality have led to accreditation procedures for a variety of educational distance delivery systems, topics of interest for ASHE members' research.

James J. Van Patten

See also Affirmative Action; Civil Rights Movement; Fourteenth Amendment; Intellectual Property

Further Readings

Baldwin, R. G., & Thelin, J. R. (1990). Thanks for the memories: The fusion of quantitative and qualitative research on college students and the college experience. *Higher Education: Handbook of Theory and Research, 6,* 337–360.

Berdahl, R. (2001). Apologia pro vita mia. *Higher Education: Handbook of Theory and Research, 16,* 1–24.

Fife, J. D., & Goodchild, L. F (1991). Administration as a profession. *New Directions for Higher Education, 76,* 103–114.

President's Commission on Higher Education. (1947). *Higher education for a democracy, a report.* New York: Harper.

A test of leadership: Charting the future of U.S. higher education. (2006). A report of the Commission appointed by Secretary of Education Margaret Spellings. Washington, DC: U.S. Department of Education.

Townsend, B. K. (1990). Doctoral study in the field of higher education. *Higher Education: Handbook of Theory and Research, 6,* 161–199.

Legal Citations

Parents Involved in Community Schools v. Seattle School District No. 1, 127 S. Ct. 2738 (2007).

Regents of the University of California v. Bakke, 438 U.S. 265 (1978).

B

BEREA COLLEGE V. KENTUCKY

Berea College v. Kentucky (1908) is a significant civil rights case in higher education that paved the way for subsequent judicial decisions that struck down segregated educational facilities as unconstitutional. Even so, the U.S. Supreme Court did not take an integrationist stance in *Berea*. Instead, the Court upheld a law from Kentucky that prohibited individuals and corporations from operating schools that taught both African American and White students.

Since its founding in 1855, Berea College had educated both African American and White students in a nondiscriminatory manner. However, in 1904, the Kentucky legislature passed the Day Law, which prohibited African American and White students from receiving an education at the same school or in schools that were located less than 25 miles apart. Insofar as Berea College was the only integrated educational institution school in Kentucky, it was clearly the target of the Day Law. Not surprisingly, Berea College was soon found to be in violation of the new legislation. Accordingly, Berea College was criminally convicted and fined $1,000 for violating the Day Law. Berea College appealed to the Court of Appeals of Kentucky, which decided that the law had the legitimate purpose of preventing racial violence and interracial marriage. Thus, the law and Berea College's fine were permitted to stand.

On further review, in 1908, in a seven-to-two judgment, the Supreme Court affirmed the decision of the Kentucky Court of Appeals, which had ruled in favor of the commonwealth. The *Berea* Court majority was careful not to overrule its earlier opinion in *Plessy v. Ferguson* (1896), which maintained that separate but equal facilities for Blacks and Whites were constitutional under the Fourteenth Amendment to the U.S. Constitution. In fact, the Court extended *Plessy's* rationale to include institutions of higher education. In order to follow precedent, the *Berea* Court did not base its judgment on Fourteenth Amendment grounds. Rather, the Court was of the view that Kentucky was legally able to change a past charter of one of its corporations. In other words, even though Berea College was still legally incorporated, the Court asserted that officials in Kentucky could amend the institution's original charter through the subsequent legislation. In this way, then, the Day Law made it illegal for Berea College to admit both Black and White students. In essence, the *Berea* majority ignored the college's argument that because voluntary and private association was protected by the Due Process Clause of the Fourteenth Amendment, it was beyond the scope of governmental regulation. To the contrary, the Court determined that because Kentucky could create Berea College as a corporation, commonwealth officials also had the legal authority to limit the activities of such corporations.

Two justices concurred with the majority's decision, and two justices dissented. Justice John Marshall Harlan strongly dissented, arguing that the purpose of the Kentucky legislature in passing the Day Law was not simply to amend Berea College's charter. Rather, he reasoned that the title of the law, "An Act to Prohibit White and Colored Persons from Attending the Same School," made it clear that its purpose was to segregate students on the basis of race. In light of this clear discriminatory legislative intent, Justice Harlan thought that it was unconstitutional under the Fourteenth Amendment's Due Process Clause. Specifically, he pointed out that the right to teach was a protected property right and a fundamental liberty. Harlan warned that by allowing Kentucky to prohibit teaching Black and White students in the same school, the Court was opening the door to allow jurisdictions to regulate whether Blacks and Whites could voluntary worship next to one another. Harlan vehemently opposed the government's intrusion on private and voluntary association among the races. Almost 50 years after it resolved *Berea*, in *Brown v. Board of Education, Topeka* (1954), the Supreme Court adopted a position that was not unlike Justice Harlan's in striking down racially segregated educational facilities as unconstitutional.

Janet R. Rumple

See also Due Process, Substantive and Procedural; Fourteenth Amendment; *McLaurin v. Oklahoma State Regents for Higher Education; Sweatt v. Painter*

Further Readings

Hacker, H. J., & Blake, W. D. (2006). The neutrality principle: The hidden yet powerful legal axiom at work in Brown versus Board of Education. *Berkeley Journal of African-American Law & Policy, 8,* 5–59.

Legal Citations

Berea College v. Kentucky, 211 U.S. 45 (1908).
Brown v. Board of Education, Topeka, 347 U.S. 483 (1954).
Plessy v. Ferguson, 163 U.S. 537 (1896).

BEREA COLLEGE V. KENTUCKY

In *Berea College,* the Supreme Court upheld a criminal conviction against a private college in Kentucky for violating a commonwealth statute against teaching African American and White students together.

Supreme Court of the United States

BEREA COLLEGE

v.

COMMONWEALTH OF KENTUCKY

211 U.S. 45

Argued April 10, 13, 1908

Decided November 9, 1908

Statement by Mr. Justice Brewer:

On October 8, 1904, the grand jury of Madison county, Kentucky, presented in the circuit court of that county an indictment, charging:

The said Berea College, being a corporation duly incorporated under the laws of the state of Kentucky, and owning, maintaining, and operating a college, school, and institution of learning, known as 'Berea College,' located in the town of Berea, Madison county, Kentucky, did unlawfully and wilfully permit and receive both the white and negro races as pupils for instruction in said college, school, and institution of learning.

This indictment was found under an act of March 22, 1904 whose 1st section reads:

Sec. 1. That it shall be unlawful for any person, corporation, or association of persons to maintain or operate any college, school, or institution where persons of the white and negro races are both received as pupils for instruction, and any person or corporation who shall operate or maintain any such college, school, or institution shall be fined $1,000, and any person or corporation who may be convicted of violating the provisions of this act shall be fined $100 for each day they may operate said school, college, or institution after such conviction.

On a trial the defendant was found guilty and sentenced to pay a fine of $1,000. This judgment was, on June 12, 1906, affirmed by the court of appeals of the state and from that court brought here on writ of error.

Mr. Justice Brewer delivered the opinion of the court:

There is no dispute as to the facts. That the act does not violate the Constitution of Ketucky is settled by the decision of its highest court, and the single question for our consideration is whether it conflicts with the Federal Constitution. The court of appeals discussed at some length the general power of the state in respect to the separation of the two races. It also ruled that 'the right to teach white and negro children in a private school at the same time and place is not a property right. Besides, appellant, as a corporation created by this state, has no natural right to teach at all. Its right to teach is such as the state sees fit to give to it. The state may withhold it altogether, or qualify it.

. . . when a state court decides a case upon two grounds, one Federal and the other non-Federal, this court will not disturb the judgment if the non-Federal ground, fairly construed, sustains the decision.

Again, the decision by a state court of the extent and limitation of the powers conferred by the state upon one of its own corporations is of a purely local nature. In creating a corporation a state may withhold powers which may be exercised by and cannot be denied to an individual. It is under no obligation to treat both alike. In granting corporate powers the legislature may deem that the best interests of the state would be subserved by some restriction, and the corporation may not plead that, in spite of the restriction, it has more or greater powers because the citizen has. "The granting of such right or privilege [the right or privilege to be a corporation] rests entirely in the discretion of the state, and, of course, when granted, may be accompanied with such conditions as its legislature may judge most befitting to its interests and policy." The act of 1904 forbids "any person, corporation, or association of persons to maintain or operate any college," etc. Such a statute may conflict with the

Federal Constitution in denying to individuals powers which they may rightfully exercise, and yet, at the same time, be valid as to a corporation created by the state.

It may be said that the court of appeals sustained the validity of this section of the statute, both against individuals and corporations. It ruled that the legislation was within the power of the state, and that the state might rightfully thus restrain all individuals, corporations, and associations. But it is unnecessary for us to consider anything more than the question of its validity as applied to corporations.

The statute is clearly separable, and may be valid as to one class while invalid as to another. Even if it were conceded that its assertion of power over individuals cannot be sustained, still it must be upheld so far as it restrains corporations.

There is no force in the suggestion that the statute, although clearly separable, must stand or fall as an entirety on the ground the legislature would not have enacted one part unless it could reach all. That the legislature of Kentucky desired to separate the teaching of white and colored children may be conceded; but it by no means follows that it would not have enforced the separation so far as it could do so, even though it could not make it effective under all circumstances. In other words, it is not at all unreasonable to believe that the legislature, although advised beforehand of the constitutional question, might have prohibited all organizations and corporations under its control from teaching white and colored children together, and thus made at least uniform official action....

. . .

Further, inasmuch as the court of appeals considered the act separable, and, while sustaining it as an entirety, gave an independent reason which applies only to corporations, it is obvious that it recognized the force of the suggestions we have made. And when a state statute is so interpreted, this court should hesitate before it holds that the supreme court of the state did not know what was the thought of the legislature in its enactment.

While the terms of the present charter are not given in the record, yet it was admitted on the trial that the defendant was a corporation organized and incorporated under the general statutes of the state of Kentucky, and of course the state courts, as well as this court on appeal, take judicial notice of those statutes. Further, in the brief of counsel for the defendant is given a history of the incorporation proceedings, together with the charters. From that it appears that Berea College was organized under the authority of an act for the incorporation of voluntary associations, which act was amended by an act of March 10, 1856 and which in terms reserved to the general assembly "the right to alter or repeal the charter of any associations formed under the provisions of this act, and the act to which this act is an amendment, at any time hereafter." After the Constitution of 1891 was adopted by the state of Kentucky, and on June 10, 1899, the college was reincorporated under the provisions of [state law], the charter defining its business in these words: "Its object is the education of all persons who may attend its institution of learning at Berea, and, in the language of the original articles, 'to promote the cause of Christ.' The Constitution of 1891 provided in § 3 of the Bill of Rights that 'every grant of a franchise, privilege, or exemption shall remain, subject to revocation, alteration, or amendment.' So that the full power of amendment was reserved to the legislature."

It is undoubtedly true that the reserved power to alter or amend is subject to some limitations, and that, under the guise of an amendment, a new contract may not always be enforceable upon the corporation or the stockholders; but it is settled 'that a power reserved to the legislature to alter, amend, or repeal a charter authorizes it to make any alteration or amendment of a charter granted subject to it, which will not defeat or substantially impair the object of the grant, or any rights vested under it, and which the legislature may deem necessary to secure either that object or any public right.

Construing the statute, the court of appeals held that "if the same school taught the different races at different times, though at the same place, or at different times at the same place, it would not be unlawful." Now, an amendment to the original charter, which does not destroy the power of the college to furnish education to all persons, but which simply separates them by time or place of instruction, cannot be said to "defeat or substantially impair the object of the grant." The language of the statute is not in terms and

amendment, yet its effect is an amendment, and it would be resting too much on mere form to hold that a statute which in effect works a change in the terms of the charter is not to be considered as an amendment, because not so designated. The act itself, being separable, is to be read as though it, in one section, prohibited any person, in another section any corporation and, in a third, any association of persons to do the acts named. Reading the statute as containing a separate prohibition on all corporations, at least, all state corporations, it substantially declares that any authority given by previous charters to instruct the two races at the same time and in the same place is forbidden, and that prohibition, being a departure from the terms of the original charter in this case, may properly be adjudged an amendment.

Again, it is insisted that the court of appeals did not regard the legislation as making an amendment, because another prosecution instituted against the same corporation under the 4th section of the act, which makes it a misdemeanor to teach pupils of the two races in the same institution, even although one race is taught in one branch and another in another branch, provided the two branches are within 25 miles of each other, was held could not be sustained, the court saying: "This last section, we think, violates the limitations upon the police power: it is unreasonable and oppressive." But, while so ruling, it also held that this section could be ignored and that the remainder of the act was complete notwithstanding. Whether the reasoning of the court concerning the 4th section be satisfactory or not is immaterial, for no question of its validity is presented, and the court of appeals, while striking it down, sustained the balance of the act. We need concern ourselves only with the inquiry whether the 1st section can be upheld as coming within the power of a state over its own corporate creatures.

We are of opinion, for reasons stated, that it does come within that power, and, on this ground, the judgment of the Court of Appeals of Kentucky is

Affirmed.

BILL OF RIGHTS

The framers of the U.S. Constitution were concerned that the individual rights of Americans in the new republic were not adequately protected in the original Constitution. Because the framers were fearful that the Constitution would not be

ratified by the states, James Madison composed 12 amendments to the Constitution, 10 of which were ratified by the states. Congress passed the amendments on September 25, 1789, and they became effective when the ratification process was completed on December 15, 1791.

The first ten amendments to the federal constitution, now known as the Bill of Rights, protect many of the rights that Americans hold most dear. In light of the significance that the Bill of Rights has had on the world of higher education, this entry examines the First, Fourth, Fifth, and Tenth Amendments, which have had the greatest impact on the rights and freedoms of faculty members, staff, and students in colleges and universities.

The First Amendment

In a 1960 Justice Hugo Black concluded a presentation on the Bill of Rights by observing that

> the First Amendment is truly the heart of the Bill of Rights. The framers balanced its freedoms of religion, speech, press, assembly and petition against the needs of a powerful central government, and decided that in those freedoms lies this nation's only true security. They were not afraid for men to be free. We should not be. (Black, 1960, p. 881)

The First Amendment guarantees five rights—freedom of religion, speech, press, assembly, and petition—the first four of which have had a major role on the campuses of American colleges and universities.

Freedom of Religion

Religious freedom was important to Americans, because many colonists had left Great Britain and other regions of Europe partly in order to be able to practice their own religions freely. The impact of this desire for religious freedom was enshrined in Article VI of the Constitution, which forbade any religious test of any officeholder. However, because many feared that Article VI was not strong enough, the First Amendment was ratified, beginning with the key words that "Congress shall make no law respecting an establishment of religion, or prohibiting the free exercise thereof." In a matter of importance to colleges and universities, the U.S. Supreme Court later extended the reach of the First Amendment to the states in *Cantwell v. Connecticut* (1940), wherein it invalidated the convictions of Jehovah's Witnesses for violating a law against soliciting funds for religious, charitable, or philanthropic purposes without prior approval of public officials.

In *Everson v. Board of Education* (1947), a dispute from New Jersey, the Supreme Court upheld the constitutionality of a law that allowed parents to be reimbursed for the cost of transporting their children to religiously affiliated nonpublic K–12 schools. Writing for the Court, Justice Hugo Black's opinion introduced a metaphor from Thomas Jefferson calling for a "wall of separation" between church and state. Although these words are not enshrined in the Constitution, they are frequently used to refer to the position most frequently associated with the contemporary Court on matters involving religion.

The Supreme Court has reached mixed results on aid to religiously affiliated institutions of higher learning and their students. To this end, in *Tilton v. Richardson* (1971), *Hunt v. McNair* (1973), and *Roemer v. Board of Public Works of Maryland* (1976), the Court allowed public funds to be used for construction projects in public colleges and universities on the basis that the programs satisfied the tripartite test that it enunciated in a K–12 case, *Lemon v. Kurtzman* (1971), and it invalidated publicly funded salary supplements to teachers in religiously affiliated nonpublic schools. Under the *Lemon* test, a governmental action must have a secular legislative purpose and a principal or primary effect that neither advances nor inhibits religion, and it cannot result in excessive entanglement between religion and government. Further, in *Witters v. Washington Department of Services for the Blind* (1986), the Court upheld the constitutionality of extending a general vocational program to a blind man who was studying to become a clergyman at a religious college. Yet the Supreme Court of Washington, in a later iteration of *Witters* (1989), invalidated the plan under the more restrictive provisions in its state constitution, which prohibited aid in support of religious instruction. Similarly, in *Locke v. Davey* (2004), the Supreme Court held that because the state constitution in Washington forbade funding for religious education, a student was not entitled to a grant that would have helped to defray tuition costs for his dual major in pastoral studies and business administration.

In a case that overlaps with free speech concerns, *Rosenberger v. Rector and Visitors of the University of Virginia* (1995), the Supreme Court decided that university officials could not deny funding of a publication due to its religious content. According to the Court, the university's program was neutral toward religion, insofar as the fund used to pay for student publications—including the religious publication—supported an open forum for speech and supported officially recognized student groups on campus. Therefore, officials would not have violated the Establishment Clause had they made the monies available to the religious group.

Freedom of Speech and the Press

"Congress shall make no law . . . abridging the freedom of speech, or of the press." The freedom of speech involved in academic freedom is of special concern for individuals in higher education, including both students and faculty. Academic freedom, a concept that emerged in the middle of the 19th century, is alive and well in the 21st century. Among the Supreme Court cases involving academic freedom, perhaps the most notable are *Sweezy v. New Hampshire* (1957) and *Keyishian v. Board of Regents* (1967). In both of these cases, the Court recognized that academic freedom is a special concern in higher education, noting in *Keyishian* that the First Amendment "does not tolerate laws that cast a pall of orthodoxy over classrooms" (p. 603).

Among others, a trio of cases from the Supreme Court dealing with speech by public employees is relevant for faculty members at public college and universities. In *Pickering v. Board of Education* (1968), the Court sought to balance the free speech rights of educators in public schools to address matters of public concern with the needs of their employers to ensure that educational operations are not disrupted. Acknowledging the rights of employees, the Court indicated that educators in public institutions maintain their right to speak as long as they truthfully address matters of public concern. In *Connick v. Myers* (1983), a dispute involving an assistant district attorney, the Court clarified the place of speech by employees on matters of personal concern in the workplace. When the attorney sought to distribute a questionnaire to peers surveying their attitudes about specified office policies, the Court determined that her private speech was unprotected, because it had nothing to do with a matter of public concern.

Finally, in *Garcetti v. Ceballos* (2006), another case involving an assistant district attorney, the Court distinguished between speech by officials in their job-related capacity and speech by officials as private citizens. At issue was a memorandum in which the attorney expressed his concern that there were serious misrepresentations in an affidavit that had been used to obtain a search warrant. In further refining the parameters of employee speech, the Court held that the attorney could be disciplined for making his views known in public, because when he was speaking in his official capacity, his speech was not protected, even though it dealt with a matter of public concern.

In its only case involving a student newspaper in higher education, *Papish v. Board of Curators of the University of Missouri* (1973), the Supreme Court reasoned that officials at a state university violated the First Amendment rights of a graduate student whom they expelled for distributing an off-campus newspaper that violated the institution's policy against "indecent speech." The Court pointed out that the dissemination of ideas could not be shut off solely in the name of conventions of decency, regardless of how offensive the ideas may have been, on a state university campus.

Freedom of Assembly

A case in which freedom of assembly overlapped with free speech, *Lehnert v. Ferris Faculty Association* (1991), helped set the standards under which unions of public education employees may charge fair share fees to nonmembers. As a general rule, the Supreme Court specified that fees must be germane to collective bargaining activities, be justifiable, and not add significantly to the burdening of free speech.

Previously, in *National Labor Relations Board v. Yeshiva University* (1980), the leading case on judicial involvement in faculty unionization, at least in private colleges and universities, the Supreme Court posited that faculty members in a private, religiously affiliated university did not have the right to organize and form unions. Basing its judgment on its belief that faculty members performed some duties that were considered managerial in nature, the Court prohibited the NLRB from intervening in a labor dispute between faculty members and the university.

The Fourth Amendment

The founders wrote the Fourth Amendment as a direct result of the Writs of Assistance that the

British used to justify searches of colonists' homes at any time. Over the ensuing years, a myriad of cases examined the Fourth Amendment in criminal cases. However, it was not until 1985 that the Supreme Court, in *New Jersey v. T.L.O.*, applied the Fourth Amendment in K–12 schools. Under the *T.L.O.* test, officials may search students' persons or property if they have "reasonable suspicion" that students violated school rules or the law; this measure is significantly lower than the "probable cause" requirement that applies to the police for searches. The Court added that the area searched must also be reasonable in terms of what officials are hoping to locate. In the years since, the judiciary has applied *T.L.O.* with some regularity to disputes in higher education.

In *O'Connor v. Ortega* (1987), the Supreme Court applied the *T.L.O.* test to searches of the offices of public employees. *Ortega* involved a dispute over a search of the office of a faculty member at a state university hospital in pursuit of evidence that he engaged in professional impropriety. In *Ortega*, the Court explained that under *T.L.O.*, such an action by supervisory officials needed only to be grounded in reasonable suspicion. The Court noted that a probable cause requirement would have been impractical in such circumstances, where employers conduct searches to determine whether employees have been involved in work-related misconduct.

The Supreme Court's only case involving the Fourth Amendment rights of students, *Washington v. Chrisman* (1982), predated *T.L.O.* In *Chrisman*, a campus police officer stood in the doorway of a student's room and observed marijuana seeds and a pipe on the desk that belonged to the student's roommate. After a second officer arrived, and the students voluntarily waived their rights orally and in writing, a search of the room led to the discovery of more marijuana and another controlled substance. On further review of the roommate's conviction for possession of controlled substances, the Court agreed that because the first officer had justification for accompanying the student to the dormitory and the marijuana had been in plain view, the search did not violate the student's Fourth Amendment rights.

The Fifth Amendment

Two key provisions in the Fifth Amendment state that an individual may not be "compelled in any criminal case to be a witness against himself, nor be deprived of life, liberty, or property without due process of law. . . ." The first part of this excerpt from the Fifth Amendment came into play after fears of communist infiltration in the United States after World War II led to the introduction of loyalty oaths for public employees. In *Slochower v. Board of Higher Education of New York City* (1956), the Supreme Court invalidated a law that led to the dismissal of a faculty member at a public college because he refused to answer questions from a federal legislative committee about his allegedly communist activities due to his fear of self-incrimination. The Court held that the statute would have essentially eviscerated the Fifth Amendment privilege against self-incrimination and thus was unconstitutional.

The most significant case wherein the Supreme Court applied the Due Process Clause of the Fifth Amendment in an educational dispute was in a K–12 setting. Even so, the Fifth Amendment retains the potential to be significant for colleges and universities. In *Bolling v. Sharp* (1954), handed down on the same day as *Brown v. Board of Education, Topeka* (1954), the Court invalidated the segregation of public schools in Washington, D.C., because the practice of segregation there was implemented through action by the federal government, and the Fourteenth Amendment applies only to the states. Therefore, the *Bolling* Court instead invoked the Fifth Amendment's Due Process Clause. While there are no federal institutions of higher learning other than the military academies, the Fifth Amendment continues to have the potential to impact higher education, especially with regard to investigation of faculty and student activities.

The Tenth Amendment

Pursuant to the Tenth Amendment, the "powers not delegated to the United States by the Constitution, nor prohibited by it to the States, are reserved to the States respectively or to the people." The most significant dimension of the Tenth Amendment for this encyclopedia is that the Supreme Court has ruled that K–12 education is not a fundamental right protected under the U.S. Constitution but instead falls under the authority vested in the states. However, insofar as higher education is voluntary, the scope of the Tenth Amendment at this level remains open to some debate.

The first federal document on education was the Northwest Ordinance of 1787. Congress established land grant colleges and universities through the Morrill Acts of 1862 and 1890, and enacted later statutes in the 20th century dealing with postsecondary education, including the Higher Education Act and the Stafford Act. Congress has also overseen a wide array of issues in higher education through legislation such as Title IX of the Education Amendments of 1972, which helped to ensure gender equity in higher education. As the federal government has taken an increasingly active role in higher education, some have questioned whether the Tenth Amendment is serving the purpose for which it was enacted.

Robert J. Safransky

See also Academic Freedom; Drug Testing of Students; Fourth Amendment Rights of Faculty; Fourth Amendment Rights of Students; Free Speech and Expression Rights of Students; *Hunt v. McNair; Keyishian v. Board of Regents of the University of the State of New York; Lehnert v. Ferris Faculty Association; Locke v. Davey*; Loyalty Oaths; Morrill Acts; *National Labor Relations Board v. Yeshiva University*; Political Activities and Speech of Faculty; *Roemer v. Board of Public Works of Maryland*; Stafford Act; State Aid and the Establishment Clause; *Sweezy v. New Hampshire; Tilton v. Richardson*

Further Readings

Black, H. L. (1960). The Bill of Rights. James Madison Lecture, New York University School of Law. *New York University Law Review, 35*, 865–881.

O'Connor, K., & Sabato, L. J. (2006). *American government: Continuity and change.* New York: Pearson Longman.

Legal Citations

Agricultural College Act of 1890 (Second Morrill Land Grant Act), ch. 841, 26 Stat. 417, 7 U.S.C. §§ 322 *et seq.*

Augustus F. Hawkins–Robert T. Stafford Elementary and Secondary School Improvement Amendments of 1988, Pub. L. No. 100-297.

Bolling v. Sharp, 347 U.S. 497 (1954).

Brown v. Board of Education, Topeka, 347 U.S. 483 (1954).

Cantwell v. Connecticut, 310 U.S. 296 (1940).

Connick v. Myers, 461 U.S. 138 (1983).

Everson v. Board of Education, 330 U.S. 1 (1947), *reh'g denied*, 330 U.S. 855 (1947).

Garcetti v. Ceballos, 547 U.S. 410 (2006).

Higher Education Act, Pub. L. No. 89-329 (1965).

Hunt v. McNair, 413 U.S. 734 (1973).

Keyishian v. Board of Regents, 385 U.S. 589 (1967).

Lehnert v. Ferris Faculty Association, 500 U.S. 507 (1991).

Lemon v. Kurtzman, 403 U.S. 602 (1971).

Locke v. Davey, 540 U.S. 712 (2004).

Morrill Land Grant Act of 1862, ch. 130, 12 Stat. 503, 7 U.S.C. §§ 301 *et seq.*

National Labor Relations Board v. Yeshiva University, 444 U.S. 672 (1980).

New Jersey v. T.L.O., 469 U.S. 325 (1985).

O'Connor v. Ortega, 480 U.S. 709 (1987).

Papish v. Board of Curators of the University of Missouri, 410 U.S. 667 (1973).

Pickering v. Board of Education, 391 U.S. 563 (1968).

Roemer v. Board of Public Works of Maryland, 426 U.S. 736 (1976).

Rosenberger v. Rector and Visitors of the University of Virginia, 515 U.S. 819 (1995).

Slochower v. Board of Higher Education of New York City, 350 U.S. 551 (1956).

Sweezy v. New Hampshire, 354 U.S. 234 (1957).

Tilton v. Richardson, 403 U.S. 672 (1971).

Title IX of the Education Amendments of 1972, 20 U.S.C. § 1681.

Washington v. Chrisman, 455 U.S. 1 (1982).

Witters v. Washington Department of Services for the Blind, 474 U.S. 481 (1986), 771 P.2d 1119 (Wash. 1989), *cert. denied*, 493 U.S. 850 (1989).

BOARD OF CURATORS OF THE UNIVERSITY OF MISSOURI V. HOROWITZ

In *Board of Curators of the University of Missouri v. Horowitz* (1978), the U.S. Supreme Court reviewed the issue of whether officials at a public university's medical school afforded one of their students procedural due process when they took steps to dismiss her from an academic program. According to the Court, university officials satisfied the constitutional requirements of procedural due process for academic dismissals when it acted in a two-stage process. First, the Court pointed out, officials had notified the student of her academic deficiencies and identified potential outcomes in the event that she failed to remedy these deficiencies, including the possibility that she could be dismissed from the program. Second, the Court acknowledged that because the student had been fully informed about her academic standing and the consequences of failing to improve, the decision to dismiss her occurred only after a careful and deliberate review of her academic performance.

Facts of the Case

During the fall of 1971, Charlotte Horowitz entered the University of Missouri, Kansas City (UMKC) Medical School with advanced standing that would have required her to spend only two years in medical school. The final two years of the student's study were to be dedicated to rotational units of academic and clinical experiences on a variety of specialized areas. During Horowitz's first of two years at UMKC, several faculty members evaluated her clinical performance, indicating that her work did not measure up to that of her peers. At the end of that first year, the academic review team, known as the Council on Evaluation, which was composed of both faculty and students, recommended Horowitz's continuation in the program on a probationary basis. During the first half of Horowitz's second year, faculty members expressed additional concerns about her capacity to perform the required clinical skills, rating her work as unsatisfactory. In the middle of that year, the Council again reviewed her academic progress. This time, the Council recommended that Horowitz not be considered for graduation at the end of the academic year. Further, the Council indicated that unless Horowitz displayed dramatic improvement in her poor clinical performance, she should be dismissed from the medical school.

Affording Horowitz another opportunity to demonstrate her academic competencies, officials at the medical school allowed her to participate in a set of oral and clinical examinations. As part of the examinations, seven well-regarded practicing physicians evaluated Horowitz's performance. The evaluations drew mixed results: Two medical doctors recommended graduation that year, two suggested immediate dismissal, and three called for deferring graduation and revisiting her academic

review when the other evaluations of her clinical experiences were received. Later that academic year, the Council reconvened after receiving additional poor ratings of Horowitz's clinical requirements. On reviewing Horowitz's performance, the Council unanimously recommended that she be dismissed from the medical school. A committee of the faculty known as the Coordinating Board affirmed that recommendation to the dean. The dean agreed and notified Horowitz of her academic dismissal from the medical school. Horowitz appealed to the university provost for health sciences. On review, the provost upheld the medical school's decision. Subsequently, Horowitz unsuccessfully filed suit against the UMKC Medical School in federal trial court based on constitutional claims, including one alleging violation of her rights to procedural due process.

In dismissing her claim, the trial court was convinced that Horowitz received due process. On appeal, the Eighth Circuit reversed in favor of the student, and the University of Missouri appealed. On final appeal, the Supreme Court reversed in favor of the UMKC.

The Supreme Court's Ruling

The Supreme Court began by identifying the issue at hand as the procedures that university officials had to perform in the face of challenges filed by students who were about to be dismissed when they claimed that they were being denied their rights to due process. In its analysis, the Court declared that institutions of higher education and their faculty have far more flexibility in dealing with procedural due process for academic dismissals than for student dismissals based on conduct.

On the merits of the case, the Supreme Court was of the opinion that even though university officials had no obligation to afford Horowitz a formal hearing, they did not violate her right to procedural due process, because they had fully informed her of her academic standing and the possibility of academic dismissal if her work did not improve. Further, the Court found that the eventual decision to dismiss the student was not arbitrary or capricious, because it occurred after careful and deliberate review of Horowitz's inability to improve her academic performance. Accordingly, the UMKC prevailed in a case that helped to establish the legal guidelines for procedural due process of academic dismissals of students.

Jeffrey C. Sun

See also Academic Abstention; Due Process, Substantive and Procedural; Due Process Rights in Faculty and Staff Dismissal; Fourteenth Amendment; *Regents of the University of Michigan v. Ewing*

Further Readings

Berger, C. J., & Berger, V. (1999). Academic discipline: A guide to fair process for the university student. *Columbia Law Review, 99*(2), 289–364.

Ford, D. L., & Strope, J. L., Jr. (1996). Judicial responses to adverse academic decisions affecting public postsecondary institution students since "Horowitz" and "Ewing." *West's Education Law Quarterly, 5*(4), 649–674.

Poteet, G. W., & Pollok, C. S. (1981). The legal side: When a student fails clinical. *American Journal of Nursing, 81*(10), 1889–1890.

Legal Citations

Board of Curators of the University of Missouri v. Horowitz, 435 U.S. 78 (1978).

BOARD OF CURATORS OF THE UNIVERSITY OF MISSOURI V. HOROWITZ

Horowitz stands out because in it, the Supreme Court addressed the due process requirements for students who are dismissed due to academic deficiencies.

Supreme Court of the United States

BOARD OF CURATORS OF THE UNIVERSITY OF MISSOURI

v.

HOROWITZ

435 U.S. 78

Argued Nov. 7, 1977

Decided March 1, 1978

Mr. Justice REHNQUIST delivered the opinion of the Court.

Respondent, a student at the University of Missouri-Kansas City Medical School, was dismissed by petitioner officials of the school during her final year of study for failure to meet academic standards. Respondent sued petitioners under 42 U.S.C. § 1983 in the United States District Court for the Western District of Missouri alleging, among other constitutional violations, that petitioners had not accorded her procedural due process prior to her dismissal. The District Court, after conducting a full trial, concluded that respondent had been afforded all of the rights guaranteed her by the Fourteenth Amendment to the United States Constitution and dismissed her complaint. The Court of Appeals for the Eighth Circuit reversed and a petition for rehearing en banc was denied by a divided court. We granted certiorari to consider what procedures must be accorded to a student at a state educational institution whose dismissal may constitute a deprivation of "liberty" or "property" within the meaning of the Fourteenth Amendment. We reverse the judgment of the Court of Appeals.

I

Respondent was admitted with advanced standing to the Medical School in the fall of 1971. During the final years of a student's education at the school, the student is required to pursue in "rotational units" academic and clinical studies pertaining to various medical disciplines such as obstetrics-gynecology, pediatrics, and surgery. Each student's academic performance at the school is evaluated on a periodic basis by the Council on Evaluation, a body composed of both faculty and students, which can recommend various actions including probation and dismissal. The recommendations of the Council are reviewed by the Coordinating Committee, a body composed solely of faculty members, and must ultimately be approved by the Dean. Students are not typically allowed to appear before either the Council or the Coordinating Committee on the occasion of their review of the student's academic performance.

In the spring of respondent's first year of study, several faculty members expressed dissatisfaction with her clinical performance during a pediatrics rotation. The faculty members noted that respondent's "performance was below that of her peers in all clinical patient-oriented settings," that she was erratic in her attendance at clinical sessions, and that she lacked a critical concern for personal hygiene. Upon the recommendation of the Council on Evaluation, respondent was advanced to her second and final year on a probationary basis.

Faculty dissatisfaction with respondent's clinical performance continued during the following year. For example, respondent's docent, or faculty adviser, rated her clinical skills as "unsatisfactory." In the middle of the year, the Council again reviewed respondent's academic progress and concluded that respondent should not be considered for graduation in June of that year; furthermore, the Council recommended that, absent "radical improvement," respondent be dropped from the school.

Respondent was permitted to take a set of oral and practical examinations as an "appeal" of the decision not to permit her to graduate. Pursuant to this "appeal," respondent spent a substantial portion of time with seven practicing physicians in the area who enjoyed a good reputation among their peers. The physicians were asked to recommend whether respondent should be allowed to graduate on schedule and, if not, whether she should be dropped immediately or allowed to remain on probation. Only two of the doctors recommended that respondent be graduated on schedule. Of the other five, two recommended that she be immediately dropped from the school. The remaining three recommended that she not be allowed to graduate in June and be continued on probation pending further reports on her clinical progress. Upon receipt of these recommendations, the Council on Evaluation reaffirmed its prior position.

The Council met again in mid-May to consider whether respondent should be allowed to remain in school beyond June of that year. Noting that the report on respondent's recent surgery rotation rated her performance as "low-satisfactory," the Council unanimously recommended that "barring receipt of any reports that Miss Horowitz has improved radically, [she] not be allowed to re-enroll in the . . . School of Medicine." The Council delayed making its recommendation official until receiving reports on other rotations; when a report on respondent's emergency rotation also turned out to be negative, the Council unanimously reaffirmed its recommendation that respondent be dropped from the school. The Coordinating Committee and the Dean approved the recommendation and notified respondent, who appealed the decision in writing to the University's Provost for Health Sciences. The Provost sustained the school's actions after reviewing the record compiled during the earlier proceedings.

II

A

To be entitled to the procedural protections of the Fourteenth Amendment, respondent must in a case such as this demonstrate that her dismissal from the school deprived her of either a "liberty" or a "property" interest. Respondent has never alleged that she was deprived of a property interest. Because property interests are creatures of state law, respondent would have been required to show at trial that her seat at the Medical School was a "property" interest recognized by Missouri state law. Instead, respondent argued that her dismissal deprived her of "liberty" by substantially impairing her opportunities to continue her medical education or to return to employment in a medically related field.

The Court of Appeals agreed . . .

We have recently had an opportunity to elaborate upon the circumstances under which an employment termination might infringe a protected liberty interest. In *Bishop v. Wood* we upheld the dismissal of a policeman without a hearing; we rejected the theory that the mere fact of dismissal, absent some publicizing of the reasons for the action, could amount to a stigma infringing one's liberty . . .

The opinion of the Court of Appeals, decided only five weeks after we issued our opinion in *Bishop*, does not discuss whether a state university infringes a liberty interest when it dismisses a student without publicizing allegations harmful to the student's reputation. Three judges of the Court of Appeals for the Eighth Circuit dissented from the denial of rehearing en banc on the ground that "the reasons for Horowitz's dismissal were not released to the public but were communicated to her directly by school officials." Citing *Bishop*, the judges concluded that "[a]bsent such public disclosure, there is no deprivation of a liberty interest." Petitioners urge us to adopt the view of these judges and hold that respondent has not been deprived of a liberty interest.

B

We need not decide, however, whether respondent's dismissal deprived her of a liberty interest in pursuing a medical career. Nor need we decide whether respondent's dismissal infringed any other interest constitutionally protected against deprivation without procedural due process. Assuming the existence of a liberty or property interest, respondent has been awarded at least as much due process as the Fourteenth Amendment requires. The school fully informed respondent of the faculty's dissatisfaction with her clinical progress and the danger that this posed to timely graduation and continued enrollment. The ultimate decision to dismiss respondent was careful and deliberate. These procedures were sufficient under the Due Process Clause of the Fourteenth Amendment. . . .

In *Goss v. Lopez* we held that due process requires, in connection with the suspension of a student from public school for disciplinary reasons, "that the student be given oral or written notice of the charges against him and, if he denies them, an explanation of the evidence the authorities have and an opportunity to present his side of the story." The Court of Appeals apparently read *Goss* as requiring some type of formal hearing at which respondent could defend her academic ability and performance. All that *Goss* required was an "informal give-and-take" between the student and the administrative body dismissing him that would, at least, give the student "the opportunity to characterize his conduct and put it in what he deems the proper context." But we have frequently emphasized that "[t]he very nature of due process negates any concept of inflexible procedures universally applicable to every imaginable situation." The need for flexibility is well illustrated by the significant difference between the failure of a student to meet academic standards and the violation by a student of valid rules of conduct. This difference calls for far less stringent procedural requirements in the case of an academic dismissal.

Since the issue first arose 50 years ago, state and lower federal courts have recognized that there are distinct differences between decisions to suspend or dismiss a student for disciplinary purposes and similar actions taken for academic reasons which may call for hearings in connection with the former but not the latter. Thus, in *Barnard v. Inhabitants of Shelburne,* the Supreme Judicial Court of Massachusetts rejected an argument, based on several earlier decisions requiring a hearing in disciplinary contexts, that school officials must also grant a hearing before excluding a student on academic grounds. . . .

A similar conclusion has been reached by the other state courts to consider the issue. Indeed, until the instant decision by the Court of Appeals for the Eighth Circuit, the Courts of Appeals were also unanimous in concluding that dismissals for academic (as opposed to disciplinary) cause do not necessitate a hearing before the school's decision making body. These prior decisions of state and federal courts, over a period of 60 years, unanimously holding that formal hearings before decision making bodies need not be held in the case of academic dismissals, cannot be rejected lightly.

Reason, furthermore, clearly supports the perception of these decisions. A school is an academic institution, not a courtroom or administrative hearing room. In *Goss,* this Court felt that suspensions of students for disciplinary reasons have a sufficient resemblance to traditional judicial and administrative factfinding to call for a "hearing" before the relevant school authority. While recognizing that school authorities must be afforded the necessary tools to maintain discipline, the Court concluded:

> "[I]t would be a strange disciplinary system in an educational institution if no communication was sought by the disciplinarian with the student in an effort to inform him of his dereliction and to let him tell his side of the story in order to make sure that an injustice is not done.

Even in the context of a school disciplinary proceedineg, however, the Court stopped short of requiring a *formal* hearing since "further formalizing the suspension process and escalating its formality and adversary nature may not only make it too costly as a regular disciplinary tool but also destroy its effectiveness as a part of the teaching process."

Academic evaluations of a student, in contrast to disciplinary determinations, bear little resemblance to the judicial and administrative fact-finding proceedings to which we have traditionally attached a full-hearing requirement. In *Goss,* the school's decision to suspend the students rested on factual conclusions that the individual students had participated in demonstrations that had disrupted classes, attacked a police officer, or caused physical damage to school property. The requirement of a hearing, where the student could present his side of the factual issue, could under such circumstances "provide a meaningful hedge against erroneous action." The decision to dismiss respondent, by comparison, rested on the academic judgment of school officials that she did not have the necessary clinical ability to perform adequately as a medical doctor and was making insufficient progress toward that goal. Such a judgment is by its nature more subjective and evaluative than the typical factual questions presented in the average disciplinary decision. Like the decision of an individual professor as to the proper grade for a student in his course, the determination whether to dismiss a student for academic reasons requires an expert evaluation of cumulative information and is not readily adapted to the procedural tools of judicial or administrative decision making.

Under such circumstances, we decline to ignore the historic judgment of educators and thereby formalize the academic dismissal process by requiring a hearing. The educational process is not by nature adversary; instead it centers around a continuing relationship between faculty and students, "one in which the teacher must occupy many roles—educator, adviser, friend, and, at times, parent-substitute." This is especially true as one advances through the varying regimes of the educational system, and the instruction becomes both more individualized and more specialized. In *Goss,* this Court concluded that the value of some form of hearing in a disciplinary context outweighs any resulting harm to the academic environment. Influencing this conclusion was clearly the belief that disciplinary proceedings, in which the teacher must decide whether to punish a student for disruptive or insubordinate behavior, may automatically bring an adversary flavor

to the normal student-teacher relationship. The same conclusion does not follow in the academic context. We decline to further enlarge the judicial presence in the academic community and thereby risk deterioration of many beneficial aspects of the faculty-student relationship. We recognize, as did the Massachusetts Supreme Judicial Court over 60 years ago, that a hearing may be "useless or harmful in finding out the truth as to scholarship."

"Judicial interposition in the operation of the public school system of the Nation raises problems requiring care and restraint. . . . By and large, public education in our Nation is committed to the control of state and local authorities." We see no reason to intrude on that historic control in this case.

III

In reversing the District Court on procedural due process grounds, the Court of Appeals expressly failed to "reach the substantive due process ground advanced by Horowitz. Respondent urges that we remand the cause to the Court of Appeals for consideration of this additional claim. In this regard, a number of lower courts have implied in dictum that academic dismissals from state institutions can be enjoined if "shown to be clearly arbitrary or capricious." Even assuming that the courts can review under such a standard an academic decision of a public educational institution, we agree with the District Court that no showing of arbitrariness or capriciousness has been made in this case. Courts are particularly ill-equipped to evaluate academic performance. The factors discussed in Part II with respect to procedural due process speak *a fortiori* here and warn against any such judicial intrusion into academic decision making.

The judgment of the Court of Appeals is therefore *Reversed.*

BOARD OF REGENTS OF STATE COLLEGES V. ROTH

Board of Regents of State Colleges v. Roth is one of two key 1972 decisions from the U.S. Supreme Court that helped to establish the parameters of federal due process for employees in higher education. The Court's rulings in *Roth* and in *Perry v. Sindermann* considered the due process requirements

when employees are facing the nonrenewal of their employment contracts.

The last half of the 20th century witnessed a great expansion of individual rights in the workplace, including federal procedural due process protections for public employees. Even so, the protections of the Due Process Clause of the Fourteenth Amendment do not apply universally to all employment situations. One area of dispute involves the due process rights of faculty members whose contracts are not renewed. In *Roth,* a faculty member who had been hired under a one-year contract and not reemployed was not given reasons his employment was terminated or an opportunity for a hearing. The Supreme Court ruled that public institutions of higher education must provide due process to employees facing the nonrenewal of their contracts only if they have liberty or property interests that trigger Fourteenth Amendment protections.

Facts of the Case

Wisconsin State University–Oshkosh employed David Roth as an assistant professor of political science under a one-year contract for 1967–1968. He completed that academic year, but university officials informed him prior to February 1, 1968, that they would not renew his contract for another year. Under Wisconsin law, faculty members could earn tenure, with accompanying due process protections for nonrenewal, after serving four years under one-year contracts. Until then, faculty members served without tenure, meaning that they lacked due process rights, including the right to receive statements of reasons their contracts were not renewed or hearings when their employment was terminated.

Roth filed suit in a federal trial court in Wisconsin, alleging that officials violated his Fourteenth Amendment substantive due process rights by not renewing his contract because of his constitutionally protected criticism of the university's administration. However, because the trial court stayed proceedings on this issue, the Supreme Court did not have to consider this question. Roth also alleged that the university's administration violated his right to procedural due process when officials elected not to renew his contract without providing him with either reasons for their decision or an opportunity to challenge their action at a hearing. The federal trial court and Seventh Circuit both entered judgments in favor of Roth, directing university officials to provide him with reasons and a hearing. The university appealed on the procedural issue. The question before the Supreme Court was whether a faculty member who was employed under a one-year agreement had a right to federal procedural due process when facing the nonrenewal of his contract.

The Supreme Court's Ruling

The Supreme Court reversed in favor of the university, finding that officials had not violated Roth's procedural due process rights. Justice Potter Stewart, delivering the opinion of the Court, began by recognizing that the Fourteenth Amendment guarantees liberty and property generally, but that it provides procedural due process protections only when there is a deprivation of a liberty or property interest. According to the Court, liberty interests exist when an employer's actions place the worker's good name, honor, and integrity at stake or create a stigma that blocks the employee from other employment opportunities. Insofar as the actions of university officials in not renewing Roth's contract did not damage his reputation, his standing in the community, or his ability to procure future employment opportunities even within the Wisconsin state university system, the Court was satisfied that the their actions did not deprive Roth of a liberty interest such that he lacked a right to due process. The Court noted that when Roth's contract was simply not renewed and while he was free to seek other employment, the actions of officials did not violate a protected liberty interest.

The Supreme Court added that the Fourteenth Amendment also guarantees due process protections to those who are deprived of property interests, a specific benefit that employees do not necessarily possess as a condition of employment. In order to have property interests, the Court explained that employees must have more than abstract needs, desires, or unilateral expectations of such interests. Rather, the Court pointed out that the individuals must have "a legitimate claim of entitlement to it" (p. 577). The Court held that faculty members in higher education facing dismissal have property interests only through tenure and their contracts. In this regard, the Court indicated that independent sources, such as state laws, rules, and understandings, not the U.S. Constitution, create property interests. The Court reasoned that Roth's only property interests were secured in his employment agreement, which ended on June 30, 1969, and that the agreement provided no due process provisions with respect to renewal. The Court concluded that because no state statute or university regulation created any legitimate claim to reemployment or procedural due process, Roth lacked a property interest that would have required university officials to afford him a hearing when they chose not to renew his employment contract.

Implications

Roth has three key implications for due process rights of educators in higher education. First, *Roth* underscores the vital role that state statutes and university policies play in determining whether, and to what extent, educators possess due process protections. In *Perry v. Sindermann*, which was resolved on the same day as *Roth*, the Supreme Court also recognized that a university's de facto, rather than formal, tenure policy may create a property interest for employees.

Second, *Roth* stands for the proposition that employees who have liberty or property interests must be provided with procedural due process, typically including statements of the reasons their contracts are not being renewed along with opportunities for hearings to challenge such actions. After *Roth*, in *Cleveland Board of Education v. Loudermill* (1985), the Supreme Court extended due process protections to the pretermination stage for employees with property interests.

Third, *Roth* is important because it highlights the fact that although employees may have due process guarantees created by their employment contracts, these normally exist only for the duration of their contracts. Moreover, when employees do not have contractual rights or liberty or property interests, officials at their universities or colleges may choose to not rehire them without providing explanations or opportunities to present their arguments at hearings. While a sense of fairness might dictate that employers provide due process, and a denial of due process may encourage grievances along with litigation, the Supreme Court made it clear that *Roth* enables employers to withhold due process in contract nonrenewal situations when employees have neither liberty nor property interests at stake.

Ralph Sharp

See also Due Process, Substantive and Procedural; Due Process Rights in Faculty and Staff Dismissal; Fourteenth Amendment; *Perry v. Sindermann*; Tenure

Legal Citations

Board of Regents of State Colleges v. Roth, 408 U.S. 564 (1972).
Cleveland Board of Education v. Loudermill, 470 U.S. 532 (1985).
Perry v. Sindermann, 408 U.S. 593 (1972).

BOARD OF REGENTS OF STATE COLLEGES V. ROTH

In *Roth*, decided on the same day as *Perry v. Sindermann*, the Supreme Court addressed the due process rights of non-tenured faculty members whose employment contracts are not renewed.

Supreme Court of the United States

BOARD OF REGENTS OF STATE COLLEGES

v.

ROTH

408 U.S. 564

Argued Jan. 18, 1972

Decided June 29, 1972

Mr. Justice STEWART delivered the opinion of the Court.

In 1968 the respondent, David Roth, was hired for his first teaching job as assistant professor of political science at Wisconsin State University-Oshkosh. He was hired for a fixed term of one academic year. The notice of his faculty appointment specified that his employment would begin on September 1, 1968, and would end on June 30, 1969. The respondent completed that term. But he was informed that he would not be rehired for the next academic year.

The respondent had no tenure rights to continued employment. Under Wisconsin statutory law a state university teacher can acquire tenure as a "permanent" employee only after four years of year-to-year employment. Having acquired tenure, a teacher is entitled to continued employment "during efficiency and good behavior." A relatively new teacher without tenure, however, is under Wisconsin law entitled to nothing beyond his one-year appointment. There are no statutory or administrative standards defining eligibility for re-employment. State law thus clearly leaves the decision whether to rehire a nontenured teacher for another year to the unfettered discretion of university officials.

The procedural protection afforded a Wisconsin State University teacher before he is separated from the University corresponds to his job security. As a matter of statutory law, a tenured teacher cannot be "discharged except for cause upon written charges" and pursuant to certain procedures. A nontenured teacher, similarly, is protected to some extent during his one-year term. Rules promulgated by the Board of Regents provide that a nontenured teacher "dismissed" before the end of the year may have some opportunity for review of the "dismissal." But the Rules provide no real protection for a nontenured teacher who simply is not re-employed for the next year. He must be informed by February 1 "concerning retention or non-retention for the ensuing year." But "no reason for non-retention need be given. No review or appeal is provided in such case."

In conformance with these Rules, the President of Wisconsin State University-Oshkosh informed the respondent before February 1, 1969, that he would not be rehired for the 1969–1970 academic year. He gave the respondent no reason for the decision and no opportunity to challenge it at any sort of hearing.

The respondent then brought this action in Federal District Court alleging that the decision not to rehire him for the next year infringed his Fourteenth Amendment rights. He attacked the decision both in substance and procedure. . . .

The District Court granted summary judgment for the respondent on the procedural issue, ordering the University officials to provide him with reasons and a hearing. The Court of Appeals, with one judge dissenting, affirmed this partial summary judgment. We granted certiorari. The only question presented to us at this stage in the case is whether the respondent had a constitutional right to a statement of reasons and a hearing on the University's decision not to rehire him for another year. We hold that he did not.

I

The requirements of procedural due process apply only to the deprivation of interests encompassed by the Fourteenth Amendment's protection of liberty and property. When protected interests are implicated, the right to some kind of prior hearing is paramount. But the range of interests protected by procedural due process is not infinite.

The District Court decided that procedural due process guarantees apply in this case by assessing and balancing the weights of the particular interests involved. It concluded that the respondent's interest in re-employment at Wisconsin State University-Oshkosh outweighed the University's interest in denying him re-employment summarily. Undeniably, the respondent's re-employment prospects were of major concern to him—concern that we surely cannot say was insignificant. And a weighing process has long been a part of any determination of the form of hearing required in particular situations by procedural due process. But, to determine whether due process requirements apply in the first place, we must look not to the "weight" but to the nature of the interest at stake. We must look to see if the interest is within the Fourteenth Amendment's protection of liberty and property.

"'Liberty' and 'property' are broad and majestic terms. They are among the '(g)reat (constitutional) concepts . . . purposely left to gather meaning from experience. . . . (T)hey relate to the whole domain of social and economic fact, and the statesmen who founded this Nation knew too well that only a stagnant society remains unchanged.'" For that reason, the Court has fully and finally rejected the wooden distinction between "rights" and "privileges" that once seemed to govern the applicability of procedural due process rights. The Court has also made clear that the property interests protected by procedural due process extend well beyond actual ownership of real estate, chattels, or money. By the same token, the Court has required due process protection for deprivations of liberty beyond the sort of formal constraints imposed by the criminal process.

Yet, while the Court has eschewed rigid or formalistic limitations on the protection of procedural due process, it has at the same time observed certain boundaries. For the words "liberty" and "property" in the Due Process Clause of the Fourteenth Amendment must be given some meaning.

II

"While this court has not attempted to define with exactness the liberty . . . guaranteed (by the Fourteenth Amendment), the term has received much consideration and some of the included things have been definitely stated. Without doubt, it denotes not merely freedom from bodily restraint but also the right of the individual to contract, to engage in any of the common occupations of life, to acquire useful knowledge, to marry, establish a home and bring up children, to worship God according to the dictates of his own conscience, and generally to enjoy those privileges long recognized . . . as essential to the orderly pursuit of happiness by free men." In a Constitution for a free people, there can be no doubt that the meaning of "liberty" must be broad indeed.

There might be cases in which a State refused to re-employ a person under such circumstances that interests in liberty would be implicated. But this is not such a case.

The State, in declining to rehire the respondent, did not make any charge against him that might seriously damage his standing and associations in his community. It did not base the nonrenewal of his contract on a charge, for example, that he had been guilty of dishonesty, or immorality. Had it done so, this would be a different case. . . .

Similarly, there is no suggestion that the State, in declining to re-employ the respondent, imposed on him a stigma or other disability that foreclosed his freedom to take advantage of other employment opportunities. The State, for example, did not invoke any regulations to bar the respondent from all other public employment in state universities. Had it done so, this, again, would be a different case. For "(t)o be deprived not only of present government employment but of future opportunity for it certainly is no small injury. . . ." The Court has held, for example, that a State, in regulating eligibility for a type of professional employment, cannot foreclose a range of opportunities "in a manner . . . that contravene(s) . . . Due Process," and, specifically, in a manner that denies the right to a full prior hearing. In the present case, however, this principle does not come into play.

To be sure, the respondent has alleged that the non-renewal of his contract was based on his exercise of his right to freedom of speech. But this allegation is not now before us. The District Court stayed proceedings on this issue, and the respondent has yet to prove that the decision not to rehire him was, in fact, based on his free speech activities.

Hence, on the record before us, all that clearly appears is that the respondent was not rehired for one year at one university. It stretches the concept too far to suggest that a person is deprived of "liberty" when he simply is not rehired in one job but remains as free as before to seek another.

III

The Fourteenth Amendment's procedural protection of property is a safeguard of the security of interests that a person has already acquired in specific benefits. These interests—property interests—may take many forms.

Thus, the Court has held that a person receiving welfare benefits under statutory and administrative standards defining eligibility for them has an interest in continued receipt of those benefits that is safeguarded by procedural due process. Similarly, in the area of public employment, the Court has held that a public college professor dismissed from an office held under tenure provisions and college professors and staff members dismissed during the terms of their contracts have interests in continued employment that are safeguarded by due process. Only last year, the Court held that this principle "proscribing summary dismissal from public employment without hearing or inquiry required by due process" also applied to a teacher recently hired without tenure or a formal contract, but nonetheless with a clearly implied promise of continued employment.

Certain attributes of "property" interests protected by procedural due process emerge from these decisions. To have a property interest in a benefit, a person clearly must have more than an abstract need or desire for it. He must have more than a unilateral expectation of it. He must, instead, have a legitimate claim of entitlement to it. It is a purpose of the ancient institution of property to protect those claims upon which people rely in their daily lives, reliance that must not be arbitrarily undermined. It is a purpose of the constitutional right to a hearing to provide an opportunity for a person to vindicate those claims.

Property interests, of course, are not created by the Constitution. Rather they are created and their dimensions are defined by existing rules or understandings that stem from an independent source such as state law—rules or understandings that secure certain benefits and that support claims of entitlement to those benefits. Thus, the welfare recipients in *Goldberg v. Kelly,* had a claim of entitlement to welfare payments that was grounded in the statute defining eligibility for them. The recipients had not yet shown that they were, in fact, within the statutory terms of eligibility. But we held that they had a right to a hearing at which they might attempt to do so.

Just as the welfare recipients' "property" interest in welfare payments was created and defined by statutory terms, so the respondent's "property" interest in employment at Wisconsin State University-Oshkosh was created and defined by the terms of his appointment. Those terms secured his interest in employment up to June 30, 1969. But the important fact in this case is that they specifically provided that the respondent's employment was to terminate on June 30. They did not provide for contract renewal absent "sufficient cause." Indeed, they made no provision for renewal whatsoever.

Thus, the terms of the respondent's appointment secured absolutely no interest in re-employment for the next year. They supported absolutely no possible claim of entitlement to re-employment. Nor, significantly, was there any state statute or University rule or policy that secured his interest in re-employment or that created any legitimate claim to it. In these circumstances, the respondent surely had an abstract concern in being rehired, but he did not have a property interest sufficient to require the University authorities to give him a hearing when they declined to renew his contract of employment.

IV

Our analysis of the respondent's constitutional rights in this case in no way indicates a view that an opportunity for a hearing or a statement of reasons for nonretention would, or would not, be appropriate or wise in public colleges and universities. For it is a written Constitution that we apply. Our role is confined to interpretation of that Constitution.

We must conclude that the summary judgment for the respondent should not have been granted, since the respondent has not shown that he was deprived of liberty or property protected by the Fourteenth Amendment. The judgment of the Court of Appeals, accordingly, is reversed and the case is remanded for further proceedings consistent with this opinion.

It is so ordered.

Reversed and remanded.

BOARD OF REGENTS OF THE UNIVERSITY OF WISCONSIN SYSTEM V. SOUTHWORTH

Board of Regents of the University of Wisconsin System v. Southworth (2000) is a U.S. Supreme Court case that addresses funding of student groups by a public university. Specifically, according to *Southworth,* if officials at state institutions of higher learning allocate funds in a viewpoint-neutral manner, they may impose mandatory student fees and distribute those fees to student organizations. Because *Southworth* validates the common practice of administrators at most public institutions of higher learning while providing guidance for compliance with the Constitution, this entry reviews its background and the Court's rationale.

Facts of the Case

Southworth arose as a constitutional challenge to the method of financing student organizations in the University of Wisconsin system. Wisconsin imposes a mandatory student fee, a portion of which officials use to fund student activities, including various political and ideological groups. Some of the students objected to this practice, because they feared that they were being forced to subsidize the promotion of controversial viewpoints with which they disagreed. In particular, the students claimed that the First Amendment precluded such forced subsidization. Outside the context of higher education, particularly in disputes concerning labor unions in education, the Court has ruled that individuals may not be compelled to support political and ideological positions with which they disagree. The students sought to extend the same principle to higher education.

A federal trial court, in an unpublished order, agreed with the students, but a sharply divided Seventh Circuit rejected their claim. The Seventh Circuit was of the opinion that because providing funding to private organizations that engaged in political activities, speech, and advocacy violated the free speech rights of the objecting students, and the injunctive relief that the trial court's order was inadequate, further proceedings were necessary. In light of the conflict between the federal trial court and the Seventh Circuit, the Supreme Court agreed to hear an appeal.

The Supreme Court's Ruling

On further review, a unanimous Supreme Court, in a judgment authored by Justice Kennedy, reversed and remanded in favor of university officials. The justices agreed that as long as the fee allocation system was viewpoint-neutral, meaning that funds were distributed in a manner that did not favor one group over another, officials at state colleges and universities could impose mandatory student fees and use the proceeds to fund student organizations.

At the outset of its analysis, the Supreme Court noted that the speech of the challenged student organizations was not the speech of the university or the government. Rather, the Court observed that the speech at issue was that of private organizations. As such, the Court viewed the question as to whether students could be forced to subsidize the speech of private organizations with which they disagreed.

The Supreme Court pointed out that under its own precedent, the students could not have been forced to subsidize speech that was not germane to the purpose for which they were being taxed. The Court rejected the extension of that rule to the context of higher education. In this way, the Court recognized that university officials had the authority to evaluate whether the institution's mission was well served if students had the means to engage in dynamic discussions of philosophical, religious, scientific, social, and political subjects in their extracurricular campus life outside of lecture halls.

At the same time, the Supreme Court emphasized that university officials did not have absolute discretion with regard to the use of the funds that they collected. The Court explained that university officials had to continue to provide some protection to the First Amendment interests of their students. The Court posited that officials could have

met this responsibility by using viewpoint neutrality in the allocation of funding support just as it had ordered in *Rosenberger v. Rector and Visitors of the University of Virginia* (1995), wherein it directed officials to pay for the costs of printing a publication of a religious group on campus, because their failure to do so would have been impermissible viewpoint discrimination. Insofar as the parties had stipulated that the University of Wisconsin's financing system was viewpoint-neutral, meaning that they agreed to this at an earlier phase in the litigation, the Court found that the overall system was constitutional.

In rounding out its judgment, the Supreme Court remained troubled by one aspect of the funding system that was employed in the state university system. The Court acknowledged that in some instances the student body could vote in a referendum to deny funds to particular organizations. However, because the judicial record had not yet developed on this issue, the Court remanded the dispute for a further consideration as to whether such a system was viewpoint-neutral.

Justice Souter, joined by Justice Stevens and Justice Breyer, concurred in the judgment. Even so, these justices disagreed to the extent that they would not have imposed the requirement of viewpoint neutrality. Rather, these justices would have concluded that the interests of the objecting students were not sufficient to overcome the university's interests.

Almost a decade after it was resolved, *Southworth* remains the cornerstone of the Supreme Court's jurisprudence on funding student organizations. Its basic holding, that officials at public colleges and universities may impose mandatory student fees as long as they distribute the proceeds in a viewpoint-neutral manner, is largely uncontroversial. Still, because there is much dispute as to what is viewpoint-neutral, it can be expected that litigation will continue to emerge on this topic.

William E. Thro

See also Free Speech and Expression Rights of Students; *Rosenberger v. Rector and Visitors of the University of Virginia*

Further Readings

Wood, R. C., & Schilling, A. J. (2000). The legal dilemma created by mandatory student activity fees:

The Supreme Court offers a resolution in *Wisconsin v. Southworth*. *Education Law Reporter, 147*, 413–428.

Legal Citations

Board of Regents of the University of Wisconsin System v. Southworth, 529 U.S. 217 (2000), *on remand,*

221 F.3d 1339 (7th Cir. 2000), *on remand,* 132 F. Supp. 2d 740 (W.D. Wis. 2000), 132 F. Supp. 2d 744 (W.D. Wis. 2000), *aff'd in part, rev'd in part,* 307 F.3d 566 (7th Cir. 2002).

Rosenberger v. Rector and Visitors of University of Virginia, 515 U.S. 819 (1995).

BOARD OF REGENTS OF THE UNIVERSITY OF WISCONSIN SYSTEM V. SOUTHWORTH

According to *Southworth,* if officials at state institutions of higher learning allocate funds in a viewpoint-neutral manner, they may impose mandatory student fees and distribute those monies to campus organizations.

Supreme Court of the United States

BOARD OF REGENTS OF THE UNIVERSITY OF WISCONSIN SYSTEM

v.

SOUTHWORTH

529 U.S. 217

Argued Nov. 9, 1999

Decided March 22, 2000

Justice KENNEDY delivered the opinion of the Court.

For the second time in recent years we consider constitutional questions arising from a program designed to facilitate extracurricular student speech at a public university. Respondents are a group of students at the University of Wisconsin (hereinafter University). They brought a First Amendment challenge to a mandatory student activity fee imposed by petitioner Board of Regents of the University of Wisconsin System and used in part by the University to support student organizations engaging in political or ideological speech. Respondents object to the speech and expression of some of the student organizations. Relying upon our precedents which protect members of unions and bar associations from being required to pay fees used for speech the members find objectionable, both the District Court and the Court of Appeals invalidated the University's student fee program. The University contends that its mandatory student activity fee and the speech which it supports are appropriate to further its educational mission.

We reverse. The First Amendment permits a public university to charge its students an activity fee used to fund a program to facilitate extracurricular student speech if the program is viewpoint neutral. We do not sustain, however, the student referendum mechanism of the University's program, which appears to permit the exaction of fees in violation of the viewpoint neutrality principle. As to that aspect of the program, we remand for further proceedings.

I

The University of Wisconsin is a public corporation of the State of Wisconsin. State law defines the University's mission in broad terms: "to develop human resources, to discover and disseminate knowledge, to extend knowledge and its application beyond the boundaries of its campuses and to serve and stimulate society by developing in students heightened intellectual, cultural and humane sensitivities . . . and a sense of purpose." . . .

The responsibility for governing the University of Wisconsin System is vested by law with the board of regents. The same law empowers the students to share in aspects of the University's governance. One of those functions is to administer the student activities fee program. . . . The students do so, in large measure, through their student government, called the Associated Students of Madison (ASM), and various ASM subcommittees. The program the University maintains to support the extracurricular activities undertaken by many of its student organizations is the subject of the present controversy.

It seems that since its founding the University has required full-time students enrolled at its Madison campus to pay a nonrefundable activity fee. For the 1995–1996 academic year, when this suit was commenced, the activity fee amounted to $331.50 per year. The fee is segregated from the University's tuition charge. Once collected, the activity fees are deposited by the University into the accounts of the State of Wisconsin. The fees are drawn upon by the University to support various campus services and extracurricular student activities. . . .

The board of regents classifies the segregated fee into allocable and nonallocable portions. The nonallocable portion approximates 80% of the total fee and covers expenses such as student health services, intramural sports, debt service, and the upkeep and operations of the student union facilities. Respondents did not challenge the purposes to which the University commits the nonallocable portion of the segregated fee.

The allocable portion of the fee supports extracurricular endeavors pursued by the University's registered student organizations or RSO's. To qualify for RSO status students must organize as a not-for-profit group, limit membership primarily to students, and agree to undertake activities related to student life on campus. During the 1995–1996 school year, 623 groups had RSO status on the Madison campus. To name but a few, RSO's included the Future Financial Gurus of America; the International Socialist Organization; the College Democrats; the College Republicans; and the American Civil Liberties Union Campus Chapter. As one would expect, the expressive activities undertaken by RSO's are diverse in range and content, from displaying posters and circulating newsletters throughout the campus, to hosting campus debates and guest speakers, and to what can best be described as political lobbying.

RSO's may obtain a portion of the allocable fees in one of three ways. Most do so by seeking funding from the Student Government Activity Fund (SGAF), administered by the ASM. SGAF moneys may be issued to support an RSO's operations and events, as well as travel expenses "central to the purpose of the organization." As an alternative, an RSO can apply for funding from the General Student Services Fund (GSSF), administered through the ASM's finance committee. During the 1995–1996 academic year, 15 RSO's received GSSF funding. . . .

These RSO's included a campus tutoring center, the student radio station, a student environmental group, a gay and bisexual student center, a community legal office, an AIDS support network, a campus women's center, and the Wisconsin Student Public Interest Research Group (WISPIRG). The University acknowledges that, in addition to providing campus services (*e.g.,* tutoring and counseling), the GSSF-funded RSO's engage in political and ideological expression.

The GSSF, as well as the SGAF, consists of moneys originating in the allocable portion of the mandatory fee. The parties have stipulated that, with respect to SGAF and GSSF funding, "[t]he process for reviewing and approving allocations for funding is administered in a viewpoint-neutral fashion" and that the University does not use the fee program for "advocating a particular point of view."

A student referendum provides a third means for an RSO to obtain funding. While the record is sparse on this feature of the University's program, the parties inform us that the student body can vote either to approve or to disapprove an assessment for a particular RSO. One referendum resulted in an allocation of $45,000 to WISPIRG during the 1995–1996 academic year. At oral argument, counsel for the University acknowledged that a referendum could also operate to defund an RSO or to veto a funding decision of the ASM. In October 1996, for example, the student body voted to terminate funding to a national student organization to which the University belonged. Both parties confirmed at oral argument that their stipulation regarding the program's viewpoint neutrality does not extend to the referendum process.

With respect to GSSF and SGAF funding, the ASM or its finance committee makes initial funding decisions. The ASM does so in an open session, and interested students may attend meetings when RSO funding is discussed. It also appears that the ASM must approve the results of a student referendum. Approval appears *pro forma,* however, as counsel for the University advised us that the student government "voluntarily views th[e] referendum as binding." Once the ASM approves an RSO's funding application, it forwards its decision to the chancellor and to the board of regents for their review and approval. Approximately 30% of the University's RSO's received funding during the 1995–1996 academic year.

RSO's, as a general rule, do not receive lump-sum cash distributions. Rather, RSO's obtain funding support on a reimbursement basis by submitting receipts or invoices to the University. Guidelines identify expenses appropriate for reimbursement. Permitted expenditures include, in the main, costs for printing, postage, office supplies, and use of University facilities and equipment. Materials printed with student fees must contain a disclaimer that the views expressed are not those of the ASM. The University also reimburses RSO's for fees arising from membership in "other related and non-profit organizations."

The University's policy establishes purposes for which fees may not be expended. RSO's may not receive reimbursement . . . The same policy adds that an RSO "shall not use [student fees] for any lobbying purposes." At one point in their brief respondents suggest that the prohibition against expenditures for "politically partisan" purposes renders the program not viewpoint neutral. In view of the fact that both parties entered a stipulation to the contrary at the outset of this litigation, which was again reiterated during oral argument in this Court, we do not consider respondents' challenge to this aspect of the University's program.

The University's Student Organization Handbook has guidelines for regulating the conduct and activities of RSO's. In addition to obligating RSO's to adhere to the fee program's rules and regulations, the guidelines establish procedures authorizing any student to complain to the University that an RSO is in noncompliance. An extensive investigative process is in place to evaluate and remedy violations. The University's policy includes a range of sanctions for noncompliance, including probation, suspension, or termination of RSO status.

One RSO that appears to operate in a manner distinct from others is WISPIRG. For reasons not clear from the record, WISPIRG receives lump-sum cash distributions from the University. University counsel informed us that this distribution reduced the GSSF portion of the fee pool. The full extent of the uses to which WISPIRG puts its funds is unclear. We do know, however, that WISPIRG sponsored on-campus events regarding homelessness and environmental and consumer protection issues. It coordinated community food drives and educational programs and spent a portion of its activity fees for the lobbying efforts of its parent organization

and for student internships aimed at influencing legislation.

In March 1996, respondents, each of whom attended or still attend the University's Madison campus, filed suit in the United States District Court for the Western District of Wisconsin against members of the board of regents. Respondents alleged, *inter alia*, that imposition of the segregated fee violated their rights of free speech, free association, and free exercise under the First Amendment. They contended the University must grant them the choice not to fund those RSO's that engage in political and ideological expression offensive to their personal beliefs. Respondents requested both injunctive and declaratory relief. On cross-motions for summary judgment, the District Court ruled in their favor, declaring the University's segregated fee program invalid under *Abood v. Detroit Bd. of Ed.*, and *Keller v. State Bar of Cal.* The District Court decided the fee program compelled students "to support political and ideological activity with which they disagree" in violation of respondents' First Amendment rights to freedom of speech and association. The court did not reach respondents' free exercise claim. The District Court's order enjoined the board of regents from using segregated fees to fund any RSO engaging in political or ideological speech.

The United States Court of Appeals for the Seventh Circuit affirmed in part, reversed in part, and vacated in part. As the District Court had done, the Court of Appeals found our compelled speech precedents controlling. After examining the University's fee program under the three-part test outlined in *Lehnert v. Ferris Faculty Assn.*, it concluded that the program was not germane to the University's mission, did not further a vital policy of the University, and imposed too much of a burden on respondents' free speech rights. "[L]ike the objecting union members in *Abood*," the Court of Appeals reasoned, the students here have a First Amendment interest in not being compelled to contribute to an organization whose expressive activities conflict with their own personal beliefs. It added that protecting the objecting students' free speech rights was "of heightened concern" following our decision in *Rosenberger v. Rector and Visitors of Univ. of Va.*, because "[i]f the university cannot discriminate in the disbursement of funds, it is imperative that students not be compelled to fund organizations which engage in political and ideological activities—that is the only way to protect the individual's rights." The Court of Appeals extended the District Court's order and enjoined the board of regents from requiring objecting students to pay that portion of the fee used to fund RSO's engaged in political or ideological expression.

Three members of the Court of Appeals dissented from the denial of the University's motion for rehearing en banc. . . .

Other courts addressing First Amendment challenges to similar student fee programs have reached conflicting results. . . . These conflicts, together with the importance of the issue presented, led us to grant certiorari. We reverse the judgment of the Court of Appeals.

II

It is inevitable that government will adopt and pursue programs and policies within its constitutional powers but which nevertheless are contrary to the profound beliefs and sincere convictions of some of its citizens. The government, as a general rule, may support valid programs and policies by taxes or other exactions binding on protesting parties. Within this broader principle it seems inevitable that funds raised by the government will be spent for speech and other expression to advocate and defend its own policies. The case we decide here, however, does not raise the issue of the government's right, or, to be more specific, the state-controlled University's right, to use its own funds to advance a particular message. The University's whole justification for fostering the challenged expression is that it springs from the initiative of the students, who alone give it purpose and content in the course of their extracurricular endeavors.

The University having disclaimed that the speech is its own, we do not reach the question whether traditional political controls to ensure responsible government action would be sufficient to overcome First Amendment objections and to allow the challenged program under the principle that the government can speak for itself. If the challenged speech here were financed by tuition dollars and the University and its officials were responsible for its content, the case might be evaluated on the premise that the government itself is the speaker. That is not the case before us.

The University of Wisconsin exacts the fee at issue for the sole purpose of facilitating the free and open exchange of ideas by, and among, its students. We conclude the objecting students may insist upon certain safeguards with respect to the expressive activities which they are required to support. Our public forum cases are instructive here by close analogy. This is true even though

the student activities fund is not a public forum in the traditional sense of the term and despite the circumstance that those cases most often involve a demand for access, not a claim to be exempt from supporting speech. The standard of viewpoint neutrality found in the public forum cases provides the standard we find controlling. We decide that the viewpoint neutrality requirement of the University program is in general sufficient to protect the rights of the objecting students. The student referendum aspect of the program for funding speech and expressive activities, however, appears to be inconsistent with the viewpoint neutrality requirement.

We must begin by recognizing that the complaining students are being required to pay fees which are subsidies for speech they find objectionable, even offensive. The *Abood* and *Keller* cases, then, provide the beginning point for our analysis. While those precedents identify the interests of the protesting students, the means of implementing First Amendment protections adopted in those decisions are neither applicable nor workable in the context of extracurricular student speech at a university.

In *Abood*, some nonunion public school teachers challenged an agreement requiring them, as a condition of their employment, to pay a service fee equal in amount to union dues. The objecting teachers alleged that the union's use of their fees to engage in political speech violated their freedom of association guaranteed by the First and Fourteenth Amendments. The Court agreed and held that any objecting teacher could "prevent the Union's spending a part of their required service fees to contribute to political candidates and to express political views unrelated to its duties as exclusive bargaining representative." The principles outlined in *Abood* provided the foundation for our later decision in *Keller*. There we held that lawyers admitted to practice in California could be required to join a state bar association and to fund activities "germane" to the association's mission of "regulating the legal profession and improving the quality of legal services." The lawyers could not, however, be required to fund the bar association's own political expression.

The proposition that students who attend the University cannot be required to pay subsidies for the speech of other students without some First Amendment protection follows from the *Abood* and *Keller* cases. Students enroll in public universities to seek fulfillment of their personal aspirations and of their own potential. If the University conditions the opportunity to receive a college education, an opportunity comparable in importance to joining a labor union or bar association, on an agreement to support objectionable, extracurricular expression by other students, the rights acknowledged in *Abood* and *Keller* become implicated. It infringes on the speech and beliefs of the individual to be required, by this mandatory student activity fee program, to pay subsidies for the objectionable speech of others without any recognition of the State's corresponding duty to him or her. Yet recognition must be given as well to the important and substantial purposes of the University, which seeks to facilitate a wide range of speech.

In *Abood* and *Keller*, the constitutional rule took the form of limiting the required subsidy to speech germane to the purposes of the union or bar association. The standard of germane speech as applied to student speech at a university is unworkable, however, and gives insufficient protection both to the objecting students and to the University program itself. Even in the context of a labor union, whose functions are, or so we might have thought, well known and understood by the law and the courts after a long history of government regulation and judicial involvement, we have encountered difficulties in deciding what is germane and what is not. The difficulty manifested itself in our decision in *Lehnert v. Ferris Faculty Assn.* where different Members of the Court reached varying conclusions regarding what expressive activity was or was not germane to the mission of the association. If it is difficult to define germane speech with ease or precision where a union or bar association is the party, the standard becomes all the more unmanageable in the public university setting, particularly where the State undertakes to stimulate the whole universe of speech and ideas.

The speech the University seeks to encourage in the program before us is distinguished not by discernable limits but by its vast, unexplored bounds. To insist upon asking what speech is germane would be contrary to the very goal the University seeks to pursue. It is not for the Court to say what is or is not germane to the ideas to be pursued in an institution of higher learning.

Just as the vast extent of permitted expression makes the test of germane speech inappropriate for intervention, so too does it underscore the high potential for intrusion on the First Amendment rights of the objecting students. It is all but inevitable that the fees will result in subsidies to speech which some students find objectionable and offensive to their personal beliefs. If the standard of germane speech is inapplicable, then, it might be argued the remedy is to allow each student to

list those causes which he or she will or will not support. If a university decided that its students' First Amendment interests were better protected by some type of optional or refund system it would be free to do so. We decline to impose a system of that sort as a constitutional requirement, however. The restriction could be so disruptive and expensive that the program to support extracurricular speech would be ineffective. The First Amendment does not require the University to put the program at risk.

The University may determine that its mission is well served if students have the means to engage in dynamic discussions of philosophical, religious, scientific, social, and political subjects in their extracurricular campus life outside the lecture hall. If the University reaches this conclusion, it is entitled to impose a mandatory fee to sustain an open dialogue to these ends.

The University must provide some protection to its students' First Amendment interests, however. The proper measure, and the principal standard of protection for objecting students, we conclude, is the requirement of viewpoint neutrality in the allocation of funding support.

Viewpoint neutrality was the obligation to which we gave substance in *Rosenberger v. Rector and Visitors of Univ. of Va.* There the University of Virginia feared that any association with a student newspaper advancing religious viewpoints would violate the Establishment Clause. We rejected the argument, holding that the school's adherence to a rule of viewpoint neutrality in administering its student fee program would prevent "any mistaken impression that the student newspapers speak for the University." While *Rosenberger* was concerned with the rights a student has to use an extracurricular speech program already in place, today's case considers the antecedent question, acknowledged but unresolved in *Rosenberger*: whether a public university may require its students to pay a fee which creates the mechanism for the extracurricular speech in the first instance. When a university requires its students to pay fees to support the extracurricular speech of other students, all in the interest of open discussion, it may not prefer some viewpoints to others. There is symmetry then in our holding here and in *Rosenberger*: Viewpoint neutrality is the justification for requiring the student to pay the fee in the first instance and for ensuring the integrity of the program's operation once the funds have been collected. We conclude that the University of Wisconsin may sustain the extracurricular dimensions of its programs by using mandatory student fees with viewpoint neutrality as the operational principle.

The parties have stipulated that the program the University has developed to stimulate extracurricular student expression respects the principle of viewpoint neutrality. If the stipulation is to continue to control the case, the University's program in its basic structure must be found consistent with the First Amendment.

We make no distinction between campus activities and the off-campus expressive activities of objectionable RSO's. Those activities, respondents tell us, often bear no relationship to the University's reason for imposing the segregated fee in the first instance, to foster vibrant campus debate among students. If the University shares those concerns, it is free to enact viewpoint neutral rules restricting off-campus travel or other expenditures by RSO's, for it may create what is tantamount to a limited public forum if the principles of viewpoint neutrality are respected. We find no principled way, however, to impose upon the University, as a constitutional matter, a requirement to adopt geographic or spatial restrictions as a condition for RSOs' entitlement to reimbursement. Universities possess significant interests in encouraging students to take advantage of the social, civic, cultural, and religious opportunities available in surrounding communities and throughout the country. Universities, like all of society, are finding that traditional conceptions of territorial boundaries are difficult to insist upon in an age marked by revolutionary changes in communications, information transfer, and the means of discourse. If the rule of viewpoint neutrality is respected, our holding affords the University latitude to adjust its extracurricular student speech program to accommodate these advances and opportunities.

Our decision ought not to be taken to imply that in other instances the University, its agents or employees, or—of particular importance—its faculty, are subject to the First Amendment analysis which controls in this case. Where the University speaks, either in its own name through its regents or officers, or in myriad other ways through its diverse faculties, the analysis likely would be altogether different. The Court has not held, or suggested, that when the government speaks the rules we have discussed come into play.

When the government speaks, for instance to promote its own policies or to advance a particular idea, it is, in the end, accountable to the electorate and the political process for its advocacy. If the citizenry objects, newly elected officials later could espouse some different or contrary position. In the instant case, the speech is not that of the University or its agents. It is not, furthermore, speech by an instructor or a professor in the academic context, where principles applicable to government speech would have to be considered.

III

It remains to discuss the referendum aspect of the University's program. While the record is not well developed on the point, it appears that by majority vote of the student body a given RSO may be funded or defunded. It is unclear to us what protection, if any, there is for viewpoint neutrality in this part of the process. To the extent the referendum substitutes majority determinations for viewpoint neutrality it would undermine the constitutional protection the program requires. The whole theory of viewpoint neutrality is that minority views are treated with the same respect as are majority views. Access to a public forum, for instance, does not depend upon majoritarian consent. That principle is controlling here. A remand is necessary and appropriate to resolve this point; and the case in all events must be reexamined in light of the principles we have discussed.

The judgment of the Court of Appeals is reversed, and the case is remanded for further proceedings consistent with this opinion. In this Court, the parties shall bear their own costs.

It is so ordered.

BOARDS OF TRUSTEES

The phrase *board of trustees* is synonymous with governance in higher education and is the most common name for groups of individuals who serve as the legal agents for and have authority over two-year colleges, four-year colleges, and universities in the United States. While several other types of boards provide similar governance, depending on their own unique institutional histories, they may have different names. Some examples of the other most common terms for these structures are *board of visitors*, as used by the Commonwealth of Virginia; *board of regents*, as used by New York, California, and several other states; *board of curators,* as used in Missouri; and *board of governors,* as used in North Carolina to describe the management of the entire university system even though each campus of the system has a separate board of trustees. The term *board of trustees* is also used to describe boards that serve related educational governance functions, such as the governing boards of quasi-independent, nonprofit foundations that raise money for institutional advancement. The term *boards* is used throughout this entry to refer to all such instances of governing structures. The entry focuses on describing the selection of members for boards, the responsibilities of boards, and the legal controversies involving boards.

Membership of Boards

The process of selection of board members varies among the many types of institutions of higher education operating in the United States. The means for selecting members is generally set out in the governing documents of colleges or universities, in the form of statutes or similar legislative provisions for state institutions, or in some form of charter if the institution is private in nature. For both public and private institutions, the governing documents contain rules about the number and length of terms board members may serve. Additionally, the number of members can range from less than 10 to more than 30.

For public institutions, selection is often made by the governor of the state or by the state legislature. In some cases, members are selected by the board of governors of the entire university system, while in other situations, members are directly elected by the public. Over the years, efforts have been made to remove the appearance of conflicts of interest in membership by prohibiting persons or their spouses from being board members if they occupy specified public offices or are employed by the state. Exceptions to this general rule are often made for ex officio members, such as student government presidents, presidents or former presidents of institutions, and other high-ranking public officials whose agencies have direct involvement with colleges or universities.

The majority of members come from the world of business; academics are rarities on boards. Board members tend to be prominent individuals with substantial leadership and executive management experience; also, many members are often distinguished alumni. The representation of women and minority groups has improved in recent decades but still lags behind equitable demographic representation. Insofar as membership on boards is seen as a great honor, members are rarely compensated for serving and receive reimbursement only for expenses related to board business.

For private institutions, some similarities to public institutions exist in the selection process, such as looking for prospective members from a pool of individuals who have connections to the institution. For instance, being a graduate or being a prominent member of the community is often a criterion for board membership for private institutions. However, many other considerations of the process are quite different due to the different missions of public and private institutions. In other words, private institutions may not have the same type of pressure to appoint political elites that may exist at public institutions, but that is not to say that officials at private colleges and universities do not have other outside pressures related to their institutional traditions in the appointment process.

Responsibilities of Boards

Boards are charged with overseeing the institution through the selection of a president or chancellor and the continuation of the institution's mission through policy development. Additionally, boards serve as the legal entities responsible for the overall operations of colleges and universities. As a result, boards often find themselves at the forefront of legal confrontations regarding higher education.

The key function of boards is the selection of a president or chancellor for single institutions or for an entire public college and/or university system. Here, again, there are differences between public and private institutions. Because they generally have more alumni, public systems have to get more extensive public input to reflect their larger constituencies; however, the diverse constituencies of private institutions can also create pressures during the selection process. One approach to this complicated process of selecting a president, which is utilized by both public and private institutions, is the use of executive search firms that specialize in finding higher education leaders. This outsourcing of a key function of board responsibility is often met with criticism; nevertheless, it has become almost standard procedure for boards, as it insulates them from the minutiae of the search and partially from the final outcome if the presidential choice does not work out as expected. Additionally, the use of search firms has been justified as a matter of confidentiality that is needed to attract high-profile leaders who do not want their names released to the public unless they are offered the position.

Boards' relationships with presidents can be contentious, especially when different visions for the institutions come into conflict. Further, new presidents with mandates from boards can come into conflict with faculties that are resistant to moves away from shared governance. These tensions often come from the differences in the backgrounds of board members and faculty, who often see the future of the institutions in quite different ways. Unfortunately, this type of tension can lead to votes of no confidence and, possibly, litigation.

In addition to hiring presidents, because boards are ultimately responsible for the operations of the campuses that they oversee, they typically make final decisions with regard to granting tenure to faculty members. Acting on input from chief academic officers, particularly in public colleges and universities, faculty members usually cannot be awarded tenure without an affirmative vote of institutional boards.

Setting institutional policies is another essential element of board governance. Institutions have different mandates depending on their nature, but the mechanism of adopting policies that regulate the campus environment finds its origin in board policy development. The development of these policies can be quite complex, technical, and implicative of considerable legal considerations. Therefore, many boards make use of committees to divide the work and institutional staff structures to provide professional legal or accounting advice.

Some of the most contentious aspects of board membership deal with the costs of attending their institutions. In these cases, board members have considerable challenges in weighing enrollment growth with increased costs for everything from instructional services to new technologies. Further, all boards across the country are concerned with increasing their institutions' national competitiveness and

prestige; this goal must be counterbalanced with the fact that improving one's reputation often requires increases in student fees and tuition. In states with constitutional mandates for low-cost public higher education, boards are undoubtedly concerned with possible litigation to cap rising costs.

Boards are also often tasked both formally and informally with serving as major fund-raising arms of their institutions. This function has increased in importance in the last few decades, as institutions seek to raise their endowments for new buildings and prestigious professorships. Of course, much of this fund-raising is also directed toward athletic programs and the scholarships that are needed to support them.

Litigation Involving Boards

Serving as the legal entities of record or agents of their institutions, boards have been at the nexus of many of the most important cases involving higher education and the law. The U.S. Supreme Court's first case addressing education on any level was *Trustees of Dartmouth College v. Woodward* (1819). In *Woodward* the Court upheld the authority of the board at a private college to engage in self-governance and maintenance without interference from state legislatures and other public entities.

The most prominent, controversial, and ongoing area in which boards have been involved in litigation has been access and admission to colleges and universities at both the undergraduate and graduate levels. The majority of these cases rely on claims under the Equal Protection Cause of the Fourteenth Amendment. For example, in *Sipuel v. Board of Regents of University of Oklahoma* (1948) the Supreme Court held that students could not be barred admission because of race. Similarly, in *McLaurin v. Oklahoma State Regents for Higher Education* (1950) and *Sweatt v. Painter* (1950), the Court found that students in higher education could not be educated in different ways based exclusively on the criterion of race. Each of these cases of expanding access to equitable higher education was of substantial importance as a precursor to the more well-known K–12 case of *Brown v. Board of Education, Topeka* (1954).

In another important Fourteenth Amendment case in higher education, *Regents of the University of California v. Bakke* (1978), the Supreme Court concluded that while educational programs that required quotas based on race were unconstitutional, efforts to diversify student bodies through affirmative action did not violate the Equal Protection Clause of the Fourteenth Amendment. The Court subsequently reached mixed results in cases involving diversity on campus, upholding such a plan for law school admissions at the University of Michigan in *Grutter v. Bollinger* (2003) on the basis that an admissions plan that took race into consideration was constitutional because it was narrowly tailored to achieve a compelling governmental interest and engaged in individualistic, holistic reviews of applicants. Conversely, in *Gratz v. Bollinger* (2003), resolved on the same day, the Court invalidated the admissions policy for an undergraduate program at the University of Michigan, because it was not was narrowly tailored to achieve a compelling governmental interest.

Many other issues have led to litigation against boards. Some brief examples follow. In *Keyishian v. Board of Regents of the University of the State of New York* (1967), the Supreme Court decided that state officials could not condition employment on loyalty oaths and that mere membership in organizations could not be judged to be subversive. In *Board of Regents of State Colleges v. Roth* (1972), the Court posited that a nontenured faculty member with a limited term contract was not entitled to the Fourteenth Amendment protection of procedural due process for contract renewal and rehiring. In *Board of Curators of the University of Missouri v. Horowitz* (1978), the Court indicated that a student could be dismissed for academic reasons without the due process protections that may be afforded for disciplinary actions, provided that such academic dismissal processes were not arbitrary and the institution had provided notice to the student for the need to improve. Further, in *Board of Regents of the University of Wisconsin System v. Southworth* (2000), the Court observed that required student activity fees could be used to support all types of student organizations regardless of their ideas and the speech they supported.

An incident that showcases the complicated nature of governance by boards is the battle between the University of Colorado and Ward Churchill, who was a faculty member in the Department of Ethnic Studies and the author of a controversial 2001 essay about the September 11 attacks. Following publicity about the essay, in which Churchill argued that the September 11 attacks were provoked by U.S. foreign policy, his employment was terminated by the regents of the university. However, the university agreed that his comments were protected by the First Amendment, and instead asserted that his firing was based on findings of research misconduct. Churchill successfully challenged his termination by the regents of the university, and in April 2009 he won a civil suit in which the jury awarded him one dollar in damages (Frosch, 2009). Churchill sought a court order to order his reinstatement, and in April 2009, the American Association of University Professors issued a statement supporting his claim. However, in July 2009, a trial court judge set aside the jury verdict, basically relying on the doctrine of academic abstention and recognizing that the decision to dismiss Churchill was a matter best left to university officials. In addition, though immunity was not discussed at trial, the Court had reserved this issue for further review. In its July ruling, the Court agreed that the Board was entitled to Eleventh Amendment immunity, absolving it from liability because it was acting as a public institution in a quasi-judicial capacity. Churchill plans to appeal.

Conclusion

Boards will undoubtedly continue as the structures governing and leading institutions of higher education into the future. Citizens and alumni of institutions should be keenly aware of the role these bodies have in shaping the direction of higher education policy in the United States. Conversely, boards must be aware of the legal implications of their decisions and draft policies that support the mission of their institution while seeking to understand the constituencies they serve.

Aaron Cooley

See also Academic Abstention; Academic Freedom; *Board of Curators of the University of Missouri v. Horowitz; Board of Regents of State Colleges v. Roth; Board of Regents of the University of Wisconsin System v. Southworth*; Eleventh Amendment; Equal Protection Analysis; Fourteenth Amendment; *Gratz v. Bollinger; Grutter v. Bollinger*; Loyalty Oaths; *McLaurin v.*

Oklahoma State Regents for Higher Education;
Political Activities and Speech of Faculty Members;
Regents of the University of California v. Bakke;
Sweatt v. Painter; Tenure; *Trustees of Dartmouth College v. Woodward*

Further Readings

Altbach, P., Berdahl, R., & Gumport, P. (Eds.). (2005). *American higher education in the twenty-first century: Social, political, and economic challenges* (2nd ed.). Baltimore: Johns Hopkins University Press.

Association of Governing Boards of Universities and Colleges: http://www.agb.org

Frosch, D. (2009, April 10). Campus still split after jury sides with professor. *The New York Times*, p. A16.

Ingram, R. T. (1993). *Governing public colleges and universities: A handbook for trustees, chief executives, and other campus leaders.* San Francisco: Jossey-Bass.

International Association of University Presidents: http://www.iaups.org

Kaplin, W., & Lee, B. (2006). *The law of higher education: A comprehensive guide to legal implications of administrative decision making* (4th ed.). New York: Jossey-Bass.

Olivas, M. (2006). *The law and higher education: Cases and materials on colleges in court.* Durham, NC: Carolina Academic Press.

Roth, J. (Ed.). (2007). *Higher education law in America.* Malvern, PA: Center for Education & Employment Law.

Smith, D. H. (1995). *Entrusted: The moral responsibilities of trusteeship.* Bloomington: Indiana University Press.

Southeastern Community College Board of Directors: http://www.scciowa.edu/about/board

University of North Carolina Board of Governors: http://www.northcarolina.edu/content.php/bog/index.htm

Legal Citations

Board of Curators of the University of Missouri v. Horowitz, 435 U.S. 78 (1978).

Board of Regents of State Colleges v. Roth, 408 U.S. 564 (1972).

Board of Regents of the University of Wisconsin System v. Southworth, 529 U.S. 217 (2000), *on remand,* 221 F.3d 1339 (7th Cir. 2000), *on remand,* 132 F. Supp. 2d 740 (W.D. Wis. 2000), 132 F. Supp. 2d 744 (W.D. Wis. 2000), *aff'd in part, rev'd in part,* 307 F.3d 566 (7th Cir. 2002).

Brown v. Board of Education, Topeka, 347 U.S. 483 (1954).

Gratz v. Bollinger, 539 U.S. 244 (2003).

Grutter v. Bollinger, 539 U.S. 306 (2003).

Keyishian v. Board of Regents of the University of the State of New York, 385 U.S. 589 (1967).

McLaurin v. Oklahoma State Regents for Higher Education, 339 U.S. 637 (1950).

Regents of the University of California v. Bakke, 438 U.S. 265 (1978).

Sipuel v. Board of Regents of Univ. of Oklahoma, 332 U.S. 631 (1948), *mandate denied sub nom. Fisher v. Hurst,* 333 U.S. 147 (1948).

Sweatt v. Painter, 339 U.S. 629 (1950).

Trustees of Dartmouth College v. Woodward, 17 U.S. 518 (1819).

BOB JONES UNIVERSITY V. UNITED STATES

The U.S. Supreme Court's 1983 opinion in *Bob Jones University v. United States, Goldsboro Christian School v. United States,* was a landmark decision in companion cases on tax exemptions for charitable giving to colleges and universities as well as K–12 schools. Institutions of higher education, whether public or private, are exempt from most forms of taxation, because they provide an essential public service for society. At issue in *Bob Jones* was whether nonprofit private universities that prescribe and enforce racially discriminatory admission standards on the basis of religious doctrine qualify as tax-exempt organizations under Section 501(c)(3) of the Internal Revenue Code. Ultimately, the Supreme Court ruled that such institutions do not qualify as tax-exempt organizations, because discriminatory policies and practices do not serve a public purpose and are contrary to established public policy.

Facts of the Case

According to Section 501(c)(3) of the Internal Revenue Code (IRC) of 1954, "Corporations . . . organized and operated exclusively for religious, charitable . . . or educational purposes" are entitled to tax exemption. Until 1970, the Internal Revenue Service (IRS) granted tax-exempt status to all private institutions independent of their racial admissions policies and permitted charitable deductions for contributions to such institutions under Section 170 of the IRC. However, in July 1970, the IRS announced that it could no longer justify extending tax exemptions to private colleges and universities that practiced racial discrimination. The IRS notified Bob Jones University officials on November 30, 1970, of the pending challenge to its tax exemption, and in early 1971, the IRS issued Revenue Ruling 71-447 requiring all "charitable" institutions to adopt and publish a nondiscrimination policy in compliance with the common law concepts in sections 501(c)(3) and 170 of the IRC.

In 1970, Bob Jones University was a nonprofit religious and educational institution serving 5,000 students from kindergarten through graduate school. The university was not affiliated with any particular religious denomination but was committed to the teaching and propagation of fundamentalist religious doctrine. All courses in the curriculum were taught from the Biblical perspective, and all teachers were required to be devout Christians as determined by university leaders. University benefactors and administrators maintained that the Bible forbade interracial dating and marriage, and African Americans were denied admission based solely on their race prior to 1971.

After the IRS published Ruling 71-447, university officials accepted applications from African Americans who were married to spouses of the same race but continued to deny admission to unmarried African Americans. Following the Fourth Circuit's 1975 decision in *McCrary v. Runyon* prohibiting private institutions from excluding minorities, Bob Jones University again revised its policy and permitted single Black students to enroll while implementing a strict rule that prohibited interracial dating and marriage. Students who violated the rule or even advocated its violation were expelled immediately. The university did not adopt and publish a nondiscriminatory admission policy in compliance with Ruling 71-447 directives.

After failing to restore its tax exemption through administrative procedures, Bob Jones University sought to enjoin the IRS from revoking its exemption, but the Supreme Court dismissed the claim. The IRS officially revoked the university's tax-exempt status on January 19, 1976, making its order effective retroactively to December 1, 1970, the day after the university officials were first informed that the institution's tax-exemption was in jeopardy. Subsequently, university officials filed suit against the IRS, demanding a $21.00 refund for unemployment taxes paid on one employee in 1975. The federal government counterfiled immediately for approximately $490,000 (plus interest) in unpaid unemployment taxes.

The federal trial court in South Carolina, in ruling that the IRS exceeded its authority, ordered it to pay the refund and dismissed the IRS's claims, prompting the IRS to appeal. The Fourth Circuit reversed in favor of the IRS, concluding that the university's admission policy violated federal law and public policy. The Fourth Circuit held that because Bob Jones University could not be considered "charitable," contributions to it were not deductible under IRC provisions, and the IRS acted legally and appropriately in revoking the tax exemption. The court added that extending the university's tax-exempt status would have been tantamount to subsidizing racial discrimination with public tax money. The Fourth Circuit remanded the dispute with instructions to dismiss the university's suit and reinstate the government's claim for back taxes.

In a companion case involving Goldsboro Christian Schools, the Fourth Circuit rejected the school's request for tax-exempt status and its claim that denial of a tax exemption would violate its First Amendment rights. Like Bob Jones University, Goldsboro Christian Schools had a racially discriminatory admissions policy against Black students based on its interpretation of the scriptures. As in the Bob Jones case, the Fourth Circuit found that the petitioner did not qualify for tax-exempt status under Section 501(c)(3) of the IRC. The U.S. Supreme Court granted certiorari in both cases and affirmed the Fourth Circuit in each.

The Supreme Court's Ruling

In its review of the cases, the Supreme Court sought to balance the interests of sincerely held religious beliefs and related First Amendment concerns with federal law and public policy prohibiting racial discrimination. The Court traced the history of tax exemptions for charitable institutions, quoting from its landmark 1861 decision in

Perin v. Carey, "It has now become an established principle of American law, that courts of chancery will sustain and protect . . . a gift . . . to public charitable uses, provided the same is consistent with local laws and public policy."

The Supreme Court's analysis in *Bob Jones* revealed the following key facts. First, tax-exempt institutions must serve a public purpose through practices that do not violate public policy. The Court pointed out that Bob Jones University's admission policy clearly discriminated against African Americans in a direct violation of public policy. Second, under IRC provisions, sectarian institutions cannot be tax-exempt if their religious doctrines lead to violations of law. Third, the IRS did not exceed its authority in denying tax exemptions to Bob Jones University and Goldsboro Christian Schools. Indeed, the Court reasoned that the IRS's ruling was entirely consistent with previous declarations from the legislative, executive, and judicial branches of government. Fourth, the government's interest in eliminating racial discrimination outweighs a private institution's exercise of its religious beliefs. Clearly, the Court maintained, the religious interests of Bob Jones University were contrary to the interests and rights of the government and the general public.

In sum, the Supreme Court's opinion in *Bob Jones* stands for the proposition that because non-profit, private universities and schools that enforce discriminatory admission policies based on religious doctrine do not qualify for tax exemptions, contributions to such institutions are not deductible as charitable donations within the meaning of the Internal Revenue Code. As a statement on its Web site shows, in 2000, Bob Jones University acknowledged that it had been wrong in not admitting African American students and lifted its ban on interracial dating.

Robert C. Cloud

See also Religious Colleges and Universities; U.S. Supreme Court Cases in Higher Education

Legal Citations

Bob Jones University v. United States, Goldsboro Christian School v. United States, 461 U.S. 574 (1983).
Internal Revenue Code, 20 U.S.C.A. §§ 170, 501(c)(3).
McCrary v. Runyon, 515 F.2d 1082 (4th Cir. 1975), *aff'd,* 427 U.S. 160 (1976).
Perin v. Carey, 24 How. 465, 501 (1861).

C

CANNON V. UNIVERSITY OF CHICAGO

Cannon v. University of Chicago (1979) stands out as the first case in which the U.S. Supreme Court recognized an implied cause of action for monetary damages under Section 901 of the Education Amendments of 1972, more commonly referred to as Title IX, in response to discrimination based on sex. The Court's judgment in *Cannon* paved the way for the subsequent application of Title IX in a wide array of cases involving gender equity for students in the world of higher education.

Facts of the Case

In 1975, Geraldine Cannon, a 39-year-old female, applied for but was denied admission to two private medical schools in Illinois, the University of Chicago and Northwestern University. Both medical schools, which were recipients of federal financial assistance, had formal policies of not admitting candidates who were over the age of 30 unless they had already earned advanced degrees. In addition, Northwestern University had a policy of denying applicants who were over 35 years of age. When Cannon learned that the admissions policies were more difficult for persons over 30 years of age than for younger, traditional candidates, she claimed they were more likely to be discriminatory against women, whose educations were typically more interrupted than those of men. She filed a legal complaint with the Department of Health, Education, and Welfare alleging that university officials engaged in sex discrimination in violation of Title IX. Cannon's primary legal argument against the admission policies was that women often need to interrupt their studies in higher education to give birth and raise families, which increases the percentage of female applicants over the age of 30 when compared to their male counterparts in the same age category.

Three months later, Cannon unsuccessfully filed suit in a federal trial court in Illinois against both universities alleging that the schools discriminated against her on the basis of sex in violation of the Fourteenth Amendment to the U.S. Constitution, the Civil Rights Act of 1871, and Title IX; in a distinction worth noting, when addressing the rights of employees and gender equity, cases are filed under Title VII of the Civil Rights Act of 1964, a statute that is beyond the scope of this entry. The court dismissed the complaint for failure to allege purposeful discrimination and granted the universities' motions to dismiss the complaint, because Title IX did not expressly authorize or properly imply a private right of action for alleged victims of sex discrimination.

Shortly after the Seventh Circuit affirmed in favor of the defendants, Congress passed the Civil Rights Attorney's Fee Awards Act of 1976, which authorized the awarding of fees to prevailing private parties in suits seeking to enforce Title IX. After having granted a rehearing, the Seventh Circuit again affirmed that even in light of the new statute, the 1976 act did not intend to create a remedy that did not previously exist.

Undaunted, Cannon appealed the dismissal of her claims to the Supreme Court. In so doing, she challenged the dismissal of her claims in asserting that Congress had acted in light of similar language in Title VI of the Civil Rights Act of 1964, under which the Supreme Court had ruled that the act implied a private remedy was available and that Congress allowed awards of attorney fees for successful claimants in such disputes.

The Supreme Court's Ruling

The primary issue before the Supreme Court in *Cannon* was whether Congress intended a private remedy to be implied from Title IX for institutions that were recipients of federal financial assistance. Reversing in favor of the plaintiff, the Supreme Court relied on the similarity between Title VI and Title IX in finding that an implied private right of action did exist pursuant to Title IX. In reaching its decision, the Court found it necessary to rely on the four-part test that it had enunciated in *Cort v. Ash* (1975), a case that addressed corporate expenses in connection with federal election campaigns when a statute is silent or unclear about private remedies.

In *Cannon*, the Supreme Court held that in evaluating whether Congress meant for a law to be enforceable privately or individually, all four of the *Cort* factors applied in granting her an implied right of action. The four-part test first addresses whether a plaintiff is a member of a special class for whose benefit a statute was enacted. Second, the test examines whether a statute's legislative history supports the intent to create or deny private rights of action. Third, the test reviews whether a private remedy frustrates or furthers the underlying purpose of the legislation. Fourth, the test considers whether a right basically involves an area of concern to the states. Having reviewed the four-part test, the Court determined that because all of its elements applied to the plaintiff, it was unnecessary to weigh the factors insofar as all of them supported the same result. The Court thus concluded that it had no choice but to reverse the Seventh Circuit's judgment in determining that Cannon could proceed with her private claim against the universities. As such, the Court remanded the dispute for further proceedings consistent with its opinion, thereby opening the door for later litigation under Title IX aimed at eradicating discrimination on the basis of sex in higher education and beyond.

Darlene Y. Bruner

See also Title VI; Title VII

Legal Citations

Cannon v. University of Chicago, 441 U.S. 677 (1979).
Civil Rights Act of 1871, Section 1983, 42 U.S.C. § 1983.
Civil Rights Attorney's Fees Awards Act of 1976, Pub. L. No. 94-559.
Cort v. Ash, 422 U. S. 66 (1975).
Title VI of the Civil Rights Act of 1964, 42 U.S.C. § 2000d.
Title IX of the Education Amendments of 1972, 20 U.S.C. § 1681.

CANNON V. UNIVERSITY OF CHICAGO

Cannon is important because it is the first case in which the Supreme Court recognized an implied cause of action for monetary damages under Title IX, in response to discrimination based on sex.

Supreme Court of the United States

CANNON

v.

UNIVERSITY OF CHICAGO

441 U.S. 677

Argued Jan. 9, 1979

Decided May 14, 1979

Mr. Justice STEVENS delivered the opinion of the Court.

Petitioner's complaints allege that her applications for admission to medical school were denied by the respondents because she is a woman. Accepting the truth of those allegations for the purpose of its decision, the Court of Appeals held that petitioner has no right of action against respondents that may be asserted in a federal court. We granted certiorari to review that holding.

Only two facts alleged in the complaints are relevant to our decision. First, petitioner was excluded from participation in the respondents' medical education programs because of her sex. Second, these education programs were receiving federal financial assistance at the time of her exclusion. These facts, admitted *arguendo* by respondents' motion to dismiss the complaints, establish a violation of § 901(a) of Title IX of the Education Amendments of 1972 (hereinafter Title IX). . . .

The statute does not, however, expressly authorize a private right of action by a person injured by a violation of § 901. For that reason, and because it concluded that no private remedy should be inferred, the District Court granted the respondents' motions to dismiss.

The Court of Appeals agreed that the statute did not contain an implied private remedy. Noting that § 902 of Title IX establishes a procedure for the termination of federal financial support for institutions violating § 901, the Court of Appeals concluded that Congress intended that remedy to be the exclusive means of enforcement. It recognized that the statute was patterned after Title VI of the Civil Rights Act of 1964 (hereinafter Title VI), but rejected petitioner's argument that Title VI included an implied private cause of action.

After the Court of Appeals' decision was announced, Congress enacted the Civil Rights Attorney's Fees Awards Act of 1976, 90 Stat. 2641, which authorizes an award of fees to prevailing private parties in actions to enforce Title IX. The court therefore granted a petition for rehearing to consider whether, in the light of that statute, its original interpretation of Title IX had been correct. After receiving additional briefs, the court concluded that the 1976 Act was not intended to create a remedy that did not previously exist. The court also noted that the Department of Health, Education, and Welfare had taken the position that a private cause of action under Title IX should be implied, but the court disagreed with that agency's interpretation of the Act. In sum, it adhered to its original view.

The Court of Appeals quite properly devoted careful attention to this question of statutory construction. As our recent cases—particularly *Cort v. Ash*—demonstrate, the fact that a federal statute has been violated and some person harmed does not automatically give rise to a private cause of action in favor of that person. Instead, before concluding that Congress intended to make a remedy available to a special class of litigants, a court must carefully analyze the four factors that *Cort* identifies as indicative of such an intent. Our review of those factors persuades us, however, that the Court of Appeals reached the wrong conclusion and that petitioner does have a statutory right to pursue her claim that respondents rejected her application on the basis of her sex. After commenting on each of the four factors, we shall explain why they are not overcome by respondents' countervailing arguments.

I

First, the threshold question under *Cort* is whether the statute was enacted for the benefit of a special class of which the plaintiff is a member. That question is answered by looking to the language of the statute itself. Thus, the statutory reference to "any employee of any such common carrier" in the 1893 legislation requiring railroads to equip their cars with secure "grab irons or handholds" made "irresistible" the Court's earliest "inference of a private right of action"—in that case in favor of a railway employee who was injured when a grab iron gave way.

Similarly, it was statutory language describing the special class to be benefited by § 5 of the Voting Rights Act of 1965 that persuaded the Court that private parties within that class were implicitly authorized to seek a declaratory judgment against a covered State. The dispositive language in that statute—"no person shall be denied the right to vote for failure to comply with [a new state enactment covered by, but not approved under, § 5]"—is remarkably similar to the language used by Congress in Title IX.

The language in these statutes—which expressly identifies the class Congress intended to benefit—contrasts sharply with statutory language customarily found in criminal statutes, such as that construed in *Cort* and other laws enacted for the protection of the general public. There would be far less reason to infer a private remedy in favor of individual persons if Congress, instead of drafting Title IX with an unmistakable focus on the benefited class, had written it simply as a ban on discriminatory conduct by recipients of federal funds or as a prohibition against the disbursement of public funds to educational institutions engaged in discriminatory practices.

Unquestionably, therefore, the first of the four factors identified in *Cort* favors the implication of a private cause of action. Title IX explicitly confers a benefit on persons discriminated against on the basis of sex, and petitioner is clearly a member of that class for whose special benefit the statute was enacted.

Second, the *Cort* analysis requires consideration of legislative history. We must recognize, however, that the legislative history of a statute that does not expressly create or deny a private remedy will typically be equally silent or ambiguous on the question. Therefore, in situations such as the present one "in which it is clear that federal law has granted a class of persons certain rights, it is not necessary to show an intention to *create* a private cause of action, although an explicit purpose to *deny* such cause of action would be controlling" (emphasis in original). But this is not the typical case. Far from evidencing any purpose to *deny* a private cause of action, the history of Title IX rather plainly indicates that Congress intended to create such a remedy.

Title IX was patterned after Title VI of the Civil Rights Act of 1964. Except for the substitution of the word "sex" in Title IX to replace the words "race, color, or national origin" in Title VI, the two statutes use identical language to describe the benefited class. Both statutes provide the same administrative mechanism for terminating federal financial support for institutions engaged in prohibited discrimination. Neither statute expressly mentions a private remedy for the person excluded from participation in a federally funded program. The drafters of Title IX explicitly assumed that it would be interpreted and applied as Title VI had been during the preceding eight years.

In 1972 when Title IX was enacted, the critical language in Title VI had already been construed as creating a private remedy. Most particularly, in 1967, a distinguished panel of the Court of Appeals for the Fifth Circuit squarely decided this issue in an opinion that was repeatedly cited with approval and never questioned during the ensuing five years. In addition, at least a dozen other federal courts reached similar conclusions in the same or related contexts during those years. It is always appropriate to assume that our elected representatives, like other citizens, know the law; in this case, because of

their repeated references to Title VI and its modes of enforcement, we are especially justified in presuming both that those representatives were aware of the prior interpretation of Title VI and that that interpretation reflects their intent with respect to Title IX.

Although 42 U.S.C. § 1983 might have provided an alternative and express cause of action in some of these cases—had it been relied upon, that section was certainly not available in *Kenbridge, supra*, involving a private defendant. Moreover, § 1983 was clearly unavailable (and no other express cause of action such as is provided in the Administrative Procedure Act was relied upon) in four other pre-1972 cases that either expressly or impliedly found causes of action under Title VI in a somewhat different context than is involved in this case. Thus, private plaintiffs successfully sued officials of the Federal Government under Title VI, and secured orders requiring those officials either to aid recipients of federal funds in devising nondiscriminatory alternatives to presently discriminatory programs, or to cut off funds to those recipients.

Moreover, in 1969, in *Allen v. State Board of Elections*, this Court had interpreted the comparable language in § 5 of the Voting Rights Act as sufficient to authorize a private remedy. Indeed, during the period between the enactment of Title VI in 1964 and the enactment of Title IX in 1972, this Court had consistently found implied remedies—often in cases much less clear than this. It was *after* 1972 that this Court decided *Cort v. Ash* and the other cases cited by the Court of Appeals in support of its strict construction of the remedial aspect of the statute. We, of course, adhere to the strict approach followed in our recent cases, but our evaluation of congressional action in 1972 must take into account its contemporary legal context. In sum, it is not only appropriate but also realistic to presume that Congress was thoroughly familiar with these unusually important precedents from this and other federal courts and that it expected its enactment to be interpreted in conformity with them.

It is not, however, necessary to rely on these presumptions. The package of statutes of which Title IX is one part also contains a provision whose language and history demonstrate that Congress itself understood Title VI, and thus its companion, Title IX, as creating a private remedy. Section 718 of the Education Amendments authorizes federal courts to award attorney's fees to the prevailing parties, other than the United States, in private actions brought against public educational agencies to enforce Title VI in the context of elementary and secondary education. The language of this provision explicitly presumes the availability of private suits to enforce Title VI in the education context. For many such suits, no express cause of action was then available; hence Congress must have assumed that one could be implied under Title VI itself. That assumption was made explicit during the debates on § 718. It was also aired during the debates on other provisions in the Education Amendments of 1972 and on Title IX itself, and is consistent with the Executive Branch's apparent understanding of Title VI at the time.

Finally, the very persistence—before 1972 and since, among judges and executive officials, as well as among litigants and their counsel, and even implicit in decisions of this Court—of the assumption that both Title VI and Title IX created a private right of action for the victims of illegal discrimination and the absence of legislative action to change that assumption provide further evidence that Congress at least acquiesces in, and apparently affirms, that assumption. We have no doubt that Congress intended to create Title IX remedies comparable to those available under Title VI and that it understood Title VI as authorizing an implied private cause of action for victims of the prohibited discrimination.

Third, under *Cort,* a private remedy should not be implied if it would frustrate the underlying purpose of the legislative scheme. On the other hand, when that remedy is necessary or at least helpful to the accomplishment of the statutory purpose, the Court is decidedly receptive to its implication under the statute.

Title IX, like its model Title VI, sought to accomplish two related, but nevertheless somewhat different, objectives. First, Congress wanted to avoid the use of federal resources to support discriminatory practices; second, it wanted to provide individual citizens effective protection against those practices. Both of these purposes were repeatedly identified in the debates on the two statutes.

The first purpose is generally served by the statutory procedure for the termination of federal financial support for institutions engaged in discriminatory practices. That remedy is, however, severe and often may not provide an appropriate means of accomplishing the second purpose if merely an isolated violation has occurred. In that situation, the violation might be remedied more efficiently by an order requiring an institution to accept an applicant who had been improperly excluded. Moreover, in that kind of situation it makes little sense to impose on an individual, whose only interest is in obtaining a benefit for herself, or on HEW, the burden of demonstrating that an institution's practices are so pervasively discriminatory that a complete cut-off of federal funding is appropriate. The award of individual relief to a private litigant who has prosecuted her own suit is not only sensible but is also fully consistent with—and in some cases even necessary to—the orderly enforcement of the statute.

The Department of Health, Education, and Welfare, which is charged with the responsibility for administering Title IX, perceives no inconsistency between the private remedy and the public remedy. On the contrary, the agency takes the unequivocal position that the individual remedy will provide effective assistance to achieving the statutory purposes. The agency's position is unquestionably correct.

Fourth, the final inquiry suggested by *Cort* is whether implying a federal remedy is inappropriate because the subject matter involves an area basically of concern to the States. No such problem is raised by a prohibition against invidious discrimination of any sort, including that on the basis of sex. Since the Civil War, the Federal Government and the federal courts have been the "*primary and powerful reliances*" in protecting citizens against such discrimination (emphasis in original). Moreover, it is the expenditure of federal funds that provides the justification for this particular statutory prohibition. There can be no question but that this aspect of the *Cort* analysis supports the implication of a private federal remedy.

In sum, there is no need in this case to weigh the four *Cort* factors; all of them support the same result. Not only the words and history of Title IX, but also its subject matter and underlying purposes, counsel implication of a cause of action in favor of private victims of discrimination.

II

Respondents' principal argument against implying a cause of action under Title IX is that it is unwise to subject admissions decisions of universities to judicial scrutiny at the behest of disappointed applicants on a case-by-case basis. They argue that this kind of litigation is burdensome and inevitably will have an adverse effect on the independence of members of university committees.

This argument is not original to this litigation. It was forcefully advanced in both 1964 and 1972 by the congressional opponents of Title VI and Title IX, and squarely rejected by the congressional majorities that passed the two statutes. In short, respondents' principal contention is not a legal argument at all; it addresses a policy issue that Congress has already resolved.

History has borne out the judgment of Congress. Although victims of discrimination on the basis of race, religion, or national origin have had private Title VI remedies available at least since 1965, respondents have not come forward with any demonstration that Title VI litigation has been so costly or voluminous that either the academic community or the courts have been unduly burdened. Nothing but speculation supports the argument that university administrators will be so concerned about the risk of litigation that they will fail to discharge their important responsibilities in an independent and professional manner.

III

Respondents advance two other arguments that deserve brief mention. Starting from the premise that Title IX and Title VI should receive the same construction, respondents argue (1) that a comparison of Title VI with other Titles of the Civil Rights Act of 1964 demonstrates that Congress created express private remedies whenever it found them desirable; and (2) that certain excerpts from the legislative history of Title VI foreclose the implication of a private remedy.

Even if these arguments were persuasive with respect to Congress' understanding in 1964 when it passed Title VI, they would not overcome the fact that in 1972 when it passed Title IX, Congress was under the impression that Title VI could be enforced by a private action and that Title IX would be similarly enforceable. "For the relevant inquiry is not whether Congress correctly perceived the then state of the law, but rather what its perception of the state of the law was." But each of respondents' arguments is, in any event, unpersuasive.

The fact that other provisions of a complex statutory scheme create express remedies has not been accepted as a sufficient reason for refusing to imply an otherwise appropriate remedy under a separate section. Rather, the Court has generally avoided this type of "excursion into extrapolation of legislative intent" unless there is other, more convincing, evidence that Congress meant to exclude the remedy.

With one set of exceptions, the excerpts from the legislative history cited by respondents as contrary to implication of a private remedy under Title VI, were all concerned with a procedure for terminating federal funding. None of them evidences any hostility toward an implied private remedy to terminate the offending dis-

crimination. They are consistent with the assumption expressed frequently during the debates that such a judicial remedy—either through the kind of broad construction of state action under § 1983 adopted by the Court of Appeals for the Fourth Circuit . . . or through an implied remedy would be available to private litigants regardless of how the fund-cutoff issue was resolved.

The only excerpt relied upon by respondents that deals precisely with the question whether the victim of discrimination has a private remedy under Title VI was a comment by Senator Keating. In it, he expressed disappointment at the administration's failure to include his suggestion for an express remedy in its final proposed bill. Our analysis of the legislative history convinces us, however, that neither the administration's decision not to incorporate that suggestion expressly in its bill, nor Senator Keating's response to that decision, is indicative of a rejection of a private right of action against recipients of federal funds. Instead, the former appears to have been a compromise aimed at protecting individual rights without subjecting the Government to suits, while the latter is merely one Senator's isolated expression of a preference for an express private remedy. In short, neither is inconsistent with the implication of such a remedy. Nor is there any other indication in the legislative history that any Member of Congress voted in favor of the statute in reliance on an understanding that Title VI did not include a private remedy.

IV

When Congress intends private litigants to have a cause of action to support their statutory rights, the far better course is for it to specify as much when it creates those rights. But the Court has long recognized that under certain limited circumstances the failure of Congress to do so is not inconsistent with an intent on its part to have such a remedy available to the persons benefited by its legislation. Title IX presents the atypical situation in which *all* of the circumstances that the Court has previously identified as supportive of an implied remedy are present. We therefore conclude that petitioner may maintain her lawsuit, despite the absence of any express authorization for it in the statute.

The judgment of the Court of Appeals is reversed, and the case is remanded for further proceedings consistent with this opinion.

It is so ordered.

CATALOGS AS CONTRACTS

The courts have constantly refined the relationship between institutions of higher learning and their students since the nascence of American higher education. As societal expectations have evolved, new demands have been placed on colleges and universities by their primary constituency, students, for less paternalism and more accountability for services rendered. This dynamic relationship can be characterized by a judicial evolution from a time during which universities stood *in loco parentis,* or in the place of the parent, to the current contractual perspective, one in which students represent consumers, and universities act as providers. This entry examines the contractual relationship between students and educational institutions, particularly as embodied in college and university publications, before reviewing the most important cases addressing this relationship.

The Institution–Student Contract

Over time, courts have considered institutional publications that describe policies or procedures as the bases of agreements between students and institutions. Courts have made use of any number of official college and university publications such as catalogs, bulletins, and course syllabi, a topic over which there is an amazing dearth of litigation, as well as oral communications by faculty members, deans, and advisors, in order to assess the mutually obligatory relationship between institutions and students. In fact, a 1972 study noted that provisions of the student–institution contract could be uncovered in statements from documents, including applications, catalogs, bulletins, and formal policy statements.

Scholars have noted that, in their basic form, contracts between students and institutions of higher learning are established by the oral and written representations made by the parties from the point of application and throughout students' tenure at colleges and universities. These representations can be included in such publications as application forms, brochures, catalogs, and course descriptions as well as in oral representations. Although courts have addressed numerous types of

university publications such as applications, housing contracts, and even oral statements with varying degrees of scrutiny, the primary document examined is the college or university catalog.

While contract law is applicable to both the public and private sector, the majority of cases concerning representations in college catalogs have emanated from the private sector, because their students are typically precluded from the protection of constitutional due process. For this reason, these students must rely heavily on representations made in institutional catalogs or other publications as bases for definitions of their relationships with institutions.

Some scholars posit that the breadth of contract theory precludes uniform application to higher education because of the multifaceted nature of college and university operations. Courts adhere closely to contract theory in some areas and apply it more liberally in others. For example, legal scholars have pointed out that in academic and disciplinary actions, courts tend to defer to institutions while simultaneously regarding the relationship between student and institution as contractual. Some critics interpret this dichotomy as precluding adequate protection for students, because it permits institutions to base their obligations to students on assertions made in collegiate literature. Others have suggested that because materials such as catalogs and bulletins are not drafted to be contracts, they are vague and amended with ease at the will of institutional decision makers. Still others assert that although catalogs may describe the mutual expectations of institutions and students, they do not capture the entire relationship or adequately reflect the totality of students' expectations.

Insofar as catalogs and bulletins are used to communicate important information to students about institutions and their policies, they can be used as recruiting tools to attract new students. As such, catalogs include disclaimers of obligations while indicating that students, by following delineated sequences of events, can enjoy continuing relationships with the institutions leading to the conferral of degrees. Some scholars maintain that students and institutions do not enter into arm's-length agreements, meaning that the parties are not in objective, disinterested relationships, because not all potential students have the wherewithal to attend colleges or universities of their choice. Some of these scholars also recognize that students are unable to negotiate the terms indicated in institutional bulletins or catalogs.

Litigation

As reflected by the fact that disputes over the status of catalogs as contracts did not emerge until the 1970s, it all but goes without saying that this is a relatively recent legal development. In *Babcock v. New Orleans Baptist Theological Seminary* (1989), an appellate court in Louisiana affirmed that because a university catalog was part of the contract between a student and the institution, the seminary was bound to follow its own regulations. The plaintiff, who was a student in the master of divinity program and an ordained minister, was dismissed from the seminary for separating from his wife and considering divorce. Officials based their action on a university policy that directed students who separated from or divorced their spouses to withdraw. The plaintiff, arguing that he and his wife were not separated, obtained an injunction preventing the seminary from dismissing him subject to provisions in the institution's student handbook. While the case was pending, the student completed his degree. However, because seminary officials refused to award the student his degree, he filed suit.

On appeal, the court found that this dispute turned on the seminary's role as an educational institution, not a church, and that by delineating a policy regarding divorce and describing due process procedures in its catalog, the institution departed the arena of religious doctrine and entered the realm of contract. The court concluded, through the application of contract principles, that the student was entitled to receive his degree in spite of the seminary's disciplinary actions. The court ruled that because the dispute involved contractual interpretation, rather than First Amendment religious issues, and did not involve matters of faith, custom, or the appointment (or removal) of ministers, the court had the authority to act. More specifically, the court decided that by placing the divorce and separation policy in the student handbook along with a description of applicable due process procedures, university officials removed the dispute from the realm of religious controversy, making it a matter of contractual application.

The precise language of university publications can also be construed in favor of students when institutions do not follow their own published procedures. Tax-supported institutions are bound constitutionally to abide by provisions concerning due process rights in disciplinary matters. While private institutions are permitted more freedom, courts look to the explicit language of institutional publications, regardless of whether a college or university is public or private, in addressing whether their actions were arbitrary or violated a contract between themselves and their students.

In *Fellheimer v. Middlebury College Corp.* (1994), a student was suspended from a private college after disciplinary proceedings for the alleged sexual assault of a fellow student. Prior to the hearing, the student was informed that he was being charged with "rape/disrespect for persons." The student contacted the dean, expressed confusion over the charge, and was told to concentrate on the rape charge. After the hearing, the student received a letter informing him that the university had found him not guilty of rape but guilty of disrespect for persons. The student filed suit for breach of contract, alleging that university officials failed to provide him adequate notice of all of the charges.

The federal trial court in Vermont entered a judgment in favor of the student, noting that the handbook specifically stated that the charges against a student "shall state the nature of the charges with sufficient particularity to permit the accused party to prepare to meet the charges." Yet, in treating the student's claim as contractual rather than constitutional, because this was the way in which he presented his case, the court rejected his challenge that the charge "disrespect of persons" as mentioned in the handbook was impermissibly vague such that it did not afford him sufficient preparation to defend himself against such a charge. Consequently, the court reasoned that college officials breached the institution's contract with the student by failing to provide him with adequate notice of the charges he faced.

The notion of the offer and acceptance of tuition and fees as creating a binding admissions contract was delineated in *Steinberg v. Chicago Medical School* (1977), a dispute that is considered the benchmark case in the application of contract theory to the admissions process. Here a student applied for admission to medical school and paid the application fee. When the student's application was rejected, he filed suit, claiming breach of contract. The student's suit alleged that officials had not evaluated his application according to the criteria stated in the school's bulletin. Instead, he charged that school officials used nonacademic criteria, namely, his ability or his family's ability to make substantial financial contributions to the medical school. The Supreme Court of Illinois held that because the publication of the criteria created a contractual relationship between the student and institution, its terms obligated officials at the medical school to evaluate applicants according to the criteria published in its catalog.

The judiciary may favor students in cases where plaintiffs reasonably and justifiably relied on statements made in catalogs concerning course requirements and curricular issues. In the issue addressed in *University of Texas Health Science Center at Houston v. Babb* (1982), a student enrolled in a nursing program under the terms of the 1979 catalog, according to which students whose grade point averages fell below a 2.0 would be placed on probation, and the grade for courses repeated would be their final grades. In addition, the catalog stated that students would be held to the requirements of the catalog under which they entered the institution. During her studies, the plaintiff received "D" grades in two classes. Then, the 1981 catalog promulgated a new regulation that students who accumulated more than "two D's" would be terminated from the program.

The student filed suit, contending that she should be subject to the provisions of the catalog under which she entered the institution and should not be bound by the new provision. When a trial court issued an injunction on her behalf, the university sought further review. An appellate court in Texas affirmed in favor of the student. According to the court, the catalog created a binding contract between the student and the institution, even though the university was free to modify its academic standards. Still, the court ruled that in light of the wording of the original catalog, which expressly stated that students would be allowed to progress through their programs under the terms of the catalogs that were in effect at the time of their enrollment, she was entitled to complete her studies.

On occasion, the judiciary has determined that institutional catalogs and bulletins do not constitute binding contractual agreements. In *Love v. Duke University* (1991), a Hispanic doctoral student whose academic performance was unsatisfactory challenged his subsequent dismissal from the program. The student unsuccessfully filed suit, alleging that he had been removed from the program due to his ethnicity and that officials breached a contractual agreement with him that was clearly specified in the university bulletin.

A federal trial court in North Carolina echoed the familiar sentiment of judicial deference to academia, refusing to find the existence of a contract between the student and the university, particularly because it did not consider the academic bulletin as a binding contract. It is interesting to note, though, that the court ruled in favor of the university on the ground that the student did not perform to the level of the guidelines delineated in the bulletin. While the court refused to treat the agreement as a contract, it looked to the specific language printed in the university publication in rendering its judgment. Put another way, in deciding that the student failed to prove that he was dismissed due to his race, it acknowledged that pursuant to handbook provisions, he was not treated differently from similarly situated students who failed their preliminary examinations in accord with programmatic guidelines, and there was no evidence that university officials acted arbitrarily or capriciously in dismissing him from the program.

The contract theory applicable to higher education has undergone an evolutionary process through which it has become firmly ensconced as a viable legal descriptor of the relationship between institutions of higher learning and students. In its nascent period, contracts existed as simple written agreements through which students pledged to uphold the rules, regulations, and codes of their college or universities. Today, these agreements have developed into legally recognized contracts for goods and services established between two parties. In its contemporary manifestation, contract theory provided students an outlet to seek redress against their colleges and universities that was previously unavailable. Now characterized as consumers, students have certain and precise expectations of collegiate performance and can actively seek judicial relief through contract theory for perceived violations of these expectations.

Kerry Brian Melear

See also Disciplinary Sanctions and Due Process Rights

Further Readings

Beh, H. G. (1998). Downsizing higher education and derailing student educational objectives: When should student claims for program closures succeed? *Georgia Law Review, 33,* 155–195.

Bickel, R. D., & Lake, P. F. (1999). *The rights and responsibilities of the modern university.* Durham, NC: Carolina Academic Press.

Hirshberg, P. M. (1994). The college's emerging duty to supervise students: *In loco parentis* in the 1990's. *Journal of Urban and Contemporary Law, 46,* 189–223.

Melear, K. B. (2003). The contractual relationship between student and institution: Disciplinary, academic, and consumer contexts. *Journal of College & University Law, 30*(1), 175–208.

Ratliff, R. C. (1972). *Constitutional rights of college students: A study in case law.* Metuchen, NJ: Scarecrow Press.

Shur, G. M. (1988). Contractual agreements: Defining relationships between students and institutions. In M. J. Barr (Ed.), *Student services and the law: A handbook for practitioners* (pp. 74–97). San Francisco: Jossey-Bass.

Stamatakos, T. C. (1990). The doctrine of *in loco parentis*, tort liability, and the student–college relationship. *Indiana Law Journal, 65,* 471–490.

Legal Citations

Babcock v. New Orleans Baptist Theological Seminary, 554 So. 2d 90 (La. Ct. App. 1989).

Fellheimer v. Middlebury College Corp., 869 F. Supp. 238 (D. Vt. 1994).

Love v. Duke University, 776 F. Supp. 1070 (M.D.N.C. 1991).

Steinberg v. Chicago Medical School, 371 N.E. 2d 634 (Ill. 1977).

University of Texas Health Science Center at Houston v. Babb, 646 S.W. 2d 502 (Tex. Ct. App. 1982).

Catholic Higher Education

See *Ex Corde Ecclesiae* and American Catholic Higher Education

Central Virginia Community College v. Katz

In *Central Virginia Community College v. Katz* (2006), the U.S. Supreme Court held that Eleventh Amendment sovereign immunity, which protects states and their agencies from litigation, did not bar adversarial proceedings brought by a Chapter 11 bankruptcy trustee to set aside alleged preferential payments that operators of a bankrupt bookstore made to public institutions of higher education. In other words, the Court affirmed an earlier order that when four colleges in Virginia received funds from a bookstore that was operating under the protection of a federal bankruptcy court, they were not immune from litigation to recover these monies in an action filed by the judicially appointed liquidating supervisor. The Court rejected the colleges' argument that their Eleventh Amendment immunity protected them from such claims as "arms of the state." In light of the impact that this case may have on the sovereign immunity of public colleges and universities, this entry examines the background and rationale in *Katz*.

Facts of the Case

Katz arose when a bookstore that engaged in business with four public institutions of higher education in Virginia sought bankruptcy protection under Chapter 11. Chapter 11 bankruptcy actions ordinarily involve corporations or partnerships that file petitions seeking to reorganize their businesses so that they can survive and to repay their creditors over time. Individual debtors can also rely on Chapter 11. Entities that seek the protection of Chapter 11 bankruptcy courts ordinarily work with court-appointed trustees in determining repayment schedules and preferences in repaying their debts.

When the owner of the bookstore sought bankruptcy protection, the judicially appointed liquidating supervisor attempted to recover allegedly preferential payments that bookstore officials had made to the institutions of higher education in Virginia when it was insolvent. However, public institutions of higher learning are arms of the state, meaning that those in *Katz* were created by officials of the Commonwealth of Virginia to carry out the public function of education. College officials therefore refused to comply with the order that they return the payments that they received, on the ground that they had sovereign immunity from the litigation initiated by the liquidating supervisor under the Eleventh Amendment. A federal bankruptcy court in Kentucky, home to the bookstore, refused to dismiss the proceedings despite the claim of sovereign immunity that the colleges advanced. Subsequently, the Sixth Circuit, based on its own precedent that Congress abrogated the states' sovereign immunity in bankruptcy proceedings, affirmed its order, leading the colleges to appeal to the Supreme Court.

The Supreme Court's Ruling

On further review, in *Katz,* in a five-to-four opinion written by Justice Stevens, the Supreme Court affirmed that when states ratified the Bankruptcy Clause in Article 1, Section 8, Clause 4 of the U.S. Constitution, they acquiesced in the subordination of whatever sovereign immunity defense that they might otherwise have raised in proceedings necessary to effectuate the jurisdiction of bankruptcy courts. In this context, *in rem* (literally "the things" as opposed to persons) jurisdiction refers to judicial powers over the assets of entities that declare bankruptcy rather than over their persons. This judicial authority includes the power to recover assets that were fraudulently transferred to others or to recover payments that improperly favored some creditors at the expense of others.

At the outset of its analysis, the Supreme Court found that the Bankruptcy Clause granted Congress the authority to establish uniform laws regulating bankruptcy in the United States. Because some jurisdictions went so far as to imprison debtors, while others seized their assets to repay their debts, the framers sought to establish a uniform system for the treatment of debtors, and the Bankruptcy Clause was intended to accomplish this. At this point, the Court conceded that it had not resolved the question of whether the Bankruptcy Clause conferred the ability on Congress to abrogate the immunity of states from such private suits. Even so, the Court noted that in *Tennessee Student Assistance Corporation v. Hood* (2004), it had upheld the application of the Bankruptcy Code to proceedings initiated by debtors against state

agencies to evaluate whether student loans could be so discharged, ruling that doing so did not infringe on state sovereignty. The Court explained that regardless of whether states choose to participate in actions, they are bound by the orders of bankruptcy courts and since they are not entitled to any special treatment, they must wait their turns to be paid like other creditors.

Turning to the nature of bankruptcy proceedings as *in rem,* the Supreme Court maintained that these actions did not allow immunity to states to the same degree that other types of legal proceedings did. Therefore, the Court thought that the framers would have interpreted the authority of the Bankruptcy Clause as including the congressional right to adopt laws addressing more than the status of rights in the *res,* or thing, namely money or other assets. To this end, the Court observed that judges resolving bankruptcy disputes have the power to issue ancillary orders enforcing their *in rem* adjudications, an interplay that the justices believed was evident in *Katz.* Regardless of whether actions such as the one at issue were properly characterized as *in rem,* the Court was convinced that the framers would have interpreted the Bankruptcy Clause as granting Congress the authority to permit the judiciary to forbid preferential transfers and to recover properties that were transferred under such circumstances.

In addressing the *in rem* jurisdiction of bankruptcy courts and their ancillary powers over matters such as preferential transfers, the Supreme Court examined the history of the Bankruptcy Clause, as well as early federal statutes. This led the Court to decide that while this judicial *in rem* authority implicated the states' sovereign immunity from litigation, the states agreed with the plan that was adopted at the Constitutional Convention that they would not raise this defense in such litigation, essentially subordinating, or abrogating, their sovereignty to the bankruptcy courts in this limited manner.

The Supreme Court found it unnecessary to address the question of whether the Bankruptcy Clause granted Congress the authority to abrogate states' immunity from such private suits that it addressed earlier in its analysis of *Hood.* Instead, the Court identified the key question not as whether Congress intended to abrogate sovereign immunity in actions to recover preferential treatments but as whether the congressional determination that states should be subject to preferential transfer proceedings was within the scope of its power to enact laws addressing bankruptcy.

Insofar as the Supreme Court was of the view that because the Bankruptcy Clause granted Congress the authority to enact statutes regulating bankruptcy, it added that Congress could either treat states in the same way as other creditors or could exempt them from the operation of such laws. In thus concluding that the relevant abrogation of judicial authority that essentially allowed states to subject themselves to the jurisdiction of the bankruptcy courts was the one identified in the plan enunciated at the Constitutional Convention, not by statute, the Court affirmed the judgment of the Sixth Circuit.

Justice Thomas's dissent, which was joined by Chief Justice Roberts as well as Justices Scalia and Kennedy, essentially maintained that the majority ignored the long-established principles that states are not subject to suit by private parties for monetary relief absent their consent or a valid congressional abrogation. The dissent reasoned that the outcome in *Katz* could not have been justified by the text, structure, or history of the Constitution and that it failed to comport with the Court's settled jurisprudence with regard to the sovereign immunity of the states.

Conclusion

In sum, *Katz* stands for the proposition that public colleges and universities do not enjoy sovereign immunity for suits seeking the recovery of preferential transfers that are necessary to effectuate the *in rem* jurisdictional authority of bankruptcy courts. Yet the Supreme Court failed to address whether sovereign immunity bars claims for breach of contract that are unnecessary to effectuate the jurisdiction of bankruptcy courts. Unlike its other sovereign immunity cases, *Katz* is significant because it turned not on whether Congress has the power to abrogate sovereign immunity but on whether the states surrendered their immunity when they ratified the Constitution.

Charles J. Russo

See also *College Savings Bank v. Florida Prepaid*; Eleventh Amendment; *Florida Prepaid v. College Savings Bank*; *Kimel v. Florida Board of Regents*

Further Readings

College Savings Bank v. Florida Prepaid, 527 U.S. 666 (1999).
Florida Prepaid v. College Savings Bank, 527 U.S. 627 (1999).
Kimel v. Florida Board of Regents, 528 U.S. 62 (2000).
Seminole Tribe of Florida v. Florida, 517 U.S. 44 (1996).
Thro, W. E. (2000). The education lawyer's guide to the sovereign immunity revolution. *Education Law Reporter, 146,* 951–981.
Thro, W. E. (2007). The future of sovereign immunity. *Education Law Reporter, 215,* 1–31.

Legal Citations

Central Virginia Community College v. Katz, 546 U.S. 356 (2006).
Tennessee Student Assistance Corp. v. Hood, 541 U.S. 440 (2004).

CHEATING AND ACADEMIC DISCIPLINE

Student cheating on college and university campuses includes taking credit for work completed by others, sharing answers on course assignments, failing to complete work on team projects, completing examinations for others, and plagiarizing term papers. Often referred to as academic dishonesty, student cheating is common on college campuses. Unfortunately, instances of cheating appear to be on the rise. Further, the advent of new technologies coupled with the electronic delivery of courses and programs (Internet-based programs) exacerbate the problem of academic dishonesty, particularly with regard to written assignments.

Students, faculty, and administrators indicate the need for action once students are found to have cheated. More specifically, students are troubled when cheating by peers is not addressed. At the same time, faculty members express concern about the lack of administrative support when they are addressing instances of cheating. In turn, administrators describe an increase in faculty indifference to cheating by students. In essence, all parties on campuses are aware of the need to address cheating, but there is disagreement regarding the assignment of responsibility and how to react.

Responses to cheating often result in disciplinary actions or academic sanctions. When instituting disciplinary sanctions, officials at institutions of higher education subject themselves to legal review. However, the courts have given considerable deference to postsecondary institutions that impose academic sanctions on students for academic dishonesty.

Disciplinary Sanctions

When confronted with disciplinary actions such as expulsions from academic programs or institutions, students attending public colleges and universities have alleged that officials violated their rights to substantive and procedural due process. Yet the courts are unsettled on the question of substantive rights for students in higher education. In instances where the courts have agreed that students do possess substantive due process rights, students bear the burden of showing that institutional actions were arbitrary or capricious.

The courts have consistently required officials at public institutions to adhere to the general principles of procedural due process. However, the extent to which due process must be provided is vague. For example, in *Board of Curators of the University of Missouri v. Horowitz* (1978), the U.S. Supreme Court determined that medical school faculty provided adequate notice to a student who was being dismissed for her poor performance even though the faculty did not provide her with a formal hearing, which is a necessary element of procedural due process.

Private institutions, on the other hand, are not subject to constitutional due process requirements and have a great deal more latitude in the development and regulation of disciplinary rules related to cheating. Because claims of due process violations are not available to students in private institutions, these institutions are often challenged with contract law violations in instances of disciplinary sanctions. In essence, disciplinary sanctions for cheating at private institutions depend greatly on the language in university catalogs and supporting documentation such as class syllabi.

Although some might allege that disciplinary sanctions occurred for malicious reasons, the courts have certainly agreed that the vast majority of these sanctions have been for legitimate reasons.

Academic Discipline

The courts typically treat sanctions for cheating as an internal problem not subject to judicial review. They are reluctant to question the academic sanctions that university officials and faculty members impose on students who have engaged in academic dishonesty. In fact, the courts tend to limit their inquiries into awards of academic grades to considerations of whether educators acted arbitrarily or capriciously. In the academic cases, the courts have generally agreed that hearings are not required unless college and university rules require such proceedings as part of their appeal procedures. Still, officials must follow institutional procedures unless the processes exceed a college or university's own procedures as publicized in handbooks, catalogs, and the like (*Schuler v. University of Minnesota*, 1986).

Guidelines for Higher Education Institutions

Officials in higher education institutions continue to struggle with effective ways to combat academic cheating. The most common strategy used to address cheating, particularly in large institutions, is the judicial process of rule compliance. According to this approach, institutional officials should clearly define cheating, the consequences of cheating, and the process for appeal of subsequent penalties. Certainly, in instances of disciplinary sanctions, institutional officials should provide adequate notice to students, conduct hearings that are presided over by fair and impartial third-party decision makers, allow students to present evidence on their own behalf, and provide at least one level of appeal. Although the criteria of due process need not exist in instances of academic discipline, institutional officials should ensure that decisions are carefully considered and are not arbitrary or capricious.

Another strategy used to combat cheating is the implementation of academic honor codes or the integrity strategy. Not surprisingly, academic honor codes are used far less often than rule compliance. While the data do not support the contention that there are fewer instances of cheating when academic honor codes are utilized, such an approach attempts to promote responsible student behavior. The underlying principle of academic honor codes is that institutions are responsible for developing a sense of moral responsibility in their students. Discipline is a part of the integrity strategy, but only as an aspect of the developmental process.

In order for academic honor codes to be effective, the concept of academic integrity must be constantly and consistently communicated to students. For example, student handbooks and course syllabi should include detailed information on course expectations, while faculty members should initiate discussions of academic integrity frequently in class. Additionally, students play a large, and important, role in both the educational and judicial processes, whether as judges or by encouraging peers to refrain from engaging in acts of academic dishonesty.

Mark Littleton

See also Academic Dishonesty; *Board of Curators of the University of Missouri v. Horowitz*; Catalogs as Contracts; Due Process, Substantive and Procedural

Further Readings

Beckham, J., & Dagley, D. (2005). *Contemporary issues in higher education law.* Dayton, OH: Education Law Association.

Dutile, F. (2001). Students and due process in higher education: Of interests and procedures. *Florida Coastal Law Journal, 2,* 243–290.

McCabe, D. (2005). It takes a village: Academic dishonesty. *Liberal Education, 91*(3), 26–31.

Sinson, S. (1997). Judicial intervention of private university expulsions: Traditional remedies and a solution sounding in tort. *Drake Law Review, 46,* 195–232.

Legal Citations

Board of Curators of the University of Missouri v. Horowitz, 435 U.S. 78 (1978).

Schuler v. University of Minnesota, 788 F.2d 610 (8th Cir. 1986).

Civil Rights Act of 1871, Section 1983

Individuals who are associated with colleges and universities, whether students, faculty, staff, or guests visiting on campuses, whose civil rights have been violated may sue for equitable relief or monetary damages under Section 1983 of the Civil Rights Act of 1871. According to Section 1983,

> Every person who, under color of any statute, ordinance, regulation, custom, or usage, of any State or Territory or the District of Columbia, subjects, or causes to be subjected, any citizen of the United States or other person within the jurisdiction thereof to the deprivation of any rights, privileges, or immunities secured by the Constitution and laws, shall be liable to the party injured in an action at law, suit in equity, or other proper proceeding for redress, except that in any action brought against a judicial officer for an act or omission taken in such officer's judicial capacity, injunctive relief shall not be granted unless a declaratory decree was violated or declaratory relief was unavailable. (42 U.S.C. § 1983)

Section 1983 is a powerful legal tool insofar as it allows plaintiffs to sue individuals for monetary damages if such individuals violated plaintiffs' constitutional and statutory rights "under the color of state law" or in the performance of their official duties. Thus, state and local government officials, including those in higher education, can be liable for their actions if courts find that their actions had the effect of depriving individuals of their civil rights. As such, Section 1983 gives aggrieved plaintiffs a vehicle for redress of constitutional or statutory violations of their rights when the statute itself does not contain a comprehensive remedial scheme. In this respect, officials can be sued in their individual capacities as well as their official capacities, meaning that they can be held individually liable for committing civil rights violations. This entry first discusses the historical context and purpose of Section 1983 and then describes some of the legal cases that have defined its scope. The cases outlined here trace the development of the scope of Section 1983's reach to entities other than the state or federal government and its application as a form of relief for statutory violations.

Purpose

Originally passed shortly after the Civil War to provide a legal remedy for former slaves whose civil rights were being violated, particularly by members of the Ku Klux Klan as well as state officials, Section 1983 does not create any new civil rights. Rather, it provides a means of enforcement for the federal courts in that it permits individuals to sue public officials for constitutional and statutory violations. As such, Section 1983 provides a powerful remedy against discrimination based on race, national origin, sex, sexual orientation, disability, and religion as well as against violations of the Fourth Amendment's prohibition on unreasonable search and seizure. Also known as the Ku Klux Klan Act, Section 1983 was introduced by Benjamin Franklin Butler, U.S. Representative from Massachusetts, early in 1871 and was signed into law by President Ulysses S. Grant later that year.

As its wording indicates, Section 1983 imposes liability on persons. Consequently, plaintiffs may file damages claims against government officers in their official capacities. In this respect, plaintiffs must show that the officers acted "under the color of state law" or in their official capacity if the plaintiffs' suits are to be successful. Although federal and state governments cannot be liable for damages under Section 1983 pursuant to Eleventh Amendment immunity, they may be sued for declaratory relief (seeking a clarification of individuals' rights) or for prospective (future) relief. On the other hand, municipal and local governments do not enjoy the same Eleventh Amendment immunity and may be sued for both damages and prospective relief by individuals who claim that their constitutional or statutory rights have been violated.

It is important to recognize that Section 1983 does not confer substantive rights on individuals. Rather, it is used only to enforce the rights already granted by, or to provide redress for violations of, the Constitution or federal statutes. Put another way, in order to succeed under Section 1983, litigants must show that they had constitutional or statutory rights and were deprived of those rights by an action, policy, or custom carried out by government authorities.

Defenses

Although federal and state governments and their agencies can claim Eleventh Amendment immunity, individual officials within those entities cannot. As indicated above, municipal and local governments do not enjoy the protection of the Eleventh Amendment nor do their officials. However, all officials may be protected by qualified immunity. Qualified immunity can generally be used as a defense when officials acted in discretionary capacities (i.e., exercised their judgment in using their decision-making authority) unless their actions clearly violated well-established constitutional or statutory rights or were obviously wrong. It goes without saying that qualified immunity cannot be used when officials knowingly violated the law.

Significant Litigation

The use of Section 1983 to redress federal constitutional and statutory violations came into prominence in 1961 following the U.S. Supreme Court's decision in *Monroe v. Pape*. In *Monroe*, homeowners sued the City of Chicago after police officers conducted a warrantless search of their premises as part of a murder investigation. The Court dismissed the suit against the city on the ground that Congress had not intended the term "person" as used in the act to include municipalities. Even so, the Court upheld the jurisdiction of the federal courts to compensate individuals who were the victims of civil rights violations committed by state officials under the color of law. More important, the Court emphasized that the purposes of Section 1983 were to override a variety of state laws, offer remedies where state laws were inadequate, and afford federal remedies where state remedies were unavailable in practice.

More than a decade and a half later, in *Monell v. Department of Social Services* (1978), the Court reversed one of its positions in *Monroe* in holding that municipalities fell within Section 1983's definition of "person," thereby allowing individuals to sue local governments and their officers. Still, the Court limited the circumstances under which local governments could be liable to situations where the wrong resulted from official policies. Subsequently, in *Maine v. Thiboutot* (1980), the Court observed that because Section 1983 applies to federal statutory laws and well as constitutional laws, it not strictly limited to civil rights or equal protection laws.

In *Wood v. Strickland* (1975), the Supreme Court ascertained that members of school boards could be sued under Section 1983. Even though the Court recognized that board members must be able to exercise judgment, it countered that those who act with disregard for the law could be held liable if they did so with an impermissible motivation or in bad faith. While Wood involved a dispute that arose in the public schools, its judgment may be applied to situations involving higher education, especially where board members, faculty, and staff must exercise their independent judgments in decision making.

As pointed out, the intent of Section 1983 is to provide a remedy in situations where individuals have been deprived of their constitutional or statutory civil rights. Yet many remedial statutes provide their own remedies. In a series of cases, the Supreme Court ruled that in these situations, where statutory remedies are comprehensive, Section 1983 may be unavailable. In the first case, *Middlesex County Sewerage Authority v. National Sea Clammers Association* (1983), a noneducation dispute, the Court declared that the existence of express remedies in the statutes at issue in the suit demonstrated Congress's intention to supplant any remedy that otherwise might be available under Section 1983 for violations of those statutes by any governmental entities.

Later, in *Smith v. Robinson* (1984), the Court interpreted the Education for All Handicapped Children Act (EHCA), now known as the Individuals with Disabilities Education Act (IDEA), as the exclusive avenue through which the rights of a student with disabilities to a free appropriate public education could be brought. Here the parents of a student with disabilities prevailed against a school board in a dispute over the financial responsibility for the child's special education program. After prevailing in their suit, the parents sought reimbursement of their legal expenses. In maintaining that such reimbursement was not available under the IDEA, the Court examined the interplay between Section 1983 and the IDEA. The Court concluded that Congress intended that students who had constitutional claims to a free appropriate public education pursue those claims through the EHCA's carefully tailored administrative and judicial scheme. In view of the EHCA's comprehensive nature and remedies, the Court concluded that Congress intended to preclude reliance on Section 1983 to remedy equal protection

claims that were essentially identical to plaintiffs' EHCA claims. Interestingly, Congress later essentially overturned this decision in enacting the Handicapped Children's Protection Act (1986), awarding attorney fees to prevailing plaintiffs based on the notion that they should have been compensated for procuring services that their children were already entitled to receive.

Similarly, in another noneducation case, *City of Rancho Palos Verdes v. Abrams* (2005), the Supreme Court reasoned that the provision of an express, private means of redress in a statute itself was an indication that Congress did not intend to establish a separate remedy under Section 1983. In addition, the Court, citing its own precedent, wrote that even though Section 1983 authorizes suits to enforce individual rights under the Constitution and federal statutes, it does not provide a means of relief every time a state actor violates a federal law. The Court emphasized that Section 1983 allows the enforcement of rights, not benefits or interests. In the end, the Court explained that a defendant may defeat the presumption that a right is enforceable under Section 1983 by showing that Congress did not intend that remedy for a newly created right. The evidence of such intent could be found directly in the statute, the Court added, or it could be inferred from the act's creation of a comprehensive enforcement scheme.

In its most recent case involving Section 1983, *Fitzgerald v. Barnstable School Committee* (2009), the Supreme Court clarified that the mere existence of a remedy within a statute is insufficient to reveal congressional intent for a remedy to be exclusive. The Court elaborated that the remedy must be comprehensive. Contrasting earlier cases with the situation here, which involved Title IX of the Education Amendments of 1972, the Court was of the view that Title IX did not have an enforcement scheme that required plaintiffs to comply with specified procedures or resort to an administrative process before taking their grievances to a judicial forum.

On the basis of *Rancho Palos Verdes*, lower courts are now examining various federal and state statutes to evaluate whether their own remedial schemes are sufficient to preclude redress under Section 1983. For example, citing the Supreme Court's precedent, the Third Circuit has concluded that the remedy under Section 504 of the

Rehabilitation Act is exclusive, and nothing within that statute indicates that Congress intended to allow Section 1983 to remedy Section 504 violations (*A. W. v. Jersey City Public Schools,* 2007).

Conclusion

Section 1983 provides litigants from institutions of higher learning with a powerful tool to enforce their rights under constitutional and statutory law. Administrators and other officials in colleges and universities could be personally liable under Section 1983, particularly when actions they have taken in their official capacities have the effect of discriminating against protected individuals. The old adage that ignorance of the law is no excuse is particularly relevant in regard to Section 1983 suits, because officials can be liable not only for knowingly violating the law but also when their actions violated clearly established rights, even when no ill intent was present. Unlike federal and state agencies, individual officials do not enjoy Eleventh Amendment immunity to suit under Section 1983.

An area worth closely watching is whether Section 1983 can be used to redress violations of all federal and state laws. Recently, based on Supreme Court precedent, lower courts have agreed that a number of statutes contain their own exclusive remedies and, therefore, preclude suits under Section 1983. This does not mean that officials would be immune to liability, as they could be subject to suits under the statutes in question themselves. However, the remedies provided under the statutes themselves may not be as severe as those that could be imposed under Section 1983.

Allan G. Osborne, Jr.

See also Eleventh Amendment; Rehabilitation Act, Section 504

Legal Citations

A. W. v. Jersey City Public Schools, 486 F.3d 791 (3d Cir. 2007).

City of Rancho Palos Verdes v. Abrams, 544 U.S. 113 (2005).

Civil Rights Act of 1871, Section 1983, 42 U.S.C. § 1983.

Fitzgerald v. Barnstable School Committee, 129 S. Ct. 788 (2009).

Handicapped Children's Protection Act of 1986, Pub. L. No. 99-372.

Individuals with Disabilities Education Act, 20 U.S.C. § 1400 *et seq.*

Maine v. Thiboutot, 448 U.S. 1 (1980).

Middlesex County Sewerage Authority v. National Sea Clammers Association, 453 U.S. 1 (1983).

Monell v. Department of Social Services, 436 U.S. 658 (1978).

Monroe v. Pape, 365 U.S. 167 (1961).

Rehabilitation Act of 1973, Section 504, 29 U.S.C. §§ 794 *et seq.*

Smith v. Robinson, 468 U.S. 992 (1984).

Title IX of the Education Amendments of 1972, 20 U.S.C. § 1681.

Wood v. Strickland, 420 U.S. 308 (1975).

CIVIL RIGHTS ACT OF 1964

The Civil Rights Act of 1964 is one of the most well-known and far-reaching contemporary civil rights statutes enacted by Congress. The act's impact on colleges and universities has been immense in that it prohibits discrimination against students, employees, and prospective employees or applicants on the basis of race, color, national origin, religion, and sex.

A decade after *Brown v. Board of Education, Topeka* (1954), and following on the heels of the assassination of President John F. Kennedy, his successor Lyndon B. Johnson worked with a wide array of civic groups to ensure that civil rights for African Americans and other minority groups would be codified into American law. Following a 54-day filibuster in the Senate, Congress approved the Civil Rights Act on July 2, 1964. Responding with haste, a mere five hours after the passage of the Civil Rights Act, President Johnson signed this monumental bill into law.

The Civil Rights Act of 1964 consists of 11 extensive titles that have impacted virtually every aspect of American life. Insofar as the act includes titles with special relevance for colleges and universities, this entry reviews the four titles that are most germane to higher education, highlighting how the law has fulfilled its mission of prohibiting discrimination in public facilities, in government, and in employment.

Title II

Title II addresses injunctive relief against discrimination in places of public accommodation. This title, in its provisions against discrimination, made it possible for minority groups to travel and have access to the same accommodations as Whites. As an extension of Title II, university cafeterias and dining halls had to be made open to all students regardless of their race. As with other provisions of the law, aggrieved parties can look to the Attorney General for relief or can file private claims for relief.

Title III

Title III concerns the desegregation of public facilities. Pursuant to Title II, the attorney general of the United States has the authority to initiate legal proceedings on behalf of a person or a group of persons who were denied the use of public facilities and who were unable to bring suit against their states due to the lack of funds necessary to obtain effective legal representation. The attorney general can thus file suit in the appropriate federal trial court. As a result of Title III, minority students cannot be denied opportunities to live in on-campus or off-campus housing and facilities.

Title VI

Title VI covers the prohibition against discrimination in programs receiving federal financial assistance. Titles VI and VII are the two most litigated titles of the Civil Rights Act, producing many changes in the operations of colleges and universities. According to Title VI, "No person in the United States shall, on the ground of race, color, or national origin, be excluded from participation in, be denied the benefits of, or be subjected to discrimination in any program receiving Federal financial assistance" (42 U.S.C. § 2000d).

The reach of Title VI is coextensive with judicial interpretation of the Equal Protection Clause of the Fourteenth Amendment to the U.S. Constitution (*Guardians Association v. Civil Service Commission of the City of New York*, 1983). However, even though the Fourteenth Amendment is triggered by state action, Title VI does have a practical effect on private institutions of higher education to the extent that their students qualify to receive federal financial assistance in the form of federal loans and grants. In this way, Title VI plays an important role in extending the protections of the Equal Protection Clause to private institutions of higher education. However, if private institutions do not receive any federal benefits whatsoever, Title VI has no impact on their operations.

The first of two enforcement provisions in Title VI authorize the federal government to threaten the withdrawal of financial assistance if federal officials or the courts determine that institutional officials engaged in unlawful discrimination. The second enforcement method is for individuals to sue colleges and universities, even though there is no specific language in the act granting awards of monetary damages. Moreover, although Title VI does not contain a provision for monetary awards, the U.S. Supreme Court has interpreted it as allowing an implied right of private action for damages, meaning that plaintiffs can recover compensatory but not punitive damages (*Barnes v. Gorman*, 2002).

Arguably, the impact of Title VI has been most significant in cases seeking to ensure equal educational opportunities for students of all races. To this end, the Supreme Court has ruled that officials at institutions of higher education may not employ racial classifications in student admissions unless their plans are narrowly tailored to achieve compelling governmental interests.

The three most significant cases dealing with racial classifications in student admissions are *Regents of the University of California v. Bakke* (1978), *Gratz v. Bollinger* (2003), and *Grutter v. Bollinger* (2003). In *Bakke*, the Court decided that even though the consideration of race was constitutionally permissible in admissions, the use of racial quotas such as the one employed by university officials in this case violated Title VI. More recently, in *Grutter* and *Gratz*, the Court reached mixed results in disputes involving racial classifications in admissions policies at the University of Michigan. In *Grutter*, the Court ruled that the use of race in the law school's policy was acceptable, because the policy helped maintain student body diversity—a compelling state interest—and was sufficiently narrowly tailored to meet this goal. Conversely, in *Gratz*, the Court struck down an undergraduate admissions policy as impermissible, because in assigning an automatic 20 points, the equivalent of one-fifth of the required points for admission, to members of the underrepresented minority groups of African Americans, Hispanics, and Native Americans, it was insufficiently narrowly tailored in pursuit of achieving a compelling governmental interest.

Title VII

Title VII, which covers equal employment opportunities, forbids employers, public and private, with 15 or more employees from discriminating against employees and prospective employees or applicants on the basis of race, color, national origin, religion, and sex. Title VII applies to hiring, discharge, transfer, promotion, demotion, compensation, and "terms, conditions, or privileges of employment" while also addressing other employment issues, including sexual harassment, maternity and religious leave, and retaliation for filing Title VII complaints. At the same time, Title VII does permit officials at colleges or universities to employ individuals on the basis of sex, national origin, or religion if such characteristics are a bona fide occupational qualification (BFOQ) necessary for their normal operations.

Title VII is enforced through the auspices of the Equal Employment Opportunity Commission (EEOC). In other words, before aggrieved parties may file suits, they must exhaust administrative remedies by filing claims with the EEOC within 180 days from the time the alleged discriminatory acts occurred. Once employers receive actual notice, and unless the parties reach a conciliation agreement or the EEOC files suit against the educational institution, its officials must notify the complainants, who then have 90 days to bring civil actions. Pursuant to Title VII, courts can award an array of remedies ranging from reinstatement to back pay and attorney fees.

Perhaps the two most significant employment areas in which the Supreme Court has applied Title VII in higher education are sexual harassment and religion. In relying on judicially created principles that evolved in the noneducational workplace in the fight against racial discrimination, the Supreme Court developed a three-step test of shifting burdens and order of proof for Title VII cases. It is interesting to note that the Court has not addressed a Title VII case involving discrimination based on race in a college or university setting.

As to religion, Title VII recognizes the authority of religious officials to operate institutions in a manner consistent with bona fide occupational qualifications that include hiring members of their own faiths in key positions. For example, in *Amos v. Corporation of Presiding Bishop* (1987) the Supreme Court upheld the authority of institutional officials who dismissed a building engineer who worked in a gymnasium open to the public because he failed to meet the church's religious "temple recommend" requirement.

In reviewing a wide array of claims involving university employees, because students are covered by Title IX of the Educational Amendments of 1972, the courts have been of the opinion that colleges and universities can be liable for same-sex sexual harassment; quid pro quo or literally "this for that" sexual harassment; and hostile or abusive work environment harassment.

Conclusion

In sum, the antidiscrimination provisions of the Civil Rights Act of 1964 have had a profound impact on the operations of American colleges and universities on a multitude of levels. In the wake of the many changes that the Civil Rights Act of 1964 has effected in higher education, it may be hoped that campuses have become more open learning and working environments in which all are free to interact for their mutual benefit and that of the wider society.

Robert J. Safransky

See also Equal Employment Opportunity Commission; Equal Protection Analysis; Fourteenth Amendment; *Gratz v. Bollinger*; *Grutter v. Bollinger*; Hostile Work Environment; *Regents of the University of California v. Bakke*; Religious Colleges and Universities; Sexual Harassment, Quid Pro Quo; Sexual Harassment, Same-Sex; Title VI; Title VII

Further Readings

Davis, D. D., III. (2005). Feedback loop: The Civil Rights Act of 1964 and its progeny. *St. Louis University Law Review, 49,* 981–1005.

Ishimaru, S. J. (2005). Fulfilling the promise of Title VII of the Civil Rights Act of 1964. *University of Memphis Law Review, 26,* 25–38.

Legal Citations

Amos v. Corporation of Presiding Bishop, 483 U.S. 327 (1987).
Barnes v. Gorman, 536 U.S. 181 (2002).
Brown v. Board of Education, Topeka, 347 U.S. 483 (1954).
Civil Rights Act of 1964, 42 U.S.C. § 2000 *et seq.*
Gratz v. Bollinger, 539 U.S. 244 (2003).
Grutter v. Bollinger, 539 U.S. 306 (2003).
Guardians Association v. Civil Service Commission of the City of New York, 463 U.S. 582 (1983).
Regents of the University of California v. Bakke, 438 U.S. 265 (1978).
United States Code, as cited.

CIVIL RIGHTS MOVEMENT

Following World War II, the United States experienced unprecedented public sentiment against the oppression of African Americans and other minorities. This public outcry presented itself in the form of boycotts, freedom rides, national rallies, and marches. These protests focused on ending discrimination and on protecting civil rights. Although not focusing on higher education per se, this entry examines the significance of the civil rights movement in the United States while discussing its background, highlighting relevant civil rights legislation, and reviewing key court cases in light of the impact that the movement had on American colleges and universities.

Background

Under the U.S. Constitution, civil rights are afforded to persons by reason of citizenship or personhood and include rights to free speech, freedom of the press, voting, due process, and equal protection of the laws. Discrimination occurs, in part, when these rights are denied. In order to prevent such discrimination, Congress has passed statutes recognizing these rights, while the Supreme Court has decided cases focused on these areas.

Court Cases

During the civil rights movement, opponents of segregation made continuing efforts to challenge it through the courts. Although the Supreme Court focused on equal rights broadly, this entry highlights major cases in particular, because they paved the road to the civil rights movement. In its 1857 decision in *Dred Scott v. Sanford,* the Supreme Court held that because slaves did not become free when they were taken into free states, they lacked the right to file judicial actions. The Court also maintained that Congress could not bar slavery from territories and that Blacks could not become citizens. Frederick Douglass, an African American abolitionist, commented that although the outcome was very troublesome, it gave him high hopes. Specifically, Douglass believed that the national conscience would overwhelmingly reject this problematic situation.

In *Plessy v. Ferguson* (1896), the Supreme Court determined that facilities for African Americans could be "separate but equal," setting a precedent that lasted until 1954, when the Supreme Court decided the case of *Brown v. Board of Education, Topeka.* The Court's ruling in *Brown* that separate was inherently unequal began a tide of litigation, legislation, and resistance that defined the civil rights movement.

Constitutional Rights and Civil Rights Legislation

Civil rights are protected primarily through the Thirteenth and Fourteenth Amendments to the Constitution and through congressional enactment of a variety of statutes. The Thirteenth Amendment, adopted in 1865, abolished slavery in the United States. The Fourteenth Amendment prohibited any state from depriving any person of "life, liberty, or property without due process of law" and from denying "to any person within its jurisdiction the equal protection of the laws" In addition, Section 5 of the Fourteenth Amendment gave Congress the power to pass any laws needed for its enforcement. The Fifteenth Amendment banned race-based voting qualifications.

Along with constitutional amendments, Congress passed civil rights statutes during the Reconstruction era after the Civil War. Two of the most noteworthy were Section 1981, which protects one from discrimination based on race in contracts and when participating in lawsuits (42 U.S.C. § 1981), and the Civil Rights Act of 1971, more commonly known as Section 1983

(42 U.S.C. § 1983). Section 1983 protects individuals whose civil rights have been violated by individuals who were acting under color of state law.

The Civil Rights Act of 1964 is the best-known modern statute passed by Congress to protect civil rights. Under this statute, one may not discriminate based on "race, color, religion, or national origin" in public establishments that participate in interstate commerce (42 U.S.C. § 2000a). Title VI of the Civil Rights Act also prohibits discrimination in federally funded programs. Agencies that violate Title VI risk the loss of federal funding. Title VII of the Civil Rights Act forbids employment discrimination where employers are engaged in interstate commerce; further, states may offer additional civil rights protections beyond the federal protections provided in this act.

Civil Rights Movement: Early Efforts

Although the commonly recalled events of the civil rights movement took place in the 1950s and 1960s, earlier civil rights efforts should be recognized. Some scholars maintain that an organized movement began in the 1700s, when Massachusetts outlawed slavery within its borders, and continued in 1808 when the importation of slaves was banned. Still other scholars cite the revolt of Nat Turner, who in 1831 led a slave rebellion in Virginia. Finally, in 1863, President Lincoln issued the Emancipation Proclamation freeing all slaves, clearly a major turning point in civil rights history.

Another significant development was the foundation of the Niagara Movement, a civil rights group, in 1905. This group, which was led by W. E. B. Du Bois, openly opposed racial segregation. The Niagara Movement eventually became known as the National Association for the Advancement of Colored People. Even so, most observers agree that the civil rights movement reached its peak from the mid-1950s through the mid-1960s.

Civil Rights Movement: The 1950s and 1960s

A major catalyst for the civil rights movement came in 1955, when Rosa Parks refused to give her seat to a White passenger on a bus in Montgomery, Alabama. After she was arrested, leaders of the Black community in Montgomery, including Dr. Martin Luther King, Jr., staged a boycott of the Montgomery bus system that eventually led to its desegregation a year later. This protest helped make King a national figure. Shortly after the bus boycott, Emmett Till, a 14-year-old Black boy from Chicago who was visiting relatives in Mississippi, was killed for allegedly whistling at a White woman. This case became an international outrage, as the two men accused of the murder were acquitted by an all-White jury.

In 1957, the Southern Christian Leadership Conference (SCLC) was formed with Dr. King as its first president. SCLC emphasized nonviolent mass action as a central form of resistance and became a major force in the civil rights movement. Also in 1957 came the desegregation of Central High School in Little Rock, Arkansas, an event that was put in the national spotlight when Governor Orval Faubus and crowds of angry students and parents barred nine Black students from the school. Faubus ordered the Arkansas National Guard to prevent the Black students from entering the school. In response, President Dwight D. Eisenhower sent the National Guard and federal troops to escort the Black students into the building. The Little Rock school system closed the public schools for a time instead of integrating the student body.

Around 1960, the growing civil rights momentum reached college students, as they began to join in the protests that were spreading across the south. In 1960, four Black students from North Carolina Agricultural and Technical College began a sit-in at a segregated Woolworth's lunch counter in Greensboro, North Carolina. Although the students were not served, they returned continuously to the counter and insisted on being served. This action prompted more sit-ins around the country, and these four students became icons of the civil rights movement. Shortly after this event, the Student Nonviolent Coordinating Committee (SNCC) was founded at Shaw University as a group that helped to organize Black youth in the civil rights movement.

Student involvement continued into the summer of 1961, when almost 1,000 Black and White students and volunteers from across the country joined in "freedom rides" that tested the desegregation of the transportation system in the United States. The freedom rides were sponsored by both SNCC and the Congress of Racial Equality (CORE). These students were often met with stiff resistance; for example, mobs in Alabama burned a bus that held the student volunteers. In Mississippi freedom riders were arrested for breaching the peace in White facilities. Several of these students were jailed.

In 1962, riots broke out at the University of Mississippi when the first Black student, James Meredith, was enrolled. Governor Ross Barnett had said that he would never allow the university to become integrated, prompting the riots in which two students were killed. Even so, Meredith was protected by the National Guard and went on to graduate from the university in 1964.

Earlier in 1963, Martin Luther King, Jr., was arrested and jailed while participating in an anti-segregation protest in Birmingham, Alabama. During this time, he wrote a "Letter from Birmingham Jail," stressing that unjust laws should be disobeyed. Another significant development in 1963 was the murder of Medgar Evers, the NAACP's field secretary for Mississippi; his murderer was convicted 30 years later. Finally, deadly riots also broke out in 1963 when four Black girls attending Sunday school in Birmingham, Alabama, were killed by a bomb that exploded at their church. It took 40 years to convict those responsible for the bombing.

Perhaps the most remembered event of the civil rights movement is Dr. King's famous "I have a dream" speech at the culmination of the 1963 march on Washington, D.C. More than 200,000 people attended this nonviolent event. Soon after the march, President John F. Kennedy, who had been quietly in favor of the movement, came out with his full support. President Kennedy began to work on getting the Civil Rights Act through Congress but ran into significant resistance.

When Kennedy was assassinated in November, only months after the 1963 march, President Lyndon B. Johnson took up the cause of the civil rights movement in Kennedy's name. Using the memory of the assassinated president, Johnson was able to get the Civil Rights Act into, and through, Congress. When Southern Democrat senators staged a filibuster that lasted a record 57 days, Johnson was able to sway the majority and win the vote to end it only by convincing a senator from Illinois who controlled several votes. Johnson did so by invoking the memory of President Lincoln, who opposed slavery and was from Illinois. President Johnson signed the act into law in 1964 and made segregation in all public facilities and employment discrimination illegal.

Shortly after the Civil Rights Act was enacted, three civil rights workers in Mississippi who were registering Black voters disappeared. The three workers had been arrested by the police on speeding charges, jailed for several hours, and murdered by the Ku Klux Klan shortly after being released. Six months later, Malcolm X, the founder of the Organization of Afro-American Unity, was shot to death in Harlem. Amidst this post–Civil Rights Act chaos, the Voting Rights Act became law in 1965, thereby enabling more Blacks to vote by banning literacy laws. Before this act was passed, Blacks who marched to Montgomery, Alabama, in support of voting rights were beaten by police at the Edmund Pettus Bridge. The event became known as "Bloody Sunday."

In further contrast to the victories of the civil rights movement, Dr. Martin Luther King, Jr., was assassinated in 1968 on the balcony of his Memphis, Tennessee, hotel room. Not long thereafter, escaped convict James Earl Ray pleaded guilty to murder and was sentenced to 99 years in prison. Yet three days after his sentencing Ray recanted his statement and maintained his innocence until his death in 1998. As a result, questions about Dr. King's death still remain.

Proponents of the movement employed a variety of approaches to bring about equality during the civil rights movement. For example, the NAACP, CORE, and SCLC endorsed peaceful methods for change, while other groups such as the Black Panthers, the Nation of Islam, and the Black Nationalist movement advocated a more aggressive approach for change.

It is also important to note that the Mexican American Legal Defense and Education Fund (MALDEF) was founded in 1968. MALDEF's mission was to safeguard the civil rights of Latinos. Moreover, the American Indian Movement (AIM) was founded in 1968 and advocated on the behalf of the interests of indigenous Americans. The women's movement had a significant presence during the civil rights movement as well, advocating for a variety of issues from equal pay to reproductive rights.

Although there is more to achieve in ending discrimination, it is unquestionable that the civil rights movement brought about important advances toward this goal with the result that its impact has been felt in the world of higher education and beyond.

Suzanne E. Eckes

See also Civil Rights Act of 1871, Section 1983; Civil Rights Restoration Act of 1987; Title VI; Title VII

Further Readings

Eckes, S. (2006). The civil rights movement. In F. English (Ed.), *Encyclopedia of educational leadership and administration* (Vol. 1, pp. 138–141). Thousand Oaks, CA: Sage.
Hampton, H., & Fayer, S. (1991). *Voices of freedom.* New York: Bantam Books.

Legal Citations

Brown v. Board of Education, Topeka, 347 U.S. 497 (1954).
Civil Rights Act of 1964, Pub. L. No. 88-352.
Dred Scott v. Sanford, 60 U.S. 393 (1857).
Plessy v. Ferguson, 163 U.S. 537 (1896).
United States Code, as cited.
Voting Rights Act of 1965, Pub. L. No. 89-110.

CIVIL RIGHTS RESTORATION ACT OF 1987

In *Grove City College v. Bell* (1984), the U.S. Supreme Court ruled that the U.S. Department of Education could sanction only part of the college for refusing to comply with the requirements of Title IX of the Education Amendments of 1972 (Title IX), a federal statute that was designed to provide gender equity in athletic programming in higher education. Dissatisfied with this outcome, Congress basically superseded the Court's judgment by enacting the Civil Rights Restoration Act of 1987 over the veto of President Ronald Reagan. This act extended the protections of Title IX and Title VI of the Civil Rights Act of 1964 to institution-wide operations rather than just those departments, programs, or components receiving federal financial aid. In light of the impact that the act has had on American colleges and universities, this entry examines the litigation in *Grove City* that led up to the act's enactment and discusses its key features.

Background

Grove City College is a private coeducational institution that was founded in 1876 by Isaac Ketler, a conservative Christian clergyman and educator. It has retained its conservative religious orientation, independence, and dedication to the freedom of individuals as well as to the free market economy. Because the college operates on a balanced budget, it remains virtually debt-free. The college seeks to maintain institutional autonomy by refusing to accept state and federal financial assistance. It thus seeks to demonstrate that institutions of higher education can offer affordable programs without government funding or mandates. Arguing that Title IX constituted an unconstitutional imposition of federal control on its students, college officials challenged federal oversight in *Grove City College v. Bell* (1984).

The dispute in *Grove City* arose because some of its students received Basic Educational Opportunity Grants (BEOGs), a form of federal financial assistance. Officials at the United States Department of Education (ED) determined that the acceptance of these grants by students constituted federal financial assistance to the college, thereby triggering the application of Title IX's nondiscrimination requirements. Consequently, officials at the ED asked administrators at the college to sign an Assurance of Compliance form ensuring that they would meet the requirements of Title IX.

College officials refused to sign the Assurance of Compliance form, because they believed that the institution did not directly receive federal financial support. However, many of the colleges' students received BEOGs through its athletic department's alternative disbursement system. When college officials continued to refuse to sign the compliance forms, the ED initiated administrative proceedings to declare the college and its students ineligible to receive BEOGs.

As a result of the administrative proceeding, the ED terminated financial assistance until such time as college officials signed the Assurance of Compliance form. In response to a suit filed by college officials and four of their students, a federal trial court in Pennsylvania held that while the students' BEOGs constituted federal financial assistance, the ED could not terminate the aid due to institutional refusal to sign the Assurance of Compliance form. However, the Third Circuit Court of Appeals reversed in favor of the ED. The court decided that the funds could be withheld in order to force college officials to sign the Assurance of Compliance. Unhappy with the result, the college appealed to the Supreme Court.

The Supreme Court's judgment in *Grove City*, affirming the Third Circuit's judgment in favor of the ED, created an all but immediate firestorm of controversy. However, although the Court found that the ED could terminate funding, its analysis maintained that funds could be withheld only for the grant program that was subject to Title IX if institutional officials refused to sign the Assurance of Compliance form indicating their willingness to follow the dictates of the statute. In so doing, the Court left itself open to criticism by its opponents for its refusal to allow the ED to sanction to the entire institution. Displeased by the outcome in *Grove City*, Congress essentially superseded it three years later with the enactment of the Civil Rights Restoration Act of 1987, thereby interpreting Title IX as it was originally written rather than the way in which the Court had narrowed its otherwise broad institution-wide application.

The Civil Rights Restoration Act

The Civil Rights Restoration Act was the culmination of decades of legislation and the work of activist groups who used the controversy that *Grove City College* generated to further prohibit the discrimination that Title VI sought to outlaw in programs receiving federal financial assistance. Although introduced in 1984, the bill was unable to gain congressional approval due to political factors; the Democratic-led House of Representatives passed the bill, but it was stalled in the Republican-controlled Senate. Further, Roman Catholic bishops lobbied against its passage, fearing that provisions in the original version of the bill dealing with abortion would apply to educational institutions and Catholic hospitals. When the Democrats regained control of the Senate in 1987, they again sought to pass the Civil Rights Restoration Act.

The Civil Rights Restoration Act began with the acknowledgment that the Supreme Court's decision in *Grove City* unduly narrowed or cast doubt on the broad application of Title IX and three additional federal laws with considerable impact on colleges and universities—Section 504 of the Rehabilitation Act of 1973, the Age Discrimination Act of 1975 (ADA), and Title VI—that were designed to fight discrimination involving recipients of federal financial assistance. Section 504 forbids discrimination against otherwise qualified individuals with impairments who can participate if they receive reasonable accommodations. The ADA outlaws discrimination based on age. Title VI, the broadest of the three laws, prohibits discrimination based on race, color, or national origin in schools, public places, and employment.

Aware of the extent of these statutes, Congress found it necessary to take legislative action to restore their prior consistent and long-standing support of broad, institution-wide application of those laws, as reflected in federal regulations administered by the executive branch. The act passed both houses and was sent to President Reagan, who promptly vetoed the law. However, the Senate voted 73–24 to override the veto while the House voted similarly 292–133. The act went into effect on March 22, 1988. The act is enforced through the authority of the Office of Civil Rights in the ED.

The Civil Rights Restoration Act makes it clear that all departments and elements of institutions or organizations that receive federal financial funds must comply, without exception, with its antidiscrimination provisions. In this way, Congress was essentially able to protect Title VI and extend its coverage to such important statutes for colleges and universities as Title IX, Section 504, and the Age Discrimination in Employment Act. Even so, it is important to recognize that the act does not change any of these statutes. Rather, it returns their coverage to the original scope that was intended when each was enacted.

Since the enactment of the Civil Rights Restoration Act, the federal government has created new federal agencies that have issued many regulations requiring institutions of higher education receiving federal funds to sign compliance forms ensuring that they are satisfying its provisions. To the extent that officials at colleges and universities follow the law, then the act's most significant impact has been on Title IX by restoring its far-reaching provisions to campuswide programming.

Robert J. Safransky

See also *Grove City College v. Bell*; Higher Education Act; Loans and Federal Aid; Rehabilitation Act, Section 504; U.S. Department of Education

Further Readings

Graham, H. D. (1988). The storm over *Grove City College:* Civil rights regulation, higher education and the Reagan administration. *History of Education Quarterly, 38*(4), 407–429.

Hendrickson, R. M., Lee, B., & Olswang, S. G. (1990). The impact of the Civil Rights Act of 1987 on higher education. *Education Law Reporter, 60,* 671–690.

Legal Citations

Age Discrimination Act of 1975, 42 U.S.C. § 6107.
Civil Rights Restoration Act of 1987, Pub. L. No. 100-259, 102 Stat. 28.
Grove City College v. Bell, 465 U.S. 555 (1984).
Rehabilitation Act of 1973, Section 504, 29 U.S.C. §§ 794 *et seq.*
Title VI of the Civil Rights Act of 1964, 42 U.S.C. § 2000d(4a).
Title IX of the Education Amendments of 1972, 20 U.S.C. § 1681.

CLERY ACT

The Jeanne Clery Disclosure of Campus Security Policy and Campus Crime Statistics Act, commonly called the Clery Act, is a federal law enacted in 1990 for the purpose of providing college and university students with important information about campus crime and security policies at the higher education institutions they attend. This entry reviews the purpose and provisions of the act and the amendments to it as well as the limited litigation that has dealt with it.

Purposes of the Clery Act

As one scholarly commentary described the Clery Act, the law's main goal

was to ensure that when selecting an [institution of higher education] to attend, current and prospective students, as well as their parents, would be able to obtain accurate "official" statistics about how much crime had occurred on a respective [college or university] campus.

In addition, students and their parents "could gain knowledge of the security procedures that each school had in place. This information would then allow students and their parents to weigh crime issues when making college enrollment decisions" (Fisher, Hartman, Cullen, & Turner, 2002, pp. 63–64).

All postsecondary institutions that participate in federal student aid programs are required to comply with the Clery Act. The law's passage was due in large part to the efforts of Howard and Connie Clery, whose daughter Jeanne was raped and murdered in her dormitory room at Lehigh University in 1986. Originally titled the Crime Awareness and Campus Security Act of 1990, the law was renamed in 1998 to commemorate Jeanne Clery.

Provisions of the Act

Under the law, officials at higher education institutions are required to collect and publish crime statistics pertaining to certain types of crime that occur on campus and in adjacent areas and noncampus buildings, including fraternity and sorority houses. Specifically, officials are required to report annually about crime activity that occurred during the preceding calendar year and the two preceding calendar years.

The Clery Act lists the following crimes or campus disciplinary offenses that are covered by the law's reporting provisions: murder, forcible and nonforcible sex offenses, robbery, aggravated assault, burglary, motor vehicle theft, manslaughter, arson, and "arrests or persons referred for campus disciplinary action for liquor law violations, drug-related violations, and weapons possession" (20 U.S.C. § 1092(f)(1)(F)(i)). Institutional officials are also required to collect and disseminate information about hate crimes that result in bodily injury if "the victim is intentionally selected because of the actual or perceived race, gender, religion, sexual orientation, ethnicity, or disability" (20 U.S.C. § 1092(f)(1)(F)(ii)).

As originally enacted, the Clery Act required only that officials at colleges and universities report crimes that occurred on their own campuses. However, the law was subsequently amended to require officials to report crimes that occur in certain noncampus buildings or on noncampus property as well as crimes that take place in certain public areas that are adjacent to a reporting institution. The law defines "noncampus building or property" as meaning "any building or property owned or controlled by a student organization recognized by the institution," as well as

> any building or property . . . owned or controlled by [the institution] that is used in direct support of, or in relation to, the institution's educational purposes, is used by students, and is not within the same reasonably contiguous geographic area of the institution. (20 U.S.C. § 1092(f)(6)(A)(ii))

Institutional officials are also required to report about crimes that occur on "public property," which the act defines as

> all public property that is within the same reasonably contiguous geographic area of the institution, such as a sidewalk, a street, or thoroughfare, or parking facility, and is adjacent to a facility owned or controlled by the institution if the facility is used by the institution in direct support of, or in a manner related to, the institution's educational purposes. (20 U.S.C. § 1092(f)(6)(A)(iii))

One of the most important provisions of the Clery Act is the law's requirement that officials at higher education institutions give their campus communities "timely warnings" of any criminal activity on campus that may pose an ongoing threat to campus employees or students. As a result of this legal requirement, officials at colleges and universities now commonly notify campus students and employees of crime incidents that pose an ongoing threat to students and employees by a variety of methods, including the student newspaper, dormitory bulletins, and e-mail alerts.

The Clery Act requires higher education institutions that operate police or security departments to maintain public crime logs that describe "any crime that occurred on campus or within the patrol jurisdiction of the campus police or the campus security

department and is reported to the campus police or security department." The Clery Act specifies that logs should include information about the "nature, date, time, and general location of each crime" and the outcome of any investigation of the crime if the outcome is known. The logs must be updated with regard to crime incidents within two business days after a new incident occurs.

College and university officials who are responsible for maintaining crime logs must make them available to students, campus employees, parents, and the press during normal business hours. All logs of campus crime incidents must remain open for 60 days after events occur. After the 60-day period expires, logs must be made available on request within two business days of when requests are made.

Amendments to the Clery Act

In 1992, the Clery Act was amended to identify certain basic rights for victims of sexual assaults, including students who were victims of date rape. The 1992 amendment, which was titled the Campus Sexual Assault Victims' Bill of Rights and is sometimes referred to as the Ramstad Act, requires officials at colleges and universities to notify sexual assault victims of their right to file criminal charges with local law enforcement authorities. Moreover, the sexual assault provision requires institutional officials to notify victims about college or university counseling services that are available and about the importance of preserving evidence of sexual assault in the event of subsequent criminal proceedings. In addition, the 1992 amendment requires officials at higher education institutions to allow both the accuser and the accused to have others present at on-campus disciplinary hearings involving sexual assault allegations and to notify the accuser of the outcome of any on-campus disciplinary proceeding involving sexual assault accusations. Officials in higher education institutions must also inform sexual assault victims of available options for changing their academic schedule or living arrangements (20 U.S.C. §1092 (f)(8)).

In the wake of the tragedy at Virginia Tech University in 2007, Congress amended the Cleary Act again in 2008. The 2008 amendment added a "campus emergency response plan" provision to the act and requires higher education institutions to "immediately notify" the campus community of a campus emergency unless notification would compromise efforts to respond effectively to the emergency. In addition, the 2008 amendment added a "whistleblower" provision to protect individuals from retaliation for actions taken pursuant to the Cleary Act while expanding on the list of the types of threats that require notification.

Litigation

Since its enactment in 1990, the Clery Act has been the subject of very little published litigation. *Havlik v. Johnson & Wales University* (2007) is the only published case at the federal appellate level that has discussed the Clery Act in any detail. In that case, Christopher Havlik sued a Rhode Island university after university officials released a crime report stating that he had been involved in a sidewalk altercation with another student and that it had been reported that he had a knife in his possession during the incident. Prior to the report's release, a university disciplinary hearing concluded that Havlik had violated university policy by his conduct but did not find that he had possessed a knife during the incident. Havlik was later acquitted by a jury of assault charges that arose from the incident.

Havlik sued the university and a variety of officials for defamation, claiming that the crime incident report was false. A federal trial court dismissed the case on the ground that the university enjoyed a qualified immunity under Rhode Island law to publish the crime incident report based on its reasonable belief that it was obligated by the Clery Act to do so. On appeal, the First Circuit affirmed the dismissal in favor of the university.

Richard Fossey

See also Cyberbullying; Hate Crimes

Further Readings

Fisher, B. S., Hartman, J. L., Cullen, F. T., & Turner, M. G. (2002). Making campuses safer for students: The Clery Act as a symbolic legal reform. *Stetson Law Review, 32*, 61–89.

Security on Campus, Inc. (n.d.). *Complying with the Jeanne Clery Act.* Retrieved February 11, 2009, from http://www.securityoncampus.org/index.php?option=com_content&view=article&id=271&Itemid=81

Legal Citations

Campus Sexual Assault Victims' Bill of Rights, Pub. L. No. 102-325, § 486(c) (1992).

Havlik v. Johnson & Wales University, 509 F.3d 25, 35 (1st Cir. 2007).

Jeanne Clery Disclosure of Campus Security Policy and Campus Crime Statistics Act, 20 U.S.C. § 1092(f).

COLLECTIVE BARGAINING

Collective bargaining involves the practice of negotiating salaries, benefits, and other terms and conditions of employment between employers and the representatives of their employees. In the bargaining process, employees select their sole bargaining representatives according to state and/or federal procedural requirements. Although some organizations are referred to as employee associations instead of unions, the terms *association* and *union* are used interchangeably for the purposes of this entry, because both groups represent their members when negotiating labor contracts. This entry presents a brief history of collective bargaining in the United States that identifies and discusses key federal legislation related to collective bargaining along with relevant cases related to negotiations in higher education. The entry concludes by identifying current key issues in collective bargaining in higher education.

History

Collective bargaining in the United States had a limited history in the private sector dating back to before the industrial revolution. Even so, a major development, the National Labor Relations Act (NLRA) of 1935, also known as the Wagner Act, which guaranteed the rights of private citizens to organize, form unions, and bargain collectively in the private sector and established the National Labor Relations Board (NLRB) to oversee unionization and labor relations in the private sector. In 1947, Congress enacted the Taft-Hartley Act and in 1959 the Landrum-Griffin Act, each amending the NLRA. These acts served to clarify which groups fell under the auspices of the NLRA's authority, allowed the federal government through the judicial system the ability to issue injunctions against prohibited union and management activities, and established requirements for union governance. Collective bargaining in the public sector began a generation after the passage of the NLRA.

Public sector collective bargaining is subject to state laws and is not regulated by the NLRA. As of 2009, 34 states require collective bargaining, while at least 3 expressly prohibit the practice. Individual states set requirements for the recognition of the exclusive representatives for employees for the purpose of collective bargaining. States may also identify specific areas that are subject to mandatory bargaining, such as terms and conditions of employment; areas that are prohibited from bargaining (referred to as management rights); and permissive areas that may be bargained subject to mutual agreement. Of course, as with bargaining in K–12 educational systems, faculty, nonprofessional employees on the support staff, and maintenance workers cannot be members of the same bargaining unions, insofar as they do not share a common community of interest. Accordingly, this entry focuses on the rights of faculty and, as noted, teaching assistants and researchers.

Federal employees gained the right to form unions and engage in collective bargaining after President Kennedy authorized the practice in 1962 via Executive Order 10988. Unionization of public school teachers began about the same time but made great strides starting in the 1970s. Employees in public colleges and universities began collective bargaining in the late 1960s with the majority of the movement in two-year community colleges. While collective bargaining and union membership have been in decline in the private sector largely due to the loss of manufacturing jobs, in education, public and private, K–12 and postsecondary, there appears to be growth in union representation and collective bargaining where the practice is not prohibited by law.

Collective bargaining at private institutions of higher education has a more recent history due mostly to the view of the NLRB that faculty occupy supervisory or managerial positions that are ordinarily exempt from participating in negotiations. Further, in *National Labor Relations Board v. Yeshiva University* (1980) the Supreme Court classified faculty members in private institutions of higher education as managerial based on the input or influence that they have with regard to

the employment of other faculty, tenure, economic decisions, and self-governance.

In light of the orders of the NLRB and the Supreme Court, it appears that the greater the influence and the higher the level of ability to engage in self-government that faculty members have, the less likely they are to be able to organize to engage in collective bargaining. At the same time, *Yeshiva* impacted public institutions in some states, causing the dissolution of existing faculty unions.

In 1997, the NLRB revisited the classification of higher education faculties at private institutions as management in a dispute from the University of Great Falls, allowing its faculty to organize and bargain collectively. Three years later, in 2000, the NLRB found that the faculty at Manhattan College had the right to organize and bargain collectively. In both instances the NLRB considered the actual influence of faculty members on employment and fiscal decisions. The NLRB granted both faculties the right to organize and bargain, because it was convinced that the majority of recommendations that faculty members made were advisory rather than dispositive in the decision-making processes on their campuses.

Key legislation from the 110th Congress and not yet introduced in the 111th Congress is the National Right-to-Work Act, a law that seeks to prohibit the requirement that workers be union members as a condition of employment in all states. According to the U.S. Department of Labor, 23 states have right-to-work laws and constitutional amendments as of January 2009. The National Right-to-Work Act would repeal some federal laws that allow dismissal for nonpayment of dues or lack of union membership and would apply to all states meaning mandatory union membership could not be a condition of employment. Although this proposed law focuses specifically on unions, its impact on collective bargaining would be immediate. Educators at colleges and universities would be wise to keep abreast of the status of this law as the 111th Congress addresses labor issues.

Graduate Students and Adjunct Faculty

Two additional groups in higher education, graduate teaching assistants and graduate researchers, have asserted the right to organize and bargain collectively with some success. The earliest union of graduate students was formed in 1969 at the University of Wisconsin. Because state laws cover public employees, state agencies responsible for labor or state courts decide whether these groups are eligible to form unions and bargain collectively. Consequently, since the late 1990s there has been an increase in collective bargaining agreements between public universities and their graduate teaching and research assistants. This spread in collective bargaining among these groups is due in large part to the NLRB's order involving New York University in 2000.

Collective bargaining typically requires full-time employment for membership in a union or employee association in both the public and private sectors. More specifically, in higher education, adjunct faculty members are not ordinarily covered by unions, because they are part-time employees. This classification may result in conflict, as some colleges and universities are moving toward part-time and adjunct faculty as a cost savings measure, because these adjunct faculty would be ineligible for benefits. In addition, institutions currently operating under collective bargaining agreements that include dismissal and reduction-in-force procedures may opt not to fill open full-time positions in favor of hiring less expensive adjunct faculty members.

Online Learning

In recent years, online education has become an issue related to faculty at institutions offering classes through this medium. These classes are becoming popular not only because they afford institutions larger pools of students without substantial increases in overhead, but also because they provide a more convenient way for many students to participate in higher education at both the graduate and undergraduate levels.

The Internet has clearly increased the availability of postsecondary education to a multitude of people. However, the lack of specific guidelines in many colleges and universities as far as the number of courses that individuals may teach, enrollment cap sizes, time dedicated to preparation of materials and actual online time, and even ownership of course content are all issues that may be subject to bargaining. Additionally, absent the direct contact with students, faculty members may have greater teaching loads than in traditional classes that must

be addressed in negotiations. Faculty at all levels undoubtedly will not disagree with the value of enabling greater numbers of students to experience college educations, but they expect regulation, perhaps through bargaining, to ensure employment equity is maintained with regard to workload and commensurate compensation. Viewing online teaching and bargaining from this perspective is likely to garner support by unions and professional associations on campuses as labor contracts are negotiated and renegotiated. In fact, as the United States moves further toward an information economy and away from a manufacturing economy, the delivery of education via electronic devices and online programs may become even more prominent in bringing this means of learning into the forefront of collective bargaining.

In sum, as legislation and litigation continue to declare more groups of employees eligible to participate in collective bargaining, administration, faculty, graduate teaching assistants, and graduate researchers on college and university campuses need to remain up-to-date with respect to constitutional requirements, statutes, regulations, and case law associated with union representation.

Michael J. Jernigan

See also National Labor Relations Act; *National Labor Relations Board v. Yeshiva University*; Unions on Campus

Further Readings

Johnson, S. M., Nelson, N. C. W., & Potter, J. (1985). *Teacher unions, school staffing, and reform.* Washington, DC: National Institute for Education. ERIC Document Reproduction Service No. ED274108. Retrieved January 25, 2009, from http://www.eric.ed.gov

Kaplan, W. A., & Lee, B. A. (2006). *The law of higher education: A comprehensive guide to legal implications of administrative decision making.* San Francisco: Jossey-Bass.

Palmer, S. (1999). *A brief history of collective bargaining in higher education.* Retrieved January 27, 2009, from http://members.home.net/eoozycki/HECollectBar.html

Russo, C. J., Gordon, W. M., & Miles, A. S. (1992). Agency shop fees and the Supreme Court: Union control and academic freedom. *Education Law Reporter, 73*(3), 609–615.

U.S. General Accounting Office. (2002, September). *Collective bargaining rights: Information on the number of workers with and without bargaining rights*. Report to Congressional Requestors, U.S. Senate, GAO-02-835. Washington, DC: Author.

Further Readings

Employee Free Choice Act of 2007, S. 1041, H.R. 800. 110th Congress (2007–08). Retrieved January 25, 2009, from http://www.govtrack.us

U.S. Department of Labor. (2009). *State right-to-work laws and constitutional amendments*. Retrieved January 25, 2009, from http://www.dol.gov/esa/whd/state/righttowork.htm

Legal Citations

Labor-Management Relations Act (Taft-Hartley Act), Pub. L. No. 80-101 (1947).

Labor-Management Reporting and Disclosure Act (Landrum-Griffin Act), Pub. L. No. 86-257 (1959).

Manhattan College and Manhattan College Faculty Coalition, New York State United Teachers a/w American Federation of Teachers, AFL-CIO. NLRB Case 2-RC-21735 (November 9, 1999). Retrieved January 25, 2009, from http://www.nlrb.gov/shared_files/Regional%20Decisions/1999/2-RC-21735.pdf

National Labor Relations Act (Wagner Act), 29 U.S.C. §§ 151-169 (1935).

National Labor Relations Board v. Yeshiva University, 444 U.S. 672 (1980).

National Right-to-Work Act. H.R. 697, S. 1301. 110th Congress (2007–08). Retrieved January 25, 2009, from http://www.govtrack.us

New York University and International Union, United Automobile, Aerospace and Agricultural Implement Workers of America, AFL-CIO. NLRB Case 2-RC-22082 (October 31, 2000). Retrieved January 25, 2009, from http://www.nlrb.gov/shared_files/Board%20Decisions/332/332-111.pdf

University of Great Falls and Montana Federation of Teachers, AFT, AFL–CIO, Petitioner. NLRB Case 19-RC-13114 (November 8, 1997). Retrieved January 25, 2009, from http://www.nlrb.gov/shared_files/Board%20Decisions/325/3253.pdf

COLLEGE SAVINGS BANK V. FLORIDA PREPAID

College Savings Bank v. Florida Prepaid Postsecondary Education Expense Board (1999) is a landmark U.S. Supreme Court case dealing with the ability of Congress to exact waivers of sovereign immunity. The Eleventh Amendment confirms that the states retain sovereign immunity from being sued by citizens. However, this immunity is not absolute. For instance, Congress, in exercising its powers to enforce the Fourteenth Amendment, may abrogate the states' immunity. In *College Savings*, the U.S. Supreme Court addressed the issue of whether public institutions could be liable for claims arising under the Trademark Act of 1946 (the Lanham Act) alleging false and misleading advertising. The Supreme Court overruled a prior landmark case in unequivocally clarifying that there are no constructive waivers of sovereign immunity. Put another way, if a litigant wishes to claim that a state has waived sovereign immunity, the litigant must point to an explicit statement of waiver by the state. To the extent that most public institutions are considered to be arms of the state for purposes of Eleventh Amendment immunity, *College Savings* has significant consequences for institutions of higher education, because it protects them from the risk of waiving sovereign immunity and exposing themselves to the threat of litigation unless officials make a conscious choice in this regard.

College Savings Bank is often confused with *Florida Prepaid Postsecondary Education Expense Board v. College Savings Bank* (1999), a case involving the same parties that resolved on the same day and addressed similar issues. However, the two cases are distinct. *College Savings* deals primarily with states' waivers of sovereign immunity and, pursuant to the precedent that it set, there are no constructive waivers of sovereign immunity. In contrast, *Florida Prepaid* is primarily about when Congress may abrogate, or abolish, a state's sovereign immunity; in that case, the Supreme Court held that Congress may not abrogate sovereign immunity for intellectual property claims.

Facts of the Case

As in the companion case of *Florida Prepaid*, the litigation in *College Savings* arose out of a dispute between the state agency in Florida that administered a prepaid tuition program and a bank in New Jersey that, in addition to marketing and selling certificates of deposit designed to finance the costs of college education for borrowers, patented a methodology for administering these funds. The bank in New Jersey sued the agency in Florida for false advertising under the Lanham Act, a federal statute that affords private rights of action against persons who use false descriptions or make false representations in commerce. Although the state agency in Florida would ordinarily have been immune from litigation, the bank argued that Congress had enacted a statute that abrogated the states' sovereign immunity for such claims. The bank also argued that by participating in interstate commerce, the agency implicitly waived its sovereign immunity. The agency contended that the purported abrogation was unconstitutional and that there was no implied waiver of sovereign immunity. After both a federal trial court in New Jersey and the Third Circuit adopted the same position as the state agency, the Supreme Court then agreed to hear an appeal that the bank filed.

The Supreme Court's Ruling

The Supreme Court, in a five-to-four judgment, affirmed in favor of the state agency from Florida. In an opinion written by Justice Scalia and joined by Chief Justice Rehnquist, as well as Justices O'Connor, Kennedy, and Thomas, the Court held that both the attempt at abrogation and the invitation to waive were unconstitutional.

In addressing the abrogation issue first, the Supreme Court began by noting that while Congress made its intention to abrogate clear, Congress could not use its Article I powers to abrogate sovereign immunity. Consequently, the critical issue was whether Congress properly used its power to enforce the Fourteenth Amendment. The answer to this inquiry turned on the application of the test from the 1997 landmark case of *City of Boerne v. Flores,* wherein the Court invalidated the Religious Freedom Restoration Act in a suit over historical preservation at a church in Texas. The *Flores* test focuses on whether Congress had identified a pattern of constitutional violations by the states, and if so, whether abrogating sovereign immunity was an appropriate response to that pattern. In a brief analysis, the Court concluded that because there was no finding of a pattern of constitutional violations by the states, the attempt at abrogation was invalid.

Having disposed of the abrogation issue, the Supreme Court turned to the much more complex question of waiver. Under the 1964 decision in *Parden v. Terminal R. of Alabama Docks Department,* a state constructively waives its sovereign immunity for specified federal claims if it chooses to participate in interstate commerce. However, as the Court acknowledged, in the years since *Parden* was handed down, the Court had cast doubt on constructive waivers of sovereign immunity, actually requiring explicit statements with respect to congressional attempts to abrogate sovereign immunity. In *College Savings Bank,* then, the Court explicitly overruled *Parden,* reasoning that there were no constructive waivers of sovereign immunity.

At the same time, the Supreme Court pointed out that recognizing a congressional power to exact constructive waivers of sovereign immunity was inconsistent with the limitations imposed on Congress's power to abrogate sovereign immunity. If Congress may not use its general Article I powers to abrogate sovereign immunity, the Court observed that Congress may not use its general Article I powers to exact a constructive waiver of sovereign immunity. Yet the Court did concede that in some instances, such as interstate compact or imposing conditions on the receipt of federal funds, Congress might be able to use its Article I powers to exact a waiver of sovereign immunity, but the Court emphasized that Congress could not require states to choose between immunity and participation in lawful activities.

Justice Stevens wrote a short dissent emphasizing his belief that sovereign immunity should not apply when a state engages in commercial activity. He added that Congress's power to abrogate sovereign immunity is much broader than the Court held.

Justice Breyer, joined by Justices Stevens, Souter, and Ginsburg, vigorously dissented. In their view, *Parden* should not have been overruled. More importantly, these justices espoused the position that ever since the Court affirmed that Congress may not use its Article I powers to abrogate sovereign immunity in *Seminole Tribe v. Florida* (1996), its jurisprudence with respect to sovereign immunity had been flawed. Rather, these dissenters contended that any abrogation of sovereign immunity must involve the Fourteenth Amendment enforcement power.

A decade after *College Savings* was resolved, while the Supreme Court has chosen not to limit its holding, lower courts have refused to expand its opinion. Indeed, every circuit has refused to impose any limits on the ability of Congress to require the states to waive sovereign immunity for certain claims as a condition of receiving federal funds. Nevertheless, for state universities that are considered an arm of the state, *College Savings* remains a foundational case.

William E. Thro

See also *Central Virginia Community College v. Katz;* Eleventh Amendment; *Florida Prepaid v. College Savings Bank; Kimel v. Florida Board of Regents*

Further Readings

Alden v. Maine, 527 U.S. 706, 713 (1999).

Board of Trustees of the University of Alabama v. Garrett, 531 U.S. 356 (2001).

Central Virginia Community College v. Katz, 126 S. Ct. 990 (2006).

Chisholm v. Georgia, 2 U.S. (2 Dall.) 419 (1793).

Ex Parte Young, 209 U.S. 123 (1908).

Federal Maritime Commission v. South Carolina State Ports Authority, 535 U.S. 743 (2002).

Kimel v. Florida Board of Regents, 528 U.S. 62 (2000).

Noonan, J. T., Jr. (2002). *Narrowing the nation's power: The Supreme Court sides with the states.* Berkeley: University of California Press.

Tennessee v. Lane, 541 U.S. 509 (2004).

Thro, W. E. (2000). The education lawyer's guide to the sovereign immunity revolution. *Education Law Reporter, 146,* 951–981.

Thro, W. E. (2007). The future of sovereign immunity. *Education Law Reporter, 215,* 1–31.

Thro, W. E. (2007). *Why you cannot sue State U: A guide to sovereign immunity* (2nd ed.). Washington, DC: National Association of College and University Attorneys.

Legal Citations

City of Boerne v. Flores, 521 U.S. 507 (1997).

College Savings Bank v. Florida Prepaid, 527 U.S. 666 (1999).

Florida Prepaid v. College Savings Bank, 527 U.S. 627 (1999).

Parden v. Terminal R. of Alabama Docks Department, 377 U.S. 184 (1964).

Seminole Tribe v. Florida, 517 U.S. 44 (1996).

Trademark Act of 1946, as amended (15 U.S.C. §§ 1051-1127).

COMMUNITY OR JUNIOR COLLEGES

Community and junior colleges are unique to American education, and no form of higher education is more varied than these institutions, all of which must comply with the same array of laws as other postsecondary educational institutions whether dealing with students, faculty, or staff. According to the American Association of Community Colleges, nearly 1,200 two-year colleges serve an average of 11.5 million students annually. Their benefits are enormous: Each year, community colleges award some 555,000 associate degrees and 295,000 certificates; 59% of new nurses and the majority of other new health care workers are educated at community colleges; close to 80% of firefighters, law enforcement officers, and EMTs are credentialed at community colleges; 95% of businesses and organizations that employ community college graduates recommend community college workforce education and training programs. The most democratic of American higher education institutions because of their open-door admission policies, community colleges include 987 public, 177 independent, and 31 tribal colleges. This entry reviews the history of these institutions, describes their contemporary status, and notes some controversies about their role in U.S. education today.

History

For more than a century, two-year colleges have been part of the American higher education landscape. J. Stanley Brown, superintendent of Joliet Township High School, and William Rainey Harper, president of the University of Chicago, urged the creation of the first two-year junior college in 1901, arguing that a separate and discrete junior college providing the first two years of collegiate education or vocational training might attract students who otherwise would not continue their education beyond high school and further might induce some students to terminate their collegiate tenure after two years of study to enter the workforce. These educators theorized that this approach might also appeal to graduate and professional schools, because the student body from which they could then recruit would be more select. Brown and Harper's vision took hold in America, and over the ensuing decades, two-year colleges began to proliferate around the nation.

In the years following World War II, more two-year institutions were established when Congress passed the Servicemen's Readjustment Act of 1944, or G. I. Bill, to support returning veterans who required retraining to prepare for civilian jobs. The massive influx of nontraditional students entering the higher education system as a result of this legislation required a substantive expansion of the system, thus stimulating the need for additional community colleges. According to Frederick Rudolph, the implementation of the G. I. Bill in the postwar United States demonstrated the relationship between education and employment and thus helped to generate support for the junior college not only as an institution providing general education but also as a source of vocational training.

In 1947, a study by the President's Commission on Higher Education (the Truman Commission) suggested that half of the country's young people could benefit from formal education through Grade 14 and further popularized the term "community college," a new title developed due to the expanded role of the institution. The 1960s witnessed the most significant expansion of two-year colleges, as the notion of accessible higher education for all who aspired to pursue it took root across the nation. During the decade enrollments skyrocketed with participation by baby boomers, and 457 two-year colleges were created at an astounding average of one new college per week. A series of grants through the Kellogg Junior College Leadership Programs helped train many community college leaders during this decade. Growth continued during the 1970s, when many young men enrolled to escape the Vietnam-era draft. The 1970s also marked a shift to faculty development that focused on more instructional training for the unique student body and mission of community colleges. During the 1980s, community colleges began to work more closely with high schools to prepare students for vocational and technical two-year programs.

The Community College Today

Today's two-year colleges share a philosophy and commitment to serving all segments of society through open admission, low cost, and extra academic and personal support. They are generally commuter colleges located within 35 miles (the national average) of their respective student populations. The implementation of the two-year college's focus on ensuring access to and opportunity for higher education services varies by institution, but the basic elements include academic transfer in preparation for subsequent transition to baccalaureate institutions (formerly provided exclusively by two-year institutions known as "junior colleges"), career and technical education (formerly provided exclusively by two-year institutions formerly known as "technical schools," "technical colleges," or "vocational technical institutes"), developmental or remedial education for students without the academic preparation necessary to be successful at the college level (formerly the exclusive domain of the K–12 education system), noncredit training of incumbent workers ("customized training"), and noncredit personal enrichment classes ("lifelong learning"). Two-year colleges that offer all of these elements are commonly known as "comprehensive community colleges" or "consolidated colleges." Community-based two-year colleges are designed to focus on meeting the academic, workforce-development, lifelong learning, and other education needs of the local region or district; accordingly, their mix of programs may vary enormously.

Frequently known as "second-chance colleges," community colleges provide utility that other levels of education cannot or will not. For example, the democratic open-door admissions policy of community colleges allows students who did not fare well in high school to enter postsecondary education; community colleges admit students without high school diplomas or GED certificates. Such students, without appropriate academic preparation, frequently cannot enter more selective "meritocratic" or "aristocratic" four-year colleges and universities. Community colleges help traditionally underserved students without adequate academic preparation, including inadequate English-language skills, through extensive personalized academic and student-support services. Where four-year colleges and universities serve the traditional 18- to 22-year-old student, the average age of community college students is 29; 60% are female, and 35% are ethnic or racial minorities. As a reflection of the significant contribution that they make to American life, as many as 39% of students who are enrolled in community colleges are the first members of their families to attend postsecondary educational institutions. Research on students transferring from community colleges to universities consistently shows that such students typically fare as well academically as their counterparts who began their postsecondary education at the more selective university.

The soaring popularity of community colleges (46% of all undergraduates in the United States and growing) is in part a product of their accessibility and affordability. Most community colleges serve commuter populations that live within 35 miles of campus; only a few (24%) provide student housing, because students can reduce costs by staying at and commuting from their family's home. The average cost of tuition at a public two-year college ($2,361) is only 38% of tuition at a public four-year college or university ($6,185).

Debate over the role and value of community colleges has emerged in recent years. Advocates argue that community colleges serve the needs of society by offering postsecondary opportunities to students who otherwise could not go to college, by training and retraining mid-level skilled workers, and by preserving the academic excellence of four-year colleges and universities. In contrast, critics argue that community colleges continue a culture of privilege through training business workers at public expense, restricting working-class learners from advancing in social class, protecting selective admissions at four-year institutions for the nation's elite, and discouraging transfer to four-year colleges and universities. Whether community colleges offer opportunities for social mobility or protect privilege, their century-long history has developed a distinctive aspect of higher education that is truly American.

Terrence Leas

See also Higher Education Act

Further Readings

American Association of Community Colleges: http://www.aacc.nche.edu/Pages/default.aspx

Brint, S., & Karabel, J. (1989). *The diverted dream: Community colleges & the promise of educational opportunity in America, 1900–1985*. New York: Oxford University Press.

Brubacher, J. S., & Rudy, W. (1976). *Higher education in transition: A history of American colleges and universities, 1636–1976* (3rd ed.). New York: Harper & Row.

Cohen, A. M., & Brawer, F. B. (2003). *The American community college* (4th ed.). San Francisco: Jossey-Bass.

Dougherty, K. J. (1994). *The contradictory college: The conflicting origins, impacts, and futures of the community college*. Albany: State University of New York Press.

Kaplin, W. A., & Lee, B. A. (2006). *The law of higher education: A comprehensive guide to legal implications of administrative decision making*. San Francisco: Jossey-Bass.

Melear, K. B., & Leas, T. (2006). *Community college governance: A compendium of state organizational structures*. Asheville, NC: College Administration Publications.

President's Commission on Higher Education. (1947). *A report of the President's Commission on Higher Education* (6 vols.). Washington, DC: U.S. Government Printing Office.

Rudolph, F. (1977). *Curriculum: A history of the American undergraduate curriculum since 1636*. San Francisco: Jossey-Bass.

University of Texas at Austin. (2009, May 31). *U.S. community colleges* [alphabetical list]. Retrieved June 25, 2009, from http://www.utexas.edu/world/comcol/alpha

Legal Citations

Servicemen's Readjustment Act (G. I. Bill), Pub. L. No. 78-346 (1944).

Conflict of Commitment

Conflict of commitment is a complex and controversial concept with potentially significant legal consequences that generally refers to those work-related situations in which the outside activities of college and university employees interfere with the time and effort that they are supposed to be providing for their employers. In higher education, conflicts of commitment commonly arise when faculty members or any other employees engage in outside work that, while related to their assigned duties, may reduce their ability to meet their contractual obligations to their primary employers. As such, conflicts of commitment may overlap with conflicts of interest when personal finances are involved; in the broader sense, *conflict of commitment* refers to conflicts of employees' time and energy. This entry describes several institutional approaches, reviews some of the main cases in this area, and considers proposals to address ongoing policy issues.

Institutional Policies

Various organizations have begun to address the ethical issues surrounding conflicts of commitment. According to the Association of American Medical Colleges (AAMC), for example, "conflict of commitment" refers to an individual faculty member's distribution of effort between obligations to his or her academic appointment and his or her commitment to outside activities. The AAMC stipulates that a conflict of commitment exists when outside activities interfere with the employee's obligations to students, colleagues, and the primary missions of the academic institution at which he or she is employed (AAMC, 1990).

At the same time, guidelines from the Association of Academic Health Centers (AAHC) emphasize the legal obligation of faculty members or other academic staff members to devote their primary effort and allegiance to their employers. The guidelines caution that any effort to divert to other entities or institutions opportunities for research, education, clinical care, or financial support that might come to the employer constitutes an inappropriate conflict of commitment (Euben, 2004).

The American Association of University Professors (AAUP) has not issued a specific statement on conflicts of commitment. However, AAUP policies do address the issue. For instance, in its *Statement on Professional Ethics,* the AAUP asserts that "Professors give due regard to their paramount responsibilities within their institution in determining the amount and character of work done outside it" (AAUP, 1987, ¶ 4). As early as 1965, the AAUP and the American Council on Education recommended that universities develop guidelines to help individual staff members understand how to conduct outside interests that might generate conflicts of interest ("On Preventing Conflicts," 1965).

Employers in higher or postsecondary education have attempted to manage conflicts of commitment by establishing institutional definitions, policies, and procedures. A simple Internet search of "conflict of commitment" on Google reveals literally thousands of references to institutional definitions, policies, and procedures governing conflicts of commitment at universities and colleges. All of these references include elements of faculty and staff members' obligations to their students and employers and the need to balance outside activities to permit fulfillment of their work obligations. They also acknowledge employees' rights to conduct outside work such as consulting, holding public office, publishing, researching, serving on the board of directors of an outside organization, serving as an elected officer of an academic organization, serving as an editor of a scholarly publication, starting an outside company, and teaching. More specifically, employees in institutions of higher learning in some states are prohibited from holding public office at the same time that they hold teaching appointments due to state restrictions against receiving dual compensation from public funding.

Legal Cases

Court challenges to outside faculty activities generally have involved the grounds of constitutional and contractual law. In constitutional cases, the Fifth Circuit upheld the right of two part-time faculty members to work with a legal services group, because their outside work did not hamper their contracted instructional activities (*Trister v. University of Mississippi,* 1969). The same court also found in favor of a faculty member from a marketing department in upholding his First Amendment right to serve as an expert witness for the defense in a case where the state was suing a tobacco company (*Hoover v. Morales,* 1998). Further, the Supreme Court of Arkansas was of the opinion that state restrictions on outside consulting were unreasonable when they were based on distinctions among faculty rank (*Atkinson v. Board of Trustees of the University of Arkansas,* 1977). Yet the Eighth Circuit affirmed a grant of summary judgment in favor of a university in rejecting a faculty member's claim that officials violated his First Amendment rights to free speech and association, among other charges, when they refused to grant him a salary increase based on research that he conducted at his home laboratory (*Day v. University of Nebraska,* 1995, 1996).

Courts have rejected claims that institutional restrictions were unconstitutional, including upholding a provision in an employer's collective bargaining agreement that prohibited outside full-time employment (*Kaufman v. Board of Trustees*, 1982), institutional restrictions on private practice revenue for medical doctors (*Adamsons v. Wharton*, 1985; *Kountz v. State University of New York*, 1983), and a university's restriction on the amount of outside practice a faculty member could engage in (*Gross v. University of Tennessee*, 1980).

On another issue, the Supreme Court of Appeals of West Virginia upheld the contractual right of a faculty member to "moonlight" (*Graf v. West Virginia University*, 1992). Even so, where contracts and faculty handbooks prohibit concurrent full-time employment at other institutions, courts have ruled in favor of colleges and universities (*Marks v. New York University*, 1999; *Morgan v. American University*, 1987; *Moshtaghi v. The Citadel*, 1994). In addition, failure to disclose a dual appointment has been upheld as just cause for termination (*Zahavy v. University of Minnesota*, 1996).

Ongoing Policy Issues

Online teaching has created novel issues for employers and faculty members alike, because the faculty member may teach for other institutions while using institutional resources to create, maintain, and deliver the outside online courses. Institutions commonly address this dilemma by enacting policies that restrict the faculty member from teaching online courses for other institutions without first obtaining permission from the employer. Euben (2004) engages in a more thorough review and analysis of issues surrounding intellectual property rights and electronic moonlighting.

Euben notes another concern for colleges and universities when faculty members use students in their own outside employment opportunities. In this regard, Euben points out that such relationships can raise questions about so-called student exploitation, the overlapping effects of evaluating student work and classroom performance, the fairness of treatment for students not included in faculty members' outside activities, the potential effects of student–faculty member relationships that sour, and possible restrictions by the outside activities on the research interests of the students.

In crafting practical solutions to the issues associated with conflict of commitment, Harrington (2001) identifies three basic elements to include in any policy: clear guidance about the minimum requirements of employees, requirements to disclose to employers all potentially relevant outside activity, and appropriate procedures for the review and resolution of conflicts.

Euben elaborates on additional elements, including the requirement of an explanation about how rules can protect faculty members, defining "conflict of commitment" in the context of the institution, differentiating between paid and unpaid outside commitments, distinguishing what activities do not constitute conflicts, articulating to whom policies apply—such as to part-time versus full-time faculty, differentiating the application of policies to the term of employment—such as 12-month versus 9-month employees, explaining how leave options may permit outside activities that otherwise might constitute conflicts of commitment, disclosing the impact that conflicts may have on tenure or promotion opportunities, and stipulating the effects of conflicts on indemnification coverage by employers. Employees and employers in higher education may also receive guidance from organizations that set professional standards for their disciplines, such as disciplinary associations and accreditation and licensing bodies.

Terrence Leas

See also Conflict of Interest

Further Readings

American Association of University Professors. (1987). *Statement on professional ethics*. Retrieved June 3, 2009, from http://www.aaup.org/AAUP/pubsres/policydocs/contents/statementonprofessionalethics.htm

Association of American Medical Colleges. (1990). Guidelines for dealing with faculty conflicts of commitment and conflicts of interest in research. *Academic Medicine, 65*, 487–490.

Boyer, C., & Lewis, D. R. (1984). Faculty consulting: Responsibility or promiscuity. *Journal of Higher Education, 55*(5), 637–659.

Euben, D. R. (2004, March 5). *Faculty employment outside of the university: Conflicts of commitment.* Presentation to the National Association of College and University Attorneys, Atlanta, Georgia. Retrieved April 17, 2009, from http://www.aaup.org/AAUP/protect/legal/topics/conflicts.htm

Gregory, D. L. (1991). The assault on scholarship. *William & Mary Law Review, 32*, 993–1004.

Harrington, P. J. (2001). Faculty conflicts of interest in an age of academic entrepreneurialism: An analysis of the problem, the law and selected university policies. *Journal of College & University Law, 27*, 775–831.

Kaplin, W. A., & Lee, B. A. (2006). *The law of higher education: A comprehensive guide to legal implications of administrative decision making.* San Francisco: Jossey-Bass.

On preventing conflicts of interest in government-sponsored research at universities. (1965). *AAUP Bulletin, 51*(42–43).

Rabban, D. M. (1998). Does academic freedom limit faculty autonomy? *Texas Law Review, 66*, 1405–1430.

Weston, M. C. (1980–1981). Outside activities of faculty members. *Journal of College & University Law, 7*, 68–77.

Legal Citations

Adamsons v. Wharton, 771 F.2d 41 (2d Cir. 1985).

Atkinson v. Board of Trustees of the University of Arkansas, 559 S.W.2d 473 (Ark. 1977).

Day v. University of Nebraska, 911 F. Supp. 1228 (D. Neb. 1995), aff'd 83 F.3d 1040 (8th Cir. 1996).

Graf v. West Virginia University, 329 S.E.2d 496 (1992).

Gross v. University of Tennessee, 620 F.2d 109 (6th Cir. 1980).

Hoover v. Morales, 164 F.3d 221 (5th Cir. 1998).

Kaufman v. Board of Trustees, 552 F. Supp. 1143 (N.D. Ill. 1982).

Kountz v. State University of New York, 450 N.Y.S.2d 416 (N.Y. App. Div. 1983).

Marks v. New York University, 61 F. Supp. 2d 81 (S.D.N.Y. 1999).

Morgan v. American University, 534 A.2d 323 (D.C. Ct. App. 1987).

Moshtaghi v. The Citadel, 443 S.E.2d 915 (S.C. Ct. App. 1994).

Trister v. University of Mississippi, 420 F.2d 499 (5th Cir. 1969).

Zahavy v. University of Minnesota, 544 N.W.2d 32 (Minn. Ct. App. 1996).

CONFLICT OF INTEREST

Conflict of interest, like its sibling conflict of commitment, is a complex and important branch of employee ethics in higher education that can have significant legal ramifications for individuals and institutions. In their most common context, conflicts of interest refer to situations in which the judgment and actions of employees may be influenced by personal financial considerations or the potential to benefit personally from their decisions. As such, conflicts of interest interfere with the ideal of independent, fair, and impartial judgment of employees.

In higher education, conflicts of interest may arise in different contexts, including accepting gifts related to decisions made in connection with employees' official duties; acting as, or making specific recommendations for, agents or attorneys; using or profiting from confidential information acquired during the course of work; accepting bribes; engaging in nepotism or inappropriate romantic relationships; soliciting for charitable, personal, political, or social purposes; accepting outside employment; using students or state property for personal benefit or the benefit of friends or family members; and improperly influencing the outcome of research for personal gain. Conflicts of interest are not limited to employees' actions on their own behalf insofar as these conflicts may be created by officers of institutions of higher learning on behalf of their colleges or universities.

Attorneys representing colleges and universities are subject to ethical standards that prohibit conflicts of interest in the client–attorney relationship. The American Bar Association has promulgated a document titled "Model Rules of Professional Conduct in Client–Lawyer Relationship" to help attorneys avoid conflicts of interest in the course of representing multiple clients, engaging in business relationships with clients, using confidential client information, accepting gifts from clients, providing financial assistance to a client, accepting compensation, and engaging in a sexual relationship with a client. Higher education faculty and staff members are generally subject to the same standards as attorneys.

In further attempts to deal with conflicts, states have adopted codes of employee conduct governing situations in which there is a conflict of interest for public employees. Public and private colleges and universities may also rely on state codes, institutional policies, collective bargaining agreements, and contract language to manage faculty and staff members' conduct and minimize potential conflicts of interest. In addition, federal laws and rules for conflicts of interest may extend to employees of institutions receiving federal funding.

Kaplan and Lee (2006) note that a special area of concern for higher education related to conflicts of interest is the relationships that may arise between colleges and universities, faculty researchers, and corporations that sponsor research. As state and federal funding for research declines, institutions may seek funding from business and industry. Other factors, such as lagging faculty salaries, pressure to meet standards for promotion or tenure, the need for specialized equipment, and demands to place graduate students in corporate positions may lead faculty researchers to form their own collaborations with the private sector.

The high stakes and complex combinations of institutional and faculty researchers' entrepreneurial relationships with business and industry raise equally complex policy, legal, and managerial issues. Beyond the financial considerations, issues of loyalty and effort give rise to conflicts of commitment. Kaplan and Lee emphasize the need for officials in institutions of higher learning to scrutinize carefully institutional or faculty members' involvement in such entrepreneurial research relationships. Special care in managing such complex relationships includes devising structural and contractual agreements carefully; appointing high-level officials to supervise sponsored research, technology transfer, and patent management; assigning trustees to a special committee to oversee the institution's outside research ventures; securing legal counsel and risk managers with expertise in these esoteric fields; adopting formal written policies governing conflicts of interest, patent ownership, and licensing rights; and keeping a focus on institutional missions to avoid compromising their values and standards.

Strategies for managing conflicts of interest in general include promulgating codes of conduct or ethics for employees, requiring disclosure of personal interests in a manner such as occurs with elected officials, removing decision makers when potential conflicts exist such as when judges recuse themselves, and seeking assurances from an impartial third party such as an auditor with expertise in the area of the potential conflict. Moreover, codes of ethics and conduct, the most common

strategy employed by institutions of higher learning as revealed by an Internet search for "conflict of interest," afford institutional officials and their employees with guidance regarding potential conflicts and constructive notice of behavior that employers will not tolerate.

Terrence Leas

See also Conflict of Commitment

Further Readings

American Bar Association, Center for Professional Development. (n.d.). *Model rules of professional conduct*. Client–Lawyer Relationship, Rule 1.7 Conflict of Interest: Current Clients. Retrieved April 17, 2009, from http://www.abanet.org/cpr/mrpc/rule_1_7.html

American Bar Association, Center for Professional Development. (n.d.). *Model rules of professional conduct*. Client–Lawyer Relationship, Rule 1.8 Conflict of Interest: Current Clients: Specific Rules. Retrieved April 17, 2009, from http://www.abanet.org/cpr/mrpc/rule_1_8.html

Carboni, R. A. (1992). *Planning and managing industry-university research collaborations*. Westport, CT: Quorum Books.

Davis, M. (1991). University research and the wages of commerce. *Journal of College & University Law, 18,* 29–38.

Euben, D. R. (2004, March 5). *Faculty employment outside of the university: Conflicts of commitment.* Presentation to the National Association of College and University Attorneys, Atlanta, Georgia. Retrieved April 17, 2009, from http://www.aaup.org/AAUP/protect/legal/topics/conflicts.htm

Kaplan, W. A., & Lee, B. A. (2006). *The law of higher education: A comprehensive guide to legal implications of administrative decision making.* San Francisco: Jossey-Bass.

COPYRIGHT

Copyrights, a topic of considerable interest to faculty, staff, and students at institutions of higher learning, are intangible rights granted by the federal Copyright Act to authors or creators of original artistic or literary works that can be fixed in tangible media of expression such as hard copy, electronic files, videos, or audio recordings. In copyright law, originality is not difficult to establish; any modicum of originality suffices. For example, question items on examinations are original works of authorship for copyright law purposes. Important to the concept of "fixed," the act defines "medium of expression" broadly to include expression made with the aid of a machine or device.

Provisions of the Copyright Act

Works prepared by students, staff, or faculty at colleges and universities on computers or word processors are not protected until they are saved as files on computers or disks or printed in hard copy. In higher educational settings, speeches and lectures given by instructors are not generally protected under copyright law, because they are not typically fixed in a tangible medium. Speakers' notes, however, either in hard copy or saved on computers, are copyrightable as items in their own rights. Further, speeches and lectures themselves become protected by law if they are original and recorded verbatim under speakers' authority. These recordings may be more regular today with the prevalence of online teaching and distance education.

Copyrightable works created on or after January 1, 1978, the effective date of the Copyright Act of 1976, are protected from the time they are fixed in tangible media of expression until 70 years after the death of their authors/creators. If the works have corporate authorship, copyrights last 95 years from publication or 120 years from creation, whichever is shorter. The duration of copyright for works created before 1978 is dependent on several factors (Gasaway, 2003). Once copyright terms expire, works go into the public domain, and advance permission to use them is no longer necessary.

The Copyright Act protects literary, musical, dramatic, choreographic, pictorial, sculptural, and architectural works as well as motion pictures and sound recordings. Each copyrightable work has several "copyrights," including exclusive rights to make copies of the works, distribute them, and perform or display the works publicly.

The subject matter of copyright includes compilations or collective works and "derivative works." Copyrights in compilations or derivative works extend only to the materials contributed by the authors of such works as distinguished from the preexisting material employed in the works. Examples of collective works include periodical issues, anthologies, and encyclopedias in which each contribution is a separate and independent work compiled into a collective whole. Derivative works are based on one or more preexisting works such as translations, musical arrangements, dramatizations, fictionalizations, motion picture versions, sound recordings, art reproductions, abridgments, condensations, or any other forms in which works may be recast, transformed, or adapted. Each author or creator may transfer one or more of these copyrights to others. For example, authors who wish their books to be used in classes at colleges and universities sell the copying and distribution rights to publishers in return for royalties gained from sales.

Limits on Exclusive Rights

The Copyright Act imposes limits on exclusive rights, three of which apply in educational settings. The act provides criteria for fair use, provides criteria according to which libraries and archives may make copies of copyrighted works, and addresses the use of copyrighted material for classroom instruction. In addition, the act addresses works for hire created by employees of educational institutions.

Fair Use

According to Section 107 of the Copyright Act, fair use of copyrighted works "for purposes such as criticism, comment, news reporting, teaching (including multiple copies for classroom use), scholarship, or research, is not an infringement of copyright." Fair use balances the rights of the owners and creators of copyrighted works with the needs of those who use such works. If uses are fair use, then users need not obtain consent of the owners. Determining whether uses are fair requires the application of four factors, articulated explicitly in the act: the purpose and character of a use, including whether such use is of a commercial nature or is for nonprofit educational purposes; the nature of the copyrighted work; the amount and substantiality of the portion used in relation to the copyrighted work as a whole; and the effect of the use upon the potential market for or value of the copyrighted work.

The fair use doctrine is often applied successfully in educational settings, because most educational uses are not commercial. Still, some guidelines are necessary. Pursuant to a report of the Ad Hoc Committee of Educational Institutions and Organizations on the Copyright Law Revision of 1976, instructors may make single copies of the following items for use in teaching or preparation to teach classes: a chapter from a book; an article from a newspaper or periodical; a short story, essay, or poem; and a chart, diagram, graph, or picture from a book, periodical, or newspaper.

The fact that students are the ultimate users of the copyrighted works notwithstanding does not automatically dictate findings of fair use. One of the biggest controversies arises in cases of course packet copies of multiple works for students to purchase. The courts largely agree that commercial copying services must obtain the copyright holders' permission before including copies of protected works in compiled course packets.

On the nature of the copyrighted works, courts generally look at whether such works are published or unpublished and whether they are fiction or fantasy versus nonfiction, factual, or scientific in nature. The use of fantasy and fiction works leans toward unfair more often than the use of nonfiction, factual, or scientific works. This noted, the determination of fair use in cases involving copyrighted informational works must also consider the controversial line between ideas that are not protected and their expression, which is protected. In nonfiction writing, scientific writing, legal writing, history, and biography, all of which are very common in higher education, multiple authors may interpret the same sets of facts and often engage similar treatment of the topics. This does not dictate that later works are infringements of all of those efforts that preceded them. It is important, then, to recognize that because the expression of facts and ideas is protected, authors retain the first right of publication of this expression.

In considering the third factor for fair use, the more material others take from copyrighted works, the more likely the courts are to treat uses as unfair. However, the measure of the material taken is made both quantitatively and qualitatively. For instance, the same number of words taken from a novel as from a short poem could certainly give way to different fair use outcome. On the quantitative end of the principle, if the quantity used is high, the fourth fair use factor, effect on the market, may play a role and dictate a finding of unfair use. On the qualitative end of the principle, the key inquiry is whether the "heart" of the original work was taken.

For the final fair use factor, the effect of the allegedly infringing use on the market for the original work, the copyright holder must demonstrate the existence of a connection between the infringement and loss of revenue, not only for the current market, but also for the future. In response, alleged infringers must show that the damages would have occurred even without this use. Important to the inquiry is the effect not only on the market for the original work, but also the markets for derivative works. With respect to academic activities, fair use is generally recognized so long as uses do not adversely affect the copyright holders' markets.

Libraries and Archives

The second limitation on exclusive rights provides that it is not an infringement of copyright for staff members in libraries to reproduce one copy or phonorecord of works or to distribute the copies or phonorecords if these activities take place without intentional commercial advantage, if libraries are open to the public, and if the reproduction includes a notice of copyright. This provision allows libraries and archives to replace lost, stolen, damaged, or deteriorating works and to preserve unpublished works.

Classroom Use

The third limitation on exclusive rights addresses classroom use of copyrighted materials. Under Section 110(1) of the Copyright Act, teachers and students in nonprofit educational institutions may perform or display copyrighted works "in the course of face-to-face teaching activities." Section 110(2), which codifies the Technology, Education, and Copyright Harmonization Act of 2002, permits essentially these same activities in distance education or online environments, but with five additional requirements:

1. Performances or displays must be at the direction of or under the supervision of instructors.

2. Such uses must be integral parts of class session offered as part of the "systematic mediated instructional activities" of educational institution.

3. Performances or displays must be directly related and of material assistance to the teaching content of the transmissions.

4. Transmissions must be available only to students enrolled in the courses and those employed to teach or assist in teaching the classes.

5. Institutions must implement policies and practices to educate instructional staff and students about copyright law while applying technological measures that prevent the retention and accessibility of copyrighted works for longer than the class sessions.

Works for Hire

Initially, ownership in works that are copyrighted vests in their authors or creators. Educational institutions may deal with "works for hire," which are works created by employees within the scope of their employment. In such cases, employers become the copyright holders. At the same time, there is a solid legal argument for a "teacher exception" to the work-for-hire doctrine (Daniel & Pauken, 1999). Under this exception, it can be argued that college and university administrative officials do not directly supervise their faculty in the preparation of academic books and articles and teaching materials.

Copyright Infringement

There are three types of infringement: direct, contributory, and vicarious. Direct infringements are those by persons or services that actually engage in the infringement of protected copyrights. Contributory infringement occurs where one "with the knowledge of the infringing activity, induces, causes, or materially contributes to the infringing conduct of another" even though she or he has "not committed or participated in the infringing acts." In order to be liable, alleged infringers must have actual or constructive knowledge of, and must have participated in, the infringing conduct (*A & M Records, Inc. v. Napster, Inc.*, 2001; *In re Aimster*, 2003). Universities must be particularly careful here, because students allegedly commonly engage in unlawful downloading and sharing of copyrighted works online. University officials must enact and enforce policies that remove infringing content and conduct from their campuses; these policies must also contain provisions advocating education for students, staff, and faculty on copyright law. Finally, vicarious infringement may be imposed on persons or entities that have the right and ability to supervise infringing activities and have direct financial interests in the exploitations of the copyrights, even though they may not have the intent to infringe or the knowledge of the infringements.

The Supreme Court's recent unanimous decision in *Metro-Goldwyn-Mayer Studios v. Grokster* (2005) may be instructive for members of college and university communities. In *Grokster*, the Court held that software distributors could be liable for indirect copyright infringement when they market software with the intention and the knowledge that computer users will infringe copyrights by downloading and sharing protected works. *Grokster* is not directly applicable to higher educational settings, because institutions are rarely software distributors. Even so, the fact that evidence of a defendant's knowledge in *Grokster* and encouragement of infringement can lead to contributory or vicarious liability under copyright law ought to convince officials to be vigilant in their policy formation and enforcement when they allow faculty, staff, and students to use their computer systems.

Remedies

Remedies available to successful copyright infringement claims include injunctive relief, impoundment or disposal of infringing works, monetary damages including actual damages and lost profits, statutory damages as provided by the Copyright Act and decided by the courts, and attorney fees. Copyright infringement need not be intentional for copyright holders to succeed in their claims.

Patrick D. Pauken

See also Digital Millennium Copyright Act; Fair Use; Intellectual Property

Further Readings

Daniel, P. T. K., & Pauken, P. D. (1999). The impact of the electronic media on instructor creativity and institutional ownership within copyright law. *Education Law Reporter, 132*, 1–43.

Daniel, P. T. K., & Pauken, P. D. (2005). Intellectual property. In J. Beckham & D. Dagley (Eds.), *Contemporary issues in higher education law* (pp. 347–393). Dayton, OH: Education Law Association.

Daniel, P. T. K., & Pauken, P. D. (2008). Copyright laws in the age of technology and their applicability to the K–12 environment. In K. E. Lane, J. F. Mead, M. A. Gooden, S. Eckes, & P. D. Pauken (Eds.), *The principal's legal handbook* (4th ed., pp. 507–519). Dayton, OH: Education Law Association.

Gasaway, L. (2003). *When U.S. works pass into the public domain.* Retrieved June 9, 2009, from http://www.unc.edu/~unclng/public-d.htm

National Association of College Stores and The Association of American Publishers. (1991). *Questions and answers on copyright for the campus community.* Oberlin, OH: National Association of College Stores.

Sperry, D. J., Daniel, P. T. K., Huefner, D. S., & Gee, E. G. (1998). *Education law and the public schools: A compendium* (pp. 191–203). Norwood, MA: Christopher-Gordon.

Legal Citations

A & M Records, Inc. v. Napster, Inc., 239 F.3d 1004 (9th Cir. 2001).

The Copyright Act, 17 U.S.C. § 101 *et seq.*

Copyright Law Revision, H.R. Rep. No. 94-1476 (1976), at 65–74.

In re Aimster, 334 F.3d 643 (7th Cir. 2003).

Metro-Goldwyn-Mayer Studios v. Grokster, 545 U.S. 913 (2005).

Technology, Education, and Copyright Harmonization Act (TEACH Act), Pub. L. No. 107–273 (2002).

CRIME AWARENESS AND CAMPUS SECURITY ACT

In 1990, Congress enacted the Crime Awareness and Campus Security Act (CACSA), a law that requires officials at all colleges and universities to implement policies concerning security and access to campus facilities; procedures for students and others to report crimes; and programs to inform students about the prevention of crimes, the relationship between campus security and local law enforcement, and collection and reporting procedures for criminal offenses.

The duty to report crimes applies to officials on campuses and at facilities owned by institutions of higher learning as well as to public property such as sidewalks, streets, or parking lots that are in the reasonably contiguous area of campuses. The crimes that must be reported include homicide, murder and non-negligent manslaughter, negligent manslaughter, sex offenses whether forcible or nonforcible, robbery, aggravated assault, burglary, motor vehicle theft, manslaughter, arson, and arrests of persons referred for disciplinary action involving liquor law violations or weapons possession (Institutional Security Policies and Crime Statistics Regulations (*Regulations*), 34 C.F.R. § 668.46 (c)) (CACSA, § 1092 (f)(2)(F)(i)). If institutions have more than one campus, then reporting must be done separately for each campus (*Regulations,* § 668.46 (d)).

The requirements for reporting crimes to students are comprehensive. In addition to reporting the numbers of crimes per category listed above, higher education authorities must report crimes by category of prejudice if victims appeared to have been intentionally selected because of their actual or perceived race, gender, religion, sexual orientation, ethnicity, or disability (*Regulations,* § 668.46 (c)(3)). Crimes must be reported by the locations where they occurred, specifically on campus, in student dormitories or other residential facilities, in or noncampus buildings or properties, or on public properties (*Regulations,* § 668.46 (c)(4)). Reporting statistics must be done using the Federal Bureau of Investigation's *Uniform Crime Reporting Handbook* (*Regulations,* § 668.46 (c)(7)).

Higher education officials are permitted to use maps as a means of reporting crime areas as long as the maps accurately "depicts its campus, noncampus buildings or property, and public property areas" (*Regulations,* § 668.46 (c)(8)). Finally, officials at higher education institutions are required to make "a reasonable, good faith effort to obtain the required statistics" from local or state police agencies, and, as long as the request is made in good faith, "It is not responsible for the failure of the local or State police agency to supply the required statistics" (*Regulations*, § 668.46 (c)(9)).

Educational institutions also have a preventive function under CACSA. This duty requires officials to provide timely warnings of crimes reported to campus security authorities as well as any activities "considered by the institution to represent a threat to students and employees" (*Regulations*, § 668.46 (e)(1)(iii)). However, "an institution is not required to provide a timely warning with respect to crimes reported to a pastoral or professional counselor" (*Regulations*, § 668.46 (e)(2)).

The regulations incident to CACSA require that institutional annual security reports include more than crime statistics. More specifically, these reports must include

- encouragements for "pastoral counselors and professional counselors, if and when they deem it appropriate, to inform the persons they are counseling of any procedures to report crimes on a voluntary, confidential basis for inclusion in the annual disclosure of crime statistics" (*Regulations*, § 668.46 (b)(3)(iii));
- "a description of programs designed to inform students and employees about the prevention of crimes" (*Regulations*, § 668.46 (b)(6));
- institutional policies "regarding the possession, use, and sale of alcoholic beverages and enforcement of State underage drinking laws" (*Regulations*, § 668.46 (b)(8));
- institutional policies "regarding the possession, use, and sale of illegal drugs and enforcement of Federal and State drug laws" (*Regulations*, § 668.46 (b)(9));
- descriptions of any institutional drug or alcohol-abuse education programs (*Regulations*, § 668.46 (b)(10));
- institutional policies regarding the awareness and reporting of sexual assault as well as counseling for victims of sexual assault and disciplinary actions concerning those charged with sex offenses (*Regulations*, § 668.46 (b)(11); CACSA, 20 U.S.C. § 1092 (B)(vi)); and
- notification to students "of options for, and available assistance in, changing academic and living situations after an alleged sexual assault incident, if so requested by the victim and if such changes are reasonably available" (*Regulations*, § 668.46 (b)(8)(B)(vii)).

On a final note, the Crime Awareness and Campus Security Act expressly denies a private cause of action to individuals to enforce its provisions (CACSA, § 1092 (8)(c)).

Congress enacted the Campus Sex Crimes Prevention Act (CSCPA) in 1994 as part of the Violent Crime Control and Law Enforcement Act. Also referred to as the Jacob Wetterling Crimes Against Children and Sexually Violent Offender Registration Program Act, this act applies to sexual offenses against any full-time or part-time students "in any public or private educational institution, including any secondary school, trade, or professional institution, or institution of higher education" (CSCPA, § 14071 (a) (3)(G)).

Under the provisions of the CSCPA, any persons required to register as sex offenders under state laws as having committed

- aggravated sexual abuses, or
- sexual abuses similar to those described under federal law (Aggravated Sexual Abuse, 18 U.S.C. § 2241), or
- any offenses that have as their elements engaging in physical contact with other persons with intent to commit aggravated sexual abuses or sexual abuses

must, among other requirements of their "release, parole, supervised release, or probation" (CSCPA, § 14071 (b)),

- report to appropriate state officials and provide fingerprints, a photograph, and information about residency (CSCPA, § 14071 (b)(1)(A) (i–iv));
- report changes in address, including moving to another state (CSCPA, § 14071 (b)(3)(B)); and
- provide "notice of enrollment at or employment by institutions of higher education" (CSCPA, § 14071 (j)). This notice, which is governed by state law, applies to each institution of higher education in a "State at which the person is employed, carries on a vocation, or is a student; and [applies to] each change in enrollment or employment status of such person at an institution of higher education in that State" (CSCPA, § 14071 (j)(1)(A)).

In response to these federal statutes, many states now require that the names of sex offenders be entered on the Internet. In *Smith v. Doe* (2003), the U.S. Supreme Court upheld the constitutionality of Alaska's Sex Offender Registration Act (SORA, 1994), which required sex offenders to register and which placed their names on the Internet. In *Smith,* the Court was of the opinion that applying Alaska's registration statute to two persons who had been released from prison prior to the state statute's enactment did not violate the Constitution's Ex Post Facto Clause, because the requirement to register was civil rather than criminal in nature. In a companion case to *Smith, Connecticut Department of Public Safety v. Doe* (2003), the Court rejected the Fourteenth Amendment Liberty Clause and Due Process claims of a convicted sex offender who objected, on the ground that he considered himself no longer to be dangerous, to a state agency posting his name on the Internet. As to the Due Process Clause claim, the Supreme Court observed that

> due process does not entitle [plaintiff] to establish a fact—that he is not currently dangerous—that is not material under the statute. . . . [T]he law's requirements turn on an offender's conviction alone—a fact that a convicted offender has already had a procedurally safeguarded opportunity to contest. (p. 7)

Similarly, in *Connecticut* the Supreme Court found that because mandatory reporting of all sexual offenders for 10 years did not amount to stigmatization under the Liberty Clause, it did not entitle a claimant to a name-clearing hearing. Subsequently, the Ninth Circuit, in *Doe v. Tandeske* (2004), applied the rationale from *Connecticut* in pointing out that persons who have been convicted of serious sex offenses do not have a fundamental right protected under the Due Process Clause to be free from the registration and notification requirements set forth in the Alaska Sex Offender Registration Act.

Other federal appellate courts have supported stringent registration requirements. In *Doe v. Smith* (*Doe,* 2005), the Eighth Circuit upheld an Iowa statute that forbade registered sex offenders from residing "within two thousand feet of the real property comprising a public or nonpublic

elementary or secondary school or a child care facility" (Iowa Code, § 692A.2A(2)). To the extent that postsecondary institutions have day care facilities on campus for the children of employees and students, statutes such as those in Iowa would be applicable, at least within the Eighth Circuit. The Eleventh Circuit, in *Doe v. Moore* (*Moore,* 2005) upheld a comprehensive Florida registration statute (Fl. Stat. Ann. § 943.043, 944.406) that requires fingerprints, photo, and a DNA sample, with the photo and description being placed on the Internet.

Most recently Congress amended the Family Educational Rights and Privacy Act specifically to permit postsecondary institutions to disclose information regarding registered sex offenders provided to those institutions under state law. FERPA declares that nothing in the statute prevents the disclosure of any information provided to the institution pursuant to the CSCPA. Although not expressly addressed in the federal statutes, where information about specific sex offenders has been made public through release to the Internet, postsecondary institutions, arguably, would seem to have a duty to make students aware of offenders on campus. In balancing the benefits to convicted sexual offender felons who would like to pursue an education in postsecondary institutions and the rights of other students in those institutions to be informed of the presence on campus of those offenders, the balance has been struck in states to require information about sex offenders to be made public. The multitude of privacy issues on campuses makes the CSCPA even more remarkable.

The elements of a crime prevention checklist prepared by Nathan Roberts, Richard Fossey, and Todd DeMitchell in *Contemporary Issues in Higher Education Law* (2005) are worth noting in terms of the guidance that they can provide for officials at colleges and universities. According to these authors, campus security plans should be comprehensive; they should

- address "lighting, shrubbery, police patrols, escort services, call boxes in isolated areas, and residence hall security";
- establish routine procedures providing notice to students of serious criminal activity in areas;

- have adequate reporting procedures in place to permit complaints about serious sexual misconduct;
- identify which sexual offenses are to be handled internally and which are to be turned over to outside law enforcement agencies; and
- develop routine processes for collecting crime data that are consistent with federal and state mandates. (Roberts, Fossey, & DeMitchell, 2005, pp. 196–197)

Ralph D. Mawdsley

See also Clery Act; Family Educational Rights and Privacy Act

Further Readings

Federal Bureau of Investigation. (2004). *Uniform crime reporting handbook*. Clarksburg, WV: U.S. Department of Justice.

Roberts, N., Fossey, R., & DeMitchell, T. (2005). Tort liability. In J. Beckham & D. Dagley (Eds.), *Contemporary issues in higher education law* (pp. 183–207). Dayton, OH: Education Law Association.

Legal Citations

Aggravated Sexual Abuse Definition, 18 U.S.C. § 2241.

Alaska Statutes, § 12.63.010 *et seq.* (Sex Offender Registration Act).

Campus Sex Crimes Prevention Act, 42 U.S.C. § 14071.

Code of Federal Regulations (C.F.R.), as cited.

Connecticut Department of Public Safety v. Doe, 538 U.S. 1 (2003).

Crime Awareness and Campus Security Act, 20 U.S.C. § 1092 (f).

Doe v. Moore, 410 F.3 1337 (11th Cir. 2005).

Doe v. Smith, 405 F.3d 700 (8th Cir. 2005).

Doe v. Tandeske, 361 F.3d 594 (9th Cir. 2004).

Family Educational Rights and Privacy Act, 20 U.S.C. § 1232g.

Florida Statutes Annotated, § 943.043, 944.406 (sexual offender information and notification).

Institutional Security Policies and Crime Statistics Regulations, 34 C.F.R. § 668.46(f).

Iowa Code Annotated, § 692A.2A (residency restrictions—child care facilities and schools).

Smith v. Doe, 538 U.S. 84 (2003).

United States Code (U.S.C.), as cited.

CYBERBULLYING

Members of today's college and university communities have unprecedented access to a wide range of technology, including e-mail, blogs, cell phones, and social networking Web sites. Faced with these technologies, an emerging legal challenge confronting today's students, faculty, staff, and community members in the world of higher education is how to address legal issues relating to cyberbullying, a relatively new form of high-tech incivility and harassment using the Internet. Consequently, this entry focuses on the issue of cyberbullying and its growing impact on the higher educational community.

Cyberbullying Defined

Cyberbullying is defined as the use of communication-based technologies, including cell phones, e-mail, instant messaging, text messaging, and social networking sites, to engage in deliberate harassment or intimidation of other individuals or groups of persons using online speech or expression. Student bullying and harassment are considerably more common at the elementary, middle, and high school levels. Even so, a recent study of bullying on college and university campuses reveals that more than 60% of students indicate that they have personally observed a student bullying or harassing another student.

The online cruelty and harassment uniquely associated with cyberbullying has recently become popular among college students due largely to the virtual anonymity of online communication, which makes it extremely difficult to identify bullies or instigators of online bullying or harassment. Also, the limitless reach of the Internet allows the online content of cyberbullying to well surpass the confines of college and university campuses when compared to traditional bullying, with which the impact is considerably more controlled.

One of the most popular and publicly accessible online venues for cyberbullying in college and university communities was a Web site called Juicy Campus. Until it was officially shut down in February 2009, this popular Web site was designed exclusively for students in higher education for posting online, anonymous, and uncensored gossip about their classmates and instructors. Advocates of the Juicy Campus Web site argued that it fostered student free speech and expression. However, critics of the Web site maintained that it actively encouraged cyberbullying against other students and faculty members in the form of negative smear campaigns, threats, and racist and sexist remarks targeting other students. During its short existence of less than two years, the Juicy Campus Web site was the subject of numerous instances of violent, online threats.

Nancy E. Willard, executive director of the Center for Safe and Responsible Internet Use, has identified the following seven major types of cyberbullying activities:

1. *Flaming:* short but intense online communications characterized by offensive, rude, or vulgar language.

2. *Harassment:* repeatedly sending someone mean, insulting, and offensive online messages.

3. *Denigration:* sending or posting online gossip or rumors about a person designed to damage that person's reputation or friendships; this is often the most popular form of cyberbullying used by students against faculty members or employees at colleges and universities.

4. *Impersonation:* impersonating the target of the bullying; for example, a cyberbully may steal the target's e-mail account and send offensive e-mail messages under that person's identity.

5. *Outing and trickery:* fooling others into revealing secrets or embarrassing information about themselves; this information is shared online.

6. *Exclusion:* intentionally restricting someone from being able to participate in a certain online group, such as a social networking site.

7. *Cyberstalking:* sending repeated, unwanted online messages that often include threats that make some victims fear for their personal safety; this represents the most serious form of cyberbullying.

In the wake of recent school shootings on the college campuses of Virginia Tech University and Northern Illinois University, researchers and college officials have begun to reexamine legal and policy issues surrounding cyberbullying and disciplining students who engage in online bullying and harassment behaviors; it is hoped that such discipline will prevent cyberbullying from escalating into violent physical behavior.

Litigation

The widespread use of the Internet by students specifically to verbally harass and even threaten the physical harm of other students, faculty, and staff has led educational officials at the elementary through postsecondary levels to examine how they discipline students for primarily off-campus, Internet-based speech. Despite a significant increase in Internet usage among young people across the country, the U.S. Supreme Court has yet to expressly address Internet-based student speech and expression. As a result, lower courts provide varying and often inconsistent legal guidance to school and higher education officials regarding how to address legal issues associated with cyberbullying. Moreover, courts are presently experiencing a sharp increase in the number of student cyberbullying suits based on a wide range of legal violations, including civil rights deprivations, First Amendment free speech violations, and numerous violations of state and federal antiharassment statutory laws. As such, even though these cases are set in elementary and secondary education, they should be informative for officials in institutions of higher learning.

Compared to traditional forms of student speech, the Internet is not limited by geographical boundaries. For this reason, an increasingly difficult legal issue for officials in institutions of higher learning as well as in elementary and secondary schools when reacting to student cyberbullying is whether there is enough evidence to link Internet-based cyberbullying to campus-based activities. This situation is further complicated by virtue of the fact that the legal authority of these officials is typically restricted mainly to the on-campus behaviors of their students. It is thus often difficult for officials to determine whether cyberbullying occurred on or off campus, or both.

The prevalence of cyberbullying among today's college students notwithstanding, the leading cases involving this practice occur at the elementary and secondary school levels. One of the first published legal cases involving student cyberbullying, *Beussink v. Woodland R-IV School District* (1998), involved a high school student who created a Web site that he used to criticize school officials. Once school officials became aware of the student's Web site, the principal suspended him initially for five days and subsequently increased the suspension to ten days. In its analysis, a federal trial court in Missouri applied the legal standard from *Tinker v. Des Moines Independent Community School District* (1969), holding that the content of the student's Web site did not "materially or substantially interfere with the school's operation," and the student's suspension was overruled. Ultimately, the court held that the principal's suspension was unjustified, because simply disliking or being upset by the student's Web site did not rise to the level of a being a substantial disruption in the operation of the school.

In the issue addressed in *Emmett v. Kent School District* (2000), a high school senior created a Web site that included mock obituaries of some of his friends; the student created the site entirely from home without using any school resources. The Web site asked visitors to vote on who would "die" next. A federal trial court in Washington was of the opinion that because the Web site was entirely created off-campus, the disturbing speech expressed on it was beyond the legal control of school officials and entitled to First Amendment protections.

J. S. v. Bethlehem Area School District (2002), the first of four cases from Pennsylvania, involved a student who created a Web site on his home computer that contained derogatory, profane, and threatening comments targeting his algebra teacher and principal. In one particularly troubling caption of the Web site, the student stated, "Why Should She Die?" The school board conducted an expulsion hearing for the student, because the Web site had such an emotional impact on one of the teachers that she applied for a medical leave, and the site had a demoralizing impact on the entire school community. The Supreme Court of Pennsylvania relied on *Tinker* in deciding that school officials had the right to expel the student and that doing so did not violate his First Amendment rights.

The issue in *Killion v. Franklin Regional School District* (2001) was that a high school student had created a "top ten list" on his Web site that specifically targeted the school's athletic director. The facts revealed that the student was apparently angry at the athletic director because the student had been refused a student parking permit and because of new rules and regulations impacting the school's track team. From his home computer, the student e-mailed a copy of the list to his friends. Several weeks later, copies of the list were distributed at the high school. The court reasoned that while the student's Web site was both derogatory and insulting, school officials failed to provide the required evidence that the Web site caused a substantial threat to the operation of the school. Based on this lack of evidence of a major disruption in the operation of the school, a federal trial court in Pennsylvania concluded that the student's suspension was not valid.

When a high school senior created a fictitious, online parody of his principal and posted it on the popular social networking Web site, MySpace.com, soon afterward classmates and school officials became aware of the online parody. The student was suspended for ten days, placed in an alternative curriculum program, banned from participating in school-sponsored events, and prohibited from attending graduation. In *Layshock v. Hermitage School District* (2007), a federal trial court in Pennsylvania observed that because school officials had the necessary evidence that the student's online parody caused a substantial disruption in school operations, they had the authority to discipline him for his behavior.

In *A. B. v. State of Indiana* (2008), the issue was that a student had posted several derogatory statements about her principal on a Web site that the principal purportedly created. Initially, officials filed a delinquency petition against the student, alleging that the minor's acts would have been criminal if they had been committed by an adult. On further review of a dismissal in favor of the student, the Supreme Court of Indiana reinstated her being adjudicated delinquent, because she intended to harass, annoy, or alarm her former middle school principal.

In *Doninger v. Niehoff* (2008), a high school junior in Connecticut was disqualified from running for senior class secretary after she posted vulgar and inaccurate online statements on a publicly accessible Web site. In light of the student's

Web site postings, administrators received many e-mails and phone calls from concerned students, parents, and community members who worried about the cancellation of an upcoming school event. As a result, officials had to reschedule events due to the controversy created by the student's online statements. The Second Circuit upheld the authority of school officials to discipline the student, insofar as the student's online statements created a foreseeable risk of substantial disruption at the school.

Responses to Cyberbullying

Legislation

An increasing number of jurisdictions are introducing legislation aimed at assisting college officials to address student cyberbullying issues on college campuses. As of 2009, legislatures in Florida, Oregon, Pennsylvania, South Carolina, Utah, and Washington have policies addressing student cyberbullying. The primary goal of these state-level legislative policies is the development of legal language that allows officials to intervene in cyberbullying incidents if the incidents have an impact on the college or university environment.

College and University Responsibilities

College and university officials must take proactive steps to monitor their students' use of technology. Despite the current legal limitations associated with the disciplining of students involved in cyberbullying, officials on college and university campuses must develop climates in which the victims of cyberbullying feel safe reporting these incidents. Additionally, college and university officials must educate themselves on how students, and others on campus, may be using current and emerging technologies as a means to harass, intimidate, and potentially physically harm other unsuspecting members of their academic communities.

Kevin P. Brady

See also Distance Learning

Further Readings

Brady, K. P. (2008). Student bullying and harassment in a cyberage: The legal ambiguity of disciplining students for cyberbullying. *International Journal of Educational Reform, 17*(2), 92–106.

Center for Safe and Responsible Internet Use: http://www.cyberbully.org

Dickerson, D. (2005). Cyberbullies on campus. *University of Toledo Law Review, 37*(1), 12–45.

Myers, J. J., & Carper, G. T. (2008). Cyberbullying: The legal challenges for educators. *West's Education Law Reporter, 238,* 1–16.

Willard, N. E. (2007). *Educator's guide to cyberbullying and cyberthreats.* Retrieved April 17, 2009, from http://www.cyberbully.org/cyberbully/docscbct educator.pdf

Legal Citations

A. B. v. State, 885 N.E.2d 1223 (Ind. 2008).

Beussink v. Woodland R-IV School District, 30 F. Supp. 2d 1175 (E.D. Mo. 1998).

Doninger v. Niehoff, 527 F.3d 41 (2d Cir. 2008).

Emmett v. Kent School District, 92 F. Supp. 2d 1088 (W.D. Wash. 2000).

J. S. v. Bethlehem Area School District, 807 A.2d 847 (Pa. 2002).

Killion v. Franklin Regional School District, 136 F. Supp. 2d 446 (W.D. Pa. 2001).

Layshock v. Hermitage School District, 496 F. Supp. 2d 587 (W.D. Pa. 2007).

Tinker v. Des Moines Independent Community School District, 393 U.S. 503 (1969).

D

DeFunis v. Odegaard

Affirmative action, which was introduced at the national level by President John F. Kennedy's Executive Order 10925, called for the creation of the Committee of Equal Employment Opportunity in order to promote access and equity for minorities in programs utilizing federal funds. More specifically, this order directed public officials to "take affirmative action" to eliminate racial discrimination in employment practices.

Educational institutions have relied on affirmative action to provide access to and increase the number of minorities in colleges and universities. Since its implementation, the constitutionality of affirmative action has been challenged vigorously in higher education. Insofar as *DeFunis v. Odegaard* (1974) was the first case challenging the constitutionality of affirmative action in higher education to reach the Supreme Court, this entry reviews its background and rationale.

Facts of the Case

DeFunis arose when Marco DeFunis, Jr., a White Jewish student of Spanish-Portuguese descent, applied for admission to the state-operated law school at the University of Washington in 1971. While the law school received around 1,600 applications, admission officials chose to limit admissions to 150 students.

During the time in which the plaintiff applied to the law school, its admissions committee calculated all applicants' predicted first-year averages (PFYAs) using their scores on the Law School Admissions Test (LSAT) as well as their junior- and senior-year grade point averages from undergraduate school. The admissions committee assigned less weight to the minority students' PFYA scores and reviewed their applications separately from those of other applicants. Further, the admissions committee accepted minority students whose PFYA scores were lower than those of their White counterparts. Admittedly, the committee did not establish quotas; it sought the inclusion of a reasonable number of minority students.

At the time when the plaintiff's application was under review, 37 minority students were admitted. Of these, 36 had PFYA scores below the plaintiff's, and 30 had scores that were below the minimal threshold needed to meet the law school's admission requirements. Of the 37, only 18 enrolled in the law school. Forty-eight nonminorities were admitted, who also had PFYA scores below the plaintiff. Another 23 of these were veterans, and 25 were admitted presumably for other factors despite their low PFYA scores.

Initially, the plaintiff was placed on a waiting list and subsequently notified that he was denied admissions to the law school. Consequently, the plaintiff filed a suit against the law school claiming that its admissions policy violated the Equal Protection Clause of the Fourteenth Amendment. A state trial court agreed with the plaintiff and ordered officials to admit him in the fall of 1971. However, after the plaintiff started his studies, the Supreme Court of Washington reversed in favor of the law school, explaining that its affirmative action program was a constitutionally permissible admissions tool justified by several state interests. The court found that the law school's affirmative action program served the state's interest in helping to diversify public education. The court thought that the law school's affirmative action policy would enable officials to attain a racially diverse student body while also helping to alleviate the shortage of minority attorneys, prosecutors, judges, and public officials.

The Supreme Court's Ruling

As the plaintiff sought further review at the U.S. Supreme Court, he was permitted to remain in school pending the outcome of his appeal. When the Court heard the case, in a five-to-four per curiam judgment, meaning that none of the justices was named as its author, it vacated the case as moot, because DeFunis was in his last quarter of law school, and law school officials decided that regardless of the final outcome of the case, he would be able to complete his studies. In so ruling, Court essentially sidestepped the merits of the case, discussing only the standards that it applied in evaluating whether to accept the suit, and remanded it for further consideration.

In the first of two dissents, Justice Douglas argued that the Supreme Court should have addressed the substance of the plaintiff's claim in light of the importance of the equity issues that it presented. Similarly, the second dissent, written by Justice Brennan and joined by Justices Douglas, White, and Marshall, maintained that insofar as it was possible that the student might not have completed his studies, the Court should have examined the issue in detail.

On remand, the Supreme Court of Washington rejected the plaintiff's attempt to intervene on behalf of a group of other applicants who alleged that they were denied admission to the law school in favor of less qualified minorities. The court was of the opinion that the plaintiff should not have been allowed to become involved in the litigation insofar as he lacked the ability to represent the interests of the class properly. The court asserted that any interests that the plaintiff might have had in such a case would have been too small, because he had already graduated from law school. Furthermore, the court reexamined its previous judgment, concluding that in light of its broad public import, it was necessary to reinstate its initial order upholding the law school's admissions policy that employed affirmative action.

Impact of the Ruling

The net result of *DeFunis* is that while the Supreme Court basically deferred having to address the constitutional merits of affirmative action admissions policies in higher education, it paved the way for additional litigation that did get to the heart of the matter. Consequently, these later cases, most notably *Regents of the University of California v. Bakke* (1978), wherein a plurality of the Court upheld the use of an affirmative action admissions plan in a case involving a medical school; *Gratz v. Bollinger* (2003), in which the Court upheld such a plan in a law school; and *Grutter v. Bollinger* (2003), wherein it invalidated a plan in undergraduate admissions, have set the parameters for the use of affirmative action in student admissions in colleges and universities.

Robert T. Palmer

See also Affirmative Action; Equal Protection Analysis; *Gratz v. Bollinger; Grutter v. Bollinger; Regents of the University of California v. Bakke*

Further Readings

Eckes, S. (2008). *Grutter v. Bollinger*. In C. J. Russo (Ed.), *Encyclopedia of education law* (Vol. 1, pp. 412–414). Thousand Oaks, CA: Sage.

Office of Affirmative Action, Equal Opportunity and Diversity. (n.d.). *Glossary of affirmative actions terms*. Retrieved December 14, 2005, from http://www.uri .edu/affirmative_action/definitions.html

Russo, C. J., & Thro, W. E. (2009). Higher education implications of *Parents Involved in Community Schools. Journal of College & University Law, 35*, 239–270.

Legal Citations

DeFunis v. Odegaard, 416 U.S. 312 (1974), *on remand*, 514 P.2d 438 (Wash. 1974).

Gratz v. Bollinger, 539 U.S. 244 (2003).

Grutter v. Bollinger, 539 U.S. 306 (2003).

Regents of the University of California v. Bakke, 438 U.S. 265 (1978).

DeFunis v. Odegaard

DeFunis is noteworthy because it is the first Supreme Court case to address affirmative action in higher education.

Supreme Court of the United States

DeFUNIS

v.

ODEGAARD

416 U.S. 312

Argued Feb. 26, 1974

Decided April 23, 1974

PER CURIAM.

In 1971 the petitioner Marco DeFunis, Jr., applied for admission as a first-year student at the University of Washington Law School, a state-operated institution. The size of the incoming first-year class was to be limited to 150 persons, and the Law School received some 1,600 applications for these 150 places. DeFunis was eventually notified that he had been denied admission. He thereupon commenced this suit in a Washington trial court, contending that the procedures and criteria employed by the Law School Admissions Committee invidiously discriminated against him on account of his race in violation of the Equal Protection Clause of the Fourteenth Amendment to the United States Constitution.

DeFunis brought the suit on behalf of himself alone, and not as the representative of any class, against the various respondents, who are officers, faculty members, and members of the Board of Regents of the University of Washington. He asked the trial court to issue a mandatory injunction commanding the respondents to admit him as a member of the first-year class entering in September 1971, on the ground that the Law School admissions policy had resulted in the unconstitutional denial of his application for admission. The trial court agreed with his claim and granted the requested relief. DeFunis was, accordingly, admitted to the Law School and began his legal studies there in the fall of 1971. On appeal, the Washington Supreme Court reversed the judgment of the trial court and held that the Law School admissions policy did not violate the Constitution. By this time DeFunis was in his second year at the Law School.

He then petitioned this Court for a writ of certiorari, and Mr. Justice Douglas, as Circuit Justice, stayed the judgment of the Washington Supreme Court pending the "final disposition of the case by this Court." By virtue of this stay, DeFunis has remained in law school, and was in the first term of his third and final year when this Court first considered his certiorari petition in the fall of 1973. Because of our concern that DeFunis' third-year standing in the Law School might have rendered this case moot, we requested the parties to brief the question of mootness before we acted on the petition. In response, both sides contended that the case was not moot. The respondents indicated that, if the decision of the Washington Supreme Court were permitted to stand, the petitioner could complete the term for which he was then enrolled but would have to apply to the faculty for permission to continue in the school before he could register for another term.

We granted the petition for certiorari on November 19, 1973. The case was in due course orally argued on February 26, 1974.

In response to questions raised from the bench during the oral argument, counsel for the petitioner has informed the Court that DeFunis has now registered 'for his final quarter in law school.' Counsel for the respondents have made clear that the Law School will not in any way seek to abrogate this registration. In light of DeFunis' recent registration for the last quarter of his final law school year, and the Law School's assurance that his registration is fully effective, the insistent question again arises whether this case is not moot, and to that question we now turn.

The starting point for analysis is the familiar proposition that "federal courts are without power to decide questions that cannot affect the rights of litigants in the case before them." The inability of the federal judiciary "to review moot cases derives from the requirement of Art. III of the Constitution under which the exercise of judicial power depends upon the existence of a case or controversy." Although as a matter of Washington state law it appears that this case would be saved from mootness by "the great public interest in the continuing issues raised by this appeal," the fact remains that under Art. III "(e)ven in cases arising in the state courts, the question of mootness is a federal one which a federal court must resolve before it assumes jurisdiction."

The respondents have represented that, without regard to the ultimate resolution of the issues in this case, DeFunis will remain a student in the Law School for the duration of any term in which he has already enrolled. Since he has now registered for his final term, it is evident that he will be given an opportunity to complete all academic and other requirements for graduation, and, if he does so, will receive his diploma regardless of any decision this Court might reach on the merits of this case. In short, all parties agree that DeFunis is now entitled to complete his legal studies at the University of Washington and to receive his degree from that institution. A determination by this Court of the legal issues tendered by the parties is no longer necessary to compel that result, and could not serve to prevent it. DeFunis did not cast his suit as a class action, and the only remedy he requested was an injunction commanding his admission to the Law School. He was not only accorded that remedy, but he now has also been irrevocably admitted to the final term of the final year of the Law School course. The controversy between the parties has thus clearly ceased to be "definite and concrete" and no longer "touch(es) the legal relations of parties having adverse legal interests."

It matters not that these circumstances partially stem from a policy decision on the part of the respondent Law School authorities. The respondents, through their counsel, the Attorney General of the State, have professionally represented that in no event will the status of DeFunis now be affected by any view this Court might express on the merits of this controversy. And it has been the settled practice of the Court, in contexts no less significant, fully to accept representations such as these as parameters for decision.

There is a line of decisions in this Court standing for the proposition that the "voluntary cessation of allegedly illegal conduct does not deprive the tribunal of power to hear and determine the case, i.e., does not make the case moot." These decisions and the doctrine they reflect would be quite relevant if the question of mootness here had arisen by reason of a unilateral change in the admissions procedures of the Law School. For it was the admissions procedures that were the target of this litiga-

tion, and a voluntary cessation of the admissions practices complained of could make this case moot only if it could be said with assurance that "there is no reasonable expectation that the wrong will be repeated."

Otherwise, "(t)he defendant is free to return to his old ways" and this fact would be enough to prevent mootness because of the "public interest in having the legality of the practices settled." But mootness in the present case depends not at all upon a "voluntary cessation" of the admissions practices that were the subject of this litigation. It depends, instead, upon the simple fact that DeFunis is now in the final quarter of the final year of his course of study, and the settled and unchallenged policy of the Law School to permit him to complete the term for which he is now enrolled.

It might also be suggested that this case presents a question that is "capable of repetition, yet evading review," and is thus amenable to federal adjudication even though it might otherwise be considered moot. But DeFunis will never again be required to run the gantlet of the Law School's admission process, and so the question is certainly not "capable of repetition" so far as he is concerned.

Moreover, just because this particular case did not reach the Court until the eve of the petitioner's graduation from Law School, it hardly follows that the issue he raises will in the future evade review. If the admissions procedures of the Law School remain unchanged, there is no reason to suppose that a subsequent case attacking those procedures will not come with relative speed to this Court, now that the Supreme Court of Washington has spoken. This case, therefore, in no way presents the exceptional situation in which the Southern Pacific Terminal doctrine might permit a departure from "(t)he usual rule in federal cases . . . that an actual controversy must exist at stages of appellate or certiorari review, and not simply at the date the action is initiated."

Because the petitioner will complete his law school studies at the end of the term for which he has now registered regardless of any decision this Court might reach on the merits of this litigation, we conclude that the Court cannot, consistently with the limitations of Art. III of the Constitution, consider the substantive constitutional issues tendered by the parties. Accordingly, the judgment of the Supreme Court of Washington is vacated, and the cause is remanded for such proceedings as by that court may be deemed appropriate.

It is so ordered.

Vacated and remanded.

DIGITAL MILLENNIUM COPYRIGHT ACT

The Digital Millennium Copyright Act (DMCA), enacted in 1998 and effective in 2000, updated federal copyright law to meet the demands of the electronic age, particularly with regard to copyright infringement on the Internet. The DMCA contains two pieces of legislation: the World Intellectual Property Organization (WIPO) Copyright and Performances and Phonograms Implementation Act and the Online Copyright Infringement Liability Limitation Act.

WIPO Copyright and Performances and Phonograms Implementation Act

The WIPO Copyright and Performances and Phonograms Implementation Act prohibits the circumvention of technologies, also known as digital rights management, or DRMs, that have been installed to prevent online infringement. For example, copyright holders often install programs requiring computer users to enter passwords in order to access specified files or applications. Copyright holders may also encrypt data or files to prohibit access by outsiders. The DMCA prohibits circumvention of these "technological protection measures." Section 1201 of the DMCA distinguishes between technological measures that restrict *access* to copyrighted works and those that restrict *copying*. This categorization is designed to ensure that fair use continues. In some cases, copying works is considered fair use, while in others unauthorized access may be deemed unfair.

The DMCA targets the manufacture, distribution, and use of computer programs designed to circumvent or decrypt protection devices. Even so, the DMCA includes several prominent exceptions, many of which are applicable in higher educational settings. Insofar as the DMCA does not forbid the following circumvention activities, they are fair uses of copyrighted works:

1. Circumvention by nonprofit library, archive, and educational institutions solely for the purpose of determining, in good faith, whether or not they wish to obtain authorized access to the works. Since this exception applies only

when libraries are open to the public, it most likely covers institutions of higher education.

2. Law enforcement, intelligence, or other governmental activities.

3. Encryption research.

4. Testing technological devices that are designed to prevent access by minors to certain material on the Internet.

5. The collection or dissemination of personally identifying information about the online activities of a person.

6. Testing the security of a computer, computer system, or computer network with the permission of its owner or operator.

Persons who are injured by violations of Section 1201 may bring civil actions for equitable and monetary damages. Violations may also be subject to criminal sanctions. However, the DMCA exempts nonprofit libraries, archives, and educational institutions from criminal liability. Furthermore, the DMCA affords special protection to nonprofit libraries, archives, and educational institutions that may be entitled to complete remission of damages in circumstances where violators prove that they were unaware and had no reason to believe the alleged acts were infringing.

Online Copyright Infringement Liability Limitation Act

The second element in the DMCA is the Online Copyright Infringement Liability Limitation Act, which protects Internet service providers (ISPs) against infringement liability for the acts of their subscribers. For instance, if computer users who are given access to the Internet through service providers access, store (long term or short term), or transmit material that is unlawfully obtained, the users face liability for infringement rather than the ISPs. To the extent that most, if not all, colleges and universities offer Internet access to their students, staff, faculty, and sometimes visitors, they may qualify for these limitations on liability. Still, the burden of proof is on institution leaders to establish that officials lacked actual knowledge or awareness that the infringing activity was occurring, and institutions must not play substantive roles in identifying the infringing content or directing or communicating the transmission of the infringing material. ISPs also must act to remove infringing material or disable infringing conduct on notification of claimed infringements (also called "take-down notice"). Limitations on liability apply only to those ISPs that have established and implemented policies, such as university acceptable use policies that provide for the termination of accounts, subscriptions, and/or computer use privileges of repeat violators. Officials at colleges and universities must continue to provide access to sites that are pay-per-access or password protected.

The special provision limiting the liability of non-profit educational institutions contains one significant point necessary for elaboration. This provision makes a distinction between faculty and graduate students on the one hand and the institutions themselves on the other. In order to limit the liability of institutions for the infringing activities of their faculty members and graduate student employees, the act maintains that when such users are performing teaching or research functions, they are considered to be persons other than the institutions. In these circumstances, knowledge or awareness of the infringing activities is not to be attributed to institutions if they meet the following three conditions:

1. Faculty members or graduate students are engaged in infringing activities that do not involve the provision of online access to instructional materials that are or were required or recommended, within the preceding three-year period, for a course taught at the institution by such faculty member or graduate student.

2. Institutions have not, within the preceding three-year period, received more than two notifications described of claimed infringement by covered faculty members or graduate students, and such notifications of claimed infringement have not been actionable as knowing material misrepresentations of copyright infringement.

3. Institutions provide all users of their systems or networks with informational materials that accurately describe, and promote compliance with, the laws of the United States relating to copyright.

There is no corresponding reference in these provisions to undergraduate students who engage in teaching and research.

Substantive litigation under the DMCA is limited, especially in educational settings. For the most part, the challenges have been from computer programmers and software developers who argue that the DMCA violates First Amendment free speech. Moreover, while courts have agreed that the development, distribution, and use of circumvention software constitutes speech, they have held that the provisions of the DMCA are valid restrictions on that speech. In *Universal City Studios v. Corley* (2001), the movie industry sued individuals and organizations for distributing a computer program (DeCSS) designed to circumvent the content scramble system (CSS), an encryption system that prevents copying DVDs. The Second Circuit affirmed a grant of a permanent injunction prohibiting the defendants from posting the DeCSS program on their Web site and from posting hyperlinks to other Web sites containing the DeCSS. The court was of the opinion that the DMCA was designed to target the program's functional attributes, not its expressive ones. In other words, the court interpreted the DMCA as not prohibiting the making of lawful copies of DVDs; it simply prohibited the decryption method of copying.

Online copyright infringement is most certainly a concern for colleges and universities as Internet service providers, regardless of whether they are aware of the infringing conduct of users. Put another way, university officials should pay attention to the provisions of the DMCA insofar as technologically savvy students may take advantage of their institutions as Internet service providers. Unauthorized copying and downloading of material such as music and movies is rampant among students, as the facts revealed in the well-known *Napster* case (*A & M Records v. Napster*, 2001) and in *Aimster* (*In re Aimster Copyright Litigation*, 2003). Only ISPs actively enforcing policies to promote compliance with copyright laws will be able to take advantage of the limitations on liability that the DMCA provides.

Litigation Under the DMCA

Section 512(h) of the DMCA affords copyright holders "subpoena power" to compel ISPs to disclose the identities of infringing subscribers. Copyright holders are particularly active in using this provision in higher education settings where large numbers of students are presumed to be engaging in unlawful downloading and sharing of copyrighted works.

In litigation, though, the DMCA's subpoena provision has met with mixed results. In *Recording Industry Association of America v. Verizon Internet Services* (2003), by way of illustration, the defendant ISP (Verizon) refused to disclose the name of an alleged infringer who downloaded 600 copyrighted songs in one day using peer-to-peer software. Verizon argued that the DMCA applied only when the infringing materials are stored on the provider's space and not when the service provider's space is used as a mere conduit for the alleged infringing material. The circuit court for the District of Columbia agreed with Verizon, reasoning that it is impossible for Internet service providers to take advantage of the limits on liability such as the removal of infringing materials or the disabling of access to such materials when the materials are not stored online. When infringing materials merely travel through the provider's space without storage, the court explained that because providers have no way of identifying the materials or user, they cannot notify the users of the infringing conduct. Similar results may be possible for universities, which often provide only transmission, routing, or connections to digital online communications but do not modify or store content (*Arista Records LLC v. Does 1–19*, 2008; *Recording Industry Association of America v. University of North Carolina at Chapel Hill*, 2005). Still, subpoenas have not been quashed based on the argument that providing identities of computer users would violate the Family Educational Rights and Privacy Act (FERPA) (*Arista Records LLC v. Does 1–19*, 2008; *Zomba Recording LLC v. Does 1–15*, 2008). This interpretation is based on the notion that the information requested in subpoenas amounts to "directory information," which is not subject to the nondisclosure rules of FERPA.

While there may be cases of undue burdens on college and university officials to provide names and contact information for alleged copyright infringers, especially when the copyrighted materials are not stored on institutional servers, it remains critically important that colleges and universities employ as many policies and practices as necessary to promote compliance with copyright laws.

In *Aimster Copyright Litigation* (2003), similar to the peer-to-peer file-sharing case in *Napster,* the Seventh Circuit upheld an injunction against Aimster, a file-sharing service that facilitates the transfer of files between users. Record companies and composers sought preliminary injunctions to shut down Aimster, arguing that its operation constituted contributory and vicarious infringement. Instead of adopting an "actual knowledge of infringement" test as the Ninth Circuit did in *Napster,* the Seventh Circuit adopted an "economic balancing test":

> If the infringing uses are substantial, then to avoid liability as a contributory infringer, the provider of the service must show that it would have been disproportionately costly for him to eliminate or at least reduce substantially the infringing uses. (p. 653)

The Seventh Circuit thus likened Aimster's response to the infringing uses to "willful blindness." Clearly, college and university officials must actively enforce policies and practices that promote compliance with copyright laws in order to avoid liability in the ever-changing technological world of higher education.

Patrick D. Pauken

See also Copyright; Family Educational Rights and Privacy Act; Intellectual Property

Further Readings

Arista Records LLC v. Does 1–17, No. 07–6197-HO, 2008 U.S. Dist. LEXIS 106461 (D. Ore. Sept. 26, 2008).

Copyright Act, 17 U.S.C. § 101, *et seq.*

Daniel, P. T. K., & Pauken, P. D. (1999). The impact of the electronic media on instructor creativity and institutional ownership within copyright law. *Education Law Reporter, 132,* 1–43.

Daniel, P. T. K., & Pauken, P. D. (2005). Intellectual property. In J. Beckham & D. Dagley (Eds.), *Contemporary issues in higher education law* (pp. 347–393). Dayton, OH: Education Law Association.

Daniel, P. T. K., & Pauken, P. D. (2008). Copyright laws in the age of technology and their applicability to the

K–12 environment. In K. E. Lane, J. F. Mead, M. A. Gooden, S. Eckes, & P. D. Pauken (Eds.), *The principal's legal handbook* (4th ed., pp. 507–519). Dayton, OH: Education Law Association.

Harris, E. M. (2004). School houses rock: University response to the threat of contributory copyright infringement and forced compliance of the Digital Millennium Copyright Act: The entertainment industry may have won the battle against Napster, but can it win the war against universities? *Rutgers Computer & Technology Law Journal, 31,* 187–215.

Metro-Goldwyn-Mayer Studios, Inc. v. Grokster, 545 U.S. 913 (2005).

Legal Citations

A & M Records v. Napster, 239 F.3d 1004 (9th Cir. 2001).

Arista Records LLC v. Does 1–19, 551 F. Supp. 2d 1 (D.D.C. 2008).

Digital Millennium Copyright Act Pub. L. No. 105-304 (1998).

In re Aimster Copyright Litigation, 334 F.3d 643 (7th Cir. 2003).

Online Copyright Infringement Liability Limitation Act, 17 U.S.C. § 512.

Recording Industry Association of America v. University of North Carolina, 367 F. Supp. 2d 945 (M.D.N.C. 2005).

Recording Industry Association of America v. Verizon Internet Services, 351 F.3d 1229 (2003), *cert. denied,* 543 U.S. 924) (2004).

Universal City Studios v. Corley, 273 F.3d 429 (2d Cir. 2001).

WIPO Copyright and Performances and Phonograms Implementation Act, 17 U.S.C. §§ 1201–1204.

Zomba Recording LLC v. Does 1–15, 2008 U.S. Dist. LEXIS 106500 (E.D. Ky. June 2, 2008).

DISCIPLINARY SANCTIONS AND DUE PROCESS RIGHTS

Due process is a central concept in American jurisprudence, rooted in the U.S. Constitution and elaborated in numerous cases involving the discipline of students in higher educational settings. The Constitution guarantees that the government cannot take away a person's basic right to "life, liberty or property, without due process of law." With respect to the discipline of students in institutions of higher education, particularly those that are public in nature (private institutions are ordinarily governed by contracts), due process guards against human error and bias while ensuring fairness in governmental actions that threaten students' lives, liberty, and/ or property interests.

Officials in institutions of higher education have the authority to promulgate and implement their own rules, policies, and procedures. Institutional officials also have the responsibility to ensure that the rules, policies, and procedures are reasonably related to fair and just purposes and are administered in an impartial and unbiased manner. Due process provides the conduit through which the liberty and property rights of students are protected as well as the legal mechanism by which institutions of higher education can be held accountable for violations of the constitutional rights of students.

This entry reviews the development and application of due process in the context of higher education, focusing on the requirements of due process in the context of disciplinary sanctions against students.

Historical Background

Historically, courts (and parents) bestowed significant independent discretion on officials in institutions of higher education regarding student discipline. As early as *Gott v. Berea College* (1913), college and university administrators were seen as standing *in loco parentis* to students; their authority was considered similar to that of educators in K–12. From the early 1900s to the late 1960s, administrators in higher education had autocratic authority over students. During this time, courts rarely, if ever, examined the propriety of administrative decision making, institutional policies, or the fairness of disciplinary actions.

The broad discretionary authority exerted over students by higher education administrators has diminished significantly since the 1960s. The seminal case establishing the requisite due process that officials have to provide to students in higher education in connection with disciplinary hearings is *Dixon v. Alabama State Board of Education* (1961).

In *Dixon*, the Fifth Circuit held that the Fourteenth Amendment's right to due process extended to university students who were involved in disciplinary situations. *Dixon* involved a group of African American college students who were expelled for protesting racial segregation by participating in marches and demonstrations. On the basis of an institutional regulation authorizing expulsion for "conduct prejudicial to the school and for conduct unbecoming a student . . . for insubordination and insurrection, or for inciting other pupils to like conduct," university officials expelled the students. The Fifth Circuit found that officials violated the students' due process rights, because the regulation itself was vague, and they did not receive a hearing prior to their expulsion. The court thus applied the due process standard of notice and a hearing to protect the rights of the students.

Substantive Versus Procedural Due Process

There are two types of due process. *Substantive due process* requires the content of legislation and regulations to be fair and to advance reasonable governmental objectives. Within the realm of higher education, substantive due process ensures basic fairness of regulations and policies that institutional officials establish and implement. Additionally, disciplinary consequences must have a rational relationship to the facts of cases and must stem from information and evidence presented at hearings. Moreover, administrators who preside over hearings must act in an impartial manner. *Procedural due process*, which promotes systematic decision making, requires at a minimum notice and a hearing if a significant life, liberty, or property interest is threatened. Deciding how much due process must be afforded to students depends largely on the specific facts of cases and increases as the severity of harm to their liberty or property interests increases. For example, student suspensions or expulsions are serious deprivations of liberty, and therefore they require a higher degree of due process protection. Procedural due process equates to the series of safeguards erected to protect students' interests before and during disciplinary actions that are taken against them.

Defining Due Process

The Fourteenth Amendment to the Constitution prohibits the taking away of liberty or property without due process of law. Courts recognize due process claims only if there are recognized liberty or property interests at stake. Protected property interests can include personal or real property as well as tangible or intangible property. By way of illustration, in higher education, a property right may encompass the right to continue a specific area of study, the right to pursue an education, or the right to a room in a residence hall. Before revoking such "property" rights, institutional officials in higher education must afford students adequate due process.

Similarly, if students' liberty interests are threatened, they are entitled to due process. In the context of higher education, students possess certain liberty rights, including the right to contract, to acquire useful information, to pursue specified professions, to pursue opportunities for continued education such as admission to law or medical school, and to protect their good names or reputations.

Dixon extended due process protections to students in higher education. However, there is no bright-line rule denoting what constitutes the requisite due process. Rather, courts frequently apply a balancing test that weighs student interests against the state's or private interests. The Supreme Court created a three-part balancing test in *Mathews v. Eldridge* (1976) that requires consideration of

1. the nature of the student's interests that stand to be affected by the official actions,

2. the potential consequence to the student balanced with additional steps taken to ensure a fair decision-making process, and

3. the potential impact to the college or university balanced with additional procedural steps to be taken.

Accordingly, the degree of due process that higher education students are entitled to varies based on the facts of specific cases and is more the product of judicial inclusion and exclusion than the application of any clear-cut legal rule.

Based on the precedent established in *Board of Curators, University of Missouri v. Horowitz*

(1978), there is a distinction made between academic and disciplinary due process. Pursuant to this distinction, academic due process results primarily from academic deficiencies, while disciplinary due process involves nonacademic violations of policies and procedure. Academic due process requires far less due process than disciplinary due process. Thus, when an institutional action is blurred, it is recommended that officials apply the higher standards for disciplinary procedures.

The higher education case that best describes the available due process inclusions and exclusions is *Esteban v. Missouri State College* (1969). In *Esteban*, a federal trial court in Missouri maintained the oral notice officials provided regarding the reason for disciplinary action against the students and the limited opportunity that they had to present their side of the events did not constitute sufficient due process prior to their being suspended. The court pointed out that students in higher education should be given written notice setting forth the charges against them at least 10 days prior to their disciplinary hearings. The court also observed that students should be permitted to inspect the documents to be used at hearings and allowed to present their own evidence and versions of the facts. The court was of the opinion that the hearing had to be conducted before a designated administrator who was required to evaluate the facts based on the evidence and render a written decision. Cases following *Esteban* routinely look to it for guidance in determining higher education students' due process rights.

Elements of Procedural Due Process

Notice

Notice is a mandatory element of due process even though the manner in which it is to be provided is flexible. However, the underlying objective of notice is to advise students of the specific charges being brought against them and to allow them to prepare for hearings adequately. Notice may be oral or written depending on the circumstances. Typically, notice includes references to institutional regulations or policies that students are accused of violating while setting forth the facts forming the basis for the charges against them, including the date, time, and place that the violations allegedly occurred.

According to *Weidemann v. State University of New York College* (1992), a second essential consideration with respect to notice is timing. This means that students should be given sufficient time to prepare adequate defenses against pending charges. Typically, two to ten days is considered to be reasonable depending on the complexity of a case and the severity of the potential sanctions facing students.

Legal Right to a Hearing

Another essential element of due process is the right to a hearing. Hearings are required for both substantive and procedural due process. In the context of higher education, procedural due process means that students must be given opportunities for hearings before tribunals such as administrative adjudicating bodies. Even though hearings are mandatory, the composition of adequate hearings varies considerably. Hearings may range from informal to more formal, often depending on the severity of the charges.

The timing of hearings may also depend on the degree of severity involved in cases. Typically, hearings should precede disciplinary actions. Yet in situations where students alleged committed substantial threats or significant disruption of the academic process, officials may invoke emergency suspensions prior to hearings. In such instances, hearing should occur within several days following suspensions. Full hearings are then required to evaluate whether students are responsible for the alleged actions and in order to impose appropriate sanctions.

In terms of substantive due process, hearings must proceed before impartial arbitrators. Students charged with violations of institutional rules or regulations should receive fair and unbiased hearings. If adjudicating administrators display bias or partiality, students have the right to challenge the adequacy of hearings. Still, hearing administrators are not rendered as biased solely on their positions within institutions; neither are hearing officers deemed to be partial simply because they have personal knowledge regarding the facts of the cases they review.

Right to Legal Counsel

There is no definitive rule regarding a student's right to legal counsel with respect to disciplinary hearings conducted within the context of higher education. Rather, the right to attorney representation depends largely on the nature of the proceeding and the severity of the consequences. Court cases such as *Gorman v. University of Rhode Island* (1986) and *Osteen v. Henley* (1993) agreed that banning the participation of attorneys in student discipline hearings does not violate their right to due process.

While there is no inherent due process right to counsel in higher education, there are situations in which counsel is permitted to advocate on behalf of students. In cases involving additional potential civil or criminal charges, for example, counsel is deemed proper, if not necessary. Similarly, legal representation has also been found to be appropriate in cases where the consequences could result in revocation of students' advanced academic degrees or where their free speech rights were implicated. Even in disputes where counsel is present, attorneys generally do not exercise the full legal representation typically afforded clients in formal court hearings such as direct questioning or cross-examining of witnesses.

Evidence

Based on *Goldberg v. Regents of University of California* (1967), the formal rules of evidence are not applicable in student discipline cases arising in higher education, because hearings are administrative rather than judicial proceedings. Even so, students should be able to present evidence to support their positions and refute the charges they face. Again, the extent to which evidence is permitted depends largely on the nature and facts of specific cases. Typically, it is left to the discretion of presiding officers to choose whether evidence is admissible. For example, in *Osteen*, the Seventh Circuit upheld a presiding officer's exclusion of unnecessarily repetitive evidence that was not pertinent to the facts at hand and evidence that was not useful to the outcome of the proceedings.

Witnesses

The right to know the identities of witnesses and to confront and cross-examine them is largely dependent on the particular facts involved in a situation. If students contest the charges they face,

they have the right to be informed of the names of witnesses. If students do not contest the charges, officials need not disclose the identity of potential witnesses. Similarly, officials need not disclose whether students are capable of defending the pending charges without such knowledge, even if the students contest the charges. With respect to the right to cross-examine witnesses, the Eleventh Circuit ruled in *Nash v. Auburn University* (1987) that there was no violation of the due process rights of two students who were expelled from veterinary school for violating the Student Code of Professional Ethics. The court affirmed that officials did not violate the students' due process rights, both because the students were present when witnesses were questioned, and because, although they did not have an opportunity to cross-examine the witnesses, they were permitted to present statements responding to the charges that they faced. The court was satisfied that there was substantial evidence supporting the students' expulsion for misconduct in connection with an examination. On the other hand, a federal trial court in New York, in *Donahue v. Baker* (1997), treated the right to cross-examine witnesses as an essential element to due process where the outcome of the hearing depended on the creditability of a sole witness.

Aimee Vergon Gibbs

See also Board of Curators of the University of Missouri v. Horowitz; Due Process, Substantive and Procedural; Fourteenth Amendment

Further Readings

Friedl, J. (2000). Punishing students for non-academic misconduct. *Journal of College & University Law, 26*(4), 710–726.

Stevens, E. (1999). *Due process and higher education: A systematic approach to fair decision-making.* Washington, DC: George Washington University.

Legal Citations

Board of Curators, University of Missouri v. Horowitz, 435 U.S. 78 (1978).

Dixon v. Alabama State Board of Education, 294 F.2d 150 (5th Cir. 1961), *cert. denied,* 368 U.S. 930 (1961).

Donahue v. Baker, 976 F. Supp. 136 (N.D.N.Y. 1997).

Esteban v. Missouri State College, 415 F.2d 1077 (1969).

Goldberg v. Regents of University of California, 57 Cal. Rptr. 463 (1967).

Gorman v. University of Rhode Island, 646 F. Supp. 799 (D.R.I. 1986).

Gott v. Berea College, 161 S.W. 204 (Ky. 1913).

Mathews v. Eldridge, 424 U.S. 319 (1976).

Nash v. Auburn University, 812 F.2d 655 (11th Cir. 1987).

Osteen v. Henley, 13 F.3d 221 (7th Cir. 1993).

Weidemann v. State University of New York College, 592 N.Y.S.2d 99 (N.Y. App. Div. 1992).

DISPARATE IMPACT

The theory of disparate impact, also known as "adverse impact," allows challenges to employment or educational practices that are nondiscriminatory on their face but that have a disproportionately negative effect on members of legally protected groups. When the U.S. Supreme Court first recognized the theory, it was hailed as a breakthrough for civil rights. However, civil rights advocates have been disappointed as federal courts have limited how and when plaintiffs may file disparate impact claims. Disparate impact suits have become less successful over time.

Evolution of Disparate Impact Theory

The theory of disparate impact arose out of the Supreme Court's landmark decision in *Griggs v. Duke Power Company* (1971), which challenged the company's requirement that employees pass an intelligence test and complete their high school diplomas to transfer out of the lowest-paying department at a power plant. Prior to 1965, African Americans had been limited to the lowest paying department and were not allowed to transfer out. When the company officially abandoned the limitation on African Americans, it instituted the high school diploma requirement for transfers.

In *Griggs*, the Supreme Court held that in analyzing employment practices that cause a disparate impact, "The touchstone is business necessity. If an employment practice which operates to exclude [members of a protected group] cannot be shown to be related to job performance, the practice is prohibited." The Court found that the two requirements were not related to job performance, noting that many White employees who had not graduated from high school were performing well in the higher-paying departments. Further, the Court thought that the intelligence test, on which African Americans tended not to perform as well as Whites, did not bear a demonstrable relationship to any of the jobs for which it was used.

The first case that significantly limited the disparate impact theory was *Washington v. Davis* (1976), in which the Supreme Court held that the theory of disparate impact did not apply to constitutional claims unless plaintiffs could show that the facially neutral standards were adopted with discriminatory intent. The court reasoned that Title VII of the Civil Rights Act of 1964 "involves a more probing judicial review of, and less deference to, the seemingly reasonable acts of administrators and executives than is appropriate under the Constitution where special racial impact, without discriminatory purpose, is claimed." In addition, the court expressed its concern that extending the theory of disparate impact to constitutional claims would open the floodgates and "would raise serious questions about, and perhaps invalidate, a whole range of tax, welfare, public service, regulatory, and licensing statutes that may be more burdensome to the poor and to the average black than to the more affluent white."

The following year, the Supreme Court, in *Dothard v. Rawlinson* (1977), addressed the "bona fide occupational qualification" exception in sex discrimination cases. Here a class of women challenged a state's height and weight requirements for prison guards at male correctional facilities. The requirements excluded approximately 40% of all women but only 1% of men. The Court decided that the disparate impact was justifiable, because strength and size constituted bona fide occupational requirements for a job that required guards to maintain order in prisons.

In *Ward's Cove Packing Company v. Antonio* (1989), the Supreme Court imposed some of its most significant limitations on the theory of disparate impact. The Court switched the burden of proof to plaintiffs, requiring that they demonstrate that employers' practices causing disparate impacts were not business necessities. Moreover, the Court indicated that plaintiffs had the burden of identifying which specific business practices generated the disparate impacts and that employers had refused to adopt alternative practice that met their needs.

Congress responded to *Ward's Cove Packing Company* in the Civil Rights Act of 1991, providing a partial victory to proponents of the theory of disparate impact. On the one hand, the statute finally codified the theory in the Title VII context and essentially superseded the Court's opinion that plaintiffs had the ultimate burden of proving a selection practice was not a business necessity. On the other hand, the Civil Rights Act of 1991 required plaintiffs to identify with specificity the challenged business practices except for a very narrow exception. The act also failed to clarify how to evaluate whether disparate impacts exist, the adequacy of employers' stated business necessities, and what plaintiffs needed to show in terms of alternative practices with lesser disparate impacts. The resulting uncertainty has made it difficult for plaintiffs to prevail in disparate impact cases.

Expansion of Disparate Impact Theory to Other Statutes

The judiciary has expanded the theory of disparate impact beyond Title VII to other federal, nondiscrimination statutes. Title VI prohibits discrimination on the basis of race to any institution receiving as little as one dollar in federal funds. The U.S. Department of Education promulgated Title VI regulations that prohibit "criteria or methods of administration which have the effect of subjecting individuals to discrimination because of their race, color, or national origin." In a fractured decision, the Supreme Court, in *Guardians Association v. Civil Service Commission of the City of New York* (1983), reached the anomalous conclusion that while Title VI itself required discriminatory intent, the federal regulations prohibiting discriminatory effects were valid.

Title IX of the Education Amendments of 1972, a sister statute to Title VI, prohibits discrimination on the basis of sex at institutions that receive federal funds. For example, Title IX prohibits the use of gender as a criterion for college admissions if use of this criterion has a disparate impact, unless the criterion is shown to predict success and no alternative criteria are available.

Disability laws also prohibit disparate impacts. Even so, plaintiffs have rarely prevailed, because the accommodation process examines each person individually, while the theory of disparate impact is designed to look at the effects on a group. In *Alexander v. Choate* (1985), the Supreme Court assumed but did not resolve whether Section 504 of the Rehabilitation Act of 1973 "reaches at least some conduct that has an unjustifiable disparate impact upon the handicapped." A similar statute, the Americans with Disabilities Act, prohibits the use of "standards, criteria, or methods of administration that have the effect of discrimination on the basis of disability."

Antidiscrimination statutes including Title VI and Title IX can be enforced administratively when federal agencies threaten to deny federal funds from institutions for noncompliance. Yet in *Alexander v. Sandoval* (2001), the Supreme Court closed the door on disparate suits brought by individuals under Title VI, ruling that although the agency regulations were valid, no private right of action existed for individuals to enforce them. *Sandoval's* precedent has been applied to Title IX because of its similarity in wording to Title VI. Still, the *Sandoval* application to Section 504 is uncertain in light of the Court's earlier judgment in *Alexander v Choate*.

The Supreme Court has determined that disparate impact claims can be brought under the Age Discrimination in Employment Act (ADEA), but it imposed significant limitations on those suits. In *Smith v. City of Jackson* (2005), the Court pointed out that when age is an issue in personnel actions, employers do not need to demonstrate the existence of business necessities. Instead, the Court was satisfied that employers could demonstrate that disparate impacts were caused simply by a "reasonable factor other than age," the less demanding standard allowed by the ADEA. The Court added that future ADEA claims should be analyzed under the restrictive guidelines established in *Ward's Cove*, because the Civil Rights Act of 1991 had overruled *Ward's Cove* with respect to Title VII but not the ADEA.

Application of Disparate Impact to Higher Education

Only a small number of disparate impact claims have been filed against institutions of higher education, and of these, few have been successful. In one notable case, a federal trial court upheld a university's requirement that applicants had to have had a doctoral degree in order to obtain positions as assistant professors, even though doing so had a disparate impact on African Americans. In *Scott v. University of Delaware* (1978), the court explained that the experience, skills, and knowledge required to obtain a doctoral were reasonably related to the important academic functions of scholarship and teaching graduate students. In another case, *Cureton v. NCAA* (1999), the Third Circuit observed that the NCAA could not be sued on the ground that its minimum standardized test scores had an unjustified disparate impact on African American student athletes in violation of Title VI. Even one of the few victories for a plaintiff, *Leftwich v. Harris-Stowe State College* (1983), now has limited value as precedent. The Eighth Circuit, in a discrimination case, established a tough business necessity standard, but the Supreme Court's judgment in *City of Jackson* eliminated the need to show business necessity in age discrimination cases.

Future of Disparate Impact Theory

The prospects for future disparate impact litigation appear bleak. Legal scholar Michael Selmi's empirical analysis of almost 300 federal appellate and trial court disparate impact cases demonstrated that plaintiffs prevailed less than 20% of the time, a rate far lower than that in other types of employment discrimination cases. Further, Selmi's analysis showed that plaintiffs have been less successful over time, as courts have further limited the use of the disparate impact theory.

In the context of higher education, one legal commentator suggests that the best hope for the disparate impact theory is voluntary compliance efforts by colleges rather than successful disparate impact litigation. Another commentator on higher education offered the opinion that *City of Jackson* means that the application of disparate impact theory in age discrimination cases will be "limited and remote." Even so, the theory of disparate impact is still frequently discussed in the legal literature, but it appears unlikely that it will play a significant role in future higher education litigation, unless courts become more receptive to its application.

D. Frank Vinik

See also Age Discrimination; Age Discrimination in Employment Act; Americans with Disabilities Act; Rehabilitation Act, Section 504; Title VI

Further Readings

Beckham, J. (2006). Disparate impact analysis under the ADEA: A standard of 'reasonableness' for college and university employees. *Education Law Reporter, 201,* 409.

Hart, M. (2007). Disparate impact discrimination: The limits of litigation, the possibilities for internal compliance. *Journal of College & University Law, 33,* 547–569.

Selmi, M. (2006). Was the disparate impact theory a mistake? *UCLA Law Review, 53,* 701–733.

Legal Citations

Age Discrimination in Employment Act, Pub. L. No. 90-202 (1967).

Alexander v. Choate, 469 U.S. 287 (1985).

Alexander v. Sandoval, 532 U.S. 275 (2001).

Americans with Disabilities Act, Pub. L. No. 101-336 (1990).

Cureton v. NCAA, 198 F.3d 107 (3d Cir. 1999).

Dothard v. Rawlinson, 433 U.S. 321 (1977).

Education Amendments of 1972, 20 U.S.C. §§ 1681 *et seq.* (1972).

Griggs v. Duke Power Company, 401 U.S. 424 (1971).

Guardians Association v. Civil Service Commission of the City of New York, 463 U.S. 582 (1983).

Leftwich v. Harris-Stowe State College, 702 F.2d 831 (8th Cir. 1983).

Rehabilitation Act of 1973, Section 504 29 U.S.C. §§ 794 *et seq.*

Scott v. University of Delaware, 455 F. Supp. 1102 (D. Del. 1978).

Smith v. City of Jackson, 544 U.S. 228 (2005).

Ward's Cove Packing Company v. Antonio, 490 U.S. 642 (1989).

Washington v. Davis, 426 U.S. 229 (1976).

DISTANCE LEARNING

Distance learning is defined as any formal instructional approach in which the majority of instruction occurs when educators and students are not in the physical presence of one another. Today's colleges and universities constitute the fastest-growing market of online distance learning courses offered to students. At the same time, postsecondary institutions use the Internet for distance learning courses more than any other mode of communication.

In light of the changing educational environment, this entry discusses emerging legal-technological issues in the cyber age related to copyright infringement liability associated with distance learning courses delivered in Internet-based environments. Copyright laws protect the creators or owners of original works, such as movies, plays, music, computer programs, photos, or paintings. Insofar as today's administrators and instructors face an increasing risk of litigation as well as the potential of paying large amounts of monetary damages and substantial legal fees for noncompliance with existing copyright laws when dealing with new platforms for the delivery of education via the spread of distance learning, this entry reviews legal issues with this approach to learning.

This entry focuses on what can be described as the more technological developments in higher education, rather than other issues such as cheating and other forms of academic dishonesty, academic freedom, or the ownership of course content. Because it is important to consider how the use of technology interfaces with existing copyright laws in the world of distance learning, the entry highlights issues in this area.

Background

Contrary to popular belief, distance learning is not a new educational development. Rather, distance learning has existed for more than a century, beginning with the development of correspondence courses in the late 1880s. Unlike today's distance learning courses, which are delivered online, lessons from correspondence courses were mailed to students who completed them and mailed them back; they were then graded and mailed back to students. The delivery method of distance learning courses changed dramatically with the advent of distance learning on the Internet in the mid-1990s. Based on the instructional development and delivery of online, or Web-based courses, the geographic location of students and faculty has become increasingly irrelevant, because online distance learning courses can be taken anywhere or at any time as long as instructors and students have Internet access.

The Digital Millennium Copyright Act (DMCA)

As with any type of instruction, access to instructional materials and making copies of these sources of information present legal issues to be considered. Under Section 110(1) of the 1976 Copyright Act, often referred to as the "classroom exception," the use of copyrighted works and materials without formal copyright permission is permitted in face-to-face instructional course settings if faculty members meet three criteria. First, the display and reproduction of copyrighted materials must take place in a nonprofit educational organization. Second, both faculty members and students must be present in the same location. Third, if materials are audiovisual works, lawful copies of the copyrighted materials must be made. Unfortunately, because this broad classroom exception under Section 110(1) of the 1976 Copyright Act did not include a consideration of the evolving new category of online distance learning courses that were incorporating emerging technologies as the primary method of instructional delivery, questions remain.

The Digital Millennium Copyright Act (DMCA), which amended the 1976 Copyright Act, became law on October 28, 1998. The primary legal directive of the DMCA was to provide a balance between the promotion of distance learning through technology while simultaneously maintaining the legal rights of copyright holders and users.

Since the DMCA's enactment, six categories of copyrighted work exemptions have developed that can be specifically applied to online distance learning courses. These six categories provide exemptions and allow persons to use selected copyrighted work without permission. These categories are the following:

1. Audiovisual works that are located in institutional educational libraries or the film or media studies department of colleges and universities, if compilations or copies of these works are made exclusively for educational use in the classroom by faculty members who teach in the area of media or film.

2. Computer programs and video games that are distributed in media formats that have become obsolete and are used exclusively for the purpose of preservation or archival reproduction by a college or university library.

3. Computer programs that are no longer manufactured, or where repairing these programs is no longer reasonably available in the commercial marketplace.

4. Literary publications that are distributed in an e-book format.

5. Computer programs that allow wireless telephone handsets to connect to a wireless telephone communication network.

6. Sound recordings and audiovisual works distributed in compact disc format and protected by measures that control access to lawfully purchased works.

The TEACH Act

The need for expanding the provision of copyright exemptions provided to students and teachers through online distance learning courses was recognized with the passage of the Technology, Education, and Copyright Harmonization Act, or the TEACH Act, on November 2, 2002. The TEACH act updated distance learning provisions to both the 1976 Copyright Act and the Digital Millennium Copyright Act (DMCA). Specifically, the TEACH Act amended both sections 110(2) and 112 of the 1976 Copyright Act. With the passage of the TEACH Act, the amount of copyrighted materials an instructor in an online distance learning course can now use without formal copyright permission has expanded. This expansion includes instructional content and materials transmitted to students to any location other than the classroom as well as the ability to digitize certain types of copyrighted works.

In order to qualify for these copyright exemptions under the TEACH Act, colleges and universities must comply with a number of technological and legal requirements. One of the major technological requirements in this regard includes the implementation of a computer system that prevents unauthorized access to or copying of educational online broadcasts by persons not formally enrolled in a particular distance learning course. The primary legal requirement of the TEACH Act is that educational institutions, such as colleges and universities, must formally establish copyright policies describing and requesting compliance with copyright law provisions, and they must distribute this information to faculty, students, and staff members.

Conclusion

In sum, the enactment of the TEACH Act has resulted in the most change in the field of copyright law as it applies to distance learning environments. Unlike previous copyright law provisions, such as the Digital Millennium Copyright Act (DMCA), which focuses almost exclusively on individual instructors, the TEACH Act holds educational institutions directly accountable for compliance with copyright usage laws. Insofar as educational institutions face liability under the TEACH Act, there are incentives for faculty members and administrators at colleges and universities to follow the act's requirements. To date, there has been no reported legal case involving the application of copyright laws to distance learning. As such, the legal connection between copyright law and digital learning is a new and evolving legal field. Undoubtedly, as new technologies emerge and are used instructionally in distance learning, issues of potential copyright infringement will arise.

Kevin P. Brady

See also Academic Dishonesty; Academic Freedom; Copyright; Digital Millennium Copyright Act

Further Readings

Armatas, S. A. (2008). *Distance learning and copyright: A guide to legal issues.* Chicago: American Bar Association.

Mehrotra, C. H., Hollister, C. D., & McGahey, L. (2001). *Distance learning: Principles for effective design, delivery, and evaluation.* Thousand Oaks, CA: Sage.

Legal Citations

Copyright Act, Pub. L. No. 94-553 (1976).

Digital Millennium Copyright Act, Pub. L. No. 105-304 (1998).

Technology, Education, and Copyright Harmonization Act (TEACH Act), Pub. L. No. 107–273 (2002).

DRUG TESTING OF STUDENTS

As officials in colleges and universities seek ways to discourage and eliminate drug use on campus, testing students for drugs has become increasingly common. Beginning in the military, private and public sector employment, and drug rehabilitation programs, drug testing had worked its way into educational institutions by the mid-1980s. Even though drug use is not uncommon on many campuses, the reported litigation involving student drug testing in higher education has all been within the realm of intercollegiate athletics. While the U.S. Supreme Court has not addressed the issue of drug testing student-athletes in higher education, it has resolved two cases on point in high school settings. This entry examines judicial opinions on the constitutionality of drug testing of student-athletes who voluntarily participate in intercollegiate sports.

Historical Background

Drug testing of student-athletes has routinely been done through urinalysis. Institutional officials have relied on urinalysis, because tests of hair, saliva, and even blood have been demonstrated to be less reliable than urinalysis. Moreover, obtaining blood samples is more invasive than collecting urine samples. As long as urine samples are precisely collected and handled, the reliability of these tests is extremely high. While most of the inaccuracy of urine samples is due to handling, college and university officials who utilize drug testing typically conduct second checks on samples that produce positive outcomes for banned substances in order to help to ensure the accuracy of results. In institutions of higher learning that employ drug testing, student-athletes are generally asked to produce urine samples at least once in the course of a sport season. Other random samples of urine may be taken throughout the remainder of the season.

In higher education, drug testing started with the National Collegiate Athletic Association (NCAA). In the early 1970s, NCAA officials adopted a policy that restricted drug use by student-athletes. However, after the United States Olympic Committee (USOC) implemented drug testing in the 1980s, the NCAA followed the USOC's lead and created its own drug-testing policy for student-athletes in member institutions. Pursuant to the NCAA's policy, student-athletes must agree to urinalysis drug testing as a precondition to qualify for participating in intercollegiate athletic competitions. Student-athletes who test positive for banned substances are banned from participating in athletic events for one calendar year from the time of the positive test.

At the same time, the NCAA policy requires student-athletes to sign consent forms agreeing to submit to random, suspicionless drug testing prior to participating in intercollegiate athletic competitions. Student-athletes who refuse to sign consent forms can be barred from participating in intercollegiate athletic competitions and practices. While one court interpreted this consent requirement as being unconstitutional, most cases agree that testing is constitutional insofar as student-athletes lack constitutional rights under the Fourteenth Amendment to participate in intercollegiate athletics. Other college athletic associations—the National Association of Intercollegiate Athletics and the National Junior College Athletic Association—do not require drug testing in the intercollegiate sports programs operated by their member institutions.

Constitutional Issues

Two U.S. Supreme Court cases addressing drug testing of high school students have helped to clarify judicial standards with regard to student privacy when confronted with search and seizure issues in this contentious area. Given the relative lack of litigation involving higher education, the judicial analyses in the Supreme Court cases can be adapted in colleges and universities to help clarify the reasonable expectations of officials who are responsible for administering drug-testing policies.

Challenges to drug-testing policies typically involve the Fourth Amendment's protection against unreasonable searches and seizures. Students have also occasionally, but unsuccessfully, raised concerns under the Fourteenth Amendment's Due Process Clause. The Supreme Court has decided that urinalysis drug testing constitutes a search within the meaning of the Fourth Amendment. Even so, the Court ruled that such searches can be justified based on the need for educational officials to prevent and deter drug use for the physical protection of their students rather than on probable cause. To this end, the Court has twice upheld random suspicionless drug testing of student athletes in high school settings in *Vernonia School District v. Acton* (1995) and *Board of Education of Pottawatomie County v. Earls* (2002).

In *Earls,* the Supreme Court essentially applied the same test as in *Vernonia* in reasoning that the policy passed the three-part test that it had devised. First, the Court remarked that because the privacy interests of students in schools are limited to begin with, the policy was constitutional. Second, as to the character of the intrusion, the Court maintained that because the urine samples were collected in a minimally intrusive manner and the test results had limited uses, meaning that officials used them for rehabilitative purposes in helping students to overcome their substance abuse problems, the infringement on their privacy was constitutionally acceptable. Third, as to the nature and immediacy of the school board's concerns and the policy's efficacy in meeting them, the Court concluded that the in light of a growing national epidemic involving drug use and the effectiveness of testing, the policy passed constitutional muster; the Court slightly modified the third prong of the test in *Earls,* making it easier for officials to justify random suspicionless drug-testing policies for student-athletes.

In the aftermath of *Earls,* lower courts continue to uphold policies that call for drug testing of student-athletes in K–12 settings. Even though both of these cases predated the key litigation in higher education, they should be informative to officials who are involved in drug testing of student-athletes in colleges and universities.

Drug-Testing Litigation in Higher Education

The two highest-profile notable cases, both of which reached state high courts, to examine drug testing of student-athletes in higher education are *University of Colorado v. Derdeyn* (1993) and *Hill v. NCAA* (1994). While both cases involve drug testing of student athletes pursuant to NCAA policies, they reach significantly different outcomes.

In *Derdeyn,* student-athletes contested the requirement that they sign forms consenting to drug testing, claiming that there was no evidence that anyone had ever used drugs while practicing

for or participating in intercollegiate sports on campus. The student-athletes argued that absent evidence of drug use or abuse, the consent requirement was an unreasonable search that violated their rights to privacy. On further review of an injunction that prevented university officials from enforcing the policy, the Supreme Court of Colorado affirmed in favor of the student-athletes. The court ruled that in the absence of voluntary consent by the student-athletes, the university's random suspicionless drug-testing policy was unconstitutional under both the federal and state constitutions. At the heart of its analysis, the court was of the opinion that the privacy rights of the student-athletes outweighed the state's interest, because the underlying policy was not supported by an important governmental interest.

Conversely, a year later in *Hill,* the Supreme Court of California rejected a challenge to the NCAA's drug-testing requirements that was filed by students and institutional officials at Stanford University primarily on the ground that it violated their state constitutional rights to privacy. As an initial matter, the court conceded that although the NCAA is a private, nonstate actor, a principle that the Supreme Court enunciated in *NCAA v. Tarkanian* (1988), this was an insufficient basis on which to resolve the case. In rejecting the NCAA's attempt to have the case dismissed because it was not a state actor subject to the Fourth Amendment, the Court found it necessary to address the merits of the claim.

In language presaging *Vernonia* and *Earls,* the *Hill* court indicated that because student-athletes must submit to physical examinations before being declared fit to compete, testing did not infringe on their already diminished expectations of privacy. The Court added that because the student-athletes had advance notice that they were to be tested or disqualified from participation if they refused to submit to doing so, their consent was not rendered involuntary. As part of this rationale, the Court pointed out that because students simply did not have a right to participate in interscholastic sports insofar as such activity is a privilege, their claim was without merit. The Court explained that because drug testing was designed to protect the integrity of both intercollegiate sports programs and the safety of their participants, the NCAA's policy was constitutional.

Other courts have reached outcomes that agree with *Hill* rather than *Derdeyn*. For example, in an earlier case, the highest court in Massachusetts relied on a commonwealth civil rights statute in rejecting a challenge to drug testing of student-athletes (*Bally v. Northeastern University*, 1989). Subsequently, an appellate court in Louisiana reviewed two issues in *Brennan v. Board of Trustees for University of Louisiana Systems* (1997). First, the court rejected the student's Fourteenth Amendment claim in observing that he did not have a Fourteenth Amendment property or liberty interest in participating in interscholastic sports. Second, the court declared that in view of a student-athlete's diminished expectation of privacy, coupled with the significant interests of his university and the NCAA, the drug-testing policy was constitutional.

Conclusion

As noted, there is some disagreement among the courts as to whether drug testing of student-athletes is constitutionally permissible in higher education. However, insofar as the Supreme Court has upheld random suspicionless drug testing under the Fourth Amendment in the context of K–12 schooling, policies promulgated by the NCAA, other similar athletic associations, colleges, and universities should be able to survive constitutional challenges to the extent that they adopt rationales similar to those in *Hill, Vernonia,* and *Earls*.

Nanette Schmitt

See also Extracurricular Activities, Law, and Policy; Fourth Amendment Rights of Students; National Collegiate Athletic Association; *National Collegiate Athletic Association v. Tarkanian*; Privacy Rights of Students

Further Readings

Giglio, E. (1991). Drug testing: Constitutional and policy implications. *Criminal Justice Policy Review, 5*(1), 1–16.

Legal Citations

Bally v. Northeastern University, 532 N.E.2d 49 (Mass. 1989).
Board of Education of Independent School District No. 92 of Pottawatomie County v. Earls, 536 U.S. 822 (2002).
Brennan v. Board of Trustees for University of Louisiana Systems, 691 So. 2d 324 (La. Ct. App. 1997).
Hill v. NCAA, 865 P.2d 633 (Cal. 1994).
NCAA v. Tarkanian, 488 U.S. 179 (1988).
University of Colorado v. Derdeyn, 863 P.2d 929 (Colo. 1993).
Vernonia School Dist. 47J v. Acton, 515 U.S. 646 (1995).

Due Process, Substantive and Procedural

Affording persons or organizations "due process" basically means to conduct legal proceedings with fairness in both content and procedure. In private colleges and universities, the principles of due process are usually governed by standards of good faith in adherence to provisions of contracts and handbooks. In contrast, as arms of state governments, public institutions of higher education are subject to the constraints of the U.S. Constitution. The Fifth Amendment to the Constitution states, as a command to the federal government, that no person shall be "deprived of life, liberty, or property, without due process of law." This phrase is, essentially, the only command that appears twice in the Constitution. Section 1 of the Fourteenth Amendment extends the same principles of due process to state governments in its stipulation that ". . . nor shall any state deprive any person of life, liberty, or property, without due process of law; . . ." The Fourteenth Amendment's relationship to state governments connects the due process clause to the work of public colleges and universities. Over the years, courts have defined what is meant by life, liberty, and property and have interpreted the due process clauses of both the Fifth and Fourteenth Amendments to contain two kinds of due process rights: substantive and procedural. In light of the great significance of substantive and procedural due process in the day-to-day activities on college and university campuses, this entry examines key issues on this topic.

Due Process Rights

In order to present viable claims for violations of due process, plaintiffs, whether they are faculty members, staff workers, administrators, or students, must allege that they were deprived of life, liberty, or property interests in connection with their activities. Due process claims alleging deprivations of life in higher education settings are very rare, because life interests under the due process clause are just what they sound like. Although there are some examples involving life interests, such as deaths of students as a result of accidents on campuses stemming from hazing, binge drinking, or athletics, these are beyond the scope of this entry.

Claims involving liberty and property interests are much more common. In higher education, liberty interests are implicated in a wide variety of cases involving student admissions, discipline, academics, degree revocation, and employment. As to faculty members, staff, and administrators, litigation typically involves hiring, dismissals, and promotion and tenure decisions. Traditional liberty interests include rights to speech, religion, assembly, and privacy. Yet much of the discussion of liberty interests in due process analysis involves the interest in persons' good names, reputations, honor, and integrity. For example, stigmatizing statements made by college or university officials about faculty members or students may damage their reputations enough to implicate liberty interests. If the damages were to harm the faculty members' or students' ability to obtain employment or other lucrative opportunities, then the injured parties may have successful due process claims. Property interests for faculty and staff are found in employment contracts. For students, property interests include the right to an earned benefit such as a course grade or degree or the right to stay in school.

Substantive Due Process

The words *due process* probably most often convey thought related to what might be described as procedural due process. The rights protected by the due process clauses—life, liberty, and property— also serve as proxies for substantive rights not explicitly named in the Constitution but nonetheless protected by its provisions. Examples here include the right to bodily integrity such as freedom from abuse and harassment at the hands of government, parents' rights to raise their families and to direct the education of their children, and the right to enter into contracts and to work. As a result, actions by governmental decision makers that deprive persons of one or more of these unnamed rights may be subject to substantive due process claims.

Substantive due process also prevents governments and governmental actors, meaning public officials with the actual or apparent ability to act in their official capacities, from acting arbitrarily, capriciously, and outside the scope of their authority. Substantive due process asks whether the government's exercise of authority "is a fair, reasonable and appropriate exercise of the police power of the State, or is it an unreasonable, unnecessary, and arbitrary interference with the right of the individual in his personal liberty . . . ?" (*Lochner v. New York,* 1905, p. 56). In effect, due process puts substantive limits on what lawmakers, judges, and government executives may do. In higher education, substantive due process regulates the activities of boards of trustees, presidents, and other administrators who make decisions in enacting policies that affect students, faculty, and staff.

State actors, including those in public higher education, are afforded a great deal of leeway in their work. In other words, courts ordinarily do not reverse the decisions made by university faculty, staff, and administrators without clear reasons for doing so. In *Regents of the University of Michigan v. Ewing* (1985), for instance, the Supreme Court upheld the decision of university officials to dismiss a medical student for poor academic performance and for failing the National Board of Medical Examiners' examination. In an important statement favoring judicial deference to the decisions of academic leaders, the Court explained that when judges are asked to review the substance of academic decisions, they ought to demonstrate great respect for the professional judgment of faculty members; this deference is rooted in the concept of academic abstention. The Court added that the judiciary may not override the judgment of academicians unless the academicians' actions are such substantial departures from accepted norms as to show that they failed to exercise appropriate professional judgment.

At the same time, substantive due process places limits on this discretion, for both individuals and institutions as a whole, particularly when the conduct of college and university officials is so arbitrary and capricious as to "shock the conscience." The limits on discretion are particularly noteworthy for college and university officials, who, as individual state actors, may be personally liable for actions they undertake while performing their official duties. The Supreme Court addressed this point in *Wood v. Strickland* (1975), a K–12 case, wherein it ruled that school board members were not immune from liability under Section 1983 of the Civil Rights Act of 1871 when they disciplined students. The Court noted that such public officials could face personal liability if they knew or reasonably should have known that the actions they took within the sphere of their official duties would violate the constitutional rights of the people affected or if they acted with malicious intent to cause a deprivation of constitutional rights or other injuries.

Procedural Due Process

Procedural due process requires officials to employ fair and appropriate procedures when restricting persons' life, liberty, or property interests. Most often, when people think of procedural due process, regardless of whether they are in higher education, they probably focus on the procedures required in cases of student discipline or faculty and staff dismissal. These procedures usually include notice of the charges against the persons or of the judgments to be made along with opportunities for the persons to be heard or appeal adverse decisions, either informally or formally.

In procedural due process analyses involving public institutions of higher education, there are two important questions to ask. The first examines whether the Fourteenth Amendment's Due Process Clause applies. Put another way, this inquiry addresses whether life, liberty, or property interests are implicated by institutional decision making, such as decisions made to discipline students or faculty members. As indicated earlier, life interests are rarely implicated in the actions of college and university officials. However, liberty and property interests are commonly present, such as the liberty interests in reputation and the opportunity to graduate or obtain employment in addition to the property interests associated with faculty and staff contracts.

The Supreme Court's opinion in *Board of Regents v. Roth* (1972) offers a fine illustration of liberty and property interests related to procedural due process. In *Roth*, the Court decided that university officials did not violate the due process rights of a nontenured faculty member when they chose not to renew his contract after it expired. As to the liberty interests at stake in *Roth*, the Court reasoned that because officials did not make any charges against Roth that might have seriously damaged his standing and associations in his community when they chose not to renew his contract, his good name, reputation, honor, and integrity were not at stake. Further, the Court thought that the dismissal did not impose a stigma on the faculty member that foreclosed his freedom to take advantage of other employment opportunities. Turning to the faculty member's property interest, the Court was of the opinion that because the property interest had expired, leaving Roth no legitimate entitlement to property, the actions of university officials did not impair his reputation or his ability to obtain employment elsewhere.

The second question to be asked in procedural due process analyses concerns the amount of process that individuals are due if the actions of university officials implicate due process rights. The level or amount of procedural due process afforded depends directly on the severity of the deprivations or losses. For example, student suspensions or losses of privileges such as participating in extracurricular activities would require less formal processes than expulsions or revocations of degrees. In like fashion, the nonrenewal of the contracts of faculty members, as in *Roth*, even when implicating due process rights, requires less process than the termination of contracts or denials of tenure.

Courts usually make distinctions between due process for discipline, which is formal, and due process for academic decisions, which is most often less formal. In *Board of Curators of the University of Missouri v. Horowitz* (1978), for example, the Supreme Court found that, in academic disputes, the degree of due process afforded students is less rigorous than that afforded them in disciplinary disputes. In academic contexts, the Constitution mandates only informal notice and reviews. In disciplinary contexts, particularly those involving suspensions or expulsions, procedural due process is ordinarily more formal, likely including provisions requiring such elements as fact-finding committees, appeals panels, recorded transcripts, and opportunities to present witnesses' testimony and written evidence.

In order to answer the question of how much process is due, courts generally engage in a balancing of rights. On one hand, courts review the interests of the students or faculty members or other staff who are being impacted by the allegedly adverse decision. For instance, students who are subject to a degree revocation would almost certainly have liberty and property interests implicated. On the other hand, courts also look at the interests of the colleges or universities. In the same example of a degree revocation, institutional interests may include academic integrity, academic standards, consistency of policy, safety of students and staff, and so on. In this balance, it is important to consider the risk of wrongful deprivation of due process rights. If college or university officials were to fail to afford procedural due process and erroneously revoke the degrees of graduates, the graduates' due process rights would certainly have been violated. The provision of procedural due process, which ensures that all sides of a story are heard, is designed to minimize this risk.

In sum, it is important to keep in mind that procedural due process, as outlined by cases such as *Roth,* highlights individuals' rights as interpreted generally by the courts. Moreover, interested readers should consult local laws and, especially, their institutional policies for the required due process procedures for academic and disciplinary decisions taken against students, staff, and faculty members.

Patrick D. Pauken

See also Academic Abstention; *Board of Curators of the University of Missouri v. Horowitz; Board of Regents of State Colleges v. Roth*; Civil Rights Act of 1871, Section 1983; Due Process Rights in Faculty and Staff Dismissal; *Regents of the University of Michigan v. Ewing*

Further Readings

Beckham, J. (2005). Faculty. In J. Beckham & D. Dagley (Eds.), *Contemporary issues in higher education law* (pp. 89–130). Dayton, OH: Education Law Association.

Legal Information Institute. (n.d.). *Due process.* Retrieved June 26, 2009, from http://topics.law.cornell.edu/wex/due_process

Russo, C. J., & Thro, W. (2005). Student equal protection and due process. In J. Beckham & D. Dagley (Eds.), *Contemporary issues in higher education law* (pp. 257–275). Dayton, OH: Education Law Association.

Legal Citations

Board of Curators of the University of Missouri v. Horowitz, 435 U.S. 78 (1978).

Board of Regents v. Roth, 408 U.S. 564 (1972).

Civil Rights Act of 1871, Section 1983, 42 U.S.C. § 1983.

Lochner v. New York, 198 U.S. 45 (1905).

Regents of the University of Michigan v. Ewing, 474 U.S. 214 (1985).

Wood v. Strickland, 420 U.S. 308 (1975).

DUE PROCESS RIGHTS IN FACULTY AND STAFF DISMISSAL

The Fifth Amendment to the U.S. Constitution states, as a command to the federal government, that no person shall be "deprived of life, liberty, or property, without due process of law." Similarly, Section 1 of the Fourteenth Amendment extends the same principles of due process to state governments. Affording individuals or organizations "due process" basically means to conduct legal proceedings with fairness in both content and procedure. It is the Fourteenth Amendment and its connection to state governments that connects the due process clause to the work of public colleges and universities. In private colleges and universities, the principles of due process are usually governed by standards of good faith in adherence to provisions of contracts and handbooks. In light of the importance of due process protections for faculty and staff members who may be facing the loss of their jobs, this entry reviews the key legal dimensions of this topic.

Faculty and staff dismissals in higher education can be initiated by a variety of events. For example, dismissals for cause may be based on academics, such as the denial of tenure or being fired for academic misconduct in teaching or research. Dismissals may also be based on disciplinary misconduct, including such activities as embezzlement, misuse of institutional or grant-related funds, insubordination, neglect of duty, unprofessional conduct, immorality, or other good cause. Finally, dismissals may be caused not by the actions or inactions of faculty members and staff persons themselves but by the necessity of layoffs in times of financial hardship; this is commonly known as a reduction in force.

In all cases involving the dismissal of faculty members and staff persons, due process is a must. Due process at dismissal requires officials to employ fair and appropriate procedures when restricting the liberty or property of employees. While the particulars may vary depending on institutions and their policies, procedures typically include notice of the charges against the persons or statements of reasons for their dismissals, notification of the decision(s) to be made, and opportunities for faculty members or staff persons to be heard and to appeal resulting adverse employment actions.

Elements of Due Process

In due process analyses involving public institutions of higher education, two important questions apply. The first question considers whether the Fourteenth Amendment's Due Process Clause applies, while the second addresses the level or amount of due process required.

Liberty and Property Interests

In determining whether the Due Process Clause applies, the question is whether liberty or property interests are implicated when institutional decision makers terminate contracts. In cases involving dismissal, both liberty and property should be involved. In higher education, traditional liberty interests include rights to speech, religion, assembly, and privacy. Yet much of the discussion of liberty interests in due process analyses involves the interest in persons' good names, reputations, honor, and integrity. For example, stigmatizing statements made by college and university officials about faculty members may damage their reputations enough to implicate liberty interests. If the damages were to harm the faculty members' ability to obtain employment or other lucrative opportunities, then the injured parties may have successful due process claims.

Property interests for faculty and staff can also be found in employment contracts. Moreover, when contracts are terminated, property rights are implicated, because employees who are in the middle of employment contracts have legitimate claims as to the salary and benefits attached to their jobs. Therefore, when college or university officials terminate contracts, they would, indeed, implicate property rights.

The Supreme Court's analysis in *Board of Regents of State College v. Roth* (1972) offers a fine explanation of liberty and property. In *Roth,* the Court held that university officials did not violate the due process rights of a nontenured faculty member when they chose not to renew his contract after it expired. Concerning the liberty interests at stake in *Roth,* the Court explained that because in not rehiring the faculty member they did not make any charges against him that might have seriously damaged his standing and associations in his community, his good name, reputation, honor, and integrity were not at stake. The Court added that the dismissal did not impose a stigma on the faculty member that foreclosed his freedom to take advantage of other employment opportunities.

With respect to the property interest, the Supreme Court observed that because the faculty member's contract had expired, leaving him no legitimate entitlement to property, the actions of university officials did not impair his reputation or his ability to obtain employment elsewhere. In contrast, in *Perry v. Sindermann* (1972), the Court affirmed that a faculty member who had been employed for 10 years on successive one-year contracts had a legitimate property interest and was denied due process when his contract was not renewed without an opportunity for a hearing. According to the Court, having such a written contract that included an explicit tenure provision was clearly evidence of a formal understanding in support of the faculty member's claim of entitlement to continued employment unless officials could demonstrate sufficient cause to dismiss him from his position. The Court also pointed out that the absence of such an explicit provision in an employment contract may not always foreclose the possibility that faculty members have property interests in their positions. In this context, statements made by administrators, whether in writing or in oral conversation, for example, even outside the explicit terms of contract, may be enough to create a property right.

The Amount of Due Process

The second due process question to be asked considers the amount of process that is due in the event that the actions of university decision makers implicate the due process rights of faculty members. The level or amount of procedural due process afforded depends directly on the severity of the deprivation or loss. For example, the nonrenewal of a contract such as in *Roth* requires less formal process than the termination of employment, because the loss of liberty and property would be noticeably higher in cases of dismissal, especially if a firing were for some wrongdoing such as academic misconduct or sexual harassment of a student. Traditionally, courts distinguish between due process for discipline, which is formal, and due process for academic decisions, which is more often less formal and in which courts grant deferential treatment to decision makers in higher education under the doctrine of academic abstention. However, when contract termination is involved, due process generally tends to be detailed and formal.

To answer the question of how much process is due, courts engage in a balancing of rights. On one hand, courts examine the interests of the faculty members or staff affected by allegedly adverse employment actions, because the interests impacted in dismissals are more substantial than those involving the nonrenewal of contracts. On the other hand, courts also look at the interests of colleges or universities. In an example of a denial of tenure, institutional interests may include academic integrity, academic standards, and deference to the expertise of faculty committees that offered negative recommendations and reviews of the affected faculty member. As to dismissals for disciplinary infractions, institutional interests may include safety of students and staff, appropriate public responses, and consistency of policy application from one case to the next.

In this overall balance, it is important to consider the risk of wrongful deprivation of due process rights of those whose employment is at stake. For instance, if university officials were to

fail to afford procedural due process and then erroneously terminate the employment of a faculty member, they will undoubtedly have violated the person's rights to due process. The provision of procedural due process, which ensures that all sides of a story are heard, minimizes this risk. In cases of employment termination, due process usually entails notice of the reasons for the dismissals and meaningful opportunities to be heard in the presence of fair and impartial third-party decision makers. The hearings are most often formal, allowing faculty members or staff persons the opportunity to present witnesses and evidence to fact-finding committees or appeals panels before considering whether to pursue judicial relief.

Alternatives to Termination

Employment termination is, of course, not the only option available to college and university officials. Usually outlined in specific institutional policies, disciplinary options available to officials include written reprimands, restitution, reassignment of duties, denials of merit raises, suspension without pay and/or benefits, and demotion in rank or salary. Sometimes, institutional policies adopt systems of "progressive discipline" where, barring extreme or egregious incidents, a single instance of misconduct usually results in a written reprimand, and penalties increase only on successive infractions involving the same employee. These policies might also include definitions or examples of misconduct that could result in dismissals. Policies might list activities such as neglect of duty, incompetence, unprofessional conduct, insubordination, and immorality as grounds for contract termination. These grounds should be sufficiently defined so as to guide conduct of faculty members, staff, and administrators. Moreover, policies should include a general phrase such as "other good or just cause," because it is all but impossible to identify all forms of inappropriate employee behavior in advance.

Courts most often grant college and university officials deference in the administration of their policies as long as the definitions are not vague or overbroad and the application of policies is not arbitrary, capricious, reckless, or in bad faith. Examples of terminable conduct on the part of faculty members and staff include a lack of collegiality, harassment, refusal to follow reasonable rules and regulations, intellectual dishonesty, concealed and exploited conflicts of interest, neglect of job responsibilities, and lack of competency in teaching and research (Beckham, 2005).

Advance Notice

Due process is important not only once decisions to terminate employment are made but also well in advance of such judgments. To this end, dismissals for repeated failures to follow rules and regulations may not be warranted if faculty members or staff persons never received notice of their original failures or opportunities to correct their behaviors. This example assumes that each failure was not extreme in and of itself, but the collection of misdeeds was substantial enough to warrant dismissal. Such a situation might arise; for example, a faculty member's failure to submit grading materials at the end of a semester may not be a terminable offense, but not having done so after several semesters of requests may be sufficient to warrant dismissal. On the other hand, a single instance of sexually harassing conduct with a student could be sufficient for dismissal without more evidence justifying, if possible, an individual's behavior. In any event, due process demands that college and university officials offer employees notice of alleged rule violations and, where possible, opportunities to correct their behavior.

Another situation where advance notice of rules violations or employment deficiencies is important for due process is annual reviews of employee performances. This is important because college and university officials typically employ some practice of annual review for faculty members and staff such as those used during probationary periods for individuals who are on the tenure track. Often, faculty members on probationary tenure track appointments are involved in mentoring programs and have senior colleagues visit their classrooms to give feedback on job performance. In addition, annual reviews and merit reviews ordinarily involve committees of senior faculty who review work performance. Without a process in place to guide such performance, such as annual suggestions for improvement of teaching, research, or service, the ability of university officials to defend the denial of tenure several years later is greatly diminished.

Negative summative evaluation without decent, detailed formative evaluation could be met with successful legal challenges if officials render adverse tenure decisions at a later date.

Dismissals Not for Cause

Not all contract dismissals are targeted to misconduct on the part of faculty members and staff. In some cases, dismissal is necessary due to financial exigency, loss of program funding, reconfigurations, or other program cuts. Under these circumstances, due process is still important and necessary, because property interests are still implicated even if liberty interests are not. Aware of these principles, college and university officials should draft institutional policies to afford due process to those who may be affected by such reductions in force. Of course, these policies should also be kept up-to-date by periodic reviews. It is important that college and university officials apply financial exigency policies and other reduction-in-force provisions closely. Finally, readers should consult their institutional policies for the due process provisions contained therein regardless of whether they are dealing with dismissals for cause or not for cause.

Patrick D. Pauken

See also Academic Abstention; *Board of Regents of State Colleges v. Roth*; Due Process, Substantive and Procedural; Equal Protection Analysis; Fourteenth Amendment; *Perry v. Sindermann*; *Regents of the University of Michigan v. Ewing*

Further Readings

Beckham, J. (2005). Faculty. In J. Beckham & D. Dagley (Eds.), *Contemporary issues in higher education law* (pp. 89–130). Dayton, OH: Education Law Association.

Legal Information Institute. (n.d.). *Due process.* Retrieved from http://topics.law.cornell.edu/wex/due_process

Regents of the University of Michigan v. Ewing, 474 U.S. 214 (1985).

Legal Citations

Board of Regents of State College v. Roth, 408 U.S. 564 (1972).

Perry v. Sindermann, 408 U.S. 593 (1972).

E

EDUCATIONAL MALPRACTICE

Educational malpractice is a tort cause of action. Essentially, a claim of educational malpractice asserts that educational institutions and their employees breached their duty to educate plaintiffs adequately. Although educational malpractice has been the subject of much scholarly commentary (see, for example, DeMitchell & DeMitchell, 2003), it has been almost universally rejected by the judiciary. As one federal court observed, the theory is "beloved by commentators, but not the courts" (*Ross v. Creighton University*, 1990, p. 1327). On the whole, courts have rejected causes of action for educational malpractice against colleges and universities. However, courts have recognized charges of breach of contract against educational institutions when plaintiffs demonstrate that educational institutions failed to carry out specific promises. In light of the legal concerns arising under educational malpractice, this entry gives an overview of judicial reasoning on educational malpractice, briefly discusses the influence of malpractice claims in elementary and secondary education, and then examines the application of this tort to colleges and universities.

Reasons for Judicial Rejection of Educational Malpractice Claims

Courts generally reject educational malpractice claims for one of three reasons. First, it is very difficult to define the duty to educate, a necessary predicate for pursuing a cause of action. In general, the courts have not recognized claims of malpractice that rest on an assertion of the general inadequacy in educational programs, although they have recognized charges for breach of contract against educational institutions when claims are pleaded with particularity. Second, causation is also difficult to determine. In fact, it is almost impossible to identify all of the reasons why students fail to achieve specified levels of education; the causes could be "physical, neurological, emotional, cultural [or] environmental (*Peter W. v. San Francisco Unified School District*, 1976, p. 861). Further, the persons responsible for the failure to educate could include teachers, parents, or students themselves. Thus, the courts have acknowledged the difficulty of determining whether officials or other parties, including the students, may have caused the bad educational outcomes. Third, some courts have indicated a strong reluctance to insert themselves into such a contentious issue of public policy as the quality of education. The courts almost universally express strong public policy concerns as a basis for rejecting causes of action for educational malpractice against colleges and universities. The judiciary has also expressed the fear that recognizing a cause of action for educational malpractice would open a floodgate of litigation, particularly at the level of primary and secondary schools, but also in higher education.

Educational Malpractice Claims Against Public Schools

Although numerous cases have been decided in the context of elementary and secondary education, two leading suits that have been influential in setting a strong judicial trend against recognizing a cause of action for educational malpractice in higher education are worth reviewing.

In *Peter W. v. San Francisco Unified School District* (1976), a high school graduate sued his school board for failing to educate him properly during the 12 years he attended its schools. The student claimed, for example, that he could only read at the fifth-grade level and was unqualified for any kind of skilled job that required an ability to read and write.

An appellate court in California affirmed the rejection of the student's educational malpractice claim, finding it almost impossible to articulate a standard of care for the purpose of defining the school board's duty to educate. "Unlike the activity of the highway or the marketplace," the court observed, "classroom methodology affords no readily acceptable standards of care, or cause, [or] injury" (p. 860). The court also acknowledged its strong reluctance to recognize a tort that would have exposed school boards to massive litigation. The court thought that holding boards to an actionable duty of care would have exposed them to suits from "disaffected students and parents in countless numbers" (p. 861). Moreover, the court rejected the plaintiff's claims for fraud and intentional misrepresentation.

Likewise, in *Donohue v. Copiague Union Free School District* (1979), New York's highest court rejected the tort of educational malpractice on public policy grounds. While the court was confident that a workable standard of care could have been established for educational malpractice, it feared that recognizing such a cause of action "would constitute blatant interference with the responsibility for the administration of the public school system lodged by Constitution and statute in school administrative agencies" (p. 1354).

Educational Malpractice Claims Against Colleges and Universities

Plaintiffs have filed suits for educational malpractice against colleges and universities with little success. Perhaps the leading case on the topic is *Ross v. Creighton University* (1992), a decision of the Seventh Circuit.

Ross v. Creighton University

In *Ross*, a high school student with an "academically disadvantaged background" accepted an athletic scholarship to study at Creighton University and to play on its varsity basketball team. Although he studied at the university from 1978 until 1982, he left there with the language skills of a fourth grader and the reading skills of a seventh grader. Creighton paid for a year of remedial education at a school in Chicago, where he attended classes with grade school students. Ross then attended a university in Chicago, but he was forced to withdraw for financial reasons.

Ross sued Creighton for educational malpractice, negligent admission, and negligent infliction of emotional distress. The plaintiff also claimed that Creighton officials breached their contract to provide him with meaningful educational opportunities in exchange for his promise to play varsity basketball for the university. After a federal trial court dismissed his suit, Ross appealed.

Citing a host of precedents from other jurisdictions, including *Peter W.* and *Donohue*, the Seventh Circuit reasoned that the state of Illinois, where Ross brought suit, would reject a cause of action for educational malpractice. The court cited problems with defining a standard of care and determining causation, expressing major public policy concerns about recognizing a tort that would embroil the judiciary in the day-to-day operational actions of educational institutions. This last concern was particularly troubling in the university setting, because the court pointed out that "it necessarily implicates considerations of academic freedom and autonomy" (p. 415). Similarly, the court rejected Ross's negligent admission claim, in which he argued that university officials had a duty to admit only students who were reasonably qualified and able to perform academically. The court saw serious public policy problems with recognizing a tort for negligent admission.

The Seventh Circuit next rejected Ross's claim for negligent infliction of emotional distress. Because it had already refused to recognize a cause of action for negligent conduct, the court maintained that the claim for negligent infliction of emotional distress must be dismissed as well.

Turning to Ross's breach of contract charge, the court observed that he could not repackage his educational malpractice claim as one for breach of contract if he was simply attacking the university's general quality of education. However, the court decided that Ross had alleged a violation of a specific promise to provide specified academic services to him so that he could participate in a meaningful way in the university's academic program. Accordingly, the Seventh Circuit ruled that Ross's "specific and narrow claim that he was barred from *any* participation in and benefit from the University's academic program" could be resolved by the trial court "without second-guessing the professional judgment of the University faculty on academic matters" (p. 417). The court thus remanded the breach of contract claim to the trial court for further adjudication.

Other Educational Malpractice Suits Against Colleges and Universities

In addition to *Ross,* other plaintiffs filed educational malpractice suits against colleges and universities with courts dismissing virtually all of the claims. For instance, at issue in *Blane v. Alabama Commercial College* (1991) was an educational loan that a woman took out to enroll in a computer and clerical course at a for-profit business college. The woman charged that college officials offered a course to provide her with the skills she would need to compete in the computer and clerical job market but that after completing the course, she was unable to find employment in those fields. In her suit, the woman sued the college for fraud, breach of contract, and educational malpractice. Affirming an earlier dismissal of the claims, the Supreme Court of Alabama agreed that because there was no evidence that college officials guaranteed her a job, the woman could not file suit for fraud or breach of contract. As for her educational malpractice claim, the court refused to recognize such a cause of action.

In *Hendricks v. Clemson University* (2003), the Supreme Court of South Carolina refused to recognize a negligence claim that a former student filed against his university for erroneous advice that he received from an academic advisor. As a result of the advisor's mistake, the student was unable to obtain NCAA eligibility to play varsity baseball. The court declined to recognize a duty of care flowing from academic advisors to students, citing educational malpractice cases from other jurisdictions (including *Peter W.* and *Ross*).

Previously, the Supreme Court of Kansas rejected claims by former students against their university for allegedly violating state consumer protection law by falsely stating in its catalog that its court reporting program was accredited. In addition, the plaintiffs brought claims against the university for the allegedly poor quality of the court reporting program. In rejecting both claims, the court decided that there was no evidence that the plaintiffs relied on the university's inaccurate statement about the court reporting program's accreditation status (*Finstad v. Washburn University of Topeka,* 1993). As for the claims that the program was inadequately conducted and supervised, the court characterized the allegations as educational malpractice, a cause of action that it refused to recognize.

In *Miller v. Loyola University of New Orleans* (2002), a law student sued a university for negligence and breach of contract based on the manner in which a faculty member taught a course. The student charged that the instructor failed to order course materials in a timely manner, that she changed the course time without the permission of law school officials, that she had students make class presentations on subjects she was obligated to teach, that she gave a final examination that consisted partly of materials from the National Conference of Bar Examiners, and that her original questions contained errors. After law school officials looked into the allegations, concluding that at least some of them had merit, the student filed suit, seeking to recover the cost of taking the course and reimbursement for the cost of taking the course a second time from a different instructor. An appellate court affirmed the rejection of all of the student's claims, declaring flatly that "Louisiana law does not recognize a cause of action for educational malpractice under contract or tort law" (p. 1061). The court also rejected the claim against the university for unjust enrichment and the claim of detrimental reliance.

Other courts have rejected educational malpractice claims regardless of whether they were filed as breach of contract or tort actions. Even so, in this regard, courts have shown themselves willing to entertain breach of contract actions against educational institutions when students were able to show that the institutions breached specific promises that qualified as contractual obligations. For example, in *Till v. Delta School of Commerce* (1986), a student successfully sued her for-profit business college after she enrolled based on representations that she would receive a degree in accounting that would have been equivalent to a two-year associate's degree from a college or university and that the degree would have been transferable to another college or university. Later, the student learned that she would receive a degree in occupational studies, not accounting, and that admission to another college or university was at the option of the transferee school. At some point, the student was dismissed from the school, allegedly for "excessive tardiness and attitude problems" (p. 182).

The student then successfully sued the college for restitution of the tuition she paid. On further review, an appellate court in Louisiana affirmed in favor of the student. The panel was satisfied that the trial record provided a basis for concluding that the student had not received the educational opportunities that led her to enroll at the school. The court added that a degree in occupational studies was not even listed in the school's catalog at the time the student enrolled.

Educational Malpractice Suit Against an Accrediting Association

Along with suits against colleges, universities, and for-profit vocational schools, at least one educational malpractice action has been filed against an accrediting association. *Ambrose v. New England Association of Colleges and Schools* (NEACE) (2001) was filed by seven former students against NEACE, the accrediting association for Thomas College, the institution where they obtained associate degrees in "medical assisting." The plaintiffs enrolled in the medical assisting program expecting it to qualify them for entry-level positions as medical assistants. According to the court, the medical assisting program had no clinical component. Because clinical tasks form a large part of a medical assistant's job, six of the seven plaintiffs were unable to find employment as medical assistants. The seventh plaintiff obtained a job but lost it due her inadequate knowledge and training.

In their suit, the plaintiffs charged NEACE with fraud, misrepresentation, and deceptive business practices based on the association's accreditation of the college. On further review of the dismissal of all of the students' claims, the First Circuit affirmed in favor of the defendants. In essence, the court observed that the misrepresentation claims were for negligent accreditation, a cause of action that it refused to entertain. In the court's view, there were strong policy arguments against recognizing such a cause of action, including "the lack of a satisfactory standard of care by which to evaluate professional judgments and the patent undesirability of having courts attempt to assess the efficacy of the operations of academic institutions" (p. 499). On just such policy grounds, the panel noted, courts rejected students' claims of educational malpractice against schools.

Richard Fossey

See also Catalogs as Contracts

Further Readings

DeMitchell, Todd A., & DeMitchell, Terri A. (2003). Statutes and standards: Has the door to educational malpractice been opened? *Brigham Young University of Education and Law Journal, 2003,* 485–518.

Legal Citations

Ambrose v. New England Association of Schools and Colleges, 252 F.3d 488 (1st Cir. 2001).

Blane v. Alabama Commercial College, 585 So. 2d 866 (Ala. 1991).

Donohue v. Copiague Union Free School District, 391 N.E.2d 1352 (N.Y. 1979).

Finstad v. Washburn University of Topeka, 845 P.2d 685 (Kan. 1993).

Hendricks v. Clemson University, 578 S.E.2d 711 (S.C. 2003).

Miller v. Loyola University of New Orleans, 829 So. 2d 1057 (La. Ct. App. 2002).

Peter W. v. San Francisco Unified School District, 131 Cal. Rptr. 854 (Cal. Ct. App. 1976).

Ross v. Creighton University, 740 F. Supp. 1319 (N.D. Ill. 1990), *aff'd,* 957 F.2d 410 (7th Cir. 1992).

Till v. Delta School of Commerce, 487 So. 2d 180 (La. Ct. App. 1986).

EDUCATION LAW ASSOCIATION

Established in 1954, the Education Law Association (ELA) is a 501(c)(3) nonprofit, nonadvocacy member association that seeks to improve education by promoting interest in and understanding of the legal framework of education as well as the rights of students, parents, school boards, and school employees. ELA's vision is to be known as the premier source of information on education law. Its mission statement reads as follows:

ELA brings together educational and legal scholars and practitioners to inform and advance educational policy and practice through knowledge of the law. Together, our professional community anticipates trends in educational law and supports scholarly research through the highest-value print and electronic publications, conferences, and professional forums. (ELA, 2009)

Beginnings

In the mid-1940s, at the urging of Frank Heinisch, an attorney from Omaha, Nebraska, Madaline Kinter Remmlein, then an employee of the National Education Association (NEA), asked NEA leadership to establish a department on school law issues at the NEA. However, her request was denied due to a perception of a lack of interest in such a topic. Edward C. Bolmeier, president of Duke University, and Lee O. Garber, professor at the University of Pennsylvania, suggested to Remmlein that they create a school law organization independent of the NEA.

In February 1954, school law research appeared for the first time as one of the topics for a roundtable discussion at the annual convention of the American Educational Research Association (AERA). The eight discussants' report urged organizing a school law national conference in order to facilitate communication between school law specialists and their colleagues. In the meanwhile, Garber's suggestion of forming a school law organization for the exchange of ideas in the school law newsletter that he wrote garnered significant support.

In June 1954, the first school law conference took place at Duke University due, in large part, to Bolmeier's influence. During the proceedings of the conference, what would soon be known as the National Organization on Legal Problems of Education (NOLPE) emerged as an independent organization. Its membership of 57 came from the District of Columbia and 15 states: Alabama, Delaware, Georgia, Maryland, Massachusetts, Missouri, Nebraska, New Jersey, New York, North Carolina, Ohio, Pennsylvania, South Carolina, Virginia, and West Virginia. Remmlein became NOLPE's first chairman. The support for the running of the organization during the organizational year came from dues, which amounted to the grand sum of $1.00, and NEA's research division provided clerical help (Remmlein, 1966).

In order to spread its membership across the country, NOLPE sent out invitations addressed to its members, to Duke conference attendees who did not join the organization, to school administrators from the 100 largest school districts in the country, and to 70 officers of state board associations, 103 deans of law schools, and 100 deans of schools of education and presidents of teacher-training institutions. Within six weeks of its creation, the "buddy system" (Remmlein, 1966, pp. 2–3) NOLPE used to promote membership succeeded in increasing its membership number to 205, with representatives from 40 states, the District of Columbia, and Guam. More than one-fifth were lawyers connected with school affairs or law schools; more than one-fifth were county or city school superintendents; one-third were professors of educational administration; and the remaining were educators on the staffs of state departments of education, the federal Department of Education, the National Education Association, and state education associations. In addition, NOLPE asked many organizations, such as the National School Boards Association, the American Association of School Administrators, AERA, and NEA to announce its creation.

A committee of four members—Lehan Tunks, dean of the law school at Rutgers University; Edward Bolmeier; Ward Keesecker; and O. H. English, a school superintendent in Pennsylvania—framed a tentative constitution, which they submitted to the membership for criticism. In September 1954, the members were asked to vote for one of two options with regard to the constitution: One was to adopt it, another was to suggest changes and defer adoption until the first annual business meeting, and a third was against adoption. The overwhelming majority responded in favor of adopting the constitution, while 47 members suggested changes to clarify ambiguities in the text. The committee made the changes and notified the members of these changes, and the constitution was immediately adopted.

For the selection of the first executive board, all members had the opportunity to name their choices for president, secretary-treasurer, and each of four spots on the executive committee. The four executive members represented different categories of members: faculty members of schools of education and teacher training institutions, law school faculty members, professional staffs of elementary and secondary school systems, and those otherwise engaged in educational activities of official or advisory natures.

On January 3, 1955, the following results were announced: Madaline Kinter Remmlein, president; Lee O. Garber, secretary-treasurer; Edward C. Bolmeier, executive committee member to represent schools of education and teacher training institutions; Robert R. Hamilton, executive committee member to represent law-school faculties; Nolan D. Pulliam, executive committee member to represent professional staffs of elementary or secondary school systems; and Edgar Fuller, executive committee member to represent those otherwise engaged in educational activities of an official or advisory nature. The terms of service were one year, with the exception of that of the secretary-treasurer, who was to serve three years. The board hired an executive director; one longtime executive director (1962–1982) was Marion McGhehey, who also served as the head of the Kansas School Boards Association (Remmlein, 1966).

NOLPE had four standing committees: research, publications, membership, and relationships with other disciplines. The president appointed the chairs of each committee with the approval of the executive board. NOLPE published a quarterly newsletter that contained digests of important cases, and relationships with other organizations were established. The first annual meeting took place in fall of 1955 at the University of Chicago, with 50 participants representing 17 states.

Organizational Maturity

In 1997, NOLPE changed its name to ELA and moved its headquarters from Topeka, Kansas, to the campus of the University of Dayton in Dayton, Ohio, where it is affiliated with the University of Dayton's School of Education and Allied Professions. ELA has come a long way since its modest beginnings. Yet ELA still serves three divergent constituency groups from across the country: attorneys, professors, and school administrators. Since its inception, the ELA's common goal has been to stay informed and up-to-date on laws that are shaping the educational future in the United States by providing unbiased information about current legal issues affecting education and the rights of those involved in education in both public and private K–12 schools, universities, and colleges. ELA membership has grown to a robust size of more than 1,200 members who include faculty in schools of education and law, public and private school administrators and teachers, administrators, school board members, attorneys, staff members of state and federal education agencies, government officials, and state and federal professional associations.

ELA is governed by the board of directors, which consists of the president, president-elect, vice president, immediate past president, and nine directors. The executive committee, which comprises the president, president-elect, vice president, immediate past president, and executive director (ex officio) has ultimate responsibility in the administration and supervision of ELA activities, including the authority to enter into contracts on behalf of ELA. Each office is held by a different person, who must be a member of ELA. The nominating committee selects the slate of candidates for vice president and directors for election at the annual meeting. The slate is announced prior to the election, and at the meeting additional nominations are accepted from the floor. The president appoints an elections subcommittee to count the ballots, and the nominees with the highest numbers of votes are elected to office.

At the conclusion of the president's term of office, the president-elect automatically assumes the office of president, at which time the vice president automatically assumes the office of the president-elect. ELA members elect the vice president at the annual business meeting of the membership. Eligible candidates must be current ELA members who have completed at least one year on the ELA board of directors. Each officer serves a one-year term starting at the time of the election, while directors serve three-year terms. In addition, ELA has four standing committees: Membership

Committee, Publications Committee, Convention Program Committee, and Nominating Committee. Last, ELA has the following committees: McGhehey Award Committee, Joseph C. Beckham Dissertation of the Year Committee, Professional Partnership Committee, Ambassadors Committee, Seminar Committee, Education Law Into Practice (ELIP) Committee, Development Committee, Steven S. Goldberg Award for Distinguished Scholarship in Education Law Committee, and George Jay Joseph Education Law Writing Award Committee.

For more than 50 years, the ELA has hosted an annual conference each year with as many as 350 people attending. The ELA annual conference provides an opportunity for members and education law professionals to stay abreast of current issues and to network with peers from across the world. The conference's format is designed to stimulate dialogue among educational and legal scholars and practitioners to inform and advance educational policy and practice through knowledge of the law. This four-day event features experts from around the country speaking on a wide range of current topics. Themes in recent years included "*Brown* and ELA at 50: The Journey Continues" (2004); "The Courts, the Congress, and Education: A New Look at Accountability and Responsibility" (2005); "Accountability and Equal Opportunity on the Line" (2006); "Education and Society: Accountability, Safety, and Climate" (2007); "Relevance and Reform: Building the Bridge Between Theory and Practice" (2008); and "Education Law in a Time of Change: Federal, State, and Local Policy" (2009). In addition, the ELA sponsors regional seminars and webinars throughout the year.

Publications have also grown since the early beginnings. Currently, the ELA keeps its members informed of current cases, decisions, and relevant information by publishing monographs and books on a wide variety of topics within education law. Typically, ELA publishes three to four new titles and the *Yearbook of Education Law* annually. At the same time, the ELA publishes two newsletters: *ELA Notes* and the *School Law Reporter*.

ELA books and monographs provide thorough and authoritative analyses of issues in education law. Many of these publications contain practical suggestions and sample policies and forms that are useful to education administrators and to attorneys who practice education law. These publications cover a myriad of topics on education law, such as school discipline; special education; discrimination based on color, national origin, sex, and disability; implementation of the Educational Opportunities Act, Title IX, the No Child Left Behind Act, the Americans with Disabilities Act, and the Individuals with Disabilities Education Act; First Amendment issues; Fourth Amendment issues; and school violence. Some of the recent book and monograph titles include the following: *The Principal's Legal Handbook; Law of Student Expulsions and Suspensions; Legal Problems of Religious and Private Schools; Educational Finance Law: Constitutional Challenges to State Aid Plans—An Analysis of Strategies; Research Methods on Legal Issues; Sexual Orientation, Public Schools, and the Law; The Law of Teacher Evaluation; Death Threats by Students: The Law and Its Implications; Contemporary Issues in Higher Education Law; School Law for Busy Administrators;* and *Students, Colleges, and Disability Law.* Many of these publications are adopted as course texts in education law classrooms. On the other hand, the *Yearbook of Education Law,* which serves as a reference work, contains analyses of the previous year's federal and state court decisions affecting private and public elementary and secondary schools and higher education. Each volume covers all phases of education law and includes a detailed index and table of cases.

The ELA publishes the *School Law Reporter* monthly and *ELA Notes* quarterly. *The School Law Reporter* is a compilation of recent court decisions affecting education. Topics covered include elementary and secondary education (tort liability; students with disabilities; teacher and administrator employment; and dismissal, nonrenewal, and reductions in force), higher education (students, faculty members, and administrator employment), and the Supreme Court docket. *ELA Notes* keeps members informed on education-law-related conferences and seminars as well as on member activities. *ELA Notes* also contains reprints of articles from the special section of West's *Education Law Reporter* known as "Education Law Into Practice" or ELIP, shorter scholarly pieces focusing on practical issues in education law, letters to the editor, and new member updates, as well as supplemental articles that appear only in its online version.

Zorka Karanxha

Further Readings

Education Law Association. (2009). *About ELA.* Retrieved May 20, 2009, from http://educationlaw.org/aboutELA.php

Remmlein, M. K. (1966). *NOLPE: The first 10 years.* Retrieved May 18, 2009, from http://educationlaw.org/images/PDFs/NOLPE%20History.pdf

ELEVENTH AMENDMENT

Most state-supported institutions of higher education are considered to be arms of the state for purposes of the Eleventh Amendment. Consequently, an understanding of the Eleventh Amendment and the U.S. Supreme Court's interpretation of it is particularly important for higher education attorneys, administrators, and legal scholars when confronted by the threat of litigation.

Essentially, "sovereign immunity of the states" means that private individuals or corporations cannot sue the states, state agencies, state institutions, or state officials in their official capacities. Therefore, if state colleges and universities are considered "arms of the state," then both the entities and their administrators generally are immune from litigation. Yet, contrary to popular belief, sovereign immunity does not mean that the states may violate federal law, that federal law is inapplicable to the states, or that the federal government cannot enforce federal law. Rather, sovereign immunity simply prevents *private parties* from enforcing certain federal claims against states. Sovereign immunity does not bar a suit by the federal government or another state. By ratifying the Constitution, the states surrendered their sovereign immunity for these claims.

Moreover, even with respect to private parties, sovereign immunity is not absolute. There are three exceptions. First, as discussed in more detail below, Congress may abrogate sovereign immunity in some limited circumstances—notably whenever a statutory claim also involves a violation of the Fourteenth Amendment. Second, a state—in the exercise of its sovereignty—may choose to waive its sovereign immunity for certain claims. However, such waivers must be clear and unambiguous and may include limitations as to both the amount that can be recovered and the forum where suits must be brought. Third, under the doctrine of a 1908 U.S. Supreme Court case, *Ex Parte Young*, private parties generally—but not always—can obtain an injunction to stop state officials from engaging in ongoing violations of *federal* law. The *Young* doctrine rests on the theory that no state would violate federal law, and any official who does so is no longer acting as the state, but is in fact a rogue officer who must be stopped. The availability of injunctive relief under the *Young* doctrine effectively means that sovereign immunity is limited to damages claims. As long as private parties are able to enforce a federal law, the parties will be able to obtain injunctive relief.

Under the terms of the Eleventh Amendment "the Judicial power of the United States shall not be construed to extend to any suit in law or equity commenced or prosecuted against one of the United States by Citizens of another State, or by Citizens or Subjects of any Foreign State." In the past, many scholars and the Supreme Court itself used the term "Eleventh Amendment immunity" to describe this immunity. Yet "sovereign immunity" is the more accurate term. As the Supreme Court recently observed,

> the sovereign immunity of the States neither derives from nor is limited by the terms of the Eleventh Amendment. Rather, as the Constitution's structure, and its history, and the authoritative interpretations by this Court make clear, the States' immunity from suit is a fundamental aspect of the sovereignty which the States enjoyed before the ratification of the Constitution, and which they retain today. (*Alden v. Maine,* 1999, p. 713)

Early History

In the founding years of the United States, there was widespread acceptance of the proposition that states had immunity from private suits. In 1793, the Supreme Court held in *Chisholm v. Georgia* that private citizens from one state could sue another state. In reaction, and almost immediately,

Congress passed and the states subsequently ratified the Eleventh Amendment, effectively overturning *Chisholm*.

While the text of the Eleventh Amendment is limited to the concerns raised in those ratification debates, the Eleventh Amendment confirms a much broader proposition, namely that the states are immune from suits. It is important to note that sovereign immunity does not exist solely in order to prevent judgments in federal courts from being paid out of state treasuries. Instead, the Eleventh Amendment allows the states to avoid being subjected to "the indignity of . . . the coercive process of judicial tribunals at the instance of private parties" (*Puerto Rico Aqueduct & Sewer Authority v. Metcalfe & Eddy*, 1993, p. 146).

The immunity confirmed by the Eleventh Amendment, then, bars suits against the states by Indian tribes, foreign nations, and corporations created by the national government. Moreover, the Eleventh Amendment applies to proceedings in state court, federal administrative proceedings, admiralty proceedings, and situations where state treasuries are not implicated.

Changing Standards

The long history of the Eleventh Amendment notwithstanding, there was a period when the Supreme Court created so many exceptions that it effectively nullified sovereign immunity. In 1976, the Court reasoned that Congress could abolish states' sovereign immunity by exercising its powers to enforce the Fourteenth Amendment, which allows the federal government to intervene if states abridge the rights of U.S. citizens. In 1989, the Court extended that holding in declaring that Congress could use any of its powers to limit state sovereign immunity, thereby giving it virtually unlimited power to strip the states of their sovereign immunity. Not surprisingly, Congress took advantage of these rulings and proceeded to cancel state sovereign immunity for most federal statutes.

All of this changed in 1996, in *Seminole Tribe v. Florida*, when the Supreme Court reversed itself in ruling that congressional power to abrogate sovereign immunity was limited to its efforts to enforce the Fourteenth Amendment. Although this case was constitutionally significant in that it technically limited congressional power to nullify

sovereign immunity, it had little practical effect, because at the time, congressional powers to enforce the Fourteenth Amendment were almost unlimited. Consequently, Congress could still abrogate sovereign immunity for most federal statutes.

A year later, in *City of Boerne v. Flores* (1997), the Supreme Court imposed significant limitations on the power of Congress to enforce the Fourteenth Amendment. *Flores* declares that Congress may enforce only the actual substantive guarantees of the Fourteenth Amendment, which include equal protection of the laws, the privileges or immunities of national citizenship, and due process.

When *Flores* and *Seminole Tribe* are combined, congressional abrogation of sovereign immunity becomes extremely difficult. In order to have a valid abrogation, Congress must first make a specific finding that states are violating the substantive guarantees of the Constitution. Once there are such findings, Congress must then demonstrate that abrogation of sovereign immunity for a particular class of claims is a proportionate response to the violations.

Recent Application

Recent Supreme Court cases—particularly those involving higher education—illustrate the points made above. For example, in *Florida Prepaid v. College Savings Bank* (1999), the Court decided that Congress could not abrogate sovereign immunity for intellectual property claims. In *Kimel v. Florida Board of Regents* (2000), the Court noted that Congress could not abrogate sovereign immunity for Age Discrimination in Employment Act claims. In 2001, in *Board of Trustees of the University of Alabama v. Garrett,* the Court pointed out that Congress could not abrogate sovereign immunity for employment claims under the Americans with Disabilities Act. In 2002, in *Federal Maritime Commission v. South Carolina State Ports Authority,* the Court maintained that sovereign immunity extended not only to judicial proceedings but to federal administrative proceedings.

In the final years of the Rehnquist Court, the justices suddenly became reluctant to expand sovereign immunity. In 2003, in *Nevada Department of Human Resources v. Hibbs,* the Court observed that sovereign immunity was abrogated for family care provisions of the Family and Medical Leave

Act. In 2004, in *Tennessee Student Assistance Corp. v. Hood*, the Court noted that sovereign immunity did not bar an action against a higher education entity to discharge a student loan. That same year, in *Tennessee v. Lane*, the Court held that sovereign immunity had been abrogated for claims under Title II of the Americans with Disabilities Act that involved the fundamental constitutional right of access to the courts. This reluctance continued during the first term of the Roberts Court. In *United States v. Georgia* (2006), the Court unanimously determined that Congress could abrogate sovereign immunity for a claim under Title II of the Americans with Disabilities Act that was also a constitutional claim. In effect, the Court held that Congress always could abrogate sovereign immunity for claims that involve actual Fourteenth Amendment violations.

Finally, in *Central Virginia Community College v. Katz* (2006), the Court declared that by ratifying the Constitution, the states had surrendered their sovereign immunity "in proceedings necessary to effectuate the in rem jurisdiction of the bankruptcy courts." As a practical matter, this means that the states may be subjected to suits to recover alleged preferential transfers. However, the Court did not address the immunity for other bankruptcy proceedings, such as a contract claim. Moreover, *Katz* should be understood not as an expansion of Congress's power to abrogate sovereign immunity, but as an expansion of the scope of sovereignty that was surrendered when the states ratified the Constitution.

William E. Thro

See also Federalism

Further Readings

College Savings Bank v. Florida Prepaid, 527 U.S. 666 (1999).

Noonan, J. T., Jr. (2002). *Narrowing the nation's power: The Supreme Court sides with the states.* Berkeley: University of California Press.

Thro, W. E. (1999). The Eleventh Amendment revolution in the lower federal courts. *Journal of College & University Law, 25,* 501–526.

Thro, W. E. (2000). The education lawyer's guide to the sovereign immunity revolution. *Education Law Reporter, 146,* 951–981.

Thro, W. E. (2007). The future of sovereign immunity. *Education Law Reporter, 215,* 1–31.

Thro, W. E. (2007). *Why you cannot sue State U: A guide to sovereign immunity* (2nd ed.). Washington, DC: National Association of College University Attorneys.

Legal Citations

Alden v. Maine, 527 U.S. 706, 713 (1999).

Board of Trustees of the University of Alabama v. Garrett, 531 U.S. 356 (2001).

Central Virginia Community College v. Katz, 126 S. Ct. 990 (2006).

Chisholm v. Georgia, 2 U.S. (2 Dall.) 419 (1793).

City of Boerne v. Flores, 521 U.S. 507 (1997).

Ex Parte Young, 209 U.S. 123 (1908).

Federal Maritime Commission v. South Carolina State Ports Authority, 535 U.S. 743 (2002).

Florida Prepaid v. College Savings Bank, 527 U.S. 627 (1999).

Kimel v. Florida Board of Regents, 528 U.S. 62 (2000).

Nevada Department of Human Resources v. Hibbs, 538 U.S. 721 (2003).

Puerto Rico Aqueduct & Sewer Authority v. Metcalf & Eddy, 539 U.S. 139 (1993).

Seminole Tribe v. Florida, 517 U.S. 44 (1996).

Tennessee v. Lane, 541 U.S. 509 (2004).

Tennessee Student Assistance Corp. v. Hood, 541 U.S. 440 (2004)

United States v. Georgia, 126 S. Ct. 877 (2006).

EQUAL EDUCATIONAL OPPORTUNITIES ACT

The struggle for equality and nondiscrimination in education at all levels has a long history in the United States. Following *Brown v. Board of Education* (1954) and the ensuing civil rights struggles of the 1950s and 1960s, Congress passed Title VI of the Civil Rights Act of 1964, which prohibits discrimination based on race, color, age, creed, or national origin in any federally funded activity or program. In addition, the Fourteenth Amendment to the U.S. Constitution, adopted in 1868, declares that no state may deny any person the equal protection of the laws. This amendment protects the privileges of all citizens, provides equal protection under the law, and gives Congress the power to enforce this amendment through legislation.

In 1974, Congress enacted the Equal Educational Opportunities Act (EEOA) to champion the rights of all children to have equal educational opportunities. Insofar as the EEOA addresses the rights of students who may hope to continue their studies in colleges and universities, this entry reviews the act's background and impact in K–12 settings. While focusing largely on K–12 issues, this entry is designed to provide educators and others who are interested in higher education with the ability to understand how the EEOA might impact the rights of the students with whom they interact on their campuses.

Background

In 1968, the Department of Health, Education and Welfare (HEW), now the U.S. Department of Education, which has authority to disseminate regulations prohibiting discrimination in federally assisted school systems, issued a guideline clarifying that school officials are responsible for ensuring that students are not denied educational opportunities that are equal to those of their peers due to their race, color, or national origin. Later, HEW issued a memorandum on May 25, 1970, in an attempt to clarify the responsibilities of school board officials to provide equal educational opportunities to English language learners under Title VI. According to the memorandum, programs for students whose English is less than proficient should be designed to teach them English as soon as possible. The memorandum added that this approach should be carried out in a meaningful way that affords students who are non-English speakers the academic and social language skills that they need to succeed in school and life. The memorandum further stipulated that school boards have the duty to communicate with parents regarding their children's education in a language the parents can understand. The memorandum also explained that students could not be placed in special education programs based solely on their inability to speak English.

In March 1972, President Nixon addressed the nation on two companion proposals. The proposals were aimed at providing the judiciary with a new and broader base on which to review future cases relating to equal educational opportunities, to place the emphasis on providing better education for all children, and to set forth alternatives to busing. The president's definition of equal educational opportunity set the stage for what in 1974 would become the EEOA. The alternatives to busing were intended to preserve "neighborhood" schools.

In its landmark decision on the rights of language minorities, the Supreme Court in *Lau v. Nichols* (1974) held that students with limited English proficiency (LEP) who were not provided with special programs to help them learn English were being denied their rights under Title VI of the Civil Rights Act of 1964. In *Lau*, the Court held that the San Francisco Unified School District should have provided instruction in English to non-English-speaking Chinese students or provided them with instruction in their native language. The Court also pointed out that merely providing students with the same facilities, textbooks, teachers, and curriculum does not constitute equal treatment. In other words, the Court reasoned that students who do not understand English are effectively foreclosed from any meaningful education. At the same time, the Court upheld HEW's 1970 memorandum as a valid interpretation of the requirements of Title VI. *Lau v. Nichols* was also important because it renewed interest in Nixon's proposal to focus on equal educational opportunity for all students.

Provisions of the Equal Educational Opportunities Act

Shortly after *Lau*, Congress passed the EEOA. This act, along with the Bilingual Education Act, was part of the 1974 amendments to the Elementary and Secondary Education Act. The EEOA affirms that no state shall deny educational opportunity based on race, color, sex, or national origin by engaging in deliberate segregation by an educational agency; failing to remedy deliberate segregation; assigning a student, other than to a school closest to his or her residence, that results in a greater degree of segregation of students on the basis of race, color, sex, or national origin; discriminating by an educational agency on the basis of race, color, or national origin in the employment of faculty or staff; transferring students from one school to another, voluntarily or otherwise, if the purpose and effect of doing so would have increased segregation on the basis of race, color, or national origin; or failing to take appropriate action to overcome language barriers that impede equal participation by its students in its instructional programs.

The EEOA allows individuals who have been denied equal educational opportunities to file civil suits in appropriate federal trial courts against such parties as may be appropriate. In addition, the attorney general of the United States may institute civil actions on behalf of individuals. However, this power is rarely implemented, because most challenges emanate from parents and advocacy organizations. Despite the intent of the law, the vague language of the EEOA has left it to the courts to decide and shape the concept of equality in education for LEP students. The constitutional issue is the right of national origin minorities to have equal educational opportunities, a question that is making its presence felt in many institutions of higher education, because a significant number of enrolling students are lacking in basic skills.

Litigation

In 1981, in *Castañeda v. Pickard* the Fifth Circuit established a three-prong test to evaluate whether educational officials have violated the rights of students who were LEP. The first prong inquires whether officials are pursuing a program informed by educational theory that is recognized by experts as sound. The second examines the steps that officials are taking to implement the approach, including whether they are providing the resources necessary to implement it effectively. The third question concerns whether, after a "legitimate trial" period, officials have examined the results of the program for results and modified it if results were not forthcoming. Furthermore, the court determined that students who are LEP should have not only the opportunity to learn English but also full access to the school system's educational program.

When evaluating programs for students who are LEP, the courts require educators to meet all three of *Castaneda's* prongs for both the teaching of English and the teaching of the entire curriculum. Although most courts relied on the *Castañeda* standard, the three-prong test is not without its judicial critics, as illustrated in *Teresa P. v. Berkeley*

Unified School District (1989). This case also raised the issue of discrimination against Mexican Americans in the hiring and promotion of teachers and administrators.

Using the *Castañeda* standard in *Keyes v. School District Number 1* (1983), the federal trial court in Colorado was of the opinion that traditional bilingual educational programs that taught English and provided understandable instruction in content areas was a sound educational theory. Nevertheless, the court remarked that the implementation system was inadequate due to a lack of emphasis on reading and writing, an apparent lack of regard for the curriculum needs of students who are LEP, and a lack of testing. Because school board officials had not provided the mandated program, the court did not address the third prong, holding that evaluating results at that point would be premature. The *Keyes* court decided that although the facts of the case did not require bilingual education as an exclusive means of access to students who were LEP, it might be required in specified circumstances. The court concluded that the issue was not whether bilingual programs were the least reparative manner for providing language instruction but whether the degree of separation is necessary to achieve the educational goal of the program in light of the fact that the students spoke Spanish.

State education agencies have been included in the enforcement of the EEOA. In 1982, in *United States v. State of Texas*, the Fifth Circuit required state education agencies to adopt guidelines regarding services provided to students who were LEP and to ensure that these guidelines were monitored and enforced. Previously the Ninth Circuit had posited, in *Idaho Migrant Council v. Board of Education* (1981), that state educational agencies have a duty to supervise local school boards to ensure compliance with federal mandates ensuring that the needs of students who are LEP are being met.

A current long-running case, *Flores v. Arizona,* was filed in the federal trial court in 1992 as parents and others alleged that state officials failed to provide students who were LEP with instruction making them proficient in English and enabling them to master the standard academic curriculum. In 2000, the court ruled that officials neither adequately funded the program nor provided enough teachers, paraprofessionals, classrooms, resources, or tutors for students who were LEP. The court thus ordered state officials to complete a cost study to establish the needed funding to implement programs for students who were LEP. As a result, the parties entered into a consent decree on nonmonetary issues, including a requirement that the state board and the department of education adopt rules and regulations for English language instruction, compensatory instruction, and monitoring by the department to ensure that students who were LEP had equal educational opportunities.

During the next phase of the litigation, in 2001, the cost study was released. However, because the study was of limited usefulness, the court ordered the state to provide adequate resources to educate students who were LEP by January 31, 2002, or by the end of any special session, whichever came first. After the legislature failed to appropriate sufficient funds, additional litigation ensued, culminating in the Ninth Circuit's ultimately affirming that the state of Arizona was required to fund programs for English language learners fully in order to comply with the EEOA. On further review in *Flores v. Arizona* (2009), the Supreme Court reversed and remanded the dispute for further consideration. In other words, the Court ruled that in light of legal and factual changes, such as Arizona's shift away from bilingual education to structured immersion for ELL students and changes mandated by the No Child Left Behind Act with regard to the finding and programs for these children that took place since the lower courts agreed that state officials violated the EEOA, the state was entitled to present its position that it was entitled to relief from those earlier judgments.

Since the enactment of the EEOA, litigation has addressed issues of proper identification of LEP students for services, oversight and monitoring of programs, teacher quality and training, and funding. As more litigation ensues, it appears that because local and state educational agencies have continued to fall short of providing adequate services to LEP students, the responsibility of better educating these students will be felt when they enter institutions of higher learning, from community colleges through research universities, because these students are very likely to need remedial instruction in order to ensure their access to equal educational opportunities.

Darlene Y. Bruner

See also Fourteenth Amendment; Title VI; U.S. Department of Education

Further Readings

Berenyi, J. R. (2008). "Appropriate action" inappropriately defined: Amending the Equal Educational Opportunities Act of 1974. *Washington and Lee Law Review, 65,* 639–674.

Nixon, R. (1972, March 16). Address to the nation on equal educational opportunities and school busing. *Public Papers, 90,* 425, 426.

Sorensen, G. P. (1998). Selected chronology of U.S. legislative and judicial documents enhancing equal educational opportunity for at-risk diverse learners in the last half-century. *Education Law Reporter, 124,* 17–19.

Legal Citations

Brown v. Board of Education, Topeka, 347 U.S. 483 (1954).

Castañeda v. Pickard, 648 F.2d 989 (5th Cir. 1981).

Equal Educational Opportunities Act, 20 U.S.C. § 1701 *et seq.*

Flores v. Arizona, 516 F.3d 1140 (9th Cir. 2008), *cert. granted,* 129 S. Ct. 893 (2009).

Idaho Migrant Council v. Board of Education, 647 F.2d 60 (9th Cir. 1981).

Keyes v. School District Number 1, 576 F. Supp. 1503 (D. Colo. 1983).

Lau v. Nichols, 414 U.S. 563 (1974).

Teresa P. v. Berkeley Unified School District, 724 F. Supp. 698, 713 (N.D. Cal. 1989)

Title VI of the Civil Rights Act of 1964, 42 U.S.C.A. § 2000 *et seq.*

United States v. State of Texas, 680 F.2d 356 (5th Cir. 1982).

Equal Employment Opportunity Commission

The Equal Employment Opportunity Commission (EEOC) is an agency of the United States government dedicated to eradicating unlawful inequity in the workplace. The commission is bipartisan; appointed by the president of the United States, five commissioners and a general counsel set policy and endorse legal actions to prevent discrimination based on age, national origin, race, religion, sex, and, beginning in November 2009, genetic information. For many years, EEOC staff attorneys have been litigating cases that have had a major impact on concepts, theories, and legal principles relating to higher education. In light of the impact that the EEOC has on American higher education, this entry examines how it impacts activities at colleges and universities.

The EEOC enforces a variety of federal laws, including the Equal Pay Act of 1963 (EPA), Title VII of the Civil Rights Act of 1964, the Age Discrimination in Employment Act of 1967 (ADEA), Sections 501 and 505 of the Rehabilitation Act of 1973, Titles I and V of the Americans with Disabilities Act of 1990 (ADA), the Civil Rights Act of 1991, and Title II of the Genetic Information Nondiscrimination Act of 2008. Some of these laws apply to private and public employers, educational institutions, and governments at both the state and local levels; others apply to American corporations operating overseas as well as multinational corporations operating in the United States; still others apply to the federal government itself.

Individuals can file charges alleging discrimination on the basis of race, color, religion, sex, national origin, disability, or age, and charges can include disparate impact, retaliation, harassment, or hostile work environment. After preliminary review to determine administrative eligibility, EEOC staff members investigate the matter by conducting equal protection analyses; if warranted, the staff members may recommend mediation or legal action.

In many ways, the history of the EEOC ties directly to the history of the civil rights movement of the 1960s. Consequently, some of the nation's most important advances dealing with affirmative action have come through EEOC-initiated litigation. From its establishment in July 1965, and throughout its history, the EEOC has been involved in groundbreaking litigation, much of it setting notable legal precedent. Furthermore, in some of the earlier cases in the 1960s, the role of the EEOC was secondary insofar as it filed so-called amicus curiae (literally, "friend of the court") briefs seeking to influence the outcome of litigation. The congressional desire for voluntary compliance with 1960s legislation designed to create an equitable work environment for all proved insufficient,

because employers continued to discriminate against workers. In response, the Congress approved the Equal Employment Opportunity Act of 1972, which gave the EEOC authority to litigate.

EEOC Litigation

The EEOC grew in size and strength as it undertook direct litigation. Some cases involved entire industries and led to multimillion-dollar settlements that, along the way, established significant and long-lasting effects on corporate, economic, and social environments. In the early 1970s, for example, the EEOC joined forces with two other departments of the federal government in a major case against steel manufacturers and a union, obtaining not only tens of millions of dollars in back pay for tens of thousands of workers but also mandating hiring goals and timetables.

Other cases have had a much smaller impact, involving only one company and a few workers. By way of illustration, in the early 1980s, the EEOC obtained several hundred thousand dollars for just over a dozen workers forced to retire because of age; in the mid-2000s, it obtained more than $200,000 from two companies for three female produce workers victimized by sexual harassment and retaliation, and more than $50,000 from another company for one technology worker for pregnancy discrimination. Other cases have involved foreign nationals in a class action; in the late 1990s, the EEOC obtained a settlement for nurses from overseas who had been recruited to work in the United States for a specified amount of pay and then paid less than they were promised after they arrived.

Still other cases have been brought against other government entities within the United States. The EEOC has sued different levels of government, including the federal, state, city and local levels, as well as school boards, in cases dealing with desegregation of school systems and institutions of higher learning. The cases have concerned a variety of cases on discrimination and other forms of inequity, and the EEOC has been successful in securing consent decrees as well as monetary or other relief.

The EEOC also has been involved in a number of Supreme Court cases related to higher education, including cases dealing with the ADEA. This litigation has addressed important constitutional matters such as equal protection analysis, the Eleventh Amendment, and the Fourteenth Amendment. Some of the most important cases here include *EEOC v. Wyoming* (1983), *University of Pennsylvania v. Equal Employment Opportunity Commission* (1990), *Florida Prepaid v. College Savings Bank* (1999), *Kimel v. Florida Board of Regents* (2000), and *Ledbetter v. Goodyear Tire and Rubber Company* (2007). Other cases involving the EEOC as a direct party relate to a range of issues including disparate impact, hostile work environment, and religious activities on campus. These suits have involved educational organizations such as the National Education Association and universities across the nation.

Other EEOC Action

Despite a different public perception in some quarters, the EEOC is involved in much more than just litigation. For example, in 1997 officials expanded the EEOC's approach by initiating an alternative dispute resolution program that has received a great deal of popular support as a result of its success. Moreover, EEOC officials carry out administrative duties, conducting monthly meetings at which commissioners not only plan litigation but also launch initiatives, issue memoranda of understanding, respond to national matters such as September 11 and Katrina, and administer internal matters such as considering recommendations, funding authorizations, and making budget allocations.

Along with its other responsibilities, the EEOC engages in numerous other activities including data gathering, education, publishing, and other forms of communication. EEOC officials collect and promulgate a wide range of information, such as statistics on legislation, charges, enforcement, and employment in such areas as job patterns for minorities and women. EEOC officials regularly conduct trainings, institutes, workshops, and seminars while simultaneously hosting conferences and other types of outreach gatherings. Additionally, the EEOC provides speakers on a variety of topics, such as the ADA. The EEOC's special initiatives include Youth@Work, E-RACE (Eradicating Racism and Colorism in Employment), and LEAD (Leadership for the Employment of Americans with Disabilities). The EEOC produces a wide range of publications, including those covering statistics and best practices, annual and other reports, news releases, manuals, fact sheets, resource lists, brochures, and other informational materials. At the same time, the EEOC produces posters and audiovisual materials such as public service announcements. Most of these resources are available in English, and many are obtainable in Arabic, Chinese, Korean, Russian, Spanish, Vietnamese, and several other languages. They also are accessible for download in electronic format from the agency's Web site. The EEOC even hosts a Fellows Program through which individuals can contribute to research on both discrimination and the workplace.

Based in Washington, D.C., the EEOC has a network of district, field, area, and local offices throughout the nation. The EEOC also collaborates with dozens of Tribal Employment Rights Offices on Native American lands around the country. All of these user-friendly strategies increase public access, thereby making it easy for both employees and employers to get specific information, learn about their rights and responsibilities, and seek resolution to problems or conflicts by filing claims or by engaging in conflict mediation. All these approaches help the EEOC move toward its vision of a "strong and prosperous nation secured through a fair and inclusive workplace" that includes colleges and universities.

Raúl Fernández-Calienes

See also Academic Freedom; Affirmative Action; Age Discrimination; Age Discrimination in Employment Act; Americans with Disabilities Act; Civil Rights Act of 1964; Civil Rights Movement; *College Savings Bank v. Florida Prepaid*; Disparate Impact; Eleventh Amendment; Equal Educational Opportunities Act; Equal Pay Act; Equal Protection Analysis; Fourteenth Amendment; Hostile Work Environment; *Kimel v. Florida Board of Regents*; Rehabilitation Act, Section 504; Sexual Harassment, Quid Pro Quo; Sexual Harassment, Same-Sex; Title VII; *University of Pennsylvania v. Equal Employment Opportunity Commission*; U.S. Supreme Court Cases in Higher Education

Further Readings

College Savings Bank v. Florida Prepaid, 527 U.S. 666 (1999).

Equal Employment Opportunity Commission. (2000). *35 years of ensuring the promise of opportunity.* Washington, DC: Author.

Legal Citations

Age Discrimination in Employment Act, Pub. L. No. 90-202 (1967).

Americans with Disabilities Act, Pub. L. No. 101-336 (1990).

Civil Rights Act of 1964, Pub. L. No. 88-352.

Civil Rights Act of 1991, Pub. L. 102-166.

EEOC v. Wyoming, 460 U.S. 226 (1983).

Equal Employment Opportunity Commission: http://www.eeoc.gov

Equal Pay Act, Pub. L. No. 88-38 (1963).

Florida Prepaid v. College Savings Bank, 527 U.S. 627 (1999).

Genetic Information Nondiscrimination Act of 2008, Pub. L. No. 110-233.

Kimel v. Florida Board of Regents, 528 U.S. 62 (2000).

Ledbetter v. Goodyear Tire & Rubber Co., 550 U.S. 618 (2007).

Rehabilitation Act of 1973, Sections 501 and 505, 29 U.S.C. §§ 791 *et seq.*

University of Pennsylvania v. EEOC, 493 U.S. 182 (1990).

EQUAL PAY ACT

The Equal Pay Act of 1963 amended the Fair Labor Standards Act (FLSA), making it illegal to pay different wages to employees of different sexes for equal work or jobs requiring equal skill, effort, or responsibility performed under similar working conditions. The act prohibits paying employees of one sex at a rate less than that paid to workers of the opposite sex for substantially equal work.

The act applies to employers in industries engaged in commerce or in the production of goods for commerce. It specifically covers elementary and secondary schools as well as institutions of higher education, regardless of whether they are public or private or are operated for profit or not for profit. Essentially, the act covers the same employees as the FLSA but, in addition, covers executives, administrators, and other professional employees who are normally exempted from the FLSA. In addition, the act covers most state

and local government employees, unless they are specifically exempted from its provisions. While most cases under the act involve claims by females, it also protects men. Proof of discriminatory intent is not required in order to prevail on a claim under the act. This entry reviews the provisions of the Equal Pay Act and defenses to claims of discrimination in violation of the act. It then discusses the implementation of the act in higher education, particularly with respect to coaching, teaching, and other academic assignments.

Provisions of the Act

According to the act,

> no employer having employees subject to any provision of [the Act] shall discriminate, within any establishment in which such employees are employed, between employees on the basis of sex by paying wages to employees in such establishment at a rate less than the rate at which he paid wages to employees of the opposite sex in such establishment for equal work on jobs the performance of which requires equal skill, effort and responsibility, and which are performed under similar working conditions.

A fundamental premise of the act is the concept of "equal pay for equal work" performed by employees of either sex. In order to recover under the act, plaintiffs must prove that employers are paying or paid different wages to employees of the opposite sex for equal work. The act defines equal work by stipulating that the performance of jobs must require "equal skill, effort and responsibility and which are performed under similar working conditions." The term *equal* has been judicially defined as "substantially equal," which means that the jobs being compared must be either "closely related" or "very much alike."

In the face of an Equal Pay Act claim, plaintiffs must make appropriate comparisons of two jobs in light of all the circumstances. The focus of inquiries in evaluating whether jobs are substantially equal is on their overall job content. Courts typically look beyond job classifications, job titles, and job descriptions to the basic substance of the work being performed. Wages are differential when they are justified in order to compensate for appreciable variations in skill, effort, responsibility, or working conditions between otherwise comparable work activities. When claimants are able to establish common cores of tasks between two jobs, courts must consider whether any additional tasks make the jobs "substantially different."

The skill, effort, and responsibility associated with a job are factors to be evaluated separately in determining whether work is equal. Plaintiffs must demonstrate that jobs are equal with respect to each of these factors in order for the equal pay requirement to apply. "Skill" is based on job performance requirements for the positions involved and considers experience, training, education, and ability. "Effort" is based on the physical and/or mental exertion required for a position. "Responsibility" is evaluated in the context of the importance of a job's duties and degree of accountability involved, such as the responsibility to supervise and direct other employees. "Working conditions" refers to physical working conditions, including surroundings and hazards.

The act permits the payment of different wages for equal work if those payments are made pursuant to seniority systems, merit systems, systems that measure earnings by quantity or quality of production, or pay differentials based on any other factors other than sex. Salary differentials based on length of time that employees have worked for employers are permissible, even where there is no formal seniority system in effect and even if this may result in generally higher salaries for men.

Violations of the Equal Pay Act

Employees may seek to file charges with the Equal Employment Opportunity Commission (EEOC) or may elect to file suit directly in court to enforce the act. The EEOC may also file suit against employers for alleged violations of the act. Jury trials are permitted under the act. Damages available include back wages, liquidated or double damages, attorney fees, and costs.

The act contains a two-year statute of limitations. However, each time an employer issues a paycheck to a woman for lower pay than a man receives (or vice versa) for performing equal work, a separate act of discrimination occurs and provides a separate basis for liability. The limitations period is increased to three years for willful violations. In addition, willful violations may be prosecuted criminally with conviction possibly resulting in fines and, for second willful violations, imprisonment.

Defenses to Discrimination Claims

Merit system defenses must be grounded in bona fide merit systems. Job descriptions that differentiate between positions but provide no means for advancement or reward based on merit do not constitute bona fide merit systems. Generally, courts require employers to demonstrate objective, written standards.

Employers must validate bona fide incentive systems based on either the amount of labor or the quality of work produced for a defense based on quantity or quality of production in order to apply. The quantity test refers to compensation rates of equal dollars per unit. As such, there is no discrimination if two employees receive the same rate of pay for producing the same product but one receives more total compensation because of his or her ability to produce more of the product. Employers may not pay lesser rates per unit to females in order to equalize total compensation between men and women where there are no qualitative differences between the work being performed, such as teaching at colleges and universities.

The "factors other than sex" defense is a broad exception encompassing the right of employers to change and revise their job evaluation and pay systems. Basing wages on sex-neutral objective measures is an example of the "factors other than sex" defense. If differentials in pay would have been the same regardless of an employee's sex, there is no violation under the act.

Equal Pay in Higher Education

Coaching

Issues regarding equal pay often arise in the context of coaching assignments. Whether two coaching assignments are considered substantially equal is a question of fact. Each position must be analyzed to determine whether they are, in fact, substantially equal, generally considering whether equal skills, equal effort, equal responsibility, and similar working conditions are involved.

The EEOC has issued a publication, *Enforcement Guidance on Sex Discrimination in the Compensation of Sports Coaches in Educational Institutions* ("EEOC Guidance") that contains numerous examples of how coaches are compensated and provides a useful framework for analysis of equal pay claims. At the same time, though, the EEOC has acknowledged that what constitutes equal skill, equal effort, or equal responsibility cannot be precisely defined. The EEOC Guidance emphasizes that insignificant or inconsequential differences do not prevent jobs from being considered equal. The guide states that focus should be on overall job content.

The EEOC Guidance states as follows:

> To determine whether the coaching jobs require equal effort, the Commission will look at the actual requirements of the jobs being compared, 29 C.F.R. § 1620.16(a), and will not limit its analysis to coaches of like sports. Coaches, regardless of the sport, typically are required to perform the following duties at both the high school and college level; (1) teaching/training; (2) counseling/advising of student athletes; (3) general program management; (4) budget management; (5) fundraising; (6) public relations; and (7) at the college level, recruiting. Some coaching jobs will require other duties, such as management of staff and event management.

Representative litigation highlights how this operates in intercollegiate athletic settings. In *Horn v. University of Minnesota* (2004), a male former assistant women's hockey team coach failed to establish that his position was substantially equal to that of a female assistant coach. The Eighth Circuit pointed out that the male accepted the second assistant position and the female was required to also serve as a public representative of the hockey team as well as its administrative assistant. In *Lewis v. Smith* (2003), the federal trial court in Arizona maintained that assistant coaching positions were not substantially equal where the respective coaches had substantially different levels of responsibility and effort regarding the very significant duties of off-campus recruiting, scouting, and dealing with the medical staff. Likewise, in *Stanley v. University of Southern California* (1999), the Ninth Circuit was of the opinion that the head

coach of the women's basketball team did not establish an equal pay violation as compared to the head coach of the men's basketball team. The court observed that the coach of the men's team had substantially different responsibilities and superior qualifications related to public relations and promotional activities designed to generate revenues. Similarly, in *Weaver v. Ohio State University* (1999), a federal trial court in Ohio ruled that differences in wage rates between the female field hockey coach and the male ice hockey coach were based on merit and seniority factors and on market rate, which were factors other than sex used to differentiate their pay.

Teaching and Other Academic Assignments

Issues of equal pay may also arise with respect to teaching and other professional academic assignments. These issues are particularly difficult to assess where the special characteristics of an academic community are involved. Although the overall objective of collegiate educators may well be the same, each educator brings unique qualities that are not easily compared.

In *Hein v. Oregon College of Education* (1983), for example, the Ninth Circuit found that the proper test for establishing a prima facie case of discrimination under the act in a professional setting, such as that of a college, is whether the plaintiff is receiving lower wages than the average wages paid to all employees of the opposite sex performing substantially equal work and similarly situated with respect to other factors, such as seniority, that affect the wage scale. The court explained that this standard recognizes that variations in professional settings may result from a multitude of factors that may not implicate sex discrimination. The court indicated that its analysis was further complicated insofar as educational institutions may reward professional experience and education without violating the act.

In *Winkes v. Brown University* (1984), the First Circuit rejected the claim that a university violated the act when a female faculty member received a larger raise than a male colleague. The court noted that university officials were required to match the offer of another institution to retain the female faculty member. Further, in another case from the First Circuit, *Donnelly v. Rhode Island Board of Governors for Higher Education*, *et al.* (1997), the court was satisfied that because a male faculty member was paid more based on his choice of academic field and the workings of the national market, not sex, university officials did not violate the act.

Jon E. Anderson

See also Title VII

Further Readings

Equal Employment Opportunity Commission. (1997). *Enforcement guidance on sex discrimination in the compensation of sports coaches in educational institutions.* EEOC Notice 915.002. Washington, DC: Author.

Gaal, J. M., Glazier, M. S., & Evans, T. S. (2002). Gender-based pay disparities: Intercollegiate coaching, the legal issues. *Journal of College & University Law, 28,* 519–568.

Keohane, L. (1997). Universities, colleges and the Equal Pay Act: The Fourth Circuit analyzes a salary dispute in *Strag v. Board of Trustees. Campbell Law Review, 19,* 333–348.

Perez-Arrieta, A. (2005). Defenses to sex-based wage discrimination claims at educational institutions: Exploring "equal work" and "any other factor other than sex" in the faculty context. *Journal of College & University Law, 31,* 393–415.

Legal Citations

Donnelly v. Rhode Island Board of Governors for Higher Education, et al. 929 F. Supp. 583 (D.R.I. 1996), *aff'd,* 110 F.3d 2 (1st Cir. 1997).

Equal Pay Act, 29 U.S.C. § 206(d) (2000).

Hein v. Oregon College of Education, 718 F.2d 910 (9th Cir. 1983).

Horn v. University of Minnesota, 362 F.3d 1042 (8th Cir. 2004).

Lewis v. Smith, 255 F. Supp. 2d 1054 (D. Ariz. 2003).

Stanley v. University of Southern California, 178 F.3d 1069 (9th Cir. 1999).

Weaver v. Ohio State University, 71 F. Supp. 2d 789 (S.D. Ohio, 1999).

Winkes v. Brown University, 747 F.2d 792 (1st Cir. 1984).

EQUAL PROTECTION ANALYSIS

Although the concept of equal protection of the laws is not mentioned in the original U.S. Constitution as drafted and ratified, this idea has become an important constitutional concept, especially in the world of higher education. Equal protection does not require identical treatment of all people in all situations. Instead, when the federal or state governments, through their officials, make distinctions between and among individuals, the courts employ equal protection analysis by looking at the specific distinctions and applying a corresponding level of scrutiny to determine whether the government action is constitutional.

Courts employ equal protection analysis when governmental officials treat people differently based on specified characteristics such as race, gender, or age. Courts also rely on equal protection analysis when governmental entities create distinctions among people who exercise fundamental rights such as those identified in the Constitution. In light of the significant impact that equal protection analysis has had on the world of higher education and beyond, this entry highlights its application in specific cases and factual circumstances involving colleges and universities.

History and Structure of Equal Protection Analysis

In 1868, following the Civil War, the Equal Protection Clause became a part of the Constitution with the ratification of the Fourteenth Amendment, the first section of which states that "No state shall make or enforce any law which shall . . . deny to any person within its jurisdiction the equal protection of the laws." Equal protection applies to the federal government through the Due Process Clause of the Fifth Amendment. Equal protection analysis includes three tiers of classification: strict scrutiny, intermediate scrutiny, and rational basis review. Rational basis review is the minimum level of scrutiny for equal protection challenges, while intermediate scrutiny and strict scrutiny are heightened levels of scrutiny. At its heart, this analysis recognizes that because no governmental action is neutral—all acts of government have an impact on the rights of persons (the Constitution distinguishes between persons and citizens)—varying degrees of scrutiny are necessary if these actions are to withstand judicial analysis.

When the government, acting in and through public officials, treats individuals differently due to their race, national origin, religion, or citizenship status, with some exception, courts employ strict scrutiny in their equal protection analyses. Strict scrutiny is also used when governmental actors make distinctions between and among people based on their exercise of fundamental rights, such as those identified in the Constitution. Strict scrutiny has not been applied to higher education cases directly, because the U.S. Supreme Court has not identified education, at any level, for that matter, as a fundamental constitutional right. Under strict scrutiny, governmental actions are upheld as constitutional only if such classifications are narrowly tailored to further compelling governmental interests (for example, when policies such as affirmation action discriminate among racial or ethnic groups). In most cases, the result of strict scrutiny equal protection analysis is the invalidation of the governmental actions or policies.

When the government or its officials treat individuals differently due to their gender or legitimacy, courts apply intermediate scrutiny in their equal protection analysis. Under intermediate scrutiny, courts sustain discriminatory governmental actions only if they are substantially related to the achievement of important governmental interests. With respect to discriminatory gender classifications, the Supreme Court requires governmental entities to demonstrate exceedingly persuasive justification for their actions.

All other discriminatory governmental classifications of individuals result in judicial application of rational basis review for their equal protection analysis. This analysis applies to the work of public higher education, where officials are in colleges and universities, institutions that are considered "arms of their states." Under rational basis review, which usually examines day-to-day institutional concerns, such as course requirements for specific degrees in public institutions of higher learning, officials' actions are ordinarily upheld as constitutional as long as their actions or classifications are rationally related to the attainment of legitimate institutional interests. Typically, when courts apply rational basis scrutiny, governmental or institutional actions are upheld. As noted in the following sections, the Supreme Court has applied equal protection analysis in key cases associated with race and gender that remain highly relevant to higher education.

Race and Higher Education

The Supreme Court resolved three key cases, *State of Missouri ex rel. Gaines v. Canada* (1938), *Sweatt v. Painter* (1950) and *McLaurin v. Oklahoma State Regents for Higher Education* (1950), which involved discriminatory racial classifications in higher education, prior to its expressly articulating the strict scrutiny standard for these types of disputes. *Gaines, Sweatt,* and *McLaurin* provided a vital foundation for the Court's treatment of cases involving governmental distinctions based on race in higher education. While these cases did not reverse the "separate but equal" precedent of *Plessy v. Ferguson* (1896), they did illustrate the Court's developing equal protection analysis and foreshadowed the dismantling of *Plessy* in *Brown v. Board of Education, Topeka* (1954).

In *Gaines,* Lloyd L. Gaines, an African American Missourian, applied to the State University of Missouri School of Law but was denied admission solely on the basis of his race. Insofar as Missouri did not have a state-supported law school that admitted African Americans, the Supreme Court found that this denial of admission violated the Equal Protection Clause. As a result, the Court directed officials to admit Gaines to the law school due to the lack of substantially equal legal training for him in the state.

In *Sweatt,* Hemon Marion Sweatt, an African American Texan, applied to the University of Texas Law School, which denied him admission based solely on his race. When Sweatt sued the law school and various officials, the state responded by attempting to establish a substantially equal law school for African Americans. Yet, Sweatt argued, ultimately successfully, that this attempt did not satisfy his right to equal protection under the law, and a unanimous Supreme Court agreed. The Court held that the Equal Protection Clause required that Sweatt be admitted to the University of Texas Law School, because a separate law school would not have provided him with an equivalent legal education.

In *McLaurin,* George W. McLaurin, an African American living in Oklahoma, unsuccessfully applied to the University of Oklahoma to pursue a doctorate in education. After McLaurin was denied admission based solely on his race, he sought assistance from the federal trial court, which ordered university officials to admit him as a student. Eventually, officials at the graduate school admitted McLaurin, but on a segregated basis, which meant that he was required to sit apart from the Caucasian students in classrooms, the library, and the cafeteria. McLaurin turned to the federal courts again, and the case eventually was appealed to the Supreme Court. The Court determined that the actions of university officials violated his right to equal protection, because the Fourteenth Amendment prohibited such differential treatment based on race. The Court ordered university officials to treat McLaurin the same as the other students.

The Supreme Court did not address governmental distinctions based on race in higher education again until 1978, when it resolved *Regents of the University of California v. Bakke* (1978). In *Bakke*, Allan Bakke, a Caucasian, applied twice to the Medical School of the University of California at Davis and was rejected twice. Thereafter, Bakke filed suit, claiming that the medical school's special admissions program, which was designed to increase student diversity and which set aside a certain number of slots for minority students, was a violation of Title VI of the Civil Rights Act of 1964 and the Equal Protection Clause. On appeal to the Supreme Court, the justices authored separate opinions in a plurality judgment, with no majority opinion on whether strict scrutiny was appropriate for affirmative action racial classifications in higher education. Instead, a plurality of the Court decided that the consideration of race was constitutionally permissible in admissions. However, the Court added in a separate plurality opinion that racial quotas like the one employed by the University of California at Davis were illegal under Title VI, resulting in an order to admit Bakke.

Bakke left key equal protection questions unresolved, including whether strict scrutiny was the appropriate level of scrutiny for affirmative action classifications in higher education and, if so, whether student body diversity could be a compelling government interest to satisfy strict scrutiny. In *Adarand Constructors v. Pena* (1995), the Supreme Court ruled that strict scrutiny was appropriate for federal affirmative action programs such as those involving building projects. The Court followed *Adarand* in providing a firm answer to the final question left open by Bakke in *Gratz v. Bollinger* (2003) and *Grutter v. Bollinger* (2003).

The Supreme Court applied strict scrutiny analysis to the affirmative action policies in effect at the University of Michigan School of Law in *Grutter* and in an undergraduate program in *Gratz*. The law school policy used race as a plus factor, meaning that it could be taken into account as a kind of bonus for minority students, alongside individualized consideration of applicants. In *Grutter*, the Court ruled that the law school's interest in maintaining student body diversity was a compelling state interest. Finding that the law school's admissions policy furthered student body diversity and was sufficiently narrowly tailored to meet this compelling interest, the Court concluded that the law school's policy did not violate the Equal Protection Clause.

Conversely, in *Gratz*, the Supreme Court reasoned that the University of Michigan's undergraduate admissions policy violated the Equal Protection Clause. Unlike officials in the law school, the Court noted that officials in the undergraduate program assigned an automatic 20 points, which was the equivalent of one-fifth of the required points for admission, to members of the underrepresented minority groups of African Americans, Hispanics, and Native Americans. The Court observed that the policy met the first prong of strict scrutiny, that the undergraduate program's classification's objective of increasing student diversity was a compelling government interest. However, the Court struck the undergraduate policy down as unconstitutional insofar as it was not narrowly tailored to meet this compelling interest due to its failure to provide for individualized consideration of applicants.

Gender and Higher Education

The judiciary employs intermediate scrutiny with respect to discriminatory gender classifications. The Supreme Court has handed down two key opinions in the area of equal protection analysis with respect to higher education: *Mississippi University for Women v. Hogan* (1982) and *United States v. Virginia* (1996).

In *Hogan,* Joe Hogan, a male nurse, applied to the Mississippi University for Women School of Nursing. After he was denied admission solely based on his gender, Hogan filed suit, alleging that officials violated his rights to equal protection. When the case was appealed to the Supreme Court, it applied intermediate scrutiny, requiring the state to show an exceedingly persuasive justification for its gender-based classification. The Court pointed out that the state's officials failed to show that the school met the requirements of either prong of the requisite intermediate scrutiny test. The Court was of the view that the alleged purpose for the classification, namely compensating for past discrimination against women, was an insufficient justification, because the state legislature failed to prove that its intended single-sex policy served to compensate anyone for perceived gender-based discrimination. Insofar as the actions of state officials failed to survive intermediate scrutiny, the Court concluded that the university's policy of denying men admission to its nursing school was an unconstitutional violation of the Equal Protection Clause.

In *Virginia,* the United States brought suit against the Commonwealth of Virginia, claiming that the policy of the publicly supported Virginia Military Institute of admitting only men was a violation of the Equal Protection Clause. Applying intermediate scrutiny in its analysis, the Supreme Court agreed. The Court explained that Virginia's proffered rationale for the gender-based distinction—that the importance of same-sex education justified the complete exclusion of women—failed to satisfy the heightened scrutiny required to pass constitutional muster. In its analysis, the Court rejected Virginia's attempt to offer military education for women at the separate facility of the Virginia Women's Institute for Leadership as a cure for the constitutional infirmity, because the programs would not have offered the same level of prestige to both men and women.

Conclusion

As demonstrated by the review of litigation in this entry, equal protection analysis has played a significant role in helping to shape contemporary higher education. Furthermore, there is no reason to believe that equal protection will play any less a role in shaping activities on college and university campuses in the future.

Amanda Harmon Cooley

See also Affirmative Action; Fourteenth Amendment; *Gratz v. Bollinger; Grutter v. Bollinger; McLaurin v. Oklahoma State Regents for Higher Education; Mississippi University for Women v. Hogan; Regents of the University of California v. Bakke; Sweatt v. Painter;* Title VI; *United States v. Virginia*

Legal Citations

Adarand Constructors v. Pena, 515 U.S. 200 (1995).
Brown v. Board of Education, Topeka, 347 U.S. 483 (1954).
Civil Rights Act of 1964, Pub. L. No. 88-352.
Gratz v. Bollinger, 539 U.S. 244 (2003).
Grutter v. Bollinger, 539 U.S. 306 (2003).
McLaurin v. Oklahoma State Regents for Higher Education, 339 U.S. 637 (1950).
Mississippi University for Women v. Hogan, 458 U.S. 718 (1982).
Plessy v. Ferguson, 163 U.S. 537 (1896).
Regents of the University of California v. Bakke, 438 U.S. 265 (1978).
State of Missouri ex rel. Gaines v. Canada, 305 U.S. 337 (1938).
Sweatt v. Painter, 339 U.S. 629 (1950).
United States v. Virginia, 518 U.S. 515 (1996).

Ex Corde Ecclesiae and American Catholic Higher Education

Discussions over the extent to which Roman Catholic colleges and universities can maintain their religious identities in a secular world have been ongoing for well over half a century. The more than 200 Catholic colleges and universities that are spread throughout the United States, many of which trace their origins back to the 19th century, represent the single largest single block of religiously affiliated institutions of higher learning in the United States. As these institutions seek to preserve their religious identities, the Vatican entered the debate on August 15, 1990, when Pope John Paul II promulgated *Ex Corde Ecclesiae* (*Ex Corde*), literally, "from the heart of the

Church." In writing *Ex Corde,* Pope John Paul II sought to reinvigorate the debate over how Catholic colleges and universities can remain true to their religious missions while being viable institutions of higher learning, wherein faculty members are free to work as researchers and teachers who meet the same criteria as their professional colleagues in other institutions of higher learning.

This entry examines how *Ex Corde* and its accompanying documents focus on the obligation of Roman Catholic theologians at Catholic colleges and universities to obtain a *mandatum,* or statement from their local bishops, attesting to their fidelity to Roman Catholic teachings. At the same time, the entry reviews *Ex Corde*'s application to faculty members who are non-Catholics who are expected to demonstrate respect for these teachings. The entry also considers *Ex Corde*'s impact on the academic freedom rights of academicians, acknowledging by its own terms its centrality in higher education and making clear that it is not so much intended to limit academic freedom as it is to ensure that Catholic theologians are faithful to Roman Catholic Church teachings.

At the heart of *Ex Corde,* which is to be implemented by local bishops, is its requirement that all Catholic theologians obtain a mandate or, more properly, a mandatum, a statement from their local bishops acknowledging that the Catholic theologians are in full communion with the teachings of the Roman Catholic Church. This requirement does not apply to faculty in other disciplines or to administrators. This entry examines the content of Roman Catholic Church documents, focusing particularly on the mandatum requirement. The firestorm of controversy in the academic community that accompanied the adoption by U.S. bishops of *The Application of Ex Corde Ecclesiae for the United States* (*The Application*) in 1999 and their acceptance of *The Guidelines Concerning the Academic Mandatum in Catholic Universities* (*The Guidelines*) (2001) two years later is beyond the scope of this descriptive entry.

Ex Corde Ecclesiae

Ex Corde consists of an introduction, two major parts, and a brief conclusion. Part 1 discusses the identity and mission of Catholic universities, typically referring only to universities, because outside

of the United States, many nations use the term *college* to refer to what are either secondary or postsecondary institutions that are not on the same level as universities. Part 2 discusses general norms associated with implementing *Ex Corde*.

At the outset of Part 1, *Ex Corde* notes that it is not a tool to convert academicians to the Catholic faith (or drive them from campus) or an instrument designed to return Catholic colleges and universities to a pre–Vatican II intellectual ghetto, wherein academic inquiry was often viewed as suspect. Instead, *Ex Corde Ecclesiae* expresses the requirement that all faculty members who work in Catholic environments, regardless of their personal value or faith systems, respect the Church's teachings and traditions. In other words, while *all* faculty members must respect the Church's teachings, only those teaching theology must obtain a mandatum. *The Application* echoed this stance in asserting that academic freedom is an essential component of a Catholic university.

After discussing the role of theology in the search for a synthesis of knowledge along with the dialogue between faith and reason, *Ex Corde* reflects on the roles of the various members of the university community, namely teachers, students, directors and administrators, and lay people. As to the place of Catholic universities in the Church, *Ex Corde* declares that members of the Catholic Church are called to a personal fidelity to the Church with all that this implies. Further, non-Catholics are required to respect the Catholic character of the universities while institutions respect their religious liberty.

In Part 2, General Norms, *Ex Corde* returns to the role of faculty and administrators at Catholic institutions, requiring that at the time of their appointment they are to be informed of the Catholic identity of the institution and its implications. Further, *Ex Corde* states that Catholic theologians, who should be aware that they mandate that they received from the Church, are to be faithful to the magisterium, or teaching authority, of the Church as the authentic interpreter of sacred scripture and sacred tradition. This language is largely consistent with the Roman Catholic Church's code of canon law, which requires those who teach theological disciplines to have a mandate from the competent ecclesiastical authority.

Ex Corde is not designed to stifle legitimate dissent in the Catholic Church or to limit academic freedom. Rather, *Ex Corde* is designed to ensure that even if, or when, theologians, who occupy special places in Catholic universities, disagree with Church teaching, they must do their best to explain the Roman Catholic Church's official magisterial position accurately, making it clear that they speak in their own names. As to non-Catholics, *Ex Corde* maintains that they must recognize and respect the distinct Catholic identity of the university. This part adds that in order not to endanger the Catholic identity of institutions, the number of non-Catholic faculty members should not be permitted to achieve majority status.

Ex Corde's approach is consistent with Title VII of the Civil Rights Act of 1964 (2008) which recognizes the right of religious institutions to grant preferences to members of their own faiths. Moreover, courts have relied on Title VII in upholding the actions of Catholic universities that preserved positions in a philosophy department for Jesuit priests (*Pime v. Loyola University,* 1986), the denial of a nun's tenure application in a department of canon law by relying on the law's ministerial exceptions clause (*EEOC v. Catholic University of America,* 1996), and the dismissal of a faculty member in a Catholic seminary who signed a petition supporting the ordination of women, because her doing so violated canon law (*McEnroy v. St. Meinrad School of Theology,* 1999).

Insofar as the Vatican left the implementation of *Ex Corde* up to local bishops, acting in concert with their national conferences and learned societies, the implementation process in the United States spawned significant controversy when the bishops set about the task of developing and implementing norms to effectuate its terms.

The American Catholic Bishops and *Ex Corde Ecclesiae*

The Application

Following years of contentious debate and a variety of drafts, on November 17, 1999, the bishops adopted the proposed set of norms, *The Application,* by the overwhelming margin of 233 to 31.

The Application is divided into two major parts, an introduction, and a conclusion. Part 1,

Theological and Pastoral Principles, examines issues surrounding the nature and role of American Catholic colleges and universities. Part 2, Particular Norms, is designed to assist Catholic institutions of higher learning in their internal processes of reviewing their identities while clarifying their missions and goals. Part 2 also highlights the role of the various aspects of the university community, including boards of trustees; administration and staff; faculty, who must exhibit academic competence, good character, and respect for Catholic doctrine; and students (Part 2, Art. 4.5). Insofar as *The Guidelines* expanded on requirements in *The Application,* the next section focuses on the details of *Ex Corde*'s requirements with regard to the mandatum.

When the bishops adopted the norms, the Vatican's Congregation for Bishops recognized *The Application* on May 3, 2000; the norms took effect a year later. After *The Application* was approved, the bishops conferred with learned academic societies, most notably the Catholic Theological Society of America, to protect academic freedom in adopting *The Guidelines* that were issued on June 15, 2001.

The Guidelines

The Guidelines consist of nine sections, not including a brief preface and introductory remarks, the most important of which address the nature of a mandatum, who should have one, who grants one, how one is granted, grounds for denying a mandatum, and appeals and dispute resolution. Beginning with the nature of a mandatum, *The Guidelines* explain that it designed to serve as an acknowledgment by church officials that Catholic faculty members in theological disciplines are teaching in accord with the position of the Catholic Church. It is important to note that *The Guidelines* recognize faculty members' lawful freedom of inquiry as well as their commitment and responsibility to teach Catholic doctrine while refraining from putting forth as Catholic teaching anything contrary to the Church's position.

In order to obtain a mandatum, which is an obligation of individual faculty members, not their universities, those who teach full- or part-time (Section 2.3) in the theological disciplines must make requests in writing to their local bishops including declarations that they will teach in full communion with the Catholic Church. Church officials are expected to respond to these requests in writing and may offer a mandatum on their own initiative. Once granted, a mandatum remains in effect for as long as an individual teaches unless or until it is removed by church officials. *The Guidelines* stipulate that if individuals do not obtain a mandatum, local church authorities should notify the appropriate officials in their colleges or universities.

Bishops who consider denying requests for or withdrawal of an already granted mandatum must discuss the cases informally with the theologian concerned, setting forth the reason they are contemplating such an action. Bishops who withhold or withdraw a mandatum must specify reasons for doing so in writing and afford theologians who think that their rights were violated opportunities for redress. In rendering negative judgments about the objectionable publications of theologians, *The Guidelines* require bishops to assess the theologians' efforts on three levels: their significance within the context of theologians' overall theological contribution; their relationship to the larger Catholic tradition; and their implications for the life of the Church.

The portion of *The Guidelines* addressing appeals stipulates that because the withdrawal of a previously issued mandatum or the denial of a request for a mandatum impacts the rights of theologians, the resolution process must comply with all of the relevant norms of canon law. In suggesting that both parties have competent canonical and theological counsel, *The Guidelines* acknowledge that canon law requires contact between a bishop and a theologian and that the rights of all parties to a good reputation must always be honored. Consistent with canon law, *The Guidelines* permit the parties to employ other means of conflict resolution, whether on the diocesan, regional, or provincial level, and they do not preclude the use of local mediation. Finally, while expressing a preference for the use of informal dispute resolution procedures, *The Guidelines* recognize that a theologian always has the right to formal recourse to the procedures contained in canon law. However, the best intentions of *The Guidelines* and canon law aside, the latter falls far short of the due process requirements that American academicians have come to expect. Insofar as the American Catholic bishops have been largely reluctant to enforce *Ex Corde*'s requirements, its status in the United States is unclear.

Charles J. Russo

See also Academic Freedom

Further Readings

Burtchaell, J. T. (1999). Out of the heartburn of the church. *Journal of College & University Law, 25*(4), 653–695.

Code of Canon Law. (1983). London: Collins Liturgical.

Gregory, D. L., & Russo, C. J. (2000). Proposals to counter continuing resistance to the implementation of *Ex Corde Ecclesiae. St. John's Law Review, 74*(3), 629–654.

McMurtrie, B. (2000, June 16). Vatican backs Catholic-colleges rules that spur fears over academic freedom. *Chronicle of Higher Education*, p. A18.

Reese, T. J. (1999, December 4). The bishops' mandatum. *America*, p. 3.

Russo, C. J. (1989). Academic freedom and theology at the Catholic University of America: An oxymoron? *Education Law Reporter, 55*(1), 1–6.

Russo, C. J., & Gregory, D. L. (1997). Some reflections on the Catholic university's tenure prerogatives. *Loyola Law Review, 43*, 181–213.

Tokasz, J., & Rey, J. (2006, October 29). Can colleges stay Catholic? Area's seven institutions confront future with fewer clergy, members of religious orders. *Buffalo News*, p. A1.

U.S. Catholic Conference of Bishops. (1999). *The application of* Ex Corde Ecclesiae *for the United States.* Retrieved May 27, 2009, from http://www .nccbuscc.org/bishops/application_of_excordeecclesiae .shtml

U.S. Catholic Conference of Bishops. (2001). *Guidelines concerning the academic mandatum in Catholic universities.* Retrieved May 27, 2009, from http:// www.nccbuscc.org/bishops/mandatumguidelines.shtml

Legal Citations

Civil Rights Act of 1964, 42 U.S.C. § 2000e-1 (2008).

EEOC v. Catholic University of America, 83 F.3d 455 (D.C. Cir. 1996).

McEnroy v. St. Meinrad School of Theology, 713 N.E.2d 334 (Ind. Ct. App. 1999), *transfer denied*, 726 N.E.2d 313 (Ind. 1999), *cert. denied*, 529 U.S. 1068 (2000).

Pime v. Loyola University, 803 F.2d 351 (7th Cir. 1986).

Extracurricular Activities, Law, and Policy

The legal relationship between college and university officials and their students is often defined by institutional regulations, rules, and policies that impact extracurricular activities as well as the places in and around campuses where these activities occur. Traditionally, the law has accorded officials at postsecondary institutions extensive autonomy in their daily operations. This academic autonomy has included institutional relationships with students that have been parental in nature. However, over time, the doctrine of *in loco parentis*, literally, "in the place of the parent," which applied to the relationship between college and university officials and their students, has diminished, as the relationship has increasingly been viewed as contractual in nature. Of course, to the extent that institutional officials promulgate policies that are incorporated by reference into enrollment agreements, students are expected to comply with their terms. In light of the manner in which the relationship between officials at institutions of higher learning and their students have evolved, this entry examines the parameters of control that college and university administrators can exert over extracurricular activities on and near campuses.

Gott v. Berea and the Evolution of In Loco Parentis

Gott v. Berea College (1913) exemplifies how *in loco parentis* functioned between students and officials in institutions of higher learning. Officials at Berea College distributed a manual containing rules and regulations for students. One section of the manual, titled "Forbidden Places," forbade students from entering any place of ill repute, liquor saloons, gambling houses, and the like. Other forbidden places included eating houses and places of amusement in the city of Berea that were not controlled by the college. Students were warned that if they entered these places, they would face immediate dismissal. This policy was based on the rationale that because college officials provided for recreation and ample accommodations for meals and refreshment, they would not permit outside parties to solicit student patronage for profit.

After two students were expelled for entering a restaurant across the street from the college, its owner filed suit. The owner claimed that the rules had the effect of materially injuring, if not ruining, his business, because the students were afraid to patronize his restaurant. On further review of a judgment in favor of the college, Kentucky's highest court affirmed the earlier order. The court held that because college officials stood *in loco parentis* with respect to students' mental training and physical and moral welfare, however widely defined, college officials could adopt rules just as parents might have done. In addition, the court noted that whether the rules or regulations were wise or their aims worthy was a matter left to the discretion of the authorities or parents. The court explained that in the exercise of the discretion that officials enjoyed, the judiciary should not interfere, unless college rules were unlawful or violated public policy.

Cases such as *Gott* established the basic principles of law regarding extracurricular activities and their relationship to college and university students. The courts generally agreed that the power of institutional officials over their students was not confined to classes or grounds. Rather, the courts maintained that rules extended to any student acts that may have been detrimental to institutional good order and best interest, regardless of whether the student acts were committed during school hours or while individuals were on their way to or from campus. The courts acknowledged that while these rules and regulations were not meant to interfere with parental control of their children in their homes, they were designed to direct the actions of student bodies. Accordingly, the courts determined that institutional officials were well within their authority when, in cases such as *Gott*, they directed students as to what to eat and where they could get it, where they could go, and what forms of amusement were forbidden.

Limitations of In Loco Parentis

Over the course of the 20th century, the *in loco parentis* relationship between institutions of higher education and their students has become more limited in nature. Two factors contributing to this change are the increased number of students who move directly into graduate study and the lowering of the age of majority of students from 21 to 18, making the *in loco parentis* relationship between institution and student less and less tenable. Further, as military veterans returned to school in the post–World War II years, *in loco parentis* was seen as increasingly anachronistic. The move away from *in loco parentis* in higher education was evident in *Dixon v. Alabama State Board of Education* (1961). Although the U.S. Supreme Court refused to hear an appeal from the Fifth Circuit in *Dixon*, this case marked the shift away from *in loco parentis* as an approach to student–institution relationships in higher education, as the Fifth Circuit found that officials improperly exercised their authority in disciplining the students in this case, because they lacked the authority to expel students for misconduct without due process hearings.

Rights of Student Organizations

As the legal relationship between institutions of higher learning and their students evolved, student organizations and extracurricular activities entered the mix. For example, in *Gay Student Services v. Texas A&M University* (1984), the Fifth Circuit examined whether officials at a public university violated the First Amendment rights of a gay student organization and three of its members by refusing to grant the group official recognition. University officials argued that their refusal was not based on the content of the group's ideas but rather on the university's long-standing policy of refusing to recognize fraternal organizations whose principal purpose is to engage in social gatherings to encourage friendship and personal affinity. In disagreeing, the court found that the refusal of officials to recognize the gay student organization as an on-campus extracurricular organization impermissibly denied its members their First Amendment rights to freedom of speech.

In *Healy v. James* (1972), the Supreme Court examined whether the refusal of college officials in Connecticut to grant recognition to those who wished to start a local chapter of Students for a Democratic Society (SDS) violated the students' First Amendment rights. The stated goals of SDS were to provide a forum for discussion and self-education for students, to bring about constructive social changes, and to provide a coordinating body for addressing the problems of leftist students and other interested groups on campus and in the community. The dispute arose in 1969, when a climate of unrest prevailed on many campuses, as widespread student civil disobedience was often accompanied by vandalism, arson, and seizure of buildings. Some institutions shut down altogether, while others had files looted and manuscripts destroyed. On some campuses, SDS chapters had been a catalytic force during the period. Based on these concerns, college officials refused to recognize the proposed SDS chapter.

In a unanimous decision authored by Justice Marshall, in *Healy*, the Supreme Court balanced the lawful exercise of First Amendment rights by the few with the concomitant rights of the majority of students. The Court decided that the mere disagreement of the college's president with SDS's philosophy did not afford a reason to deny it recognition absent clear evidence that it would have been a disruptive influence at the campus.

Other Issues

Cases regarding other efforts by college and university officials to regulate and control extracurricular activities have grown as the courts have examined a significant number of issues. In one such case, a student successfully challenged her dismissal for being a disruptive influence when she suggested a petition and signed it, along with others, charging the school's administration with overcharging them and misappropriating government loans and grants (*Fussell v. Louisiana Business College of Monroe*, 1988). The court held that the student's voicing her complaints to a newspaper reporter was not a violation of her obligation to avoid disruptive behavior.

Hazing

Other legal issues arise related to fraternities and student use of alcohol. In general, if the actions of students who are involved in fraternities contribute to alcohol abuse by their members and others, they and their organizations can be liable for this abuse. Moreover, as reflected by a case from South Carolina where a student who was seeking to join a fraternity died of being forced to consume large amounts of alcoholic beverages, its members were liable for his death, because they had a duty to provide aid to students who are inebriated (*Ballou v. Sigma Nu*, 1986). Consequently, in order to regulate alcohol abuse and consumption, campus officials commonly take steps to monitor fraternity activities more closely.

Hazing on college campuses, particularly in the context of fraternities and sororities, has resulted in litigation. Students have been injured in hazing incidents during school-sanctioned extracurricular activities, exposing institutions to financial liability. Based on these concerns, state laws regarding hazing by fraternities and sororities are typically upheld and often lead to having fraternities and sororities on campuses becoming decertified if their officials are unable to control the activities of their members (*Phelps v. Colby College*, 1991). College and university officials continue to be concerned that they have a duty to exercise reasonable care when they know or should have known that fraternities haze prospective members. As a result, due to the large number of injuries that prospective fraternity members and others sustain during hazing, legislatures in a growing number of states have joined colleges and universities in enacting antihazing laws to control the behavior of students.

Status of Constitutional Claims by Students

As a final matter, in the context of events that transpire on college and university campuses, students cannot always rely on constitutional claims, such as deprivations of their First Amendment rights as in *Healy*, to overturn charges that they have violated institutional rules, especially because constitutional constraints typically are inapplicable at private institutions. Furthermore, insofar as college or university attendance is considered a privilege and not a right, courts do not often allow constitutional claims to supersede institutional rules, particularly when students are subject to discipline. Participation in voluntary extracurricular activities is even less like a right than a privilege, and thus it is even further removed from constitutional protection than attendance at colleges and universities; as a result, there is even greater judicial reluctance to intervene in disputes over such activities. Moreover, while some courts conceded that students entered into contractual relationships with their institutions,

officials typically have virtually unlimited power to dictate contractual terms. Not surprisingly, courts routinely uphold rules that are promulgated by college and university officials.

Conclusion

In general, courts agree that because attendance at colleges and universities is a privilege and not a right, officials have the authority not to accept students for admission. However, once admitted as students at institutions of higher learning, students are required to comply with rules and regulations that are related to academics as well as to their deportment during school hours and extracurricular activities. To this end, institutional officials promulgate rules and policies affording them the authority to dismiss students whose behavior they determine is unacceptable.

Colleges and university officials have also implemented rules aimed at regulating the prevalent moral environment, however widely defined as following institutional policies. In attempting to regulate student morality, institutions often oversee extracurricular activities and accepted behaviors. As a result, officials must be able to refer to rules, regulations, or reasons related to students' academic performances or deportment that the students allegedly violated before the students can be expelled for disciplinary infractions. At the same time, once accused, students bear legal burden of proving that they have followed institutional rules and regulations. If officials find that students failed to comply with the established norms, the students may be dismissed. In this way, college and university officials preserve their authority over students outside of classrooms as they engage in extracurricular activities.

Vivian Hopp Gordon

See also Due Process, Substantive and Procedural; Hazing; Privacy Rights of Students; Student Moral Development

Further Readings

Melear, K. B. (2005). Contracts with students. In J. Beckham & D. Dagley (Eds.), *Contemporary issues in higher education law* (pp. 209–234). Dayton, OH: Education Law Association.

Russo, C. J., & Thro, W. E. (2005). Student equal protection and due process. In J. Beckham & D. Dagley (Eds.), *Contemporary issues in higher education law* (pp. 257–275). Dayton, OH: Education Law Association.

Legal Citations

Ballou v. Sigma Nu, 352 S.E.2d 499 (S.C. Ct. App. 1986).

Dixon v. Alabama State Board of Education, 294 F.2d 150 (1961), *cert. denied*, 368 U.S. 930 (1961).

Fussell v. Louisiana Business College of Monroe, 519 So.2d 384 (La. Ct. App. 1988).

Gay Student Services v. Texas A&M University, 737 F.2d 1317 (5th Cir. 1984).

Gott v. Berea College, 161 S.W. 204 (1913).

Healy v. James, 408 U.S. 169 (1972).

Phelps v. Colby College, 595 A.2d 403 (Me. 1991).

F

FAIR USE

The cornerstone of the Copyright Act is the concept of fair use, a practice that is common on college and university campuses, particularly in their libraries. Under the act, copyright attaches as soon as the original works of authors are placed into tangible media. Neither registering works with the U.S. Copyright Office nor placing copyright notices is required in order to create copyright protection for original works. Even so, placing copyright notices on works is beneficial, because notice to the public is necessary in most cases in order to claim statutory damages and attorney fees for copyright infringements.

Determinations as to whether the copying or reproduction of the original works of others is a Copyright Act violation begins with the act's broad exemption that "criticism, comment, news reporting, teaching (including multiple copies for classroom use), scholarship or research is not an infringement of copyright" (Copyright Act, § 107). While the act allows for the use of copyright protected material for these purposes, these functions are still subject to the act's four fair use factors:

the purpose and character of the use, including whether it is of a commercial nature or is for nonprofit educational purposes;

the nature of the copyrighted work;

the amount and substantiality of the portion used; and

the effect of the use upon the potential market for or value of the copyrighted work. (Copyright Act, § 102)

Considerable litigation, frequently involving publishing houses, has resulted in the sharpening of the definition of these four factors for the purpose of calculating the appropriate balancing of the factors where some, but not all, have been violated.

The Copyright Act permits instructors and students at nonprofit educational institutions to perform and display copyrighted material in face-to-face teaching activities. Excluded from this exemption are audiovisual works that are not "lawfully made under this title, and that the person responsible for the performance knew or had reason to believe was not lawfully made" (Copyright Act, § 110(1)). The definition of face-to-face instruction has been extended to include e-mail courses and classes transmitted by means of interactive digital networks by instructors at "accredited nonprofit educational institutions" (Copyright Act, § 110(2)(A)). Accreditation is defined for postsecondary institutions as certification provided by regional or national accreditation organizations approved by the Council of Higher Education Accreditation or the U.S. Department of Education.

The e-course exemption allows instructors both to perform and display, by means of digital technology, entire nondramatic literary and musical works as reasonable, and limited portions of any type of audiovisual work. This expanded range of educational use of materials is inapplicable to material designed for the distance-learning market or works not lawfully made or acquired; materials not directly related to teaching content and limited to reception for students in classes for which the transmission is being made; materials that are not analogous to those of a typical classroom; transmissions that lack safeguards to prevent student retention and redistribution of transmitted material; or the making of digital copies that are used for other than authorized transmissions. While the Copyright Act permits the making of digital works and digitizing them to portions of analog works, the conversions of analog or print works into digital formats is impermissible unless no digital version of the analog version is available or the "digital version of the work that is available to the institution is subject to technological protection measures that prevent its use for "lawful transmission under section 110(2)" (Copyright Act, § 112 (f)(2)).

Whether educational institutions are entitled to exemptions under the copyright act has been subject to fairly continuous congressional action over the years regarding music and other electronic programming. In evaluating fair use, the act addresses not only whether educational institutions impose charges for seeing or hearing copyrighted electronic reproduction but whether audiences include only students or can be expanded to cover members of the general public.

The classic fair use and copyright infringement case is *Marcus v. Rowley* (1983), wherein a high school teacher (Marcus) who developed a 35-page booklet, "Cake Decorating Made Easy," found herself in the awkward position of being charged with plagiarism by her own students after another teacher (Rowley) had copied portions of Marcus's booklet without permission or attribution and distributed them to students. A student who had been given the booklet while enrolled in one of the courses taught by the copyright infringing teacher (Rowley) refused to buy the booklet from Marcus when the student enrolled in one of Marcus's courses, believing that Marcus had impermissibly copied Rowley's work. Worth noting is that plaintiff, Eloise Marcus, had placed in each booklet the copyright symbol © followed by "1973 Eloise Marcus." In the plaintiff's subsequent suit under the Copyright Act resulting from the defendant's unauthorized copying, the Ninth Circuit held that a copyright violation occurred and remanded for damages. Regarding the four fair use factors, the court asserted that the defendant violated the first

element, because her use had been "for the same intrinsic purpose for which the copyright owner intended" (*Marcus,* p. 1175). The court added that the defendant violated the third factor, because it was inconceivable that "the copying of all, or substantially all, of a copyrighted [item] can be held to be a fair use" (*Marcus,* p. 1176).

Defining a Copyrightable Interest

The basic aspect of fair use is that it protects only against unlawful copying and extends only to the copyrightable portions of the author's output (*Nazer v. Stein*, 1954). The Copyright Act protects only the medium of expression and protection but does not extend to "any idea, procedure, process, method of operation, concept, principle, or discovery" (Copyright Act, § 102(b)). In addition, copyright infringement applies only to substantial similarity in copying (*Twentieth Century–Fox v. MCA*, 1983). Thus, the threshold question in considering whether a defendant has exceeded fair use and, as a result, violated the Copyright Act, is always whether that which has been copied was copyrightable.

In *Clark v. Crues* (2008), the Federal Circuit court held that a teacher who developed a hall pass system did not have a copyrightable interest in that system for purposes of an infringement action against the school's development of a similar system, because he had only a "business idea" that is excluded from Copyright Act protection. In essence, the Federal Circuit court did not have to reach the question of fair use, because it was of the opinion that the teacher's idea did not display the originality to be copyrightable. However, the court went even further to declare that even if school officials intentionally copied the teacher's ideas, he still would have lacked a claim, because the two hall pass systems displayed a "limited use of similar functional language" that cannot support a copyright infringement action (*Clark,* p. 294).

Photocopying

An especially contentious issue in education is the use of photocopied materials for classes. Although Section 107 of the Copyright Act indicates that multiple photocopying for classroom distribution is fair use, such photocopying has been clarified by a separate agreement negotiated by groups representing authors, publishers, and educators (Guidelines for Classroom Copying in Not-For-Profit Educational Institutions, Copyright Act, § 107). Unfortunately, the agreement's guidelines for multiple classroom copies based on the criteria of brevity, spontaneity, and cumulative effect are far from clear. Guidelines negotiated separately between music educators and music publishers regarding the copying of music (Guidelines for Educational Uses of Music, Copyright Act, § 107) are much more narrowly drawn and much more readily understandable.

Section 108 of the Copyright Act limits library photocopying to one copy of items so that they can be used for "private study, scholarship, or research" (Copyright Act, § 108(d)(1)). In addition, libraries are required to have, at locations where copies are made, "a warning of copyright in accordance with requirements that the Register of Copyrights shall prescribe by regulation" (Copyright Act, § 108(e)(2)). In *Basic Books, Inc. v. Kinko's Graphics Corporation* (1991) a federal trial court in New York awarded a book publishing company statutory damages, injunctive relief, attorney fees, and costs in a dispute over copying. The court recognized that when employees of a Kinko's located adjacent to a higher education campus made copies of a book without permission, they were not engaged in fair use. According to the court, "The copying was just that—copying—and did not 'transform' the works in suit, that is, interpret them or add any value to the material copied, as would a biographer's or critic's use of a copyrighted quotation or excerpt" (*Basic Books*, p. 1530).

Employment Relationships

Fair use and copyright ownership can become intertwined issues involving employment relationships. Works that are created as part of employment relationships, especially at colleges and universities, are considered "works for hire." Moreover, under the Copyright Act, "The employer or other person for whom the work was prepared is considered the author . . . unless the parties have expressly agreed otherwise in a written instrument signed by them, [the employer] owns all of the rights comprised in the copyright" (Copyright Act,

§ 201(b)). In *Pavlica v. Behr* (2005), a federal trial court in New York thought that a triable question of fact existed as to whether a high school teacher owned the copyright to a manual he developed to teach a new course to his students; he distributed the manual to other teachers as part of a university professor's National Science Foundation research project. When the teacher's involvement with the project was terminated, he claimed copyright ownership of the manual. In ordering the case to trial, the court was unwilling to grant motions for summary judgment in favor of the defendant professor and the university on their theory that the teacher lacked copyright interest in a manual. The court thus rejected the defendants' argument that the manual was a work for hire based on his employment relationship at the high school.

Remedies

The civil remedies for copyright infringement are daunting and can involve injunctive relief and damages. Copyright owners have the option of proving actual damages or using the statutory damages provided in the act. If copyright owners elect the former, actual damages may include lost profits and lost royalties. In *Applied Innovations v. Regents of the University of Minnesota* (1989), the university and its licensee recovered $226,598 in lost profits for the licensee and $162,161 in lost royalties for the university as copyright owner.

In an important distinction, the Copyright Act makes it clear that the range of statutory damages depends on the willfulness of the infringement violation. Damages for infringements that are not willful range from a minimum of $750 to a maximum of $30,000 for each violation (Copyright Act, § 504(c)(1)). Awards for willful violations can be as high as $150,000 for each violation (Copyright Act, § 504(c)(2)). In cases of copyright infringements where the "infringer was not aware and had no reason to believe that his or her acts constituted an infringement of copyright" (Copyright Act, § 504(c)(2)), courts have the discretion to reduce awards of statutory damages to sums not less than $200 for each violation. Furthermore, if agents or employees of institutions of higher learning who were acting in the scope of their employment, and believed or had reasonable grounds for believing that their use of copyrighted work was fair use, then courts have the authority to remit statutory damages.

Ralph D. Mawdsley

See also Digital Millennium Copyright Act

Further Readings

Abramson, E. M. (1988). How much copying under copyright? Contradictions, paradoxes, inconsistencies. *Temple Law Review, 61,* 153–196.

Legal Citations

Applied Innovations v. Regents of the University of Minnesota, 876 F.2d 626 (8th Cir. 1989).
Basic Books v. Kinko's Graphics Corporation, 758 F. Supp. 1522 (S.D.N.Y. 1991).
Clark v. Crues, 260 Fed. App'x. 292 (Fed. Cir. 2008).
Copyright Act of 1976, 17 U.S.C. § 102 (Fair Use); § 107 (Exemption); § 107 (Historical and Statutory Notes—Guidelines for Classroom Copying in Not-For-Profit Educational Institutions); § 107 (Historical and Statutory Notes—Guidelines for Educational Uses of Music); § 108 (Reproduction by Libraries and Archives); § 110 (Performance Exemptions); § 112 (Limitations on Exemptions); § 201(b) (Works for Hire); § 412 (Damages and Attorney Fees); § 504(c) (Statutory Damages).
Marcus v. Rowley, 695 F.2d 1171 (9th Cir. 1983).
Nazer v. Stein, 347 U.S. 201 (1954).
Pavlica v. Behr, 397 F. Supp. 2d 519 (S.D.N.Y 2005).
Twentieth Century–Fox Film Corporation, et al. v. MCA Inc., et al., 715 F.2d 1327 (9th Cir. 1983).

FAMILY AND MEDICAL LEAVE ACT

The Family and Medical Leave Act (FMLA), which became law in 1993, requires educational employers, including both public and private colleges and universities, to provide generally unpaid leave for covered faculty and staff to care for their medical needs and those of specified family members. Moreover, insofar as there are no special provisions for institutions of higher learning, they are subject to all of the FMLA's requirements, including those for record keeping, except that special rules apply to instructional employees of K–12 schools who wish to take leave near the end of school terms (29 C.F.R. § 825.600a). The FMLA defines covered employers, including public agencies such as institutions of higher learning, as those engaged in commerce or industry with 50 or more eligible employees each working day during 20 or more calendar weeks in the current or preceding calendar year.

In order to be covered by the FMLA, faculty and staff members, regardless of whether they work on a full- or part-time basis, must have been employed by their colleges or universities for at least 12 months, providing at least 1,250 hours of service during the year immediately preceding the start of leave. As noted below, subject to greater protections that they may have under other federal or state laws or collective bargaining contracts, individuals are entitled to 12 weeks of unpaid leave during any 12-month period as provided for in the FMLA policies adopted by their institutions. If colleges and universities offer paid leave for fewer than 12 weeks, then the remainder of leaves may be without pay. Even so, if individuals have accrued paid vacation, personal, or family leave, they may elect, or employers may require, these to be substituted for unpaid leave. If institutional leave plans do not allow for substitutions, then they are not permitted.

When college and university officials create one-year policies, they may use the calendar year, any 12-month leave period such as a fiscal year, or a 12-month span measured forward or backward from the first FMLA leave date. Institutions may modify their policies as long as they afford workers 60 days' notice.

Types of FMLA Leave

Faculty and staff at colleges and universities can request FMLA leave under two broad categories. The first type of FMLA leave, child care, covers the birth, adoption, or foster care assumption of a child within 12 months of the event. The second kind of FMLA leave, a "serious health condition," pertains to the illnesses of spouses, children, or parents, or one rendering employees unable to perform their own job functions (29 C.F.R. § 2612 (1)(D)). The FMLA defines a serious health condition as one requiring treatment from or under the direction of health care providers such as doctors of medicine and osteopathy, podiatrists, dentists, clinical psychologists, optometrists, and nurse practitioners. The three categories of serious health conditions are those requiring inpatient care; those necessitating absences from work, school, or other daily activities in order to obtain continuing treatment; and those including prenatal care or continuing treatments for chronic or long-term conditions that are incurable or so serious that if left untreated would likely result in incapacities for more than three days. In a case from a noneducational setting that is relevant to institutions of higher learning, a federal trial court in Pennsylvania rejected the claim of a pharmacy technician that her single medical treatment for bronchitis met the definition of a chronic health condition. The court granted the employer's motion for summary judgment in the face of the plaintiff's claim that her employment was terminated in retaliation for seeking FMLA leave (*Phinizy v. Pharmacare*, 2008).

Faculty and staff members may take leave for 12 consecutive weeks or may seek intermittent or reduced leave. Intermittent leave is taken in separate blocks of time for single illnesses or injuries rather than over continuous periods of time. Reduced leave occurs when employees seek changes to part-time or flexible scheduling after childbirth. In the event that this occurs, officials at colleges and universities may temporarily transfer qualified employees, typically those other than faculty and instructional personnel, as long as there are no reductions in salary and benefits. Spouses who work for the same institution may take up to 12 weeks each for childbirth or to care for sick parents, and each may take 12 weeks of unpaid leave to look after children who are ill.

Notice and Certification

Individuals who request FMLA leave for child care or serious medical conditions must provide 30 days' notice or as much as is practicable. Individuals who request FMLA leave for foreseeable treatments due to serious medical conditions must make reasonable efforts to schedule them so as not to cause undue disruptions at work. While

FMLA leave policies are free to waive notice requirements, if such provisions remain in effect but employees do not comply, employers may deny leave requests for up to 30 days so they have time to get replacement workers to meet institutional requirements.

Officials at colleges and universities may require certification from health care providers before granting FMLA leaves. Certification should include the dates when conditions started, their likely duration, and statements of inability to perform job functions. Leaves to care for family matters should include estimates of how long individuals will be absent while providing care. If institutional officials doubt the validity of certifications, they may, at their own expense, obtain second opinions. If the two opinions conflict, institutional officials may seek a third, again at their own expense, from a health care provider that is mutually acceptable to both parties. A third opinion binds both parties.

Faculty and staff members who are asked to provide certification must be given at least 15 days to comply. Institutional officials may seek recertification at reasonable intervals of not less than 30 days. If employees request extensions or are unable to return to work after 30 days, or if employers doubt the continuing validity of certifications, they need not wait 30 days before seeking to be recertified for leave. In order to address circumstances of this nature, FMLA leave policies should address consequences for employees who fail to provide certification of the reasons for their absences.

Health Insurance

Subject to the conditions identified below, institutions of higher learning must continue to provide preexisting group health plans to employees who are on leave on the same basis as if the employees had worked continuously. Moreover, faculty and staff members are entitled to new plans, benefits, or changes in group coverage to the same extent as if they were not on leave, along with notification of any opportunities to change plans or benefits.

If institutional health care plans require faculty and staff members to contribute to the cost of their insurance premiums, FMLA leave policies should include terms on how payments will be made during absences. If employers choose not to pay premiums for employees on leave, they have two options: They can either continue making payments to keep absent employees' policies active and collect from employees when the employees return to work, or they may discontinue coverage after 30 days. If coverage for health lapses while they are away from work, returning faculty and staff members are entitled to reinstatement without qualifying periods. If individuals fail to return to work due to serious health conditions or situations beyond their control, employers may not recover contributions that they made for health care. Institutional employers may seek reimbursements from faculty and staff members who do not return to work due to changing their jobs.

Return to Employment

The key protection available under the FMLA is that employees returning from leaves must be restored to their same or similar positions with equivalent pay and benefits. Still, if institutional employers have good faith reasons to eliminate the jobs of individuals who are on leaves and do not act out of retaliation, then, subject to proving that they acted with proper motives, positions may be terminated. At the same time, as reflected by a case from the Tenth Circuit in which an employee was dismissed for poor job performance, the court held that she was not entitled to relief on her claim that officials fired her in retaliation for her for having requested, and taken, FMLA leave (*Gray v. Baker*, 2005).

Officials at colleges and universities may require faculty and staff members to provide certification of fitness to return to work following FMLA leave. Returning employees who are no longer qualified to perform their jobs must ordinarily be afforded reasonable opportunities to meet new standards. Even so, a case from New York highlights the fact that the FMLA, in a manner that is similar to that of the Americans with Disabilities Act, does not confer an absolute right to return to employment, especially if individuals cannot meet basic job requirements due to circumstances such as having to deal with substance abuse problems. The court ruled that because a former nurse at a university hospital was unable to perform essential job functions when she returned to work after completing an approved FMLA leave to deal with her substance abuse problem, she was not entitled to reinstatement (*Geromanos v. Columbia University*, 2004).

Along with protecting employees from being fired for claiming their rights, the FMLA requires employers to make, keep, and preserve records demonstrating their compliance. To this end, the Department of Labor has an annual right to review the FMLA records of employers and may examine them more frequently if necessary to investigate alleged violations.

Faculty and staff members who allege that their rights have been violated may file suit in federal or state court within two years of alleged violations. Individuals who can prove that officials at their colleges or universities willfully or intentionally failed to comply with the FMLA have three years within which to file suit. Institutions that violate the FMLA may have to reinstate or promote employees and may be liable for up to 12 weeks of wages, benefits, and reasonable attorney fees. However, in at least one case, a federal trial court in Mississippi rejected the FMLA claim of a medical technologist who had been employed by a university on the basis that the Eleventh Amendment barred her claim for alleged violations of the statute's self-care provisions (*Bryant v. Mississippi State University*, 2004). The court explained that while claims are viable for caring for family members, they may not proceed for self-care under the Eleventh Amendment.

Of course, nothing in the FMLA is meant to supersede any greater leave protections that employees at colleges and university may have received subject to collective bargaining agreements (29 C.F.R. § 825.700), state law (29 C.F.R. § 825.701), or federal and state anti-discrimination laws (29 C.F.R. § 825.702).

Charles J. Russo

See also Americans with Disabilities Act; Eleventh Amendment

Legal Citations

Americans with Disabilities Act, 42 U.S.C.A. §§ 12101 *et seq.*

Bryant v. Mississippi State University, 329 F. Supp. 2d 818 (N.D. Miss. 2004).

Code of Federal Regulations, as cited.

Family and Medical Leave Act, 29 U.S.C.A. §§ 2601 *et seq.*

Geromanos v. Columbia University, 322 F. Supp. 2d 420 (S.D.N.Y. 2004).

Gray v. Baker, 399 F.3d 1241 (10th Cir. 2005).

Phinizy v. Pharmacare, 569 F. Supp. 2d 512 (W.D. Pa. 2008).

FAMILY EDUCATIONAL RIGHTS AND PRIVACY ACT

The content of and access to student records in higher education are governed primarily by the Family Educational Rights and Privacy Act (FERPA). Also known as the Buckley Amendment after its primary sponsor, New York State Senator James Buckley, FERPA was enacted into law in 1974. The two primary goals of FERPA, which applies to institutions receiving federal financial assistance, are to grant access to their records to eligible students, meaning those who are over the age of 18, and their parents, for those who are younger, while limiting the access of third parties. While FERPA applies equally to parents and eligible students who are over the age of 18 or who attend postsecondary schools, most litigation over FERPA has been filed by parents on behalf of their children rather than by students in postsecondary institutions. Even so, FERPA should be of great interest to all in institutions of higher learning.

FERPA covers educational records containing personally identifiable information about students that are preserved by educational agencies or by those acting on their behalf. Insofar as educational records may include information about more than one student, individuals reviewing records may examine only that portion of group data that is specific to themselves.

Another form of records that educational institutions preserve is so-called directory information, which includes each student's "name, address, telephone listing, date and place of birth, major field of study, participation in officially recognized activities and sports, weight and height of members of athletic teams, degrees and awards received, and the most recent previous educational agency or institution attended by the student" (20 U.S.C. § 1232g(a)(5)(A)). Before educational officials may release directory information about students, they must provide the students (or their parents) with public notice of the categories of records that are designated as directory information while affording them a reasonable time to request that materials not be released without their consent.

Pursuant to FERPA, educational officials must annually inform parents and students over the age of 18 of their rights under FERPA before educational institutions may disclose any directory information, such as a student's age or academic standing, to third parties. Parents and students ordinarily receive notice by a means that is reasonably likely to inform them of their rights, such as in newsletters, student handbooks, or other means designed to ensure that they receive notice. In addition to rights of access, FERPA requires educational officials to provide individuals with reasonable interpretations and explanations of information contained in their records.

FERPA includes four major exceptions for information that is not classified as educational records subject to its disclosure provisions. First, records made by educational personnel that remain in the sole possession of their makers, such as class notes and private notebooks, and that are not accessible to others except temporary instructors, are not subject to release. Second, parties may not access records kept separately by the law enforcement units of educational agencies that are used only for the agencies' own purposes. Third, records that are made in the ordinary course of events relating to individuals who work at, but who do not attend, educational institutions, and which refer solely to their staff capacities, are not subject to disclosure. Fourth, records of students who are 18 or older or who attend postsecondary institutions that are made by physicians, psychiatrists, psychologists, or other professionals for use in treatment are not available to others except at the requests of the students.

As noted, under FERPA, parental permission or consent is transferred to eligible students who reach their 18th birthdays or who attend postsecondary institutions. Another restriction of interest is that that officials at institutions of higher learning do not have to permit students to inspect financial records in their files that include information about the resources of the students' parents or letters of recommendation for which students have waived their rights of access. Further, officials are not required to grant access to records pertaining to individuals who are not or never have been students at their institutions, such as in cases where students applied for admission but never enrolled in a school.

FERPA permits third parties to access educational records, other than directory information, only if eligible individuals provide written consent or if the third parties qualify for one of the following nine major exceptions, for which approval is not required before they may review records.

First, officials with legitimate educational interests may access student records such as transcripts.

Second, officials representing institutions to which students have applied for admission may access records, as long as parents (or students over the age of 18) receive proper notice that the information has been sent to the receiving institutions.

Third, authorized representatives of the U.S. comptroller general, the secretary of the Department of Education, and state and local education officials with authority under state law may view student records for law enforcement purposes.

Fourth, persons who are responsible for evaluating student eligibility for financial aid may review appropriate educational records.

Fifth, members of organizations conducting studies on behalf of educational agencies or institutions developing predictive tests or administering aid programs and improving instruction may view records if doing so does not lead to the release of personal information.

Sixth, those acting in the course of their duties for accrediting organizations may review student records.

Seventh, parents of dependent children may access student records.

Eighth, in emergencies, persons who protect the health and safety of students or other persons may view records. Following the tragic shootings at Virginia Tech University, the federal Department of Education modified the regulation on this eighth point with regard to student safety. According to this modification, staff at the Department of Education will defer to the judgment of campus officials as to what constitutes an emergency as long as the officials have a rational justification for acting (34 C.F.R. § 99.32(a)(5)).

Ninth, written permission is not necessary if student records are subpoenaed or otherwise obtained through judicial orders except that individuals must be notified in advance of compliance by educational officials.

Third parties seeking disclosure of student records must have written consent from qualified individuals specifying the record(s) to be released, the reason(s) for the requested release, and to whom the information is being given. FERPA specifies that students whose records are released (or their parents) have the right to receive copies of the released materials. Educational officials must keep records of all, except exempted parties, who request or obtain access to records; these records must both explain the legitimate interests of those who were granted access and be kept with student records.

Educational agencies that maintain student records must comply with requests for reviews without unnecessary delays. Unless parties agree to the contrary, they must be granted access no later than 45 days after making requests. Agencies may not charge fees to search for or to retrieve student records, but they may require payment for copies as long as this does not effectively prevent individuals from exercising their rights to inspect and review these materials.

Individuals who disagree with the contents of educational records may ask officials to amend the files. If officials refuse to amend records within a reasonable time, parties are entitled to hearings at which hearing officers decide whether the challenged materials are accurate and appropriately included in student files. Hearings must take place within a reasonable time. If hearing officers agree that contested materials are inaccurate, misleading, or otherwise violate student rights to privacy, educators must amend them and inform the parents (or students over the age of 18) in writing of their actions. However, if hearing officers find that materials are acceptable, the materials need not be removed or amended. Individuals who have concerns over the contents of their educational records, even after hearing officers find them permissible, may add statements explaining their objections; these statements must be kept with the contested information for as long as it is maintained.

If interested parties are denied the opportunity to review their records, they may file written complaints detailing the specifics of alleged violation with the federal Department of Education's Family Policy Compliance Office (FPCO). Complaints must be filed within 180 days of alleged violations or the date when parties knew or reasonably should have known about claimed violations. When the FPCO receives a complaint, its staff must notify officials at the offending educational institution in writing, detailing the substance of the alleged violations and asking the officials to respond, before considering whether to proceed with investigations. If, after investigations are completed, officials at the FPCO agree that violations occurred, the Department of Education can sanction institutions by withholding payments, issue orders to compel compliance, or terminate the institution's eligibility for funding if officials refuse to comply within a reasonable time.

Litigation Relating to FERPA

The Supreme Court addressed its only two cases involving FERPA in 2002. In *Owasso Independent School District v. Falvo*, the Court, in permitting a private claim to proceed, held that peer grading, whereby teachers in K–12 schools permit students to grade the papers of classmates, does not turn the student papers into educational records covered by FERPA. The Court was of the opinion that school board officials did not violate FERPA by permitting teachers to use the practice over a mother's objection, insofar as grades do not become official records until they are maintained or saved by educational staff.

Four months later, in *Gonzaga University v. Doe*, a student unsuccessfully challenged a university official's unauthorized release of information about him that led to the denial of his request for certification as a public school teacher. The dispute arose when a certification specialist in the administrative offices of the dean in the School of Education,

on overhearing a conversation about the student's alleged inappropriate conduct with a female friend, conducted an unauthorized investigation, contacted the state agency for teacher certification, and discussed the situation with officials in that office. Based on the improper release of information without the student's knowledge or permission, the student filed suit, challenging the actions of the university officials.

In *Doe*, the Supreme Court essentially repudiated that part of its decision in *Falvo* that allowed a private claim to proceed, ruling that FERPA's nondisclosure provisions do not permit aggrieved parties to file suits against institutions in disputes over access to, or impermissible release of, their educational records. Instead, in a point that should be of great significance for postsecondary institutions, the Court concluded that the only remedy available to parties with FERPA-related grievances is to petition the Department of Education, asking it to impose sanctions.

Charles J. Russo

See also Grading Practices; Student Teachers, Rights of

Further Readings

Individuals with Disabilities Act 20 U.S.C. §§ 1400 (2004).

Legal Citations

Code of Federal Regulations, 34 C.F.R. §§ 99.1 *et seq.*
Family Educational Rights and Privacy Act, 20 U.S.C. § 1232g.
Gonzaga University v. Doe, 536 U.S. 273 (2002).
Owasso Independent School District v. Falvo, 534 U.S. 426 (2002).

FEDERALISM

The term *federalism* refers to the division of power and responsibility between the states and the national government. Implicit in the structure of the U.S. Constitution and reaffirmed by the Tenth Amendment, the principles of dual sovereignty, commonly called federalism, limit the powers of the national government in three significant ways. First, as the Eleventh Amendment confirms, the states retain their immunity from lawsuits. Second, dual sovereignty limits Congress's power to enforce the Fourteenth Amendment. Third, federalism limits Congress's ability to regulate interstate commerce.

Federalism is enormously important for state-supported higher education institutions, which are generally considered to be state actors or arms of the state for constitutional and legal purposes. Thus, federalism limits the ability of the national government to interfere with state universities and preserves their power to make to certain policy decisions. The origins of federalism in the Constitution and early court rulings are discussed in this entry along with the limitations the U.S. Supreme Court has placed on Congress's power to enforce the Fourteenth Amendment and to regulate interstate commerce.

Background

In *The Federalist No. 51,* James Madison wrote, "In the compound republic of America, the power surrendered by the people is first divided between two distinct governments." Madison believed that by dividing sovereignty between the national government and the states, the Constitution ensured that "a double security arises to the rights of the people. The different governments will control each other, at the same time that each will be controlled by itself." Thus, as the Supreme Court said in *Texas v. White* (1868),

> The preservation of the States, and the maintenance of their governments, are as much within the design and care of the Constitution as the preservation of the Union and the maintenance of the National Government. The Constitution, in all its provisions, looks to an indestructible Union, composed of indestructible States.

According to a more recent decision of the Supreme Court, this division of sovereignty between the states and the national government "is a defining feature of our Nation's constitutional blueprint" (*Federal Maritime Commission v. South Carolina State Ports Authority,* 2002). The division of power between *dual sovereigns,* the states and the national government, is reflected throughout the Constitution's text, as well as its structure. The Supreme Court said, in *Gregory v. Ashcroft* (1991),

> Just as the separation and independence of the coordinate branches of the Federal Government serve to prevent the accumulation of excessive power in any one branch, a healthy balance of power between the States and the Federal Government will reduce the risk of tyranny and abuse from either front.

In other words, although the Constitution gives vast power to the national government, the national government remains one of enumerated, hence limited, powers. Indeed, "that these limits may not be mistaken, or forgotten, the constitution is written," according to the landmark *Marbury v. Madison* (1803) ruling.

Because the federal balance of powers is so important, the Court has intervened to maintain the sovereign prerogatives of both the states and the national government. In order to preserve the sovereignty of the national government, the Court has prevented the states from imposing term limits on members of Congress and instructing members of Congress as to how to vote on certain issues. Similarly, it has invalidated state laws that infringe on the right to travel, that undermine the nation's foreign policy, and that exempt a state from generally applicable regulations of interstate commerce.

Conversely, recognizing that "the States retain substantial sovereign powers under our constitutional scheme, powers with which Congress does not readily interfere" (*Gregory,* 1991) and that "the erosion of state sovereignty is likely to occur a step at a time" (*South Carolina v. Baker,* 1988), the Court declared that the national government may not compel the states to pass particular legislation, to require state officials to enforce federal law, to dictate the location of state capitols, to regulate purely local matters, or to abrogate the state's sovereign immunity.

Development of the Concept

Adopted at the time of the Civil War, the Fourteenth Amendment included several clauses that diminished the states' sovereign authority while enhancing the power of the national government. First, both the Equal Protection Clause and the Privileges or Immunities Clause imposed substantive restrictions on the states. Moreover, although the Bill of Rights originally did not apply to the states, the Due

Process Clause incorporated most of the provisions of the Bill of Rights. *Incorporation* in this context means that the Fourteenth Amendment gave Congress the authority to enact legislation that enforced the substantive guarantees of the Fourteenth Amendment against the states; this power was provided by the amendment's Enforcement Clause. Consequently, if the states have engaged in conduct that violates the Fourteenth Amendment, Congress can take remedial action to correct the violation and to prevent future violations.

However, there are limits on Congress's power to enforce the Fourteenth Amendment. In *City of Boerne v. Flores* (1997), the Court applies the "congruence and proportionality" test, which involves three questions. First, the Court must identify the scope of the constitutional right at issue. Second, after identifying the right at issue, the Court must determine whether Congress identified a history and pattern of unconstitutional discrimination by the states. Third, if there is a pattern of constitutional violations by the states, the Court determines whether Congress's response is proportionate to the finding of constitutional violations.

The Court has identified three broad categories of activity that Congress may regulate under the Commerce Clause in Article 1 of the Constitution. First, Congress may regulate the use of the channels of interstate commerce. Second, Congress is empowered to regulate and protect the instrumentalities of interstate commerce, or persons or things in interstate commerce, even though the threat may come only from intrastate activities. Third, Congress may regulate intrastate activities having a substantial relation to interstate commerce. The Court has stated that this last category includes only activities that are economic in nature.

The test for determining whether an intrastate activity substantially affects interstate commerce varies depending on whether the regulated activity is economic in nature. If the intrastate activity is economic in nature, the impact of all similar activity nationwide is considered. Conversely, if the intrastate activity is not economic in nature, its impact on interstate commerce must be evaluated on an individualized, case-by-case basis, in which the focus is on preventing disruption and maintaining a stable economic environment. In other words, does the activity have anything to do with "commerce" or any sort of economic enterprise? Is

it an essential, or indeed any, part of a larger regulation of economic activity?

While Congress may regulate the states when the states engage in general commercial activities, Congress may not regulate the states when the states act in their sovereign capacities:

Even where Congress has the authority under the Constitution to pass laws requiring or prohibiting certain acts, it lacks the power directly to compel the States to require or prohibit those acts. . . . The Commerce Clause, for example, authorizes Congress to regulate interstate commerce directly; it does not authorize Congress to regulate state governments' regulation of interstate commerce. (*Printz v. United States*, 1997)

William E. Thro

See also Eleventh Amendment; Equal Protection Analysis

Further Readings

Hamilton, A. (1788, June 25 and 28). The federalist no. 81. The judiciary continued, and the distribution of judicial authority. *The Independent Journal.*
Madison, J. (1788, January 16). The federalist no. 39. Conformity of the plan to republican principles. *The Independent Journal.*
Madison, J. (1788, February 16). The federalist no. 51. The structure of the government must furnish the proper checks and balances between the different departments. *The Independent Journal.*
Thro, W. E. (2003). That those limits may not be forgotten: An explanation of dual sovereignty. *Widener Law Journal, 12,* 567–583.
Wilkinson, J. H., III. (2001). Federalism for the future. *Southern California Law Review, 74,* 523–541.

Legal Citations

City of Boerne v. Flores, 521 U.S. 507 (1997).
Federal Maritime Commission v. South Carolina State Ports Authority, 525 U.S. 743 (2002).
Gregory v. Ashcroft, 501 U.S. 452 (1991).
Marbury v. Madison, 5 U.S. 137 (1803).
Printz v. United States, 521 U.S. 898 (1997).
South Carolina v. Baker, 485 U.S. 505 (1988).
Texas v. White 74 U.S. 700 (1868).

FLORIDA PREPAID V. COLLEGE SAVINGS BANK

Florida Prepaid Postsecondary Education Expense Board v. College Savings Bank (1999) is a landmark U.S. Supreme Court case dealing with the ability of Congress to abrogate sovereign immunity for claims involving intellectual property.

The Eleventh Amendment confirms that the states retain sovereign immunity from lawsuits. However, this immunity is not absolute. Congress, in exercising its powers to enforce the Fourteenth Amendment, may abrogate the states' immunity. Moreover, states may voluntarily waive their immunity. Finally, when there are ongoing violations of federal law, the doctrine established in the landmark case *Ex Parte Young* (1908) generally allows federal courts to enjoin state officials from engaging in unlawful behavior. *Florida Prepaid* involved the abrogation exception to sovereign immunity. The U.S. Supreme Court's ruling in *Florida Prepaid* established that Congress has not abrogated the states' sovereign immunity for claims involving intellectual property; thus, states and state agencies remain immune from intellectual property claims. Insofar as most public institutions, including colleges and universities, are considered arms of their states for purposes of the Eleventh Amendment immunity claims, this entry reviews the analysis in *Florida Prepaid* and its significance for higher education.

Facts of the Case

The litigation arose out of a dispute between a state agency in Florida that administered a prepaid tuition program and a bank in New Jersey. After the bank in New Jersey had secured a patent for a particular financing methodology, it claimed that the state agency in Florida violated its patent. Although the Florida agency normally would have been immune from such a claim, Congress had enacted a statute purporting to abrogate the states' sovereign immunity for intellectual property claims. In light of this, the agency in Florida contended that this purported abrogation was unconstitutional. Even so, both the federal trial court in New Jersey and the court of appeals for the Federal Circuit, a specialized court with jurisdiction over

patent claims, rejected the Florida agency's position. The Supreme Court then agreed to hear an appeal.

The Supreme Court's Ruling

On further review, in a five-to-four decision authored by Chief Justice Rehnquist and joined by Justices O'Connor, Scalia, Kennedy, and Thomas, the Court reversed in favor of the agency from Florida on the basis that Congress's attempt to abrogate sovereign immunity was unconstitutional. The Court began by noting that Congress had made its intention to abrogate clear and that Congress could not use its Article I powers to abrogate sovereign immunity. To this end, the Court identified the critical issue as whether Congress had properly used its power to enforce the Fourteenth Amendment.

The dispute before the Supreme Court in *Florida Prepaid* turned on the application of the test from the 1997 landmark case of *City of Boerne v. Flores,* wherein the Supreme Court invalidated the federal Religious Freedom Restoration Act in a suit over historical preservation at a church in Texas. Reformulating the *Flores* test, the Court focused on whether Congress had identified a pattern of constitutional violations by the states and if so, whether abrogating sovereign immunity was an appropriate response to that pattern. The Court pointed out that Congress failed on both inquiries. First, the Court ruled that Congress had never identified a pattern of patent infringement, much less a pattern of constitutional violations. Second, the Court reasoned that the broad remedy imposed by Congress, namely abrogating sovereign immunity for all patent claims against all states for an indefinite period, was not the type of limited remedy required by the Constitution. Accordingly, the Court struck down as unconstitutional the statute that purported to abrogate sovereign immunity.

Justice Stevens, joined by Justices Souter, Ginsburg, and Breyer, vigorously dissented. In their view, Congress had the power to establish national uniformity with respect to patents, and that included the ability to abrogate the states' sovereign immunity. At the same time, the dissent was of the opinion that the congressional findings of potential patent violations were more than sufficient to satisfy the *Flores* standard. The dissent also emphasized its disagreement with the Court's recent reaffirmation of sovereign immunity principles.

A decade after it was decided, the Court has not limited its judgment in *Florida Prepaid*. Indeed, in later cases the Court has expanded this rationale in other substantive areas of the law. For state universities that are considered an arm of the state, *Florida Prepaid* and its progeny remains a foundational case protecting them from liability.

William E. Thro

See also *Central Virginia Community College v. Katz*; Eleventh Amendment; *Kimel v. Florida Board of Regents*

Further Readings

Board of Trustees of the University of Alabama v. Garrett, 531 U.S. 356 (2001).

Central Virginia Community College v. Katz, 126 S. Ct. 990 (2006).

Chisholm v. Georgia, 2 U.S. (2 Dall.) 419 (1793).

College Savings Bank v. Florida Prepaid, 527 U.S. 666 (1999).

Federal Maritime Commission v. South Carolina State Ports Authority, 535 U.S. 743 (2002).

Kimel v. Florida Board of Regents, 528 U.S. 62 (2000).

Nevada Department of Human Resources v. Hibbs, 538 U.S. 721 (2003).

Noonan, J. T., Jr. (2002). *Narrowing the nation's power: The Supreme Court sides with the states*. Berkeley: University of California Press.

Puerto Rico Aqueduct & Sewer Authority v. Metcalf & Eddy, 539 U.S. 139 (1993).

Seminole Tribe v. Florida, 517 U.S. 44 (1996).

Tennessee Student Assistance Corporation v. Hood, 541 U.S. 440 (2004).

Tennessee v. Lane, 541 U.S. 509 (2004).

Thro, W. E. (1999). The Eleventh Amendment revolution in the lower federal courts. *Journal of College & University Law, 25*, 501–525.

Thro, W. E. (2000). The education lawyer's guide to the sovereign immunity revolution. *Education Law Reporter, 146*, 951–931.

Thro, W. E. (2007). The future of sovereign immunity. *Education Law Reporter, 215*, 1–31.

Thro, W. E. (2007). *Why you cannot sue State U: A guide to sovereign immunity* (2nd ed.). Washington, DC:

National Association of College and University Attorneys.

United States v. Georgia, 126 S. Ct. 877 (2006).

Legal Citations

City of Boerne v. Flores, 521 U.S. 507 (1997).

Ex Parte Young, 209 U.S. 123 (1908).

Florida Prepaid v. College Savings Bank, 527 U.S. 627 (1999).

FOR-PROFIT COLLEGES AND UNIVERSITIES

See Proprietary or For-Profit Colleges and Universities

FOURTEENTH AMENDMENT

The Fourteenth Amendment to the U.S. Constitution emerged as the result of a congressional debate about how to deal with integrating the southern states into the Union after the Civil War. The amendment was designed to grant slaves citizenship rights and to eliminate the economic and political system that had supported slavery. Further, in addition to ensuring equal protection to all persons, the Fourteenth Amendment guarantees that no person may be deprived of life, liberty, or property without due process of law. In light of the significant impact that the Fourteenth Amendment has had on legal developments in higher education, this entry reviews its key features along with examples of how it has been applied in specific cases.

Historical Background

Efforts to heal the nation began in 1868 when the states ratified the Fourteenth Amendment to the Constitution. Congress had passed the Fourteenth Amendment in 1866, but it did not become the law of the land until it was ratified two years later. In fact, the Fourteenth Amendment was the result of a compromise between radicals and moderates regarding treatment of former Confederates. Previously, Republicans in the 39th Congress formed a Joint Committee of Fifteen to resolve the difficulties associated with former Confederate state congressmen by granting citizenship to all persons born or naturalized in the United States.

The first section of the Fourteenth Amendment has been the focus of a great amount of litigation. According to this section, no state, which the courts have interpreted as including public officials acting on behalf of states, may abridge the privileges and immunities of citizens; deprive any person of life, liberty, or property without due process of law; or deny any person within its jurisdiction their equal protection of the law. The Fourteenth Amendment Due Process and Equal Protection Clauses shield all individuals from unfair and unjust treatment, protection that has been extended to all regardless of race, sex, religion, or age.

Section 2 of the Fourteenth Amendment provides for representation in Congress, changing the three-fifths compromise, wherein five slaves were counted as equal to three free persons in determining a state's representation in the House of Representatives, into the provision that all persons in a state counted individually for representation except Indians, who were not taxed. Section 3 calls for removing from Congress all of those who fought against the United States in the Civil War. Section 4 validates the debt of the United States, voids all debts incurred to support the rebellion, and expunges all claims for slave compensation. Section 5 grants Congress the authority to pass legislation to enforce the provisions of the Fourteenth Amendment.

Judicial Interpretation

The Fourteenth Amendment's Due Process and Equal Protection Clauses ensure that persons are protected from all forms of discrimination. The Amendment was designed to give civil rights protection to minorities and the voiceless. Early Supreme Court cases after the Fourteenth Amendment was adopted limited the scope of the law, clarifying its provisions.

The *Slaughterhouse Cases* in 1873 examined a monopoly in Louisiana, wherein the Supreme Court adopted a limited view of the scope of the Fourteenth Amendment with regard to state action.

When independent butchers sought protection for their occupation, the Court reiterated the principle that state legislatures have always exercised the power of granting exclusive rights when necessary to protect the public good. While such power is not forbidden by the Thirteenth Amendment in conjunction with the first section of the Fourteenth Amendment, the Court explained that the main purpose of these articles was to protect the due process rights of all individuals. Even so, in the late 1890s, southern and border states implemented Jim Crow laws and Black Codes that led to mandatory segregation of Blacks in all public places and private businesses, including cemeteries and institutions of higher learning.

In *Plessy v. Ferguson* (1896) the Supreme Court institutionalized a Jim Crow law from Louisiana in maintaining that the notion of "separate but equal" was constitutional. At issue was a law that mandated separation of passengers in public railway cars based on their races. In so doing, the Court upheld established state segregation customs and usage practices, allowing officials to use partitions to keep the races apart when there were not enough railroad cars to separate the races. In the Court's majority analysis, Justice Henry Brown noted that the Fourteenth Amendment was undoubtedly enacted to enforce absolute equality of the two races before the law. Yet, in the nature of things, he contended that it could not have been intended to abolish all distinctions based on color or to enforce social, as distinct from political, equality or to require a commingling of the two races unsatisfactory to either race.

The sole dissenter, Justice John Harlan, whose position essentially presaged the majority judgment in *Brown v. Board of Education, Topeka* (1954), noted that the Constitution is color-blind, neither knowing nor tolerating classes among citizens. In the matter of civil rights, he maintained that all citizens are equal before the law. Further, Harlan's observation that *Plessy* would, in time, prove only to stimulate brutal and irritating aggressions on the rights of African Americans was borne out, as states and the judiciary relied on it as legal justification for segregating students based on race in education at all levels of schooling. For example, in *Berea College v. Kentucky* (1908) the Court upheld a criminal conviction against a private college for teaching African Americans and Whites together.

As challenges mounted to *Plessy*, initially from the world of higher education, the Supreme Court incrementally undercut the basis of "separate but equal." In the issue in *Sweatt v. Painter* (1950), a Black student was denied admission to the University of Texas Law School. Because there were no law schools for Blacks, a lower court in Texas ordered officials to create a law school for Blacks. However, the Supreme Court agreed with Sweatt's position that because the segregated law school was inadequate, officials had to admit him to the University of Texas Law School. In *McLaurin v. Oklahoma State Regents for Higher Education* (1950), the issue was that a Black graduate student at the University of Oklahoma was allowed to enroll but required to sit in the designated areas for Blacks in all areas of the university. The Court invalidated this treatment as an unconstitutional violation of the Equal Protection Clause.

The seminal case dealing with the application of the Fourteenth Amendment Equal Protection Clause is *Brown v. Board of Education, Topeka* (*Brown I*, 1954). In a unanimous decision, the Supreme Court ruled that that because segregation of students solely on the basis of race deprived minority children of equal educational opportunities, the doctrine of "separate but equal" had no place in public education. The Court added that because separate educational facilities are inherently unequal, state officials violated the Fourteenth Amendment equal protection rights of all children who had been subjected to racial segregation in their schooling.

While *Brown* did not address remedies, in *Brown v. Board of Education II* (*Brown II*, 1955), the Supreme Court directed officials to integrate the schools "with all deliberate speed." Yet state and local officials made persistent efforts to delay or circumvent the Court's mandate. Subsequently, the Civil Rights Act of 1964, which became law during the presidency of Lyndon Baines Johnson, reinforced the importance of safeguarding the due process and equal protection rights of all. More specifically, Title VI of the act prohibited discrimination on the basis of race, color, or national origin in any program receiving federal aid.

The Supreme Court narrowed the scope of affirmative action over time. *Regents of the University of California v. Bakke* (1978) was the Court's first case dealing with the merits of affirmative action as applied to admissions in higher education. In a

plurality, meaning that the Court was unable to reach an opinion on which five justices agreed, it rejected the use of quotas but was willing to treat race as legitimate factor in consideration for admission to a public university's medical school. Still, because the judgment left key questions unanswered, additional litigation ensued.

Adarand Constructors v. Pena (1995) involved affirmative action remedies with regard to a publicly funded construction project. The Supreme Court ruled that because strict scrutiny and narrow tailoring were the appropriate criteria when dealing with affirmative action, the case had to be remanded for a consideration of whether the program met these standards in its attempt to correct historical injustices.

The Supreme Court's two most recent cases involving affirmative action in higher education arose at the University of Michigan, and the Court applied strict scrutiny (see definition of this term below) in both cases. In *Gratz v. Bollinger* (2003) the court ruled that the admissions policy at the University of Michigan School of Law, which was designed to encourage racial diversity in the student body, was constitutional. In reaching its judgment, the Court was satisfied that the law school's interest in having a diverse student body was a compelling governmental interest that was sufficiently narrowly tailored to achieve the goal of student body diversity, because all applicants were subjected to highly individualized holistic reviews.

On the other had, in *Grutter v. Bollinger* (2003) the Supreme Court invalidated an undergraduate admissions policy at the University of Michigan that granted preferences to members of identified minority groups. While conceding that having a diverse student body was a compelling governmental interest, the Court struck down the program as unconstitutional in noting that admissions officials could not use student numerical quota systems or grant points to individual applicants based on their race. Instead, the Court explained that officials had to accept applicants in light of their individual qualifications.

Levels of Scrutiny

Equal protection analysis recognizes that no governmental action is neutral and that all acts of government impact the rights of persons. In its contemporary equal protection analysis, the Supreme Court has identified three levels of scrutiny to which governmental actions, through their officials, can be subjected. To this end, three degrees of scrutiny emerged in reviewing challenges to these actions. The highest level, *strict scrutiny,* applies when the government or its officials treat individuals differently due to their race, national origin, religion, or citizenship status. When government action disadvantages members of these "suspect" classes, such actions must be shown to serve a compelling government interest. Government actions that impact fundamental rights such as those identified in the Constitution also trigger strict scrutiny. When the courts apply strict scrutiny, asking whether actions are narrowly tailored to further compelling governmental interests, most governmental actions are struck down as unconstitutional.

Courts apply *intermediate scrutiny* when governmental actions in educational settings treat individuals differently typically due to their gender or legitimacy. Although not as stringent as strict scrutiny, this test upholds governmental actions if they are substantially related to achieving important governmental interests.

The third level, *rational basis scrutiny,* is applied to day-to-day governmental actions, such as those dealing with health and safety. These are ordinarily upheld as constitutional as long as officials can demonstrate that their actions are rationally related to legitimate governmental purposes.

In sum, in light of the history of slavery, it was some time before the implementation of due process and equal protection actually occurred, because officials in states with histories of segregation used a variety of tactics, such as Jim Crow laws, to forestall such action. Yet, over the years, the Fourteenth Amendment has been the source of expanded civil rights in gender, racial, ethnic, civil rights, age, and religion conflicts.

The authors of the Fourteenth Amendment worked through conflicting views to achieve a workable compromise to expanded rights for future generations. Civil rights laws will continue to expand equal access and opportunity for the nation's growing diverse population. At the same time, the judiciary, in its deliberations, will continue to clarify and expand Fourteenth Amendment due process and equal protection rights for a diverse multicultural, multiracial, multiethnic population in American colleges and universities.

James J. Van Patten

See also Affirmative Action; Civil Rights Movement; Equal Protection Analysis; *Gratz v. Bollinger; Grutter v. Bollinger; McLaurin v. Oklahoma State Regents for Higher Education; Regents of the University of California v. Bakke; Sweatt v. Painter;* Title VI

Further Readings

Kaplan, W. A., & Lee, B. A. (2006). *The law of higher education* (4th ed.). San Francisco: Jossey-Bass.

Knudson, S., & Sorenson, A. (1984). *The guide to American law* (Vol. 4). New York: West.

Legal Citations

Adarand Constructors v. Pena, 515 U.S. 200 (1995).
Berea College v. Kentucky, 211 U.S. 45 (1908).
Brown v. Board of Education, Topeka, 347 U.S. 483 (1954).
Brown v. Board of Education II, 349 U.S. 294 (1955).
Civil Rights Act of 1964, Pub. L. No. 88-352.
Gratz v. Bollinger, 539 U.S. 244 (2003).
Grutter v. Bollinger, 539 U.S. 306 (2003).
McLaurin v. Oklahoma State Regents for Higher Education, 339 U.S. 637 (1950).
Plessy v. Ferguson, 163 U.S. 537 (1896).
Regents of the University of California v. Bakke, 438 U.S. 265 (1978).
Slaughterhouse Cases, 83 U.S. 36 (1873).
Sweatt v. Painter, 339 U.S. 629 (1950).
Title VI of the Civil Rights Act of 1964, 42 U.S.C. § 2000d.

FOURTH AMENDMENT RIGHTS OF FACULTY

The Fourth Amendment to the U.S. Constitution protects persons from "unreasonable searches and seizures." Searches can be physically invasive or may invade individuals' legitimate expectation of privacy. Physical invasions, such as being forcibly restrained and ordered to strip for decontamination, seem clearly to invoke Fourth Amendment protection. However, the question of whether a search has taken place under less physically invasive circumstances, such as when a campus security officer looks into an open dormitory room, can be less clear. To make successful claims for protection under the Fourth Amendment for nonphysical invasions, individuals must have genuine beliefs not only that they have expectations of privacy but also that these expectations are reasonable in the view of an ordinary, reasonably prudent person experiencing the same circumstances. If challenges fail either prong of this test, then individuals lack legitimate expectations of privacy and are not entitled to protection under the Fourth Amendment.

At the same time, it is important to note that the right to be free from unreasonable searches or invasions of privacy under the Fourth Amendment cannot be casually conflated with the right of privacy under the Fourteenth Amendment. Moreover, faculty First Amendment and academic freedom concerns over access to material that is sexually explicit on the Internet via university-owned computers and systems, as was the issue in *Urofsky v. Gilmore* (2000), should not be confused with issues relating to searches. In light of the significant implications involving the rights of faculty members, particularly those at public colleges and universities, this entry examines the parameters of their Fourth Amendment rights, even though many of the cases are presented as nonbinding precedent due to the relative dearth of litigation in this important arena.

The General Rule for Searches: Probable Cause

The Fourth Amendment prohibits only unreasonable searches. Law enforcement officials often conduct investigations that obviously invade legitimate expectations of privacy, such as searches of the persons and homes of criminal suspects. In most such cases, searches of homes may occur only following the presentation of evidence to judges or magistrates and the issuance of warrants. This process ensures that searches are conducted following showings of probable cause that persons, places, or things to be searched will yield evidence of crimes. As a general rule, then, warrantless searches are deemed to be unreasonable and are prohibited

by the Fourth Amendment. Yet not every investigative effort by governmental officials involves the enforcement of state or federal laws. Hence, the courts have recognized important exceptions to the general prohibition on warrantless searches. While searches of students in K–12 settings do not directly implicate the rights of faculty members in higher education, the U.S. Supreme Court's rationale in its only case on this point is instructive for higher education.

Lesser Standard for Searches

Searches of Public School Students

In *New Jersey v. T.L.O.* (*T.L.O.*, 1985), after a high school student was accused of smoking and a subsequent search of her purse by an assistant principal revealed that she possessed marijuana, she was ultimately unsuccessful in her attempt to suppress the evidence based on her claim that the warrantless search violated her rights under the Fourth Amendment. Although acknowledging that a search occurred within the meaning of the Fourth Amendment, the Supreme Court held that the Fourth Amendment's warrant requirement was unsuited for school environments, because it would interfere with the need of educational officials to take swift and informal disciplinary action. The Court then determined that public school officials possess "special needs" and that these needs justify the application of a reasonableness standard for searches rather than the traditional probable cause standard that applies to the police.

The Supreme Court decided that under ordinary circumstances, searches of students, either by teachers or other educational officials, are justified as constitutional at their inception if educators have reasonable cause for suspecting that such searches will turn up evidence that students have violated either the law or school rules, and if the searches as actually conducted are reasonably related in scope to the circumstances that justified the searches in the first place. Even if officials have met both the subjective and objective requirements necessary to establish a legitimate expectation of privacy, warrantless searches may still be permissible if special needs are at issue. This deferential approach created an exception to the general probable cause rule and conceded that while public school students enjoy some protection under the Fourth Amendment, these safeguards are diminished within the educational environment, including at colleges and universities.

Searches of Employees of Public Universities

Diminished Fourth Amendment rights such as those identified in *T.L.O.* have since been extended to others within educational environments. Two years after *T.L.O.*, in *O'Connor v. Ortega* (1987), the Supreme Court applied a reduced standard to public employees, including university faculty members. At issue in *Ortega* was a search of the office of a physician–faculty member at a state university hospital that was conducted in order to gather evidence of professional impropriety. The physician unsuccessfully filed suit, alleging that the search of his office and desk violated the Fourth Amendment.

In *Ortega*, the Supreme Court again conceded that a search had occurred, but citing *T.L.O.* as precedent, explained that a workplace search conducted by supervisory public officials in their capacity as employers is a special need that requires only reasonable cause. The Court noted that because a probable cause requirement would be impractical in circumstances involving work-related, noninvestigatory intrusions as well as employee misconduct, the reasonableness standard under the circumstances applied. The Court was of the opinion that public employment represents another context in which public officials may face fewer restrictions with regard to the privacy rights of employees.

When a Search May Occur: Reasonable Cause

Whether a search is reasonable is a determination made by balancing the rights of individuals against public interests. This balancing test is often discussed in terms of intrusiveness by considering whether the special need for a search justifies the resulting intrusion. If this seems less than clear, it is. The Supreme Court has found that an absolute definition of reasonableness in this balancing test is not possible. However, what is clear is that reasonable cause is a lesser standard than probable cause and that any search conducted under the

reasonable cause standard must be objectively reasonable in both inception and in execution.

In order to evaluate whether there is reasonable cause to conduct a search, one must consider the factual circumstances and balance the interests of the individual and the public accordingly. This asks whether a reasonable person would find the motivation for and purpose of a search to be reasonable. If so, then the inception of the search is likely to have satisfied constitutional parameters. The next inquiry is into whether a reasonable person would think that that, in light of the purposes for a search, it was conducted in a reasonable manner. If so, then the execution of the search was likely permissible. The presence of protection for both the purpose and execution of the search reflects a recognition that even a search that is permissibly motivated may become impermissible if it becomes unreasonable in execution.

When Searches Begin and Why It Matters

Although searches can be benign intrusions, such as entry into an office to water potted plants, they can also be utilized to gather evidence of misconduct or criminal behavior. Consistent with the *T.L.O.* standard, searches that are conducted to investigate allegations of misconduct are usually justified at their inception if there are reasonable grounds for suspecting that they will uncover evidence that employees are guilty of having engaged in work-related misconduct (*Wasson v. Sonoma County Junior College*, 1997). To this end, any evidence that is collected in connection with such searches has been "seized" within the meaning of the Fourth Amendment. In this way, it is critical that information collected during searches be collected lawfully so that subsequent criminal prosecutions are not jeopardized.

In *United States v. Butler* (2001), for example, a student in Maine was expelled and charged with receiving child pornography over the Internet via the public university's computers. The student left a pornographic image of a child frozen on at least one computer, and a university employee observed the image. The incident led to an investigation by university officials that revealed many more such images on computers that the student used. The student unsuccessfully argued that all the evidence collected was the product of an illegal search, and therefore inadmissible at trial. The court specified that insofar as a search must be permissible in purpose and execution, if one is impermissible at inception, any evidence subsequently seized will be inadmissible in a criminal proceeding. The court concluded that when it is known that evidence collected during a search is likely to be used for criminal prosecution, it may be prudent to consider whether a warrant should be sought. The same type of analysis would likely apply in cases involving faculty members.

Searches Outside the Scope of the Fourth Amendment

As should be clear, not all searches are protected by the Fourth Amendment. In determining whether searches are protected, the courts consider whether the searches were conducted with consent, whether the searches involved the observation of something that was readily apparent, and/or whether the searches took place in the context of regulations that affected whether there were reasonable expectations of privacy.

Consent

When individuals grant meaningful consent to searches, the general rule is that they have waived their protection. As a result, consent may play an important part in the efforts of employers to conduct suspicionless searches, those that are carried out despite the absence of reasons to believe that evidence of wrongdoing will be uncovered. Adopting this approach, the Supreme Court has consistently treated drug testing, which is often random and therefore suspicionless, as constituting a search within the meaning of the Fourth Amendment (*Georgia v. Randolph*, 2006). Under some circumstances, such as those with government employees who are responsible for enforcing antidrug laws (*National Treasury Employees Union v. Von Raab*, 1989), the Court has upheld the use of drug testing under the special needs exception. However, the Court has noted that permitting drug testing under such an exception is rare, because testing violates legitimate privacy expectations of most private citizens and public employees. In some circumstances, therefore, meaningful consent is likely to be the only means by which to remove warrantless searches from the protection of the Fourth Amendment.

Observable

Searches that consist of no more than observing that which is readily observable, such as items that are in plain view, are not considered searches within the protection of the Fourth Amendment on the basis that what individuals knowingly expose to the public, even in their homes or offices, is not subject to the protection of the Fourth Amendment. The application of this principle can be seen in two similar surveillance cases that produced different results.

In *United States v. Knotts* (1983), the Supreme Court addressed whether using a radio transmitter, which was placed inside a container used in a suspected illegal drug laboratory, constituted a search within the meaning of the Fourth Amendment. The transmitter permitted law enforcement to follow an automobile to a secluded location, where the activities of the suspects could be observed. The Court ruled that no warrant was necessary, because no search occurred insofar as the transmitter only aided officials in observation by adding to the sensory faculties. Yet, in *United States v. Karo* (1984), a case with similar facts, the Court thought that a search did occur when a transmitter was used to track a container not on public roads but on private property out of public view. The Court pointed out that because a private residence creates an expectation of privacy in individuals, government intrusion may occur only with proof of probable cause supported by a warrant.

Regulatory Context

The regulatory context of the workplace may also render a search outside the protection of the Fourth Amendment. Put another way, a work environment with no custom or policy of conducting searches may create a reasonable expectation of privacy on the part of employees. However, where employee surveillance is regularly and transparently conducted, employees are unlikely to have reasonable expectations of privacy. In *United States v. Maxwell* (1996), a federal military court indicated that an air force officer had a legitimate expectation of privacy where the officer composed and dispatched messages on employer computers but during the officer's personal time and through a private Internet service provider. According to the court, the officer had a reasonable expectation that the e-mail communication was private. In contrast, in *United States v. Monroe* (1999), another military court affirmed that a sergeant who had a pornographic e-mail solicitation in his computer files had no reasonable expectation of privacy where the government owned both the computer and the e-mail system. In overruling the individual's privacy claim, the court asserted that unlike the system involved in *Maxwell,* the electronic mail host system in this dispute was owned by the government and, as such, carried no expectation of privacy.

When employers monitor workplace e-mail, employees are often aware of what is taking place. In *McLaren v. Microsoft Corp.* (1999), an appellate court in Texas affirmed that that e-mail messages stored on employer-owned computers were not the employee's personal property, nor were they private, because the employer was free to observe any communication passing through the account. The court reached this outcome despite the fact that the information was stored in a password-protected "personal" folder on the computer. Similarly, a federal trial court in Pennsylvania granted a private employer's motion to dismiss a wrongful discharge claim that was filed by an employee who was fired for making inappropriate and unprofessional comments in e-mail messages. The court wrote that a reasonable person would conclude that a company's interest in preventing inappropriate communication outweighs any employee privacy interest in work-related e-mail communication. The court reached this judgment even though officials of the employer broke an explicit promise to their employees that communication occurring through the employer-provided e-mail system would remain private and confidential and would not be used for the purposes of discharging an employee (*Smyth v. Pillsbury Co.,* 1996).

In order to ensure that employees do not have any expectation of e-mail privacy, many employers require that employees acknowledge in writing their awareness of e-mail surveillance by the employers or even that their e-mail communications are not private. This practice has been successful in persuading courts to find no legitimate

expectation of privacy in employee e-mail (*Biby v. University of Nebraska at Lincoln,* 2005). This success has usually been grounded in the objective prong of the expectation of privacy test. Insofar as it is widely known that employers, including public colleges and universities, routinely intercept and review employee e-mail, even if individuals genuinely think that the e-mail is private, such a belief may well not be reasonable.

Increasing Impact of Technology on Fourth Amendment Jurisprudence

Finally, it is important to keep in mind that most of the evolution in Fourth Amendment workplace legal analysis is being generated by technological advances, particularly on college and university campuses. To the extent that technology is expanding the scope of observable activity, and further because states can reduce the protections of public employees—including faculty members at institutions of higher learning—through regulation, an argument can be made that technological progress serves to shrink the realm of guaranteed privacy. As technology develops, a pattern or cycle may emerge in which what was once unobservable becomes observable. Once it is widely known that what was once unobservable is now observable, elements of society will cease to recognize it as private, and once there appears to be some societal acceptance of this shift, employers, including institutions of higher learning, are likely to implement regulatory policies to prevent faculty members from claiming legitimate expectations of privacy over that which was once private. Theoretically, this cycle results in fewer individuals satisfying both the subjective and objective prongs of the test necessary to place a search within the protections of the Fourth Amendment.

Philip T. K. Daniel

See also Fourteenth Amendment

Legal Citations

Biby v. University of Nebraska at Lincoln, 419 F.3d 845 (8th Cir. 2005).
Georgia v. Randolph, 547 U.S. 103 (2006).
McLaren v. Microsoft Corp., 1999 WL 339015 (Tex. App. 1999).

National Treasury Employees Union v. Von Raab, 489 U.S. 656 (1989).

New Jersey v. T.L.O., 469 U.S. 325, 341 (1985).

O'Connor v. Ortega, 480 U.S. 709 (1987).

Smyth v. Pillsbury Co., 914 F. Supp. 97 (E.D. Pa. 1996).

United States v. Butler, 151 F. Supp. 2d 82 (D. Me. 2001).

United States v. Karo, 468 U.S. 705 (1984).

United States v. Knotts, 460 U.S. 276, 282 (1983).

United States v. Maxwell, 45 M.J. 406 (C.A.A.F. 1996).

United States v. Monroe, 50 M.J. 550 (A.F.C.C.A. 1999).

Urofsky v. Gilmore, 216 F.3d 401 (4th Cir. 2000), *cert. denied*, 531 U.S. 1070 (2001).

Wasson v. Sonoma County Junior College, 4 F. Supp. 2d 893, 905 (N.D. Cal. 1997).

FOURTH AMENDMENT RIGHTS OF STUDENTS

According to the Fourth Amendment to the United States Constitution,

> The right of the people to be secure in their persons, houses, papers, and effects, against unreasonable searches and seizures shall not be violated; and no Warrants shall issue but upon probable cause . . . and particularly describing the place to be searched, and the persons or things to be seized.

The Fourth Amendment has far-reaching ramifications in higher education with respect to searches of students' dormitory rooms or their persons incident to drug testing of participants in intercollegiate athletics, whether in public or private institutions of higher learning. This entry reviews litigation in which courts have examined the Fourth Amendment rights of college and university students.

Dormitory Searches at Public Colleges and Universities

The Supreme Court's only case involving the Fourth Amendment rights of college students was *Washington v. Chrisman* (1982). *Chrisman* dealt with a search of a dormitory room that took place after a police officer at a public university watched a student who appeared to be under the legal drinking age of 21 leave his dormitory while carrying a bottle of gin. The officer stopped the student and asked for identification and then accompanied the student to his room so that the student could obtain his identification. While the officer was standing in the doorway, he noticed what he thought were marijuana seeds and a pipe on the desk. The officer then entered the room, confirmed that the seeds were marijuana, decided that the pipe smelled of marijuana, and informed both the student and his roommate of their rights. When asked whether there were other drugs in the room, the roommate gave the officer a box containing more marijuana and cash. Once a second police officer arrived, both students waived their Miranda rights to remain silent or to have an attorney present and voluntarily consented, orally and in writing, to a search of the room. The search yielded more marijuana and another controlled substance, leading to the roommate's being charged with two counts of possessing the controlled substances.

After the Supreme Court of Washington invalidated the search that led to the roommate's criminal conviction, the U.S. Supreme Court reversed in favor of the state. The Court held that it was not unreasonable for the police officer to have accompanied the student to the dormitory and to have remained in the doorway. Given that the officer was present lawfully and that the marijuana had been "in plain view," meaning that it was openly visible in the room from the doorway, the Court held that the seizure of the drugs did not violate the Fourth Amendment.

As reflected by the illustrative cases reviewed in this entry, lower courts, both before and after *Chrisman*, addressed the Fourth Amendment rights of college and university students in disputes involving searches of dormitory rooms that led to their facing criminal charges for possessing illegal drugs. Such cases have had mixed results. *Moore v. Student Affairs Committee of Troy State University* (1968), an early dormitory search case, involved the search of a student's dormitory room by two state narcotics agents and the university's dean of men. When the search turned up a matchbox containing a small amount of marijuana, the student was suspended indefinitely. Although a federal trial court found that the hearing process denied the student of his constitutional right to due process, a second hearing resulted in his again being suspended.

When the student challenged his second suspension based on an unreasonable search and seizure under the Fourth Amendment, he was unsuccessful. A federal trial court, relying in part on a university regulation that granted institutional officials the right to enter dormitory rooms for inspection purposes, ruled against the student. In the court's view, the student waived his right to object to reasonable searches that were conducted pursuant to the university's regulations. Moreover, the court thought that the regulation was a reasonable exercise of university's responsibility to maintain discipline.

In *State v. Hunter* (1992), a later case in which a view much the same as that in Moore was expressed, an appellate court in Utah upheld the search of a student's dormitory room at a state university by the director of housing, a custodian, a football coach, and a university police officer. The search, which had been prompted by incidents of vandalism in the dormitory, proceeded from room to room. When the searchers entered the plaintiff's room, they saw a sign and a banner in plain view, both of which were stolen university property. This evidence was seized, and the student was later charged with misdemeanor theft. The student then succeeded in having the evidence of the stolen property suppressed at his criminal trial on the ground that the warrantless search of his dormitory room violated his Fourth Amendment rights.

On further review, an appellate court upheld the legality of the search under the Fourth Amendment, citing *Moore* with approval. As in *Moore,* the court ruled that the officials legitimately exercised their authority to maintain the educational environment. The court pointed out that the student had both signed a housing contract that gave officials right of reasonable inspection and had waived Fourth Amendment objections to the university's exercise of that right. The court was untroubled by the fact that a university police officer participated in the search, because the housing director initiated the search without input from the police, who took part for the sole purpose of assisting the director with any problems that he might not have been able to handle on his own.

Other courts have been more protective of students' Fourth Amendment rights. In *Piazzola v. Watkins* (1971), the Fifth Circuit considered the constitutionality of a dormitory search at a state university that was similar to the one in *Moore.*

State narcotics agents and university officials discovered marijuana in dormitory rooms occupied by two students, who were later convicted for the possession of marijuana and sentenced to five years in an Alabama prison. Upholding a federal trial court's grant of habeas corpus in favor of the two former students, the Fifth Circuit determined that students who occupied college dormitory rooms enjoy the protection of the Fourth Amendment despite the existence of a university regulation reserving the right to search dormitory rooms. The court observed that such a regulation could not have been construed as giving consent to a search pursued primarily for the purpose of gathering evidence for a criminal prosecution. Otherwise, the court wrote, the regulation would have been an illegal attempt to force students to waive their constitutional right to be free from unreasonable searches and seizures as a condition of residing in college dormitories.

In an interesting case from the same era, *Smyth v. Lubbers* (1975), a federal trial court in Michigan considered the constitutionality of disciplinary proceedings instituted against two students who were discovered to possess marijuana during searches of their dormitory rooms. College officials and two campus police officers who were also county deputy sheriffs participated in the searches, which had been conducted without warrants. As a result of the disciplinary hearing, both students were suspended. College officials had not filed criminal charges against the students at the time of the court's decision, which solely concerned the college's disciplinary process.

The court began its analysis by clearly endorsing the principle that college students have an important privacy interest in their dormitory rooms, an interest that is protected by the Fourth Amendment. To this end, the court posited that because student dormitory rooms are, for all practical purposes, their homes, they have the same interests in the privacy of their rooms as any adults in the privacy of their dwellings. The court refused to interpret the fact that students agreed to allow officials to search their rooms in their housing contracts as waivers of their constitutional rights under the Fourth Amendment. In the court's view, the search was unreasonable, because authorities had not obtained a warrant issued on probable cause, and therefore the students were entitled to have the evidence seized during the unconstitutional search excluded from admission in the disciplinary proceedings.

Finally, in a more recent case, *United States v. Heckenkamp* (2007), a graduate student in Wisconsin was charged with a federal crime based on allegations that he hacked into the university's computer system. University officials were working with FBI agents on an investigation of the hacking activities, and the FBI was in the process of obtaining a warrant to further its investigation. A university employee was concerned that the student might damage the computer system before a warrant could be obtained. Accompanied by university police officers, the employee entered the student's room and disconnected the computer there from the university's network. The employee also wanted to run commands on the student's computer but did not have the access password. An officer located the student, who voluntarily provided his computer password so that the employee could run the commands. The student was later charged with a federal crime and sought to suppress the evidence against him on the grounds that the searches involved in the investigation, including the search of his computer, violated his rights under the Fourth Amendment. While recognizing that the student had a constitutionally protected privacy interest in his computer, the Seventh Circuit upheld the search. The court concluded that a limited warrantless remote search of the computer was justified under the "special needs" exception to the warrant requirement because of the harm that the student could have caused by his unauthorized access to a protected computer without authorization.

Dormitory Searches at Private Colleges and Universities

Officials at private institutions of higher education are not subject to Fourth Amendment constraints when they search students' dormitory rooms unless they act in concert with law enforcement authorities. For example, in *State v. Burroughs* (1996), when a student occupied a dormitory room in a private college, as a condition of living in campus housing, he and others were required to consent to unannounced and unscheduled searches by campus officials. After the college's director of residential life learned that illegal drugs might be in the student's room, he searched it and discovered a white

powdery substance resembling cocaine. The director then notified a dean who contacted the local police, leading to the student's being charged with a drug offense.

The student unsuccessfully sought to exclude evidence of his dormitory search on the grounds both that the director acted as an agent of the police and that the search was conducted without a warrant in violation of the Fourth Amendment. The Supreme Court of Tennessee conceded that a relationship between college officials and the police might have made the officials police agents who were subject to the Fourth Amendment's warrant requirement. However, the court refused to treat the director as an agent of the police when he conducted the search, because his authority to search the room was in furtherance of college policy, not police business. Moreover, the court noted that the director searched the room before college officials contacted the police and that the search did not take place at the request of law enforcement authorities.

Other Searches in College or University Environments

Most cases involving the Fourth Amendment rights of college students involve dormitory searches. Even so, at least one published case involved other kinds of searches such as of student purses, mail, or briefcases. In *People v. Lanthier* (1971), the Supreme Court of California reviewed the constitutionality of a warrantless search of a student's library carrel locker by library employees at a private university; the search was triggered by a noxious odor emanating from the locker. When a library maintenance worker opened a briefcase in the locker, he found 38 packets of marijuana, which apparently gave off an odor because of a preservative that had been added to it. The court upheld a criminal conviction that stemmed from the search on the basis that the smell coming from the locker constituted an emergency.

Drug Testing in Intercollegiate Athletes

In *Vernonia School District 47J v. Acton* (1995), the Supreme Court upheld the constitutionality of a school board's random drug-testing program for student athletes against a Fourth Amendment challenge. Further, in *Board of Education of Independent School District No. 92 of Pottawatomie County v. Earls* (2002), the Court upheld a random drug-testing program for high school students engaged in extracurricular activities. At the college level, the Supreme Court of Colorado ruled that a state university's drug-testing program for varsity athletes violated the Fourth Amendment and state constitution (*University of Colorado v. Derdeyn*, 1993). Conversely, in *Hill v. NCAA* (1994), the Supreme Court of California reasoned that the NCAA's drug-testing policies for college varsity athletes did not violate the privacy provision of California's constitution. The court ruled that while the privacy provision applied to the NCAA, the privacy interests of intercollegiate athletes were outweighed by the NCAA's interest in preserving the integrity of competitive athletics as well as the health and safety of student athletes. Earlier, in *Bally v. Northeastern University* (1989), the Massachusetts Supreme Judicial Court rejected a claim that a private university's drug-testing program for varsity athletes violated the commonwealth's civil rights act and privacy legislation.

Conclusion

As the litigation discussed in this entry reflects, lower courts have upheld warrantless searches even when security personnel participated in searches, notwithstanding the fact that the Supreme Court has not articulated constitutional guidelines regarding the Fourth Amendment rights of college and university students in their dormitory rooms. An important element in these cases concerns the motivation for the searches. The prime consideration for courts in upholding searches was whether officials acted in furtherance of their own policies or whether they were in concert with the police to advance criminal investigations. In the event of the former, courts usually upheld the constitutionality of the searches.

Students who are searched outside their dormitory rooms generally have the Fourth Amendment rights of other citizens who are searched and enjoy no special status arising from the fact that they are students. Although lower courts reached mixed results on drug testing of athletes, in light of the Supreme Court's rationale in both *Acton* and *Earls*, it seems likely that any federal challenge to random drug testing of intercollegiate student athletes would fail.

Richard Fossey

See also Drug Testing of Students; Due Process, Substantive and Procedural; National Collegiate Athletic Association; Privacy Rights of Students

Further Readings

Jones, E. O. (2007). The Fourth Amendment and dormitory searches. *Journal of College & University Law, 33*, 597–623.

Smith, M. C., & Fossey, R. (1995). *Crime on campus: Legal issues and campus administration.* Phoenix, AZ: American Council on Education & Oryx Press.

Legal Citations

Bally v. Northeastern University, 532 N.E.2d 49 (Mass. 1989).

Board of Education of Independent School District No. 92 of Pottawatomie County v. Earls, 536 U.S. 822 (2002).

Hill v. NCAA, 865 P.2d 633 (Cal. 1994).

Moore v. Student Affairs Committee of Troy State University, 284 F. Supp. 725 (M.D. Ala. 1968).

People v. Lanthier, 448 P.2d 625 (Cal. 1971).

Piazzola v. Watkins, 442 F.2d 284 (5th Cir. 1971).

Smyth v. Lubbers, 398 F. Supp. 777 (W.D. Mich. 1975).

State v. Burroughs, 926 S.W.2d 243 (Tenn. 1996).

State v. Hunter, 831 P.2d 1033 (Utah. App. 1992).

United States v. Heckenkamp, 482 F.3d 1142 (9th Cir. 2007).

University of Colorado v. Derdeyn, 863 P.2d 929 (Colo. 1993).

Vernonia School District 47J v. Acton, 515 U.S. 646 (U.S. 1995).

Washington v. Chrisman, 455 U.S. 1 (1982).

FREE SPEECH AND EXPRESSION RIGHTS OF STUDENTS

Students in public colleges and universities enjoy a constitutional right to free speech under the First Amendment. Even so, the nature of this right varies greatly depending on the context in which students raise speech claims. Student organizations also enjoy First Amendment protection. Once public institutions create limited open forums for student groups, officials may not deny recognition to particular groups based on the groups' viewpoints. Yet because the right to freedom of expression is not absolute in higher education, the courts have permitted officials to impose reasonable time, manner, and place regulations on the speech of students and their organizations. In light of the array of issues that have arisen on campuses, this entry highlights key litigation dealing with the First Amendment speech and expression rights of students in public colleges and universities.

Free Speech Rights of Student Organizations

In *Healy v. James* (1972), the Supreme Court addressed its first case on the constitutional rights of student organizations in public colleges and universities. Officials at Central Connecticut State College refused to recognize a local chapter of Students for a Democratic Society (SDS) due to their concern that the group's philosophy was contrary to the college's official policy. Recognition would have entitled the group to a variety of privileges, including access to campus bulletin boards and the right to use campus facilities for meetings. After a federal trial court upheld the action of officials denying SDS recognition, a divided Second Circuit affirmed. On further review, the U.S. Supreme Court reversed in favor of SDS, observing that state colleges and universities are not enclaves immune from the sweep of the First Amendment. The Court ruled that college officials could not restrict a group's speech or right to associate simply because they found the group's views to be abhorrent. Still, the Court added that administrators in public institutions may require student groups seeking official recognition to affirm in advance their willingness to abide by reasonable regulations to prevent campus disruptions.

Almost a decade later, in *Widmar v. Vincent* (1981), a Christian student group at the University of Missouri at Kansas City challenged officials who denied them the use of campus facilities for their meetings. Officials denied access on the ground that granting it would have run afoul of the Establishment Clause. After a trial court granted

the university's motion for summary judgment, the Eighth Circuit reversed in favor of the group. The Supreme Court then affirmed in favor of the group. The Court reasoned that because university officials recognized more than 100 campus groups, they created an open forum whereby student groups expressing all sorts of views were permitted to use campus facilities. Having created such a forum, the Court declared, officials could not deny recognition to a group based on the content of its views. Further, the Court decided that university officials would not have violated the Establishment Clause simply by granting the religious group the same privileges and benefits that it offered other organizations.

Together, *Healy* and *Widmar* set the stage for constitutional litigation by student groups that were banned from participating in campus life based on their viewpoints. In particular, a string of federal cases resolved during the 1970s and 1980s agreed that once administrators at public colleges and universities officially recognized other student groups, they were required to grant the same benefits to organizations of gay students.

In *Gay Student Services v. Texas A&M University* (1984), for example, a gay group sued Texas A&M University (TAMU) after officials rejected its application for official recognition. Citing *Healy*, the Fifth Circuit stated that disagreement with the group's philosophy did not provide officials at TAMU with a legal basis for denying official recognition to the organization. Citing *Widmar*, the court noted that because TAMU officials had created a forum of student groups, they could not exclude the gay student group due to the content of its speech.

Expression of Controversial Views

In addition to cases involving officials' refusal to recognize selected student groups, litigation has addressed the constitutionality of regulations restricting the expressive activities of student groups with controversial views. In such a case, *Justice for All v. Faulkner* (2005), officials at the University of Texas refused to allow a recognized antiabortion student group to distribute flyers unless the material identified the sponsoring group by name. Affirming an earlier order in favor of the group, the Fifth Circuit pointed out not only that the First Amendment protects anonymous speech but also that the university policy was not narrowly tailored to minimize infringement on the group's constitutional right to engage in anonymous speech.

Pro-Life Cougars v. University of Houston (2003), another dispute between a prolife student group and university officials, arose when the organization sued the University of Houston, alleging that its "Disruption of University Operations and Events" policy violated the group's First Amendment rights. Under the policy, student groups requesting permits to conduct an expressive event were required to apply for permission from the dean of students, who had sole discretion to evaluate whether an event was "potentially disruptive"; in such a situation, the dean could assign the group to one of two relatively remote sites. After the dean directed the group to meet in a remote location because its meeting was "potentially disruptive," the students filed suit, causing officials to amend the policy in an attempt to have the litigation dismissed as moot. In rejecting the university motion to dismiss, a federal trial court in Texas invalidated the policy as unconstitutional on the grounds that it was overbroad and gave the dean of students unfettered discretion to evaluate which student groups' expressive events were "potentially disruptive."

"Fighting Words"

College and university officials are not required to tolerate "fighting words" on their campuses, even in public outdoor areas that are generally open for expressive activities. In *Gilles v. Davis* (2005), campus police officers arrested a nonstudent "campus evangelist" for directing comments to a woman who identified herself as a "Christian and a lesbian." According to the Third Circuit, the evangelist's epithets and statements to the woman, including "Christian lesbo," "lesbian for Jesus," "Do you lay down with dogs?" and "Are you a bestiality lover?" were "fighting words." As such, the court affirmed that the police could arrest the man for disorderly conduct even though other parts of his speech were less provocative.

First Amendment Right of Association

As illustrated by *Pi Lambda Phi v. University of Pittsburgh* (2000), student groups have challenged restrictions on their activities on the grounds that institutional policies infringed on their constitutional right to association. In *Pi Lambda Phi,* a fraternity sued university officials for revoking its status as a recognized student organization after a police raid led to the arrest of fraternity members for possession of illegal drugs. The fraternity unsuccessfully argued that university officials and the police had violated its First Amendment right of association. The Third Circuit affirmed that the fraternity was neither an intimate association such as a family nor an expressive association formed to advance a political or social viewpoint or to engage in the free exercise of religion. Rather, the court viewed the fraternity as merely a social group that enjoyed no associational rights under the First Amendment. In any event, the court added that the revocation of the fraternity's charter was triggered by its members' drug activities, which had no constitutionally protected expressive element.

Two cases illustrate that courts do not always agree even in similar factual situations. In *Christian Legal Society v. Walker* (2006), a student group at a public law school in Illinois sued the dean for revoking its recognition due to the group's rule against admitting students who engage in homosexual activity; the law school saw this rule as a violation of university nondiscrimination policies. The Seventh Circuit ruled that because the group was an expressive association that believed that sexual activity outside of marriage between a man and a woman was immoral, it was constitutionally entitled to exclude individuals whose views were contrary to its core beliefs. Conversely, the Ninth Circuit upheld the action of the dean at a public law school in California who denied funding to the local chapter of the Christian Legal Society because of restrictions in its by-laws related to religion and sexual orientation that violated the university's nondiscrimination policy (*Christian Legal Society Chapter of University of California v. Kane*, 2009). Insofar as splits such as these between Federal Circuit courts often make their way to the Supreme Court, it bears watching to see whether the justices will accept an appeal to resolve the disagreement between the federal circuits.

Student Activity Fees and University Regulation of Extracurricular Activities

Mandatory student activity fees raise two types of First Amendment concerns at public colleges or universities. The initial First Amendment issue arises when public institutions require students to pay activities fees to fund student organizations engaged in activities or speech with which they disagree. Another First Amendment issue concerns when public institutions use activities fees to benefit student religious organization. The Supreme Court has addressed and resolved both of these issues.

In *Board of Regents of the University of Wisconsin System v. Southworth* (2000), the Supreme Court ruled that it was allowable for a university to institute mandatory student fees and to distribute this money to a variety of student organizations as long as resource allocations are viewpoint-neutral. From the Court's perspective, institutional interests in fostering a wide variety of extracurricular groups outweighed any burden that might fall on students' First Amendment rights. The Court rejected allegations that students may have been compelled to fund organizations that they did not support.

Earlier, in *Rosenberger v. Rector and Visitors of the University of Virginia* (1995), a student group had filed suit after university officials refused to pay its printing bill for a publication on the ground that doing so would have violated the Establishment Clause. Ruling in favor of the group, the Supreme Court explained that paying for the printing did not violate the Establishment Clause as long as the activity funding program was viewpoint-neutral and benefited a wide spectrum of student organizations.

In the issue addressed in *Flint v. Dennison* (2007), officials at the University of Montana disqualified a candidate for a student senate seat for exceeding the $100 limit on campaign expenditures. In rejecting the student's First Amendment challenge, the Ninth Circuit affirmed that because the election process was a limited public forum, the campaign expenditure limitation was a reasonable, viewpoint-neutral regulation.

Hate Speech Codes and Sanctions for Derogatory Speech

Students have had some success challenging hate speech codes. In *Doe v. University of Michigan* (1989), a federal trial court agreed with a graduate student who argued that the university's speech code, which prohibited behavior, whether verbal or physical, that stigmatizes or victimizes

individuals due to their of race, ethnicity, religion, sex, sexual orientation, creed, national origin, ancestry, age, marital status, handicap, or Vietnam-era veteran status, was unconstitutionally overbroad. Similarly, in *UWM Post v. Board of Regents of the University of Wisconsin System* (1991), a federal trial court struck down an antidiscrimination policy as overbroad and vague. More recently, in *DeJohn v. Temple University* (2008), the Third Circuit affirmed that a sexual harassment policy was unconstitutional because it was facially overbroad, meaning that it did not make clear what was prohibited.

Dambrot v. Central Michigan University (1995) is the case that ensued when university officials dismissed a basketball coach for using a racial epithet in a motivational talk to players, a majority of whom were African Americans. When the coach sued university officials, arguing that his choice of the "N word" was constitutionally protected, team members joined the suit, alleging that the harassment policy under which the coach was fired was unconstitutionally vague. While the Sixth Circuit agreed with the players that the policy was unconstitutionally vague, it upheld the coach's dismissal, because he lacked a constitutional right to use a racial slur as his chosen means of motivating basketball players.

At issue in *Murakowski v. University of Delaware* (2008) was the appropriateness of disciplining a student for posting messages with violent themes about women on a Web site he maintained on the university's computer system. The federal court observed that while university officials afforded the student a full due process hearing prior to imposing discipline, because his Web-based prose was not a "true threat" for purposes of constitutional analysis and it had not caused a material or substantial disruption, the officials had violated his rights. The court concluded that because the student's Web site musings were constitutionally protected by the First Amendment, he was entitled to $10 in nominal damages.

At issue in *Iota Xi Chapter of Sigma Chi Fraternity v. George Mason University* (1993) was a fraternity's "Ugly Woman" contest that campus officials deemed hostile to women. Although fraternity officials later apologized, university administrators imposed a two-year restriction on the group's social activities. The Fourth Circuit was convinced that officials violated the fraternity's rights in asserting that the low quality of the entertainment did not necessarily weigh in First Amendment inquiries.

Student Speech in the Academic Setting

Courts have often looked to litigation involving K–12 schools when addressing the free speech rights of college and university students. This trend is evident in a dispute from the Ninth Circuit, *Brown v. Li* (2002), perhaps the leading case on the speech rights of university students in academic settings. The dispute arose when a graduate student placed a two-page "Disacknowledgements" section in his master's thesis after it had been approved by his committee. The Disacknowledgements made negative comments about various individuals, including university library staff, university administrators, the Regents of the University of California, and a former state governor. When faculty committee members learned of what the student had done, they refused to approve his thesis with the Disacknowledgements included. After several rounds of hearings, the student was allowed to graduate, but his thesis was not placed in the university library. Later, the student unsuccessfully sought an order directing officials to put his thesis in the university library, including the Disacknowledgements.

In a divided opinion, the Ninth Circuit upheld the actions of university officials. In its analysis, the court relied heavily on the Supreme Court's judgment in *Hazelwood School District v. Kuhlmeier* (1988), in which it approved a school board's placing restrictions on the content of a newspaper that students produced as part of a journalism class. In *Hazelwood,* the Court posited that educators may limit student speech in curricular activities as long as their actions are reasonably related to legitimate pedagogical concerns. To this end, the court interpreted *Hazelwood* as affording educators in public institutions the right to determine curricular content and to require students to comply with the terms of academic assignments. The court explicitly rejected the argument that *Hazelwood* was inapplicable in higher education.

A later case, *Pugel v. Board of Trustees of the University of Illinois* (2004), involved allegations of academic misconduct against a graduate student who also served as a teaching assistant. The student was accused of fabricating data for a research presentation at an academic conference. After an investigation and a hearing led to the student's dismissal, she filed suit in a federal trial court, arguing that she was sanctioned in violation of her First Amendment right to free speech. In analyzing the case, the Seventh Circuit applied the balancing test articulated in *Pickering v. Board of Education* (1969), a dispute involving the free speech rights of public school teachers to speak out as citizens on matters of public concern. The court weighed the student's First Amendment rights against the university's interest in maintaining the integrity of academic research and concluded that the university's interests outweighed any constitutional interest that the student might have had in making a research presentation that officials determined to be fraudulent.

Conclusion

College students have brought free speech claims against officials at public colleges and universities in a wide range of factual contexts. Student have claimed a constitutional right to association and to official recognition of their student organizations by public universities, have challenged the manner in which officials disburse student activity fees, have disputed hate-speech policies, and have complained about the policies that officials have applied to regulate on-campus expressive events. Many of the cases involving college students' free speech rights have been brought by student organizations rather than individual students, while only a few have involved a student's free speech rights in the academic setting. In addressing the free speech claims of individual students, judges have frequently relied on Supreme Court cases that arose from constitutional disputes in the K–12 school environments, a trend that is likely to continue.

Richard Fossey

See also Board of Regents of the University of Wisconsin System v. Southworth; Healy v. James; Papish v. Board of Curators of the University of Missouri; Rosenberger v. Rector and Visitors of the University of Virginia; Student Press; Widmar v. Vincent

Further Readings

Pauken, P. (2005). Student speech. In J. Beckham & D. Dagley (Eds.), *Contemporary issues in higher education law* (pp. 235–255). Dayton, OH: Education Law Association.

Legal Citations

Board of Regents of the University of Wisconsin System v. Southworth, 529 U.S. 217 (2000).

Brown v. Li, 308 F. 3d 939 (9th Cir. 2002), *cert. denied*, 538 U.S. 908 (2003).

Christian Legal Society Chapter of University of California v. Kane, No. 06-15956, 2009 WL 693391 (9th Cir. March 17, 2009).

Christian Legal Society v. Walker, 453 F.3d 853 (7th Cir. 2006).

Dambrot v. Central Michigan University, 55 F.3d 1177 (6th Cir. 1995).

DeJohn v. Temple University, 537 F.3d 301 (3d Cir. 2008).

Doe v. University of Michigan, 721 F. Supp. 852 (E.D. Mich. 1989).

Flint v. Dennison, 488 F.3d 816 (9th Cir. 2007).

Gay Student Services v. Texas A&M University, 737 F.2d 1317 (5th Cir. 1984).

Gilles v. Davis, 427 F.3d 197 (3d Cir. 2005).

Hazelwood School District v. Kuhlmeier, 484 U.S. 260 (1988).

Healy v. James, 408 U.S. 169 (1972).

Iota Xi Chapter of Sigma Chi Fraternity v. George Mason University, 993 F.2d 386 (4th Cir. 1993).

Justice for All v. Faulkner, 410 F.3d 760 (5th Cir. 2005).

Murakowski v. University of Delaware, 575 F. Supp. 2d 571 (D. Del. 2008).

Pickering v. Board of Education, 391 U.S. 563 (1969).

Pi Lambda Phi v. University of Pittsburgh, 229 F.3d 435 (3d Cir. 2000).

Pro-Life Cougars v. University of Houston, 259 F. Supp. 2d 575 (S.D. Tex. 2003), *appeal dismissed*, 67 Fed. App'x. 251 (5th Cir. 2003).

Pugel v. Board of Trustees of the University of Illinois, 378 F.3d 659 (7th Cir. 2004).

Rosenberger v. Rector and Visitors of the University of Virginia, 515 U.S. 819 (1995).

UWM Post v. Board of Regents of the University of Wisconsin System, 774 F. Supp. 1163 (E.D. Wis. 1991).

Widmar v. Vincent, 454 U.S. 263 (1981).

GRADING PRACTICES

Grading policies and practices are time-honored traditions in higher education. Most universities and colleges, departments, and programs have policies that suggest or require grading scales (90–100 = A, 80–89 = B, etc.) for graded courses. Similarly, institutions have guidelines on courses such as seminars, internships, qualifying examinations, theses, or dissertations that are graded on a "pass/fail" or "satisfactory/unsatisfactory" basis. In addition, many programs, departments, and colleges require faculty members to adopt specified textbooks, syllabi, or specific language related to assessment and grading. At the same time, many academic units such as education, architecture, law, social work, health, and medicine are guided by external accreditation or licensing organizations that dictate academic standards. In some cases, these external organizations require that particular assignments, assessments, or student experiences be included in academic programs. Internal and external forces of this kind have potentially profound legal implications for the work of university faculty members, because they are expected to comply with grading policies or risk losing privileges, promotions, and even continued employment.

Against these forces are claims from faculty members that overly restrictive grading policies and practices violate their individual rights to freedom of speech or academic freedom. However, by and large, officials in institutions of higher learning succeed in their defenses of these grading policies and practices. The one notable exception in this trend favoring colleges and universities came in one of the earlier cases, *Parate v. Isibor* (1989). In *Parate*, the Sixth Circuit held that forcing a university faculty member to sign a memorandum changing a student's grade unlawfully constituted compelled speech. The court ruled that the "assignment of a letter grade is a symbolic communication intended to send a specific message to the student . . . [and] is entitled to some measure of First Amendment protection" (p. 827). According to the court, because an instructor's assignment of grades is central to an individual's teaching methods, faculty members should retain wide discretion over the evaluation of students.

The trend favoring colleges and universities in faculty challenges to grading practices can be traced, in part, to important language in *Sweezy v. New Hampshire* (1957), a case that is widely known for its arguments in favor of the rights of individual faculty members. In *Sweezy*, the Supreme Court acknowledged that colleges and universities have four essential freedoms: the right to determine who may teach, what may be taught, how it shall be taught, and who may be admitted to study. Following this approach, recent courts have reasoned that academic freedom belongs to institutions rather than to individuals (*Urofsky v. Gilmore*, 2000). For example, a federal trial court in Virginia was of the opinion that a department chair utilizing his authority as chair to alter the course grade of a student did not infringe the First Amendment rights of the faculty member who taught the course, because academic freedom rested with the institution, not with individual faculty members (*Stronach v. Virginia State University*, 2008).

A review of illustrative cases highlights the point that courts remain deferential to university grading practices, barring a significant infringement on free speech. In *Brown v. Armenti* (2001), a tenured faculty member, who had been teaching for almost three decades and had been tenured since 1972, was suspended from teaching after he refused to follow an order to change a student's grade. The faculty member assigned the student a failing grade in a practicum class after the student attended only three of fifteen required meetings even though the president of the university ordered that the grade be changed to an "incomplete." The faculty member was later dismissed for writing a letter to the board of trustees criticizing the president's action. On the allegation that the initial suspension was in retaliation for refusing to change the grade, the Third Circuit entered a judgment in favor of the university in explaining that

> "In the classroom" refers to those settings where the professor is acting as the university's proxy, fulfilling one of the functions involved in the university's "four essential freedoms": choosing "who may teach, what may be taught, how it shall be taught, and who may be admitted to study." (p. 75)

The court pointed out that had the faculty member been speaking generally on the issue of grade inflation, then his speech that was critical of the president might have been protected. Yet the court found that because the faculty member was essentially expressing his dissatisfaction with the internal office decision of his supervisor, his speech was not protected.

In *Wozniak v. Conry* (2001), when a long-time faculty member submitted his semester grades, he refused to include grading materials despite requests to do so. In response, the dean of the faculty member's college barred him from teaching any more classes, canceled his research funds, and reassigned him to manage the departmental Web site. The Seventh Circuit affirmed that the faculty member's refusal to follow reasonable university rules and such insubordination was unprotected by the Constitution: "No person has a fundamental right to teach undergraduate engineering classes without following the university's grading rules" (p. 891). The court added that in the area of grades, academic freedom is an institutional concern, because it is a university's name that is entered on diplomas, and the university's officials certify to employers, graduate schools, and accrediting bodies that their students have successfully completed the program of study: "Universities are entitled to assure themselves that their evaluation systems have been followed; otherwise, their credentials are meaningless" (p. 891).

Often, the grading practices at issue in legal disputes stem from course syllabi and not merely final assigned grades. In *Johnson-Kurek v. Abu-Absi* (2005), for instance, the Sixth Circuit affirmed that it is not a constitutional violation to require instructors to provide detailed advice to students on how to meet course requirements. A nontenured faculty member filed suit, alleging that her teaching assignments were reduced in retaliation for her refusal to comply with a request to provide detailed advice to students about what was required to complete a course she had taught. Further, the plaintiff assigned grades of "incomplete" to 13 of the 17 students who were enrolled in the course. In an electronic communication to the class listserv, the plaintiff listed three reasons the students would have received incompletes, namely formatting, citations, and text changes in papers they had written for the class, informing them that it was their responsibility to discover for themselves what problems they had to resolve.

When the faculty member's immediate supervisor requested that she provide the students with more guidance, she refused to do so. After receiving complaints from students, the supervisor made the request a second time and reduced the plaintiff's teaching assignment, causing her to file an unsuccessful suit against her university. Upholding an earlier order in favor of the university, the court observed that the faculty member was not compelled to speak or to believe ideas that were not her own and that she was not told what grades to assign her students. Instead, because "she was simply required, as one might be in preparing a syllabus, to spell out in detail the requirements she had devised" (p. 595), the court agreed that her claim was without merit.

In most of the cases involving disputes over grading practices, the courts defer to university policy, determining that disputes rarely concern speech protected by the First Amendment. Rather, courts tend to view the question as to whether a policy is reasonable and whether it has been applied reasonably. Such was the case in *Keen v. Penson* (1992), where the Seventh Circuit affirmed a university's decision to demote a faculty member in both salary and rank after he refused to change a student's grade and offer her an apology for the way he treated her in class and in written communication. Ironically, the dispute escalated when the faculty member directed his student to apologize for her alleged unprofessional behavior in class. When the faculty member ultimately failed the student in the course, the university's chancellor initiated the required procedures designed to resolve such matters. A faculty rights advocate was assigned to the case initially and recommended to the chancellor that he require the faculty member to change the grade to at least a "C" and to offer a written apology to the student. Two faculty subcommittees reviewed these findings and agreed that the plaintiff violated faculty policies on professional conduct. The faculty member argued that the penalties violated his First Amendment rights, but the court held otherwise. The court was of the view that the plaintiff's refusal to comply with the committees' requests was not the reason for the penalties. To the contrary, the court interpreted that the faculty member's sanctionable misconduct in the way he treated the student and abused his discretion led to his being directed to change the grade.

Legal complaints about grading practices in higher education are not reserved for faculty alone. Students have also raised issues regarding the actions of faculty and administrators regarding the assessment of their work. In such an illustrated dispute, *Brown v. Li* (2002), a student chose to include a "Disacknowledgments" section at the end of his master's thesis in which he insulted academic and political leaders whom he considered to be hindrances during his graduate career. In response, his thesis committee did not accept the thesis, withheld the degree, and placed the student on academic probation for failing to complete the degree in a timely manner. After the student had been on probation, the university relented and granted the degree when the student agreed to submit the thesis without the offending section.

The student then unsuccessfully filed suit, arguing that the withholding of his degree violated his free speech rights. The Ninth Circuit affirmed an earlier order in favor of the university and its administrators. The majority opinion applied the principles set forth in *Hazelwood Independent School District v. Kuhlmeier* (1988), a K–12 case involving student speech in school-sponsored, academic settings. The court in *Brown* deferred to the authority of an educational institution to establish its curricular standards:

> An educator can, consistent with the First Amendment, require that a student comply with the terms of an academic assignment. . . . The First Amendment does not require an educator to change the assignment to suit the student's opinion or to approve the work of a student that, in his or her judgment, fails to meet a legitimate academic standard. (p. 949)

Applying the *Hazelwood* standard, the court agreed that because a master's thesis is part of a university's curriculum, its applicable procedural and substantive rules were reasonably related to legitimate pedagogical concerns. In fact, the majority opinion indicated that as their "learning progresses," students in higher education, in particular, need a stronger guiding hand when it comes to oral and written expression.

On the subject of guidance offered to a college student, in *Axson-Flynn v. Johnson* (2004), the Tenth Circuit considered the question of whether universities may compel certain speech as part of academic programs. The dispute arose when a former student in a university theater program who, instead of using profane language to make her points, wished to refrain from doing so. The former student filed suit against the program faculty, alleging that they violated her rights to free speech and free exercise of religion when they required her to perform monologues and other scenes that contained what she student argued were offensive words. While she received very good grades on assignments, instructors told the student that she would have to "get over" her misgivings if she wished to grow as an actor. At the student's semester review, faculty members told her that she would have to modify her values or consider leaving the program. The student left the program voluntarily and filed suit, alleging violation of her rights to both free speech and free exercise of religion. While the court agreed that compulsion to speak is intimately related to professional work in theater and was necessary in this instance, it held that there was a factual dispute over whether the compulsion to speak was reasonably related to a legitimate pedagogical concern or was a pretext for religious discrimination. As a result, the court denied the defendants' motion to dismiss the student's claim.

Patrick D. Pauken

See also Academic Freedom; *Sweezy v. New Hampshire; Urofsky v. Gilmore*

Further Readings

Pauken, P. D. (2005). Faculty speech. In J. Beckham & D. Dagley (Eds.), *Contemporary issues in higher education law* (pp. 151–182). Dayton, OH: Education Law Association.

Legal Citations

Axson-Flynn v. Johnson, 356 F.3d 1277 (10th Cir. 2004).
Brown v. Armenti, 247 F.3d 69 (3d Cir. 2001).
Brown v. Li, 308 F.3d 939 (9th Cir. 2002), *cert. denied,* 538 U.S. 908 (2003).
Hazelwood Independent School District v. Kuhlmeier, 484 U.S. 260 (1988).
Johnson-Kurek v. Abu-Absi, 423 F.3d 590 (6th Cir. 2005).
Keen v. Penson, 970 F.2d 252 (7th Cir. 1992).
Parate v. Isibor, 868 F.2d 821 (6th Cir. 1989).
Stronach v. Virginia State University, 2008 W.L. 161304 (E.D. Va. Jan. 15, 2008).
Sweezy v. New Hampshire, 354 U.S. 234 (1957).
Urofsky v. Gilmore, 261 F.3d 401 (4th Cir. 2000).
Wozniak v. Conry, 236 F.3d 888 (7th Cir. 2001).

GRADUATION REQUIREMENTS

Graduation requirements for students in colleges and universities are established as part of the interrelationship between accrediting organizations, the federal and state governments, the courts, and institutional boards of trustees. This entry reviews the role of these groups in defining graduation requirements and then examines the legal framework for dismissing students who fail to meet these standards.

Defining Graduation Requirements

Accrediting organizations are national governing organizations that provide accreditation to colleges and universities. Institutions of higher education seek admission into and approval of accrediting organizations that often have universal graduation requirements for their students. Member colleges and universities of accrediting organizations routinely complete the process of seeking accreditation and, in doing so, must meet the accrediting bodies' delineated requirements.

States also have help in defining graduation requirements and guidelines for institutions of higher education via detailed statutes as well as rules and regulations for state certifications and endorsements that students may seek. At the same time, colleges and universities offering these certifications and endorsements must develop programs of course offerings that meet the state requirements and must apply to the state for approval of their programs. On receipt of approval, institutions are able to offer their students the course offerings concomitant for the certifications and endorsements.

Historically, the federal government has not been directly involved in regulating college and university graduation requirements. However, the federal government has provided other support for colleges and universities. Significant federal legislation that affected public higher education in the 18th and 19th centuries included the Northwest Ordinance of 1787, which required states to provide public higher education with proceeds from the sale of public lands, and the Morrill Land Grant Acts, which established funding sources for the study of agricultural and technical education. The G. I. Bill of 1944, the Federal Work-Study Program established with the Economic Opportunity Act of 1964, and the Higher Education Act of 1965 all reflect federal commitments to student financial aid, grant programs, and support for higher education. In addition, the Smith-Lever Act of 1914 and the National Defense Education Act of 1958 provided federal research funds to institutions of higher learning. Moreover, the Higher Education Facilities Act of 1963 offered help for facilities, while the Higher Education Act of 1965 provided federal guidelines on institutional aid that ultimately helped to raise graduation rates to the extent that the aid to students made it easier for individuals to complete a college education.

By the 1950s, public institutions of higher learning and many states moved to centralize their control and governance of institutions of higher learning. States did so through the establishment of higher education boards or coordinating agencies. These evolving state efforts have helped define graduation requirements and institutional accreditation.

Colleges and universities also define graduation requirements through their respective boards of trustees or other named governing bodies. In general, the structure of colleges and universities includes boards of trustees that implement charters of incorporation. As part of their governing authority, these boards have the power to appoint and remove faculty members, to fix salaries, to direct the courses of study to be pursued by the students, and to fill vacancies created in their own bodies. Moreover, boards of trustees define and vote on graduation requirements in their role as the legal decision-making entities of their colleges or universities.

Types of Dismissals

Insofar as determining whether students should graduate or be dismissed from academic programs short of graduation has always been controversial, the judiciary has played a key role in reviewing some of these cases. In general, there are two types of dismissals from colleges and universities that impact student graduation: academic dismissals and disciplinary dismissals.

Academic Dismissals

Academic dismissals from colleges, universities, graduate schools, and professional schools have triggered litigation. The issues often have been whether students were owed due process before being dismissed for academic reasons and whether institutional officials, rather than courts, decide whether students should graduate or be dismissed. Generally, absent significant faculty misconduct or institutional negligence, students may be dismissed from colleges and universities for academic reasons.

The U.S. Supreme Court first addressed the issue of academic dismissal in the seminal case of

Board of Curators of the University of Missouri v. Horowitz in 1978. At issue was whether a medical school had to provide procedural due process prior to a student's academic dismissal and whether officials had authority to evaluate whether she failed to meet the institution's academic standards. More specifically, the Court considered whether the student was entitled to procedural protections under the Fourteenth Amendment and whether officials deprived her of either a liberty or a property interest. The student contended that her dismissal deprived her of liberty by substantially impairing her opportunities to continue her medical education or to return to employment in a medically related field.

In *Horowitz*, the Supreme Court found that it did not have to resolve whether the student's dismissal deprived her of a liberty interest in pursing a medical career, nor did it have to evaluate whether her dismissal infringed any other interest constitutionally protected against deprivation without due process. Instead, the Court ruled that assuming there was a liberty or property interest, the student received at least as much due process as the Fourteenth Amendment required. The Court was satisfied that officials informed the student of their dissatisfaction and the danger it posed to timely graduation or continued enrollment in a manner that was careful and deliberate.

As part of its analysis in *Horowitz,* the Supreme Court held that academic evaluations of students, in contrast to disciplinary reviews, do not necessarily require full hearings. To this end, the Court pointed out that the dismissal rested on the academic judgment of school officials that the student lacked the necessary clinical ability to perform adequately as a medical doctor and that she was making insufficient progress toward that goal. According to the Court, such judgments are, by nature, subjective and evaluative. By analogy, it is fair to say that like the actions of faculty members as to the proper grades to assign to students in their courses, evaluating whether to dismiss a student for academic reasons requires expert evaluation and is not readily adapted to judicial or administrative decision making. In this way the Court declined to substitute its judgment for that of the faculty members at the medical school, declaring that education was committed to the control of state and local authorities. The Court suggested that only perhaps under a showing or arbitrariness or capriciousness could academic dismissals from state institutions of higher education be enjoined. Thus, absent a showing of arbitrariness or capriciousness, the Court concluded with a warning against judicial intrusion into academic decision making.

Other courts have examined graduation requirements and academic dismissals. In *University of Texas Health Science Center v. Babb* (1982), an appellate court addressed whether a student could return to complete her nursing degree after being dismissed from the university due to her poor academic performance. The catalog under which the student entered the nursing program indicated that if, at the end of any semester, a student's grade point average fell below 2.0, he or she would be placed on scholastic probation. When the student was notified that she was failing a course, her counselor advised her to withdraw, send a letter asking for readmission, and reenter under a new quarter program. The student did as advised and was readmitted, but received a grade of WF, meaning that she withdrew failing. The new catalog existing when she reentered indicated that students with more than two Ds in their programs would be required to withdraw. After the student subsequently received two Ds, she was sent a notice informing her that her participation in the program was being terminated.

On review of the student's suit, an appellate court in Texas interpreted the school's catalog as constituting a written contract between it and the student. In noting that the student had the right to rely on its terms, the court pointed out that the first catalog allowed students to complete degrees within a six-year period and maintain 2.0 grade point averages. Therefore, the court directed officials to permit the student to return to school and complete her degree.

Three years later the Supreme Court returned to the question of academic dismissals in *Regents of University of Michigan v. Ewing* (1985). In dispute in *Ewing* was the claim of a student in a six-year medical school program who was dismissed after failing an important written examination. At issue was whether officials deprived the student of a property interest without due process in refusing to allow him to retake the examination.

Ruling in favor of university officials in *Ewing*, the Supreme Court held that when the student

enrolled in the special six-year program offering a joint undergraduate college degree and medical degree, he was required to complete four years of study and pass the written examination administered by the National Board of Medical Examiners. The facts revealed that although the student completed the courses of study, he failed five of the seven subjects on the examination. In light of this, the Court upheld the action of the university's Promotion and Review Board, which voted unanimously to drop the student from the program, because it agreed that officials acted in accordance with the institution's promulgated procedures. In upholding the academic dismissal, the Court observed that because the dismissal rested on the sound academic judgment of university officials, absent improper notice or arbitrary or capricious conduct, there was no basis on which it could interfere with such an academic dismissal.

Disciplinary Dismissals

Disciplinary dismissals that impact the ability to graduate have other constitutional requirements. For example, in *Goss v. Lopez* (1975), a case from K–12, the U.S. Supreme Court, in reviewing disciplinary dismissals, including suspensions and expulsions, explained that students have rights to procedural and, in some instances, substantive due process prior to be excluded from school, consistent with the Fourteenth Amendment. In its judgment, the Court commented that procedural due process requires notice, a timely hearing, right to counsel, a decision based on the record of a proceeding or hearing, and such other procedures as would allow the student an opportunity for a full and fair hearing. Substantive due process involves the provision of basic fairness.

Disciplinary dismissals usually involve student conduct that violates college or university rules, regulations, or policies as well as the law. Violations of these provisions may result in dismissals from academic programs and the failure to graduate. Under this approach, student behavior is generally examined not just in classroom settings but also in academic or other circumstances including laboratories, libraries, and/or off-campus activities.

Common student behaviors that have triggered disciplinary dismissals include cheating, participating in hazing, and taking part in events involving the impermissible use of alcohol. In some cases, there have been mixed academic and behavior fact patterns, such as when a graduate student tinkered with thesis research and was challenged about the authenticity of data. Students who failed courses and were involved in behavior issues have also incurred dismissal.

Professional schools such as those for careers in education and law often have the additional requirement that students be certified as being of good character. Dismissals or refusals to stipulate the good character of students that may restrict their ability to graduate or enter their chosen professions may require the existence of promulgated institutional rules and regulations. In disciplinary dismissal cases, due process hearing is required prior to dismissals. As a result of such due process hearings, other students who were convicted of felonies, including credit card fraud, were dismissed. Institutional officials have considered other behaviors, such as where skills related to professional competence were lacking, in determining whether students should be allowed to graduate.

Conclusion

Graduation requirements, then, are defined by accrediting agencies, states, federal law and court decisions, and boards of trustees. Even so, academic and disciplinary dismissals based on college or university rules and regulations are subject to faculty and administration review. In the end, there is something of a dichotomy when students are denied the opportunity to graduate. On the one hand, if students are unable to graduate due to academic infractions, the courts generally defer to the expert judgment of institutions and their faculty, without reliance on full hearings, based on appropriate academic standards. On the other hand, if students are unable to graduate due to disciplinary infractions, courts are more careful to ensure that institutions act based on promulgated school rules that may well entitle students to due process hearing before they may be subject to the penalty of dismissal.

Vivian Hopp Gordon

See also Academic Dishonesty; Academic Freedom; *Board of Curators of the University of Missouri v. Horowitz*; Catalogs as Contracts; *Regents of the University of Michigan v. Ewing*

Further Readings

Melear, K. B. (2008). Academic grade appeals: Legally sound policies and procedures. *Education Law Reporter, 237*, 557–564.

Legal Citations

Agricultural College Act of 1890 (Second Morrill Land Grant Act), ch. 841, 26 Stat. 417, 7 U.S.C. §§ 322 *et seq.*

Board of Curators of the University of Missouri v. Horowitz, 435 U.S. 78 (1978).

Economic Opportunity Act of 1964, Pub. L. No. 88-452.

Goss v. Lopez, 419 U.S. 565 (1975).

Higher Education Act, Pub. L. No. 89-329 (1965).

Higher Education Facilities Act, Pub. L. No. 88-204 (1963).

Morrill Land Grant Act of 1862, ch. 130, 12 Stat. 503, 7 U.S.C. §§ 301 *et seq.*

National Defense Education Act, Pub. L. No. 85-864 (1958).

Regents of the University of Michigan v. Ewing, 474 U.S. 214 (1985).

Servicemen's Readjustment Act (G. I. Bill), Pub. L. No. 78-346 (1944).

Smith-Lever Act, 7 U.S.C. § 343 (1914).

University of Texas Health Science Center v. Babb, 646 S.W. 2d 502 (Tex. App. 1982).

GRATZ V. BOLLINGER

Gratz v. Bollinger is a landmark 2003 judgment of U.S. Supreme Court that together with its companion case, *Grutter v. Bollinger* (2003), defines the circumstances under which officials at colleges and universities may consider race in making admissions decisions. On the one hand, in *Grutter* the Court ruled that achieving the educational benefits of a diverse student body is a compelling governmental interest and articulated a multifactored standard for determining narrow tailoring. On the other hand, in *Gratz* the Court found that the use of race in a university's undergraduate admissions was not narrowly tailored to achieve a compelling governmental interest. This entry reviews the Court's analysis in *Gratz* in some detail.

Facts of the Case

Gratz arose out of a challenge to the University of Michigan's undergraduate admissions policies. Unlike the University of Michigan Law School admissions policy, which was addressed in *Grutter* and called for all applicants to be evaluated individually, officials in the undergraduate college used a point system based on such criteria as test scores, grades, recommendations, and activities. Under this system, applicants had to accumulate 100 points in order to guarantee admission. Applicants who were members of designated minority groups were automatically given 20 points simply because of their race. As a practical matter, this meant that members of the minority groups had to accumulate only 80 points under the other criteria, while nonminority applicants had to accumulate 100 points from those sources.

After a federal trial court in Michigan partially granted a motion for summary judgment entered on behalf of students who challenged the admissions policy, and while an appeal was pending at the Sixth Circuit, the Supreme Court agreed to hear *Gratz* in light of its having already having accepted a challenge to the outcome in *Grutter*.

The Supreme Court's Ruling

The Supreme Court, in a six-to-three judgment written by Chief Justice Rehnquist, reasoned that because the university's admissions policy was not narrowly tailored to achieve a compelling governmental interest, it was unconstitutional. In reaching its judgment, the Court made three key points. First, the Court explained that such a bureaucratic approach was inconsistent with individualized consideration, because the potential for each applicant to contribute to diversity had to be judged on a case-by-case basis. To this end, the Court noted that one cannot assume that individuals will contribute to diversity simply because of their races.

Second, the Supreme Court pointed out that the educational benefits of diversity must encompass more than simple racial diversity. The Court maintained that because other characteristics may well give applicants unique perspectives that constitute contributions to diversity, officials had to take these into consideration.

Third, the Court indicated that administrative convenience did not justify the bureaucratic application of race. More specifically, the Court wrote that if officials intend to rely on race as an admissions criterion, then they must read each application. It almost goes without saying that this point has enormous practical consequences for large institutions or officials in highly competitive colleges and universities that receive thousands of applications.

Justice O'Connor, the author of the majority opinion in *Grutter*, penned a short concurrence. She emphasized the differences between the unconstitutional policy for undergraduate admissions in *Gratz* and the constitutional approach that the law school used in making admissions decisions in *Grutter*.

Justice Stevens, joined by Justice Souter, dissented. He asserted that the plaintiffs lacked standing because they enrolled in other schools after being rejected by the University of Michigan. Justice Souter filed a dissent in which Justice Ginsburg joined in part, arguing that *Gratz* should have been rejected because the plaintiffs never raised the narrow tailoring issue in the lower courts. He also was of the view that the admissions policy was sufficiently narrowly tailored. Justice Ginsburg filed a dissenting opinion in which Justice Souter joined and Justice Breyer joined in part. This dissent declared that classifications designed to help racial minorities should have been subjected to a lesser degree of scrutiny.

Impact of *Gratz*

Gratz rejects the notion that officials at colleges and universities may use bureaucratic rather than individualized approaches, emphatically rejecting the idea of separate admissions tracks for racial minorities and automatic assumptions about what racial minorities might contribute. Instead, the Court focused on the importance of considering each applicant as an individual, assessing all of the person's qualities before reviewing the person's ability to contribute to the unique setting of higher education. The Supreme Court added that just as growing up in a specific region or having particular professional experiences was likely to impact an applicant's views, so too did the applicant's unique experience as a member of a racial minority still matter. Of course, such examinations must include evaluations of other factors that may shape applicants' attitudes and experiences, such as religion, cultural background, socioeconomic class, or home life. In other words, if applicants are to be judged on the experiences and attitudes that they would bring to the intellectual life of institutions, then their races, like any other factor that shapes attitudes and experiences, becomes relevant.

Put another way, while *Gratz* rejects the direct consideration of race, it embraces the indirect consideration of race, a subtle but crucial distinction. This represents the difference between judging individuals on the content of their character and conferring benefits based on their skin color. It is the difference between individual consideration and group rights, the difference between the holistic evaluation of all aspects of applications that the Supreme Court called for in *Grutter* and a bureaucratic sorting of applications into various categories. Further, this is the difference between an objective detailed examination of what applicants can contribute to the intellectual life of institutions and stereotypical assumptions. Most important from the perspective of education policy makers, this is the difference between an admissions process being upheld as constitutional as in *Grutter* and being invalidated as in *Gratz*.

William E. Thro

See also Affirmative Action; Equal Protection Analysis; *Grutter v. Bollinger; Regents of the University of California v. Bakke*; U.S. Supreme Court Cases in Higher Education

Further Readings

Jenkins, J. K. (2004). *Grutter*, diversity, & K–12 public schools. *Education Law. Reporter, 182*, 353–370.

Mawdsley, R. D., & Russo, C. J. (2003). Supreme Court dissenting opinions in *Grutter*: Has the majority created a nation divided against itself? *Education Law Reporter, 180*, 417–435.

Meers, E. B., & Thro, W. E. (2004). *Race conscious admissions & financial aid after the University of Michigan decisions*. Washington, DC: National Association of College and University Attorneys.

Regents of the University of California v. Bakke, 438 U.S. 265 (1978).

Thro, W. E. (2005). No direct consideration of race: The lessons of the University of Michigan decisions. *Education Law Reporter, 196*, 755–764.

Legal Citations

Gratz v. Bollinger, 539 U.S. 244 (2003).

Grutter v. Bollinger, 539 U.S. 306 (2003).

GRATZ V. BOLLINGER

In *Gratz*, the Supreme Court struck down a race-conscious admissions plan because it was insufficiently narrowly tailored to achieve the university's goal of a diverse student body.

Supreme Court of the United States

GRATZ

v.

BOLLINGER

539 U.S. 244

Argued April 1, 2003

Decided June 23, 2003

Chief Justice REHNQUIST delivered the opinion of the Court.

We granted certiorari in this case to decide whether "the University of Michigan's use of racial preferences in undergraduate admissions violate[s] the Equal Protection Clause of the Fourteenth Amendment, Title VI of the Civil Rights Act of 1964." Because we find that the manner in which the University considers the race of applicants in its undergraduate admissions guidelines violates these constitutional and statutory provisions, we reverse that portion of the District Court's decision upholding the guidelines.

I

A

Petitioners Jennifer Gratz and Patrick Hamacher both applied for admission to the University of Michigan's (University) College of Literature, Science, and the Arts (LSA) as residents of the State of Michigan. Both petitioners are Caucasian. Gratz, who applied for admission for the fall of 1995, was notified in January of that year that a final decision regarding her admission had been delayed until April. This delay was based upon the University's determination that, although Gratz was "well qualified," she was "less competitive than the students who ha[d] been admitted on first review." Gratz was notified in April that the LSA was unable to offer her admission. She enrolled in the University of Michigan at Dearborn, from which she graduated in the spring of 1999.

Hamacher applied for admission to the LSA for the fall of 1997. A final decision as to his application was also postponed because, though his "academic credentials [were] in the qualified range, they [were] not at the level needed for first review admission." Hamacher's application was subsequently denied in April 1997, and he enrolled at Michigan State University.

In October 1997, Gratz and Hamacher filed a lawsuit in the United States District Court for the Eastern District of Michigan against the University, the LSA, James Duderstadt, and Lee Bollinger. Petitioners' complaint was a class-action suit alleging "violations and threatened violations of the rights of the plaintiffs and the class they represent to equal protection of the laws under the Fourteenth Amendment . . . , and for racial discrimination in violation of 42 U.S.C. §§ 1981, 1983 and 2000d *et seq.*" Petitioners sought, *inter alia*, compensatory and punitive damages for past violations, declaratory relief finding that respondents violated petitioners' "rights to nondiscriminatory treatment," an injunction prohibiting respondents from "continuing to discriminate on the basis of race in violation of the Fourteenth Amendment," and an order requiring the LSA to offer Hamacher admission as a transfer student.

The District Court granted petitioners' motion for class certification after determining that a class action was appropriate pursuant to Federal Rule of Civil Procedure 23(b)(2). The certified class consisted of "those individuals who applied for and were not granted admission to the College of Literature, Science & the Arts of the University of Michigan for all academic years from 1995 forward and who are members of those racial or ethnic groups, including Caucasian, that defendants treat[ed] less favorably on the basis of race in considering their application for admission." And Hamacher, whose claim the District Court found to challenge a "practice of racial discrimination pervasively applied on a classwide basis," was designated as the class representative. The court also granted petitioners' motion to bifurcate the proceedings into a liability and damages phase. The liability phase was to determine "whether [respondents'] use of race as a factor in admissions decisions violates the Equal Protection Clause of the Fourteenth Amendment to the Constitution."

B

The University has changed its admissions guidelines a number of times during the period relevant to this litigation, and we summarize the most significant of these changes briefly. The University's Office of Undergraduate Admissions (OUA) oversees the LSA admissions process. In order to promote consistency in the review of the large number of applications received, the OUA uses written guidelines for each academic year. Admissions counselors make admissions decisions in accordance with these guidelines.

OUA considers a number of factors in making admissions decisions, including high school grades, standardized test scores, high school quality, curriculum strength, geography, alumni relationships, and leadership. OUA also considers race. During all periods relevant to this litigation, the University has considered African-Americans, Hispanics, and Native Americans to be "underrepresented minorities," and it is undisputed that the University admits "virtually every qualified . . . applicant" from these groups.

During 1995 and 1996, OUA counselors evaluated applications according to grade point average combined with what were referred to as the "SCUGA" factors. These factors included the quality of an applicant's high school (S), the strength of an applicant's high school curriculum (C), an applicant's unusual circumstances (U), an applicant's geographical residence (G), and an applicant's alumni relationships (A). After these scores were combined to produce an applicant's "GPA 2" score, the reviewing admissions counselors referenced a set of

"Guidelines" tables, which listed GPA 2 ranges on the vertical axis, and American College Test/Scholastic Aptitude Test (ACT/SAT) scores on the horizontal axis. Each table was divided into cells that included one or more courses of action to be taken, including admit, reject, delay for additional information, or postpone for reconsideration.

In both years, applicants with the same GPA 2 score and ACT/SAT score were subject to different admissions outcomes based upon their racial or ethnic status. For example, as a Caucasian in-state applicant, Gratz's GPA 2 score and ACT score placed her within a cell calling for a postponed decision on her application. An in-state or out-of-state minority applicant with Gratz's scores would have fallen within a cell calling for admission.

In 1997, the University modified its admissions procedure. Specifically, the formula for calculating an applicant's GPA 2 score was restructured to include additional point values under the "U" category in the SCUGA factors. Under this new system, applicants could receive points for underrepresented minority status, socioeconomic disadvantage, or attendance at a high school with a predominantly underrepresented minority population, or underrepresentation in the unit to which the student was applying (for example, men who sought to pursue a career in nursing). Under the 1997 procedures, Hamacher's GPA 2 score and ACT score placed him in a cell on the in-state applicant table calling for postponement of a final admissions decision. An underrepresented minority applicant placed in the same cell would generally have been admitted.

Beginning with the 1998 academic year, the OUA dispensed with the Guidelines tables and the SCUGA point system in favor of a "selection index," on which an applicant could score a maximum of 150 points. This index was divided linearly into ranges generally calling for admissions dispositions as follows: 100–150 (admit); 95–99 (admit or postpone); 90–94 (postpone or admit); 75–89 (delay or postpone); 74 and below (delay or reject).

Each application received points based on high school grade point average, standardized test scores, academic quality of an applicant's high school, strength or weakness of high school curriculum, in-state residency, alumni relationship, personal essay, and personal achievement or leadership. Of particular significance here, under a "miscellaneous" category, an applicant was entitled to 20 points based upon his or her membership in an underrepresented racial or ethnic minority group. The

University explained that the "development of the selection index for admissions in 1998 changed only the mechanics, not the substance, of how race and ethnicity [were] considered in admissions."

In all application years from 1995 to 1998, the guidelines provided that qualified applicants from underrepresented minority groups be admitted as soon as possible in light of the University's belief that such applicants were more likely to enroll if promptly notified of their admission. Also from 1995 through 1998, the University carefully managed its rolling admissions system to permit consideration of certain applications submitted later in the academic year through the use of "protected seats." Specific groups—including athletes, foreign students, ROTC candidates, and underrepresented minorities—were "protected categories" eligible for these seats. A committee called the Enrollment Working Group (EWG) projected how many applicants from each of these protected categories the University was likely to receive after a given date and then paced admissions decisions to permit full consideration of expected applications from these groups. If this space was not filled by qualified candidates from the designated groups toward the end of the admissions season, it was then used to admit qualified candidates remaining in the applicant pool, including those on the waiting list.

During 1999 and 2000, the OUA used the selection index, under which every applicant from an underrepresented racial or ethnic minority group was awarded 20 points. Starting in 1999, however, the University established an Admissions Review Committee (ARC), to provide an additional level of consideration for some applications. Under the new system, counselors may, in their discretion, "flag" an application for the ARC to review after determining that the applicant (1) is academically prepared to succeed at the University, (2) has achieved a minimum selection index score, and (3) possesses a quality or characteristic important to the University's composition of its freshman class, such as high class rank, unique life experiences, challenges, circumstances, interests or talents, socioeconomic disadvantage, and underrepresented race, ethnicity, or geography. After reviewing "flagged" applications, the ARC determines whether to admit, defer, or deny each applicant.

C

The parties filed cross-motions for summary judgment with respect to liability.

Petitioners asserted that the LSA's use of race as a factor in admissions violates Title VI of the Civil Rights Act of 1964, and the Equal Protection Clause of the Fourteenth Amendment.

Respondents relied on Justice Powell's opinion in *Regents of Univ. of Cal. v. Bakke* to respond to petitioners' arguments. As discussed in greater detail in the Court's opinion in *Grutter v. Bollinger,* Justice Powell, in *Bakke,* expressed the view that the consideration of race as a factor in admissions might in some cases serve a compelling government interest. Respondents contended that the LSA has just such an interest in the educational benefits that result from having a racially and ethnically diverse student body and that its program is narrowly tailored to serve that interest. Respondent-intervenors asserted that the LSA had a compelling interest in remedying the University's past and current discrimination against minorities.

The District Court began its analysis by reviewing this Court's decision in *Bakke.*

Although the court acknowledged that no decision from this Court since *Bakke* has explicitly accepted the diversity rationale discussed by Justice Powell it also concluded that this Court had not, in the years since *Bakke,* ruled out such a justification for the use of race. The District Court concluded that respondents and their *amici curiae* had presented "solid evidence" that a racially and ethnically diverse student body produces significant educational benefits such that achieving such a student body constitutes a compelling governmental interest.

The court next . . . determined that the admissions program the LSA began using in 1999 is a narrowly tailored means of achieving the University's interest in the educational benefits that flow from a racially and ethnically diverse student body. The court emphasized that the LSA's current program does not utilize rigid quotas or seek to admit a predetermined number of minority students. The award of 20 points for membership in an underrepresented minority group, in the District Court's view, was not the functional equivalent of a quota because minority candidates were not insulated from review by virtue of those points. Likewise, the court rejected the assertion that the LSA's program operates like the two-track system Justice Powell found objectionable in *Bakke* on the grounds that LSA applicants are not competing for different groups of seats. The court also dismissed petitioners' assertion that the LSA's current system is nothing more than a means by which to achieve racial balancing. The court explained that the LSA does not seek to achieve a certain proportion of minority students, let alone a proportion that represents the community.

The District Court found the admissions guidelines the LSA used from 1995 through 1998 to be more problematic. . . . This system, the court concluded, operated as the functional equivalent of a quota and ran afoul of Justice Powell's opinion in *Bakke.*

. . . the court granted petitioners' motion for summary judgment with respect to the LSA's admissions programs in existence from 1995 through 1998, and respondents' motion with respect to the LSA's admissions programs for 1999 and 2000. Accordingly, the District Court denied petitioners' request for injunctive relief.

The District Court issued an order consistent with its rulings and certified two questions for interlocutory appeal to the Sixth Circuit pursuant to 28 U.S.C. § 1292(b). Both parties appealed aspects of the District Court's rulings, and the Court of Appeals heard the case en banc on the same day as *Grutter v. Bollinger.* The Sixth Circuit later issued an opinion in *Grutter,* upholding the admissions program used by the University of Michigan Law School, and the petitioner in that case sought a writ of certiorari from this Court. Petitioners asked this Court to grant certiorari in this case as well, despite the fact that the Court of Appeals had not yet rendered a judgment, so that this Court could address the constitutionality of the consideration of race in university admissions in a wider range of circumstances. We did so.

II

As they have throughout the course of this litigation, petitioners contend that the University's consideration of race in its undergraduate admissions decisions violates § 1 of the Equal Protection Clause of the Fourteenth Amendment, Title VI, and 42 U.S.C. § 1981. We consider first whether petitioners have standing to seek declaratory and injunctive relief, and, finding that they do, we next consider the merits of their claims.

A

. . .

. . . . After being denied admission, Hamacher demonstrated that he was "able and ready" to apply as a transfer student should the University cease to use race in undergraduate admissions. He therefore has standing to seek prospective relief with respect to the University's continued use of race in undergraduate admissions.

. . .

From the time petitioners filed their original complaint through their brief on the merits in this Court, they have consistently challenged the University's use of race in undergraduate admissions and its asserted justification of promoting "diversity." Consistent with this challenge, petitioners requested injunctive relief prohibiting respondents "from continuing to discriminate on the basis of race." They sought to certify a class consisting of all individuals who were not members of an underrepresented minority group who either had applied for admission to the LSA and been rejected or who intended to apply for admission to the LSA, for all academic years from 1995 forward. The District Court determined that the proposed class satisfied the requirements of the Federal Rules of Civil Procedure, including the requirements of numerosity, commonality, and typicality. The court further concluded that Hamacher was an adequate representative for the class in the pursuit of compensatory and injunctive relief for purposes of Rule 23(a)(4) and found "the record utterly devoid of the presence of . . . antagonism between the interests of . . . Hamacher, and the members of the class which [he] seek[s] to represent." Finally, the District Court concluded that petitioners' claim was appropriate for class treatment because the University's "practice of racial discrimination pervasively applied on a classwide basis." The court certified the class pursuant to Federal Rule of Civil Procedure 23(b)(2), and designated Hamacher as the class representative.

. . .

In the present case, the University's use of race in undergraduate transfer admissions does not implicate a significantly different set of concerns than does its use of race in undergraduate freshman admissions. Respondents challenged Hamacher's standing at the certification stage, but *never* did so on the grounds that the University's use of race in undergraduate transfer admissions involves a different set of concerns than does its use of race in freshman admissions.

Respondents' failure to allege any such difference is simply consistent with the fact that no such difference exists. Each year the OUA produces a document entitled "COLLEGE OF LITERATURE, SCIENCE AND THE ARTS GUIDELINES FOR ALL TERMS," which sets forth guidelines for all individuals seeking admission to the LSA, including freshman applicants, transfer applicants, international student applicants, and the like. The guidelines used to evaluate transfer applicants specifically cross-reference factors and qualifications considered in assessing freshman applicants. In fact, the criteria used to determine whether a transfer applicant will contribute to the University's stated goal of diversity are *identical* to that used to evaluate freshman applicants. For example, in 1997, when the class was certified and the District Court found that Hamacher had standing to represent the class, the transfer guidelines contained a separate section entitled "CONTRIBUTION TO A DIVERSE STUDENT BODY." This section explained that any transfer applicant who could "*contribut[e] to a diverse student body*" should "generally be admitted" even with substantially lower qualifications than those required of other transfer applicants. (emphasis added). To determine whether a transfer applicant was capable of "contribut[ing] to a diverse student body," admissions counselors were instructed to determine whether that transfer applicant met the "criteria as defined in Section IV of the 'U' category of [the] SCUGA" factors used to assess freshman applicants. Section IV of the "U" category, entitled "Contribution to a Diverse Class," explained that "[t]he University is committed to a rich educational experience for its students. A diverse, as opposed to a homogenous, student population enhances the educational experience for all students. To insure a diverse class, significant weight will be given in the admissions process to indicators of students contribution to a diverse class." These indicators, used in evaluating freshman and transfer applicants alike, list being a member of an underrepresented minority group as establishing an applicant's contribution to diversity. Indeed, the *only* difference between the University's use of race in considering freshman and transfer applicants is that all underrepresented minority freshman applicants receive 20 points and "virtually" all who are minimally qualified are admitted, while "generally" all minimally qualified minority transfer applicants are admitted outright. While this difference might be relevant to a narrow tailoring analysis, it clearly has no effect on petitioners' standing to challenge the University's use of race in undergraduate admissions and its assertion that diversity is a compelling state interest that justifies its consideration of the race of its undergraduate applicants.

Particularly instructive here is our statement in *General Telephone Co. of Southwest v. Falcon* that "[i]f [defendant-employer] used a biased testing procedure to evaluate both applicants for employment and incumbent employees, a class action on behalf of every applicant or employee who might have been prejudiced by the test clearly would satisfy the . . . requirements of Rule 23(a)." Here, the District Court found that the sole rationale the University had provided for any of its race-based preferences in undergraduate admissions was the interest in "the educational benefits that result from having a diverse student body." And petitioners argue that an interest in "diversity" is not a compelling state interest that is ever capable of justifying the use of race in undergraduate admissions. In sum, the same set of concerns is implicated by the University's use of race in evaluating all undergraduate admissions applications under the guidelines. We therefore agree with the District Court's carefully considered decision to certify this class-action challenge to the University's consideration of race in undergraduate admissions. Indeed, class-action treatment was particularly important in this case because "the claims of the individual students run the risk of becoming moot" and the "[t]he class action vehicle . . . provides a mechanism for ensuring that a justiciable claim is before the Court." Thus, we think it clear that Hamacher's personal stake, in view of both his past injury and the potential injury he faced at the time of certification, demonstrates that he may maintain this class-action challenge to the University's use of race in undergraduate admissions.

B

Petitioners argue, first and foremost, that the University's use of race in undergraduate admissions violates the Fourteenth Amendment. Specifically, they contend that this Court has only sanctioned the use of racial classifications to remedy identified discrimination, a justification on which respondents have never relied. Petitioners further argue that "diversity as a basis for employing racial preferences is simply too open-ended, ill-defined, and indefinite to constitute a compelling interest capable of supporting narrowly-tailored means." But for the reasons set forth today in *Grutter v. Bollinge*, the Court has rejected these arguments of petitioners.

Petitioners alternatively argue that even if the University's interest in diversity can constitute a compelling state interest, the District Court erroneously concluded that the University's use of race in its current freshman admissions policy is narrowly tailored to achieve

such an interest. Petitioners argue that the guidelines the University began using in 1999 do not "remotely resemble the kind of consideration of race and ethnicity that Justice Powell endorsed in *Bakke*." Respondents reply that the University's current admissions program *is* narrowly tailored and avoids the problems of the Medical School of the University of California at Davis program (U.C. Davis) rejected by Justice Powell. They claim that their program "hews closely" to both the admissions program described by Justice Powell as well as the Harvard College admissions program that he endorsed. Specifically, respondents contend that the LSA's policy provides the individualized consideration that "Justice Powell considered a hallmark of a constitutionally appropriate admissions program." For the reasons set out below, we do not agree.

It is by now well established that "all racial classifications reviewable under the Equal Protection Clause must be strictly scrutinized." This "standard of review . . . is not dependent on the race of those burdened or benefited by a particular classification." Thus, "any person, of whatever race, has the right to demand that any governmental actor subject to the Constitution justify any racial classification subjecting that person to unequal treatment under the strictest of judicial scrutiny."

To withstand our strict scrutiny analysis, respondents must demonstrate that the University's use of race in its current admissions program employs "narrowly tailored measures that further compelling governmental interests." Because "[r]acial classifications are simply too pernicious to permit any but the most exact connection between justification and classification," our review of whether such requirements have been met must entail "a most searching examination." We find that the University's policy, which automatically distributes 20 points, or one-fifth of the points needed to guarantee admission, to every single "underrepresented minority" applicant solely because of race, is not narrowly tailored to achieve the interest in educational diversity that respondents claim justifies their program.

In *Bakke*, Justice Powell reiterated that "[p]referring members of any one group for no reason other than race or ethnic origin is discrimination for its own sake." He then explained, however, that in his view it would be permissible for a university to employ an admissions program in which "race or ethnic background may be deemed a 'plus' in a particular applicant's file." He explained that such a program might allow for "[t]he file of a particular black applicant [to] be examined for his potential contribution to diversity without the factor of race being decisive when compared, for example, with that of an applicant identified as an Italian-American if the latter is thought to exhibit qualities more likely to promote beneficial educational pluralism." Such a system, in Justice Powell's view, would be "flexible enough to consider all pertinent elements of diversity in light of the particular qualifications of each applicant."

Justice Powell's opinion in *Bakke* emphasized the importance of considering each particular applicant as an individual, assessing all of the qualities that individual possesses, and in turn, evaluating that individual's ability to contribute to the unique setting of higher education. The admissions program Justice Powell described, however, did not contemplate that any single characteristic automatically ensured a specific and identifiable contribution to a university's diversity. Instead, under the approach Justice Powell described, each characteristic of a particular applicant was to be considered in assessing the applicant's entire application.

The current LSA policy does not provide such individualized consideration. The LSA's policy automatically distributes 20 points to every single applicant from an "underrepresented minority" group, as defined by the University. The only consideration that accompanies this distribution of points is a factual review of an application to determine whether an individual is a member of one of these minority groups. Moreover, unlike Justice Powell's example, where the race of a "particular black applicant" could be considered without being decisive the LSA's automatic distribution of 20 points has the effect of making "the factor of race . . . decisive" for virtually every minimally qualified underrepresented minority applicant.

Also instructive in our consideration of the LSA's system is the example provided in the description of the Harvard College Admissions Program, which Justice Powell both discussed in, and attached to, his opinion in *Bakke.* The example was included to "illustrate the kind of significance attached to race" under the Harvard College program. It provided as follows:

"The Admissions Committee, with only a few places left to fill, might find itself forced to choose between A, the child of a successful black physician in an academic community with promise of superior academic performance, and B, a black who grew up in an inner-city ghetto of semi-literate parents whose academic achievement was lower but who had demonstrated energy and leadership as well as an apparently abiding interest in black power. If a good number of black students much like A but few like B had already been admitted, the Committee might prefer B; and vice versa. If C, a white student with extraordinary artistic talent, were also seeking one of the remaining places, his unique quality might give him an edge over both A and B. Thus, the critical criteria are often individual qualities or experience *not dependent upon race but sometimes associated with it.*

This example further demonstrates the problematic nature of the LSA's admissions system. Even if student C's "extraordinary artistic talent" rivaled that of Monet or Picasso, the applicant would receive, at most, five points under the LSA's system. At the same time, every single underrepresented minority applicant, including students A and B, would automatically receive 20 points for submitting an application. Clearly, the LSA's system does not offer applicants the individualized selection process described in Harvard's example. Instead of considering how the differing backgrounds, experiences, and characteristics of students A, B, and C might benefit the University, admissions counselors reviewing LSA applications would simply award both A and B 20 points because their applications indicate that they are African-American, and student C would receive up to 5 points for his "extraordinary talent."

Respondents emphasize the fact that the LSA has created the possibility of an applicant's file being flagged for individualized consideration by the ARC. We think that the flagging program only emphasizes the flaws of the University's system as a whole when compared to that described by Justice Powell. Again, students A, B, and C illustrate the point. First, student A would never be flagged. This is because, as the University has conceded, the effect of automatically awarding 20 points is that virtually every qualified underrepresented minority applicant is admitted. Student A, an applicant "with promise of superior academic performance," would certainly fit this description. Thus, the result of the automatic distribution of 20 points is that the University would never consider student A's individual background, experiences, and characteristics to assess his individual "potential contribution to diversity," Instead, every applicant like student A would simply be admitted.

It is possible that students B and C would be flagged and considered as individuals. This assumes that student B was not already admitted because of the automatic 20-point distribution, and that student C could muster at least 70 additional points. But the fact that the "review committee can look at the applications individually and ignore the points," once an application is flagged is of little comfort under our strict scrutiny analysis. The record does not reveal precisely how many applications are flagged for this individualized consideration, but it is undisputed that such consideration is the exception and not the rule in the operation of the LSA's admissions program. Additionally, this individualized review is only provided *after* admissions counselors automatically distribute the University's version of a "plus" that makes race a decisive factor for virtually every minimally qualified underrepresented minority applicant.

Respondents contend that "[t]he volume of applications and the presentation of applicant information make it impractical for [LSA] to use the . . . admissions system" upheld by the Court today in *Grutter*. But the fact that the implementation of a program capable of providing individualized consideration might present administrative challenges does not render constitutional an otherwise problematic system. Nothing in Justice Powell's opinion in *Bakke* signaled that a university may employ whatever means it desires to achieve the stated goal of diversity without regard to the limits imposed by our strict scrutiny analysis.

We conclude, therefore, that because the University's use of race in its current freshman admissions policy is not narrowly tailored to achieve respondents' asserted compelling interest in diversity, the admissions policy violates the Equal Protection Clause of the Fourteenth Amendment. We further find that the admissions policy also violates Title VI and 42 U.S.C. § 1981. Accordingly, we reverse that portion of the District Court's decision granting respondents summary judgment with respect to liability and remand the case for proceedings consistent with this opinion.

It is so ordered.

GROVE CITY COLLEGE V. BELL

Grove City College v. Bell (1984) stands out as a dispute in which the U.S. Supreme Court restricted the application of Title IX of the Education Amendments of 1972 at a private college that accepted no direct federal funding on its own but had large number of students who received federally funded grants. *Grove City* created a firestorm of controversy, because the Court maintained that while the U.S. Department of Education (ED) could terminate funding, it could do so only for the grant program that was subjected to Title IX if college officials refused to sign a form indicting their compliance with the statute. In so ruling, the Court refused to allow the ED to sanction to the entire institution. Dissatisfied by the outcome in *Grove City*, Congress essentially superseded it three years later with the enactment of the Civil Rights Restoration Act of 1987, thereby interpreting Title IX more expansively.

Facts of the Case

The dispute began when officials at Grove City College refused to accept state and federal financial assistance in an effort to preserve institutional autonomy. However, the college admitted a large number of students who received Basic Educational Opportunity Grants (BEOGs). As a result, the ED determined that the college was a recipient of federal financial assistance, which triggered the application of Title IX of the Education Amendments of 1972. Consequently, officials at the ED asked administrators at the college to sign an Assurance of Compliance that they would comply with the requirements of Title IX.

When officials at the college refused to sign the assurance form, the ED initiated an administrative proceeding. As a result, the ED terminated financial assistance to students at Grove City College until such time as college officials signed the Assurance of Compliance. In response to a suit filed by the college and four of its students, a federal trial court in Pennsylvania ruled that while the students' BEOGs constituted federal financial assistance, the ED could not terminate the aid due to institutional refusal to sign the Assurance of Compliance. However, the Third Circuit reversed in favor of the ED, finding that the funds could be withheld in order to force college officials to sign the Assurance of Compliance. Displeased with the result, the college appealed to the Supreme Court.

The Supreme Court's Ruling

On further review, in a seven-to-two decision authored by Justice White, the Supreme Court affirmed that Title IX's coverage was triggered because some students received BEOGs to pay for their education, and thus the ED had the authority to act. At the same time, though, the Court pointed out that the receipt of BEOGs did not trigger institution-wide coverage of Title IX. Rather, the Court thought that because the BEOGs were assistance to the college's financial aid program, only the program that was directly affected could be regulated under Title IX. In fact, even though the BEOG funds eventually reached the college's general operating funds, the Court was of the opinion that this was not enough to subject the entire institution to the scope of Title IX.

As part of its analysis, the Supreme Court engaged in a lengthy discussion of the legislative history of Title IX, noting that it was closely modeled after Title VI of the Civil Rights Act of 1964, a far-reaching antidiscrimination statute. To this end, the Court interpreted Title VI's legislative history to show that an institution's receipt of student aid funds triggered coverage under Title VI. The Court added that because the language of Title VI is identical to that of Title IX, Congress intended for Title IX to be applied in the same manner as Title VI. Moreover, the Court observed that Title VI contained a list of programs covered by the law, including BEOGs.

Acknowledging that Congress had had the opportunity to invalidate parts of regulations that it deemed inconsistent with Title IX but chose not do so, the Supreme Court held that this was strong proof of congressional intent that BEOGs were considered "federal financial assistance." Furthermore, the Court posited that because Congress reauthorized the statute governing BEOGs three times, it was well aware of the administrative interpretation that the grants were thought to trigger Title IX coverage.

In evaluating which educational program of the College received federal assistance, the Supreme Court looked to how the funds were disbursed. The Court explored the disbursement mechanism though the Regular Disbursement System, under which the Secretary of Education estimated the amount that an institution needs for grants and sends that amount directly to it; institutional officials are then free to identify eligible students. The Court commented that if college officials used this program, then it would have had "no doubt" that the program that received federal assistance was only the financial aid program. Yet the record reflected that the college used the Alternative Disbursement System, under which the grants were awarded directly to the students, bypassing the financial aid department. However, even though the BEOGs were disbursed through the Alternate Disbursement System and therefore did not go to the college for the financial aid department to disburse, the Court still decided that because the BEOGs expand the resources that the college could devote to financial aid, the financial aid program was subject to regulation under Title IX.

The Court made short work of the plaintiffs' final challenge, namely that signing a form indicating that college officials would comply with Title IX as a condition for the receipt of federal financial assistance infringed on their First Amendment rights. Declaring that Congress is free to attach conditions to federal financial assistance that institutions are not obligated to accept, the Court affirmed there were no First Amendment infringements, because college officials could have refused to participate in the program, and the students could have taken the funds elsewhere.

Justice Powell's concurrence remarked that while he agreed with the majority's holding, he did so only reluctantly, because he believed that it represented an example of "overzealousness" on the part of the federal government. Powell wrote that it was undisputed that Grove City College had never discriminated against anyone on the basis of sex and that the ED demanded the Assurance of Compliance to be signed even in light of the lack of any claims of discrimination.

Justice Stevens's partial concurrence maintained that the majority addressed an issue that was not in dispute, describing it as an advisory opinion, in finding that the college was not required to refrain from discrimination on the basis of sex in any program other than financial aid. Further, he was of the view that the record was inadequate to answer all of the questions at bar and that a factual inquiry was necessary to have resolved which programs actually benefited from federal financial assistance.

In dissent, Justice Brennan contended that the majority completely disregarded the remedial purposes of Title IX while ignoring congressional intent surrounding the statute. He argued that the majority mistakenly limited the scope of Title IX even though the federal funds were benefiting the entire college. This position was later essentially vindicated by congressional enactment of the Civil Rights Restoration Act of 1987, which stated that if any part of an institution receives federal aid, the institution as a whole must comply with Title IX.

Megan L. Rehberg

See also Higher Education Act; Loans and Federal Aid

Further Readings

Villalobos, P. M. (1990). The Civil Rights Restoration Act of 1987: Revitalization of Title IX. *Marquette Sports Law Journal, 1,* 149–169.

Legal Citations

Civil Rights Restoration Act of 1987, Pub. L. No. 100-259, 102 Stat. 28 (1988).
Grove City College v. Bell, 465 U.S. 555 (1984).
Title IX of the Education Amendments of 1972, 20 U.S.C. § 1681.

GROVE CITY COLLEGE V. BELL

In *Grove City,* the Supreme Court's restriction of the application of Title IX created a firestorm of controversy leading to Congress's enactment of the Civil Rights Restoration Act of 1987. This legislation interpreted Title IX more expansively, essentially superseding the Court's holding in *Grove City.*

Supreme Court of the United States

GROVE CITY COLLEGE

v.

BELL

465 U.S. 555

Argued Nov. 29, 1983

Decided Feb. 28, 1984

Justice WHITE delivered the opinion of the Court.

Section 901(a) of Title IX of the Education Amendments of 1972 prohibits sex discrimination in "any education program or activity receiving Federal financial assistance" and § 902 directs agencies awarding most types of assistance to promulgate regulations to ensure that recipients adhere to that prohibition. Compliance with departmental regulations may be secured by termination of assistance "to the particular program, or part thereof, in which . . . noncompliance has been . . . found" or by "any other means authorized by law." § 902.

This case presents several questions concerning the scope and operation of these provisions and the regulations established by the Department of Education. We must decide, first, whether Title IX applies at all to Grove City College, which accepts no direct assistance but enrolls students who receive federal grants that must be used for educational purposes. If so, we must identify the "education program or activity" at Grove City that is "receiving Federal financial assistance" and determine whether federal assistance to that program may be terminated solely because the College violates the Department's regulations by refusing to execute an Assurance of Compliance with Title IX. Finally, we must consider whether the application of Title IX to Grove City infringes the First Amendment rights of the College or its students.

I

Petitioner Grove City College is a private, coeducational, liberal arts college that has sought to preserve its institutional autonomy by consistently refusing state and federal financial assistance. Grove City's desire to avoid federal oversight has led it to decline to participate, not only in direct institutional aid programs, but also in federal student assistance programs under which the College would be required to assess students' eligibility and to determine the amounts of loans, work-study funds, or grants they should receive. Grove City has, however, enrolled a large number of students who receive Basic Educational Opportunity Grants (BEOGs) under the Department of Education's Alternate Disbursement System (ADS).

The Department concluded that Grove City was a "recipient" of "Federal financial assistance" as those terms are defined in the regulations implementing Title IX and, in July 1977, it requested that the College execute the Assurance of Compliance. . . . If Grove City had signed the Assurance, it would have agreed to "[c]omply, to the extent applicable to it, with Title IX . . . and all applicable requirements imposed by or pursuant to the Department's regulation . . . to the end that . . . no person shall, on the basis of sex, be . . . subjected to discrimination under any education program or activity for which [it] receives or benefits from Federal financial assistance from the Department."

When Grove City persisted in refusing to execute an Assurance, the Department initiated proceedings to declare the College and its students ineligible to receive BEOGs. The Administrative Law Judge held that the federal financial assistance received by Grove City obligated it to execute an Assurance of Compliance and entered an order terminating assistance until Grove City "corrects its noncompliance with Title IX and satisfies the Department that it is in compliance" with the applicable regulations.

Grove City and four of its students then commenced this action in the District Court for the Western District of Pennsylvania, which concluded that the students' BEOGs constituted "Federal financial assistance" to Grove City but held, on several grounds, that the Department could not terminate the students' aid because of the College's refusal to execute an Assurance of Compliance. The Court of Appeals reversed. It first examined the language and legislative history of Title IX and held that indirect, as well as direct, aid triggered coverage under § 901(a) and that institutions whose students financed their educations with BEOGs were recipients of federal financial assistance within the meaning of Title IX. Although it recognized that Title IX's

provisions are program-specific, the court likened the assistance flowing to Grove City through its students to nonearmarked aid, and, with one judge dissenting, declared that "[w]here the federal government furnishes indirect or non-earmarked aid to an institution, it is apparent to us that the institution itself must be the 'program.'" Specifically, the Court of Appeals concluded that the Department could condition financial aid upon the execution of an Assurance of Compliance and that the Department had acted properly in terminating federal financial assistance to the students and Grove City despite the lack of evidence of actual discrimination.

We granted certiorari, and we now affirm the Court of Appeals' judgment that the Department could terminate BEOGs received by Grove City's students to force the College to execute an Assurance of Compliance.

II

In defending its refusal to execute the Assurance of Compliance required by the Department's regulations, Grove City first contends that neither it nor any "education program or activity" of the College receives any federal financial assistance within the meaning of Title IX by virtue of the fact that some of its students receive BEOGs and use them to pay for their education. We disagree.

Grove City provides a well-rounded liberal arts education and a variety of educational programs and student services. The question is whether any of those programs or activities "receiv[es] Federal financial assistance" within the meaning of Title IX when students finance their education with BEOGs. The structure of the Education Amendments of 1972, in which Congress both created the BEOG program and imposed Title IX's nondiscrimination requirement, strongly suggests an affirmative conclusion. BEOGs were aptly characterized as a "centerpiece of the bill" and Title IX "relate[d] directly to [its] central purpose." In view of this connection and Congress' express recognition of discrimination in the administration of student financial aid programs, it would indeed be anomalous to discover that one of the primary components of Congress' comprehensive "package of federal aid" was not intended to trigger coverage under Title IX.

It is not surprising to find, therefore, that the language of § 901(a) contains no hint that Congress perceived a substantive difference between direct institutional assistance and aid received by a school through its students. The linchpin of Grove City's argument that none of its programs receives any federal assistance is a perceived distinction between direct and indirect aid, a distinction that finds no support in the text of § 901(a). Nothing in § 901(a) suggests that Congress elevated form over substance by making the application of the nondiscrimination principle dependent on the manner in which a program or activity receives federal assistance. There is no basis in the statute for the view that only institutions that themselves apply for federal aid or receive checks directly from the federal government are subject to regulation. As the Court of Appeals observed, "by its all inclusive terminology appears to encompass *all* forms of federal aid to education, direct or indirect." (emphasis in original). We have recognized the need to "accord [Title IX] a sweep as broad as its language," and we are reluctant to read into § 901(a) a limitation not apparent on its face.

Our reluctance grows when we pause to consider the available evidence of Congress' intent. The economic effect of direct and indirect assistance often is indistinguishable and the BEOG program was structured to ensure that it effectively supplements the College's own financial aid program. Congress undoubtedly comprehended this reality in enacting the Education Amendments of 1972. The legislative history of the amendments is replete with statements evincing Congress' awareness that the student assistance programs established by the amendments would significantly aid colleges and universities. In fact, one of the stated purposes of the student aid provisions was to "provid[e] assistance to institutions of higher education."

Congress' awareness of the purpose and effect of its student aid programs also is reflected in the sparse legislative history of Title IX itself. Title IX was patterned after Title VI of the Civil Rights Act of 1964. The drafters of Title VI envisioned that the receipt of student aid funds would trigger coverage, and, since they approved identical language, we discern no reason to believe that the Congressmen who voted for Title IX intended a different result.

. . .

Persuasive evidence of Congress' intent concerning student financial aid may also be gleaned from its subsequent treatment of Title IX. . . .

With the benefit of clear statutory language, powerful evidence of Congress' intent, and a longstanding and coherent administrative construction of the phrase "receiving Federal financial assistance," we have little trouble concluding that Title IX coverage is not foreclosed because federal funds are granted to Grove City's students rather than directly to one of the College's educational programs. There remains the question, however, of identifying the "education program or activity" of the College that can properly be characterized as "receiving" federal assistance through grants to some of the students attending the College.

III

An analysis of Title IX's language and legislative history led us to conclude in *North Haven Board of Education v. Bell* that "an agency's authority under Title IX both to promulgate regulations and to terminate funds is subject to the program-specific limitations of §§ 901 and 902." Although the legislative history contains isolated suggestions that entire institutions are subject to the nondiscrimination provision whenever one of their programs receives federal assistance, we cannot accept the Court of Appeals' conclusion that in the circumstances present here Grove City itself is a "program or activity" that may be regulated in its entirety.

Nevertheless, we find no merit in Grove City's contention that a decision treating BEOGs as "Federal financial assistance" cannot be reconciled with Title IX's program-specific language since BEOGs are not tied to any specific "education program or activity."

If Grove City participated in the BEOG program through the RDS, we would have no doubt that the "education program or activity receiving Federal financial assistance" would not be the entire College; rather, it would be its student financial aid program. RDS institutions receive federal funds directly, but can use them only to subsidize or expand their financial aid programs and to recruit students who might otherwise be unable to enroll. In short, the assistance is earmarked for the recipient's financial aid program. Only by ignoring Title IX's program-specific language could we conclude that funds received under the RDS, awarded to eligible students, and paid back to the school when tuition comes due represent federal aid to the entire institution.

We see no reason to reach a different conclusion merely because Grove City has elected to participate in the ADS. Although Grove City does not itself disburse students' awards, BEOGs clearly augment the resources that the College itself devotes to financial aid. As is true of the RDS, however, the fact that federal funds eventually reach the College's general operating budget cannot subject Grove City to institutionwide coverage. Grove City's choice of administrative mechanisms, we hold, neither expands nor contracts the breadth of the "program or activity"—the financial aid program—that receives federal assistance and that may be regulated under Title IX.

To the extent that the Court of Appeals' holding that BEOGs received by Grove City's students constitute aid to the entire institution rests on the possibility that federal funds received by one program or activity free up the College's own resources for use elsewhere, the Court of Appeals' reasoning is doubly flawed. First, there is no evidence that the federal aid received by Grove City's students results in the diversion of funds from the College's own financial aid program to other areas within the institution. Second, and more important, the Court of Appeals' assumption that Title IX applies to programs receiving a larger share of a school's own limited resources as a result of federal assistance earmarked for use elsewhere within the institution is inconsistent with the program-specific nature of the statute. Most federal educational assistance has economic ripple effects throughout the aided institution, and it would be difficult, if not impossible, to determine which programs or activities derive such indirect benefits. Under the Court of Appeals' theory, an entire school would be subject to Title IX merely because one of its students received a small BEOG or because one of its departments received an earmarked federal grant. This result cannot be squared with Congress' intent.

The Court of Appeals' analogy between student financial aid received by an educational institution and nonearmarked direct grants provides a more plausible justification for its holding, but it too is faulty. Student financial aid programs, we believe, are *sui generis*. In neither purpose nor effect can BEOGs be fairly characterized as unrestricted grants that institutions may use for whatever purpose they desire. The BEOG program was designed, not merely to increase the total resources available to educational institutions, but to enable them to offer their services to students who had previously been unable to afford higher education. It is true, of course, that substantial portions of the BEOGs received by Grove City's students ultimately find their way into the College's general operating budget and are used to

provide a variety of services to the students through whom the funds pass. However, we have found no persuasive evidence suggesting that Congress intended that the Department's regulatory authority follow federally aided students from classroom to classroom, building to building, or activity to activity. In addition, as Congress recognized in considering the Education Amendments of 1972, the economic effect of student aid is far different from the effect of nonearmarked grants to institutions themselves since the former, unlike the latter, increases both an institution's resources and its obligations. In that sense, student financial aid more closely resembles many earmarked grants.

We conclude that the receipt of BEOGs by some of Grove City's students does not trigger institution-wide coverage under Title IX. In purpose and effect, BEOGs represent federal financial assistance to the College's own financial aid program, and it is that program that may properly be regulated under Title IX.

IV

Since Grove City operates an "education program or activity receiving Federal financial assistance," the Department may properly demand that the College execute an Assurance of Compliance with Title IX. Grove City contends, however, that the Assurance it was requested to sign was invalid, both on its face and as interpreted by the Department, in that it failed to comport with Title IX's program-specific character. Whatever merit that objection might have had at the time, it is not now a valid basis for refusing to execute an Assurance of Compliance.

The Assurance of Compliance regulation itself does not, on its face, impose institution-wide obligations. Recipients must provide assurance only that "each education program or activity operated by . . . [them] *and to which this part applies* will be operated in compliance with this part" (emphasis added). The regulations apply, by their terms, "to every recipient and to *each education program or activity* operated by such recipient *which receives or benefits from Federal financial assistance*" (emphasis added). These regulations, like those at issue in *North Haven Board of Education v. Bell* "conform with the limitations Congress enacted in §§ 901 and 902." Nor does the Department now claim that its regulations reach beyond the College's student aid program. Furthermore, the Assurance of Compliance currently in use, like the one Grove City refused to execute, does not on its face purport to reach the entire College; it certifies compliance with respect to those "education programs and activities receiving Federal financial assistance." Under this opinion, consistent with the program-specific requirements of Title IX, the covered education program is the College's financial aid program.

A refusal to execute a proper program-specific Assurance of Compliance warrants termination of federal assistance to the student financial aid program. The College's contention that termination must be preceded by a finding of actual discrimination finds no support in the language of § 902, which plainly authorizes that sanction to effect "[c]ompliance with any requirement adopted pursuant to this section." Regulations authorizing termination of assistance for refusal to execute an Assurance of Compliance with Title VI had been promulgated, long before Title IX was enacted, and Congress no doubt anticipated that similar regulations would be developed to implement Title IX. We conclude, therefore, that the Department may properly condition federal financial assistance on the recipient's assurance that it will conduct the aided program or activity in accordance with Title IX and the applicable regulations.

V

Grove City's final challenge to the Court of Appeals' decision—that conditioning federal assistance on compliance with Title IX infringes First Amendment rights of the College and its students—warrants only brief consideration. Congress is free to attach reasonable and unambiguous conditions to federal financial assistance that educational institutions are not obligated to accept. Grove City may terminate its participation in the BEOG program and thus avoid the requirements of § 901(a). Students affected by the Department's action may either take their BEOGs elsewhere or attend Grove City without federal financial assistance. Requiring Grove City to comply with Title IX's prohibition of discrimination as a condition for its continued eligibility to participate in the BEOG program infringes no First Amendment rights of the College or its students.

Accordingly, the judgment of the Court of Appeals is *Affirmed.*

GRUTTER V. BOLLINGER

Grutter v. Bollinger (2003) is a landmark judgment of the U.S. Supreme Court that together with its companion case, *Gratz v. Bollinger*, clarifies the circumstances under which college and university officials may consider race in admissions actions. More specifically, the Court in *Grutter* held that obtaining the educational benefits of a diverse student body is a compelling governmental interest for equal protection purposes and that the admissions policy of the University of Michigan Law School was narrowly tailored to meet this goal and thus was constitutional. In light of the controversy that *Grutter* engendered, this entry examines the background of this decision, the Supreme Court's rationale in *Grutter*, and its ramifications for admissions in higher education.

Facts of the Case

Grutter arose out of a challenge to the admissions policy at the University of Michigan. Law school officials sought to obtain the educational benefits of a diverse student body by considering race as one factor among many. *Grutter* was filed by an unsuccessful 43-year-old White female applicant who was in the 86th percentile nationally on the Law School Admissions Test. The applicant challenged the law school's use of race as a factor in admissions. During the litigation, university officials conceded that the plaintiff probably would have been admitted had she been a member of one of the underrepresented minority groups, which the policy defined as African Americans, Hispanics, and Native Americans.

The Supreme Court's Ruling

Ultimately, the Supreme Court, in a five-to-four judgment authored by Justice O'Connor, upheld the law school's policy. The Court was convinced that the policy was constitutional because it was narrowly tailored to achieve the law school's goal of a diverse student body.

Compelling Governmental Interest

The Supreme Court has established repeatedly and with great clarity that classifications based on racial and ethnic distinctions are inherently suspect and are subject to the most exacting judicial examination of strict scrutiny under Fourteenth Amendment equal protection analysis. Moreover, the Court noted that the government, and by extension, officials at public colleges and universities, bear the burden of proving that racial classifications are narrowly tailored measures that further compelling governmental interests. The fact that racial classifications may be used to help racial minorities has not changed the Court's analysis. If anything, the Court has insisted on strict scrutiny in every context, even for so-called "benign" racial classifications such as race-conscious university admissions policies.

In *Grutter*, the Supreme Court recognized that context matters in the review of race-based governmental policies, because not all actions are equally objectionable; strict scrutiny is designed to provide a framework for carefully examining the importance of the reasons advanced by governmental decision makers for their use. The *Grutter* Court did not hold that obtaining racial diversity by correcting the underrepresentation of specified racial groups was a compelling governmental interest. In fact, university officials had never argued that it was. Rather, the university's lawyers emphasized that enrolling specified racial groups was only part of a goal of assembling a class of students that was both exceptionally academically qualified and broadly diverse.

The Supreme Court, then, found that public institutions of higher education have a compelling interest in obtaining the educational benefits that flow from diverse student bodies. In so ruling, the Court explained that it was embracing the concept of diversity articulated 25 years earlier by Justice Powell in *Regents of the University of California v. Bakke* (1978). Yet because no other justice joined the diversity portion of Justice Powell's opinion in *Bakke*, lower courts were divided on whether it constituted binding precedent. However, in *Grutter*, the majority expressly endorsed Justice Powell's view that diversity is not an "aesthetic" quality to be judged by the mosaic of skin tones composing a student body. Instead, for Powell, diversity arises from students who can contribute the most to the robust exchange of ideas on their campuses. In this way, Powell was emphatic that programs focusing solely on ethnic diversity would hinder rather than further the attainment of genuine diversity.

The difference between obtaining the educational benefits of diversity and correcting the underrepresentation of specified racial groups is demonstrated by comparing the approach that officials took in the University of Michigan Law School with the one followed by the undergraduate school, where students with the highest point totals were admitted, and points were awarded to applicants simply for being members of particular races. Relying on *Bakke*, the Supreme Court pointed out that preferring members of any one group for no reason other than race or ethnic origin was impermissible, because it was discriminatory.

While the Supreme Court did not specify how much emphasis could be given to race or ethnicity, it is clear that race and ethnic origin may not be the sole diversity factors that officials use. If such factors are considered, the Court explained that they may be no more than part of a broad array of qualifications and characteristics. Given this language, admissions programs are likely to be invalid if, when they are considered as a whole, race and ethnicity predominate over other diversity factors. Similarly, the Court indicated that the compelling interest it approved did not mean that student bodies must include specified percentages of particular groups merely because of their races or ethnic origins, because such an approach would amount to racial balancing, a patently unconstitutional practice.

Narrow Tailoring

Turning to the issue of narrow tailoring in higher education admissions, the Supreme Court stated in *Grutter* that such programs must provide for individualized consideration, may be undertaken only after officials engage in serious good faith considerations of the viability of nonracial alternatives, must not unduly burden nonminorities, must be periodically reviewed, and must be of limited duration.

Individualized Consideration of Each Applicant

The Supreme Court began its four-part analysis by declaring that if institutional officials wish to utilize race in admissions decisions to foster diversity, they must provide for truly individualized consideration by reviewing all pertinent elements of diversity in light of the qualifications of each applicant. Officials must take such an approach in order to place all applicants on the same footing for consideration even if they do necessarily treat each criterion as having the same weight. Essentially, the Court specified that individualized consideration involves two elements—that no applicant is isolated from competition and that the person's race is not the defining feature of an application.

If race-conscious programs are to pass the narrow tailoring test, institutional officials may not insulate applicants who belong to specified racial or ethnic groups from the competition for admission, may not establish quotas for members of certain racial groups, and may not have separate admissions tracks for different races. However, the Supreme Court recognized a legally significant difference between the use of quotas and the goal of attaining critical masses of underrepresented students. While the former is prohibited, the latter is allowed. Although the dissent took issue with this distinction, the majority expounded on its understanding of this difference. According to the Court, quotas impose a fixed number or percentage that must be attained and insulates individuals from comparisons with all other candidates. Conversely, the Court thought that permissible goals require only good faith efforts to achieve a range demarcated by the goals themselves, while permitting the consideration of race as a "plus" factor with regard to particular candidates while ensuring that individuals compete with all other qualified applicants.

The Supreme Court further observed that race-conscious admissions programs that operate as quotas do not, by themselves, meet the requirement of individualized consideration. Rather, the Court asserted that institutional officials must demonstrate that race is not the decisive or defining feature of applications. In order to satisfy this requirement, officials must demonstrate not only that applicants had the opportunity to highlight their contributions to a diverse educational environment but also that their applications were read individually as part of a highly individualized, holistic review of their files.

In evaluating the contributions that individuals can make to diversity, the Supreme Court indicated that officials must not assume that a single characteristic would automatically guarantee a specific and identifiable contribution to diversity.

To this end, the Court rejected the notion of an automatic acceptance or rejection based on any single "soft" variable such as the enthusiasm of recommenders, the quality of the undergraduate institutions that applicants attended, their essays, and the areas and difficulty of their undergraduate course selection. Instead, the Court directed officials to consider how and whether applicants will contribute to diversity based on their own unique characteristics. Moreover, if institutional officials consider race in order to obtain the educational benefits of diverse student bodies, the Court expects decision makers to give substantial weight to diversity factors other than race.

Consideration of Race-Neutral Alternatives

Second, in order to show that the use of race is narrowly tailored, the Supreme Court maintained that university officials must be able to demonstrate that they employed serious, good faith considerations of workable race-neutral alternatives to achieve diversity. At this point the Court assumed without deciding that "percentage plans," which ensure admission to all students above specified class-rank thresholds, are race-neutral even though such policies could be subject to legal challenges if they were adopted for a racially discriminatory purposes. In applying these standards to the law school, the Court discussed three specific race-neutral alternatives suggested during the litigation: lottery systems, decreasing the emphasis for applicants on undergraduate GPA and LSAT scores, and employing percentage plans such as those adopted by public institutions in Texas, California, and Florida. Still, the Court accepted the law school's assertion that none of these options was an adequate alternative to race-conscious measures.

No Undue Burden

Third, the Supreme Court acknowledged that because racial preferences pose serious problems of justice, race-conscious admissions programs must not unduly burden individuals who are not members of the favored racial and ethnic groups. The Court held that the admissions policy met this standard, because officials chose nonminority applicants with greater potential to enhance student body diversity over underrepresented minority applicants.

Limited Duration

Fourth, the Supreme Court wrote that race-conscious admissions policies must be of a limited time duration, because all governmental uses of race must have logical end points. The Court suggested that officials can meet this requirement by developing sunset provisions in race-conscious admissions programs and periodic reviews to evaluate whether racial preferences are still necessary to achieve student body diversity. The Court concluded that it expected that racial preferences would no longer be necessary in 25 years but did not offer a justification as to how it developed this time line.

Dissenting Opinions

Three different dissenting opinions, by Justices Scalia and Thomas and Chief Justice Rehnquist, raised a variety of concerns with the Supreme Court's rationale. Among the questions that the dissents raised were judicial deference to academic decision making as reflected in the concept of academic abstention and calculating when a critical mass of minority students is sufficient.

William E. Thro

See also Affirmative Action; Equal Protection Analysis; *Gratz v. Bollinger; Regents of the University of California v. Bakke*; U.S. Supreme Court Cases in Higher Education

Further Readings

Jenkins, J. K. (2004). *Grutter*, diversity, & K–12 public schools. *Education Law Reporter, 182*, 353–370.

Mawdsley, R. D., & Russo, C. J. (2003). Supreme Court dissenting opinions in *Grutter*: Has the majority created a nation divided against itself? *Education Law Reporter, 180*, 417–435.

Meers, E. B., & Thro, W. E. (2004). *Race conscious admissions & financial aid after the University of Michigan decisions*. Washington, DC: National Association of College and University Attorneys.

Thro, W. E. (2005). No direct consideration of race: The lessons of the University of Michigan decisions. *Education Law Reporter, 196*, 755–764.

Legal Citations

Gratz v. Bollinger, 539 U.S. 244 (2003).
Grutter v. Bollinger, 539 U.S. 306 (2003).
Regents of the University of California v. Bakke, 438 U.S. 265 (1978).

GRUTTER V. BOLLINGER

In *Grutter*, the Supreme Court upheld a race-conscious admissions plan because it was sufficiently narrowly tailored to achieve the university's goal of a diverse student body.

Supreme Court of the United States

GRUTTER

v.

BOLLINGER

539 U.S. 306

Argued April 1, 2003

Decided June 23, 2003

Rehearing Denied Aug. 25, 2003

Justice O'CONNOR delivered the opinion of the Court.

This case requires us to decide whether the use of race as a factor in student admissions by the University of Michigan Law School (Law School) is unlawful.

I

A

The Law School ranks among the Nation's top law schools. It receives more than 3,500 applications each year for a class of around 350 students. Seeking to "admit a group of students who individually and collectively are among the most capable," the Law School looks for individuals with "substantial promise for success in law school" and "a strong likelihood of succeeding in the practice of law and contributing in diverse ways to the well-being of others." More broadly, the Law School seeks "a mix of students with varying backgrounds and experiences who will respect and learn from each other." In 1992, the dean of the Law School charged a faculty committee with crafting a written admissions policy to implement these goals. In particular, the Law School sought to ensure that its efforts to achieve student body diversity complied with this Court's most recent ruling on the use of race in university admissions. Upon the unanimous adoption of the committee's report by the Law School faculty, it became the Law School's official admissions policy.

The hallmark of that policy is its focus on academic ability coupled with a flexible assessment of applicants' talents, experiences, and potential "to contribute to the learning of those around them." The policy requires admissions officials to evaluate each applicant based on all the information available in the file, including a personal statement, letters of recommendation, and an essay describing the ways in which the applicant will contribute to the life and diversity of the Law School. In reviewing an applicant's file, admissions officials must consider the applicant's undergraduate grade point average (GPA) and Law School Admission Test (LSAT) score because they are important (if imperfect) predictors of academic success in law school. The policy stresses that "no applicant should be admitted unless we expect that applicant to do well enough to graduate with no serious academic problems."

The policy makes clear, however, that even the highest possible score does not guarantee admission to the Law School. Nor does a low score automatically disqualify an applicant. Rather, the policy requires admissions officials to look beyond grades and test scores to other criteria that are important to the Law School's educational objectives. So-called "'soft' variables" such as "the enthusiasm of recommenders, the quality of the undergraduate institution, the quality of the applicant's essay, and the areas and difficulty of undergraduate course selection" are all brought to bear in assessing an "applicant's likely contributions to the intellectual and social life of the institution."

The policy aspires to "achieve that diversity which has the potential to enrich everyone's education and thus make a law school class stronger than the sum of its parts." The policy does not restrict the types of diversity contributions eligible for "substantial weight" in the admissions process, but instead recognizes "many possible bases for diversity admissions." The policy does, however, reaffirm the Law School's longstanding commitment to "one particular type of diversity," that is, "racial and ethnic diversity with special reference to the inclusion of students from groups which have been historically discriminated against, like African-Americans, Hispanics and Native Americans, who without this commitment might not be represented in our student body in meaningful numbers." By enrolling a "'critical mass' of [underrepresented] minority students," the Law School seeks to "ensur[e] their ability to make unique contributions to the character of the Law School."

The policy does not define diversity "solely in terms of racial and ethnic status." Nor is the policy "insensitive to the competition among all students for admission to the [L]aw [S]chool." Rather, the policy seeks to guide admissions officers in "producing classes both diverse and academically outstanding, classes made up of students who promise to continue the tradition of outstanding contribution by Michigan Graduates to the legal profession."

B

Petitioner Barbara Grutter is a white Michigan resident who applied to the Law School in 1996 with a 3.8 GPA and 161 LSAT score. The Law School initially placed petitioner on a waiting list, but subsequently rejected her application. In December 1997, petitioner filed suit in the United States

District Court for the Eastern District of Michigan against the Law School, the Regents of the University of Michigan, Lee Bollinger (Dean of the Law School from 1987 to 1994), and [others] . . . Petitioner alleged that respondents discriminated against her on the basis of race in violation of the Fourteenth Amendment; Title VI of the Civil Rights Act of 1964.

Petitioner further alleged that her application was rejected because the Law School uses race as a "predominant" factor, giving applicants who belong to certain minority groups "a significantly greater chance of admission than students with similar credentials from disfavored racial groups." Petitioner also alleged that respondents "had no compelling interest to justify their use of race in the admissions process." Petitioner requested compensatory and punitive damages, an order requiring the Law School to offer her admission, and an injunction prohibiting the Law School from continuing to discriminate on the basis of race. Petitioner clearly has standing to bring this lawsuit.

The District Court granted petitioner's motion for class certification and for bifurcation of the trial into liability and damages phases. . . .

The District Court heard oral argument on the parties' cross-motions for summary judgment on December 22, 2000. . . .

During the 15-day bench trial, the parties introduced extensive evidence concerning the Law School's use of race in the admissions process. . . .

. . .

In the end, the District Court concluded that the Law School's use of race as a factor in admissions decisions was unlawful. Applying strict scrutiny, the District Court determined that the Law School's asserted interest in assembling a diverse student body was not compelling because "the attainment of a racially diverse class . . . was not recognized as such by *Bakke* and it is not a remedy for past discrimination." The District Court went on to hold that even if diversity were compelling, the Law School had not narrowly tailored its use of race to further that interest. The District Court granted petitioner's request for declaratory relief and enjoined the Law School from using race as a factor in its admissions decisions. The Court of Appeals entered a stay of the injunction pending appeal.

Sitting en banc, the Court of Appeals reversed the District Court's judgment and vacated the injunction. The Court of Appeals first held that Justice Powell's opinion in *Bakke* was binding precedent establishing diversity as a compelling state interest. According to the Court of Appeals, Justice Powell's opinion with respect to diversity constituted the controlling rationale for the judgment of this Court under the analysis set forth in *Marks v. United States,* the Court of Appeals also held that the Law School's use of race was narrowly tailored because race was merely a "potential 'plus' factor" and because the Law School's program was "virtually identical" to the Harvard admissions program described approvingly by Justice Powell and appended to his *Bakke* opinion.

Four dissenting judges would have held the Law School's use of race unconstitutional. . . .

We granted certiorari to resolve the disagreement among the Courts of Appeals on a question of national importance: Whether diversity is a compelling interest that can justify the narrowly tailored use of race in selecting applicants for admission to public universities.

II

A

We last addressed the use of race in public higher education over 25 years ago. In the landmark *Bakke* case, we reviewed a racial set-aside program that reserved 16 out of 100 seats in a medical school class for members of certain minority groups. The decision produced six separate opinions, none of which commanded a majority of the Court. Four Justices would have upheld the program against all attack on the ground that the government can use race to "remedy disadvantages cast on minorities by past racial prejudice." Four other Justices avoided the constitutional question altogether and struck down the program on statutory grounds. Justice Powell provided a fifth vote not only for invalidating the set-aside program, but also for reversing the state court's injunction against any use of race whatsoever. The only holding for the Court in *Bakke* was that a "State has a substantial interest that legitimately may be served by a properly devised admissions program involving the competitive consideration of race and ethnic origin." Thus, we reversed that part of the lower court's judgment that enjoined the university "from any consideration of the race of any applicant."

Since this Court's splintered decision in *Bakke,* Justice Powell's opinion announcing the judgment of the Court has served as the touchstone for constitutional analysis of race-conscious admissions policies. Public and private universities across the Nation have modeled their own admissions programs on Justice Powell's views on permissible race-conscious policies. . . .

. . .

In the wake of our fractured decision in *Bakke,* courts have struggled to discern whether Justice Powell's diversity rationale, set forth in part of the opinion joined by no other Justice, is nonetheless binding precedent. . . .

We do not find it necessary to decide whether Justice Powell's opinion is binding . . . It does not seem "useful to pursue the . . . inquiry to the utmost logical possibility when it has so obviously baffled and divided the lower courts that have considered it." More important, for the reasons set out below, today we endorse Justice Powell's view that student body diversity is a compelling state interest that can justify the use of race in university admissions.

B

The Equal Protection Clause provides that no State shall "deny to any person within its jurisdiction the equal protection of the laws." Because the Fourteenth Amendment "protect[s] *persons*, not *groups*," all "governmental action based on race—a *group* classification long recognized as in most circumstances irrelevant and therefore prohibited—should be subjected to detailed judicial inquiry to ensure that the *personal* right to equal protection of the laws has not been infringed." We are a "free people whose institutions are founded upon the doctrine of equality." It follows from that principle that "government may treat people differently because of their race only for the most compelling reasons."

We have held that all racial classifications imposed by government "must be analyzed by a reviewing court under strict scrutiny." This means that such classifications are constitutional only if they are narrowly tailored to further compelling governmental interests. "Absent searching judicial inquiry into the justification for such race-based measures," we have no way to determine what "classifications are 'benign' or 'remedial' and what classifications are in fact motivated by illegitimate notions of racial inferiority or simple racial politics." We apply strict scrutiny to all racial classifications to "'smoke out' illegitimate uses of race by assuring that [government] is pursuing a goal important enough to warrant use of a highly suspect tool."

Strict scrutiny is not "strict in theory, but fatal in fact." Although all governmental uses of race are subject to strict scrutiny, not all are invalidated by it. As we have explained, "whenever the government treats any person unequally because of his or her race, that person has suffered an injury that falls squarely within the language and spirit of the Constitution's guarantee of equal protection." But that observation "says nothing about the ultimate validity of any particular law; that determination is the job of the court applying strict scrutiny." When race-based action is necessary to further a compelling governmental interest, such action does not violate the constitutional guarantee of equal protection so long as the narrow-tailoring requirement is also satisfied.

Context matters when reviewing race-based governmental action under the Equal Protection Clause. In *Adarand Constructors, Inc. v. Peña*, we made clear that strict scrutiny must take "'relevant differences' into account." Indeed, as we explained, that is its "fundamental purpose." Not every decision influenced by race is equally objectionable, and strict scrutiny is designed to provide a framework for carefully examining the importance and the sincerity of the reasons advanced by the governmental decisionmaker for the use of race in that particular context.

III

A

With these principles in mind, we turn to the question whether the Law School's use of race is justified by a compelling state interest. Before this Court, as they have throughout this litigation, respondents assert only one justification for their use of race in the admissions process: obtaining "the educational benefits that flow from a diverse student body." In other words, the Law School asks us to recognize, in the context of higher education, a compelling state interest in student body diversity.

We first wish to dispel the notion that the Law School's argument has been foreclosed, either expressly or implicitly, by our affirmative-action cases decided since *Bakke*. It is true that some language in those opinions might be read to suggest that remedying past discrimination is the only permissible justification for race-based governmental action. But we have never held that the only governmental use of race that can survive strict scrutiny is remedying past discrimination. Nor, since *Bakke*, have we directly addressed the use of race in the context of public higher education. Today, we hold that the Law School has a compelling interest in attaining a diverse student body.

The Law School's educational judgment that such diversity is essential to its educational mission is one to which we defer. The Law School's assessment that diversity will, in fact, yield educational benefits is substantiated by respondents and their *amici*. Our scrutiny of the interest asserted by the Law School is no less strict for taking into account complex educational judgments in an area that lies primarily within the expertise of the university. Our holding today is in keeping with our tradition of giving a degree of deference to a university's academic decisions, within constitutionally prescribed limits.

We have long recognized that, given the important purpose of public education and the expansive freedoms of speech and thought associated with the university environment, universities occupy a special niche in our constitutional tradition. In announcing the principle of student body diversity as a compelling state interest, Justice Powell invoked our cases recognizing a constitutional dimension, grounded in the First Amendment, of educational autonomy: "The freedom of a university to make its own judgments as to education includes the selection of its student body." From this premise, Justice Powell reasoned that by claiming "the right to select those students who will contribute the most to the 'robust exchange of ideas,'" a university "seek[s] to achieve a goal that is of paramount importance in the fulfillment of its mission." Our conclusion that the Law School has a compelling interest in a diverse student body is informed by our view that attaining a diverse student body is at the heart of the Law School's proper institutional mission, and that "good faith" on the part of a university is "presumed" absent "a showing to the contrary."

As part of its goal of "assembling a class that is both exceptionally academically qualified and broadly diverse," the Law School seeks to "enroll a 'critical mass' of minority students." The Law School's interest is not simply "to assure within its student body some specified percentage of a particular group merely because of its race or ethnic origin." That would amount to outright racial balancing, which is patently unconstitutional. Rather, the Law School's concept of critical mass is defined by reference to the educational benefits that diversity is designed to produce.

These benefits are substantial. As the District Court emphasized, the Law School's admissions policy promotes "cross-racial understanding," helps to break down racial stereotypes, and "enables [students] to better understand persons of different races." These benefits are "important and laudable," because "classroom discussion is livelier, more spirited, and simply more enlightening and interesting" when the students have "the greatest possible variety of backgrounds."

The Law School's claim of a compelling interest is further bolstered by its *amici*, who point to the educational benefits that flow from student body diversity. In addition to the expert studies and reports entered into evidence at trial, numerous studies show that student body diversity promotes learning outcomes, and "better prepares students for an increasingly diverse workforce and society, and better prepares them as professionals."

These benefits are not theoretical but real, as major American businesses have made clear that the skills needed in today's increasingly global marketplace can only be developed through exposure to widely diverse people, cultures, ideas, and viewpoints. What is more, high-ranking retired officers and civilian leaders of the United States military assert that, "[b]ased on [their] decades of experience," a "highly qualified, racially diverse officer corps ... is essential to the military's ability to fulfill its principle mission to provide national security." ...

We have repeatedly acknowledged the overriding importance of preparing students for work and citizenship, describing education as pivotal to "sustaining our political and cultural heritage" with a fundamental role in maintaining the fabric of society. This Court has long recognized that "education . . . is the very foundation of good citizenship. For this reason, the diffusion of knowledge and opportunity through public institutions of higher education must be accessible to all individuals regardless of race or ethnicity. The United States, as *amicus curiae*, affirms that "[e]nsuring that public institutions are open and available to all segments of American society, including people of all races and ethnicities, represents a paramount government objective." And, "[n]owhere is the importance of such openness more acute than in the context of higher education." Effective participation by members of all racial and ethnic groups in the civic life of our Nation is essential if the dream of one Nation, indivisible, is to be realized.

Moreover, universities, and in particular, law schools, represent the training ground for a large number of our Nation's leaders. Individuals with law degrees occupy roughly half the state governorships, more than half the seats in the United States Senate, and more than a third of the seats in the United States House of Representatives. The pattern is even more striking when it comes to highly selective law schools. . . .

In order to cultivate a set of leaders with legitimacy in the eyes of the citizenry, it is necessary that the path to leadership be visibly open to talented and qualified individuals of every race and ethnicity. All members of our heterogeneous society must have confidence in the openness and integrity of the educational institutions that provide this training. As we have recognized, law schools "cannot be effective in isolation from the individuals and institutions with which the law interacts." Access to legal education (and thus the legal profession) must be inclusive of talented and qualified individuals of every race and ethnicity, so that all members of our heterogeneous society may participate in the educational institutions that provide the training and education necessary to succeed in America.

The Law School does not premise its need for critical mass on "any belief that minority students always (or even consistently) express some characteristic minority viewpoint on any issue." To the contrary, diminishing the force of such stereotypes is both a crucial part of the Law School's mission, and one that it cannot accomplish with only token numbers of minority students. Just as growing up in a particular region or having particular professional experiences is likely to affect an individual's views, so too is one's own, unique experience of being a racial minority in a society, like our own, in which race unfortunately still matters. The Law School has determined, based on its experience and expertise, that a "critical mass" of underrepresented minorities is necessary to further its compelling interest in securing the educational benefits of a diverse student body.

B

Even in the limited circumstance when drawing racial distinctions is permissible to further a compelling state interest, government is still "constrained in how it may pursue that end: [T]he means chosen to accomplish the [government's] asserted purpose must be specifically and narrowly framed to accomplish that purpose." The purpose of the narrow tailoring requirement is to ensure that "the means chosen 'fit' th[e] compelling goal so closely that there is little or no possibility that the motive for the classification was illegitimate racial prejudice or stereotype."

Since *Bakke,* we have had no occasion to define the contours of the narrow-tailoring inquiry with respect to race-conscious university admissions programs. That inquiry must be calibrated to fit the distinct issues raised by the use of race to achieve student body diversity in public higher education. Contrary to Justice KENNEDY's assertions, we do not "abando[n] strict scrutiny." Rather, as we have already explained, we adhere to *Adarand's* teaching that the very purpose of strict scrutiny is to take such "relevant differences into account."

To be narrowly tailored, a race-conscious admissions program cannot use a quota system-it cannot "insulat[e] each category of applicants with certain desired qualifications from competition with all other applicants." Instead, a university may consider race or ethnicity only as a "'plus' in a particular applicant's file," without "insulat[ing] the individual from comparison with all other candidates for the available seats." In other words, an admissions program must be "flexible enough to consider all pertinent elements of diversity in light of the particular qualifications of each applicant, and to place

them on the same footing for consideration, although not necessarily according them the same weight."

We find that the Law School's admissions program bears the hallmarks of a narrowly tailored plan. . . .

We are satisfied that the Law School's admissions program, like the Harvard plan described by Justice Powell, does not operate as a quota. Properly understood, a "quota" is a program in which a certain fixed number or proportion of opportunities are "reserved exclusively for certain minority groups." Quotas "impose a fixed number or percentage which must be attained, or which cannot be exceeded" and "insulate the individual from comparison with all other candidates for the available seats." In contrast, "a permissible goal . . . require[s] only a good-faith effort . . . to come within a range demarcated by the goal itself" and permits consideration of race as a "plus" factor in any given case while still ensuring that each candidate "compete[s] with all other qualified applicants." Justice Powell's distinction between the medical school's rigid 16-seat quota and Harvard's flexible use of race as a "plus" factor is instructive. Harvard certainly had minimum *goals* for minority enrollment, even if it had no specific number firmly in mind. What is more, Justice Powell flatly rejected the argument that Harvard's program was "the functional equivalent of a quota" merely because it had some "plus" for race, or gave greater "weight" to race than to some other factors, in order to achieve student body diversity.

The Law School's goal of attaining a critical mass of underrepresented minority students does not transform its program into a quota. As the Harvard plan described by Justice Powell recognized, there is of course "some relationship between numbers and achieving the benefits to be derived from a diverse student body, and between numbers and providing a reasonable environment for those students admitted." "[S]ome attention to numbers," without more, does not transform a flexible admissions system into a rigid quota. Nor, as Justice Kennedy posits, does the Law School's consultation of the "daily reports," which keep track of the racial and ethnic composition of the class (as well as of residency and gender), "sugges[t] there was no further attempt at individual review save for race itself" during the final stages of the admissions process. To the contrary, the Law School's admissions officers testified without contradiction that they never gave race any more or less weight based on the information contained in these reports. . . .

. . . .

That a race-conscious admissions program does not operate as a quota does not, by itself, satisfy the requirement of individualized consideration. When using race as a "plus" factor in university admissions, a university's admissions program must remain flexible enough to ensure that each applicant is evaluated as an individual and not in a way that makes an applicant's race or ethnicity the defining feature of his or her application. The importance of this individualized consideration in the context of a race-conscious admissions program is paramount.

Here, the Law School engages in a highly individualized, holistic review of each applicant's file, giving serious consideration to all the ways an applicant might contribute to a diverse educational environment. The Law School affords this individualized consideration to applicants of all races. There is no policy, either *de jure* or *de facto*, of automatic acceptance or rejection based on any single "soft" variable. Unlike the program at issue in *Gratz v. Bollinger*, the Law School awards no mechanical, predetermined diversity "bonuses" based on race or ethnicity. Like the Harvard plan, the Law School's admissions policy "is flexible enough to consider all pertinent elements of diversity in light of the particular qualifications of each applicant, and to place them on the same footing for consideration, although not necessarily according them the same weight."

We also find that, like the Harvard plan Justice Powell referenced in *Bakke*, the Law School's race-conscious admissions program adequately ensures that all factors that may contribute to student body diversity are meaningfully considered alongside race in admissions decisions. With respect to the use of race itself, all underrepresented minority students admitted by the Law School have been deemed qualified. By virtue of our Nation's struggle with racial inequality, such students are both likely to have experiences of particular importance to the Law School's mission, and less likely to be admitted in meaningful numbers on criteria that ignore those experiences.

The Law School does not, however, limit in any way the broad range of qualities and experiences that may be considered valuable contributions to student body diversity. To the contrary, the 1992 policy makes clear "[t]here are many possible bases for diversity admissions," and provides examples of admittees who have lived or traveled widely abroad, are fluent in several languages, have overcome personal adversity and family hardship, have exceptional records of extensive community service, and have had successful careers in other fields. The Law School seriously considers each "applicant's promise of making a notable contribution to the class by way of a particular strength, attainment, or characteristic—*e.g.*, an unusual

intellectual achievement, employment experience, non-academic performance, or personal background." All applicants have the opportunity to highlight their own potential diversity contributions through the submission of a personal statement, letters of recommendation, and an essay describing the ways in which the applicant will contribute to the life and diversity of the Law School.

What is more, the Law School actually gives substantial weight to diversity factors besides race. The Law School frequently accepts nonminority applicants with grades and test scores lower than underrepresented minority applicants (and other nonminority applicants) who are rejected. This shows that the Law School seriously weighs many other diversity factors besides race that can make a real and dispositive difference for nonminority applicants as well. By this flexible approach, the Law School sufficiently takes into account, in practice as well as in theory, a wide variety of characteristics besides race and ethnicity that contribute to a diverse student body. . . .

Petitioner and the United States argue that the Law School's plan is not narrowly tailored because race-neutral means exist to obtain the educational benefits of student body diversity that the Law School seeks. We disagree. Narrow tailoring does not require exhaustion of every conceivable race-neutral alternative. Nor does it require a university to choose between maintaining a reputation for excellence or fulfilling a commitment to provide educational opportunities to members of all racial groups. Narrow tailoring does, however, require serious, good faith consideration of workable race-neutral alternatives that will achieve the diversity the university seeks.

We agree with the Court of Appeals that the Law School sufficiently considered workable race-neutral alternatives. The District Court took the Law School to task for failing to consider race-neutral alternatives such as "using a lottery system" or "decreasing the emphasis for all applicants on undergraduate GPA and LSAT scores." But these alternatives would require a dramatic sacrifice of diversity, the academic quality of all admitted students, or both.

The Law School's current admissions program considers race as one factor among many, in an effort to assemble a student body that is diverse in ways broader than race. Because a lottery would make that kind of nuanced judgment impossible, it would effectively sacrifice all other educational values, not to mention every other kind of diversity. So too with the suggestion that the Law School simply lower admissions standards for all students, a drastic remedy that would require the Law School to become a much different institution and sacrifice a vital component of its educational mission. The United States advocates "percentage plans," recently adopted by public undergraduate institutions in Texas, Florida, and California, to guarantee admission to all students above a certain class-rank threshold in every high school in the State. The United States does not, however, explain how such plans could work for graduate and professional schools. Moreover, even assuming such plans are race-neutral, they may preclude the university from conducting the individualized assessments necessary to assemble a student body that is not just racially diverse, but diverse along all the qualities valued by the university. We are satisfied that the Law School adequately considered race-neutral alternatives currently capable of producing a critical mass without forcing the Law School to abandon the academic selectivity that is the cornerstone of its educational mission.

We acknowledge that "there are serious problems of justice connected with the idea of preference itself." Narrow tailoring, therefore, requires that a race-conscious admissions program not unduly harm members of any racial group. Even remedial race-based governmental action generally "remains subject to continuing oversight to assure that it will work the least harm possible to other innocent persons competing for the benefit." To be narrowly tailored, a race-conscious admissions program must not "unduly burden individuals who are not members of the favored racial and ethnic groups."

We are satisfied that the Law School's admissions program does not. Because the Law School considers "all pertinent elements of diversity," it can (and does) select nonminority applicants who have greater potential to enhance student body diversity over underrepresented minority applicants. As Justice Powell recognized in *Bakke*, so long as a race-conscious admissions program uses race as a "plus" factor in the context of individualized consideration, a rejected applicant "will not have been foreclosed from all consideration for that seat simply because he was not the right color or had the wrong surname. . . . His qualifications would have been weighed fairly and competitively, and he would have no basis to complain of unequal treatment under the Fourteenth Amendment."

We agree that, in the context of its individualized inquiry into the possible diversity contributions of all applicants, the Law School's race-conscious admissions program does not unduly harm nonminority applicants.

We are mindful, however, that "[a] core purpose of the Fourteenth Amendment was to do away with all governmentally imposed discrimination based on race." Accordingly, race-conscious admissions policies must be limited in time. This requirement reflects that racial classifications, however compelling their goals, are potentially so dangerous that they may be employed no more broadly than the interest demands. Enshrining a permanent justification for racial preferences would offend this fundamental equal protection principle. We see no reason to exempt race-conscious admissions programs from the requirement that all governmental use of race must have a logical end point. The Law School, too, concedes that all "race-conscious programs must have reasonable durational limits."

In the context of higher education, the durational requirement can be met by sunset provisions in race-conscious admissions policies and periodic reviews to determine whether racial preferences are still necessary to achieve student body diversity. Universities in California, Florida, and Washington State, where racial preferences in admissions are prohibited by state law, are currently engaged in experimenting with a wide variety of alternative approaches. Universities in other States can and should draw on the most promising aspects of these race-neutral alternatives as they develop.

The requirement that all race-conscious admissions programs have a termination point "assure[s] all citizens that the deviation from the norm of equal treatment of all racial and ethnic groups is a temporary matter, a measure taken in the service of the goal of equality itself."

We take the Law School at its word that it would "like nothing better than to find a race-neutral admissions formula" and will terminate its race-conscious admissions program as soon as practicable. It has been 25 years since Justice Powell first approved the use of race to further an interest in student body diversity in the context of public higher education. Since that time, the number of minority applicants with high grades and test scores has indeed increased. We expect that 25 years from now, the use of racial preferences will no longer be necessary to further the interest approved today.

IV

In summary, the Equal Protection Clause does not prohibit the Law School's narrowly tailored use of race in admissions decisions to further a compelling interest in obtaining the educational benefits that flow from a diverse student body. Consequently, petitioner's statutory claims based on Title VI and 42 U.S.C. § 1981 also fail. The judgment of the Court of Appeals for the Sixth Circuit, accordingly, is affirmed.

It is so ordered.

H

HATE CRIMES

The presence of bias-motivated crime, or hate crime, on college and university campuses is a reality in today's cultural landscape. Hate crime is a criminal offense that is motivated, in whole or in part, by the offender's bias against a particular race, color, religion, disability, ethnicity/national origin, or sexual orientation. Officials at institutions of higher learning may be asked to deal with these types of offenses on many different levels, ranging from cultural education to the campus judicial system to the criminal justice system. This entry outlines the attributes of current hate crime legislation on both the federal and state levels and describes currently pending federal hate crime legislation. The goals of hate crime legislation are then reviewed, along with arguments for the view that hate crime statutes are not in the public's best interest. The entry then briefly discusses the differences between hate crime and hate speech and the legal relationship they play to harassment. Finally, the entry examines the potential of campus speech codes and codes of conduct in regulating hate crime.

Hate Crime Statutes

Hate crime statutes vary from jurisdiction to jurisdiction. The regulations enacted pursuant to the major federal hate crime statute, the Violent Crime Control and Law Enforcement Act of 1994, allow for more severe sentences in cases where "the defendant intentionally selected any victim or any property as the object of the offense because of the actual or perceived race, color, religion, national origin, ethnicity, gender, disability, or sexual orientation of any person" (60 *Federal Register* 25,082, Application Notes 4). Other major federal statutes include the Hate Crime Statistics Act of 1990 and the Campus Hate Crimes Right to Know Act of 1997 (also known as the Clery Act).

The Hate Crime Statistics Act recognizes the classes of race, religion, disability, sexual orientation, and ethnicity, but it excludes color, national origin, and gender, three classes that were later included in the Violent Crime Control and Law Enforcement Act of 1994. Based on these classifications, the latter act directs the attorney general to collect data on hate crimes occurring in the United States. These data are then made available through a joint report by the FBI and Department of Justice.

Reporting Requirements

The Campus Hate Crimes Right to Know Act of 1997 amended the Higher Education Act of 1965 to include a requirement to report all crimes "based on race, gender, religion, sexual orientation, ethnicity, and disability." This act does not include the classes of color and national origin. The Campus Hate Crimes Right to Know Act is formally codified in 20 U.S.C. § 1092(f) with other reporting provisions of the Clery Act. The annual reporting of hate crime statistics by university officials is just one of the crime statistics that must be reported by college officials. In addition to annual crime reports, institutional officials must issue timely warnings about crimes, have a public crime log, and ensure that established rights of the victims of campus sexual assault are respected.

State Laws

The three pieces of federal hate crime legislation do not use the same categories or classes of membership to define victims of hate crime, and state statutory views are equally uneven. All but five states currently have some form of hate crime statutes, but the included classes differ. Some classes that are included in state statutes but not included in federal statutes are political affiliation (5 states), age (13 states), and transgender/gender identity (12 states). Additionally, states vary on reporting requirements, ability to bring civil suits, required training for law enforcement, and vandalism statutes.

The effect of this rugged legal landscape for the education community is that for most parties, the application of state law to the facts at hand is the most important element. However, state law also has the most variability; thus, institutions operating in multiple states will have to deal with potentially disparate laws, especially if one of the states in which they operate has no hate crime statutes at all. The Anti-Defamation League keeps a comprehensive list of state-by-state hate crime statutes and can provide a valuable starting place for becoming familiar with state hate crime statutes.

Proposed Legislation

In light of the incongruence in state hate crime legislation, there is currently proposed federal legislation, the Local Law Enforcement Hate Crimes Prevention Act of 2007, also known as the Matthew Shepard Act, which would broaden the federally protected classes of membership to include gender identity. The current version of H.R. 1592 would also expand the classifications to include actual or perceived membership, thus resulting in the inclusion of people who do not actually meet the requirements for membership but whose alleged violators mistakenly believed that they did. This legislation was under consideration as of mid-2009 but had yet to pass both houses of Congress. In addition to broadening the included protected classes, the act is designed to harmonize the existing federal statute classes.

Arguments for and Against Hate Crime Laws

Hate crime laws are intended to provide harsher punishment for crimes that are committed with an element of bias than for comparable crimes committed without such bias. In *Wisconsin v. Mitchell* (1993), the U.S. Supreme Court acknowledged that state officials may want to enact such laws, because hate crimes inflict greater individual and societal harm than other crimes. For example, such crimes may increase the likelihood of retaliatory crimes, cause a distinct kind of emotional harm to the victim, and contribute to community unrest. The Court held that these state interests amounted to more than just disagreement with the offender's beliefs or biases and that hate crime laws did not violate defendants' rights to free speech by purportedly punishing their biased beliefs.

In addition to these reasons for hate crime legislation, others have argued that only through codified hate crime laws can the government send a clear message that bigotry is not accepted or valued. Proponents of this position assert that because it is impossible for the government to take a neutral stance toward hate crimes, a governmental entity that fails to enact hate crimes is expressing a value judgment of acceptance through doing nothing.

Opposition to hate crime laws are grounded in two different concepts—government discrimination and First Amendment violations. The first concept asserts that increased sanctions due to the victim's membership in a governmentally selected class results in preferred treatment of these classes by the government, to the detriment of other classes of people. The argument is that by using hate crime laws to combat bigotry and intolerance, the government is discriminating against other classes of citizens. The second argument that opponents raise is grounded in the First Amendment and maintains that hate crime laws increase punishments simply for "thought crimes" or for being a bigot.

Opponents of this position criticize the outcome of *Wisconsin v. Mitchell* (1993), wherein the Supreme Court upheld an enhanced punishment where the victim was intentionally selected because he was White. The Court rejected the notion that the statute violated the defendant's First Amendment right to free speech by purportedly punishing him for biased beliefs, because violence or other potentially expressive activities that result in special harm are distinct from their communicative impact and thus are not entitled to constitutional protection. Even so, these critics have questioned this legal reasoning as nothing more than an attempt to avoid the protections of the Free Speech Clause of the First Amendment.

Hate Speech

Regardless of purpose, the application of hate crime legislation is frequently confused and intermingled with hate speech. Hate crime legislation provides for increased sanctions and reporting mechanisms for bias-motivated crimes. The underlying requirement, then, is that a crime be committed. Hate speech, on the other hand, is speech that is directed toward one of the protected classes such as individuals of a certain race, gender, or sexual orientation, and it may or may not be protected.

Due to this distinction, hate speech can end up being protected by constitutional and state law guarantees of free speech. What qualifies as protected speech is very fact specific and can vary based on many factors. What may be protected speech under one set of facts may qualify as harassment in a different situation. Speech may generally qualify as harassment if a reasonable person finds it is "severe or pervasive," if it creates a hostile work environment, or if it is based on a trait of a protected class of people. This definition leaves a great deal of discretion as to what speech qualifies as harassment. The resulting legal outcome is one that requires careful attention to whether a crime is being committed other than violating a hate crime statute, if the behavior is harassment rather than a hate crime, or if the speech (or expressive behavior) qualifies as protected speech.

Campus Behavior and Speech Codes

Many campuses may want to create campus behavior or speech codes aimed at a variety of different nontolerated behaviors, including bias-motivated crimes. Such a restriction is more easily enacted at a private higher education institution. However, officials at public institutions of higher learning, as actors on behalf of state entities, need to ensure that their behavior and speech codes are content-neutral and designed to meet a narrow government interest. These types of campus rules, while not singling out specific classes of protected people, express a clear value stance that bigotry will not be tolerated by any member of the campus community. Such codes can provide campus officials with greater flexibility in enforcement and the needed judicial reach to preserve harmonious campus cultures.

Clayton H. Slaughter

See also Clery Act; Crime Awareness and Campus Security Act; Disciplinary Sanctions and Due Process Rights; Free Speech and Expression Rights of Students; Higher Education Act

Further Readings

Gellman, S. (1991). Sticks and stones can put you in jail, but words increase your sentence? Constitutional and policy dilemmas of ethnic intimidation laws. *UCLA Law Review, 39,* 333–397.

R. A. V. v. City of St. Paul, 505 U.S. 377 (1992).

Robinson, P. H. (2005). Hate crimes. In P. H. Robinson (Ed.), *Criminal law: Case studies and controversies* (pp. 833–860). New York: Aspen.

Legal Citations

Campus Hate Crimes Right to Know Act, 20 U.S.C. § 1092 (1997).

Hate Crime Statistics Act of 1990, 28 U.S.C. § 994 (2006).

Higher Education Act, 20 U.S.C. §§ 1001 *et seq.* (1965).

Local Law Enforcement Hate Crimes Prevention Act of 2007, H.R. 1592, 110th Cong. § 8 (2007).

Violent Crime Control and Law Enforcement Act of 1994, Pub. L. No. 103-322, 108 Stat. 1796, 2042 (1994).

Wisconsin v. Mitchell, 508 U.S. 476 (1993).

HAZING

"I don't think parents are aware of what their kids are being asked to navigate, particularly when they go to college." These words were spoken by Leslie Lanahan, mother of Gordie Bailey, a University of Colorado student who died in September 2004 as a result of alcohol poisoning after a fraternity hazing ritual. Gordie was a freshman pledge in Chi Psi fraternity. Several months following Bailey's death, the university's chapter of the fraternity was shut down. Furthermore, the university's interfraternity council lost its affiliation with the university after its leaders refused to agree to a series of reforms demanded by institutional administrators. Among the disputed reforms was a delay in recruitment until the spring semester and a requirement that each fraternity and sorority have a live-in adviser. Lanahan filed suit against the fraternity and some of its members, alleging negligence in the death of her son. In March 2009, the parties reached an out-of-court settlement (*Lanahan v. Chi Psi Fraternity*, 2008). The settlement acknowledged that the Chi Psi fraternity brothers hazed Bailey up until his death. The Lanahans then formed the Gordie Foundation, which is designed to raise awareness and raise funds for antihazing activities and initiatives. Subsequently, the foundation joined documentary filmmaker Pete Schuermann and produced the 2008 film *Haze* to bring further attention to Gordie's story and others of a similar nature. This entry examines scope of hazing and the legal issues surrounding it.

According to the antihazing group StopHazing .org, hazing is defined as "any activity expected of someone joining a group (or to maintain full status in a group) that humiliates, degrades or risks emotional and/or physical harm, regardless of the person's willingness to participate." The nature and effects of hazing vary greatly. Examples of subtle hazing include deception, assigning demerits, silence periods or other social isolation, deprivation of privileges, and assigning tasks to newcomers that are not assigned to others. More harassing forms of hazing include verbal abuse, threats of abuse, sleep deprivation, requiring new members to wear embarrassing or humiliating attire, obligating them to perform skits or stunts, and mandating that they perform tasks for veteran members. According to StopHazing.org, the most serious and violent hazing activities includes sexual misconduct, public nudity, forced or coerced drug and alcohol consumption, branding, paddling or other physical assault, burning, and engaging in illegal activity. While hazing activities are most commonly connected with fraternities, sororities, and athletics teams, hazing does occur elsewhere,

including in performing arts, academics, and other activities. Moreover, today, hazing and its effects have spread to cyberspace, where hazing activities themselves, like harassment and threats, occur online, and where photographs and videos of those activities are posted to social networking sites and to YouTube.

Criminal and Civil Liability

According to StopHazing.org, 44 states have enacted antihazing laws that apply to K–12 schools as well as colleges and universities. For example, Ohio's law defines hazing as "doing any act or coercing another, including the victim, to do any act of initiation into any student or other organization that causes or creates a substantial risk of causing mental or physical harm to any person" (Ohio Rev. Code Ann. § 2903.31; see also Ohio Rev. Code Ann. § 2307.44). Ohio's law, like the antihazing laws of many other states, imposes both criminal and civil liability on offenders, who are most often other students, and it is important to note that liability is imposed on administrators, staff members, and faculty members who permit such hazing to occur, either recklessly or negligently by failing to prevent it from happening.

Criminal penalties against those who commit hazing or permit it to take place range from low-degree misdemeanors to felonies. It is likely more common that the students who directly participate in hazing activities would be the ones criminally charged. However, in at least one recent case, a dean of students and a director of Greek life were also indicted in a hazing incident that led to the death of a student, although charges against the administrators were later dismissed.

Civil liability, most often in the form of substantial monetary damages, can attach to colleges or universities as a whole, the local and national fraternities or other associated organizations with which they are affiliated, and to the individuals involved, both students who engaged in hazing and employees. Such a situation arose in Louisiana, where a student and his parents successfully filed suit to recover for the injuries that he sustained as a result of being hazed by fraternity members (*Morrison v. Kappa Alpha Psi*, 1999). For an example of a civil liability standard from state statutory law, consider the following:

If the hazing involves students in a primary, secondary, or post-secondary school, university, college, or any other educational institution, an action may also be brought against any administrator, employee, or faculty member of the school, university, college, or other educational institution who knew or reasonably should have known of the hazing and who did not make reasonable attempts to prevent it and against the school, university, college, or other educational institution. If an administrator, employee, or faculty member is found liable in a civil action for hazing, then . . . the school, university, college, or other educational institution that employed the administrator, employee, or faculty member may also be held liable. (Ohio Rev. Code Ann. § 2307.44)

The prospect of civil and criminal liability against colleges and universities along with individual officials ought to act as an incentive for institutions to enact and enforce strong in institutional antihazing policies. In fact, the best defense that college or university officials can offer against claims for civil liability in hazing incidents is that administrators were actively enforcing policies against hazing when incidents transpired. Furthermore, enforcement must not be arbitrary, capricious, or against the weight of the offenses. In other words, punishments, often including the closing of fraternity chapters, the denial of recognition of student organizations or athletics teams, and suspension and expulsion of student participants, must fit the severity of the alleged infractions. At the same time, it is important that university officials follow all internal procedural requirements. For instance, if a college or university has a student judicial panel that is designated to hear such cases, then officials must ensure that all procedures associated with such hearings are followed.

When students or others who have been injured file suit, their negligence or consent is rarely a viable defense, even though most victims of hazing in institutions of higher education are, legally, adults. Additionally, while the existence of antihazing policies is a powerful tool for colleges and universities, their existence is useful for plaintiffs in liability suits insofar as they can assert the policies in their arguments that defendants had duties of care to keep students safe.

A leading case making this point with regard to liability is *Furek v. University of Delaware* (1991). In *Furek,* pledges to the Sigma Phi Epsilon fraternity were expected to undergo a series of initiation rituals, the culmination of which was a secret ritual known as Hell Night. As part of Hell Night, Jeffrey Furek, a pledge in the fraternity, was escorted while blindfolded into the kitchen of the fraternity house. Fraternity members then proceeded to pour pancake batter, ketchup, and other food onto the heads of the pledges. One member also poured a lye-based liquid on the back of the plaintiff's neck, causing him to suffer from first and second degree burns. The plaintiff was permanently scarred and subsequently withdrew from the university, forfeiting his athletic scholarship. The national fraternity withdrew the local chapter's registration. The plaintiff filed suit against the university, both the local and national chapters of the fraternity, and individual members of the local chapter.

The jury in *Furek* awarded the plaintiff $30,000 in damages, apportioning 93% of the liability to the university and 7% to the upperclass fraternity member who poured the chemicals on the plaintiff. On further review of the university's appeal, its lawyers argued that its officials did not owe a duty of care to supervise the actions of adult students living in fraternity houses even though the land was owned by the university and the building was owned and operated by the fraternity. The Supreme Court of Delaware disagreed with the university's arguments. In its analysis, the court cited the university's own antihazing policy as evidence. To this end, the court was of the opinion that the existence of the policy, which defined hazing and gave university officials the authority to deny recognition and registration to any student groups that engaged in such activities, helped establish a special relationship between the institution and its students that gave rise to the duty of care.

Although university officials did not regulate the day-to-day living conditions in the fraternity house, the house was located within the campus boundaries and was subject to the university's security department and disciplinary provisions. The court acknowledged that the students involved in the activities were legal adults and that the university would not be liable on an application of the *in loco parentis* doctrine as if its officials were acting "in place of the parents." The court added that the university, through its officials, did have a duty to regulate and supervise the foreseeable and dangerous activities of its students on campus.

The Supreme Court of Delaware ultimately upheld the dismissal of the local fraternity for procedural reasons while sustaining the jury's findings in favor of the national fraternity, because its officials exercised reasonable care in controlling the local chapter's activities. With respect to the university, the court engaged in a detailed discussion of the duty of care that officials owed in such circumstances, ultimately concluding that institutional administrators were liable, because they had assumed such a duty. The court thus remanded the dispute for a trial on the amount of damages that the university would owe the injured student.

In response to the incidents in *Furek* and other hazing cases, the national fraternity adopted the "Balanced Man Program" in 1993. This is an intensive four-year experience that shifts fraternity life from "beer-soaked blowouts" to healthy living, self-respect, and academic and professional development.

The court in *Furek* noted the importance of the existence of a university antihazing policy in the establishment of a duty of care. Yet liability often depends not merely on the duty of care but on how university officials react to knowledge of hazing incidents. For example, university officials who act with deliberate indifference to known and reported acts of hazing would likely be found liable, at least in part, for the damages suffered by the victims. On the other hand, if university officials have no knowledge of the incidents, and the victims deny that they ever occurred, then liability may not be imputed to the university or its leaders (*Alton v. Texas A&M University*, 1999). As stated earlier, the best defense for universities and their leaders to hazing claims is actively enforced antihazing policies and cultures that encourage healthy, professional group activity and prevent hazing from occurring in the first place. Readers are strongly encouraged to consult their local laws and university policies for antihazing provisions and other initiatives designed to eliminate hazing as well as its dangerous effects on the wide array of stakeholders who are engaged in day-to-day activities in institutions of higher learning.

Patrick D. Pauken

See also Cyberbullying; Disciplinary Sanctions and Due Process Rights; Extracurricular Activities, Law, and Policy; Hate Crimes; Sexual Harassment, Peer-to-Peer; Sexual Harassment, Quid Pro Quo; Sexual Harassment, Same-Sex; Student Suicides

Further Readings

Anas, B. (2009, March 17). Lawsuit over Gordie Bailey's death in CU frat settled. *Boulder Daily Camera* [Electronic version]. Retrieved June 21, 2009, from http://www.dailycamera.com/news/2009/mar/17/lawsuit-over-gordie-baileys-death-cu-frat-settled

Coughlan, A. (2008, December 17). Hazing death sentence: No booze for frat prez. *The Trentonian* [Electronic version]. Retrieved June 23, 2009, from http://www.trentonian.com/articles/2008/12/17/news/doc4948af457d301602765230.txt

Goldwert, L. (2007, August 28). Charges dropped in college drinking death. *CBS News*. Retrieved June 23, 2009, from http://www.cbsnews.com/stories/2007/08/28/national/main3213819.shtml

Johnson, J., & Holman, M. (Eds.). (2004). *Making the team: Inside the world of sport initiations and hazing*. Toronto, ON: Canadian Scholars' Press.

Lanahan, M., Lanahan, L., & Watt, R. (Producers), & Schuermann, P. (Director). (2008). *Haze* [Motion picture]. United States: Pete Schuermann in association with the Gordie Foundation. Available at http://www.hazethemovie.com

Lipka, S. (2008, March 21). Student-affairs meeting: Hazing extends beyond fraternities. *Chronicle of Higher Education, 54*(28), A21.

Mullan, E. (2007, September). *Administrators indicted after student death*. Retrieved June 21, 2009, from http://www.thefreelibrary.com/Administrators+indicted+after+student+death.-a0169088123

O'Toole, T. (2006, May 19). Internet revives hazing issue. *USA Today*, p. 9C.

StopHazing.org: Educating to eliminate hazing. http://www.stophazing.org

Thornburgh, N., & Sanders, E. (2006, February 20). Taming the toga. *Time, 167*(8), 52.

Legal Citations

Alton v. Texas A&M University, 168 F.3d 196 (5th Cir. 1999).

Furek v. University of Delaware, 594 A.2d 506 (Del. 1991).

Lanahan v. Chi Psi Fraternity, 175 P.3d (Colo. 2008).

Morrison v. Kappa Alpha Psi Fraternity, 738 So. 2d 1105
  (La. Ct. App. 1999).
Ohio Rev. Code Ann. §§ 2307.44, 2903.31.

HEALY V. JAMES

Often seen as the analogue in public higher education to *Tinker v. Des Moines Independent
Community School District* (1969), the Supreme
Court's decision in *Healy v. James* (1972) differs
in four significant respects. First, the Court had
less unanimity in *Tinker,* where Justice Stewart's
concurrence only partially agreed with the majority opinion, and Justices Black and Harlan dissented altogether. Second, perhaps because colleges
and universities at the time were, particularly in
comparison to elementary and secondary schools,
a hotbed of militant demonstrations, the *Healy*
Court was more deferential to the defendant public institutions, leaving the administrators a viable
alternative upon remand to sustain their original
decision. Third, *Tinker* relied on First Amendment
freedom of expression, while *Healy* relied more
specifically on First Amendment freedom of association. Finally, *Healy* expressly referred to "academic freedom," reflecting the ambiguity and,
ultimately in this case, the irony, of this concept.
Nevertheless, *Healy* is a comparable landmark
decision in higher education, serving as the most
famous in the panoply of First Amendment case
law concerning public colleges and universities.

Facts of the Case

During the era of civil unrest in the late 1960s, a
group of students at Central Connecticut State
College organized a local chapter of Students for
Democratic Society (SDS), which was a militant
national "anti-establishment" organization that
promoted not only civil disobedience but also violent disruption in higher education. The students
filed an application for official recognition from
the college's committee for campus organizations.
The committee expressed concern about the activities of the national SDS organization, to which the
chapter representatives replied that their group
would remain completely independent and unaffiliated. In response to the committee's inquiries as

to whether they would engage in violent or other
disruptive activities, the representatives gave no
assurances, stating that it would depend on the
circumstances.

After a second hearing, the committee recommended, on a six-to-two vote, that the college's
president approve the group's recognition application. However, several days later, the president
rescinded the approval, explaining that he found
the group's philosophy antithetical to the institution's policies (including their repudiation of academic freedom) and that he doubted the group's
avowed independence. When the members of the
group met in the campus center's coffee shop to
discuss the rejection, the president had them disbanded due to their lack of official recognition.

Dissatisfied with the outcome, the students subsequently filed suit in federal court, claiming that the
rejection of recognition violated their First Amendment right to freedom of expression. Ruling that the
president had denied the plaintiff-students procedural due process by basing his decision on conclusions about the group's affiliation that were outside
the record before him, the federal trial court in
Connecticut ordered him to hold a hearing to explore
this matter. At the hearing, the students reaffirmed
their lack of connection to the national organization.
After reviewing the expanded record, the president
reaffirmed his prior decision for reasons paralleling
his original explanation, including what he characterized as the group's "disruptive influence." The
court then summarily ruled in the college's favor, and
the Second Circuit affirmed on a two-to-one vote.
The Supreme Court granted certiorari.

The Supreme Court's Ruling

Justice Powell's opinion, on behalf of eight members of the Supreme Court, held that public institutions of higher education must not refuse
recognition of student groups based on unsupported fear of disruption but instead bear a heavy
burden to justify a "prior restraint," that is, a governmental content-based prohibition of expression, on account of First Amendment protection.
The majority first made clear that its 1969 judgment in *Tinker* applied at least as strongly in
higher education.

Finding the denial of recognition to have had a
substantial effect, the majority relied specifically on

the First Amendment freedom of association, which various precedents have established to be implicit in the freedoms of speech, assembly, and petition. However, reading the "ambiguous state of the record" as providing four possible justifications for recognition, including one that met the requisite burden, the majority remanded the case for further proceedings. The three unacceptable justifications were the group's relationship to the national SDS, the president's disagreement with the group's philosophy, and the unsupported perception of substantially disruptive conduct. The acceptable justification would be the group's unwillingness to be bound by reasonable institutional rules regarding conduct. The Court found that a remand was necessary to determine whether the College's recognition procedures required the group to affirm the intent to comply with reasonable campus rules and whether the group was willing to make said affirmation. "The critical line for First Amendment purposes," according to the majority, "must be drawn between advocacy which is entitled to full protection, and action, which is not."

Justice Burger's concurrence merely added the importance of higher education institutions as the primary forum to resolve such competing interests, emphasizing that the courts should be a last resort. Justice Douglas inveighed against the sick state of higher education in terms of academic freedom, concluding: "Without ferment of one kind or another, a college or university . . . becomes a useless appendage to a society which traditionally has reflected the spirit of rebellion."

Only Justice Rehnquist refused to subscribe to the entire majority opinion, carefully concurring only in the result. Specifically, he expressed serious doubt whether the precedents dealing with criminal sanctions and prior restraints, on which the majority relied in notable part, properly applied to public colleges. For example, Rehnquist noted that it is permissible for government employers or school administrators to impose reasonable regulations on students, which would not be permissible if such regulations were placed on all citizens.

Perry A. Zirkel

See also Free Speech and Expression Rights of Students

Further Readings

Zirkel, P. A. (2000). The first amendment and higher education: Part II: The secular cases. *West's Education Law Reporter, 141,* 947–966.

Legal Citations

Healy v. James, 408 U.S. 169 (1972).
Tinker v. Des Moines Independent Community School District, 393 U.S. 503 (1969).

HEALY V. JAMES

Healy is noteworthy because it is the first Supreme Court case to address the free speech rights of students in higher education.

Supreme Court of the United States

HEALY

v.

JAMES

408 U.S. 169

Argued March 28, 1972

Decided June 26, 1972

Mr. Justice POWELL delivered the opinion of the Court.

This case, arising out of a denial by a state college of official recognition to a group of students who desired to form a local chapter of Students for a Democratic Society (SDS), presents this Court with questions requiring the application of well-established First Amendment principles. While the factual background of this particular case raises these constitutional issues in a manner not heretofore passed on by the Court, and only infrequently presented to lower federal courts, our decision today is governed by existing precedent.

As the case involves delicate issues concerning the academic community, we approach our task with special caution, recognizing the mutual interest of students, faculty members, and administrators in an environment free from disruptive interference with the educational process. We also are mindful of the equally significant interest in the widest latitude for free expression and debate consonant with the maintenance of order. Where these interests appear to compete, the First Amendment, made binding on the States by the Fourteenth Amendment, strikes the required balance.

I

We mention briefly at the outset the setting in 1969–1970. A climate of unrest prevailed on many college campuses in this country. There had been widespread civil disobedience on some campuses, accompanied by the seizure of buildings, vandalism, and arson. Some colleges had been shut down altogether, while at others files were looted and manuscripts destroyed. SDS chapters on some of those campuses had been a catalytic force during this period. Although the causes of campus disruption were many and complex, one of the prime consequences of such activities was the denial of the lawful exercise of First Amendment rights to the majority of students by the few. Indeed, many of the most cherished characteristics long associated with institutions of higher learning appeared to be endangered. Fortunately, with the passage of time, a calmer atmosphere and greater maturity now pervade our campuses. Yet, it was in this climate of earlier unrest that this case arose.

Petitioners are students attending Central Connecticut State College (CCSC), a state-supported institution of higher learning. In September 1969 they undertook to organize what they then referred to as a "local chapter" of SDS. Pursuant to procedures established by the College, petitioners filed a request for official recognition as a campus organization with the Student Affairs Committee, a committee composed of four students, three faculty members, and the Dean of Student Affairs. The request specified three purposes for the proposed organization's existence. It would provide "a forum of discussion and self-education for students developing an analysis of American society"; it would serve as "an agency for

integrating thought with action so as to bring about constructive changes"; and it would endeavor to provide "a coordinating body for relating the problems of leftist students" with other interested groups on campus and in the community. The Committee, while satisfied that the statement of purposes was clear and unobjectionable on its face, exhibited concern over the relationship between the proposed local group and the National SDS organization. In response to inquiries, representatives of the proposed organization stated that they would not affiliate with any national organization and that their group would remain "completely independent."

In response to other questions asked by Committee members concerning SDS' reputation for campus disruption, the applicants made the following statements, which proved significant during the later stages of these proceedings:

"Q. How would you respond to issues of violence as other S.D.S. chapters have?

"A. Our action would have to be dependent upon each issue.

"Q. Would you use any means possible?

"A. No I can't say that; would not know until we know what the issues are.

"Q. Could you envision the S.D.S. interrupting a class?

"A. Impossible for me to say."

With this information before it, the Committee requested an additional filing by the applicants, including a formal statement regarding affiliations. The amended application filed in response stated flatly that "CCSC Students for a Democratic Society are not under the dictates of any National organization." At a second hearing before the Student Affairs Committee, the question of relationship with the National organization was raised again. One of the organizers explained that the National SDS was divided into several "factional groups," that the national-local relationship was a loose one, and that the local organization accepted only "certain ideas" but not all of the National organization's aims and philosophies.

By a vote of six to two the Committee ultimately approved the application and recommended to the President of the College, Dr. James, that the organization be accorded official recognition. In approving the application, the majority indicated that its decision was premised on the belief that varying viewpoints should be represented on campus and that since the Young Americans for Freedom, the Young Democrats, the

Young Republicans, and the Liberal Party all enjoyed recognized status, a group should be available with which "left wing" students might identify. The majority also noted and relied on the organization's claim of independence. Finally, it admonished the organization that immediate suspension would be considered if the group's activities proved incompatible with the school's policies against interference with the privacy of other students or destruction of property. The two dissenting members based their reservation primarily on the lack of clarity regarding the organization's independence.

Several days later, the President rejected the Committee's recommendation, and issued a statement indicating that petitioners' organization was not to be accorded the benefits of official campus recognition. His accompanying remarks, which are set out in full in the margin, indicate several reasons for his action. He found that the organization's philosophy was antithetical to the school's policies, and that the group's independence was doubtful. He concluded that approval should not be granted to any group that "openly repudiates" the College's dedication to academic freedom.

Denial of official recognition posed serious problems for the organization's existence and growth. Its members were deprived of the opportunity to place announcements regarding meetings, rallies, or other activities in the student newspaper; they were precluded from using various campus bulletin boards; and—most importantly—nonrecognition barred them from using campus facilities for holding meetings. This latter disability was brought home to petitioners shortly after the President's announcement. Petitioners circulated a notice calling a meeting to discuss what further action should be taken in light of the group's official rejection. The members met at the coffee shop in the Student Center ("Devils' Den") but were disbanded on the President's order since nonrecognized groups were not entitled to use such facilities.

Their efforts to gain recognition having proved ultimately unsuccessful, and having been made to feel the burden of nonrecognition, petitioners resorted to the courts. They filed a suit in the United States District Court for the District of Connecticut, seeking declaratory and injunctive relief against the President of the College, other administrators, and the State Board of Trustees. Petitioners' primary complaint centered on the denial of First Amendment rights of expression and association arising from denial of campus recognition. The cause was submitted initially on stipulated facts,

and, after a short hearing, the judge ruled that petitioners had been denied procedural due process because the President had based his decision on conclusions regarding the applicant's affiliation which were outside the record before him. The court concluded that if the President wished to act on the basis of material outside the application he must at least provide petitioners a hearing and opportunity to introduce evidence as to their affiliations. While retaining jurisdiction over the case, the District Court ordered respondents to hold a hearing in order to clarify the several ambiguities surrounding the President's decision. One of the matters to be explored was whether the local organization, true to its repeated affirmations, was in fact independent of the National SDS. And if the hearing demonstrated that the two were not separable, the respondents were instructed that they might then review the "aims and philosophy" of the National organization.

Pursuant to the court's order, the President designated Dean Judd, the Dean of Student Affairs, to serve as hearing officer and a hearing was scheduled. The hearing, which spanned two dates and lasted approximately two hours, added little in terms of objective substantive evidence to the record in this case. . . . This failure of the hearing to advance the litigation was, at bottom, the consequence of a more basic failure to join issue on the considerations that should control the President's ultimate decision, a problem to which we will return in the ensuing section.

Upon reviewing the hearing transcript and exhibits, the President reaffirmed his prior decision to deny petitioners recognition as a campus organization. The reasons stated, closely paralleling his initial reasons, were that the group would be a "disruptive influence" at CCSC and that recognition would be "contrary to the orderly process of change" on the campus.

After the President's second statement issued, the case then returned to the District Court, where it was ordered dismissed. The court concluded, first, that the formal requisites of procedural due process had been complied with, second, that petitioners had failed to meet their burden of showing that they could function free from the National organization, and, third, that the College's refusal to place its stamp of approval on an organization whose conduct it found "likely to cause violent acts of disruption' did not violate petitioners" associational rights.

Petitioners appealed to the Court of Appeals for the Second Circuit where, by a two-to-one vote, the District

Court's judgment was affirmed. The majority purported not to reach the substantive First Amendment issues on the theory that petitioners had failed to avail themselves of the due process accorded them and had failed to meet their burden of complying with the prevailing standards for recognition. Judge Smith dissented, disagreeing with the majority's refusal to address the merits and finding that petitioners had been deprived of basic First Amendment rights. This Court granted certiorari and, for the reasons that follow, we conclude that the judgments of the courts below must be reversed and the case remanded for reconsideration.

II

At the outset we note that state colleges and universities are not enclaves immune from the sweep of the First Amendment. "It can hardly be argued that either students or teachers shed their constitutional rights to freedom of speech or expression at the schoolhouse gate." Of course, as Mr. Justice Fortas made clear in Tinker, First Amendment rights must always be applied "in light of the special characteristics of the . . . environment" in the particular case. And, where state-operated educational institutions are involved, this Court has long recognized "the need for affirming the comprehensive authority of the States and of school officials, consistent with fundamental constitutional safeguards, to prescribe and control conduct in the schools." Yet, the precedents of this Court leave no room for the view that, because of the acknowledged need for order, First Amendment protections should apply with less force on college campuses than in the community at large. Quite to the contrary, "(t)he vigilant protection of constitutional freedoms is nowhere more vital than in the community of American schools." The college classroom with its surrounding environs is peculiarly the "marketplace of ideas," and we break no new constitutional ground in reaffirming this Nation's dedication to safeguarding academic freedom.

Among the rights protected by the First Amendment is the right of individuals to associate to further their personal beliefs. While the freedom of association is not explicitly set out in the Amendment, it has long been held to be implicit in the freedoms of speech, assembly, and petition. There can be no doubt that denial of official recognition, without justification, to college organizations burdens or abridges that associational right. The primary impediment to free association flowing from

nonrecognition is the denial of use of campus facilities for meetings and other appropriate purposes. The practical effect of nonrecognition was demonstrated in this case when, several days after the President's decision was announced, petitioners were not allowed to hold a meeting in the campus coffee shop because they were not an approved group.

Petitioners' associational interests also were circumscribed by the denial of the use of campus bulletin boards and the school newspaper. If an organization is to remain a viable entity in a campus community in which new students enter on a regular basis, it must possess the means of communicating with these students. Moreover, the organization's ability to participate in the intellectual give and take of campus debate, and to pursue its stated purposes, is limited by denial of access to the customary media for communicating with the administration, faculty members, and other students. Such impediments cannot be viewed as insubstantial.

Respondents and the courts below appear to have taken the view that denial of official recognition in this case abridged no constitutional rights. . . .

We do not agree with the characterization by the courts below of the consequences of nonrecognition. We may concede, as did Mr. Justice Harlan in his opinion for a unanimous Court in *NAACP v. Alabama ex rel. Patterson*, that the administration "has taken no direct action . . . to restrict the rights of (petitioners) to associate freely. . . ." But" the Constitution's protection is not limited to direct interference with fundamental rights. The requirement in *Patterson* that the NAACP disclose its membership lists was found to be an impermissible, though indirect, infringement of the members' associational rights. Likewise, in this case, the group's possible ability to exist outside the campus community does not ameliorate significantly the disabilities imposed by the President's action. We are not free to disregard the practical realities. Mr. Justice Stewart has made the salient point: "Freedom such as these are protected not only against heavy-handed frontal attack, but also from being stifled by more subtle governmental interference."

The opinions below also assumed that petitioners had the burden of showing entitlement to recognition by the College. While petitioners have not challenged the procedural requirement that they file an application in conformity with the rules of the College, they do question the view of the courts below that final rejection could rest on their failure to convince the administration that their organization was unaffiliated with the National SDS. For reasons to be stated later in this opinion, we do not consider the issue of affiliation to be a controlling one. But, apart from any particular issue, once petitioners had filed an application in conformity with the requirements, the burden was upon the College administration to justify its decision of rejection. It is to be remembered that the effect of the College's denial of recognition was a form of prior restraint, denying to petitioners' organization the range of associational activities described above. While a college has a legitimate interest in preventing disruption on the campus, which under circumstances requiring the safeguarding of that interest may justify such restraint, a "heavy burden" rests on the college to demonstrate the appropriateness of that action.

III

These fundamental errors—discounting the existence of a cognizable First Amendment interest and misplacing the burden of proof—require that the judgments below be reversed. But we are unable to conclude that no basis exists upon which nonrecognition might be appropriate.

Indeed, based on a reasonable reading of the ambiguous facts of this case, there appears to be at least one potentially acceptable ground for a denial of recognition. Because of this ambiguous state of the record we conclude that the case should be remanded and, in an effort to provide guidance to the lower courts upon reconsideration, it is appropriate to discuss the several bases of President James' decision. Four possible justifications for nonrecognition, all closely related, might be derived from the record and his statements. Three of those grounds are inadequate to substantiate his decision: a fourth, however, has merit.

A

From the outset the controversy in this case has centered in large measure around the relationship, if any, between petitioners' group and the National SDS. The Student Affairs Committee meetings, as reflected in its minutes, focused considerable attention on this issue; the court-ordered hearing also was directed primarily to this question. Despite assurances from petitioners and their counsel that the local group was in fact independent of the National organization, it is evident that President James was significantly influenced by his apprehension that there was a connection. Aware of the fact that some

SDS chapters had been associated with disruptive and violent campus activity, he apparently considered that affiliation itself was sufficient justification for denying recognition.

Although this precise issue has not come before the Court heretofore, the Court has consistently disapproved governmental action imposing criminal sanctions or denying rights and privileges solely because of a citizen's association with an unpopular organization. In these cases it has been established that "guilt by association alone, without (establishing) that an individual's association poses the threat feared by the Government," is an impermissible basis upon which to deny First Amendment rights. The government has the burden of establishing a knowing affiliation with an organization possessing unlawful aims and goals, and a specific intent to further those illegal aims. Students for a Democratic Society, as conceded by the College and the lower courts, is loosely organized, having various factions and promoting a number of diverse social and political views only some of which call for unlawful action. Not only did petitioners proclaim their complete independence from this organization, but they also indicated that they shared only some of the beliefs its leaders have expressed. On this record it is clear that the relationship was not an adequate ground for the denial of recognition.

B

Having concluded that petitioners were affiliated with, or at least retained an affinity for, National SDS, President James attributed what he believed to be the philosophy of that organization to the local group. He characterized the petitioning group as adhering to "some of the major tenets of the national organization," including a philosophy of violence and disruption. Understandably, he found that philosophy abhorrent. In an article signed by President James in an alumni periodical, and made a part of the record below, he announced his unwillingness to "sanction an organization that openly advocates the destruction of the very ideals and freedoms upon which the academic life is founded." He further emphasized that the petitioners' "philosophies" were "counter to the official policy of the college."

The mere disagreement of the President with the group's philosophy affords no reason to deny it recognition. As repugnant as these views may have been, especially to one with President James' responsibility, the mere expression of them would not justify the denial of

First Amendment rights. Whether petitioners did in fact advocate a philosophy of "destruction" thus becomes immaterial. The College, acting here as the instrumentality of the State, may not restrict speech or association simply because it finds the views expressed by any group to be abhorrent. . . .

C

As the litigation progressed in the District Court, a third rationale for President James' decision—beyond the questions of affiliation and philosophy—began to emerge. His second statement, issued after the court-ordered hearing, indicates that he based rejection on a conclusion that this particular group would be a "disruptive influence at CCSC." This language was underscored in the second District Court opinion. In fact, the court concluded that the President had determined that CCSC-SDS' "prospective campus activities were likely to cause a disruptive influence at CCSC."

If this reason, directed at the organization's activities rather than its philosophy, were factually supported by the record, this Court's prior decisions would provide a basis for considering the propriety of nonrecognition. The critical line heretofore drawn for determining the permissibility of regulation is the line between mere advocacy and advocacy "directed to inciting or producing imminent lawless action and . . . likely to incite or produce such action." In the context of the "special characteristics of the school environment," the power of the government to prohibit "lawless action" is not limited to acts of a criminal nature. Also prohibitable are actions which "materially and substantially disrupt the work and discipline of the school." Associational activities need not be tolerated where they infringe reasonable campus rules, interrupt classes, or substantially interfere with the opportunity of other students to obtain an education.

The "Student Bill of Rights" at CCSC, upon which great emphasis was placed by the President, draws precisely this distinction between advocacy and action. It purports to impose no limitations on the right of college student organizations "to examine and discuss all questions of interest to them." (Emphasis supplied.) But it also states that students have no right (1) "to deprive others of the opportunity to speak or be heard," (2) "to invade the privacy of others," (3) "to damage the property of others," (4) "to disrupt the regular and essential operation of the college," or (5) "to interfere with the rights of others." The line between permissible speech and impermissible conduct tracks the constitutional requirement, and if there were an evidential basis to support the conclusion that CCSC-SDS posed a substantial threat of material disruption in violation of that command the President's decision should be affirmed.

The record, however, offers no substantial basis for that conclusion. The only support for the view expressed by the President, other than the reputed affiliation with National SDS, is to be found in the ambivalent responses offered by the group's representatives at the Student Affairs Committee hearing, during which they stated that they did not know whether they might respond to "issues of violence" in the same manner that other SDS chapters had on other campuses. Nor would they state unequivocally that they could never "envision . . . interrupting a class."

Whatever force these statements might be thought to have is largely dissipated by the following exchange between petitioners' counsel and the Dean of Student Affairs during the court-ordered hearing. . . .

D

These same references in the record to the group's equivocation regarding how it might respond to "issues of violence" and whether it could ever "envision . . . interrupting a class," suggest a fourth possible reason why recognition might have been denied to these petitioners. These remarks might well have been read as announcing petitioners' unwillingness to be bound by reasonable school rules governing conduct. The College's Statement of Rights, Freedoms, and Responsibilities of Students contains, as we have seen, an explicit statement with respect to campus disruption. The regulation, carefully differentiating between advocacy and action, is a reasonable one, and petitioners have not questioned it directly. Yet their statements raise considerable question whether they intend to abide by the prohibitions contained therein.

As we have already stated in Parts B and C, the critical line for First Amendment purposes must be drawn between advocacy, which is entitled to full protection, and action, which is not. Petitioners may, if they so choose, preach the propriety of amending or even doing away with any or all campus regulations. They may not, however, undertake to flout these rules. . . .

Just as in the community at large, reasonable regulations with respect to the time, the place, and the manner in which student groups conduct their speech-related activities must be respected. A college administration may impose a requirement, such as may have been imposed in this case, that a group seeking official recognition affirm in advance its willingness to adhere to reasonable campus law. Such a requirement does not impose an impermissible condition on the students' associational rights. Their freedom to speak out, to assemble, or to petition for changes in school rules is in no sense infringed. It merely constitutes an agreement to conform with reasonable standards respecting conduct. This is a minimal requirement, in the interest of the entire academic community, of any group seeking the privilege of official recognition.

Petitioners have not challenged in this litigation the procedural or substantive aspects of the College's requirements governing applications for official recognition. Although the record is unclear on this point, CCSC may have, among its requirements for recognition, a rule that prospective groups affirm that they intend to comply with reasonable campus regulations. Upon remand it should first be determined whether the College recognition procedures contemplate any such requirement. If so, it should then be ascertained whether petitioners intend to comply. Since we do not have the terms of a specific prior affirmation rule before us, we are not called on to decide whether any particular formulation would or would not prove constitutionally acceptable. Assuming the existence of a valid rule, however, we do conclude that the benefits of participation in the internal life of the college community may be denied to any group that reserves the right to violate any valid campus rules with which it disagrees.

IV

We think the above discussion establishes the appropriate framework for consideration of petitioners' request for campus recognition. Because respondents failed to accord due recognition to First Amendment principles, the judgments below approving respondents' denial of recognition must be reversed. Since we cannot conclude from this record that petitioners were willing to abide by reasonable campus rules and regulations, we order the case remanded for reconsideration. We note, in so holding, that the wide latitude accorded by the Constitution to the freedoms of expression and association is not without its costs in terms of the risk to the maintenance of civility and an ordered society. Indeed, this latitude often has resulted, on the campus and elsewhere, in the infringement of the rights of others. Though we deplore the tendency of some to abuse the very constitutional privileges they invoke, and although the infringement of rights of others certainly should not be tolerated, we reaffirm this Court's dedication to the principles of the Bill of Rights upon which our vigorous and free society is founded.

Reversed and remanded.

HIGHER EDUCATION ACT

The Higher Education Act of 1965 (HEA), Public Law 89-329, was initiated and passed as a part of President Lyndon Johnson's ambitious social policy programs, which were known as the "Great Society." The many subsequent reauthorizations and various amendments of the HEA have continued to provide means for greater access to higher education. This entry discusses the most noteworthy sections of original law and of the legislative changes chronologically. In addition, the entry reviews relevant cases that have emerged in court and that challenged applications of the law.

The main impetus for the HEA was President's Johnson's desire to use education as a tool for economic growth and development, an approach that fit within his broader social policy agenda. For example, Johnson sought to push the United States toward greater opportunities for the disenfranchised through governmental action, such as the Civil Rights Act of 1964, the Voting Rights Act of 1965, and the Elementary and Secondary Education Act of 1965. The HEA was designed to make higher education more accessible to populations of persons who were previously unable to attend these educational institutions because of economic circumstances. The HEA provided grants to institutions of higher learning for research, allocated need-based aid to students in the form of scholarships and loans, and attempted to link improvements in higher education with K–12 education through support for teacher preparation and advancement.

In the decades after its passage, the HEA has been amended to further support its original intent of providing greater opportunities for individuals to attend higher education and supplying resources to improve the facilities of colleges and universities. One of the most significant changes related to the HEA came in the passage of the omnibus Education Amendments of 1972 (Public Law 92-318), which included the Patsy T. Mink Equal Opportunity in Education Act (now commonly referred to as Title IX). This provision prohibited discrimination based on sex in any educational program that was to receive federal support and funding; it is now codified at 20 U.S.C. § 1681. Today, the term *Title IX* is seemingly synonymous with equality in athletics, but the legislation was not specifically written to remedy inequality in this area. Athletics just happened to provide the most egregious example of discrimination.

The Title IX provisions of the HEA have been repeatedly litigated. Specifically, in *Cannon v. University of Chicago* (1979), the U.S. Supreme Court held that individuals had the right to bring suit under Title IX. Further, in *Grove City College v. Bell* (1984), the Court ruled that Title IX could also be applied to private colleges that do not get direct grants from the federal government but whose students use federal financial aid. However, the Court restricted the scope of the regulations so that they did not have to be applied to the entire institution—therefore exempting athletics in the eyes of some critics. Eventually, through further litigation, near parity was achieved, and Title IX is now seen as a great success for equal rights.

In the Higher Education Amendments of 1992 (Public Law 102-325), which included Title IV, Congress attempted to crack down on technical schools, colleges, and universities that provided financial incentives to admissions officers based on a commission system in the recruiting of students. This step to combat the enrollment of academically underprepared students into programs of marginal quality and value succeeded for some time. However, this success was fleeting, culminating in the filing of a rash of lawsuits against the for-profit education sector. In many of these cases, employees sought relief under the False Claims Act for violations of Title IV, which prohibits such unscrupulous tactics. One of these prominent cases was *United States of America ex rel. Hendow v. University of Phoenix* (2008). Eventually, the Apollo Group reached a settlement agreement with the U.S. Department of Education by paying a $9.8

million fine after a review of the University of Phoenix recruiter and admissions officer compensation packages found them to be problematic.

During the next set of discussions around the reauthorization of the Higher Education Amendments of 1998 (Public Law 105-245), there was congressional debate on the Riggs Amendment, which many saw as a frontal assault on affirmative action policies in higher education institutions. The amendment sought to add a new Title XI, which would have eliminated federal funding for any education program subject to the HEA that used any preference or discrimination in admissions. The amendment was not adopted, and the Supreme Court eventually stepped in to address race and admission issues in the cases of *Gratz v. Bollinger* (2003) and *Grutter v. Bollinger* (2003), striking down the use of race-conscious admissions policies in undergraduate programs at the University of Michigan but upholding its use in the university's law school.

Chapter 2 of the final bill that emerged in 1998 included a new program called Gaining Early Awareness and Readiness for Undergraduate Programs (GEAR UP). This provision was created to grant greater access to higher education by teaching the skills necessary for admission and success in higher education to underserved students. The provision is designed to accomplish its goal by affording precollege students access to mentoring relationships with college students and to college preparatory programs often conducted on college campuses.

Another important and controversial change in the Higher Education Amendments of 1998 and to the HEA was a small addition to the Free Application for Federal Student Aid (FAFSA). This form must be completed by students to be eligible for financial assistance through federal loan guaranty programs, such as the Perkins and Stafford programs, as well as aid in the form of Pell grants. What has become known as "Question 31" asks, "Have you been convicted for the possession or sale of illegal drugs for an offense that occurred while you were receiving federal student aid (grants, loans, and/or work-study)?" This provision led to a case, *Students for Sensible Drug Policy Foundation v. Spellings* (2006, 2008), in which a federal trial court in South Dakota rejected the plaintiff's claims that the question and penalties for an affirmative answer violated Fifth and Eighth Amendment protections. The case was dismissed on the ground that the plaintiff failed to state a claim. The Eighth Circuit affirmed the dismissal on the bases that the statute demonstrated congressional intent that the penalties were designed to be civil in nature and that the law was not so punitive in its purpose or effect as to transform a civil penalty into criminal penalty.

The most recent reauthorization of the HEA was enacted on August 14, 2008, after many extensions and a half-decade past the expiration of the previous reauthorization. The bill finally materialized, with a slightly different title, as the Higher Education Opportunity Act of 2008 (Public Law 110-315). While the legislation is set to expire on September 30, 2014, it will undoubtedly be reauthorized after much political wrangling. The following sections highlight some of the most crucial changes to the existing statutes.

An often overlooked issue in higher education is the continued proliferation of "diploma mills" throughout this country and, with the rise of the Internet, around the world. Many students are taken advantage of by proprietors of fake colleges and universities that provide degrees for a fee and little or no academic work. Most of the previous federal legislative efforts in this area have been directed at protecting the interests of the government in terms of loan guarantees, but in the 2008 reauthorization, the term *diploma mill* is defined for the first time along with several related provisions to increase public awareness about these illegal activities (§ 109). Further, this section urges greater cooperation between the law enforcement agencies that are responsible for investigating and prosecuting crimes related to diploma mills.

Many policy makers sought to include accountability measures in the 2008 reauthorization inspired by the No Child Left Behind Act of 2001 in an attempt to make higher education institutions more responsible for student learning outcomes and for the public money invested in educational programming. Needless to say, resistance to these efforts from higher education institutions resulted in contentious debate around the bill. In the end, the institutions prevailed on defining student success for themselves and not having to apply an external standard for judging success of the institution (§ 495).

One of the most pressing issues facing students and parents planning for higher education is the continuing increase in the cost of tuition and fees well above typical rates of inflation. As a part of the 2008 legislation, the U.S. Department of Education is supposed to provide an increased level of public information regarding higher education costs and their rates of increase. These measures include information about the most expensive colleges (§ 132c), net price calculators (§ 132h), state allocations (§ 132g), and four-year tuition calendars (§ 132j). All of this data is geared to provide the public with better information to plan for higher education costs.

Another section of the legislation also addresses rising costs of higher education. Here, the federal government increases the amount of the Pell grants and makes them available in the summer (§ 401). This is to allow students to complete their programs and degrees in a timelier manner. Also, reform in the area of access to student aid comes in the form of an attempt to streamline the process to apply for aid (§ 110).

Other additional sections of the 2008 legislation are worth noting. The revisions changed the ways in which student loan programs could be managed in the wake of scandals (§ 1001); teacher education programs received some guidance about teaching in a digital age (§ 230); international education programs continued to stress the need to increase the number of area specialists and area studies centers (§ 601); and there was funding provided for numerous studies, including research on bias in student achievement tests (§ 1110) and minority male achievement (§ 1109).

Other provisions added to the HEA seem to be more ideologically driven rather than simple expansions of higher educational opportunities. One of the first of these provisions is § 104, which provides the sense of the Congress that higher education should be a forum for the free exchange of ideas as well as a place where "students should not be intimidated, harassed, [or] discouraged from speaking out."

In the years since Napster was started on a college campus, peer-to-peer music sharing has continued to evolve; the law and owners of intellectual property have tried to catch up with both students and their technology. In the recent legislation, § 488 compels college and university officials to offer advice to students with regard to relevant statutes that prohibit unauthorized sharing as well as the means that may be used to track down the biggest perpetrators, including checking on bandwidth usage.

The last noteworthy provision is § 805, "American History for Freedom." This section offers grant money for institutions and programs that teach and promote the values and history of free institutions; such an institution is defined by the legislation as "an institution that emerged out of Western civilization, such as democracy, constitutional government, individual rights, market economics, religious freedom and religious tolerance, and freedom of thought and inquiry." It is not difficult to assume that this insertion and funding is another looming dispute in the culture wars over higher education's historical canon and related issues around multiculturalism.

Aaron Cooley

See also Affirmative Action; American Association of University Professors; *Cannon v. University of Chicago*; *Gratz v. Bollinger*; *Grove City College v. Bell*; *Grutter v. Bollinger*; Historically Black Colleges and Universities; Stafford Act

Further Readings

Altbach, P., Berdahl, R., & Gumport, P. (Eds.). (2005). *American higher education in the twenty-first century: Social, political, and economic challenges* (2nd ed.). Baltimore: Johns Hopkins University Press.

Kaplin, W., & Lee, B. (2006). *The law of higher education: A comprehensive guide to legal implications of administrative decision making* (4th ed.). New York: Jossey-Bass.

Lucas, C. (2006). *American higher education: A history* (2nd ed.). New York: Palgrave Macmillan.

Olivas, M. (2006). *The law and higher education: Cases and materials on colleges in court*. Durham, NC: Carolina Academic Press.

Roth, J. (Ed.). (2007). *Higher education law in America*. Malvern, PA: Center for Education & Employment Law.

U.S. Department of Education. (n.d.). *Policy: Higher education—legislation*. Retrieved April 24, 2009, from http://www.ed.gov/policy/highered/leg/edpicks.jhtml

Woolley, J. T., & Peters, G. (n.d.). *The American presidency project* [online]. Santa Barbara: University of California (hosted), Gerhard Peters (database). Retrieved April 24, 2009, from http://www.presidency.ucsb.edu/ws/?pid=27356

Legal Citations

Cannon v. University of Chicago, 441 U.S. 677 (1979).

Civil Rights Act of 1964, Pub. L. No. 88-352.

Elementary and Secondary Education Act of 1965, Pub. L. No. 89-10.

False Claims Act, Pub. L. No. 99-562 (1986).

Gratz v. Bollinger, 539 U.S. 244 (2003).

Grove City College v. Bell, 465 U.S. 555 (1984).

Grutter v. Bollinger, 539 U.S. 306 (2003).

Higher Education Act of 1965, 20 U.S.C. §§ 1001 *et seq.* (2008).

Higher Education Amendments of 1992, Pub. L. No. 102-325.

Higher Education Amendments of 1998, Pub. L. No. 105-245.

Higher Education Opportunity Act of 2008, Pub. L. No. 110-315.

No Child Left Behind Act, Pub. L. No. 107-110 (2001).

Students for Sensible Drug Policy Foundation v. Spellings, 523 F.3d 896 (8th Cir. 2008).

Title IX of the Education Amendments of 1972, 20 U.S.C. § 1681.

United States of America ex rel. Hendow v. University of Phoenix, 2008 WL 4542252 (E.D. Cal. 2008).

Voting Rights Act of 1965, Pub. L. No. 89-110.

HISTORICALLY BLACK COLLEGES AND UNIVERSITIES

The Higher Education Act of 1965 defined Black colleges and universities (HBCUs) as those founded before 1964 with the mission of educating African Americans. At the outset, it is worth keeping in mind that HBCUs are distinct from predominantly Black colleges and universities, which serve large numbers of Black students but were not founded with the unique mission of HBCUs and do not share their federal designation. This entry reviews the history and status of HBCUs in the world of American higher education.

History of HBCUs

HBCUs were established to educate Blacks who could not gain admission to White colleges. Three HBCUs opened prior to the Civil War and are generally considered the first colleges established for African Americans: Cheyney University (1837) and

Lincoln University (1854) in Pennsylvania and Wilberforce University (1856) in Ohio. The remainder were established after 1865 and operated as segregated institutions until segregation was dismantled in higher education by U.S. Supreme Court rulings in *Sweatt v. Painter* (1950) and *McLaurin v. Oklahoma State Regents for Higher Education* (1950), cases that forbade inter- and intrainstitutional racial segregation, respectively. Subsequently, due to *Brown v. Board of Education, Topeka* (1954) and the civil rights movement, more Black students enrolled in White colleges and universities.

Cheyney University in Pennsylvania, which opened in 1837, was the first Black institution to educate Blacks beyond elementary school and was founded through a bequest from a Quaker philanthropist, Richard Humphreys. It was followed by Lincoln University in 1854 in Pennsylvania and in 1856 by Wilberforce University in Ohio. The other HBCUs were established after 1865 as religious or teaching training institutions that required advanced elementary education and later secondary education at a time when most states offered only three years of public education. Support for these colleges came from African American benevolent societies, especially those of the Baptist and African Methodist Episcopal churches; northern White benevolent and denominational societies; and wealthy corporate philanthropists such as John D. Rockefeller, Sr.

A small number of HBCUs began as private schools and are now public. For example, in 1925 Thurgood Marshall enrolled in Lincoln University in Chester, Pennsylvania, a Black school for male students founded in 1854 by a White Presbyterian minister. Today, Lincoln University is a public college enrolling both males and females.

Among the senior colleges, 16 are land grant colleges under the Morrill Land Grant Acts to help educate farmers, scientists, and teachers; Alcorn State University in Mississippi was the first. Each state was required to provide this education for all races, and the Southern states established one for Whites and one for Blacks in each of these states. These institutions became these states' A&M and A&T colleges.

Early Examples

Butler's (1977) history of three distinctive Black colleges provides an illustrative history of the origin of Black colleges. She cited Talladega, Tuskegee, and Morehouse as the best HBCUs in 1977. While most HBCUs were organized by Whites for the education of Blacks during the days of segregation, one was organized by a Black person, Booker T. Washington; this was something rare in the 1880s and after. The schools under White direction were able to raise funds and maintain staff, faculty, and administration while drawing top academically prepared students. For example, Thurgood Marshall enjoyed such an environment at Lincoln University and at Howard Law School. At Howard Law School, Marshall's mentor was the Black dean Charles Hamilton Houston, who graduated from Amherst College as class valedictorian and later graduated from Harvard Law School. Also on the Howard Law faculty was William Henry Hastie, a Harvard Law graduate and editor of the *Harvard Law Review* (Davis & Clark, 1994). During this period, the best of Black intellectuals taught at Black colleges, for example, W. E. B. Du Bois, the first Black to earn a doctorate from Harvard University, was never offered a job at or taught in a White university. He and others like him taught at HBCUs.

Talladega College

Talladega College is located in a small rural community in Alabama. It is a denominationally supported college that was founded by the American Missionary Association (AMA), and its graduates have made outstanding achievements. Like other AMA schools, Talladega was operated by Whites who also did the teaching in what began as elementary schools before progressing to secondary education years later. Most AMA schools opened college departments in 1870s and taught three courses: Latin, Greek, and higher mathematics. The school offered its first bachelor of arts and science degrees in 1907. Talladega hired its first Black dean, James T. Cater, in 1932. In 1953, it named its first Black president, Rev. Arthur Douglass Gray, an alumnus of the college.

Tuskegee University

Tuskegee University was founded in 1881, when the state of Alabama allocated funds to establish a normal school for Blacks in Macon

County. Tuskegee was to be headed by a White principal and asked Hampton Institute's White principal, General Samuel C. Armstrong, for help in finding a candidate (Butler, 1977). However, when the general informed officials that he was unaware of any White who wanted the job, they hired Booker T. Washington, a graduate of Hampton and the first Black to teach at Hampton to prepare school teachers. Insofar as Washington was Black, and Whites could not work under the direction of a Black person, Tuskegee was unique among the Black colleges in that all of its faculty and administrators were Black until the 1960s. Under Washington's leadership, Tuskegee added industrial education with a grant from a private foundation. Even so, Tuskegee Normal and Industrial Institute operated primarily as a teacher training program. In 1928 Tuskegee opened a college department and in 1944 began a school of veterinary medicine.

Morehouse College

Morehouse College was established by a White church group in Augusta, Georgia, in order to prepare Black males; it moved to Atlanta in 1878 as the Atlanta Baptist Seminary (Butler, 1977). The institution became Morehouse College in 1913 after receiving a gift from Henry Morehouse, secretary of the Atlanta Baptist Home Mission Society. John Hope became the school's first African American president in 1906. In 1940, 19 years after beginning his teaching career there, Benjamin E. Mays, a distinguished Black educator, became the fifth president of Morehouse College. Today, the college educates students from more than 40 states and 18 countries and is home to the Andrew Young Center for International Affairs and to the King Papers, a 10,000-piece collection that includes handwritten notes and unpublished sermons of its best-known alumnus, Rev. Martin Luther King, Jr.

Changing Enrollments

Although most African Americans attended and graduated from HBCUs prior to the 1950s, this pattern began to change after 1960 due to desegregation efforts ushered in by the Supreme Court in the cases noted above. Since the 1960s, more African Americans have enrolled in White colleges than in HBCUs. In 1964 more than half of Black college students in the United States attended HBCUs. Yet by 1970 only one-third of these students attended HBCUs. Also, although HBCUs were established to serve African Americans, they began admitting students of all races in the 1970s amid the social changes of the era. Today, all HBCUs have non-Blacks in their student bodies. In addition to serving students of all races, HCBUs include faculty and administrators of different races.

In 1970 there were more than 100 HBCUs, of which 51 were private senior colleges and 11 were two-year private colleges; another 36 were public senior colleges, while another 4 were public two-year colleges; total enrollment was 168,000. Most of the HBCUs are located in the South; two are in Pennsylvania and two in Ohio. North Carolina leads the way with 11 HBCUs, followed by Alabama with 9; Georgia and South Carolina each have 8, and Texas has 7 HBCUs.

HBCUs Today

Today's approximately 103 HBCUs, down from the 123 that existed in 1960, represent about 3% of all colleges and universities in the United States; the number declined due to mergers, closings, and the desegregation of some institutions. More specifically, HBCUs include 41 four-year public colleges, 49 private four-year colleges, 11 two-year public colleges, and 2 two-year private colleges (*List of HBCUs*, n.d.).

In 2005, HBCUs enrolled 311,768 students and conferred 3,819 associate degrees, 30,548 bachelor's degrees, 6,778 master's degrees, 1,723 first professional degrees, and 444 doctoral degrees. The average fee for attendance at an HBCU was about $6,000 (U.S. Department of Education, 2007).

At present, HBCUs provide students with opportunities to earn undergraduate and graduate degrees in a wide range of academic disciplines and professional fields, including law, medicine, dentistry, engineering, education, and nursing. Among the distinguished graduate degree programs are law schools at North Carolina Central University, Texas Southern University, Howard University, and Florida A&M University and medical schools at Howard University, Meharry Medical College, and Morehouse School of Medicine.

Table I   Historically Black Colleges and Universities in the United States

Institution	State	Organization
Alabama A&M University http://www.aamu.edu	Alabama	4-year public
Alabama State University http://www.alasu.edu	Alabama	4-year public
University of Arkansas at Pine Bluff http://www.uapb.edu	Arkansas	4-year public
Delaware State University http://www.desu.edu	Delaware	4-year public
Howard University http://www.howard.edu	District of Columbia	4-year public
University of the District of Columbia http://www.udc.edu	District of Columbia	4-year public
Florida A&M University http://www.famu.edu	Florida	4-year public
Albany State University http://www.asurams.edu/index.php	Georgia	4-year public
Fort Valley State University http://www.fvsu.edu	Georgia	4-year public
Savannah State University http://www.savstate.edu	Georgia	4-year public
Kentucky State University http://www.kysu.edu	Kentucky	4-year public
Grambling State University http://www.gram.edu	Louisiana	4-year public
Southern University A&M College http://www.subr.edu	Louisiana	4-year public
Southern University at New Orleans http://www.suno.edu	Louisiana	4-year public
Bowie State University http://www.bowiestate.edu	Maryland	4-year public
Coppin State College http://www.coppin.edu	Maryland	4-year public
Morgan State University http://www.morgan.edu	Maryland	4-year public
University of Maryland Eastern Shore http://www.umes.edu	Maryland	4-year public
Alcorn State University http://www.alcorn.edu	Mississippi	4-year public
Jackson State University http://www.jsums.edu	Mississippi	4-year public
Mississippi Valley State University http://www.mvsu.edu	Mississippi	4-year public
Harris-Stowe State University http://www.hssu.edu	Missouri	4-year public
Lincoln University http://www.lincolnu.edu	Missouri	4-year public
Elizabeth City State University http://www.ecsu.edu	North Carolina	4-year public
Fayetteville State University http://www.uncfsu.edu	North Carolina	4-year public

Institution	State	Organization
North Carolina A&T State University http://www.ncat.edu	North Carolina	4-year public
North Carolina Central University http://www.nccu.edu	North Carolina	4-year public
Winston-Salem State University http://www.wssu.edu	North Carolina	4-year public
Central State University http://www.centralstate.edu	Ohio	4-year public
Langston University http://www.lunet.edu	Oklahoma	4-year public
Cheyney University of Pennsylvania http://www.cheyney.edu	Pennsylvania	4-year public
Lincoln University http://www.lincoln.edu	Pennsylvania	4-year public
South Carolina State University http://www.scsu.edu	South Carolina	4-year public
Tennessee State University http://www.tnstate.edu	Tennessee	4-year public
Prairie View A&M University http://www.pvamu.edu	Texas	4-year public
Texas Southern University http://www.tsu.edu	Texas	4-year public
University of the Virgin Islands http://www.uvi.edu	U.S. Virgin Islands	4-year public
Norfolk State University http://www.nsu.edu	Virginia	4-year public
Virginia State University http://www.vsu.edu	Virginia	4-year public
Bluefield State College http://www.bluefieldstate.edu	West Virginia	4 year public
West Virginia State University http://www.wvstateu.edu	West Virginia	4-year public

Institution	State	Organization
Concordia College Selma http://www.concordiaselma.edu	Alabama	4-year private
Miles College http://www.miles.edu	Alabama	4-year private
Oakwood University http://www.oakwood.edu	Alabama	4-year private
Selma University http://www.selmauniversity.org	Alabama	4-year private
Stillman College http://www.stillman.edu	Alabama	4-year private
Talladega College http://www.talladega.edu	Alabama	4-year private
Tuskegee University http://www.tuskegee.edu	Alabama	4-year private
Arkansas Baptist College http://www.arkansasbaptist.edu	Arkansas	4-year private

(Continued)

Table I (Continued)

Institution	State	Organization
Philander Smith College http://www.philander.edu	Arkansas	4-year private
Bethune-Cookman University http://www.bethune.cookman.edu	Florida	4-year private
Edward Waters College http://www.ewc.edu	Florida	4-year private
Florida Memorial University http://www.fmuniv.edu	Florida	4-year private
Clark Atlanta University https://www.cau.edu	Georgia	4-year private
Interdenominational Theological Center http://www.itc.edu	Georgia	4-year private
Morehouse College http://www.morehouse.edu	Georgia	4-year private
Morehouse School of Medicine http://www.msm.edu	Georgia	4-year private
Morris Brown College http://www.morrisbrown.edu	Georgia	4-year private
Paine College http://www.paine.edu	Georgia	4-year private
Spelman College http://www.spelman.edu	Georgia	4-year private
Dillard University http://www.dillard.edu	Louisiana	4-year private
Xavier University of Louisiana http://www.xula.edu	Louisiana	4-year private
Rust College http://www.rustcollege.edu	Mississippi	4-year private
Tougaloo College http://www.tougaloo.edu	Mississippi	4-year private
Bennett College http://www.bennett.edu	North Carolina	4-year private
Johnson C. Smith University http://www.jcsu.edu	North Carolina	4-year private
Livingstone College http://www.livingstone.edu	North Carolina	4-year private
Shaw University http://www.shawuniversity.edu	North Carolina	4-year private
St. Augustine's College http://www.st-aug.edu	North Carolina	4-year private
Wilberforce University http://www.wilberforce.edu	Ohio	4-year private
Allen University http://www.allenuniversity.edu	South Carolina	4-year private
Benedict College http://www.benedict.edu	South Carolina	4-year private
Claflin University http://www.claflin.edu	South Carolina	4-year private

Institution	State	Organization
Morris College http://www.morris.edu/default.aspx	South Carolina	4-year private
Voorhees College http://www.voorhees.edu	South Carolina	4-year private
Fisk University http://www.fisk.edu	Tennessee	4-year private
Knoxville College http://www.knoxvillecollege.edu	Tennessee	4-year private
Lane College http://www.lanecollege.edu	Tennessee	4-year private
Lemoyne-Owen College http://www.loc.edu	Tennessee	4-year private
Meharry Medical College http://www.mmc.edu	Tennessee	4-year private
Huston-Tillotson University http://www.htu.edu	Texas	4-year private
Jarvis Christian College http://www.jarvis.edu	Texas	4-year private
Paul Quinn College http://www.pqc.edu	Texas	4-year private
Southwestern Christian College http://www.swcc.edu	Texas	4-year private
Texas College http://www.texascollegeonline.net	Texas	4-year private
Wiley College http://www.wileyc.edu	Texas	4-year private
Hampton University http://www.hamptonu.edu	Virginia	4-year private
Saint Paul's College http://www.saintpauls.edu	Virginia	4-year private
Virginia Union University http://www.vuu.edu	Virginia	4-year private
Virginia University of Lynchburg http://www.vulonline.us	Virginia	4-year private

Institution	State	Organization
Bishop State Community College http://www.bscc.cc.al.us	Alabama	2-year public
Shelton State Community College, C. A. Fredd Campus http://www.sheltonstate.edu	Alabama	2-year public
Gadsden State Comm. College, Valley Street http://www.gadsdenstate.edu	Alabama	2-year public
J. F. Drake State Technical College http://www.dstc.cc.al.us	Alabama	2-year public
Lawson State Community College http://www.ls.cc.al.us	Alabama	2-year public
Trenholm State Technical College http://www.trenholmtech.cc.al.us	Alabama	2-year public

(Continued)

Table I (Continued)

Institution	State	Organization
Southern University at Shreveport http://www.susla.edu	Louisiana	2-year public
Coahoma Community College http://www.ccc.cc.ms.us	Mississippi	2-year public
Hinds Community College, Utica http://www.hindscc.edu	Mississippi	2-year public
Denmark Technical College http://www.denmarktech.edu	South Carolina	2-year public
St. Philip's College http://www.accd.edu/spc	Texas	2-year public

Institution	State	Organization
Lewis College of Business http://www.lewiscollege.edu	Michigan	2-year private
Clinton Junior College http://www.clintonjuniorcollege.edu	South Carolina	2-year private

Source: List of HBCUs. (n.d.).

Note: HBCUs that have ceased operation include Storer College (founded 1865); Barber-Scotia College (founded 1867); Mount Hermon Female Seminary (founded 1875); and Bishop College (founded 1881). West Virginia State University and Bluefield State University, both in West Virginia, are not listed because the majority of their students are currently non-Black.

Noted Graduates of HBCUs

Graduates of HBCUs have distinguished themselves in many fields. Among the most illustrious of graduates from HBCUs are the renowned civil rights leader Dr. Martin Luther King, Jr.; Supreme Court justice Thurgood Marshall; educator and scientist Booker T. Washington; sociologist, historian, and activist W. E. B. Du Bois; authors Toni Morrison, Alex Haley, and Alice Walker; movie director Spike Lee; actors Ossie Davis and Samuel L. Jackson; historian John Hope Franklin; television host and media personality Oprah Winfrey; poet Nikki Giovanni; radio host Tom Joyner; and many leading politicians, pastors, and civil rights leaders, including Andrew Young, Jesse Jackson, and Calvin O. Butts III.

Future of HBCUs

Allen (1992) found that Black students who attend HBCUs perform better academically and have higher aspirations than Black students who attended White colleges and universities. However, extensive research on Black college attendance prior to 1970 was rare. It appears that the population at Black colleges then was significantly different from the population after 1970, when many academically gifted Black students enrolled in White colleges. Despite the opportunity of Black students to attend White colleges, many continue to attend HBCUs, along with White and other minority students.

Some observers argue that when Blacks enroll in White colleges and universities, they do not enjoy the same advantages in gaining elected leadership positions as they may have had at an HCBU. Conversely, one may argue that the campus environments at White institutions may be a better representation of America. Also, many Black students who have opted to enroll in White colleges have taken certain elements found on HBCUs, such as Black fraternities and sororities, onto those campuses.

HBCUs fare well when rated against similarly classified White colleges, but ratings among the

HBCUs are constantly changing. In 1977, Butler rated the top HBCUs as Tuskegee, Talladega, and Morehouse universities. In 2009, *U.S. News & World Report* listed its top 10 HBCUs in the following order: Spelman, Howard, Morehouse, Hampton, Fisk, Tuskegee, Claflin, Dillard, Xavier, and Johnson C. Smith.

Even as debate and concerns surface about low college graduation rates for African American students at HBCUs, these institutions, in general, have a bright future. Not surprisingly, the public HBCUs are in better financial shape than the private colleges, many of which are having difficulty with fund-raising and recruiting more students who can afford the cost of attending a private college or university with a higher tuition cost than public HBCUs. Still, the top academically rated private HBCUs will continue to attract African American students along with the public HBCUs.

Frank Brown

See also McLaurin v. Oklahoma State Regents for Higher Education; Morrill Acts; Sweatt v. Painter

Further Readings

Allen, W. R. (1992). The color of success: African-American college student outcomes at predominantly white and historically black college. *Harvard Educational Review, 6*(2), 26–44.

Black student college graduation rates inch higher but a large racial gap persists. (2007). *Journal of Black Higher Education.* Retrieved April 24, 2009, from http://www.jbhe.com/preview/winter07preview.html

Brown, F., & Stent, M. D. (1977). *Minorities enrolled in institutions of higher education.* New York: Praeger Press.

Brown, M. C., II. (1999). *The quest to define collegiate desegregation: Black colleges, Title VI compliance, and post-Adams litigation.* Westport, CT: Bergin & Garvey.

Browning, J., & Williams, J. B. (1978). History and goals of black institutions of higher learning. In C. V. Willie & R. R. Edmonds (Eds.), *Black colleges in America: Challenge, development, and survival* (pp. 127–142). New York: Teachers College Press.

Butler, A. L. J. (1977). *The distinctive black college: Talladega, Tuskegee and Morehouse.* Metuchen, NJ: Scarecrow Press.

Crossland, F. E. (1971). *Minority access to college: A Ford Foundation report.* New York: Schocken Books.

Davis, M. D., & Clark, H. R. (1994). *Thurgood Marshall: Warrior at the bar, rebel on the bench.* New York: Citadel Press.

Freeman, K. (1999). HBCs or PWIs? African American high school students' consideration of higher education institution types. *The Review of Higher Education, 23*(1), 91–106.

Hill, S. (1985). *Traditionally black institutions of higher education: Their development and status: 1860 to 1982.* Washington, DC: National Center for Education Statistics.

List of HBCUs. (n.d.). U.S. Department of Education, The White House Initiative Office on HBCUs. Retrieved May 20, 2009, from http://www.ed.gov/about/inits/list/whhbcu/edlite-list.html

Myrdal, G. (1944). *An American dilemma: The negro problem and modern democracy.* New York: Harper & Row.

U.S. Department of Education. (2007). *Digest of educational statistics.* Washington, DC: Author.

Legal Citations

Agricultural College Act of 1890 (Second Morrill Land Grant Act), ch. 841, 26 Stat. 417, 7 U.S.C. §§ 322 *et seq.*

Brown v. Board of Education, Topeka, 347 U.S. 483 (1954).

McLaurin v. Oklahoma State Regents for Higher Education, 339 U.S. 637 (1950).

Morrill Land Grant Act of 1862, ch. 130, 12 Stat. 503, 7 U.S.C. §§ 301 *et seq.*

Sweatt v. Painter, 339 U.S. 629 (1950).

HOSTILE WORK ENVIRONMENT

Hostile work environment is a category of sexual discrimination prohibited by Title VII of the Civil Rights Act of 1964 (Title VII) and Title IX of the Education Amendments of 1972 (Title IX). Title VII protects employees from discrimination on the basis of race, sex, religion, color, and national origin, and it applies to employers with 15 or more employees. Title VII is enforced by the Equal Employment Opportunity Commission (EEOC). Title IX applies to recipients of federal aid and is enforced by the Office for Civil Rights (OCR) in the U.S. Department of Education. This entry describes the application of the law on hostile work environment in the context of higher education.

Hostile work environment can apply to any of the protected classes under Title VII, which covers race, sex, religion, color, and national origin. Regulations from the EEOC, published in 1980, supplied definitions for harassment on the basis of sex:

Harassment on the basis of sex is a violation of Sec. 703 of Title VII. Unwelcome sexual advances, requests for sexual favors, and other verbal or physical conduct of a sexual nature constitute harassment when (1) submission to such conduct is made explicitly or implicitly a term or condition of an individual's employment, (2) submission to or rejection of such conduct by an individual is sued as a basis for employment affecting such individual, (3) such conduct has the purpose or effect of unreasonably interfering with an individual's work performance or creating an intimidating, hostile, or offensive working environment. (29 C.F.R. § 1604.11(a))

As case law developed under Title VII, the first two categories of behaviors in the regulations became identified with quid pro quo (literally, "this for that") sexual harassment, while the third category became identified with hostile work environment sexual harassment. Quid pro quo sexual harassment occurs when an agent for an employer uses supervisory status or power to induce a subordinate to grant sexual favors in exchange for employment benefits.

Through a series of cases, especially the U.S. Supreme Court's judgment in *Harris v. Forklift Systems* (1993), hostile work environment sexual harassment has required the showing of four elements: severity, pervasiveness, subjectively unwelcome behavior, and objectively unwelcome behavior. Severity and pervasiveness operate together, so that a severe action, occurring only once, could foster a claim. A single minor action, such as utterance of an epithet or asking someone for a date, no matter how subjectively unwelcome to the target of the speech, would not be sufficient to create a hostile work environment. However, repeated utterances of an epithet or requests for a date can become objectionable or irritating enough that a reasonable person would objectively view it as unwelcome behavior. To a certain extent, the legal theories defining hostile work environment

sexual harassment under Title VII have become applicable to claims under Title IX as well.

Title VII Cases

The theory of hostile work environment was first advanced in *Rogers v. EEOC* (1971), which involved a claim based on race. Hostile work environment theory was subsequently applied for the first time for religious discrimination in *Compston v. Borden* (1976), for national origin discrimination in *Cariddi v. Kansas City Chiefs Football Club* (1977), and finally for sexual discrimination in *Henson v. Dundee* (1982). Hostile work environment discrimination law can theoretically apply to all five protected classes under Title VII, but its application is apparently more fully developed for the protected class of sex, with more cases before the Supreme Court. Consequently, the expression "hostile work environment" in higher education tends to apply largely to the protected class of sex.

The first hostile work environment sexual discrimination case to reach the Supreme Court was *Meritor Savings Bank FSB v. Vinson* (1986). In *Meritor*, the Supreme Court rejected the utility of an inquiry into whether sex-related behavior had been voluntarily entered into by the victim; instead, the court required an inquiry into whether the alleged sexual advances were "unwelcome." The Court further emphasized that the "totality of the circumstances" must be used in determining whether sexual harassment exists, thus permitting the entry of details such as manner of dress and sex-related behaviors of the victim into the record.

In *Harris v. Forklift Systems* (1993), the Supreme Court held that it was not necessary to show psychological injury to support a claim of hostile work environment. On the other hand, merely offensive jokes or comments would be insufficient for proving a hostile work environment. The Court suggested that lower courts follow what it called a middle path between allowing an action for any conduct that is merely offensive and allowing an action only when the conduct causes a tangible psychological injury. In *Oncale v. Sundowner Offshore Services* (1998), the Court ruled that nothing in Title VII necessarily bars a claim of discrimination because of sex merely because the plaintiff and the defendant are of the same sex. In *Oncale*, the Supreme Court also stressed that sexual harassment law was not intended to create a code of civility in the workplace.

In *Faragher v. City of Boca Raton* (1998) and *Burlington Industries v. Ellerth* (1998), the Supreme Court addressed the question of what legal standard to apply for imputing liability against an employer when a supervisory employee is the harasser. In these companion cases, the Court established that employers could be strictly liable for the misuse of supervisory authority by their employees. However, the Court also balanced this standard by providing a means for employers to raise an affirmative defense against liability. Absent tangible employment actions such as demotions, discharges, or other adverse employment actions, employers may not be liable when they exercised reasonable care to prevent and promptly correct any sexually harassing behavior and when victimized employees unreasonably failed to avail themselves of any preventive or corrective opportunities provided by their employers.

Title IX Cases

Grove City College had the distinction of being a postsecondary institution that wanted to retain its sectarian focus and remain independent from governmental control, and thus it did not directly accept federal funds. In *Grove City College v. Bell* (1984), the Supreme Court upheld a requirement that college officials must sign a form ensuring compliance with Title IX as a condition for students to receive federally sponsored Basic Educational Opportunity Grants. However, the Court limited the application of Title IX to the financial assistance program and refused to extend its application across all campus activities. In reversing this rule, Congress passed the Civil Rights Restoration Act of 1988, which expanded the remedy for noncompliance under Title IX (as well as Title VI of the Civil Rights Act of 1964, Section 504 of the Rehabilitation Act of 1973, and the Age Discrimination Act of 1975) to include systemwide withdrawal of federal funds.

Franklin v. Gwinnett County Public Schools (1992), the first of a trio of K–12 cases, involved teacher-to-student sexual harassment. Although not dealing directly with hostile work environment, these cases are reviewed because of the profound impact they had on the law dealing with sexual harassment in the workplace, including educational institutions. Here the Supreme Court reasoned that money damages were available under Title IX on the ground that a statute without a remedy would otherwise have served little purpose. The Court revisited teacher-to-student sexual harassment in *Gebser v. Lago Vista Independent School District* (1998), determining that a school board that receives federal funds cannot be liable for damages for teacher-to-student sexual harassment, unless officials with the authority to stop the harassment had actual notice of it and were deliberately indifferent to the behavior of the harasser.

In a case involving student-to-student sexual harassment, *Davis v. Monroe County Board of Education* (1999), the Supreme Court noted that school boards are liable under Title IX only if their officials are deliberately indifferent to sexual harassment of which they have actual knowledge, and if the harassment is so severe, pervasive, and objectively offensive that it deprives the victim of equal educational opportunities.

Finally, in *Jackson v. Birmingham Board of Education* (2005), the Supreme Court was of the opinion that a male basketball coach for a girls' team had a private right of action against a school board under Title IX for retaliation, because he had alleged discrimination against the girls' basketball team.

Application to Colleges and Universities

Even though most hostile work environment sexual harassment cases brought to the Supreme Court under Title VII involve private employers and most cases brought under Title IX originated in K–12 education, the principles from case law under both acts extend to universities and colleges.

Both *Burlington Industries* and *Faragher* instruct that colleges and universities may avoid strict liability under Title VII and raise an affirmative defense against claims that do not involve loss of tangible employment benefits. The first thing that college and university officials must do is to be vigilant while providing reasonable care to prevent and promptly correct any behavior that might be sexually harassing. The second thing that officials must do is to make certain that they have in place an effective sexual harassment policy.

Most colleges and universities have sexual harassment policies with comparable components: a commitment to fight discrimination on the basis of sex; a definition of sexual harassment, usually based on the 1980 EEOC regulations; identification of an official who stands ready to receive complaints; procedures for dealing with the complaint; and an explanation of the potential penalties (usually stated broadly, up to and including termination of employment) for violating the policy. While such policies are necessary for raising an affirmative defense to hostile work environment sex discrimination claims, they can be problematic in their administrative implementation. For example, the EEOC regulations use a definition of sexual harassment focusing upon the victim's viewpoint and the unwanted nature of the perpetrator's behavior. This definition is broader than that fashioned subsequently by the Supreme Court. Consequently, based on the language in many sexual harassment policies in institutions of higher learning, a first-year student who finds a painting of naked figures in an art history class to be "unwelcome" could allege sexual harassment under the policy and demand an adverse employment action against the faculty member. Insofar as a policy definition probably does not include the elements of both subjective and objective offense, it may not comport with the definition of hostile work environment sexual harassment recognized by the courts. Accordingly, a university administrative proceeding against the faculty member may find that the sexual harassment policy, not the faculty member, created a significant problem due to its lack of clarity.

Title IX also provides potential claims against universities and colleges for hostile work environment sexual harassment. The private right of action under Title IX supplied by *Franklin* allows a plaintiff to proceed directly against the body corporate of the university or college upon a showing of deliberate indifference to the alleged discrimination. In contrast, proceeding against the body corporate of the university or college under Title VII is problematic in light of the affirmative defense provided by *Burlington Industries* and *Faragher*, namely, that officials acted reasonably and an employee did not seek to use institutional remedies. Thus, a Title VII claim, coupled with an allegation of a violation of civil rights under

Section 1983, would usually be more likely to provide recovery against an individual postsecondary administrator than against the body corporate of the university or college.

Under *Davis,* student-to-student harassment is actionable when university or college officials know or should have known about the harassment and were deliberately indifferent to it. Further, the harassment must occur under the operations of a recipient of federal funds, and the harassment must take place in a context subject to the recipient's control. This last provision, under *Davis,* provides an additional challenge for colleges and universities. There is probably no greater area of control exerted by a university or college over students than in the area of interscholastic athletics. Consequently, student-to-student hostile work environment sexual harassment involving student-athletes is an area where university and college administrators must exert extraordinary oversight.

David L. Dagley

See also *Grove City College v. Bell*; Sexual Harassment, Peer-to-Peer; Sexual Harassment, Quid Pro Quo; Sexual Harassment, Same-Sex; Sexual Harassment of Students by Faculty Members; Title VII

Further Readings

Dagley, D. L. (1998). When does protected speech become sexual discrimination? *Education Law Reporter, 129,* 565–581.

DeMitchell, T. A. (2000). Peer sexual harassment: More than teasing. *Davis v. Monroe County Board of Education. International Journal of Educational Reform, 9,* 180–186.

Miles, A., Dagley, D., & Russo, C. (1999). University student-athlete conduct codes after *Davis v. Monroe County Board of Education. Education Law Reporter, 138,* 969–981.

Legal Citations

Age Discrimination Act, 42 U.S.C. §§ 6101 *et seq.*

Burlington Industries v. Ellerth, 524 U.S. 742 (1998).

Cariddi v. Kansas City Chiefs Football Club, 568 F.2d 87 (8th Cir. 1977).

Civil Rights Act of 1871, Section 1983, 42 U.S.C. § 1983.

Civil Rights Restoration Act of 1988, 20 U.S.C. § 1687.

Compston v. Borden, 424 F. Supp. 157 (S.D. Ohio 1976).

Davis v. Monroe County Board of Education, 526 U.S. 629 (1999), *on remand*, 206 F.3d 1377 (11th Cir. 2000).

Faragher v. City of Boca Raton, 524 U.S. 775 (1998).

Franklin v. Gwinnett County Public Schools, 503 U.S. 60 (1992).

Gebser v. Lago Vista Independent School District, 524 U.S. 274 (1998).

Grove City College v. Bell, 465 U.S. 555 (1984).

Harris v. Forklift Systems, 510 U.S. 17 (1993).

Henson v. Dundee, 682 F.2d 897 (11th Cir. 1982).

Jackson v. Birmingham Board of Education, 544 U.S. 167 (2005).

Meritor Savings Bank FSB v. Vinson, 477 U.S. 57 (1986).

Oncale v. Sundowner Offshore Services, 523 U.S. 75 (1998).

Rehabilitation Act of 1973, Section 504, 29 U.S.C. §§ 794 *et seq.*

Rogers v. EEOC, 454 F.2d 234 (5th Cir. 1971).

Title VI of the Civil Rights Act of 1964, 42 U.S.C. § 2000d.

Title VII of the Civil Rights Act of 1964, 78 Stat. 257, *as amended*, 86 Stat. 109, 42 U.S.C. § 2000e.

Title IX of the Education Amendments of 1972, 20 U.S.C. § 1681.

HUNT V. MCNAIR

At issue in *Hunt v. McNair* (1973) was the constitutionality of a program in South Carolina that provided support for religious institutions of higher learning. When federal, state, or local governments undertake to provide financial or other support for private postsecondary education, the question arises whether this aid, insofar as it benefits religious institutions, constitutes government support for religion. If governmental aid does constitute such support, then it may well violate the Establishment Clause, because the state would have departed from its position of neutrality. In higher education, *Hunt v. McNair* stands out as a leading case, along with *Tilton v. Richardson* (1971), *Roemer v. Board of Public Works* (1976), and *Witters v. Washington Department of Services for the Blind* (1986), in suggesting that a wide range of postsecondary support programs can be devised to be compatible with the Establishment Clause and that a wide range of religious institutions can be eligible to receive government support. This entry reviews *Hunt* and its background.

Background

In a series of cases, the U.S. Supreme Court provided the foundation for the modern law on government support for church-related schools both in K–12 and higher education settings. The most far-reaching of the cases, *Lemon v. Kurtzman* (1971), invalidated programs from Pennsylvania and Rhode Island that would have provided aid in the form of salary supplements for religiously affiliated nonpublic K–12 schools. In *Lemon*, the Court developed a three-pronged test for evaluating when a governmental support program passes muster under the Establishment Clause. The three prongs are that a program or statute's purpose must be secular, its principal or primary effect must be one that neither advances nor inhibits religion, and it must not foster excessive entanglement between state and religion. Further, in *Tilton v. Richardson* (1971), a decision that was handed down on the same day as *Lemon*, the Court applied the *Lemon* test in upholding the constitutionality of a state program that provided construction grants to higher education institutions, including those that were church related, thus opening the door to later litigation described in the previous paragraph.

Facts of the Case

The South Carolina Educational Facilities Authority Act established an Educational Facilities Authority ("the Authority"), the purpose of which was to assist institutions of higher education in the construction, financing, and refinancing of projects primarily through the issuance of revenue bonds. Under the terms of the act, projects could encompass buildings, facilities, site preparation, and related items but could not include facilities used or to be used for sectarian instruction or as places of religious worship. Additionally, the act forbade funding for facilities that were used or to be used primarily in connection with any parts of programs of schools or departments of divinity for religious denominations. As such, the act accorded the Authority specified powers over projects, including the power to determine the amount of fees to be charged for the use of projects and to establish regulations for their use.

On January 6, 1970, the Baptist College at Charleston, South Carolina, submitted a request for preliminary approval for the issuance of revenue bonds to the Authority. The college intended to use the funds to complete its dining hall facilities. In return, the college would convey the project, without cost, to the Authority, which would then lease the property back to the college. After payment in full of the bonds, the project would be reconvened to the college. The Authority granted preliminary approval that same month. A state taxpayer challenged the Authority, seeking declaratory and injunctive relief against the operation of the act insofar as it authorized a proposed financing transaction involving the issuance of revenue bonds for the benefit of the Baptist College at Charleston.

In the initial round of litigation, a state trial court denied relief, and the Supreme Court of South Carolina affirmed in favor of the Authority. On further review, the U.S. Supreme Court vacated and remanded the case for reconsideration in light of its intervening decisions in *Lemon v. Kurtzman* and *Tilton v. Richardson*. Following the Supreme Court of South Carolina's adherence to its earlier position, the U.S. Supreme Court, in turn, affirmed in favor of the Authority.

The Supreme Court's Ruling

Writing for the Supreme Court in a six-to-three decision, Justice Powell affirmed that the proposed transaction did not violate the Establishment Clause of the First Amendment under the three-pronged *Lemon* tests of purpose, effect, and entanglement. The Court explained that the act creating the Authority had a secular purpose in seeking to aid all institutions of higher education, regardless of whether they were religiously affiliated. Using *Tilton* for its effect argument, the Court held that the college's operations were not oriented significantly toward sectarian rather than secular education, because there were no religious qualifications for faculty membership or student admission and the percentage of Baptist students was roughly equal to the percentage of Baptists in that area of the state. The Court added that the bond issuance would not have the primary effect of advancing or inhibiting religion, because the

project would not include any buildings or facilities used for religious purposes.

The Supreme Court concluded that the issuance of bonds would not have fostered excessive entanglement with religion merely because the college had a formalistic relationship with it or because the Authority might have foreclosed on the debt if the college failed to make the prescribed rental payments or otherwise defaulted on its obligations.

In a dissent joined by Justices Douglas and Marshall, Justice Brennan maintained that the act should have been struck down as unconstitutional, because religious entanglement was present. More specifically, he argued that under the college's proposed plan, the state's policing could have become so extensive that the state would be in complete control of the college's operations, with college officials surrendering their comprehensive and continuing surveillance of the institution's educational, religious, and fiscal affairs to the state. Justice Brennan also argued that through the plan, the state would be aiding a religiously affiliated institution by permitting college officials to take advantage of the state's unique ability to borrow money at low interest rates. He ended the dissent by declaring that his position was compelled, because it involved the state in the religious activities of religious institutions while employing the organs of government for essentially religious purposes.

Zorka Karanxha

See also State Aid and the Establishment Clause; *Witters v. Washington Department of Services for the Blind*

Further Readings

Kaplin, W. A., & Lee, B. A. (2006). *The law of higher education: A comprehensive guide to legal implications of administrative decision making* (4th ed.). San Francisco: Jossey-Bass.

Legal Citations

Hunt v. McNair, 413 U.S. 734 (1973).
Lemon v. Kurtzman, 403 U.S. 602 (1971).
Roemer v. Board of Public Works, 426 U.S. 736 (1976).
South Carolina Educational Facilities Authority Act, S. C. Code Ann. 22-41.
Tilton v. Richardson, 403 U.S. 672 (1971).
Witters v. Washington Department of Services for the Blind, 474 U.S. 481 (1986).

HUNT V. MCNAIR

In *Hunt*, the Supreme Court upheld the constitutionality of a bond program that provided support for religious institutions of higher learning, on the basis that the program was consistent with the Establishment Clause.

Supreme Court of the United States

HUNT

v.

McNAIR

413 U.S. 734

Argued Feb. 21, 1973

Decided June 25, 1973

Mr. Justice POWELL delivered the opinion of the Court.

Appellant, a South Carolina taxpayer, brought this action to challenge the South Carolina Educational Facilities Authority Act (the Act) as violative of the Establishment Clause of the First Amendment insofar as it authorizes a proposed financing transaction involving the issuance of revenue bonds for the benefit of the Baptist College at Charleston (the College). The trial court's denial of relief was affirmed by the Supreme Court of South Carolina. This Court vacated the judgment and remanded the case for reconsideration in light of the intervening decisions in *Lemon v. Kurtzman, Earley v. DiCenso* and *Robinson v. DiCenso* and *Tilton v. Richardson.*

On remand, the Supreme Court of South Carolina adhered to its earlier position. We affirm.

I

We begin by setting out the general structure of the Act. The Act established an Educational Facilities Authority (the Authority), the purpose of which is "to assist institutions for higher education in the construction, financing and refinancing of projects . . ." primarily through the issuance of revenue bonds. Under the terms of the Act, a project may encompass buildings, facilities, site preparation, and related items, but may not include "any facility used or to be used for sectarian instruction or as a place of religious worship nor any facility which is used or to be used primarily in connection with any part of the program of a school or department of divinity for any religious denomination."

Correspondingly, the Authority is accorded certain powers over the project, including the powers to determine the fees to be charged for the use of the project and to establish regulations for its use.

While revenue bonds to be used in connection with a project are issued by the Authority, the Act is quite explicit that the bonds shall not be obligations of the State, directly or indirectly . . . :

Moreover, since all of the expenses of the Authority must be paid from the revenues of the various projects in which it participates, none of the general revenues of South Carolina is used to support a project.

On January 6, 1970, the College submitted to the Authority for preliminary approval an application for the issuance of revenue bonds. Under the proposal, the Authority would issue the bonds and make the proceeds available to the College for use in connection with a portion of its campus to be designated a project (the Project) within the meaning of the Act. In return, the College would convey the Project, without cost, to the Authority, which would then lease the property so conveyed back to the College. After payment in full of the bonds, the Project would be reconveyed to the College. The Authority granted preliminary approval on January 16, 1970.

In its present form, the application requests the issuance of revenue bonds totaling $1,250,000, of which $1,050,000 would be applied to refund short-term financing of capital improvements and $200,000 would be applied to the completion of dining hall facilities. The advantage of financing educational institutions through a state-created authority derives from relevant provisions of federal and South Carolina state income tax laws which provide in effect that the interest on such bonds is not subject to income taxation. The income-tax-exempt status of the interest enables the Authority, as an instrumentality of the State, to market the bonds at a significantly lower rate of interest than the educational institution would be forced to pay if it borrowed the money by conventional private financing.

Because the College's application to the Authority was a preliminary one, the details of the financing arrangement have not yet been fully worked out. But Rules and Regulations adopted by the Authority govern certain of its aspects. Every lease agreement between the Authority and an institution must contain a clause "obligating the Institution that neither the leased land, nor the facility located thereon, shall be used for sectarian instruction or as a place of religious worship, or in connection with any part of the program of a school or department of divinity of any religious denomination."

To insure that this covenant is honored, each lease agreement must allow the Authority to conduct inspections, and any reconveyance to the College must contain a restriction against use for sectarian purposes. The Rules further provide that simultaneously with the execution of the lease agreement, the Authority and the trustee bank would enter into a Trust Indenture which would create, for the benefit of the bondholders, a foreclosable mortgage lien on the Project property including a mortgage on the "right, title and interest of the Authority in and to the Lease Agreement." Our consideration of appellant's Establishment Clause claim extends only to the proposal as approved preliminarily with such additions as are contemplated by the Act, the Rules, and the decisions of the courts below.

II

As we reaffirm today in *Committee for Public Education & Religious Liberty v. Nyquist*, the principles which govern our consideration of challenges to statutes as violative of the Establishment Clause are three: "First, the statute must have a secular legislative purpose; second, its principal or primary effect must be one that neither advances nor inhibits religion . . . ; finally, the statute must not foster 'an excessive government entanglement with religion.'" With full recognition that these are no more than helpful signposts, we consider the present statute and the proposed transaction in terms of the three "tests": purpose, effect, and entanglement.

A

The purpose of the statute is manifestly a secular one. The benefits of the Act are available to all institutions of higher education in South Carolina, whether or not having a religious affiliation. While a legislature's declaration of purpose may not always be a fair guide to its true intent, appellant makes no suggestion that the introductory paragraph of the Act represents anything other than a good-faith statement of purpose. . . .

The College and other private institutions of higher education provide these benefits to the State. As of the academic year 1969–1970, there were 1,548 students enrolled in the College, in addition to approximately 600 night students. Of these students, 95% are residents of South Carolina who are thereby receiving a college education without financial support from the State of South Carolina.

B

To identify "primary effect," we narrow our focus from the statute as a whole to the only transaction presently before us. Whatever may be its initial appeal, the proposition that the Establishment Clause prohibits any program which in some manner aids an institution with a religious affiliation has consistently been rejected. Stated another way, the Court has not accepted the recurrent argument that all aid is forbidden because aid to one aspect of an institution frees it to spend its other resources on religious ends.

Aid normally may be thought to have a primary effect of advancing religion when it flows to an institution in which religion is so pervasive that a substantial portion of its functions are subsumed in the religious mission or when it funds a specifically religious activity in an otherwise substantially secular setting. In *Tilton v. Richardson*, the Court refused to strike down a direct federal grant to four colleges and universities in Connecticut. Mr. Chief Justice Burger, for the plurality, concluded that despite some institutional rhetoric, none of the four colleges was pervasively sectarian, but held open that possibility for future cases. . . .

Appellant has introduced no evidence in the present case placing the College in such a category. It is true that the members of the College Board of Trustees are elected by the South Carolina Baptist Convention, that the approval of the Convention is required for certain financial transactions, and that the charter of the College may be amended only by the Convention. But it was likewise true of the institutions involved in *Tilton* that they were "governed by Catholic religious organizations." What little there is in the record concerning the College establishes that there are no religious qualifications for faculty membership or student admission, and that only 60% of the College student body is Baptist, a percentage roughly equivalent to the percentage of Baptists in that area of South Carolina. On the record in this case there is no basis to conclude that the College's operations are oriented significantly towards sectarian rather than secular education.

Nor can we conclude that the proposed transaction will place the Authority in the position of providing aid to the religious as opposed to the secular activities of the College. The scope of the Authority's power to assist institutions of higher education extends only to "projects," and the Act specifically states that a project "shall not include" any buildings or facilities used for religious purposes. In the absence of evidence to the contrary, we must assume that all of the proposed financing and refinancing relates to buildings and facilities within a properly delimited project. It is not at all clear from the record that the portion of the campus to be conveyed by the College to the Authority and leased back is the same as that being financed, but in any event it too must be part of the Project and subject to the same prohibition against use for religious purposes. In addition, as we have indicated, every lease agreement must contain a clause forbidding religious use and another allowing inspections to enforce the agreement. For these reasons, we are satisfied that implementation of the proposal will not have the primary effect of advancing or inhibiting religion.

C

The final question posed by this case is whether under the arrangement there would be an unconstitutional degree of entanglement between the State and the College. Appellant argues that the Authority would become involved in the operation of the College both by inspecting the project to insure that it is not being used for religious purposes and by participating in the management decisions of the College.

The Court's opinion in *Lemon* and the plurality opinion in *Tilton* are grounded on the proposition that the degree of entanglement arising from inspection of facilities as to use varies in large measure with the extent to which religion permeates the institution. In finding excessive entanglement, the Court in Lemon relied on the "substantial religious character of these church-related" elementary schools. Mr. Chief Justice Burger's opinion for the plurality in *Tilton* placed considerable emphasis

on the fact that the federal aid there approved would be spent in a college setting: "Since religious indoctrination is not a substantial purpose or activity of these church-related colleges and universities, there is less likelihood than in primary and secondary schools that religion will permeate the area of secular education."

. . .

A majority of the Court in *Tilton*, then, concluded that on the facts of that case inspection as to use did not threaten excessive entanglement. As we have indicated above, there is no evidence here to demonstrate that the College is any more an instrument of religious indoctrination than were the colleges and universities involved in *Tilton*.

A closer issue under our precedents is presented by the contention that the Authority could become deeply involved in the day-to-day financial and policy decisions of the College. . . .

As the South Carolina Supreme Court pointed out, the Act was patterned closely after the South Carolina Industrial Revenue Bond Act, and perhaps for this reason appears to confer unnecessarily broad power and responsibility on the Authority. The opinion of that court, however, reflects a narrow interpretation of the practical operation of these powers: "Counsel for plaintiff argues that the broad language of the Act causes the State, of necessity, to become excessively involved in the operation, management and administration of the College. We do not so construe the Act. . . . (T)he basic function of the Authority is to see . . . that fees are charged sufficient to meet the bond payments."

As we read the College's proposal, the Lease Agreement between the Authority and the College will place on the College the responsibility for making the detailed decisions regarding the government of the campus and the fees to be charged for particular services. Specifically, the proposal states that the Lease Agreement "will unconditionally obligate the College (a) to pay sufficient rentals to meet the principal and interest requirements as they become due on such bonds, (and) (b) to impose an adequate schedule of charges and fees in order to provide adequate revenues with which to operate and maintain the said facilities and to make the rental payments. . . ."

In short, under the proposed Lease Agreement, neither the Authority nor a trustee bank would be justified in taking action unless the College fails to make the prescribed rental payments or otherwise defaults in its obligations. Only if the College refused to meet rental payments or was unable to do so would the Authority or the trustee be obligated to take further action. In that event, the Authority or trustee might either foreclose on the mortgage or take a hand in the setting of rules, charges, and fees. It may be argued that only the former would be consistent with the Establishment Clause, but we do not now have that situation before us.

III

This case comes to us as an action for injunctive and declaratory relief to test the constitutionality of the Act as applied to a proposed—rather than an actual—issuance of revenue bonds. The specific provisions of the Act under which the bonds will be issued, the Rules and Regulations of the Authority, and the College's proposal—all as interpreted by the South Carolina Supreme Court—confine the scope of the assistance to the secular aspects of this liberal arts college and do not foreshadow excessive entanglement between the State and religion.

Accordingly, we affirm the holding of the court below that the Act is constitutional as interpreted and applied in this case.

Affirmed.

I

IMMIGRATION REFORM AND CONTROL ACT

The Immigration Reform and Control Act (IRCA) was enacted in 1974 to provide assistance to the Immigration and Naturalization Service (INS) in identifying those persons who were in the United States illegally. In effect, the IRCA makes all employers, including institutions of higher learning, part of the INS enforcement process by denying employment to those persons who lack appropriate documentation and by requiring employers to maintain records of documentation for those persons hired. Basically, the IRCA makes it unlawful for a person to knowingly hire or recruit an unauthorized alien for work, or to refer such a person for a fee. It also prohibits hiring someone without complying with the IRCA documentation requirements (IRCA, § 1324a (1) (A) and B)).

The Homeland Security Act of 2002 transferred the functions of the INS to the Department of Homeland Security (DHS), with overall control vested in the Department of Justice's (DOJ) Executive Office for Immigration Review (EOIR). This arrangement has resulted in identical sets of regulations regarding employment verification requirements, one for INS/DHS and the other for EOIR/DOJ. In light of the many legal issues surrounding the immigration of students and employees, then, this entry focuses on the primary federal law on point, the Immigration Reform and Control Act.

Employees

The key item necessary in the verification process for new employee work authorization is the I-9 Employment Eligibility Verification Form that is available either in paper format from the Superintendent of Documents in Washington, D.C., or in electronic format from the Web site of U.S. Citizenship and Immigration Services (http://www.uscis.gov). The documentation is divided into three categories: documents that establish both identity and work authorization, those that establish identity only, and those that establish work authorization only.

Documents That Establish Identity and Work Authorization

The federal regulations identify the following documents as establishing both identity and work authorization:

(1) U.S. passport (unexpired or expired);

(2) Alien registration receipt card or permanent resident card, Form I-551;

(3) An unexpired foreign passport that contains a temporary I-551 stamp;

(4) An unexpired employment authorization document issued by the Immigration and Naturalization Service which contains a photograph, Form I-766, Form I-688, Form I-688A, or Form I-688B;

(5) In the case of a nonimmigrant alien authorized to work for a specific employer incident to

status, an unexpired foreign passport with an Arrival-Departure Record, Form I-94, bearing the same name as the passport and containing an endorsement of the alien's nonimmigrant status, so long as the period of endorsement has not yet expired and the proposed employment is not in conflict with any restrictions or limitations identified on the Form I-94.

The regulations further identify the following documents as establishing identity only:

(1) For individuals 16 years of age or older:

   (i) A driver's license or identification card containing a photograph, issued by a state (as defined in section 101(a)(36) of the Act) or an outlying possession of the United States (as defined by section 101(a)(29) of the Act). If the driver's license or identification card does not contain a photograph, identifying information shall be included such as: name, date of birth, sex, height, color of eyes, and address;

   (ii) School identification card with a photograph;

   (iii) Voter's registration card;

   (iv) U.S. military card or draft record;

   (v) Identification card issued by federal, state, or local government agencies or entities. If the identification card does not contain a photograph, identifying information shall be included such as: name, date of birth, sex, height, color of eyes, and address;

   (vi) Military dependent's identification card;

   (vii) Native American tribal documents;

   (viii) United States Coast Guard Merchant Mariner Card;

   (ix) Driver's license issued by a Canadian government authority.

(2) For individuals under age 18 who are unable to produce a document listed in paragraph (b)(1)(v)(B)(1) of this section, the following documents are acceptable to establish identity only:

   (i) School record or report card;

   (ii) Clinic doctor or hospital record;

   (iii) Daycare or nursery school record.

(3) Minors under the age of 18 who are unable to produce one of the identity documents listed in paragraph (b)(1)(v)(B)(1) or (2) of this section are exempt from producing one of the enumerated identity documents if:

   (i) The minor's parent or legal guardian completes on the Form I-9 Section 1—"Employee Information and Verification" and in the space for the minor's signature, the parent or legal guardian writes the words, "minor under age 18."

   (ii) The minor's parent or legal guardian completes on the Form I-9 the "preparer/translator certification."

   (iii) The employer or the recruiter or referrer for a fee writes in Section 2—"Employer Review and Verification" under List B in the space after the words "Document Identification #" the words, "minor under age 18."

(4) Individuals with handicaps, who are unable to produce one of the identity documents listed in paragraph (b)(1)(v)(B)(1) or (2) of this section, who are being placed into employment by a nonprofit organization, association or as part of a rehabilitation program, may follow the procedures for establishing identity provided in this section for minors under the age of 18, substituting where appropriate, the term "special placement" for "minor under age 18," and permitting, in addition to a parent or legal guardian, a representative from the nonprofit organization, association or rehabilitation program placing the individual into a position of employment, to fill out and sign in the appropriate section, the Form I-9. For purposes of this section the term individual with handicaps means any person who

   (i) Has a physical or mental impairment which substantially limits one or more of such person's major life activities,

   (ii) Has a record of such impairment, or

   (iii) Is regarded as having such impairment.

Finally, the regulations identify the following documents as establishing work authorization only:

(1) A social security number card other than one which has printed on its face "not valid for employment purposes";

(2) A Certification of Birth Abroad issued by the Department of State, Form FS-545;

(3) A Certification of Birth Abroad issued by the Department of State, Form DS-1350;

(4) An original or certified copy of a birth certificate issued by a State, county, municipal authority or outlying possession of the United States bearing an official seal;

(5) Native American tribal document;

(6) United States Citizen Identification Card, INS Form I-197;

(7) Identification card for use of resident citizen in the United States, INS Form I-179;

(8) An unexpired employment authorization document issued by the Immigration and Naturalization Service.

This verification process must occur for every new employee who is hired.

The IRCA has special rules for determining the kinds of employment decisions that do not constitute new employment. Employees are considered to be involved in continuing employment where an individual

(1) takes approved paid or unpaid leave on account of study, illness or disability of a family member, illness or pregnancy, maternity or paternity leave, vacation, union business, or other temporary leave approved by the employer;

(2) is promoted, demoted, or gets a pay raise;

(3) is temporarily laid off for lack of work;

(4) is on strike or in a labor dispute;

(5) is reinstated after disciplinary suspension for wrongful termination found unjustified by any court, arbitrator, or administrative body, or otherwise resolved through reinstatement or settlement;

(6) transfers from one distinct unit of an employer to another distinct unit of the same employer (the employer may transfer the individual's Form I-9 to the receiving unit);

(7) continues his or her employment with a related, successor, or reorganized employer, provided that the employer obtains and maintains from the previous employer records and Forms I-9 where applicable. For this purpose, a related, successor, or reorganized employer includes:

(i) The same employer at another location;

(ii) An employer who continues to employ some or all of a previous employer's workforce in cases involving a corporate reorganization, merger, or sale of stock or assets;

(iii) An employer who continues to employ any employee of another employer's workforce where both employers belong to the same multi-employer association and the employee continues to work in the same bargaining unit under the same collective bargaining agreement. For purposes of this subsection, any agent designated to complete and maintain the Form I-9 must record the employee's date of hire and/or termination each time the employee is hired and/or terminated by an employer of the multi-employer association; or

(8) is engaged in seasonal employment.

At the same time, the IRCA imposes a number of requirements pertaining to the storage and inspection of documents requirement for employment. Employers must retain I-9 forms along with verification documents for at least three years or for one year after individuals are discharged, whichever is longer (IRCA, § 1324a(b)(3)). Moreover, the I-9 forms are subject to inspection by agents of INS or the Department of Labor upon no more than three days' notice without their having to secure a subpoena or warrant. Civil penalties for failure to comply with the IRCA include progressive fines from a maximum of a $2,000 fine for a first-time offense for each unauthorized alien up to a maximum of a $10,000 fine for repeat employer offenders. Criminal penalties can include fines up to $3,000 and a six-month imprisonment for each violation.

The IRCA and Discrimination

It is worth noting that the IRCA prohibits discrimination based on national origin or citizenship status. To this end, employers of more than three employees are prohibited from discriminating in hiring or discharge of workers because of their national origin or because applicants are U.S. citizens or intend to become citizens. In interpreting this nondiscrimination policy, a federal trial court in Texas, in a case from K–12 education, rendered a judgment that should be of interest to officials at colleges and universities. In *League of United Latin American Citizens v. Pasadena Independent School District* (1987), in enjoining the enforcement of such a policy, the court was of the opinion that a school board's policy of terminating the employment of undocumented aliens for the sole reason that they gave their employers false social security numbers constituted an unfair immigration-related employment practice under the IRCA.

Students

The IRCA also addresses issues attendant to student reception of Title IV funds, also known as Pell Grants. In order to be eligible for Title IV funds, all students must declare, under penalty of perjury, whether they are U.S. citizens, and if they are not U.S. citizens, that they are in an immigrant status that does not render them ineligible for grants, loans, or work assistance under Title IV. The act mandates that officials in institutions of higher learning follow a three-step procedure:

First, officials must collect documents that verify the immigration status of individuals; these do not have to be the same documents that verify identity and work employability under the IRCA.

Second, where documentation is not immediately presented or, if presented, has not been verified, students must be afforded reasonable opportunities to submit evidence to institutional officials documenting their satisfactory immigration status,

and until such a reasonable opportunity is provided, their eligibility for Title IV funds cannot be delayed, denied, reduced, or terminated.

Third, if institutional officials received documentation that they deem satisfactory to constitute reasonable evidence of employment status, they must send photostatic copies to the INS for verification and, pending verification, students' Title IV eligibility cannot be delayed, denied, reduced, or terminated.

If alien students have improperly received Title IV funds, educational institutions are protected from imposition of penalties by the U.S. secretary of education if their officials relied on INS verification of eligibility or were awaiting either student documentation or INS verification. In the case of guaranteed student loans, guarantees are not voided nor are payments nullified if college and university officials notify loan-making entities promptly when they learn of a student's ineligibility.

Another issue relating to immigration and higher education is whether undocumented students can be granted residency status in order to qualify for in-state tuition at public colleges and universities. Although Section 505 of the Illegal Immigration Reform and Immigrant Responsibility Act of 1996 prohibits states from "providing a postsecondary education to an alien not lawfully present unless any citizen or national is eligible for such benefit," the states have interpreted this in various ways, with some states seeking to prevent students who are undocumented immigrants from receiving state tuition benefits and others granting them access to in-state tuition rates. Congress is currently considering legislation that would allow states to grant in-state tuition and financial aid to undocumented students. This bill, the Development, Relief, and Education for Alien Minors (S. 729 and H.R. 1751, known as the DREAM Act), would repeal Section 505 of the IIRIRA and make undocumented students eligible for some forms of federal aid.

Ralph D. Mawdsley

Legal Citations

Code of Federal Regulations, 8 C.F.R. §§ 274.1 *et seq.* (IRCA employment verification requirements).

Homeland Security Act, 6 U.S.C. §§ 101 *et seq.*

Illegal Immigration Reform and Immigrant Responsibility Act of 1996, Pub. L. No. 104-208.

Immigration Reform and Control Act, 8 U.S.C. §§ 1324, 1324(a).

League of United Latin American Citizens v. Pasadena Independent School District, 662 F. Supp. 443 (S.D. Tex. 1987).

Title IV Basic Educational Opportunity Grants, 20 U.S.C. §§ 1070–1091.

INTELLECTUAL PROPERTY

Intellectual property includes literary or artistic works, inventions, business methods, industrial processes, logos, and product designs. Nearly every activity engaged in by students, staff, and faculty in colleges and universities involves the production or use of intellectual property. Among the activities involving intellectual property are research projects, books, journal articles, musical compositions, lesson plans, student assignments, speeches and lectures, videos, university Web sites, newspapers, reports, concerts, and plays. Most items used in education are legally protected intellectual property, often owned by someone other than the user. All members of university communities are permitted to use protected intellectual property, but they must engage in "fair use" or get advanced permission of the owners. Accordingly, faculty, staff, and students must be careful not to use intellectual property unlawfully, or they risk having to pay damages, fines, and court costs. Items that are in the public domain are, of course, free to use without cost to the users or consent of the owners. This entry examines the variety of legal issues associated with the topic of intellectual property.

Legal issues relating to intellectual property in education involve both the creation and use of intellectual works. Intellectual property law balances the rights of individuals to make, own, distribute, and profit from their creations with the rights of the public to make use of knowledge and inventions. Examples of the law of intellectual property in education include copyright and patent protection for the products of teaching and scholarship, copyright and patent infringement for improper use of protected works, and trademark licensing and protection of names, logos, symbols, and pictures used to identify colleges and universities. Readers are strongly encouraged to consult intellectual property policies enacted by individual colleges and universities for details on how particular institutions work with copyrights, patents, and trademarks.

Copyright

Copyrights are intangible rights granted through the federal Copyright Act to authors or creators of original artistic or literary works that can be fixed in tangible means of expression such as hard copies, electronic files, videos, or audio recordings. Copyright law protects literary, musical, dramatic, choreographic, pictorial, sculptural, and architectural works as well as motion pictures and sound recordings. Each copyrightable work has a variety of "copyrights," including the exclusive rights to make copies of the work, distribute the work, prepare "derivative works," and perform or display the work publicly.

With some important exceptions, two of which are highlighted here, teachers and students may not use the copyrighted works of others without permission of the copyright holders. The first exception, fair use, is the most important and most often cited. Under the Copyright Act, the fair use of a copyrighted work, "for purposes such as criticism, comment, news reporting, teaching (including multiple copies for classroom use), scholarship, or research, is not an infringement of copyright." If a use is a fair use, then the user need not obtain advance consent of the copyright holder. Evaluating whether a use is fair requires the application of four factors: purpose and character of the use; nature of the copyrighted work; amount and substantiality of the portion used in relation to the work as a whole; and effect of the use on the potential market for or value of the work. The second exception is also fairly common in educational institutions: It is not an infringement for faculty members and students to perform or display copyrighted works in the course of face-to-face or online/distance education teaching activities. For electronic displays or performances, institutions must comply with additional requirements.

Initially, ownership in a work's copyrights vests in the authors or creators of the work. However, educational institutions may deal with "works for hire" that are created by employees within the scope of their employment. In such instances, employers become the copyright holders. Daniel and Pauken (2005, 2008) maintain that there is a solid legal argument for a "teacher exception" to the work-for-hire doctrine. Under this exception, it can be argued that because college and university administrative officials do not directly supervise their faculty in the preparation of academic books and articles and teaching materials, these faculty members' work does not fall within the definition of work for hire under this principle.

Remedies available to successful copyright infringement claims include injunctive relief, impoundment or disposal of infringing works, monetary damages in the form of actual damages and lost profits, statutory damages as provided by the Copyright Act and decided by the courts, and attorney fees.

Copyrightable works created today are protected from the time that works are fixed in a tangible medium of expression until 70 years after the death of the author/creator. Once a copyright term expires, the work goes into the public domain.

Patents

Under federal patent law, patents for "novel, useful, and nonobvious" inventions are granted for a nonrenewable 20-year term, granting inventors the right to exclude others from making, using, or selling their inventions during that time. At the expiration of the terms, inventions enter the public domain.

In applications for patents, applicants must provide a "specification" describing how the invention works and offer "claims" stating what is new, useful, and nonobvious that makes their inventions patentable. When multiple applications, including recently granted patents, make identical or nearly identical claims, staff at the U.S. Patent Office must conduct investigations to determine which applicants first conceived and reduced the patents to practice. Effectively, a patent can be thought of as belonging to the winner of a race, the one who first brings the invention from conception to patent application and then to practice.

Patentees have the right, just as they would with any personal property, to assign property rights to other persons or entities, including the rights to make, sell, and use patented articles. Assigning these rights, in whole or in part, is popular in colleges and universities as educational institutions draft and enforce intellectual property policies. For example, a university policy may require the taking of 50% of the net income from the invention of a faculty researcher or may adopt a sliding scale where the university takes various percentages of the income depending on the dollar amount.

Patent litigation in higher education often involves the relationships between faculty members, student researchers, and their institutions. An important lesson to be learned here is that all faculty members, and student employees who engage in the production of intellectual property as part of their employment, sign on to their universities' intellectual property policies when they sign their contracts. In a case involving alleged violations of university patent policy, a faculty member sued Yale University for conversion, theft, tortious interference with business relationships, and violation of Connecticut unfair trade laws (*Fenn v. Yale University,* 2006). Yale counterclaimed with an action for breach of contract. The suit stemmed from an invention developed while the faculty member worked at Yale. Under Yale policy, all researchers were required to notify Yale first of any invention. Yale then worked with the University's Office of Cooperative Research to carry out the patent and commercialization processes. Pursuant to university policy, unless otherwise agreed between the parties, Yale gained ownership of the inventions, the Office of Cooperative Research received the titles to the patents, and the inventors were able to share in the licensing royalties.

When the faculty member developed his invention in mass spectrometry, he did not give the university first notice. Instead, he presented it in a paper at a national convention. Further, the faculty member discouraged university officials from pursuing the patent and significantly downplayed the commercial value of the invention. All the while, the faculty member applied for and received the patent with the support of private companies with whom he was to license the invention. After the federal trial court in Connecticut rejected the faculty member's claims, ruling in favor of Yale on its breach of contract counterclaim, the Second Circuit affirmed that the university, not the plaintiff, owned the patent.

Under Section 154 of the Patent Act, patentees have "the right to exclude others from making, using, offering for sale, or selling the invention throughout the United States or importing the invention into the United States." In patent infringement cases, defendants may argue that plaintiffs' patents were unwarranted for such reasons as they failed to meet the novelty, utility, or nonobviousness requirements. Further, there is no defense for good faith or ignorance of the patent. Patent owners are required to mark the product with a notice of patent or provide actual notice of the patent to the infringer. Still, defendants may produce evidence that, acting in good faith, they put the products or process into practice at least one year in advance of the patent owner's application.

Trademarks

Under the federal Lanham Act, a "trademark" includes "any word, name, symbol, or device, or any combination thereof used . . . to identify and distinguish [a person's] goods . . . from those manufactured or sold by others and to indicate the source of the goods" (15 U.S.C. § 1127). Trademarks are also protected under state law. The intent of trademark law is to make

actionable the deceptive and misleading use of marks in commerce; to protect persons engaged in such commerce against unfair competition; [and] to prevent fraud and deception in such commerce by the use of reproductions, copies, counterfeits, or colorable imitations of registered marks.

The primary requirement for trademarks is distinctiveness, to identify the goods and services and avoid confusion or deception. Trademark law protects trademark owners from losing their markets. Key factors are analyzed in trademark infringement claims: the degree of similarity between the two marks, the strength of the owner's mark, evidence of actual confusion, the length of time the defendant has used the alleged similar mark without evidence of actual confusion, intent of the alleged infringer, the degree to which the two marks and associated goods and services are in the same competitive market, and the similarity of the goods and services in the minds of the public. The more similar to one another the competing marks are, the more likely that there will be findings of confusion and infringement. In addition, the more distinctive and recognizable a registered mark is in the market (i.e., identifiable as a particular good or service), the more likely there will be findings of infringement in cases involving a competing mark. There is likely no trademark infringement when later use of similar marks is established in different geographical markets where the second users have no notice of the first mark, they acted in good faith, and there is no confusion or other deception.

Collegiate trademarking and licensing of goods and services is a booming business. Without trademark protection for its words, symbols, and slogans, this business would not be nearly as lucrative for higher education institutions. With such protection, this business, like any in a similar competitive arena, remains rather litigious. There are, generally, four types of marks: generic, descriptive, suggestive, and arbitrary or fanciful. Suggestive and arbitrary marks are the easiest to register and protect, because they are typically the most distinctive. For example, in *Board of Trustees of the University of Arkansas v. Razorback Sports and Physical Therapy Clinic* (1995), university officials sued the clinic alleging trademark infringement, unfair competition, and dilution of trademark. In finding for the university, a federal trial court held, in part, that the term "Razorback" was not a geographic term. In fact, the court was of the opinion the term "Razorback" was "arbitrary" for trademark purposes in the sense that it was not directly descriptive of the goods and services provided, giving the term more strength as a trademark.

The law more often provides trademark protection for "fanciful or arbitrary" words or phrases that, in words alone, are distinctive than it does for words or phrase common to everyday language such as the word "Columbia" (*Trustees of Columbia University v. Columbia/HCA Healthcare Corporation*, 1997). Of course, marks that are similar in sound, design, appearance, or impression may not be infringing when the goods or services offered are not at all similar. The real test is whether marks will confuse relevant consumers.

Protection of trademarks and service marks used by colleges and universities has recently moved into cyberspace. In 1999, Congress passed the Anti-Cybersquatting Consumer Protection Act (ACPA). The ACPA amended the Lanham Act to protect registered domain names as part of an electronic address on the Internet. Under the ACPA, persons who register domain names that are identical or substantially and confusingly similar to the name of other living persons, without the consent of those persons, and with the specific intent to profit from such names, are liable in civil actions. There is an exception for persons who register the names as part of copyrighted work protected under copyright law.

Patrick D. Pauken

See also Copyright; Digital Millennium Copyright Act

Further Readings

Daniel, P. T. K., & Pauken, P. D. (2005). Intellectual property. In J. Beckham & D. Dagley (Eds.), *Contemporary issues in higher education law* (pp. 347–393). Dayton, OH: Education Law Association.

Daniel, P. T. K., & Pauken, P. D. (2008). Copyright laws in the age of technology and their applicability to the K–12 environment. In K. E. Lane, J. F. Mead, M. A. Gooden, S. Eckes, & P. D. Pauken (Eds.), *The principal's legal handbook* (4th ed., pp. 507–519). Dayton, OH: Education Law Association.

Sperry, D. J., Daniel, P. T. K., Huefner, D. S., & Gee, E. G. (1998). Copyright law. In *Education law and the public schools: A compendium* (pp. 191–203). Norwood, MA: Christopher-Gordon.

Legal Citations

Anti-Cybersquatting Consumer Protection Act, 15 U.S.C. § 1129.

Board of Trustees of the University of Arkansas v. Razorback Sports and Physical Therapy Clinic, 873 F. Supp. 1280 (1995).

Copyright Act, 17 U.S.C. §§ 101 *et seq.*

Fenn v. Yale University, 184 Fed. App'x. 21 (2d Cir. 2006).

Lanham Act, 15 U.S.C. §§ 1051 *et seq.*

Patent Act, 35 U.S.C. §§ 1 *et seq.*

Trustees of Columbia University v. Columbia/HCA Healthcare Corporation, 964 F. Supp. 733 (S.D.N.Y. 1997).

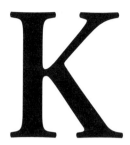

KEYISHIAN V. BOARD OF REGENTS OF THE UNIVERSITY OF THE STATE OF NEW YORK

Keyishian v. Board of Regents of the University of the State of New York (1967) arose at a time when it was common for public employers to require their employees, including educators, to subscribe to loyalty oaths. These oaths, which included possible criminal sanctions, were often more concerned with what educators should not have done, such as avoiding membership in specified organizations, rather than what activities they should have pursued.

The U.S. Supreme Court considered two major issues in *Keyishian*. The first issue was whether Regents of the State University of New York (SUNY) could require faculty and staff members to sign a loyalty oath as a condition of employment. This question arose because Section 3022 of New York State's Education Law, known as the Feinberg Law, required all employees to certify that they were not members of the Communist Party and to notify the president of SUNY if they ever had been members. Under the statute, membership in the Communist Party was prima facie cause to deny or terminate employment of university employees. The second issue in *Keyishian* concerned whether references to "treasonable or seditious speech or acts" in Section 3021 of the Education Law and Section 105, Subdivision 3, of the Civil Service Law threatened the First Amendment freedoms of speech and press that are fundamental to academic freedom in colleges and universities.

Facts of the Case

Harry Keyishian and others were employees of the University of Buffalo (UB), then a private institution in New York; they became state employees in 1962 when UB joined the SUNY system. In accordance with New York law, the plaintiffs were required to sign the "Feinberg Certificate," disavowing any association with the Communist Party and declaring their loyalty to state and federal governments. When Keyishian and his colleagues refused to sign on principle, his one-year contract was not renewed. SUNY officials also announced that the contracts of Keyishian's colleagues would not be extended.

When their contracts were not renewed, the plaintiffs filed suit, alleging violations of their First Amendment rights to free speech and assembly. Subsequently, on remand from an earlier round of litigation, a three-judge federal trial court upheld sections 3021 and 3022 of the Education Law and Section 105 of the Civil Service Law as constitutional. In addition, the court dismissed Keyishian's claims that the statutes were too vague, lacked a proper legal objective, or violated the plaintiff's right to due process.

The Supreme Court's Ruling

On further review, in a five-to-four judgment authored by Justice Brennan, the Supreme Court reversed in favor of Keyishian on the basis that the statutes were unconstitutionally vague, in violation of the First Amendment. At the outset of its analysis, the Court focused on two questions. First, did

Section 3022 violate the constitutional rights of higher education faculty and staff? Second, were the provisions in Section 3021 and Section 105 outlawing treasonable or seditious utterances or acts unconstitutionally vague and overbroad and, therefore, likely to infringe the free speech and academic freedom rights of faculty?

After considering the first question pursuant to existing case law, the Supreme Court ruled that membership in a subversive organization in and of itself was not sufficient cause to deny employment at a public college or university. According to the Court, "a law which applies to membership [only] without the specific intent to further the illegal aims of the organization infringes unnecessarily on protected freedoms. It rests on the doctrine of guilt by association which has no place here." The Court added that mere knowing membership in a subversive organization like the Communist Party, without intent or action to further its aims, is not a justifiable reason for termination from a university faculty appointment. The Court thus concluded that Section 3022 infringed on the First Amendment rights of faculty to speak and assemble. After the *Keyishian* decision, public colleges and universities could not require faculty and staff to sign loyalty oaths as a condition of employment.

Having rejected the constitutionality of Section 3022, the Supreme Court turned to an analysis of Section 3021 and Section 105 that mandated removal of faculty and staff for "treasonable or seditious" utterances or actions. While commending New York State's efforts to protect its educational system from subversive persons, the Court cautioned the legislators and SUNY regents that constitutional rights could not be violated in the process. Indeed, the Court noted that it is important to provide an opportunity for political discussion in democratic institutions.

To the Supreme Court, governmental sanctions for vaguely defined "treasonable or seditious" speech or actions could easily have a chilling effect on the free and open discussion that is absolutely essential in a democratic society. The Court held that nowhere was free and open dialogue more important than on college and university campuses, where faculty must have the academic freedom to research, write, teach, and publish free from the fear of retribution based on the unpopularity of their ideas. In fact, the *Keyishian* Court described academic freedom as "a special concern of the First Amendment which does not tolerate laws that cast a pall of orthodoxy over the classroom" while characterizing the university classroom as "a marketplace of ideas."

In the end, it was clear to the Supreme Court that the Section 3021 provisions proscribing treasonous and seditious actions were far too vague and overbroad to meet constitutional muster. The Court feared that such provisions could easily have created an atmosphere of suspicion and mistrust on college and university campuses that posed a real and present threat to the academic freedom of faculty in New York state universities. The Court worried that Section 3021 would surely "cast a pall of orthodoxy" over classrooms in the SUNY system if these provisions were not amended and clarified or eliminated entirely. Accordingly, the Supreme Court declared Sections 3021 and 3022 of the Education Law of New York to be unconstitutional. Since being resolved, *Keyishian v. Board of Regents*, including its description of academic freedom, has been perhaps the most frequently cited decision in jurisprudence dealing with academic freedom.

Robert C. Cloud

See also Loyalty Oaths; Political Activities and Speech of Faculty Members; *Slochower v. Board of Higher Education of New York City; Sweezy v. New Hampshire*

Further Readings

Elfbrandt v. Russell, 384 U.S. 11 (1966).
Shelton v. Tucker, 364 U.S. 479 (1960).
Slochower v. Board of Higher Education of New York City, 350 U.S. 551 (1956).
Sweezy v. New Hampshire, 354 U.S. 234 (1957).
Wieman v. Updegraff, 344 U.S. 183 (1952).

Legal Citations

Keyishian v. Board of Regents, 385 U.S. 589 (1967).

KEYISHIAN V. BOARD OF REGENTS OF THE UNIVERSITY OF THE STATE OF NEW YORK

In *Keyishian*, the Supreme Court invalidated a regulatory scheme designed to prevent individuals who were involved in "subversive" organizations from teaching in higher education, on the basis that because its requirements were vague, they violated the First Amendment.

Supreme Court of the United States

KEYISHIAN

v.

BOARD OF REGENTS OF THE UNIVERSITY OF THE STATE OF NEW YORK

385 U.S. 589

Argued Nov. 17, 1966

Decided Jan. 23, 1967

Mr. Justice BRENNAN delivered the opinion of the Court.

Appellants were members of the faculty of the privately owned and operated University of Buffalo, and became state employees when the University was merged in 1962 into the State University of New York, an institution of higher education owned and operated by the State of New York. As faculty members of the State University their continued employment was conditioned upon their compliance with a New York plan, formulated partly in statutes and partly in administrative regulations, which the State utilizes to prevent the appointment or retention of "subversive" persons in state employment.

Appellants Hochfield and Maud were Assistant Professors of English, appellant Keyishian an instructor in English, and appellant Garver, a lecturer in Philosophy. Each of them refused to sign, as regulations then in effect required, a certificate that he was not a Communist, and that if he had ever been a Communist, he had communicated that fact to the President of the State University of New York. Each was notified that his failure to sign the certificate would require his dismissal. Keyishian's one-year-term contract was not renewed because of his failure to sign the certificate. Hochfield and Garver, whose contracts still had time to run, continue to teach, but subject to proceedings for their dismissal if the constitutionality of the New York plan is sustained. Maud has voluntarily resigned and therefore no longer has standing in this suit.

Appellant Starbuck was a nonfaculty library employee and part-time lecturer in English. Personnel in that classification were not required to sign a certificate but were required to answer in writing under oath the question, "Have you ever advised or taught or were you ever a member of any society or group of persons which taught or advocated the doctrine that the Government of the United States or of any political subdivisions thereof should be overthrown or overturned by force, violence or any unlawful means?" Starbuck refused to answer the question and as a result was dismissed.

Appellants brought this action for declaratory and injunctive relief, alleging that the state program violated the Federal Constitution in various respects. A three-judge federal court held that the program was constitutional. We noted probable jurisdiction of appellants' appeal. We reverse.

I

We considered some aspects of the constitutionality of the New York plan 15 years ago in *Adler v. Board of Education.* That litigation arose after New York passed the Feinberg Law which added § 3022 to the Education Law. The Feinberg Law was enacted to implement and enforce two earlier statutes. The first was a 1917 law, now § 3021 of the Education Law, under which "the utterance of any treasonable or seditious word or words or the doing of any treasonable or seditious act" is a ground for dismissal from the public school system. The second was a 1939 law which was § 12-a of the Civil Service Law when *Adler* was decided and, as amended, is now § 105 of that law. This law disqualifies from the civil service and from employment in the educational system any person who advocates the overthrow of government by force, violence, or any unlawful means, or publishes material advocating such overthrow or organizes or joins any society or group of persons advocating such doctrine.

The Feinberg Law charged the State Board of Regents with the duty of promulgating rules and regulations providing procedures for the disqualification or removal of persons in the public school system who violate the 1917 law or who are ineligible for appointment to or retention in the public school system under the 1939 law. The Board of Regents was further directed to make a list, after notice and hearing, of "subversive" organizations, defined as organizations which advocate the doctrine of overthrow of government by force, violence, or any unlawful means. Finally, the Board was directed to provide in its rules and regulations that membership in any listed organization should constitute prima facie evidence of disqualification for appointment to or retention in any office or position in the public schools of the State.

The Board of Regents thereupon promulgated rules and regulations containing procedures to be followed by appointing authorities to discover persons ineligible for appointment or retention under the 1939 law, or because of violation of the 1917 law. The Board also announced its intention to list "subversive" organizations after requisite notice and hearing, and provided that membership in a listed organization after the date of its listing should be regarded as constituting prima facie evidence of disqualification, and that membership prior to listing should be presumptive evidence that membership has continued, in the absence of a showing that such membership was terminated in good faith. Under the regulations, an appointing official is forbidden to make an appointment until after he has first inquired of an applicant's former employers and other persons to ascertain whether the applicant is disqualified or ineligible for appointment. In addition, an annual inquiry must be made to determine whether an appointed employee has ceased to be qualified for retention, and a report of findings must be filed.

Adler was a declaratory judgment suit in which the Court held, in effect, that there was no constitutional infirmity in former § 12-a or in the Feinberg Law on their faces and that they were capable of constitutional application. But the contention urged in this case that both § 3021 and § 105 are unconstitutionally vague was not heard or decided. Section 3021 of the Education Law was challenged in *Adler* as unconstitutionally vague, but because the challenge had not been made in the pleadings or in the proceedings in the lower courts, this Court refused to consider it. Nor was any challenge on grounds of vagueness made in *Adler* as to subdivisions 1(a) and (b) of § 105 of the Civil Service Law. Subdivision 3 of § 105 was not added until 1958.

Appellants in this case timely asserted below the unconstitutionality of all these sections on grounds of vagueness and that question is now properly before us for decision. Moreover, to the extent that *Adler* sustained the provision of the Feinberg Law constituting membership in an organization advocating forceful overthrow of government a ground for disqualification, pertinent constitutional doctrines have since rejected the premises upon which that conclusion rested. *Adler* is therefore not dispositive of the constitutional issues we must decide in this case.

II

A 1953 amendment extended the application of the Feinberg Law to personnel of any college or other institution of higher education owned and operated by the State or its subdivisions. In the same year, the Board of Regents, after notice and hearing, listed the Communist Party of the United States and of the State of New York as "subversive organizations." In 1956 each applicant for an appointment or the renewal of an appointment was required to sign the so-called "Feinberg Certificate" declaring that he had read the Regents Rules and understood that the Rules and the statutes constituted terms of employment, and declaring further that he was not a member of the Communist Party, and that if he had ever been a member he had communicated that fact to the President of the State University. This was the certificate that appellants Hochfield, Maud, Keyishian, and Garver refused to sign.

In June 1965, shortly before the trial of this case, the Feinberg Certificate was rescinded and it was announced that no person then employed would be deemed ineligible for continued employment "solely" because he refused to sign the certificate. In lieu of the certificate, it was provided that each applicant be informed before assuming his duties that the statutes, §§ 3021 and 3022 of the Education Law and § 105 of the Civil Service Law, constituted part of his contract. He was particularly to be informed of the disqualification which flowed from membership in a listed "subversive" organization. The 1965 announcement further provides: "Should any question arise in the course of such inquiry such candidate may request . . . a personal interview. Refusal of a candidate to answer any question relevant to such inquiry by such officer shall be sufficient ground to refuse to make or recommend appointment." A brochure is also given new applicants. It outlines and explains briefly the legal effect of the statutes and invites any applicant who may have any question about possible disqualification to request an interview. The covering announcement concludes that "a prospective appointee who does not believe himself disqualified need take no affirmative action. No disclaimer oath is required."

The change in procedure in no wise moots appellants' constitutional questions raised in the context of their refusal to sign the now abandoned Feinberg Certificate. The substance of the statutory and regulatory complex remains and from the outset appellants' basic claim has been that they are aggrieved by its application.

III

Section 3021 requires removal for "treasonable or seditious" utterances or acts. The 1958 amendment to § 105 of the Civil Service Law, now subdivision 3 of that section, added such utterances or acts as a ground for removal under that law also. The same wording is used in both statutes—that "the utterance of any treasonable or seditious word or words or the doing of any treasonable or seditious act or acts" shall be ground for removal. But there is a vital difference between the two laws. Section 3021 does not define the terms "treasonable or seditious" as used in that section; in contrast, subdivision 3 of § 105 of the Civil Service Law provides that the terms "treasonable word or act" shall mean "treason" as defined in the Penal Law and the terms "seditious word or act" shall mean "criminal anarchy" as defined in the Penal Law.

Our experience under the Sedition Act of 1798 taught us that dangers fatal to First Amendment freedoms inhere in the word "seditious." And the word "treasonable," if left undefined, is no less dangerously uncertain. Thus it becomes important whether, despite the omission of a similar reference to the Penal Law in § 3021, the words as used in that section are to be read as meaning only what they mean in subdivision 3 of § 105. Or are they to be read more broadly and to constitute utterances or acts "seditious" and "treasonable" which would not be so regarded for the purposes of § 105?

Even assuming that "treasonable" and "seditious" in § 3021 and § 105, subd. 3 have the same meaning, the uncertainty is hardly removed. The definition of 'treasonable' in the Penal Law presents no particular problem. The difficulty centers upon the meaning of "seditious."

Subdivision 3 equates the term "seditious" with "criminal anarchy" as defined in the Penal Law. Is the reference only to Penal Law, § 160, defining criminal anarchy as "the doctrine that organized government should be overthrown by force or violence, or by assassination of the executive head or of any of the executive officials of government, or by any unlawful means"? But that section ends with the sentence "The advocacy of such doctrine either by word of mouth or writing is a felony." Does that sentence draw into § 105, Penal Law § 161, proscribing "advocacy of criminal anarchy"? If so, the possible scope of "seditious" utterances or acts has virtually no limit. For under Penal Law § 161, one commits the felony of advocating criminal anarchy if he ". . . publicly displays any book . . . containing or advocating, advising or teaching the doctrine that organized government should be overthrown by force, violence or any unlawful means." Does the teacher who carries a copy of the Communist Manifesto on a public street thereby advocate criminal anarchy? It is no answer to say that the statute would not be applied in such a case. We cannot gainsay the potential effect of this obscure wording on "those with a conscientious and scrupulous regard for such undertakings." Even were it certain that the definition referred to in § 105 was solely Penal Law § 160, the scope of § 105 still remains indefinite. The teacher cannot know the extent, if any, to which a "seditious" utterance must transcend mere statement about abstract doctrine, the extent to which it must be intended to and tend to indoctrinate or incite to action in furtherance of the defined doctrine. The crucial consideration is that no teacher can know just where the line is drawn between "seditious" and nonseditious utterances and acts.

Other provisions of § 105 also have the same defect of vagueness. Subdivision 1(a) of § 105 bars employment of any person who "by word of mouth or writing willfully and deliberately advocates, advises or teaches the doctrine" of forceful overthrow of government. This provision is plainly susceptible of sweeping and improper application. It may well prohibit the employment of one who merely advocates the doctrine in the abstract without any attempt to indoctrinate others, or incite others to action in furtherance of unlawful aims. And in prohibiting "advising" the "doctrine" of unlawful overthrow does the statute prohibit mere "advising" of the existence of the doctrine, or advising another to support the doctrine? Since "advocacy" of the doctrine of forceful overthrow is separately prohibited, need the person "teaching" or "advising" this doctrine himself "advocate" it? Does the teacher who informs his class about the precepts of Marxism or the Declaration of Independence violate this prohibition?

Similar uncertainty arises as to the application of subdivision I(b) of § 105. That subsection requires the disqualification of an employee involved with the distribution of written material "containing or advocating, advising or teaching the doctrine" of forceful overthrow, and who himself "advocates, advises, teaches, or embraces the duty, necessity or propriety of adopting the doctrine contained therein." Here again, mere advocacy of abstract doctrine is apparently included. And does the prohibition of distribution of matter "containing" the doctrine bar histories of the evolution of Marxist doctrine or tracing the background of the French, American, or Russian revolutions? The additional requirement, that the person participating in distribution of the material be one who "advocates, advises, teaches, or embraces the duty, necessity or propriety of adopting the doctrine" of forceful overthrow, does not alleviate the uncertainty in the scope of the section, but exacerbates it. Like the language of § 105, subd. I(a), this language may reasonably be construed to cover mere expression of belief. For example, does the university librarian who recommends the reading of such materials thereby "advocate . . . the . . . propriety of adopting the doctrine contained therein"?

We do not have the benefit of a judicial gloss by the New York courts enlightening us as to the scope of this complicated plan. In light of the intricate administrative machinery for its enforcement, this is not surprising. The very intricacy of the plan and the uncertainty as to the scope of its proscriptions make it a highly efficient in terrorem mechanism. It would be a bold teacher who would not stay as far as possible from utterances or acts which might jeopardize his living by enmeshing him in

this intricate machinery. The uncertainty as to the utterances and acts proscribed increases that caution in "those who believe the written law means what it says." The result must be to stifle "that free play of the spirit which all teachers ought especially to cultivate and practice. . . ." That probability is enhanced by the provisions requiring an annual review of every teacher to determine whether any utterance or act of his, inside the classroom or out, came within the sanctions of the laws. For a memorandum warns employees that under the statutes "subversive" activities may take the form of "(t)he writing of articles, the distribution of pamphlets, the endorsement of speeches made or articles written or acts performed by others," and reminds them "that it is a primary duty of the school authorities in each school district to take positive action to eliminate from the school system any teacher in whose case there is evidence that he is guilty of subversive activity. School authorities are under obligation to proceed immediately and conclusively in every such case."

There can be no doubt of the legitimacy of New York's interest in protecting its education system from subversion. But "even though the governmental purpose be legitimate and substantial, that purpose cannot be pursued by means that broadly stifle fundamental personal liberties when the end can be more narrowly achieved." The principle is not inapplicable because the legislation is aimed at keeping subversives out of the teaching ranks. . . .

Our Nation is deeply committed to safeguarding academic freedom, which is of transcendent value to all of us and not merely to the teachers concerned. That freedom is therefore a special concern of the First Amendment, which does not tolerate laws that cast a pall of orthodoxy over the classroom. "The vigilant protection of constitutional freedoms is nowhere more vital than in the community of American schools." The classroom is peculiarly the "marketplace of ideas." The Nation's future depends upon leaders trained through wide exposure to that robust exchange of ideas which discovers truth "out of a multitude of tongues, (rather) than through any kind of authoritative selection." . . .

We emphasize once again that "(p)recision of regulation must be the touchstone in an area so closely touching our most precious freedoms," "(f)or standards of permissible statutory vagueness are strict in the area of free expression. . . . Because First Amendment freedoms need breathing space to survive, government may regulate in the area only with narrow specificity." New York's complicated and intricate scheme plainly violates that standard. When one must guess what conduct or utterance may lose him his position, one necessarily will "steer far wider of the unlawful zone. . . ." For "(t)he threat of sanctions may deter . . . almost as potently as the actual application of sanctions." The danger of that chilling effect upon the exercise of vital First Amendment rights must be guarded against by sensitive tools which clearly inform teachers what is being proscribed.

The regulatory maze created by New York is wholly lacking in "terms susceptible of objective measurement." It has the quality of "extraordinary ambiguity" found to be fatal to the oaths considered in *Cramp* and *Baggett v. Bullitt.* "(M)en of common intelligence must necessarily guess at its meaning and differ as to its application. . . ." Vagueness of wording is aggravated by prolixity and profusion of statutes, regulations, and administrative machinery, and by manifold cross-references to interrelated enactments and rules.

We therefore hold that § 3021 of the Education Law and subdivisions I(a), I(b) and 3 of § 105 of the Civil Service Law as implemented by the machinery created pursuant to § 3022 of the Education Law are unconstitutional.

IV

Appellants have also challenged the constitutionality of the discrete provisions of subdivision I(c) of § 105 and subdivision 2 of the Feinberg Law, which make Communist Party membership, as such, prima facie evidence of disqualification. The provision was added to subdivision I(c) of § 105 in 1958 after the Board of Regents, following notice and hearing, listed the Communist Party of the United States and the Communist Party of the State of New York as "subversive" organizations. Subdivision 2 of the Feinberg Law was, however, before the Court in *Adler* and its constitutionality was sustained. But constitutional doctrine which has emerged since that decision has rejected its major premise. That premise was that public employment, including academic employment, may be conditioned upon the surrender of constitutional rights which could not be abridged by direct government action. Teachers, the Court said in *Adler,* "may work for the school system upon the reasonable terms laid down by the proper authorities of New York. If they do not

choose to work on such terms, they are at liberty to retain their beliefs and associations and go elsewhere." The Court also stated that a teacher denied employment because of membership in a listed organization "is not thereby denied the right of free speech and assembly. His freedom of choice between membership in the organization and employment in the school system might be limited, but not his freedom of speech or assembly, except in the remote sense that limitation is inherent in every choice."

However, the Court of Appeals for the Second Circuit correctly said in an earlier stage of this case, ". . . the theory that public employment which may be denied altogether may be subjected to any conditions, regardless of how unreasonable, has been uniformly rejected."

Indeed, that theory was expressly rejected in a series of decisions following *Adler.* In *Sherbert v. Verner,* we said: "It is too late in the day to doubt that the liberties of religion and expression may be infringed by the denial of or placing of conditions upon a benefit or privilege."

We proceed then to the question of the validity of the provisions of subdivision I of § 105 and subdivision 2 of § 3022, barring employment to members of listed organizations. Here again constitutional doctrine has developed since *Adler.* Mere knowing membership without a specific intent to further the unlawful aims of an organization is not a constitutionally adequate basis for exclusion from such positions as those held by appellants.

In *Elfbrandt v. Russell* we said, "Those who join an organization but do not share its unlawful purposes and who do not participate in its unlawful activities surely pose no threat, either as citizens or as public employees." We there struck down a statutorily required oath binding the state employee not to become a member of the Communist Party with knowledge of its unlawful purpose, on threat of discharge and perjury prosecution if the oath were violated. We found that "(a)ny lingering doubt that proscription of mere knowing membership, without any showing of 'specific intent,' would run afoul of the Constitution was set at rest by our decision in *Aptheker v. Secretary of State.*" In *Aptheker* we held that Party membership, without knowledge of the Party's unlawful purposes and specific intent to further its unlawful aims, could not constitutionally warrant deprivation of the right to travel abroad. As we said in *Schneiderman v. United States,* "(U)nder our traditions beliefs are personal and not a matter of mere association, and . . . men in adhering to a political party or other organization . . . do not subscribe unqualifiedly to all of its platforms or asserted principles." "A law which applies to membership without the 'specific intent' to further the illegal aims of the organization infringes unnecessarily on protected freedoms. It rests on the doctrine of 'guilt by association' which has no place here." Thus mere Party membership, even with knowledge of the Party's unlawful goals, cannot suffice to justify criminal punishment, nor may it warrant a finding of moral unfitness justifying disbarment.

These limitations clearly apply to a provision, like § 105, subd. I(c), which blankets all state employees, regardless of the "sensitivity" of their positions. But even the Feinberg Law provision, applicable primarily to activities of teachers, who have captive audiences of young minds, are subject to these limitations in favor of freedom of expression and association; the stifling effect on the academic mind from curtailing freedom of association in such manner is manifest, and has been documented in recent studies. *Elfbrandt* and *Aptheker* state the governing standard: legislation which sanctions membership unaccompanied by specific intent to further the unlawful goals of the organization or which is not active membership violates constitutional limitations.

Measured against this standard, both Civil Service Law § 105, subd. I(c), and Education Law § 3022, subd. 2 sweep overbroadly into association which may not be proscribed. The presumption of disqualification arising from proof of mere membership may be rebutted, but only by (a) a denial of membership, (b) a denial that the organization advocates the overthrow of government by force, or (c) a denial that the teacher has knowledge of such advocacy. Thus proof of nonactive membership or a showing of the absence of intent to further unlawful aims will not rebut the presumption and defeat dismissal. This is emphasized in official administrative interpretations. For example, it is said in a letter addressed to prospective appointees by the President of the State University, "You will note that . . . both the Law and regulations are very specifically directed toward the elimination and nonappointment of 'Communist' from or to our teaching ranks . . . ." The Feinberg Certificate was even more explicit: "Anyone who is a member of the Communist Party or of any organization that advocates the violent overthrow of the Government of the United States or of the State of New York or any political subdivision thereof cannot be employed by the State University." This official administrative interpretation is supported by the legislative preamble to the Feinberg Law, § I, in which the legislature concludes as a result of its findings that "it is essential that the laws prohibiting persons who are members of subversive groups, such as the Communist Party and its affiliated organizations, from obtaining or retaining employment in the public schools, be rigorously enforced."

Thus § 105, subd. I(c), and § 3022, subd. 2, suffer from impermissible "overbreadth." They seek to bar employment both for association which legitimately may be proscribed and for association which may not be proscribed consistently with First Amendment rights. Where statutes have an overbroad sweep, just as where they are vague, "the hazard of loss or substantial impairment of those precious rights may be critical" since those covered by the statute are bound to limit their behavior to that which is unquestionably safe. As we said in *Shelton v. Tucker,* "The breadth of legislative abridgment must be viewed in the light of less drastic means for achieving the same basic purpose."

We therefore hold that Civil Service Law § 105, subd. I(c), and Education Law § 3022, subd. 2, are invalid insofar as they proscribe mere knowing membership without any showing of specific intent to further the unlawful aims of the Communist Party of the United States or of the State of New York.

The judgment of the District Court is reversed and the case is remanded for further proceedings consistent with this opinion.

Reversed and remanded.

KIMEL V. FLORIDA BOARD OF REGENTS

Kimel v. Florida Board of Regents (2000) is a landmark U.S. Supreme Court case dealing with congressional ability to abrogate the sovereign immunity of states from lawsuits charging violation of the Age Discrimination in Employment Act (ADEA), a federal statute that protects workers over the age of 40 from discrimination. The Eleventh Amendment gives states sovereign immunity from suits, but this immunity is not absolute. For instance, when exercising its power to enforce the Fourteenth Amendment, Congress may abrogate the states' immunity. In *Kimel,* the Court held that

Congress did not have the power to abolish state immunity to ADEA claims and thereby enable individuals to sue states and state agencies in federal court for age discrimination. Because most public institutions of higher education are considered to be arms of their states for the purposes of the Eleventh Amendment, *Kimel* meant that public colleges and universities were immune from lawsuits filed under the ADEA.

Congress has the power to abrogate sovereign immunity to enforce claims of discrimination brought under the Fourteenth Amendment. Also, when ongoing violations of federal law are present, according to Supreme Court precedent in *Ex Parte Young* (1908), a dispute involving criminal proceedings, federal courts may generally enjoin state officials from continuing to break the law. Moreover, states may voluntarily waive their immunity. The question in *Kimel* was whether claims under the ADEA could be considered further exceptions to the Eleventh Amendment prohibition of lawsuits in federal court against the states.

Facts of the Case

Kimel arose out of a dispute between the Florida Board of Regents and faculty members who sued for age discrimination in federal court. Although the governing board ordinarily would have been immune from liability as an arm of the state, Congress had enacted a provision in the ADEA purporting to abrogate sovereign immunity. The board contended that this purported abrogation was unconstitutional, but a federal trial court rejected its argument and ruled against the board. However, after the Eleventh Circuit reversed in favor of the board on the basis that the ADEA did not abrogate Eleventh Amendment immunity, the Supreme Court agreed to hear an appeal.

The Supreme Court's Ruling

On further review, in a judgment written by Justice O'Connor wherein the justices reached divergent opinions, the Supreme Court affirmed both that Congress had expressed its intention to abrogate sovereign immunity for ADEA claims and that the attempted abrogation was unconstitutional. The first holding, that Congress expressed its intention to abrogate, received the support of all justices

except Kennedy and Thomas. The second holding, that the attempt to abrogate was unconstitutional, was joined by Chief Justice Rehnquist as well as Justices Scalia, Kennedy, and Thomas.

Insofar as Congress may only abrogate sovereign immunity when it expresses its intention in a clear and unambiguous manner, the first issue was whether Congress had done so in the ADEA. The Supreme Court observed that, unlike other statutes, the ADEA did not explicitly mention a desire to abrogate sovereign immunity. Nevertheless, seven justices agreed that the generalized language referring to suits and enforcement along with the inclusion of the states in certain definitions meant that Congress intended to abrogate the states' sovereign immunity.

Having determined that Congress had intended to abrogate states' immunity, the Supreme Court turned to the more critical question of whether its attempt to do so was successful. The Court began by reaffirming a basic point, namely that Congress may not use its general Article I powers to abrogate sovereign immunity, because any abrogation must come from the power to enforce the Fourteenth Amendment. In evaluating whether Congress acted properly to enforce the Fourteenth Amendment, the Court applied the test articulated in *City of Boerne v. Flores* (1997), wherein it explained that Congress exceeded its enforcement powers in enacting the Religious Freedom Restoration Act. Under this test, Congress must establish a pattern of actual constitutional violations by the states and must demonstrate that its remedy of abrogating sovereign immunity is proportionate to the pattern of constitutional violations.

The Supreme Court ruled that Congress failed in both tasks. First, the Court decided that Congress had not identified a pattern of unconstitutional violations of the ADEA by the states. The Court noted that violations of the ADEA are not necessarily violations of the Constitution. The Court also indicated that what evidence Congress did have of age discrimination by the states was anecdotal and limited to a few jurisdictions. Further, the Court did not think that discrimination by the private sector could form the basis for a finding of discrimination by the states. Because the findings were inadequate, the Court viewed the remedy, namely the abrogation of sovereign immunity, as also clearly inadequate. Thus, the Court invalidated the statutory attempt to abrogate the board's sovereign immunity.

Justice Stevens, joined by Justices Souter, Ginsburg, and Breyer, vigorously dissented. In their view, the Court's current sovereign immunity jurisprudence was fundamentally flawed and imposed unnecessary restrictions on the powers of Congress. The dissent criticized the Court's decision in *Seminole Tribe of Florida v. Florida* (1996), wherein it maintained that Congress lacked the authority under the Indian Commerce clause to abrogate the states' Eleventh Amendment immunity.

Justice Thomas, joined by Justice Kennedy, dissented on the issue of whether Congress clearly and unambiguously had expressed its intention to abrogate.

A decade after the case was resolved, the Supreme Court has yet to limit *Kimel*. If anything, the Court subsequently expanded the scope of Kimel in substantive areas of the law, such as in *Federal Maritime Commission v. South Carolina State Ports Authority* (2002), wherein it concluded that sovereign immunity forbade the commission from adjudicating a dispute over whether a private cruise ship could berth at a state-run port. For state universities that are considered arms of the state, *Kimel* remains a foundational case.

William E. Thro

See also Age Discrimination; Age Discrimination in Employment Act; *Central Virginia Community College v. Katz*; Eleventh Amendment; *Florida Prepaid v. College Savings Bank*

Further Readings

Alden v. Maine, 527 U.S. 706, 713 (1999).

Board of Trustees of the University of Alabama v. Garrett, 531 U.S. 356 (2001).

Central Virginia Community College v. Katz, 546 U.S. 356 (2006).

Chisholm v. Georgia, 2 U.S. (2 Dall.) 419 (1793).

Florida Prepaid v. College Savings Bank, 527 U.S. 627 (1999).

Noonan, J. T., Jr. (2002). *Narrowing the nation's power: The Supreme Court sides with the states.* Berkeley: University of California Press.

Thro, W. E. (1999). The Eleventh Amendment revolution in the lower federal courts. *Journal of College & University Law, 25,* 501–526.

Thro, W. E. (2000). The education lawyer's guide to the sovereign immunity revolution. *Education Law Reporter, 146,* 951–981.

Thro, W. E. (2007). The future of sovereign immunity. *Education Law Reporter, 215,* 1–31.

United States v. Georgia, 546 U.S. 151 (2006).

Legal Citations

Age Discrimination in Employment Act, Pub. L. No. 90-202 (1967).

City of Boerne v. Flores, 521 U.S. 507 (1997).

Ex Parte Young, 209 U.S. 123 (1908)

Federal Maritime Commission v. South Carolina State Ports Authority, 535 U.S. 743 (2002).

Kimel v. Florida Board of Regents, 528 U.S. 62 (2000).

Religious Freedom Restoration Act, Pub. L. No. 103-141 (1993).

Seminole Tribe of Florida v. Florida, 517 U.S. 44 (1996).

Knight v. Board of Regents of the University of the State of New York

At issue in *Knight v. Board of Regents of the University of the State of New York* (1967, 1968) was a state law mandating that all instructors at public schools and at tax-exempt, private schools, including institutions of higher learning, had to sign a loyalty oath. Unlike other cases in which the U.S. Supreme Court invalidated loyalty oaths because they were not sufficiently clear in forbidding individuals from engaging in particular activities, the Supreme Court upheld the oath in *Knight*, holding that it was not too vague. *Knight* stands for the proposition that state laws may require faculty members in colleges and universities, as well as in K–12 schools, to sign affirmative loyalty oaths in support of the national and state constitutions in the fulfillment of their professional obligations, as long as the oaths neither place restrictions on political or philosophical expressions nor are impermissibly vague. Insofar as the issue in *Knight*, which was whether the state law calling for the loyalty oath violated the constitutional rights of faculty members, remains of significance to this day, this entry examines its facts and the judicial rationale in upholding the law.

In effect since 1934, a New York state law required faculty members in public schools and tax-exempt, private schools, including colleges and universities, to sign an oath indicating that individuals would support the federal and state constitutions in the faithful execution of their professional duties. In October 1966, state officials realized that faculty members at Adelphi University, a nonprofit, tax-exempt university in New York, had not signed the oath. When the administrators at Adelphi asked the faculty members to sign and return the oath, 27 of them declined to do so. Instead, the faculty members brought an action contesting the constitutional legitimacy of the state law. Specifically, the faculty members claimed that the law violated their rights under the First, Fifth, Ninth, and Fourteenth Amendments of the U.S. Constitution.

In initiating their claims, the faculty members filed a motion for a provisional injunction known as an injunction pendente lite, which requested a temporary, legal hold on the loyalty oath requirement until the litigation was resolved. Pursuant to a hearing regarding the motion, a three-judge panel in a federal trial court in New York conducted a hearing to determine whether requiring the faculty members to sign the loyalty oath violated their constitutional rights.

The faculty raised three main arguments in their motion. First, the faculty members claimed that obligating them to take an oath as to the performance of their professional duties violated their constitutional rights. In support of this position, the faculty relied on the Supreme Court's analysis in *West Virginia State Board of Education v. Barnette* (1943), in which the parents of students challenged a state requirement that their children were required to salute and pledge their allegiance to the American flag. In *Barnette*, the Supreme Court held that the students' expulsion and school's threat of criminal juvenile penalties for failing to salute the flag and pledge allegiance were violations of the students' First Amendment rights.

According to the faculty members at Adelphi, the requirement of the loyalty oath was similar to saluting and pledging of allegiance to the flag. The three-judge panel disagreed on the basis that the pledge in *Barnette* was far more elaborate than the oath that the faculty members were challenging. The judges noted that *Barnette* involved a challenge to the religious freedom of the children in *Barnette*, because

they were Jehovah's Witnesses whose religious beliefs prohibited expressions of reverence to images such as a flag. In *Knight,* the court pointed out that because the oath neither compelled individuals to act against their religious beliefs nor threatened the faculty members with criminal sanctions as in *Barnette,* its precedent was inapplicable.

Second, the faculty argued that the statute was unconstitutionally vague, which was precisely the reason the Supreme Court had struck down earlier loyalty oaths. The court disagreed on this argument, too. Here the faculty members relied on cases that invalidated negative loyalty oaths because the oaths required individuals to refrain from acts and associational memberships and because the individuals were subject to criminal penalties if they disobeyed. In those cases, the court observed that the laws were not precise enough to enable ordinary persons to decide what acts and associational memberships they had to avoid. Consequently, the court noted, the earlier laws had been struck down for vagueness. By contrast, the court held that *Knight* presented a loyalty oath that required only affirmative support for the national and state constitutions in the fulfillment of faculty members' professional obligations. Insofar as the language in the disputed statute was clear and reasonable, the court ruled that the law was not constitutionally vague.

Third, the faculty asserted a public policy argument that educators needed a work environment that was free from outside interferences. In response, the court was of the opinion that because the loyalty oath did not restrict the political or philosophical expressions of the faculty members, it did not interfere with their work.

In sum, taking the three arguments that the faculty presented, the court denied their motion for an injunction. Dissatisfied with the outcome, the faculty members sought further review. On appeal, the U.S. Supreme Court summarily affirmed the order of the three-judge panel in a brief one-sentence order that simply stated, "The motion to affirm is granted and the judgment is affirmed" (p. 36).

Jeffrey C. Sun

See also Academic Freedom; Bill of Rights; *Keyishian v. Board of Regents of the University of the State of New York*; Loyalty Oaths; Political Activities and Speech of Faculty Members

Further Readings

Notes and comments: Loyalty oaths. (1968). *Yale Law Journal, 77*(4), 739–766.

Sun, J. C. (2008). Loyalty oaths. In C. J. Russo (Ed.). *Encyclopedia of education law* (Vol. 2, pp. 521–523). Thousand Oaks, CA: Sage.

Legal Citations

Knight v. Board of Regents of the University of the State of New York, 269 F. Supp. 339 (S.D.N.Y. 1967), aff'd, 390 U.S. 36 (1968).

West Virginia State Board of Education v. Barnette, 319 U.S. 624 (1943).

L

LEHNERT V. FERRIS FACULTY ASSOCIATION

At issue in *Lehnert v. Ferris Faculty Association* (1991) was whether the union representing faculty members at a college could compel dissenting members in an agency shop to subsidize legislative lobbying and other political activities not directly related to standard collective bargaining activities such as contract negotiation and grievance adjudication. Ultimately, in *Lehnert* the U.S. Supreme Court ruled that the unions of public employees may charge dissenting employees the cost of activities that are clearly germane to collective bargaining as are justified by the government's vital policy interest in labor peace. In addition, the Court sought to avoid having "freeloaders," those who did not pay for benefits that unions gained on their behalf, typically in the form of salary increases and benefits. At the same time, the Court did not wish to limit the First Amendment rights of dissenters by essentially compelling them to support speech with which they disagree. Further, the Court added that the government and unions cannot compel nonmember employees to support political lobbying efforts as a condition of public employment.

Lehnert v. Ferris Faculty Association stands out, because in it the Supreme Court balanced the First Amendment rights of faculty members who do not wish to join unions with the rights of unions to collect fair compensation for the services that they provide to all employees, regardless of whether they are members.

Background

The State of Michigan's Public Employment Relations Act provides that a duly selected union shall serve as the exclusive representative of public employees in a particular bargaining unit. The act, which applied to faculty members in all educational institutions in Michigan, permitted unions and state employers to enter into "agency shop" arrangements in which the unions acted as agent for all employees regardless of their union membership status. Employees in agency shops are not required to join unions but are compelled to pay service fees that almost equal union dues, because nonmembers benefit from union collective bargaining efforts as much as members. The primary purpose of such policies, of course, is to prevent nonmembers from freeloading on union efforts without sharing the attendant costs. However, agency shop arrangements in public sector unions raise First Amendment concerns, because they require nonmembers to contribute money to unions as a condition of government employment.

In *Abood v. Detroit Board of Education,* a 1977 case from K–12 education, the Supreme Court first upheld the constitutionality of the agency shop provision in Michigan's Public Employment Relations Act that related to *Lehnert,* while emphasizing that unions in the public sector may not use the fees of dissenting nonmembers for political purposes. The justices also highlighted important guidelines for lower courts to consider in the adjudication of future agency shop disputes. First, the Court explained that compelling employees to pay a service fee prompts First Amendment concerns, because unions support a wide range of social, political, and ideological viewpoints, any one of which might bring disapproval from individual employees. Under the First Amendment, employees have the right to speak and associate or not to speak and associate regarding union political activities.

Second, in *Abood* the Supreme Court noted that compulsory financial support of a public employee union does not in and of itself violate the First Amendment rights of nonmembers, because the advantage of peaceful labor relations fostered by agency shops normally supersede constitutional infringements that may occur. Third, because the Court was of the opinion that states may not condition public employment upon professed religious allegiance or association with a political party, it concluded that public employers may not require "an employee to contribute to the support of an ideological cause he may oppose as a condition of holding a job" as a public educator.

Facts of the Case

Following the Supreme Court's decision in *Abood,* the faculty association in *Lehnert* entered into an agency shop arrangement with Ferris State College in Michigan whereby nonmembers were required to pay a service fee equal to union dues. James P. Lehnert and other members of the Ferris State College faculty filed suit, claiming that the union's use of their agency fees to pay for lobbying and other political activities not directly related to collective bargaining violated their First and Fourteenth Amendment rights. The plaintiffs also claimed that the procedures that the union used to establish the amount of, collect, and account for their service fees were inadequate. A federal trial court ruled that some, but not all, of the union expenditures were constitutionally chargeable to the plaintiffs. The plaintiffs appealed following a partial settlement, and, on further review, the Sixth Circuit affirmed.

The Supreme Court's Ruling

After agreeing to hear an appeal, the Supreme Court partially affirmed the earlier judgments in clarifying the relationship between dissenting nonmembers and the unions representing educational employees. First, the Court reasoned that faculty members, including those who did not belong to the union, could be charged a pro rata share of the costs associated with activities of state and national union affiliates even if those activities did not directly benefit the bargaining unit at Ferris State College. Second, the Court pointed out that union members could be charged for expenses that the union incurred in preparing for a proposed strike even though it would have been illegal under Michigan state law.

Third, in accordance with existing agency shop jurisprudence, the Supreme Court determined that the union could not charge dissenting nonmembers for lobbying, electoral, and other political activities that did not relate to the collective bargaining agreement. In this regard, the Court found that the state may not compel its employees to subsidize lobbying or other political activities that are outside the context of contract ratification. In order to ensure proper accounting and distribution of agency shop fees in the future, then, the Court emphasized that unions in agency shops bear the burden of proving the proportion of chargeable expenses to total expenses for purposes of determining the amount the union may charge dissenters for services.

Robert C. Cloud

See also Collective Bargaining; Political Activities and Speech of Faculty Members; Unions on Campus; U.S. Supreme Court Cases in Higher Education

Further Readings

Chicago Teachers Union, Local No. 1 v. Hudson, 475 U.S. 292 (1986).
Davenport v. Washington Education Association, 127 S. Ct. 2372 (2007).
Russo, C. J., Gordon, W. M., & Miles, A. S. (1992). Agency shop fees and the Supreme Court: Union control and academic freedom. *Education Law Reporter, 73*(3), 609–615.

Legal Citations

Abood v. Detroit Board of Education, 431 U.S. 209 (1977).
Lehnert v. Ferris Faculty Association, 500 U.S. 507 (1991).

LEHNERT V. FERRIS FACULTY ASSOCIATION

In *Lehnert*, the Supreme Court clarified the parameters of the types of aid that non-union employees in the public sector could be required to pay as part of their "fair share" or representation fees.

Supreme Court of the United States

LEHNERT

v.

FERRIS FACULTY ASSOCIATION

Argued Nov. 5, 1990

Decided May 30, 1991

Rehearing Denied June 24, 1991

Justice BLACKMUN announced the judgment of the Court and delivered the opinion of the Court with respect to Parts I, II, III-B, III-C, IV-B (except for the final paragraph), IV-D, IV-E, and IV-F, and an opinion with respect to Parts III-A and IV-A, the final paragraph of Part IV-B, and Parts IV-C and V, in which THE CHIEF JUSTICE, Justice WHITE, and Justice STEVENS join.

This case presents issues concerning the constitutional limitations, if any, upon the payment, required as a condition of employment, of dues by a nonmember to a union in the public sector.

I

Michigan's Public Employment Relations Act (Act), provides that a duly selected union shall serve as the exclusive collective-bargaining representative of public employees in a particular bargaining unit. The Act, which applies to faculty members of a public educational institution in Michigan, permits a union and a government employer to enter into an "agency-shop" arrangement under which employees within the bargaining unit who decline to become members of the union are compelled to pay a "service fee" to the union.

Respondent Ferris Faculty Association (FFA), an affiliate of the Michigan Education Association (MEA) and the National Education Association (NEA), serves, pursuant to this provision, as the exclusive bargaining representative of the faculty of Ferris State College in Big Rapids, Mich. Ferris is a public institution established under the Michigan Constitution and is funded by the State. Since 1975, the FFA and Ferris have entered into successive collective-bargaining agreements containing agency-shop provisions. Those agreements were the fruit of negotiations between the FFA and respondent Board of Control, the governing body of Ferris.

Subsequent to this Court's decision in *Abood v. Detroit Board of Education*, in which the Court upheld the constitutionality of the Michigan agency-shop provision and outlined permissible uses of the compelled fee by public-employee unions, Ferris proposed, and the FFA agreed to, the agency-shop arrangement at issue here. That agreement required all employees in the bargaining unit who did not belong to the FFA to pay a service fee equivalent to the amount of dues required of a union member. Of the $284 service fee for 1981–1982, the period at issue, $24.80 went to the FFA, $211.20 to the MEA, and $48 to the NEA.

Petitioners were members of the Ferris faculty during the period in question and objected to certain uses by the unions of their service fees. Petitioners instituted this action in the United States District Court for the Western District of Michigan, claiming that the use of their fees for purposes other than negotiating and administering a collective-bargaining agreement with the Board of Control violated rights secured to them by the First and Fourteenth Amendments to the United States Constitution. Petitioners also claimed that the procedures implemented by the unions to determine and collect service fees were inadequate.

After a 12-day bench trial, the District Court issued its opinion holding that certain union expenditures were chargeable to petitioners, that certain other expenditures were not chargeable as a matter of law, and that still other expenditures were not chargeable because the unions had failed to sustain their burden of proving that the expenditures were made for chargeable activities.

Following a partial settlement, petitioners took an appeal limited to the claim that the District Court erred in holding that the costs of certain disputed union activities were constitutionally chargeable to the plaintiff faculty members. Specifically, petitioners objected to the District Court's conclusion that the union constitutionally could charge them for the costs of (1) lobbying and electoral politics; (2) bargaining, litigation, and other activities on behalf of persons not in petitioners' bargaining unit; (3) public-relations efforts; (4) miscellaneous professional activities; (5) meetings and conventions of the parent unions; and (6) preparation for a strike which, had it materialized, would have violated Michigan law.

The Court of Appeals, with one judge dissenting in large part, affirmed. After reviewing this Court's cases in the area, the court concluded that each of the challenged activities was sufficiently related to the unions' duties as the exclusive bargaining representative of petitioners' unit to justify compelling petitioners to assist in subsidizing it. The dissenting judge concurred with respect to convention expenses but disagreed with the majority's resolution of the other items challenged. Because of the importance of the issues, we granted certiorari.

II

This is not our first opportunity to consider the constitutional dimensions of union-security provisions such as the agency-shop agreement at issue here. . . .

. . .

It was not until the decision in *Abood* that this Court addressed the constitutionality of union-security provisions in the public-employment context. There, the Court upheld the same Michigan statute which is before us today against a facial First Amendment challenge. At the same time, it determined that the claim that a union has utilized an individual agency-shop agreement to force dissenting employees to subsidize ideological activities could establish, upon a proper showing, a First Amendment violation. In so doing, the Court set out several important propositions:

First, it recognized that "[t]o compel employees financially to support their collective-bargaining representative has an impact upon their First Amendment interests." Unions traditionally have aligned themselves with a wide range of social, political, and ideological viewpoints, any number of which might bring vigorous disapproval from individual employees. To force employees to contribute, albeit indirectly, to the promotion of

such positions implicates core First Amendment concerns.

Second, the Court in *Abood* determined that, as in the private sector, compulsory affiliation with, or monetary support of, a public-employment union does not, without more, violate the First Amendment rights of public employees. Similarly, an employee's free speech rights are not unconstitutionally burdened because the employee opposes positions taken by a union in its capacity as collective-bargaining representative. "[T]he judgment clearly made in *Hanson* and *Street* is that such interference as exists is constitutionally justified by the legislative assessment of the important contribution of the union shop to the system of labor relations established by Congress."

In this connection, the Court indicated that the considerations that justify the union shop in the private context—the desirability of labor peace and eliminating "free riders"—are equally important in the public-sector workplace. Consequently, the use of dissenters' assessments "for the purposes of collective bargaining, contract administration, and grievance adjustment," approved under the RLA, is equally permissible when authorized by a State vis-a-vis its own workers.

Third, the Court established that the constitutional principles that prevent a State from conditioning public employment upon association with a political party, or upon professed religious allegiance, similarly prohibit a public employer "from requiring [an employee] to contribute to the support of an ideological cause he may oppose as a condition of holding a job" as a public educator.

The Court in *Abood* did not attempt to draw a precise line between permissible assessments for public-sector collective bargaining activities and prohibited assessments for ideological activities. It did note, however, that, while a similar line must be drawn in the private sector under the RLA, the distinction in the public sector may be "somewhat hazier." This is so because the "process of establishing a written collective-bargaining agreement prescribing the terms and conditions of public employment may require not merely concord at the bargaining table, but subsequent approval by other public authorities; related budgetary and appropriations decisions might be seen as an integral part of the bargaining process."

Finally, in *Ellis*, the Court considered, among other issues, a First Amendment challenge to the use of dissenters' funds for various union expenses including union conventions, publications, and social events. Recognizing that by allowing union-security arrangements at all, it has necessarily countenanced a significant burdening of First

Amendment rights, it limited its inquiry to whether the expenses at issue "involve[d] *additional* interference with the First Amendment interests of objecting employees, and, if so, whether they are nonetheless adequately supported by a governmental interest."

Applying that standard to the challenged expenses, the Court found all three to be properly supportable through mandatory assessments. The dissenting employees in *Ellis* objected to charges relating to union social functions, not because those activities were inherently expressive or ideological in nature, but purely because they were sponsored by the union.

Because employees may constitutionally be compelled to affiliate with a union, the Court found that forced contribution to union social events that were open to all imposed no additional burden on their First Amendment rights. Although the challenged expenses for union publications and conventions were clearly communicative in nature, the Court found them to entail little additional encroachment upon freedom of speech, "and none that is not justified by the governmental interests behind the union shop itself."

Thus, although the Court's decisions in this area prescribe a case-by-case analysis in determining which activities a union constitutionally may charge to dissenting employees, they also set forth several guidelines to be followed in making such determinations. *Hanson* and *Street* and their progeny teach that chargeable activities must (1) be "germane" to collective-bargaining activity; (2) be justified by the government's vital policy interest in labor peace and avoiding "free riders"; and (3) not significantly add to the burdening of free speech that is inherent in the allowance of an agency or union shop.

III

In arguing that these principles exclude the charges upheld by the Court of Appeals, petitioners propose two limitations on the use by public-sector unions of dissenters' contributions. First, they urge that they may not be charged over their objection for lobbying activities that do not concern legislative ratification of, or fiscal appropriations for, their collective-bargaining agreement. Second, as to nonpolitical expenses, petitioners assert that the local union may not utilize dissenters' fees for activities that, though closely related to collective bargaining generally, are not undertaken directly on behalf of the bargaining unit to which the objecting employees belong. We accept the former proposition but find the latter to be foreclosed by our prior decisions.

A

The Court of Appeals determined that unions constitutionally may subsidize lobbying and other political activities with dissenters' fees so long as those activities are "pertinent to the duties of the union as a bargaining representative." . . . the court relied upon the inherently political nature of salary and other workplace decisions in public employment. . . .

This observation is clearly correct. Public-sector unions often expend considerable resources in securing ratification of negotiated agreements by the proper state or local legislative body. Similarly, union efforts to acquire appropriations for approved collective-bargaining agreements often serve as an indispensable prerequisite to their implementation. It was in reference to these characteristics of public employment that the Court in *Abood* discussed the "somewhat hazier" line between bargaining-related and purely ideological activities in the public sector. The dual roles of government as employer and policymaker in such cases make the analogy between lobbying and collective bargaining in the public sector a close one.

This, however, is not such a case. Where, as here, the challenged lobbying activities relate not to the ratification or implementation of a dissenter's collective-bargaining agreement, but to financial support of the employee's profession or of public employees generally, the connection to the union's function as bargaining representative is too attenuated to justify compelled support by objecting employees.

We arrive at this result by looking to the governmental interests underlying our acceptance of union-security arrangements. We have found such arrangements to be justified by the government's interest in promoting labor peace and avoiding the "free-rider" problem that would otherwise accompany union recognition. Neither goal is served by charging objecting employees for lobbying, electoral, and other political activities that do not relate to their collective-bargaining agreement.

Labor peace is not especially served by allowing such charges because, unlike collective-bargaining negotiations between union and management, our national and state legislatures, the media, and the platform of public discourse are public fora open to all. Individual employees are free to petition their neighbors and government in opposition to the union which represents them in the workplace. Because worker and union cannot be said to speak with one voice, it would not further the cause of harmonious industrial relations to compel objecting employees to finance union political activities as well as their own.

Similarly, while we have endorsed the notion that non-union workers ought not be allowed to benefit from the terms of employment secured by union efforts without paying for those services, the so-called "free-rider" concern is inapplicable where lobbying extends beyond the effectuation of a collective-bargaining agreement. The balancing of monetary and other policy choices performed by legislatures is not limited to the workplace but typically has ramifications that extend into diverse aspects of an employee's life.

Perhaps most important, allowing the use of dissenters' assessments for political activities outside the scope of the collective-bargaining context would present "additional interference with the First Amendment interests of objecting employees." There is no question as to the expressive and ideological content of these activities. Further, unlike discussion by negotiators regarding the terms and conditions of employment, lobbying and electoral speech are likely to concern topics about which individuals hold strong personal views. Although First Amendment protection is in no way limited to controversial topics or emotionally charged issues, the extent of one's disagreement with the subject of compulsory speech is relevant to the degree of impingement upon free expression that compulsion will effect.

The burden upon freedom of expression is particularly great where, as here, the compelled speech is in a public context. By utilizing petitioners' funds for political lobbying and to garner the support of the public in its endeavors, the union would use each dissenter as "an instrument for fostering public adherence to an ideological point of view he finds unacceptable." The First Amendment protects the individual's right of participation in these spheres from precisely this type of invasion. Where the subject of compelled speech is the discussion of governmental affairs, which is at the core of our First Amendment freedoms, the burden upon dissenters' rights extends far beyond the acceptance of the agency shop and is constitutionally impermissible.

Accordingly, we hold that the State constitutionally may not compel its employees to subsidize legislative lobbying or other political union activities outside the limited context of contract ratification or implementation.

B

Petitioners' contention that they may be charged only for those collective-bargaining activities undertaken directly on behalf of their unit presents a closer question. While we consistently have looked to whether nonideological expenses are "germane to collective bargaining," we have never interpreted that test to require a direct relationship between the expense at issue and some tangible benefit to the dissenters' bargaining unit.

We think that to require so close a connection would be to ignore the unified-membership structure under which many unions, including those here, operate. Under such arrangements, membership in the local union constitutes membership in the state and national parent organizations.

The essence of the affiliation relationship is the notion that the parent will bring to bear its often considerable economic, political, and informational resources when the local is in need of them. Consequently, that part of a local's affiliation fee which contributes to the pool of resources potentially available to the local is assessed for the bargaining unit's protection, even if it is not actually expended on that unit in any particular membership year.

The Court recognized as much in *Ellis.* There it construed the RLA to allow the use of dissenters' funds to help defray the costs of the respondent union's national conventions. It reasoned that "if a union is to perform its statutory functions, it must maintain its corporate or associational existence, must elect officers to manage and carry on its affairs, and may consult its members about overall bargaining goals and policy." We see no reason why analogous public-sector union activities should be treated differently.

We therefore conclude that a local bargaining representative may charge objecting employees for their pro rata share of the costs associated with otherwise chargeable activities of its state and national affiliates, even if those activities were not performed for the direct benefit of the objecting employees' bargaining unit. This conclusion, however, does not serve to grant a local union *carte blanche* to expend dissenters' dollars for bargaining activities wholly unrelated to the employees in their unit. The union surely may not, for example, charge objecting employees for a direct donation or interest-free loan to an unrelated bargaining unit for the purpose of promoting employee rights or unionism generally. Further, a contribution by a local union to its parent that is not part of the local's responsibilities as an affiliate but is in the nature of a charitable donation would not be chargeable to dissenters. There must be some indication that the payment is for services that may ultimately inure to the benefit of the members of the local union by virtue of their membership in the parent organization. And, as always, the union bears the burden of proving the proportion of chargeable expenses to total expenses. We conclude merely that the union need not demonstrate a direct and tangible impact upon the dissenting employee's unit.

C

. . .

We turn to the union activities at issue in this case.

IV

A

The Court of Appeals found that the union could constitutionally charge petitioners for the costs of a Preserve Public Education (PPE) program designed to secure funds for public education in Michigan, and that portion of the MEA publication, the Teacher's Voice, which reported these activities. Petitioners argue that, contrary to the findings of the courts below, the PPE program went beyond lobbying activity and sought to affect the outcome of ballot issues and "millages" or local taxes for the support of public schools. Given our conclusion as to lobbying and electoral politics generally, this factual dispute is of little consequence. None of these activities was shown to be oriented toward the ratification or implementation of petitioners' collective-bargaining agreement. We hold that none may be supported through the funds of objecting employees.

B

Petitioners next challenge the Court of Appeals' allowance of several activities that the union did not undertake directly on behalf of persons within petitioners' bargaining unit. This objection principally concerns NEA "program expenditures" destined for States other than Michigan, and the expenses of the Teacher's Voice listed as "Collective Bargaining" and "Litigation." Our conclusion that unions may bill dissenting employees for their share of general collective-bargaining costs of the state or national parent union is dispositive as to the bulk of the NEA expenditures. The District Court found these costs to be germane to collective bargaining and similar support services and we decline to disturb that finding. No greater relationship is necessary in the collective-bargaining context.

This rationale does not extend, however, to the expenses of litigation that does not concern the dissenting employees' bargaining unit or, by extension, to union literature reporting on such activities. While respondents are clearly correct that precedent established through litigation on behalf of one unit may ultimately be of some use to another unit, we find extraunit litigation to be more akin to lobbying in both kind and effect. We long have recognized the important political and expressive nature of litigation. Moreover, union litigation may cover a diverse range of areas from bankruptcy proceedings to employment discrimination. When unrelated to an objecting employee's unit, such activities are not germane to the union's duties as exclusive bargaining representative. Just as the Court in *Ellis* determined that the RLA, as informed by the First Amendment, prohibits the use of dissenters' fees for extra-unit litigation, we hold that the Amendment proscribes such assessments in the public sector.

C

The Court of Appeals determined that the union constitutionally could charge petitioners for certain public relations expenditures. In this connection, the court said: "Public relations expenditures designed to enhance the reputation of the teaching profession . . . are, in our opinion, sufficiently related to the unions' duty to represent bargaining unit employees effectively so as to be chargeable to dissenters." We disagree. Like the challenged lobbying conduct, the public relations activities at issue here entailed speech of a political nature in a public forum. More important, public speech in support of the teaching profession generally is not sufficiently related to the union's collective-bargaining functions to justify compelling dissenting employees to support it. Expression of this kind extends beyond the negotiation and grievance-resolution contexts and imposes a substantially greater burden upon First Amendment rights than do the latter activities.

Nor do we accept the Court of Appeals' comparison of these public relations expenses to the costs of union social activities held in *Ellis* to be chargeable to dissenters. In *Ellis*, the Court found the communicative content of union social activities, if any, to derive solely from the union's involvement in them. "Therefore," we reasoned, "the fact that the employee is forced to contribute does not increase the infringement of his First Amendment rights already resulting from the compelled contribution to the union." The same cannot be said of the public relations charges upheld by the Court of Appeals which covered "informational picketing, media exposure, signs, posters and buttons."

D

The District Court and the Court of Appeals allowed charges for those portions of the Teachers' Voice that concern teaching and education generally, professional development, unemployment, job opportunities, award programs of the MEA, and other miscellaneous matters. Informational support services such as these are neither political nor public in nature. Although they do not directly concern the members of petitioners' bargaining unit, these expenditures are for the benefit of all and we discern no additional infringement of First Amendment rights that they might occasion. In short, we agree with the Court of Appeals that these expenses are comparable to the *de minimis* social activity charges approved in *Ellis.*

E

The Court of Appeals ruled that the union could use the fees of objecting employees to send FFA delegates to the MEA and the NEA conventions and to participate in the 13E Coordinating Council, another union structure. Petitioners challenge that determination and argue that, unlike the national convention expenses found to be chargeable to dissenters in *Ellis,* the meetings at issue here were those of affiliated parent unions rather than the local, and therefore do not relate exclusively to petitioners' unit.

We need not determine whether petitioners could be commanded to support all the expenses of these conventions. The question before the Court is simply whether the unions may constitutionally require petitioners to subsidize the participation in these events of delegates from the local. We hold that they may. That the conventions were not solely devoted to the activities of the FFA does not prevent the unions from requiring petitioners' support. We conclude above that the First Amendment does not require so close a connection. Moreover, participation by members of the local in the formal activities of the parent is likely to be an important benefit of affiliation. This conclusion is supported by the District Court's description of the 13E Coordinating Council meeting as an event at which "bargaining strategies and representational policies are developed for the UniServ unit composed of the Ferris State College and Central Michigan University bargaining units." As was held in *Ellis,* "[c]onventions such as those at issue here are normal events . . . and seem to us to be essential to the union's discharge of its duties as bargaining agent."

F

The chargeability of expenses incident to preparation for a strike which all concede would have been illegal under Michigan law is a provocative question. At the beginning of the 1981–1982 fiscal year, the FFA and Ferris were engaged in negotiating a new collective-bargaining agreement. The union perceived these efforts to be ineffective and began to prepare a "job action" or, in more familiar terms, to go out on strike. These preparations entailed the creation by the FFA and the MEA of a "crisis center" or "strike headquarters." . . .

Had the FFA actually engaged in an illegal strike, the union clearly could not have charged the expenses incident to that strike to petitioners. We can imagine no legitimate governmental interest that would be served by compelling objecting employees to subsidize activity that the State has chosen to disallow. Similarly, one might expect the State to prohibit unions from using dissenters' funds to threaten or prepare for such conduct. The Michigan Legislature, however, has chosen not to impose such a restriction, and we do not find the First Amendment to require that limitation.

Petitioners can identify no determination by the State of Michigan that mere preparation for an illegal strike is itself illegal or against public policy, and we are aware of none. Further, we accept the rationale provided by the Court of Appeals in upholding these charges that such expenditures fall "within the range of reasonable bargaining tools available to a public sector union during contract negotiations." The District Court expressly credited trial testimony by an MEA representative that outward preparations for a potential strike serve as an effective bargaining tool and that only one out of every seven or eight "job action investigations" actually culminates in a strike. The Court of Appeals properly reviewed this finding for clear error.

In sum, these expenses are substantively indistinguishable from those appurtenant to collective-bargaining negotiations. The District Court and the Court of Appeals concluded, and we agree, that they aid in those negotiations and inure to the direct benefit of members of the dissenters' unit. Further, they impose no additional burden upon First Amendment rights. The union may properly charge petitioners for those costs.

V

The judgment of the Court of Appeals is affirmed in part and reversed in part, and the case is remanded for further proceedings consistent with this opinion.

It is so ordered.

LOANS AND FEDERAL AID

The costs associated with obtaining higher education make financial aid a necessity for many students. While now best known for its student loan programs, the federal government has offered various forms of aid to higher education throughout its history. This entry traces the history of federal financial assistance to higher education from the early use of land grants to promote the establishment of postsecondary institutions to the extensive loan programs implemented in the late 20th and early 21st centuries.

Early Institutional Aid

Early on, the federal government expressed only minute interest in higher education. Prior to the adoption of the U.S. Constitution, the Northwest Ordinance of 1787 supplied land grants to fund the establishment of a university in the territory that became the State of Ohio in 1803. Even so, the federal government did not return to the issue until near the middle of the 19th century. During the Civil War, Congress passed the Morrill Act of 1862, which helped promote two government initiatives. On the one hand, the sale of land grants of unoccupied territory in the West helped encourage settlement as homesteaders purchased and took up residence on the unused land. At the same time, the revenues from the sale of the lands went to support postsecondary schooling by funding institutions and promoting curricular offerings in agricultural and mechanical arts.

In 1890, Congress enacted the Second Morrill Act, which provided direct federal financial appropriations to support agriculture and mechanical curricula. Also known as the Agricultural College Act of 1890, the Second Morrill Act allowed racial segregation to continue in higher education by requiring states either to admit freed slaves to existing land grant institutions or to establish new postsecondary schools to provide these citizens with agricultural and other training.

Established between the passage of the First and Second Morrill Acts, the Hatch Act of 1887 also helped the federal government to promote the cause of agriculture. The Hatch Act provided the first source of direct federal funding to higher education for agricultural experimentation, research in agricultural science, and the establishment of agriculture stations to export agricultural research and curricula to the farmers throughout participating states. Under the Smith-Lever Act of 1914, the agricultural stations created in the Hatch Act became the cooperative extension system within the land grant institutions.

Student Aid and the Cold War

Despite agricultural support, direct student aid did not receive attention from Congress until well into the 20th century. Commonly known as the G. I. Bill, the Servicemen's Readjustment Act of 1944 is the earliest example of federal direct student aid. Under this act, World War II veterans received both stipends and tuition assistance because of their service to the country. Designed to prevent a postwar economic decline, the funds provided an incentive for veterans to delay entering the labor market while also making it easier for them to attend college.

Continuing to focus on national security, the National Defense of Education Act (NDEA, 1958) provided both institutional and student aid to higher education. To institutions, the NDEA offered financial support for academic priorities in science, mathematics, and foreign languages useful in the cold war effort. Further, the NDEA made funds available to provide students with graduate fellowships to pursue degrees in the areas identified as high need. Additionally, the NDEA created the National Defense Student Loan (NDSL), a low-interest loan program for qualified students in areas highlighted by the act. Congress renamed the NDSL as the Federal Perkins Loan under the 1986 reauthorization of the Higher Education Act.

Aid, Expansion, and Social Equity

In the 1960s, federal education legislation shifted attention to social equity issues. Part of President Lyndon B. Johnson's "Great Society," the Economic Opportunity Act of 1964 (EOA) generated a range of new programs focused on helping children and families burdened by poverty. Three of these programs had direct relationship to higher education: Upward Bound, VISTA, and College Work-Study.

Now part of the federal government's TRIO Programs, Upward Bound helps to prepare low-income students to transition to and succeed in postsecondary schools. Volunteers in Service to America, or VISTA, focuses on training volunteers to serve impoverished communities by working with local government agencies or nonprofit organizations.

Developed in 1993, the AmeriCorps Program is a more recent rendition of VISTA that focuses on service to public schools. In fact, AmeriCorps survived a challenge alleging that it violated the Establishment Clause, because some participants taught religion along with secular subjects in religious schools. The circuit court for the District of Columbia ruled that AmeriCorps was constitutional, because as a governmental program that was neutral with regard to religion, it offered assistance directly to individuals who independently chose to use the aid in religious schools (*American Jewish Congress v. Corporation for National and Community Service*, 2005, 2006).

The College Work-Study Program provides part-time employment for students during their enrollment to help them earn money while pursuing an education. Now known as the Federal Work-Study Program, this program continues to support student employment at approximately 3,400 participating institutions at levels equal to or higher than the federal minimum wage.

A year after the EOA was enacted, President Johnson further advanced his Great Society with the passage of the Higher Education Act of 1965, which included several new and consolidated federal provisions related to financial aid. Building on previous legislation, the Higher Education Act (HEA) created the Guaranteed Student Loan (GSL) Program. The act also expanded federal aid offerings with the Educational Opportunity Grant (EOG) Program, which targeted students with high established financial need. Moreover, the EOG is earliest form of gift aid that the federal government provided to students. Unlike other forms of aid, the EOG did not require repayment or previous government service, and it did not have curricular restrictions. Rather, the EOG Program distributed funds to institutions, which could then award the aid to eligible students. In 1972, the Educational Opportunity Grant Program became the Supplemental Educational Opportunity Grant (SEOG) Program. That same year, the federal government created the Basic Educational Opportunity Grant (BEOG) Program. While the SEOG allocates financial aid to institutions, the BEOG awards funds to students who can use the money to attend an appropriate institution of their own choice. Called the Pell Grant since 1980, the BEOG Program offers a maximum award value as set by Congress based on calculated level of student financial need.

Stemming from the Great Society, 1960s legislation helped to expand access to higher education by offering new types of aid to categories of students who received little consideration under previous acts. While the G. I. Bill and the NDEA focused on financial aid to support national priorities, the higher education legislation of the 1960s and early 1970s centered on getting students into postsecondary schools to help address domestic concerns.

Universal Aid

In contrast to the 1960s, legislation of the late 1970s and 1980s shifted to a broader population. Beginning with the 1976 reauthorization of the HEA, the federal government began to both increase the categories of students eligible for aid and add more conditions on students in order to become and remain eligible to receive financial support. Most notably, the 1976 reauthorization added the condition that students make satisfactory academic progress to continue to receive federal financial aid.

Following the 1976 reauthorization legislation, Congress made additional steps toward offering universal financial aid for all college students. In 1978, Congress passed the Middle Income Student Assistance Act (MISAA), which removed the income eligibility requirements from the GSL Program. Renamed the Stafford Loan in 1988, the GSL became the first form of federal aid that was truly available to all college students regardless of family income. Additionally, the MISAA also expanded the eligibility guidelines for the Pell Grant, giving access to more students.

Building on the MISAA, the 1980 and 1986 reauthorizations of the HEA provided the foundation for the development of more aid with fewer eligibility restrictions. In the 1980 reauthorization, Congress created the Parent Loan for Undergraduate Students (PLUS), which gave parents the opportunity to borrow money to cover college costs. Later, the 1986 reauthorization refined the PLUS program by restricting it to parents, thus removing the need to consider a student's ability to repay these loans. In addition, the 1986 reauthorization established the Supplemental Loan to Students (SLS) for graduate, professional, and independent students, thus providing additional resources to these students.

The universal aid movement of the late 1970s and 1980s gave more students access to more money. With each of these loans, the federal government offered student and parent borrowers more ways to finance an education. Likewise, the different interest rates and policies attached to these loan programs placed new burdens on borrowers. Unlike previous loan programs, some loans created during this period accumulated interest while students remained enrolled in higher education. The PLUS program both charges interest and requires repayment while students are still attending postsecondary school.

Loans and Limits

Since the 1980s, loans have been the dominant form of federal financial aid available to postsecondary students at all levels. In order to further entrench loans into the financial aid landscape, the federal government devised the Federal Family Education Loan (FFEL) Program in 1986. The FFEL Program included all existing federal loans and sought to make it easier for students and parents to repay education loans by putting them all together. Yet, the creation of a consolidation program illustrated how loan-driven federal aid had become. Other changes in the 1990s and 2000s further demonstrate the federal government's desire to limit and control its investment in higher education.

In the 1992 reauthorization of the HEA, Congress streamlined the financial aid process by creating the Free Application for Federal Student Aid (FAFSA). With the FAFSA, Congress created one form for all students to use when applying for federal aid. That same year, the federal government made additional changes to the student loan programs in an effort to reduce the nationwide default rate. These changes included extending the grace period to 270 days for students to begin repayment after leaving college, deeming institutions ineligible to distribute federal aid if 25% of their graduates default over a three-year period or 40% default in a single year, and reducing the interest rates to make repayment easier.

Continuing to focus on loans, the Student Loan Reform Act of 1993 increased the federal government's involvement in the programs by having the government take on the role of direct lender. At the same time, this act created the income-contingent repayment option. Later, in 1997, the federal government passed the Taxpayer Relief Act, which provides a range of relief measures related to college costs, including making interest paid on student loans tax deductible. The following year, the 1998 HEA reauthorization created loan cancellation for teachers, made students with drug conviction ineligible to receive federal aid, and authorized FAFSA verification with federal tax records to eliminate fraud in aid applications. More recently, the College Cost Reduction and Access Act (2007) cut payments to student loan lenders, increased the maximum Pell Grant award, and established loan forgiveness opportunities for graduates in a range of public service employment. Clearly, student loans will continue to be the primary form of federal aid available to students and their families for many years to come.

Saran Donahoo

See also Morrill Acts

Further Readings

Baum, S. (2007). It's time for serious reform to the student-aid system. *Change, 39*(2), 15–20.

Beaver, W. (2008). The student loan scandal. *Society, 45*(3), 216–221.

Flint, T. A. (1997). Predicting student loan defaults. *The Journal of Higher Education, 68*(3), 322–354.

Perna, L. (2008). Understanding high school students' willingness to borrow to pay college prices. *Research in Higher Education, 49*(7), 589–606.

Schrag, P. G. (2007). Federal student loan repayment assistance for public interest lawyers and other employees of governments and nonprofit organizations. *Hofstra Law Review, 36*, 27–63.

Legal Citations

Agricultural College Act of 1890 (Second Morrill Act), ch. 841, § 4, 26 Stat. 419 (1890).

American Jewish Congress v. Corporation for National and Community Service, 399 F.3d 351 (D.C. Cir. 2005), *cert. denied*, 546 U.S. 1130 (2006).

College Cost Reduction and Access Act of 2007, Pub. L. No. 110-84, 121 Stat. 784 (2007).

Economic Opportunity Act of 1964, Pub. L. No. 88-452, 78 Stat. 508 (1964).

Hatch Act of 1887, 7 U.S.C. §§ 361a *et seq.*

Higher Education Act of 1965, Pub. L. No. 110-315 (2008).

Middle Income Student Assistance Act, Pub. L. No. 95-561 (1978).

Morrill Act of 1862, ch. 130, § 1, 12 Stat. 503 (1862).

National Defense of Education Act of 1958, Pub. L. No. 85-864, Title I, § 101, 72 Stat. 1581 (1958).

Servicemen's Readjustment Act of 1944 (G. I. Bill), ch. 268, 58 Stat. 284 (1944).

Smith-Hughes National Vocational Education Act of 1917, ch. 114, 39 Stat. 929 (1917).

Smith-Lever Act, 7 U.S.C. §§ 341 *et seq.* (1914).

Taxpayer Relief Act of 1997, Pub. L. No. 105-34 (1997).

Locke v. Davey

Locke v. Davey (2004) concerned the question of whether a state scholarship program violated the Free Exercise Clause of the First Amendment when, in accordance with a state constitutional provision, it explicitly barred funding for students pursuing degrees in theology. In upholding the program, the Supreme Court discussed the relationship between the Free Exercise and Establishment Clauses of the First Amendment. The Court found that the state's policy of refusing to fund theological degrees did not violate students' free exercise rights and that the policy reflected the state's interest against the establishment of religion. As such, *Davey* has important implications for state-sponsored scholarship programs in higher education, because it recognizes that states can impose limits on the amount of scholarship aid that they provide to students who attend religiously affiliated institutions of higher learning.

Facts of the Case

The Washington State Legislature established the Promise Scholarship Program to assist eligible postsecondary students with education-related expenses. The scholarship, which was renewable for one year, was paid for out of the state's general fund, prorated among all eligible students. In 1999–2000, the scholarship awarded $1,125 to each student. In order to qualify, students had to meet specified requirements. First, the student had to have graduated from a high school in Washington State. Second, the student must have graduated in the top 15% of his or her class or have achieved a score of at least 1,200 on the SAT I or 27 on the ACT. Third, the income of the student's family could not be higher than 135% of the state average. Fourth, the student had to enroll at least half time in an eligible institution of higher education in Washington State. Eligible institutions included religiously affiliated, accredited colleges and universities. However, consistent with the state constitution's anti–religious establishment provision, the statute further required that no scholarship could be awarded to a student pursuing a degree in theology. Students using scholarship funds were permitted to attend classes in theology, provided that they were seeking degrees in different fields.

Jonathan Davey received a Promise Scholarship and enrolled in Northwest College (now Northwest University), a private, accredited institution located near Seattle that was associated with the Assemblies of God Church. Davey, whose ambition was to become a church pastor, chose to pursue a double major in pastoral studies and business administration. At a meeting with the college's financial aid director, Davey discovered that he would be unable to receive his Promise Scholarship unless he signed a form stating that he would not use the money to pursue a theological degree. When he refused to sign the form, Davey did not receive any of the funds. Davey then filed suit against state officials based on the theory that their refusal to disburse the scholarship funds to him violated the Free Speech, Establishment, and Free Exercise Clauses of the First Amendment as well as the Equal Protection Clause of the Fourteenth Amendment.

A federal trial court in Washington State denied Davey's request for a preliminary injunction that would have prevented officials from withholding the scholarship funds before granting the defendants' motion for summary judgment, essentially dismissing his claim. On appeal, the Ninth Circuit reversed in favor of Davey in reasoning that the state impermissibly singled out religion for unfavorable treatment. Because the state's concerns about preventing the establishment of religion did not amount to a compelling state interest, the court held that the state had infringed on Davey's right to free exercise of religion. Dissatisfied with the outcome, state officials sought further review.

The Supreme Court's Ruling

The U.S. Supreme Court reversed the judgment of the Ninth Circuit, declaring that the restrictions on funding under the Promise Scholarship Program did not violate either the Free Exercise or Free Speech Clauses. Chief Justice Rehnquist, writing for the majority, rejected the plaintiff's assertion that the scholarship's lack of facial neutrality toward religion necessarily meant that the restrictions violated the First Amendment. The Court explained that excluding funding for theological degrees was not presumptively unconstitutional, because the state was neither criminalizing nor penalizing the study of theology. Instead, the Court pointed out that the state merely refused to pay for the student's study of theology. To this end, the Court maintained that the state was not obligated to provide funding for such degrees simply because it offered scholarships for degrees in secular subjects.

In rejecting Davey's free speech claims, the Supreme Court posited that because the scholarship was not a forum for speech, the state's refusal to fund theological degrees could not be considered viewpoint discrimination. If anything, the Court interpreted the state's purpose in establishing the scholarship program as being designed to assist lower-income college students, not to promote diverse viewpoints on campus. The Court next rejected Davey's assertion that the state constitutional provision in question was motivated by antireligious, particularly anti-Catholic, bias, finding no evidence to suggest that the prohibition on funding theological degrees was motivated by an animus toward religion. Because the state's actions did not violate Davey's free exercise rights, the

Court required only that the state show a rational basis for the different treatment afforded to theology students. The Court added that the state had a substantial interest in not funding degrees in theology, because the state constitution forbade such aid. Further, the Court was convinced that the lack of such funding placed a relatively minor burden on students. As such, the Court concluded that the state did not violate Davey's rights to equal protection.

Justice Scalia, joined by Justice Thomas, dissented. Scalia asserted that the state's establishment of a new benefit through the Promise Scholarship created a new baseline against which the Court ought to have measured burdens on religion. According to Scalia, the state, in its assessment, was seeking to replace one benefit, namely money to pursue students' chosen areas of study, with lesser benefits of money to pursue courses of study that individuals would not have chosen. Scalia thus rejected the majority's claim that the lack of animus toward religion on the part of the authors of the state constitution was relevant to the case at bar. In cases dealing with other varieties of facial discrimination, Scalia observed, such as discrimination on the basis of sex or race, the Court considered primarily the present-day effects of the law and only secondarily the motives of the legislators. In Justice Scalia's view, when the state chose to withhold the full benefit of the scholarship only from those students who wished to study theology, its doing so violated the Free Exercise Clause.

James Mawdsley

See also Equal Protection Analysis; State Aid and the Establishment Clause

Further Readings

Russo, C. J., & Mawdsley, R. D. (2004). *Locke v. Davey:* The Supreme Court limits state aid to students in religious institutions. *School Business Affairs, 70*(7), 36–38.

Legal Citations

Locke v. Davey, 540 U.S. 712 (2004).

LOCKE V. DAVEY

In *Locke*, the Supreme Court found that a student who was studying for the ministry was ineligible to participate in a state scholarship program that barred funding to theology, because the program restriction was consistent with the First Amendment's Establishment Clause and did not violate the a student's right to free exercise of religion.

Supreme Court of the United States

LOCKE

v.

DAVEY

540 U.S. 712

Argued Dec. 2, 2003

Decided Feb. 25, 2004

Chief Justice REHNQUIST delivered the opinion of the Court.

The State of Washington established the Promise Scholarship Program to assist academically gifted students with postsecondary education expenses. In accordance with the State Constitution, students may not use the scholarship at an institution where they are pursuing a degree in devotional theology. We hold that such an exclusion from an otherwise inclusive aid program does not violate the Free Exercise Clause of the First Amendment.

The Washington State Legislature found that "[s]tudents who work hard . . . and successfully complete high school with high academic marks may not have the financial ability to attend college because they cannot obtain financial aid or the financial aid is insufficient." In 1999, to assist these high-achieving students, the legislature created the Promise Scholarship Program, which provides a scholarship, renewable for one year, to eligible students for postsecondary education expenses. Students may spend their funds on any education-related expense, including room and board. The scholarships are funded through the State's general fund, and their amount varies each year depending on the annual appropriation, which is evenly prorated among the eligible students. The scholarship was worth $1,125 for academic year 1999–2000 and $1,542 for 2000–2001.

To be eligible for the scholarship, a student must meet academic, income, and enrollment requirements. A student must graduate from a Washington public or private high school and either graduate in the top 15% of his graduating class, or attain on the first attempt a cumulative score of 1,200 or better on the Scholastic Assessment Test I or a score of 27 or better on the American College Test. The student's family income must be less than 135% of the State's median. Finally, the student must enroll "at least half time in an eligible postsecondary institution in the state of Washington," and may not pursue a degree in theology at that institution while receiving the scholarship. Private institutions, including those religiously affiliated, qualify as "[e]ligible postsecondary institution[s]" if they are accredited by a nationally recognized accrediting body. A "degree in theology" is not defined in the statute, but, as both parties concede, the statute simply codifies the State's constitutional prohibition on providing funds to students to pursue degrees that are "devotional in nature or designed to induce religious faith."

A student who applies for the scholarship and meets the academic and income requirements is notified that he is eligible for the scholarship if he meets the enrollment requirements. Once the student enrolls at an eligible institution, the institution must certify that the student is enrolled at least half time and that the student is not pursuing a degree in devotional theology. The institution, rather than the State, determines whether the student's major is devotional. *Id.*, at 126, 131. If the student meets the enrollment requirements, the scholarship funds are sent to the institution for distribution to the student to pay for tuition or other educational expenses.

Respondent, Joshua Davey, was awarded a Promise Scholarship, and chose to attend Northwest College. Northwest is a private, Christian college affiliated with the Assemblies of God denomination, and is an eligible institution under the Promise Scholarship Program. Davey had "planned for many years to attend a Bible college and to prepare [himself] through that college training for a lifetime of ministry, specifically as a church pastor." To that end, when he enrolled in Northwest College, he decided to pursue a double major in pastoral ministries and business management/administration. There is no dispute that the pastoral ministries degree is devotional and therefore excluded under the Promise Scholarship Program.

At the beginning of the 1999–2000 academic year, Davey met with Northwest's director of financial aid. He learned for the first time at this meeting that he could not use his scholarship to pursue a devotional theology degree. He was informed that to receive the funds appropriated for his use, he must certify in writing that he was not pursuing such a degree at Northwest. He refused to sign the form and did not receive any scholarship funds.

Davey then brought an action under . . . 42 U.S.C. § 1983, against various state officials (hereinafter State) in the District Court for the Western District of Washington to enjoin the State from refusing to award the scholarship solely because a student is pursuing a devotional theology degree, and for damages. He argued the denial of his scholarship based on his decision to pursue a theology degree violated, *inter alia*, the Free Exercise, Establishment, and Free Speech Clauses of the First Amendment, as incorporated by the Fourteenth Amendment, and the Equal Protection Clause of the Fourteenth Amendment. After the District Court denied Davey's request for a preliminary injunction, the parties filed cross-motions for summary judgment. The District Court rejected Davey's constitutional claims and granted summary judgment in favor of the State.

A divided panel of the United States Court of Appeals for the Ninth Circuit reversed. The court concluded that the State had singled out religion for unfavorable treatment and thus under our decision in *Church of Lukumi Babalu Aye, Inc. v. Hialeah*, the State's exclusion of theology majors must be narrowly tailored to achieve a compelling state interest. Finding that the State's own antiestablishment concerns were not compelling, the court declared Washington's Promise Scholarship Program unconstitutional. We granted certiorari and now reverse.

The Religion Clauses of the First Amendment provide: "Congress shall make no law respecting an establishment of religion, or prohibiting the free exercise thereof." These two Clauses, the Establishment Clause and the Free Exercise Clause, are frequently in tension. Yet we have long said that "there is room for play in the

joints" between them. In other words, there are some state actions permitted by the Establishment Clause but not required by the Free Exercise Clause.

This case involves that "play in the joints" described above. Under our Establishment Clause precedent, the link between government funds and religious training is broken by the independent and private choice of recipients. As such, there is no doubt that the State could, consistent with the Federal Constitution, permit Promise Scholars to pursue a degree in devotional theology and the State does not contend otherwise. The question before us, however, is whether Washington, pursuant to its own constitution, which has been authoritatively interpreted as prohibiting even indirectly funding religious instruction that will prepare students for the ministry, can deny them such funding without violating the Free Exercise Clause.

Davey urges us to answer that question in the negative. He contends that under the rule we enunciated in *Church of Lukumi Babalu Aye, Inc. v. Hialeah*, the program is presumptively unconstitutional because it is not facially neutral with respect to religion. We reject his claim of presumptive unconstitutionality, however; to do otherwise would extend the *Lukumi* line of cases well beyond not only their facts but their reasoning. In *Lukumi*, the city of Hialeah made it a crime to engage in certain kinds of animal slaughter. We found that the law sought to suppress ritualistic animal sacrifices of the Santeria religion. In the present case, the State's disfavor of religion (if it can be called that) is of a far milder kind. It imposes neither criminal nor civil sanctions on any type of religious service or rite. It does not deny to ministers the right to participate in the political affairs of the community. And it does not require students to choose between their religious beliefs and receiving a government benefit. The State has merely chosen not to fund a distinct category of instruction.

Justice SCALIA argues, however, that generally available benefits are part of the "baseline against which burdens on religion are measured." Because the Promise Scholarship Program funds training for all secular professions, Justice SCALIA contends the State must also fund training for religious professions. But training for religious professions and training for secular professions are not fungible. Training someone to lead a congregation is an essentially religious endeavor. Indeed, majoring in devotional theology is akin to a religious calling as well as an academic pursuit. And the subject of religion is one in which both the United States and state constitutions embody distinct views—in favor of free exercise, but opposed to establishment—that find no counterpart with respect to other callings or professions. That a State would deal differently with religious education for the ministry than with education for other callings is a product of these views, not evidence of hostility toward religion.

Even though the differently worded Washington Constitution draws a more stringent line than that drawn by the United States Constitution, the interest it seeks to further is scarcely novel. In fact, we can think of few areas in which a State's antiestablishment interests come more into play. Since the founding of our country, there have been popular uprisings against procuring taxpayer funds to support church leaders, which was one of the hallmarks of an "established" religion.

Most States that sought to avoid an establishment of religion around the time of the founding placed in their constitutions formal prohibitions against using tax funds to support the ministry. The plain text of these constitutional provisions prohibited *any* tax dollars from supporting the clergy. We have found nothing to indicate, as Justice SCALIA contends, that these provisions would not have applied so long as the State equally supported other professions or if the amount at stake was *de minimis*. That early state constitutions saw no problem in explicitly excluding *only* the ministry from receiving state dollars reinforces our conclusion that religious instruction is of a different ilk.

Far from evincing the hostility toward religion which was manifest in *Lukumi*, we believe that the entirety of the Promise Scholarship Program goes a long way toward including religion in its benefits. The program permits students to attend pervasively religious schools, so long as they are accredited. As Northwest advertises, its "concept of education is distinctly Christian in the evangelical sense." It prepares *all* of its students, "through instruction, through modeling, [and] through [its] classes, to use . . . the Bible as their guide, as the truth," no matter their chosen profession. And under the Promise Scholarship Program's current guidelines, students are still eligible to take devotional theology courses. Davey notes all students at Northwest are required to take at least four devotional courses, "Exploring the Bible," "Principles of Spiritual Development," "Evangelism in the Christian Life," and "Christian Doctrine," and some students may have additional religious requirements as part of their majors.

In short, we find neither in the history or text of Article I, § I I, of the Washington Constitution, nor in the operation of the Promise Scholarship Program, anything that suggests animus toward religion. Given the historic and substantial state interest at issue, we therefore cannot conclude that the denial of funding for vocational religious instruction alone is inherently constitutionally suspect.

Without a presumption of unconstitutionality, Davey's claim must fail. The State's interest in not funding the pursuit of devotional degrees is substantial and the exclusion of such funding places a relatively minor burden on Promise Scholars. If any room exists between the two Religion Clauses, it must be here. We need not venture further into this difficult area in order to uphold the Promise Scholarship Program as currently operated by the State of Washington.

The judgment of the Court of Appeals is therefore *Reversed.*

LOYALTY OATHS

In the aftermath of World War II, amid concerns about communist infiltration in the United States, employers in government, education, and other arenas began to make use of loyalty oaths, a widespread practice with an extensive history tracing its origins to the ancient world. Educators and other public employees in the government and educational systems were required to sign such oaths as a condition of employment. As oaths became increasingly far reaching in nature, some forbade educators from joining specified organizations, while others required individuals to attest that they did not engage in specified (typically political) activities or belong to particular organizations. Although such activities and memberships would not ordinarily make applicants subject to criminal sanctions, failure to attest to the required oaths resulted in the applicants being rendered ineligible for teaching (Hyman, 1959).

Black's Law Dictionary describes an oath as "Any form of attestation by which a person signifies that he is bound in conscience to perform an act faithfully and truthfully." *Black's* also defines a loyalty oath as

> an oath by which a person promises and binds himself to bear true allegiance to a particular sovereign or government and to support its Constitution, administered generally to certain public officers or officials, to members of the armed services, to attorneys on being admitted to the bar, to aliens applying for naturalization. (p. 966)

Article II, Section 1 of the U.S. Constitution, for example, states that the president, "before he enter on the execution of his office, he shall take the following oath or affirmation," and Article VI addresses office holders who "shall be bound by oath or affirmation, to support this Constitution." Likewise, personnel in higher education have been asked to sign loyalty oaths that have often been challenged, with mixed results. In light of the role that loyalty oaths continue to play, this entry examines the history of loyalty oaths in American higher education, including cases from the world of K–12 schooling because of the precedential role that these disputes played in reviewing the constitutionality of such affirmations.

As loyalty oaths proliferated in post–World War II America, litigation began to emerge over their constitutionality. *Wieman v. Updegraff* (1952) arose when the state legislature in Oklahoma enacted a statute requiring state employees to take an oath affirming that they were not, nor had they been in the preceding five years, members of organizations that were named on the U.S. attorney general's list of "communist" or "subversive" groups. After a group of employees refused to take the oath, the Supreme Court struck down the law as unconstitutional. The Court held that the statute violated the Fourteenth Amendment, because its indiscriminate classification of innocent persons without their full knowledge of whether their activities may have been against the law when they engaged in the conduct contravened their right to due process.

Adler v. Board of Education of New York City (1952), which reached the opposite outcome from *Wieman*, was litigated in a K–12 setting. *Adler* involved a statute that while, like *Sweezy* (see below), not requiring a loyalty oath per se, was designed to implement and enforce older laws to

the same effect. Under the new law, educators who were members of subversive organizations were disqualified from working in public schools. In upholding the statute, the Supreme Court found that there was "no constitutional infirmity" in its wording that would have rendered educators in public school ineligible to work if they belonged to organizations that advocated the overthrow of the government by force. The Court decided that the law was constitutional because it did not limit the freedom of speech or assembly of the plaintiffs insofar as once they were notified of the statutory requirements, they had the choice of retaining their memberships in the organizations or discontinuing their jobs as public employees.

In a second case from New York City, a faculty member at a public college filed suit after he was dismissed for refusing to answer questions from a federal legislative committee about his communist activities because of his fear of self-incrimination. In *Slochower v. Board of Education* (1956), the Supreme Court maintained that because such a requirement would have essentially eviscerated the privilege against self-incrimination and was squarely within the prohibition that it established in *Wieman*, it was unconstitutional.

Sweezy v. New Hampshire (1957) involved a faculty member's challenge of a contempt conviction for refusing to respond to inquiries about his knowledge of political parties and their members. In a case that did not concern a loyalty oath per se, the Supreme Court thus invalidated the conviction on the basis that the questions that he refused to answer violated his rights to academic freedom and political expression. *Shelton v. Tucker* (1960) dealt with a law from Arkansas that required educators in public institutions, including faculty at colleges and universities, to file annual affidavits listing the organizations they had belonged to or contributed to within the past five years. The contracts of educators who refused to file the affidavits were not renewed. In invalidating the statute, the Supreme Court ruled that while state officials could investigate the competence and experience of the educators that they hired, the statute unconstitutionally impaired the rights of employees both to free association and freedom of speech.

In *Cramp v. Board of Public Instruction* (1961), a teacher from Florida who refused to sign an oath nine years after he was hired filed suit when his action led to his dismissal from his job. While recognizing the right of states to expect loyalty from their employees, the Supreme Court invalidated the underlying statute for vagueness and for being overly broad, because it failed to describe the forbidden behavior adequately.

In 1932, Washington State enacted a law requiring individuals who applied for teaching licenses or license renewals to swear an oath respecting the American flag and pledging their allegiance to the United States. A 1955 law required state employees to swear that they were not subversive persons or member of the Communist Party or subversive organizations. Teachers, other public employees, and students subsequently filed suit, challenging the constitutionality of the law. In *Baggett v. Bullitt* (1964), the Supreme Court vitiated the statutes that authorized both oaths as unconstitutional, because they were so vague that individuals had to guess as to their meanings and whether they complied with the laws.

Elfbrandt v. Russell (1966), involving an oath not unlike the one in *Adler,* concerned a challenge to a statute that required individuals to take a loyalty oath and that denied public employment to those who ever belonged to or were associated with organizations with unlawful ends, even if individuals were unaware of what the group believed in or whether they actually subscribed to those beliefs. The Supreme Court observed that the statute was unconstitutional to the extent that the Court was convinced that the law was based on the impermissible inference that individuals necessarily shared the unlawful goals of organizations to which they belonged.

Keyishian v. Board of Regents of the State of New York (1967) involved litigation by faculty members who challenged their loss of employment for refusing to sign an oath stating that they were not members of the Communist Party (O'Neill, 2008). The Supreme Court ruled that the statute was unconstitutionally vague, not only because it lacked objective measures to evaluate the actions of individuals but also because it unlawfully abridged the faculty members' right to freedom of association.

Conversely, a year later, in another case from New York, the Supreme Court reached the opposite result in summarily affirming an order of a federal trial court. In *Knight v. Board of Regents of the University of the State of New York* (1967,

1968), the Court upheld an oath requiring employees to support the federal and state constitutions in performing their duties. The trial court was of the opinion that the oath passed constitutional muster insofar as it neither placed restrictions on political or philosophical expressions nor was it impermissibly vague.

In the first of two cases relying on *Knight,* the Supreme Court upheld a similar statute from Florida in *Connell v. Higginbotham* (1971). The Court pointed out that the statute was constitutional, because it did not treat state employees any differently from federal employees. In *Biklen v. Board of Education* (1972), the Court essentially upheld the constitutionality of the oath from *Knight* in the face of a challenge from a teacher who objected for religious reasons. The Court affirmed that because the teacher had the opportunity to take the oath and keep her job, she was not entitled to a hearing before officials terminated her employment contract. In the same year, in *Cole v. Richardson* (1972), the Court upheld a similar oath from Massachusetts. According to the Court, the statute was constitutional, because wording that required individuals to uphold and defend the federal and commonwealth constitutions from being overthrown violently did not violate the First Amendment speech or Fourteenth Amendment due process rights of public employees.

Disagreements over loyalty oaths continue to generate controversy. In a 2008 incident that did not involve litigation, a mathematics teacher at California State University–Hayward refused, on the basis that it violated her Quaker religious beliefs against bearing arms, to sign an oath that she would "support and defend" the U.S. and California constitutions against their enemies. University officials refused to allow her to modify the language to state that she would do so "nonviolently." She was fired for her refusal to sign but was later reinstated (Hendricks, 2008). In allowing the faculty member to return to work, university officials cited a 1946 U.S. Supreme Court case affirming that public employees need not violate their religious beliefs in their defense of the government and noted that they had never intended to force the employee to violate her religious beliefs by engaging in acts of violence.

Robert J. Safransky

See also Academic Freedom; *Keyishian v. Board of Regents of the University of the State of New York*

Further Readings

Black, H. C. (1979). *Black's law dictionary* (5th ed.). St. Paul, MN: West.

Euben, D. R. (2001). *Legal watch: Academic freedom, loyalty oaths, and diversity in academe.* Retrieved April 27, 2009, from http://www.aaup.org/AAUP/pubsres/academe/2001/MJ/Cols/lw.htm

Hendricks, T. (2008, March 8). Pacifist Cal State teacher gets job back. *San Francisco Chronicle*, p. B8. Retrieved April 27, 2009, from http://www.sfgate.com/cgi-bin/article.cgi?f=/c/a/2008/03/08/BADRVG6CI.DTL

Hyman, H. M. (1959). *To try men's souls: Loyalty oaths in American history.* Berkeley: University of California Press.

O'Neill, R. M. (2008). The story of *Keyishian v. Board of Regents:* Loyalty oaths, academic freedom and free speech in the university community. In M. A. Olivas & R. G. Olivas (Eds.), *Education law stories* (pp. 285–302). New York: Foundation Press.

Schrecker, E. (1999, October 7). *Political tests for professors: Academic freedom during the McCarthy years.* Talk delivered as part of the University Loyalty Oath: A 50th Anniversary Perspective Symposium, University of California at Berkeley. Retrieved April 27, 2009, from http://sunsite.berkeley.edu/uchistory/archives_exhibits/loyaltyoath/symposium/schrecker.html

Legal Citations

Adler v. Board of Education of the City of New York, 342 U.S. 485 (1952).

Baggett v. Bullitt, 377 U.S. 360 (1964).

Biklen v. Board of Education, 406 U.S. 951 (1972).

Cole v. Richardson, 405 U.S. 676 (1972).

Connell v. Higginbotham, 403 U.S. 207 (1971).

Cramp v. Board of Public Instruction, 368 U.S. 278 (1961).

Elfbrandt v. Russell, 384 U.S. 11 (1966).

Keyishian v. Board of Regents of the University of the State of New York, 385 U.S. 589 (1967).

Knight v. Board of Regents of the University of the State of New York, 269 F. Supp. 339 (S.D.N.Y. 1967), *aff'd*, 390 U.S. 36 (1968).

Shelton v. Tucker, 364 U.S. 479 (1960).

Slochower v. Board of Higher Education of New York City, 350 U.S. 551 (1956).

Sweezy v. New Hampshire, 354 U.S. 234 (1957), *reh'g denied*, 355 U.S. 852 (1957).

Wieman v. Updegraff, 344 U.S. 183 (1952).

M

MCLAURIN V. OKLAHOMA STATE REGENTS FOR HIGHER EDUCATION

McLaurin v. Oklahoma State Regents for Higher Education (1950) was one of the key cases that invalidated intra- and interinstitution racial segregation in colleges and universities that helped to pave the way for *Brown v. Board of Education, Topeka* (1954). In *McLaurin* and its companion case, *Sweatt v. Painter* (1950), the U.S. Supreme Court held that African American students must receive the same treatment as all other students in the realm of higher education.

Facts of the Case

The litigation in *McLaurin* began to take shape when an African American student with a master's degree applied for admission to the University of Oklahoma in pursuit of a doctorate in education but was denied entry solely due to his race. At the time, an Oklahoma law made it a misdemeanor to operate, teach at, or attend an educational institution that admitted both White and African American students. The student filed a complaint for injunctive relief, claiming that the statute was unconstitutional, because it deprived him of equal protection of the laws.

A three-judge federal trial court determined that officials in Oklahoma had a constitutional duty to provide the plaintiff with the education he wanted as soon as they offered the same to students of any other race. Although the court declared that the statute allowing officials to deny the student

admission to the program was null and void, it refused to grant his request for an injunction based on the assumption that officials would follow the constitutional mandate in its order. Even so, the court retained jurisdiction of the case in order to provide the student with equal protection of the laws with regard to his education.

In response, legislators in Oklahoma amended the statute, permitting African Americans to be admitted to institutions provided that the education was "upon a segregated basis." The student was then admitted to the Graduate School of the University of Oklahoma, a state-funded institution, where he was permitted to use the same cafeteria, library, and classrooms as White students. However, he was not allowed to eat at the same time as all other students

As a result of the amended Oklahoma law, though, the plaintiff was assigned to a row of seats in the classroom reserved for African American students, had to sit at an assigned table in the library, and while he was allowed to eat in the cafeteria, he had a designated table and was assigned to eat at a different time from other students. After the plaintiff unsuccessfully filed a motion to amend the earlier order and judgment of the trial court, he appealed to the Supreme Court.

During the time between the student's having filed his appeal and the Supreme Court's having conducted oral arguments, university officials modified their treatment of the plaintiff. The sign that hung around the student's sites in the classroom stating "Reserved For Colored" was removed, and he was assigned to a table on the main floor of the library; his previous table was on the mezzanine level.

The Supreme Court's Ruling

On appeal, the Supreme Court focused on the question of whether officials could treat a student at a state university differently from other students based solely on his race. In a unanimous decision authored by Chief Justice Vinson, the Court reversed in favor of the student. The Court reasoned that under the Fourteenth Amendment's Equal Protection Clause, state officials had the legal duty to treat the plaintiff in the same manner as students of other races.

Using sweeping language, the Supreme Court acknowledged that because American society was changing, discrimination based on race had no place in education. In addition, the Court ruled that insofar as the restrictions that officials imposed on the student impaired and inhibited his ability to study and to engage in discussions and debates with other students as well as faculty, this treatment had a detrimental impact on his overall educational experience.

In its defense, attorneys for the State of Oklahoma argued that the restrictions that officials imposed on African American students were nominal, because the facilities were made available to all students and the rooms that he was assigned had no disadvantages when compared to those used by all other students. The Court summarily dismissed this argument, noting that the treatment set the plaintiff apart from other students even if he had been allowed to use the same facilities, because he was still restricted as to where he could sit. In fact, the Court responded that the restrictions were designed to comply with the state statute that ordered officials in institutions of higher education to treat students differently based on their races. As a result, the Court pointed out that the plaintiff was held back in pursuit of his education, because he was unable to debate and discuss his ideas with other students and faculty with the result that his ability to learn his chosen profession, teaching, was hampered.

As part of its analysis, the Supreme Court recognized that because society was becoming more diverse and complex, the country needed a greater number of well-educated teachers. To this end, the Court observed that by pursuing his doctorate in education, the plaintiff endeavored to become a teacher and leader whose students would reflect the education that he received. In this regard, the Court was convinced that the plaintiff deserved an education that was equal to that of his peers in order to provide future generations of students with proper education and development. As a result, the Court asserted that any state-imposed restriction that produced inequalities could not be continued.

At the same time, the Supreme Court addressed the State's argument that the restrictions might have benefited the plaintiff by enabling him to avoid discriminatory acts by his fellow students. The Court rejected this argument as holding no weight, indicating there is a vast difference between the state-imposed discrimination that resulted from the admissions policy based on race and the discrimination of private individuals. While the Court conceded that the removal of the restrictions would not necessarily have eliminated the prejudices of some students, it was still inappropriate for the state, through institutional officials and the weight that their actions carried, to have deprived the plaintiff and other students of opportunities afforded to other students.

Rounding out its opinion, the Supreme Court ruled that officials at the University of Oklahoma violated the student's right to equal protection of the law by denying him an education that was equal to that of his peers. The Court thus concluded that the Fourteenth Amendment precluded the enforcement of the Oklahoma statute that required African American students to be treated differently and that because the plaintiff had been admitted to a state-supported school, he had to be treated like every other student, regardless of his race.

Megan L. Rehberg

See also Equal Protection Analysis; Fourteenth Amendment; *Sweatt v. Painter*

Legal Citations

Brown v. Board of Education, Topeka, 347 U.S. 483 (1954).

McLaurin v. Oklahoma State Regents for Higher Education, 339 U.S. 637 (1950).

Sweatt v. Painter, 339 U.S. 629 (1950).

McLAURIN V. OKLAHOMA STATE REGENTS FOR HIGHER EDUCATION

McLaurin, decided on the same day as *Sweatt v. Painter*, stands out because in it, the Supreme Court invalidated racial segregation in higher education.

Supreme Court of the United States

McLAURIN

v.

OKLAHOMA STATE REGENTS FOR HIGHER EDUCATION

339 U.S. 637

Argued April 3, 4, 1950

Decided June 5, 1950

Mr. Chief Justice VINSON delivered the opinion of the Court.

In this case, we are faced with the question whether a state may, after admitting a student to graduate instruction in its state university, afford him different treatment from other students solely because of his race. We decide only this issue.

Appellant is a Negro citizen of Oklahoma. Possessing a Master's degree, he applied for admission to the University of Oklahoma in order to pursue studies and courses leading to a Doctorate in Education. At that time, his application was denied, solely because of his race. The school authorities were required to exclude him by the Oklahoma statutes which made it a misdemeanor to maintain or operate, teach or attend a school at which both whites and Negroes are enrolled or taught. Appellant filed a complaint requesting injunctive relief, alleging that the action of the school authorities and the statutes upon which their action was based were unconstitutional and deprived him of the equal protection of the laws. Citing our decisions in *State of Missouri ex rel. Gaines v. Canada* and *Sipuel v. Board of Regents,* a statutory three-judge District Court held that the State had a constitutional duty to provide him with the education he sought as soon as it provided that education for applicants of any other group. It further held that to the extent the Oklahoma statutes denied him admission they were unconstitutional and void. On the assumption, however, that the State would follow the constitutional mandate, the court refused to grant the injunction, retaining jurisdiction of the cause with full power to issue any necessary and proper orders to secure McLaurin the equal protection of the laws.

Following this decision, the Oklahoma legislature amended these statutes to permit the admission of Negroes to institutions of higher learning attended by white students, in cases where such institutions offered courses not available in the Negro schools. The amendment provided, however, that in such cases the program of instruction "shall be given at such colleges or institutions of higher education upon a segregated basis." Appellant was thereupon admitted to the University of Oklahoma Graduate School. In apparent conformity with the amendment, his admission was made subject to "such rules and regulations as to segregation as the President of the University shall consider to afford Mr. G. W. McLaurin substantially equal educational opportunities as are afforded to other persons seeking the same education in the Graduate College," a condition which does not appear to have been withdrawn. Thus he was required to sit apart at a designated desk in an anteroom adjoining the classroom; to sit at a designated desk on the mezzanine floor of the library, but not to use the desks in the regular reading room; and to sit at a designated table and to eat at a different time from the other students in the school cafeteria.

To remove these conditions, appellant filed a motion to modify the order and judgment of the District Court. That court held that such treatment did not violate the provisions of the Fourteenth Amendment and denied the motion. This appeal followed.

In the interval between the decision of the court below and the hearing in this Court, the treatment afforded appellant was altered. For some time, the section of the classroom in which appellant sat was surrounded by a rail on which there was a sign stating, "Reserved For Colored," but these have been removed. He is now assigned to a seat in the classroom in a row specified for colored students; he is assigned to a table in the library on the main floor; and he is permitted to eat at the same time in the cafeteria as other students, although here again he is assigned to a special table.

It is said that the separations imposed by the State in this case are in form merely nominal. McLaurin uses the same classroom, library and cafeteria as students of other races; there is no indication that the seats to which he is assigned in these rooms have any disadvantage of location. He may wait in line in the cafeteria and there stand and talk with his fellow students, but while he eats he must remain apart.

These restrictions were obviously imposed in order to comply, as nearly as could be, with the statutory requirements of Oklahoma. But they signify that the State, in administering the facilities it affords for professional and graduate study, sets McLaurin apart from the other students. The result is that appellant is handicapped in his pursuit of effective graduate instruction. Such restrictions impair and inhibit his ability to study, to engage in discussions and exchange views with other students, and, in general, to learn his profession.

Our society grows increasingly complex, and our need for trained leaders increases correspondingly. Appellant's case represents, perhaps, the epitome of that need, for he is attempting to obtain an advanced degree in education, to become, by definition, a leader and trainer of others. Those who will come under his guidance and influence must be directly affected by the education he receives. Their own education and development will necessarily suffer to the extent that his training is unequal to that of his classmates. State-imposed restrictions which produce such inequalities cannot be sustained.

It may be argued that appellant will be in no better position when these restrictions are removed, for he may still be set apart by his fellow students. This we think irrelevant. There is a vast difference—a Constitutional difference—between restrictions imposed by the state which prohibit the intellectual commingling of students, and the refusal of individuals to commingle where the state presents no such bar. The removal of the state restrictions will not necessarily abate individual and group predilections, prejudices and choices. But at the very least, the state will not be depriving appellant of the opportunity to secure acceptance by his fellow students on his own merits.

We conclude that the conditions under which this appellant is required to receive his education deprive him of his personal and present right to the equal protection of the laws. We hold that under these circumstances the Fourteenth Amendment precludes differences in treatment by the state based upon race. Appellant, having been admitted to a state-supported graduate school, must receive the same treatment at the hands of the state as students of other races. The judgment is

Reversed.

MISSISSIPPI UNIVERSITY FOR WOMEN V. HOGAN

In *Mississippi University for Women v. Hogan* (1982), the U.S. Supreme Court explored the applicability of the Fourteenth Amendment's Equal Protection Clause within the context of admissions and gender. In a five-to-four decision, the Court held that officials at the publicly funded women's university, in denying admission to a male nursing applicant on the basis of his gender, violated the Equal Protection Clause, because the admission policy was not substantially related to a compelling governmental interest. The Court also reasoned that exemptions provided to single-sex institutions within the text of Title IX of the Education Amendments of 1972 did not exempt university officials from compliance with constitutional obligations. *Hogan* stands out as significant, because the Court relied on it in subsequent gender admissions cases in higher education, including, perhaps most notably, *United States v. Virginia* (1996), in which it found that the Virginia Military Institute's refusal to admit women violated the Equal Protection Clause.

Facts of the Case

Established in Columbus, Mississippi, in 1884, Mississippi University for Women (MUW)

historically limited its enrollment to female students. In 1974, the university instituted a four-year baccalaureate program in nursing. Five years later, the plaintiff, Joe Hogan, applied for admission. The plaintiff, a registered nurse in Columbus, Mississippi, did not possess a bachelor's degree. Although he otherwise met enrollment requirements, the plaintiff was denied admission to the nursing program on the basis of his gender. Officials at MUW informed the plaintiff that he could audit courses in which he was interested but could not enroll for credit.

The plaintiff filed suit in a federal trial court, arguing that the nursing school's single-sex admission policy violated the Equal Protection Clause. The court rejected the plaintiff's claim, deciding that maintaining MUW as a single-sex public institution bore a rational relationship to Mississippi's stated interest in providing the greatest practical range of educational opportunities for females.

On further review, the then Fifth, now Eleventh, Circuit reversed in favor of the plaintiff. The court was of the opinion that because the admissions policy discriminated on the basis of gender, the trial court improperly analyzed the case using the rational relationship test rather than the higher intermediate scrutiny standard. This higher standard of review required the state to carry the more substantive burden of demonstrating that the gender classification was substantially related to an important governmental concern.

On rehearing, the university argued that through enacting Section 901(a)(5) of Title IX of the Education Amendments of 1972, which provides some exemptions from Title IX's gender prohibitions for single-sex institutions, Congress expressly authorized officials at MUW to continue the single-sex admission policy. The Fifth Circuit rejected that argument, pointing out that Congress could not authorize states to continue practices that otherwise violated the Fourteenth Amendment.

The Supreme Court's Ruling

In 1982, the Supreme Court affirmed the Fifth Circuit's judgment in an opinion authored by Justice Sandra Day O'Connor. The majority determined that MUW's single-sex admission policy violated the Equal Protection Clause and that Title

IX's exemptions did not nullify constitutional obligations owed by the university.

At the heart of its rationale, the Supreme Court ruled that the case should have been analyzed through the frame of intermediate scrutiny, not the lower level of rational basis scrutiny, because the admission policy discriminated on the basis of gender. The Court was thus of the view that university officials were required to demonstrate an "exceedingly persuasive justification" for the gender classification that served an important governmental objective. In addition, the Court expected officials to show that the single-sex admission policy was substantially related to achieving the aforementioned objective.

The record reflected that MUW's primary objective for maintaining the single-sex admission policy was that it compensated for prior discrimination against women, thereby constituting educational affirmative action. Yet, the Supreme Court posited that Mississippi made no showing that women lacked opportunities to obtain nursing education and training. Rather, the Court interpreted the exclusion of males from admission to the nursing program as perpetuating the perception of nursing as the exclusive province of females.

The Supreme Court added that the policy also failed the second prong of the equal protection test, noting that Mississippi did not demonstrate that a gender-based admission classification was substantially or directly related to the proposed compensatory intent. Instead, the Court observed that allowing men to audit classes, but not enroll for credit, undermined officials' claim that separating the genders benefited female students. The Court quickly dispensed with MUW's Title IX argument, finding it unclear that Congress intended to exempt MUW from any constitutional obligation through Section 901(a)'s exemptions.

In his dissent, Justice Powell argued that the case required only rational basis analysis, not intermediate scrutiny, because it was grounded on the mere inconvenience of travel to another public institution for the student. Justice Burger agreed, but wrote separately to emphasize that the majority's holding was limited to the context of a public nursing program. As a result of *Hogan,* in 1982 MUW changed its admission policy and so began admitting men to all programs.

Courts have applied *Hogan* in later challenges to male-only admission policies at public military institutions. For example, in *Faulkner v. Jones* (1995), the Fourth Circuit held that The Citadel's exclusion of women also violated the Equal Protection Clause; accordingly, the court ordered officials at the institution to admit women. Moreover, in *United States v. Virginia* (1996), in an opinion authored by Justice Ginsburg, the Supreme Court asserted that Virginia Military Institute's exclusion of women violated the Equal Protection Clause, couching its analysis in intermediate scrutiny in a fashion akin to that of *Hogan*.

Kerry Brian Melear

See also Equal Protection Analysis; Fourteenth Amendment; Single-Sex Colleges; U.S. Supreme Court Cases in Higher Education; *United States v. Virginia*

Further Readings

Kaplin, W. A., & Lee, B. A. (2006). *The law of higher education: A comprehensive guide to legal implications of administrative decision making*. (4th ed.). San Francisco: Jossey-Bass.

Olivas, M. A., & Denison, K. M. (1984). Legalization in the academy: Higher education and the Supreme Court. *Journal of Law and Higher Education, 11*, 1–50.

Legal Citations

Faulkner v. Jones, 51 F.3d 440 (4th Cir. 1995), *motion to stay denied*, 66 F.3d 661 (4th Cir. 1995), *cert. dismissed*, 516 U.S. 910 (1995), *cert. denied*, 516 U.S. 938 (1995).

Mississippi University for Women v. Hogan, 458 U.S. 718 (1982).

Title IX of the Education Amendments of 1972, 20 U.S.C. §§ 1681 *et seq.* (1972).

United States v. Virginia, 518 U.S. 515 (1996).

MISSISSIPPI UNIVERSITY FOR WOMEN V. HOGAN

In *Hogan*, the Supreme Court ruled that officials at a publicly funded women's university violated the Equal Protection Clause when they denied admission to a male nursing applicant due to his gender, because the institution's single-sex admissions policy was not substantially related to a compelling governmental interest.

Supreme Court of the United States

MISSISSIPPI UNIVERSITY FOR WOMEN

v.

HOGAN

458 U.S. 718

Argued March 22, 1982

Decided July 1, 1982

Justice O'CONNOR delivered the opinion of the Court.

This case presents the narrow issue of whether a state statute that excludes males from enrolling in a state-supported professional nursing school violates the Equal Protection Clause of the Fourteenth Amendment.

I

The facts are not in dispute. In 1884, the Mississippi Legislature created the Mississippi Industrial Institute and College for the Education of White Girls of the State of Mississippi, now the oldest state-supported all-female college in the United States. The school, known today as Mississippi University for Women (MUW), has from its inception limited its enrollment to women.

In 1971, MUW established a School of Nursing, initially offering a 2-year associate degree. Three years later, the school instituted a 4-year baccalaureate program in nursing and today also offers a graduate program. The School of Nursing has its own faculty and administrative officers and establishes its own criteria for admission.

Respondent, Joe Hogan, is a registered nurse but does not hold a baccalaureate degree in nursing. Since 1974, he has worked as a nursing supervisor in a medical center in Columbus, the city in which MUW is located. In 1979, Hogan applied for admission to the MUW School of Nursing's baccalaureate program. Although he was otherwise qualified, he was denied admission to the School of Nursing solely because of his sex. School officials informed him that he could audit the courses in which he was interested, but could not enroll for credit.

Hogan filed an action in the United States District Court for the Northern District of Mississippi, claiming the single-sex admissions policy of MUW's School of Nursing violated the Equal Protection Clause of the Fourteenth Amendment. Hogan sought injunctive and declaratory relief, as well as compensatory damages.

Following a hearing, the District Court denied preliminary injunctive relief. The court concluded that maintenance of MUW as a single-sex school bears a rational relationship to the State's legitimate interest "in providing the greatest practical range of educational opportunities for its female student population." . . .

The Court of Appeals for the Fifth Circuit reversed, holding that, because the admissions policy discriminates on the basis of gender, the District Court improperly used a "rational relationship" test to judge the constitutionality of the policy. Instead, the Court of Appeals stated, the proper test is whether the State has carried the heavier burden of showing that the gender-based classification is substantially related to an important governmental objective. Recognizing that the State has a significant interest in providing educational opportunities for all its citizens, the court then found that the State had failed to show that providing a unique educational opportunity for females, but not for males, bears a substantial relationship to that interest. Holding that the policy excluding Hogan because of his sex denies him equal protection of the laws, the court vacated the summary judgment entered against Hogan as to his claim for monetary damages, and remanded for entry of a declaratory judgment in conformity with its opinion and for further appropriate proceedings.

On rehearing, the State contended that Congress, in enacting § 901(a)(5) of Title IX of the Education Amendments of 1972, expressly had authorized MUW to continue its single-sex admissions policy by exempting public undergraduate institutions that traditionally have used single-sex admissions policies from the gender discrimination prohibition of Title IX. Through that provision, the State argued, Congress limited the reach of the Fourteenth Amendment by exercising its power under § 5 of the Amendment. The Court of Appeals rejected the argument, holding that § 5 of the Fourteenth Amendment does not grant Congress power to authorize States to maintain practices otherwise violative of the Amendment.

We granted certiorari and now affirm the judgment of the Court of Appeals.

II

We begin our analysis aided by several firmly established principles. Because the challenged policy expressly discriminates among applicants on the basis of gender, it is subject to scrutiny under the Equal Protection Clause of the Fourteenth Amendment. That this statutory policy discriminates against males rather than against females does not exempt it from scrutiny or reduce the standard of review. Our decisions also establish that the party seeking to uphold a statute that classifies individuals on the basis of their gender must carry the burden of showing an "exceedingly persuasive justification" for the classification. The burden is met only by showing at least that the classification serves "important governmental objectives and that the discriminatory means employed" are "substantially related to the achievement of those objectives."

Although the test for determining the validity of a gender-based classification is straightforward, it must be applied free of fixed notions concerning the roles and abilities of males and females. Care must be taken in ascertaining whether the statutory objective itself reflects archaic and stereotypic notions. Thus, if the statutory objective is to exclude or "protect" members of one gender because they are presumed to suffer from an inherent handicap or to be innately inferior, the objective itself is illegitimate.

If the State's objective is legitimate and important, we next determine whether the requisite direct, substantial relationship between objective and means is present. The purpose of requiring that close relationship is to assure that the validity of a classification is determined through reasoned analysis rather than through the mechanical application of traditional, often inaccurate, assumptions about the proper roles of men and women. The need for the requirement is amply revealed by reference to the broad range of statutes already invalidated by this Court, statutes that relied upon the simplistic, outdated assumption that gender could be used as a "proxy for other, more germane bases of classification" to establish a link between objective and classification.

Applying this framework, we now analyze the arguments advanced by the State to justify its refusal to allow males to enroll for credit in MUW's School of Nursing.

III

A

The State's primary justification for maintaining the single-sex admissions policy of MUW's School of Nursing is that it compensates for discrimination against women and, therefore, constitutes educational affirmative action. As applied to the School of Nursing, we find the State's argument unpersuasive.

In limited circumstances, a gender-based classification favoring one sex can be justified if it intentionally and directly assists members of the sex that is disproportionately burdened. However, we consistently have emphasized that "the mere recitation of a benign, compensatory purpose is not an automatic shield which protects against any inquiry into the actual purposes underlying a statutory scheme." The same searching analysis must be made, regardless of whether the State's objective is to eliminate family controversy, to achieve administrative efficiency, or to balance the burdens borne by males and females.

It is readily apparent that a State can evoke a compensatory purpose to justify an otherwise discriminatory classification only if members of the gender benefited by the classification actually suffer a disadvantage related to the classification. . . .

. . .

In sharp contrast, Mississippi has made no showing that women lacked opportunities to obtain training in the field of nursing or to attain positions of leadership in that field when the MUW School of Nursing opened its door or that women currently are deprived of such opportunities. In fact, in 1970, the year before the School of Nursing's first class enrolled, women earned 94 percent of the nursing baccalaureate degrees conferred in Mississippi and 98.6 percent of the degrees earned nationwide. That year was not an aberration; one decade earlier, women had earned all the nursing degrees conferred in Mississippi and 98.9 percent of the degrees conferred nationwide. As one would expect, the labor force reflects the same predominance of women in nursing. When MUW's School of Nursing began operation, nearly 98 percent of all employed registered nurses were female.

Rather than compensate for discriminatory barriers faced by women, MUW's policy of excluding males from admission to the School of Nursing tends to perpetuate the stereotyped view of nursing as an exclusively woman's job. By assuring that Mississippi allots more openings in its state-supported nursing schools to women than it does to men, MUW's admissions policy lends credibility to the old view that women, not men, should become nurses, and makes the assumption that nursing is a field for women a self-fulfilling prophecy. Thus, we conclude that, although the State recited a "benign, compensatory purpose," it failed to establish that the alleged objective is the actual purpose underlying the discriminatory classification.

The policy is invalid also because it fails the second part of the equal protection test, for the State has made no showing that the gender-based classification is substantially and directly related to its proposed compensatory objective. To the contrary, MUW's policy of permitting men to attend classes as auditors fatally undermines its claim that women, at least those in the School of Nursing, are adversely affected by the presence of men.

MUW permits men who audit to participate fully in classes. Additionally, both men and women take part in continuing education courses offered by the School of Nursing, in which regular nursing students also can enroll. The uncontroverted record reveals that admitting men to nursing classes does not affect teaching style, that the presence of men in the classroom would not affect the performance of the female nursing students, and that men in coeducational nursing schools do not dominate the classroom. In sum, the record in this case is flatly inconsistent with the claim that excluding men from the School of Nursing is necessary to reach any of MUW's educational goals.

Thus, considering both the asserted interest and the relationship between the interest and the methods used by the State, we conclude that the State has fallen far short of establishing the "exceedingly persuasive justification" needed to sustain the gender-based classification.

Accordingly, we hold that MUW's policy of denying males the right to enroll for credit in its School of Nursing violates the Equal Protection Clause of the Fourteenth Amendment.

B

In an additional attempt to justify its exclusion of men from MUW's School of Nursing, the State contends that MUW is the direct beneficiary "of specific congressional legislation which, on its face, permits the institution to exist as it has in the past." The argument is based upon the language of § 901(a) in Title IX of the Education Amendments of 1972. Although § 901(a) prohibits gender discrimination in education programs that receive federal financial assistance, subsection 5 exempts the admissions policies of undergraduate institutions "that traditionally and continually from [their] establishment [have] had a policy of admitting only students of one sex" from the general prohibition. See n. 5, *supra.* Arguing that Congress enacted Title IX in furtherance of its power to enforce the Fourteenth Amendment, a power granted by § 5 of that Amendment, the State would have us conclude that § 901(a)(5) is but "a congressional limitation upon the broad prohibitions of the Equal Protection Clause of the Fourteenth Amendment."

The argument requires little comment. Initially, it is far from clear that Congress intended, through § 901(a)(5), to exempt MUW from any constitutional obligation. Rather, Congress apparently intended, at most, to exempt MUW from the requirements of Title IX.

Even if Congress envisioned a constitutional exemption, the State's argument would fail. Section 5 of the Fourteenth Amendment gives Congress broad power indeed to enforce the command of the Amendment and "to secure to all persons the enjoyment of perfect equality of civil rights and the equal protection of the laws against State denial or invasion. . . ." Congress' power under § 5, however, "is limited to adopting measures to enforce the guarantees of the Amendment; § 5 grants Congress no power to restrict, abrogate, or dilute these guarantees."

Although we give deference to congressional decisions and classifications, neither Congress nor a State can validate a law that denies the rights guaranteed by the Fourteenth Amendment.

The fact that the language of § 901(a)(5) applies to MUW provides the State no solace: "[A] statute apparently governing a dispute cannot be applied by judges, consistently with their obligations under the Supremacy Clause, when such an application of the statute would conflict with the Constitution."

IV

Because we conclude that the State's policy of excluding males from MUW's School of Nursing violates the Equal Protection Clause of the Fourteenth Amendment, we affirm the judgment of the Court of Appeals.

It is so ordered.

MORAL DEVELOPMENT

See Student Moral Development

MORRILL ACTS

The Morrill Acts of 1862 and 1890 provided funding for the establishment of land grant colleges and universities in the United States. Under the Morrill Act of 1862, each state received 30,000 acres of land for each senator and representative in the House of Representatives it had been awarded by the census of 1860. States were then able to sell the land and create trust funds to finance educational programming. Thus, the act not only made land available for homesteaders who would help to populate expanding parts of the United States but also provided some funding for states to establish colleges and universities. The Morrill Land Grant Act of 1890, also known as the Agricultural College Act of 1890, provided greater funding for the schools established by the 1862 act and also led to the establishment of a number of colleges for African American students. This entry reviews the history and legacy of this legislation.

The Morrill Act of 1862

The Morrill Act of 1862 was spearheaded by Justin S. Morrill, a U.S. Representative from Vermont during the Civil War. Initially, he had advocated legislation to create a national agricultural school similar to West Point, but it was vetoed by President Buchanan. This defeat was a temporary setback, because Morrill went on to labor long and hard to bring a revised version of his bill to the next president's desk.

On July 2, 1862, President Abraham Lincoln signed the first Morrill Land Grant Act. This act would initiate a revolution in American higher education, as it provided states with the funds they would use for

> the endowment, support, and maintenance of at least one college where the leading object shall be, without excluding other scientific and classical studies, and including military tactics, to teach such branches of learning as are related to agriculture and the mechanic arts . . . to promote the liberal and practical education of the industrial classes in the several pursuits and professions in life.

Justin S. Morrill, the author of the act, was born in Vermont and had to leave school at age 15. He never attended college but was involved in agriculture and other businesses. As his entrepreneurship flourished, he was able to build a magnificent residence and, in 1854, he was elected to the U.S. House of Representatives, where he served for 12 years. Morrill, who was elected to the U.S. Senate in 1867 and served until his death in 1898, was also involved in the creation of the Library of Congress and the Washington Monument. Further, he was instrumental in the enactment of the Morrill Land Grant of 1890, the Second Morrill Act, which provided funds for colleges for Black students.

The Morrill Land Grant Act of 1890

The Morrill Land Grant Act of 1890, also known as the Agricultural College Act of 1890, helped with the creation of agricultural colleges and mechanical curricula while being designed to bring higher education to former slaves, as they were unable to gain entrance to colleges and universities for Whites. This act led to the creation of 17 historically Black land grant colleges in the former Confederate states, which had the apparently unintended consequence of buttressing racial segregation in higher education, insofar as the act called on states either to admit freed slaves to their existing land grant colleges and universities or to create new postsecondary institutions for qualified students.

As institutions of higher learning were created for Blacks under the Second Morrill Act, there was

a significant difference of opinion between two leading Black educators as to the benefits of the agricultural and mechanical colleges. Booker T. Washington was a proponent of the agricultural and mechanical college concept as a way for Black people to achieve prosperity through learning and practicing the trades. Conversely, W. E. B. Du Bois was not in favor of having Black students study to become skilled tradespeople, because he wanted them to pursue leadership roles by obtaining a college education.

Impact of the Morrill Acts

The Morrill Land Grant Acts changed American higher education insofar as Morrill wanted land grant colleges and universities to offer both liberal education and training not only for the leisure class but for people who wanted and needed instruction in the pursuits of life. In addition, Morrill believed that these institutions of higher learning should focus on improving American agriculture. Morrill thus had a vision of these colleges becoming partners in the growth and development of America. The Morrill Acts led to great changes in American society by opening up higher education to working-class men, women, minorities, and immigrants and giving them the education to succeed in a changing society.

At the same time, it is important to note that the Hatch Act of 1887 created agricultural experimentation stations that would bring theory into the fields of agriculture and improve the yield per acre as the agents worked with farmers to show them ways to increase production. During the last third of the 19th century, almost 60% of the U.S. population was engaged in agriculture. By way of stark contrast, in 2009 about 2% of the U.S. population produces the food and fiber for a nation of more than 300 million people and exports its surplus to other nations.

The Smith-Lever Act of 1914 created cooperative extensions that "shall consist of instruction and practical demonstration in agriculture and home economics to persons not attending or resident in said colleges in the several communities, and imparting to such persons information on said subjects through field demonstrations, publications and otherwise. . . ." The impact of this legislation can be seen in the work of the extension agents with and for farmers and the production of food in this country. The cooperative extension helped expand the number of acres devoted to the raising of wheat from 47 million acres in 1913 to 74 million acres in 1919. The cooperative extension agents still are at work with farmers, as productivity per person has continued to increase. It is also worth observing that 20 Native American tribal colleges gained land grant status. They did not receive land but received federal funds.

At present, 105 land grant colleges, products of the Morrill Acts, operate in the United States and its territories. These opportunities for higher education for many Americans were made possible by a person who never had a formal degree but who has a stamp issued in his memory and buildings at many colleges and universities named for him. Morrill's vision of higher education benefits American students in the 21st century.

Robert J. Safransky

See also Historically Black Colleges and Universities; Loans and Federal Aid

Legal Citations

Agricultural College Act of 1890 (Second Morrill Land Grant Act), ch. 841, 26 Stat. 417, 7 U.S.C. §§ 322 *et seq.*

Hatch Act of 1887, ch. 314, 24 Stat. 440, 7 U.S.C. §§ 361a *et seq.*

Morrill Land Grant Act of 1862, ch. 130, 12 Stat. 503, 7 U.S.C. §§ 301 *et seq.*

Smith-Lever Act of 1914, 7 U.S.C. §§ 343 *et seq.*

NATIONAL ASSOCIATION OF COLLEGE AND UNIVERSITY ATTORNEYS

The National Association of College and University Attorneys (NACUA) was founded in 1960 by a group of attorneys who frequently handled cases involving colleges and universities; they also had the assistance of officials of the University of Michigan, the University of Alabama, Northwestern University, and several Ivy League institutions. NACUA, the premier organization in the field of higher education law, is currently composed of more than 3,600 members representing 700 non-profit, accredited institutions of higher education located at 1,500 campuses in the United States, Canada, and abroad. Approximately two-thirds of NACUA members are public and private colleges and universities with student enrollment above 5,000 and annual expenditures between $50 million and $4 billion. The remaining one-third of the association's members are private colleges and universities with student enrollment below 5,000 and annual expenditures below $50 million per year.

NACUA's mission is to advance the effective practices of attorneys for the benefit of the colleges and universities they serve. Attorneys for institutions of higher education may encounter legal issues such as those surrounding student discipline, civil rights, animal rights, intellectual property, and employment. Therefore, NACUA offers its members a wide range of services that can help members identify, analyze, resolve, and prevent legal problems at institutions of higher education. The services that NACUA offers its members are rooted in the core values of quality, service, civility, collegiality, diversity, inclusiveness, and respect. The association seeks to assist officials on college and university campuses by educating and informing attorneys through publications, educational programs, and online resources.

Publications

NACUA publishes *The Journal of College & University Law* (*JCUL*) jointly with the University of Notre Dame School of Law as the only national journal focused exclusively on the law of higher education. *JCUL,* which has been published since 1973 and has a circulation of approximately 3,800, provides information of interest to those involved with higher education law, including reflections on recent cases involving higher education, legislative updates, book reviews, papers from NACUA's annual conference, and other articles of interest to college and university attorneys. Contributors to the publication include college and university counsel and education law specialists in the academic community. *JCUL* is published three times a year and is available electronically or in print to members of NACUA.

NACUA also publishes pamphlets, monographs, and compendia available for purchase that cover a broad range of topics that are of interest to higher education administrators, faculty, and legal counsel. Pamphlets and monographs are brief, concise reference guides that focus on specific topics of interest to administrators, faculty, and attorneys.

Topics such as background checks for faculty, privacy acts, and sovereign immunity are examined in the NACUA pamphlets and monographs. Among the items compiled into compendia are general articles, public statements, law review articles, and information on government regulations. Topics of compendia include free speech issues, information for new attorneys in higher education, and academic freedom and tenure.

In addition to monographs, NACUA members have published books under its auspices; the organization's Web site (www.nacua.org) provides information on these books. Titles such as *Academic Freedom in the Wired World* by Robert O'Neill; *Computer and Internet Use on Campus: A Legal Guide to Issues of Intellectual Property, Free Speech, and Privacy* by Constance S. Hawke; *The Law of Higher Education* by William A. Kaplin and Barbara A. Lee; and *The Law of Higher Education: Cases and Materials on Colleges in Court* by Michael Olivas are examples of books written by NACUA members. NACUA's Web site also provides information and resources for using Kaplin and Lee's *The Law of Higher Education* as a textbook in courses focused on higher education law.

Educational Programs

Since 1960, NACUA has conducted an annual conference attended by college and university attorneys from around the United States and Canada. The conference focuses on current issues and legal developments in higher education law. Sessions at the conference examine broad topics in larger sessions, while small discussion sessions examine specific issues of importance to attorneys and their institutions. Topics such as student affairs, litigation strategies, technology, trademark licensing, and employment law as well as numerous others are examined throughout the four-day conference.

NACUA offers continuing legal education workshops in various locations around the country featuring experienced attorneys who provide participants with current legal information. In addition, these workshops offer the opportunity for attorneys from different institutions to share their challenges and concerns with one another. The topics of these workshops include faculty discipline, patent case law, animal research, terminating

employees, discrimination issues, and academic freedom as well as other topics of current interest.

At the same time, NACUA offers interactive virtual seminars in which participants listen to presenters via telephone and other types of connections while viewing presentations online. These virtual seminars allow participants to "attend" the presentation without the need to spend time or expense on traveling. Participants at a site are charged one flat fee, regardless of the number of participants "attending" the seminar. Prior to the seminars, session handouts are delivered by mail or downloaded electronically for participants to review and use during the seminar. During sessions, participants are able to ask questions of presenters, to participate in live polling, and to examine other seminar participants' responses. These seminars, which focus on topics of current interest such as examining new regulations, are designed for both attorneys and their clients.

Online Resources

NACUA provides its members with numerous online resources, including its Legal Reference Service. NACUA's Web site and weekly e-mail newsletter, the *Higher Education Case Highlights*, offers members current information and recent developments on legal issues of interest to members. In addition, NACUA's Legal Reference Service acts as a clearinghouse for information on topics of interest to college and university attorneys. This information is collected from members and other sources and is made available online. Documents such as legal policies and agreements, conference/workshop outlines, and articles published in *JCUL* can be accessed through the Legal Reference Service. Members can search for information, or a member of the Legal Reference Service staff, which includes two law clerks, can conduct searches for members at no cost. While the Legal Reference Service does not provide legal advice, it can be a valuable resource when researching topics in higher education law.

The organization's Web site also offers links to additional Web sites of interest to college and university attorneys, such as sites of federal courts, federal statutes and regulations, state courts, state statutes and regulations, other legal associations, legal search engines, and legal blogs. NACUA maintains an e-mail discussion list intended to facilitate communication among NACUA members. Known as NACUANET, this service is free to NACUA member attorneys and has over 2,100 members. Subscribers to this service can receive 10 to 20 messages per day on topics such as recent legislation, sample policies, legal briefs, relevant Web sites, administrative issues, and position announcements. Moreover, these messages are archived so that members can search from the over 40,000 messages contained in NACUA's archive.

Carolyn L. Carlson

See also Education Law Association; U.S. Supreme Court Cases in Higher Education

Further Readings

Bickel, R. D., & Lake, P. F. (1999). *The rights and responsibilities of the modern university: Who assumes the risk of college life?* Durham, NC: Carolina Academic Press.

Hawke, C. (2001). *Computer and internet use on campus: A legal guide to issues of intellectual property, free speech, and privacy.* San Francisco: Jossey-Bass.

Journal of College & University Law. http://www.nd.edu/~jcul

Kaplin, W. A., & Lee, B. A. (2006). *The law of higher education: A comprehensive guide to legal implications of administrative decision making.* (4th ed.). San Francisco: Jossey-Bass.

National Association of College and University Attorneys. http://www.nacua.org

Olivas, M. A. (2006). *The law and higher education: Case materials on colleges in court* (3rd ed.). Durham, NC: Carolina Academic Press.

O'Neill, R. (2008). *Academic freedom in the wired world: Political extremism, corporate power, and the university.* Cambridge, MA: Harvard University Press.

NATIONAL COLLEGIATE ATHLETIC ASSOCIATION

The National Collegiate Athletic Association (NCAA) is a voluntary, unincorporated association that organizes the intercollegiate athletic programs of its membership, which includes more than 1,200 colleges and universities. As the governing body of intercollegiate sports in the United States, the NCAA's objectives include regulation and promotion of playing rules, of standards of amateurism and academic eligibility, and of various relationships between student-athletes, coaches, and the institutions on whose behalf they compete. This is accomplished by classifying the 1,200-plus-member institution sports programs into Divisions I, II, and III, which reflect the scale and stature of a given institution's athletic programs. This entry addresses the history and impact of the NCAA on intercollegiate athletics in the United States.

Historical Background

The beginning of intercollegiate athletics in the United States dates to the Harvard–Yale rivalry of the 19th century, which was modeled after competitions between Oxford and Cambridge in England. During these early years, students were in charge of every aspect of athletics, including coaching. One of the earliest such events was a major rowing regatta between Harvard and Yale, sponsored by the Elkins Rail Line, in which Harvard is purported to have tried to gain an advantage by using a coxswain who was not a student. In the first collegiate football game, Rutgers beat Princeton with a football team that included three freshmen who were failing algebra. Cheating and gambling were known to be rampant during the latter part of this era.

The early commercialization and popularity of these athletic competitions caused much debate among academics about the role of sports on campuses. When students requested financial support from their schools for coaching professionals and facilities, it was viewed by a good many people as an opportunity for universities to have greater influence over the sports activities of their students. However, with official support from schools and alumni, the beginning of the 20th century saw intercollegiate athletics become far more organized and competitive. Despite official support, as more and more institutions began play, schools struggled with their oversight and policing of collegiate athletics, especially in the sport of football.

One result of this growth was the development of new, aggressive styles of play that led to new types of injuries and, in some cases, deaths. In 1905 alone, there were 18 deaths and more than

100 major injuries attributed to college football. This prompted President Theodore Roosevelt to call for a White House conference on football. The needs for safety and oversight were two of the driving concerns that prompted Henry M. MacCracken, chancellor of New York University, to convene a meeting of 13 academic institutions for the purpose of modifying, unifying, and updating football rules. Within a few weeks after this late 1905 meeting, the Intercollegiate Athletic Association of the United States (IAAUS) was founded. Before the decade was out, the IAAUS had become the NCAA and had grown to include 62 member schools.

Early and Modern-Day Development

During its early years, the NCAA did not assume an increased role in the governance of college athletics. Rather, the NCAA helped expand the catalog of athletic offerings of member schools by developing championships in a variety of sports. At the same time, the NCAA struggled with a litany of abuses, including overcommercialization, cheating, academic fraud, student-athlete welfare, and gambling. A report issued in 1929 by the Carnegie Foundation for the Advancement of Education acknowledged that these abuses were the results of the increasing popularity of college sports.

Things began to change rapidly in the years following World War II, as access to higher education increased, and college enrollments reached historic levels. With more people attending college than ever before, the popularity of college sports also increased. Accordingly, the NCAA had to take action. In 1948, the NCAA made its first attempt to govern and investigate college sports, by issuing the so-called Sanity Code. The code was intended to stem the rise of immoral recruiting practices, and it created a Constitutional Compliance Committee to interpret rules and investigate possible violations. Another important transformation took place in 1951, when Walter Byers became the first full-time executive director of the NCAA. With Byers in a leadership role, a position he held until his retirement in 1988, the NCAA established its headquarters in Kansas City. From there, Byers and the NCAA began a significant period of organizational growth, power, and independence. Among the NCAA's first interests was to establish

a significant revenue stream. This much was accomplished through their negotiating a series of national broadcast contracts for college football.

Thanks to several sports betting scandals, Byers also found that he had the capacity and opportunity to expand the organization's investigative and enforcement powers. By the 1970s, the NCAA had increased its authority, and it began to come under criticism for the unfair and arbitrary exercise of its power. In response to this criticism, the NCAA formed a committee in 1973 that was charged with examining the enforcement process; the eventual result of this committee's work was the division of the investigative and prosecutorial roles of the Committee on Infractions.

Still, the NCAA continued to expand its staff charged with investigation and prosecution and broadened its authority to adjudicate complaints. During this period, however, the NCAA was subject to complaints, from all manner of critics, over enforcement practices. Some in the media and academic community argued the NCAA was doing too little to curb the abuses in collegiate sports; on the other side of the criticism were some who believed the NCAA was grossly overstepping any authority it had and that expanded investigative and enforcement powers threatened the independence of universities to administer their own athletic programs.

By the late 1970s, universities in the South and Southwest complained of unfair targeting compared to older schools in the East and Midwest, which prompted the U.S. House of Representatives to hold hearings on alleged inequities of the NCAA's enforcement process. This criticism continued to be leveled at the NCAA into the 1980s and 1990s, a period during which the NCAA's most severe sanction, the so-called Death Penalty, called for a ban on competition for repeated major rules infractions, such as was applied in 1985 against the football team at Southern Methodist University.

The NCAA addressed another competitive and economic imbalance in governance in the early 1970s when its membership split into three divisions. The divisions were reflective of the competitive orientation of each institution; that is, they grouped similar institutions based on their sizes. The grouping also resolved a primary complaint among major college sports programs that their representation and power inside the NCAA had become diluted by schools with far more modest athletic ambitions. Under the terms of the division, the NCAA created Division I for universities offering numerous and well-funded sports programs, Division II for regional schools with more modest funding and competitive goals, and Division III for universities and colleges not offering athletic scholarships. These divisions were further stratified when Division I was split into three subdivisions in the 1990s.

Among the other significant transformations concerning the modern development of the NCAA was a change in the organization's governing structure during the 1980s. In June 1985, university presidents, whose prior involvement in the NCAA's activities was often spotty at best, called a special convention. Over the course of the better part of the next decade, the Presidents Commission restructured the NCAA's governance, adding an executive committee and board of directors for each division. The last 25 years have seen university presidents take a much more active role in the administration of the NCAA, largely supplanting athletic administrators as the driving force inside the organization. Yet, this period of increased power of university presidents within the NCAA has been legally tumultuous, with several major court controversies delimiting the legal and economic reach of the organization.

NCAA v. Board of Regents

One of the most significant legal decisions related to the NCAA took place in the early-to-mid-1980s, when the U.S. Supreme Court ruled on *NCAA v. Board of Regents of the University of Oklahoma and University of Georgia Athletic Association*. In 1981, the NCAA sought to limit the number of games that universities could have televised as part of its contract with the American Broadcasting Company (ABC). The NCAA also prohibited universities from selling the television rights of their other football games to other broadcast entities. This was a significant impediment, because a number of schools had, by then, become reliant on both the revenue and the publicity their programs received from these television appearances.

In response, the members of almost 60 major college football schools formed the College Football Association (CFA). The CFA, which was originally organized to promote the interests of major football-playing colleges within the NCAA structure, claimed that it should have a weightier part in the formulation of football television policy than it had at that time. It consequently negotiated a contract with the National Broadcasting Company (NBC) that would have permitted the opportunity for more colleges to appear on television and, thereby, increased revenues for CFA members.

The NCAA responded with an announcement that it would take disciplinary action against any CFA member that complied with the CFA–NBC contract. This reaction led to the beginning of a long period of legal wrangles, starting with the naming of the Universities of Oklahoma and Georgia as plaintiffs in a federal trial court action. The court maintained that the NCAA controls over televised college football games violated Section 1 of the Sherman Antitrust Act.

A federal trial court in Oklahoma decided that the NCAA restrained competition in the relevant market, that is, "live college football television," by price fixing for particular telecasts, because it viewed exclusive network contracts as equivalent to a group boycott of other potential broadcasters. The court explained that the NCAA's threat of sanctions against its member institutions embodied a threatened boycott of potential competitors, and its television plan artificially limited the production of televised college football.

On further review, the Tenth Circuit affirmed that the NCAA violated the Sherman Act, because its television plan constituted some form of price fixing that, even if not illegal, placed an anticompetitive limitation on price. The court added that any procompetitive attributes of the plan did not qualify as sufficient justifications for its continuation. Subsequently, the Supreme Court affirmed in favor of the plaintiffs, causing the NCAA to lose economic control of its college football television revenues. By the end of its trial run, *NCAA v. Board of Regents of the University of Oklahoma and University of Georgia Athletic Association* demonstrated that the NCAA possessed very limited antitrust protection, which did little to stave off future suits over its exercise of power or exclusivity against its members.

Without the control over the football television revenue it previously had, the NCAA became more dependent on the funds produced by its basketball tournament. The NCAA therefore undertook a major program of television rights sales and tournament sponsorship. However, as the NCAA became more dependent on basketball revenue, it came under greater criticism for being inequitable in its treatment of African Americans. One significant controversy in this area involved the freshman eligibility of student-athletes who scored poorly on standardized tests. Issues involving recruiting, amateurism, gambling, and enforcement have continued to confront the NCAA, as the presidents moved toward cost control as a way of keeping these runaway processes in check.

Title IX

The other topic that has consumed the NCAA as a body is the subject of gender equity and compliance with Title IX. While not directly an NCAA matter, no more controversial issue has emerged in the context of collegiate athletics than the discussion surrounding Title IX of the Education Amendments of 1972. Title IX, a federal statute, was signed into law in order to prohibit sex discrimination in education programs that receive financial assistance from the federal government. Despite the popular link between Title IX and athletics programs, the statute did not originally address or otherwise reference athletics. Following a two-year comment period on Title IX, during which a majority of the nearly 10,000 comments received referred to athletics, Congress passed Section 844 of the Education Amendments of 1974. This so-called Javits Amendment included intercollegiate athletics as part of Title IX. At the same time, in a decision that would have profound consequences in later years, the Senate dropped an amendment to exempt revenue-producing sports from Title IX.

By the 1980s, in part due to the social implications of Title IX, issues surrounding opportunities and equity in expenditures across women's sports began to heat up. In the interim, despite a series of new regulations and refinements, the expanded opportunities afforded to women have been controversial, because the cost of women's programs is disproportionate to the revenue generated by a majority of women's teams, even in prominent sports such as basketball. Most of the disagreement concerns whether all athletic programs should

be self-sufficient within the institution or whether revenue-producing male sports should have to distribute their funds to women's sports. Other court cases have led to other controversies; for example, *Grove City College v. Bell* (1984) and *NCAA v. Smith* (1999) raised new questions about the relationship between federal funding and Title IX coverage.

Current Controversies

The reach and role of athletics in the academy is at least as old as ancient Greece, where athletic competition was as important as rhetoric and mathematics as a means to strength and health, and ancient Rome, where it was believed that athletics was but a means to developing and maintaining capable soldiers. Today, an increased concern over the declining scholastic progress of student-athletes, especially those in high-profile sports like football and basketball, has led a growing number of universities and colleges to increase institutional oversight of their athletic departments. Today's college sports atmosphere is defined by a balance between offering quality educational opportunities for student-athletes and offering quality sports teams for students and alumni. It is a balance between college athletics as a part of business and of society.

As the NCAA has grown in size and stature, it has had to confront many judicial hurdles. In this way, the NCAA experienced much progress, such as when the Supreme Court reasoned that the NCAA was not a state actor in *NCAA v. Tarkanian* (1988) and when the Court approved the NCAA's ability to perform drug testing of student-athletes in its championship contests in *Hill v. NCAA* (1994). Still, the NCAA has also been on the losing side of a number of key antitrust suits, the most significant of which was *Law v. NCAA* (1998), which involved a rule capping the pay of assistant basketball coaches.

Payment to college athletes has been another thorny issue for the NCAA in recent years, and there have been attempts to organize and elevate student-athletes into collective bargaining entities. Although largely unsuccessful, the calls have continued as revenues from sponsorship, bowl games, and television viewership have grown. The arguable inequity of an athlete receiving no direct financial benefit, apart from a scholarship, while schools and the NCAA itself collect all revenues, has become a topic of increasing conversation.

Lee H. Igel and Robert A. Boland

See also Civil Rights Act of 1964; *Grove City College v. Bell*; National Collegiate Athletic Association v. Tarkanian; Sports Programming and Scheduling; Title IX and Athletics

Further Readings

Smith, R. K. (2000). A brief history of the NCAA's role in regulating intercollegiate athletics. *Marquette Sports Law Journal, 11*(1), 9–22.

Sperber, M. (1998). *Onward to victory: The crises that shaped college sports*. New York: Henry Holt.

Yaeger, D. (1991). *Undue process: The NCAA's injustice for all*. Champaign, IL: Sagamore.

Zimbalist, A. (1999). *Unpaid professionals: Commercialism and conflict in big-time college sports*. Princeton, NJ: Princeton University Press.

Legal Citations

Grove City College v. Bell, 465 U.S. 555 (1984).

Hill v. NCAA, 7 Cal. 4th 1 (1994).

Law v. NCAA, 134 F.3d 1010 (10th Cir. 1998).

NCAA v. Board of Regents of the University of Oklahoma and University of Georgia Athletic Association, 468 U.S. 85 (1984).

NCAA v. Smith, 525 U.S. 459 (1999).

NCAA v. Tarkanian, 488 U.S. 179 (1988).

Title IX of the Education Amendments of 1972, 20 U.S.C. § 1681 *et seq.* (1972).

NATIONAL COLLEGIATE ATHLETIC ASSOCIATION V. TARKANIAN

In *National Collegiate Athletic Association (NCAA) v. Tarkanian* (1988), the U.S. Supreme Court held that threatened NCAA sanctions against the head basketball coach of a public university did not constitute state action, even though the university was a member of the NCAA, and thus the NCAA's actions did not violate the coach's civil rights. In light of the potential ramifications that *Tarkanian* has for the relationship between institutions of higher education and the NCAA with regard to intercollegiate athletics, this entry reviews the case in detail. *Tarkanian* is noteworthy, because although the NCAA was ultimately unsuccessful in its attempted disciplining of the coach, the case appears to limit the ability of individuals to sue the NCAA for violation of their civil rights, because the NCAA is not a "state actor" whose actions would trigger protections of due process under the Fourteenth Amendment. Moreover, although federal actions cannot be filed, nothing prevents states from permitting such claims under their own laws.

Facts of the Case

Jerry Tarkanian was hired as the head basketball coach at the University of Nevada, Las Vegas (UNLV) in 1973. He was also a professor of physical education at the same campus.

The NCAA is an unincorporated association, which at that time had approximately 960 members, including nearly all public and private universities and four-year colleges with major athletic programs in the United States. One of the NCAA's basic policies is to "maintain intercollegiate athletics as an integral part of the education program and the athlete as an integral part of the student body, and by so doing, retain a clear line of demarcation between college athletics and professional sports." In an effort to promote this policy, the NCAA has adopted rules or "legislation" governing the conduct of the programs of its members. The NCAA's rules apply to a variety of issues, including academic eligibility, financial aid, and recruiting of students. When members join the NCAA, they agree to abide by and enforce the association's rules.

In 1972, the NCAA notified the UNLV that it was initiating a preliminary inquiry into the university's athletic recruiting practices. After three years, the NCAA decided an "Official Inquiry" was needed and instructed the UNLV to investigate a series of allegations, many of which implicated basketball coach Tarkanian.

When officials at the UNLV conducted an investigation, they concluded that Tarkanian was innocent of any wrongdoing. However, the NCAA convened a four-day hearing at the UNLV at which university officials challenged the credibility of the NCAA's informants with regard to the alleged recruiting violations. The NCAA's Committee on Infractions ultimately found that officials at the UNLV committed 38 rules violations, including 10 by Tarkanian, one of which was his lack of full cooperation with the investigation.

As a result of its investigation, the committee proposed sanctions, including a two-year probation for the university and a request for it to show cause as to why the UNLV should not suffer greater penalties if officials failed to discipline Tarkanian by removing him from his coaching position during the two-year probation. In response, UNLV officials determined they had three options: reject the NCAA sanctions and risk heavier penalties, including a longer probation; accept the NCAA sanctions and reassign Tarkanian, all the while believing that the NCAA was wrong; and withdraw from the NCAA completely. The president of the UNLV chose to pursue the second option.

In response, Tarkanian filed for an injunction in state court, alleging that the NCAA deprived him of property and liberty without due process. The trial court enjoined the UNLV from suspending Tarkanian on the basis that he had been deprived of both procedural and substantive due process.

Tarkanian then filed suit against the university before amending his filing to include the NCAA. A trial court ruled that because the NCAA's conduct constituted state action for jurisdictional and constitutional purposes, the university was forbidden to take any other action against the coach. On further review, the Supreme Court of Nevada, agreeing that the NCAA engaged in state action, affirmed that because the NCAA violated Tarkanian's substantive and procedural due process rights, the association could not enforce the sanctions that it had intended to impose on the coach. Dissatisfied with the outcome, the NCAA appealed, and the Supreme Court agreed to hear the case. Tarkanian never missed a day of work during the course of the litigation, because the trial court had enjoined the university from suspending him from coaching.

The Supreme Court's Ruling

In an opinion authored by Justice Stevens, the Supreme Court, in a five-to-four judgment, reversed in favor of the NCAA. As described by the Court, at issue was whether the NCAA's conduct constituted state action. At the outset, the Court rejected Tarkanian's assertion that the NCAA was a state actor because it misused the power that the UNLV, a state actor, had conferred on it. Instead, the Court decided that the NCAA was a private party that could only recommend that its members take actions such as sanctioning coaches. The Court explained that insofar as officials at the UNLV retained the authority to withdraw from the NCAA, the association was not acting under color of Nevada law when it created rules governing recruitment, eligibility, and academic requirements. While the UNLV may have played a minor role in creating some of the NCAA legislation, the Court rejected the notion that it actions were sufficient to have made the NCAA a state actor.

The Supreme Court also pointed out that the NCAA had no governmental assistance to further its investigation, because it lacked subpoena power, had no way to impose contempt sanctions, and could not have imposed sovereign authority over any individual. In this regard, the Court observed that the only power that the NCAA had was to threaten the UNLV with sanctions, the greatest of which would have been to expel the UNLV from NCAA membership. Moreover, the Court noted that insofar as the UNLV and the NCAA were adversaries throughout all the proceedings, it would be difficult to describe the association's behaviors as those of a state actor.

The Supreme Court also rejected Tarkanian's argument that the NCAA's power was so great that the UNLV had no real choice but to comply with its sanctions and recommendations. The Court disagreed, reasoning that even if the NCAA could impose its will on a state actor such as the UNLV, it did not follow that the NCAA operated under color of state law.

The dissent, written by Justice White, maintained that because the NCAA had hoped to have Tarkanian suspended for violations of association rules, which the UNLV had accepted as a member of the association, the NCAA and the university acted jointly. In addition, the dissent acknowledged that in other cases, the Supreme Court recognized that private parties became state actors when they acted jointly with state officials. Subsequently, the Court reached this outcome in *Brentwood Academy v. Tennessee Secondary School Athletic Association* (2001), wherein it found that a state association in a K–12 setting that imposed sanctions on a non-public school had engaged in state action. The dissent focused on the fact that the UNLV contractually agreed to carry out its athletic program in accordance with the NCAA's rules.

Rounding out its analysis, the dissenting justices commented that the UNLV had allowed the NCAA to conduct the hearings that were found by the Nevada Supreme Court to have violated Tarkanian's right to procedural due process. In addition, they remarked that the UNLV agreed to be bound by the results of the NCAA hearings, doing more than giving a mere "promise to cooperate" with the association. The dissent was convinced that because the NCAA's determinations that Tarkanian violated its rules were made at NCAA-conducted hearings, all of which the UNLV agreed to in its membership agreement, and which resulted in Tarkanian's suspension, this meant that the NCAA was jointly engaged with UNLV officials as a state actor.

In sum, the Supreme Court's later holding in *Brentwood Academy v. Tennessee Secondary School Athletic Association* casts some doubt on the proposition that the NCAA was not a state actor. Even so, because *Brentwood* can be distinguished from the UNLV case because it was set in K–12 education, *Tarkanian* remains an important case in the world of higher education, because it addresses the boundaries of the relationship between the NCAA and its member institutions.

Megan L. Rehberg

See also National Collegiate Athletic Association

Further Readings

Goplerud, C. P., III. (1991). NCAA enforcement process: A call for procedural fairness. *Capitol University Law Review, 20*, 543–650.

Legal Citations

Brentwood Academy v. Tennessee Secondary School Athletic Association, 531 U.S. 288 (2001), *on remand*, 262 F.3d 543 (6th Cir. 2001), *reh'g en banc denied, cert. denied*, 535 U.S. 971 (2002).

NCAA v. Tarkanian, 488 U.S. 179 (1988), *on remand*, 810 P.2d 343 (Nev. 1989), *appeal after remand*, 879 P.2d 1180 (Nev. 1994).

NATIONAL LABOR RELATIONS ACT

In July 1935, the United States Congress enacted the National Labor Relations Act (NLRA) in order to regulate labor–management relations in organizations involved in interstate commerce. Through the NLRA, the executive and legislative branches sought to equalize bargaining power between employers and employees to protect the rights of workers who chose to organize and bargain collectively.

Commonly known as the Wagner Act, the NLRA was enacted during the Great Depression, a time of high unemployment, labor management strife, and a stagnant economy. Historically, the federal government had not supported the growth of labor unions or collective bargaining over wages and working conditions. However, President Franklin Roosevelt and Congress were sympathetic to the plight of the unions and working class as a result of the severely depressed economy. The NLRA was enacted with the strong and coordinated support of the administration and Congress, marking a significant change in the government's position on labor–management relations. In light of the impact that the NLRA continues to have on the life of labor relations in American colleges and universities, this entry examines key aspects of the act.

Provisions of the NLRA

The primary purpose of the NLRA is to guarantee employees "the right to self-organization, to bargain collectively through representatives of their own choosing, and to engage in concerted activities for the purpose of collective bargaining or other mutual aid or protection. . . ." Under the act, employers cannot restrain or coerce employees in their exercise of these rights. The NLRA also ensures the right of employees to refrain from joining unions, collective bargaining, and related activities "except to the extent that such right may be affected by an agreement requiring membership in a labor organization as a condition of employment as authorized in section 8(a)(3)." The federal government, states and their political subdivisions, and labor organizations except when they are acting as employers were not included as employers under NLRA. In order to enforce the NLRA, Congress created a three-member National Labor Relations Board (NLRB) to arbitrate labor–management disputes, ensure democratic union elections, penalize specified unfair labor practices by employers (but not unions), and administer all components of the law.

Impact and Evolution of the NLRA

Stated simply, the NLRA was intended to improve wages, hours, and conditions of employment for American workers in both public and private sectors. When enacted in 1935, management viewed the NLRA as biased and one sided, because it listed unfair labor practices for employers but did not include unfair labor practices for which the unions would be sanctioned. From the perspective of many in corporate management, the NLRA was blatantly prolabor, and its passage prompted a contentious debate about the fairness and constitutionality of the act. Differences of opinion about the NLRA notwithstanding, it did provide the legal framework necessary for civil and productive labor–management dialogue and cooperation.

Ultimately, the NLRA fostered reasonably peaceful labor relations during the tumultuous period between 1935 and the end of World War II. In 1937, the Supreme Court upheld the constitutionality of the NLRA in *NLRB v. Jones & Laughlin Steel Corp.*, ruling that the statute did not violate the constitutional rights of employers or employees. The American Federation of Labor (AFL) and Congress of Industrial Organizations (CIO) responded to the NLRA with aggressive, nationwide membership campaigns, and the number of unionized workers increased from about 3.5 million in 1935 to approximately 15 million in 1947.

The Taft-Hartley Act

By 1947, the federal government's attitude toward organized labor had changed. Congress, then dominated by a conservative Republican majority, sought to curb the power of the unions by amending the NLRA. The Labor-Management

Relations Act of 1947, also known as the Taft-Hartley Act, amended the NLRA by listing unfair labor practices for unions and empowering the NLRB to secure injunctions for using such practices. Both unions and management were banned from restraining or coercing employees in organization activities. Unions could not refuse to bargain in good faith, and check-off of union dues was prohibited without written consent of the employees. Union-shop agreements were permitted only with the approval of a majority of employees in a secret-ballot election. At this time, the NLRB membership was increased from three to five.

Above all, Taft-Hartley emphasized the right of all employees *not* to join a union and *not* to bargain collectively. Taft-Hartley prompted a fierce controversy between its supporters, who insisted that it was necessary to restore a proper balance between labor and management in the workplace, and its opponents, who asserted that it was intended to destroy the labor movement. Detractors described Taft-Hartley as the "slave labor law." In the end, the Taft-Hartley Act did not destroy the labor movement, but union leaders claimed (and still claim) that Section 14(b) of the act, permitting states to adopt right-to-work laws, impeded union activity in those states enacting such legislation.

Other Amendments

Additional amendments to the NLRA followed those in Taft-Hartley. In 1951, for example, Congress permitted union-shop agreements without approval of the majority of employees in a secret-ballot election, but employees could petition the NLRB for a secret-ballot election to rescind union-shop initiatives. The Labor-Management Reporting and Disclosure (Landrum-Griffin) Act of 1959 amended the NLRA to preclude secondary boycotts, control union corruption, and prevent picketing by a union if a valid bargaining agreement was in effect with another union. In the 1970s, Congress expanded the NLRA to include employees in the U.S. Postal Service, private health care facilities, colleges and universities, and law firms.

NLRA and Higher Education

Federal labor law creates three distinct categories of employee organizations in higher education.

The NLRA left states free to regulate labor relationships with their public employees. Consequently, public colleges and universities, as subdivisions of the state, are excluded from NLRA coverage. Public institutions are governed by state laws regarding employee rights to organize and bargain collectively. Some jurisdictions have extended organization rights to employees of public institutions, while other states, particularly those in the South, have not done so. As a general rule, states with right-to-work laws, most of which are in the South, have maintained their statutory exemption from mandatory collective bargaining and have made organized activity and strikes illegal.

The NLRA impacts private institutions differently than it does public colleges and universities. In 1970, the NLRB extended the reach of the NLRA to private colleges and universities when it ensured the recognition of employee bargaining units at Cornell and Syracuse universities. Consequently, employees in private secular institutions retain the right to organize, bargain collectively, pursue grievances, and conduct strikes to achieve union goals. However, the Supreme Court's ruling in *NLRB v. Catholic Bishop of Chicago* (1979), a case that was concerned with unionization in Catholic secondary schools, may have indirectly limited the NLRA's applicability to religiously affiliated colleges and universities as persuasive precedent. *In dicta* (meaning that this precise issue was not before it), the Court suggested that imposing federal labor law on religious institutions might have created entangling conflicts between church and state. Even so, because it was able to resolve the case on the basis of statutory interpretation of the NLRA, the Court was able to sidestep the difficult questions associated with the First Amendment religion clauses. Lacking a clear intent by Congress to apply the NLRA to religious institutions, the Court concluded that the NLRB was barred from extending its authority into Catholic high schools.

A year later, in *National Labor Relations Board v. Yeshiva University* (1980), the Supreme Court affirmed an earlier order of the Second Circuit with regard to faculty unionization. The Court observed that insofar as full-time faculty members in a religiously affiliated university could be considered managerial employees, they were not entitled to the protections of the NLRA that would have allowed them to form unions in order to engage in collective bargaining with their employer. As a result of *Yeshiva*, faculty members in private colleges and universities are not entitled to the protections that the NLRA affords with regard to unionization and collective bargaining. Consequently, bargaining is an internal labor relations issue that faculty members must resolve with the leadership of their institutions free from the dictates of federal labor laws.

Robert C. Cloud

See also Collective Bargaining; *National Labor Relations Board v. Yeshiva University*; Political Activities and Speech of Faculty Members; Unions on Campus

Further Readings

Gregory, D. L. (1990). The right to unionize as a fundamental human and civil right. *Mississippi College Law Review, 9,* 136–154.

Legal Citations

Labor-Management Relations (Taft-Hartley) Act, 29 U.S.C. §§ 141 *et seq.*
Labor-Management Reporting and Disclosure (Landrum-Griffin) Act, 29 U.S.C. §§ 401 *et seq.*
National Labor Relations Act, 29 U.S.C. §§ 151 *et seq.*
NLRB v. Catholic Bishop of Chicago, 440 U.S. 490 (1979).
NLRB v. Jones & Laughlin Steel Corp., 301 U.S. 1 (1937).
NLRB v. Yeshiva University, 443 U.S. 672 (1980).

NATIONAL LABOR RELATIONS BOARD V. YESHIVA UNIVERSITY

National Labor Relations Board v. Yeshiva University (1980) stands out as perhaps the U.S. Supreme Court's most significant ruling on whether faculty members may organize and bargain collectively with officials representing their private colleges and universities. In *Yeshiva*, a closely divided Court affirmed that because full-time faculty members at a private university exercised what it described as absolute authority in helping to establish guidelines with regard to such academic matters as scheduling classes, selecting teaching methods, setting grading policies, determining teaching loads, establishing pay scales and benefits packages, and deciding who is awarded tenure, promotion, and sabbaticals, they essentially exercised managerial duties. The controlling consideration in this case is that the faculty of Yeshiva University exercises authority that in any other context unquestionably would be managerial. Thus, consistent with general principles of labor law that managers or supervisors and regular employees should not be in the same bargaining unit because they represent significantly different communities of interest, faculty were not entitled to the protections afforded by the National Labor Relations Act (NLRA) with regard to forming collective bargaining units. In light of the impact that *Yeshiva* had on labor relations for faculty members in higher education, this entry reviews the case in detail.

Facts of the Case

The litigation in *Yeshiva* traces its origins to the fall of 1974, when the Faculty Association at Yeshiva University filed a petition with the National Labor Relations Board (NLRB), the federal body governing private-sector labor relations. The association filed its petition in an attempt to gain recognition as the exclusive bargaining representative for full-time faculty members at the religiously affiliated private university. University officials opposed the petition, arguing that the faculty members were not employees within the meaning of the NLRA. University officials maintained that because faculty members were policy-setting employees, their status was more closely associated with that of managers, so they were not permitted to engage in bargaining. Nevertheless, the NLRB directed university officials to conduct an election under its supervision in which voters selected the Faculty Association as its bargaining representative. After university officials refused to recognize or bargain with the association, the NLRB filed suit over its refusal.

The Second Circuit denied the NLRB's petition to enforce its order on the basis that because the full-time faculty members served as managers, they were not employees within the meaning of the NLRA. The court did not review their status as

supervisors. (*Managers* and *supervisors* are terms with significantly different legal meanings.)

The Supreme Court's Ruling

On further review, the Supreme Court affirmed in favor of the university. Writing for the majority in the Court's five-to-four judgment, Justice Powell began his review by noting that because employees who perform supervisory and managerial functions are generally excluded from an entitlement to participate in collective bargaining, the question was whether the full-time faculty members at Yeshiva University were covered by the NLRA. After reviewing the facts of the dispute as outlined above, the Court began its substantive analysis with the observation that there was no evidence that Congress addressed whether it intended the NLRA to cover full-time faculty members in higher education. However, the Court was quick to add that the absence of clear congressional direction denied the NLRB jurisdiction over the dispute. In fact, the Court acknowledged that the NLRB began to assert jurisdiction in higher education for the first time in 1970, finding that because full-time faculty members were professional employees, they were covered by the NLRA.

As part of its rationale, the Supreme Court acknowledged that university officials did not challenge the status of faculty members as professional employees under the NLRA. Instead, university officials based their claim on the allegation that faculty members were managerial or supervisory employees who were not covered by the NLRA. According to the NLRA, professional employees are those whose work is predominantly intellectual and varied in character as opposed to routine mental, manual, mechanical, or physical work. These efforts also involve the consistent exercise of discretion and judgment in their performance, are of such a character that the output produced or the results accomplished cannot be standardized in relation to set periods of time, and require knowledge of an advanced type that is customarily acquired by a prolonged course of specialized intellectual instruction and study in an institution of higher learning as opposed to general academic education, apprenticeships, or training in the performance of routine mental, manual, or physical processes. The Court itself, relying on its own precedent, defined managerial employees are those who "formulate and effectuate management policies by expressing and making operative the decisions of their employer" (p. 882).

In contrast, the act defines supervisors as individuals with authority who, in the interest of the employer, must exercise independent judgment in hiring, transferring, suspending, laying off, recalling, promoting, discharging, assigning, rewarding, or disciplining other staff or to direct them in their duties. Interestingly, insofar as the Second Circuit limited its judgment to the status of faculty as managerial, rather than supervisory, employees, the Court focused its holding in the same way.

The Supreme Court then turned to the statutory definition of managers as individuals who apply independent professional judgment in establishing policies and acting on behalf of their employers, finding that this placed faculty members within the managerial structure. To this end, without even considering the concepts of academic freedom and academic abstention that go to the heart of intellectual endeavors at American colleges and universities, the Court described the "controlling consideration" as whether the faculty members engaged in duties that in other contexts would have been treated as managerial. The Court reached this position in positing that this was so, because faculty members exercised what it described as nearly absolute power over academic affairs vis-à-vis the matters identified above, such as promotion and tenure decisions, selecting methodologies, and the like.

At the heart of its opinion, then, the Supreme Court rejected the NLRB's assertion that the decision-making authority of faculty members was not managerial in the ordinary sense of the word because they exercised independent professional judgment in engaging in routine academic tasks. Further, the Court rebuffed the notion that the faculty members may have been acting in their own interests rather than those of the university in pointing out that if this were the case, then the NLRB might have opened a Pandora's Box that would have created more problems than it would have solved. In fact, in again acknowledging the role that faculty members play in academic governance, the Court maintained that it had no choice but to affirm the order of the Second Circuit.

As author of a strongly worded dissent, Justice Brennan argued that the NLRB's enforcement order was consistent with the terms of the NLRB, and thus he and his three colleagues would have reversed in its favor. They were convinced that Congress had intended to permit collective bargaining by faculty members in higher education. They also argued that faculty in higher education differ significantly from managers in other work settings, because individual faculty members do not represent the interests of the administration in the same way that managers in an industrial setting represent the interests of their employers.

Yeshiva has had a long-term impact on labor relations with regard to faculty bargaining in private colleges and universities in the United States. In the wake of *Yeshiva*, then, the number of faculty unions on private campuses is less than in public institutions of higher education and is likely to remain so at the federal level, unless or until the Supreme Court or Congress intervenes to change this situation. Of course, as reflected in subsequent litigation on faculty unions, nothing forbids states from granting faculty members, especially those in private colleges and universities, the right to bargain collectively with officials of their universities.

Charles J. Russo

See also Academic Abstention; Academic Freedom; Collective Bargaining; Unions on Campus

Further Readings

Gregory, D. L., & Russo, C. J. (1990). Overcoming *NLRB v. Yeshiva University* by the implementation of Catholic labor theory. *Labor Law Journal, 41*(1), 51–64.

Metchick, R. H., & Singh, P. (2003). *Yeshiva* and faculty unionization in higher education. *Labor Studies Journal, 28*(4), 45–65.

Nagle, P. (1994). *Yeshiva's* impact on collective bargaining in public-sector higher education. *Journal of College & University Law, 20*, 383–403.

Russo, C. J. (1990). Yeshiva and public education: A tempest in a teapot. *Record in Educational Administration and Supervision, 11*(1), 90–93.

Legal Citations

National Labor Relations Act, 49 Stat. 449, as amended, 61 Stat. 136, 73 Stat. 519, 29 U.S.C. §§ 151 *et seq.* (2008).

National Labor Relations Board v. Yeshiva University, 444 U.S. 672 (1980).

NATIONAL LABOR RELATIONS BOARD V. YESHIVA UNIVERSITY

In *NLRB*, the Supreme Court ruled that insofar as faculty members are managerial employees, they were excluded from engaging in the collective bargaining process with their universities.

Supreme Court of the United States

NATIONAL LABOR RELATIONS BOARD

v.

YESHIVA UNIVERSITY

444 U.S. 672

Argued Oct. 10, 1979

Decided Feb. 20, 1980

Mr. Justice POWELL delivered the opinion of the Court.

Supervisors and managerial employees are excluded from the categories of employees entitled to the benefits of collective bargaining under the National Labor Relations Act. The question presented is whether the full-time faculty of Yeshiva University fall within those exclusions.

Yeshiva is a private university which conducts a broad range of arts and sciences programs at its five undergraduate and eight graduate schools in New York City. On October 30, 1974, the Yeshiva University Faculty Association (Union) filed a representation petition with the National Labor Relations Board (Board). The Union sought certification as bargaining agent for the full-time faculty members at 10 of the 13 schools. The University opposed the petition on the ground that all of its faculty members are managerial or supervisory personnel and hence not employees within the meaning of the National Labor Relations Act (Act). A Board-appointed hearing officer held hearings over a period of five months, generating a voluminous record.

The evidence at the hearings showed that a central administrative hierarchy serves all of the University's schools. Ultimate authority is vested in a Board of Trustees, whose members (other than the President) hold no administrative positions at the University. The President sits on the Board of Trustees and serves as chief executive officer, assisted by four Vice Presidents who oversee, respectively, medical affairs and science, student affairs, business affairs, and academic affairs. An Executive Council of Deans and administrators makes recommendations to the President on a wide variety of matters.

University-wide policies are formulated by the central administration with the approval of the Board of Trustees, and include general guidelines dealing with teaching loads, salary scales, tenure, sabbaticals, retirement, and fringe benefits. The budget for each school is drafted by its Dean or Director, subject to approval by the President after consultation with a committee of administrators. The faculty participate in University-wide governance through their representatives on an elected student-faculty advisory council. The only University-wide faculty body is the Faculty Review Committee, composed of elected representatives who adjust grievances by informal negotiation and also may make formal recommendations to the Dean of the affected school or to the President. Such recommendations are purely advisory.

The individual schools within the University are substantially autonomous. Each is headed by a Dean or Director, and faculty members at each school meet formally and informally to discuss and decide matters of institutional and professional concern. At four schools, formal meetings are convened regularly pursuant to written bylaws. The remaining faculties meet when convened by the Dean or Director. Most of the schools also have faculty committees concerned with special areas of educational policy. Faculty welfare committees negotiate with administrators concerning salary and conditions of employment. Through these meetings and committees, the faculty at each school effectively determine its curriculum, grading system, admission and matriculation standards, academic calendars, and course schedules.

Faculty power at Yeshiva's schools extends beyond strictly academic concerns. The faculty at each school make recommendations to the Dean or Director in every case of faculty hiring, tenure, sabbaticals, termination and promotion. Although the final decision is reached by the central administration on the advice of the Dean or Director, the overwhelming majority of faculty recommendations are implemented. Even when financial problems in the early 1970's restricted Yeshiva's budget, faculty recommendations still largely controlled personnel decisions made within the constraints imposed by the administration. Indeed, the faculty of one school recently drew up new and binding policies expanding their own role in these matters. In addition, some faculties make final decisions regarding the admission, expulsion, and graduation of individual students. Others have decided questions involving teaching loads, student absence policies, tuition and enrollment levels, and in one case the location of a school.

II

A three-member panel of the Board granted the Union's petition in December 1975, and directed an election in a bargaining unit consisting of all full-time faculty members at the affected schools. The unit included Assistant Deans, senior professors, and department chairmen, as well as associate professors, assistant professors, and instructors. Deans and Directors were excluded. The Board summarily rejected the University's contention that its entire faculty are managerial, viewing the claim as a request for reconsideration of previous Board decisions on the issue. Instead of making findings of fact as to Yeshiva, the Board referred generally to the record and found no "significan[t]" difference between this faculty and others it had considered. The Board concluded that the faculty are professional employees entitled to the protection of the Act because "faculty participation in collegial decision making is on a collective rather than individual basis, it is exercised in the faculty's own interest rather than 'in the interest of the employer,' and final authority rests with the board of trustees."

The Union won the election and was certified by the Board. The University refused to bargain, reasserting its view that the faculty are managerial. In the subsequent unfair labor practice proceeding, the Board refused to reconsider its holding in the representation proceeding and ordered the University to bargain with the Union. When the University still refused to sit down at the negotiating table, the Board sought enforcement in the Court of Appeals for the Second Circuit, which denied the petition.

Since the Board had made no findings of fact, the court examined the record and related the circumstances in considerable detail. It agreed that the faculty are professional employees under § 2(12) of the Act. But the court found that the Board had ignored "the extensive control of Yeshiva's faculty" over academic and personnel decisions as well as the "crucial role of the full-time faculty in determining other central policies of the institution." The court concluded that such power is not an exercise of individual professional expertise. Rather, the faculty are, "in effect, substantially and pervasively operating the enterprise." Accordingly, the court held that the faculty are endowed with "managerial status" sufficient to remove them from the coverage of the Act. We granted certiorari and now affirm.

III

There is no evidence that Congress has considered whether a university faculty may organize for collective bargaining under the Act. Indeed, when the Wagner and Taft-Hartley Acts were approved, it was thought that congressional power did not extend to university faculties because they were employed by nonprofit institutions which did not "affect commerce." Moreover, the authority structure of a university does not fit neatly within the statutory scheme we are asked to interpret. The Board itself has noted that the concept of collegiality "does not square with the traditional authority structures with which th[e] Act was designed to cope in the typical organizations of the commercial world."

The Act was intended to accommodate the type of management-employee relations that prevail in the pyramidal hierarchies of private industry. In contrast, authority in the typical "mature" private university is divided between a central administration and one or more collegial bodies. This system of "shared authority" evolved from the medieval model of collegial decisionmaking in which guilds of scholars were responsible only to themselves. At early universities, the faculty were the school. Although faculties have been subject to external control in the United States since colonial times, traditions of collegiality continue to play a significant role at many universities, including Yeshiva. For these reasons, the Board has recognized that principles developed for use in the industrial setting cannot be "imposed blindly on the academic world."

The absence of explicit congressional direction, of course, does not preclude the Board from reaching any particular type of employment. Acting under its responsibility for adapting the broad provisions of the Act to differing workplaces, the Board asserted jurisdiction over a university for the first time in 1970. The Board reasoned that faculty members are "professional employees" within the meaning of § 2(12) of the Act and therefore are entitled to the benefits of collective bargaining.

Yeshiva does not contend that its faculty are not professionals under the statute. But professionals, like other employees, may be exempted from coverage under the Act's exclusion for "supervisors" who use independent judgment in overseeing other employees in the interest of the employer, or under the judicially implied exclusion for "managerial employees" who are involved in developing and enforcing employer policy. Both exemptions grow out of the same concern: That an employer is entitled to the undivided loyalty of its representatives. Because the Court of Appeals found the faculty to be managerial employees, it did not decide the question of their supervisory status. In view of our agreement with that court's application of the managerial exclusion, we also need not resolve that issue of statutory interpretation.

IV

Managerial employees are defined as those who "formulate and effectuate management policies by expressing and making operative the decisions of their employer." These employees are "much higher in the managerial structure" than those explicitly mentioned by Congress, which "regarded [them] as so clearly outside the Act that no specific exclusionary provision was thought necessary." Managerial employees must exercise discretion within, or even independently of, established employer policy and must be aligned with management. Although the Board has established no firm criteria for determining when an employee is so aligned, normally an employee may be excluded as managerial only if he represents management interests by taking or recommending discretionary actions that effectively control or implement employer policy.

The Board does not contend that the Yeshiva faculty's decision making is too insignificant to be deemed managerial. Nor does it suggest that the role of the faculty is merely advisory and thus not managerial. Instead, it contends that the managerial exclusion cannot be applied in a straightforward fashion to professional employees because those employees often appear to be exercising managerial

authority when they are merely performing routine job duties. The status of such employees, in the Board's view, must be determined by reference to the "alignment with management" criterion. The Board argues that the Yeshiva faculty are not aligned with management because they are expected to exercise "independent professional judgment" while participating in academic governance, and because they are neither "expected to conform to management policies [nor] judged according to their effectiveness in carrying out those policies."

Because of this independence, the Board contends there is no danger of divided loyalty and no need for the managerial exclusion. In its view, union pressure cannot divert the faculty from adhering to the interests of the university, because the university itself expects its faculty to pursue professional values rather than institutional interests. The Board concludes that application of the managerial exclusion to such employees would frustrate the national labor policy in favor of collective bargaining.

This "independent professional judgment" test was not applied in the decision we are asked to uphold. The Board's opinion relies exclusively on its previous faculty decisions for both legal and factual analysis. But those decisions only dimly foreshadow the reasoning now proffered to the Court. Without explanation, the Board initially announced two different rationales for faculty cases, then quickly transformed them into a litany to be repeated in case after case: (i) faculty authority is collective, (ii) it is exercised in the faculty's own interest rather than in the interest of the university, and (iii) final authority rests with the board of trustees. In their arguments in this case, the Board's lawyers have abandoned the first and third branches of this analysis, which in any event were flatly inconsistent with its precedents, and have transformed the second into a theory that does not appear clearly in any Board opinion.

V

The controlling consideration in this case is that the faculty of Yeshiva University exercise authority which in any other context unquestionably would be managerial. Their authority in academic matters is absolute. They decide what courses will be offered, when they will be scheduled, and to whom they will be taught. They debate and determine teaching methods, grading policies, and matriculation standards. They effectively decide which students will be admitted, retained, and graduated. On occasion their views have determined the size of the student body, the tuition to be charged, and the location of a school. When one considers the function of a university, it is difficult to imagine decisions more managerial than these. To the extent the industrial analogy applies, the faculty determines within each school the product to be produced, the terms upon which it will be offered, and the customers who will be served.

The Board nevertheless insists that these decisions are not managerial because they require the exercise of independent professional judgment. We are not persuaded by this argument. There may be some tension between the Act's exclusion of managerial employees and its inclusion of professionals, since most professionals in managerial positions continue to draw on their special skills and training. But we have been directed to no authority suggesting that that tension can be resolved by reference to the "independent professional judgment" criterion proposed in this case. Outside the university context, the Board routinely has applied the managerial and supervisory exclusions to professionals in executive positions without inquiring whether their decisions were based on management policy rather than professional expertise.

Indeed, the Board has twice implicitly rejected the contention that decisions based on professional judgment cannot be managerial. Since the Board does not suggest that the "independent professional judgment" test is to be limited to university faculty, its new approach would overrule *sub silentio* this body of Board precedent and could result in the indiscriminate recharacterization as covered employees of professionals working in supervisory and managerial capacities.

Moreover, the Board's approach would undermine the goal it purports to serve: To ensure that employees who exercise discretionary authority on behalf of the employer will not divide their loyalty between employer and union. In arguing that a faculty member exercising independent judgment acts primarily in his own interest and therefore does not represent the interest of his employer, the Board assumes that the professional interests of the faculty and the interests of the institution are distinct, separable entities with which a faculty member could not simultaneously be aligned. The Court of Appeals found no justification for this distinction, and we perceive none. In fact, the faculty's professional interests—as applied to governance at a university like Yeshiva—cannot be separated from those of the institution.

In such a university, the predominant policy normally is to operate a quality institution of higher learning that will accomplish broadly defined educational goals within the limits of its financial resources. The "business" of a university is education, and its vitality ultimately must depend on academic policies that largely are formulated and generally are implemented by faculty governance decisions. Faculty members enhance their own standing and fulfill their professional mission by ensuring that the university's objectives are met. But there can be no doubt that the quest for academic excellence and institutional distinction is a "policy" to which the administration expects the faculty to adhere, whether it be defined as a professional or an institutional goal. It is fruitless to ask whether an employee is "expected to conform" to one goal or another when the two are essentially the same.

The problem of divided loyalty is particularly acute for a university like Yeshiva, which depends on the professional judgment of its faculty to formulate and apply crucial policies constrained only by necessarily general institutional goals. The university requires faculty participation in governance because professional expertise is indispensable to the formulation and implementation of academic policy. It may appear, as the Board contends, that the professor performing governance functions is less "accountable" for departures from institutional policy than a middle-level industrial manager whose discretion is more confined. Moreover, traditional systems of collegiality and tenure insulate the professor from some of the sanctions applied to an industrial manager who fails to adhere to company policy. But the analogy of the university to industry need not, and indeed cannot, be complete. It is clear that Yeshiva and like universities must rely on their faculties to participate in the making and implementation of their policies. The large measure of independence enjoyed by faculty members can only increase the danger that divided loyalty will lead to those harms that the Board traditionally has sought to prevent.

We certainly are not suggesting an application of the managerial exclusion that would sweep all professionals outside the Act in derogation of Congress' expressed intent to protect them. The Board has recognized that employees whose decision making is limited to the routine discharge of professional duties in projects to which they have been assigned cannot be excluded from coverage even if union membership arguably may involve some divided loyalty. Only if an employee's activities fall outside the scope of the duties routinely performed by similarly situated professionals will he be found aligned with management. We think these decisions accurately capture the intent of Congress, and that they provide an appropriate starting point for analysis in cases involving professionals alleged to be managerial.

VI

Finally, the Board contends that the deference due its expertise in these matters requires us to reverse the decision of the Court of Appeals. The question we decide today is a mixed one of fact and law. But the Board's opinion may be searched in vain for relevant findings of fact. The absence of factual analysis apparently reflects the Board's view that the managerial status of particular faculties may be decided on the basis of conclusory rationales rather than examination of the facts of each case. The Court of Appeals took a different view, and determined that the faculty of Yeshiva University, "in effect, substantially and pervasively operat[e] the enterprise." We find no reason to reject this conclusion. As our decisions consistently show, we accord great respect to the expertise of the Board when its conclusions are rationally based on articulated facts and consistent with the Act. In this case, we hold that the Board's decision satisfies neither criterion.

Affirmed.

P

Papish v. Board of Curators of the University of Missouri

Papish v. Board of Curators of the University of Missouri (1973) was the first case from the U.S. Supreme Court to address student press on campus. At issue in *Papish* was whether university officials could expel a graduate student for distributing a newspaper on campus because they disapproved of its content. Given the significant implications of *Papish* for the First Amendment rights of students in colleges and universities and the extent to which institutional officials can limit speech that may be perceived as offensive, this entry reviews its background and judicial analysis.

Facts of the Case

Barbara Papish, a 32-year-old graduate student majoring in journalism at the University of Missouri, was expelled for distributing an issue of the *Free Press Underground* newspaper, published by the nonprofit Columbia Free Press Corporation. According to university officials, the paper contained forms of what they described as indecent speech. The newspaper had been sold on campus for more than four years with authorization from officials in the university's business office. The issue of the newspaper in question was unacceptable to university officials, because it included a political cartoon depicting police officers raping the Statue of Liberty and the *Goddess of Justice* and an article with the title "M— f— Acquitted." Papish was a staff member of the *Free Press Underground*.

The student, who had been pursuing a graduate degree for five and one-half years when the newspaper episode occurred, was on academic probation for prolonged submarginal academic progress. After the Faculty Committee on Student Conduct decided that the student violated a university bylaw prohibiting "indecent conduct or speech," she was placed on disciplinary probation. The student subsequently exhausted her rights to review within the university as its chancellor and board of curators affirmed her expulsion. Although the student was allowed to remain on campus until the end of the semester, she was not given credit for the one course she passed.

The student unsuccessfully filed suit in a federal trial court in Missouri, seeking declaratory and injunctive relief pursuant to 42 U.S.C. § 1983, also commonly known as Section 1983 of the Civil Rights Act of 1871 (a law that was enacted to fight discrimination against Blacks during Reconstruction), asserting that she was expelled for activities protected by the First Amendment. Based on the university's defense that focused on the time and place of distributing the newspaper issue, the student's being on academic probation, and the issue of indecent speech, the Eighth Circuit affirmed in its favor. The court was convinced that the student's freedom of expression could be subordinated to the "conventions of decency" with regard to the language and pictures on the campus of a public university.

The Supreme Court's Ruling

On further review, in a six-to-three judgment, in a relatively brief per curiam opinion that was not signed by any of the members of the majority, the Supreme Court reversed in favor of the student. In its deliberations, the Court noted that the Eighth Circuit's ruling came just before the Court's judgment in *Healy v. James* (1972), wherein it held that officials at public colleges and universities are not without the ability and responsibility to enforce reasonable rules governing student conduct. Yet, acknowledging its recent judgment in *Tinker v. Des Moines Independent School District* (1969), in which it upheld the free speech rights of high school students who wore black armbands to protest American involvement in Vietnam, the Court pointed out that college and university campuses are not closed societies that are immune to the sweep of the First Amendment.

In *Healy,* the Court ruled that officials had overstepped their bounds by forbidding students from organizing a local chapter of Students for a Democratic Society on the grounds that such an organization might have caused a disruption on campus. In the light of *Healy,* the Supreme Court determined that the mere dissemination of offensive ideas is an insufficient ground on which to bar student groups from campuses. Put another way, the Court made it clear that the propagation of ideas on a state university campus, regardless of their offensiveness, cannot be prohibited simply in the name of "conventions of decency." The Court, relying on its own precedent in free speech cases in noneducation contexts, was clear that neither the political cartoon nor the title was obscene or unprotected under the First Amendment. The Court thus concluded that officials acted unconstitutionally in expelling the student because of the content of the newspaper rather than the time, place, or manner of its distribution on campus.

In his dissent, Chief Justice Burger disagreed with the majority in observing that the cases on which the majority relied arose in the context of criminal cases rather than on campuses, where university officials had the right to control unacceptable speech. Justice Rehnquist also dissented, contending that the Court should not have ignored evidence presented at trial on how unacceptable the student's behavior had been before she was expelled for distributing the newspaper.

As the first case to address the free speech rights of students in higher education to distribute newspapers on campuses, even if the content of such papers may have been perceived as offensive, *Papish* has opened the door to ongoing litigation on the boundaries of the First Amendment on college and university campuses. As institutions of higher learning have entered the cyber age, college and university officials should consider the ramifications that *Papish* might have when attempting to limit the content of student publications.

Darlene Y. Bruner

See also Civil Rights Act of 1871, Section 1983; Free Speech and Expression Rights of Students; *Healy v. James*; Student Press

Further Readings

Brownstein, A. E. (1986). Regulating hate speech at public universities: Are First Amendment values functionally incompatible with equal protection principles? *Buffalo Law Review, 39,* 1–52.

Legal Citations

Civil Rights Act of 1871, Section 1983, 42 U.S.C. § 1983.
Healy v. James, 408 U.S. 169 (1972).
Papish v. Board of Curators of the University of Missouri, 410 U.S. 667 (1973).
Tinker v. Des Moines Independent School District, 393 U.S. 503 (1969).

PAPISH V. BOARD OF CURATORS OF THE UNIVERSITY OF MISSOURI

Papish is important because it is the only case in which the Supreme Court addressed the rights of a student who was involved with a newspaper in higher education.

Supreme Court of the United States

PAPISH

v.

BOARD OF CURATORS OF THE UNIVERSITY OF MISSOURI

410 U.S. 672

Decided March 19, 1973

PER CURIAM.

Petitioner, a graduate student in the University of Missouri School of Journalism, was expelled for distributing on campus a newspaper "containing forms of indecent speech" in violation of a bylaw of the Board of Curators. The newspaper, the Free Press Underground, had been sold on this state university campus for more than four years pursuant to an authorization obtained from the University Business Office. The particular newspaper issue in question was found to be unacceptable for two reasons. First, on the front cover the publishers had reproduced a political cartoon previously printed in another newspaper depicting policemen raping the Statue of Liberty and the Goddess of Justice. The caption under the cartoon read: " . . . With Liberty and Justice for All." Secondly, the issue contained an article entitled "M—-f—-Acquitted," which discussed the trial and acquittal on an assault charge of a New York City youth who was a member of an organization known as "Up Against the Wall, M—-f—-." Following a hearing, the Student Conduct Committee found that petitioner had violated Par. B of Art. V of the General Standards of Student Conduct which requires students "to observe generally accepted standards of conduct" and specifically prohibits "indecent conduct or speech." Her expulsion, after affirmance first by the Chancellor of the University

and then by its Board of Curators, was made effective in the middle of the spring semester. Although she was then permitted to remain on campus until the end of the semester, she was not given credit for the one course in which she made a passing grade.[3]

After exhausting her administrative review alternatives within the University, petitioner brought an action for declaratory and injunctive relief pursuant to 42 U.S.C. § 1983 in the United States District Court for the Western District of Missouri. She claimed that her expulsion was improperly premised on activities protected by the First Amendment. The District Court denied relief, and the Court of Appeals affirmed, one judge dissenting. Rehearing en banc was denied by an equally divided vote of all the judges in the Eighth Circuit.

The District Court's opinion rests, in part, on the conclusion that the banned issue of the newspaper was obscene. The Court of Appeals found it unnecessary to decide that question. Instead, assuming that the newspaper was not obscene and that its distribution in the community at large would be protected by the First Amendment, the court held that on a university campus "freedom of expression" could properly be "subordinated to other interests such as, for example, the conventions of decency in the use and display of language and pictures." The court concluded that "(t)he Constitution does not compel the University . . . (to allow) such publications as

---

FN3. Miss Papish, a 32-year-old graduate student, was admitted to the graduate school of the University in September 1963. Five and one-half years later, when the episode under consideration occurred, she was still pursuing her graduate degree. She was on "academic probation" because of "prolonged submarginal academic progress," and since November 1, 1967, she also had been on disciplinary probation for disseminating Students for a Democratic Society literature found at a university hearing to have contained "pornographic, indecent and obscene words." This dissemination had occurred at a time when the University was host to high school seniors and their parents. But disenchantment with Miss Papish's performance, understandable as it may have been, is no justification for denial of constitutional rights.

the one in litigation to be publicly sold or distributed on its open campus."

This case was decided several days before we handed down *Healy v. James* in which, while recognizing a state university's undoubted prerogative to enforce reasonable rules governing student conduct, we reaffirmed that "state colleges and universities are not enclaves immune from the sweep of the First Amendment." We think *Healy* makes it clear that the mere dissemination of ideas—no matter how offensive to good taste—on a state university campus may not be shut off in the name alone of "conventions of decency." Other recent precedents of this Court make it equally clear that neither the political cartoon nor the headline story involved in this case can be labeled as constitutionally obscene or otherwise unprotected. There is language in the opinions below which suggests that the University's action here could be viewed as an exercise of its legitimate authority to enforce reasonable regulations as to the time, place, and manner of speech and its

dissemination. While we have repeatedly approved such regulatory authority, the facts set forth in the opinions below show clearly that petitioner was expelled because of the disapproved content of the newspaper rather than the time, place, or manner of its distribution.

Since the First Amendment leaves no room for the operation of a dual standard in the academic community with respect to the content of speech, and because the state University's action here cannot be justified as a nondiscriminatory application of reasonable rules governing conduct, the judgments of the courts below must be reversed. Accordingly the petition for a writ of certiorari is granted, the case is remanded to the District Court, and that court is instructed to order the University to restore to petitioner any course credits she earned for the semester in question and, unless she is barred from reinstatement for valid academic reasons, to reinstate her as a student in the graduate program.

Reversed and remanded.

PERRY V. SINDERMANN

At issue in *Perry v. Sindermann* (1972) was whether the Fourteenth Amendment required college officials to provide procedural due process when they choose not to renew the contract of a faculty member who lacked tenure. In *Perry*, the U.S. Supreme Court ruled that faculty members who lack tenure and whose contracts are not renewed may have a right to procedural due process if they can establish that they had property interests in continued employment. In light of the significant questions that *Perry* raises for nontenured faculty members whose employment contracts are not renewed, this entry examines the case in detail.

Facts of the Case

Robert Sindermann was employed as a nontenured faculty member in the Texas state college system from 1959 to 1969. During the last four years of his time there, Sindermann served as a professor of government and social science at Odessa Junior College (OJC) under consecutive one-year contracts. While Sindermann also served briefly as

cochair of the social sciences department, officials at OJC dismissed him from that position, because he circulated lengthy letters to members of the department criticizing its actions. Moreover, Sindermann's being elected president of the Texas Junior College Teachers Association in February 1969 led to further controversy between him and the OJC administration. Serving in his capacity as president of the association, Sindermann was absent several times from his teaching duties, even though the administration denied his requests to testify in the state capitol before committees of the Texas legislature. In addition, Sindermann publicly supported the elevation of OJC to four-year status, a change that its board of regents opposed.

In May 1969, when the board of regents voted not to renew Sindermann's contract for the 1969–1970 academic year, it issued a press release citing his insubordination and the deterioration of their relationship. The board did not provide him with an official statement of the reasons for nonrenewal and did not give him an opportunity for a hearing in which to respond to the allegations. At the time, OJC had no formal tenure system that gave any faculty member the assurance of continued employment beyond the present year. However, a statement published in its Faculty Guide stipulated that while OJC did not have a tenure system, its administration wanted faculty members "to feel" that they had permanent tenure as long as their teaching was satisfactory, they were cooperative with coworkers and their superiors, and they were happy in their work.

Sindermann filed suit in a federal trial court in Texas, alleging that because his contract was not renewed as a result of his public criticism of the OJC administration, officials violated his First Amendment right to freedom of expression. He also contended that the board's failure to provide a hearing violated his Fourteenth Amendment rights to procedural due process. The board, in denying that its actions were retaliatory, responded that it had no obligation to provide a hearing, because Sindermann's contract had expired, and he lacked a property interest in continued employment.

The court, determining that the plaintiff's contract expired and that OJC had not adopted a tenure system, ruled in the board's favor. The Fifth Circuit reversed in favor of the plaintiff, finding that the board violated his Fourteenth Amendment rights in denying his request for a hearing to resolve whether the nonrenewal of his contract was due to his protected free speech and whether he had an "expectancy" of reemployment. Dissatisfied with the outcome, OJC appealed; the Supreme Court agreed to hear an appeal and considered Perry along with *Board of Regents of State Colleges v. Roth* (1972), wherein a faculty member in Wisconsin who was hired under a one-year contract challenged the nonrenewal of his contract after he was provided neither with reasons that his employment was terminated nor an opportunity for a hearing.

The Supreme Court's Ruling

In a five-to-three judgment, with Justice Powell not participating, the Supreme Court affirmed the order of the Fifth Circuit. The Court first considered whether the plaintiff's lack of contractual or tenure rights defeated his claim that the nonrenewal of his contract violated his First Amendment rights of free speech and expression. The plaintiff claimed that his contract was not renewed because of his controversial testimony about the OJC board of regents both publicly and before the legislative committees. Insofar as the trial court granted the board's motion for summary judgment

on this issue, the justices were unable to decide whether his free speech and expression were the sole reason for its action and so did not enter a judgment for either party on this issue. Even so, the Court reiterated the principle that the government, in the form of boards of regents at public institutions of higher education, cannot deny benefit to individuals on grounds that infringe on their constitutionally protected right to free speech. To this end, the Court was satisfied that because the plaintiff presented a bona fide claim based on First Amendment freedom of expression, the trial court erred in granting the board's motion for summary judgment on the issue of whether he was entitled to a hearing.

The Supreme Court next turned to the plaintiff's claim that OJC's refusal to provide him with a hearing violated his right to procedural due process. The Court noted that in *Roth*, which it handed down on the same day, faculty members who lack tenure have a right to a hearing only if they are deprived of liberty or property interests. The Court thus considered this claim in light of the plaintiff's allegation that although OJC had no official tenure policy, the de facto tenure provision in its Faculty Guide created an understanding or expectancy for continued employment and thereby created a property interest. The Court, in recognizing that rules and understandings may entitle faculty members to continued employment, did not order the plaintiff's reinstatement to his job. However, the Court reasoned that officials at OJC had to provide him with an opportunity to show he had a property interest that entitled him, not to automatic reinstatement, but to a due process hearing.

In his short, partial dissent, Justice Marshall agreed with the Court that the plaintiff presented a valid First Amendment claim but would have granted his motion for summary judgment, rather than the board's, and required the board to provide him with a reason that his contract was not renewed.

Justice Brennan's brief partial dissent, which was joined by Justice Douglas, also agreed with the majority on the First Amendment claim but disagreed to the extent that he would have modified the judgment of the Fifth Circuit in the same way as Justice Marshall.

Perry raises key five implications for the rights of faculty members in higher education. First, officials cannot fail to renew their contracts because of constitutionally protected expression by employees, even if the employees lack tenure. Second, when facing the nonrenewal of their contacts, faculty members with liberty or property interests in their jobs are entitled to procedural due process, including an opportunity for a hearing. Third, within the terms of their contracts or tenure policies, tenured faculty members have due process rights, while those who are not tenured must demonstrate an expectancy of continued employment in order to receive procedural due process rights. Fourth, because de facto tenure systems may create property interests that entitle faculty members to due process, college and university officials should carefully word their contracts and policies to trigger only the employee protections that they wish to provide. Finally, because not renewing employment contracts often leads to legal challenges, officials should provide opportunities for due process hearings to ensure that all faculty, both those with tenure and those without it, receive due process. In sum, *Perry* and *Board of Regents of State Colleges v. Roth* stand out as important cases that helped to establish the parameters of when faculty members in higher education who are facing the nonrenewal of their employment contracts have rights to due process protections.

Marilyn Denison

See also *Board of Regents of State Colleges v. Roth*; Due Process Rights in Faculty and Staff Dismissal; Due Process, Substantive and Procedural; Fourteenth Amendment; Tenure

Further Readings

Beckham, J. (2005). Faculty. In J. Beckham & D. Dagley (Eds.), *Contemporary issues in higher education law* (pp. 89–130). Dayton, OH: Education Law Association.
Cleveland Board of Education v. Loudermill, 470 U.S. 532 (1985).

Legal Citations

Board of Regents of State Colleges v. Roth, 408 U.S. 564 (1972).
Perry v. Sindermann, 408 U.S. 593 (1972).

PERRY V. SINDERMANN

In *Perry*, decided on the same day as *Board of Regents v. Roth*, the Supreme Court addressed the due process rights of non-tenured faculty members whose employment contracts are not renewed.

Supreme Court of the United States

PERRY

v.

SINDERMANN

408 U.S. 593

Argued Jan. 18, 1972

Decided June 29, 1972

Mr. Justice STEWART delivered the opinion of the Court.

From 1959 to 1969 the respondent, Robert Sindermann, was a teacher in the state college system of the State of Texas. After teaching for two years at the University of Texas and for four years at San Antonio Junior College, he became a professor of Government and Social Science at Odessa Junior College in 1965. He was employed at the college for four successive years, under a series of one-year contracts. He was successful enough to be appointed, for a time, the cochairman of his department.

During the 1968–1969 academic year, however, controversy arose between the respondent and the college administration. The respondent was elected president of the Texas Junior College Teachers Association. In this capacity, he left his teaching duties on several occasions to testify before committees of the Texas Legislature, and he became involved in public disagreements with the policies of the college's Board of Regents. In particular, he aligned himself with a group advocating the elevation of the college to four-year status—a change opposed by the Regents. And, on one occasion, a newspaper advertisement appeared over his name that was highly critical of the Regents.

Finally, in May 1969, the respondent's one-year employment contract terminated and the Board of Regents voted not to offer him a new contract for the next academic year. The Regents issued a press release setting forth allegations of the respondent's insubordination. But they provided him no official statement of the reasons for the nonrenewal of his contract. And they allowed him no opportunity for a hearing to challenge the basis of the nonrenewal.

The respondent then brought this action in Federal District Court. He alleged primarily that the Regents' decision not to rehire him was based on his public criticism of the policies of the college administration and thus infringed his right to freedom of speech. He also alleged that their failure to provide him an opportunity for a hearing violated the Fourteenth Amendment's guarantee of procedural due process. The petitioners—members of the Board of Regents and the president of the college—denied that their decision was made in retaliation for the respondent's public criticism and argued that they had no obligation to provide a hearing. On the basis of these bare pleadings and three brief affidavits filed by the respondent, the District Court granted summary judgment for the petitioners. It concluded that the respondent had "no cause of action against the (petitioners) since his contract of employment terminated May 31, 1969, and Odessa Junior College has not adopted the tenure system."

The Court of Appeals reversed the judgment of the District Court. First, it held that, despite the respondent's lack of tenure, the nonrenewal of his contract would violate the Fourteenth Amendment if it in fact was based on his protected free speech. Since the actual reason for the Regents' decision was "in total dispute" in the pleadings, the court remanded the case for a full hearing on this contested issue of fact. Second, the Court of Appeals held that, despite the respondent's lack of tenure, the failure to allow him an opportunity for a hearing would violate the constitutional guarantee of procedural due process if the respondent could show that he had an "expectancy" of re-employment. It, therefore, ordered that this issue of fact also be aired upon remand. We granted a writ of certiorari, and we have considered this case along with *Board of Regents v. Roth.*

I

The first question presented is whether the respondent's lack of a contractual or tenure right to re-employment, taken alone, defeats his claim that the nonrenewal of his contract violated the First and Fourteenth Amendments. We hold that it does not.

For at least a quarter-century, this Court has made clear that even though a person has no "right" to a valuable governmental benefit and even though the government may deny him the benefit for any number of reasons, there are some reasons upon which the government may not rely. It may not deny a benefit to a person on a basis that infringes his constitutionally protected interests—especially, his interest in freedom of speech. For if the government could deny a benefit to a person because of his constitutionally protected speech or associations, his exercise of those freedoms would in effect be penalized and inhibited. This would allow the government to "produce a result which (it) could not command directly." Such interference with constitutional rights is impermissible.

We have applied this general principle to denials of tax exemptions and unemployment benefits. But, most often, we have applied the principle to denials of public employment. We have applied the principle regardless of the public employee's contractual or other claim to a job.

Thus, the respondent's lack of a contractual or tenure "right" to re-employment for the 1969–1970 academic year is immaterial to his free speech claim. Indeed, twice before, this Court has specifically held that the nonrenewal of a nontenured public school teacher's one-year contract may not be predicated on his exercise of First and Fourteenth Amendment rights. We reaffirm those holdings here.

In this case, of course, the respondent has yet to show that the decision not to renew his contract was, in fact, made in retaliation for his exercise of the constitutional right of free speech. The District Court foreclosed any opportunity to make this showing when it granted summary judgment. Hence, we cannot now hold that the Board of Regents' action was invalid.

But we agree with the Court of Appeals that there is a genuine dispute as to "whether the college refused to renew the teaching contract on an impermissible basis—as a reprisal for the exercise of constitutionally protected rights." The respondent has alleged that his nonretention was based on his testimony before legislative committees and his other public statements critical of the Regents' policies. And he has alleged that this public criticism was within the First and Fourteenth Amendments' protection of freedom of speech. Plainly, these allegations present a bona fide constitutional claim. For this Court has held that a teacher's public criticism of his superiors on matters of public concern may be constitutionally protected and may, therefore, be an impermissible basis for termination of his employment.

For this reason we hold that the grant of summary judgment against the respondent, without full exploration of this issue, was improper.

II

The respondent's lack of formal contractual or tenure security in continued employment at Odessa Junior College, though irrelevant to his free speech claim, is highly relevant to his procedural due process claim. But it may not be entirely dispositive.

We have held today in *Board of Regents v. Roth* that the Constitution does not require opportunity for a hearing before the nonrenewal of a nontenured teacher's contract, unless he can show that the decision not to rehire him somehow deprived him of an interest in "liberty" or that he had a "property" interest in continued employment, despite the lack of tenure or a formal contract. In *Roth* the teacher had not made a showing on either point to justify summary judgment in his favor.

Similarly, the respondent here has yet to show that he has been deprived of an interest that could invoke procedural due process protection. As in *Roth*, the mere showing that he was not rehired in one particular job, without more, did not amount to a showing of a loss of liberty. Nor did it amount to a showing of a loss of property.

But the respondent's allegations—which we must construe most favorably to the respondent at this stage of the litigation—do raise a genuine issue as to his interest in continued employment at Odessa Junior College. He alleged that this interest, though not secured by a formal contractual tenure provision, was secured by a no less binding understanding fostered by the college administration. In particular, the respondent alleged that the college had a de facto tenure program, and that he had tenure under that program. He claimed that he and others legitimately relied upon an unusual provision that had been in the college's official Faculty Guide for many years: "Teacher Tenure: Odessa College has no tenure system. The Administration of the College wishes the faculty member to feel that he has permanent tenure as long as his teaching services are satisfactory and as long as he displays a cooperative attitude toward his co-workers and his superiors, and as long as he is happy in his work."

Moreover, the respondent claimed legitimate reliance upon guidelines promulgated by the Coordinating Board of the Texas College and University System that provided that a person, like himself, who had been employed as a teacher in the state college and university system for seven years or more has some form of job tenure. Thus, the respondent offered to prove that a teacher with his long period of service at this particular State College had no less a "property" interest in continued employment than a formally tenured teacher at other colleges, and had no less a procedural due process right to a statement of reasons and a hearing before college officials upon their decision not to retain him.

We have made clear in *Roth* that "property" interests subject to procedural due process protection are not limited by a few rigid, technical forms. Rather, "property" denotes a broad range of interests that are secured by "existing rules or understandings." A person's interest in a benefit is a "property" interest for due process purposes if there are such rules or mutually explicit understandings that support his claim of entitlement to the benefit and that he may invoke at a hearing.

A written contract with an explicit tenure provision clearly is evidence of a formal understanding that supports a teacher's claim of entitlement to continued employment unless sufficient "cause" is shown. Yet absence of such an explicit contractual provision may not always foreclose the possibility that a teacher has a "property" interest in reemployment. For example, the law of contracts in most, if not all, jurisdictions long has employed a process by which agreements, though not formalized in writing, may be "implied." Explicit contractual provisions may be supplemented by other agreements implied from "the promisor's words and conduct in the light of the surrounding circumstances." And, "(t)he meaning of (the promisor's) words and acts is found by relating them to the usage of the past."

A teacher, like the respondent, who has held his position for a number of years, might be able to show from the circumstances of this service—and from other relevant facts—that he has a legitimate claim of entitlement to job tenure. Just as this Court has found there to be a "common law of a particular industry or of a particular plant" that may supplement a collective-bargaining agreement, so there may be an unwritten "common law" in a particular university that certain employees shall have the equivalent of tenure. This is particularly likely in a college or university, like Odessa Junior College, that has no explicit tenure system even for senior members of its faculty, but that nonetheless may have created such a system in practice.

In this case, the respondent has alleged the existence of rules and understandings, promulgated and fostered by state officials, that may justify his legitimate claim of entitlement to continued employment absent "sufficient cause." We disagree with the Court of Appeals insofar as it held that a mere subjective "expectancy" is protected by procedural due process, but we agree that the respondent must be given an opportunity to prove the legitimacy of his claim of such entitlement in light of "the policies and practices of the institution." Proof of such a property interest would not, of course, entitle him to reinstatement. But such proof would obligate college officials to grant a hearing at his request, where he could be informed of the grounds for his nonretention and challenge their sufficiency.

Therefore, while we do not wholly agree with the opinion of the Court of Appeals, its judgment remanding this case to the District Court is

Affirmed.

Mr. Justice POWELL took no part in the decision of this case.

Personnel Records

Personnel records are the records maintained by employers such as colleges or universities to document the employment history of individual employees. Personnel records can be in any form, such as paper, electronic, and audio or video files in a variety of formats. What establishes the nature of personnel files is the quality of the information in them, not their physical nature. In other words, personnel files are important more for the information they contain than for the form they take, whether written or electronic. Personnel records may include application materials, college transcripts, resumes or curriculum vitae, evaluation and merit materials, tenure and promotion files, and disciplinary information about individual employees. Traditionally, personnel files have been considered to be property of employers, information maintained in them was private, and even the subjects of the files were not given access. Presumably, only those with a "need to know," usually supervisors of employees, were permitted access. The law of personnel records for institutions of higher learning and their employees has become increasingly sophisticated. As such, this area of law largely depends on a combination of common law and statutory law that differs across jurisdictions. In light of the important legal issues associated with such files, this entry reviews key legal issues associated with personnel files.

The information in college and university personnel records represent competing values. On one hand, individual employees who are subjects of personnel files have an expectation of privacy with regard to certain information in their files, an expectation that is buttressed by potential judicial claims. On the other hand, because employees of public colleges and universities are governmental employees, the people of the jurisdictions within which they work have expectations of transparency in government's businesses, including education.

Privacy Interests in Personnel Records

Judge Thomas Cooley famously described the right to privacy as "the right to be let alone" (Cooley, 1888, p. 29). The expectations that individuals have to privacy in many matters is supported by federal and state constitutional law, federal and state statutory law, and common law.

Under the U.S. Constitution, there are two types of privacy. The first type, usually called "information privacy," deals with the federal government's release of private information about individuals.

The second type, often referred to as "constitutional autonomy," deals with situations in which the federal government interferes with highly private individual decisions. In addition, many jurisdictions have explicit privacy protections in their state constitutions. For example, Montana's state constitution provides a guarantee as follows: "The right of individual privacy is essential to the well-being of a free society and shall not be infringed without the showing of a compelling state interest."

Federal statutory law also recognizes certain privacy interests in personnel records. The Privacy Act of 1974, now incorporated into the federal Freedom of Information Act, controls the extent and uses of information about individuals that is maintained by federal agencies. The Americans with Disabilities Act (ADA) requires employers covered by its provisions to secure information obtained by post–job offer medical examinations in places separate from general personnel files while maintaining their confidentiality. Insofar as colleges and universities are providers of health care or purchase group health insurance, they are subject to the privacy provisions in the Health Insurance Portability and Accountability Act. At least one employee claimed that the college transcripts in her personnel file were covered by the Family Education Rights and Privacy Act (FERPA). However, the Fifth Circuit affirmed that once transcripts had become part of an individual's personnel file, they were no longer educational records as defined by FERPA and therefore were subject to disclosure under state law (*Klein Independent School District v. Mattox,* 1988).

Individual state statutory provisions related to privacy can implicate college or university personnel files in odd ways. By way of illustration, the Texas Education Code prohibits institutions of higher education from releasing oral interviews for historical purposes if the materials were obtained through confidentiality agreements between interviewees and representatives of state institutions, such as faculty members and students who are engaged in gathering data for their dissertations. For example, a history department's oral history project that focused on the memories of university employees might trigger privacy interests in audio or video files that find their way into personnel files.

The common law recognizes four separate tort claims concerned with individual rights to privacy.

The four potential claims are intrusion on seclusion, public disclosure of a private fact, being placed in a false light in the public eye, and appropriation of another's name or image. All states have adopted one or more of these common law claims, while damages and injunctive relief are available for impairing the privacy interests of individuals at common law.

The Public's Right to Know

The public's interest in transparency in government is supported by various sunshine laws related to records. In 1974, the Congress enacted the Freedom of Information Act, which applies to federal agencies. This act creates a presumption that all records produced by the federal government must be disclosed to the general public, unless they are subject to a specific exemption in its provisions. It is worth noting that personnel files are the sixth specific exemption provided in this act. Consequently, personnel files in federal institutions of higher education such as the military academies are categorically exempt from disclosure.

By 1981, all states except Mississippi had adopted state-level freedom of information acts (Braverman & Hepler, 1981). Mississippi added its own open records law in 1983. Many states adopted open records laws that were structurally similar to the federal act, beginning with a presumption in favor of disclosing all state governmental records but providing a specific exemption related to personnel files, sometimes with variations. Administrators in college and universities in states with freedom of information acts that provide a full exemption for personnel files, without modifying language, can likely presume that personnel files in their institutions are categorically exempt from disclosure. However, modifications in the language of the exemptions may modify the duty to disclose. For example, Colorado's exemption is for personnel files except applications and performance ratings.

A number of states have no exemption language in their freedom of information acts. For instance, in a situation not unlike the federal case involving FERPA, the Supreme Court of North Dakota affirmed that absent a specific exemption for the personnel files of educators, the contents of such files were subject to disclosure (*Hovet v. Hebron Public School District,* 1988). Consequently, whether personnel files must be disclosed is subject to case-by-case analyses balancing the public's right to know against individual employees' privacy interests to be let alone.

In Pari Materia Analysis

Freedom of information acts and privacy acts are statutes treated as *in pari materia*, literally, "relating to the same person or thing or having a common purpose." This rule of statutory construction requires courts to read, construe, and apply both statutes together so that they can gather legislative intent from the whole of both laws. The application of this rule can be seen in *University of Pennsylvania v. EEOC* (1990), wherein the Equal Employment Opportunity Commission (EEOC) sought tenure review files of male faculty members on behalf of an unsuccessful female applicant for tenure. The U.S. Supreme Court held that in the face of the female's claim that she was subjected to discrimination based on sex under Title IX of the Education Amendments of 1972, university officials were required to release otherwise confidential peer-review materials that were contained in the tenure dossiers to the EEOC in order to evaluate her allegations. This case is important for higher education, because it stands for the proposition that the EEOC has the power to enforce its statutory duty to investigate discrimination, here involving gender, and to issue subpoenas while not granting institutions of higher learning any special exemptions as it goes about its job.

Another example of this rule of construction arose when an appellate court in Colorado ruled that documents placed in the personnel file of a former university chancellor, including an employment termination settlement agreement, were subject to disclosure. The court reached this outcome despite the general prohibition under state law against disclosing personnel files except for applications and performance ratings. The court held that granting university officials unfettered discretion to prevent the disclosure of documents that did not implicate privacy rights and that contained information that was routinely disclosed to others was not entitled to blanket nondisclosure under state law, because granting such a wide exception would have been contrary to public policy (*Denver Publishing Co. v. University of Colorado*, 1990).

In sum, insofar as personnel files occupy a central role for campus employees, including administrators, faculty members, and staff, all of those interested in higher education should be mindful of their rights under federal and state laws.

David L. Dagley

See also Family Educational Rights and Privacy Act; Privacy Rights of Faculty Members; *University of Pennsylvania v. Equal Employment Opportunity Commission*

Further Readings

Braverman, B. A., & Hepler, W. R. (1981). A practical review of state open records laws. *George Washington Law Review, 49*, 720–760.

Cooley, T. M. (1888). *A treatise on torts.* Chicago: Callaghan & Co.

Dagley, D. L. (1994). Privacy interests of school personnel in district personnel files. *Illinois School Law Quarterly, 14*, 81–105.

Russo, C. J., Ponterotto, J. G., & Jackson, B. L. (1990). Confidential peer review: A Supreme Court update and implications for university personnel. *Initiatives, 53*(2), 11–17.

Legal Citations

Americans with Disabilities Act, 42 U.S.C. §§ 12101 *et seq.*

Colo. Rev. Stat. § 24-72-204(3)(a)(II) (Bradford, 1988).

Denver Publishing Co. v. University of Colorado, 812 P.2d 682 (Colo. Ct. App. 1990).

Family Education Rights and Privacy Act, 20 U.S.C. § 1232g.

Freedom of Information Act, 5 U.S.C. § 552A.

Health Insurance Portability and Accountability Act (HIPAA), 29 §§ U.S.C. 1181 *et seq.*; 42 U.S.C. § 200gg; 42 U.S.C. §§ 1320d, 1320d 1-8; 26 U.S.C. §§ 9801 *et seq.*

Hovet v. Hebron Public School District, 419 N.W.2d 189 (N.D. 1988).

Klein Independent School District v. Mattox, 830 F.2d 576 (5th Cir. 1987), *cert. denied*, 485 U.S. 1008 (1988).

Miss. Public Record Act of 1983, Miss. Code Ann. § 25-61-1 to § 25-61-17.

Montana Constitution of 1972, art. II, § 10 (1972).

Privacy Act of 1974, 5 U.S.C. § 552A.

Texas Education Code, § 51.910.

Title IX of the Education Amendments of 1972, 20 U.S.C. § 1681.

University of Pennsylvania v. EEOC, 493 U.S. 182 (1990).

POLITICAL ACTIVITIES AND SPEECH OF FACULTY MEMBERS

While institutions of higher education serve as venues for participation in the marketplace of ideas, college and university officials sometimes restrict or regulate the political activities and speech of faculty members. The legal parameters pertaining to political activities and speech of college and university faculty members typically emerge as an issue of whether individuals' expression, association, or service qualifies as their rights as citizens to engage in such activities. Because public colleges and universities represent state actors, policies or actions restricting or regulating the political speech or activities of faculty members generally implicate First Amendment issues and other constitutional rights. In order to present the legal parameters pertaining to political speech of faculty, this entry examines U.S. Supreme Court cases elaborating on the legal limits pertaining to adverse actions arising from public faculty speech, controls restraining faculty activities and speech, and limits on faculty political associations.

Political Speech Leading to Adverse Action

At public colleges and universities, political speech of faculty conveys an expression of individuals speaking as citizens. These expressions may include delivering speeches, protesting, publishing editorials, wearing buttons, or displaying signs. In order to evaluate whether faculty speech qualifies for constitutional protections when officials at public institutions take adverse actions based on that speech, the courts generally apply a two-part test.

Matter of Public Concern

The first line of inquiry poses the issue of whether faculty speech qualifies as a matter of legitimate public concern. If so, the expression qualifies as protected speech under the First Amendment. In *Pickering v. Board of Education* (1968), the Supreme Court established a balancing test between educators' interests to speak freely as citizens on matters of public concern and their public employers' interests to promote the efficient performance of the services that they provide. *Pickering* emerged after a school board dismissed a teacher for writing an editorial in a local newspaper criticizing its dealings regarding a municipal bond proposal. The Court emphasized that public employees enjoy First Amendment rights as citizens, ruling that the teacher's editorial questioning whether the board managed past funds appropriately and now needed additional resources raised a matter of legitimate public concern worthy of protection under the First Amendment.

When public employees speak on matters of public concern, their speech qualifies for First Amendment protections even if the statements were made not in public settings such as newspapers but in private settings. In the actions that led to *Givhan v. Western Line Consolidated School District* (1979), a teacher was dismissed primarily for criticizing her school's policies and practices regarding a desegregation order. As the Court noted, the teacher's remarks did not deal with matters pertaining strictly to her; rather, her speech questioned the school's policies and practices, which impact the public and are of public interest. However, unlike *Pickering*, the teacher in *Givhan* expressed her comments privately to her principal. Despite that setting, the Court recognized the teacher's speech still dealt with a matter of public concern warranting First Amendment protection.

More fully, the legal determination of whether speech by public employees qualifies as a matter of public concern requires a review of the content, form, and context of the expression as well as an examination of the entire record. In *Connick v. Myers* (1983), an assistant district attorney reacted to her office transfer by circulating a questionnaire about office policies, procedures, and morale. Examining the record as a whole, the Supreme Court ruled that except for one survey item, which inquired about whether staff members ever felt pressured to work in political campaigns on behalf of office-supported candidates, the items in the questionnaire did not qualify as matters of public concern. The Court wrote that because the items dealt with an individual employment dispute regarding a transfer policy, they reflected a matter of a personal interest that is typically is not a matter of public concern. The Court thus concluded that the employee lacked constitutional protections as a form of protected political speech.

When public employee speech is made pursuant to the employee's official duties, it does not rise to a matter of public concern and is generally not protected under the First Amendment. In *Garcetti v. Ceballos* (2006), after a county prosecutor investigated concerns about an affidavit used to obtain a search warrant, he decided that it contained serious misrepresentations and sent a memorandum to his supervisors regarding his concerns. In the memorandum, the prosecutor also recommended the dismissal of the case. After receiving the information, the supervisor still chose to move forward with the case. The prosecutor spoke publicly about his position regarding the discrepancy in the affidavit. In fact, the defense attorney called the prosecutor as a witness for the defense to testify about his findings regarding the discrepancy. The prosecutor then claimed that due to his expressions about the affidavit, he faced retaliatory employment actions. The Supreme Court noted that the prosecutor's expressions were based on an employer's commissioned memo and that he was not acting on his own accord in making his statements. The Court indicated that when public employees speak in furtherance of their job responsibilities, their speech is not protected, because they are speaking as employees rather than citizens.

The general rule is that public employee speech made pursuant to the employee's official duties is unprotected under the First Amendment. Yet, *in dicta* in *Garcetti,* Justice Kennedy, writing for the majority, pointed out that this analysis might not apply to academic scholarship and teaching. He added that faculty members might not fall under traditional public employee speech analysis. While Justice Kennedy's statements do not represent legal mandates, they likely serve as persuasive legal guides. If so, in evaluating whether the speech of college or university faculty members qualifies as a matter of public concern, courts might inquire as to whether the faculty members' speech was made pursuant to their official duties, excluding responsibilities connected with teaching or scholarly activities, but covering matters related to administrative

and organizational functions within their institutions (*Garcetti,* 2006). If the answer is yes, because the faculty speech likely falls outside of the scope of a matter of public concern, it is unprotected.

Efficient Governmental Operations

The second line of inquiry asks whether employer interests in regulating faculty members' speech to avoid disruption in the workplace and maintain institutional efficiency outweigh the free speech rights of faculty members. As the Court has articulated, speech connected with disputes over employment policies, particularly under close working relationships, may rise to the level of disruptive speech; in such cases, public employers may curb such speech in order to fulfill their responsibilities to provide public service. Further, as revealed in *Connick v. Myers,* deference should be given to supervisors when employees threaten the authority of supervisors to manage the workplace.

Applying a standard of reasonableness, public employers decide the meaning of employee speech and its impact on the workplace. In *Waters v. Churchill* (1994), when a nurse at a public hospital informed a coworker about problems within her unit while in the break room, another nurse overheard the comments and reported them to their supervisor. The supervisor interviewed other hospital staff who overheard the nurse's comments in the break room and, based on those findings, terminated her employment. The Supreme Court enunciated two standards reflecting the meaning derived from and the impact of the public employee's speech. First, the Court addressed the manner of understanding the message that an individual employee sought to convey, noting that this derived from what the employer reasonably believed was stated. This standard establishes a "reasonable manager" to interpret the message. Second, the Court posited that public employment disruption does not have to be actual disruption, that potential disruptiveness is sufficient for a public employer's interest for efficient operations. The Court posited that the potential disruptiveness of an employee's speech may render it unprotected in the light of a public employer's interest in efficient operations, even when no actual disruption has occurred.

In sum, when officials at public colleges or universities take adverse actions against faculty members based on alleged political speech, courts typically apply a two-part test in evaluating whether the speech warrants constitutional protections. First, the court asks whether the speech qualifies as a matter of public concern. Reviewing the record as a whole, courts examine the context, content, and form of the speech to decide whether the expression pertains to a public concern, even if the expression occurred in a private setting. Courts agree that speech addressing personal matters regarding one's employment situation or matters pursuant to one's official duties do not pertain to matters of public concern. However, if speech qualifies as a matter of public concern, the second part of the test asks whether the government's interest in efficient operations outweighs the faculty member's right to free speech, when such speech actually or potentially disrupts the work environment. If the faculty speech is not disruptive, it likely qualifies for constitutional protections.

Bans on Political Activities and Speech

If a public employee's expression is summarily barred outside of the workplace, such a penalty may violate the First Amendment. As the Supreme Court ruled in *United States v. National Treasury Employees Union* (*NTEU*, 1995), governmental policies on the speech of public employees that involve broad sweeping restrictions entail a greater burden for the government to demonstrate how the policies further its interest in efficient operations. *NTEU* dealt with a federal law that prohibited federal employees from receiving honoraria for speaking and writing engagements. According to the Court, the law served as a disincentive for federal employees to participate in expressions outside of the workplace on matters potentially of public concern. Insofar as this restriction blocked speech from ever happening, the Court analyzed public employee speech by distinguishing all public employee speech from speech that took place before adverse actions followed. The Court explained that unlike the adverse action cases, the balancing of interests is not simply between public employees and employers. Instead, the Court recognized that the needs and interests of both employees and the government as employer regarding the expression extend

to potential audiences as well as current and future employees, on the one hand, and to public employers regarding their interest for efficient operations, on the other hand. Balancing those interests, the Court found that the government failed to demonstrate sufficiently how the ban on compensation furthers its efficient operations as an interest that outweighs the large-scale disincentive to the expressive rights of public employees. In other words, the Court thought that the potential value of the public employees' expressions to the audience outweighed the government's interests.

At the same time, governmental officials may restrict public employees from actively engaging in political activities such as lobbying and campaigning at work or engaging in activities that may imply that a public employer is endorsing positions or candidates. In particular, government actors may limit or prohibit faculty members' political activities that involve public resources or endorsements. The source of law for state employees derives from respective state statutes and regulations. In addition, faculty members at private institutions who are working under special arrangements with the federal government may be classified as federal employees when they work at federal laboratories on campus, such as those that are government owned or contractor operated and held to the statutory guidelines within the Hatch Act. Generally, these laws prohibit the use of public resources such as public funds, the use of employee time during work hours for activities such as making campaign calls, and favoring one candidate or political group by allowing physical resources such as classrooms and auditoriums to be used for political gatherings.

Similarly, governmental actors have no obligation to facilitate programs or systems such as payroll deduction options for political action committees. In *Ysursa v. Pocatello Education Association* (2009), the Supreme Court declared that a state's payroll deduction system, which permits deductions for state employee union dues, may prohibit deduction processing for the union's political action committee. The Court maintained that this prohibition does not limit political speech. Instead, the Court interpreted the state law as simply not promoting public employee speech through political activities.

Finally, governmental actors may indirectly restrict political activities of faculty members at private colleges and universities. Under Section 501(c)(3) of the Internal Revenue Code and its accompanying regulations, in order for private colleges and universities as well as foundations of either public or private institutions to keep their tax-exempt status, these organizations, or the faculty members representing them in their official capacities, may not participate or intervene in political campaigns supporting candidates, engage in substantial propaganda activities, or behave in manners largely reflecting political action organizations.

Political Associations

As the Supreme Court has ruled, absent governmental interests outweighing individuals' interest to associate freely, public employers, including faculty members at colleges and universities, may not make employment decisions such as hiring, dismissing, transferring, promoting, or rehiring of faculty based solely on organizational associations or allegiances.

The Supreme Court reasoned that mandating political membership as a basis for employment decisions deprives the negatively impacted employees of their First and Fourteenth Amendments of the Constitution. In *Elrod v. Burns* (1976), a newly elected sheriff replaced non–civil servant employees who were members of the Republican Party with individuals in the Democratic Party. While laws protected civil servants from arbitrary dismissal, legal protections did not exist for public employees who were not civil servants. The Court observed that dismissals based solely on political patronage violate the constitutional rights of the dismissed employees. Moreover, the Court declared that dismissals applied in a "wholesale replacement" manner do not further the efficient operations of government. As the Court acknowledged, the practice of political patronage did not necessarily serve a particular governmental interest as opposed to serving the interest of a political organization. The Court was thus convinced that the government did not demonstrate that staff replacement from political patronage enhanced employee motivation or performance, nor did the practice of political patronage bring in more qualified candidates. Similarly, in *Branti v. Finkel* (1980), the Court decided that public employment practices

that condition political allegiances to particular organizations violate the First Amendment.

The opposite is true, too. The Supreme Court held that mandating nonassociation as the basis for public employment actions deprives negatively impacted employees of their constitutional rights. In *Elfbrandt v. Russell* (1966), a statute from Arizona placed penalties including those associated with perjury and employment dismissal based on an organizational association. The statute explicitly prohibited association with the Communist Party and other organizations that support the overthrow of government. While subversive activity that could lead to the overthrow of the government qualifies as a legitimate reason to make public employment decisions including hiring and firing, mere membership in an organization that subscribes to those beliefs is not a sufficient ground for basis of a public employment decision. Here the Court conceded that mere membership in an organization does not necessarily translate into all members subscribing to the unlawful beliefs or behaviors of the organization; individuals may not be punished on the basis of membership alone. Consequently, the Court invalidated the statute.

Likewise, placing restrictions on associational activities and political speech that do not clearly convey acceptable and unacceptable behaviors often violates constitutional standards, because such restrictions are overbroad or vague. For example, *Keyishian v. Board of Regents* (1967) addressed a loyalty oath that was enacted pursuant to a statute from New York that included provisions in which educators would be removed from their jobs if they participated in subversive activities. Pursuant to an internal memorandum to state employees, examples of subversive activities included writing articles, distributing pamphlets, and endorsing speeches made or articles written or acts performed by others whether inside or outside of classrooms. Because these expressive and speech acts are protected for common citizens under the First Amendment as well as within legitimate educational and scholarly applications protected under constitutional interpretations of academic freedom, the Court noted that the loyalty oath impermissibly classified protected speech as prohibited acts.

Finally, public employers may place restrictions based on association when governmental interests prevail. For instance, public employers may prohibit employees' associational activities if organizations have specific intent to further illegal actions and employees subscribe to those beliefs.

Jeffrey C. Sun

See also *Keyishian v. Board of Regents of the University of the State of New York*; Loyalty Oaths

Further Readings

American Association of University Professors. (2001). Statement on professors and political activity. In *Policy and document reports* (9th ed., pp. 33–34). Washington, DC: Author.

Hogan & Hartson, LLP. (2007). *Political campaign-related activities of and at colleges and universities.* Washington, DC: American Council on Education.

Pauken, P. (2005). Faculty speech. In J. Beckham & D. Dagley (Eds.), *Contemporary issues in higher education law* (pp. 151–182). Dayton, OH: Education Law Association.

Legal Citations

Branti v. Finkel, 445 U.S. 507 (1980).
Connick v. Myers, 461 U.S. 138 (1983).
Elfbrandt v. Russell, 384 U.S. 11 (1966).
Elrod v. Burns, 427 U.S. 347 (1976).
Garcetti v. Ceballos, 547 U.S. 410 (2006).
Givhan v. Western Line Consolidated School District, 439 U.S. 410 (1979).
Hatch Act, 15 U.S.C. § 1501 et seq. (2008).
Internal Revenue Code, 26 U.S.C. § 501(c)(3) (2008) and its regulations, 26 C.F.R. §§ 1.501(c)(3)-1(3) (2008).
Keyishian v. Board of Regents, 385 U.S. 589 (1967).
Pickering v. Board of Education, 391 U.S. 563 (1968).
United States v. National Treasury Employees Union, 513 U.S. 454 (1995).
Waters v. Churchill, 511 U.S. 661 (1994).
Ysursa v. Pocatello Education Association, 129 S. Ct. 1093 (2009).

Privacy Rights of Faculty Members

Privacy, as Judge Thomas Cooley described it, is "the right to be let alone" (1888, p. 29). Faculty members, as well as all university employees, may look to several sources—constitutional, statutory, and common law—as a basis for asserting their privacy rights. Insofar as the entry on the Fourth Amendment rights of faculty members focuses on issues surrounding searches of their persons, offices, and property, this entry highlights other concerns associated with the privacy rights of faculty members and other employees in institutions of higher education.

Constitutional privacy claims under the U.S. Constitution consist of two types. The first is informational privacy, which is breached when governmental officials release private information about individuals. Because a substantial number of federal laws address release of private information, claims for constitutional informational privacy are few, with potential plaintiffs apparently opting for specified claims under federal statutes. The second type of federal constitutional privacy is constitutional autonomy, a breech of which occurs when governmental actions interfere with highly private individual decisions.

Constitutional Autonomy

The concept of constitutional autonomy emerged from two Supreme Court cases in the 1920s, both of which were set in K–12 education: *Meyer v. Nebraska* (1923) and *Pierce v. Society of Sisters* (1925). In these cases, the Court recognized a constitutional privacy right for parents to direct the upbringing of their children to learn a foreign language (*Meyer*) or to satisfy compulsory attendance laws by choosing to send their children to religiously affiliated nonpublic schools (*Pierce*). From these cases, constitutional autonomy grew to include many types of situations where the courts were convinced that the government had gone too far in interfering with highly private, personal decisions, such as whether one could marry a person of another race (*Loving v. Virginia*, 1967), whether one could have access to contraceptive devices (*Eisenstadt v. Baird*, 1972; *Griswold v. Connecticut*, 1965), whether a public school board as an employer could decide when pregnant faculty members could take their maternity leaves (*Cleveland Board of Education v. LaFleur*, 1974), whether one could have access to an abortion (*Roe v. Wade*, 1973), and whether states could prosecute persons for violating state antisodomy laws (*Lawrence and Garner v. Texas*, 2003). Where states have privacy clauses in their state constitutions, there is also potential for state claims for constitutional privacy. However, cases involving university personnel asserting violation of state constitutional privacy are rare.

Statutory Privacy

Statutory privacy, as its name implies, arises from legislative actions by the federal Congress and the state legislatures. Statutory privacy at the federal level is exemplified by protections provided by such measures as the Health Insurance Portability and Accountability Act of 1996, the Privacy Act of 1974, the Equal Employment Opportunity Act, and the Family Educational Rights and Privacy Act. Examples of state-level statutory privacy statutes include Connecticut's Privacy Act, which prohibits state agencies from collecting personal data beyond what is necessary for the agency's function and prohibits agencies from releasing personal data. In like fashion, North Carolina's Privacy Act prohibits public agencies from denying individuals rights, benefits, or privileges because they refuse to disclose their social security numbers.

Common Law Privacy

Common law privacy arises from tort claims that the judiciary has recognized. In fact, common law privacy is actually composed of four separate intentional tort claims: intrusion on seclusion, public disclosure of a private fact, placing another in a false light, and appropriation of another's name or image.

Intrusion on Seclusion

Intrusion on seclusion occurs when one intrudes on another's solitude or private affairs, where the other person had a reasonable expectation of privacy and others would agree that the intrusion is highly offensive. Most intrusion on seclusion claims in university settings come from investigations, and most are unsuccessful. For example, when a university administrator confiscated a researcher's university-owned laptop to investigate a plagiarism charge, an appellate court in California affirmed the denial of the intrusion claim on the basis that the laptop was university property (*Baughman v. State*, 1995). In addition, the court was of the opinion that the officials did not violate the researcher's rights, because the officials did not access or disclose any private information from the computer files. Another unsuccessful intrusion claim addressed the placement by campus security of a surveillance camera in an office area where a secretary had changed clothes and applied sunburn medication when she thought she was alone. Massachusetts's highest court denied the secretary's claim that officials invaded her privacy, because she did not have a reasonable expectation of privacy in the office area (*Nelson v. Salem State College*, 2006).

Public Disclosure of Private Fact

Public disclosure of private fact claims arise where one can prove that another gave publicity to a matter that would be highly offensive to a reasonable person, and the subject matter was not of legitimate public concern. Such a case arose when university officials informed the student newspaper that a facilities supervisor was one of three people who resigned after an investigation revealed use of university equipment for personal gain. When the supervisor sued a variety of defendants claiming publication of a private fact, an appellate court in New Jersey affirmed the denial of his claim on the basis that the investigation was not a private matter (*Gallo v. Princeton University*, 1995).

Placing Another in a False Light

False light privacy claims occur when one publicizes a matter in the private life of another, when the matter publicized would be highly offensive to the reasonable person, and when the actor had knowledge of or acted in reckless disregard concerning the falsity of the matter. An example of an unsuccessful false light claim involved a university faculty member who supposedly made anti-American comments in a political science course. A student alleged that the faculty member directed him to leave class; the student left the class because the instructor would not allow him to express an opinion that did not agree with the one the instructor espoused. The student subsequently contested the faculty member's in-class statements by contacting a local newspaper, which published the student's account. The faculty member then unsuccessfully filed a false light privacy claim against the newspaper and others. An appellate court in Georgia upheld the denial of the faculty member's claim, because he had been unable to demonstrate that staff at the newspaper acted with actual malice in publishing the student's version of the event (*Sewell v. Trib Publications*, 2005).

Appropriation of Another's Name or Image

Appropriation occurs when one makes use of another person's name or likeness for the first person's benefit or purposes. The first of three cases of unsuccessful appropriations occurred in a relatively early dispute, where a faculty member objected to the use of his name on an updated version of a legal treatise. An appellate court in New York rejected the claim, noting that it was insufficient to state a claim for a prima facie tort or other form of intentional harm absent an allegation that the faculty member suffered any losses as a result of being named as editor of the book (*Clevenger v. Baker Voorhis & Co.*, 1960). Similarly, in another early case, a university and its president unsuccessfully objected to the use of its name in a book and movie. New York's highest court affirmed an earlier judgment denying the university's request for an injunction seeking to prevent the release and distribution of a movie and book about its football team on the ground that appropriating its name, symbols, and reputation constituted commercial misappropriation, concluding that if any claim had been present, it should have been filed as libel (*University of Notre Dame Du Lac v. Twentieth Century–Fox Film Corp.*, 1965). A final example of an unsuccessful claim against a university is supplied by *Nemani v. St. Louis University* (2000). The Supreme Court of Missouri rejected the claim of a faculty member who alleged that university officials submitted a grant in his name without his express knowledge or consent. Reversing an earlier order awarding the faculty member $300,000 in damages, the court ruled that a "collaborative research" clause in his employment contract implied that he granted university officials permission to use his name in the grant process.

As can be seen by the sampling of relevant litigation, most common law privacy claims brought against colleges and universities fail, because plaintiffs fail to prove each of the elements of their charges, or because the court recognizes public interest that outweighed their private interests.

David L. Dagley

See also Family Educational Rights and Privacy Act; Personnel Records

Further Readings

Cooley, T. M. (1888). *A treatise on torts.* Chicago: Callaghan & Co.

Legal Citations

Baughman v. State, 45 Cal. Rptr. 2d 82 (Cal. Ct. App. 1995).
Cleveland Board of Education v. LaFleur, 414 U.S. 632 (1974).
Clevenger v. Baker Voorhis & Co., 199 N.Y.S.2d 358 (N.Y. App. Div. 1960).
Connecticut Privacy Act, Conn. Gen Stat. § 4-193.
Eisenstadt v. Baird, 405 U.S. 438 (1972).
Equal Employment Opportunity Act, 42 U.S.C. §§ 2000e *et seq.*
Family Educational Rights and Privacy Act, 20 U.S.C. § 1232g.
Gallo v. Princeton University, 656 A.2d 1267 (N.J. Super. Ct. App. Div. 1995).
Griswold v. Connecticut, 381 U.S. 479 (1965).
Health Insurance Portability and Accountability Act of 1996 (HIPAA), 29 U.S.C. §§ 1181 *et seq.*
Lawrence and Garner v. Texas, 539 U.S. 558 (2003).
Loving v. Virginia, 388 U.S. 1 (1967).
Meyer v. Nebraska, 262 U.S. 390 (1923).
Nelson v. Salem State College, 845 N.E.2d 338 (Mass. 2006).
Nemani v. St. Louis University, 33 S.W.3d 184 (Mo. 2000).
North Carolina Privacy Act, N.C. Gen. Stat. § 143-64.60.
Pierce v. Society of Sisters, 268 U.S. 510 (1925).
Privacy Act of 1974, 5 U.S.C. § 552a.
Roe v. Wade, 410 U.S. 113 (1973).
Sewell v. Trib Publications, 622 S.E.2d 919 (Ga. Ct. App. 2005).
University of Notre Dame Du Lac v. Twentieth Century–Fox Film Corp., 259 N.Y.S.2d 832 (N.Y. 1965).

Privacy Rights of Students

Emerging technologies, ranging from genetic testing to data mining to online social networking, have given rise to privacy concerns that affect not only students but society generally. With millions of students using sites such as Facebook and MySpace, the boundaries between public and private have shifted. As privacy is redefined in the light of scientific innovations, college students may look to several sources to assert their privacy rights, including federal and state constitutions, federal and state statutes, and the common law. This entry reviews the constitutional rights, legislation, and common law that provide the foundation for privacy claims that relate to issues of students at institutions of higher education.

Constitutional Privacy Claims

Privacy claims under the U.S. Constitution are of two types. Informational privacy is breached when government officials release private information about individuals. Insofar as a substantial number of federal statutes now protect against the release of private information, claims for informational privacy under the federal Constitution are relatively few. Related constitutional claims arise out of concerns associated with student privacy under the Fourth Amendment in areas such as drug testing of student athletes, video surveillance, and possibly student use of social networking sites. The second type of federal privacy claim is constitutional autonomy, a breach of which occurs when governmental officials interfere with highly private, individual decisions.

The legal construct of constitutional autonomy emerged from two U.S. Supreme Court cases in the 1920s, both of which were set in K–12 education, *Meyer v. Nebraska* (1923), and *Pierce v. Society of Sisters* (1925). In these cases, the Court recognized a constitutional privacy right for parents to direct the upbringing of their children, whether to learn a foreign language, which was addressed by the former case, or to satisfy compulsory attendance laws by choosing to send their children to religiously affiliated nonpublic schools, addressed in the latter. From these cases, constitutional autonomy grew to include many types of situations where the courts were

convinced that the government had gone too far in interfering with highly private, personal decisions, such as whether one could marry a person of another race (*Loving v. Virginia*, 1967), whether one could have access to contraceptive devices (*Eisenstadt v. Baird*, 1972; *Griswold v. Connecticut*, 1965), whether a school employer could decide when pregnant faculty members could take their maternity leaves (*Cleveland Board of Education v. LaFleur*, 1974), whether one could have access to an abortion (*Roe v. Wade*, 1973), or whether states could prosecute persons for violating state antisodomy laws (*Lawrence and Garner v. Texas*, 2003). Although there apparently has been no reported litigation on this topic, students could certainly make a constitutional claim opposing the release of any records, especially to their parents, relating to health services that they might obtain on campus, such as for pregnancy, sexually transmitted diseases, or alcohol abuse. Such a dispute would probably be litigated as a constitutional rather than statutory claim under the Family Educational Rights and Privacy Act (FERPA), which controls educational records, because it is unlikely that such information would be viewed or treated as educational in nature.

In the world of intercollegiate sports, student athletes have, with limited success, challenged the use of drug testing as a condition for participation. In the one case where students successfully challenged the use of drug testing, *University of Colorado Through Regents of University of Colorado v. Derdeyn* (1993), they did so on the basis that the practice violated their constitutional right to privacy, because no important governmental interest supported the underlying policy.

In an emerging area where law, technology, and campus life intersect, growing numbers of colleges and universities are adopting video surveillance as a means to ensure safety for faculty, staff, and students. As the practice becomes more widespread, it is likely that some will raise privacy issues in the event that institutional officials are not careful in terms of where they place such equipment.

There have been few claims filed to date over social networking sites that are so commonly used by college students and others. In one such case, *Snyder v. Millersville University* (2008), a student teacher was dismissed from her assignment due to what university and school district officials deemed were inappropriate postings on her MySpace page.

The teacher challenged her dismissal as an alleged violation of her First Amendment right to free speech, but it is possible that privacy issues will emerge in this growing area.

In addition to federal claims, many jurisdictions include privacy clauses in their state constitutions. For example, the constitution of the State of Washington promises that "no person shall be disturbed in his private affairs, or his home invaded, without authority of law." Although there is potential for state claims for constitutional privacy under state constitutional provisions, claims involving college and university students are rare.

Statutory Privacy

Statutory privacy originates in actions by the U.S. Congress and the state legislatures. Statutory privacy at the federal level is exemplified by protections provided by such measures as the Health Insurance Portability and Accountability Act of 1996, which governs medical records; the Americans with Disabilities Act, which addresses the extent to which individuals with disabilities must inform college and university officials about how to accommodate their needs; and FERPA.

Examples of state-level statutory privacy laws include Utah's Governmental Internet Information Privacy Act, which limits the collection of personally identifiable information by postsecondary institutions and other governmental entities. Similarly, Connecticut's Privacy Act, which prohibits state agencies from collecting personal data beyond what is necessary for their function, also forbids agencies from releasing personal data.

Common Law Privacy

Common law privacy arises from tort claims that judges have recognized. Common law privacy is actually composed of four separate intentional tort claims: intrusion on seclusion, public disclosure of a private fact, placing another in a false light, and appropriation of another's name or image.

Intrusion on seclusion occurs when one intrudes on another's solitude or private affairs, where the other person had a reasonable expectation of privacy and others would agree that the intrusion is highly offensive. A successful intrusion claim occurred in *Doe v. High-Tech Institute* (1998), in which a student filed suit after consenting to a blood test for rubella but was instead given a test for AIDS, which confirmed that he had the latter disease. An appellate court in Colorado ruled that the student could recover damages for both intrusion on seclusion and unreasonable disclosure of private facts, insofar as he was subjected to a test without his knowledge, and the results were made available to others without his consent.

Conversely, a federal trial court in North Carolina rejected the intrusion claim that a student filed against a coach in *Jennings v. University of North Carolina* (2004). In granting a motion for summary judgment in favor of the coach and university officials, a federal trial court was of the opinion that the coach's asking members of the soccer team about their sex lives neither violated the plaintiff's right to privacy not was actionable under Title IX of the Education Amendments of 1972 as a form of sexual harassment. However, on further review, the Fourth Circuit found that if proven, the coach's actions could serve as the basis for liability under Title IX (*Jennings v. University of North Carolina*, 2007). At the same time, three courts rejected motions for summary judgment in disputes in which there were allegations of rape or sexual harassment because they were satisfied that there was sufficient evidence on which to permit the cases to proceed to trial (*Kelley v. Troy State University*, 1996; *Liu v. Striuli*, 1999; *Simon v. Morehouse School of Medicine*, 1995).

Public disclosure of private fact claims occur where one can prove that another publicized a matter that would be highly offensive to a reasonable person and that is not of legitimate concern to the public. In *Cantu v. Rocha* (1996), a student unsuccessfully sued university officials for public disclosure of a private fact arising out of events that occurred at a party that was conducted by the criminal justice club at a university in Texas. When the student alleged that she was sexually assaulted at the party, and university police were called to the scene, she claimed that the investigating officer violated her rights by commenting to witnesses at the party about his summarized impressions of her testimony. Insofar as the witnesses were in the process of disclosing the same information to the investigator, the court decided that he did not commit a public disclosure of a private fact.

False light privacy claims occur when one publicizes a matter in the private life of another, when the matter that was disclosed would be highly offensive to a reasonable person, and when the actor had knowledge of or acted in reckless disregard concerning the falsity of the matter. An example of an unsuccessful false light claim was included in a counterclaim in a dispute wherein a graduate student in Illinois filed suit against a faculty member for sexual harassment. In response, the faculty member counterclaimed that the student may have engaged in an affair with a colleague. The Seventh Circuit affirmed that because the faculty member who filed the report acted within the scope of his employment in reporting the possibility of the affair, there was no basis for the graduate student's invasion of privacy claim (*Shockley v. Svoboda*, 2003). The court added that the student could not try to sue under Section 1983, which is designed to protect those whose civil rights have been violated, to enforce the nondisclosure provisions of FERPA, because the latter statute simply does not allow for such claims to proceed.

Appropriation occurs when one makes use of another person's name or likeness for the first person's benefit or purposes. An example of appropriation occurred in a relatively early case where a faculty member objected to the use of his name on an updated version of a legal treatise. An appellate court in New York rejected the claim, pointing out that it was insufficient to state a claim for a prima facie tort or other form of intentional harm absent an allegation that the faculty member suffered any losses as a result of being named as editor of the book (*Clevenger v. Baker Voorhis & Co.*, 1960). Apparently no appropriation cases involving college or university students have been reported. However, in light of the increasing use of technology for teaching and for student social networking, it is possible that appropriation claims will become more common on college and university campuses.

David L. Dagley

See also Drug Testing of Students; Family Educational Rights and Privacy Act; Fourth Amendment Rights of Students; Video Surveillance

Further Readings

Jones, H., & Soltren, J. H. (2005). *Facebook: Threats to privacy.* Retrieved May 27, 2009, from http://groups .csail.mit.edu/mac/classes/6.805/student-papers/fall05-papers/facebook.pdf

Russo, C. J. (2009). Social networking sites and the free speech rights of school employees. *School Business Affairs, 75*(4), 38–41.

Legal Citations

Americans with Disabilities Act (ADA), 42 U.S.C. §§ 12101 *et seq.*

Cantu v. Rocha, 77 F.3d 795 (5th Cir. 1996).

Civil Rights Act of 1871, Section 1983, 42 U.S.C. § 1983.

Cleveland Board of Education v. LaFleur, 414 U.S. 632 (1974).

Clevenger v. Baker Voorhis & Co., 199 N.Y.S.2d 358 (N.Y. App. Div. 1960).

Connecticut Privacy Act, Conn. Gen. Stat. § 4-193.

Doe v. High-Tech Institute, 972 P.2d 1060 (Colo. Ct. App. 1998).

Eisenstadt v. Baird, 405 U.S. 438 (1972).

Family Educational Rights and Privacy Act, 20 U.S.C. § 1232g.

Griswold v. Connecticut, 381 U.S. 479 (1965).

Health Insurance Portability and Accountability Act of 1996, 29 U.S.C. §§ 1181 *et seq.*

Jennings v. University of North Carolina, 340 F. Supp. 2d 666 (M.D.N.C. 2004), 482 F.3d 686 (4th Cir. 2007), *cert. denied,* 128 S. Ct. 247 (2007).

Kelley v. Troy State University, 923 F. Supp. 1494 (M.D. Ala. 1996).

Lawrence and Garner v. Texas, 539 U.S. 558 (2003).

Liu v. Striuli, 36 F. Supp. 2d 452 (D.R.I. 1999).

Loving v. Virginia, 388 U.S. 1 (1967).

Meyer v. Nebraska, 262 U.S. 390 (1923).

Pierce v. Society of Sisters, 268 U.S. 510 (1925).

Roe v. Wade, 410 U.S. 113 (1973).

Shockley v. Svoboda, 342 F.3d 736 (7th Cir. 2003).

Simon v. Morehouse School of Medicine, 908 F. Supp. 959 (N.D. Ga. 1995).

Snyder v. Millersville University, 2008 WL 5093140 (E.D. Pa. 2008).

University of Colorado Through Regents of University of Colorado v. Derdeyn, 863 P.2d 929 (Colo. 1993).

Utah Governmental Internet Information Privacy Act, Utah Stat. 63D-2-101 *et seq.* (1953).

Wash. Const. Article I, Section 7 (1889).

Proprietary or For-Profit Colleges and Universities

In the United States, the postsecondary educational landscape has been dominated historically by the existence of nonprofit public and private degree-granting colleges and universities. Over the past two decades, however, for-profit or proprietary colleges and universities have emerged as one of the fastest growing sectors of postsecondary institutions in U.S. higher education, with student enrollments continuing to grow at a rapid pace of nearly 10% a year. This entry examines possible legal issues that may arise in connection with proprietary or for-profit institutions of higher education in the United States.

Background

For-profit colleges and universities rely largely on student tuition to cover operating expenses and maintain a profit. Currently, for-profit colleges and universities enroll nearly 2 million of the approximately 20 million students enrolled at accredited two- and four-year colleges and universities throughout the United States. While for-profit colleges and universities in the U.S. still account for only a relatively small percentage of the total postsecondary student enrollment, publicly traded higher education corporations, such as the University of Phoenix, founded in 1976, are using the Internet on a large scale to deliver courses in their degree programs to students in the United States and abroad.

According to the U.S. Department of Education, students at for-profit colleges and universities are eligible to receive Title IV funds if the institutions provide at least a six-month degree or certificate program preparing students for employment in a recognized occupation, have been legally providing instruction in such capacities for a minimum of two years, and derive at least 10% of their revenues from non–Title IV funds, mainly tuition. At the same time, for-profit or proprietary colleges and universities are distinguished from traditional, not-for-profit higher education institutions in two major ways. First, the primary student outcome focus of for-profit colleges and universities is the employment of their student graduates, while traditional institutions tend to place a much greater emphasis on student learning and academic development even while preparing them for gainful employment. Second, compared to traditional public and private colleges and universities, for-profit colleges and universities receive less funding from Title IV governmental sources, such as the federal Pell Grant, Supplemental Educational Opportunity Grant (SEOG), and Perkins Loan programs.

Student Characteristics

Recent studies reveal significant differences in average student enrollment characteristics between traditional public and private postsecondary institutions and for-profit colleges and universities. For example, students enrolled at for-profit colleges and universities tend to be much older. The 2000 Futures Project study from Brown University indicated that the average age of a University of Phoenix student was 35 years, compared to the average student age of 23 years for those enrolled at a traditional public or private postsecondary institution. Additionally, student enrollment statistics reveal that for-profit colleges and universities disproportionately serve minority, low-income, and other traditionally underserved postsecondary student populations. Statistics from the College Board indicate that students attending for-profit colleges and universities incur significantly more student loan debt compared to students at public or private colleges and universities. For example, the average student attending a for-profit college or university for an associate's degree incurs two-and-a-half times as much student loan debt as a student who attended a public community college. Students earning a bachelor's degree and attending a for-profit college or university incurred 58% more student loan debt than students who attended a public four-year postsecondary institution, and 26% more loan debt than students who attended a private, four-year institution.

The Higher Education Act and For-Profit Colleges

Since 1972, for-profit colleges and universities have been eligible for federal student aid under Title IV of the Higher Education Act (HEA) of 1965. Eligibility for federal student aid under Title IV has spurred controversy concerning whether for-profit colleges and universities should be classified alongside other accredited, nonprofit public and private postsecondary institutions recognized by the federal government. Subsequent reauthorizations of the HEA have given for-profit colleges and universities both heightened credibility and visibility within the U.S. higher educational system.

At a time when for-profit colleges and universities are experiencing student enrollment levels at their highest levels and receiving billions of dollars in federal aid, largely targeting low-income students, competition among higher education institutions to recruit and enroll students is intense. One particularly negative legal consequence of this fervent competition for students has been the adoption of unethical student recruiting practices. For example, some of the more well-known for-profit colleges and universities, including the University of Phoenix, have been sued and accused of violating the provisions of the HEA, based largely on allegations of fraudulently providing financial incentives to some of their admissions employees to enroll students. Among these cases concerned with for-profit institutions of higher education, the one with the highest profile involves the University of Phoenix.

United States ex rel. Hendow v. University of Phoenix

In 2003, in *United States ex rel. Hendow v. University of Phoenix,* former enrollment counselors sued the University of Phoenix under the False Claims Act (FCA), a federal statute that renders anyone liable who "knowingly makes, uses, or causes to be made or used, a false record or statement to get a false or fraudulent claim paid or approved by the Government" (31 U.S.C. § 3729(a)(2)). The two former employees alleged that officials at the for-profit university violated the Higher Education Act's incentive compensation plan by knowingly offering them financial incentives to recruit students. Moreover, the plaintiffs alleged that officials at the University of Phoenix falsely obtained hundreds of millions of dollars in federal financial aid after making false statements to officials at the Department of Higher Education in order to obtain financial aid in the form of Pell Grants and other programs.

After a federal trial court in California initially dismissed the suit as baseless, the former admissions representatives sought further review. In *United States ex rel. Hendow v. University of Phoenix* (2006), the Ninth Circuit reversed in favor of the plaintiffs. The court was of the opinion that because the former employees presented evidence that university officials had made the claims that the plaintiffs alleged, the former employees had presented a valid claim under the FCA. Although the Ninth Circuit did not explicitly remand the dispute to the trial court, the case is set to go to trial in 2010, subject to any settlement agreement that the parties may reach in the interim.

The Future of For-Profit Colleges and Universities

Most recently, there have been discussions about imposing tougher federal regulations on for-profit colleges and universities. However, officials at the U.S. Department of Education have reassured investors in for-profit colleges that these institutions serve a valuable role in today's competitive and growing higher education marketplace. While it is clear that for-profit colleges and universities are not without controversy, they have firmly established themselves in the modern era of higher education as a growing component of the U.S. postsecondary landscape. As for-profit colleges and universities continue to expand their use of technology to deliver their courses, compete with traditional public and private postsecondary institutions for students, and provide admission opportunities for less traditional postsecondary students, all indications are that student enrollments at for-profit colleges and universities will continue to increase.

Kevin P. Brady

See also Higher Education Act; Loans and Federal Aid

Further Readings

Berg, G. A. (2005). *Lessons from the edge: For-profit and non-traditional higher education in America.* Westport, CT: Praeger.

Lederman, D. (2009). Ferment over for-profit colleges. *Inside Higher Education.* Retrieved June 16, 2009, from http://www.insidehighered.com/layout/set/print/news/2009/06/16/cca

Ruth, R. S. (2001). *Higher Ed. Inc.: The rise of the for-profit university*. Baltimore: Johns Hopkins University Press.

Tierney, W. G., & Hentschke, G. C. (2007). *New players, different game: Understanding the rise of for-profit colleges and universities*. Baltimore: Johns Hopkins University Press.

Legal Citations

False Claims Act, Pub. L. No. 99-562 (1986).

United States ex rel. Hendow v. University of Phoenix, 461 F.3d 1166 (9th Cir. 2006).

R

REGENTS OF THE UNIVERSITY OF CALIFORNIA V. BAKKE

Regents of the University of California v. Bakke (1978) was a landmark case in which the U.S. Supreme Court first addressed the merits of a claim on affirmative action, also identified by critics as race-conscious admissions policies or reverse discrimination (the term used in the plaintiff's complaint), an extremely controversial topic with regard to admissions programs in higher education. At issue in *Bakke* was whether the separate admissions policy that officials at the medical school of the University of California at Davis used for disadvantaged minorities violated the Fourteenth Amendment Equal Protection Clause and/or Title VI of the Civil Rights Act of 1964. The challenge for the Court was to balance the rights of individuals who sought equal treatment by officials at a public medical school and the state's obligation to cultivate equality among its citizens. In light of the impact that *Bakke* has had on affirmative action plans in higher education, this entry reviews the case in detail.

Facts of the Case

In 1968, the UC Davis School of Medicine had opened with 50 students; in 1971, officials admitted a class of 100 students. There was no admissions program in place for minority or disadvantaged students when the school opened, and the first class included only three Asian Americans and no other minority or disadvantaged students. In response, the faculty devised a special admissions program in order to increase the number of minority and disadvantaged students in each subsequent class.

From 1971 to 1974, the special admissions program at UC Davis resulted in 63 minority students (21 African Americans, 30 Mexican Americans, and 12 Asian Americans) being admitted to the medical school, while the regular admissions program admitted 44 minority students (1 African American student, 6 Mexican Americans, and 37 Asian Americans). During this time, disadvantaged white students also applied through the special admission program, but none were admitted.

Alan Bakke, a white male, applied to UC Davis medical school in 1973 for consideration under the general admissions program and received an interview. Although considered a strong candidate with a benchmark score of 468 out of 500, he was rejected because his application was late coupled with the fact that no applicants in the general admissions process with scores below 470 were accepted. He was not considered for four unfilled special admissions slots. Bakke wrote to the associate dean and chair of the Admissions Committee protesting that the special admissions program functioned as a racial and ethnic quota system. He reapplied in 1974 and met the application deadline. The student interviewer scored him 94, commenting that he was "well tempered" and "conscientious." By chance, the faculty interviewer was the same person he had written to in protest of the special admissions program. The faculty interviewer commented that Bakke was limited in his approach to problems of the medical field and based solutions on personal opinions rather a reliance on a study of the problems; this interviewer gave him the lowest of six ratings, 86. Bakke's total was 549 out of 600 for the general admissions process, and he was again denied admission. At the discretion of the chair of the Admissions Committee, Bakke was not placed on the waiting list either year he applied for admission.

After his second rejection, Bakke filed a suit in a trial court in California seeking injunctive and declaratory relief requiring his admission to UC Davis. The suit alleged that the special admissions program operated to exclude the plaintiff on the basis of race, in violation of the Equal Protection Clause of the Fourteenth Amendment and Section 601 of Title VI of the Civil Rights Act of 1964. The trial court, in an unpublished order, invalidated the UC Davis admission policy as unconstitutional. However, the court did not order the plaintiff's admission, because he had not proven that he would have been admitted if the special admissions process did not exist.

On further review, the Supreme Court of California affirmed the unconstitutionality of the special admissions policy, because it violated the rights of nonminorities. The court explained that the program was unacceptable, because it granted minority applicants a race-based advantage in the admissions process even though, in light of the university's criteria, they were not as qualified for the study of medicine as nonminorities who were denied admission. In addition, the court directed officials to admit the plaintiff. University officials appealed to the U.S. Supreme Court. Having side-stepped the merits of such a claim in *DeFunis v. Odegaard* (1974), wherein it decided that that a white law student's challenge to an affirmative policy was moot because he was in his final year of study, and after granting an initial stay of the order of the Supreme Court of California, the Supreme Court agreed to hear an appeal.

The U.S. Supreme Court's Ruling

In *Bakke,* two important conclusions were reached by a divided Supreme Court in a plurality decision, meaning that five justices were unable to agree on a single rationale with regard to the place of race in admissions that would render their judgment binding precedent in other cases.

More specifically, the first plurality, led by Justice Stevens and joined by Chief Justice Burger along with Justices Stewart and Rehnquist, affirmed the Supreme Court of California's rejection of the UC Davis admissions policy because it violated Title VI of the Civil Rights Act of 1964. Justice Powell, in helping to create the plurality, viewed the policy as having violated the Equal Protection Clause of the Fourteenth Amendment. These justices maintained that Bakke should have been admitted to the medical school.

A second plurality consisting of Justices Brennan, White, Marshall, and Blackmun was formed by Justice Powell's joining his colleagues to reverse the judgment of the Supreme Court of California insofar as it barred any consideration of race as a factor in admissions actions. Justice Powell's separate analysis upheld the use of race in admissions as a "plus" factor in indicating that the goal of having a diverse student body is a compelling governmental interest that could justify its consideration as one of numerous factors in the application process. The Court also vacated its earlier stay in the case. The dissenting justices feared that such an affirmative action policy was discriminatory.

Although the *Bakke* decision was made by a plurality, it stands out as the first case in a steady stream of litigation over affirmative action plans in a variety of settings in higher education and beyond. *Bakke's* most direct application to higher education was in the companion cases of *Grutter v. Bollinger* and *Gratz v. Bollinger* (both decided in 2003). The Court upheld affirmative action policies used in the University of Michigan School of Law (*Grutter*) but rejected such policies in the same university's undergraduate programs (*Gratz*). Perhaps most notably, in *Grutter,* the majority essentially endorsed Justice Powell's rationale that diversity is a compelling governmental interest, because the Court found it unnecessary to review his perspective. The Court thus concluded that race can be used as a "plus" factor in admissions decisions as long as applicants are subjected to highly individualized, holistic reviews of their credentials.

Darlene Y. Bruner

See also Affirmative Action; *DeFunis v. Odegaard*; Equal Protection Analysis; Fourteenth Amendment; *Gratz v. Bollinger*; *Grutter v. Bollinger*; Title VI

Further Readings

Ball, H. (2000). *The Bakke case: Race, education, and affirmative action.* Lawrence: University Press of Kansas.

Jeffries, J. C., Jr. (2004). *Bakke* revisited. *Supreme Court Review, 55,* 1–21.

Liu, G. (2002). The causation fallacy: *Bakke* and the basic arithmetic of selective admissions. *Michigan Law Review, 100,* 1045–1107.

Rosman, M. (2002). Thoughts on *Bakke* and its effect on race-conscious decision-making. *University of Chicago Legal Forum, 2002,* 45–71.

Tribe, L. H. (1979). Perspectives on *Bakke:* Equal protection, procedural fairness, or structural justice? *Harvard Law Review, 92,* 864–877.

Legal Citations

DeFunis v. Odegaard, 416 U.S. 312 (1974), *on remand,* 514 P.2d 438 (Wash. 1974).

Gratz v. Bollinger, 539 U.S. 244 (2003).

Grutter v. Bollinger, 539 U.S. 306 (2003).

Regents of the University of California v. Bakke, 438 U.S. 265 (1978).

Title VI of the Civil Rights Act of 1964, 42 U.S.C. § 2000d (1964).

REGENTS OF THE UNIVERSITY OF CALIFORNIA V. BAKKE

In *Bakke,* a highly divided Supreme Court, in a lengthy opinion of which only brief excerpts are included, reached two important outcomes. The first plurality, Chief Justice Burger along with Justices Stewart, Rehnquist, Stevens, and Powell, affirmed the ruling of the Supreme Court of California insofar as it rejected the medical school's admissions policy because it violated either Title VI of the Civil Rights Act of 1964 or the Equal Protection Clause of the Fourteenth Amendment. The second plurality, Justices Brennan, White, Marshall, Blackmun, and Powell, reversed the judgment of the Supreme Court of California insofar as that court affirmed an earlier order that had barred any consideration of race as a factor in admissions decisions as a matter of constitutional law. This excerpt is limited to Justice Powell's opinion because it is the most widely cited part of the case.

Supreme Court of the United States

REGENTS OF THE UNIVERSITY OF CALIFORNIA

v.

BAKKE

438 U.S. 265

Argued Oct. 12, 1977

Decided June 28, 1978

Mr. Justice POWELL announced the judgment of the Court.

This case presents a challenge to the special admissions program of the petitioner, the Medical School of the University of California at Davis, which is designed to assure the admission of a specified number of students from certain minority groups. The Superior Court of California sustained respondent's challenge, holding that petitioner's program violated the California Constitution, Title VI of the Civil Rights Act of 1964 and the Equal Protection Clause of the Fourteenth Amendment. The court enjoined petitioner from considering respondent's race or the race of any other applicant in making admissions decisions. It refused, however, to order respondent's admission to the Medical School, holding that he had not carried his burden of proving that he would have been admitted but for the constitutional and statutory violations. The Supreme Court of California affirmed those portions of the trial court's judgment declaring the special admissions program unlawful and enjoining petitioner from considering the race of any applicant. It modified that portion of the judgment denying respondent's requested injunction and directed the trial court to order his admission.

For the reasons stated in the following opinion, I believe that so much of the judgment of the California court as holds petitioner's special admissions program unlawful and directs that respondent be admitted to the Medical School must be affirmed. For the reasons expressed in a separate opinion, my Brothers THE CHIEF JUSTICE, Mr. Justice STEWART, Mr. Justice REHNQUIST and Mr. Justice STEVENS concur in this judgment.

I also conclude for the reasons stated in the following opinion that the portion of the court's judgment enjoining petitioner from according any consideration to race in its admissions process must be reversed. For reasons expressed in separate opinions, my Brothers Mr. Justice BRENNAN, Mr. Justice WHITE, Mr. Justice MARSHALL, and Mr. Justice BLACKMUN concur in this judgment.

Affirmed in part and reversed in part.

REGENTS OF THE UNIVERSITY OF MICHIGAN V. EWING

In *Regents of the University of Michigan v. Ewing* (1985), the U.S. Supreme Court faced the issue of whether university officials acted arbitrarily in violation of a student's substantive due process rights when a faculty board dismissed him from a program without granting him an opportunity to retake a medical board examination that he failed. The Court noted the judicial deference to academic professionals on matters of substantive due process that it had granted seven years earlier in *Board of Curators of the University of Missouri v. Horowitz* (1978), another case involving the academic dismissal of a student in a medical school. Given this deference and the faculty's conscientious and deliberate review, the Court concluded that university officials, vis-à-vis the program faculty, did not violate the student's substantive due process rights. In light of the Court's essentially reiterating that deference, this entry examines the history and judicial analyses in *Ewing*.

Facts of the Case

In 1975, the plaintiff, Ewing, began his studies at the University of Michigan in a six-year combined undergraduate and medical program known as Inteflex. The Inteflex program consisted of four years of course work followed by two years of clinical training. The record demonstrated that, as a result of academic and personal challenges, the student had difficulty completing courses on time and achieving satisfactory grades in several courses. In an attempt to support his academic progress, officials placed the student on an irregular program sequence. Eventually, in the spring of

1981, six years after his initial entry into the program, the student completed his coursework.

As a condition of entering the clinical portion of the program, students were required to pass the first part of the National Board of Medical Examiners test (NBME Part 1). When the student took the examination in the spring of 1981, he failed five of the seven subjects on the NBME Part 1 and received a score of 235; a passing score was 345. In fact, at the time, the student received the lowest score within the Inteflex program's short history. In the summer of 1981, the Inteflex program's nine-member Promotion and Review Board reviewed the files of a group of students including the plaintiff regarding their academic progress. After examining the student's file, the board voted unanimously to dismiss him from the Inteflex program. When the student was notified and appealed, the board met with him over his request that he be permitted to reenter the program. The student argued that the NBME Part 1 did not accurately reflect his academic progress or capacity. Following this discussion, the board voted again and decided unanimously again to dismiss the student from the program. Subsequently, the student met on three different occasions with the executive committee of the medical school, which denied his appeals for reentry into the program.

In 1982, the student commenced legal action in a federal trial court against the university, alleging that under state law, the actions attempted by university officials breached his contract and therefore were barred by promissory estoppel, meaning that because there was the good faith expectation and reliance that they would carry through on their word, they were bound to do so. In addition, the student filed a federal claim in which he alleged that he had a property interest in continued enrollment in the Inteflex program and that the university had violated his right to substantive due process by arbitrarily and capriciously dismissing him from the program. A federal trial court in Michigan rejected the breach of contract and promissory estoppel claims due to a lack of evidence supporting the student's claims. In addition, the court ruled that although the student had substantive due process rights at stake, university officials did not violate them, because they acted in a fair and impartial manner, after careful and deliberate consideration of his academic performance, in excluding him from the program.

On appeal, the Sixth Circuit, also acknowledging the student's constitutionally protected right to continued enrollment in the program, reversed in his favor on the basis that officials violated his substantive due process right. The court grounded its judgment in the fact that at trial the student entered evidence demonstrating that officials permitted other students to retake the NBME Part I, and he was the only person not given an opportunity to retake the test between 1975 and 1982. The court thus ordered university officials to provide the student with an opportunity to retake the examination and, if he passed, to reinstate him into the Inteflex program. The case was then appealed to the U.S. Supreme Court.

The Supreme Court's Ruling

On further review before the Supreme Court, at issue was whether university officials acted arbitrarily by behaving in a manner that substantially deviated from their academic practices when they dropped the student from the program without an opportunity to retake the examination. Viewed another way, because the legal question centered on the student's substantive due process rights, the Court inquired as to whether university officials misjudged the student's fitness to remain in the Inteflex program. It is interesting that the Court never addressed whether the student had a constitutionally protected right to continued enrollment in the program.

In examining the record, the Supreme Court, in an opinion written by Justice Stevens, unanimously reversed in favor of university officials. The Court recognized that the evidence demonstrated serious concerns about the student's academic performance, including his troubles with coursework, his placement on an irregular course pattern in order to try to help him to succeed, and his poor NBME Part 1 score. Further, the Court pointed out that the record demonstrated that officials engaged in regular academic reviews to evaluate the student's academic status. Taking these factors into consideration, the Court reasoned that because university officials, vis-à-vis the faculty, exercised their professional judgment in a fair and impartial manner after careful and deliberate consideration, it had no choice but to uphold their action.

Justice Powell, in a brief concurring opinion, agreed with the outcome but explained that he had thought it unnecessary to have even assumed that the student had a substantive due process right at stake, insofar as, at most, he had a state law contract claim over being able to retake the examination. Justice Powell also specified that he supported the Supreme Court's granting deference to university officials on academic matters.

Simply put, *Ewing* stands for the proposition that on matters of substantive due process regarding academic program decisions, courts examine whether university officials, in this case via the faculty, exercised their professional judgment in a fair and impartial manner after careful and deliberate consideration. If so, and absent other events, the courts generally defer to the faculty's academic judgment and refuse to find violations of students' substantive due process rights.

Jeffrey C. Sun

See also Academic Abstention; *Board of Curators of the University of Missouri v. Horowitz*; Due Process, Substantive and Procedural; Due Process Rights in Faculty and Staff Dismissal; Fourteenth Amendment

Further Readings

Berger, C. J., & Berger, V. (1999). Academic discipline: A guide to fair process for the university student. *Columbia Law Review, 99,* 289–364.

Ford, D. L., & Strope, J. L., Jr. (1996). Judicial responses to adverse academic decisions affecting public postsecondary institution students since *Horowitz* and *Ewing. Education Law Reporter, 110,* 517–542.

Melear, K. B. (2003). Judicial intervention in postsecondary academic decisions: The standards of arbitrary and capricious conduct. *West's Education Law Reporter, 177,* 1–13.

Legal Citations

Board of Curators of the University of Missouri v. Horowitz, 435 U.S. 78 (1978).

Regents of the University of Michigan v. Ewing, 474 U.S. 214 (1985).

REGENTS OF THE UNIVERSITY OF MICHIGAN V. EWING

Ewing helped to clarify the due process requirements when college and university students are excluded from programs due to poor academic performance.

Supreme Court of the United States

REGENTS OF THE UNIVERSITY OF MICHIGAN

v.

EWING

474 U.S. 214

Argued Oct. 8, 1985

Decided Dec. 12, 1985

Justice STEVENS delivered the opinion of the Court.

Respondent Scott Ewing was dismissed from the University of Michigan after failing an important written examination. The question presented is whether the University's action deprived Ewing of property without due process of law because its refusal to allow him to retake the examination was an arbitrary departure from the University's past practice. The Court of Appeals held that his constitutional rights were violated. We disagree.

I

In the fall of 1975 Ewing enrolled in a special 6-year program of study, known as "Inteflex," offered jointly by the undergraduate college and the Medical School. An undergraduate degree and a medical degree are awarded upon successful completion of the program. In order to qualify for the final two years of the Inteflex program, which consist of clinical training at hospitals affiliated with the University, the student must successfully complete four years of study including both premedical courses and courses in the basic medical sciences. The student must also pass the "NBME Part I"—a 2-day written test administered by the National Board of Medical Examiners.

In the spring of 1981, after overcoming certain academic and personal difficulties, Ewing successfully completed the courses prescribed for the first four years of the Inteflex program and thereby qualified to take the NBME Part I. Ewing failed five of the seven subjects on that examination, receiving a total score of 235 when the passing score was 345. (A score of 380 is required for state licensure and the national mean is 500.) Ewing received the lowest score recorded by an Inteflex student in the brief history of that program.

On July 24, 1981, the Promotion and Review Board individually reviewed the status of several students in the Inteflex program. After considering Ewing's record in some detail, the nine members of the Board in attendance voted unanimously to drop him from registration in the program.

In response to a written request from Ewing, the Board reconvened a week later to reconsider its decision. Ewing appeared personally and explained why he believed that his score on the test did not fairly reflect his academic progress or potential. After reconsidering the matter, the nine voting members present unanimously reaffirmed the prior action to drop Ewing from registration in the program.

In August, Ewing appealed the Board's decision to the Executive Committee of the Medical School. After giving Ewing an opportunity to be heard in person, the Executive Committee unanimously approved a motion to deny his appeal for a leave of absence status that would enable him to retake Part I of the NBME examination. In the following year, Ewing reappeared before the Executive Committee on two separate occasions, each time unsuccessfully seeking readmission to the Medical School. On August 19, 1982, he commenced this litigation in the United States District Court for the Eastern District of Michigan.

II

Ewing's complaint against the Regents of the University of Michigan asserted a right to retake the NBME Part I test on three separate theories, two predicated on state law and one based on federal law. As a matter of state law, he alleged that the University's action constituted a breach of contract and was barred by the doctrine of promissory estoppel. As a matter of federal law, Ewing alleged that he had a property interest in his continued enrollment in the Inteflex program and that his dismissal was arbitrary and capricious, violating his "substantive due process rights" guaranteed by the Fourteenth Amendment and entitling him to relief under 42 U.S.C. § 1983.

The District Court held a 4-day bench trial at which it took evidence on the University's claim that Ewing's dismissal was justified as well as on Ewing's allegation that other University of Michigan medical students who had failed the NBME Part I had routinely been given a second opportunity to take the test. The District Court described Ewing's unfortunate academic history in some detail. Its findings, set forth in the margin, reveal that Ewing "encountered immediate difficulty in handling the work," and that his difficulties—in the form of marginally passing grades and a number of incompletes and makeup examinations, many experienced while Ewing was on a reduced course load—persisted throughout the 6-year period in which he was enrolled in the Inteflex program.

Ewing discounted the importance of his own academic record by offering evidence that other students with even more academic deficiencies were uniformly allowed to retake the NBME Part I. The statistical evidence indicated that of the 32 standard students in the Medical School who failed Part I of the NBME since its inception, all 32 were permitted to retake the test, 10 were allowed to take the test a third time, and 1 a fourth time. Seven students in the Inteflex program were allowed to retake the test, and one student was allowed to retake it twice. Ewing is the only student who, having failed the test, was not permitted to retake it. Dr. Robert Reed, a former Director of the Inteflex program and a member of the Promotion and Review Board, stated that students were "routinely" given a second chance. Ewing argued that a promotional pamphlet released by the Medical School approximately a week before the examination had codified this practice. . . .

The District Court concluded that the evidence did not support either Ewing's contract claim or his promissory estoppel claim under governing Michigan law. There was "no sufficient evidence to conclude that the defendants bound themselves either expressly or by a course of conduct to give Ewing a second chance to take Part I of the NBME examination." . . .

With regard to Ewing's federal claim, the District Court determined that Ewing had a constitutionally protected property interest in his continued enrollment in the Inteflex program and that a state university's academic decisions concerning the qualifications of a medical student are "subject to substantive due process review" in federal court. The District Court, however, found no violation of Ewing's due process rights. The trial record, it emphasized, was devoid of any indication that the University's decision was "based on bad faith, ill will or other impermissible ulterior motives"; to the contrary, the "evidence demonstrate[d] that the decision to dismiss plaintiff was reached in a fair and impartial manner, and only after careful and deliberate consideration." To "leave no conjecture" as to his decision, the District Judge expressly found that "the evidence demonstrate[d] no arbitrary or capricious action since [the Regents] had good reason to dismiss Ewing from the program."

Without reaching the state-law breach-of-contract and promissory-estoppel claims, the Court of Appeals reversed the dismissal of Ewing's federal constitutional claim. The Court of Appeals agreed with the District Court that Ewing's implied contract right to continued enrollment free from arbitrary interference qualified as a property interest protected by the Due Process Clause, but it concluded that the University had arbitrarily deprived him of that property in violation of the Fourteenth Amendment because (1) "Ewing was a 'qualified' student, as the University defined that term, at the time he sat for NBME Part I"; (2) "it was the consistent practice of the University of Michigan to allow a qualified medical student who initially failed the NBME Part I an opportunity for a retest"; and (3) "Ewing was the only University of Michigan medical student who initially failed the NBME Part I between 1975 and 1982, and was not allowed an opportunity for a retest." The Court of Appeals therefore directed the University to allow Ewing to retake the NBME Part I, and if he should pass, to reinstate him in the Inteflex program.

We granted the University's petition for certiorari to consider whether the Court of Appeals had misapplied the doctrine of "substantive due process." We now reverse.

III

In *Board of Curators, Univ. of Mo. v. Horowitz*, we assumed, without deciding, that federal courts can review an academic decision of a public educational institution under a substantive due process standard. In this case Ewing contends that such review is appropriate because he had a constitutionally protected property interest in his continued enrollment in the Inteflex program. But remembering Justice Brandeis' admonition not to " 'formulate a rule of constitutional law broader than is required by the precise facts to which it is to be applied,'" we again conclude, as we did in *Horowitz*, that the precise facts disclosed by the record afford the most appropriate basis for decision. We therefore accept the University's invitation to "assume the existence of a constitutionally protectible property right in [Ewing's] continued enrollment," and hold that even if Ewing's assumed property interest gave rise to a substantive right under the Due Process Clause to continued enrollment free from arbitrary state action, the facts of record disclose no such action.

As a preliminary matter, it must be noted that any substantive constitutional protection against arbitrary dismissal would not necessarily give Ewing a right to retake the NBME Part I. The constitutionally protected interest alleged by Ewing in his complaint, App. 15, and found by the courts below, derives from Ewing's implied contract right to continued enrollment free from arbitrary dismissal. The District Court did not find that Ewing had any separate right to retake the exam and, what is more, explicitly "reject[ed] the contract and promissory estoppel claims, finding no sufficient evidence to conclude that the defendants bound themselves either expressly or by a course of conduct to give Ewing a second chance to take Part I of the NBME examination." The Court of Appeals did not overturn the District Court's determination that Ewing lacked a tenable contract or estoppel claim under Michigan law and we accept its reasonable rendering of state law, particularly when no party has challenged it.

The University's refusal to allow Ewing to retake the NBME Part I is thus not actionable in itself. It is, however, an important element of Ewing's claim that his dismissal was the product of arbitrary state action, for under proper analysis the refusal may constitute evidence of arbitrariness even if it is not the actual legal wrong alleged. The question, then, is whether the record compels the conclusion that the University acted arbitrarily in dropping Ewing from the Inteflex program without permitting a reexamination. It is important to remember that this is not a case in which the procedures used by the University were unfair in any respect; quite the contrary is true. Nor can the Regents be accused of concealing

nonacademic or constitutionally impermissible reasons for expelling Ewing; the District Court found that the Regents acted in good faith. Ewing's claim, therefore, must be that the University misjudged his fitness to remain a student in the Inteflex program. The record unmistakably demonstrates, however, that the faculty's decision was made conscientiously and with careful deliberation, based on an evaluation of the entirety of Ewing's academic career. When judges are asked to review the substance of a genuinely academic decision, such as this one, they should show great respect for the faculty's professional judgment. Plainly, they may not override it unless it is such a substantial departure from accepted academic norms as to demonstrate that the person or committee responsible did not actually exercise professional judgment.

. . .

Added to our concern for lack of standards is a reluctance to trench on the prerogatives of state and local educational institutions and our responsibility to safeguard their academic freedom, "a special concern of the First Amendment." If a "federal court is not the appropriate forum in which to review the multitude of personnel decisions that are made daily by public agencies," far less is it suited to evaluate the substance of the multitude of academic decisions that are made daily by faculty members of public educational institutions—decisions that require "an expert evaluation of cumulative information and [are] not readily adapted to the procedural tools of judicial or administrative decisionmaking."

This narrow avenue for judicial review precludes any conclusion that the decision to dismiss Ewing from the Inteflex program was such a substantial departure from accepted academic norms as to demonstrate that the faculty did not exercise professional judgment.

Certainly his expulsion cannot be considered aberrant when viewed in isolation. The District Court found as a fact that the Regents "had good reason to dismiss Ewing from the program." Before failing the NBME Part I, Ewing accumulated an unenviable academic record characterized by low grades, seven incompletes, and several terms during which he was on an irregular or reduced course load. Ewing's failure of his medical boards, in the words of one of his professors, "merely culminate[d] a series of deficiencies. . . . In many ways, it's the straw that broke the camel's back." Moreover, the fact that Ewing was "qualified" in the sense that he was eligible to take the examination the first time does not weaken this conclusion, for after Ewing took the NBME Part I it was entirely reasonable for the faculty to reexamine his entire record in the light of the unfortunate results of that examination. Admittedly, it may well have been unwise to deny Ewing a second chance. Permission to retake the test might have saved the University the expense of this litigation and conceivably might have demonstrated that the members of the Promotion and Review Board misjudged Ewing's fitness for the medical profession. But it nevertheless remains true that his dismissal from the Inteflex program rested on an academic judgment that is not beyond the pale of reasoned academic decision-making when viewed against the background of his entire career at the University of Michigan, including his singularly low score on the NBME Part I examination.

The judgment of the Court of Appeals is reversed, and the case is remanded for proceedings consistent with this opinion.

It is so ordered.

REHABILITATION ACT, SECTION 504

The Rehabilitation Act of 1973, which traces its origins in the U.S. government's efforts to provide rehabilitative services to military veterans after World War I, was the first civil rights law explicitly ensuring the rights of individuals with disabilities to employment and services. Section 504 of the Rehabilitation Act specifically prohibits discrimination against individuals with disabilities in programs receiving federal funds. Insofar as most postsecondary institutions either directly or indirectly receive federal funds in the form of grants or financial assistance to students, they are required to adhere to Section 504's antidiscrimination requirements. Further, courts have interpreted the term "recipient of federal funds" broadly, so that institutions are subject to Section 504's mandates if any of their programs receive governmental aid (*Bob Jones University v. United States,* 1983). Section 504 paved the way for the passage of the Americans with Disabilities Act in 1990, a statute that extended many of the Rehabilitation Act's protections to the private sector. This entry reviews the provisions of the act, describes key cases that have interpreted it, and discusses its implications both for employees and for students.

Provisions of the Rehabilitation Act

Section 504's provisions are similar to those in Titles VI and VII of the Civil Rights Act of 1964, both of which forbid employment discrimination in programs that receive federal financial assistance on the basis of race, color, religion, sex, or national origin. Section 504 covers individuals who have physical or mental impairments that substantially limit one or more major life activities, have a record of such impairments, or are regarded as having such impairments. This definition was amended by the Americans with Disabilities Act Amendments Act of 2008, which made it clear that individuals who suffer from epilepsy, diabetes, cancer, multiple sclerosis, and other ailments are protected even when measures may be taken to mitigate the effects of their conditions. Even so, the amendments specifically offer an exception so that entities can consider the mitigating effects of, for example, ordinary eyeglasses or contact lenses in determining whether visual impairments substantially limit major life activities. Major life activities include everyday tasks such as caring for oneself and performing manual tasks along with actions such as walking, seeing, hearing, speaking, breathing, learning, and working. Specifically, Section 504 states that

no otherwise qualified individual with a disability in the United States . . . shall, solely by reason of her or his disability, be excluded from the participation in, be denied the benefits of, or be subjected to discrimination under any program or activity receiving Federal financial assistance or under any program or activity conducted by any Executive agency or by the United States Postal Service. (29 U.S.C. § 794)

Two major U.S. Supreme Court cases, the second of which was set in a postsecondary institution, have made it clear that individuals are otherwise qualified under Section 504's terms if they are capable of meeting all of a program's requirements in spite of their disabilities (*School Board of Nassau County v. Arline,* 1987; *Southeastern Community College v. Davis,* 1979). In order to be otherwise qualified, then, individuals with disabilities need to be able, with reasonable accommodations, to take part in programs or activities in spite of their impairments.

When individuals are otherwise qualified to participate, recipients of federal funds must make reasonable accommodations that allow those individuals to take part in desired programs or activities, unless doing so would create undue hardships on the programs. Reasonable accommodations may require adaptations to allow access—such as constructing wheelchair ramps or making doors wider, providing sign language interpreters in class, or providing extra time to complete examinations, but program officials are not required to eliminate essential prerequisites to participation or to lower their standards. In the educational context, Section 504 applies to employees, students, and others, such as parents and the general public, who may access buildings on campuses of postsecondary institutions or participate in programs that the institutions offer.

Employees

In order to succeed in discrimination claims under Section 504, employees with disabilities must prove that they were treated differently than other workers or that they were subjected to adverse employment actions because of their impairments. Employees with disabilities are unsuccessful in their discrimination claims if they cannot show that they have the skills to perform the jobs in question even when they are provided with reasonable accommodations or if their alleged disabilities are not covered by Section 504. For example, Maine's highest court rejected the discrimination suit filed by an instructor who was dismissed for violating his college's sexual harassment policy but claimed to have a sexual behavior disorder (*Winston v. Maine Technical College System,* 1993). The court was not convinced that a sexual behavior disorder was a covered disability. For the most part, courts do not uphold discrimination claims when employers can establish that they took adverse employment actions for nondiscriminatory

reasons. Even so, the burden generally is on employers to show that they took the adverse actions for legitimate nondiscriminatory reasons.

Individuals with disabilities are considered to be otherwise qualified if they can perform all essential job requirements in spite of their impairments. Accordingly, individuals who cannot perform essential functions of their positions, such as showing up on time for teaching assignments, even with reasonable accommodations, are not otherwise qualified. For example, in the educational context, failure to meet prerequisite requirements for teaching positions would disqualify applicants even if their failures are allegedly due to their disabilities. A case from Virginia where a teacher who claimed to be learning disabled failed to pass the communications section of the National Teachers Examination after several tries is illustrative. Insofar as the plaintiff did not meet the requirements for certification, a basic condition of employment for a teacher, a federal trial court found that she was not otherwise qualified (*Pandazides v. Virginia Board of Education,* 1992). In its analysis, the court pointed out that the skills measured by the communications part of the examination were necessary for competent performance as a classroom teacher.

At the same time, Section 504 does not protect misconduct, even when it can be attributed to worker disabilities. In this respect courts have supported the discharges of employees who committed acts of egregious or criminal misconduct (*Maddox v. University of Tennessee,* 1995) or exhibited excessive absenteeism, because appropriate conduct and being present are essential functions of most positions (*Linares v. City of White Plains,* 1991).

Under Section 504, employers are required to provide reasonable accommodations that afford otherwise qualified employees with disabilities the opportunities to work and compete with employees who do not have disabilities. The purpose of providing accommodations is to grant employees with disabilities opportunities to lead normal lives, not provide them with special advantages. Accommodations may include minor adjustments in the employee's job responsibilities, alterations to their schedules, or changes in their physical work environment. On the other hand, employers are not required to supply accommodation if doing so would place undue burdens on the employers. However, it is the responsibility of employers to prove that requested accommodations would create an undue financial or administrative burden.

At the same time, employers are not required to make accommodations that would fundamentally alter the nature of their programs or the work duties of employees. Even so, employers could be required to reassign employees with disabilities to other vacant positions that involve tasks that they are able to carry out (*Ransom v. State of Arizona Board of Regents*, 1997). Still, employers need not make reassignments if no other positions are available for which employees with disabilities are qualified. Further, employers are under no obligation to create new positions or to accommodate employees with disabilities by eliminating essential aspects of their positions.

Students

Otherwise qualified students with disabilities are entitled to reasonable accommodations that will allow them to access the programs and services available in institutions of higher education. In this respect, accommodations may need to be made in how courses of study are presented, and alterations may be necessary to allow physical access to buildings. As is the situation with providing accommodations to employees, the purpose of providing accommodations for students is to allow them to compete on an equal footing with their peers who do not have disabilities.

Institutions of higher education are not required to lower their admissions standards to accept students with disabilities. In one case, the federal trial court in Maine sustained the action of university officials who denied a transfer admission to a student with a learning disability, because he did not meet the institution's minimum grade point average requirements (*Halasz v. University of New England*, 1993).

Many students with disabilities have filed suits after they were dismissed from postsecondary schools for a variety of reasons, such as misconduct or failing to meet academic standards. For the most part, students have been unsuccessful where college and university officials could demonstrate the existence of legitimate, nondiscriminatory reasons for dismissing students. By way of illustration, the

Fourth Circuit upheld the dismissal of a premedical university student who failed to maintain a minimum grade point average even though he had received accommodations for his disability (*Betts v. Rector and Visitors of the University of Virginia*, 2005). Similarly, the Eighth Circuit was convinced that university officials had a legitimate nondiscriminatory reason for barring a student with disabilities who threatened a faculty member's life (*Mershon v. St. Louis University*, 2006).

Students with disabilities frequently request testing accommodations, such as having extra time to complete examinations or being provided with quiet spaces in which to take the tests. The purpose of testing accommodations is to allow students with disabilities to be tested effectively on their knowledge. In order to be granted accommodations, students first must establish that they have disabilities and consequently need accommodations. Students may also be required to show that the requested accommodations are actually necessary because of their disabilities.

Allan G. Osborne, Jr.

See also Americans with Disabilities Act; *Bob Jones University v. United States*; Civil Rights Act of 1964; *Southeastern Community College v. Davis*

Further Readings

Russo, C. J., & Osborne, A. G. (2009). *Section 504 and the ADA*. Thousand Oaks, CA: Corwin.

Legal Citations

Americans with Disabilities Act, 42 U.S.C. §§ 12101 *et seq.*
Americans with Disabilities Amendments Act of 2008, Pub. L. No. 110-325, 122 Stat. 3553 (2008).
Betts v. Rector and Visitors of the University of Virginia, 145 Fed. App'x 7 (4th Cir. 2005).
Bob Jones University v. United States, 461 U.S. 574 (1983).
Halasz v. University of New England, 816 F. Supp. 37 (D. Me. 1993).
Linares v. City of White Plains, 773 F. Supp. 559 (S.D.N.Y. 1991).
Maddox v. University of Tennessee, 62 F.3d 843 (6th Cir. 1995).
Mershon v. St. Louis University, 442 F.3d 1069 (8th Cir. 2006).

Pandazides v. Virginia Board of Education, 804 F. Supp. 794 (E.D. Va. 1992), *reversed on other grounds,* 13 F.3d 823 (4th Cir. 1994).

Ransom v. State of Arizona Board of Regents, 983 F. Supp. 895 (D. Ariz. 1997).

Rehabilitation Act of 1973, Section 504, 29 U.S.C. § 794 (1973).

School Board of Nassau County v. Arline, 480 U.S. 273 (1987).

Southeastern Community College v. Davis, 442 U.S. 397 (1979).

Winston v. Maine Technical College System, 631 A.2d 70 (Me. 1993).

RELIGIOUS ACTIVITIES ON CAMPUS

Student expressive rights in higher education reflect the U.S. Supreme Court's landmark decision in *Tinker v. Des Moines Community School District* (1969). In *Tinker,* the justices declared, in response to public school students wearing black arm bands to express their opposition to the Vietnam war, that "neither students [nor] teachers shed their constitutional rights to freedom of speech or expression at the schoolhouse gate" (p. 506). Unlike free expression litigation in K–12 settings that have often involved individual or classroom expressive activities, issues in higher education deal primarily with the expressive activities of student groups outside of classroom settings or with student organizations. Virtually all of the higher education law in the area of campus expressive rights has been distilled from litigation involving the interpretation of college or university regulations. This entry examines the parameters of student religious activity on college and university campuses as a subset of free expression litigation.

Three years after *Tinker,* the Supreme Court, in *Healy v. James* (1972), overturned the refusal of officials at a state college to permit students to form a local chapter of Students for a Democratic Society based on the fear that it would have been disruptive to campus life. In the process, the Court set the foundational principle for determining when it is acceptable to limit the speech of students at colleges and universities. The Court found that college officials, acting as instrumentalities of the state, may not restrict student free speech or association rights simply because they find the perspectives expressed by any group abhorrent.

Nine years later, in *Widmar v. Vincent* (1981), the Supreme Court reviewed the free expression claims of a religious student group for the first time. The litigation began when officials denied the group permission to meet in university facilities pursuant to an institutional regulation prohibiting the use of campus buildings or grounds for religious worship or religious teaching. In rejecting the university's claim that its position was required by the Establishment Clause, the Court, citing both *Tinker* and *Healy,* held that the First Amendment rights of speech and association extend to the campuses of state universities and that once officials extended the university's forum to the expression of other student groups, they had to do the same for the religious groups. To this end, the Court asserted that the issue was no longer whether the university was advancing religion under the Establishment Clause by permitting the religious groups to meet, but whether officials could have excluded groups based on the content of their speech. In balancing the university's responsibilities under the Establishment Clause not to advance religion, and under the Free Speech Clause not to make content-based restrictions of student expression, the Court determined that content-based discrimination against the group's religious speech was neither required by the Establishment Clause nor permitted under the Free Speech Clause.

In essence, the *Widmar* Court ruled that once university officials opened facilities for use by student groups, attempted restrictions of the expressive religious views of the organizations under the Establishment Clause was trumped by the organizations' expressive rights under the Free Speech Clause. It is worth noting, though, that the Court was careful to specify that it had no intention of undermining the authority of officials to enact reasonable regulations concerning the time, place, and manner of use. At the same time, the Court made it clear that it had no desire to question the authority of officials to make academic judgments about the allocation of scarce resources or to decide independently on academic bases who may teach, what may be taught, how it shall be taught, and who may be admitted to study.

Fourteen years after *Widmar,* the Supreme Court, in *Rosenberger v. Rector and Visitors of the*

University of Virginia (1995), addressed whether the Free Speech Clause required equal access to university funding to finance a religious organization's publication. The university's written policy was to use a portion of mandatory student fees to fund the printing costs of student organizations' publications. Even so, officials denied funds for the student publication, *Wide Awake: A Christian Perspective at the University of Virginia,* pursuant to a provision in its policy prohibiting the use of funds for any group that primarily promoted or manifested a particular belief in or about a deity or an ultimate reality. Insofar as the Court, in invalidating the policy, viewed the denial of funds as being the same as the denial of facilities in *Widmar,* it treated the dispute as one involving viewpoint discrimination under the Free Speech Clause rather than as promoting or advancing religion under the Establishment Clause. In effect, as long as a university rule applies in a neutral manner to all student organizations, the Court concluded that the Establishment Clause's prohibition on advancing religion could not be used as a basis to justify viewpoint discrimination.

Five years after *Rosenberger,* the Supreme Court, in *Board of Regents of the University of Wisconsin System v. Southworth* (2000), revisited university funding of student organizations. This time students alleged that the university's allocation of mandatory fees to organizations with which they disagreed violated their free speech and free exercise of religion rights under the First Amendment. In rejecting the students' claims, the Court held that the viewpoint neutrality requirement of the university program in terms of eligibility for funds was sufficient to protect the rights of the objecting students. The Court maintained that while university officials could not object under viewpoint neutrality to the funding of the viewpoints of religious student groups as in *Rosenberger,* neither can students object to a university's allocation of funds pursuant to a viewpoint-neutral policy of encouraging different viewpoints as in the case at bar. However, the Court remarked that a part of the university's funding policy allowing a student referendum to defund a student organization presented free expression problems, because insofar as a referendum substituted the majority's choice for viewpoint neutrality, it would have undermined the constitutional protection that the program required. The Court commented that the theory of viewpoint neutrality is that minority views are to be treated with the same respect as majority perspectives.

The effect of *Widmar* and *Rosenberger* has been to solidify the principles that the Free Speech Clause's viewpoint neutrality requirement obligates officials to treat religious organizations the same as other nonreligious groups and that permitting student religious expression on campuses pursuant to such viewpoint neutrality does not violate the Establishment Clause. Still, as *Southworth* recognizes, neutrality can be used to further university purposes even when it is at odds with religious beliefs. Consequently, while colleges and universities enact nondiscrimination policies prohibiting discriminatory practices by student organizations, it is unclear how officials can resolve disputes when the actions of one protected category affect those of individuals in another category.

In *Christian Legal Society v. Walker* (2006), a religious student organization in a law school was granted injunctive relief against efforts to revoke its official recognition for excluding homosexuals from voting membership on religious grounds. The Seventh Circuit ruled that the law school's antidiscrimination policy protecting students from discrimination based on sexual orientation, among other categories, was not sufficiently compelling to outweigh the organization's interest in expressing its disapproval of homosexual activity. The court observed both that law school officials violated the organization's free speech rights by excluding it from a speech forum that they had created and that they had not excluded other student groups with restrictive membership requirements based on race, national origin, and gender. In effect, the court acknowledged that the application of the university's antidiscrimination policy to force inclusion of those who engaged in, or affirmed, homosexual conduct would have significantly affected the ability of the student organization to express its disapproval of homosexual activity, because it could not have conveyed its disapproval of certain types of conduct if it had to accept members who engaged in that conduct. Yet, as reflected by a case from the Ninth Circuit with the opposite outcome, *Christian Legal Society Chapter of University of California v. Kane* (2009), not all courts agree that universities lack a compelling interest in enforcing their antidiscrimination policies against the religious speech claims of student organizations.

The balancing process described above has been applied in other situations regarding the use of college or university property for expressive activities. In *Orin v. Barclay* (2001), the Ninth Circuit addressed the use of public community college property by three members of a right-to-life advocacy group. College officials permitted the group to gather in the quad that was used by other groups to advocate their causes but imposed three requirements on its use of the quad. Under the conditions, the group could not breach the peace or cause a disturbance, interfere with campus activities or access to school buildings, or engage in religious worship or instruction. When the participants began stating their right-to-life claims in religious terms and were removed from the campus, they promptly filed suit, alleging that the conditions were unconstitutional. In reversing a grant of summary judgment that had been entered on behalf of the college, the Ninth Circuit explained that while the first two conditions represented constitutionally permissible limitations on free expression, the third was an unconstitutional restriction and, therefore, the official responsible for imposing it could be sued individually under Section 1983 of the Civil Rights Act. In addition, because religious expression was an established constitutional right at the time the restriction was imposed, the court added that the official was not entitled to qualified immunity.

The authority of college and university officials to enact regulations limiting expression has not fared well in the courts, which have generally required that any restrictions must reflect a compelling interest and must be narrowly tailored to reach that compelling interest. In *Khademi v. South Orange County Community College* (2002), for example, a federal trial court in California struck down, as a prior restraint on speech, a regulation that delegated complete and unfettered discretion to the campus president to permit or prohibit expression that might be considered offensive. The lack of objective guidelines to define whether speech was offensive led the court to find that the requirement was not narrowly tailored to reach a compelling governmental interest. On the other hand, the court conceded that college officials did have a compelling interest in preventing

the campus from being used for unlawful acts, such as using, distributing, or selling illegal substances, and in prohibiting substantial disruption to campus operations. Similarly, the court thought that officials could restrict expressive activities on college lawns during maintenance or on facilities for which preexisting reservations existed. Also, the court was convinced that college officials could not prohibit the posting of materials advertising student activities nor could they forbid individuals from placing leaflets on windshields, in parking lots, and inside buildings.

The protective attitude taken by federal courts toward student expression has been manifested in efforts by higher education institutions to prohibit hate speech. Federal trial courts in *Doe v. University of Michigan* (1989) and *UWM Post v. Board of Regents of the University of Wisconsin System* (1991) struck down policies prohibiting physical or verbal behavior that stigmatized or victimized individuals as to a broad list of protected categories, reasoning that the policies were so broad as to make distinguishing among classroom speech, academic discussions, and research impossible to accomplish. In *Iota Xi Chapter of Sigma Chi Fraternity v. George Mason University* (1993), the Fourth Circuit affirmed a grant of summary judgment in favor of a fraternity regarding its "ugly woman contest." According to the court, the activity constituted protected speech, even though it was a form of low-grade entertainment. The Court therefore held that officials could not silence speech simply to further the university's interest in providing gender-neutral education free of discrimination and racism.

Further, in *Saxe v. State College Area School District* (2001), the Third Circuit invalidated a local school board policy prohibiting the creation of an intimidating, hostile, or offensive environment on the ground that it was overbroad and unconstitutional, because it included teasing, name-calling, joke-telling, and mimicking. In sum, it is important to keep in mind that because colleges and universities are for adult students, courts are far less willing to restrict expressive rights than they might in K–12 schools.

Ralph D. Mawdsley

See also Civil Rights Act of 1871, Section 1983; *Healy v. James; Rosenberger v. Rector and Visitors of the University of Virginia; Widmar v. Vincent*

Further Readings

Mawdsley, R. D. (2007). Sailing the uncharted waters of free speech rights in public schools: The rocky shoals and uncertain currents of student t-shirt expression. *Education Law Reporter, 219,* 1–23.

Legal Citations

Board of Regents of the University of Wisconsin System v. Southworth, 529 U.S. 217 (2000).

Christian Legal Society Chapter of University of California v. Kane, 2006 WL 997217 (N.D. Cal. Apr. 17, 2006), *aff'd without opinion,* 2009 WL 693391 (9th Cir. 2009).

Christian Legal Society v. Walker, 453 F.3d 853 (7th Cir. 2006).

Civil Rights Act of 1964, Section 1983, 42 U.S.C. § 1983.

Doe v. University of Michigan, 721 F. Supp. 852 (E.D. Mich. 1989).

Healy v. James, 408 U.S. 169 (1972).

Iota Xi Chapter of Sigma Chi Fraternity v. George Mason University, 993 F.2d 386 (4th Cir. 1993).

Khademi v. South Orange County Community College, 194 F. Supp. 2d 1011 (C.D. Cal. 2002).

Orin v. Barclay, 272 F.3d 1207 (9th Cir. 2001).

Rosenberger v. Rector and Visitors of the University of Virginia, 515 U.S. 819 (1995).

Saxe v. State College Area School District, 240 F.3d 200 (3d Cir. 2001).

Tinker v. Des Moines Community School District, 393 U.S. 503 (1969).

UWM Post v. Board of Regents of the University of Wisconsin System, 774 F. Supp. 1163 (E.D. Wis. 1991).

Widmar v. Vincent, 454 U.S. 263 (1981).

RELIGIOUS COLLEGES AND UNIVERSITIES

Religious colleges and universities can be distinguished from nonsectarian private institutions by their commitment to religious rituals, traditions, and/or core religious beliefs. Yet, the extent to which the governance of postsecondary institutions is controlled by these rituals, traditions, or beliefs differs significantly. The clear trend among religious colleges and universities is to dilute, or separate from, their religious origins.

The first three institutions of higher education that were founded in what became the United States—Harvard in 1636, William and Mary in 1693, and Yale in 1701—were religious in character and organized to train men for the ministry. Today, William and Mary is public, and although the other two remain private, they no longer are identified with their religious roots. Moreover, many colleges and universities that have continued their religious identifications struggle to maintain their religious intensity while integrating secular influences such as accreditation, academic freedom, and due process into the religious matrices of their founding charters. In light of the many issues that they confront, this entry examines the status of religious colleges and universities in the United States.

Exemption From Statutory Requirements

Religious postsecondary institutions can enjoy exemptions from some but not all federal and state statutory requirements. Pervasively sectarian institutions are generally exempt from state unemployment laws (*Bleich v. Maimonides School,* 2006; *Czigler v. Bureau of Employment Services,* 1985), and church-controlled universities can be exempt from Social Security and ERISA requirements. However, in *Bob Jones University v. U.S.* (1983), the U.S. Supreme Court upheld the constitutionality of the Internal Revenue Service's revocation of the university's tax-exempt status when it refused to eliminate its religiously based, racially segregated dating and marriage policies. In so ruling, the Court declared that its acting in furtherance of the fundamental national public policy aimed at the eradication of racial discrimination warranted the denial of the federal benefit in the form of tax-exempt status. While the Court has not applied this "fundamental national public policy" rationale to other protected categories, the federal trial court in the nation's capital used a similar rationale in finding that a Jesuit institution, Georgetown University, violated a District of Columbia ordinance prohibiting discrimination based on sexual orientation when it refused to recognize a gay/lesbian rights student group (*Gay Rights Coalition v. Georgetown University,* 1987). According to the court, although officials did not have to recognize the group because of the university's religion-based opposition to homosexuality, its religious beliefs would not be violated by permitting the gay/lesbian student group to use its facilities and services.

Charters and Accreditation

Religious colleges and universities are like all other institutions of higher education in that they must have state charters authorizing them to adopt rules and regulations. Usually, the granting of such charters is done pursuant to the process of state incorporation, which identifies the broad authority of college or university boards to act in the interest of their institutions as well as imposing state limits on that authority. While state legislatures can impose requirements on the formation and operation of religious colleges and universities, the Supreme Court long ago recognized in *Trustees of Dartmouth College v. Woodward* (1819) that states cannot change unilaterally institutional structures so as to alter the private nature of colleges or universities. Nonetheless, states may impose requirements that are perceived by officials at religious colleges or universities as contrary to their rights protected under the Free Exercise or Establishment Clauses.

As long as states have compelling interests and the method for furthering their interests is the least restrictive means, states may require postsecondary private institutions to be accredited (*Newport International University v. Wyoming*, 2008). In *New Jersey State Board of Education v. Board of Directors of Shelton College* (1982), the Supreme Court of New Jersey upheld a requirement of the state board of education that all institutions of higher education had to secure licenses from the state in order to confer degrees. The court was of the opinion that this requirement did not violate the Free Exercise Clause, because the church's religious beliefs supporting the college did not require attendance at the college. Even though the requirement imposed some burden on the college, the court was satisfied that the state had a compelling interest in maintaining minimum academic standards while ensuring the integrity of the degrees that it conferred.

Fiduciary Duty and Standard of Care

Board members of religious colleges and universities, like members of all boards in higher education, have a fiduciary duty in their dealings with their institutions. In *Jarvis Christian College v. National Union Fire Insurance Company* (1999), members of the college's board were unsuccessful in recovering $2 million from its liability insurer following the loss of that sum due to speculative investments by an investment company with which one of the board members had an undisclosed financial interest. In upholding the insurer's position that it was not liable for the wrongful acts of one of the board members, the Fifth Circuit reasoned that the board's liability policy exempted any claim that arose out of gaining a personal profit or advantage and that even though the errant board member had realized no profit, the opportunity to realize a profit was sufficient to exempt the insurer from liability.

The standard of care owed by board members for the decisions they make, then, is generally a corporate standard of care rather than the higher charitable trust standard. In *Corporation of Mercer University v. Smith* (1988), the Supreme Court of Georgia upheld an action of the university's board of directors to close the campus of a women's college with which it had recently merged, where both institutions were affiliated with the Georgia Baptist Convention. The court agreed with the board that because universities are businesses, their officials need administrative flexibility to make day-to-day decisions, including the ability to acquire and sell assets.

Faculty Rights

Faculty at religious colleges and universities, in the absence of state action, do not have constitutional rights. The Fourteenth Amendment's Due Process Clause, through which substantive constitutional rights are applied to public colleges and universities, does not apply to religiously affiliated institutions of higher education. A higher education institution's relationship with a state must be something other than reception of funds, accreditation, filing of forms, tax exemption, or state inspection or regulation in order to invoke state action (*Corporation of Mercer University v. Smith*, 1986; *Logan v. Bennington College*, 1995). The leading case concerning state action continues to be the Supreme Court's judgment in *Rendell-Baker v. Kohn* (1982) a case from K–12 education that is informative for colleges and universities. The

Court refused to find state action to support the free speech claims of faculty members who were dismissed for disagreeing with the board's hiring policy, even though the school received 905 of its funds from the federal government, received all student referrals from public schools, and complied with a variety of public regulations.

Courts can intervene when officials at religious college and universities have contractual disputes with faculty members. However, insofar as contractual disputes in religious postsecondary institutions can also involve religious functions that are part of institutional expectations, courts have limited their judgments to issues in which faculty members are involved in secular or nonreligious functions, such as terms and conditions of employment, including disagreements over salaries and benefits. Generally, as reflected in *Alicea v. New Brunswick Theological Seminary* (1992) and *EEOC v. Southwestern Baptist Theological Seminary* (1981), courts have protected them from governmental intrusion into their religious beliefs when employee responsibilities are involved with ministerial functions. On the other hand, where employees are not involved in ministerial functions, as discussed below, courts apply the same legal principles as in disagreements in secular colleges and universities. In such a case, *Welter v. Seton* (1992), the Supreme Court of New Jersey upheld $45,000 breach of contract awards for two nuns in rejecting a university's claim that the awards intruded into the Catholic Church's control over those involved in religious service. The court noted that because the nuns were computer science instructors and not involved in a ministerial function at the university, it could apply common law contract principles without intruding into the university's religious tenets.

Title VII and Religious Institutions

Religious colleges and universities enjoy some exemptions from nondiscrimination statutes. The workhorse of federal discrimination litigation, Title VII of the Equal Employment Opportunity Act prohibits employment practices that discriminate in hiring, discharging, or classifying individuals based on race, color, religion, sex, or national origin. Moreover, Title VII contains three exemptions for religious employers to protect employment actions that are based on religious beliefs.

The first Title VII exemption involves the hiring, discharging, and classifying of employees where "religion is a bona fide [occupational qualification] [BFOQ] reasonably necessary to the operations of that particular business or enterprise" (§ 2000e-2(e)(1)). In *Pime v. Loyola University of Chicago* (1984), a federal trial court permitted a university to hire a Jesuit over a female applicant for a position teaching philosophy where fixing the number of Jesuits at 7 of 31 was a reasonable BFOQ.

Title VII's second exemption concerns the employment of persons of a particular religion if an institution is

in whole or in substantial part, owned, supported, controlled or managed by a particular religious corporation, association, or society or if the curriculum of such school, college, university, or other educational institution or institution of learning is directed toward the propagation of a particular religion. (§ 2000e-3(e)(2))

In *Wirth v. College of Ozarks* (2000), the Eighth Circuit affirmed the actions of officials at a nondenominational Christian college in terminating the employment of a tenured Catholic faculty member whose religious views were different from those of the college.

The third Title VII exemption applies to

a religious corporation, association, educational institution, or society with respect to the employment of individuals of a particular religion to perform work connected with the carrying on by such corporation, association, educational institution, or society of its activities. (§ 2000e-1(a))

In *Amos v. Corporation of Presiding Bishop* (1987), the Supreme Court upheld the constitutionality of this exemption against an Establishment Clause challenge. In the underlying dispute, officials of the Church of Jesus Christ of Latter-Day Saints discharged a building engineer working in a gymnasium that was open to the public, because he failed to meet the church's religious requirement that he have a "temple recommend"—a certificate that he was a member of the Church who was eligible to attend its temple services.

Student Rights

The rights of students at religious colleges and universities parallel those of faculty members. Unless courts can find state action, students have no substantive or procedural constitutional due process rights. Despite efforts by students to allege state action because of a variety of connections between religious colleges and universities and the state, courts typically have refused to find state action to support constitutional theories of recovery. Thus, in *Ben-Yonatan v. Concordia College* (1994), the federal trial court in Minnesota decided that a student who was suspended had no right to constitutional due process protection even though the college was the recipient of considerable amounts of state and federal funds. The process to which students are entitled depends on rights accorded students in their student handbooks or other postsecondary documents, such as enrollment contracts. At the very least, though, students must have an opportunity to present their version of the facts (*Galiani v. Hofstra University*, 1986). Consequently, the failure of officials at postsecondary institutions to follow their handbooks can result in breach of contract actions (*Morehouse College v. McGaha*, 2005). Still, once the courts are satisfied that college or university officials followed the procedures in their handbooks, they are unwilling to second-guess officials' disciplinary actions (*Lyon College v. Gray*, 1999).

Ralph D. Mawdsley

See also Academic Freedom; Due Process, Substantive and Procedural; Due Process Rights in Faculty and Staff Dismissal; Equal Employment Opportunity Act; Equal Employment Opportunity Commission; *Ex Corde Ecclesiae* and American Catholic Higher Education; Title VI; Title VII; *Trustees of Dartmouth College v. Woodward*

Further Readings

Edwards, H. T., & Nordin, V. (1979). *Higher education and the law*. Cambridge, MA: Institute for Educational Management, Harvard University.

Mawdsley, R. D. (2005). Private colleges and universities. In J. Beckham & D. Dagley (Eds.), *Contemporary issues in higher education law* (pp. 35–61). Dayton, OH: Education Law Association.

Mawdsley, R. D. (2005). Religious colleges and universities. In J. Beckham & D. Dagley (Eds.), *Contemporary issues in higher education law* (pp. 63–87). Dayton, OH: Education Law Association.

Legal Citations

Alicea v. New Brunswick Theological Seminary, 608 A.2d 218 (N.J. 1992).

Amos v. Corporation of Presiding Bishop, 483 U.S. 327 (1987).

Ben-Yonatan v. Concordia College, 863 F. Supp. 983 (D. Minn. 1994).

Bleich v. Maimonides School, 849 N.E.2d 185 (Mass. 2006).

Bob Jones University v. U.S., 461 U.S. 574 (1983).

Church ERISA Exemption, 29 U.S.C. §§1002 (A)(33); 1321 (B); 26 U.S.C. § 414(e)(3)(B).

Corporation of Mercer University v. Smith, 371 S.E.2d 858 (Ga. 1988).

Corporation of Mercer University v. Smith, 612 F. Supp. 72 (W.D. Pa. 1985), *aff'd*, 787 F.2d 583 (3d Cir. 1986).

Czigler v. Bureau of Employment Services, 501 N.E.2d 56 (Ohio Ct. App. 1985).

EEOC v. Southwestern Baptist Theological Seminary, 651 F.2d 277 (5th Cir. 1981).

Galiani v. Hofstra University, 499 N.Y.S.2d 182 (N.Y. App. Div. 1986).

Gay Rights Coalition v. Georgetown University, 536 A.2d 1 (D.C. 1987).

Jarvis Christian College v. National Union Fire Insurance Company, 197 F.3d 742 (5th Cir. 1999).

Logan v. Bennington College, 72 F.3d 1017 (2d Cir. 1995).

Lyon College v. Gray, 999 S.W.2d 213 (Ark. Ct. App. 1999).

Morehouse College v. McGaha, 627 S.E.2d 39 (Ga. Ct. App. 2005).

New Jersey State Board of Education v. Board of Directors of Shelton College, 448 A.2d 988 (N.J. 1982).

Newport International University v. Wyoming, 186 P.3d 382 (Wyo. 2008).

Pime v. Loyola University of Chicago, 585 F. Supp. 435 (N.D. Ill. 1984).

Rendell-Baker v. Kohn, 457 U.S. 830 (1982).

Social Security Exemption, 42 U.S.C. § 410(a)(8)(B).

Title VII of the Equal Employment Opportunities Act, 42 U.S.C. §§ 2000e-2.

Trustees of Dartmouth College v. Woodward, 4 Wheat. (U.S.) 518 (1819).

Welter v. Seton, 608 A.2d 206 (N.J. 1992).

Wirth v. College of Ozarks, 208 F.3d 219 (8th Cir. 2000).

RELIGIOUS FREEDOM RESTORATION ACT

Acting in response to the U.S. Supreme Court's judgment in *Employment Division, Department of Human Resources v. Smith* (1990), Congress enacted the Religious Freedom Restoration Act (RFRA) in 1993 pursuant to the Necessary and Proper Clause in the federal Constitution. In *Employment Division*, the Court held that the Free Exercise Clause of the First Amendment would no longer be a defense to government statutes or regulations that were neutral and generally applicable. In light of the potential impact that the RFRA may have on religious colleges and universities, particularly with regards to zoning and land uses, this entry examines the act's key provisions along with cases interpreting its application in the event that such litigation should arise. This entry also reviews the Religious Land Use and Institutionalized Persons Act, which applies the principles of the RFRA to local and state governments.

When Congress enacted the RFRA, it noted in its findings that the free exercise of religion is an unalienable right protected by the First Amendment and that "laws 'neutral' toward religion may burden religious exercise as surely as laws intended to interfere with religious exercise" (RFRA § 2000bb(a)(1), (2)). In emphasizing that it was essentially reversing the Supreme Court's judgment in *Employment Division*, Congress identified its two purposes for enacting RFRA. Congress's first goal in enacting the RFRA was the restoration "of the compelling interest test as set forth in *Sherbert v. Verner* (1963) and *Wisconsin v. Yoder* (1972)" that applies when the government action affects religious freedom. The second aim of the act was providing "a claim or defense to persons whose religious exercise is substantially burdened by government" (RFRA, § 2000bb(b)).

In the RFRA, Congress allowed the government to place a substantial burden on the free exercise of religion only if it demonstrated that the burden was "(1) in furtherance of a compelling governmental interest; and (2) [was] the least restrictive means of furthering that compelling governmental interest (RFRA, § 2000bb-1(b))." At the same time, the RFRA specifically directed that its terms could not be applied to alleged violations of the

Establishment Clause, stipulating that "granting government funding, benefits, or exemptions, to the extent permissible under the Establishment Clause, shall not constitute a violation of this chapter" (RFRA, § 2000bb-4).

In 1997, the Supreme Court, in *City of Boerne v. Flores*, found that the application of the RFRA to a city zoning ordinance in Texas over a dispute on a wall located on church property was overreaching in terms of its impact on the relationship between states and the federal government under the Tenth Amendment. To this end, the Court invalidated the RFRA as it applied to states. While the Court acknowledged that Congress has authority under Section 5 of the Fourteenth Amendment to legislate rights protected under the Fourteenth Amendment, it may exercise this power in a manner that forbids constitutional state action in an effort to limit unconstitutional actions by state officials.

In response to *City of Boerne*, Congress amended the RFRA in 2000 by limiting the application of its 1997 version to the federal government. Congress also added a new statute, the Religious Land Use and Institutionalized Persons Act (RLUIPA). Although RLUIPA is not technically an amendment to RFRA, it immediately follows the RFRA in the United States Code (the official compilation of federal statutes) and applies the principles of the RFRA to local and state governments. Insofar as the RLUIPA prohibits any government from imposing or implementing land use regulations that treat religious assemblies or institutions any differently from nonreligious ones or from discriminating against religious assemblies or institutions, it should be of significant interest to officials in religiously affiliated colleges and universities. However, the RLUIPA, unlike the RFRA, is grounded in Congress's spending power and prohibits government at any level from imposing substantial burdens on the religious exercise of individuals in programs or activities that receive federal financial assistance. In addition, the RLUIPA prohibits a substantial burden on religious exercise that affects interstate commerce. The RLUIPA imposes the same "compelling government interest" and "least restrictive means" tests that are required under the RFRA on all levels of government.

The impact of RLUIPA on education has mainly involved issues relating to zoning requirements that prohibit religious educational institutions from expanding their facilities, an issue that should be of interest to religious colleges and universities. For example, in *Westchester Day School v. Village of Mamaroneck* (2007), the Second Circuit affirmed that a zoning board in New York had improperly denied a religious school's request for a permit to expand its facilities. The court viewed this as an impermissible governmental prohibition within the meaning of the statute, because it substantially burdened the school's religious exercise, in violation of the RLUIPA. Conversely, in *Ehlers-Renzi v. Connelly School of the Holy Child* (2000), the Fourth Circuit upheld a county building code exception from Maryland for schools that were located on land owned or leased by churches or religious organizations, ruling that the code did not violate the Establishment Clause. The court maintained that nonreligious educational institutions, on the other hand, were required to file petitions explaining in detail how the special exception would operate. Relying on the Supreme Court's decision in *Amos v. Corporation of the Presiding Bishop* (1987), the Fourth Circuit reasoned that the zoning code did not violate the Establishment Clause's tripartite *Lemon v. Kurtzman* (1971) test, observing that at times the government is entitled to, and must, accommodate religion without violating the Establishment Clause.

In the years since Congress passed the 2000 amendment to the RFRA in response to *Boerne*, the Supreme Court has not addressed another challenge to the act's constitutionality on its face, meaning as it is written but not applied. However, in *Hankins v. Lyght* (2006), the Second Circuit upheld the RFRA's constitutionality against a separation of powers claim that Congress had imposed greater protection from federal actors and statutes for religious entities than the Supreme Court required. According to the court, Congress may provide more individual liberties on the federal level than the Constitution requires without violating the vital separation of powers principles. *Hankins* is an interesting case, because although the Second Circuit remanded the case for trial, it indicated that the RFRA could serve as a church's defense to a former bishop's Age Discrimination Employment Act (ADEA) claim that church officials had compelled him to retire at the age of 70, a somewhat extraordinary position, because the RFRA protects against federal, not individual,

actions. Subsequently, the Second Circuit in *Rweyemamu v. Cote* (2008), without reaching the merits of the claim, suggested that although the RFRA would be a defense against discrimination claims where the Equal Educational Opportunities Commission was a plaintiff, it should not apply to claims based on federal discrimination statutes brought by individuals.

Both *Hankins* and *Rweyemamu* leave open the extent to which the federal government may negatively impact religious claimants. In *Holy Land Foundation for Relief and Development v. Ashcroft* (2003), the District of Columbia Circuit upheld the designation of a Muslim-related charitable foundation as a Specially Designated Global Terrorist Organization, pursuant to two Presidential Executive Orders issued under a federal statute. The court was satisfied that the RFRA technically did not apply to the foundation, because the RFRA makes no reference to religion in its purposes. Even so, the court was of the view that, even had the foundation stated that the fomenting and spread of terrorism was mandated by the religion of Islam, the Free Exercise Clause does not create a right to fund terrorists, and there was no evidence that Congress intended to create such a right within the RFRA.

The RFRA has been extensively litigated by inmates in state and federal prisons, alleging that prison rules and regulations violate the exercise of their religious beliefs. The Seventh Circuit, in *O'Bryan v. Bureau of Prisons* (2003), posited that because the RFRA applied to Bureau of Prisons personnel, it governed a federal prison inmate's action challenging the bureau's rule against "casting of spells/curses" that effectively prohibited him from practicing his Wiccan religion. *O'Bryan* is a useful case, because it clarified the reach of *City of Boerne*. The Seventh Circuit remarked in *O'Bryan* that in *City of Boerne*, the Supreme Court had not declared the RFRA violated any substantive constitutional rights. Rather, the court recognized that the RFRA allowed Congress to determine how the national government would conduct its own affairs but did not offer a source of authority to apply the RFRA to both state and local governments. More recently, the District of Columbia Circuit affirmed, in *Webman v. Federal Bureau of Prisons* (2006), that the RFRA waived sovereign immunity to private enforcement to the extent that it allowed parties whose rights were violated to obtain appropriate relief against the government. However, the court acknowledged that the waiver did not extend to monetary damages, because insofar as the RFRA's reference to appropriate relief was susceptible to more than one interpretation, it did not amount to the kind of unambiguous waiver that is necessary in order for governmental entities to be sued.

To date, the RFRA has produced no reported cases involving higher education, although nothing in its provisions would prohibit its application to religious colleges and universities. Issues have arisen under the RLUIPA involving religious entities such as churches, where the focus is a local zoning ordinance requiring special use permits to build public assembly buildings in an area zoned as residential. Courts have generally rejected claims of RLUIPA violations where ordinances are facially neutral, do not unfairly target religions, and provide no evidence that any nonreligious groups were treated more favorably (*Vision Church v. Village of Long Grove*, 2006). Presumably, because courts would reach the same outcome if the litigation concerned challenges by religious colleges or universities to local restrictive zoning code requirements, this is a topic that should be of interest to officials and attorneys in institutions of higher education.

Ralph D. Mawdsley

See also Age Discrimination in Employment Act; Eleventh Amendment; Equal Educational Opportunity Commission; Federalism; Religious Colleges and Universities; Zoning

Legal Citations

Age Discrimination in Employment Act, 29 U.S.C. § 621.

Amos v. Corporation of the Presiding Bishop, 483 U.S. 327 (1987).

City of Boerne v. Flores, 521 U.S. 507 (1997).

Ehlers-Renzi v. Connelly School of the Holy Child, 224 F.3d 283 (4th Cir. 2000).

Employment Division, Department of Human Resources v. Smith, 494 U.S. 872 (1990).

Hankins v. Lyght, 441 F.3d 96 (2d Cir. 2006).

Holy Land Foundation for Relief and Development v. Ashcroft, 333 F.3d 156 (D.C. Cir. 2003).

Lemon v. Kurtzman, 403 U.S. 602 (1971).

O'Bryan v. Bureau of Prisons, 349 F.3d 399 (7th Cir. 2003).

Religious Freedom Restoration Act, 42 U.S.C. §§ 2000bb-2000bb-4.

Religious Land Use and Institutionalized Persons Act, 42 U.S.C. §§ 2000cc-2000cc-5.

Rweyemamu v. Cote, 520 F.3d 198 (2d Cir. 2008).

Sherbert v. Verner, 374 U.S. 398 (1963).

Vision Church v. Village of Long Grove, 468 F.3d 975 (7th Cir. 2006).

Webman v. Federal Bureau of Prisons, 441 F.3d 1022 (D.C. Cir. 2006).

Westchester Day School v. Village of Mamaroneck, 504 F.3d 338 (2d Cir. 2007).

Wisconsin v. Yoder, 406 U.S. 205 (1972).

ROEMER V. BOARD OF PUBLIC WORKS OF MARYLAND

In *Roemer v. Board of Public Works of Maryland* (1976), the U.S. Supreme Court upheld the constitutionality of a program from Maryland that made public funds available to religiously affiliated institutions of higher education. *Roemer* is a relatively obscure case in the academic literature, because not a single law review article has been devoted exclusively to an analysis of the Court's judgment, even though it is cited frequently in these writings. Nevertheless, *Roemer* remains important, because it reinforced earlier precedent approving state and federal funding programs that are neutral on their face but provide aid to religious colleges and universities so long as such programs are not "pervasively sectarian."

In 1971, the Supreme Court resolved *Lemon v. Kurtzman,* in which it struck down statutes from Pennsylvania and Rhode Island that authorized governmental financial aid for the benefit of private elementary and secondary schools in the form of salary supplements for teachers, including those who taught in Roman Catholic schools. At the heart of its rationale, the Court articulated its now well-known three-part *Lemon* test for analyzing Establishment Clause challenges to government programs that aid religious institutions. In order to pass constitutional muster, the *Lemon* Court decreed, government programs that aid religious institutions must have secular legislative purposes, must not have the principal or primary effect of advancing (or inhibiting) religion, and must not excessively entangle states in religious affairs.

On the same day as it handed down *Lemon*, in *Tilton v. Richardson* (1971), the Supreme Court upheld the constitutionality of the Higher Education Facilities Act of 1963 against an Establishment Clause challenge, in spite of the fact that the statute allowed religious colleges and universities to participate in a funding program for the construction of facilities. Two years later, in *Hunt v. McNair* (1973), the Supreme Court upheld the constitutionality of the South Carolina Educational Facilities Act, a state law authorizing the issuance of revenue bonds for construction of college and university buildings in the state, including those built by religious institutions. In *Roemer*, the Supreme Court again addressed the issue of governmental aid for religious colleges as a plurality upheld a program from Maryland that allowed such assistance.

Facts of the Case

At issue in *Roemer* was a law authorizing the Maryland Council for Higher Education to award state funds to private in-state institutions of higher education that met statutory criteria and that maintained one or more "associate of arts or baccalaureate degree" programs and that refrained from awarding "only seminarian or theological degrees" (*Roemer*, p. 740). Under the law, participating colleges and universities were required to use the state funds for secular purposes only and to report to the council on how they used the money. The law authorized the council to make appropriations to Maryland's private colleges and universities on an annual basis. In 1971, 17 private colleges and universities, including four Catholic colleges and one Methodist institution, received a total of $1.7 million in state aid.

Taxpayers sued the Maryland Board of Public Works and the five religious colleges that received money pursuant to the statute, challenging its constitutionality under the Establishment Clause and seeking the return of money that had been awarded to the religious colleges. The Methodist college was subsequently dismissed from the suit, because its officials chose to disassociate from its religious leadership, and one of the Catholic institutions ceased operations. A divided three-judge federal trial court upheld the law after applying the three-part *Lemon* test.

The Supreme Court's Ruling

On further review, the Supreme Court affirmed the constitutionality of the statute in a plurality opinion (meaning that it did not achieve the five-justice majority needed to become binding precedent). The opinion was written by Justice Blackmun, with Justices Burger and Powell joining.

Citing its own precedent, a plurality of the Supreme Court observed that "religious institutions need not be quarantined from public benefits that are neutrally available to all" (p. 746). The Court then applied the three-part *Lemon* test for evaluating whether the statute passed constitutional muster. With respect to the first prong of the test, which required that the legislature have secular purposes for awarding the funds, the plurality noted that the taxpayers had not challenged the earlier judgment that the statute had the secular purpose of aiding private higher education generally. Thus, the result of the first prong of the test was not in dispute.

The plurality devoted considerable discussion to the second prong of the *Lemon* test. The plurality noted that the religious colleges that had received funding under the law were not "pervasively sectarian" and that religion courses, although mandatory, were mere supplements to their liberal arts curricula, which were offered in an atmosphere of academic freedom. Moreover, the plurality reasoned that the state funding extended only to the colleges' secular activities. Thus, the plurality had no difficulty upholding the ruling that the primary effect of the law was secular.

Turning to the third prong of the *Lemon* test— the question of whether the law created excessive entanglement between the state and religious institutions—the plurality agreed with the trial court that it did not. Acknowledging that gauging whether entanglement is present between church and state is not an exact science, the plurality affirmed the trial court's emphasis on the character of the Catholic colleges that had been aided by the law, concluding that their officials were capable of separating their secular and religious functions.

Justice White, joined by Justice Rehnquist, agreed with *Roemer*'s outcome but filed a concurring opinion emphasizing that it was unnecessary to analyze whether the law created excessive entanglement between the state and religious institutions, professing that this prong of the *Lemon* test was both curious and mystifying. Justice Brennan, joined by Justice Marshall, filed a dissenting opinion. Justices Stewart and Justice Stevens each filed separate dissents.

In addition to the dissenters having filed relatively short opinions detailing why they believed that the statute violated the *Lemon* test, Justice Stevens expressed his concern about what he described as "the pernicious tendency of a state subsidy to tempt religious schools to compromise their religious mission without wholly abandoning it" (p. 775).

In *Roemer,* then, the Supreme Court approved governmental aid for religious colleges and universities for the third time. In so ruling, the Court made it clear that the Establishment Clause was not a constitutional barrier to government aid programs that were properly constructed and that provided benefits to both religious and secular institutions as long as the religious colleges and universities were not "pervasively sectarian" in character.

Richard Fossey

See also *Hunt v. McNair*; Religious Colleges and Universities; State Aid and the Establishment Clause; *Tilton v. Richardson*

Legal Citations

Higher Education Facilities Act, Pub. L. No. 88-204 (1963).
Hunt v. McNair, 413 U.S. 734 (1973).
Lemon v. Kurtzman, 403 U.S. 602 (1971).
Roemer v. Board of Public Works of Maryland, 426 U.S. 736 (1976).
Tilton v. Richardson, 403 U.S. 672 (1971).

ROSENBERGER V. RECTOR AND VISITORS OF THE UNIVERSITY OF VIRGINIA

In *Rosenberger v. Rector and Visitors of the University of Virginia* (1995), the U.S. Supreme Court held that the actions of university officials in denying funding to help pay for the publishing costs of *Wide Awake: A Christian Perspective at the University of Virginia* constituted viewpoint discrimination in violation of the Free Speech Clause of the First Amendment. In light of the significance of *Rosenberger* with regard to the treatment of religious speech as a subset of free speech, this entry examines its background and judicial analyses.

Facts of the Case

The Student Activities Fund at the University of Virginia was built from mandatory student fees and was designed to support a variety of extracurricular student activities. Any organization that wished to receive funds had to become a "Contracted Independent Organization" (CIO) and had to include in all written materials to third parties that the group was independent of the university and that the university was not responsible for the CIO. Fund guidelines governed and controlled the disbursement of monies to CIOs. The guidelines stated that the purpose of the fund was to support a range of extracurricular activities and that the money had to be administered in a manner consistent with the education purpose of the university as well as with state and federal law.

Ronald Rosenberger was a University of Virginia student who created Wide Awake Productions as a CIO. The group published a magazine of religious and philosophical expression in order to facilitate discussion within an atmosphere of tolerance of Christian viewpoints. In addition, the group published a newspaper, the Christian viewpoint of which was clear from the first issue. The fact that Wide Awake Productions was a valid CIO is important, because if the group had been a religious organization, it would not have qualified for CIO status under fund guidelines. These guidelines stipulated that religious organizations were those whose purposes were to practice devotion to acknowledge ultimate realities or deities.

When the student requested monies from the fund to subsidize the publication of *Wide Awake,* officials rejected his application for aid on the ground that the magazine was a religious activity pursuant to its guidelines. The student then filed suit on behalf of Wide Awake Productions, claiming that the denial of funding solely on the basis of the publication's religious editorial viewpoint violated the group's rights to freedom of the press and speech, the right to free exercise of religion, and equal protection of the law.

A federal trial court, in granting the university's motion for summary judgment, was of the opinion that that the denial of support was not viewpoint discrimination and that officials' concern about the group's religious activities was a sufficient justification to deny the request for funds. On appeal, the Fourth Circuit affirmed that university officials did not violate the group's rights, because they had a compelling interest in preserving strict separation of church and state.

The Supreme Court's Ruling

On further review, in a five-to-four judgment authored by Justice Kennedy, the Supreme Court reversed in favor of the Wide Awake Productions. The Court ruled that the denial of funding for the publication imposed a financial burden on the group's speech amounting to viewpoint discrimination. Acknowledging that the fund was a forum, the Court compared this case with a similar situation in *Lamb's Chapel v. Center Moriches Union Free School District* (1993), wherein it found that a school board that made meeting space available to a large variety of groups could not exclude religious organizations based on the religious nature of their speech, because this amounted to viewpoint discrimination. The Court reasoned in *Rosenberger* that because funding was made available to groups for other journalistic pursuits, it had to do the same for the publications of other organizations whose content and subject matter were religious in nature.

The Supreme Court next rejected the university's claim that the guidelines and the accompanying restrictions were based on content, not viewpoint. The Court responded that with regard to religion, while the distinction between content and viewpoint is difficult to distinguish, religion served as a perspective and a standpoint for discussion. Consequently, the Court was convinced that university officials discriminated against the group due to its views, not the content of its publication. In discussing this distinction between content and viewpoint discrimination, the Court explained that content discrimination could be permissible if it preserved the purposes of the limited open forum but that viewpoint discrimination is impermissible when the speech is within the forum's limitation.

The Supreme Court then reviewed the university's claim that because *Rosenberger* dealt with funds and not facilities, its officials should have been afforded substantial discretion as to the allocation of resources to accomplish the institution's educational mission. The Court distinguished this situation from one where the University was the speaker and was controlling the message. Insofar as all CIOs had to sign waivers acknowledging that they were neither agents of the university nor its responsibility, the Court determined that because the groups were private speakers, the university officials could not silence the viewpoints of selected groups. Even if the case had dealt with facilities, the Court suggested that university officials would have been prohibited from acting as they did in denying funds.

Turning to the Establishment Clause issue, the Supreme Court pointed out that the university's program was neutral toward religion, because the purpose of the fund was to open a forum for speech and to support valid student groups. Deciding that the mandatory fee to support the fund was not a tax, the Court concluded that because the program furthered its neutrality by ensuring that each CIO was considered a private group and was not part of the university, officials would not have violated the Establishment Clause had they made the funds available.

Justice O'Connor's concurrence commented that there were four considerations that led her to believe that there was no Establishment Clause violation. She identified these as the facts that the CIOs remained independent of the university, that money from the fund was distributed only after publication and to outside vendors, that *Wide Awake* was competing with 15 other campus publications, and that students were involved in both the contribution and distribution of the funds.

Justice Thomas also concurred, explaining the historical context of the Establishment Clause. He remarked that the Establishment Clause does not require the exclusion of religious groups from all government benefits.

The dissent, authored by Justice Souter, and joined by Justices Stevens, Ginsburg, and Breyer, maintained that the university would have been directly subsidizing religion by paying printing costs for the newspaper. Further, he contended that the student activity fee was a tax, much like those imposed on the colonists for church support before the Constitution was enacted. As a result, he viewed the fee as a blatant violation of the Establishment Clause, because it provided a direct aid to religion.

In the wake of *Rosenberger*, the free speech rights of students on college and university campuses were strengthened even while the Supreme Court protected the ability of religiously affiliated organizations to use public facilities. Moreover, *Rosenberger* stands out, because it ensures that groups with differing viewpoints can be afforded equal access to funding, thereby promoting diversity of perspectives on college and university campuses.

Megan L. Rehberg

See also Free Speech and Expression Rights of Students; Religious Activities on Campus

Further Readings

Mawdsley, R. D., & Russo, C. J. (1995). Religion in public education: *Rosenberger* fuels an ongoing debate. *Education Law Reporter, 103,* 13–31.

Morris, A. A. (1995). Separation of church and state— Remarks on *Rosenberger v. University of Virginia. Education Law Reporter, 103,* 553–571.

Schimmel, D. (1995). Discrimination against religious viewpoints prohibited in public colleges and universities: An analysis of *Rosenberger v. University of Virginia. Education Law Reporter, 102,* 911–927.

Legal Citations

Lamb's Chapel v. Center Moriches Union Free School District, 508 U.S. 384 (1993).

Rosenberger v. Rector and Visitors of the University of Virginia, 515 U.S. 819 (1995).

ROSENBERGER V. RECTOR AND VISITORS OF THE UNIVERSITY OF VIRGINIA

Rosenberger stands out because in it, the Supreme Court treated religious speech as a subset of free speech, thereby helping to eliminate discrimination based on the viewpoint of speakers on campuses.

Supreme Court of the United States

ROSENBERGER

v.

RECTOR AND VISITORS OF THE UNIVERSITY OF VIRGINIA

515 U.S. 819

Argued March 1, 1995

Decided June 29, 1995

Justice KENNEDY delivered the opinion of the Court.

The University of Virginia, an instrumentality of the Commonwealth for which it is named and thus bound by the First and Fourteenth Amendments, authorizes the payment of outside contractors for the printing costs of a variety of student publications. It withheld any authorization for payments on behalf of petitioners for the sole reason that their student paper "primarily promotes or manifests a particular belie[f] in or about a deity or an ultimate reality." That the paper did promote or manifest views within the defined exclusion seems plain enough. The challenge is to the University's regulation and its denial of authorization, the case raising issues under the Speech and Establishment Clauses of the First Amendment.

I

The public corporation we refer to as the "University" is denominated by state law as "the Rector and Visitors of the University of Virginia" and it is responsible for governing the school. Founded by Thomas Jefferson in 1819, and ranked by him, together with the authorship of the Declaration of Independence and of the Virginia Act for Religious Freedom, as one of his proudest achievements, the University is among the Nation's oldest and most respected seats of higher learning. . . . An understanding of the case requires a somewhat detailed description of the program the University created to support extracurricular student activities on its campus.

Before a student group is eligible to submit bills from its outside contractors for payment by the fund described below, it must become a "Contracted Independent Organization" (CIO). CIO status is available to any group the majority of whose members are students, whose managing officers are full time students, and that complies with certain procedural requirements. A CIO must file its constitution with the University; must pledge not to discriminate in its membership; and must include in dealings with third parties and in all written materials a disclaimer, stating that the CIO is independent of the University and that the University is not responsible for the CIO. CIO's enjoy access to University facilities, including meeting rooms and computer terminals. A standard agreement signed between each CIO and the University provides that the benefits and opportunities afforded to CIO's "should not be misinterpreted as meaning that those organizations are part of or controlled by the University, that the University is responsible for the organizations' contracts or other acts or omissions, or that the University approves of the organizations' goals or activities."

All CIO's may exist and operate at the University, but some are also entitled to apply for funds from the Student Activities Fund (SAF). Established and governed by University Guidelines, the purpose of the SAF is to support a broad range of extracurricular student activities that "are related to the educational purpose of the University." The SAF is based on the University's "recogni[tion] that the availability of a wide range of opportunities" for its students "tends to enhance the University environment." The Guidelines require that it be administered "in a manner consistent with the educational purpose of the University as well as with state and federal law." The SAF receives its money from a mandatory fee of $14 per semester assessed to each full-time student. The Student Council, elected by the students, has the initial authority to disburse the funds, but its actions are subject to review by a faculty body chaired by a designee of the Vice President for Student Affairs.

Some, but not all, CIO's may submit disbursement requests to the SAF. The Guidelines recognize 11 categories of student groups that may seek payment to third-party contractors because they "are related to the educational purpose of the University of Virginia." One of these is "student news, information, opinion, entertainment, or academic communications media groups." The Guidelines also specify, however, that the costs of

certain activities of CIO's that are otherwise eligible for funding will not be reimbursed by the SAF. The student activities that are excluded from SAF support are religious activities, philanthropic contributions and activities, political activities, activities that would jeopardize the University's tax-exempt status, those which involve payment of honoraria or similar fees, or social entertainment or related expenses. The prohibition on "political activities" is defined so that it is limited to electioneering and lobbying. . . . A "religious activity," by contrast, is defined as any activity that "primarily promotes or manifests a particular belie[f] in or about a deity or an ultimate reality."

The Guidelines prescribe these criteria for determining the amounts of third-party disbursements that will be allowed on behalf of each eligible student organization: the size of the group, its financial self-sufficiency, and the University-wide benefit of its activities. If an organization seeks SAF support, it must submit its bills to the Student Council, which pays the organization's creditors upon determining that the expenses are appropriate. No direct payments are made to the student groups. During the 1990–1991 academic year, 343 student groups qualified as CIO's. One hundred thirty-five of them applied for support from the SAF, and 118 received funding. Fifteen of the groups were funded as "student news, information, opinion, entertainment, or academic communications media groups."

Petitioners' organization, Wide Awake Productions (WAP), qualified as a CIO. Formed by petitioner Ronald Rosenberger and other undergraduates in 1990, WAP was established "[t]o publish a magazine of philosophical and religious expression," "[t]o facilitate discussion which fosters an atmosphere of sensitivity to and tolerance of Christian viewpoints," and "[t]o provide a unifying focus for Christians of multicultural backgrounds." WAP publishes Wide Awake: A Christian Perspective at the University of Virginia. The paper's Christian viewpoint was evident from the first issue, in which its editors wrote that the journal "offers a Christian perspective on both personal and community issues, especially those relevant to college students at the University of Virginia." The editors committed the paper to a two-fold mission: "to challenge Christians to live, in word and deed, according to the faith they proclaim and to encourage students to consider what a personal relationship with Jesus Christ means." The first issue had articles about racism, crisis pregnancy, stress, prayer, C.S. Lewis' ideas about evil and free will, and reviews of religious music. In the next two issues, Wide Awake featured stories about homosexuality, Christian missionary work, and eating disorders, as well as music reviews and interviews with University professors. Each page of Wide Awake, and the end of each article or review, is marked by a cross. The advertisements carried in Wide Awake also reveal the Christian perspective of the journal. For the most part, the advertisers are churches, centers for Christian study, or Christian bookstores. By June 1992, WAP had distributed about 5,000 copies of Wide Awake to University students, free of charge.

WAP had acquired CIO status soon after it was organized. This is an important consideration in this case, for had it been a "religious organization," WAP would not have been accorded CIO status. As defined by the Guidelines, a "[r]eligious [o]rganization" is "an organization whose purpose is to practice a devotion to an acknowledged ultimate reality or deity." At no stage in this controversy has the University contended that WAP is such an organization.

A few months after being given CIO status, WAP requested the SAF to pay its printer $5,862 for the costs of printing its newspaper. The Appropriations Committee of the Student Council denied WAP's request on the ground that Wide Awake was a "religious activity" within the meaning of the Guidelines, *i.e.*, that the newspaper "promote[d] or manifest[ed] a particular belie[f] in or about a deity or an ultimate reality." It made its determination after examining the first issue. WAP appealed the denial to the full Student Council, contending that WAP met all the applicable Guidelines and that denial of SAF support on the basis of the magazine's religious perspective violated the Constitution. The appeal was denied without further comment, and WAP appealed to the next level, the Student Activities Committee. In a letter signed by the Dean of Students, the committee sustained the denial of funding.

Having no further recourse within the University structure, WAP, Wide Awake, and three of its editors and members filed suit in the United States District Court for the Western District of Virginia, challenging the SAF's action as violative of . . . 42 U.S.C. § 1983. They alleged that refusal to authorize payment of the printing costs of the publication, solely on the basis of its religious editorial viewpoint, violated their rights to freedom of speech and press, to the free exercise of religion, and to equal protection of the law. They relied also upon

Article I of the Virginia Constitution and the Virginia Act for Religious Freedom, but did not pursue those theories on appeal. The suit sought damages for the costs of printing the paper, injunctive and declaratory relief, and attorney's fees.

On cross-motions for summary judgment, the District Court ruled for the University, holding that denial of SAF support was not an impermissible content or viewpoint discrimination against petitioners' speech, and that the University's Establishment Clause concern over its "religious activities" was a sufficient justification for denying payment to third-party contractors. The court did not issue a definitive ruling on whether reimbursement, had it been made here, would or would not have violated the Establishment Clause.

The United States Court of Appeals for the Fourth Circuit, in disagreement with the District Court, held that the Guidelines did discriminate on the basis of content. It ruled that, while the State need not underwrite speech, there was a presumptive violation of the Speech Clause when viewpoint discrimination was invoked to deny third-party payment otherwise available to CIO's. The Court of Appeals affirmed the judgment of the District Court nonetheless, concluding that the discrimination by the University was justified by the "compelling interest in maintaining strict separation of church and state." We granted certiorari.

II

It is axiomatic that the government may not regulate speech based on its substantive content or the message it conveys. Other principles follow from this precept. In the realm of private speech or expression, government regulation may not favor one speaker over another. Discrimination against speech because of its message is presumed to be unconstitutional. These rules informed our determination that the government offends the First Amendment when it imposes financial burdens on certain speakers based on the content of their expression. When the government targets not subject matter, but particular views taken by speakers on a subject, the violation of the First Amendment is all the more blatant. Viewpoint discrimination is thus an egregious form of content discrimination. The government must abstain from regulating speech when the specific motivating ideology or the opinion or perspective of the speaker is the rationale for the restriction.

These principles provide the framework forbidding the State to exercise viewpoint discrimination, even when the limited public forum is one of its own creation. In a case involving a school district's provision of school facilities for private uses, we declared that "[t]here is no question that the District, like the private owner of property, may legally preserve the property under its control for the use to which it is dedicated." The necessities of confining a forum to the limited and legitimate purposes for which it was created may justify the State in reserving it for certain groups or for the discussion of certain topics. Once it has opened a limited forum, however, the State must respect the lawful boundaries it has itself set. The State may not exclude speech where its distinction is not "reasonable in light of the purpose served by the forum," nor may it discriminate against speech on the basis of its viewpoint. Thus, in determining whether the State is acting to preserve the limits of the forum it has created so that the exclusion of a class of speech is legitimate, we have observed a distinction between, on the one hand, content discrimination, which may be permissible if it preserves the purposes of that limited forum, and, on the other hand, viewpoint discrimination, which is presumed impermissible when directed against speech otherwise within the forum's limitations.

The SAF is a forum more in a metaphysical than in a spatial or geographic sense, but the same principles are applicable. The most recent and most apposite case is our decision in *Lamb's Chapel*. There, a school district had opened school facilities for use after school hours by community groups for a wide variety of social, civic, and recreational purposes. The district, however, had enacted a formal policy against opening facilities to groups for religious purposes. Invoking its policy, the district rejected a request from a group desiring to show a film series addressing various child-rearing questions from a "Christian perspective." There was no indication in the record in *Lamb's Chapel* that the request to use the school facilities was "denied, for any reason other than the fact that the presentation would have been from a religious perspective." . . .

The University does acknowledge (as it must in light of our precedents) that "ideologically driven attempts to suppress a particular point of view are presumptively unconstitutional in funding, as in other contexts," but insists that this case does not present that issue because the Guidelines draw lines based on content, not viewpoint. As we have noted, discrimination against one set of views or ideas is but a subset or particular instance of the more general phenomenon of content discrimination. And, it must be acknowledged, the distinction is not a precise one. It is, in a sense, something of an understatement to speak of religious thought and discussion as just a viewpoint, as distinct from a comprehensive body of thought. The nature of our origins and destiny and their dependence upon the existence of a divine being have been subjects of philosophic inquiry throughout human history. We conclude, nonetheless, that here, as in *Lamb's Chapel*, viewpoint discrimination is the proper way to interpret the University's objections to Wide Awake. By the very terms of the SAF prohibition, the University does not exclude religion as a subject matter but selects for disfavored treatment those student journalistic efforts with religious editorial viewpoints. Religion may be a vast area of inquiry, but it also provides, as it did here, a specific premise, a perspective, a standpoint from which a variety of subjects may be discussed and considered. The prohibited perspective, not the general subject matter, resulted in the refusal to make third-party payments, for the subjects discussed were otherwise within the approved category of publications.

. . . If the topic of debate is, for example, racism, then exclusion of several views on that problem is just as offensive to the First Amendment as exclusion of only one. It is as objectionable to exclude both a theistic and an atheistic perspective on the debate as it is to exclude one, the other, or yet another political, economic, or social viewpoint. . . .

The University's denial of WAP's request for third-party payments in the present case is based upon viewpoint discrimination not unlike the discrimination the school district relied upon in *Lamb's Chapel* and that we found invalid. The church group in *Lamb's Chapel* would have been qualified as a social or civic organization, save for its religious purposes. Furthermore, just as the school district in *Lamb's Chapel* pointed to nothing but the religious views of the group as the rationale for excluding its message, so in this case the University justifies its denial of SAF participation to WAP on the ground that the contents of Wide Awake reveal an avowed religious perspective. It bears only passing mention that the dissent's attempt to distinguish *Lamb's Chapel* is entirely without support in the law. . . . There is no indication in the opinion of the Court (which, unlike an advocate's statements at oral argument, is the law) that exclusion or inclusion of other religious or antireligious voices from that forum had any bearing on its decision.

The University tries to escape the consequences of our holding in *Lamb's Chapel* by urging that this case involves the provision of funds rather than access to facilities. The University begins with the unremarkable proposition that the State must have substantial discretion in determining how to allocate scarce resources to accomplish its educational mission. Citing our decisions in *Rust v. Sullivan, Regan v. Taxation with Representation of Wash.*, and *Widmar v. Vincent*, the University argues that content-based funding decisions are both inevitable and lawful. Were the reasoning of *Lamb's Chapel* to apply to funding decisions as well as to those involving access to facilities, it is urged, its holding "would become a judicial juggernaut, constitutionalizing the ubiquitous content-based decisions that schools, colleges, and other government entities routinely make in the allocation of public funds."

To this end the University relies on our assurance in *Widmar v. Vincent.* There, in the course of striking down a public university's exclusion of religious groups from use of school facilities made available to all other student groups, we stated: "Nor do we question the right of the University to make academic judgments as to how best to allocate scarce resources." The quoted language in *Widmar* was but a proper recognition of the principle that when the State is the speaker, it may make content-based choices. When the University determines the content of the education it provides, it is the University speaking, and we have permitted the government to regulate the content of what is or is not expressed when it is the speaker or when it enlists private entities to convey its own message. In the same vein, in *Rust v. Sullivan*, we upheld the government's prohibition on abortion-related advice applicable to recipients of federal funds for family planning counseling. There, the government did not create a program to encourage private speech but instead used private speakers to transmit specific information pertaining to its own program. We recognized that when the government appropriates public funds to promote a particular policy of its own it is entitled to say what it wishes. When the government disburses public funds to private entities to convey a governmental message, it may take legitimate and appropriate steps to ensure that its message is neither garbled nor distorted by the grantee.

It does not follow, however, and we did not suggest in *Widmar*, that viewpoint-based restrictions are proper when the University does not itself speak or subsidize transmittal of a message it favors but instead expends funds to encourage a diversity of views from private

speakers. A holding that the University may not discriminate based on the viewpoint of private persons whose speech it facilitates does not restrict the University's own speech, which is controlled by different principles. For that reason, the University's reliance on *Regan v. Taxation with Representation of Wash.* is inapposite as well. *Regan* involved a challenge to Congress' choice to grant tax deductions for contributions made to veterans' groups engaged in lobbying, while denying that favorable status to other charities which pursued lobbying efforts. Although acknowledging that the Government is not required to subsidize the exercise of fundamental rights, we reaffirmed the requirement of viewpoint neutrality in the Government's provision of financial benefits by observing that "[t]he case would be different if Congress were to discriminate invidiously in its subsidies in such a way as to 'ai[m] at the suppression of dangerous ideas.'" *Regan* relied on a distinction based on preferential treatment of certain speakers—veterans' organizations—and not a distinction based on the content or messages of those groups' speech. The University's regulation now before us, however, has a speech-based restriction as its sole rationale and operative principle.

The distinction between the University's own favored message and the private speech of students is evident in the case before us. The University itself has taken steps to ensure the distinction in the agreement each CIO must sign. The University declares that the student groups eligible for SAF support are not the University's agents, are not subject to its control, and are not its responsibility. Having offered to pay the third-party contractors on behalf of private speakers who convey their own messages, the University may not silence the expression of selected viewpoints.

The University urges that, from a constitutional standpoint, funding of speech differs from provision of access to facilities because money is scarce and physical facilities are not.

Beyond the fact that in any given case this proposition might not be true as an empirical matter, the underlying premise that the University could discriminate based on viewpoint if demand for space exceeded its availability is wrong as well. The government cannot justify viewpoint discrimination among private speakers on the economic fact of scarcity. Had the meeting rooms in *Lamb's Chapel* been scarce, had the demand been greater than the supply, our decision would have been no different. It would have been incumbent on the State, of course, to ration or allocate the scarce resources on some acceptable neutral principle; but nothing in our decision indicated that scarcity would give the State the right to exercise viewpoint discrimination that is otherwise impermissible.

Vital First Amendment speech principles are at stake here. The first danger to liberty lies in granting the State the power to examine publications to determine whether or not they are based on some ultimate idea and, if so, for the State to classify them. The second, and corollary, danger is to speech from the chilling of individual thought and expression. That danger is especially real in the University setting, where the State acts against a background and tradition of thought and experiment that is at the center of our intellectual and philosophic tradition. In ancient Athens, and, as Europe entered into a new period of intellectual awakening, in places like Bologna, Oxford, and Paris, universities began as voluntary and spontaneous assemblages or concourses for students to speak and to write and to learn. The quality and creative power of student intellectual life to this day remains a vital measure of a school's influence and attainment. For the University, by regulation, to cast disapproval on particular viewpoints of its students risks the suppression of free speech and creative inquiry in one of the vital centers for the Nation's intellectual life, its college and university campuses.

The Guideline invoked by the University to deny third-party contractor payments on behalf of WAP effects a sweeping restriction on student thought and student inquiry in the context of University sponsored publications. The prohibition on funding on behalf of publications that "primarily promot[e] or manifes[t] a particular belie[f] in or about a deity or an ultimate reality," in its ordinary and commonsense meaning, has a vast potential reach. The term "promotes" as used here would comprehend any writing advocating a philosophic position that rests upon a belief in a deity or ultimate reality. And the term "manifests" would bring within the scope of the prohibition any writing that is explicable as resting upon a premise that presupposes the existence of a deity or ultimate reality. Were the prohibition applied with much vigor at all, it would bar funding of essays by hypothetical student contributors named Plato, Spinoza, and Descartes. And if the regulation covers, as the University says it does, those student journalistic efforts that primarily manifest or promote a belief that there is no deity and no ultimate reality, then undergraduates named Karl Marx, Bertrand Russell, and Jean-Paul Sartre

would likewise have some of their major essays excluded from student publications. If any manifestation of beliefs in first principles disqualifies the writing, as seems to be the case, it is indeed difficult to name renowned thinkers whose writings would be accepted, save perhaps for articles disclaiming all connection to their ultimate philosophy. Plato could contrive perhaps to submit an acceptable essay on making pasta or peanut butter cookies, provided he did not point out their (necessary) imperfections.

Based on the principles we have discussed, we hold that the regulation invoked to deny SAF support, both in its terms and in its application to these petitioners, is a denial of their right of free speech guaranteed by the First Amendment. It remains to be considered whether the violation following from the University's action is excused by the necessity of complying with the Constitution's prohibition against state establishment of religion. We turn to that question.

III

Before its brief on the merits in this Court, the University had argued at all stages of the litigation that inclusion of WAP's contractors in SAF funding authorization would violate the Establishment Clause. Indeed, that is the ground on which the University prevailed in the Court of Appeals. We granted certiorari on this question: "Whether the Establishment Clause compels a state university to exclude an otherwise eligible student publication from participation in the student activities fund, solely on the basis of its religious viewpoint, where such exclusion would violate the Speech and Press Clauses if the viewpoint of the publication were nonreligious." The University now seems to have abandoned this position, contending that "[t]he fundamental objection to petitioners' argument is not that it implicates the Establishment Clause but that it would defeat the ability of public education at all levels to control the use of public funds." That the University itself no longer presses the Establishment Clause claim is some indication that it lacks force; but as the Court of Appeals rested its judgment on the point and our dissenting colleagues would find it determinative, it must be addressed.

. . .

A central lesson of our decisions is that a significant factor in upholding governmental programs in the face of Establishment Clause attack is their neutrality towards religion. We have decided a series of cases addressing the receipt of government benefits where religion or religious views are implicated in some degree. The first case in our modern Establishment Clause jurisprudence was *Everson v. Board of Ed. of Ewing*. There we cautioned that in enforcing the prohibition against laws respecting establishment of religion, we must "be sure that we do not inadvertently prohibit [the government] from extending its general state law benefits to all its citizens without regard to their religious belief." We have held that the guarantee of neutrality is respected, not offended, when the government, following neutral criteria and evenhanded policies, extends benefits to recipients whose ideologies and viewpoints, including religious ones, are broad and diverse. More than once have we rejected the position that the Establishment Clause even justifies, much less requires, a refusal to extend free speech rights to religious speakers who participate in broad-reaching government programs neutral in design.

The governmental program here is neutral toward religion. There is no suggestion that the University created it to advance religion or adopted some ingenious device with the purpose of aiding a religious cause. The object of the SAF is to open a forum for speech and to support various student enterprises, including the publication of newspapers, in recognition of the diversity and creativity of student life. The University's SAF Guidelines have a separate classification for, and do not make third-party payments on behalf of, "religious organizations," which are those "whose purpose is to practice a devotion to an acknowledged ultimate reality or deity." The category of support here is for "student news, information, opinion, entertainment, or academic communications media groups," of which Wide Awake was 1 of 15 in the 1990 school year. WAP did not seek a subsidy because of its Christian editorial viewpoint; it sought funding as a student journal, which it was.

The neutrality of the program distinguishes the student fees from a tax levied for the direct support of a church or group of churches. A tax of that sort, of course, would run contrary to Establishment Clause concerns dating from the earliest days of the Republic. The apprehensions of our predecessors involved the levying of taxes upon the public for the sole and exclusive purpose of establishing and supporting specific sects. The exaction here, by contrast, is a student activity fee designed to reflect the reality that student life in its many

dimensions includes the necessity of wide-ranging speech and inquiry and that student expression is an integral part of the University's educational mission. The fee is mandatory, and we do not have before us the question whether an objecting student has the First Amendment right to demand a pro rata return to the extent the fee is expended for speech to which he or she does not subscribe. We must treat it, then, as an exaction upon the students. But the $14 paid each semester by the students is not a general tax designed to raise revenue for the University. The SAF cannot be used for unlimited purposes, much less the illegitimate purpose of supporting one religion. Much like the arrangement in *Widmar*, the money goes to a special fund from which any group of students with CIO status can draw for purposes consistent with the University's educational mission; and to the extent the student is interested in speech, withdrawal is permitted to cover the whole spectrum of speech, whether it manifests a religious view, an antireligious view, or neither. Our decision, then, cannot be read as addressing an expenditure from a general tax fund. Here, the disbursements from the fund go to private contractors for the cost of printing that which is protected under the Speech Clause of the First Amendment. This is a far cry from a general public assessment designed and effected to provide financial support for a church.

Government neutrality is apparent in the State's overall scheme in a further meaningful respect. The program respects the critical difference "between *government* speech endorsing religion, which the Establishment Clause forbids, and *private* speech endorsing religion, which the Free Speech and Free Exercise Clauses protect." In this case, "the government has not fostered or encouraged" any mistaken impression that the student newspapers speak for the University. The University has taken pains to disassociate itself from the private speech involved in this case. The Court of Appeals' apparent concern that Wide Awake's religious orientation would be attributed to the University is not a plausible fear, and there is no real likelihood that the speech in question is being either endorsed or coerced by the State.

The Court of Appeals (and the dissent) are correct to extract from our decisions the principle that we have recognized special Establishment Clause dangers where the government makes direct money payments to sectarian institutions. The error is not in identifying the principle, but in believing that it controls this case. Even assuming that WAP is no different from a church and that its speech is the same as the religious exercises conducted in *Widmar* (two points much in doubt), the Court of Appeals decided a case that was, in essence, not before it, and the dissent would have us do the same. We do not confront a case where, even under a neutral program that includes nonsectarian recipients, the government is making direct money payments to an institution or group that is engaged in religious activity. . . .

It does not violate the Establishment Clause for a public university to grant access to its facilities on a religion-neutral basis to a wide spectrum of student groups, including groups that use meeting rooms for sectarian activities, accompanied by some devotional exercises. This is so even where the upkeep, maintenance, and repair of the facilities attributed to those uses are paid from a student activities fund to which students are required to contribute. The government usually acts by spending money. Even the provision of a meeting room, as in *Mergens* and *Widmar*, involved governmental expenditure, if only in the form of electricity and heating or cooling costs. The error made by the Court of Appeals, as well as by the dissent, lies in focusing on the money that is undoubtedly expended by the government, rather than on the nature of the benefit received by the recipient. If the expenditure of governmental funds is prohibited whenever those funds pay for a service that is, pursuant to a religion-neutral program, used by a group for sectarian purposes, then *Widmar, Mergens,* and *Lamb's Chapel* would have to be overruled. Given our holdings in these cases, it follows that a public university may maintain its own computer facility and give student groups access to that facility, including the use of the printers, on a religion neutral, say first-come-first-served, basis. If a religious student organization obtained access on that religion-neutral basis and used a computer to compose or a printer or copy machine to print speech with a religious content or viewpoint, the State's action in providing the group with access would no more violate the Establishment Clause than would giving those groups access to an assembly hall. There is no difference in logic or principle, and no difference of constitutional significance, between a school using its funds to operate a facility to which students have access, and a school paying a third-party contractor to operate the facility on its behalf. The latter occurs here. The University provides printing services to a broad spectrum of student newspapers qualified as CIO's by reason of their officers and membership. Any benefit to

religion is incidental to the government's provision of secular services for secular purposes on a religion-neutral basis. Printing is a routine, secular, and recurring attribute of student life.

By paying outside printers, the University in fact attains a further degree of separation from the student publication, for it avoids the duties of supervision, escapes the costs of upkeep, repair, and replacement attributable to student use, and has a clear record of costs. As a result, and as in *Widmar*, the University can charge the SAF, and not the taxpayers as a whole, for the discrete activity in question. It would be formalistic for us to say that the University must forfeit these advantages and provide the services itself in order to comply with the Establishment Clause. It is, of course, true that if the State pays a church's bills it is subsidizing it, and we must guard against this abuse. That is not a danger here, based on the considerations we have advanced and for the additional reason that the student publication is not a religious institution, at least in the usual sense of that term as used in our case law, and it is not a religious organization as used in the University's own regulations. It is instead a publication involved in a pure forum for the expression of ideas, ideas that would be both incomplete and chilled were the Constitution to be interpreted to require that state officials and courts scan the publication to ferret out views that principally manifest a belief in a divine being. . . .

* * *

To obey the Establishment Clause, it was not necessary for the University to deny eligibility to student publications because of their viewpoint. The neutrality commanded of the State by the separate Clauses of the First Amendment was compromised by the University's course of action. The viewpoint discrimination inherent in the University's regulation required public officials to scan and interpret student publications to discern their underlying philosophic assumptions respecting religious theory and belief. That course of action was a denial of the right of free speech and would risk fostering a pervasive bias or hostility to religion, which could undermine the very neutrality the Establishment Clause requires. There is no Establishment Clause violation in the University's honoring its duties under the Free Speech Clause.

The judgment of the Court of Appeals must be, and is, reversed.

It is so ordered.

RUMSFELD V. FORUM FOR ACADEMIC AND INSTITUTIONAL RIGHTS

Rumsfeld v. Forum for Academic and Institutional Rights (2006) concerned a constitutional challenge to the Solomon Amendment, a modification in a federal statute that required the U.S. Department of Defense (DoD) to deny funding to institutions of higher education that refused to give military representatives access and assistance for recruiting purposes. In a unanimous opinion, with Justice Alito not participating, the Supreme Court held that the Solomon Amendment did not impose an unconstitutional condition on the receipt of federal funds, did not compel educational institutions to speak the government's message, did not regulate inherently expressive conduct, and did not violate the plaintiffs' First Amendment freedom of association. In light of the implications that *Rumsfeld* raises for colleges and universities, this entry reviews the case in detail.

Facts of the Case

When some law schools began restricting the access of military recruiters to their students because of disagreement with the federal government's "don't ask, don't tell" policy on homosexuals in the military, Congress responded in 1994 by adding the Solomon Amendment to the DoD's appropriations bill, with further changes to the amendment in 1997, 1999, and 2004. Named after its sponsor, New York Representative Gerald B. H. Solomon, the amendment denied funds to institutions of higher education that did not allow military recruiters access to their campuses equal to that accorded other recruiters or that prohibited or in effect prevented students from enrolling in reserve military units on their campuses. The prohibition applied to funds distributed through five different federal agencies.

After September 11, 2001, the DoD began applying an informal policy of requiring access equal to what other recruiters received. The DoD apparently anticipated that this approach would lead law schools to suspend their policies banning discrimination related to sexual orientation and allow access for military recruitment. In September 2003, an association of law schools and law faculties functioning under the title Forum for Academic and Institutional Rights (FAIR) filed suit in a federal trial court in New Jersey, seeking to enjoin the enforcement of the Solomon Amendment. All the members of the association had adopted policies prohibiting discrimination based on sexual orientation. The court denied FAIR's request for a preliminary injunction, finding that the plaintiffs were unlikely to prevail on the merits of their claims that the amendment infringed their First Amendment free speech and association rights to oppose sexual orientation discrimination, constituted viewpoint discrimination, and was unconstitutionally vague. On appeal, the Third Circuit reversed in a two-to-one judgment, holding that plaintiffs had a reasonable likelihood of success, and remanded the case to the trial court with order to grant a preliminary injunction.

The Supreme Court's Ruling

On further review, a unanimous Supreme Court, in an opinion authored by Chief Justice Roberts, reversed the judgment of the Third Circuit. The Court reasoned that Congress could require law schools to provide equal access to military recruiters without violating their First Amendment speech and expressive association rights. As to the authority of Congress to enact and enforce the Solomon Amendment, the Court observed that the First Amendment did not prohibit Congress from imposing directly the amendment's access requirement on law schools.

In terms of compliance with the Solomon Amendment's equal access requirement, the law schools had argued that they could comply with the law by denying access equally to all recruiters who violated their sexual orientation nondiscrimination policies, not just military recruiters. However, the Supreme Court rejected that position in determining that because the amendment focused not on the content of policies but rather on the results they achieved, the law schools could not be in compliance if the enforcement of their policies resulted in a greater level of access for other recruiters than for those from the military.

Turning to the law schools' most substantial claim—that enforcement of the Solomon Amendment violated their rights of speech and expressive association, the Supreme Court noted that the amendment regulated conduct, not speech. Being required to provide the same services for military recruiters as for others, including sending e-mails to students about the presence of recruiters on campus, was not, according to the Court, the kind of compelled speech that the Court addressed in *West Virginia Board of Education v. Barnette* (1943). In that case, the Court held that students could not be required to pledge allegiance to the U.S. flag in violation of their religious beliefs as Jehovah's Witnesses. Roberts explained that to equate a requirement that law schools send e-mails on behalf of all recruiters, including military ones, with compelling students to violate their sincerely held religious beliefs trivialized the freedom protected in *Barnette*.

At the same time, Roberts acknowledged that the government cannot compel speech that changes a complaining party's own expressive message, as the Court had decided in *Hurley v. Irish-American Gay, Lesbian and Bisexual Group of Boston* (1995). In *Hurley,* the Court held that officials in the city of Boston who sought to enforce a sexual orientation nondiscrimination policy by denying a permit to the organizers of the St. Patrick's Day parade violated the organizers' rights to free speech. The Court pointed out that such a result would have violated the First Amendment, because requiring the parade organizers to allow participation by gay/lesbian/bisexual groups seeking to project their own message about sexual orientation would have forced the organizers to accommodate a message different from the parade's purpose of recognizing the Irish tradition. The Court was satisfied that no such change of message occurred in *Rumsfeld,* because nothing in the recruiting process would suggest that that the law schools were in agreement with the expressive views of the recruiters. In fact, the Court added that the amendment in no way restricted the freedom of law school officials and faculty members to express their own views about the military's policies.

In rounding out its analysis, the Supreme Court rejected any comparison of *Rumsfeld* to *Boy Scouts of America v. Dale* (2000), wherein it agreed that a state law violated the right to expressive association of the Boy Scouts, because it required the organization to accept a homosexual scoutmaster. The Court maintained that even though military recruiters might interact with law school personnel, the recruiters were not part of the schools, and thus the Solomon Amendment did not violate the First Amendment.

Rumsfeld stands out because it is at the intersection of the relationship between the power of the federal government to impose conditions of the receipt of aid that it provides and the First Amendment and academic freedom rights of faculty members in law schools and other parts of campus communities. Insofar as the Supreme Court upheld the authority of Congress to impose conditions on the receipt of federal funds, it opens the door to other potential conflicts in this contentious arena.

Ralph D. Mawdsley

See also Academic Freedom

Further Readings

van Dalen, M. (2007). Rumsfeld v. FAIR, A free speech setback or strategic victory for the military? *Journal of the Legal Profession, 31,* 75–96.

Legal Citations

Boy Scouts of America v. Dale, 530 U.S. 640 (2000).
Hurley v. Irish-American Gay, Lesbian and Bisexual Group of Boston, 515 U.S. 557 (1995).
Rumsfeld v. Forum for Academic and Institutional Rights, 547 U.S. 47 (2006).
Solomon Amendment, 10 U.S.C. § 983.
West Virginia Board of Education v. Barnette, 319 U.S. 624 (1943).

Rumsfeld v. Forum for Academic and Institutional Rights

In *Rumsfeld,* the Supreme Court ruled that granting military recruiters access to law schools under the Solomon Amendment did not impose an unconstitutional condition on the receipt of federal funds, did not compel educational institutions to speak the government's message, did not regulate inherently expressive conduct, and did not violate the plaintiffs' First Amendment rights to freedom of association.

Supreme Court of the United States

RUMSFELD

v.

FORUM FOR ACADEMIC AND INSTITUTIONAL RIGHTS

547 U.S. 47

Argued Dec. 6, 2005

Decided March 6, 2006

Chief Justice ROBERTS delivered the opinion of the Court.

When law schools began restricting the access of military recruiters to their students because of disagreement with the Government's policy on homosexuals in the military, Congress responded by enacting the Solomon Amendment. That provision specifies that if any part of an institution of higher education denies military recruiters access equal to that provided other recruiters, the entire institution would lose certain federal funds. The law schools responded by suing, alleging that the Solomon Amendment infringed their First Amendment freedoms of speech and association. The District Court disagreed but was reversed by a divided panel of the Court of Appeals for the Third Circuit, which ordered the District Court to enter a preliminary injunction against enforcement of the Solomon Amendment. We granted certiorari.

I

Respondent Forum for Academic and Institutional Rights (FAIR), is an association of law schools and law faculties. Its declared mission is "to promote academic freedom, support educational institutions in opposing discrimination and vindicate the rights of institutions of higher education." FAIR members have adopted policies expressing their opposition to discrimination based on, among other factors, sexual orientation. They would like to restrict military recruiting on their campuses because

they object to the policy Congress has adopted with respect to homosexuals in the military. The Solomon Amendment, however, forces institutions to choose between enforcing their nondiscrimination policy against military recruiters in this way and continuing to receive specified federal funding.

In 2003, FAIR sought a preliminary injunction against enforcement of the Solomon Amendment, which at that time—it has since been amended—prevented the Department of Defense (DOD) from providing specified federal funds to any institution of higher education "that either prohibits, or in effect prevents" military recruiters "from gaining entry to campuses." FAIR considered the DOD's interpretation of this provision particularly objectionable. Although the statute required only "entry to campuses," the Government—after the terrorist attacks on September 11, 2001—adopted an informal policy of "requir[ing] universities to provide military recruiters access to students equal in quality and scope to that provided to other recruiters." Prior to the adoption of this policy, some law schools sought to promote their nondiscrimination policies while still complying with the Solomon Amendment by having military recruiters interview on the undergraduate campus. But under the equal access policy, military recruiters had to be permitted to interview at the law schools, if other recruiters did so.

FAIR argued that this forced inclusion and equal treatment of military recruiters violated the law schools' First Amendment freedoms of speech and association.

According to FAIR, the Solomon Amendment was unconstitutional because it forced law schools to choose between exercising their First Amendment right to decide whether to disseminate or accommodate a military recruiter's message, and ensuring the availability of federal funding for their universities.

The District Court denied the preliminary injunction on the ground that FAIR had failed to establish a likelihood of success on the merits of its First Amendment claims. The District Court held that inclusion "of an unwanted periodic visitor" did not "significantly affect the law schools' ability to express their particular message or viewpoint." The District Court based its decision in large part on the determination that recruiting is conduct and not speech, concluding that any expressive aspect of recruiting "is entirely ancillary to its dominant economic purpose." The District Court held that Congress could regulate this expressive aspect of the conduct under the test set forth in *United States v. O'Brien.*

In rejecting FAIR's constitutional claims, the District Court disagreed with "the DOD's proposed interpretation that the statute requires law schools to 'provide military recruiters access to students that is at least equal in quality and scope to the access provided other potential employers.' In response to the District Court's concerns, Congress codified the DOD's informal policy. The Solomon Amendment now prevents an institution from receiving certain federal funding if it prohibits military recruiters "from gaining access to campuses, or access to students . . . on campuses, for purposes of military recruiting in a manner that is at least equal in quality and scope to the access to campuses and to students that is provided to any other employer."

FAIR appealed the District Court's judgment, arguing that the recently amended Solomon Amendment was unconstitutional for the same reasons as the earlier version. A divided panel of the Court of Appeals for the Third Circuit agreed. According to the Third Circuit, the Solomon Amendment violated the unconstitutional conditions doctrine because it forced a law school to choose between surrendering First Amendment rights and losing federal funding for its university. Unlike the District Court, the Court of Appeals did not think that the *O'Brien* analysis applied because the Solomon Amendment, in its view, regulated speech and not simply expressive conduct. The Third Circuit nonetheless determined that if the regulated activities were properly treated as expressive conduct rather than speech, the Solomon

Amendment was also unconstitutional under *O'Brien.* As a result, the Court of Appeals reversed and remanded for the District Court to enter a preliminary injunction against enforcement of the Solomon Amendment. A dissenting judge would have applied *O'Brien* and affirmed.

We granted certiorari.

II

The Solomon Amendment denies federal funding to an institution of higher education that "has a policy or practice . . . that either prohibits, or in effect prevents" the military "from gaining access to campuses, or access to students . . . on campuses, for purposes of military recruiting in a manner that is at least equal in quality and scope to the access to campuses and to students that is provided to any other employer." The statute provides an exception for an institution with "a longstanding policy of pacifism based on historical religious affiliation." The Government and FAIR agree on what this statute requires: In order for a law school and its university to receive federal funding, the law school must offer military recruiters the same access to its campus and students that it provides to the nonmilitary recruiter receiving the most favorable access.

Certain law professors participating as *amici,* however, argue that the Government and FAIR misinterpret the statute. According to these *amici,* the Solomon Amendment's equal access requirement is satisfied when an institution applies to military recruiters the same policy it applies to all other recruiters. On this reading, a school excluding military recruiters would comply with the Solomon Amendment so long as it also excluded any other employer that violates its nondiscrimination policy.

In its reply brief, the Government claims that this question is not before the Court because it was neither included in the questions presented nor raised by FAIR. But our review may, in our discretion, encompass questions "'fairly included'" within the question presented, and there can be little doubt that granting certiorari to determine whether a statute is constitutional fairly includes the question of what that statute says. Nor must we accept an interpretation of a statute simply because it is agreed to by the parties. After all, "[o]ur task is to construe what Congress has enacted." We think it appropriate in the present case to consider whether institutions can comply with the Solomon Amendment by applying a general nondiscrimination policy to exclude military recruiters.

We conclude that they cannot and that the Government and FAIR correctly interpret the Solomon Amendment. The statute requires the Secretary of Defense to compare the military's "access to campuses" and "access to students" to "the access to campuses and to students that is provided to *any other employer.*" (Emphasis added.) The statute does not call for an inquiry into why or how the "other employer" secured its access. Under *amici*'s reading, a military recruiter has the same "access" to campuses and students as, say, a law firm when the law firm is permitted on campus to interview students and the military is not. We do not think that the military recruiter has received equal "access" in this situation—regardless of whether the disparate treatment is attributable to the military's failure to comply with the school's nondiscrimination policy.

The Solomon Amendment does not focus on the *content* of a school's recruiting policy, as the *amici* would have it. Instead, it looks to the *result* achieved by the policy and compares the "access . . . provided" military recruiters to that provided other recruiters. Applying the same policy to all recruiters is therefore insufficient to comply with the statute if it results in a greater level of access for other recruiters than for the military. Law schools must ensure that their recruiting policy operates in such a way that military recruiters are given access to students at least equal to that "*provided* to any other employer." (Emphasis added.)

Not only does the text support this view, but this interpretation is necessary to give effect to the Solomon Amendment's recent revision. Under the prior version, the statute required "entry" without specifying how military recruiters should be treated once on campus. The District Court thought that the DOD policy, which required equal access to students once recruiters were on campus, was unwarranted based on the text of the statute. Congress responded directly to this decision by codifying the DOD policy. Under *amici*'s interpretation, this legislative change had no effect—law schools could still restrict military access, so long as they do so under a generally applicable nondiscrimination policy. Worse yet, the legislative change made it *easier* for schools to keep military recruiters out altogether: Under the prior version, simple access could not be denied, but under the amended version, access could be denied altogether, so long as a nonmilitary recruiter would also be denied access. That is rather clearly *not* what Congress had in mind in codifying the DOD policy. We refuse to interpret the Solomon Amendment in a way that negates its recent revision, and indeed would render it a largely meaningless exercise.

We therefore read the Solomon Amendment the way both the Government and FAIR interpret it. It is insufficient for a law school to treat the military as it treats all other employers who violate its nondiscrimination policy. Under the statute, military recruiters must be given the same access as recruiters who comply with the policy.

III

The Constitution grants Congress the power to "provide for the common Defence," "[t]o raise and support Armies," and "[t]o provide and maintain a Navy." Congress' power in this area "is broad and sweeping" and there is no dispute in this case that it includes the authority to require campus access for military recruiters. That is, of course, unless Congress exceeds constitutional limitations on its power in enacting such legislation. But the fact that legislation that raises armies is subject to First Amendment constraints does not mean that we ignore the purpose of this legislation when determining its constitutionality; as we recognized in *Rostker*, "judicial deference . . . is at its apogee" when Congress legislates under its authority to raise and support armies.

Although Congress has broad authority to legislate on matters of military recruiting, it nonetheless chose to secure campus access for military recruiters indirectly, through its Spending Clause power. The Solomon Amendment gives universities a choice: Either allow military recruiters the same access to students afforded any other recruiter or forgo certain federal funds. Congress' decision to proceed indirectly does not reduce the deference given to Congress in the area of military affairs. Congress' choice to promote its goal by creating a funding condition deserves at least as deferential treatment as if Congress had imposed a mandate on universities.

Congress' power to regulate military recruiting under the Solomon Amendment is arguably greater because universities are free to decline the federal funds. . . .

Other decisions, however, recognize a limit on Congress' ability to place conditions on the receipt of funds. We recently held that "the government may not deny a benefit to a person on a basis that infringes his constitutionally protected . . . freedom of speech even if he has no entitlement to that benefit." Under this principle, known as the unconstitutional conditions doctrine, the Solomon Amendment would be unconstitutional if Congress could not directly require universities to provide military recruiters equal access to their students.

This case does not require us to determine when a condition placed on university funding goes beyond the "reasonable" choice . . . and becomes an unconstitutional condition. It is clear that a funding condition cannot be unconstitutional if it could be constitutionally imposed directly. Because the First Amendment would not prevent Congress from directly imposing the Solomon Amendment's access requirement, the statute does not place an unconstitutional condition on the receipt of federal funds.

A

The Solomon Amendment neither limits what law schools may say nor requires them to say anything. Law schools remain free under the statute to express whatever views they may have on the military's congressionally mandated employment policy, all the while retaining eligibility for federal funds. As a general matter, the Solomon Amendment regulates conduct, not speech. It affects what law schools must *do*—afford equal access to military recruiters—not what they may or may not *say*.

Nevertheless, the Third Circuit concluded that the Solomon Amendment violates law schools' freedom of speech in a number of ways. First, in assisting military recruiters, law schools provide some services, such as sending e-mails and distributing flyers that clearly involve speech. The Court of Appeals held that in supplying these services law schools are unconstitutionally compelled to speak the Government's message. Second, military recruiters are, to some extent, speaking while they are on campus. The Court of Appeals held that, by forcing law schools to permit the military on campus to express its message, the Solomon Amendment unconstitutionally requires law schools to host or accommodate the military's speech. Third, although the Court of Appeals thought that the Solomon Amendment regulated speech, it held in the alternative that, if the statute regulates conduct, this conduct is expressive and regulating it unconstitutionally infringes law schools' right to engage in expressive conduct. We consider each issue in turn.

1

Some of this Court's leading First Amendment precedents have established the principle that freedom of speech prohibits the government from telling people what they must say. . . .

The Solomon Amendment does not require any similar expression by law schools.

Nonetheless, recruiting assistance provided by the schools often includes elements of speech. For example, schools may send e-mails or post notices on bulletin boards on an employer's behalf. Law schools offering such services to other recruiters must also send e-mails and post notices on behalf of the military to comply with the Solomon Amendment. As FAIR points out, these compelled statements of fact ("The U.S. Army recruiter will meet interested students in Room 123 at 11 a.m."), like compelled statements of opinion, are subject to First Amendment scrutiny.

This sort of recruiting assistance, however, is a far cry from the compelled speech in *Barnette* and *Wooley*. The Solomon Amendment, unlike the laws at issue in those cases, does not dictate the content of the speech at all, which is only "compelled" if, and to the extent, the school provides such speech for other recruiters. There is nothing in this case approaching a Government-mandated pledge or motto that the school must endorse.

The compelled speech to which the law schools point is plainly incidental to the Solomon Amendment's regulation of conduct, and "it has never been deemed an abridgment of freedom of speech or press to make a course of conduct illegal merely because the conduct was in part initiated, evidenced, or carried out by means of language, either spoken, written, or printed." Congress, for example, can prohibit employers from discriminating in hiring on the basis of race. The fact that this will require an employer to take down a sign reading "White Applicants Only" hardly means that the law should be analyzed as one regulating the employer's speech rather than conduct. Compelling a law school that sends scheduling e-mails for other recruiters to send one for a military recruiter is simply not the same as forcing a student to pledge allegiance, or forcing a Jehovah's Witness to display the motto "Live Free or Die," and it trivializes the freedom protected in *Barnette* and *Wooley* to suggest that it is.

2

Our compelled-speech cases are not limited to the situation in which an individual must personally speak the government's message. We have also in a number of instances limited the government's ability to force one speaker to host or accommodate another speaker's message. Relying on these precedents, the Third Circuit concluded that the Solomon Amendment unconstitutionally compels law schools to accommodate the military's message "[b]y requiring schools to include military recruiters in the interviews and recruiting receptions the schools arrange."

The compelled-speech violation in each of our prior cases, however, resulted from the fact that the complaining speaker's own message was affected by the speech it was forced to accommodate. The expressive nature of a parade was central to our holding in *Hurley*. We concluded that because "every participating unit affects the message conveyed by the [parade's] private organizers," a law dictating that a particular group must be included in the parade "alter[s] the expressive content of th[e] parade." As a result, we held that the State's public accommodation law, as applied to a private parade, "violates the fundamental rule of protection under the First Amendment, that a speaker has the autonomy to choose the content of his own message."

The compelled-speech violations in *Tornillo* and *Pacific Gas* also resulted from interference with a speaker's desired message. In *Tornillo*, we recognized that "the compelled printing of a reply . . . tak[es] up space that could be devoted to other material the newspaper may have preferred to print" and therefore concluded that this right-of-reply statute infringed the newspaper editors' freedom of speech by altering the message the paper wished to express. The same is true in *Pacific Gas*. There, the utility company regularly included its newsletter, which we concluded was protected speech, in its billing envelope. Thus, when the state agency ordered the utility to send a third-party newsletter four times a year, it interfered with the utility's ability to communicate its own message in its newsletter. A plurality of the Court likened this to the situation in *Tornillo* and held that the forced inclusion of the other newsletter interfered with the utility's own message.

In this case, accommodating the military's message does not affect the law schools' speech, because the schools are not speaking when they host interviews and recruiting receptions. Unlike a parade organizer's choice of parade contingents, a law school's decision to allow recruiters on campus is not inherently expressive. Law schools facilitate recruiting to assist their students in obtaining jobs. A law school's recruiting services lack the expressive quality of a parade, a newsletter, or the

editorial page of a newspaper; its accommodation of a military recruiter's message is not compelled speech because the accommodation does not sufficiently interfere with any message of the school.

The schools respond that if they treat military and nonmilitary recruiters alike in order to comply with the Solomon Amendment, they could be viewed as sending the message that they see nothing wrong with the military's policies, when they do. We rejected a similar argument in *PruneYard Shopping Center v. Robins*. In that case, we upheld a state law requiring a shopping center owner to allow certain expressive activities by others on its property. We explained that there was little likelihood that the views of those engaging in the expressive activities would be identified with the owner, who remained free to disassociate himself from those views and who was "not . . . being compelled to affirm [a] belief in any governmentally prescribed position or view."

The same is true here. Nothing about recruiting suggests that law schools agree with any speech by recruiters, and nothing in the Solomon Amendment restricts what the law schools may say about the military's policies. We have held that high school students can appreciate the difference between speech a school sponsors and speech the school permits because legally required to do so, pursuant to an equal access policy. Surely students have not lost that ability by the time they get to law school.

3

Having rejected the view that the Solomon Amendment impermissibly regulates *speech*, we must still consider whether the expressive nature of the *conduct* regulated by the statute brings that conduct within the First Amendment's protection. In *O'Brien*, we recognized that some forms of "'symbolic speech'" were deserving of First Amendment protection. But we rejected the view that "conduct can be labeled 'speech' whenever the person engaging in the conduct intends thereby to express an idea." Instead, we have extended First Amendment protection only to conduct that is inherently expressive. In *Texas v. Johnson*, for example, we applied *O'Brien* and held that burning the American flag was sufficiently expressive to warrant First Amendment protection.

Unlike flag burning, the conduct regulated by the Solomon Amendment is not inherently expressive. Prior to the adoption of the Solomon Amendment's equal access requirement, law schools "expressed" their disagreement with the military by treating military recruiters differently from other recruiters. But these actions were expressive only because the law schools accompanied their conduct with speech explaining it. For example, the point of requiring military interviews to be conducted on the undergraduate campus is not "overwhelmingly apparent." An observer who sees military recruiters interviewing away from the law school has no way of knowing whether the law school is expressing its disapproval of the military, all the law school's interview rooms are full, or the military recruiters decided for reasons of their own that they would rather interview someplace else.

The expressive component of a law school's actions is not created by the conduct itself but by the speech that accompanies it. The fact that such explanatory speech is necessary is strong evidence that the conduct at issue here is not so inherently expressive that it warrants protection under *O'Brien*. If combining speech and conduct were enough to create expressive conduct, a regulated party could always transform conduct into "speech" simply by talking about it. For instance, if an individual announces that he intends to express his disapproval of the Internal Revenue Service by refusing to pay his income taxes, we would have to apply *O'Brien* to determine whether the Tax Code violates the First Amendment. Neither *O'Brien* nor its progeny supports such a result.

Although the Third Circuit also concluded that *O'Brien* does not apply, it held in the alternative that the Solomon Amendment does not pass muster under *O'Brien* because the Government failed to produce evidence establishing that the Solomon Amendment was necessary and effective. The Court of Appeals surmised that "the military has ample resources to recruit through alternative means," suggesting "loan repayment programs" and "television and radio advertisements." As a result, the Government—according to the Third Circuit—failed to establish that the statute's burden on speech is no greater than essential to furthering its interest in military recruiting.

We disagree with the Court of Appeals' reasoning and result. We have held that "an incidental burden on speech is no greater than is essential, and therefore is permissible under *O'Brien*, so long as the neutral regulation promotes a substantial government interest that would be achieved less effectively absent the regulation." The Solomon Amendment clearly satisfies this requirement. Military recruiting promotes the substantial Government interest in raising and supporting the Armed Forces—an objective that would be achieved less

effectively if the military were forced to recruit on less favorable terms than other employers. The Court of Appeals' proposed alternative methods of recruiting are beside the point. The issue is not whether other means of raising an army and providing for a navy might be adequate. That is a judgment for Congress, not the courts. It suffices that the means chosen by Congress add to the effectiveness of military recruitment. Accordingly, even if the Solomon Amendment were regarded as regulating expressive conduct, it would not violate the First Amendment under *O'Brien*.

B

The Solomon Amendment does not violate law schools' freedom of speech, but the First Amendment's protection extends beyond the right to speak. We have recognized a First Amendment right to associate for the purpose of speaking, which we have termed a "right of expressive association." The reason we have extended First Amendment protection in this way is clear: The right to speak is often exercised most effectively by combining one's voice with the voices of others. If the government were free to restrict individuals' ability to join together and speak, it could essentially silence views that the First Amendment is intended to protect.

FAIR argues that the Solomon Amendment violates law schools' freedom of expressive association. According to FAIR, law schools' ability to express their message that discrimination on the basis of sexual orientation is wrong is significantly affected by the presence of military recruiters on campus and the schools' obligation to assist them. Relying heavily on our decision in *Dale*, the Court of Appeals agreed.

In *Dale*, we held that the Boy Scouts' freedom of expressive association was violated by New Jersey's public accommodations law, which required the organization to accept a homosexual as a scoutmaster. After determining that the Boy Scouts was an expressive association, that "the forced inclusion of Dale would significantly affect its expression," and that the State's interests did not justify this intrusion, we concluded that the Boy Scouts' First Amendment rights were violated.

The Solomon Amendment, however, does not similarly affect a law school's associational rights. To comply with the statute, law schools must allow military recruiters on campus and assist them in whatever way the school chooses to assist other employers. Law schools therefore "associate" with military recruiters in the sense that they interact with them. But recruiters are not part of the law school. Recruiters are, by definition, outsiders who come onto campus for the limited purpose of trying to hire students—not to become members of the school's expressive association. This distinction is critical. Unlike the public accommodations law in *Dale*, the Solomon Amendment does not force a law school "to accept members it does not desire." The law schools *say* that allowing military recruiters equal access impairs their own expression by requiring them to associate with the recruiters, but just as saying conduct is undertaken for expressive purposes cannot make it symbolic speech, so too a speaker cannot "erect a shield" against laws requiring access "simply by asserting" that mere association "would impair its message."

FAIR correctly notes that the freedom of expressive association protects more than just a group's membership decisions. For example, we have held laws unconstitutional that require disclosure of membership lists for groups seeking anonymity or impose penalties or withhold benefits based on membership in a disfavored group. Although these laws did not directly interfere with an organization's composition, they made group membership less attractive, raising the same First Amendment concerns about affecting the group's ability to express its message.

The Solomon Amendment has no similar effect on a law school's associational rights. Students and faculty are free to associate to voice their disapproval of the military's message; nothing about the statute affects the composition of the group by making group membership less desirable. The Solomon Amendment therefore does not violate a law school's First Amendment rights. A military recruiter's mere presence on campus does not violate a law school's right to associate, regardless of how repugnant the law school considers the recruiter's message.

* * *

In this case, FAIR has attempted to stretch a number of First Amendment doctrines well beyond the sort of activities these doctrines protect. The law schools object to having to treat military recruiters like other recruiters, but that regulation of conduct does not violate the First Amendment. To the extent that the Solomon Amendment incidentally affects expression, the law schools' effort to cast themselves as just like the schoolchildren in *Barnette*, the parade organizers in *Hurley*, and the Boy Scouts in *Dale* plainly overstates the expressive nature of their activity and the impact of the Solomon Amendment on it, while exaggerating the reach of our First Amendment precedents.

Because Congress could require law schools to provide equal access to military recruiters without violating the schools' freedoms of speech or association, the Court of Appeals erred in holding that the Solomon Amendment likely violates the First Amendment. We therefore reverse the judgment of the Third Circuit and remand the case for further proceedings consistent with this opinion.

It is so ordered.

Justice ALITO took no part in the consideration or decision of this case.

S

SEXUAL HARASSMENT, PEER-TO-PEER

Sexual harassment is pervasive on college campuses, with reports indicating that instances of harassment are on the rise. Sexually harassing behaviors take the form of calling others disparaging names of a sexual nature, touching, grabbing, pinching, and visually subjecting another to genitalia. However, students report that the most common form of sexual harassment is being subjected to vulgar comments, sexual jokes, and ogling. Although both male and female students report being sexually harassed by their peers, females are the more common victims of the harassing behavior. Further, in a report published by the American Association of University Women, one-third of victims failed to report the harassing behavior. In light of the significant legal issues that emerge, this entry examines associated questions by examining representative cases of peer-to-peer sexual harassment on the campuses of American colleges and universities before examining enforcement strategies and guidelines aimed at eliminating such behavior.

Litigation

The U.S. Supreme Court, in a K–12 case that is cited in disputes involving higher education, ruled that colleges, universities, and their officials can be liable for peer-to-peer sexually harassing behavior. In *Davis v. Monroe County Board of Education*

(1999), the Court explained that institutional officials have a duty to protect students from harassing behavior of peers. More specifically, the Court found that educational institutions can be liable in damages only when their officials act with deliberate indifference to sexual harassment that is so severe, pervasive, and objectively offensive that it can be said to deprive the victims of access to the educational opportunities or benefits provided by the institution. The Court further required that institutional officials must have actual knowledge of such harassment, meaning that they have received reports. The Court added that institutions can be liable only if officials have substantial control over both the harasser and the context in which the known harassment takes place.

A further complication of peer-to-peer sexual harassment law is that student-to-student relationships in higher education settings are not as clear as they may be in elementary and secondary schools, given that college and university students are older and act more independently than children in elementary and secondary school. Further, student participation in campus activities in sororities, fraternities, or other similar higher education settings such as those involved in military training, where a supervisor–subordinate relationship often exists between peers, calls for closer scrutiny of claims of sexual harassment.

In *Morse v. Regents of the University of Colorado* (1998), for example, female students filed suit against their university, alleging that a higher-ranking cadet in their Reserve Officers Training Corps (ROTC) unit allegedly subjected them to sexual harassment. Without reaching the merits of whether the harasser was subject to liability, the Tenth Circuit ruled that because the ROTC program was a university-sanctioned program that was under the direct supervision of institutional officials, the complaint against it could proceed. The court allowed the complaint against the university to survive the university's motion to dismiss the litigation, because it was convinced that the women had alleged the elements necessary under Title IX, most notably, deliberate indifference by officials in the face of known complaints of peer-to-peer harassment.

Conversely, in a case from the Citadel, the state-funded military academy in South Carolina, the Fourth Circuit rejected a similar claim (*Mentavlos v. Anderson*, 2001). The court affirmed that upper-class cadets were not government actors subject to liability based on their having mistreated a female first-year student who ultimately withdrew from the university. Upper-class cadets had some authority to report and correct infractions of the rules by first-year students; however, the ultimate authority for discipline rested with active military officers, not upper-class cadets. Although the plaintiff in this case asserted that upper-class cadets were acting "under color of law" in their abuse of the first-year student, the court held that the actions of the upper-class cadets were not sanctioned by the academy. Because the upper-class cadets were not exercising the state's coercive powers, they could not be regarded as "state actors." The court upheld an earlier motion for summary judgment in favor of the upper-class cadets, essentially dismissing the woman's Title IX suit for sexual harassment. The U.S. Supreme Court refused to hear an appeal.

Enforcement

Title IX of the Education Amendments of 1972 prohibits discriminatory treatment of individuals in educational institutions on the basis of sex. Under Title IX, private and public institutions receiving federal funds are liable for the sexual harassment of students or employees. Title IX, the statute most commonly utilized in the creation of policies aimed at eliminating peer-to-peer (and other forms of) sexual harassment, is enforced by the Office of Civil Rights in the U.S. Department

of Education. Individuals can also file private complaints under Title IX. The department has noted that institutions could be liable for peer sexual harassment if hostile environments existed in their programs, officials knew or should have known that the harassment existed, and officials failed to take immediate, appropriate action to remedy situations.

Office of Civil Rights Guidelines on Sexual Harassment

The Office of Civil Rights (2001) provides guidance to educational institutions to help prevent acts of sexual harassment and to address incidents of harassment. These guidelines advise institutional officials to develop sexual harassment policies that include a definition of sexual harassment, an explanation of the penalties for engaging in harassing conduct, an outline of the grievance procedures, contact information for those who receive complaints, and an expressed commitment to keep complaints confidential. The guidelines also direct officials to be prompt in the investigation of complaints of sexual harassment and to avoid ignoring the plight of alleged victims. In applying these standards directly to situations of peer-to-peer harassment in higher education, this means that college and university officials should assist with the complaint process, develop guidelines for the identification of sexually harassing behavior, and teach all employees about how to identify harassing behavior and intervene on behalf of victims by having clear guidelines for reporting sexually harassing behavior.

Mark Littleton

See also Hostile Work Environment; Sexual Harassment, Quid Pro Quo; Sexual Harassment, Same-Sex; Sexual Orientation; Title IX and Sexual Harassment; U.S. Department of Education

Further Readings

Harris, A. M., & Grooms, K. B. (2000). New lesson plan for educational institutions: Expanded rules governing Title IX liability of the Education Amendments of 1972 for student and faculty sexual harassment. *American University Journal of Gender, Social Policy, and the Law, 8,* 575–621.

Hill, C., & Silva, E. (2005). *Drawing the line: Sexual harassment on campus.* Washington, DC: AAUW Educational Foundation. Retrieved June 3, 2009, from http://www.aauw.org/research/upload/DTLFinal.pdf

Office of Civil Rights, U.S. Department of Education. (2001). *Revised sexual harassment guidance: Harassment of students by school employees, other students, or third parties.* Retrieved June 3, 2009, from http://www.ed.gov/about/offices/list/ocr/docs/shguide.pdf

Sachs, A. J. (2002). *Mentavlos v. Anderson*—One step backward: The loss of a "totality of the circumstances" approach in the Fourth Circuit's state action analysis. *Maryland Law Review, 61,* 1120–1140.

Title VII of the Civil Rights Act of 1964, 42 U.S.C. § 2000e.

Legal Citations

Davis v. Monroe County Board of Education, 526 U.S. 629 (1999), *on remand,* 206 F.3d 1377 (11th Cir. 2000).

Mentavlos v. Anderson, 249 F.3d 301 (4th Cir. 2001), *cert. denied,* 534 U.S. 952 (2001).

Morse v. Regents of the University of Colorado, 154 F.3d 1124 (10th Cir. 1998).

Title IX of the Educational Amendments of 1972, 20 U.S.C. § 1681.

SEXUAL HARASSMENT, QUID PRO QUO

When sexual harassment involves the exchange of sexual favors for desired benefits, it is referred to as "quid pro quo" ("this for that") sexual harassment. Quid pro quo harassment implies a power relationship between harassers and their victims. Usually, quid pro quo harassment involves employees and supervisors, but it may be also consist of inappropriate relationships between students and faculty members in higher education. For example, student athletes who reject sexual advances by their coaches, lose their athletic scholarships, and are prevented from practicing with their teams may raise judicial claims of quid pro quo harassment.

Unlike hostile environment sexual harassment, quid pro quo harassment is more easily recognizable.

Additionally, a single incident of quid pro quo harassment can be a sufficient basis on which to establish a sexual harassment claim, because the victim need not submit to demands for sexual favors in order for the defendant to have violated the law. In light of statutory and case law on this important topic, this entry examines the legal status of issues surrounding quid pro quo sexual harassment in American institutions of higher learning.

Statutory Provisions and Enforcement

Under Title VII of the Civil Rights Act of 1964, private and public institutions with 15 or more employees may be liable for acts of supervisors and employees who sexually harass others. Title VII is enforced by the Equal Employment Opportunity Commission. Title IX of the Education Amendments of 1972, an educational statute, prohibits discrimination on the basis of sex in educational institutions that receive federal financial aid. In addition to being able to file private complaints, aggrieved parties can seek help from the Office of Civil Rights in the U.S. Department of Education in enforcing Title IX. Title VII addresses employer-to-employee sexual harassment, while Title IX covers employee-to-employee, employee-to-student, and student-to-student quid pro quo sexual harassment.

Background

The law of quid pro quo sexual harassment emerged in U.S. Supreme Court cases dealing with the workplace starting in the 1980s; none of these cases directly involved higher education. Although quid pro quo claims are less numerous than those for hostile work environment sexual harassment, a body of case law is evolving, the vast majority of which is resolved in favor of colleges and universities. Moreover, although the two forms of harassment involve slightly different issues, they generally require plaintiffs to establish the same elements in seeking to hold individuals and/or institutions liable.

In order for plaintiffs to prevail on claims of quid pro quo sexual harassment, they must be able to establish five points. First, insofar as plaintiffs must belong to a protected category and most, although certainly not all, such claims have been filed by women, this element is satisfied on its face when women file claims (because they are part of the class that the law is designed to protect). Second, plaintiffs must have been subjected to unwelcomed sexual harassment. Third, the offending behavior must have been considered harassment because it was disproportionately offensive or demeaning to one sex, such as, for example, when humor is not directed at any one individual or group of persons but at individuals of one sex. Fourth, the harassment must affect a term, condition, or privilege of employment to such a degree that it alters working conditions to the point that it seriously affects the psychological well-being of plaintiffs. Fifth, employers, through their officials, must have known or should have known of the harassment but have failed to take prompt remedial action.

Unlike hostile environment sexual harassment, in quid pro quo sexual harassment, when supervisory employees have primary or absolute authority to hire, promote, or dismiss employees and use their power to secure sexual favors, the courts are likely to render them liable. If the harassment results in tangible employment actions, consistent with Supreme Court precedent, employers can also be liable. Both *Burlington Industries v. Ellerth* (1998) and *Faragher v. City of Boca Raton* (1998) provide examples of tangible employment actions causing significant changes in benefits and work assignments, because the women in both cases quit their jobs, as a salesperson and lifeguard, respectively, in response to sexual harassment at the hands of a supervisor in the former and coworkers in the latter. The Court imposed Title VII liability on the employers in both cases, because officials were aware of the complaints that the women filed but refused to intervene in their behalf.

On the other hand, in instances where supervisory employees have limited authority to hire, promote, or dismiss victims, then the courts may not render employers or institutions liable. If the harassment does not result in tangible employment actions, then institutions may be able to avoid liability by demonstrating both that their officials exercised reasonable care to prevent and promptly correct any harassing behaviors and that employees unreasonably failed to take advantage of any preventive or corrective opportunities that were available or to avoid harm otherwise. The prudent course for college and university officials who wish to avoid institutional liability for harassment under Title VII is to promulgate antiharassment policies and accompanying complaint procedures and to ensure that all employees are aware of these documents.

Litigation

As illustrated in the majority of cases under Title IX, because officials must have actual notice and respond with deliberate indifference, it is relatively easy for them to avoid liability under this statute. In contrast, although Title VII imposes a standard of strict liability, institutions can avoid liability if officials can demonstrate that they have taken sufficient steps to respond to complaints of quid pro quo sexual harassment. For example, in *Holly D. v. California Institute of Technology* (2003), the Ninth Circuit refused to impose Title VII liability on a university in a situation where an employee who engaged in a consensual sexual relationship with the faculty member who supervised her work activities later filed claims including one for quid pro quo sexual harassment. As a result of the incident, the faculty member resigned from his position. The court ruled that university officials were not liable, because they exercised reasonable care to prevent and correct sexual harassment, and the employee unreasonably failed to take advantage of any preventive or corrective opportunities that they had provided. More specifically, the court pointed out that officials conducted periodic training on sexual harassment, which they publicized to staff members via e-mail; that the employee admitted that she knew the training was offered and that her supervisor's conduct constituted sexual harassment; that when officials learned of the allegations of harassment, they convened an investigatory committee that interviewed witnesses and recommended she be transferred away from the supervisor; and that the committee ordered that the supervisor be "reminded" of the operative harassment policy.

Institutional Responses

As reflected in *Holly D.*, preparation and prevention are the best tools to eliminate claims of sexual harassment. Still, college and university officials can take steps to reduce or prevent the occurrence of sexually harassing behavior by establishing sexual harassment policies. Employees should be educated to understand the intent as well as the content of the policies. Appropriately devised policies should include a commitment to eradicate and prevent sexual harassment, definitions of quid pro quo (and other forms of) sexual harassment, explanations of penalties for sexually harassing conduct, outlines of grievance procedures, contact persons for consultation, and expressed commitments to keep all complaints and personnel actions confidential.

Additionally, once institutional officials are made aware of sexually harassing behavior, it is incumbent on them to act and not to be deliberately indifferent to the plight of victims. Officials are deliberately indifferent if they possess the authority to address harassing behavior, have actual knowledge of the wrongdoing, and consciously disregard the behavior. Adequate preparation is crucial to identifying signs of sexual harassment. To this end, preparation should occur on sexual harassment complaint procedures, including time frames and information on how to file formal complaints, who complaints are filed with, and how officials should respond to formal complaints.

Mark Littleton

See also Sexual Harassment, Peer-to-Peer; Sexual Harassment of Students by Faculty Members; Sexual Orientation; Title VII; Title IX and Sexual Harassment; U.S. Department of Education

Further Readings

Hill, C., & Silva, E. (2005). *Drawing the line: Sexual harassment on campus.* Washington, DC: AAUW Educational Foundation. Retrieved June 3, 2009, from http://www.aauw.org/research/upload/DTLFinal.pdf

Lewis, J. E., & Hastings, S. C. (1994). *Sexual harassment in education* (2nd ed.). Topeka, KS: National Organization on Legal Problems in Education (now Education Law Association).

Office of Civil Rights, U.S. Department of Education. (2001). *Revised sexual harassment guidance: Harassment of students by school employees, other students, or third parties.* Retrieved June 3, 2009, from http://www.ed.gov/about/offices/list/ocr/docs/ shguide.pdf

Legal Citations

Burlington Industries v. Ellerth, 524 U.S. 742 (1998), *on remand,* 165 F.3d 31 (7th Cir. 1998).

Faragher v. City of Boca Raton, 524 U.S. 775 (1998), *on remand,* 166 F.3d 1152 (11th Cir. 1999).

Holly D. v. California Institute of Technology, 339 F.3d 1158 (2003).

Title VII of the Civil Rights Act of 1964, 42 U.S.C. § 2000e.

Title IX of the Educational Amendments of 1972, 20 U.S.C. § 1681.

Sexual Harassment, Same-Sex

Sexual harassment is unwanted conduct of a sexual nature that is prohibited both by Title VII of the Civil Rights Act of 1964 and Title IX of the Educational Amendments of 1972. While Title VII applies to sexual harassment complaints involving employees, Title IX protects students from inappropriate behavior. The original purpose of sexual harassment legislation was to prohibit employers from hiring and promoting employees on the basis of their gender and from making sexual favors a condition of employment. Early sexual harassment litigation focused on male and female interaction in work and educational settings.

Unfortunately, there are numerous incidents of harassing behavior of students, faculty members, and staff at colleges and universities based on their sexual orientations. Lesbian, gay, bisexual, and transgendered students are more likely to be harassed than their heterosexual counterparts. This harassment comes primarily from their peers; however, incidents of reported *sexual* harassment by same-sex students are rare. The relatively small number of reported incidents may be a result of the fact that threats of violence often do not materialize after peers threaten or harass student victims.

As reflected by the litigation discussed below, same-sex sexual harassment is less common among college or university employees than among employees in other areas. A U.S. Supreme Court ruling specifically on same-sex harassment, together with various decisions from lower courts, has established that Title VII's prohibition of sexual harassment includes cases where the perpetrator and victim are of the same sex. This entry reviews these cases and also examines issues relating to enforcement and institutional liability for sexual harassment.

Litigation

Oncale v. Sundowner Offshore Services (1998) is the only Supreme Court case on same-sex sexual harassment. *Oncale* involved a male roustabout on an eight-man platform crew in Louisiana who alleged that he was forcibly subjected to humiliating sex-related actions by some of his male coworkers in the presence of the rest of the crew and that he was physically assaulted and threatened with rape by another worker. The Court ruled that the claim of same-sex sexual harassment was properly filed pursuant to Title VII, thus establishing that the prohibition of sexual harassment applies to same-sex incidents. In its analysis, the Court added that because the motivation for the harassing behavior need not be sexual desire, cases could proceed to trial as long as harassers had engaged in behavior that was so severe or pervasive that it created an abusive working environment.

To date, the vast majority of litigation addressing same-sex sexual harassment has occurred in settings outside of higher education. Even so, there has been litigation involving colleges and universities that is worth noting. In *Snider v. Jefferson State Community College* (2003), the Eleventh Circuit affirmed the dismissal of claims filed by male security officers who sued the president and a dean at their community college for same-sex sexual harassment by their supervisor. The court maintained that the defendants were entitled to rely on Eleventh Amendment sovereign immunity to shield them from the plaintiffs' Title VII claim, because it was not clear at the time that the alleged incidents occurred that the harassment violated the rights of the security officers.

Other courts have allowed same-sex sexual harassment complaints from both men and women to proceed. In *Mota v. University of Texas Houston Health Science Center* (2001), the Fifth Circuit affirmed that even though a faculty member did not suffer a tangible employment action such as the loss of his job, he could recover damages. The court agreed with a jury that the plaintiff had been subjected to retaliation in the form of being denied the opportunity to take paid leave from work after he filed a complaint alleging that he had been harassed by a supervisor of the same sex. The court concluded that the plaintiff presented a valid claim that he was subjected to same-sex sexual

harassment, and it therefore upheld a damages award in favor of the plaintiff.

In *Nogueras v. University of Puerto Rico* (1995), a case that predates *Oncale*, a federal trial court allowed a librarian's claim to proceed in the face of motions to dismiss that were filed by her supervisor and a female library consultant. The court held that the librarian had presented evidence that despite her asking a female supervisor and female library consultant to stop sexually harassing her by touching her, making sexually suggestive remarks about her clothing and appearance, inviting her to engage in sexual activity, and commenting that men were "not necessary for enjoyment," the harassment continued; therefore, the librarian presented a valid claim under Title VII.

At issue in *Miles v. New York University* (1997) was whether a student who was a transsexual could sue a faculty member for sexual harassment. In clarifying that Title IX prohibited both same-sex and opposite-sex sexual harassment, a federal trial court in New York rejected a faculty member's motion for summary judgment, insofar as the student presented sufficient evidence to allow the claim to proceed. The student complained that the faculty member touched her on the breasts, buttocks, and crotch while also attempting to kiss her as he made sexual propositions. The faculty member had thought that the student was a female, but the student was actually a female transsexual who was in the process of becoming female. The court refused to grant the motion for summary judgment in pointing out that although university officials put a copy of the student's letter of complaint in the faculty member's file, they did not investigate the matter any further, even though four other students had complained. In addition, the court recognized that because the student was treated in a hostile manner by other faculty members, she withdrew from the program prematurely and did not complete her studies.

Enforcement

According to Title VII, public and private educational institutions with 15 or more employees can be liable for sexual harassment by their employees. Title VII is enforced by the Equal Employment Opportunity Commission. At the same time, Title IX covers employee-to-employee, employee-to-student, and student-to-student harassment.

Pursuant to Title IX, institutions receiving federal funds can be liable for sexual harassment of students and employees. The Office of Civil Rights in the U.S. Department of Education enforces Title IX claims; individuals are also able to file private complaints with the courts or with the Office of Civil Rights.

Avoiding Liability

Primary to preventing sexual harassment on college and university campuses is the development of a clear, no-nonsense policy. Secondary to the policy development is making sure that faculty members, staff, and students know what sexually harassing behaviors are and how to adequately respond to those behaviors. Often college and university officials raise awareness through the use of brochures, seminars, e-mails, and Web-based promotions.

Along with preventative measures, college and university officials should establish formal complaint procedures to address instances of bullying and harassing behaviors. Insofar as sexually motivated harassment is frequently unreported, employees and others should be trained in how to identify and report harassing behavior.

Mark Littleton

See also Sexual Harassment, Peer-to-Peer; Sexual Harassment, Quid Pro Quo; Sexual Harassment of Students by Faculty Members; Sexual Orientation; Title VII; Title IX and Sexual Harassment; U.S. Department of Education

Further Readings

Connell, M. A., & Euben, D. (2004). Evolving law in same-sex sexual harassment and sexual orientation. *Journal of College & University Law, 31,* 193–238.

Hill, C., & Silva, E. (2005). *Drawing the line: Sexual harassment on campus.* Washington, DC: AAUW Educational Foundation. Retrieved May 28, 2009, from http://www.aauw.org/research/upload/DTLFinal.pdf

Office of Civil Rights, U.S. Department of Education. (2001). *Revised sexual harassment guidance: Harassment of students by school employees, other students, or third parties.* Retrieved May 28, 2009, from http://www.ed.gov/about/offices/list/ocr/docs/shguide.pdf

Legal Citations

Miles v. New York University, 979 F. Supp. 248 (S.D.N.Y. 1997).

Mota v. University of Texas Houston Health Science Center, 261 F.3d 512 (5th Cir. 2001).

Nogueras v. University of Puerto Rico, 890 F. Supp. 60 (D. Puerto Rico 1995).

Oncale v. Sundowner Offshore Services, 523 U.S. 75 (1998).

Snider v. Jefferson State Community College, 344 F.3d 1325 (11th Cir. 2003), *rehearing and rehearing en banc denied,* 90 Fed. App'x. 391 (11th Cir. 2003).

Title VII of the Civil Rights Act of 1964, 42 U.S.C. § 2000e.

Title IX of the Educational Amendments of 1972, 20 U.S.C. § 1681.

SEXUAL HARASSMENT OF STUDENTS BY FACULTY MEMBERS

Although not as common as peer-to-peer sexual harassment on campuses, sexual harassment of students by faculty does occur. According to a monograph published by the American Association of University Women, approximately 7% of students reported being sexually harassed by a professor. Clearly, students find faculty sexual harassment extremely objectionable. Incidents of sexual harassment by faculty are more likely to be reported to the appropriate authorities than are incidents of peer-to-peer sexual harassment.

There is no stereotypical perpetrator of sexual misconduct. In higher education, the sexual exploitation of students by faculty members is exacerbated by the close working relationships that often develop as a result of shared interests, particularly between graduate students and faculty. Students often seek to please faculty members who have the opportunity to advance their educational and career opportunities. In turn, faculty members enjoy the attention and admiration of the students, and often, unwittingly, breach appropriate professional relationships.

Officials in higher education are warned not to take students' claims of sexual harassment lightly. Inappropriate jokes, e-mails, and sexually oriented comments can place students in uncomfortable, and often hostile, situations. In addition, officials should not allow inappropriate language and illegal behavior to be justified by faculty First Amendment claims of academic freedom. In light of statutory and case law on this important topic, this entry examines the legal status of issues surrounding sexual harassment of students by faculty members in American colleges and universities.

Litigation

To date, no case of sexual harassment of students by faculty members in colleges and universities has made its way to the U.S. Supreme Court. The judiciary does look to the Court's judgment in *Gebser v. Lago Vista Independent School District* (1998) for guidance in setting the standard for liability of educational institutions and their officials. *Gebser* involved a teacher at a Texas high school who engaged in sexual relations with one of his students. In *Gebser,* the Court held that educational institutions that are the recipients of federal financial assistance are liable for damages based on sexual harassment of students by faculty members only if officials with the authority to correct the harassment had actual notice of, and were deliberately indifferent to, the actions of harassers. In other words, institutions are not likely to be liable unless officials had actual knowledge of incidents of misconduct but chose not to respond. The following cases are representative of the growing body of case law dealing with sexual harassment of college and university students by faculty members.

In *Hayut v. State University of New York* (2003), a student filed suit against a faculty member who continually addressed her as "Monica," a reference to the well-known sexual scandal involving President Bill Clinton and Monica Lewinsky. In affirming the rejection of an earlier motion for summary judgment entered by the faculty member and university, the Second Circuit permitted the case to proceed on the basis that a reasonable person could have concluded that his calling the student such a name created a hostile environment.

Along the same line, a long-running case involving a coach rather than a faculty member was litigated in a dispute from North Carolina. The Fourth Circuit held that the coach's inquiries into the sex lives of the members of the women's soccer team, if proven to be sufficiently "severe or pervasive," would have created a hostile environment in

violation of Title IX. Consequently, the court affirmed a lower court's decision that the plaintiff's claim could proceed (*Jennings v. University of North Carolina,* 2007).

A case from New York, *Miles v. New York University* (1997), concerned whether a student who was a transsexual could sue a faculty member for sexual harassment. In clarifying that Title IX prohibited both same-sex and opposite-sex sexual harassment, a federal trial court rejected a faculty member's motion for summary judgment. The court reached this outcome because it was satisfied that the student presented sufficient evidence to allow the claim to proceed. The student complained that the faculty member improperly touched her on the breasts, buttocks, and crotch while also attempting to kiss her as he made sexual propositions. The faculty member had thought that the student was a female, but the student was actually a transsexual who was in the process of becoming female. The court observed that although university officials put a copy of the student's letter of complaint in the faculty member's file, they did not investigate the matter any further, even though four other students had complained. The court also indicated that the student withdrew from the university prematurely because of hostile treatment by other faculty members.

On the other hand, when institutional officials respond to complaints by students and demonstrate that they did not act with deliberate indifference to allegations of sexual harassment, then courts are unresponsive to allegations by students. For example, in *Abramova v. Albert Einstein College of Medicine of Yeshiva University* (2008), the Second Circuit affirmed that because officials responded adequately to a student's complaint of sexual harassment by a faculty member, the trial court properly entered the defendant's motion for summary judgment, essentially dismissing her complaint.

A year earlier, the Eighth Circuit reached the same result in upholding a grant of immunity in favor of a university's president and chancellor, because they were not deliberately indifferent to offensive conduct by a faculty member who undressed a student who then refused to engage in sexual relations with him in his home (*Cox v. Sugg,* 2007). The court noted that the student failed to report the faculty member's misconduct until she met with a grievance officer and that university officials forced the faculty member to resign within a week after the student filed her report. Further, the court determined that the student had not shown that the president and chancellor had actual knowledge of the misconduct before the student reported it, that they responded inadequately to the misconduct when they learned of it, or that they had exhibited deliberate indifference to the problem of sexual harassment at the university. In addition, the Tenth Circuit affirmed that various university officials were not liable for sexual harassment by a faculty member because they were not deliberately indifferent to a student's complaints (*Escue v. Northern Oklahoma College,* 2006).

Two additional cases reflect the judicial attitude toward sexual harassment by faculty members. Although it was not the primary issue in the litigation, the Seventh Circuit affirmed a grant of summary judgment in favor of a university when a faculty member filed suit after his contract was not renewed. Among a number of grounds given by the university for not renewing the contract were complaints by students that the faculty member had sexually harassed them (*Keri v. Board of Trustees of Purdue University,* 2006). Further, a state appellate court in Minnesota affirmed a grant of summary judgment in favor of institutional officials who refused to rehire an instructor who had sexually harassed students (*Phillips v. State,* 2007).

Enforcement

Two federal statutes address incidents of sexual harassment. The first, Title VII of the Civil Rights Act of 1964, an employment statute, prohibits discrimination on the basis of race, color, national origin, religion, and sex. Under Title VII, private and public institutions with 15 or more employees are liable for acts of supervisors and employees who sexually harass. Title VII is enforced by the Equal Employment Opportunity Commission.

Title IX of the Education Amendments of 1972, which prohibits discrimination on the basis of sex in educational institutions that receive federal financial assistance, is the most commonly used statute to enforce laws forbidding sexual harassment of students by faculty. Under Title IX, private and public institutions receiving federal funds are liable for the sexual harassment of students or employees. The Office of Civil Rights (OCR) in the Department of Education enforces Title IX; in addition, individuals can file private complaints with the OCR or with the courts.

Identifying Sexual Misconduct

Identifying sexual misconduct by faculty members who seek to take advantage of students is not an easy task. Still, there are some indicators that inappropriate behavior may be occurring. One indicator is overly affectionate behavior such as hugging or touching. Related indicating behavior includes telling jokes of a sexual nature and using suggestive terms in conversation. Telephone, Internet, and social networking communication and conversations of an intimate nature between the faculty member and student are additional indicators of inappropriate relationships.

Finally, complaints of and innuendos referring to inappropriate relationships between faculty members and students can be indicative of sexual misconduct. These "rumors" should be taken seriously and properly investigated. Although consensual sexual activity may occur in some instances when a faculty member and a student are both of the age of consent, most colleges and universities have policies that prohibit inappropriate sexual conduct between faculty members and students.

Preventing Sexual Harassment

In order to combat faculty sexual harassment of students, college and university officials should establish clear written policies that delineate and prohibit inappropriate relationships. Additionally, officials in higher education should train employees in how to avoid inappropriate relationships.

Formal anti–sexual harassment policies should identify individuals to serve as investigators of allegations and rumors. Although an atmosphere of faculty guilt is implicit in many of the investigations, experts caution policy makers to avoid establishing a climate of suspicion. In such a climate, innocent employees may believe that false accusations and vendettas against demanding faculty members would become commonplace, even though studies indicate that such accusations are rare.

Mark Littleton

See also Sexual Harassment, Quid Pro Quo; Sexual Harassment, Same-Sex; Title VII; Title IX and Sexual Harassment; U.S. Department of Education

Further Readings

Hill, C., & Silva, E. (2005). *Drawing the line: Sexual harassment on campus.* Washington, DC: AAUW Educational Foundation. Retrieved June 3, 2009, from http://www.aauw.org/research/upload/DTLFinal.pdf

Office of Civil Rights, U.S. Department of Education. (2001). *Revised sexual harassment guidance: Harassment of students by school employees, other students, or third parties.* Retrieved June 3, 2009, from http://www.ed.gov/about/offices/list/ocr/docs/shguide.pdf

Shoop, R. J. (2004). *Sexual exploitation in schools: How to spot it and stop it.* Thousand Oaks, CA: Corwin.

Legal Citations

Abramova v. Albert Einstein College of Medicine of Yeshiva University, 278 Fed. App'x. 30 (2d Cir. 2008).

Cox v. Sugg, 484 F.3d 1062 (8th Cir. 2007).

Escue v. Northern Oklahoma College, 450 F.3d 1146 (10th Cir. 2006).

Gebser v. Lago Vista Independent School District, 524 U.S. 274 (1998).

Hayut v. State University of New York, 352 F.3d 733 (2d Cir. 2003).

Jennings v. University of North Carolina, 482 F.3d 686 (2007), *cert. denied,* 128 S. Ct. 247 (2007).

Keri v. Board of Trustees of Purdue University, 458 F.3d 620 (7th Cir. 2006), *cert. denied,* 549 U.S. 1210 (2007).

Miles v. New York University, 979 F. Supp. 248 (S.D.N.Y. 1997).

Phillips v. State, 725 N.W.2d 778 (Minn. Ct. App. 2007), *review denied.*

Title VII of the Civil Rights Act of 1964, 42 U.S.C. § 2000e.

Title IX of the Educational Amendments of 1972, 20 U.S.C. § 1681.

Sexual Orientation

Legal issues related to sexual orientation have affected institutions of higher education in their roles as employers, educators, and scholarly communities. As employers, college and university officials have responded to calls by lesbians, gays, bisexuals, and transgendered persons (LGBTs) for equal treatment in the workplace. Insofar as they are often in the vanguard of political debate and social change, campus officials generally have been leaders in promoting equal treatment and dignity for LGBTs. According to the Human Rights Campaign, an advocacy group for LGBTs, more than 500 institutions of higher education in the United States include sexual orientation in their nondiscrimination policies. Approximately 100 also address gender identity, which is intended to prevent discrimination against individuals who are transgendered. Besides prohibiting discrimination in employment, such policies also typically aim to protect students from discrimination or harassment that would impair their ability to pursue an education. This entry examines legal issues associated with LGBT students on campus.

Employee Benefits for Same-Sex Couples

Same-sex couples are prohibited from marrying in most states. Even so, it has become increasingly common for employers to offer health insurance and other benefits to the same-sex domestic partners of employees on the same terms as those benefits are offered to spouses. In fact, colleges and universities were among the first sectors to widely adopt domestic partner benefits; university faculty and staff members were plaintiffs in key court cases seeking such benefits in Alaska (*University of Alaska v. Tumeo,* 1997), New Jersey (*Rutgers Council of AAUP Chapters v. Rutgers,* 1997), and Oregon (*Tanner v. Oregon Health Sciences University,* 1998).

Institutions of higher education adopting domestic partner benefits usually have explained that such benefits are necessary both to advance economic justice and to remain competitive with peer institutions in attracting and retaining the best faculty and staff. Such benefits are offered at more than 300 campuses, according to the Human Rights Campaign, and typically include not only subsidized health insurance but also such perquisites as tuition discounts and access to campus libraries and recreational facilities.

Early court challenges to such benefits, based, for example, on the theory that such programs at public universities infringed on legislative prerogatives to define marriage, were generally unsuccessful. However, in *National Pride at Work v. Governor of Michigan* (2008), the state supreme court ruled that a voter-approved amendment to the state's constitution prohibiting recognition of same-sex marriages was worded broadly enough to bar public employers in the state, including universities, from offering benefits to same-sex domestic partners.

Discrimination, Harassment, and Viewpoint Neutrality

Officials at many colleges and universities have sought to prevent legal complaints over discrimination and harassment against LGBT students, as well as to improve campus climate and encourage dialogue on issues surrounding sexual orientation, through their student-services programs. To this end, more than 150 campuses maintain professionally staffed offices dedicated to providing support for LGBT students. Moreover, programs and courses devoted to the promotion of diversity typically include units devoted to sexual orientation and gender identity. In addition to addressing these issues as personal matters, such courses often include discussion of legal and political controversies surrounding LGBT rights.

In addition to promoting awareness of sexual orientation as a means of improving campus climate, higher education institutions may have legal obligations to address antigay harassment, at least when it rises to the level of physical violence. In *Love v. Morehouse College* (2007), an appellate court in Georgia refused to dismiss a personal injury suit filed by a plaintiff who was brutally assaulted by a fellow student. The plaintiff blamed the assault on what he described as a pervasive atmosphere of intolerance toward gays that the college failed to address. In letting the suit proceed under the plaintiff's tort theory, the court was of the opinion that the evidence could show that college officials knew about problems of harassment and that it was reasonably foreseeable that such harassment could escalate into the kind of violence that transpired.

Institutional desires to prevent harassment and promote debate over sexual orientation have provoked legal challenges from conservative or religious students who claim that such policies infringe on their own rights. For instance, in *Board of Regents of the University of Wisconsin System v. Southworth* (2000), a group of students challenged a public university's student activity fee that funded, among other things, an LGBT student center and an AIDS support network. University officials posited that the fee was intended to enhance the educational experiences of all students by promoting debate on diverse points of view and encouraging student participation in political activities. The plaintiffs responded that being forced to offer financial support for political and ideological activities with which they disagreed violated their First Amendment rights.

The U.S. Supreme Court decided that the activity fee was constitutional as long as the university allocated proceeds on a viewpoint-neutral basis. According to the Court, university officials may evaluate whether their institutional mission is well served if students have the means to engage in dynamic discussions of philosophical, religious, scientific, social, and political subjects in their extracurricular campus life outside the lecture hall. The Court added that if university officials reach this conclusion, then they are entitled to impose mandatory fees to sustain open dialogue to these ends.

To date, federal courts remain split on the related issue of whether colleges and university officials, pursuant to their nondiscrimination policies, may require officially recognized student groups that oppose homosexuality to nonetheless admit homosexual members. The legal controversy in these cases centers on whether such policies are viewpoint-neutral, because they simply ensure equality in membership opportunities for all students—even those who disagree with the mission of the group, or whether the policies actually reflect a certain viewpoint on homosexuality and thus would force the affected student groups to abandon their sincerely held religious beliefs. Seeking to settle or avoid litigation, officials at some public universities have exempted religious student groups from their institutional policies against sexual orientation discrimination.

When campus officials have sought to punish student speech that is perceived as demeaning toward homosexuals or other groups, they have sometimes found themselves sued for adopting "speech codes." The constitutionality of such policies appears to turn on whether they are applied to punish actual harassment or incitement to violence, as opposed to mere hurtful words or controversial opinions.

Intercollegiate Athletics

Another facet of student life where issues of sexual orientation have received increasing legal attention is intercollegiate athletics. According to legal scholar Barbara Osborne, writing in the *Marquette Sports Law Review*, both male and female "homosexual athletes suffer fear, humiliation, isolation, and sometimes physical violence" (p. 485), and they frequently have been denied access to participation in college-level athletics programs. Gay or lesbian coaches also have been fired or denied employment because of their sexual orientation. Consequently, litigation has been filed by female athletes claiming that their coaches made derogatory comments about lesbians or pressured lesbians to quit their teams (*Yost v. Board of Regents, University of Maryland*, 1993).

Although federal statutory law does not prohibit discrimination on the basis of sexual orientation, recent interpretations of Title IX of the Education Amendments of 1972, which prohibits gender discrimination in education, have suggested that such discrimination against male or female students due to their perceived sexual orientations may be actionable as a form of prohibited sexual harassment if it effectively denies students the opportunity to participate in institutional programs. Consequently, federal courts have applied Title IX to address harassment or violence against students who were perceived to be gay based on gender stereotyping (*Ray v. Antioch Unified School District*, 2000).

Military Recruitment

While colleges and universities enjoy considerable latitude to promote equality and awareness about sexual orientation within their own campuses, some institutions suffered a setback in an effort to oppose the military's "don't ask, don't tell" policy concerning gay service members. In *Rumsfeld v. Forum for Academic and Institutional Rights* (2006), a group representing law schools and law faculty members challenged the Solomon Amendment, a federal law that requires educational institutions that receive federal funding to provide military recruiters with access to their campuses equal to the access provided to recruiters from other types of employers. Citing their institutions' nondiscrimination policies, the law schools and faculty argued that forced inclusion and equal treatment of military recruiters violated their First Amendment freedoms of speech and association.

The Supreme Court rejected this argument and upheld the Solomon Amendment, reasoning that recruiting services on campus at the law schools lack the expressive qualities of activities such as parades, newsletters, or the editorial pages of newspapers. In addition, the Court refused to interpret the accommodation of the messages of military recruiters as compelled speech, because any accommodations that officials made did not sufficiently interfere with any school messages. The Court went on to observe that law schools associate with military recruiters in the sense that they share some interaction, but the recruiters are not part of the schools. The Court then acknowledged that recruiters are, by definition, outsiders who come onto campus for the limited purpose of trying to hire students and that they are not present in the hope of becoming members of the schools' expressive associations.

In the wake of the Supreme Court's upholding the Solomon Amendment, a federal court of appeals also rejected a similar claim by a group of Yale University faculty members that the Solomon Amendment impaired their academic freedom to advance normative values of equality and acceptance (*Burt v. Gates*, 2007). The court explained that seeking to bar military recruiters from campus was too attenuated from what courts have perceived as the primary purpose of First Amendment academic freedom: to ensure the free flow of ideas.

Faculty Advocates

Aside from campus policies, faculty members have increasingly contributed their expertise to assist litigants in high-profile cases involving the rights of gays and lesbians. In one notable example, a group of Iowa-based law and history professors submitted an amicus curiae, "friend of the court," brief to the Supreme Court of Iowa in a case involving same-sex marriage. In its unanimous 2009 ruling in favor of marriage equality, the court cited material, brought to its attention by the professors, that illustrated the state judiciary's history of bold decisions concerning civil rights and civil liberties.

Steve Sanders

See also Academic Freedom; *Board of Regents of the University of Wisconsin System v. Southworth*; Free Speech and Expression Rights of Students; Political Activities and Speech of Faculty Members; *Rumsfeld v. Forum for Academic and Institutional Rights*; Sexual Harassment, Same-Sex; Title IX and Sexual Harassment

Further Readings

Human Rights Campaign: http://www.hrc.org/issues/workplace/equal_opportunity.asp

Lester, T. (2008). Talking about sexual orientation, teaching about homophobia: Negotiating the divide between religious belief and tolerance for LGBT rights in the classroom. *Duke Journal of Gender Law and Policy, 15,* 399–417.

Osborne, B. (2007). No drinking, no drugs, no lesbians: Sexual orientation discrimination in intercollegiate athletics. *Marquette Sports Law Review, 17,* 481–501.

Nabozny v. Podlesny, 92 F.3d 446 (7th Cir. 1996).

Varnum v. Brien, 763 N.W.2d 822 (Iowa 2009).

Legal Citations

Board of Regents of the University of Wisconsin System v. Southworth, 529 U.S. 217 (2000).

Burt v. Gates, 502 F.3d 183 (2d Cir. 2007).

Love v. Morehouse College, 652 S.E.2d 624 (Ga. Ct. App. 2007).

National Pride at Work v. Governor of Michigan, 748 N.W.2d 524 (Mich. 2008).

Ray v. Antioch Unified School District, 107 F. Supp. 2d 1165 (N.D. Cal. 2000).

Rumsfeld v. Forum for Academic and Institutional Rights, 547 U.S. 47 (2006).

Rutgers Council of AAUP Chapters v. Rutgers, 689 A.2d 828 (N.J. Super. App. Div. 1997).

Solomon Amendment, 10 U.S.C. § 983 (1996).

Tanner v. Oregon Health Sciences University, 971 P.2d 435 (Ore. Ct. App. 1998).

Title IX of the Education Amendments of 1972, 20 U.S.C. § 1681.

University of Alaska v. Tumeo, 933 P.2d 1147 (Alaska 1997).

Yost v. Board of Regents, University of Maryland, 1993 WL 524757 (D. Md. 1993).

Single-Sex Colleges

The history of institutions of higher education includes the evolution of single-sex colleges and universities. In colonial America, private colleges often blurred the lines between church and state, creating variety in the types of colleges and universities that existed at that time. The institutions that existed during the colonial era, and which evolved into today's modern colleges and universities, had relationships with the state and were often publicly supported even though they had church affiliations. In light of legal issues surrounding their status, this entry examines contemporary legal questions involving single-sex institutions of higher learning.

History

The first generations of educated women in the United States were, with few exceptions, products of single-sex secondary and undergraduate colleges. The first all-female academies, founded in the early 1800s, reflected a commitment to traditional gender roles that reserved the public sphere for men. These schools later became an essential part of the 19th-century women's movement, which incorporated ideas such as preparing women for work outside the home. At that time, sexual segregation was considered the norm.

At the beginning of the 20th century, a significant number of colleges and universities were single-sex institutions. For example, in 1910, out of the nation's 1,083 colleges, 27% were exclusively for men, 15% were exclusively for women, and the remaining 58% were coeducational colleges. In the 1960s, the number of single-sex colleges in the United States began a precipitous decline that has continued into the current century. In the 1970s, a number of men's colleges began accepting women. In 1970, there were 230 women's colleges and 174 men's colleges; as of 2000, only 63 women's colleges remained. Between 1970 and 1980, 108 women's colleges and 101 men's colleges became coeducational, while another 46 women's colleges and 27 men's colleges closed. As of 1987, only 2% of full-time female students were enrolled in women-only colleges.

Single-Sex Colleges Today

At present, about 50 women's colleges, all of which were established in the mid-19th century, still exist, although all but a handful of this total now include male students in their full-time populations on campus (National Center for Education Statistics, 2007). The remaining colleges that were founded for women include the famed Seven Sisters in New York, Pennsylvania, and Massachusetts: Barnard College (NY), Bryn Mawr College (PA), Mount Holyoke College (MA), Radcliffe College (MA), Smith College (MA), Vassar College (NY), and Wellesley College (MA). There are also two women's colleges among historically black colleges and universities: Spelman College in Atlanta, Georgia, and Bennett College for Women, in Greensboro, North Carolina.

Today, in the United States, women outnumber men among college graduates. Yet, only a little over 1% of all women who are awarded bachelor of arts degrees graduate from single-sex colleges. However, applications and numbers of students who choose to enroll in colleges for women have increased. In fact, the data indicate about 3% of female high school seniors consider attending one of the nation's women's colleges.

When students at single-sex colleges seek funding for their education, such funds are regulated by the Higher Education Act of 1965. The U.S. Department of Education interpreted this act as requiring officials at institutions wishing to participate in federal programs for student financial aid either to have or to be about to receive accreditation from nationally recognized accrediting bodies or to show that credits earned by their students are accepted, on transfer and enrollment, by at least three accredited institutions. The Department of Education has interpreted the construction of the statute as meaning that if a college is to participate in federal aid programs, students from that college actually have to have successfully transferred to and enrolled in at least three accredited institutions. The congressional intent of the statute was to broaden the accessibility of federal financial aid funds to include students attending nontraditional or specialized postsecondary institutions. The purpose of this provision was solely to ensure that unaccredited institutions be of acceptable academic quality if they are seeking eligibility to participate in student aid programs.

When considering whether to attend single-sex colleges, applicants often review historical data and writings addressing the benefit or detriment of attending such institutions. Needless to say, these data, and researchers who helped produce them, often reach conflicting and controversial points of view. To this end, some statistical data demonstrate that students from single-sex schools outperform peers from coeducational institutions. Other studies point to the neurological and chemical differences between men and women and assert that single-sex education can better take such biological differences into account. Without the presence of the opposite sex, some researchers think that students will be less distracted from their studies. In short, some researchers argue that all males and females receive and process information differently, hear and see differently, and develop at different paces, and therefore require different teaching styles. Proponents also assert classroom structures should be adopted to accommodate both sexes separately. These studies maintain that students who attend single-sex colleges are more successful in academic development, social skill development, and career preparation.

On the other hand, defenders of the coeducational system respond that separate learning facilities are inherently unequal, reinforce gender stereotypes, and perpetuate societal inequalities related to opportunities afforded males and females. These researchers state that without the presence of the opposite sex, students are denied a learning environment that is representative of real life. From this perspective, interaction only with peers of the same sex fosters ignorance and prejudice toward the other sex.

Even though officials at most of the colleges for women have decided to admit males in recent years, new and emerging issues continue to arise. For example, officials at the Seven Sisters and undoubtedly other institutions are grappling with an array of legal questions on topics such as dormitory rooms and perhaps athletic programs in light of the fact that a number of students are becoming transgendered while completing their studies.

Litigation

Three key cases, two of which reached the U.S. Supreme Court, have addressed the constitutionality of single-sex institutions. The first dispute, *Mississippi University for Women v. Hogan* (1982), emerged when a male challenged his exclusion from a nursing program on the basis of his gender. According to the university's admissions policy, men could audit courses but could not enroll in the nursing program for credit. Affirming earlier judgments in favor of the male applicant, the Supreme Court applied intermediate scrutiny under its Fourteenth Amendment Equal Protection Clause analysis in finding that state and university officials failed to demonstrate an exceedingly persuasive justification for the gender-based classification that was applied in the admissions program. More specifically, in applying intermediate scrutiny, the Court decided that university officials had to show, at a minimum, that the classification served an important governmental objective and that the discriminatory means employed were related to achieving those objectives. The Court was of the opinion that because state and university officials were unable to prove that the policy of denying men admission to its nursing school was justified according to the judicially created standard that the Court had enunciated, the policy was unconstitutional, because it violated the Establishment Clause.

United States v. Virginia (1996) dealt with whether the Virginia Military Institute, which employed an adversarial form of military training for the 15% of its students who chose to enter the military as a career, could admit only males to its corps of cadets. After the Fourth Circuit entered a judgment that would have allowed commonwealth officials to create a parallel program for women at another public institution, the Supreme Court struck this plan down as a violation of the Equal Protection Clause. Again applying intermediate scrutiny, the Court thought that because Virginia's stated rationale for the gender-based distinction, namely that the importance of same-sex education justified the complete exclusion of women, failed to meet constitutional standards, it failed to demonstrate that there was an exceedingly persuasive justification for excluding all women. In explaining why it refused to accept Virginia's offer to create a program to provide military education for women at a separate facility, the Court reasoned that creating a new programs would not have remedied the constitutional violation, because this approach would not have offered the same level of prestige to both men and women.

A similar case arose at another military institution, the Citadel in South Carolina, when a female student successfully challenged its all-male admissions policy in *Faulkner v. Jones* (1995). Although the Fourth Circuit had approved the creation of a separate program for women, in light of the Supreme Court's striking down the admissions policy at the Virginia Military Institute in *United States v. Virginia*, the board at the Citadel voted to end the male-only admissions policy and to admit women to its corps of cadets.

In examining the law related to single-sex institutions of higher education, unless public officials can offer a separate and equal alternative for each sex, single-sex state-funded colleges and universities are likely to be forbidden on the grounds that they violate the Equal Protection Clause. Because state colleges and universities are publicly funded, then, admission policies must include both genders, unless programs offer separate but inherently equal state institutions to both male and female students.

Vivian Hopp Gordon

See also Equal Protection Analysis; Fourteenth Amendment; Higher Education Act; *Mississippi University for Women v. Hogan*; Religious Colleges and Universities; *United States v. Virginia*; U.S. Department of Education

Further Readings

Brune, A. (2007, April 8). When she graduates as he. *The Boston Globe*, p. 28. Retrieved May 22, 2009, from http://www.boston.com/news/globe/magazine/articles/2007/04/08/when_she_graduates_as_he/

Mael, F. E. (1998). Single-sex and coeducational schooling: Relationships to socioemotional and academic development. *Review of Educational Research*, 68(2), 101–129.

National Center for Educational Statistics. (2007). *Table 227. Enrollment and degrees conferred in degree-granting women's colleges, by selected characteristics and institution: Fall 2005 and 2005-06.* Retrieved May 22, 2009, from http://nces.ed.gov/programs/digest/d07/tables/dt07_227.asp

Rockler-Gladen, N. (2008). *Advantages and disadvantages of single sex education.* Retrieved May 22, 2009, from http://campuslife.suite101.com/article.cfm/all_womens_colleges_and_universities_in_the_us

Russo, C. J., & Scollay, S. J. (1993). All male state-funded military academies: Anachronism or necessary anomaly? *Education Law Reporter, 82,* 1073–1085.

Legal Citations

Faulkner v. Jones, 51 F.3d 440 (4th Cir. 1995), *motion to stay denied,* 66 F.3d 661 (4th Cir. 1995), *cert. dismissed,* 516 U.S. 910 (1995), *cert. denied,* 516 U.S. 938 (1995).

Higher Education Act, Pub. L. No. 89-329 (1965).

Mississippi University for Women v. Hogan, 458 U.S. 718 (1982).

United States v. Virginia, 518 U.S. 515 (1996).

SLOCHOWER V. BOARD OF HIGHER EDUCATION OF NEW YORK CITY

Slochower v. Board of Higher Education of New York City (1956) stands for the legal proposition that laws pertaining to public employees, including faculty members at public colleges and universities, cannot inferentially treat employees' assertions of Fifth Amendment privilege not to speak for fear of self-incrimination as automatically equivalent to legal wrongdoing. In *Slochower,* the U.S. Supreme Court invalidated a municipal law that required termination of employment for city workers who sought to raise their privilege against self-incrimination in order to avoid responding to questions relating to their official duties. The Court determined that had the law been enforced, it would have violated their right to due process. In light of the issues that *Slochower* raises about the due process rights of faculty members to refrain from answering questions about their political activities, this entry reviews the litigation and judicial analyses in the Supreme Court's ruling.

Facts of the Case

In 1952, officials at Brooklyn College, an institution of higher education under the control of New York City's Board of Higher Education, terminated the employment of Harry Slochower, a tenured faculty member with 27 years of service at Brooklyn College. The case dealt with events that took place during the anticommunist movement that originated in the 1940s. More specifically, in 1940, the New York State legislature formed the Joint Legislative Committee to Investigate the Educational System of the State of New York, also known as the Rapp-Coudert Committee. The committee was charged with investigating and uncovering the identities of public educational employees who were affiliated with the Communist Party so that its staff members could evaluate the employees' involvement and assess whether they were fit to teach in New York state public educational institutions. In 1941, a witness testified before the Rapp-Coudert Committee that Professor Slochower had ties to the Communist Party. The record indicated that Slochower testified before the Rapp-Coudert Committee and the Board of Faculty about his Communist Party affiliations in 1940 and 1941.

In 1952, the U.S. Senate's Internal Security Subcommittee of the Committee on the Judiciary also conducted an investigation of the ties that members of educational communities had to the Communist Party. When Harry Slochower was called to testify, he declared that he was not, at the time, a member of the Communist Party. Although he was willing to testify, he asserted his Fifth Amendment right not to speak about matters that might be self-incriminating. To this end, he refused to respond to inquiries about his affiliations with the Communist Party from 1940 to 1941. The Senate Committee acknowledged Slochower's constitutional right and did not compel him to testify to these matters. However, soon after, officials at Brooklyn College dismissed Slochower pursuant to a city law that called for terminating the employment of city workers who sought to raise the Fifth Amendment privilege against self-incrimination in order to avoid responding to questions relating to their official duties. Insofar as the law summarily called for dismissal of employees who asserted the Fifth Amendment privilege of not speaking for fear of self-incrimination, for all intents and purposes, the law attached wrongdoing as a foregone conclusion. After all three levels of the state court system in New York upheld the faculty member's dismissal for refusing to testify, he appealed to the Supreme Court.

The Supreme Court's Ruling

On further review, the Court reversed in favor of the faculty member in a five-to-four judgment authored by Justice Clark. Slochower's lawyer argued that officials at Brooklyn College violated his right to due process. Besides alleging that the law unfairly discharged public employees for exercising their Fifth Amendment right against self-incrimination, the plaintiff's lawyers contended that pursuant to a New York statute, officials could dismiss a tenured faculty member for cause only with proper notice, a hearing, and an opportunity to appeal the initial decision. Yet, the law permitted automatic dismissals when employees asserted their privilege against self-incrimination. Balancing the rights of the public's interest with those of individuals, the Court emphasized that while the faculty members did not have a guaranteed right to employment, officials at governmental agencies such as the college still had to comply with the U.S. Constitution, which guaranteed faculty members' right to due process.

In its analysis, the Supreme Court pointed out that absent due process, the law assumed that public employees' assertion of privilege against self-incrimination summarily translated into wrongdoing, and it did not factor in the reasons individuals might raise the Fifth Amendment privilege in their defense. The Court noted that although witnesses such as the plaintiff may have had reasonable fears of prosecution even though they were innocent of any fault, the law failed to consider any possibility other than wrongdoing. The Court found that such an approach rendered the law arbitrary. Further, the Court was troubled by the fact that although college officials had known about and failed to act on the plaintiff's Senate testimony for 12 years, they now took it as conclusive evidence of his having been at fault, even though this was a civil rather than a criminal case. The majority decided that the municipal law was unconstitutional, because it violated the plaintiff's right to due process.

Two different dissenting opinions, written by Justices Reed and Harlan, essentially maintained that the Supreme Court overstepped its authority in considering how public employers regulate the conduct of their employees, including those in higher education.

Slochower is an important case in a line of litigation that highlights the due process protections to which tenured faculty members are entitled before their employment may be terminated. In addition, *Slochower* is significant because it invalidated the New York City law that presumed fault when individuals invoke their Fifth Amendment right against self-incrimination.

Jeffrey C. Sun

See also Due Process, Substantive and Procedural; Loyalty Oaths; Political Activities and Speech of Faculty Members

Further Readings

Kilpatrick, R. N. (1976). School personnel, organized professional groups, and the law. *Urban Educator, 11*(2), 167–184.

Ratner, L. G. (1957). Consequences of exercising the privilege against self-incrimination. *University of Chicago Law Review, 24*(3), 472–511.

Legal Citations

Slochower v. Board of Higher Education of New York City, 350 U.S. 551 (1956).

SOUTHEASTERN COMMUNITY COLLEGE V. DAVIS

In *Southeastern Community College v. Davis* (1979), the U.S. Supreme Court reviewed Section 504 of the Rehabilitation Act of 1973 (Section 504) for the first time. Section 504 prohibits recipients of federal funds from discriminating against individuals with disabilities on the basis of their disabilities. The statute further requires federally funded programs to provide reasonable accommodations to otherwise qualified individuals with disabilities so that they can participate in these programs. In *Davis,* the Court defined the term *otherwise qualified* as it is used in Section 504. Under the Court's definition, institutions of higher education can consider the effects of individuals' disabilities in evaluating whether they are otherwise qualified. Further, the Court indicated that Section 504's mandate to provide reasonable accommodations does not require institutional officials to make substantial changes to the fundamental natures of their programs in order to provide individuals with accommodations. In light of the impact that *Davis* had on the development of the law with regard to Section 504 as it applies to colleges and universities as well as other educational institutions, this entry examines the case in detail.

Facts of the Case

Davis involved an individual with a history of hearing problems and dependence on a hearing aid who applied to the nursing program of a community college. When the student filed her application, she was advised to consult an audiologist. Following an examination, the audiologist made a change in her hearing aid but reported that she would still need to rely on lip reading for effective communication. College officials consulted with the executive director of the state's nursing board, who advised that the applicant not be admitted to the program, because her hearing disability would have made it unsafe for her to participate in clinical training or practice as a nurse. Consequently, the applicant was denied admission into the program.

The applicant unsuccessfully filed suit in a federal court in North Carolina, alleging that the denial of admission violated Section 504 and the Equal Protection and Due Process Clauses of the Fourteenth Amendment. The court ruled that because the applicant was not otherwise qualified under Section 504, she was not protected against discrimination. In its analysis, the court interpreted the term *otherwise qualified* to mean that an individual is able to function sufficiently in a position in spite of a disability. Insofar as the applicant's disability prevented her from functioning sufficiently in the nursing program, the court agreed that the decision denying her admission was not discriminatory. On appeal, the Fourth Circuit reversed in finding that the trial court misinterpreted Section 504. The panel explained that the trial court erred in taking the applicant's disability into account when it evaluated whether she was otherwise qualified. Moreover, the court indicated that Section 504 required affirmative conduct on the part of officials at educational institutions to modify their programs to accommodate individuals with disabilities even when such modifications are expensive.

The Supreme Court's Ruling

On further review, the U.S. Supreme Court, in a unanimous opinion written by Justice Powell, reversed the Fourth Circuit order and, in essence, confirmed the trial court's definition of *otherwise qualified*. According to the Court, the language of Section 504 does not compel officials at educational institutions to disregard disabilities or make substantial modifications to their programs in order to allow individuals with disabilities to participate. Rather, the Court wrote, Section 504 requires only that otherwise qualified individuals with disabilities not be excluded from participation in federally funded programs solely because of their disabilities. To the Court, an otherwise qualified individual with a disability was one who was able to meet all of a program's requirements in spite of the disability.

Regarding the circumstances in the case before it, the Supreme Court pointed out that it was not open to dispute that the ability to understand speech without reliance on lip reading was necessary for patient safety during the clinical phase of the college's nursing program. This ability, in the Court's judgment, was also required for many of the tasks that registered nurses perform in their daily activities. As the Court viewed it, the fundamental alterations to the program that would have been necessary to allow the applicant to participate were much more than Section 504 required as reasonable accommodations. To this end, the Court refused to interpret Section 504 as imposing a requirement on educational institutions to lower or substantially modify their standards to accommodate individuals with disabilities.

Davis is significant not only for its definition of *otherwise qualified* but also because it helped to define the parameters of Section 504's mandate to provide reasonable accommodations. Due to the similarities between the statutes, because these guidelines additionally apply to the Americans with Disabilities Act as well as to Section 504, they should be of great interest to educators and students alike on campuses of institutions of higher learning as they seek to provide equal educational and work opportunities for students, faculty members, and staff with disabilities.

Allan G. Osborne, Jr.

See also Fourteenth Amendment; Rehabilitation Act, Section 504; U.S. Supreme Court Cases in Higher Education

Further Readings

Russo, C. J., & Osborne, A. G. (2009). *Section 504 of the Rehabilitation Act of 1973 and the Americans with Disabilities Act: Implications*

for educational leaders. Thousand Oaks, CA: Corwin.

Legal Citations

Americans with Disabilities Act, 42 U.S.C. §§ 12101 *et seq.*
Rehabilitation Act, Section 504, 29 U.S.C. § 794.
Southeastern Community College v. Davis, 442 U.S. 397 (1979).

SOUTHEASTERN COMMUNITY COLLEGE V. DAVIS

Davis is significant because in reviewing Section 504 of the Rehabilitation Act for the first time in an educational setting, the Supreme Court ruled that officials do not have to make substantial changes to the fundamental natures of their programs in order to accommodate individuals who are otherwise qualified to participate in those programs.

Supreme Court of the United States

SOUTHEASTERN COMMUNITY COLLEGE

v.

DAVIS

442 U.S. 397

Argued April 23, 1979

Decided June 11, 1979

Mr. Justice POWELL delivered the opinion of the Court.

This case presents a matter of first impression for this Court: Whether § 504 of the Rehabilitation Act of 1973, which prohibits discrimination against an "otherwise qualified handicapped individual" in federally funded programs "solely by reason of his handicap," forbids professional schools from imposing physical qualifications for admission to their clinical training programs.

I

Respondent, who suffers from a serious hearing disability, seeks to be trained as a registered nurse. During the 1973–1974 academic year she was enrolled in the College Parallel program of Southeastern Community College, a state institution that receives federal funds.

Respondent hoped to progress to Southeastern's Associate Degree Nursing program, completion of which would make her eligible for state certification as a

registered nurse. In the course of her application to the nursing program, she was interviewed by a member of the nursing faculty. It became apparent that respondent had difficulty understanding questions asked, and on inquiry she acknowledged a history of hearing problems and dependence on a hearing aid. She was advised to consult an audiologist.

On the basis of an examination at Duke University Medical Center, respondent was diagnosed as having a "bilateral, sensori-neural hearing loss." A change in her hearing aid was recommended, as a result of which it was expected that she would be able to detect sounds "almost as well as a person would who has normal hearing." But this improvement would not mean that she could discriminate among sounds sufficiently to understand normal spoken speech. Her lipreading skills would remain necessary for effective communication: "While wearing the hearing aid, she is well aware of gross sounds occurring in the listening environment. However, she can only be responsible for speech spoken to her, when the talker gets her attention and allows her to look directly at the talker."

Southeastern next consulted Mary McRee, Executive Director of the North Carolina Board of Nursing. On the basis of the audiologist's report, McRee recommended that respondent not be admitted to the nursing program. In McRee's view, respondent's hearing disability made it unsafe for her to practice as a nurse. In addition, it would be impossible for respondent to participate safely in the normal clinical training program, and those modifications that would be necessary to enable safe participation would prevent her from realizing the benefits of the program: "To adjust patient learning experiences in keeping with [respondent's] hearing limitations could, in fact, be the same as denying her full learning to meet the objectives of your nursing programs."

After respondent was notified that she was not qualified for nursing study because of her hearing disability, she requested reconsideration of the decision. The entire nursing staff of Southeastern was assembled, and McRee again was consulted. McRee repeated her conclusion that on the basis of the available evidence, respondent "has hearing limitations which could interfere with her safely caring for patients." Upon further deliberation, the staff voted to deny respondent admission.

Respondent then filed suit in the United States District Court for the Eastern District of North Carolina, alleging both a violation of § 504 of the Rehabilitation Act of 1973 and a denial of equal protection and due process. After a bench trial, the District Court entered judgment in favor of Southeastern. It confirmed the findings of the audiologist that even with a hearing aid respondent cannot understand speech directed to her except through lipreading, . . .

. . .

. . .[T]he District Court concluded that respondent was not an "otherwise qualified handicapped individual" protected against discrimination by § 504. In its view, "[o]therwise qualified, can only be read to mean otherwise able to function sufficiently in the position sought in spite of the handicap, if proper training and facilities are suitable and available." Because respondent's disability would prevent her from functioning "sufficiently" in Southeastern's nursing program, the court held that the decision to exclude her was not discriminatory within the meaning of § 504.

On appeal, the Court of Appeals for the Fourth Circuit reversed. It did not dispute the District Court's findings of fact, but held that the court had misconstrued § 504. In light of administrative regulations that

had been promulgated while the appeal was pending, the appellate court believed that § 504 required Southeastern to "reconsider plaintiff's application for admission to the nursing program without regard to her hearing ability." It concluded that the District Court had erred in taking respondent's handicap into account in determining whether she was "otherwise qualified" for the program, rather than confining its inquiry to her "academic and technical qualifications." The Court of Appeals also suggested that § 504 required "affirmative conduct" on the part of Southeastern to modify its program to accommodate the disabilities of applicants, "even when such modifications become expensive."

Because of the importance of this issue to the many institutions covered by § 504, we granted certiorari. We now reverse.

II

As previously noted, this is the first case in which this Court has been called upon to interpret § 504. It is elementary that "[t]he starting point in every case involving construction of a statute is the language itself." Section 504 by its terms does not compel educational institutions to disregard the disabilities of handicapped individuals or to make substantial modifications in their programs to allow disabled persons to participate. Instead, it requires only that an "otherwise qualified handicapped individual" not be excluded from participation in a federally funded program "solely by reason of his handicap," indicating only that mere possession of a handicap is not a permissible ground for assuming an inability to function in a particular context.

The court below, however, believed that the "otherwise qualified" persons protected by § 504 include those who would be able to meet the requirements of a particular program in every respect except as to limitations imposed by their handicap. Taken literally, this holding would prevent an institution from taking into account any limitation resulting from the handicap, however disabling. It assumes, in effect, that a person need not meet legitimate physical requirements in order to be "otherwise qualified." We think the understanding of the District Court is closer to the plain meaning of the statutory language. An otherwise qualified person is one who is able to meet all of a program's requirements in spite of his handicap.

The regulations promulgated by the Department of HEW to interpret § 504 reinforce, rather than contradict, this conclusion. According to these regulations, a "[q]ualified handicapped person" is, "[w]ith respect to postsecondary and vocational education services, a handicapped person who meets the academic and technical standards requisite to admission or participation in the [school's] education program or activity. . . ."

. . .

III

The remaining question is whether the physical qualifications Southeastern demanded of respondent might not be necessary for participation in its nursing program. It is not open to dispute that, as Southeastern's Associate Degree Nursing program currently is constituted, the ability to understand speech without reliance on lipreading is necessary for patient safety during the clinical phase of the program. As the District Court found, this ability also is indispensable for many of the functions that a registered nurse performs.

Respondent contends nevertheless that § 504, properly interpreted, compels Southeastern to undertake affirmative action that would dispense with the need for effective oral communication. First, it is suggested that respondent can be given individual supervision by faculty members whenever she attends patients directly. Moreover, certain required courses might be dispensed with altogether for respondent. It is not necessary, she argues, that Southeastern train her to undertake all the tasks a registered nurse is licensed to perform. Rather, it is sufficient to make § 504 applicable if respondent might be able to perform satisfactorily some of the duties of a registered nurse or to hold some of the positions available to a registered nurse.

Respondent finds support for this argument in portions of the HEW regulations discussed above. In particular, a provision applicable to postsecondary educational programs requires covered institutions to make "modifications" in their programs to accommodate handicapped persons, and to provide "auxiliary aids" such as sign-language interpreters. Respondent argues that this regulation imposes an obligation to ensure full participation in covered programs by handicapped individuals and, in particular, requires Southeastern to make the kind of adjustments that would be necessary to permit her safe participation in the nursing program.

We note first that on the present record it appears unlikely respondent could benefit from any affirmative action that the regulation reasonably could be interpreted as requiring. Section 84.44(d)(2), for example, explicitly excludes "devices or services of a personal nature" from the kinds of auxiliary aids a school must provide a handicapped individual. Yet the only evidence in the record indicates that nothing less than close, individual attention by a nursing instructor would be sufficient to ensure patient safety if respondent took part in the clinical phase of the nursing program. Furthermore, it also is reasonably clear that § 84.44(a) does not encompass the kind of curricular changes that would be necessary to accommodate respondent in the nursing program. In light of respondent's inability to function in clinical courses without close supervision, Southeastern, with prudence, could allow her to take only academic classes. Whatever benefits respondent might realize from such a course of study, she would not receive even a rough equivalent of the training a nursing program normally gives. Such a fundamental alteration in the nature of a program is far more than the "modification" the regulation requires.

Moreover, an interpretation of the regulations that required the extensive modifications necessary to include respondent in the nursing program would raise grave doubts about their validity. If these regulations were to require substantial adjustments in existing programs beyond those necessary to eliminate discrimination against otherwise qualified individuals, they would do more than clarify the meaning of § 504. Instead, they would constitute an unauthorized extension of the obligations imposed by that statute.

The language and structure of the Rehabilitation Act of 1973 reflect a recognition by Congress of the distinction between the evenhanded treatment of qualified handicapped persons and affirmative efforts to overcome the disabilities caused by handicaps. Section 501(b), governing the employment of handicapped individuals by the Federal Government, requires each federal agency to submit "an affirmative action program plan for the hiring, placement, and advancement of handicapped individuals. . . ." These plans "shall include a description of the extent to which and methods whereby the special needs of handicapped employees are being met." Similarly, § 503(a), governing hiring by federal contractors, requires employers to "take affirmative action to employ and advance in employment qualified handicapped individuals. . . ." The President is required to promulgate regulations to enforce this section.

Under § 501(c) of the Act, by contrast, state agencies such as Southeastern are only "encourage[d] . . . to adopt and implement such policies and procedures." Section 504 does not refer at all to affirmative action, and except as it applies to federal employers it does not provide for implementation by administrative action. A comparison of these provisions demonstrates that Congress understood accommodation of the needs of handicapped individuals may require affirmative action and knew how to provide for it in those instances where it wished to do so.

Although an agency's interpretation of the statute under which it operates is entitled to some deference, "this deference is constrained by our obligation to honor the clear meaning of a statute, as revealed by its language, purpose, and history." Here, neither the language, purpose, nor history of § 504 reveals an intent to impose an affirmative-action obligation on all recipients of federal funds. Accordingly, we hold that even if HEW has attempted to create such an obligation itself, it lacks the authority to do so.

IV

We do not suggest that the line between a lawful refusal to extend affirmative action and illegal discrimination against handicapped persons always will be clear. It is possible to envision situations where an insistence on continuing past requirements and practices might arbitrarily deprive genuinely qualified handicapped persons of the opportunity to participate in a covered program. Technological advances can be expected to enhance opportunities to rehabilitate the handicapped or otherwise to qualify them for some useful employment. Such advances also may enable attainment of these goals without imposing undue financial and administrative burdens upon a State. Thus, situations may arise where a refusal to modify an existing program might become unreasonable and discriminatory. Identification of those instances where a refusal to accommodate the needs of a disabled person amounts to discrimination against the handicapped continues to be an important responsibility of HEW.

In this case, however, it is clear that Southeastern's unwillingness to make major adjustments in its nursing program does not constitute such discrimination. The uncontroverted testimony of several members of Southeastern's staff and faculty established that the purpose of its program was to train persons who could serve the nursing profession in all customary ways. This type of purpose, far from reflecting any animus against handicapped individuals is shared by many if not most of the institutions that train persons to render professional service. It is undisputed that respondent could not participate in Southeastern's nursing program unless the standards were substantially lowered. Section 504 imposes no requirement upon an educational institution to lower or to effect substantial modifications of standards to accommodate a handicapped person.

One may admire respondent's desire and determination to overcome her handicap, and there well may be various other types of service for which she can qualify. In this case, however, we hold that there was no violation of § 504 when Southeastern concluded that respondent did not qualify for admission to its program. Nothing in the language or history of § 504 reflects an intention to limit the freedom of an educational institution to require reasonable physical qualifications for admission to a clinical training program. Nor has there been any showing in this case that any action short of a substantial change in Southeastern's program would render unreasonable the qualifications it imposed.

V

Accordingly, we reverse the judgment of the court below, and remand for proceedings consistent with this opinion.

So ordered.

Sports Programming and Scheduling

The scheduling of athletic competitions and practices in higher education is addressed by U.S. federal law as well as institutional policies of intercollegiate athletics programs. Although some financial limits may restrict the scheduling of games among athletic teams, legal constraints involving the scheduling of such events in higher education are established mainly through Title IX of the Education Amendments of 1972 (Title IX). To this end, Title IX has a major impact on interscholastic, intercollegiate, club, and intramural athletics as well as on scheduling policy regulations that have been established by the National Collegiate Athletic Association (NCAA). In light of questions that can arise in this complex area, this entry reviews key legal issues associated with sports scheduling and programming in American colleges and universities.

Provisions of Title IX

According to Title IX, "No person in the United States shall, on the basis of sex, be denied the benefits of, or be subjected to discrimination under, any education program or activity receiving Federal financial assistance" (20 U.S.C. § 1681). In 1979, the U.S. Department of Health, Education, and Welfare, now the U.S. Department of Education, promulgated a policy interpretation of Title IX that led to legal limitations on sports scheduling under 34 C.F.R. § 106.41. Section 106.41 of this regulation specifically concentrates on the equitable participatory policies of athletics programs. Further, the regulation directs athletic administrators to consider the equal athletic opportunities in 10 areas, including scheduling of games and practice time (34 C.F.R. § 106.41 (c)(3)).

In order to comply with Title IX, athletic programming must meet one prong of the Title IX tripartite test. Under the first prong, institutional officials must ensure that each gender's representation in varsity athletics is substantially proportionate to its representation in the student body. Pursuant to the second prong, if institutional officials have not achieved substantial proportionality in programming, they may demonstrate that there is a continuing history of expanding opportunities for the underrepresented gender. The third prong stipulates that institutional officials may demonstrate that they are currently accommodating all interests and abilities of the underrepresented gender.

Equitable scheduling typically implicates the third prong of the tripartite test, which requires institutional officials to show that they have taken steps to ensure that the interests and abilities of the members of the underrepresented sex have been fully and effectively accommodated. The Office of Civil Rights, which investigates and enforces Title IX compliance, noted that the third prong was used in more than two-thirds of the enforcement cases brought before its enforcement staff. Institutional policies are paramount in demonstrating that an institution has met the needs of all student-athletes and has complied with federal statutes.

When evaluating scheduling policies, athletic administrators must affirmatively address two key aspects of scheduling. The first question inquires whether scheduling policies are discriminatory in their language or effect. In other words, even though a schedule may appear to be fair, its effect may not be fair if it overlaps with the season of another sport in which student-athletes may wish to participate. The second question considers whether substantial and unjustified disparities exist between males and females in benefits, services, or opportunities, such as opportunities to use practice facilities and access to training staffs derived from scheduling. If the answers to these questions reveal discriminatory actions, then litigation could ensue. In order to better address these questions, athletic scheduling policies and procedures must comply with Title IX statutory and administrative law, which depends on five principles of equitable scheduling of playing and practice seasons. These principles include the number of competitive events that occur per sport, the number and length of practice opportunities, the time of day competitive events are scheduled, the time of day when practice opportunities are scheduled, and the opportunities to engage in preseason and postseason competition.

NCAA Regulations

The NCAA addressed the preceding five principles in the institutional constitution and operating bylaws that were approved by its member institutions. Items 2.6 and 2.14 of the NCAA constitution state that the purpose of complying with these principles is to promote nondiscrimination and to minimize the time demands of sports on student-athletes to ensure that they receive a quality education. At the same time, it is important to note that the NCAA rules are not federal or state laws but regulations established to maintain order among "voluntary" member colleges and universities that belong to the NCAA. Beyond this, there are three important points to keep in mind with regard to sports programming and scheduling.

Number of Competitive Events

First, Article 17 of the NCAA operating bylaws regulates the number of competitive events per sport. The NCAA regulations categorize sports as team sports and individual sports. This distinction is important, insofar as the classifications in the policy do not categorize by gender of student-athletes but rather by the nature of the sports involved. Team sports include basketball, ice hockey, volleyball, football, softball, and baseball. The NCAA has established a maximum number of contests and dates of competition for all team and individual sports to create uniform schedules for all of its member institutions. The length of playing seasons is limited to 132 days for team sports and 144 days for individual sports. The exceptions to these limitations occur in women's rowing and men's and women's track and field, which have a playing season limitation of 156 days. Moreover, Bylaw 17.1.7 stipulates the method of calculation that member institutions are required to follow to maintain compliance with NCAA regulations. Also, each sport has specific limitations on the maximum number of competitive events during the regular season. For example, football teams in the Football Bowl Subdivision that was formerly known as Division I-A may not compete in more than 12 games in the regular season, while golf may not exceed 24 dates of competition. In this way, the NCAA has followed the guidelines for interpretation of compliant behavior in Title IX by evaluating the athletics program as a whole while recognizing the differences in types of sport in scheduling policies of the number of competitive events per sport.

Practices

Second, NCAA Bylaw 17.1.6 regulates the number and length of practice opportunities, the time of day competitive events are scheduled, and the time of day practice opportunities are scheduled. There are two major distinctions regarding the number and length of practice opportunities: outside of the playing season, and during the playing season.

In order to avoid superfluous distractions from educational experiences while increasing opportunities to share facilities for practice time, NCAA Bylaw 17.1.6 places time restrictions on the time that student-athletes use in practice and competitive events each week. During the playing season, sports, and of course, student-athletes, are subject to a 20-hour limitation per week and no more than four hours of practice per day. When calculating the number of hours each week, competitions count as only three hours despite the actual duration of the game. Various types of meetings count as athletically related activities subject to the 20-hour rule. Additionally, all student-athletes are required to take one day off each week with a few exceptions such as basketball, for which a team may have three competitions scheduled in one week or scheduled postseason competitions.

Outside of the playing season, or during the off-season, there are increased time limitations on scheduling practice and athletically related activities. Here all sports are required to limit practice time to eight hours per week with not more than two hours spent on skill-related workouts or watching game film. Moreover, outside of the playing season, all sports are required by the NCAA to have two days off each week from all athletically related activities. While the primary purpose of this NCAA legislation is to reduce interference with the opportunities that student-athletes have to complete quality educational programs in a manner consistent with what is available to the student bodies as a whole, the policies also account for nondiscriminatory language and widespread expectations of compliance regardless of the gender of student-athletes.

Pre- and Postseason Activities

Third, the NCAA's scheduling rules attend to the opportunities to engage in preseason and postseason competition. Most postseason competitions are not counted in the playing season maximum number limitations previously noted. Illustrations of such team postseason competitions include football bowl games licensed by the NCAA Championships/Sports Management Cabinet and NCAA championship events in basketball, softball, baseball, and ice hockey.

Regulations for Individual Sports

Fourth, individual sports have additional limitations and flexibility that is not afforded to team sports. For instance, competitions outside of

NCAA championship events, such as the Intercollegiate Rowing Association championship and USA Gymnastics Collegiate national championship, are exempt from an institution's declared playing season limitations. In addition, certified summer foreign tours, where student-athletes of some team and individual sports compete outside of the United States, are available to student-athletes regardless of gender. However, these opportunities are limited in the number of competitors per sport in order to avoid superfluous financial expenses incurred by travel. Even though many opportunities for student-athletes to engage in postseason and preseason competitions exist, Bylaw 17.1.7 certifies that only individuals who are relevant to or eligible for postseason competitions may continue to practice, which could cause some issues of discrimination based on the discretion of coaches. Nevertheless, the language of NCAA Article 17 policies is nondiscriminatory in scope and has not been challenged by litigation to date.

In sum, the policies of scheduling athletic playing and practice seasons are outlined in NCAA regulations and must adhere to the federal statutory laws included in Title IX as well as to administrative law contained in 34 C.F.R. § 106.41 (c)(3). The focus of compliance with sports scheduling laws and policies is to enhance the educational and athletic opportunities of all individuals within a nondiscriminatory educational environment for all who are involved in intercollegiate athletics.

Mario Torres and Robert Clark

See also National Collegiate Athletic Association; Title IX and Athletics; U.S. Department of Education

Further Readings

Carpenter, L. J., & Acosta, R. V. (2005). *Title IX*. Champaign, IL: Human Kinetics.

Reynolds, G. (2003, July 11). *Further clarification of intercollegiate athletics policy guidance regarding Title IX compliance*. Washington, DC: U.S. Department of Education. Retrieved January 6, 2009, from http://www.ed.gov/about/offices/list/ocr/title9guidanceFinal.html

Spellings, M., & Manning, J. F. (2005, March 17). *Additional clarification of intercollegiate athletics policy: Three-part test—Part three*. Washington, DC: U.S. Department of Education. Retrieved January 4, 2009, from http://www.ed.gov/about/offices/list/ocr/docs/title9guidanceadditional.pdf

2008–2009 NCAA Division I Manual. Indianapolis, IN: National Collegiate Athletic Association.

Legal Citations

Code of Federal Regulations, as cited.

Title IX of the Education Amendments of 1972, 20 U.S.C. §§ 1681 *et seq*.

STAFFORD ACT

As part of President Lyndon B. Johnson's "Great Society" initiative, the U.S. Congress passed, and he signed into law, the Higher Education Act of 1965, authorizing federal student financial aid programs including the Educational Opportunity Grant Program and the Federal Insured Student Loan Program, better known as the Guaranteed Student Loan Program (GSL). The eligibility requirements and terms and conditions of the loans are set forth in Title IV of the act and its subsequent amendments. Since its inception, the GSL Program has provided low-cost loans allowing millions of students to receive a college education that they otherwise might not have been able to afford. In 1988, the GSL Program was renamed the Stafford Loan Program in honor of Republican Senator Robert T. Stafford of Vermont for his efforts to make higher education more accessible to students regardless of their socioeconomic status.

Stafford loans from the federal government are available to students who are engaged in undergraduate, graduate, or professional school studies and are enrolled on at least a half-time basis. Undergraduate students must be enrolled for six or more credit or semester hours. Eligible students may apply for Stafford loans by completing what is known as the Free Application for Federal Student Aid (FAFSA), which may be obtained at no charge from college or university financial aid offices or online at the FAFSA government organization Web site.

Financial aid is available to both dependent and independent undergraduate students whose dependency status is determined by information that they provide on their FAFSA forms. The limit on the amount of money students may borrow varies according to their grade level and dependency status. The law does not require credit checks when students apply for loans, because individuals are generally eligible to receive the loans regardless of their credit scores or history of financial problems. Stafford loans can be direct or indirect in nature. Direct loans are those that are administered by officials at institutions chosen by borrowers, while indirect loans are handled by staff members at lending organizations such as banks.

There are two types of Stafford loans, subsidized and unsubsidized. Both types of loans are guaranteed by the U.S. Department of Education. Subsidized loans are awarded on the basis of demonstrated financial need. If students qualify for a loan, the federal government pays the interest on (subsidizes) the loans while the students are attending school as well as for a six-month grace period thereafter. The grace period commences when students graduate, leave school, or are enrolled less than half time. Interest does not accrue on a loan until the repayment period begins. No payments are due on loans until six months after graduation or until borrowers become less-than-half-time students. For example, students who borrow $10,000 to help finance their education would owe $10,000 after graduation. At one time, subsidized loans were the only type of Stafford loans available.

Unsubsidized Stafford loans are now available to students regardless of their or their parents' incomes, and these loans are not awarded on the basis of financial need. For unsubsidized Stafford loans, the government does not pay the interest on the loans; students are responsible for the payment of interest that accrues on the loans from the time the money is disbursed to them until they repay their loan debt in full. For example, a student who borrowed $10,000 on entering school would, on graduation, owe $10,000 plus interest that accrued while he or she was in school. The interest would be computed and added to the total loan amount, and after the grace period expired, the student would have to begin making payments on the principal plus the accumulated interest. To continue with the same example, if the amount of interest accrued was $1,000, then the student would owe a total of $11,000. Students have the option of making

payments while they are still in school to avoid the accrued interest.

The interest rates on Stafford loans vary according to the date when the loans were disbursed to the students. Loans disbursed prior to July 1, 2006, have variable interest rates, while those that were initially disbursed on or after July 1, 2006, have a fixed interest rate of 6.8 percent. As noted earlier, loans may be financed by a bank, another private lender, or agencies of the federal government. The amount of time that students have to repay loans can range from 10 to 25 years, depending on the amount that they owe and the type of repayment plans that they negotiated with their lending institutions. Under specified circumstances, individuals may seek to defer the repayment of their loans or to have them discharged if they suffer from disabilities; if they experience economic hardship (for example, if they successfully declare bankruptcy); or if they are employed as teachers in school systems that serve low-income students and offer such relief as an incentive in return for serving a fixed period of time.

Michael Yates

See also Higher Education Act; Loans and Federal Aid; U.S. Department of Education

Further Readings

Cloud, R. C. (2006). Offsetting Social Security benefits to repay student loans: Pay us now or pay us later. *Education Law Reporter, 208,* 11–21.

Cloud, R. C. (2006). When does repaying a student loan become an undue hardship? *Education Law Reporter, 185,* 783–804.

Legal Citations

Augustus F. Hawkins–Robert T. Stafford Elementary and Secondary School Improvement Amendments of 1988, Pub. L. No. 100-297.

Federal Student Loan Programs, http://www.staffordloan .com

Free Application for Federal Student Aid, http://www .fafsa.ed.gov

Higher Education Act of 1965, Pub. L. No. 89-329, 20 U.S.C. §§ 1001 *et seq.*

Higher Education Amendments of 1988, Pub. L. No. 100-369, 20 U.S.C. §§ 1071 *et seq.*

STATE AID AND THE ESTABLISHMENT CLAUSE

The extent to which religious colleges and universities can receive government aid is evaluated under the First Amendment's Establishment Clause. The U.S. Supreme Court's tripartite test from *Lemon v. Kurtzman* (1971) provides the standard for assessing the constitutionality of statutes, regulations, or practices that provide governmental aid to religious entities. Pursuant to this judicially crafted standard, aid must have a secular legislative purpose, its principal or primary effect must neither advance nor inhibit religion, and it must avoid excessive governmental entanglement with religion. In light of persisting questions about the parameters of constitutionally acceptable forms of governmental aid to religious institutions of higher learning and their students, this entry reviews key issues on this contentious topic.

Defining Religiously Affiliated Institutions

Courts have generally referred to educational institutions with religious connections as *sectarian*, while those with extensive religious connections or church control are identified as being *pervasively sectarian*. Whether religiously affiliated colleges or universities are pervasively sectarian can influence institutional eligibility for government aid under the Establishment Clause. Of course, whether an institution is pervasively sectarian depends on the facts of a case.

In *Tilton v. Richardson* (1971), the Supreme Court examined the constitutionality of the Higher Education Facilities Act as it applied to providing construction grants for buildings and facilities for Roman Catholic colleges and universities in Connecticut. In assessing the grants under the *Lemon* test, the Court held that the act did not have the effect of advancing religion, because the funds were not used for buildings where sectarian instruction or religious worship occurred nor would a one-time grant of funds create an excessive entanglement. The Court went further in deciding that the colleges and universities were not pervasively sectarian because they subscribed to the American Association of University Professors (AAUP) 1940 Statement of Academic Freedom and Tenure, they admitted non-Catholic students, they hired non-Catholic faculty, and they offered religion courses that were other religions other than Catholicism.

Two years later, similarly, the Supreme Court, in *Hunt v. McNair* (1973), upheld the eligibility of a Baptist college to receive funds from state tax-exempt bonds as part of a state program to assist colleges and universities as long as the monies were not used for sectarian instruction or to build places of worship. The statutory scheme in *Hunt* called for colleges receiving monies to convey the funded projects to a state authority, which would then lease them back and reconvey them on the payment of the bonds. The Court did not think that the college was pervasively sectarian, even though members of its board of trustees were elected by the South Carolina Baptist Convention, the convention's approval was required for specified financial transactions, and only the convention could amend the college's charter. The Court was satisfied that the college had no religious qualifications for faculty membership or student admission, and only 60% of its student body was Baptist; this percentage was roughly equivalent to the percentage of Baptists in that area of the state.

Three years after *Hunt*, in *Roemer v. Board of Public Works of Maryland* (1976), the Supreme Court upheld a state subsidy to four Catholic colleges. The court was satisfied that the plan for providing aid was constitutional where none of the colleges received funds from or reported to the Catholic Church, the Catholic representatives on the colleges' boards did not influence college decisions, attendance at religious services on campus was not required, mandatory religion courses were taught within the 1940 AAUP Principles of Academic Freedom, before-class prayer was miniscule and not required, and faculty members did not have to be Catholic.

Religiously Affiliated Institution and Federal Aid

More recent Supreme Court cases have cast doubt as to whether the pervasive sectarianism at religiously affiliated colleges and universities should be a bar at all to participating in governmental assistance. In *Witters v. Washington Department of Services for the Blind* (*Witters I*, 1986), the Court wrote that a state program that provided financial grants to students who attended pervasively sectarian Bible colleges for the purpose of preparing for the ministry did not violate the Establishment Clause. The Court distinguished *Witters I* from *Tilton, Hunt,* and *Roemer* where the governmental funds had been distributed directly to religious postsecondary institutions. In effect, the Court in *Witters I* circumvented the pervasively sectarian argument, because the direct recipients were individuals and not institutions. The Court applied the same rationale in later K–12 government assistance cases that should be informative for all of those who are interested in higher education.

In the first of four cases on government aid and the Establishment Clause, *Zobrest v. Catalina Foothills School District* (1993), the Supreme Court rejected a claim of an Establishment Clause violation where, under special education law, a public school provided a sign-language interpreter to a student with special needs at his religious high school, where religion permeated most of the courses in his school. In *Agostini v. Felton* (1997), the Court adopted a similar argument that permitted publicly funded teachers to provide services for poor students who attended religiously affiliated nonpublic schools. The Court explained that the aid was permissible, because it was for the benefit of students who attended the schools due to the choices of their parents, not government officials. In addition, the *Agostini* Court adopted a neutrality argument that the services that children received in the religious schools were the same as those available to their peers in public schools. Finally, in *Mitchell v. Helms* (2000), the Court stretched *Agostini* further in applying its parent choice and neutrality rationales to permit the direct loan of instructional materials to religiously affiliated nonpublic schools.

Religiously Affiliated Institutions and State Aid

An important distinction arises in light of the fact that government aid that is permissible under the federal Establishment Clause may not be allowable under more stringent state constitutions. For example, when *Witters I* was remanded to the Supreme Court of Washington (*Witters II,* 1989), the State maintained that the financial gain to the student violated the State's more restrictive state constitution. Similarly, the Supreme Court of Arizona, in *Cain v. Horne* (2008), declared that state vouchers for students with disabilities and children in foster homes that parents could use for tuition at religious schools violated the restrictive language in the state constitution.

The Supreme Court's judgment in *Locke v. Davey* (2004) serves to validate state court decisions such as *Witters II* and *Cain* by noting that permissible government assistance under the federal Establishment Clause does not create an entitlement to the aid under the First Amendment's Free Exercise Clause. In *Locke,* the Court upheld the Supreme Court of Washington's refusal to provide, under its state constitution, a grant to a student majoring in theology at a religious college over his claim that the denial of the grant violated his right to free exercise of religion. The Court conceded that some state actions may be permitted pursuant to the Establishment Clause, but they are not required under the Free Exercise Clause.

One important area where religious colleges and universities have had some success is in gaining eligibility to receive funds from tax-exempt revenue bonds and to use state grants for expenses as part of postsecondary high school option programs. In *Virginia College Building Authority v. Lynn* (2000), the Supreme Court of Virginia pointed out that a pervasively sectarian institution, Regent University, was eligible to participate in the commonwealth's tax-exempt revenue bond program even though secular courses were taught from a religious perspective at the university. Unlike the states of Arizona and Washington, which have restrictive constitutional provisions regarding state aid to religious educational institutions, Virginia's constitution stipulates that aid is permitted to institutions whose primary purpose is to offer collegiate or graduate education and not to provide religious training or theological education. Other than Regent University's School of Divinity, which was excluded under the constitution because it clearly prepared individuals for the ministry, the court was satisfied that the rest of the university's graduate programs that taught secular subjects from a religious perspective did not constitute religious training or theological education. The court thus concluded that the university, except for its School of Divinity, was entitled to participate in the tax-exempt revenue program.

An appellate court in Minnesota reached a similar result involving a state program in *Minnesota Federation of Teachers v. Mammenga* (1993). The court observed that the state could reimburse a pervasively sectarian college for tuition, textbook, and materials costs of high school students who attended its courses pursuant to the state's Post-Secondary Enrollment Options Act. The court was of the opinion that it was unnecessary to evaluate whether the college's pervasive sectarianism should have prohibited it from being reimbursed under state constitution's Establishment Clause. The court indicated that reimbursement could be considered indirect and incidental aid, because the act, in affording high school students an opportunity to take nonsectarian courses at participating colleges, effectively meant that giving students the choice of which postsecondary institution to attend eliminated control by the college over the number of students who chose to take their classes. The court added that the amount of reimbursement that the college received amounted to less than half its actual costs, and officials had separated the reimbursements from other funds in order to ensure that the state benefits were used only for nonsectarian purposes.

In another case, the Fourth Circuit, in *Columbia College v. Oliver* (2001), determined that a private four-year college affiliated with and controlled by the Seventh-Day Adventist Church was entitled to participate in Maryland's Joseph A. Sellinger Program, because it satisfied the program's six neutrality criteria. The court treated the college's participation in the program as constitutional, because the institution was a nonprofit private college or university that was established in Maryland before the statutorily mandated date of July 1, 1970; was approved by the Maryland Higher Education Commission; was accredited; had awarded baccalaureate degrees to at least one graduating class; had programs leading to degrees other than seminary or theology programs; and had submitted each new program to the commission for its approval. In affirming that the college was eligible for state funds, the court relied on *Agostini* and *Mitchell* in explaining that the program satisfied the *Lemon* tripartite test, because it had the secular legislative purpose of supporting private higher education generally; it did not advance religion, because it was founded on neutral criteria; and the

prohibition against using any Sellinger money for religious purposes avoided excessive entanglement. The court left open the issue of whether a finding that the college was pervasively sectarianism would have changed the results.

The Tenth Circuit, in *Colorado Christian University v. Weaver* (2008), has since struck down a state statute that prohibited the awarding of scholarships to students who attended institutions defined as pervasively sectarian, although scholarships remained available to those attending institutions identified as sectarian but not pervasively so. The court ruled that the statute violated the First Amendment Free Exercise and Fourteenth Amendment Due Process Clause rights of students who attended the pervasively sectarian institutions.

Conclusion

The question of whether religiously affiliated colleges and universities are eligible for governmental aid has largely shifted away from analysis under the federal Establishment Clause to comparable provisions in state constitutions. *Locke* underscores the reality that students in states with constitutional provisions more restrictive than the Establishment Clause are not likely to have the same access to public funds as their colleagues in states with less restrictive constitutional provisions.

Ralph D. Mawdsley

See also *Hunt v. McNair*; Religious Colleges and Universities; *Tilton v. Richardson*; *Witters v. Washington Department of Services for the Blind*

Further Readings

Russo, C. J., & Mawdsley, R. D. (2004). *Locke v. Davey:* The Supreme Court limits state aid to students in religious institutions. *School Business Affairs, 70*(7), 36–38.

Russo, C. J., & Mawdsley, R. D. (2005). The United States Supreme Court and aid to students who attend religiously-affiliated institutions of higher education. *Education and Law Journal, 14*, 301–311.

Legal Citations

Agostini v. Felton, 521 U.S. 203 (1997).
Cain v. Horne, 183 P.3d 1269 (Ariz. 2008).

Colorado Christian University v. Weaver, 534 F.3d 1245 (10th Cir. 2008).

Columbia College v. Oliver, 254 F.3d 496 (4th Cir. 2001).

Hunt v. McNair, 413 U.S. 734 (1973).

Lemon v. Kurtzman, 403 U.S. 602 (1971).

Locke v. Davey, 540 U.S. 712 (2004).

Minnesota Federation of Teachers v. Mammenga, 500 N.W.2d 136 (Minn. Ct. App. 1993).

Mitchell v. Helms, 530 U.S. 1296 (2000).

Roemer v. Board of Public Works of Maryland, 426 U.S. 736 (1976).

Tilton v. Richardson, 403 U.S. 672 (1971).

Virginia College Building Authority v. Lynn, 538 S.E.2d 682 (Va. 2000).

Witters v. Washington Department of Services for the Blind, 474 U.S. 481 (*Witters I*, 1986), 771 P.2d 1119 (*Witters II*, Wash. 1989).

Zobrest v. Catalina Foothills School District, 509 U.S. 1 (1993).

STUDENT MORAL DEVELOPMENT

Educators expect students to recognize and respect legal boundaries in higher education environments. Yet, sometimes educators are not prepared to understand how the complexity of students' reasoning abilities may lead to questionable or unacceptable behaviors. Moral development theories, such as those of Jean Piaget, Lawrence Kohlberg, and Carol Gilligan, explore patterns of moral judgments made by individuals that can result in moral actions. These judgments and actions are situated in cultural contexts that hold, whether implicitly or explicitly, expectations and values that are developed over time with increasing experience. To be specific, researchers on moral development suggest that conceptions of what is "right," and their potential legal ramifications, often shift from simplistic to more sophisticated as individuals interact with the world and face the challenges of dealing with conflicting information.

Better understanding these patterns of the development of moral judgment can help educators to respond to student behaviors in ways that are based on individual student perspectives and needs while maximizing their learning experiences. This entry provides basic information about major theories that are relevant to college students' moral development, ways in which these ideas can contribute to educators' understanding of how students may interpret and act on policies and the law, and implications for higher education practice.

Theoretical Background

Jean Piaget

The study of moral development originated in the work of Jean Piaget, the cognitive psychologist often credited with creating stage-based theories of intellectual and moral growth in children that served as a springboard for many to follow. Piaget's study of the moral judgment of children involved examining the "practice and consciousness of rules" (1948, p. 4) that they employed when playing a game of marbles. Piaget's premise was that children actively construct and reconstruct reality based on experiences that call into question their current understanding of reality. According to Piaget, the framework of this sensemaking changes qualitatively as new information that does not fit the current reality requires an adjustment in the framework. This progression of cognitive "structures" or modes that individuals use to reason about the world consistently across contexts is often believed to be at the center of human intellectual development, and it became the hallmark of Piaget's contributions to psychology.

Lawrence Kohlberg

Lawrence Kohlberg, in the tradition of Piaget, sought to investigate moral thinking through longitudinal studies with adolescent, mostly male, boys and adults. Kohlberg assessed moral development by asking participants to settle hypothetical moral dilemmas such as the now-classic "Heinz" scenario. In this story, individuals were asked to decide whether Heinz, whose wife was dying of a terminal illness, should have stolen a drug that may have cured his wife's condition. The scenario offers the fact that the local druggist who discovered the medicine had charged several times his cost and that Heinz had been able only to raise a portion of the needed funds. Reactions to this dilemma allowed Kohlberg to focus on how respondents came to resolutions. He viewed this process of reasoning as more important than the solution itself in the investigation of cognitive or moral development.

Kohlberg's (1976, 1981) theory of moral reasoning concluded that individuals undergo development in a three-level, six-stage sequence. Kohlberg labeled Level 1 as "preconventional"; its two stages describe individuals making moral judgments based on following rules, avoiding punishment, and finding what is "fair." The difference between the two stages in this level is that in Stage 1, deference is given to authorities to dictate what is "right," while in Stage 2, the individual recognizes that everyone may not agree on what is right and bases decisions on self-interests. At this level, rules and expectations are viewed as external to self. Level 2, named the "conventional" level, also has two stages. Stage 3 involves concern for doing what is considered characteristically "good" and having motives that appear acceptable to others. In Stage 4, the society within which individuals live and the rules within them, the larger social order, become priorities. In this level, the self has internalized the rules and expectations of others at this level. Finally, Level 3, also known as the "postconventional" level, contains Stages 5 and 6. In Stage 5, human rights, based on social agreements resulting from a democratic process, are paramount. Stage 6, viewed as a more theoretical stage, because Kohlberg found little evidence to support its existence, hinges on individuals committing to justice by supporting the spirit of "universal principles" that should apply to everyone and every situation. This level involves individuals mediating between self-chosen and others' rules and expectations to make informed judgments.

Carol Gilligan

Carol Gilligan (1982) questioned Kohlberg's emphasis on the male, privileged populations involved in his study and his assumptions about the generalizability of his findings to women. In fact, when women's moral development was measured using Kohlberg's model, they often appeared "less developed." Gilligan's research with girls and boys along with women and men uncovered some patterns related to moral development that differed from those identified by Kohlberg. While Kohlberg's research results emphasized a moral inclination toward ideal "justice" or obligation to rights, narratives from Gilligan's interviews with girls and women revealed an orientation that placed more value on relationships than justice, or,

in her words, an "ethic of care" (pp. 73–74) and obligation to others. While Gilligan did not claim such tendencies were gender exclusive, she aimed to illuminate new possibilities for understanding the various ways in which humans construct moral decision making.

Gilligan's theory was the outcome of several studies that focused on judgment making in the context of various moral conflicts, whether real or hypothetical in nature, and their relationship to the self. Her theory contains three levels and two transitions. At Level 1, individuals focus on the preservation of self and survival. The transition from the first into the second level is centered on moving away from selfish desires and toward increasing responsibility and connection to others. In Level 2, individuals' desire to be in relationships with others may override their own interests, resulting in "self-sacrifice," or putting "good" above the self. The transition between Levels 2 and 3 starts to exhibit more balance between others and self, or as Gilligan puts it, moving "from goodness to truth" (p. 82). Finally, in Level 3, individuals prioritize "nonviolence" (pp. 103–104), the avoidance of hurt to self or others, as the primary criterion for making moral decisions.

Application to Students

When applying the developmental concepts described above to the perspectives and actions of students in higher education, it becomes clear that the moral perspective of specific students provides a lens through which they can make sense of dilemmas and conflicts, thereby interpreting the role of policies and the law. Depending on students' moral orientation and developmental levels, the importance of laws may even be construed as different from university policies that are more local in nature and based on community needs and standards.

Kohlberg believed that children usually reason at Stages 1 and 2, while adults typically operate at Stages 3 and 4 (Rich & DeVitis, 1994). Therefore, it can reasonably be assumed that college students should generally be functioning between Stages 2 and 4. Take, for example, the all-too-common practice of college students obtaining fake identification cards for the purpose of getting into bars or accessing alcohol when they are under the legal drinking age. Such actions raise a series of potential questions about the impact of their possibly violating the law and institutional policies that may lead to disciplinary sanctions. Students at Kohlberg's Level 2 would be operating primarily from the perspective of self-interest. At this stage, students may view the law as conflicting with what "everybody else is doing" and thus what they should also have a right to do. Moreover, at this level, fairness is relative, and self-interests are viewed as equal in value to the interests of others. However, at Stage 4, where individuals take responsibility for upholding social obligations that include the law, purchasing invalid drivers' licenses would be inconsistent with maintaining commitment to the social contract and ideal justice. The concern for the student at this stage is not "everybody is doing it" but "what if everyone did it?" (Kohlberg, 1981, p. 411).

Another consideration is Gilligan's assertion that students may view the conditions of "rightness" in terms of relationships with others. By way of illustration, the impetus for students to turn down their stereos or to conform to policies set forth by their residence hall leaders may be based on connection with others or a commitment to "shared norms and expectations" (1982, p. 79) more than justice or the notion of the right to independent judgment.

To be sure, moral judgments do not always translate into consistent moral actions. As humans develop reasoning skills, they often come to new understandings that may take time to progress into regularized behaviors.

Implications for Higher Education Practice

Educators who desire optimal learning outcomes when dealing with student violations of laws or policies should bear in mind the moral judgment process behind student actions. Students who decide to experiment with marijuana or other drugs in their residence halls, to cheat on tests, or to destroy the property of others—actions that may carry significant legal sanctions including dismissal or prosecution—are often operating from a perspective that accepts such risks as tolerable or even justifiable. While university officials likely have obligations to address legal violations using legal parameters, additional student sanctions can be utilized for educational purposes. In addition, violations of internal community standards or

policies, such as respecting quiet hours in residence halls in the example mentioned earlier, can be dealt with creatively while taking aim at student learning and development. Finding out why students took the moral actions they did may illuminate how individuals construct what is "right." Once this information is determined, college and university officials can call for administrative and/or judicial actions that acknowledge, yet challenge, students' current approach to moral judgment, potentially prompting consideration of alternative views or more sophisticated perspectives.

Michele M. Welkener

See also Disciplinary Sanctions and Due Process Rights

Further Readings

Gilligan, C. (1982). *In a different voice: Psychological theory and women's development.* Cambridge, MA: Harvard University Press.

Kohlberg, L. (1976). Moral stages and moralization: The cognitive-developmental approach. In T. Lickona (Ed.), *Moral development and behavior: Theory, research, and social issues* (pp. 31–53). New York: Holt, Rinehart & Winston.

Kohlberg, L. (1981). *Essays on moral development: The philosophy of moral development.* San Francisco: Harper & Row.

Piaget, J. (1948). *The moral judgment of the child.* Glencoe, IL: The Free Press.

Rich, J. M., & DeVitis, J. (1994). *Theories of moral development* (2nd ed.). Springfield, IL: Charles C Thomas.

STUDENT PRESS

As tangible forms of free speech and expression, student newspapers and other publications at public colleges and universities enjoy considerable protection under the First Amendment. Student publications at these institutions, including officially recognized newspapers and other publications that students produce off campus, are entitled to First Amendment protection. Because student newspapers at private institutions have only those rights identified in institutional policies, there is a dearth of litigation in these schools.

In light of the significant question surrounding the free speech and expression rights of students who are involved with the production of newspapers, this entry examines key legal issues and representative litigation with regard to student publications at public colleges and universities.

U.S. Supreme Court's Ruling in a Higher Education Case

Papish v. Board of Curators of the University of Missouri (1973) was the U.S. Supreme Court's first, and only, case involving a newspaper on a college or university campus. In *Papish,* officials at a state university expelled a graduate student for distributing an off-campus newspaper that violated the institution's policy against "indecent speech." Specifically, the newspaper contained a cartoon depicting the Statue of Liberty being raped by a policeman and a newspaper article containing offensive language. A federal trial court and the Eighth Circuit upheld the student's expulsion, but the Supreme Court reversed in her behalf. The Court ruled that the mere dissemination of ideas on a state university campus could not be shut off in the name of conventions of decency alone, regardless of how offensive those ideas may have been.

Circuit Court Decisions in Higher Education

Less than a month after *Papish,* the Fourth Circuit, in *Joyner v. Whiting* (1973), decided that officials at a public, predominantly Black university in North Carolina had no obligation to establish student newspapers. However, the court added that if officials did allow student newspapers, the officials could not terminate the newspapers' publication on the basis of dissatisfaction with their editorial content. *Joyner* involved an editorial in which Black students criticized the admission of White students in the light of the growing population of White students on campus. Even though the president of the university disagreed with this perspective, the court directed him to restore funding to the student newspaper. The court interpreted the president's actions as abridging the students' freedom of the press in violation of the First Amendment. Likewise, in *Schiff v. Williams* (1975), the Fifth Circuit declared that a public university could not control the content of a student newspaper except under "special circumstances." The court thus affirmed that university officials could not remove students from their positions as editors of the campus newspaper due to disagreements over the way in which the students managed the newspaper.

In *Stanley v. McGrath* (1983), the Eighth Circuit reviewed the actions of officials at a public university in Minnesota who changed the funding mechanism for the student newspaper after its staff published a satire issue that contained crude sexual language and offensive remarks about religious and ethnic groups. Although the level of funding was not reduced, officials instituted a policy that allowed students who disapproved of the newspaper to receive a refund for that portion of their services fee that otherwise would have contributed to funding the newspaper. While reiterating that officials were not required to support a student newspaper, the court pointed out that the actions of university officials violated the First Amendment, because their actions were motivated by dissatisfaction with the paper's content, an impermissible violation of the newspaper staff's freedom of expression.

In other cases, courts have agreed that because campus newspapers at public colleges and universities are independent entities rather than governmental actors, student editors are free to make independent editorial comments. For instance, in *Sinn v. The Daily Nebraskan* (1987), individuals unsuccessfully sued a student newspaper in Nebraska for refusing to print advertisements in which people seeking roommates proclaimed their sexual orientations. The Eighth Circuit affirmed that because the newspaper's editors were not state actors, they could not be compelled to publish advertisements that conflicted with their advertising policy.

U.S. Supreme Court's Ruling in *Hazelwood v. Kuhlmeier*

In *Hazelwood School District v. Kuhlmeier* (1988), the U.S. Supreme Court upheld the legality of the actions of a high school principal who excluded two articles from a newspaper that students produced as part of a journalism class that was part of the school's curriculum. One of the articles involved teen pregnancy, while the other involved the impact of divorce on the children of couples who divorce. Officials were concerned that although no students were mentioned by name in the articles, the students mentioned might have been easily identified in the community. Consequently, the principal directed that the articles not be printed.

The *Hazelwood* Court found that because the student newspaper was part of the curriculum, officials could limit its style and content as long as their actions were reasonably related to a legitimate pedagogical concern. According to the ruling in *Hazelwood*, schools are not required to print material incompatible with their basic educational mission. It is interesting that in a footnote acknowledging the obvious—that the dispute at bar was set in a secondary school—the Court noted that it did not have to address whether the actions of officials in college and university settings were entitled to similar deference.

Application of *Hazelwood* to Student Publications in Higher Education

Two more recent cases, *Kincaid v. Gibson* (2001) and *Hosty v. Carter* (2005), are discussed below in light of judicial application of the Supreme Court's ruling in *Hazelwood*. Federal courts are split with regard to whether *Hazelwood* should apply in cases involving student publications at the college and university level. In *Kincaid*, the Sixth Circuit was of the opinion that *Hazelwood* was inapplicable in university settings. The issue in *Kincaid* was that university officials refused to distribute copies of the student yearbook, asserting that it was of poor quality and that the editors strayed beyond the traditional themes that the book had followed in the past. The Sixth Circuit, in an en banc decision (meaning that all of the members of the court participated in the decision), concluded that because the yearbook was a limited open forum that granted considerable deference to the free speech rights of students, the editors were free to make decisions about the yearbook's content, and officials lacked the power to direct its content.

On the other hand, in the immediate aftermath of *Hazelwood*, the Eleventh Circuit treated it as controlling precedent in *Alabama Student Party v. Student Government Association of the University of Alabama* (1989), a case involving restrictions that a student government association placed on campaign activities in student elections. The court

considered the constitutionality of university time, manner, and place rules that restricted the distribution of campus literature to three days before elections took place and only at residences or outside of campus buildings, prohibited distribution of campaign literature on election days, and limited open forums of discussion or debates to the weeks of election. In upholding the rules, the court found them to be reasonably related to the legitimate interests of university officials in minimizing the disruptive effect of campus electioneering.

More recently, the Seventh Circuit applied *Hazelwood* to a case involving a university newspaper in *Hosty*. *Hosty*, which has been subject to considerable academic commentary, arose when a dean directed staff at a printing company not to produce copies of the newspaper without his approval. The dean made this directive after student editors had published what university officials described as irresponsible and defamatory journalism; it attacked the dean's integrity in a disagreement over institutional funds and hiring practices, particularly in not renewing the employment contract of the newspaper's faculty moderator. As a result, the newspaper ceased operations for a time but did resume publication with a new editorial staff.

In declining to follow *Kincaid*, an en banc panel in *Hosty* observed that *Hazelwood* applied to the dispute. The court conceded that although the editors and context were different from those in *Hazelwood*, the *Hazelwood* precedent applied insofar as the rights of student editors in higher education were unclear. The court also thought that the editors could not sue the dean even though he violated their First Amendment rights by limiting what they could publish, because their rights were unclear at that time, especially because the costs associated with publishing the newspaper were paid for with student activity fees that university officials collected. The court determined that the dean was entitled to qualified immunity shielding him from personal liability, because he acted to prevent the students from publishing material that he deemed inappropriate while acting in his official capacity as dean rather than as a private citizen.

In light of the conflicting perspectives of federal circuits over the appropriate level of free speech to which they are entitled, it will be interesting to see whether the Supreme Court intervenes in a dispute clarifying the rights of students who are involved with campus publications.

Richard Fossey

See also Free Speech and Expression Rights of Students; *Papish v. Board of Curators of the University of Missouri*

Further Readings

Fiore, M. J. (2002). Trampling the "marketplace of ideas": The case of extending *Hazelwood* to college campuses. *University of Pennsylvania Law Review, 150,* 1915–1968.

Lyons, J. B. (2006). Defining freedom of the college press after *Hosty v. Carter. Vanderbilt Law Review, 59,* 1771–1810.

Legal Citations

Alabama Student Party v. Student Government Association of the University of Alabama, 867 F.2d 1344 (11th Cir. 1989).

Hazelwood School District v. Kuhlmeier, 484 U.S. 260 (1988).

Hosty v. Carter, 412 F.3d 731 (7th Cir. 2005), *cert. denied,* 546 U.S. 1169 (2006).

Joyner v. Whiting, 477 F.2d 456, 460 (4th Cir. 1973).

Kincaid v. Gibson, 236 F.3d 342 (6th Cir. 2001).

Papish v. Board of Curators of the University of Missouri, 410 U.S. 667 (1973).

Schiff v. Williams, 519 F.2d 257 (5th Cir. 1975), *cert. denied,* 423 U.S. 834 (1975).

Sinn v. The Daily Nebraskan, 829 F.2d 662 (8th Cir. 1987).

Stanley v. McGrath, 719 F.2d 279 (8th Cir. 1983).

STUDENT RECORDS

See Family Educational Rights and Privacy Act

STUDENT SUICIDES

In the early years of the 21st century, administrators in institutions of higher learning have become increasingly concerned about the phenomenon of student suicides on their campuses. This concern was prompted in part by a highly publicized suit between the Massachusetts Institute of Technology and the family of a student who committed suicide (*Shin v. Massachusetts Institute of Technology,* 2005) and a 2002 judgment involving Ferrum College in Virginia, in which a federal trial court ruled that the estate of a student who killed himself by hanging had made out a cause of action for negligence against the college and one of its administrators (*Schieszler v. Ferrum College,* 2002). The rising suicide rate for young people also contributed to this concern (Centers for Disease Control and Prevention, 2007). In fact, between 2000 and 2008, a variety of law review articles examined liability issues pertaining to suicide among college students. This entry reviews several legal rulings dealing with suicides by college students and discusses the liability of educational institutions for student suicides.

As of 2008, though, only a handful of published court decisions addressed the issue of institutional liability for the suicide death of college or university students. In two of these cases, state courts decided that suicide is an intervening cause that precludes third-party liability in their respective jurisdictions (*Bogust v. Iverson,* 1960; *Jain v. State,* 2000). In a third case, the Supreme Court of Wyoming found that University of Wyoming employees were immune from liability for a student's suicide (*White v. University of Wyoming,* 1998).

On the other hand, in *Wallace v. Broyles* (1998), a case involving the suicide death of a varsity athlete at the University of Arkansas, the Supreme Court of Arkansas was of the opinion that that the decedent's mother could proceed with a suit against athletic officials there on the basis of allegations that they gave her son prescription pain medication in violation of federal drug-dispensing laws. Dissenting justices argued that there was no evidence that the defendants actually gave the athlete prescription medications and that the majority had proceeded on the basis of "irrelevant, albeit unsavory, practices" in the athletic department (p. 719).

In addition, in *Schieszler,* a federal trial court in Virginia pointed out that the estate of a first-year student who committed suicide presented sufficient evidence to demonstrate that college officials were in a "special relationship" with the student, that they were aware that he was in danger of committing suicide, and that they failed to take reasonable precautions to prevent the suicide from occurring. The court reached this conclusion despite the fact that the college's dean of students responded immediately on learning that the student was suicidal by going to the student's dormitory room and talking with both him and his girlfriend. Moreover, the court was not satisfied even though the dean obtained a written promise from the student not to attempt suicide and followed up by making arrangements for a counseling agency to provide him with counseling.

The fact that only a few courts have issued published opinions addressing institutional liability for student suicides at colleges and universities notwithstanding, at least 17 court cases have considered this issue in the context of elementary or secondary schools. These courts handed down judgments that should be of interest to officials at colleges and universities. Some of these cases proceeded under common negligence principles, others alleged constitutional violations, and another group alleged both state tort claims and federal constitutional violations.

In two articles addressing the liability of school systems for student suicides, Zirkel and Fossey (2004, 2005) observed that most decisions were rendered in favor of boards. In their 2005 article, the authors wrote that educators had little to fear from suits arising from student suicides, because most courts were "generally inhospitable to plaintiffs seeking to hold educators liable for a student's suicide death," regardless of whether boards were sued in negligence or for constitutional violations (Zirkel & Fossey, 2005, p. 497). School boards prevailed in these cases on a variety of grounds, including statutory immunity and the tort principle that suicide is an intervening cause that forecloses tort liability for individuals' suicides.

Suicide by students in higher education has sometimes been described as an epidemic. Yet, the rates for the traditional college-student age group are actually lower than for older Americans. Among males, the highest rate of suicide is among individuals aged 75 and older. Among women, suicide rates are highest for individuals in their 40s and 50s (Centers for Disease Control and Prevention, 2008).

Regardless of the liability risk, commentators have urged officials in institutions of higher education to implement formal suicide-prevention policies with specific guidelines for intervention for suicidal students and for contacting their parents in appropriate circumstances (Moore, 2007; Wei, 2008). Based on analyses of student suicide cases involving elementary and secondary schools and published cases involving the suicide of college and university students, American courts do not appear particularly receptive to suits seeking to render colleges or universities liable for the suicide deaths of their students.

Richard Fossey

Further Readings

Centers for Disease Control and Prevention. (2007). Suicide trends among youths and young adults aged 10–24 years—United States, 1990–2004. *Morbidity and Mortality Weekly Report, 56,* 905–908.

Centers for Disease Control and Prevention. (2008, Summer). *Suicide: Facts at a glance.* Retrieved June 4, 2008, from http://www.cdc.gov/ncipc/dvp/Suicide/suicide_data_sheet.pdf

Fossey, R., & Zirkel, P. A. (2004). Liability for a student suicide in the wake of *Eisel. Texas Wesleyan Law Review, 10,* 403–439.

Moore, H. E. (2007). Note: University liability when students commit suicide: Expanding the scope of the special relationship. *Indiana Law Review, 40,* 423–451.

Wei, M. (2008). College and university policy and procedural responses to students at risk of suicide. *Journal of College and University Law, 34,* 285–318.

Zirkel, P. A., & Fossey, R. (2005). Liability for student suicide. *Education Law Reporter, 197,* 489–497.

Legal Citations

Bogust v. Iverson, 102 N.W.2d 228 (Wis. 1960).

Jain v. State, 617 N.W.2d 293 (Iowa 2000).

Schieszler v. Ferrum College, 236 F. Supp. 2d 602, 609 (W.D. Va. 2002).

Shin v. Massachusetts Institute of Technology, No. 020403, 2005 WL 1869101, at 13 (Mass. Super. Ct. June 27, 2005).

Wallace v. Broyles, 961 S.W.2d 712 (Ark. 1998).

White v. University of Wyoming, 954 P.2d 983 (Wyo. 1998).

STUDENT TEACHERS, RIGHTS OF

Students who seek teacher certification through university approval must successfully complete the prerequisite coursework, a field experience course, and a final student teaching internship in order to gain licensure for teaching purposes. Clearly, student teaching is a high-stakes enterprise that represents the culmination of a student's teacher preparation program and serves as the prerequisite to teacher certification. Legislation in each of the 50 states provides institutions of higher education with express or implied authority for this purpose. On occasion, the representatives of the sponsoring institutions of higher education or the cooperating school boards make decisions that deprive students from colleges or schools of education of the opportunity to begin or complete student teaching, thereby leading to litigation. In light of emerging questions surrounding this key topic, this entry examines legal issues involving the rights of student teachers.

Representative Litigation

The following four cases are representative examples of published judicial opinions that resulted when student teachers sued institutions of higher learning or school boards. The issues in these cases include fulfillment of prerequisites for participation in student teaching, faculty evaluations of student teachers' teaching skills, behavior of student teachers at student teaching sites not directly related to the classes they teach, and student teachers' behavior outside the school site or classroom.

In *Hunt v. University of Alaska* (2002), officials at a public university refused to allow an elementary education major with a 3.58 grade point average, including the prerequisite courses and practicum for student teaching, to participate in student teaching. The facts revealed that the student failed the reading and writing parts of the Praxis examination, which is usually not required until after completion of the degree. The Supreme Court of Alaska affirmed that the faculty could impose this prerequisite to the student's participation, because his application essays caused concern regarding his language skills.

Embrey v. Central State University (1991) involved another education major, at a private college, who received a final grade of "F" for student teaching without receiving any written evaluations during the semester. Although the applicable policy called for periodic meetings between the

supervising faculty member and the student teacher, the faculty member had expressed concerns about the student's performance only to the cooperating teacher. Even so, an appellate court in Ohio upheld the student's dismissal from the program, because she did not pass the course.

In *Leone v. Whitford* (2007), a student teacher in Connecticut ripped down the bulletin board she had been working on after the cooperating teacher suggested changes. A week later, a special university committee conducted a hearing with the student teacher concerning the incident and her previous pattern of confrontational behavior. The resulting decision was to withdraw her from the student teaching placement and the certification program and to offer her the opportunity to work on the department's Web page as an independent study project to fulfill the B.S. degree in art education with no certification. When the student teacher sued the university and officials on a variety of claims, the federal trial court granted their motion for summary judgment on the ground that she failed to establish that she had a fundamental right to earn her degree.

The final case, *Lai v. Board of Trustees of East Carolina University* (1971), involved a student teacher who was arrested in another state and charged with drug possession. However, the prosecution dropped the charges. Then, the student submitted a student teaching application that the director rejected. Subsequently, at the direction of the university president, the education committee provided the student with notice and a hearing wherein he admitted that he had smoked marijuana, resulting in affirming the director's decision. In the ensuing litigation, a federal trial court in North Carolina granted the university's motion for summary judgment in light of this and other factors, such as the student's overall academic status and failure to fulfill his prior assignments.

Practical Considerations for Student Teachers

A review and analysis of the published case law yields some useful points for student teachers to consider should they find themselves in similar situations. First, student teachers need to think carefully before proceeding with litigation. The costs of litigation, including not only attorney fees and court costs but also the often underestimated time commitment and the adversarial nature of proceedings are considerable and draining. Moreover, the outcomes of such suits have often been in favor of the defendant institutions. More specifically, of the 28 published cases to this point, 23 were resolved in favor of colleges and universities on all counts.

The five cases that were not completely in favor of the institutions were outliers in terms of factual or legal circumstances. In *Miller v. Dailey* (1902), the earliest published opinion on student teaching, a student successfully challenged his exclusion from a program, because officials had failed to provide any evaluation before dismissing him from the program. This case is outside the modern mainstream of the pertinent published decisions, because it is the earliest case in student teaching litigation, and the proinstitution trend is more pronounced in the current judicial climate. The second case, *Moore v. Gaston County Board of Education* (1973), was factually distinctive, because the plaintiff was substituting for a regular teacher and thus was within the role of an employee rather than in the marginal position of student teacher. The third decision, *Betts v. Ann Arbor Public Schools* (1978), interpreted "employee" in terms of state disability law, a broader view than in most student teaching cases, perhaps because of the severity of the eye injury that the plaintiff had sustained while serving as a student teacher and for which he had entered a workers' compensation claim. The fourth dispute, *Burns v. Slippery Rock University* (2007), was a limited and inconclusive victory for the student teacher in a dispute over whether she could successfully complete a field experience. Finally, the fifth case, which reached the U.S. Supreme Court, *Doe v. Gonzaga University* (2001), had a mixed outcome, where both the university and the student teacher scored partial victories in a disagreement over the release of information about the plaintiff that impacted his ability to earn certification.

Difference Between Private and Public Institutions as Defendants

The second consideration for student teachers as plaintiffs is whether the educational institution they are suing is public or private, because that represents a major contributing factor in the avenues of litigation that they might seek. The primary claims that potential plaintiffs for student teaching cases immediately identify are First Amendment freedom of speech, Fourth Amendment privacy, and the Fourteenth Amendment protections against discrimination, such as those afforded by the Equal Protection Clause, and arbitrary action under the Due Process Clause, which provides for procedural and substantive fair play. None of these constitutional rights applies to students at private colleges, universities, and cooperating schools, regardless of whether they receive federal funds. Instead, the primary claim against private institutions is for breach of contract, which is based on the official institutional policies applicable to student teaching.

Doctrine of Deference

Similarly important for student teachers to consider is the applicable deference doctrine. In general, whether it is a constitutional case or a breach of contract case, courts have consistently accorded notable latitude to educational institutions, including school districts, and even more so for colleges and universities. This deference is attributable to the traditional posture of courts in relation to administrative agencies and the additional special responsibility of school districts to protect youth in their charge and, more strongly, the ivory-tower isolation of colleges and universities. In issues of subjective academic judgment, which is often the case in student teaching litigation, the courts are particularly likely to abstain from intruding on the defendant institution's judgment based on the specialized expertise of educators. Following the lead of the Supreme Court, which concluded that the clinical phase of medical school, including issues of patient relations and personal hygiene, were academic issues (*Board of Curators of University of Missouri v. Horowitz*, 1978), the lower courts stretched the umbrella of academic abstention to cover most matters in student teaching.

Following are the two illustrative cases and the outcomes: In the first case (*Hunt v. University of Alaska*, 2002), reviewed earlier, the state Supreme Court affirmed the dismissal of the student teacher's suit, thereby summarily rejecting his constitutional and contractual claims while giving the defendant university the benefit of the doubt under the deference doctrine. The court also affirmed the earlier order directing the student teacher to pay part of the university's attorney fees under the state's rules of civil procedure, a rule he relied on erroneously.

Similarly, an appellate court in Ohio, in another case that was reviewed earlier, affirmed a judgment that was adverse to a former student teacher (*Embrey v. Central State University,* 1991). While acknowledging that the supervising faculty member was remiss in not fulfilling the periodic-meeting policy, the court was of the view that any breach was not material, because the student had reason to know of the specific performance criteria and had failed to fulfill them. Again, judicial deference to academic discretion was obvious in the outcome.

Pro Se Representation

Student teachers who are represented by attorneys who follow the nuances of the law in student teachers' respective states are more successful than those who sue "pro se," that is, without legal counsel. Although, as persons above the age of majority, student teachers have the option to proceed in court pro se, they do so at considerable risk. The complexities include not only the laws and precedents that are the basis for a student teacher's case but also the procedures of the state or federal court in which student teacher sues. For example, in one of the 28 cases published between 1902 and 2007, the court dismissed the student teacher's pro se suit against his cooperating school board (*Cornell v. Pleasant Grove Independent School District,* 2005), because his statement of the charges did not conform to the specificity requirements of the pertinent pleading process. In another case (*Holt v. Munitz,* 1996), the pro se plaintiff lost his First Amendment free-speech case against a public university, relying on the adverse precedents that apply to employees rather than the more favorable precedents that apply to students. In a third such situation (*Arko v. U.S. Air Force Reserve Officer Training Program,* 1987), a disgruntled former student teacher filed suit under two provisions of the U.S. Constitution and two federal statutes but did not get his day in court on any of them, because, without the benefit of any attorney's expertise, he filed after the applicable

limitations period for each of them had expired. The aforementioned *Hunt v. University of Alaska* (2002) was another pro se suit that ended badly for the student teacher.

The lesson for student teachers, then, is clear: If one runs into high-stakes problems with regard to student teaching, individuals need to know both their legal rights and limitations.

Institutional Considerations

Two considerations warrant attention on the institutional side. First, officials on school boards and at public universities need, as a constitutional matter, to put a priority on procedural due process, particularly when the issue is disciplinary rather than academic. Private institutions should consider the same as a matter of moral and professional imperative, legal claims under breach of contract, or sheer competitiveness for quality candidates. The particular procedures include both adequate notice, prior to depriving a student or course credits or certification, of specific charges and hearings that satisfy the rudimentary notion of fair play.

Second, whether a matter of constitutional, contractual, or common law, substantive due process also merits attention. The analog to procedural fairness is substantive reasonableness, meaning that decisions and actions are neither arbitrary nor capricious. Within these broad principles, the number and outcomes of pertinent published cases suggest that institutional officials, whether in higher education or in school districts, need not be paralyzed by fear of litigation initiated by student teachers.

Zorka Karanxha and Perry A. Zirkel

See also Academic Abstention; Academic Freedom; *Board of Curators of the University of Missouri v. Horowitz*; Due Process, Substantive and Procedural

Further Readings

Karanxha, Z., & Zirkel, P. A. (2008). The case law on student teachers' rights. *Action in Teacher Education, 30*(2), 46–58.

Karanxha, Z., & Zirkel, P. A. (2008). Student teachers' diversity rights: The case law. In C. J. Craig & L. Deretchin (Eds.), *Teacher education yearbook: Imagining a renaissance in teacher education* (pp. 201–212). Lanham, MD: Rowman & Littlefield Education.

Legal Citations

Arko v. U.S. Air Force Reserve Officer Training Program, 661 F. Supp. 31 (D. Colo. 1987).

Betts v. Ann Arbor Public Schools, 271 N.W.2d 498 (Mich. 1978).

Board of Curators of University of Missouri v. Horowitz, 435 U.S. 78 (1978).

Burns v. Slippery Rock University, 2007 WL 2317310 (W.D. Pa. 2007), *on reconsideration*, 2007 WL 2463402 (W.D. Pa. 2007).

Cornell v. Pleasant Grove Independent School District, 2005 WL 2277396 (E.D. Tex. 2005).

Doe v. Gonzaga University, 24 P.3d 390 (Wash. 2001), *rev'd in part, sub nom. Gonzaga University v. Doe*, 536 U.S. 273 (2002).

Embrey v. Central State University, 1991 WL 224228 (Ohio Ct. App. 1991).

Holt v. Munitz, 87 F.3d 1319 (9th Cir. 1996).

Hunt v. University of Alaska, 52 P.3d 739 (Alaska 2002).

Lai v. Board of Trustees of East Carolina University, 320 F. Supp. 904 (E.D.N.C. 1971).

Leone v. Whitford, 2007 WL 1191347 (D. Conn. 2007).

Miller v. Dailey, 68 P. 1029 (Cal. 1902).

Moore v. Gaston County Board of Education, 357 F. Supp. 1037 (W.D.N.C. 1973).

Sweatt v. Painter

In *Brown v. Board of Education, Topeka* (1954), the U.S. Supreme Court overruled the "separate but equal" doctrine that it had articulated in the late 19th century in *Plessy v. Ferguson* (1896). This "separate but equal" doctrine became the legal basis for racial segregation in schools, colleges, universities, and the wider American society. In *Brown*, the Court, building on its earlier precedent from disputes in higher education, declared that racially segregated schools violated the Equal Protection Clause of the Fourteenth Amendment.

Less well known than *Brown* is a series of earlier cases in which the Supreme Court undermined racial segregation in higher education: *Missouri ex rel. Gaines v. Canada* (1938) and the companion cases of *McLaurin v. Oklahoma State Regents for Higher Education* (1950) and *Sweatt v. Painter* (1950). In *Sweatt*, perhaps the most famous of these cases, the Court ruled that officials at the University of Texas had violated the Equal Protection Clause of the Fourteenth Amendment in denying admission to the law school to Heman Sweatt, an African American, because of his race. Rejecting the efforts of officials to provide a separate law school for African Americans as an acceptable alternative, the Court held that the University of Texas had to admit him to its law school. In light of the impact that *Sweatt* played in dismantling segregated higher education and beyond, this entry reviews its background and the Court's analysis in ruling.

Facts of the Case

Heman Sweatt sought admission to the University of Texas Law School in 1946, but his application was rejected solely because of his race. Sweatt then sued in state court, seeking an injunction to require law school officials to admit him to study. At the time Sweatt filed suit, there was no law school in the state of Texas for African Americans. A trial court acknowledged that Texas violated Sweatt's right to equal protection by denying him an opportunity to obtain a legal education while providing that opportunity to Whites. Even so, the court did not grant Sweatt the relief that he sought. Instead, the court continued Sweatt's suit for six months to give the State of Texas time to establish a separate law school for African Americans.

In 1947, the state legislature enacted legislation establishing the Texas State University "for the sole purpose of creating a separate but equal school of law for Negroes and to prevent Heman Sweatt's admission to the University of Texas Law School" (Butler, 1997, p. 45). The law school admitted its first class of students that same year, and in 1950 graduated its first student, Henry Doyle. Doyle later became the first African American to be appointed to a state appellate court in Texas.

When Sweatt refused to enroll in the newly created law school, a state trial court maintained that the school for African Americans offered him an opportunity for studying law that was substantially equivalent to the one provided to White students at the University of Texas Law School. Accordingly, the court denied Sweatt's request for relief, and an appellate court affirmed in favor of the law school. After the Supreme Court of Texas refused Sweatt's application for a writ of error in 1948, he appealed to the U.S. Supreme Court, which granted certiorari. In response to Sweatt's suit, the attorneys general for 11 Southern states filed amici curiae, literally, "friend of the court," briefs supporting Texas's position that it had no constitutional duty to admit the plaintiff to the University of Texas Law School.

The Supreme Court's Ruling

In a unanimous decision authored by Chief Justice Vinson, the Supreme Court reversed in favor of Sweatt, reasoning that the State of Texas had not provided him with opportunities to study law that were "substantially equal" to those afforded to White students who were eligible for admission to the University of Texas Law School. The Court ruled that on the basis of the size of the faculty, the array of courses, the opportunities for specialization in different areas of the law, the size of the student body, the scope of the library, and the availability of a scholarly law review and similar activities, the University of Texas Law School was superior to the newly established law school for African Americans. The Court added that the University of Texas Law School had a far greater degree of the qualities that were incapable of objective measurement but that made for greatness in a law school. According to the Court, the qualities that could not be measured included the reputation of the faculty, the experience of the administration, the position and influence of the school's alumni, its standing in the community, its traditions, and its prestige.

The Supreme Court elaborated on its rationale by pointing out that a law school cannot be effective if it operates in isolation from the individuals and institutions with which the law interacts. From the Court's perspective, few students would have chosen to study law in an academic vacuum wherein they were removed from the interplay of ideas and the exchange of views with which the law is concerned. As the Court observed, the law school where the State of Texas was willing to allow Sweatt to study would have excluded racial groups that made up 85% of the state's population and most of the lawyers, witnesses, jurors, judges, and other officials with whom Sweatt would inevitably have been dealing when he became a lawyer. In light of the substantial and significant segment of society that the actions of state and law school officials sought to exclude, the Court rejected the notion that the education they offered Sweatt was substantially equal to that which he would have received had he been admitted to the University of Texas Law School.

Based on a finding of inequality in educational opportunities, the Supreme Court concluded that the Equal Protection Clause required the State of Texas to admit Heman Sweatt to the University of Texas Law School. The Court's rationale considered both tangible and intangible factors, presaging similar analysis in *Brown*. In noting that the law school for African Americans was not equal to the state's premier law school, the Court implied that the establishment of professional schools solely for African Americans could never be considered equal for purposes of Fourteenth Amendment analysis by the federal courts.

The law school that the Texas legislature founded for African Americans in 1947 continued to operate and became one of the nation's leading law schools for producing African American law graduates. In 1976, the law school was renamed Thurgood Marshall School of Law in honor of Supreme Court Justice Thurgood Marshall. It is located on the campus of Texas Southern University in Houston, Texas, and has one of the most racially and ethnically diverse student bodies of any law school in the United States.

Richard Fossey

See also Equal Protection Analysis; Fourteenth Amendment; *McLaurin v. Oklahoma State Regents for Higher Education*

Further Readings

Butler, M. L. (1997). The history of Texas Southern University Thurgood Marshall School of Law: "The house that Sweatt built." *Thurgood Marshall Law Review, 23*, 45–53.

Legal Citations

Brown v. Board of Education, Topeka, 347 U.S. 483 (1954).

McLaurin v. Oklahoma State Regents for Higher Education, 339 U.S. 637 (1950).

Missouri ex rel. Gaines v. Canada, 305 U.S. 377 (1938).

Plessy v. Ferguson, 163 U.S. 537 (1896).

Sweatt v. Painter, 339 U.S. 629 (1950).

SWEATT V. PAINTER

Sweatt, decided on the same day as *McLaurin v. Oklahoma*, stands out because in it the Supreme Court invalidated racial segregation in higher education.

Supreme Court of the United States

SWEATT

v.

PAINTER

339 U.S. 629

Argued April 4, 1950

Decided June 5, 1950

Rehearing Denied Oct. 9, 1950

Mr. Chief Justice VINSON delivered the opinion of the Court.

This case and *McLaurin v. Oklahoma State Regents* present different aspects of this general question: To what extent does the Equal Protection Clause of the Fourteenth Amendment limit the power of a state to distinguish between students of different races in professional and graduate education in a state university? Broader issues have been urged for our consideration, but we adhere to the principle of deciding constitutional questions only in the context of the particular case before the Court. We have frequently reiterated that this Court will decide constitutional questions only when necessary to the disposition of the case at hand, and that such decisions will be drawn as narrowly as possible. Because of this traditional reluctance to extend constitutional interpretations to situations or facts which are not before the Court, much of the excellent research and detailed argument presented in these cases is unnecessary to their disposition.

In the instant case, petitioner filed an application for admission to the University of Texas Law School for the February, 1946 term. His application was rejected solely because he is a Negro. Petitioner thereupon brought this suit for mandamus against the appropriate school officials, respondents here, to compel his admission. At that time, there was no law school in Texas which admitted Negroes.

The State trial court recognized that the action of the State in denying petitioner the opportunity to gain a legal education while granting it to others deprived him of the equal protection of the laws guaranteed by the Fourteenth Amendment. The court did not grant the relief requested, however, but continued the case for six months to allow the State to supply substantially equal facilities. At the expiration of the six months, in December, 1946, the court denied the writ on the showing that the authorized university officials had adopted an order calling for the opening of a law school for Negroes the following February. While petitioner's appeal was pending, such a school was made available, but petitioner refused to register therein. The Texas Court of Civil Appeals set aside the trial court's judgment and ordered the cause "remanded generally to the trial court for further proceedings without prejudice to the rights of any party to this suit."

On remand, a hearing was held on the issue of the equality of the educational facilities at the newly established school as compared with the University of Texas Law School. Finding that the new school offered petitioner "privileges, advantages, and opportunities for the study of law substantially equivalent to those offered by the State to white students at the University of Texas," the trial court denied mandamus. The Court of Civil Appeals affirmed. Petitioner's application for a writ of error was denied by the Texas Supreme Court. We granted certiorari because of the manifest importance of the constitutional issues involved.

The University of Texas Law School, from which petitioner was excluded, was staffed by a faculty of sixteen full-time and three part-time professors, some of whom are nationally recognized authorities in their field. Its student body numbered 850. The library contained over 65,000 volumes. Among the other facilities available to the students were a law review, moot court facilities, scholarship funds, and Order of the Coif affiliation. The school's alumni occupy the most distinguished positions in the private practice of the law and in the public life of the State. It may properly be considered one of the nation's ranking law schools.

The law school for Negroes which was to have opened in February, 1947, would have had no independent faculty or library. The teaching was to be carried on by four members of the University of Texas Law School faculty, who were to maintain their offices at the University of Texas while teaching at both institutions. Few of the 10,000 volumes ordered for the library had arrived; nor was there any full-time librarian. The school lacked accreditation.

Since the trial of this case, respondents report the opening of a law school at the Texas State University for Negroes. It is apparently on the road to full accreditation. It has a faculty of five full-time professors; a student body of 23; a library of some 16,500 volumes serviced by a full-time staff; a practice court and legal aid association; and one alumnus who has become a member of the Texas Bar.

Whether the University of Texas Law School is compared with the original or the new law school for Negroes, we cannot find substantial equality in the educational opportunities offered white and Negro law students by the State. In terms of number of the faculty, variety of courses and opportunity for specialization, size of the student body, scope of the library, availability of law review and similar activities, the University of Texas Law School is superior. What is more important, the University of Texas Law School possesses to a far greater degree those qualities which are incapable of objective measurement but which make for greatness in a law school. Such qualities, to name but a few, include reputation of the faculty, experience of the administration, position and influence of the alumni, standing in the community, traditions and prestige. It is difficult to believe that one who had a free choice between these law schools would consider the question close.

Moreover, although the law is a highly learned profession, we are well aware that it is an intensely practical one. The law school, the proving ground for legal learning and practice, cannot be effective in isolation from the individuals and institutions with which the law interacts. Few students and no one who has practiced law would choose to study in an academic vacuum, removed from the interplay of ideas and the exchange of views with

which the law is concerned. The law school to which Texas is willing to admit petitioner excludes from its student body members of the racial groups which number 85% of the population of the State and include most of the lawyers, witnesses, jurors, judges and other officials with whom petitioner will inevitably be dealing when he becomes a member of the Texas Bar. With such a substantial and significant segment of society excluded, we cannot conclude that the education offered petitioner is substantially equal to that which he would receive if admitted to the University of Texas Law School.

It may be argued that excluding petitioner from that school is no different from excluding white students from the new law school. This contention overlooks realities. It is unlikely that a member of a group so decisively in the majority, attending a school with rich traditions and prestige which only a history of consistently maintained excellence could command, would claim that the opportunities afforded him for legal education were unequal to those held open to petitioner. That such a claim, if made, would be dishonored by the State, is no answer. "Equal protection of the laws is not achieved through indiscriminate imposition of inequalities."

It is fundamental that these cases concern rights which are personal and present. This Court has stated unanimously that "The State must provide (legal education) for (petitioner) in conformity with the equal protection clause of the Fourteenth Amendment and provide it as soon as it does for applicants of any other group." That case "did not present the issue whether a state might not satisfy the equal protection clause of the Fourteenth Amendment by establishing a separate law school for Negroes." In *State of Missouri ex rel. Gaines v. Canada* the Court, speaking through Chief Justice Hughes, declared that "petitioner's right was a personal one. It was as an individual that he was entitled to the equal protection of the laws, and the State was bound to furnish him within its borders facilities for legal education substantially equal to those which the State there afforded for persons of the white race, whether or not other Negroes sought the same opportunity." These are the only cases in this Court which present the issue of the constitutional validity of race distinctions in state-supported graduate and professional education.

In accordance with these cases, petitioner may claim his full constitutional right: legal education equivalent to that offered by the State to students of other races. Such education is not available to him in a separate law school as offered by the State. We cannot, therefore, agree with respondents that the doctrine of *Plessy v. Ferguson* requires affirmance of the judgment below. Nor need we reach petitioner's contention that *Plessy v. Ferguson* should be reexamined in the light of contemporary knowledge respecting the purposes of the Fourteenth Amendment and the effects of racial segregation.

We hold that the Equal Protection Clause of the Fourteenth Amendment requires that petitioner be admitted to the University of Texas Law School. The judgment is reversed and the cause is remanded for proceedings not inconsistent with this opinion.

Reversed.

Sweezy v. New Hampshire

At issue in *Sweezy v. New Hampshire* (1957) was whether a state investigation of alleged subversive activities deprived a speaker at a university of due process of law under the Fourteenth Amendment. Ultimately, the U.S. Supreme Court held that the New Hampshire attorney general's investigation did violate the speaker's constitutional rights. In light of the impact that *Sweezy* played in the larger realm of litigation on the constitutionality of loyalty oaths, even though it did not deal with such oaths per se, this entry reviews its history and judicial analyses in detail.

Background

In 1951, during a time of anticommunist fears, political blacklisting, and Senator Joseph McCarthy's investigations into "un-American activities," the legislature of the State of New Hampshire passed the Subversive Activities Act. Provisions in the act defined a subversive organization as one that supported activities intended to change the constitutional form of government by force or violence. The act defined a subversive person as one who aided in the commission of acts intended to alter the constitutional form of government by force or violence. The act further declared subversive organizations to be unlawful and ordered them dissolved. Under the terms of the act, subversive persons were made ineligible for state employment. Teachers and others employed by an educational institution were subject to the law's provisions. All state employees and candidates for elective offices were required to sign statements that they were not subversive persons. In 1953, the legislature adopted a joint resolution charging the attorney general with responsibility for investigating subversive activities, identifying subversive persons in the state, and prosecuting those who were deemed to have violated the law.

Facts of the Case

Paul Sweezy was an avowed classical Marxist and socialist, an active member of the Progressive Party, and coeditor of an article condemning the United States' use of violence to preserve capitalistic social orders. Sweezy had delivered guest lectures to students in a humanities course at the University of New Hampshire (UNH) on at least three occasions.

Based on Sweezy's political associations and expression, New Hampshire Attorney General Louis Wyman subpoenaed him to testify on two occasions, January 5 and June 3, 1954. Wyman's questions at the January 5 hearing focused on Sweezy's lectures at UNH and his leadership role in Henry Wallace's 1948 presidential campaign on the Progressive Party ticket. While stating emphatically that Wyman's interrogation was unjustified and unconstitutional, Sweezy answered most of the questions honestly and directly, stating that he had never been a member of the Communist Party, had never knowingly associated with communists in the state, and did not advocate violent overthrow of the government. Sweezy acknowledged that he was a moderate socialist who believed in peaceful social and political change and that he once belonged to several organizations that were being monitored by the U.S. attorney general and the House Un-American Activities Committee. Invoking his First Amendment rights to freedom of speech and association, Sweezy declined to answer specific questions about Progressive Party membership, activities of individuals who had worked in the Wallace campaign, the content of his UNH lectures, and whether he believed communism to be superior to capitalism.

Attorney General Wyman again summoned Sweezy to testify on June 3, at which time he was questioned about his relationships with known communists and about his article deploring the United States' use of violence to further its capitalistic agenda. Sweezy again acknowledged that he was a Marxist and socialist, and he confirmed that his article reflected his opinion about American imperialism. Once again, Sweezy refused to answer questions about the Progressive Party and his UNH lectures, maintaining that they were not pertinent to the matter under inquiry and that they infringed his rights to free speech and association.

Following the two hearings, the attorney general petitioned a state trial court to compel Sweezy to answer all questions. When the court agreed and called Sweezy as a witness, he again refused to answer questions that he believed were not germane to the issue. The court thus held him in contempt and ordered him jailed until the contempt charge was purged. Sweezy appealed to the Supreme Court of New Hampshire, which conceded that the attorney general's investigation violated Sweezy's constitutional rights to political association and speech. The court held that that the attorney general reasonably believed Sweezy to be a subversive who was advocating violent overthrow of the government. It affirmed the earlier contempt order, holding that the state's interest outweighed his constitutional rights to speech, association, and due process of law.

The Supreme Court's Ruling

In a plurality judgment (meaning that five Justices were unable to agree on a rationale that would render their judgment binding precedent), the U.S. Supreme Court reversed in favor of the plaintiff. The plurality, led by Chief Justice Burger and joined by Justices Black, Douglas, and Brennan, cited the lower court's acknowledgment that the plaintiff's rights had been violated. The Court found that there unquestionably was an invasion of petitioner's academic freedom and First Amendment rights, areas in which it explained that the government should be extremely reluctant to intrude. To the Court, a state's legitimate concern about subversive individuals and their activities does not trump the Bill of Rights. To this end, the Court observed that because the American

form of government is built on the notion that all citizens have the right to engage in political expression and association, mere unorthodoxy or dissent from the prevailing perspectives should not be condemned. In fact, the plurality was of the view that the absence of such voices would have been a symptom of grave illness in American society. In summarizing its analysis, the Court emphasized the vital role of academic freedom in higher education, highlighting the idea that because scholarship cannot flourish in an atmosphere of suspicion and distrust, faculty members and students must always remain free to inquire, to study, and to evaluate, to gain new maturity and understanding.

In his concurring opinion, Justice Frankfurter, joined by Justice Harlan, identified the now-famous four freedoms necessary to sustain that climate of discovery and free inquiry on university campuses. According to Frankfurter, universities are designed to provide an atmosphere that is conducive to speculation, experiment, and creation and in which four essential freedoms prevail. He identified these freedoms as the right of universities to determine for themselves on academic grounds who may teach, what may be taught, how it shall be taught, and who may be admitted to study. Justice Whittaker did not participate in the case.

Justice Clark, in a dissent that was joined by Justice Burton, essentially argued that the Court overstepped its boundaries in denying the state's legislature and its officials the authority to investigate subversive activities within its boundaries.

In sum, *Sweezy* stands out because although it did not involve a loyalty oath, per se, the Supreme Court struck down the speaker's contempt conviction because the questions he had been asked were an invasion of his rights to academic freedom and political expression, topics that the Court would return to explore in later cases.

Robert C. Cloud

See also Academic Freedom; *Keyishian v. Board of Regents of the University of the State of New York*; Loyalty Oaths; Political Activities and Speech of Faculty Members; U.S. Supreme Court Cases in Higher Education

Further Readings

Elfbrandt v. Russell, 384 U.S. 11 (1966).

Euben, D. R. (2001). *Legal watch: Academic freedom, loyalty oaths, and diversity in academe.* Retrieved April 27, 2009, from http://www.aaup.org/AAUP/pubsres/academe/2001/MJ/Cols/lw.htm

Hyman, H. M. (1959). *To try men's souls: Loyalty oaths in American history.* Berkeley: University of California Press.

Keyishian v. Board of Regents of the University of the State of New York, 385 U.S. 589 (1967).

Wieman v. Updegraff, 344 U.S. 183 (1952).

Legal Citations

Sweezy v. New Hampshire, 354 U.S. 234 (1957).

Sweezy v. New Hampshire

Sweezy stands out because in it, the Supreme Court held that an investigation of his alleged subversive activities deprived a speaker at a university of his to due process.

Supreme Court of the United States

SWEEZY

v.

NEW HAMPSHIRE

354 U.S. 234

Argued March 5, 1957

Decided June 17, 1957

Mr. Chief Justice WARREN announced the judgment of the Court and delivered an opinion, in which Mr. Justice BLACK, Mr. Justice DOUGLAS, and Mr. Justice BRENNAN join.

This case, like *Watkins v. United States,* brings before us a question concerning the constitutional limits of legislative inquiry. The investigation here was conducted under the aegis of a state legislature, rather than a House of Congress. This places the controversy in a slightly different setting from that in *Watkins.* The ultimate question here is whether the investigation deprived Sweezy of due process of law under the Fourteenth Amendment. For the reasons to be set out in this opinion, we conclude that the record in this case does not sustain the power of the State to compel the disclosures that the witness refused to make.

This case was brought here as an appeal under 28 U.S.C. § 1257(2). Jurisdiction was alleged to rest upon contentions, rejected by the state courts, that a statute of New Hampshire is repugnant to the Constitution of the United States. We postponed a decision on the question of jurisdiction until consideration of the merits. The parties neither briefed nor argued the jurisdictional question. The appellant has thus failed to meet his burden of showing that jurisdiction by appeal was properly invoked. The appeal is therefore dismissed. Treating the appeal papers as a petition for writ of certiorari, under 28 U.S.C. § 2103, the petition is granted.

The investigation in which petitioner was summoned to testify had its origins in a statute passed by the New Hampshire legislature in 1951. It was a comprehensive scheme of regulation of subversive activities. There was a section defining criminal conduct in the nature of sedition. "Subversive organizations" were declared unlawful and ordered dissolved. "Subversive persons" were made ineligible for employment by the state government. Included in the disability were those employed as teachers or in other capacities by any public educational institution. A loyalty program was instituted to eliminate "subversive persons" among government personnel. All present employees, as well as candidates for elective office in the future, were required to make sworn statements that they were not "subversive persons."

In 1953, the legislature adopted a "Joint Resolution Relating to the Investigation of Subversive Activities." It was resolved:

"That the attorney general is hereby authorized and directed to make full and complete investigation with respect to violations of the subversive activities act of 1951 and to determine whether subversive persons as defined in said act are presently located within this state. The attorney general is authorized to act upon his own motion and upon such information as in his judgment may be reasonable or reliable. . ."

* * *

"The attorney general is directed to proceed with criminal prosecutions under the subversive activities act whenever evidence presented to him in the course of the investigation indicates violations thereof, and he shall report to the 1955 session on the first day of its regular session the results of this investigation, together with his recommendations, if any, for necessary legislation."

Under state law, this was construed to constitute the Attorney General as a one-man legislative committee. He was given the authority to delegate any part of the investigation to any member of his staff. The legislature conferred upon the Attorney General the further authority to subpoena witnesses or documents. He did not have power to hold witnesses in contempt, however. In the event that coercive or punitive sanctions were needed, the Attorney General could invoke the aid of a State Superior Court which could find recalcitrant witnesses in contempt of court.

Petitioner was summoned to appear before the Attorney General on two separate occasions. On January 5, 1954, petitioner testified at length upon his past conduct and associations. He denied that he had ever been a member of the Communist Party or that he had ever been part of any program to overthrow the government by force or violence. The interrogation ranged over many matters, from petitioner's World War II military service with the Office of Strategic Services to his sponsorship, in 1949, of the Scientific and Cultural Conference for World Peace, at which he spoke.

During the course of the inquiry, petitioner declined to answer several questions. His reasons for doing so were given in a statement he read to the Committee at the outset of the hearing. He declared he would not answer those questions which were not pertinent to the subject under inquiry as well as those which transgress the limitations of the First Amendment. In keeping with this stand, he

refused to disclose his knowledge of the Progressive Party in New Hampshire or of persons with whom he was acquainted in that organization. No action was taken by the Attorney General to compel answers to these questions.

The Attorney General again summoned petitioner to testify on June 3, 1954. There was more interrogation about the witness' prior contacts with Communists. The Attorney General lays great stress upon an article which petitioner had co-authored. It deplored the use of violence by the United States and other capitalist countries in attempting to preserve a social order which the writers thought must inevitably fall. This resistance, the article continued, will be met by violence from the oncoming socialism, violence which is to be less condemned morally than that of capitalism since its purpose is to create a "truly human society." Petitioner affirmed that he styled himself a "classical Marxist" and a "socialist" and that the article expressed his continuing opinion.

Again, at the second hearing, the Attorney General asked, and petitioner refused to answer, questions concerning the Progressive Party, and its predecessor, the Progressive Citizens of America. . . .

Distinct from the categories of questions about the Progressive Party and the lectures was one question about petitioner's opinions. He was asked: "Do you believe in Communism?" He had already testified that he had never been a member of the Communist Party, but he refused to answer this or any other question concerning opinion or belief.

Petitioner adhered in this second proceeding to the same reasons for not answering he had given in his statement at the first hearing. He maintained that the questions were not pertinent to the matter under inquiry and that they infringed upon an area protected under the First Amendment.

Following the hearings, the Attorney General petitioned the Superior Court of Merrimack County, New Hampshire, setting forth the circumstances of petitioner's appearance before the Committee and his refusal to answer certain questions. The petition prayed that the court propound the questions to the witness. After hearing argument, the court ruled that the questions set out above were pertinent. Petitioner was called as a witness by the court and persisted in his refusal to answer for constitutional reasons. The court adjudged him in contempt and ordered him committed to the county jail until purged of the contempt.

The New Hampshire Supreme Court affirmed. . . .

There is no doubt that legislative investigations, whether on a federal or state level, are capable of encroaching upon the constitutional liberties of individuals. It is particularly important that the exercise of the power of compulsory process be carefully circumscribed when the investigative process tends to impinge upon such highly sensitive areas as freedom of speech or press, freedom of political association, and freedom of communication of ideas, particularly in the academic community. Responsibility for the proper conduct of investigations rests, of course, upon the legislature itself. If that assembly chooses to authorize inquiries on its behalf by a legislatively created committee, that basic responsibility carries forward to include the duty of adequate supervision of the actions of the committee. This safeguard can be nullified when a committee is invested with a broad and ill-defined jurisdiction. The authorizing resolution thus becomes especially significant in that it reveals the amount of discretion that has been conferred upon the committee.

In this case, the investigation is governed by provisions in the New Hampshire Subversive Activities Act of 1951. The Attorney General was instructed by the legislature to look into violations of that Act. In addition, he was given the far more sweeping mandate to find out if there were subversive persons, as defined in that Act, present in New Hampshire. That statute, therefore, measures the breadth and scope of the investigation before us.

"Subversive persons" are defined in many gradations of conduct. Our interest is in the minimal requirements of that definition since they will outline its reach. According to the statute, a person is a "subversive person" if he, by any means, aids in the commission of any act intended to assist in the alteration of the constitutional form of government by force or violence. The possible remoteness from armed insurrection of conduct that could satisfy these criteria is obvious from the language. The statute goes well beyond those who are engaged in efforts designed to alter the form of government by force or violence. The statute declares, in effect, that the assistant of an assistant is caught up in the definition. This chain of conduct attains increased significance in light of the lack of a necessary element of guilty knowledge in either stage of assistants. The State Supreme Court has held that the definition encompasses persons engaged in the specified conduct ". . . whether or not done 'knowingly and willfully. . . .'" The potential sweep of this definition extends to conduct which is only remotely related to actual subversion and which is done

completely free of any conscious intent to be a part of such activity.

The statute's definition of "subversive organizations" is also broad. An association is said to be any group of persons, whether temporarily or permanently associated together, for joint action or advancement or views on any subject. An organization is deemed subversive if it has a purpose to abet, advise or teach activities intended to assist in the alteration of the constitutional form of government by force or violence.

The situation before us is in many respects analogous to that in *Wieman v. Updegraff.* The Court held there that a loyalty oath prescribed by the State of Oklahoma for all its officers and employees violated the requirements of the Due Process Clause because it entailed sanctions for membership in subversive organizations without scienter. A State cannot, in attempting to bar disloyal individuals from its employ, exclude persons solely on the basis of organizational membership, regardless of their knowledge concerning the organizations to which they belonged. . . .

The sanction emanating from legislative investigations is of a different kind than loss of employment. But the stain of the stamp of disloyalty is just as deep. The inhibiting effect in the flow of democratic expression and controversy upon those directly affected and those touched more subtly is equally grave. Yet here, as in *Wieman,* the program for the rooting out of subversion is drawn without regard to the presence or absence of guilty knowledge in those affected.

The nature of the investigation which the Attorney General was authorized to conduct is revealed by this case. He delved minutely into the past conduct of petitioner, thereby making his private life a matter of public record. The questioning indicates that the investigators had thoroughly prepared for the interview and were not acquiring new information as much as corroborating data already in their possession. On the great majority of questions, the witness was cooperative, even though he made clear his opinion that the interrogation was unjustified and unconstitutional. Two subjects arose upon which petitioner refused to answer: his lectures at the University of New Hampshire, and his knowledge of the Progressive Party and its adherents.

The state courts upheld the attempt to investigate the academic subject on the ground that it might indicate whether petitioner was a "subversive person." What he taught the class at a state university was found relevant to the character of the teacher. The State Supreme Court carefully excluded the possibility that the inquiry was sustainable because of the state interest in the state university. There was no warrant in the authorizing resolution for that. The sole basis for the inquiry was to scrutinize the teacher as a person, and the inquiry must stand or fall on that basis.

The interrogation on the subject of the Progressive Party was deemed to come within the Attorney General's mandate because that party might have been shown to be a "subversive organization." The State Supreme Court held that the ". . . questions called for answers concerning the membership or participation of named persons in the Progressive Party which, if given, would aid the Attorney General in determining whether that party and its predecessor are or were subversive organizations."

The New Hampshire court concluded that the ". . . right to lecture and the right to associate with others for a common purpose, be it political or otherwise, are individual liberties guaranteed to every citizen by the State and Federal Constitutions but are not absolute rights. . . . The inquiries authorized by the Legislature in connection with this investigation concerning the contents of the lecture and the membership, purposes and activities of the Progressive Party undoubtedly interfered with the defendant's free exercise of those liberties."

The State Supreme Court thus conceded without extended discussion that petitioner's right to lecture and his right to associate with others were constitutionally protected freedoms which had been abridged through this investigation. These conclusions could not be seriously debated. Merely to summon a witness and compel him, against his will, to disclose the nature of his past expressions and associations in a measure of governmental interference in these matters. These are rights which are safeguarded by the Bill of Rights and the Fourteenth Amendment. We believe that there unquestionably was an invasion of petitioner's liberties in the areas of academic freedom and political expression—areas in which government should be extremely reticent to tread. The essentiality of freedom in the community of American universities is almost self-evident. No one should underestimate the vital role in a democracy that is played by those who guide and train our youth. To impose any strait jacket upon the intellectual leaders in our colleges and universities would imperil the future of our Nation. No field of education is so thoroughly comprehended by man that new discoveries cannot yet be made. Particularly is that true in the social sciences, where few, if any, principles are accepted as absolutes. Scholarship cannot flourish in an atmosphere of suspicion and distrust.

Teachers and students must always remain free to inquire, to study and to evaluate, to gain new maturity and understanding; otherwise our civilization will stagnate and die.

Equally manifest as a fundamental principle of a democratic society is political freedom of the individual. Our form of government is built on the premise that every citizen shall have the right to engage in political expression and association. This right was enshrined in the First Amendment of the Bill of Rights. Exercise of these basic freedoms in America has traditionally been through the media of political associations. Any interference with the freedom of a party is simultaneously an interference with the freedom of its adherents. All political ideas cannot and should not be channeled into the programs of our two major parties. History has amply proved the virtue of political activity by minority, dissident groups, who innumerable times have been in the vanguard of democratic thought and whose programs were ultimately accepted. Mere unorthodoxy or dissent from the prevailing mores is not to be condemned. The absence of such voices would be a symptom of grave illness in our society.

Notwithstanding the undeniable importance of freedom in the areas, the Supreme Court of New Hampshire did not consider that the abridgment of petitioner's rights under the Constitution vitiated the investigation. In the view of that court, "the answer lies in a determination of whether the object of the legislative investigation under consideration is such as to justify the restriction thereby imposed upon the defendant's liberties." It found such justification in the legislature's judgment, expressed by its authorizing resolution, that there exists a potential menace from those who would overthrow the government by force and violence. That court concluded that the need for the legislature to be informed on so elemental a subject as the self-preservation of government outweighed the deprivation of constitutional rights that occurred in the process.

We do not now conceive of any circumstance wherein a state interest would justify infringement of rights in these fields. But we do not need to reach such fundamental questions of state power to decide this case. The State Supreme Court itself recognized that there was a weakness in its conclusion that the menace of forcible overthrow of the government justified sacrificing constitutional rights. There was a missing link in the chain of reasoning. The syllogism was not complete. There was nothing to connect the questioning of petitioner with this fundamental interest of the State. Petitioner had been interrogated by a one-man legislative committee, not by the legislature itself. The relationship of the committee to the full assembly is vital, therefore, as revealing the relationship of the questioning to the state interest.

In light of this, the state court emphasized a factor in the authorizing resolution which confined the inquiries which the Attorney General might undertake to the object of the investigation. That limitation was thought to stem from the authorizing resolution's condition precedent to the institution of any inquiry. The New Hampshire legislature specified that the Attorney General should act only when he had information which ". . . in his judgment may be reasonable or reliable." The state court construed this to mean that the Attorney General must have something like probable cause for conducting a particular investigation. It is not likely that this device would prove an adequate safeguard against unwarranted inquiries. The legislature has specified that the determination of the necessity for inquiry shall be left in the judgment of the investigator. In this case, the record does not reveal what reasonable or reliable information led the Attorney General to question petitioner. The state court relied upon the Attorney General's description of prior information that had come into his possession.

The respective roles of the legislature and the investigator thus revealed are of considerable significance to the issue before us. It is eminently clear that the basic discretion of determining the direction of the legislative inquiry has been turned over to the investigative agency. The Attorney General has been given such a sweeping and uncertain mandate that it is his decision which picks out the subjects that will be pursued, what witnesses will be summoned and what questions will be asked. In this circumstance, it cannot be stated authoritatively that the legislature asked the Attorney General to gather the kind of facts comprised in the subjects upon which petitioner was interrogated.

Instead of making known the nature of the data it desired, the legislature has insulated itself from those witnesses whose rights may be vitally affected by the investigation.

Incorporating by reference provisions from its subversive activities act, it has told the Attorney General, in effect to screen the citizenry of New Hampshire to bring to light anyone who fits into the expansive definitions.

Within the very broad area thus committed to the discretion of the Attorney General there may be many facts which the legislature might find useful. There would also be a great deal of data which that assembly would not want or need. In the classes of information that the legislature might deem to desirable to have, there will be some which it could not validly acquire because of the effect upon the constitutional rights of individual citizens. Separating the wheat from the chaff, from the standpoint of the legislature's object, is the legislature's responsibility because it alone can make that judgment. In this case, the New Hampshire legislature has delegated that task to the Attorney General.

As a result, neither we nor the state courts have any assurance that the questions petitioner refused to answer fall into a category of matters upon which the legislature wanted to be informed when it initiated this inquiry. The judiciary are thus placed in an untenable position. Lacking even the elementary fact that the legislature wants certain questions answered and recognizing that petitioner's constitutional rights are in jeopardy, we are asked to approve or disapprove his incarceration for contempt.

In our view, the answer is clear. No one would deny that the infringement of constitutional rights of individuals would violate the guarantee of due process where no state interest underlies the state action. Thus, if the Attorney General's interrogation of petitioner were in fact wholly unrelated to the object of the legislature in authorizing the inquiry, the Due Process Clause would preclude the endangering of constitutional liberties. We believe that an equivalent situation is presented in this case. The lack of any indications that the legislature wanted the information the Attorney General attempted to elicit from petitioner must be treated as the absence of authority. It follows that the use of the contempt power, notwithstanding the interference with constitutional rights, was not in accordance with the due process requirements of the Fourteenth Amendment.

The conclusion that we have reached in this case is not grounded upon the doctrine of separation of powers. In the Federal Government, it is clear that the Constitution has conferred the powers of government upon three major branches: the Executive, the Legislative and the Judicial. No contention has been made by petitioner that the New Hampshire legislature, by this investigation, arrogated to itself executive or judicial powers. We accept the finding of the State Supreme Court that the employment of the Attorney General as the investigating committee does not alter the legislative nature of the proceedings. Moreover, this Court has held that the concept of separation of powers embodied in the United States Constitution is not mandatory in state governments. Our conclusion does rest upon a separation of the power of a state legislature to conduct investigations from the responsibility to direct the use of that power insofar as that separation causes a deprivation of the constitutional rights of individuals and a denial of due process of law.

The judgment of the Supreme Court of New Hampshire is reversed.

Reversed.

Mr. Justice WHITTAKER took no part in the consideration or decision of this case.

T

TAX EXEMPTIONS FOR COLLEGES AND UNIVERSITIES

Tax exemptions often refer to exclusions from responsibility for paying property taxes on buildings and grounds owned or used by colleges and universities. Insofar as both public and private postsecondary institutions provide an important state function, state laws usually grant them tax exemptions for property that they own or use. A threshold question in this regard considers the conditions under which state statutes grant exemptions to institutions of higher learning. A secondary inquiry examines the nature of the property interests held by postsecondary institutions. In light of the various legal issues surrounding the issue for colleges and universities, this entry examines the dimensions of tax exemptions in the world of higher education.

Statutory Language

In order to determine which properties are entitled to tax-exempt status, courts usually begin with examinations of the language of state statutes on the subject. A brief survey of tax-exemption statutes reveals that such laws typically grant exemptions for ownership, for having control over, for uses, for uses with exceptions, for ownership or use, or for ownership and use. Even so, as reflected in the following illustrative cases, the judiciary can interpret tax exemptions expansively or narrowly.

Alabama's statutory exemption is more narrowly stated than most, allowing exemptions only for property that is used "exclusively for religious worship, for schools or for purposes purely charitable." After an industrial development board built a hotel and conference center on university-owned land, the board leased the facility to the hotel, which was part of a limited partnership. The hotel company then subleased the conference center back to the university but contracted with a hotel management firm for its operation. On further review of the denial of the partnership's request for a tax exemption, an appellate court affirmed that it was not entitled to the relief it sought (*AU Hotel, Ltd. v. Eagerton,* 1996). The court explained that insofar as the hotel provided lodging for the general public, it was not reserved for an exclusive educational use within the meaning of the state tax code.

Where Georgia's tax exemption statute allows exemptions for any "seminary of learning," a challenge to an apprenticeship program in pipefitting and plumbing prompted the question of whether a trade school was a "seminary of learning." An appellate court ruled that because the term "seminary of learning" had historically been used to describe any educational enterprise, the trade school program qualified for the tax exemption (*J.A.T.T. Title Holding Corp. v. Roberts,* 1988).

At issue in a dispute from Kansas was the meaning of an exemption for property that is for "educational use." Litigation ensued when the National Collegiate Athletic Association (NCAA) created a corporation to manage the property where it located its headquarters. On further review of the reversal of the tax appeals board's denial of the NCAA's property tax-exempt status on the basis that the headquarters did not qualify as an "educational use," the state's highest court affirmed in favor of the NCAA (*National Collegiate Realty v. Board of County Commissioners*, 1984). The court applied a broad interpretation of the words "educational use" in upholding the exemption insofar as it acknowledged the NCAA's role in assuring amateurism in intercollegiate sports.

The Pennsylvania Constitution grants a tax exemption for property "used for the purposes of the institution," while a commonwealth statute extends the exemption to property "necessary for the occupancy and enjoyment of the university." When a college rented eight of approximately 50 houses it owned to central service staff at a reduced rate, officials successfully challenged the county taxation board's denial of the institution's tax-exempt status on the eight houses. The record revealed that the staff members who occupied the houses were on call around the clock for maintenance and security work. An appellate court affirmed that renting houses to staff members to answer emergency calls, even when such incidents occurred only a few times each year, was for institutional purposes that made the rental of such houses necessary, and that the university was therefore entitled to the exemption (*In re Swarthmore College*, 1994).

Tennessee provides a tax exemption for property that is owned, operated, or controlled by the state. Consequently, when a university leased five parcels for various commercial purposes, including hotels, apartments, and a service station, the state's highest court upheld the exemption in the face of what had been a possible assessment by a county tax assessor (*Lamanna v. University of Tennessee*, 1971). The court affirmed that the exemption was acceptable, because it was within the ambit of the statute that required the income derived from the leases to be applied to public uses.

Two cases on a similar issue reached different outcomes. The property tax code of Texas grants an exemption for property "used exclusively for educational functions" and "reasonably necessary for the operation of the school." In light of this provision, a tax dispute arose over an exemption for a college president's residence. In finding that the private residential use of a building met neither the standard of exclusivity nor that of necessity, an appellate court denied the request for tax-exempt

status (*Bexar Appraisal District v. Incarnate Word College*, 1992).

On the other hand, the Supreme Court of Iowa upheld a request for tax-exempt status for the house of a university's vice president of ministry (*St. Ambrose University v. Board of Review for City of Davenport*, 1993). The court interpreted the broad tax exemption in state law for "all grounds and buildings used or under construction by literary, scientific, charitable, benevolent, agricultural, and religious institutions and societies" as allowing the vice president's university-owned residence to qualify for the exemption.

In light of Wisconsin's tax exemption for property "owned and used exclusively by . . . educational or benevolent associations," town officials contested an order granting a tax exemption for lakeside property owned by a university. The university sought the exemption, because it provided a physical education course on the property early in the summer but leased it to the alumni association for use as a summer camp for the remainder of the summer. Affirming in favor of the university, an appellate court noted the educational use of the physical education course and the integration of the alumni association with the operations of the university. The court thus agreed that the property qualified for the tax exemption, even though the university was in another state (*Trustees of Indiana University v. Town of Rhine*, 1992).

Types of Property Interest

The nature of the property interests of postsecondary institutions is another aspect that can determine their tax-exempt status. The nature of an institution's interest is important, because a variety of situations can occur, in terms of contractual arrangements necessary to secure building uses, of creative financial arrangements necessary for constructing or maintaining buildings, or of changes in the management and control of buildings over time.

A case from Connecticut illustrates the nature of a university's property interest in a dispute over a tax exemption in *University of Hartford v. City of Hartford* (1984). A university leased an apartment building and used it primarily for student housing. More specifically, about two-thirds of the apartments were rented to students, while the remaining units were rented to the elderly and persons with disabilities. In declining to consider whether the usages were educational for the purposes of gaining tax-exempt status, an appellate court affirmed that the university's leasehold was not the type of interest in the property that qualified for tax-exempt status.

The fact that Illinois grants of tax exemptions for state-owned property made the nature of a university's property interest central in one dispute. Where a university foundation owned a building that was used for a conference center, an appellate court acknowledged the close relationship between the university and the foundation. However, the grantor of the property attached covenants and restrictions on the use of the property, with the possibility of a reversion to the grantor if the terms were not observed. The court was of the opinion that this type of property interest, wherein the grantor controlled so much authority and the property was not used primarily for educational purposes, meant that the conference center was not entitled to tax-exempt status (*Northern Illinois Foundation v. Sweet*, 1992).

Creative financial arrangements were at the center of a tax exemption dispute in New York, where a college corporation that operated two colleges on one campus leased land to a developer for 40 years. The college then joined in a master lease with the developer to build a dormitory on the land. During the term of the master lease, the college controlled rental levels and selected students who could live in the dormitory. At the end of the lease, ownership reverted to the college. As reflected in state law, retaining tax exemptions in lease agreements requires colleges to show that they had the incidents, or outward appearance, of ownership in the property. College officials argued successfully that the institution had all of the same incidents of ownership, because the board financed the dormitory with a mortgage. An appellate court affirmed that because the college was the owner of the dormitories for tax purposes, it was entitled to the tax exemption (*Colleges of Seneca v. City of Geneva*, 2000).

Proportional Exemptions

Proportional exemptions occur when university-owned properties have mixed uses. Commonly,

exemption disputes concern whether property is fully or partially tax exempt, proportional to the amount of use that is educational. The application of proportional exemptions, like that of full exemptions, depends on the interpretation of state law.

In the first of two cases from Ohio, a mixed-use property tax dispute arose when a university created a business incubator program. The office of the incubator program was located in a university office building that included an adjacent parking garage. The tenants in the building included three nonprofit corporations and two for-profit corporations; two of the three nonprofit corporations were directly affiliated with the university. In affirming a grant of partial tax-exempt status, an appellate court ruled that the space occupied by the two university-affiliated corporations was entitled to such relief (*Case Western Reserve University v. Tracy*, 1999). The court denied the request for the remainder of the building and the parking garage, because these spaces were used by for-profit corporations.

Insofar as Ohio law grants tax-exemption status when property is "used for the support of such [an] institution," it creates a broader exemption than usual. Where the state held title to a building on behalf of a university, its school of architecture took up 88% of the space with the remaining 12% leased for commercial use as a laundry and convenience store. Because it was satisfied that the rent from the commercial uses went into the university's general fund, the state's highest court affirmed that all of the building qualified for the tax exemption (*State for Use of University of Cincinnati v. Limbach*, 1990).

Conclusion

The law related to tax exemptions parallels the observed authority relationships between postsecondary institutions and local communities in zoning regulations, wherein the language of exemption statutes can be narrow or broad. As state-level financial support for colleges and universities continues to decline, postsecondary administrators will likely continue to seek more creative arrangements for contracting, maintaining, and operating institutional buildings. To this end, administrators will need to take care in their creativity not to compromise their facilities' status under state tax-exemption laws that have granted them significant benefits in the past.

David L. Dagley

See also Zoning

Further Readings

Dagley, D. L. (2005). Town and gown issues. In J. Beckham & D. Dagley (Eds.), *Contemporary issues in higher education law* (pp. 449–478). Dayton, OH: Education Law Association.

Legal Citations

AU Hotel, Ltd. v. Eagerton, 689 So. 2d 859 (Ala. Civ. App. 1996).

Bexar Appraisal District v. Incarnate Word College, 824 S.W.2d 295 (Tex. App. 1992).

Case Western Reserve University v. Tracy, 703 N.E.2d 1240 (Ohio 1999).

Colleges of Seneca v. City of Geneva, 709 N.Y.S.2d 493 (N.Y. App. Div. 2000).

In re Swarthmore College, 645 A.2d 470 (Pa. Commw. Ct. 1994).

J.A.T.T. Title Holding Corp. v. Roberts, 371 S.E.2d 861 (Ga. 1988).

Lamanna v. University of Tennessee, 462 S.W.2d 877 (Tenn. 1971).

National Collegiate Realty v. Board of County Commissioners, 690 P.2d 1366 (Kan. 1984).

Northern Illinois Foundation v. Sweet, 603 N.E.2d 84 (Ill. App. Ct. 1992).

St. Ambrose University v. Board of Review for City of Davenport, 503 N.W.2d 406 (Iowa 1993).

State for Use of University of Cincinnati v. Limbach, 553 N.E.2d 1056 (Ohio 1990).

Trustees of Indiana University v. Town of Rhine, 488 N.W.2d 128 (Wis. Ct. App. 1992).

University of Hartford v. City of Hartford, 477 A.2d 1023 (Conn. Ct. App. 1984).

TENURE

Tenure was designed to prevent the dismissal of educators by arbitrary or capricious actions of educational officials. At the same time, it is important to acknowledge tenure does not guarantee lifetime employment. Rather, tenure provides procedural due process when faculty members with property interests in their jobs, either in the form of tenure or set amounts of time remaining on contracts, face the threat of dismissal from their jobs for cause. When faculty members are subject to dismissal for cause, the disputes often result in litigation, with a few high-profile cases garnering much media attention.

The concept of tenure has a long history representing efforts to protect educators from job insecurity resulting from reactions to their teaching, speaking at conferences, or published works. This entry reviews the origins of tenure, its evolution in the United States in colleges and universities through the work of the American Association of University Professors (AAUP), and rulings on tenure by the U.S. Supreme Court over the years. The entry also describes the function of tenure in higher education, where it plays a central role in protecting academic freedom.

Origins of Tenure

As noted, tenure grants faculty members protection from unfair dismissal. In perhaps the earliest example of what might be considered protection akin to tenure, in 1245, Pope Innocent IV granted exemptions to scholars in the University of Paris excusing them from having to appear at ecclesiastical courts some distance from Paris. The following year, a Court of Conservation was founded to protect university faculty when the same types of issues arose. Over time, as reflected in practices such as academic abstention, universities and academicians were granted autonomy from local, civil, and ecclesiastical officials. There were some limits to these protections when attacks were made on the prevalent dogmas, but the concept of autonomy provided insulation from excessive encroachment by officials outside of the realm of the academy.

In the 1890s, Germany sought protection for educators through *Lernfreiheit,* or the freedom of university students to choose courses, move from school to school, and be free of dogmatic restrictions. *Lernfreiheit,* which essentially lies at the heart of academic freedom, also stressed faculty rights to freedom of inquiry and freedom of teaching with the right to report on findings in an unhindered, unrestricted, and unfettered environment.

Through the founding of the AAUP in 1915, John Dewey and others sought to help academicians be free from interference with their employment by external persons or groups. This protection was important, because during the 19th and early 20th centuries, faculty members were often dismissed for offending individuals or groups. Faculty members were also fired for criticizing business and corporate ethics.

During periods of international conflicts involving the expansion of feared ideologies such as communism, books by faculty members were criticized for their rhetoric, in some cases even banned. Based on fears of communism, others induced conspiracy theories that threatened academic freedom. Consequently, loyalty oaths, which had emerged earlier, became more widespread in the 1950s and 1960s with the Supreme Court reaching mixed results on their constitutionality in a variety of cases. The AAUP was a strong supporter of the rights of faculty members to academic freedom, freedom of speech, and tenure during these periods. Still, political interference was frequent, often leaving faculty members with limited recourse against unreasonable interference with their professional responsibilities.

Evolution of Tenure in the United States

In 1940, the AAUP issued a Statement of the Principles on Academic Freedom and Tenure. The principles in this statement included assumptions that tenure is a means toward freedom in teaching and research as well as in extracurricular activities. The document added that tenure is important in recruiting and retaining qualified individuals to the teaching profession, especially in higher education. Further, the document maintained that freedom and economic security for faculty members were indispensable to the success of colleges and universities in meeting their professional obligations to students and society.

Thirty years later, in 1970, a committee of the AAUP and Association of American Colleges (AAC) clarified that the 1940 statement was not a static code. Rather, the AAUP and AAC explained that the original document provided the framework for guiding future changes in the social, political, and economic climate on campuses. The groups also

observed that in *Keyishian v. Board of Regents of the University of the State of New York* (1967), the Supreme Court reiterated that the United States is committed to safeguarding academic freedom to all citizens, not just educators; this, the AAUP and AAC declared, is a freedom that is especially supported by the First Amendment.

The AAUP has since identified colleges and universities that it has censored for what it believes are infringements on academic freedom and tenure. In this regard, the AAUP encourages university officials to work to with faculty members to eliminate threats to academic freedom and tenure. In its function as a voluntary organization, the AAUP uses its censorship lists and on-campus membership in attempting to change institutional policies that threaten academic freedom and tenure.

Tenure and the U.S. Supreme Court

In *Sweezy v. New Hampshire* (1957), the Supreme Court highlighted the importance of tenure in academic freedom when it wrote:

> The essentiality of freedom in the community of American universities is almost self-evident. . . . To impose any strait jacket upon the intellectual leaders in our colleges and universities would imperil the future of our Nation. . . . Scholarship cannot flourish in an atmosphere of suspicion and distrust. Teachers and students must always remain free to inquire, to study, to evaluate, to gain new maturity and understanding; otherwise, our civilization will stagnate and die. (p. 250)

The Supreme Court has reiterated this principle in succeeding cases through the years, acknowledging the important role that tenure occupies in the lives of American colleges and universities.

In *Board of Regents v. Roth* (1972), the Supreme Court held that liberty and property rights are created by contract or state law and constitutionally protected. In order to acquire that protection, faculty members in higher education are typically required to serve for set periods of time, often seven years, meeting specified requirements in scholarship, teaching, and service before earning tenure. During their probationary periods, faculty members who are on the so-called tenure track are not entitled to employment property rights beyond the terms of their contracts. To this end, in *Perry v. Sindermann* (1972), the Court was of the opinion that procedural due process safeguards are required only for faculty members who have a property or liberty interest in employment. While public and private institutions of higher learning may operate under different provisions with regard to tenure, in the uncommon situation of reductions in force on campuses, where individuals are dismissed through no fault on their part due to such reasons as financial exigency or the termination of programs, faculty members with tenure are typically dismissed last.

As citizens, faculty members in higher education have the freedom to express their beliefs and opinions and to engage in controversial debate and inquiry. However, because faculty members have obligations and responsibilities to be professional and ethical in their work, tenure does not protect them if they fail to meet these requirements. The AAUP principles of professional ethics and responsibility also caution faculty members to avoid persistent introduction of material that has no relation to the subjects they are teaching; this is an area of increasing controversy in the politicization of many campuses.

Challenges and Controversies

The 1915 AAUP Statement of Principles reminds faculty members that when they speak as private citizens, they have obligations to inform listeners that they are not speaking as representatives of their educational institutions. This is sometimes difficult in teaching the humanities and other social sciences, where encouraging students to engage in critical inquiry often entails examining assumptions underlying policy decisions. Peer review has been used in recent years to ensure that faculty members are productive and current in their academic fields.

Critics of tenure maintain that it may make it difficult to dismiss faculty members who are incompetent, nonproductive, underprepared, or not up-to-date in their fields. The enforcement of tenure is a function of individual colleges and universities. Major institutions maintain administrative policies to ensure that faculty tenure rights are secure and followed throughout the organizations, especially when individuals are subject to dismissal for cause.

Generally, administrators in higher education, many of whom are culled from academic ranks, are not granted tenure in their administrative roles. Tenure is arguably becoming less frequent in public education; for example, it may not be part of school policy in charter schools, which operate under different governance models than other public schools. Nevertheless, tenure is usually present in colleges and universities, in part as a recruiting tool and also to facilitate retention of productive academicians. Nontenured faculty members, who have contracts for set lengths of time, generally four to seven years, may have specified property rights to employment but generally cannot receive de facto tenure absent affirmative actions by educational officials.

Tenure is a work in progress in distance learning institutions, as the Internet involves new and emerging tools for teaching. Ethical codes for the use of the Internet are being developed and updated as technology advances.

In recent years, there has been an increase in the number of faculty members who serve on a part-time basis as adjunct or contingency employees without the benefits and protection of tenure. Efforts are currently under way to extend essential tenure protections to these part-time faculty members, even though such an approach is often resisted by full-time university faculty. This distinction is important in community colleges, where more than half of faculties are typically part-time. Moreover, this issue is coming to a head as major universities increasingly rely on contingency faculty. However, accrediting agencies often criticize institutions of higher learning for over-reliance on using part-time faculty members to meet understaffed course and program needs, because they view this practice as designed to undermine the place of tenure on campuses.

James J. Van Patten

See also Academic Abstention; Academic Freedom; American Association of University Professors; *Board of Regents of State Colleges v. Roth*; Due Process Rights in Faculty and Staff Dismissal; *Keyishian v. Board of Regents of the University of the State of New York; Loyalty Oaths; Perry v. Sindermann*

Further Readings

Mawdsley, R. D. (1999). Collegiality as a factor in tenure decisions. *Journal of Personnel Evaluation in Education, 13*, 167–177.

Legal Citations

Board of Regents of State Colleges v. Roth, 408 U.S. 564 (1972).

Keyishian v. Board of Regents of the University of the State of New York, 385 U.S. 589 (1967).

Perry v. Sindermann, 408 U.S. 593 (1972).

Sweezy v. New Hampshire, 354 U.S. 234 (1957).

TILTON V. RICHARDSON

Tilton v. Richardson is a landmark 1971 decision of the U.S. Supreme Court upholding a congressional grant program that made federal funds available to private religious colleges for constructing buildings. In light of *Tilton*'s having expanded the limits of governmental aid to religiously affiliated colleges and universities, this entry reviews the Court's rationale and considers the case's implications.

Facts of the Case

Tilton involved a challenge by taxpayers to Title I of the Higher Education Facilities Act of 1963, which made available grants to colleges and universities, including those that are religiously affiliated, in order to construct buildings and facilities that are used exclusively for secular educational purposes. The taxpayers objected to grants to four institutions in Connecticut, all of which were religiously affiliated, claiming that the law granting the funds to the institutions violated the taxpayers' rights under both the Establishment and Free Exercise Clauses of the First Amendment.

A three-judge federal trial court in Connecticut upheld the act in the face of the Establishment Clause claim on the bases that it authorized grants to church-related institutions of higher learning and that it had neither the purpose nor effect of promoting religion. The court also held that

because the grants did not coerce the taxpayers in the practice of their religious beliefs, it did not violate their rights under the Free Exercise Clause. Dissatisfied with the outcome, the taxpayers appealed to the Supreme Court.

The Supreme Court's Ruling

On further review, a sharply divided Supreme Court, in a case in which no opinion commanded a majority, upheld the constitutionality of the act. The Court found that the act violated neither the Establishment nor the Free Exercise Clause. A four-justice bloc, led by Chief Justice Burger and joined by Justices Harlan, Stewart, and Blackmun, formed the plurality that announced the judgment of the Court. A fifth member of the Court, Justice White, concurred in the result, but not necessarily in the plurality's reasoning.

Chief Justice Burger, as author of the plurality opinion, began by defining the scope of the act. The plurality pointed out that Congress intended the act to apply to all colleges and universities, regardless of whether they were religiously affiliated. The plurality then applied the three-part test that it articulated in *Lemon v. Kurtzman* (1971), which has become the judicial standard in controversies involving religion in both K–12 and higher educational settings. The judgments in both *Tilton* and *Lemon* were handed down on the same day.

In applying the *Lemon* test, the plurality was satisfied that Congress had a secular purpose in enacting the statute. The plurality explained that the act was constitutional because Congress carefully designed it to ensure both that funds would be available to assist institutions to serve the rapidly growing number of young people who wished to achieve a higher education and that the federal resources would be used for defined secular purposes, while expressly forbidding the use of these monies for religious instruction, training, or worship. In its analysis, the plurality added that none of the four institutions violated the act's restrictions.

The plurality next determined that the act did not advance religion. In doing so, the plurality stressed that the money was not being used for facilities for religious purposes. Rather, the plurality acknowledged that the funds were being used to construct facilities such as libraries and performing arts centers. While upholding the statute as applied, the plurality explicitly invalidated a portion of the law that allowed buildings constructed with government funds to be used for religious purposes after a period of 20 years had expired, because this section unconstitutionally allowed a contribution of property of substantial value to religious bodies.

Finally, stressing the fundamental differences between K–12 education and higher education, the plurality posited that the act did not create excessive entanglement with religion. The plurality distinguished *Tilton* from *Lemon*, wherein the Court invalidated aid in the form of salary supplements to teachers in religiously affiliated nonpublic schools. The Court observed that the cases were significantly different, because in *Tilton*, religious indoctrination was not a substantial purpose or activity in the four institutions insofar as their student bodies were not composed of impressionable young people, the assistance was not ideological, and the one-time grants were for the single purpose of construction.

Having resolved that the act did not violate the Establishment Clause, the plurality quickly dismissed the Free Exercise challenge. The plurality rejected the taxpayers' argument that by being compelled to pay taxes, a portion of which were used to finance the disputed grants, the taxpayers were experiencing coercion that was directed at their own religious beliefs. The plurality remarked that the grants were indistinguishable from other types of aid that the Supreme Court has permitted.

Justice White, who provided the crucial fifth vote, concurred. White declared that because states and the federal government had the authority to finance the separable secular function of higher education, the act passed constitutional muster. He also commented that even though religion and private interests other than education might substantially benefit from the act, these benefits did not convert the act into an impermissible establishment of religion.

Justice Douglas, along with Justices Black and Marshall, joined in a common dissent. The dissenters emphasized their belief that any aid to religiously affiliated institutions was unconstitutional. A fourth Justice, Brennan, dissented in *Tilton* while expressing his support for *Lemon*.

Impact of *Tilton*

Tilton is significant for higher education in three respects. First, *Tilton* stands for the proposition that the government may provide money directly to religiously affiliated colleges and universities without violating the Establishment or Free Exercise Clauses. As such, *Tilton* removed any doubt that there are circumstances under which the government may provide aid directly to religiously affiliated institutions. Second, the Court drew a constitutional distinction between pervasively sectarian activities such as religious instruction, training, and worship, on the one hand, and activities that would take place at any university, such as using libraries, laboratories, or residence halls, on the other. In fact, the Court invalidated a portion of the law that allowed the buildings to be used for religious purposes after 20 years. Third, in recognizing fundamental distinctions between education at the K–12 level and higher education, the Court upheld aid where sufficient safeguards were in place to avoid First Amendment concerns.

In the almost 40 years since *Tilton*, insofar as the Supreme Court has not overruled or limited its original judgment, the principle that religiously affiliated institutions may receive government assistance for nonreligious activities remains intact. Yet, while the Court has never repudiated the distinction between pervasively sectarian and secular activities, recent cases seem to blur the distinction.

William E. Thro

See also *Hunt v. McNair*; *Locke v. Davey*; State Aid and the Establishment Clause; *Witters v. Washington Department of Services for the Blind*

Further Readings

Hunt v. McNair, 413 U.S. 734 (1973).

Locke v. Davey, 540 U.S. 712 (2004).

Note. (1991). The First Amendment and public funding of religiously controlled or affiliated higher education. *Journal of College & University Law, 17*, 381.

Roemer v. Board of Public Works, 426 U.S. 736 (1976).

Russo, C. J., & Mawdsley, R. D. (2005). The United States Supreme Court and aid to students who attend religiously-affiliated institutions of higher education. *Education and Law Journal, 14*(3), 301–311.

Witters v. Washington Department of Services for the Blind, 474 U.S. 481 (1986).

Legal Citations

Higher Education Facilities Act, Pub. L. No. 88-204 (1963).

Lemon v. Kurtzman, 403 U.S. 602 (1971).

Tilton v. Richardson, 403 U.S. 672 (1971).

TILTON V. RICHARDSON

In *Tilton*, decided the same day as *Lemon v. Kurtzman*, the Supreme Court upheld parts of a federal statute that provided aid to religiously affiliated colleges and universities on the ground that the law did not run afoul of the Establishment Clause.

Supreme Court of the United States

TILTON

v.

RICHARDSON

403 U.S. 672

Argued March 2, 3, 1971

Decided June 28, 1971

Rehearing Denied Oct. 12, 1971

Mr. Chief Justice BURGER announced the judgment of the Court and an opinion in which Mr. Justice HARLAN, Mr. Justice STEWART and Mr. Justice BLACKMUN join.

This appeal presents important constitutional questions as to federal aid for church-related colleges and universities under Title I of the Higher Education Facilities Act of 1963, which provides construction grants for buildings and facilities used exclusively for secular educational purposes. We must determine first whether the Act authorizes aid to such church-related institutions, and, if so, whether the Act violates either the Establishment or Free Exercise Clauses of the First Amendment.

I

The Higher Education Facilities Act was passed in 1963 in response to a strong nationwide demand for the expansion of college and university facilities to meet the sharply rising number of young people demanding higher education. The Act authorizes federal grants and loans to "institutions of higher education" for the construction of a wide variety of "academic facilities." But § 751(a) (2) expressly excludes "any facility used or to be used for sectarian instruction or as a place for religious worship, or . . . any facility which . . . is used or to be used primarily in connection with any part of the program of a school or department of divinity. . . ."

The Act is administered by the United States Commissioner of Education. He advises colleges and universities applying for funds that under the Act no part of the project may be used for sectarian instruction, religious worship, or the programs of a divinity school. The Commissioner requires applicants to provide assurances that these restrictions will be respected. The United States retains a 20-year interest in any facility constructed with Title I funds. If, during this period, the recipient violates the statutory conditions, the United States is entitled to recover an amount equal to the proportion of its present value that the federal grant bore to the original cost of the facility. During the 20-year period, the statutory restrictions are enforced by the Office of Education primarily by way of on-site inspections.

Appellants are citizens and taxpayers of the United States and residents of Connecticut. They brought this suit for injunctive relief against the officials who administer the Act. Four church-related colleges and universities in Connecticut receiving federal construction grants under Title I were also named as defendants. Federal funds were used for five projects at these four institutions: (1) a library building at Sacred Heart University; (2) a music, drama, and arts building at Annhurst College; (3) a science building at Fairfield University; (4) a library building at Fairfield; and (5) a language laboratory at Albertus Magnus College.

A three-judge federal court was convened under 28 U.S.C. § 2282 and § 2284. Appellants attempted to show that the four recipient institutions were "sectarian" by introducing evidence of their relations with religious authorities, the content of their curricula, and other indicia of their religious character. The sponsorship of these institutions by religious organizations is not disputed. Appellee colleges introduced testimony that they had fully complied with the statutory conditions and that their religious affiliation in no way interfered with the performance of their secular educational functions. The District Court ruled that Title I authorized grants to church-related colleges and universities. It also sustained the constitutionality of the Act, finding that it had neither the purpose nor the effect of promoting religion. We noted probable jurisdiction.

II

We are satisfied that Congress intended the Act to include all colleges and universities regardless of any affiliation with or sponsorship by a religious body. Congress defined "institutions of higher education," which are eligible to receive aid under the Act, in broad and inclusive terms. Certain institutions, for example, institutions that are neither public nor nonprofit, are expressly excluded, and the Act expressly prohibits use of the facilities for religious purposes. But the Act makes no reference to religious affiliation or nonaffiliation. Under these circumstances "institutions of higher education" must be taken to include church-related colleges and universities.

This interpretation is fully supported by the legislative history. Although there was extensive debate on the wisdom and constitutionality of aid to institutions affiliated with religious organizations, Congress clearly included them in the program. The sponsors of the Act so stated and amendments aimed at the exclusion of church-related institutions were defeated.

III

Numerous cases considered by the Court have noted the internal tension in the First Amendment between the Establishment Clause and the Free Exercise Clause. *Walz v. Tax Comm'n* is the most recent decision seeking to define the boundaries of the neutral area between these two provisions within which the legislature may legitimately act. There, as in other decisions, the Court treated the three main concerns against which the Establishment Clause sought to protect: "sponsorship, financial support, and active involvement of the sovereign in religious activity."

Every analysis must begin with the candid acknowledgment that there is no single constitutional caliper that can be used to measure the precise degree to which these three factors are present or absent. Instead, our analysis in this area must begin with a consideration of the cumulative criteria developed over many years and applying to a wide range of governmental action challenged as violative of the Establishment Clause.

There are always risks in treating criteria discussed by the Court from time to time as "tests" in any limiting sense of that term. Constitutional adjudication does not lend itself to the absolutes of the physical sciences or mathematics. The standards should rather be viewed as guidelines with which to identify instances in which the objectives of the Religion Clauses have been impaired. And, as we have noted in *Lemon v. Kurtzman* and *Earley v. DiCenso*, candor compels the acknowledgment that we can only dimly perceive the boundaries of permissible government activity in this sensitive area of constitutional adjudication.

Against this background we consider four questions: First, does the Act reflect a secular legislative purpose? Second, is the primary effect of the Act to advance or inhibit religion? Third, does the administration of the Act foster an excessive government entanglement with religion? Fourth, does the implementation of the Act inhibit the free exercise of religion?

(a)

The stated legislative purpose appears in the preamble where Congress found and declared that "the security and welfare of the United States require that this and future generations of American youth be assured ample opportunity for the fullest development of their intellectual capacities, and that this opportunity will be jeopardized unless the Nation's colleges and universities are encouraged and assisted in their efforts to accommodate rapidly growing numbers of youth who aspire to a higher education."

This expresses a legitimate secular objective entirely appropriate for governmental action.

The simplistic argument that every form of financial aid to church-sponsored activity violates the Religion Clauses was rejected long ago in *Bradfield v. Roberts.* There a federal construction grant to a hospital operated by a religious order was upheld. Here the Act is challenged on the ground that its primary effect is to aid the religious purposes of church-related colleges and universities.

Construction grants surely aid these institutions in the sense that the construction of buildings will assist them to perform their various functions. But bus transportation, textbooks, and tax exemptions all gave aid in the sense that religious bodies would otherwise have been forced to find other sources from which to finance these services. Yet all of these forms of governmental assistance have been upheld. The crucial question is not whether some benefit accrues to a religious institution as a consequence of the legislative program, but whether its principal or primary effect advances religion.

A possibility always exists, of course, that the legitimate objectives of any law or legislative program may be subverted by conscious design or lax enforcement. There is nothing new in this argument. But judicial concern about these possibilities cannot, standing alone, warrant striking down a statute as unconstitutional.

The Act itself was carefully drafted to ensure that the federally subsidized facilities would be devoted to the secular and not the religious function of the recipient institutions. It authorizes grants and loans only for academic facilities that will be used for defined secular purposes and expressly prohibits their use for religious instruction, training, or worship. These restrictions have been enforced in the Act's actual administration, and the record shows that some church-related institutions have been required to disgorge benefits for failure to obey them.

Finally, this record fully supports the findings of the District Court that none of the four church-related institutions in this case has violated the statutory restrictions. The institutions presented evidence that there had been no religious services or worship in the federally financed facilities, that there are no religious symbols or plaques in or on them, and that they had been used solely for nonreligious purposes. On this record, therefore, these buildings are indistinguishable from a typical state university facility. Appellants presented no evidence to the contrary.

Appellants instead rely on the argument that government may not subsidize any activities of an institution of higher learning that in some of its programs teaches religious doctrines. This argument rests on *Everson* where the majority stated that the Establishment Clause barred any "tax . . . levied to support any religious . . . institutions . . . whatever form they may adopt to teach or practice religion." In *Allen,* however, it was recognized that the Court had fashioned criteria under which an analysis

of a statute's purpose and effect was determinative as to whether religion was being advanced by government action. Under this concept appellants' position depends on the validity of the proposition that religion so permeates the secular education provided by church-related colleges and universities that their religious and secular educational functions are in fact inseparable. The argument that government grants would thus inevitably advance religion did not escape the notice of Congress. It was carefully and thoughtfully debated but was found unpersuasive. It was also considered by this Court in *Allen.* There the Court refused to assume that religiosity in parochial elementary and secondary schools necessarily permeates the secular education that they provide.

This record, similarly, provides no basis for any such assumption here. Two of the five federally financed buildings involved in this case are libraries. The District Court found that no classes had been conducted in either of these facilities and that no restrictions were imposed by the institutions on the books that they acquired. There is no evidence to the contrary. The third building was a language laboratory at Albertus Magnus College. The evidence showed that this facility was used solely to assist students with their pronunciation in modern foreign languages—a use which would seem peculiarly unrelated and unadaptable to religious indoctrination. Federal grants were also used to build a science building at Fairfield University and a music, drama, and arts building at Annhurst College.

There is no evidence that religion seeps into the use of any of these facilities. Indeed, the parties stipulated in the District Court that courses at these institutions are taught according to the academic requirements intrinsic to the subject matter and the individual teacher's concept of professional standards. Although appellants introduced several institutional documents that stated certain religious restrictions on what could be taught, other evidence showed that these restrictions were not in fact enforced and that the schools were characterized by an atmosphere of academic freedom rather than religious indoctrination. All four institutions, for example, subscribe to the 1940 Statement of Principles on Academic Freedom and Tenure endorsed by the American Association of University Professors and the Association of American Colleges.

Rather than focus on the four defendant colleges and universities involved in this case, however, appellants seek to shift our attention to a "composite profile" that they have constructed of the "typical sectarian" institution of higher education. We are told that such a "composite" institution imposes religious restrictions on admissions, requires attendance at religious activities, compels obedience to the doctrines and dogmas of the faith, requires instruction in theology and doctrine, and does everything it can to propagate a particular religion. Perhaps some church-related schools fit the pattern that appellants describe. Indeed, some colleges have been declared ineligible for aid by the authorities that administer the Act. But appellants do not contend that these four institutions fall within this category. Individual projects can be properly evaluated if and when challenges arise with respect to particular recipients and some evidence is then presented to show that the institution does in fact possess these characteristics. We cannot, however, strike down an Act of Congress on the basis of a hypothetical "profile."

(b)

Although we reject appellants' broad constitutional arguments, we do perceive an aspect in which the statute's enforcement provisions are inadequate to ensure that the impact of the federal aid will not advance religion. If a recipient institution violates any of the statutory restrictions on the use of a federally financed facility, § 754(b)(2) permits the Government to recover an amount equal to the proportion of the facility's present value that the federal grant bore to its original cost.

This remedy, however, is available to the Government only if the statutory conditions are violated "within twenty years after completion of construction." This 20-year period is termed by the statute as "the period of Federal interest" and reflects Congress' finding that after 20 years "the public benefit accruing to the United States" from the use of the federally financed facility "will equal or exceed in value" the amount of the federal grant.

Under § 754(b)(2), therefore, a recipient institution's obligation not to use the facility for sectarian instruction or religious worship would appear to expire at the end of 20 years. We note, for example, that under § 718(b)(7)(C), an institution applying for a federal grant is only required to provide assurances that the facility will not be used for sectarian instruction or religious worship "during at least the period of the Federal interest therein (as defined in section 754 of this title)."

Limiting the prohibition for religious use of the structure to 20 years obviously opens the facility to use

for any purpose at the end of that period. It cannot be assumed that a substantial structure has no value after that period and hence the unrestricted use of a valuable property is in effect a contribution of some value to a religious body. Congress did not base the 20-year provision on any contrary conclusion. If, at the end of 20 years, the building is, for example, converted into a chapel or otherwise used to promote religious interests, the original federal grant will in part have the effect of advancing religion.

To this extent the Act therefore trespasses on the Religion Clauses. The restrictive obligations of a recipient institution under § 751(a)(2) cannot, compatibly with the Religion Clauses, expire while the building has substantial value. This circumstance does not require us to invalidate the entire Act, however. "The cardinal principle of statutory construction is to save and not to destroy." In *Champlin Rfg. Co. v. Corporation Commission,* the Court noted "The unconstitutionality of a part of an act does not necessarily defeat . . . the validity of its remaining provisions. Unless it is evident that the Legislature would not have enacted those provisions which are within its power, independently of that which is not, the invalid part may be dropped if what is left is fully operative as a law."

Nor does the absence of an express severability provision in the Act dictate the demise of the entire statute.

We have found nothing in the statute or its objectives intimating that Congress considered the 20-year provision essential to the statutory program as a whole. In view of the broad and important goals that Congress intended this legislation to serve, there is no basis for assuming that the Act would have failed of passage without this provision; nor will its excision impair either the operation or administration of the Act in any significant respect.

IV

We next turn to the question of whether excessive entanglements characterize the relationship between government and church under the Act. Our decision today in *Lemon v. Kurtzman* and *Robinson v. DiCenso* has discussed and applied this independent measure of constitutionality under the Religion Clauses. There we concluded that excessive entanglements between government and religion were fostered by Pennsylvania and Rhode Island statutory programs under which state aid was provided to parochial elementary and secondary schools. Here, however, three factors substantially diminish the extent and the potential danger of the entanglement.

In *DiCenso* the District Court found that the parochial schools in Rhode Island were "an integral part of the religious mission of the Catholic Church." There, the record fully supported the conclusion that the inculcation of religious values was a substantial if not the dominant purpose of the institutions. The Pennsylvania case was decided on the pleadings, and hence we accepted as true the allegations that the parochial schools in that State shared the same characteristics.

Appellants' complaint here contains similar allegations. But they were denied by the answers, and there was extensive evidence introduced on the subject. Although the District Court made no findings with respect to the religious character of the four institutions of higher learning, we are not required to accept the allegations as true under these circumstances, particularly where, as here, appellants themselves do not contend that these four institutions are "sectarian."

There are generally significant differences between the religious aspects of church-related institutions of higher learning and parochial elementary and secondary schools. The "affirmative if not dominant policy" of the instruction in pre-college church schools is "to assure future adherents to a particular faith by having control of their total education at an early age." There is substance to the contention that college students are less impressionable and less susceptible to religious indoctrination. Common observation would seem to support that view, and Congress may well have entertained it. The skepticism of the college student is not an inconsiderable barrier to any attempt or tendency to subvert the congressional objectives and limitations.

Furthermore, by their very nature, college and postgraduate courses tend to limit the opportunities for sectarian influence by virtue of their own internal disciplines. Many church-related colleges and universities are characterized by a high degree of academic freedom and seek to evoke free and critical responses from their students.

The record here would not support a conclusion that any of these four institutions departed from this general pattern. All four schools are governed by Catholic religious organizations, and the faculties and student bodies at each are predominantly Catholic.

Nevertheless, the evidence shows that non-Catholics were admitted as students and given faculty appointments. Not one of these four institutions requires its students to attend religious services. Although all four schools require their students to take theology courses, the parties stipulated that these courses are taught according to the academic requirements of the subject matter and the teacher's concept of professional standards. The parties also stipulated that the courses covered a range of human religious experiences and are not limited to courses about the Roman Catholic religion. The schools introduced evidence that they made no attempt to indoctrinate students or to proselytize. Indeed, some of the required theology courses at Albertus Magnus and Sacred Heart are taught by rabbis. Finally, as we have noted, these four schools subscribe to a well-established set of principles of academic freedom, and nothing in this record shows that these principles are not in fact followed. In short, the evidence shows institutions with admittedly religious functions but whose predominant higher education mission is to provide their students with a secular education.

Since religious indoctrination is not a substantial purpose or activity of these church-related colleges and universities, there is less likelihood than in primary and secondary schools that religion will permeate the area of secular education. This reduces the risk that government aid will in fact serve to support religious activities. Correspondingly, the necessity for intensive government surveillance is diminished and the resulting entanglements between government and religion lessened. Such inspection as may be necessary to ascertain that the facilities are devoted to secular education is minimal and indeed hardly more than the inspections that States impose over all private schools within the reach of compulsory education laws.

The entanglement between church and state is also lessened here by the nonideological character of the aid that the Government provides. Our cases from *Everson* to *Allen* have permitted church-related schools to receive government aid in the form of secular, neutral, or nonideological services, facilities, or materials that are supplied to all students regardless of the affiliation of the school that they attend. In *Lemon* and *DiCenso*, however, the state programs subsidized teachers, either directly or indirectly. Since teachers are not necessarily religiously neutral, greater governmental surveillance would be required to guarantee that state salary aid would not in fact subsidize religious instruction. There we found the resulting entanglement excessive. Here, on the other hand, the Government provides facilities that are themselves religiously neutral. The risks of Government aid to religion and the corresponding need for surveillance are therefore reduced.

Finally, government entanglements with religion are reduced by the circumstance that, unlike the direct and continuing payments under the Pennsylvania program, and all the incidents of regulation and surveillance, the Government aid here is a one-time, single-purpose construction grant. There are no continuing financial relationships or dependencies, no annual audits, and no government analysis of an institution's expenditures on secular as distinguished from religious activities. Inspection as to use is a minimal contact.

No one of these three factors standing alone is necessarily controlling; cumulatively all of them shape a narrow and limited relationship with government which involves fewer and less significant contacts than the two state schemes before us in *Lemon* and *DiCenso*. The relationship therefore has less potential for realizing the substantive evils against which the Religion Clauses were intended to protect.

We think that cumulatively these three factors also substantially lessen the potential for divisive religious fragmentation in the political arena. This conclusion is admittedly difficult to document, but neither have appellants pointed to any continuing religious aggravation on this matter in the political processes. Possibly this can be explained by the character and diversity of the recipient colleges and universities and the absence of any intimate continuing relationship or dependency between government and religiously affiliated institutions. The potential for divisiveness inherent in the essentially local problems of primary and secondary schools is significantly less with respect to a college or university whose student constituency is not local but diverse and widely dispersed.

V

Finally, we must consider whether the implementation of the Act inhibits the free exercise of religion in violation of the First Amendment. Appellants claim that the Free Exercise Clause is violated because they are compelled to pay taxes, the proceeds of which in part finance grants under the Act. Appellants, however, are unable to identify any coercion directed at the practice or exercise of their religious beliefs. Their share of the cost of the grants under the Act is not fundamentally distinguishable from the impact of the tax exemption sustained in *Walz* or the provision of textbooks upheld in *Allen*.

We conclude that the Act does not violate the Religion Clauses of the First Amendment except that part of § 754(b)(2) providing a 20-year limitation on the religious use restrictions contained in § 751(a)(2). We remand to the District Court with directions to enter a judgment consistent with this opinion.

Vacated and remanded.

TITLE VI

Title VI of the Civil Rights Act of 1964 was adopted as part of the landmark civil rights law designed to outlaw racial discrimination in schools, public places, and employment. The legislation was extremely controversial at the time and survived a 54-day filibuster in the U.S. Senate before its passage. According to Title VI, "No person in the United States shall, on the ground of race, color, or national origin, be excluded from participation in, be denied the benefits of, or be subjected to discrimination in any program receiving Federal financial assistance" (42 U.S.C. § 2000d).

Eight years later, Congress enacted Title IX of the Educational Amendments of 1972, which prohibits discrimination on the basis of sex using the exact same wording as Title VI. Insofar as the two statutes contain virtually identical language, the U.S. Supreme Court has held that cases interpreting one of the laws can generally be applied to the other. This entry first reviews the scope of the statute, the mechanisms by which it is enforced, and the criteria for establishing a case under Title VI. It then considers several issues that have been litigated under Title VI, including affirmative action, race-exclusive scholarships, and academic standards for athletic eligibility.

Scope

The scope of Title VI is coextensive with judicial interpretation of the Equal Protection Clause of the Fourteenth Amendment to the U.S. Constitution (*Guardians Association v. Civil Service Commission of the City of New York*, 1983). Because the Fourteenth Amendment is triggered by state action, Title VI has no practical effect on private institutions of higher education that do not receive federal financial assistance. Even so, Title VI plays an important role in extending the protections of the Equal Protection Clause to private institutions of higher education.

In a key case involving a private institution, *Grove City College v. Bell* (1984), the Supreme Court ruled that Title VI and Title IX applied only to discrimination in a particular program receiving federal funds. Under this precedent, colleges and universities could, in theory, have engaged in widespread racial discrimination, as long as there was no discrimination in their programs receiving federal funds. In response to the Court's decision, Congress amended Title VI with the Civil Rights Restoration Act of 1987 and changed the definition of "program" to include "all of the operations" of an institution. As a result, institutions of higher education that receive as little as one dollar in federal funds are prohibited from racially discriminating anywhere on their campuses.

Enforcement

Title VI employs two enforcement mechanisms. The first is for the federal government to threaten withdrawal of federal funds if it finds that unlawful discrimination is occurring. Title VI derives its power from the Spending Clause of the U.S. Constitution, which is located in Article I, Section 8, Clause 1. Insofar as Title VI conditions receipt of federal funds on compliance with federal requirements, and courts view it as a contract, it is interpreted using regular contract principles. Consequently, institutional officials must know that actions are unlawful at the time that they agree to take the federal funds (*Gebser v. Lago Vista Independent School District*, 1998).

The second enforcement mechanism under Title VI is through suits by private individuals. While the language of Title VI contains no provision for awarding monetary damages, the Supreme Court has interpreted it as allowing an implied right of private action for damages. Accordingly, Title VI plaintiffs can recover compensatory but not punitive damages (*Barnes v. Gorman*, 2002). The prohibition on punitive damages has resulted in Title VI being primarily used in suits brought by or on behalf of college students. For employees, the

preferred statutes are Title VII of the Civil Rights Act of 1964 or 42 U.S.C. § 1981, which both allow punitive damages. Some employees prefer to file under state nondiscrimination laws, which can be more favorable to employees than federal statutes.

An additional limitation on Title VI is that it does not allow disparate impact claims. As a general rule, courts recognize two types of discrimination. Disparate treatment involves the unequal treatment of individuals because of a discriminatory motive. For example, colleges that prohibit immigrant students from playing intercollegiate sports would be engaging in disparate treatment. Disparate impact, often called "adverse impact," involves seemingly neutral standards that have disproportionately negative impacts on particular groups of individuals. For instance, colleges that require minimum scores on a test of English proficiency before students may play intercollegiate sports might be engaged in disparate impact discrimination. In *Alexander v. Sandoval* (2001), the Supreme Court was of the opinion that the implied private right of action under Title VI does not extend to disparate impact claims. Still, the Court reaffirmed that Title VI continues to apply to disparate treatment claims.

Student Harassment and Discrimination Suits

A number of students have filed suits against colleges and universities under Title VI alleging racial discrimination or harassment. In discrimination cases, the legal analysis is adapted from case law interpreting Title VII of the Civil Rights Act of 1964 (*McDonnell Douglas Corp. v. Green*, 1973). This means that plaintiffs must first establish prima facie cases of discrimination. If plaintiffs can do so, the burden shifts to defendants to show legitimate, nondiscriminatory reasons for their conduct. Plaintiffs then have the opportunity to show that the reasons offered by the defendants were not true and were actually pretexts for discrimination.

Plaintiffs may establish prima facie cases through direct evidence of discrimination, but those cases are rare. More frequently, plaintiffs offer indirect evidence to show that they were members of a protected class, that they suffered adverse actions at the hands of the defendants in pursuit of their education, that they were qualified to continue in the pursuit of their education, and that they were treated differently from similarly situated students who were not members of the protected class.

In Title VI and Title IX harassment cases, the Supreme Court has set a high bar for plaintiffs, who must show that the harassment was "so severe, pervasive, and objectively offensive that it effectively bars the victim's access to an educational opportunity or benefit" (*Davis v. Monroe County Board of Education,* 1999, p. 650). In addition, plaintiffs must show that officials acting on behalf of institutional recipients of federal funds acted with deliberate indifference to known acts of harassment in programs or activities. Ironically, this standard provides less protection to student victims of harassment than it does to employees, who must only show that the employers knew or should have known of the harassment and failed to take prompt remedial action.

Affirmative Action in Admissions

Affirmative action in student admissions involves the most controversial and high-profile Title VI litigation. Federal regulations interpreting Title VI require affirmative action to overcome the effects of past discrimination and permit it to overcome the effects of conditions that limit participation in a program by individuals of a particular race, color, or national origin. Those regulations state that

> (i) In administering a program regarding which the recipient has previously discriminated against persons on the ground of race, color, or national origin, the recipient must take affirmative action to overcome the effects of prior discrimination.
>
> (ii) Even in the absence of such prior discrimination, a recipient in administering a program may take affirmative action to overcome the effects of conditions which resulted in limiting participation by persons of a particular race, color, or national origin. (34 C.F.R. §100.3(b)(6))

Affirmative action efforts to remedy past discrimination have not fared well in the courts in recent years. Courts have required specific evidence of past discrimination and a direct nexus to present-day effects before granting relief. Further, affirmative action in higher education cannot be used to remedy the effects of societal discrimination and must be narrowly tailored to accomplish a compelling governmental interest. In contrast, the Supreme Court embraced affirmative action to promote student diversity in *Grutter v. Bollinger* (2003); the Court reached the opposite result in the companion case of *Gratz v. Bollinger* (2003) involving undergraduate admissions at the University of Michigan.

In *Grutter,* the Supreme Court upheld an affirmative action program at the University of Michigan Law School, stating that student diversity is a compelling state interest that satisfies the strict scrutiny faced by racial classifications under the Fourteenth Amendment. Since *Grutter* was decided under both the Equal Protection Clause and Title VI, it applies to both public and private colleges and universities.

Grutter explicitly permits the use of affirmative action in admissions but imposes restrictions on institutions that seek to adopt policies in this regard. First, colleges or university policies may not use quotas in the admissions process or set aside particular slots for students from a specific racial group. Second, educators may not operate separate tracks in their admissions process that evaluate minority applicants differently from other applicants. Third, officials must perform an individualized review of every student's application that considers how that individual could contribute to campus diversity. Fourth, educators must take a broad view of diversity and look at race as one of many factors that could further their diversity goals. Fifth, admissions officers may not automatically award a certain number of points to students of a particular race as a bonus in the admissions process. Sixth, policies must consider race-neutral alternatives to achieve campus diversity. Seventh, officials must periodically evaluate whether it is necessary to continue considering race in the admissions process to achieve institutional diversity goals.

Race-Exclusive Scholarships and Programs

In the wake of *Grutter,* the legality of scholarships and programs targeted toward a particular racial group is questionable. Proponents argue that they are essential to achieving student diversity, which *Grutter* held is a compelling state interest. Opponents argue that such policies violate *Grutter,* because they prevent students from specific racial groups from competing for specific benefits, use race mechanically, and effectively function as unlawful set-asides. Prior to *Grutter,* a scholarship program for African Americans at the University of Maryland that was designed to remedy past discrimination was found to violate Title VI (*Podboresky v. Kirwan,* 1994).

In 2004, opponents of affirmative action sent letters to more than 100 universities with race-exclusive scholarships or programs, threatening legal action. In response, many institutions, including Harvard, Yale, Cal Tech, and Carnegie Mellon, broadened the eligibility criteria for those programs so that they are no longer race-exclusive.

One option for officials at institutions that wish to continue race-exclusive scholarships is to fund and administer them through private foundations such as alumni associations. As long as foundations are not a branch of government and do not accept federal funds, they are unlikely to be subject to the Fourteenth Amendment and Title VI, because they will not be perceived as state actors.

Past and Future Directions

In the late 1980s and early 1990s, Title VI suits challenged the freshman academic eligibility standards adopted by the National Collegiate Athletic Association, typically based on claims that the standards had a disparate impact on African American students. All of those suits lost, and most commentators agree that they are unlikely to succeed now that disparate impact is no longer a viable legal theory under Title VI.

In contrast, in *Jackson v. Birmingham Board of Education* (2005), the Supreme Court held that the coach of a high school girls' basketball team could collect money damages under Title IX for retaliation he faced after complaining that girls' teams did not receive the same opportunities and funding as boys' teams. To the extent that Title IX and Title VI are worded almost identically, *Jackson* may open the possibility of private retaliation suits by individuals charging that they were subjected to retaliation by supervisors for complaining about

general violations of Title VI, rather than violations of an individual's Title VI rights.

D. Frank Vinik

See also Affirmative Action; Disparate Impact; Equal Protection Analysis; Fourteenth Amendment; *Gratz v. Bollinger*; *Grove City College v. Bell*; *Grutter v. Bollinger*; National Collegiate Athletic Association; Title VII; Title IX and Athletics; Title IX and Retaliation; Title IX and Sexual Harassment

Further Readings

Bruton, D. (2002). At the busy intersection: Title VI and NCAA standards. *Journal of College and University Law, 28,* 569–603.

Coleman, A., & Palmer, S. (2006). *Admissions and diversity after Michigan: The next generation of legal and policy issues.* Washington, DC: College Board. Retrieved April 30, 2009, from http://www .collegeboard.com/prod_downloads/diversity collaborative/acc-div_next-generation.pdf

Coleman, A., Palmer, S., & Richards, F. (2005). *Federal law and financial aid: A framework for evaluating diversity-related programs.* Washington, DC: College Board. Retrieved April 30, 2009, from http://www .collegeboard.com/prod_downloads/ diversitycollaborative/diversity_manual.pdf

Habenicht, A. (2003). Has the shot clock expired? *Pryor v. NCAA* and the premature disposal of a "deliberate indifference" discrimination claim under Title VI of the Civil Rights Act of 1964. *George Mason Law Review, 11,* 551–608.

Legal Citations

Alexander v. Sandoval, 532 U.S. 275 (2001).

Barnes v. Gorman, 536 U.S. 181, 189 (2002).

Civil Rights Restoration Act of 1987, Pub. L. No. 100-259.

Davis v. Monroe County Board of Education, 526 U.S. 629 (1999).

Gebser v. Lago Vista Independent School District, 524 U.S. 276, 288 (1998).

Gratz v. Bollinger, 465 U.S. 244 (2003).

Grove City College v. Bell, 465 U.S. 555 (1984).

Grutter v. Bollinger, 539 U.S. 306 (2003).

Guardians Association v. Civil Service Commission of the City of New York, 463 U.S. 582 (1983).

Jackson v. Birmingham Board of Education, 544 U.S. 167 (2005).

McDonnell Douglas Corporation v. Green, 411 U.S. 792 (1973).

Podboresky v. Kirwan, 38 F.3d 147 (4th Cir. 1994).

Title VI of the Civil Rights Act of 1964, 42 U.S.C. § 2000d.

Title IX of the Education Amendments of 1972, 20 U.S.C. § 1681.

TITLE VII

Congress enacted a series of antidiscrimination statutes in the 1960s and 1970s that were designed to combat widespread discrimination in the workplace. The most comprehensive of these laws, Title VII of the Civil Rights Act of 1964, prohibits discrimination against employees and prospective employees or applicants on the basis of race, color, national origin, religion, and sex. Title VII applies to hiring, discharge, transfer, promotion, demotion, compensation, and "terms, conditions, or privileges of employment," and also addresses other employment issues, including sexual harassment, maternity and religious leave, and retaliation for filing Title VII complaints. This entry reviews the general framework of Title VII in terms of the burden of proof required, the types of claims allowable, and the mechanisms in place for administrative enforcement and judicial relief. The entry concludes with a discussion of the application of Title VII to such specific discrimination issues as pregnancy, religion, harassment, and retaliation.

Title VII outlaws employment discrimination by both private and, since 1972, public higher educational employers with 15 or more employees. Under Title VII, colleges or universities can lawfully employ individuals on the basis of sex, national origin, or religion if such a characteristic is a bona fide occupational qualification (BFOQ) necessary for the institution's normal operations. For example, the Seventh Circuit upheld as a valid BFOQ a philosophy department's resolution that three faculty vacancies be reserved for Jesuits at a Jesuit university (*Pime v. Loyola University of Chicago,* 1986).

In addition to BFOQs, Title VII recognizes two other major exemptions that are relevant for religiously affiliated colleges and universities that are "in whole or in part, owned, supported, controlled, or managed by a particular religion or . . . religious corporation, association, or society . . ." (42 U.S.C. § 2000e-2(e)(2)(2009)). Under the so-called ministerial exemption, Title VII allows educational institutions to employ individuals of their faiths. For instance, in *EEOC v. Catholic University of America* (1996), the Federal Circuit court for the District of Columbia refused to overturn the denial of tenure to a nun in the Department of Canon Law in part because her teaching responsibilities clearly fell within this ministerial exemption (Russo, 1997). In other words, because the nun taught canon law, a discipline that went to the heart of governance in Catholic institutions, the court refused to get involved in what it perceived as a doctrinal issue. The second exemption permits colleges and universities to employ individuals of the institutions' faiths if their curricula are directed toward disseminating their religious beliefs.

Insofar as race is addressed under the types of Title VII claims that may be filed, it is not addressed in a separate category; it is interesting that because complainants can bring race-based Title VII claims, White plaintiffs have challenged the employment actions of historically Black institutions of higher education, claiming that they were discriminated against based on race.

General Framework of Title VII

Burden of Proof

The burden in Title VII cases rests on employees or prospective employees to establish that employers subjected them to unlawful discrimination. In the leading cases of *McDonnell Douglas Corp. v. Green* (1973) and *Texas Department of Community Affairs v. Burdine* (1981), the Supreme Court developed a three-step test of shifting burdens and order of proof for Title VII cases.

Under the Supreme Court's burden-shifting tests, plaintiffs must first establish prima facie cases by demonstrating that they were members of a protected group, applied for jobs for which they were qualified and for which the employer sought applicants, and were rejected. They must also demonstrate that, after the rejections, the employers continued to seek applicants with the plaintiffs' qualifications. As the burden shifts, the employer may then rebut claims by producing legitimate, nondiscriminatory reasons for rejecting plaintiffs. In the third step, the burden shifts back to plaintiffs, who have opportunities to establish that employers' proffered reasons were pretexts for actual impermissible discrimination. In *Burdine,* the Court explained that in the final stage, plaintiffs may either show directly that employers were more likely motivated by discriminatory reasons or indirectly that the employers' proffered rationales were not credible. The *McDonnell Douglas–Burdine* test is flexible, affording the judiciary the option of addressing discrimination claims in dismissal, demotion, transfer, and denial of tenure and academic promotion.

Types of Claims

Title VII claims fall into two categories. Disparate impact claims challenge facially neutral employment policies or practices that on the surface appear nondiscriminatory but nonetheless impact more harshly and significantly a protected group. The primary defense available to institutions of higher learning and other employers is that business necessities justify the policies or practices. An example of a higher education disparate impact claim is *Scott v. University of Delaware* (1978), wherein the federal trial court in Delaware upheld a university policy that required a terminal degree of a PhD or its equivalent for appointment or promotion to most positions as assistant professor or higher. While recognizing that the policy probably impacted African Americans disparately, the court nonetheless found that the terminal degree requirement was justified as a business necessity in light of the university's interest in hiring and promoting those most likely to be successful in furthering the knowledge in their disciplines (the scholarship function) and effective in teaching graduate students (the teaching function).

More common in the higher education setting are Title VII disparate treatment claims. In these cases, employees or prospective employees allege that officials at colleges and universities treated them less favorably, either individually or as a group, and with unlawful intent because of race, color, national origin, sex, or religion. Title VII higher education claims frequently challenge negative institutional decisions, based on a faculty committee's or administrative recommendation,

concerning hiring, academic promotion, tenure, and reemployment, which the plaintiffs charge were unlawfully grounded in one of Title VII's protected classifications.

One area under Title VII where the courts are reluctant to become involved in is disputes over tenure and academic promotion. Courts are hesitant to review the merits of tenure and other academic decisions absent clear evidence of unlawful discrimination. Under the concept of academic abstention, the courts generally recognize that academicians are better suited than they to make the highly subjective judgments that involve the review of scholarship, university service, and teaching. For example, in *Namenwirth v. Board of Regents of University of Wisconsin System* (1985), the Seventh Circuit accepted as not pretextual the university's assertion that the female plaintiff was denied tenure because her work showed insufficient promise, a judgment that resulted in her department's close tenure vote and equivocal recommendation. The court decided that the university's justification was sufficient to overcome past sex-based discrimination by both the department as a whole and the institution as well as questions concerning the department's potentially inconsistent treatment of tenure applicants based on gender.

Administrative Enforcement and Judicial Relief

The Equal Employment Opportunity Commission (EEOC) serves as the federal enforcement mechanism for Title VII. Before proceeding to litigation, individuals must exhaust administrative remedies by filing claims with the EEOC within 180 days from the time the alleged discriminatory acts occurred. After employers receive actual notice, and unless the parties reach agreement or the EEOC files suit against the educational institution, its officials must notify the complainants, who then have 90 days to bring civil actions.

Title VII authorizes courts to award a wide range of equitable relief to plaintiffs who establish that colleges and universities intentionally engaged in unlawful employment practices. In academic employment discrimination cases, courts commonly grant injunctive relief, ordering institutional officials to stop engaging in the unlawful discriminatory practices. Courts also often order reinstatement or other equitable relief along with back pay and attorney fees. However, only in exceptional instances have courts awarded tenure and rank promotion; because the judiciary is aware of its lack of expertise in evaluating faculty performance, judges are reluctant to intrude on institutional autonomy over academic issues.

Specific Unlawful Employment Practices

Pregnancy Discrimination

The Pregnancy Discrimination Act of 1978 (PDA), an amendment to Title VII, clarifies and protects the rights of pregnant employees and applicants for employment. The PDA outlaws discrimination against employees or prospective employees based on "pregnancy, childbirth, or related medical conditions." Further, employers must treat pregnancy-related conditions as they do other temporary disabilities in insurance, fringe benefit, and leave policies that govern the length of leave, the use of leave for disabilities, and the conditions to return to work (such as medical and administrative clearance and notice requirements). In higher education settings, questions may arise concerning the timelines for tenure or academic promotion when faculty members take maternity leave.

Harassment

Title VII outlaws harassment, typically consisting of offensive words, actions, or conditions that substantially annoy, alarm, or distress persons and that have no legitimate, official purpose. Normally, the unlawful activities must consist of more than stray remarks or isolated behaviors. By way of illustration, the Seventh Circuit affirmed that a dean's comments that a faculty member who was denied tenure was a "liberal union-oriented Jew" and that the plaintiff missed university events due to her Jewish holidays did not establish unlawful religious discrimination (*Adelman-Reyes v. Saint Xavier University*, 2007). The court was satisfied that the tenure decision involved numerous layers of review by various university committees and administrators. While harassment in the higher education workplace can be religious, racial, or ethnic, most claims are gender-based. Victims and harassers may be male or female and of the opposite or same sex.

Claims of sexual harassment of employees under Title VII fall into two general categories; Title IX of the Education Amendments of 1972 covers claims of sexual harassment against students. The first, quid pro quo, literally, "this for that," harassment occurs when employers threaten to or actually make employment decisions, such as hiring, promotion, pay raise, nonfiring, or transfer, contingent on sexual favors from a subordinate or peers.

Courts recognize a second form of harassment, hostile or abusive work environment, when employees are so severely or pervasively mistreated that the conditions exceed what reasonable persons would have been expected to tolerate or if the conditions have affected the persons' job performance. Examples may be verbal, such as offensive name-calling, description of alleged or imagined behavior, or dirty jokes; physical, such as leering, touching, or exposing oneself; or written, which might include posting offensive cartoons, pictures, or graffiti. Such abusive conditions may result from the behaviors of coworkers or superiors. In these circumstances, alleged victims must report the unwelcomed behavior to college or university officials who have the authority to correct or prevent the harassment. Liability is present if officials react to the actual notice of the alleged harassment with deliberate indifference or disregard.

Religious Discrimination

In addition to Title VII's general ban against religious discrimination, in 1972 Congress added Section 701(j), which clarifies that the statute's coverage extends to the religious beliefs, observances, and practices of employees or prospective employees. Officials at colleges or universities must make reasonable accommodations for such workers unless doing so would cause undue hardships on institutional operations. Even so, institutional officials do not have to offer employees preferred choices of reasonable accommodations and are not required to make accommodations resulting in more than minimal costs that can result in undue hardship, such as having to pay overtime to others who would replace individuals who could not work their schedules due to religious conflicts.

Courts have consistently agreed that educational employees have a right to miss work to observe their religious holy days and to maintain their employment status when doing so, but they have no right to paid leave under Title VII. Thus, a federal trial court in New York reached mixed results when a Muslim orderly filed a Title VII claim. The court partially granted the university's motion for summary judgment in the face of the employee's claim that he was subject to discrimination on religious grounds because officials at a teaching hospital required him to work on Friday mornings and later terminated his employment (*Gay v. S.U.N.Y Health Science Center of Brooklyn,* 1998). At the same time, the court rejected the hospital's motion to dismiss the plaintiff's retaliation claim, thereby allowing the dispute to proceed to trial.

Retaliation

Another provision of Title VII protects employees from retaliation if they challenge employment actions under the statute. Accordingly, Title VII prohibits college or university officials from retaliating against employees or prospective employees who oppose practices that are made unlawful under the statute by filing complaints or litigation or by participating in investigation or proceedings under the law. In this way, the statute protects complainants from reprisal provided they acted in the good-faith belief that Title VII was violated, regardless of whether their challenges were successful.

Ralph Sharp

See also Academic Abstention; Civil Rights Act of 1964; Disparate Impact; Equal Employment Opportunity Commission; Hostile Work Environment; Sexual Harassment, Quid Pro Quo

Further Readings

Mawdsley, R. D. (1996). Employment discrimination on the basis of religion: Where should the line be drawn? *Education Law Reporter, 111*(4), 1077–1090.

Russo, C. J. (1997). The camel's nose in the tent: Judicial intervention in tenure disputes at Catholic universities. *Education Law Reporter, 117*(3), 813–831.

Legal Citations

Adelman-Reyes v. Saint Xavier University, 500 F.3d 662 (7th Cir. 2007).

EEOC v. Catholic University of America, 83 F.3d 455 (D.C. Cir. 1996).

Gay v. S.U.N.Y Health Science Center of Brooklyn, 1998 WL 765190 (E.D.N.Y. 1998).

McDonnell Douglas Corp. v. Green, 411 U.S. 792 (1973).

Namenwirth v. Board of Regents of University of Wisconsin System, 769 F.2d 1235 (7th Cir. 1985).

Pime v. Loyola University of Chicago, 803 F.2d 351 (7th Cir. 1986).

Pregnancy Discrimination Act of 1978, Pub. L. No. 95-555.

Scott v. University of Delaware, 455 F. Supp. 1102 (D. Del. 1978), *aff'd in part, vacated and remanded in part,* 601 F.2d 76 (3d Cir. 1979).

Texas Department of Community Affairs v. Burdine, 450 U.S. 248 (1981).

Title VII, Civil Rights Act of 1964, 42 U.S.C. § 2000e (1964).

TITLE IX AND ATHLETICS

Title IX of the Education Amendments of 1972 prohibits public and private educational institutions that receive federal funds from discriminating because of gender in any aspect of their operations. If any aspect of a college or university's operations receives federal funds, then all aspects of their operations are subject to Title IX. Insofar as virtually all institutions of higher education receive federal funds in the form of student financial aid, just about all colleges and universities in the United States are covered by Title IX. This entry reviews the impact of Title IX with regard to intercollegiate athletics in American higher education.

The statute explicitly forbids quotas, and judicial interpretations of the law in a wide array of cases are both broader and narrower than the prohibitions against gender discrimination that are provided for by the Equal Protection Clause in the Fourteenth Amendment to the U.S. Constitution. Although there is no mention of intercollegiate or interscholastic athletics in the actual statute, its implementing regulations make it clear that athletics is covered by Title IX. The Office for Civil Rights (OCR) of the U.S. Department of Education is the agency charged with the enforcement of Title IX.

Under the OCR's interpretation, which has been universally endorsed by the federal appellate courts, institutional officials must do one of three things in order to achieve compliance with Title IX in the context of athletic participation. Officials may ensure that the representation of each gender is substantially proportionate; they may demonstrate a continuing history of expanding opportunities for students of the underrepresented gender; or they may demonstrate that they are currently accommodating the interests and abilities of the underrepresented gender.

Substantial Proportionality

The first way in which institutions may comply with Title IX is to ensure that each gender's representation in varsity athletics is substantially proportionate to its representation in the student body. Of course, the fact that the OCR expects a gender's representation among athletes to be "substantially proportionate" to that gender's representation in the student body necessarily begs the question of what is meant by "substantially proportionate." In 1996, the OCR clarified that athletic opportunities are "substantially proportionate when the number of opportunities that would be required to achieve proportionality would not be sufficient to sustain a viable team, meaning a team for which there is a sufficient number of interested and able students as well as enough available competition to sustain an intercollegiate team." In plain English, the OCR first decides how many additional opportunities must be offered to the underrepresented gender in order to achieve perfect proportionality. If this number is sufficient to field a viable team, then institutions are not considered substantially proportionate and must add a team.

As an illustration of how the OCR test works, suppose that university with a student body that is 55% female presently offers 700 athletic participation opportunities. Of these chances, men have 385 athletic participation opportunities while women have 315 participation opportunities. Under this example, this means that women represent 45% of the athletes (315 divided by 700) even though they account for 55% of the full-time undergraduate students. The first step for institutional officials would be to consider how many opportunities they must add for women in order to achieve perfect proportionality of 55%. If male participation remains constant, which is the assumption that the OCR employs, university officials must add 156 participation opportunities for women. If university officials did so, then there would be 471 female opportunities (315 current + 156 additional) and 385 male opportunities (all current). The second step is for officials to address whether the number of new participation opportunities required, 156 in this example, is sufficient to field a viable team. Clearly, this would be sufficient. In fact, a university could field seven or eight new women's teams with 156 additional opportunities.

Although the above example is purely hypothetical, the actual practice of the OCR yields similar results. In a letter dated August 24, 2000, the OCR advised officials at the University of Wisconsin that, based on its deviation of 2.89 percentage points (involving an enrollment of women of 52.96% compared with their intercollegiate athletic participation of 50.07%), it failed to comply with its commitment in a plan submitted to OCR to meet the first prong of the three-part test. In this letter, the OCR stated the deviation represented as many as 46 participation opportunities for women, which would be sufficient to sustain the addition of a viable women's team. In short, if one gender represents 50% of a student body, its representation among varsity athletes must approximate 50%.

Demonstration of Expanded Opportunities

Second, if an institution has not achieved substantial proportionality, its officials may demonstrate that it has a continuing history of expanding opportunities for the underrepresented gender. In other words, it is acceptable for female representation among athletes to be substantially below their representation in the student body if an institution has consistently added new teams for women and intends to continue to do so in the future. In evaluating "history," the OCR examines an institution's record for adding teams, its record of increasing participants on existing teams, and its response to requests to add teams. In assessing "continuing practice," the OCR looks at an institution's current policy for adding teams. In practical terms, this means that an institution must have consistently added new teams for the underrepresented gender about every three to four years, must refrain from eliminating any teams for the underrepresented gender, and must have a plan for adding new teams in the future. To be sure, the fact that the OCR demands that teams be added in the future necessarily begs the question of when an institution may cease adding teams. Apparently, the answer is that an institution is excused from adding teams when it finally achieves substantial proportionality. Until such time, an institution must add teams at the rate of about once every three years.

Accommodating Interests and Abilities

Third, institutional officials may demonstrate that they are currently accommodating all interests and abilities of the underrepresented gender. Under guidance issued in 2005, compliance with the third prong turns on the following factors: unmet interest sufficient to sustain a varsity team in the sport(s), sufficient ability to sustain an intercollegiate team in the sport(s), and reasonable expectation of intercollegiate competition for a team in the sport(s) within the institution's normal competitive region. In other words, institutions are not required to accommodate the interests and abilities of all their students or fulfill every request for the addition or elevation of particular sports, unless all three conditions are present. However, insofar as students are constantly entering and leaving the institution, survey data quickly become useless. To this end, if institutional officials are to demonstrate that they are filling all student needs and thereby meet the third requirement, they must complete surveys on a continuing basis. Presumably, this means that the institutional officials must periodically survey the underrepresented gender and add a new team every time there is an indication of an unmet interest and ability, until substantial proportionality is achieved.

Impact of the Three Options

As a practical matter, all three options eventually lead to substantial proportionality, the first option. Unless an institution has achieved substantial proportionality, its officials must add teams for the underrepresented gender periodically until such time as substantial proportionality is achieved; or cut opportunities for the overrepresented gender immediately so that substantial proportionality is achieved; or add a team every time there is an indication of an unmet interest and ability among the underrepresented gender until substantial proportionality is achieved; or some combination of the first three options. The question is not whether substantial proportionality will be reached but when.

Athletic Scholarships

In addition to mandating particular levels of participation, the federal regulations address the provision of athletic scholarships. As to athletic financial assistance, the regulation is specific. With respect to athletic scholarships, the regulation provides as follows:

(1) To the extent that a recipient awards athletic scholarships or grants-in-aid, it must provide reasonable opportunities for such awards for members of each sex in proportion to the number of students of each sex participating in interscholastic sports.

(2) Separate athletic scholarships or grants-in-aid for members of each sex may be provided as part of separate athletic teams for members of each sex to the extent consistent with this paragraph and § 106.41(c). (C.F.R. § 106.37(c))

In effect, if 45% of the athletes are female, then females should receive approximately 45% of total athletic financial assistance.

As in the case of the participation requirements, although no level of permissible deviation from exact equality in scholarship aid has been established, OCR issued a guidance letter addressing this point. According to this letter,

if any unexplained disparity in the scholarship budgets for athletes of either gender is 1% or less for the entire budget for athletic scholarships, there will be a strong presumption that such a disparity is reasonable and based on legitimate nondiscriminatory factors. Conversely, there will be a strong presumption that an unexplained disparity of more than 1% is in violation of the "substantially proportionate" requirement. (Letter to Nancy S. Footer, general counsel of Bowling Green University, July 23, 1998)

To be sure, the financial assistance regulation and the accommodating interests and abilities regulation work in tandem. As a gender's participation increases, its share of scholarship money must also increase. Thus, while adding some extra nonscholarship players may help an institution to achieve substantial proportionality in the context of participation, it may actually cause noncompliance in the financial context. Conversely, limiting nonscholarship players to achieve financial assistance compliance may cause a college or university to fail the substantial proportionality test. Since it is extremely difficult for an institution to meet both of these Title IX standards, their officials must remain vigilant.

William E. Thro

See also *Grove City College v. Bell*; National Collegiate Athletic Association; U.S. Department of Education

Further Readings

Beveridge, C. P. (1996). Title IX and intercollegiate athletics: When schools cut men's athletic teams. *University of Illinois Law Review*, pp. 809–842.

Boucher v. Syracuse University, 164 F.3d 113 (2d Cir. 1999).

Cohen v. Brown University, 809 F. Supp. 978 (D.R.I. 1992), *aff'd*, 991 F.2d 888 (1st Cir. 1993), *remanded* 879 F. Supp. 185 (D.R.I. 1995), *aff'd in part, rev'd in part*, 102 F.3d 155 (1st Cir. 1996).

Davis v. Monroe County School District, 526 U.S. 626 (1999).

Favia v. Indiana University of Pennsylvania, 812 F. Supp. 578 (W.D. Pa. 1993), *aff'd*, 7 F.3d 332 (3d Cir. 1993).

Gavora, J. (2002). *Tilting the playing field: Schools, sports, sex, & Title IX*. San Francisco: Encounter Books.

Gebser v. Lago Vista Independent School District, 524 U.S. 276 (1998).

Hollinger, C. L., Jr. (1994). Are male college sports in jeopardy? A look at *Kelly v. Board of Trustees of the University of Illinois. Seattle University Law Review*, 21, 151–169.

Kelley v. Board of Trustees, 35 F.3d 265 (7th Cir. 1994).

Neal v. Board of Trustees of the California State Universities, 198 F.3d 763 (9th Cir. 1999).

Policy interpretation. 44 *Federal Register* 71413 (1979).

Roberts v. Colorado State Board of Agriculture, 998 F.2d 824 (10th Cir. 1993).

Snow, B. A., & Thro, W. E. (1996). Still on the sidelines: Developing the non-discrimination paradigm under Title IX. *Duke Journal of Gender Law & Policy, 3*, 1–48.

Snow, B. A., Thro, W. E., & Clemente, S. (2001). The problem of determining Title IX liability. *Education Law Reporter, 154*, 1–44.

Thro, W. E., & Snow, B. A. (1993). The significance of *Cohen v. Brown University* for the future of intercollegiate and interscholastic athletics. *Education Law Reporter, 84*, 611–628.

Thro W. E., & Snow, B. A. (1998). The conflict between the Equal Protection Clause and *Cohen v. Brown University. Education Law Reporter, 123*, 1013–1037.

Title IX of the Education Amendments of 1972, 20 U.S.C. §§ 1681 *et seq.* (1972).

Legal Citations

Code of Federal Regulations, 34 C.F.R. §§ 106.37(c), 106.41.

Office for Civil Rights. (1996). *Clarification of intercollegiate athletics policy guidance: The three-part test.* Retrieved May 1, 2009, from http://www.ed.gov/about/offices/list/ocr/docs/clarific.html

Office for Civil Rights. (2005). *Additional clarification of intercollegiate athletics policy: Three-part test—part three.* Retrieved May 1, 2009, from http://www.ed.gov/about/offices/list/ocr/docs/title9guidanceadditional.html

TITLE IX AND RETALIATION

In 2005, the U.S. Supreme Court, in *Jackson v. Birmingham Board of Education*, rendered a sharply divided opinion in deciding that employees who report gender discrimination in violation of Title IX of the Education Amendments of 1972 and are retaliated against as a result of their complaints can seek redress for retaliation under Title IX. Title IX prohibits discrimination "on the basis of sex" by recipients of federal education funds. Although there is no specific reference to retaliation in the text of Title IX, *Jackson* extends the statute's protections against discrimination "on the basis of sex" to those retaliated against for reporting violations of its provisions regardless of their gender.

Until *Jackson* was resolved, lower federal courts had disagreed as to whether a private right of action existed under Title IX. *Jackson* settled the question and has stimulated litigation against colleges and universities resulting in costly damages and settlement agreements, thereby opening a new window for aggrieved employees to seek restitution from institutions of higher learning for alleged instances of retaliation under Title IX. Accordingly, this entry examines *Jackson*'s background and potential ramifications for institutions of higher leaning.

Jackson v. Birmingham Board of Education

Facts of the Case

Roderick Jackson was hired as the physical education teacher and girls' basketball coach by the public school board in Birmingham, Alabama, in 1993. Jackson was transferred to a different school in 1999, where he discovered that the girls' basketball team did not receive equal funding or access to athletic equipment and facilities. The lack of funding and equipment caused Jackson significant difficulty in coaching the girls' basketball team. Jackson complained of this unequal treatment to his supervisor beginning in December 2000, but his complaints were unheeded. Rather, Jackson began to receive negative performance evaluations and his employment as coach was terminated in May 2001; he retained his job as a teacher.

Jackson filed suit in a federal trial court in Alabama alleging, among other issues, that the school board retaliated against him because of his complaints of gender inequity in violation of Title IX. However, the trial court dismissed Jackson's claim in declaring that Title IX's private right of action did not include retaliation claims. The Eleventh Circuit affirmed on the basis that the plaintiff failed to state a claim, because Title IX did not provide for a private right of action for retaliation. The court added that even if Title IX had prohibited retaliation, Jackson would not have been entitled to relief, because he was not a member of the protected class, namely females, under Title IX.

The Supreme Court's Ruling

The Supreme Court agreed to hear an appeal in order to resolve the question of whether the private right of action under Title IX encompassed claims of retaliation for complaints of discrimination on the basis of sex. Writing for the majority in a five-to-four judgment, Justice O'Connor, writing for the Court, reversed in favor of Jackson.

At the outset of its analysis, the Supreme Court pointed out that in 1979, in *Cannon v. University of Chicago*, it had recognized that Title IX implies a private right of action to prohibit intentional discrimination on the basis of sex. The Court also noted that, over time, it had distilled the contours of this private right of action in other cases, indicating that it authorizes private parties to seek monetary damages for Title IX violations and that the private right of action encompasses intentional sex discrimination in the form of deliberate indifference to a teacher's sexual harassment of a student or to sexual harassment of a student by another student.

In *Jackson,* the Supreme Court held that retaliation against a person who complained of sex discrimination is another form of intentional discrimination on the basis of sex that is subject to Title IX's private right of action. The Court reasoned that retaliation, by definition, is an intentional act and a form of discrimination, because a complainant is treated differently on the basis of a complaint, an action that represents an intentional response to an allegation of sex discrimination that constitutes the very nature of the complaint. The Court thus indicated that if plaintiff is subject to retaliation for raising a complaint of sex discrimination, this constitutes intentional discrimination "on the basis of sex," in violation of Title IX.

The Supreme Court further explained that discrimination is a term covering a broad spectrum of disparate treatment and that Congress provided Title IX with a wide berth as a result of the breadth of its statutory language. To this end, the Court determined that Congress could have mentioned retaliation expressly in Title IX, just as it did in Title VII of the Civil Rights Act of 1964. Even so, the Court interpreted the two laws as different, insofar as Title IX's cause of action is implied, while Title VII's is explicit. According to this interpretation, the Court wrote, Title IX is a broadly constructed general prohibition of discrimination accompanied by narrow and specific exceptions to that general prohibition, while Title VII expressly denotes the conduct that constitutes illegal discrimination.

The Supreme Court went on to reject the board's argument that Jackson was not entitled to invoke Title IX because his experience of the sex discrimination was indirect. Rather, the Court posited that because Title IX's construction is sufficiently broad, it does not require victims of retaliation to also be the victims of the discrimination that was the subject of the initial complaints. In this way, the majority was of the opinion that the individuals who complained of discrimination, if retaliated against on the basis of those complaints, were to be treated as victims of discrimination regardless of whether they were parties to the original complaints.

As part of its rationale, the Supreme Court recognized that because reporting discrimination is essential to the enforcement of Title IX, the statute would have been diminished if the subjects of those reports could retaliate against persons who filed complaints alleging that discriminatory policies were in effect. The Court noted that those who teach and coach are in the best position to advocate for the rights of their students; they can effectively bring discrimination to the attention of administrators because of their closeness to situations in which discrimination might occur.

The school board's final argument centered on the notion that Title IX should not have been interpreted as prohibiting retaliation, because its officials were unaware that it could have been liable for retaliating against those who complained of Title IX violations. The Supreme Court disagreed, ruling that the board and its officials should have been placed on notice in light of earlier cases that consistently interpreted Title IX's private right of action as encompassing diverse forms of intentional sex discrimination.

According to the Court, because the regulations implementing Title IX, which clearly prohibited retaliation, had been in place for some 30 years, this fact should reasonably have informed the defendants that they were not free to retaliate against individuals who complained of gender inequity in violation of Title IX. In conclusion, the Supreme Court reversed and remanded in favor of Jackson, specifying that he should have been allowed to offer evidence to support his allegation of retaliation under Title IX. Jackson and the board subsequently reached a settlement that allowed him to return to work as head coach of a girls' team at another high school in the district under the same terms of employment as other coaches ("Coach in Title IX Case," 2006, p. 14).

The Dissent

The dissenters, in an opinion authored by Justice Thomas, characterized the majority's holding as plainly against the grain of the language of Title IX, indicating that retaliatory conduct does not constitute discrimination on the basis of sex. The dissenting justices further asserted that they would have interpreted Title IX as not referring to retaliation in its text and that the clear meaning of the phrase "on the basis of sex" is relative to the sex of the plaintiff, not the complainant. The dissent was convinced that, within this construction, Jackson's argument that the board retaliated against him failed to advance a claim for sex discrimination and that his allegation of discrimination was predicated on a tenuous connection between the alleged adverse treatment of the female basketball team and the alleged retaliation against him. The dissent rounded out its opinion with the comment that because Jackson's sex did not play a role in his adverse treatment, the language of Title IX precluded embracing his complaint as a valid retaliation claim.

Impact of *Jackson v. Birmingham* in Higher Education

Jackson has stimulated litigation against institutions of higher education that has resulted in damages and settlement agreements reaching into the millions of dollars. The first application of the retaliation standard articulated in *Jackson* to higher education took place in 2006 in *Atkinson v. Lafayette College*. In *Atkinson*, a female athletic director who alleged that her employment was terminated as a result of her complaints regarding gender inequities in her institution's sport programs successfully persuaded the Third Circuit to vacate an earlier order dismissing her case and to remand it for further proceedings consistent with *Jackson*. *Atkinson* was followed closely by *Burch v. Regents of University of California* (2006), in which a university wrestling coach publicly complained of inequities relative to the female wrestling team. His employment was subsequently terminated, which the institution held was a factor of the coach's employment record of potential NCAA violations. Yet, the coach demonstrated that there were material issues of fact as to whether he was dismissed in retaliation for his complaints of gender inequities, consistent with the *Jackson* Title IX retaliation standard. The university settled with the coach for $725,000 in 2007.

In a case described by Lipka (2007), California State University at Fresno faced steep damages and settlements as a result of Title IX retaliation litigation. In 2007, a former volleyball coach was awarded a verdict of $5.85 million, while a female basketball coach who successfully argued retaliation for her advocacy of women's athletics was awarded $19.1 million, an amount later reduced to $9 million. The university also settled a similar case with a former female athletics director for $3.5 million, while the University of California system settled for $3.5 million with a former Berkeley swimming coach who successfully contended that her layoff was discriminatory and retaliatory in nature (Lipka, 2007).

In 2008, Florida Gulf Coast University (FGCU) settled with two female coaches who argued that they had been retaliated against on the basis of their complaints concerning inequities in women's athletics at the institution (Jaschik, 2008). FGCU paid the coaches $3.4 million, and also paid $800,000 to a former general counsel who argued that she had been retaliated against while working to resolve the matter. Similarly, in 2008 two female basketball coaches filed suit under Title IX against San Diego Mesa College, alleging retaliation for their advocacy of women's sports (Stripling, 2008).

Kerry Brian Melear

See also *Cannon v. University of Chicago*; Title VII; U.S. Supreme Court Cases in Higher Education

Further Readings

Coach in Title IX case wins reinstatement. (2006, December 6). *Education Week*, p. 14.

Hausrath, C. M. (2006). *Jackson v. Birmingham Board of Education:* Expanding the class of the protected, or protecting the protectors? *University of Richmond Law Review, 40*, 613–630.

Jaschik, S. (2008, October 22). *Quick takes.* Retrieved June 23, 2008, from http://www.insidehighered.com/news/2008/10/22/qt

Lipka, S. (2007, August 3). Fresno State grapples with a spate of sex-discrimination claims. *The Chronicle of Higher Education, 53*(48), A29.

Melear, K. B. (2007). Title IX and retaliation: The impact of *Jackson v. Birmingham Board of Education on Higher Education. Journal of Personnel Evaluation in Education, 19*, 91–103.

Redden, E. (2007, December 10). *Fallout from Fresno State's multi-million dollar case(s).* Retrieved May 25, 2009, from http://www.insidehighered.com/news/2007/12/10/fresno

Russo, C. J., & Thro, W. E. (2005). The meaning of sex: *Jackson v. Birmingham School Board* and its potential implications. *Education Law Reporter, 198*, 777–792.

Stripling, J. (2008, July 28). *Lesbian basketball coaches call foul.* Retrieved May 25, 2009, from http://www.insidehighered.com/news/2008/07/28/mesa

Legal Citations

Atkinson v. Lafayette College, 460 F.3d 447 (3d Cir. 2006).

Burch v. Regents of University of California, 433 F. Supp. 2d 1110 (E.D. Cal. 2006).

Cannon v. University of Chicago, 441 U.S. 677 (1979).

Jackson v. Birmingham Board of Education, 544 U.S. 167 (2005).

Title VII of the Civil Rights Act of 1964, 42 U.S.C. § 2000e (1964).

Title IX of the Education Amendments of 1972, 20 U.S.C. §§ 1681 *et seq.* (1972).

TITLE IX AND SEXUAL HARASSMENT

Title IX of the Education Amendments of 1972 forbids gender discrimination by any educational institution, public or private, that receives federal funds, and the U.S. Supreme Court has interpreted Title IX to prohibit sexual harassment whether by individuals or institutions. Institutions, of course, can be liable due to the acts of officials who either chose to break the law or fail to enforce its provisions. After permitting private causes of action under Title IX to proceed in *Cannon v. University of Chicago* (1979) and *Franklin v. Gwinnett County Public Schools* (1992), the Court applied Title IX to sexual harassment of a student by a teacher in a public school in *Gebser v. Lago Vista Independent School District* (1998). A year later, in *Davis v. Monroe County Board of Education* (1999), the Court extended its holding to sexual harassment of a student by a peer in a public school. Based on the significant issues involved in this area, this entry examines the status of the law with regard to sexual harassment on college and university campuses, focusing on the law with respect to institutional liability for sexual harassment, not on what counts as sexual harassment in general.

With respect to faculty-student sexual harassment in the context of higher education, institutional liability can be demonstrated by showing that an "appropriate person" had actual notice of the conduct and that the individual responded, or perhaps more appropriately, failed to respond, with deliberate indifference. With respect to the first element, an appropriate person means an official "who at a minimum has authority to address the alleged discrimination and to institute corrective measures" on the school's behalf. In other words, "appropriate persons" are those who have the authority to address the misconduct by terminating or otherwise disciplining the offending party. As to the second element, deliberate indifference, this means that an educational official knows of the conduct and, as a matter of official policy, does nothing. Consequently, the courts have interpreted institutions as effectively causing continuing violations. In other words, liability results when institutional officials know of the harassment and affirmatively choose to do nothing.

When the person engaging in sexual harassment is a student, rather than a faculty member in higher education, additional requirements come into play. In *Davis*, the Supreme Court stressed that the language of Title IX, coupled with the requirement that recipients of federal financial assistance have notice of the proscriptions under the statute, requires that institutions subjected to liability must have substantial control over the harasser and the environment in which the harassment occurs before they can be liable: "Only then can the recipient be said to 'expose' its students to harassment or cause them to undergo it 'under' the recipient's programs" (*Davis*, p. 646). In reaching this outcome, the Court relied in part on the requirement in Title IX that harassment occur under the operations of a funding recipient.

However, the Court, in an apparent attempt to qualify the requirement as it might apply in higher education, emphasized that college or university officials might not

> be expected to exercise the same degree of control over its students that a grade school would enjoy [citation omitted], and it would be entirely reasonable for a school to refrain from a form of disciplinary action that would expose it to constitutional or statutory claims. (p. 649)

The Supreme Court imposed two additional conditions on its test for peer-to-peer sexual harassment that were not addressed in *Gebser*. The first provides a defense if institutional recipients of federal financial assistance can show that official responses to harassment were not "clearly unreasonable." The Court distinguished this from a "mere 'reasonableness' standard," stating that in an appropriate case, "There is no reason why courts, on a motion to dismiss, for summary judgment, or for a directed verdict, could not identify a response as 'not clearly unreasonable' as a matter of law" (p. 649). The second condition, which is based on the attachment of Title IX to "actions that occur under any program or activity," requires that damages be "available only where behavior is so severe, pervasive, and objectively offensive that it denies its victims the equal access to education that Title IX is designed to protect" (p. 652).

The *Davis* Court further sought to avoid an overly expansive application of its holding to common behavior, particularly among children, involving such things as "simple acts of teasing and name calling" (p. 676). The Court also stressed that it did not contemplate or hold that a mere decline in grades is sufficient to survive a motion to dismiss. The Court attempted to provide some general guidance as to when gender-oriented conduct rises to the level of actionable sexual harassment by declaring that it "depends on a constellation of surrounding circumstances, expectations, and relationships, including, but not limited to, the ages of the harasser and the victim and the number of individuals involved" (p. 651).

In both *Gebser* and *Davis*, the Supreme Court implicitly ruled that Title IX liability turned on a finding of intentional discrimination by the educational institution. In other words, the Court was of the opinion that before Title IX liability attaches, a plaintiff must demonstrate that institutional officials made a conscious choice to discriminate by failing to act on actual knowledge. The Court thus made it clear that it is not enough to show that an employee or agent of a college or university behaved improperly. Rather, the Court explained that a plaintiff must show that an official or officials at an educational institution endorsed such conduct or failed to stop it from continuing.

In response to the litigation at the Supreme Court, and aware of the need to eliminate or remedy incidences of sexual harassment on college and university campuses, federal regulations promulgated pursuant to Title IX require institutions to develop clearly written policies prohibiting all forms of sexual harassment. In developing and reviewing policies, officials should include representatives of faculty, staff, and students to ensure that those charged with harassment are entitled to protection under due process procedures that have been set forth for other forms of alleged policy violations. At the same time, policies should have effective and well-publicized procedures by which students, faculty, and staff can report and resolve sexual harassment complaints in a timely manner that respects the substantive and procedural due process rights of both the accused and the accuser.

William E. Thro

See also Sexual Harassment, Peer-to-Peer; Sexual Harassment, Quid Pro Quo; Sexual Harassment, Same-Sex; Sexual Harassment of Students by Faculty Members; Title IX and Retaliation

Further Readings

Russo, C. J., & Thro, W. E. (2005). Student equal protection and due process. In J. Beckham & D. Dagley (Eds.), *Contemporary issues in higher education law* (pp. 257–275). Dayton, OH: Education Law Association.

Snow B. A., & Thro, W. E. (1996). Still on the sidelines: Developing the non-discrimination paradigm under Title IX. *Duke Journal of Gender Law & Policy, 3,* 1–49.

Snow, B. A., Thro, W. E., & Clemente, S. (2001). The problem of determining Title IX liability. *Education Law Reporter, 154*(1), 1–44.

Legal Citations

Cannon v. University of Chicago, 441 U.S. 677 (1979).
Code of Federal Regulations, 34 C.F.R. § 106.8(b).
Davis v. Monroe County Board of Education, 526 U.S. 629 (1999).
Franklin v. Gwinnett County Public Schools, 503 U.S. 60 (1992), *on remand,* 969 F.2d 1022 (11th Cir. 1992).
Gebser v. Lago Vista Independent School District, 524 U.S. 274 (1998).
Title IX of the Education Amendments of 1972, 20 U.S.C. §§ 1681 *et seq.* (1972).

TRUSTEES OF DARTMOUTH COLLEGE V. WOODWARD

Trustees of Dartmouth College v. Woodward (1819) stands out not only because it was the U.S. Supreme Court's first case dealing with a dispute involving education but also because it provided constitutional protections for private contracts, albeit in an educational context. At issue in *Dartmouth* was the validity of private contracts after the New Hampshire legislature sought to overturn agreements that the college's trustees had entered. As a result of *Dartmouth,* private colleges were allowed to have self-governance and maintenance without interference from state legislatures and other public entities. This entry reviews the background, the facts, and the Court's rationale in this seminal case.

Background

By way of background to *Dartmouth,* it is worth noting that previously, in *Fletcher v. Peck* (1810), the Supreme Court reviewed the legality of contracts for the exchange of land in Georgia. Here, writing for the Court, Chief Justice Marshall pointed out that Georgia was not a single unconnected power but was a member of the American union that was bound by the federal Constitution. Marshall observed that a state law annulling the sale of public lands due to fraudulent acts, although deplorable, violated the sanctity of contracts. This judgment indicates that states are subject to the federal Constitution, which includes the provision forbidding the states from enacting laws impairing the obligation of contracts, and it serves as a necessary backdrop for *Dartmouth.*

Facts of the Case

The Board of Trustees of Dartmouth College received a corporate charter from England in 1769. Earlier, the Reverend Eleazar Wheelock had founded a charity school in 1754 for "civilizing and spreading the Christian knowledge to children of pagans." Wheelock, who sought private funds in England and New Hampshire to maintain and expand the school, received a charter from the English King George in 1769 for the education of youth including American Indians, English children, and others desirous of receiving an education. The charter granted the trustees of Dartmouth College corporate governance rights in perpetuity. The original Dartmouth trustees had contributed private funds for the college's founding and maintenance and had intended that the funds be used to spread "knowledge of the only true God and Savior among the American savages." Dartmouth was named after one of its English benefactors, the Right Honorable William, Earl of Dartmouth.

A dispute arose in 1816 when senior trustees disagreed with those seeking to expand the body's membership from 12 to 21 in order to grant control over the college to the New Hampshire state legislature, which had passed a law changing the charter from private to state control. After the Superior Court of New Hampshire ruled that control of Dartmouth was the province of the state, Wheelock and the original founders sought further review from the U.S. Supreme Court, where Daniel Webster argued the case successfully on behalf of the trustees. Webster, an alumnus, spoke of Dartmouth as a small college, emphasizing that yet there were those who loved the school.

The Supreme Court's Ruling

In a majority opinion written by Chief Justice John Marshall, the Supreme Court reversed in favor of the college. In so doing, the Court upheld the sanctity of private contracts even though the original charter was between King George and the trustees, and the United States was independent of England. The Court ruled that Article 1, Section 10 of the United States Constitution prevented states from encroaching on a private contract in its assertion that "No state shall . . . pass any . . . Law impairing the Obligation of Contracts [sic]. . . ."

In striking down the judgment of the New Hampshire court as unconstitutional, Chief Justice Marshall addressed how delicate such decisions are for the Supreme Court when reviewing cases between citizens of different states, between states and their citizens, or between two states. The Court reasoned that the issue at bar was not limited to a single college but included every college and educational institution in the country. To this end, the Court explained that all private institutions have a common principle in their existence, namely the inviolability of their charters. As such, the Court maintained that it would have been dangerous to allow these institutions be subject to the rise and fall of popular parties and the fluctuations of public opinion. The Court was of the opinion that because the college was created and maintained by private donations, its benefactors need assurances that their contributions were honored for the purposes intended. Consequently, the Court concluded that although a corporation is an artificial being, invisible, intangible, and existing only in the law, Dartmouth's charter provided for perpetuation of its educational mission.

It is important to acknowledge the role of Chief Justice John Marshall, author of the opinion in *Dartmouth*, because it is an important illustration in an educational context of his leadership role in strengthening the Supreme Court by making it a coequal partner with the executive and legislative branches of the government. Although Marshall had only one month of formal legal studies before he was admitted to the bar, he proved to be an effective chief justice who served for 34 years while authoring 574 opinions. Thus, *Dartmouth* is significant because it set an important precedent for the existence and perpetuity of private colleges and universities in America.

In sum, *Dartmouth* still serves as useful precedent for cases dealing with state interference with private schools, including the Supreme Court's 1925 decision in *Pierce v. Society of Sisters* that, in upholding the rights of parents to satisfy compulsory attendance laws by sending their children to religiously affiliated nonpublic K–12 schools, essentially upheld the right of these schools to continue operating. *Dartmouth* is important, then, because it stimulated the growth of private educational institutions at all levels while providing protection for private corporations including colleges and universities.

James J. Van Patten

See also Boards of Trustees; Federalism

Further Readings

Friedman, L. M. (2005). *A history of American law.* New York: Simon & Schuster.

Knight, E. (1951). *Education in the United States.* New York: Ginn.

Rehnquist, W. H. (1987). *The Supreme Court.* New York: Vintage Books.

Legal Citations

Fletcher v. Peck, 10 U.S. 87 (1810).
Pierce v. Society of Sisters, 268 U.S. 355 (1925).
Trustees of Dartmouth College v. Woodward, 17 U.S. 518 (1819).

TRUSTEES OF DARTMOUTH COLLEGE V. WOODWARD

In *Woodward,* the Supreme Court's first case on education at any level, the Justices upheld the right of self-governance and maintenance at private colleges and universities to be free from interference from state legislatures and other public entities. In light of *Woodward*'s historical significance, it is reprinted here in its entirety.

Supreme Court of the United States

TRUSTEES OF DARTMOUTH COLLEGE

v.

WOODWARD

Feb. 2, 1819

The opinion of the court was delivered by MARSHALL, Ch. J.

This is an action of trover, brought by the Trustees of Dartmouth College against William H. Woodward, in the state court of New Hampshire, for the book of records, corporate seal, and other corporate property, to which the plaintiffs allege themselves to be entitled. A special verdict, after setting out the rights of the parties, finds for the defendant, if certain acts of the legislature of New Hampshire, passed on the 27th of June, and on the 18th of December 1816, be valid, and binding on the trustees, without their assent, and not repugnant to the constitution of the United States; otherwise, it finds for the plaintiffs. The superior court of judicature of New Hampshire rendered a judgment upon this verdict for the defendant, which judgment has been brought before this court by writ of error. The single question now to be considered is, do the acts to which the verdict refers violate the constitution of the United States?

This court can be insensible neither to the magnitude nor delicacy of this question. The validity of a legislative act is to be examined; and the opinion of the highest law tribunal of a state is to be revised—an opinion which carries with it intrinsic evidence of the diligence, of the ability, and the integrity, with which it was formed. On more than one occasion, this court has expressed the cautious circumspection with which it approaches the consideration of such questions; and has declared, that in no doubtful case, would it pronounce a legislative act to be contrary to the constitution. But the American people have said, in the constitution of the United States, that "no state shall pass any bill of attainder, *ex post facto* law, or law impairing the obligation of contracts." In the same instrument, they have also said, "that the judicial power shall extend to all cases in law and equity arising under the constitution." On the judges of this court, then, is imposed the high and solemn duty of protecting, from even legislative violation, those contracts which the constitution of our country has placed beyond legislative control; and, however irksome the task may be, this is a duty from which we dare not shrink.

The title of the plaintiffs originates in a charter dated the 13th day of December, in the year 1769, incorporating twelve persons therein mentioned, by the name of

"The Trustees of Dartmouth College," granting to them and their successors the usual corporate privileges and powers, and authorizing the trustees, who are to govern the college, to fill up all vacancies which may be created in their own body.

The defendant claims under three acts of the legislature of New Hampshire, the most material of which was passed on the 27th of June 1816, and is entitled, "an act to amend the charter, and enlarge and improve the corporation of Dartmouth College." Among other alterations in the charter, this act increases the number of trustees to twenty-one, gives the appointment of the additional members to the executive of the state, and creates a board of overseers, with power to inspect and control the most important acts of the trustees. This board consists of twenty-five persons. The president of the senate, the speaker of the house of representatives of New Hampshire, and the governor and lieutenant-governor of Vermont, for the time being, are to be members *ex officio*. The board is to be completed by the governor and council of New Hampshire, who are also empowered to fill all vacancies which may occur. The acts of the 18th and 26th of December are supplemental to that of the 27th of June, and are principally intended to carry that act into effect. The majority of the trustees of the college have refused to accept this amended charter, and have brought this suit for the corporate property, which is in possession of a person holding by virtue of the acts which have been stated. It can require no argument to prove, that the circumstances of this case constitute a contract. An application is made to the crown for a charter to incorporate a religious and literary institution. In the application, it is stated, that large contributions have been made for the object, which will be conferred on the corporation, as soon as it shall be created. The charter is granted, and on its faith the property is conveyed. Surely, in this transaction every ingredient of a complete and legitimate contract is to be found. The points for consideration are, 1. Is this contract protected by the constitution of the United States? 2. Is it impaired by the acts under which the defendant holds?

1. On the first point, is has been argued, that the word "contract," in its broadest sense, would comprehend the political relations between the government and its citizens, would extend to offices held within a state, for state purposes, and to many of those laws concerning civil institutions, which must change with circumstances, and be modified by ordinary legislation; which deeply concern the public, and which, to preserve good government, the public judgment must control. That even marriage is a contract, and its obligations are affected by the laws respecting divorces. That the clause in the constitution, if construed in its greatest latitude, would prohibit these laws. Taken in its broad, unlimited sense, the clause would be an unprofitable and vexatious interference with the internal concerns of a state, would unnecessarily and unwisely embarrass its legislation, and render immutable those civil institutions, which are established for purposes of internal government, and which, to subserve those purposes, ought to vary with varying circumstances. That as the framers of the constitution could never have intended to insert in that instrument, a provision so unnecessary, so mischievous, and so repugnant to its general spirit, the term "contract" must be understood in a more limited sense. That it must be understood as intended to guard against a power, of at least doubtful utility, the abuse of which had been extensively felt; and to restrain the legislature in future from violating the right to property. That, anterior to the formation of the constitution, a course of legislation had prevailed in many, if not in all, of the states, which weakened the confidence of man in man, and embarrassed all transactions between individuals, by dispensing with a faithful performance of engagements. To correct this mischief, by restraining the power which produced it, the state legislatures were forbidden "to pass any law impairing the obligation of contracts," that is, of contracts respecting property, under which some individual could claim a right to something beneficial to himself; and that, since the clause in the constitution must in construction receive some limitation, it may be confined, and ought to be confined, to cases of this description; to cases within the mischief it was intended to remedy.

The general correctness of these observations cannot be controverted. That the framers of the constitution did not intend to restrain the states in the regulation of their civil institutions, adopted for internal government, and that the instrument they have given us, is not to be so construed, may be admitted. The provision of the constitution never has been understood to embrace other contracts, than those which respect property, or some object of value, and confer rights which may be asserted in a court of justice. It never has been understood to restrict the general right of the legislature to legislate on the subject of divorces. Those acts enable some tribunals, not to impair a marriage contract, but to liberate one of the parties, because it has been broken by the other. When any state legislature shall pass an act annulling all marriage contracts, or allowing either party to annul it, without the consent of the other, it will be time enough to inquire, whether such an act be constitutional.

The parties in this case differ less on general principles, less on the true construction of the constitution in the abstract, than on the application of those principles to this case, and on the true construction of the charter of 1769. This is the point on which the cause essentially depends. If the act of incorporation be a grant of political power, if it create a civil institution, to be employed in the administration of the government, or if the funds of the college be public property, or if the state of New Hampshire, as a government, be alone interested in its transactions, the subject is one in which the legislature of the state may act according to its own judgment, unrestrained by any limitation of its power imposed by the constitution of the United States.

But if this be a private eleemosynary institution, endowed with a capacity to take property, for objects unconnected with government, whose funds are bestowed by individuals, on the faith of the charter; if the donors have stipulated for the future disposition and management of those funds, in the manner prescribed by themselves; there may be more difficulty in the case, although neither the persons who have made these stipulations, nor those for whose benefit they were made, should be parties to the cause. Those who are no longer interested in the property, may yet retain such an interest in the preservation of their own arrangements, as to have a right to insist, that those arrangements shall be held sacred. Or, if they have themselves disappeared, it becomes a subject of serious and anxious inquiry, whether those whom they have legally empowered to represent them for ever, may not assert all the rights which they possessed, while in being; whether, if they be without personal representatives, who may feel injured by a violation of the compact, the trustees be not so completely their representatives, in the eye of the law, as to stand in their place, not only as respects the government of the college, but also as respects the maintenance of the college charter. It becomes then the duty of the court, most seriously to examine this charter, and to ascertain its true character.

From the instrument itself, it appears, that about the year 1754, the Rev. Eleazer Wheelock established, at his own expense, and on his own estate, a charity school for the instruction of Indians in the Christian religion. The success of this institution inspired him with the design of soliciting contributions in England, for carrying on and extending his undertaking. In this pious work, he employed the Rev. Nathaniel Whitaker, who, by virtue of a power of attorney from Dr. Wheelock, appointed the Earl of Dartmouth and others, trustees of the money, which had been, and should be, contributed; which appointment Dr. Wheelock confirmed by a deed of trust, authorizing the trustees to fix on a site for the college. They determined to establish the school on Connecticut river, in the western part of New Hampshire; that situation being suposed favorable for carrying on the original design among the Indians, and also for promoting learning among the English; and the proprietors in the neighborhood having made large offers of land, on condition, that the college should there be placed. Dr. Wheelock then applied to the crown for an act of incorporation; and represented the expediency of appointing those whom he had, by his last will, named as trustees in America, to be members of the proposed corporation. "In consideration of the premises," "for the education and instruction of the youth of the Indian tribes," &c., "and also of English youth, and any others," the charter was granted, and the trustees of Dartmouth College were, by that name, created a body corporate, with power, for the use of the said college, to acquire real and personal property, and to pay the president, tutors and other officers of the college, such salaries as they shall allow.

The charter proceeds to appoint Eleazer Wheelock, "the founder of said college," president thereof, with power, by his last will, to appoint a successor, who is to continue in office, until disapproved by the trustees. In case of vacancy, the trustees may appoint a president, and in case of the ceasing of a president, the senior professor or tutor, being one of the trustees, shall exercise the office, until an appointment shall be made. The trustees have power to appoint and displace professors, tutors and other officers, and to supply any vacancies which may be created in their own body, by death, resignation, removal or disability; and also to make orders, ordinances and laws for the government of the college, the same not being repugnant to the laws of Great Britain, or of New Hampshire, and not excluding any person on account of his speculative sentiments in religion, or his being of a religious profession different from that of the trustees. This charter was accepted, and the property, both real and personal, which had been contributed for the benefit of the college, was conveyed to, and vested in, the corporate body. From this brief review of the most essential parts of the charter, it is apparent, that the funds of the college consisted entirely of private donations. It is, perhaps, not very important, who were the donors. The probability is, that the Earl of Dartmouth, and the other trustees in England, were, in fact, the largest contributors. Yet the legal conclusion, from the facts recited in the charter, would probably be, that Dr. Wheelock was the founder of the college. The origin of the institution was, undoubtedly, the Indian charity school, established by Dr. Wheelock, at his own expense. It was at his instance, and to enlarge this school, that contributions were solicited in England. The person soliciting these contributions was his agent; and the trustees, who received the money, were appointed by, and act under, his authority. It is not too much to say, that the funds were obtained by him, in trust, to be applied by him to the purposes of his enlarged school. The charter of incorporation was granted at his instance. The persons named by him, in his last will, as the trustees of his charity-school, compose a part of the corporation, and he is declared to be the founder of the college, and its president for life. Were the inquiry material, we should feel some hesitation in saying, that Dr. Wheelock was not, in law, to be considered as the founder (1 Bl. Com. 481) of this institution, and as possessing all the rights appertaining to that character. But be this as it may, Dartmouth College is really endowed by private individuals, who have bestowed their funds for the propagation of the Christian religion among the Indians, and for the promotion of piety and learning generally. From these funds, the salaries of the tutors are drawn; and these salaries lessen the expense of education to the students. It is then an eleemosynary and so far as respects its funds, a private corporation.

Do its objects stamp on it a different character? Are the trustees and professors public officers, invested with any portion of political power, partaking in any degree in the administration of civil government, and performing duties which flow from the sovereign authority? That education is an object of national concern, and a proper subject of legislation, all admit. That there may be an institution, founded by government, and placed entirely under its immediate control, the officers of which would be public officers, amenable exclusively to government, none will deny. But is Dartmouth College such an institution? Is education altogether in the hands of government? Does every teacher of youth become a public

officer, and do donations for the purpose of education necessarily become public property, so far that the will of the legislature, not the will of the donor, becomes the law of the donation? These questions are of serious moment to society, and deserve to be well considered.

Doctor Wheelock, as the keeper of his charity-school, instructing the Indians in the art of reading, and in our holy religion; sustaining them at his own expense, and on the voluntary contributions of the charitable, could scarcely be considered as a public officer, exercising any portion of those duties which belong to government; nor could the legislature have supposed, that his private funds, or those given by others, were subject to legislative management, because they were applied to the purposes of education. When, afterwards, his school was enlarged, and the liberal contributions made in England, and in America, enabled him to extend his care to the education of the youth of his own country, no change was wrought in his own character, or in the nature of his duties. Had he employed assistant-tutors with the funds contributed by others, or had the trustees in England established a school, with Dr. Wheelock at its head, and paid salaries to him and his assistants, they would still have been private tutors; and the fact, that they were employed in the education of youth, could not have converted them into public officers, concerned in the administration of public duties, or have given the legislature a right to interfere in the management of the fund. The trustees, in whose care that fund was placed by the contributors, would have been permitted to execute their trust, uncontrolled by legislative authority.

Whence, then, can be derived the idea, that Dartmouth College has become a public institution, and its trustees public officers, exercising powers conferred by the public for public objects? Not from the source whence its funds were drawn; for its foundation is purely private and eleemosynary—not from the application of those funds; for money may be given for education, and the persons receiving it do not, by being employed in the education of youth, become members of the civil government. Is it from the act of incorporation? Let this subject be considered. A corporation is an artificial being, invisible, intangible, and existing only in contemplation of law. Being the mere creature of law, it possesses only those properties which the charter of its creation confers upon it, either expressly, or as incidental to its very existence. These are such as are supposed best calculated to effect the object for which it was created. Among the most important are immortality, and, if the expression may be allowed, individuality; properties, by which a perpetual succession of many persons are considered as the same, and may act as a single individual. They enable a corporation to manage its own affairs, and to hold property, without the perplexing intricacies, the hazardous and endless necessity, of perpetual conveyances for the purpose of transmitting it from hand to hand. It is chiefly for the purpose of clothing bodies of men, in succession, with these qualities and capacities, that corporations were invented, and are in use. By these means, a perpetual succession of individuals are capable of acting for the promotion of the particular object, like one immortal being. But this being does not share in the civil government of the country, unless that be the purpose for which it was created. Its immortality no more confers on it political power, or a political character, than immortality would confer such power or character on a natural person. It is no more a state instrument, than a natural person exercising the same powers would be. If, then, a natural person, employed by individuals in the education of youth, or for the government of a seminary in which youth is educated, would not become a public officer, or be considered as a member of the civil government, how is it, that this artificial being, created by law, for the purpose of being employed by the same individuals, for the same purposes, should become a part of the civil government of the country? Is it because its existence, its capacities, its powers, are given by law? Because the government has given it the power to take and to hold property, in a particular form, and for particular purposes, has the government a consequent right substantially to change that form, or to vary the purposes to which the property is to be applied? This principle has never been asserted or recognised, and is supported by no authority. Can it derive aid from reason?

The objects for which a corporation is created are universally such as the government wishes to promote. They are deemed beneficial to the country; and this benefit consitutes the consideration, and in most cases, the sole consideration of the grant. In most eleemosynary institutions, the object would be difficult, perhaps unattainable, without the aid of a charter of incorporation. Charitable or public-spirited individuals, desirous of making permanent appropriations for charitable or other useful purposes, find it impossible to effect their design securely and certainly, without an incorporating act. They apply to the government, state their beneficent object, and offer to advance the money necessary for its accomplishment, provided the government will confer on the instrument which is to execute their designs the capacity to execute them. The proposition is considered and approved. The benefit to the public is considered as an ample compensation for the faculty it confers, and the corporation is created. If the advantages to the public constitute a full compensation for the faculty it gives, there can be no reason for exacting a further compensation, by claiming a right to exercise over this artificial being, a power which changes its nature, and touches the fund, for the security and application of which it was created. There can be no reason for implying in a charter, given for a valuable consideration, a power which is not only not expressed, but is in direct contradiction to its express stipulations.

From the fact, then, that a charter of incorporation has been granted, nothing can be inferred, which changes the character of the institution, or transfers to the government any new power over it. The character of civil institutions does not grow out of their incorporation, but out of the manner in which they are formed, and the objects for which they are created. The right to change them is not founded on their being incorporated, but on their being the instruments of government, created for its purposes. The same institutions, created for the same objects, though not incorporated, would be public institutions, and, of course, be controllable by the legislature. The incorporating act neither gives nor prevents this control. Neither, in reason, can the incorporating act change the character of a private eleemosynary institution.

We are next led to the inquiry, for whose benefit the property given to Dartmouth College was secured? The counsel for the defendant have insisted, that the beneficial interest is in the people of New Hampshire. The charter, after reciting the preliminary measures which had been taken, and the application for an act of incorporation, proceeds thus: "Know ye, therefore, that we, considering the premises, and being willing to encourage the laudable and charitable design of spreading Christian knowledge among the savages of our American wilderness, and also that the best means of education be established in our province of New Hampshire, for the benefit of said province, do, of our special grace," &c. Do these expressions bestow on New Hampshire any exclusive right to the property of the college, any exclusive interest in the labors of the professors? Or do they merely indicate a willingness that New Hampshire should enjoy those advantages which result to all from the establishment of a seminary of learning in the neighborhood? On this point, we think it impossible to entertain a serious doubt. The words themselves, unexplained by the context, indicate, that the "benefit intended for the province" is that which is derived from "establishing the best means of education therein;" that is, from establishing in the province, Dartmouth College, as constituted by the charter. But, if these words, considered alone, could admit of doubt, that doubt is completely removed, by an inspection of the entire instrument.

The particular interests of New Hampshire never entered into the mind of the donors, never constituted a motive for their donation. The propagation of the Christian religion among the savages, and the dissemination of useful knowledge among the youth of the country, were the avowed and the sole objects of their contributions. In these, New Hampshire would participate; but nothing particular or exclusive was intended for her. Even the site of the college was selected, not for the sake of New Hampshire, but because it was "most subservient to the great ends in view," and because liberal donations of land were offered by the proprietors, on condition that the institution should be there established. The real advantages from the location of the college, are, perhaps, not less considerable to those on the west, than to those on the east side of Connecticut river. The clause which constitutes the incorporation, and expresses the objects for which it was made, declares those objects to be the instruction of the Indians, "and also of English youth, and any others." So that the objects of the contributors, and the incorporating act, were the same; the promotion of Christianity, and of education generally, not the interests of New Hampshire particularly.

From this review of the charter, it appears, that Dartmouth College is an eleemosynary institution, incorporated for the purpose of perpetuating the application of the bounty of the donors, to the specified objects of that bounty; that its trustees or governors were originally named by the founder, and invested with the power of perpetuating themselves; that they are not public officers, nor is it a civil institution, participating in the administration of government; but a charity-school, or a seminary of education, incorporated for the preservation of its property, and the perpetual application of that property to the objects of its creation.

Yet a question remains to be considered, of more real difficulty, on which more doubt has been entertained, than on all that have been discussed. The founders of the college, at least, those whose contributions were in money, have parted with the property bestowed upon it, and their representatives have no interest in that property. The donors of land are equally without interest, so long as the corporation shall exist. Could they be found, they are unaffected by any alteration in its constitution, and probably regardless of its form, or even of its existence. The students are fluctuating, and no individual among our youth has a vested interest in the institution, which can be asserted in a court of justice. Neither the founders of the college, nor the youth for whose benefit it was founded, complain of the alteration made in its charter, or think themselves injured by it. The trustees alone complain, and the trustees have no beneficial interest to be protected. Can this be such a contract, as the constitution intended to withdraw from the power of state legislation? Contracts, the parties to which have a vested beneficial interest, and those only, it has been said, are the objects about which the constitution is solicitous, and to which its protection is extended.

The court has bestowed on this argument the most deliberate consideration, and the result will be stated. Dr. Wheelock, acting for himself, and for those who, at his solicitation, had made contributions to his school, applied for this charter, as the instrument which should enable him, and them, to perpetuate their beneficent intention. It was granted. An artificial, immortal being, was created by the crown, capable of receiving and distributing for ever, according to the will of the donors, the donations which should be made to it. On this being, the contributions which had been collected were immediately bestowed. These gifts were made, not indeed to make a profit for the donors, or their posterity, but for something, in their opinion, of inestimable value; for something which they deemed a full equivalent for the money with which it was purchased. The consideration for which they stipulated, is the perpetual application of the fund to its object, in the mode prescribed by themselves. Their descendants may take no interest in the preservation of this consideration. But in this respect their descendants are not their representatives; they are represented by the corporation. The corporation is the assignee of their rights, stands in their place, and distributes their bounty, as they would themselves have distributed it, had they been immortal. So, with respect to the students who are to derive learning from this source; the corporation is a trustee for them also. Their potential rights, which, taken distributively, are imperceptible, amount collectively to a most important interest. These are, in the aggregate, to be exercised, asserted and protected, by the corporation. They were as completely out of the donors, at the instant of their being vested in the corporation, and as incapable of being asserted by the students, as at present.

According to the theory of the British constitution, their parliament is omnipotent. To annul corporate rights might give a shock to public opinion, which that government has chosen to avoid; but its power is not questioned. Had parliament, immediately after the emanation of this charter, and the execution of those conveyances which followed it, annulled the instrument, so that the living donors would have witnessed the disappointment of their hopes, the perfidy of the transaction would have been universally acknowledged. Yet, then, as now, the donors would have no interest in the property; then, as now, those who might be students would have had no rights to be violated; then, as now, it might be said, that the trustees, in whom the rights of all were combined, possessed no private, individual, beneficial interests in the property confided to their protection. Yet the contract would, at that time, have been deemed sacred by all. What has since occurred, to strip it of its inviolability? Circumstances have not changed it. In reason, in justice, and in law, it is now, what is was in 1769.

This is plainly a contract to which the donors, the trustees and the crown (to whose rights and obligations New Hampshire succeeds) were the original parties. It is a contract made on a valuable consideration. It is a contract for the security and disposition of property. It is a contract, on the faith of which, real and personal estate has been conveyed to the corporation. It is, then, a contract within the letter of the constitution, and within its spirit also, unless the fact, that the property is invested by the donors in trustees, for the promotion of religion and education, for the benefit of persons who are perpetually changing, though the objects remain the same, shall create a particular exception, taking this case out of the prohibition contained in the constitution.

It is more than possible, that the preservation of rights of this description was not particularly in the view of the framers of the constitution, when the clause under consideration was introduced into that instrument. It is probable, that interferences of more frequent occurrence,

to which the temptation was stronger, and of which the mischief was more extensive, constituted the great motive for imposing this restriction on the state legislatures. But although a particular and a rare case may not, in itself, be of sufficient magnitude to induce a rule, yet it must be governed by the rule, when established, unless some plain and strong reason for excluding it can be given. It is not enough to say, that this particular case was not in the mind of the convention, when the article was framed, nor of the American people, when it was adopted. It is necessary to go further, and to say that, had this particular case been suggested, the language would have been so varied, as to exclude it, or it would have been made a special exception. The case being within the words of the rule, must be within its operation likewise, unless there be something in the literal construction, so obviously absurd or mischievous, or repugnant to the general spirit of the instrument, as to justify those who expound the constitution in making it an exception.

On what safe and intelligible ground, can this exception stand? There is no expression in the constitution, no sentiment delivered by its contemporaneous expounders, which would justify us in making it. In the absence of all authority of this kind, is there, in the nature and reason of the case itself, that which would sustain a construction of the constitution, not warranted by its words? Are contracts of this description of a character to excite so little interest, that we must exclude them from the provisions of the constitution, as being unworthy of the attention of those who framed the instrument? Or does public policy so imperiously demand their remaining exposed to legislative alteration, as to compel us, or rather permit us, to say, that these words, which were introduced to give stability to contracts, and which in their plain import comprehend this contract, must yet be so construed as to exclude it?

Almost all eleemosynary corporations, those which are created for the promotion of religion, of charity or of education, are of the same character. The law of this case is the law of all. In every literary or charitable institution, unless the objects of the bounty be themselves incorporated, the whole legal interest is in trustees, and can be asserted only by them. The donors, or claimants of the bounty, if they can appear in court at all, can appear only to complain of the trustees. In all other situations, they are identified with, and personated by, the trustees; and their rights are to be defended and maintained by them. Religion, charity and education are, in the law of England, legatees or donees, capable of receiving bequests or donations in this form. They appear in court, and claim or defend by the corporation. Are they of so little estimation in the United States, that contracts for their benefit must be excluded from the protection of words, which in their natural import include them? Or do such contracts so necessarily require new modelling by the authority of the legislature, that the ordinary rules of construction must be disregarded, in order to leave them exposed to legislative alteration?

All feel, that these objects are not deemed unimportant in the United States. The interest which this case has excited, proves that they are not. The framers of the constitution did not deem them unworthy of its care and protection. They have, though in a different mode, manifested their respect for science, by reserving to the government of the Union the power "to promote the progress of science and useful arts, by securing for limited times, to authors and inventors, the exclusive right to their respective writings and discoveries." They have, so far, withdrawn science, and the useful arts, from the action of the state governments. Why then should they be supposed so regardless of contracts made for the advancement of literature, as to intend to exclude them from provisions, made for the security of ordinary contracts between man and man? No reason for making this supposition is perceived.

If the insignificance of the object does not require that we should exclude contracts respecting it from the protection of the constitution; neither, as we conceive, is the policy of leaving them subject to legislative alteration so apparent, as to require a forced construction of that instrument, in order to effect it. These eleemosynary institutions do not fill the place, which would otherwise be occupied by government, but that which would otherwise remain vacant. They are complete acquisitions to literature. They are donations to education; donations, which any government must be disposed rather to encourage than to discountenance. It requires no very critical examination of the human mind, to enable us to determine, that one great inducement to these gifts is the conviction felt by the giver, that the disposition he makes of them is immutable. It is probable, that no man ever was, and that no man ever will be, the founder of a college, believing at the time, that an act of incorporation constitutes no security for the institution; believing, that it is immediately to be deemed a public institution, whose funds are to be governed and applied, not by the

will of the donor, but by the will of the legislature. All such gifts are made in the pleasing, perhaps, delusive hope, that the charity will flow for ever in the channel which the givers have marked out for it. If every man finds in his own bosom strong evidence of the universality of this sentiment, there can be but little reason to imagine, that the framers of our constitution were strangers to it, and that, feeling the necessity and policy of giving permanence and security to contracts, of withdrawing them from the influence of legislative bodies, whose fluctuating policy, and repeated interferences, produced the most perplexing and injurious embarrassments, they still deemed it necessary to leave these contracts subject to those interferences. The motives for such an exception must be very powerful, to justify the construction which makes it.

The motives suggested at the bar grow out of the original appointment of the trustees, which is supposed to have been in a spirit hostile to the genius of our government, and the presumption, that if allowed to continue themselves, they now are, and must remain for ever, what they originally were. Hence is inferred the necessity of applying to this corporation, and to other similar corporations, the correcting and improving hand of the legislature. It has been urged repeatedly, and certainly with a degree of earnestness which attracted attention, that the trustees, deriving their power from a regal source, must, necessarily, partake of the spirit of their origin; and that their first principles, unimproved by that resplendent light which has been shed around them, must continue to govern the college, and to guide the students.

Before we inquire into the influence which this argument ought to have on the constitutional question, it may not be amiss to examine the fact on which it rests. The first trustees were undoubtedly named in the charter, by the crown; but at whose suggestion were they named? By whom were they selected? The charter informs us. Dr. Wheelock had represented, "that for many weighty reasons, it would be expedients, that the gentlemen whom he had already nominated, in his last will, to be trustees in America, should be of the corporation now proposed." When, afterwards, the trustees are named in the charter, can it be doubted, that the persons mentioned by Dr. Wheelock in his will were appointed? Some were probably added by the crown, with the approbation of Dr. Wheelock. Among these, is the doctor himself. If any others were appointed, at the instance of the crown, they are the governor, three members of the council, and the speaker of the house of representatives of the colony of New Hampshire. The stations filled by these persons ought to rescue them from any other imputation than too great a dependence on the crown. If, in the revolution that followed, they acted under the influence of this sentiment, they must have ceased to be trustees; if they took part with their countrymen, the imputation, which suspicion might excite, would no longer attach to them. The original trustees, then, or most of them, were named by Dr. Wheelock, and those who were added to his nomination, most probably, with his approbation, were among the most eminent and respectable individuals in New Hampshire.

The only evidence which we possess of the character of Dr. Wheelock is furnished by this charter. The judicious means employed for the accomplishment of his object, and the success which attended his endeavors, would lead to the opinion, that he united a sound understanding to that humanity benevolence which suggested his undertaking. It surely cannot be assumed, that his trustees were selected without judgment. With as little probability can it be assumed, that while the light of science, and of liberal principles, pervades the whole community, these originally benighted trustees remain in utter darkness, incapable of participating in the general improvement; that while the human race is rapidly advancing, they are stationary. Reasoning *à priori*, we should believe, that learned and intelligent men, selected by its patrons for the government of a literary institution, would select learned and intelligent men for their successors; men as well fitted for the government of a college as those who might be chosen by other means. Should this reasoning ever prove erroneous, in a particular case, public opinion, as has been stated at the bar, would correct the institution. The mere possibility of the contrary would not justify a construction of the constitution, which should exclude these contracts from the protection of a provision whose terms comprehend them.

The opinion of the court, after mature deliberation, is, that this is a contract, the obligation of which cannot be impaired, without violating the constitution of the United States. This opinion appears to us to be equally supported by reason, and by the former decisions of this court.

2. We next proceed to the inquiry, whether its obligation has been impaired by those acts of the legislature of New Hampshire, to which the special verdict refers?

From the review of this charter, which has been taken, it appears that the whole power of governing the college, of appointing and removing tutors, of fixing their salaries, of directing the course of study to be pursued by the students, and of filling up vacancies created in their own body, was vested in the trustees. On the part of the crown, it was expressly stipulated, that this corporation, thus constituted, should continue for ever; and that the number of trustees should for ever consist of twelve, and no more. By this contract, the crown was bound, and could have made no violent alteration in its essential terms, without impairing its obligation.

By the revolution, the duties, as well as the powers, of government devolved on the people of New Hampshire. It is admitted, that among the latter was comprehended the transcendent power of parliament, as well as that of the executive department. It is too clear, to require the support of argument, that all contracts and rights respecting property, remained unchanged by the revolution. The obligations, then, which were created by the charter to Dartmouth College, were the same in the new, that they had been in the old government. The power of the government was also the same. A repeal of this charter, at any time prior to the adoption of the present constitution of the United States, would have been an extraordinary and unprecedented act of power, but one which could have been contested only by the restrictions upon the legislature, to be found in the constitution of the state. But the constitution of the United States has imposed this additional limitation, that the legislature of a state shall pass no act "impairing the obligation of contracts."

It has been already stated, that the act "to amend the charter, and enlarge and improve the corporation of Dartmouth College," increases the number of trustees to twenty-one, gives the appointment of the additional members to the executive of the state, and creates a board of overseers, to consist of twenty-five persons, of whom twenty-one are also appointed by the executive of New Hampshire, who have power to inspect and control the most important acts of the trustees.

On the effect of this law, two opinions cannot be entertained. Between acting directly, and acting through the agency of trustees and overseers, no essential difference is perceived. The whole power of governing the college is transferred from trustees, appointed according to the will of the founder, expressed in the charter, to the executive of New Hampshire. The management and application of the funds of this eleemosynary institution, which are placed by the donors in the hands of trustees named in the charter, and empowered to perpetuate themselves, are placed by this act under the control of the government of the state. The will of the state is substituted for the will of the donors, in every essential operation of the college. This is not an immaterial change. The founders of the college contracted, not merely for the perpetual application of the funds which they gave, to the objects for which those funds were given; they contracted also, to secure that application by the constitution of the corporation. They contracted for a system, which should, so far as human foresight can provide, retain for ever the government of the literary institution they had formed, in the hands of persons approved by themselves. This system is totally changed. The charter of 1769 exists no longer. It is re-organized; and re-organized in such a manner, as to convert a literary institution, moulded according to the will of its founders, and placed under the control of private literary men, into a machine entirely subservient to the will of government. This may be for the advantage of this college in particular, and may be for the advantage of literature in general; but it is not according to the will of the donors, and is subversive of that contract, on the faith of which their property was given.

In the view which has been taken of this interesting case, the court has confined itself to the rights possessed by the trustees, as the assignees and representatives of the donors and founders, for the benefit of religion and literature. Yet, it is not clear, that the trustees ought to be considered as destitute of such beneficial interest in themselves, as the law may respect. In addition to their being the legal owners of the property, and to their having a freehold right in the powers confided to them, the charter itself countenances the idea, that trustees may also be tutors, with salaries. The first president was one of the original trustees; and the charter provides, that in case of vacancy in that office, "the senior professor or tutor, being one of the trustees, shall exercise the office of president, until the trustees shall make choice of, and appoint a president." According to the tenor of the charter, then, the trustees might, without impropriety, appoint a president and other professors from their own body. This is a power not entirely unconnected with an interest. Even if the proposition of the counsel for the defendant were sustained; if it were admitted, that those contracts only are protected by the constitution, a beneficial interest in which is vested in the party, who appears in court to assert that interest; yet it is by no means clear, that the trustees of Dartmouth College have no beneficial interest in themselves. But the court has deemed it unnecessary to investigate this particular point, being of opinion, on general principles, that in these private eleemosynary institutions, the body corporate, as possessing the whole legal and equitable interest, and completely representing the donors, for the purpose of executing the trust, has rights which are protected by the constitution.

It results from this opinion, that the acts of the legislature of New Hampshire, which are stated in the special verdict found in this cause, are repugnant to the constitution of the United States; and that the judgment on this special verdict ought to have been for the plaintiffs. The judgment of the state court must, therefore, be

Reversed.

U

Unions on Campus

The First Amendment to the U.S. Constitution, in part, prohibits Congress from enacting laws restricting the right of people to assemble peacefully. Consequently, the First Amendment has been interpreted as meaning that individuals are free to organize and join unions of their choosing. Unions are a collection of members who come together for the common purpose of engaging in collective bargaining or negotiations over terms and conditions of employment, such as wages, benefits, and other items for which bargaining is not prohibited by state or federal law. While the majority of public teachers in American K–12 schools belong to unions, this is not the case with regard to faculty members and other instructional staff members on the campuses of colleges and universities in the United States. This entry discusses issues associated with the status of unions on college and university campuses in both public and private institutions of higher learning.

Insofar as union leaders advocate the importance of organization and strength in numbers, labor organizers typically identify substandard working conditions, low wages, nonexistent or minimal benefits, and mistreatment of employees by employers to spark unionism in the work force. In this way, unions justify their activities as providing protection for their members from employers while negotiating benefits for workers that would otherwise be unattainable.

When organizers attempt to form unions, they must demonstrate that prospective members share a "community of interests" that, generally, includes common concerns over such matters as wages, work hours, benefits, qualifications, training and skills, and job functions. While the community of interests should be readily apparent for faculty members and other instructional personnel, as opposed to nonprofessional staff such as maintenance workers and office assistants, some view the advantages of this requirement as having to be balanced against the disadvantages of a proliferation of multiple smaller bargaining units that could reduce the strength of unions and their collective numbers.

The Negotiation Process

Once unions are organized, collective bargaining or negotiation practices vary greatly in education. The three primary types of union negotiations that have been prevalent in educational settings are meet-and-confer, good-faith bargaining, and bargaining during an unexpected crisis. The meet-and-confer approach, which largely predated bargaining but still exists in some places today, amounts to a discussion between faculty and administration, with the latter largely setting contract terms. Most states with unions in higher education rely on the traditional model of good-faith bargaining, which is characterized by mutual respect where each party approaches negotiations with the intent to resolve all issues equitably. The unexpected crisis is the beginning of the end for traditional collective bargaining due to the adversarial posturing of administrators and faculty, because in this approach neither party is willing to compromise or negotiate an equitable outcome.

A new type of negotiation has been in use recently, win-win. In win-win bargaining, each team looks at the available resources and agrees to terms that are amenable to both sides in a manner that is less confrontational, more collegial, and more professional than the tradition confrontational, zero-sum model of good faith bargaining that emerged from the industrial labor relations model. Because this model approaches compromise in its truest form, the results tend to be less stressful due to the commitment to arrive at settlements with which both sides can live.

Regardless of which model faculty members and their institutions adopt, they must bear in mind that some topics are mandatory subjects of bargaining, while other are permissible, and still others are prohibited from being the subject of negotiations, depending on state law. Academic abstention and faculty governance issues in higher education vary significantly from those of K–12 schools, and the distinctions between these three types of topics are readily blurred at colleges and universities. Typically, salary and benefits are mandatory topics of bargaining. Depending on the jurisdiction, other topics, such as placing limits on enrollment in classes and programs, may be permissible topics over which bargaining may take place. Prohibited topics of bargaining are those for which bargaining is forbidden by state law, such as setting tuition rates at public colleges and universities.

Evolution of Unions and Labor Law

As unions developed in the United States, initially in the private industrial relations sector, Congress enacted the National Labor Relations Act (NLRA), also known as the Wagner Act, in 1935. However, the NLRA affected only private industry's ability to organize, form unions, and bargain collectively under the First Amendment. At the same time, the NLRA established the National Labor Relations Board (NLRB) to oversee union activities in private industry. Subsequently, Congress enacted the Labor-Management Relations (Taft-Hartley) Act of 1947 and the Labor-Management Reporting and Disclosure (Landrum-Griffin) Act of 1959. These laws amended the NLRA by clarifying which groups were covered by the NLRA, setting requirements for union self-governance, and allowing the federal government, through the judicial system, to issue injunctions against unions for prohibited activities.

Public sector unionization began in 1959, when Wisconsin became the first state to allow its public employees to bargain. Another major push toward bargaining occurred in 1962, when President Kennedy signed Executive Order 10988 allowing federal employees to organize and engage in collective bargaining. Later in the same year, public school teachers, starting in New York City, engaged in activism leading to large-scale unionization among their ranks nationwide.

As labor law developed, the rights of public employees, including faculty members and other instructional staff at public institutions of higher education, to form unions and bargain collectively emerged largely under the aegis of state laws. To this end, jurisdictions that allow bargaining are free to set their own requirements for union recognition and bargaining practices. Moreover, right-to-work laws and state constitutions identify whether unions are permitted and whether collective bargaining is required. As unionization and collective bargaining have developed, three different workplace models have evolved.

Workplace Models

The three different types of workplace models are closed shops, fair share or agency shops, and open shops. Although the Taft-Hartley Act of 1947 officially declared them to be illegal in 1947, closed shops continue to exist in some locations and industries; they are not present in educational workplaces. Because closed shops require union membership as a condition of employment, employers hire only union members to fill vacancies. Moreover, states with right-to-work laws explicitly prohibit these types of shops. Fair share or agency shops allow employers to hire individuals who are not union members but require nonmembers to pay a fair share of the costs associated with the bargaining process that provides them with salary and other benefits. Under this approach, nonmembers ask union officials for breakdowns of the percentages of union dues that are associated with bargaining. These individuals are then required to pay only the portion of dues used for negotiating salary, benefits, and other terms and conditions of employment; even so, fair share fees can cost non-members almost as much as union dues. The third model, open shops, does not require membership in unions or paying of any portion of union dues or fair share fees by nonmembers.

Fair Share Fees

In jurisdictions with the most common approach, fair share or agency shops, state laws and local policies have established the rules governing what can be included when setting fair share fees. These rules have been supplemented by the rulings in five U.S. Supreme Court cases, only one of which was set in higher education. In *Abood v. Detroit Board of Education* (1977) and *Lehnert v. Ferris Faculty Association* (1991), a case from higher education, the Supreme Court set the standards under which unions may charge fair share fees to nonmembers. Generally, such fees must be germane to collective bargaining activities, be justifiable, and not add significantly to the burdening of free speech. Further, in *Chicago Teachers Union, Local No. 1, AFT, AFL-CIO v. Hudson* (1991), the Court disapproved of a rebate system whereby nonmembers paid the full dues and received a rebate, because this system did not avoid the risk that nonmember funds might be temporarily used for improper purposes. In *Davenport v. Washington Education Association* (2007), the Court limited the use of fair share fees of nonunion members; affirmative authorization is now required before nonmember fees may be spent for political purposes. Most recently, in *Ysura v. Pocatello Education Association* (2009), the Court placed further restrictions on the ability of unions to spend the fair share fees of nonmembers in upholding a ban on public-employee payroll deductions for local political activities, because it advanced the State of Idaho's interest in separating the operation of government from partisan politics.

Judicial Involvement in Faculty Unionization

The leading case on judicial involvement in faculty unionization, at least in private colleges and universities, is *National Labor Relations Board v. Yeshiva University* (1980). In *Yeshiva*, the Court held that faculty members in a private, religiously affiliated university did not have the right to

organize and form unions, because they performed some duties that were considered managerial in nature. In so ruling, the Court forbade the NLRB from intervening in a labor dispute between faculty members and the university. Even so, in 1997 the NLRB decided that faculty members at the University of Great Falls had the right to form a union and bargain collectively. The NLRB reached the same result in 2000 in finding that faculty members at Manhattan College were entitled to form a union based on the small amount of influence that they exerted on management when making financial or employment decisions. In the same year, the NLRB was convinced that graduate teaching assistants and graduate researchers at New York University have the right to organize as a union and bargain collectively. Previously, because these two groups had been classified as students, not employees, they were forbidden from forming unions.

Faculty Representation

At the national level, three organizations, the National Education Association (NEA), American Federation of Teachers (AFT), and American Association of University Professors (AAUP), in addition to many local groups, represent the majority of organized faculties at public and private colleges and universities. During the surge of unionization at colleges and universities in the 1960s, both the NEA and AFT were able to associate with higher education faculties. The AAUP represents only higher education faculties and has no ties to elementary or secondary education. Although the AAUP was started in 1915 in order to protect academic freedom, during the 1970s it began pursuing collective bargaining for higher education faculties. The first faculty to unionize at a public institution was that of the U.S. Merchant Marine Academy in 1967, which affiliated itself with the AFT. During the 1970s, the proliferation of community colleges led to an increase in unions on campuses across the United States. Yet, faculty members in other institutions of higher learning were less active, in part because of the impact of *Yeshiva*.

On campuses with unions, regardless of whether they are public and private, individuals select their representatives by secret ballots. Election results at public colleges and universities are reviewed by their state labor boards for certification, and boards recognize the election winners as the sole representatives for collective bargaining. The NLRB reviews and certifies votes before recognizing bargaining representatives. However, change may be in the offing with regard to the selection of unions, as Congress is considering a bill that would eliminate elections when employees choose whether to organize a union. Under the proposed Employee Free Choice Act (EFCA) that has already passed in the House and may make its way to the Senate in the 111th Congress, employees would sign cards indicating their desire to form a union rather than engage in secret ballots. If the EFCA is enacted into law, it may have a significant impact on labor relations on campuses, because it may make it easier for unions to form. It certainly bears watching to observe whether the EFCA becomes law.

Michael J. Jernigan

See also Academic Abstention; American Association of University Professors; Collective Bargaining; *Lehnert v. Ferris Faculty Association*; National Labor Relations Act; *National Labor Relations Board v. Yeshiva University*

Further Readings

American Association of University Professors. (2009). *History of the AAUP*. Retrieved February 5, 2009, from http://www.aaup.org/AAUP/about/history

Epstein, R. A. (2005). Breaking down the ivory sweatshops: Graduate student assistants and their elusive search for employee status on the private university campus. *St. John's Journal of Legal Commentary, 20,* 157–197.

Kerchner, C. T., & Mitchell, D. E. (1988). *The changing idea of a teachers' union.* Philadelphia, PA: Falmer Press.

Palmer, S. (1999). *A brief history of collective bargaining in higher education.* Retrieved January 27, 2009, from http://members.home.net/eoozycki/HECollectBar.html

Russo, C. J. (2002). Right-to-work and fair share agreements: A delicate balance. *School Business Affairs, 68*(4), 12–15.

Russo, C. J. (2007). Supreme Court update: Unions, fair share agreements, and the first amendment. *Education and the Law, 19*(3–4), 237–244.

Russo, C. J., Gordon, W. M., & Miles, A. S. (1992). Agency shop fees and the Supreme Court: Union control and academic freedom. *Education Law Reporter, 73,* 609–615.

Saltzman, G. M. (2001). Higher education collective bargaining and the law. In National Education Association, *The NEA 2001 almanac of higher education* (pp. 45–58). Retrieved January 27, 2009, from http://www2.nea.org/he/healma2k1/images/a01p45.pdf

U.S. Department of Labor. (2009). *State right-to-work laws and constitutional amendments.* Retrieved January 25, 2009, from http://www.dol.gov/esa/whd/state/righttowork.htm

Legal Citations

Abood v. Detroit Board of Education, 431 U.S. 209 (1977).

Chicago Teachers Union, Local No. 1, AFT, AFL-CIO v. Hudson, 501 U.S. 1230 (1991).

Davenport v. Washington Education Association, 127 S. Ct. 2372, 2383 (2007).

Employee Free Choice Act of 2007, H.R. 800, 110th Congress (2007–08). Retrieved May 28, 2009, from http://www.govtrack.us/congress/bill.xpd?bill=h110-800

Labor–Management Relations Act (Taft-Hartley Act), Pub. L. No. 80-101 (1947).

Labor-Management Reporting and Disclosure Act (Landrum-Griffin Act), Pub. L. No. 86-257 (1959).

Lehnert v. Ferris Faculty Association, 500 U.S. 507 (1991).

Manhattan College and Manhattan College Faculty Coalition, New York State United Teachers a/w American Federation of Teachers, AFL-CIO. NLRB Case 2-RC-21735, November 9, 1999. Retrieved January 25, 2009, from http://www.nlrb.gov/shared_files/Regional%20Decisions/1999/2-RC-21735.pdf

National Labor Relations Act, 29 U.S.C. §§ 151 *et seq.*

National Labor Relations Board v. Yeshiva University, 444 U.S. 672 (1980).

New York University and International Union, United Automobile, Aerospace and Agricultural Implement Workers of America, AFL-CIO. NLRB Case 2-RC-22082, October 31, 2000. Retrieved January 25, 2009, from http://www.nlrb.gov/shared_files/Board%20Decisions/332/332-111.pdf

University of Great Falls and Montana Federation of Teachers, AFT, AFL-CIO, Petitioner. NLRB Case 19-RC-13114, November 8, 1997. Retrieved January

25, 2009, from http://www.nlrb.gov/shared_files/
Board%20Decisions/325/3253.pdf

Ysura v. Pocatello Education Association, 129 S. Ct.
1093 (2009).

UNITED STATES V. VIRGINIA

United States v. Virginia (1996) is a landmark
U.S. Supreme Court case concerning the ability of
state officials to maintain public single-sex institutions of higher education. In *VMI*, the Court held
that, as a matter of constitutional law, the Virginia
Military Institute could not exclude women from
enrolling as students. Insofar as the Court's judgment in *VMI* took the significant step of outlawing single-sex education at public colleges and
universities, this entry examines its background,
judicial analyses, and implications.

The VMI was founded in 1839 as a state-
supported military school. Since that time, the
institute has employed a rigorous curriculum, also
referred to as the "adversative method," which is
designed to produce citizen-soldiers who become
leaders in both military and civilian life. While
VMI alumni include many prominent military generals, political leaders, and business executives, the
institute did not admit women as students during
its first 150 years of operation.

Facts of the Case

The vast majority of constitutional challenges
involve private parties suing the government. Yet,
VMI was an action by the federal government
against the government of the Commonwealth of
Virginia. In 1990, the Justice Department, responding to a complaint from a female high school student, sued Virginia, contending that having an
all-male institution of higher education violated
the Equal Protection Clause of the Fourteenth
Amendment. After a federal trial court in Virginia
decided that the single-sex admissions policy did
not violate the Fourteenth Amendment, the Fourth
Circuit disagreed. The Fourth Circuit vacated the
trial court's original order on the ground that commonwealth officials had not advanced a justification showing why they should offer a program for
men and not for women. However, the Fourth

Circuit did not order the admission of women.
Rather, the court presented officials in Virginia
with a choice: They could either admit women or
establish a parallel program that was all female.

Virginia chose to establish a parallel program,
the Virginia Women's Institute for Leadership, at
an all-female private institution, Mary Baldwin
College. Although there were significant differences in the academic quality of the two programs,
the federal trial court approved Virginia's alternative program. On appeal, a sharply divided Fourth
Circuit affirmed. The Supreme Court agreed to
hear the case.

The Supreme Court's Ruling

By a vote of seven to one, in an opinion authored by
Justice Ginsburg, with Justice Thomas not participating, the Supreme Court reversed in striking down the
Fourth Circuit's second order while reinstating its
initial determination. According to the Court, in
equal protection cases involving gender, state governments bear the burden of establishing "exceedingly
persuasive" justifications for any gender classification. The Court explained that gender classifications
are upheld only if classifications are substantially
related to important governmental interests.

The Supreme Court then proceeded to reject
each of the interests proffered by Virginia for wishing to continue to operate the VMI as an all-male
institution. First, the Court found that prohibiting
women from enrolling at the institute did not contribute to a diversity of educational opportunities
in Virginia. Second, the Court rejected the idea
that admitting women would require substantial
changes to the institute's curriculum. In this regard,
the Court noted that because women had successfully integrated into the federal service academies,
the refusal to admit females as students was
unconstitutional.

Having ruled that VMI's policy violated the
Equal Protection Clause of the Fourteenth
Amendment, the Supreme Court turned to address
the proper remedy. Even though Virginia had
implemented an all-female parallel program at
another institution, the Court rejected the alternative program, because the educational opportunities that it afforded were not equal in prestige to
those offered at the institute.

Chief Justice Rehnquist concurred in the judgment of the Court, but wrote separately to emphasize his disagreement with the standard that the Supreme Court employed. The Chief Justice posited that the Court was adding an additional requirement, namely a showing of an "exceedingly persuasive justification," to the accepted standard of a substantial relationship to an important governmental interest. To this end, he feared that adding the exceedingly persuasive justification requirement would be less precise and lead to more inconsistency.

Justice Scalia dissented. In his view, the Constitution neither compels nor prohibits single-sex education. He was of the view that because the Constitution is silent on the issue, he would have deferred to Virginia's judgment that single-sex education was necessary. Moreover, Justice Scalia believed that under the Court's pre-*VMI* precedents, the institute would have satisfied the constitutional standard.

Impact of the Ruling

While the result had a significant impact for the Virginia Military Institute and the Citadel, a similar military school in South Carolina, *VMI* has had little immediate practical effect on higher education, because every other public institution of higher education was already coeducational.

Moreover, private colleges and universities are not subject to the Constitution's command, and single-sex education explicitly is allowed under Title IX. Nevertheless, the *VMI* Court's broad rejection of any policy that excludes one gender remains a cornerstone of higher education law. In sum, then, public institutions must open all programs to all persons, regardless of gender. The first female cadets were admitted to VMI in 1997.

William E. Thro

See also Equal Protection Analysis; Single-Sex Colleges

Further Readings

Mississippi University for Women v. Hogan, 458 U.S. 718 (1982).

Russo, C. J., & Mawdsley, R. D. (1997). VMI and single-sex public schools: The end of an era? *Education Law Reporter, 114,* 999–1010.

Wood, R. C., & Cornelius, L. (1997). Public supported all-male military colleges: The Supreme Court rules in *U.S. v. Commonwealth of Virginia. Education Law Reporter, 118,* 819–833.

Legal Citations

United States v. Virginia, 518 U.S. 515 (1996).

UNITED STATES V. VIRGINIA

In what is known as the "the VMI case," the Supreme Court invalidated single-sex education at public colleges and universities.

Supreme Court of the United States

UNITED STATES

v.

VIRGINIA

518 U.S. 515

Argued Jan. 17, 1996

Decided June 26, 1996

Justice GINSBURG delivered the opinion of the Court.

Virginia's public institutions of higher learning include an incomparable military college, Virginia Military Institute (VMI). The United States maintains that the Constitution's equal protection guarantee precludes Virginia from reserving exclusively to men the unique educational opportunities VMI affords. We agree.

I

Founded in 1839, VMI is today the sole single-sex school among Virginia's 15 public institutions of higher learning. VMI's distinctive mission is to produce "citizen-soldiers," men prepared for leadership in civilian life and in military service. VMI pursues this mission through pervasive training of a kind not available anywhere else in Virginia. Assigning prime place to character development, VMI uses an "adversative method" modeled on English public schools and once characteristic of military instruction. VMI constantly endeavors to instill physical and mental discipline in its cadets and impart to them a strong moral code. The school's graduates leave VMI with heightened comprehension of their capacity to deal with duress and stress, and a large sense of accomplishment for completing the hazardous course.

VMI has notably succeeded in its mission to produce leaders; among its alumni are military generals, Members of Congress, and business executives. The school's alumni overwhelmingly perceive that their VMI training helped them to realize their personal goals. VMI's endowment reflects the loyalty of its graduates; VMI has the largest per-student endowment of all public undergraduate institutions in the Nation.

Neither the goal of producing citizen-soldiers nor VMI's implementing methodology is inherently unsuitable to women. And the school's impressive record in producing leaders has made admission desirable to some women. Nevertheless, Virginia has elected to preserve exclusively for men the advantages and opportunities a VMI education affords.

II

A

From its establishment in 1839 as one of the Nation's first state military colleges, VMI has remained financially supported by Virginia and "subject to the control of the [Virginia] General Assembly." . . . Civil War strife threatened the school's vitality, but a resourceful superintendent regained legislative support by highlighting "VMI's great potential[,] through its technical know-how," to advance Virginia's postwar recovery.

VMI today enrolls about 1,300 men as cadets. Its academic offerings in the liberal arts, sciences, and engineering are also available at other public colleges and universities in Virginia. But VMI's mission is special. It is

the mission of the school "'to produce educated and honorable men, prepared for the varied work of civil life, imbued with love of learning, confident in the functions and attitudes of leadership, possessing a high sense of public service, advocates of the American democracy and free enterprise system, and ready as citizen-soldiers to defend their country in time of national peril.'"

In contrast to the federal service academies, institutions maintained "to prepare cadets for career service in the armed forces," VMI's program "is directed at preparation for both military and civilian life"; "[o]nly about 15% of VMI cadets enter career military service."

VMI produces its "citizen-soldiers" through "an adversative, or doubting, model of education" which features "[p]hysical rigor, mental stress, absolute equality of treatment, absence of privacy, minute regulation of behavior, and indoctrination in desirable values." As one Commandant of Cadets described it, the adversative method "dissects the young student," and makes him aware of his "limits and capabilities," so that he knows "how far he can go with his anger, . . . how much he can take under stress, . . . exactly what he can do when he is physically exhausted."

VMI cadets live in spartan barracks where surveillance is constant and privacy nonexistent; they wear uniforms, eat together in the mess hall, and regularly participate in drills.

Entering students are incessantly exposed to the rat line, "an extreme form of the adversative model," comparable in intensity to Marine Corps boot camp. Tormenting and punishing, the rat line bonds new cadets to their fellow sufferers and, when they have completed the 7-month experience, to their former tormentors.

VMI's "adversative model" is further characterized by a hierarchical "class system" of privileges and responsibilities, a "dyke system" for assigning a senior class mentor to each entering class "rat," and a stringently enforced "honor code," which prescribes that a cadet "does not lie, cheat, steal nor tolerate those who do."

VMI attracts some applicants because of its reputation as an extraordinarily challenging military school, and "because its alumni are exceptionally close to the school." "[W]omen have no opportunity anywhere to gain the benefits of [the system of education at VMI]."

B

In 1990, prompted by a complaint filed with the Attorney General by a female high-school student seeking admission to VMI, the United States sued the Commonwealth of Virginia and VMI, alleging that VMI's exclusively male admission policy violated the Equal Protection Clause of the Fourteenth Amendment. Trial of the action consumed six days and involved an array of expert witnesses on each side.

In the two years preceding the lawsuit, the District Court noted, VMI had received inquiries from 347 women, but had responded to none of them. . . . The court further recognized that, with recruitment, VMI could "achieve at least 10% female enrollment"—"a sufficient 'critical mass' to provide the female cadets with a positive educational experience." And it was also established that "some women are capable of all of the individual activities required of VMI cadets." In addition, experts agreed that if VMI admitted women, "the VMI ROTC experience would become a better training program from the perspective of the armed forces, because it would provide training in dealing with a mixed-gender army."

The District Court ruled in favor of VMI, however, and rejected the equal protection challenge pressed by the United States. That court correctly recognized that *Mississippi Univ. for Women v. Hogan* was the closest guide. There, this Court underscored that a party seeking to uphold government action based on sex must establish an "exceedingly persuasive justification" for the classification. *Mississippi Univ. for Women.* . . .

The District Court reasoned that education in "a single-gender environment, be it male or female," yields substantial benefits. . . .

"Women are [indeed] denied a unique educational opportunity that is available only at VMI," the District Court acknowledged. But "[VMI's] single-sex status would be lost, and some aspects of the [school's] distinctive method would be altered," if women were admitted; "Allowance for personal privacy would have to be made"; "[p]hysical education requirements would have to be altered, at least for the women"; the adversative environment could not survive unmodified. Thus, "sufficient constitutional justification" had been shown, the District Court held, "for continuing [VMI's] single-sex policy."

The Court of Appeals for the Fourth Circuit disagreed and vacated the District Court's judgment. The appellate court held: "The Commonwealth of Virginia has not . . . advanced any state policy by which it can justify its determination, under an announced policy of diversity, to afford VMI's unique type of program to men and not to women."

The appeals court greeted with skepticism Virginia's assertion that it offers single-sex education at VMI as a facet of the Commonwealth's overarching and undisputed policy to advance "autonomy and diversity." . . . In short, the court concluded, "[a] policy of diversity which aims to provide an array of educational opportunities, including single-gender institutions, must do more than favor one gender."

The parties agreed that "*some* women can meet the physical standards now imposed on men" and the court was satisfied that "neither the goal of producing citizen soldiers nor VMI's implementing methodology is inherently unsuitable to women." The Court of Appeals, however, accepted the District Court's finding that "at least these three aspects of VMI's program—physical training, the absence of privacy, and the adversative approach—would be materially affected by coeducation." Remanding the case, the appeals court assigned to Virginia, in the first instance, responsibility for selecting a remedial course. The court suggested these options for the Commonwealth: Admit women to VMI; establish parallel institutions or programs; or abandon state support, leaving VMI free to pursue its policies as a private institution. In May 1993, this Court denied certiorari.

C

In response to the Fourth Circuit's ruling, Virginia proposed a parallel program for women: Virginia Women's Institute for Leadership (VWIL). The 4-year, state-sponsored undergraduate program would be located at Mary Baldwin College, a private liberal arts school for women, and would be open, initially, to about 25 to 30 students. Although VWIL would share VMI's mission—to produce "citizen-soldiers"—the VWIL program would differ, as does Mary Baldwin College, from VMI in academic offerings, methods of education, and financial resources.

The average combined SAT score of entrants at Mary Baldwin is about 100 points lower than the score for VMI freshmen. Mary Baldwin's faculty holds "significantly fewer Ph.D.'s than the faculty at VMI" and receives significantly lower salaries. While VMI offers degrees in liberal arts, the sciences, and engineering, Mary Baldwin, at the time of trial, offered only bachelor of arts degrees. A VWIL student seeking to earn an engineering degree could gain one, without public support, by attending Washington University in St. Louis, Missouri, for two years, paying the required private tuition.

Experts in educating women at the college level composed the Task Force charged with designing the VWIL program; Task Force members were drawn from Mary Baldwin's own faculty and staff. Training its attention on methods of instruction appropriate for "most women," the Task Force determined that a military model would be "wholly inappropriate" for VWIL.

VWIL students would participate in ROTC programs and a newly established, "largely ceremonial" Virginia Corps of Cadets, but the VWIL House would not have a military format and VWIL would not require its students to eat meals together or to wear uniforms during the schoolday. In lieu of VMI's adversative method, the VWIL Task Force favored "a cooperative method which reinforces self-esteem." In addition to the standard bachelor of arts program offered at Mary Baldwin, VWIL students would take courses in leadership, complete an off-campus leadership externship, participate in community service projects, and assist in arranging a speaker series.

Virginia represented that it will provide equal financial support for in-state VWIL students and VMI cadets and the VMI Foundation agreed to supply a $5.4625 million endowment for the VWIL program. Mary Baldwin's own endowment is about $19 million; VMI's is $131 million. Mary Baldwin will add $35 million to its endowment based on future commitments; VMI will add $220 million. The VMI Alumni Association has developed a network of employers interested in hiring VMI graduates. The Association has agreed to open its network to VWIL graduates, but those graduates will not have the advantage afforded by a VMI degree.

D

Virginia returned to the District Court seeking approval of its proposed remedial plan, and the court decided the plan met the requirements of the Equal Protection Clause. . . .

A divided Court of Appeals affirmed the District Court's judgment. . . .

. . .

The Fourth Circuit denied rehearing en banc. . . .

III

The cross-petitions in this suit present two ultimate issues. First, does Virginia's exclusion of women from the educational opportunities provided by VMI—extraordinary opportunities for military training and civilian leadership development—deny to women "capable of all of the individual activities required of VMI cadets" the equal protection of the laws guaranteed by the Fourteenth Amendment? Second, if VMI's "unique" situation—as Virginia's sole single-sex public institution of higher education—offends the Constitution's equal protection principle, what is the remedial requirement?

IV

We note, once again, the core instruction of this Court's pathmarking decisions in *J.E.B. v. Alabama ex rel. T. B.* and *Mississippi Univ. for Women:* Parties who seek to defend gender-based government action must demonstrate an "exceedingly persuasive justification" for that action.

Today's skeptical scrutiny of official action denying rights or opportunities based on sex responds to volumes of history. As a plurality of this Court acknowledged a generation ago, "our Nation has had a long and unfortunate history of sex discrimination." Through a century plus three decades and more of that history, women did not count among voters composing "We the People"; not until 1920 did women gain a constitutional right to the franchise. And for a half century thereafter, it remained the prevailing doctrine that government, both federal and state, could withhold from women opportunities accorded men so long as any "basis in reason" could be conceived for the discrimination.

In 1971, for the first time in our Nation's history, this Court ruled in favor of a woman who complained that her State had denied her the equal protection of its laws. *Reed v. Reed* (holding unconstitutional Idaho Code prescription that, among " 'several persons claiming and equally entitled to administer [a decedent's estate], males must be preferred to females' "). Since *Reed,* the Court has repeatedly recognized that neither federal nor state government acts compatibly with the equal protection principle when a law or official policy denies to women, simply because they are women, full citizenship stature—equal opportunity to aspire, achieve, participate in and contribute to society based on their individual talents and capacities.

Without equating gender classifications, for all purposes, to classifications based on race or national origin, the Court, in post-*Reed* decisions, has carefully inspected official action that closes a door or denies opportunity to women (or to men). To summarize the Court's current directions for cases of official classification based on gender: Focusing on the differential treatment or denial of opportunity for which relief is sought, the reviewing court must determine whether the proffered justification is "exceedingly persuasive." The burden of justification is demanding and it rests entirely on the State. The State must show "at least that the [challenged] classification serves 'important governmental objectives and that the discriminatory means employed' are 'substantially related to the achievement of those objectives.'" The justification must be genuine, not hypothesized or invented *post hoc* in response to litigation. And it must not rely on overbroad generalizations about the different talents, capacities, or preferences of males and females.

The heightened review standard our precedent establishes does not make sex a proscribed classification. Supposed "inherent differences" are no longer accepted as a ground for race or national origin classifications. Physical differences between men and women, however, are enduring: "[T]he two sexes are not fungible; a community made up exclusively of one [sex] is different from a community composed of both."

"Inherent differences" between men and women, we have come to appreciate, remain cause for celebration, but not for denigration of the members of either sex or for artificial constraints on an individual's opportunity. Sex classifications may be used to compensate women "for particular economic disabilities [they have] suffered" to "promot[e] equal employment opportunity," to advance full development of the talent and capacities of our Nation's people. But such classifications may not be used, as they once were, to create or perpetuate the legal, social, and economic inferiority of women.

Measuring the record in this case against the review standard just described, we conclude that Virginia has shown no "exceedingly persuasive justification" for excluding all women from the citizen-soldier training afforded by VMI. We therefore affirm the Fourth Circuit's initial judgment, which held that Virginia had violated the Fourteenth Amendment's Equal Protection Clause. Because the remedy proffered by Virginia—the Mary Baldwin VWIL program—does not cure the constitutional violation, *i.e.*, it does not provide equal opportunity, we reverse the Fourth Circuit's final judgment in this case.

V

The Fourth Circuit initially held that Virginia had advanced no state policy by which it could justify, under

equal protection principles, its determination "to afford VMI's unique type of program to men and not to women." Virginia challenges that "liability" ruling and asserts two justifications in defense of VMI's exclusion of women. First, the Commonwealth contends, "single-sex education provides important educational benefits" and the option of single-sex education contributes to "diversity in educational approaches." Second, the Commonwealth argues, "the unique VMI method of character development and leadership training," the school's adversative approach, would have to be modified were VMI to admit women. We consider these two justifications in turn.

A

Single-sex education affords pedagogical benefits to at least some students, Virginia emphasizes, and that reality is uncontested in this litigation. Similarly, it is not disputed that diversity among public educational institutions can serve the public good. But Virginia has not shown that VMI was established, or has been maintained, with a view to diversifying, by its categorical exclusion of women, educational opportunities within the Commonwealth. In cases of this genre, our precedent instructs that "benign" justifications proffered in defense of categorical exclusions will not be accepted automatically; a tenable justification must describe actual state purposes, not rationalizations for actions in fact differently grounded.

Mississippi Univ. for Women is immediately in point. There the State asserted, in justification of its exclusion of men from a nursing school, that it was engaging in "educational affirmative action" by "compensat[ing] for discrimination against women." Undertaking a "searching analysis," the Court found no close resemblance between "the alleged objective" and "the actual purpose underlying the discriminatory classification." Pursuing a similar inquiry here, we reach the same conclusion.

Neither recent nor distant history bears out Virginia's alleged pursuit of diversity through single-sex educational options. In 1839, when the Commonwealth established VMI, a range of educational opportunities for men and women was scarcely contemplated. Higher education at the time was considered dangerous for women; reflecting widely held views about women's proper place, the Nation's first universities and colleges—for example, Harvard in Massachusetts, William and Mary in Virginia—admitted only men. VMI was not at all novel in this respect: In admitting no women, VMI followed the lead of the Commonwealth's flagship school, the University of Virginia, founded in 1819.

"[N]o struggle for the admission of women to a state university," a historian has recounted, "was longer drawn out, or developed more bitterness, than that at the University of Virginia." In 1879, the State Senate resolved to look into the possibility of higher education for women, recognizing that Virginia "has never, at any period of her history," provided for the higher education of her daughters, though she "has liberally provided for the higher education of her sons." Despite this recognition, no new opportunities were instantly open to women.

Virginia eventually provided for several women's seminaries and colleges. Farmville Female Seminary became a public institution in 1884. Two women's schools, Mary Washington College and James Madison University, were founded in 1908; another, Radford University, was founded in 1910. By the mid-1970's, all four schools had become coeducational.

Debate concerning women's admission as undergraduates at the main university continued well past the century's midpoint. Familiar arguments were rehearsed. If women were admitted, it was feared, they "would encroach on the rights of men; there would be new problems of government, perhaps scandals; the old honor system would have to be changed; standards would be lowered to those of other coeducational schools; and the glorious reputation of the university, as a school for men, would be trailed in the dust."

Ultimately, in 1970, "the most prestigious institution of higher education in Virginia," the University of Virginia, introduced coeducation and, in 1972, began to admit women on an equal basis with men. A three-judge Federal District Court confirmed: "Virginia may not now deny to women, on the basis of sex, educational opportunities at the Charlottesville campus that are not afforded in other institutions operated by the [S]tate."

Virginia describes the current absence of public single-sex higher education for women as "an historical anomaly." But the historical record indicates action more deliberate than anomalous: First, protection of women against higher education; next, schools for women far from equal in resources and stature to schools for men; finally, conversion of the separate schools to coeducation. The state legislature, prior to the advent of this controversy, had repealed "[a]ll Virginia statutes

requiring individual institutions to admit only men or women." And in 1990, an official commission, "legislatively established to chart the future goals of higher education in Virginia," reaffirmed the policy "of affording broad access" while maintaining "autonomy and diversity." Significantly, the commission reported:

"Because colleges and universities provide opportunities for students to develop values and learn from role models, it is extremely important that they deal with faculty, staff, and students without regard to sex, race, or ethnic origin." . . .

Our 1982 decision in *Mississippi Univ. for Women* prompted VMI to reexamine its male-only admission policy. Virginia relies on that reexamination as a legitimate basis for maintaining VMI's single-sex character. . . .

In sum, we find no persuasive evidence in this record that VMI's male-only admission policy "is in furtherance of a state policy of 'diversity.'" No such policy, the Fourth Circuit observed, can be discerned from the movement of all other public colleges and universities in Virginia away from single-sex education. That court also questioned "how one institution with autonomy, but with no authority over any other state institution, can give effect to a state policy of diversity among institutions." A purpose genuinely to advance an array of educational options, as the Court of Appeals recognized, is not served by VMI's historic and constant plan—a plan to "affor[d] a unique educational benefit only to males." However "liberally" this plan serves the Commonwealth's sons, it makes no provision whatever for her daughters. That is not *equal* protection.

B

Virginia next argues that VMI's adversative method of training provides educational benefits that cannot be made available, unmodified, to women. Alterations to accommodate women would necessarily be "radical," so "drastic," Virginia asserts, as to transform, indeed "destroy," VMI's program. Neither sex would be favored by the transformation, Virginia maintains: Men would be deprived of the unique opportunity currently available to them; women would not gain that opportunity because their participation would "eliminat[e] the very aspects of [the] program that distinguish [VMI] from . . . other institutions of higher education in Virginia."

The District Court forecast from expert witness testimony, and the Court of Appeals accepted, that coeducation would materially affect "at least these three aspects of VMI's program-physical training, the absence of privacy, and the adversative approach." And it is uncontested that women's admission would require accommodations, primarily in arranging housing assignments and physical training programs for female cadets. It is also undisputed, however, that "the VMI methodology could be used to educate women." The District Court even allowed that some women may prefer it to the methodology a women's college might pursue. . . . The parties, furthermore, agree that "*some* women can meet the physical standards [VMI] now impose[s] on men In sum, as the Court of Appeals stated, "neither the goal of producing citizen soldiers," VMI's *raison d'être,* "nor VMI's implementing methodology is inherently unsuitable to women."

In support of its initial judgment for Virginia, a judgment rejecting all equal protection objections presented by the United States, the District Court made "findings" on "gender-based developmental differences." These "findings" restate the opinions of Virginia's expert witnesses, opinions about typically male or typically female "tendencies." . . .

The United States does not challenge any expert witness estimation on average capacities or preferences of men and women. Instead, the United States emphasizes that time and again since this Court's turning point decision in *Reed v. Reed,* we have cautioned reviewing courts to take a "hard look" at generalizations or "tendencies" of the kind pressed by Virginia, and relied upon by the District Court. State actors controlling gates to opportunity, we have instructed, may not exclude qualified individuals based on "fixed notions concerning the roles and abilities of males and females."

It may be assumed, for purposes of this decision, that most women would not choose VMI's adversative method. . . . Education, to be sure, is not a "one size fits all" business. The issue, however, is not whether "women—or men—should be forced to attend VMI"; rather, the question is whether the Commonwealth can constitutionally deny to women who have the will and capacity, the training and attendant opportunities that VMI uniquely affords.

The notion that admission of women would downgrade VMI's stature, destroy the adversative system and, with it, even the school, is a judgment hardly proved, a prediction hardly different from other "self-fulfilling prophec[ies]," once routinely used to deny rights or opportunities. When women first sought admission to the bar and access to legal education, concerns of the same order were expressed. . . .

. . .

Women's successful entry into the federal military academies, and their participation in the Nation's military forces, indicate that Virginia's fears for the future of VMI may not be solidly grounded. The Commonwealth's justification for excluding all women from "citizen-soldier" training for which some are qualified, in any event, cannot rank as "exceedingly persuasive," as we have explained and applied that standard.

. . .

The Commonwealth's misunderstanding and, in turn, the District Court's, is apparent from VMI's mission: to produce "citizen-soldiers," individuals "imbued with love of learning, confident in the functions and attitudes of leadership, possessing a high sense of public service, advocates of the American democracy and free enterprise system, and ready . . . to defend their country in time of national peril."

Surely that goal is great enough to accommodate women, who today count as citizens in our American democracy equal in stature to men. Just as surely, the Commonwealth's great goal is not substantially advanced by women's categorical exclusion, in total disregard of their individual merit, from the Commonwealth's premier "citizen-soldier" corps. Virginia, in sum, "has fallen far short of establishing the 'exceedingly persuasive justification,'" that must be the solid base for any gender-defined classification.

VI

In the second phase of the litigation, Virginia presented its remedial plan—maintain VMI as a male-only college and create VWIL as a separate program for women. The plan met District Court approval. The Fourth Circuit, in turn, deferentially reviewed the Commonwealth's proposal and decided that the two single-sex programs directly served Virginia's reasserted purposes: single-gender education, and "achieving the results of an adversative method in a military environment." Inspecting the VMI and VWIL educational programs to determine whether they "afford[ed] to both genders benefits comparable in substance, [if] not in form and detail," the Court of Appeals concluded that Virginia had arranged for men and women opportunities "sufficiently comparable" to survive equal protection evaluation. The United States challenges this "remedial" ruling as pervasively misguided.

A

A remedial decree, this Court has said, must closely fit the constitutional violation; it must be shaped to place persons unconstitutionally denied an opportunity or advantage in "the position they would have occupied in the absence of [discrimination]." The constitutional violation in this suit is the categorical exclusion of women from an extraordinary educational opportunity afforded men. A proper remedy for an unconstitutional exclusion, we have explained, aims to "eliminate [so far as possible] the discriminatory effects of the past" and to "bar like discrimination in the future."

Virginia chose not to eliminate, but to leave untouched, VMI's exclusionary policy. For women only, however, Virginia proposed a separate program, different in kind from VMI and unequal in tangible and intangible facilities. Having violated the Constitution's equal protection requirement, Virginia was obliged to show that its remedial proposal "directly address[ed] and relate[d] to" the violation, *i.e.*, the equal protection denied to women ready, willing, and able to benefit from educational opportunities of the kind VMI offers. Virginia described VWIL as a "parallel program," and asserted that VWIL shares VMI's mission of producing "citizen-soldiers" and VMI's goals of providing "education, military training, mental and physical discipline, character . . . and leadership development." If the VWIL program could not "eliminate the discriminatory effects of the past," could it at least "bar like discrimination in the future"? A comparison of the programs said to be "parallel" informs our answer. In exposing the character of, and differences in, the VMI and VWIL programs, we recapitulate facts earlier presented.

VWIL affords women no opportunity to experience the rigorous military training for which VMI is famed. Instead, the VWIL program "deemphasize[s]" military education, and uses a "cooperative method" of education "which reinforces self-esteem." VWIL students participate in ROTC and a "largely ceremonial" Virginia Corps of Cadets but Virginia deliberately did not make VWIL a military institute. The VWIL House is not a military-style residence and VWIL students need not live together throughout the 4-year program, eat meals together, or wear uniforms during the schoolday. VWIL students thus do not experience the "barracks" life "crucial to the VMI experience," the spartan living arrangements designed to foster an "egalitarian ethic." "[T]he most important aspects of the VMI educational experience

occur in the barracks," the District Court found, yet Virginia deemed that core experience nonessential, indeed inappropriate, for training its female citizen-soldiers.

VWIL students receive their "leadership training" in seminars, externships, and speaker series, episodes and encounters lacking the "[p]hysical rigor, mental stress, . . . minute regulation of behavior, and indoctrination in desirable values" made hallmarks of VMI's citizen-soldier training,. Kept away from the pressures, hazards, and psychological bonding characteristic of VMI's adversative training, VWIL students will not know the "feeling of tremendous accomplishment" commonly experienced by VMI's successful cadets.

Virginia maintains that these methodological differences are "justified pedagogically," based on "important differences between men and women in learning and developmental needs," "psychological and sociological differences" Virginia describes as "real" and "not stereotypes." The Task Force charged with developing the leadership program for women, drawn from the staff and faculty at Mary Baldwin College, "determined that a military model and, especially VMI's adversative method, would be wholly inappropriate for educating and training *most women.*" VMI's adversative method "would not be effective for *women as a group.*" The Commonwealth embraced the Task Force view, as did expert witnesses who testified for Virginia.

As earlier stated, generalizations about "the way women are," estimates of what is appropriate for *most women*, no longer justify denying opportunity to women whose talent and capacity place them outside the average description. Notably, Virginia never asserted that VMI's method of education suits *most men.* It is also revealing that Virginia accounted for its failure to make the VWIL experience "the entirely militaristic experience of VMI" on the ground that VWIL "is planned for women who do not necessarily expect to pursue military careers." By that reasoning, VMI's "entirely militaristic" program would be inappropriate for men in general or *as a group,* for "[o]nly about 15% of VMI cadets enter career military service."

In contrast to the generalizations about women on which Virginia rests, we note again these dispositive realities: VMI's "implementing methodology" is not "inherently unsuitable to women"; "some women . . . do well under [the] adversative model"; "some women, at least, would want to attend [VMI] if they had the opportunity"; "some women are capable of all of the individual activities required of VMI cadets," and "can meet the physical standards [VMI] now impose[s] on men." It is on behalf of these women that the United States has instituted this suit, and it is for them that a remedy must be crafted, a remedy that will end their exclusion from a state-supplied educational opportunity for which they are fit, a decree that will "bar like discrimination in the future."

B

In myriad respects other than military training, VWIL does not qualify as VMI's equal. VWIL's student body, faculty, course offerings, and facilities hardly match VMI's. Nor can the VWIL graduate anticipate the benefits associated with VMI's 157-year history, the school's prestige, and its influential alumni network.

. . .

Although Virginia has represented that it will provide equal financial support for in-state VWIL students and VMI cadets and the VMI Foundation has agreed to endow VWIL with $5.4625 million, the difference between the two schools' financial reserves is pronounced. Mary Baldwin's endowment, currently about $19 million, will gain an additional $35 million based on future commitments; VMI's current endowment, $131 million—the largest public college per-student endowment in the Nation—will gain $220 million.

The VWIL student does not graduate with the advantage of a VMI degree. Her diploma does not unite her with the legions of VMI "graduates [who] have distinguished themselves" in military and civilian life. "[VMI] alumni are exceptionally close to the school," and that closeness accounts, in part, for VMI's success in attracting applicants. A VWIL graduate cannot assume that the "network of business owners, corporations, VMI graduates and non-graduate employers . . . interested in hiring VMI graduates" will be equally responsive to her search for employment.

Virginia, in sum, while maintaining VMI for men only, has failed to provide any "comparable single-gender women's institution." Instead, the Commonwealth has created a VWIL program fairly appraised as a "pale shadow" of VMI in terms of the range of curricular choices and faculty stature, funding, prestige, alumni support and influence.

Virginia's VWIL solution is reminiscent of the remedy Texas proposed 50 years ago, in response to a state trial court's 1946 ruling that, given the equal protection guarantee, African-Americans could not be denied a legal education at a state facility. . . .

Before this Court considered the case, the new school had gained "a faculty of five full-time professors; a student body of 23; a library of some 16,500 volumes serviced by a full-time staff; a practice court and legal aid association; and one alumnus who ha[d] become a member of the Texas Bar." [In *Sweatt v. Painter*, t]his Court contrasted resources at the new school with those at the school from which Sweatt had been excluded. The University of Texas Law School had a full-time faculty of 16, a student body of 850, a library containing over 65,000 volumes, scholarship funds, a law review, and moot court facilities.

More important than the tangible features, the Court emphasized, are "those qualities which are incapable of objective measurement but which make for greatness" in a school, including "reputation of the faculty, experience of the administration, position and influence of the alumni, standing in the community, traditions and prestige." Facing the marked differences reported in the *Sweatt* opinion, the Court unanimously ruled that Texas had not shown "substantial equality in the [separate] educational opportunities" the State offered. Accordingly, the Court held, the Equal Protection Clause required Texas to admit African-Americans to the University of Texas Law School. In line with *Sweatt*, we rule here that Virginia has not shown substantial equality in the separate educational opportunities the Commonwealth supports at VWIL and VMI.

C

When Virginia tendered its VWIL plan, the Fourth Circuit did not inquire whether the proposed remedy, approved by the District Court, placed women denied the VMI advantage in "the position they would have occupied in the absence of [discrimination]." Instead, the Court of Appeals considered whether the Commonwealth could provide, with fidelity to the equal protection principle, separate and unequal educational programs for men and women.

The Fourth Circuit acknowledged that "the VWIL degree from Mary Baldwin College lacks the historical benefit and prestige of a degree from VMI." The Court of Appeals further observed that VMI is "an ongoing and successful institution with a long history," and there remains no "comparable single-gender women's institution." Nevertheless, the appeals court declared the substantially different and significantly unequal VWIL program satisfactory. The court reached that result by revising the applicable standard of review. The Fourth Circuit displaced the standard developed in our precedent and substituted a standard of its own invention.

We have earlier described the deferential review in which the Court of Appeals engaged, a brand of review inconsistent with the more exacting standard our precedent requires. Quoting in part from *Mississippi Univ. for Women*, the Court of Appeals candidly described its own analysis as one capable of checking a legislative purpose ranked as "pernicious," but generally according "deference to [the] legislative will." Recognizing that it had extracted from our decisions a test yielding "little or no scrutiny of the effect of a classification directed at [single-gender education]," the Court of Appeals devised another test, a "substantive comparability" inquiry, and proceeded to find that new test satisfied.

The Fourth Circuit plainly erred in exposing Virginia's VWIL plan to a deferential analysis, for "all gender-based classifications today" warrant "heightened scrutiny." Valuable as VWIL may prove for students who seek the program offered, Virginia's remedy affords no cure at all for the opportunities and advantages withheld from women who want a VMI education and can make the grade. In sum, Virginia's remedy does not match the constitutional violation; the Commonwealth has shown no "exceedingly persuasive justification" for withholding from women qualified for the experience premier training of the kind VMI affords.

VII

A generation ago, "the authorities controlling Virginia higher education," despite long established tradition, agreed "to innovate and favorably entertain[ed] the [then] relatively new idea that there must be no discrimination by sex in offering educational opportunity."

Commencing in 1970, Virginia opened to women "educational opportunities at the Charlottesville campus that [were] not afforded in other [state-operated] institutions." A

federal court approved the Commonwealth's innovation, emphasizing that the University of Virginia "offer[ed] courses of instruction . . . not available elsewhere." The court further noted: "[T]here exists at Charlottesville a 'prestige' factor [not paralleled in] other Virginia educational institutions."

VMI, too, offers an educational opportunity no other Virginia institution provides, and the school's "prestige"—associated with its success in developing "citizen-soldiers"—is unequaled. Virginia has closed this facility to its daughters and, instead, has devised for them a "parallel program," with a faculty less impressively credentialed and less well paid, more limited course offerings, fewer opportunities for military training and for scientific specialization. VMI, beyond question, "possesses to a far greater degree" than the VWIL program "those qualities which are incapable of objective measurement but which make for greatness in a . . . school," including "position and influence of the alumni, standing in the community, traditions and prestige." Women seeking and fit for a VMI-quality education cannot be offered anything less, under the Commonwealth's obligation to afford them genuinely equal protection.

A prime part of the history of our Constitution, historian Richard Morris recounted, is the story of the extension of constitutional rights and protections to people once ignored or excluded. VMI's story continued as our comprehension of "We the People" expanded. There is no reason to believe that the admission of women capable of all the activities required of VMI cadets would destroy the Institute rather than enhance its capacity to serve the "more perfect Union."

* * *

For the reasons stated, the initial judgment of the Court of Appeals is affirmed, the final judgment of the Court of Appeals is reversed, and the case is remanded for further proceedings consistent with this opinion.

It is so ordered.

Justice Thomas took no part in the consideration or decision of these cases.

UNIVERSITY OF PENNSYLVANIA V. EQUAL EMPLOYMENT OPPORTUNITY COMMISSION

In *University of Pennsylvania v. Equal Employment Opportunity Commission* (EEOC, 1990), the U.S.

Supreme Court made it clear that university officials do not have a special legal privilege that allows them to refuse to release administratively and judicially requested materials in disputes about tenure. In *EEOC*, the Court held that university officials were required to release peer review tenure documents to the EEOC. In light of the Court's having rejected the claim of university officials who refused to comply on the basis that the materials were confidential and exempt from disclosure, this entry reviews the background of the case and its analysis and reflects on its implications for faculty members in higher education.

Facts of the Case

EEOC arose as commission officials investigated a charge of alleged discrimination on the basis of race, sex, or national origin in violation of Title VII of the Civil Rights Act of 1964. When an Asian American, female associate professor was denied tenure, she filed a claim with the EEOC. Acting through the EEOC, the faculty member filed a complaint alleging that her department chairperson sexually harassed her, and when she rejected his advances, he retaliated by writing an unfavorable letter to the university committee that was responsible for making the final decision about whether she would be granted tenure. In addition, the faculty member complained that most of her colleagues had recommended her for tenure, and she had not received any reason from university officials as to why she was denied tenure. Further, the faculty member alleged that university officials claimed that they were not interested in her "China-related research," which she interpreted as a pretext for discrimination based on her national origin and race. As part of its investigation, the EEOC subpoenaed the faculty member's tenure review file along with the files of five male colleagues who allegedly received better treatment than she did in the review process.

Both a federal trial court, in an unpublished opinion, and the Third Circuit rejected the arguments advanced by university officials as to why they should not have to comply with the EEOC's subpoena. University officials then sought further review, and the Supreme Court agreed to hear an appeal.

The Supreme Court's Ruling

A unanimous Supreme Court, in an opinion authored by Justice Blackmun, affirmed in favor of the EEOC. At the outset, the Court rejected the argument of university officials who contended that they did not have to release the tenure files based on a common-law privilege. If anything, university officials claimed that the EEOC would have needed to demonstrate a specific need beyond relevance to obtain the materials. However, the Court ruled that because a university does not have a qualified privilege (meaning that officials are not exempt from liability for having made potentially defamatory remarks in the context of promotion and tenure decisions), the EEOC did not need to show anything more than relevance before obtaining peer review materials in connection with a discrimination claim.

In response to the university officials' claim for a common-law privilege, the Supreme Court reasoned that when Congress extended Title VII coverage to educational institutions, it did not create a privilege for peer review materials. The Court refused to create a new privilege for peer review materials, because they are often necessary to investigate whether "invidious discrimination" has occurred. The Court expressed its concern that if the EEOC had been required to demonstrate a particular need for disclosure, then its investigations would have been hindered. Additionally, the Court did not believe that university materials meet the requisite need for qualified privilege in the same manner as presidential communications, because the latter involve governmental operations, a situation that was not present in the case at bar. To this end, the Court explained that the extension of qualified privilege could lead to many similar requests from other employers, thereby undercutting the authority of the EEOC.

The Supreme Court was not persuaded by the academic freedom argument that university officials advanced. More specifically, in asserting that confidentiality was necessary to keep the peer review process candid, the university officials claimed that allowing peer review documents to be released on the basis of mere relevance would have infringed on the First Amendment right to academic freedom. However, the Court clarified that academic freedom protections are content based and that university officials had not provided a content-based rationale for prohibiting the release of the materials in the tenure file. The Court thus concluded that it would not expand First Amendment protection to include peer review materials, because there was no reason for it to do so.

Impact of the Ruling

By resolving the litigation in favor of the EEOC, the Supreme Court opened the door for increased disclosure in the tenure process. As a result of *EEOC*, then, discrimination that could have remained hidden in confidential peer review documents is now open to judicial scrutiny; it is hoped that it will ensure a more equitable process for all applicants for tenure.

Janet R. Rumple

See also Academic Freedom; Equal Employment Opportunity Commission; Personnel Records; Tenure; Title VII

Further Readings

Russo, C. J., Ponterotto, J. G., & Jackson, B. L. (1990). Confidential peer review: A Supreme Court update and implications for university personnel. *Initiatives,* *53*(2), 11–17.

Legal Citations

Title VII of the Civil Rights Act of 1964, 42 U.S.C. § 2000e.
University of Pennsylvania v. EEOC, 493 U.S. 182 (1990).

UNIVERSITY OF PENNSYLVANIA V. EQUAL EMPLOYMENT OPPORTUNITY COMMISSION

In *University of Pennsylvania v. EEOC*, the Supreme Court made it clear that there are circumstances under which officials can be required to release peer review tenure documents to the EEOC.

Supreme Court of the United States

UNIVERSITY OF PENNSYLVANIA

v.

EQUAL EMPLOYMENT OPPORTUNITY COMMISSION

493 U.S. 182

Argued Nov. 7, 1989

Decided Jan. 9, 1990

Justice BLACKMUN delivered the opinion of the Court.

In this case we are asked to decide whether a university enjoys a special privilege, grounded in either the common law or the First Amendment, against disclosure of peer review materials that are relevant to charges of racial or sexual discrimination in tenure decisions.

I

The University of Pennsylvania, petitioner here, is a private institution. . . .

In 1985, the University denied tenure to Rosalie Tung, an associate professor on the Wharton faculty. Tung then filed a sworn charge of discrimination with respondent Equal Employment Opportunity Commission (EEOC or Commission). As subsequently amended, the charge alleged that Tung was the victim of discrimination on the basis of race, sex, and national origin, in violation of § 703(a) of Title VII of the Civil Rights Act of 1964, which makes it unlawful "to discriminate against any individual with respect to his compensation, terms, conditions, or privileges of employment, because of such individual's race, color, religion, sex, or national origin."

In her charge, Tung stated that the department chairman had sexually harassed her and that, in her belief, after she insisted that their relationship remain professional, he had submitted a negative letter to the University's Personnel Committee which possessed ultimate responsibility for tenure decisions. She also alleged that her qualifications were "equal to or better than" those of five named male faculty members who had received more favorable treatment. Tung noted that the majority of the members of her department had recommended her for tenure, and stated that she had been given no reason for the decision against her, but had discovered of her own efforts that the Personnel Committee had attempted to justify its decision "on the ground that the Wharton School is not interested in China-related research." This explanation, Tung's charge alleged, was a pretext for discrimination: "simply their way of saying they do not want a Chinese-American, Oriental, woman in their school."

The Commission undertook an investigation into Tung's charge and requested a variety of relevant information from petitioner. When the University refused to provide certain of that information, the Commission's Acting District Director issued a subpoena seeking, among other things, Tung's tenure-review file and the tenure files of the five male faculty members identified in the charge. *Id.*, at 21. Petitioner refused to produce a number of the tenure-file documents. It applied to the Commission for modification of the subpoena to exclude what it termed "confidential peer review information," specifically, (1) confidential letters written by Tung's evaluators; (2) the department chairman's letter of evaluation; (3) documents reflecting the internal deliberations of faculty committees considering applications for tenure, including the Department Evaluation Report summarizing the deliberations relating to Tung's application for tenure; and (4) comparable portions of the tenure-review files of the five males. The University urged the Commission to "adopt a balancing approach reflecting the constitutional and societal interest inherent in the peer review process" and to resort to "all feasible methods to minimize the intrusive effects of its investigations."

The Commission denied the University's application. It concluded that the withheld documents were needed in order to determine the merit of Tung's charges. . . . The Commission indicated that enforcement proceedings might be necessary if a response was not forthcoming within 20 days.

The University continued to withhold the tenure-review materials. The Commission then applied to the United States District Court for the Eastern District of Pennsylvania for enforcement of its subpoena. The court entered a brief enforcement order.

The Court of Appeals for the Third Circuit affirmed the enforcement decision. Relying upon its earlier opinion in *EEOC v. Franklin and Marshall College,*, the court rejected petitioner's claim that policy considerations and First Amendment principles of academic freedom required the recognition of a qualified privilege or the adoption of a balancing approach that would require the Commission to demonstrate some particularized need, beyond a showing of relevance, to obtain peer review materials. Because of what might be thought of as a conflict in approach with the Seventh Circuit's decision in *EEOC v. University of Notre Dame du Lac* and because of the importance of the issue, we granted certiorari limited to the compelled-disclosure question.

II

As it had done before the Commission, the District Court, and the Court of Appeals, the University raises here essentially two claims. First, it urges us to recognize a qualified common-law privilege against disclosure of confidential peer review materials. Second, it asserts a First Amendment right of "academic freedom" against wholesale disclosure of the contested documents. With respect to each of the two claims, the remedy petitioner seeks is the same: a requirement of a judicial finding of particularized necessity of access, beyond a showing of mere relevance, before peer review materials are disclosed to the Commission.

A

Petitioner's common-law privilege claim is grounded in Federal Rule of Evidence 501. This provides in relevant part:

> "Except as otherwise required by the Constitution . . . as provided by Act of Congress or in rules prescribed by the Supreme Court . . . , the privilege of a witness . . . shall be governed by the principles of the common law as they may be interpreted by the courts of the United States in the light of reason and experience."

The University asks us to invoke this provision to fashion a new privilege that it claims is necessary to protect the integrity of the peer review process, which in turn is central to the proper functioning of many colleges and universities. These institutions are special, observes petitioner, because they function as "centers of learning, innovation and discovery."

We do not create and apply an evidentiary privilege unless it "promotes sufficiently important interests to outweigh the need for probative evidence. . . ." Inasmuch as "[t]estimonial exclusionary rules and privileges contravene the fundamental principle that 'the public . . . has a right to every man's evidence,' " any such privilege must "be strictly construed."

Moreover, although Rule 501 manifests a congressional desire "not to freeze the law of privilege" but rather to provide the courts with flexibility to develop rules of privilege on a case-by-case basis, we are disinclined to exercise this authority expansively. We are especially reluctant to recognize a privilege in an area where it appears that Congress has considered the relevant competing concerns but has not provided the privilege itself. The balancing of conflicting interests of this type is particularly a legislative function.

With all this in mind, we cannot accept the University's invitation to create a new privilege against the disclosure of peer review materials. We begin by noting that Congress, in extending Title VII to educational institutions and in providing for broad EEOC subpoena powers, did not see fit to create a privilege for peer review documents.

When Title VII was enacted originally in 1964, it exempted an "educational institution with respect to the employment of individuals to perform work connected with the educational activities of such institution." § 702, 78 Stat. 255. Eight years later, Congress eliminated that specific exemption by enacting § 3 of the Equal Employment Opportunity Act of 1972. This extension of Title VII was Congress' considered response to the widespread and compelling problem of invidious discrimination in educational institutions. The House Report focused specifically on discrimination in higher education, including the lack of access for women and minorities to higher ranking (*i.e.,* tenured) academic positions. . . . Petitioner therefore cannot seriously contend that Congress was oblivious to concerns of academic autonomy when it abandoned the exemption for educational institutions.

The effect of the elimination of this exemption was to expose tenure determinations to the same enforcement procedures applicable to other employment decisions.

This Court previously has observed that Title VII "sets forth 'an integrated, multistep enforcement procedure' that enables the Commission to detect and remedy instances of discrimination." The Commission's enforcement responsibilities are triggered by the filing of a specific sworn charge of discrimination. The Act obligates the Commission to investigate a charge of discrimination to determine whether there is "reasonable cause to believe that the charge is true." If it finds no such reasonable cause, the Commission is directed to dismiss the charge. If it does find reasonable cause, the Commission shall "endeavor to eliminate [the] alleged unlawful employment practice by informal methods of conference, conciliation, and persuasion." If attempts at voluntary resolution fail, the Commission may bring an action against the employer.

To enable the Commission to make informed decisions at each stage of the enforcement process, § 2000e-8(a) confers a broad right of access to relevant evidence . . . If an employer refuses to provide this information voluntarily, the Act authorizes the Commission to issue a subpoena and to seek an order enforcing it [§ 2000e-9].

On their face, §§ 2000e-8(a) and 2000e-9 do not carve out any special privilege relating to peer review materials, despite the fact that Congress undoubtedly was aware, when it extended Title VII's coverage, of the potential burden that access to such material might create. Moreover, we have noted previously that when a court is asked to enforce a Commission subpoena, its responsibility is to "satisfy itself that the charge is valid and that the material requested is 'relevant' to the charge . . . and more generally to assess any contentions by the employer that the demand for information is too indefinite or has been made for an illegitimate purpose." It is not then to determine "whether the charge of discrimination is 'well founded' or 'verifiable.'"

The University concedes that the information sought by the Commission in this case passes the relevance test set forth in *Shell Oil.* Petitioner argues, nevertheless, that Title VII affirmatively grants courts the discretion to require more than relevance in order to protect tenure review documents. Although petitioner recognizes that Title VII gives the Commission broad "power to seek access to all evidence that may be 'relevant to the charge under investigation,'" it contends that Title VII's subpoena enforcement provisions do not give the Commission an unqualified right to *acquire* such evidence. This interpretation simply cannot be reconciled with the plain language of the text of § 2000e-8(a), which states that the Commission *"shall . . . have* access" to "relevant" evidence (emphasis added). The provision can be read only as giving the Commission a right to obtain that evidence, not a mere license to seek it.

Although the text of the access provisions thus provides no privilege, Congress did address situations in which an employer may have an interest in the confidentiality of its records. The same § 2000e-8 which gives the Commission access to any evidence relevant to its investigation also makes it "unlawful for any officer or employee of the Commission to make public in any manner whatever any information obtained by the Commission pursuant to its authority under this section prior to the institution of any proceeding" under the Act. A violation of this provision subjects the employee to criminal penalties. To be sure, the protection of confidentiality that § 2000e-8(e) provides is less than complete. But this, if anything, weakens petitioner's argument. Congress apparently considered the issue of confidentiality, and it provided a modicum of protection. Petitioner urges us to go further than Congress thought necessary to safeguard that value, that is, to strike the balance differently from the one Congress adopted. Petitioner, however, does not offer any persuasive justification for that suggestion.

We readily agree with petitioner that universities and colleges play significant roles in American society. Nor need we question, at this point, petitioner's assertion that confidentiality is important to the proper functioning of the peer review process under which many academic institutions operate. The costs that ensue from disclosure, however, constitute only one side of the balance. As Congress has recognized, the costs associated with racial and sexual discrimination in institutions of higher learning are very substantial. Few would deny that ferreting out this kind of invidious discrimination is a great, if not compelling, governmental interest. Often, as even petitioner seems to admit, disclosure of peer review materials will be necessary in order for the Commission to determine whether illegal discrimination has taken place. Indeed, if there is a "smoking gun" to be found that demonstrates discrimination in tenure decisions, it is likely to be tucked away in peer review files. . . .

Moreover, we agree with the EEOC that the adoption of a requirement that the Commission demonstrate a "specific reason for disclosure" beyond a showing of relevance, would place a substantial litigation-producing obstacle in the way of the Commission's efforts to investigate and remedy alleged discrimination. A university faced with a disclosure request might well utilize the privilege in a way that frustrates the EEOC's mission. We are reluctant to "place a potent weapon in the hands of employers who have no interest in complying voluntarily with the Act, who wish instead to delay as long as possible investigations by the EEOC."

Acceptance of petitioner's claim would also lead to a wave of similar privilege claims by other employers who play significant roles in furthering speech and learning in society. What of writers, publishers, musicians, lawyers? It surely is not unreasonable to believe, for example, that confidential peer reviews play an important part in partnership determinations at some law firms. We perceive no limiting principle in petitioner's argument. Accordingly, we stand behind the breakwater Congress has established: unless specifically provided otherwise in the statute, the EEOC may obtain "relevant" evidence. Congress has made the choice. If it dislikes the result, it of course may revise the statute.

Finally, we see nothing in our precedents that supports petitioner's claim. In *United States v. Nixon,* upon which petitioner relies, we recognized a qualified privilege for Presidential communications. It is true that in fashioning this privilege we noted the importance of confidentiality in certain contexts: "Human experience teaches that those who expect public dissemination of their remarks may well temper candor with a concern for appearances and for their own interests to the detriment of the decisionmaking process."

But the privilege we recognized in *Nixon* was grounded in the separation of powers between the branches of the Federal Government. "[T]he privilege can be said to derive from the supremacy of each branch within its own assigned area of constitutional duties. Certain powers and privileges flow from the nature of enumerated powers; the protection of the confidentiality of Presidential communications has similar constitutional underpinnings." As we discuss below, petitioner's claim of privilege lacks similar constitutional foundation.

In *Douglas Oil Co. of Cal. v. Petrol Stops Northwest,* the Court recognized the privileged nature of grand jury proceedings. We noted there that the rule of secrecy dated back to the 17th century, was imported into our federal common law, and was eventually codified in Federal Rule of Criminal Procedure 6(e) as "an integral part of our criminal justice system." The Court recognized a privilege for the votes and deliberations of a petit jury, noting that references to the privilege "bear with them the implications of an immemorial tradition." More recently, in *NLRB v. Sears, Roebuck & Co.*, we construed an exception to the Freedom of Information Act in which Congress had incorporated a well-established privilege for deliberative intra-agency documents. A privilege for peer review materials has no similar historical or statutory basis.

B

As noted above, petitioner characterizes its First Amendment claim as one of "academic freedom." Petitioner begins its argument by focusing our attention upon language in prior cases acknowledging the crucial role universities play in the dissemination of ideas in our society and recognizing "academic freedom" as a "special concern of the First Amendment." In that case the Court said: "Our Nation is deeply committed to safeguarding academic freedom, which is of transcendent value to all of us and not merely to the teachers concerned." Petitioner places special reliance on Justice Frankfurter's opinion, concurring in the result, in *Sweezy v. New Hampshire*, where the Justice recognized that one of "four essential freedoms" that a university possesses under the First Amendment is the right to "determine for itself on academic grounds *who may teach*" (emphasis added).

Petitioner contends that it exercises this right of determining "on academic grounds who may teach" through the process of awarding tenure. A tenure system, asserts petitioner, determines what the university will look like over time. "In making tenure decisions, therefore, a university is doing nothing less than shaping its own identity."

Petitioner next maintains that the peer review process is the most important element in the effective operation of a tenure system. A properly functioning tenure system requires the faculty to obtain candid and detailed written evaluations of the candidate's scholarship, both from the candidate's peers at the university and from scholars at other institutions. These evaluations, says petitioner, traditionally have been provided with express or implied assurances of confidentiality. It is confidentiality that ensures candor and enables an institution to make its tenure decisions on the basis of valid academic criteria.

Building from these premises, petitioner claims that requiring the disclosure of peer review evaluations on a finding of mere relevance will undermine the existing process of awarding tenure, and therefore will result in a significant infringement of petitioner's First Amendment right of academic freedom. As more and more peer evaluations are disclosed to the EEOC and become public, a "chilling effect" on candid evaluations and discussions of candidates will result. And as the quality of peer review evaluations declines, tenure committees will no longer be able to rely on them. "This will work to the detriment of universities, as less qualified persons achieve tenure causing the quality of instruction and scholarship to decline." Compelling disclosure of materials "also will result in divisiveness and tension, placing strain on faculty relations and impairing the free interchange of ideas that is a hallmark of academic freedom." The prospect of these deleterious effects on American colleges and universities, concludes petitioner, compels recognition of a First Amendment privilege.

In our view, petitioner's reliance on the so-called academic-freedom cases is somewhat misplaced. In those cases government was attempting to control or direct the *content* of the speech engaged in by the university or those affiliated with it. In *Sweezy*, for example, the Court invalidated the conviction of a person found in contempt for refusing to answer questions about the content of a lecture he had delivered at a state university. Similarly, in *Keyishian*, the Court invalidated a network of state laws that required public employees, including teachers at state universities, to make certifications with respect to their membership in the Communist Party. When, in those cases, the Court spoke of "academic freedom" and the right to determine on "academic grounds who may teach" the Court was speaking in reaction to content-based regulation.

Fortunately, we need not define today the precise contours of any academic-freedom right against governmental attempts to influence the content of academic speech through the selection of faculty or by other means, because petitioner does not allege that the Commission's subpoenas are intended to or will in fact direct the content of university discourse toward or away from particular subjects or points of view. Instead, as noted above, petitioner claims that the "quality of instruction and scholarship [will] decline" as a result of the burden EEOC subpoenas place on the peer review process.

Also, the cases upon which petitioner places emphasis involved *direct* infringements on the asserted right to "determine for itself on academic grounds who may teach." In *Keyishian,* for example, government was attempting to *substitute* its teaching employment criteria for those already in place at the academic institutions, directly and completely usurping the discretion of each institution. In contrast, the EEOC subpoena at issue here effects no such usurpation. The Commission is not providing criteria that petitioner *must* use in selecting teachers. Nor is it preventing the University from using any criteria it may wish to use, except those—including race, sex, and national origin—that are proscribed under Title VII. In keeping with Title VII's preservation of employers' remaining freedom of choice, courts have stressed the importance of avoiding second-guessing of legitimate academic judgments. This Court itself has cautioned that "judges . . . asked to review the substance of a genuinely academic decision . . . should show great respect for the faculty's professional judgment." Nothing we say today should be understood as a retreat from this principle of respect for *legitimate* academic decisionmaking.

That the burden of which the University complains is neither content-based nor direct does not necessarily mean that petitioner has no valid First Amendment claim. Rather, it means only that petitioner's claim does not fit neatly within any right of academic freedom that could be derived from the cases on which petitioner relies. In essence, petitioner asks us to recognize an *expanded* right of academic freedom to protect confidential peer review materials from disclosure. Although we are sensitive to the effects that content-neutral government action may have on speech and believe that burdens that are less than direct may sometimes pose First Amendment concerns, we think the First Amendment cannot be extended to embrace petitioner's claim.

First, by comparison with the cases in which we have found a cognizable First Amendment claim, the infringement the University complains of is extremely attenuated. To repeat, it argues that the First Amendment is infringed by disclosure of peer review materials because disclosure undermines the confidentiality which is central to the peer review process, and this in turn is central to the tenure process, which in turn is the means by which petitioner seeks to exercise its asserted academic-freedom right of choosing who will teach. To verbalize the claim is to recognize how distant the burden is from the asserted right.

Indeed, if the University's attenuated claim were accepted, many other generally applicable laws might also be said to infringe the First Amendment. In effect, petitioner says no more than that disclosure of peer review materials makes it more difficult to acquire information regarding the "academic grounds" on which petitioner wishes to base its tenure decisions. But many laws make the exercise of First Amendment rights more difficult. For example, a university cannot claim a First Amendment violation simply because it may be subject to taxation or other government regulation, even though such regulation might deprive the university of revenue it needs to bid for professors who are contemplating working for other academic institutions or in industry. We doubt that the peer review process is any more essential in effectuating the right to determine "who may teach" than is the availability of money.

In addition to being remote and attenuated, the injury to academic freedom claimed by petitioner is also speculative. As the EEOC points out, confidentiality is not the norm in all peer review systems. Moreover, some disclosure of peer evaluations would take place even if petitioner's "special necessity" test were adopted. Thus, the "chilling effect" petitioner fears is at most only incrementally worsened by the absence of a privilege. Finally, we are not so ready as petitioner seems to be to assume the worst about those in the academic community. Although it is possible that some evaluators may become less candid as the possibility of disclosure increases, others may simply ground their evaluations in specific examples and illustrations in order to deflect potential claims of bias or unfairness. Not all academics will hesitate to stand up and be counted when they evaluate their peers.

The case we decide today in many respects is similar to *Branzburg v. Hayes.* In *Branzburg,* the Court rejected the notion that under the First Amendment a reporter could not be required to appear or to testify as to information obtained in confidence without a special showing that the reporter's testimony was necessary. Petitioners there, like petitioner here, claimed that requiring disclosure of information collected in confidence would inhibit the free flow of information in contravention of First Amendment principles. In the course of rejecting the First Amendment argument, this Court noted that "the First Amendment does not invalidate every incidental burdening of the press that may result from the enforcement of civil or criminal statutes of general applicability." We also indicated a reluctance to recognize a constitutional privilege where it was "unclear how often and to what extent informers are actually deterred from furnishing information when newsmen are forced to testify before a grand jury." We were unwilling then, as we are today, "to embark the judiciary on a long and difficult journey to . . . an uncertain destination." Because we conclude that the EEOC subpoena process does not infringe any First Amendment right enjoyed by petitioner, the EEOC need not demonstrate any special justification to sustain the constitutionality of Title VII as applied to tenure peer review materials in general or to the subpoena involved in this case. Accordingly, we need not address the Commission's alternative argument that any infringement of petitioner's First Amendment rights is permissible because of the substantial relation between the Commission's request and the overriding and compelling state interest in eradicating invidious discrimination.

The judgment of the Court of Appeals is affirmed.

It is so ordered.

UROFSKY V. GILMORE

The case of *Urofsky v. Gilmore* (2000) involved a statute from Virginia that forbade public employees from accessing sexually explicit material on the Internet on publicly owned or leased computers, except in conjunction with bona fide research projects. At issue were whether the statute violated the First Amendment rights of all public employees and whether the statute infringed on the academic freedom rights of faculty members. Ultimately, the Fourth Circuit ruled that the law was not unconstitutionally vague or overbroad and that it did not infringe on either the First Amendment rights of public employees in general or the academic freedom rights of faculty members in public colleges and universities in particular. In light of the significant issues that *Urofsky* raises about the academic freedom and free speech rights of faculty members in higher education during the cyber age, this entry reviews the court's rationale in detail.

Facts of the Case

In 1999, six faculty members who were employed by public institutions in Virginia filed suit, challenging the constitutionality of a commonwealth statute. The plaintiffs alleged that the law violated their right to access sexually explicit materials on the Internet for work-related purposes and that it infringed their rights to academic freedom by denying them the opportunity to determine for themselves the topics about which they would engage in research and teaching. A federal trial court granted the faculty members' motion for summary judgment on the basis that the law violated their rights to freedom of speech, because it unconstitutionally infringed on their First Amendment rights by failing to provide sufficient clarity on the kinds of Web sites to which it was regulating access.

The Fourth Circuit's Ruling

On further review, a three-judge panel of the Fourth Circuit reversed in favor of the commonwealth. The court was satisfied that the statute was constitutional, because it regulated the speech of pubic employees only in their official capacities (and not as private citizens) as they addressed "matters of public concern." The court explained that the speech of public employees involves matters of public concern and is entitled to First Amendment protection only when it addresses an issue of social, political, or other interest to the community, a situation that was not present in the case at bar.

Subsequently, the Fourth Circuit vacated the judgment of the three-judge panel, and in an en banc hearing (meaning that all of its members had the opportunity to review the dispute), again reversed in upholding the constitutionality of the statute. The Fourth Circuit viewed the faculty members' challenge as twofold. First, the court observed that the faculty members argued that the act unconstitutionally violated the rights of all state employees. Second, the court acknowledged that the faculty members claimed that the act infringed on their rights to academic freedom.

As to the first claim, the Fourth Circuit pointed out that the act restricted access to material that was sexual in nature only on public computers.

Further, the court indicated that agency heads could authorize access to information on public computers if it was necessary to do so in support of legitimate research projects. In fact, the court commented that none of the faculty members had requested or been denied access to material that was sexually explicit. In addition, the court remarked that the faculty members did not assert a constitutional right to access the materials on publicly owned or leased computers for personal use, because they challenged the restriction on their ability to view Web sites for work-related purposes. Moreover, the court thought that the faculty members conceded that the law did not impact their speech as private citizens and that they were free to access the material in question on their personal computers.

Citing First Amendment jurisprudence, the court reasoned that the commonwealth, acting as an employer through its officials, had greater authority to restrict the speech of employees than it would have had as the state, acting through its appointed and elected officials, to limit the speech of the general citizenry. Further, they applied the balancing test that the U.S. Supreme Court enunciated in *Pickering v. Board of Education* (1968), a dispute involving the free speech rights of teachers in public schools. In *Pickering,* the Supreme Court found that when the speech of public employees as private citizens does not involve matters of public concern, then public officials may regulate their speech and related conduct without infringing on the First Amendment. Insofar as *Urofsky* involved the speech of public employees in their work capacities and not as private citizens addressing matters of public concern, the court ascertained that commonwealth officials could control the manner in which they discharged their official duties. The court thus held that because the statute did not infringe on the First Amendment rights of the faculty members, it was not unconstitutional.

Turning to the second claim, the court addressed whether the statute violated the First Amendment rights of the faculty members to academic freedom by hindering their ability to perform professional duties, particularly with regard to teaching and research. The faculty members also alleged that their academic freedom was a constitutional right as well as a professional norm. In its analysis here, the court cited the American Association of University Professors' (AAUP) definition of academic freedom as

> a right claimed by the accredited educator . . . to interpret his findings and to communicate his conclusions without being subjected to any interference, molestation, or penalization because the conclusions are unacceptable to some constituted authority within or beyond the institution. (*Urofsky,* p. 411)

The court, however, interpreted the AAUP's words as conceiving of academic freedom as a professional norm to facilitate the search for truth and not as a legal manifestation of the First Amendment. Citing Supreme Court precedent, the Fourth Circuit was of the opinion that despite having many opportunities to do so, the Supreme Court had never treated faculty members as having a constitutional right to academic freedom to determine for themselves the content of their courses and scholarship. Simply put, the court wrote that academic freedom was not a constitutional right under the First Amendment. Based on its review of existing jurisprudence, the Fourth Circuit concluded that to the extent that the Constitution recognizes that faculty members have a right to academic freedom that exceeds the First Amendment rights of all citizens, it inheres to their universities and not to individual faculty members. In other words, in rejecting the challenge to the statute, the court decided that academic freedom rights belong to universities rather than to faculty members and students. To the chagrin of many in higher education, the Supreme Court refused to hear a further appeal.

Impact of the Ruling

Even though *Urofsky*'s holding is limited to the Fourth Circuit, it remains a noteworthy case. *Urofsky* is important, because it opened the door to what should be ensuing discussions about the free speech and academic rights of faculty members in colleges and universities during the cyber age. In this discussion, educators, jurists, and lawmakers will have to balance the rights of faculty members to access information that is relevant to their work as academicians in research and teaching with their rights to access materials that have little or nothing to do with their professional lives while at work. Thus, perhaps the most significant question that *Urofsky* raises is whether the academic freedom of faculty members in public colleges and universities gives them rights that are more extensive than those of other public employees, or whether their rights can be limited in the same fashion as those of other public employees.

Robert C. Cloud

See also Academic Freedom; Acceptable Use Policies; American Association of University Professors; Privacy Rights of Faculty Members

Further Readings

Keyishian v. Board of Regents of the University of the State of New York, 385 U.S. 589 (1967).
Sweezy v. New Hampshire, 354 U.S. 234 (1957).
Weidner, D. (2002). Thoughts on academic freedom: *Urofsky* and beyond. *University of Toledo Law Review, 31*, 257–268.
Williams, K. (2002). Loss of academic freedom on the Internet: The Fourth Circuit's decision in *Urofsky v. Gilmore. Review of Litigation, 21*, 493–527.

Legal Citations

Pickering v. Board of Education, 391 U.S. 563 (1968).
Urofsky v. Gilmore, 216 F.3d 401 (4th Cir. 2000), *cert. denied*, 531 U.S. 1070 (2001).

U.S. Department of Education

The United States Department of Education (ED) serves as the federal agency charged with addressing education-related issues. Unlike the structure utilized in other nations such as Brazil, France, Germany, and Japan, the ED lacks plenary power to set nationwide educational policies. Even so, the department does exercise significant influence over crucial education matters, such as the awarding and distribution of federal funds, the implementation of federal policies, and the collection of data on educational practices and outcomes at all levels. Accordingly, this entry discusses the ED's history and development, its place within the federal government, and the laws that outline and establish its duties.

Early Federal Influence on Education

Under the language of the U.S. Constitution, the federal government reserved no control over education. Indeed, according to the Tenth Amendment, "the powers not delegated to the United States by the Constitution, nor prohibited by it to the States, are reserved to the States respectively, or to the people." Thus, the early structure of the federal government did not include an agency to address education.

The Tenth Amendment notwithstanding, the federal government has used various pieces of legislation to influence education law and policy while encouraging the creation of schools at all levels to promote curricula that support initiatives of national importance. For example, while still operating under the Articles of Confederation in 1785, Congress adopted a policy that reserved land in each township as an endowment for the development of schools. Likewise, the Northwest Ordinance, which was enacted in 1787, provided support to higher education by giving land to townships to establish a university for the territory that later became the State of Ohio. This serves as the first example of federal higher education policy.

Even after the adoption of the Constitution, the federal government continued to find ways of influencing education. Although the United States repeatedly refused to establish a federal university, the U.S. Military Academy at West Point was created in 1802. Along with the other military academies, it fulfills a national mission by assisting with the training and maintenance of a standing army and other defense forces. Soon thereafter, Congress directed that 15% of the money earned from selling federal lands go to support schools in new states.

Focusing specifically on higher education, the federal government used the sale of land to encourage college and university development. In 1862, the first Morrill Act provided federal land to both new and existing states to sell and use the proceeds to support the creation or expansion of higher education. In addition, the federal government relied on the First Morrill Act to encourage greater emphasis on and access to certain curricular foci, such as mechanical arts, agriculture, military training, liberal education, and practical preparation, thus creating the land grant institutions. Later, through the Hatch Act of 1887, Congress expanded its support of higher education as a means of improving agriculture and food production by providing land grants to fund experiment stations and distribute new knowledge about growth and soil management techniques throughout the states. In many cases, the states used their land grant higher education institutions to house, manage, and deliver the services required under the Hatch Act. Later, the Second Morrill Act, passed as the Agricultural College Act of 1890, provided federal subsidies to further support agriculture research and teaching in higher education.

Formation of the Department of Education

Despite the Constitution's lack of attention to schooling in any form, the federal government has operated an office to address educational issues for several years. The first rendition of the Department of Education began in 1867, after both President James Garfield and Congress recognized the need for the federal government to provide some educational direction for the growing nation. However, in 1868, this version gave way to the Office of Education, which lasted only one year. In 1869, the Bureau of Education came into existence and functioned as the main office for federal education information until 1930. All three of these early versions of the federal education office as well as the renamed Office of Education (1930–1939) functioned as part of the Department of the Interior.

While the name remained the same until 1980, the Office of Education shifted through many governmental departments, first moving from the Department of the Interior in 1939 to the Federal Security Agency. In 1953, the office moved to the Department of Health, Education, and Welfare (HEW). In 1972, the Division of Education increased the profile of the office within HEW. In 1980, education gained enough federal attention to become a separate cabinet department as the ED. In that same year, President Jimmy Carter appointed Shirley Hufstedler to serve as the first secretary of education within his cabinet.

Purpose of the Department of Education

For the most part, the primary duty of the Department of Education is to enforce federal education policies as specified and enacted by Congress. Accordingly,

the actual tasks assigned to the ED have transitioned over the years to address contemporary federal initiatives as they develop.

As established in 1867, the Office of Education was intended to collect information on schools and teaching in order to improve learning throughout the states. Later, the various renditions of the agency became responsible for upholding federal legislation related to education. Under the Second Morrill Act (1890), the renamed Office of Education gained responsibility for distributing federal funds to land grant colleges and universities. Likewise, the Smith-Hughes Act of 1917 and the George-Barden Act of 1946 (also known as Vocational Educational Act) gave the Office of Education the task of overseeing vocational, agricultural, home economics, and industrial training within U.S. educational facilities, with special emphasis on secondary schools.

During the 1940s and early 1950s, the federal government charged the office with distributing federal money to school districts to ease the impact of the war effort under the Lanham Act (1941). Various statutes provided impact aid to districts with populations that were substantially enlarged by the attendance of children of federal employees—such as those whose parents are in the military—but which lost school tax revenues due to the federal government's being exempt from property taxes. Another well-known aid to higher education institutions to support the enrollment of veterans in postsecondary schools was the Servicemen's Readjustment Act of 1944, better known as the G. I. Bill. In response to the cold war, the National Defense Education Act of 1958 made the Office of Education responsible for ensuring that children and adults received training needed to help the nation remain internationally competitive. This training focused on science, mathematics, foreign languages, and technical fields in all levels of education.

During the civil rights era of the mid-20th century, the Office of Education (later the Department of Education) was assigned to address issues involving discrimination in education. Under the Civil Rights Act of 1964, the office expanded its activities to include enforcement of the Supreme Court's decisions in *Brown v. Board of Education, Topeka* (1954, 1955) by working to get educational institutions at all levels to end the practice of racial segregation. Indeed, the Department of Education played a significant role in many desegregation suits. Yet, it was subject to criticism both because it did not enforce Title VI of the act by denying federal funds to school systems, colleges, universities, and states that did not end segregation and because it did not initiate litigation against institutions that failed to comply with the law.

In addition to racial discrimination, the Department of Education oversees compliance related to sex and disability discrimination. As specified under Title IX of the Education Amendments of 1972, the ED works to ensure that girls and women get access to the same educational and athletic opportunities as their male counterparts. Likewise, Section 504 of the Rehabilitation Act of 1973 and the Education for All Handicapped Children Act of 1975, now known as the Individuals with Disabilities Education Act or IDEA, assign the department the task of addressing the treatment and educational opportunities available to students with a wide range of physical, mental, and learning impairments. As it was with the Civil Rights Act of 1964, the Department of Education has become party to several lawsuits due to the need to define and enforce the proper implementation of laws related to sex and disability discrimination.

Updated regularly, the Elementary and Secondary Education Act of 1965 (ESEA), now the No Child Left Behind Act, and the Higher Education Act of 1965 also direct the activities and functions of the Department of Education. While some elements of these laws reiterate initiatives originally specified in other legislation, these acts provide additional duties to the department. Generally, these laws grant the department a role in ensuring school accountability, dispersing educational research information, and distributing financial resources to assist in educating economically and academically disadvantaged students. In postsecondary education, the ED approves accreditation agencies, awards research grants and service contracts, monitors crime reporting, and supervises the distribution of federal student financial aid, including student loans, Pell grants, and work-study funding.

Oversight of Higher Education

As illustrated by the various laws, the responsibilities that the U.S. Department of Education has with respect to higher education have changed throughout the years. In 2008, Congress passed a reauthorization of the Higher Education Act of 1965 that both altered and reiterated various federal priorities for higher education. As dictated by the act, the department continues to distribute federal student aid from the government to institutions where eligible students enroll and attend. In addition, the ED helps determine institutional eligibility to accept federal aid by monitoring campus compliance with various laws and policies, such as crime reporting and limiting student default on student loans.

Outside of direct aid, the ED distributes program and research funds to institutions. This includes funds awarded to colleges and universities through competitive grants for academic research as well as service initiatives sponsored and encouraged by the federal government. Likewise, the department oversees the federally sponsored TRIO Programs, which include GEAR-UP, McNair Scholars, Talent Search, and Upward Bound. Targeting various age groups, these programs focus on increasing student preparation, participation, and success in postsecondary education.

Finally, the department serves as an education data collection and distribution agency for the federal government, higher education institutions, and the general public. As required under specific laws, the ED collects and updates information about institutional size, enrollment, and academic scope; costs associated with attendance; crime rates; and other campus facts. Much of this information assists the department in monitoring the overall status of the higher education community as well as individual institutions. More recently, the ED has started to package and distribute information on postsecondary schools to the general public, especially students who are preparing to go to college and their parents. In September 2008, the department launched a Web site, www.college.gov, that seeks to provide students with realistic information regarding what they need to do and can expect in college.

Saran Donahoo

See also Americans with Disabilities Act; Civil Rights Act of 1964; Federalism; Higher Education Act; Loans and Federal Aid; Morrill Acts; Rehabilitation Act, Section 504; Stafford Act; Title VI; Title IX and Sexual Harassment

Further Readings

Field, K. (2008, August 8). A bill that took longer than a bachelor's degree. *The Chronicle of Higher Education, 54*(48), A1–A12.

Lane, J. (2007, November/December). The spider web of oversight: An analysis of external oversight of higher education. *The Journal of Higher Education, 78*(6), 615–644.

Morgan, P. M. (1981). Academia and the federal government. *Policy Studies Journal, 10*(1), 70–84.

U.S. Department of Education. (2008). *About ED.* Retrieved November 15, 2008, from http://www.ed .gov/about/landing.jhtml?src=gu

U.S. Department of Education. (2008). *Higher education update.* Retrieved November 15, 2008, from http:// www.ed.gov/about/bdscomm/list/hiedfuture/plan/ index.html

Legal Citations

Agricultural College Act (Second Morrill Land Grant Act) of 1890, ch. 841, 26 Stat. 417, 7 U.S.C. §§ 322 *et seq.*

Brown v. Board of Education, Topeka, 347 U.S. 483 (1954), 349 U.S. 294 (1955).

Elementary and Secondary Education Act of 1965, Pub. L. No. 107-110 (2002).

George-Barden Act of 1946, remaining sections codified at 20 U.S.C. §§ 1241 *et seq.*

Hatch Act of 1887, 7 U.S.C. §§ 361(a)–(i).

Higher Education Act of 1965, Pub. L. No. 110-315 (2008).

Individuals with Disabilities Education Act, 20 U.S.C. §§ 1400 *et seq* (2004).

Lanham Act, 54 Stat. 1125.

Morrill Land Grant Act of 1862, ch. 130, 12 Stat. 503, 7 U.S.C. §§ 301 *et seq.*

National Defense Education Act of 1958, Pub. L. No. 85-864, Title I, § 101, 72 Stat. 1581 (1958).

Northwest Ordinance of 1787, 1 Stat 51.

Rehabilitation Act of 1973, Section 504, 29 U.S.C. § 794(a) (1973).

Servicemen's Readjustment Act of 1944 (G. I. Bill), 58 Stat. 284.

Smith-Hughes National Vocational Education Act of 1917, ch. 114, 39 Stat. 929 (1917).

Title VI, Civil Rights Act of 1964, 42 U.S.C. § 2000d.

Title IX of the Education Amendments of 1972, 20 U.S.C. § 1681.

U.S. Supreme Court Cases in Higher Education

The relationship between the law and higher education institutions, as well as that between the law and those institutions' faculties, students, administrations, and governing boards, has changed dramatically throughout the history of higher education in the United States. Values in the larger society have often been mirrored in cases concerning issues that have arisen on campuses. Since the first American institutions of higher learning were established, colleges and universities have seen the presence of the law grow on campus, as their autonomy has faced serious challenges, and the essential relationships between and among faculty members, students, administrators, and governing boards have evolved. During this time, themes involving authority and autonomy have emerged. This entry provides an overview of major higher education cases, focusing primarily, but not exclusively, on litigation from the U.S. Supreme Court, in areas that helped shape the nature of the relationship among institutions, their faculty, and students.

Governance and the Public–Private Dichotomy

Institutions of higher education traditionally governed themselves. Pursuant to the doctrine of academic abstention, the courts have been reluctant to interfere with the business of higher education and the judgments of institutional officials. However, the relationship between colleges, universities, and the courts depended in large part on whether institutions were public or private. While private institutions enjoy a fair amount of judicial deference, public institutions historically have not enjoyed that kind of autonomy.

The first case to address the right of private institutions to resist governmental interference came in 1819 with *Trustees of Dartmouth College v. Woodward,* a dispute that was prompted by the attempt of the State of New Hampshire to take control of Dartmouth College. The Court considered whether the state could assume control of the college even though its charter put the governing authority in the trustees. Entering a judgment in favor of the college, the Court ruled that private institutions have the right to govern themselves without state interference.

Student Issues

Issues involving the rights of students in higher education have emerged since the tumultuous days of the 1960s. Key student issues involve their relationships with institutional officials, due process, free speech, and affirmative action.

Student Autonomy

Questions of autonomy grew out of the relationship between institutions of higher education and their students. The first major case, albeit not one involving the U.S. Supreme Court, involved the nature of the relationship between institutions and their students. In *Gott v. Berea College* (1913), a local restaurant owner sued the college for prohibiting its students from patronizing eating establishments that the college did not control. The college insisted that as a private institution charged with the care of its students, officials had to take necessary measures to protect and educate their students. Agreeing, Kentucky's highest court decided that the doctrine of *in loco parentis,* literally "in the place of the parents," defined the role of college authorities over their students. The court acknowledged that college authorities could make any rule or requirement for students that parents could make for their children and that courts should not interfere or question the wisdom of those decisions. *Gott* established the legal doctrine that would define the institution–student relationship for at least half a century.

In 1928, an appellate court in New York furthered the status of *in loco parentis* in *Anthony v. Syracuse University.* The primary issue here involved contract law where university officials dismissed the plaintiff for little other than her not being "a typical Syracuse" girl. The plaintiff argued that she had a contract with the university that officials breached. The court recognized that under ordinary circumstances, students entered into contracts when they enrolled in universities. Even so, the court conceded that officials had wide discretion in evaluating which behaviors merited

dismissals of students and that the judiciary should be slow to invalidate any such judgments. Subsequently, courts continued the pattern of judicial deference to the control that college and university officials exercised over their students.

By the 1950s, changes in American society made their way to campuses. The enactment of the G. I. Bill dramatically increased access to higher education, particularly among war veterans, while increasing the diversity in student bodies. By the 1960s, the civil rights movement and social unrest outside college campuses impacted the student–institution relationship, as more students demanded greater rights and to be treated like adults. A key case involving this shift was *Dixon v. Alabama State Board of Education* (1961). Although the Supreme Court chose not to hear an appeal in *Dixon,* it is significant for two reasons: It helped to establish the due process rights owed to public university students, and it marked the shift away from *in loco parentis* as a doctrinal approach to the student–institution relationship.

Due Process

Due process is the constitutional principle that individuals who are accused of misconduct are owed substantive and procedural rights in judicial proceedings. In higher education, due process refers to the fairness of procedures used in misconduct hearings involving both academic and disciplinary infractions. While substantive due process addresses the substance of the law or rules on which actions are made, procedural due process mainly concerns the procedures themselves. A personal misconduct case, *Dixon* involved the expulsion of students and their right to be notified of and to have a hearing. After participating in a sit-in at a local lunch counter, six students were expelled from Alabama State College. The court explained that there must be a balancing of the private interest of students and the power of the government. Pointing out that attendance at public institutions of higher learning is not a constitutionally protected right, the court nonetheless found that the students had a right to remain enrolled in their public college because of the educational benefits that they gained by doing so. In addition, the court observed that the college's power was not unlimited and could not be exercised in an arbitrary way, even if there were reasonable regulations guiding the decision. Moreover, the court rejected the application of *in loco parentis* as a means of judicial deference to college and university officials who purportedly acted in the best interests of their institutions. In its analysis, the court laid out basic due process standards for college and university officials in personal misconduct cases: Officials must provide notice of the charges against students and a hearing on those charges with the opportunity for the students to refute them. Noting that different cases called for different kinds of hearings, the court concluded that these basic elements satisfied the requirements of due process.

Free Speech Rights

The social unrest on and off campus that led to the demise of *in loco parentis* also helped to enhance student free speech rights. Following on *Tinker v. Des Moines Independent School District* (1969), a secondary school case wherein the justices upheld the right of students to wear black armbands to school in protest of American activity in Vietnam, the Supreme Court turned to higher education. In *Healy v. James* (1972), the Court upheld the free speech rights of students who wished to form a local chapter of Students for a Democratic Society, even though officials feared that the group's presence would be disruptive. The Court posited that officials at the college could not restrict a group's speech or right to associate simply because they thought that the group's views were abhorrent.

Among other student free speech cases, perhaps the most notable is *Clark v. Community for Creative Non-Violence* (1984), in which the Supreme Court developed time, place, and manner restrictions for campus demonstrations. The Court further addressed hate speech regulations in cases such as *R.A.V. v. City of St. Paul* (1992) in invalidating a city ordinance designed to ban hate crimes. Relying on the Court's reasoning in *R.A.V.*, lower courts have invalidated campus hate speech regulations in cases including *Doe v. University of Michigan* (1989). In the area of free speech, courts have weighed the rights of public colleges and universities against the free speech rights of their students, reaching mixed results depending on the circumstances.

Affirmative Action

Courts continued to defer, albeit to a lesser degree, to college and university officials, especially in internal decision making. This deference changed as societal concerns over racial preferences arose on campus and questions about affirmative action arose. After sidestepping the question in *DeFunis v. Odegaard* (1974), when it held that the challenge of a White law student in Washington to an affirmative policy was moot because he was in his final year of study, the Supreme Court agreed to hear its first appeal on the merits of such a case in *Regents of the University of California v. Bakke* (1978). The plaintiff sued because he had been denied admission to a public medical school that evaluated disadvantaged students through a program using a separate admissions process. The university argued this program was necessary for a variety of reasons, including increasing the number of doctors in underserved communities and diversifying the student body. While the Supreme Court agreed that these justifications were compelling interests, it invalidated the admissions program as unconstitutional. Insofar as there were different majorities on various sections of the plurality opinion, meaning that the case did have the requisite five justices who agreed to the same point of law to render it binding precedent, the case left the status of affirmative action open for further litigation.

As legal questions surrounding affirmative action remained open for decades, later cases addressed the issue, including disputes over financial aid. For example, in *Podberesky v. Kirwan* (1994), the Fourth Circuit invalidated a race-based scholarship program as unconstitutional, because university officials failed to prove that they were trying to overcome the present effects of past discrimination or that the underlying plan was sufficiently narrowly tailored to remedy minority underrepresentation on campus. The Supreme Court refused to hear an appeal.

The two latest affirmative action cases, both of which arose at the University of Michigan, are *Gratz v. Bollinger* (2003) and *Grutter v. Bollinger* (2003). In *Grutter,* the Supreme Court upheld the law school's admissions policy that afforded additional consideration to race on the ground that seeking to diversify the student body was a compelling state interest. Conversely, in *Gratz,* the Court struck down the undergraduate admissions system as unconstitutional, because it relied on a point-based system that resembled a quota system of the type that the Court invalidated in *Bakke.*

Faculty Issues

Themes involving faculty issues, authority, and autonomy have also occupied a great deal of judicial decision making. Of particular importance are employment concerns, especially tenure. Tenure disputes typically involved interests governed by the doctrine of constitutional due process, especially procedural due process. As with issues involving students, procedural due process involves fairness in the process. For employment actions, due process requires a fair hearing when liberty or property interests protected by the Constitution are at stake.

Tenure and Due Process

The two leading Supreme Court cases involving faculty rights to tenure and due process are *Board of Regents of State Colleges v. Roth* (1972) and *Perry v. Sindermann* (1972). In *Roth,* a faculty member sued after his one-year teaching contract was not renewed, alleging both that he was not rehired because he was critical of the administration and that the failure of officials to give him notice and a hearing violated his rights to procedural due process. The Supreme Court indicated that this failure did not violate the faculty member's constitutional rights, because insofar as he lacked a property interest in the one-year contract or in state rules and regulations, he had no reasonable expectation of continued employment on which to expect notice and a hearing. In *Perry,* the Court ruled in favor of a faculty member under a different set of circumstances surrounding his procedural due process claims. Even though the plaintiff was informed that his contract was not going to be renewed and that he was not to be given a hearing, unlike the plaintiff in *Roth,* he had been employed through a series of one-year contracts. Therefore, the Court was convinced that the faculty member could raise the question of a property interest in continued employment. In other words, the Court was satisfied that the facts could reasonably have led the plaintiff to

believe that he was entitled to continued employment under the terms of his contract, the college's Faculty Guide, and state agency rules.

Academic Freedom and Free Speech

Related to the employment issue of tenure is academic freedom and related concerns over free speech. Although there are many definitions of academic freedom, the doctrine protects faculty rights in research and the classroom. Academic freedom initially protected faculty members against outside political interference, but today it protects faculty in broader contexts. In *Sweezy v. New Hampshire* (1957), the Supreme Court acknowledged the importance of academic freedom when an individual who spoke at a state university successfully challenged his contempt conviction for refusing to divulge his knowledge of political parties and their members. Subsequently, in *Keyishian v. Board of Regents of the University of the State of New York* (1967), the Court invalidated a state requirement that forced faculty members to sign certificates stating that they were not communists or members of subversive organizations, as this would have infringed on their right to academic freedom. In *Pickering v. Board of Education* (1968), a K–12 case, the Court addressed the issue of free speech in public debate. Establishing a balancing test, the Court declared that school board officials could not limit the teacher's free speech in public debate. The Court followed the *Pickering* test in *Connick v. Myers* (1983), in asserting that a speech by a public employee, an assistant district attorney, was unprotected, because it was not on a matter of public concern.

Over the years, academic freedom arguments have been used in tenure cases as well. Most recently, in *Garcetti v. Ceballos* (2006), another noneducation case, the Court maintained that because public employees, here another assistant district attorney, are not addressing matters of public concern when they speak in furtherance of their job responsibilities, their speech is unprotected.

Collective Bargaining

As to collective bargaining, the Supreme Court has handed down two noteworthy judgments. In

National Labor Relations Board v. Yeshiva University (1980), the Court determined that because faculty members in a private, religiously affiliated university performed some duties that were considered management in nature, they did not have the right to organize and form unions in order to engage in collective bargaining. In *Lehnert v. Ferris Faculty Association* (1991), the Court addressed limits on the ability of a union to collect fair share fees from nonmembers for the costs associated with obtaining their benefits in collective bargaining. The Court was of the opinion that while unions may charge nonmembers and dissenting employees for activities that are clearly germane to collective bargaining, are justified by the government's vital policy interest in labor peace and avoiding freeloaders, and do not burden the First Amendment issue inherent in public sector agency shops, they may not compel nonmember employees to support political lobbying efforts as a condition of public employment.

Conclusion

Issues of autonomy and authority have been played out on campus and in court for much of the history of American higher education. College and university boards and officials have exercised their authority as students and faculty have pushed for rights, with courts responding by applying constitutional principles to traditional areas of judicial deference. Constitutional and social issues facing courts in the broader society have appeared on campus as well. No doubt, new areas of judicial concern will arise as the nature of college and university life—for institutions, students, and faculty—changes in the future.

Catherine L. Matthews

See also Academic Abstention; Academic Freedom; Affirmative Action; *Board of Regents of State Colleges v. Roth*; Civil Rights Movement; *DeFunis v. Odegaard*; Disciplinary Sanctions and Due Process Rights; Due Process, Substantive and Procedural; Free Speech and Expression Rights of Students; *Gratz v. Bollinger*; *Grutter v. Bollinger*; *Keyishian v. Board of Regents of the University of the State of New York*; *Lehnert v. Ferris Faculty Association*; *National Labor Relations Board v. Yeshiva University*; *Perry v. Sindermann*; *Regents of the University of California v. Bakke*; *Sweezy v. New Hampshire*; Tenure; *Trustees of Dartmouth College v. Woodward*

Legal Citations

Anthony v. Syracuse University, 231 N.Y.S. 435 (N.Y. App. Div. 1928).

Board of Regents v. Roth, 408 U.S. 564 (1972).

Clark v. Community for Creative Non-Violence, 468 U.S. 288 (1984).

Connick v. Myers, 461 U.S. 138 (1983).

DeFunis v. Odegaard, 416 U.S. 312 (1974), *on remand*, 514 P.2d 438 (Wash. 1974).

Dixon v. Alabama State Board of Education, F.2d 150 (1961), *cert. denied*, 368 U.S. 930 (1961).

Doe v. University of Michigan, 721 F. Supp. 852 (E.D. Mich. 1989).

Garcetti v. Ceballos, 547 U.S. 410 (2006).

Gott v. Berea College, 161 S.W. 204 (Ky. 1913).

Gratz v. Bollinger, 539 U.S. 244 (2003).

Grutter v. Bollinger, 539 U.S. 306 (2003).

Healy v. James, 408 U.S. 169 (1972).

Keyishian v. Board of Regents of the University of the State of New York, 385 U.S. 589 (1967).

Lehnert v. Ferris Faculty Association, 500 U.S. 507 (1991).

National Labor Relations Board v. Yeshiva University, 444 U.S. 672 (1980).

Perry v. Sindermann, 408 U.S. 593 (1972).

Pickering v. Board of Education, 391 U.S. 563 (1968).

Podberesky v. Kirwan, 38 F.3d 147 (4th Cir. 1994), *amended on denial of rehearing*, 46 F.3d 5 (4th Cir. 1994), *cert. denied*, 514 U.S. 1128 (1995).

R.A.V. v. City of St. Paul, 505 U.S. 377 (1992).

Regents of the University of California v. Bakke, 438 U.S. 265 (1978).

Sweezy v. New Hampshire, 354 U.S. 234 (1957).

Tinker v. Des Moines Independent School District, 393 U.S. 503 (1969).

Trustees of Dartmouth College v. Woodward, 17 U.S. 518 (1819).

V

VIDEO SURVEILLANCE

Video surveillance uses video cameras to transmit data to monitors or recording devices and is designed to observe people in a variety of settings. Video cameras can be used as part of overall security efforts, as a tool to address theft or vandalism that has occurred, or as a tool to ensure worker productivity. Officials in institutions of higher learning who choose to use video surveillance cameras must balance concerns for safety and productivity with Fourth Amendment rights related to the privacy of students, faculty, and staff. This entry describes video surveillance technology and examines the tensions that can arise when officials approve its use on campuses. Officials at institutions desiring to use available technology must understand these issues and respect the privacy and security concerns in designing systems that will be both effective and accepted in their campus communities.

The quality of video surveillance technology has significantly improved in recent years. Technology exists to obtain video in settings where there is little or no light. Video equipment may be monitored in real time, but it is often tied to recording devices where electronic information is maintained in a computer database for review at a time after the recording is created. The collection of audio data is generally prohibited under Title I of the Electronic Communication Privacy Act (ECPA) of 2002. However, the ECPA does not regulate silent video surveillance.

Video surveillance raises a number of competing legal and philosophical issues. The mere physical presence of video cameras on campus may suggest that campuses are dangerous places and thus have the unintended effect of reinforcing a climate of fear. On the other hand, the presence of video cameras can mislead students and others into believing that campuses are safe places, thereby creating false senses of security and blurring the line of responsibility that individuals must have for ensuring their own safety. In addition, the use of video cameras raises significant political issues that must be considered by leaders in campus communities. The fact that "someone is watching" may raise criticisms from students and staff who argue that the use of such cameras threatens their privacy. Some critics may ask whether "Big Brother" is coming to campus. From this perspective, cameras may be viewed as icons of an Orwellian approach to campus security, a potentially thorny political issue that must be considered and debated on campuses.

Video cameras used as part of a surveillance effort serve both a deterrent and an enforcement purpose. Placing cameras on campus and publicizing their use will have a deterrent effect. Video cameras, and the records they produce, can be used to identify offenders and to document conduct that runs afoul of institutional rules, policies, or laws.

Cameras may be placed as part of comprehensive plans to address potential problems such as theft, assaults, vandalism, bullying, and other offenses. In such situations, placement of cameras may not be made public, at least not their locations. Under these conditions, cameras may well have little deterrent effect but are employed to identify offenders as part of law enforcement efforts. Video surveillance technology thus gives institutional officials opportunities to identify suspects after unlawful or inappropriate activities have occurred.

Privacy Concerns

Officials on both public and private college and university campuses need to take the issue of privacy seriously when evaluating the use of video surveillance technology. Careful consideration of the location to be observed should reduce the opportunity for claims of violations of privacy rights to arise. Cameras should not be placed in areas where persons likely to be observed have reasonable expectations of privacy. Placing cameras in bathroom stalls or locker rooms, for example, would likely violate reasonable expectations of privacy. On the other hand, placing cameras in areas where individuals lack a reasonable expectation of privacy, such as at entrances of buildings, in hallways, or in gymnasia, is really no different from assigning staff members to observe events at those locations, because both cameras and staff members can observe and record activities at assigned or designated locations. Even so, cameras perhaps provide better records and, in the long run, may be more cost effective and more effective initiatives while creating potentially permanent and more accurate records of what has occurred.

Addressing the expectation of privacy at the outset is important. Letting those affected know that they may be subject to video monitoring while on campus should remove the expectation of privacy that may otherwise exist. Statements in student and staff handbooks along with signs in areas where cameras are in use address the privacy issue up front by removing the privacy expectation.

Employee Relations

The placement of cameras in workplace areas may negatively impact employee morale while increasing anxiety. Video surveillance in the workplace may also raise labor relations issues in unionized settings, because the introduction of video surveillance technology into the workplace may be a mandatory subject of collective bargaining. In other words, institutional employers may have obligations to bargain with employee unions concerning decisions to use such technology, how it will be used, and the circumstances under which it will be used. Moreover, employers may have to bargain the "effects" of using such technology. That is, once records are created, questions may arise over how they are to be used and the circumstances under which they may be used, such as in disciplinary or dismissal proceedings. Ultimately, attorneys and other educational leaders on campuses will need to review state and federal laws should they consider the use of video surveillance technology.

Institutions considering video surveillance technology that are subject to the Family Educational Rights and Privacy Act (FERPA) must also consider the FERPA implications arising out of the use of such technology, including, where applicable, the records created in the process. Further, public institutions that are subject to state records laws need to consider whether the records created through the use of video surveillance technology are public records. Records created using video surveillance technology may need to be maintained and preserved if this is required by law. A case from K–12 education may be informative in this regard as to whether videotapes are treated as part of student records that may be subject to disclosure. The Supreme Court of Washington ruled that a videotape of students that was made while they were passengers on a school bus surveillance camera was subject to disclosure under state law, because it was not a record that contained personal information relating to their education (*Lindeman v. Kelso School District No. 458* (2007).

Jon E. Anderson

See also Family Educational Rights and Privacy Act; Fourth Amendment Rights of Faculty; Fourth Amendment Rights of Students; Privacy Rights of Faculty Members; Privacy Rights of Students

Further Readings

Blitz, M. J. (2004). Video surveillance and the constitution of public space: Fitting the Fourth Amendment to a world that tracks image and identity. *Texas Law Review, 82,* 1349–1422.

Carr, J. G., & Bellia, P. L. (2008–2009). *The law of electronic surveillance*. National Clearinghouse for Educational Facilities, School Security Technologies. Eagen, MN: Thomson West.

Davis, L. M. (2008). Has Big Brother moved off campus? An examination of college communities' responses to unruly student behavior. *Journal of Law and Education, 35,* 153–197.

Legal Citations

Electronic Communication Privacy Act, 18 U.S.C § 2510 (2002).

Family Education Rights and Privacy Act, 20 U.S.C. § 1232g.

Lindeman v. Kelso School District No. 458, 172 P.3d 329 (Wash. 2007).

WIDMAR V. VINCENT

In *Widmar v. Vincent* (1981), the U.S. Supreme Court considered the constitutionality of a state university regulation that prohibited the use of campus facilities by religious student groups. The Court rejected the university's contention that it could not provide facilities to religious groups without offering prohibited support to religion, holding that such a regulation violated the students' rights to free speech and free exercise of religion. *Widmar* stands out as significant, because it ensured that religious groups would have the same level of access to public facilities as nonreligious groups in both higher education and K–12 schools.

Facts of the Case

From 1973 to 1977, Cornerstone, an organization of evangelical Christian students at the University of Missouri at Kansas City, conducted group meetings in classrooms and the student center on campus. Cornerstone was just one of more than 100 officially recognized student organizations on campus; university officials routinely allowed all such groups to meet in its buildings. Moreover, students were assessed a student activity fee of $41 per semester in order to help offset the cost to the university. Cornerstone meetings included prayer, hymns, and religious discussions. While Cornerstone's active membership consisted of about 20 students, its meetings, which were open to the public, sometimes attracted up to 125 people. In

1977 university officials refused to grant Cornerstone permission to continue using the rooms, citing a regulation that barred the use of campus facilities for religious worship.

The dispute arose because the university's board of curators had adopted the regulation in question in 1972, based on its belief that the First Amendment's ban on the establishment of religion required that the university prohibit religious worship in state facilities. Even so, the regulation permitted prayer at public functions on university grounds and allowed religious groups to continue using school chapels. However, there was no chapel at the Kansas City campus. The nearest University of Missouri chapel was at the Columbia campus, approximately 125 miles away. Without access to university facilities, Cornerstone members were obligated to move their meetings off campus to rooms which were, in their view, inconvenient and uncomfortable.

Eleven student members of Cornerstone filed suit, challenging the regulation as a violation of their rights to free exercise of religion, equal protection, and freedom of speech. A federal trial court in Missouri found that the university had never knowingly allowed any religious group access to its facilities. In granting the university's motion for summary judgment, the court was of the opinion that the regulation was not merely permitted, but was, in fact, required by the Establishment Clause. The Eighth Circuit reversed in favor of Cornerstone on the basis that the university's regulation was content-based discrimination against religious speech with no compelling justification. The court explained that the

Establishment Clause did not forbid a policy of equal access to university property by all student groups. When university officials were dissatisfied with the outcome, the Supreme Court agreed to hear their appeal.

The Supreme Court's Ruling

In *Widmar,* the Supreme Court, in an eight-to-one judgment authored by Justice Powell, affirmed in favor of Cornerstone. The Court reasoned that university officials violated the fundamental principle that state regulation of speech should be content-neutral when they sought to enforce the exclusionary policy. Insofar as the state, through university officials, created a limited public forum for student speech, the Court noted that it was required to show that a policy that discriminated against religious groups was narrowly drawn to achieve a compelling state interest. While the state's interest in fulfilling its obligations under the Establishment Clause was compelling, the Court determined that the university policy went further than the First Amendment required.

The Supreme Court acknowledged that an alternative policy that allowed religious groups to meet in university buildings would not have violated the Establishment Cause under the three-pronged test created in *Lemon v. Kurtzman* (1971). The *Lemon* test was developed in the context of K–12 education but has been widely applied in disputes involving religion. In this regard, the Court added that both the trial court and the Eighth Circuit agreed that an open forum policy that allowed religious groups to meet would satisfy two of the three prongs of the *Lemon* test. According to the Court, such a policy would have had a secular purpose (thus meeting the first prong of the *Lemon* test) and would have avoided excessive government entanglement with religion (satisfying the second prong). On the question of the remaining prong of the test, the Court was satisfied that absent evidence showing that religious groups would have dominated the university's open forum, providing equal access to Cornerstone would not have had the primary effect of advancing religion. The Court observed that under these circumstances, university officials could not have been seen as endorsing religious speech, because they would merely have been providing the same

benefit to Cornerstone that they provided to non-religious groups.

Rounding out its analysis, the Supreme Court decided that the state's interest in creating a greater separation of church and state than was required by the Establishment Clause was not sufficiently compelling to justify the violation of the students' rights to free exercise of religion and free speech. The Court specified that university officials, having established a limited public forum for speech, could deny a group access only if it or its members proposed to use the forum for a purpose that was inconsistent with the purpose for which the forum was created. The Court thus concluded that allowing access to religious groups would not be inconsistent with a forum created to allow students to freely exchange ideas.

Justice Stevens concurred in the Court's judgment but authored a separate opinion, because he thought that the majority's rationale may have threatened academic freedom.

In the sole dissent, Justice White rejected what he viewed as the majority's assertion that the Free Speech Clause could be applied to student meetings that amounted to religious worship. From his perspective, the university could not treat religious worship the same as it treated non-religious speech, because the Court had already held, in cases such as *Engel v. Vitale* (1962), which struck down prayer in K–12 public schools, that the Establishment Clause placed limits on government promotion of religion. White further maintained that the actual burden that university officials imposed on Cornerstone and its members was minimal, because they were required only to move a few blocks from their former meeting site. In the absence of a free speech violation, White posited that public officials needed only to assert a permissible state end in order to withstand a constitutional challenge and that university administrators satisfied this requirement with their claim that they wished to avoid an appearance of unconstitutionally supporting religion.

James Mawdsley

See also Academic Freedom; Equal Protection Analysis;
   Free Speech and Expression Rights of Students;
   Religious Activities on Campus

Legal Citations

Engel v. Vitale, 370 U.S. 421 (1962).
Lemon v. Kurtzman, 403 U.S. 602 (1971).
Widmar v. Vincent, 454 U.S. 263 (1981).

WITTERS V. WASHINGTON DEPARTMENT OF SERVICES FOR THE BLIND

Witters v. Washington Department of Services for the Blind (1986) addressed the question of whether a student's use of state disability funds at a religious college would violate the Establishment Clause in the First Amendment to the U.S. Constitution. In a unanimous decision, the U.S. Supreme Court held that a student's receiving such financial assistance and using it at a religious college did not amount to the kind of direct subsidy prohibited by the Establishment Clause. However, the Court left open the question whether the Supreme Court of Washington, on remand, could prohibit the financial assistance under its more restrictive state constitution. In fact, Washington's high court did exactly that on remand, finding that the indirect subsidies to religious institutions, even if not prohibited by the Establishment Clause, were prohibited under the Washington constitution.

Witters also left open the question of whether Washington's denial of student aid under its more restrictive constitution would serve to deprive students of rights protected under the U.S. Constitution's Free Exercise Clause, a question that the Supreme Court addressed 18 years later in *Locke v. Davey* (2004). In that case, the Court invalidated another scholarship program from Washington State that would have helped to pay the tuition of a student with dual majors who wished to study to become a pastoral minister.

Facts of the Case

Larry Witters was a student at Inland Empire School of the Bible, a private Christian college in Spokane, Washington, where he was preparing for a career as a pastor, missionary, or youth director. Although Witters had a progressive eye condition that qualified him under state law for financial aid, when he applied for vocational rehabilitation assistance to the Washington Commission for the Blind, officials denied his request. In rejecting the student's request, the officials relied on a state policy statement prohibiting the use of state funds to assist individuals in the pursuit of degrees or careers in theology or related areas.

Disappointed with the outcome, the student appealed the commission's denial of his request to a state hearing officer, who affirmed its order in light of a state constitutional provision prohibiting public money or property being appropriated for or applied to any religious worship, exercise, or the support of any religious establishment. At this point, the plaintiff filed suit in a state superior court, seeking both declaratory and injunctive relief to receive rehabilitation assistance. The court upheld the commission's decision, relying on the same state constitutional grounds as the hearing officer.

Subsequently, the Supreme Court of Washington also upheld the commission's action but did so by relying on the Establishment Clause of the U.S. Constitution rather than its own state constitution, as the hearing officer and state superior court had done. The Supreme Court of Washington maintained that the state's providing financial rehabilitation assistance to Witters would have the primary effect of advancing religion and thus would violate the second prong of the tripartite *Lemon v. Kurtzman* (1971) test. Although the *Lemon* test was developed in the context of K–12 education to determine whether government action violated the Establishment Clause, it has had wide application in disputes involving religion and education. The second prong of the test states that the primary effect of a law or program must be one that neither advances nor inhibits religion. Applying the *Lemon* test to *Witter*, the Supreme Court of Washington held that the Establishment Clause prohibited the granting of the student's request for assistance. The student again appealed, this time to the Supreme Court.

The Supreme Court's Ruling

On further review, the U.S. Supreme Court unanimously reversed in favor of the student, holding that there was no violation of the Establishment Clause. The Court noted in passing that the

Washington law providing services to blind students clearly had a secular purpose, as required under the first prong of the *Lemon* test. To this end, the Court acknowledged that no one seriously claimed that legislators' purpose in enacting a statute that promoted the well-being of individuals with visual disabilities had been to endorse religion.

Focusing most of its analysis on the second prong of the *Lemon* test—whether providing assistance to the student would have had the impermissible effect of subsidizing religion, the Court distinguished between a state's direct financial assistance to an individual student and a state's direct financial assistance to a religious institution. Pointing out that the Establishment Clause prohibits direct rather than indirect subsidies to religion, the Court observed that nothing in the Establishment Clause forbids state employees who receive their paychecks from donating the money to religious institutions. Applying this distinction between direct and indirect subsidies to the student's reception of state financial assistance, the Court was of the opinion that any money from Washington's program that flowed to a religious institution did so only as a result of the genuinely independent and private choices of aid recipients. The Court recognized that the program did not create incentives for students to use their funds at religious as opposed to secular institutions. In fact, the Court indicated that officials from the State of Washington failed to furnish evidence that any other student had ever used such funding to finance an education at a religious institution. The Court further determined that a student's choice to use neutrally available state aid to help pay for religious education was not an endorsement of religion. Finally, the Court noted that nothing

would prevent the Supreme Court of Washington from applying its far stricter constitutional prohibitions to the facts on remand. However, the Court refused to provide advice as to whether it would be a violation of the Free Exercise Clause if, on remand, the Supreme Court of Washington decided that aid to students at religious institutions violated the state's constitution.

A Final Ruling

On remand in *Witters v. State Commission for the Blind* (1989), the Supreme Court of Washington did prevent the student from receiving aid. The court forbade granting the student assistance on the ground that doing so would have violated a prohibition in the state constitution against using public funds to pay for any type of religious instruction.

Ralph D. Mawdsley

See also *Locke v. Davey*; State Aid and the Establishment Clause; *Tilton v. Richardson*

Further Readings

Witters v. Commission for the Blind, 689 P.2d 53 (Wash. 1984).

Legal Citations

Lemon v. Kurtzman, 403 U.S. 602 (1971).
Locke v. Davey, 540 U.S. 712 (2004).
Witters v. State Commission for the Blind, 771 P.2d 1119 (Wash. 1989).
Witters v. Washington Department of Services for the Blind, 474 U.S. 481 (1986).

Z

ZONING

Zoning and land use laws promote the common good in attempting to balance the authority of officials in local municipalities to control the impact of growth and development of college and university campuses in and near their communities with the interests of the educational institutions. Postsecondary institutions, which also promote the common good by providing an educated citizenry, often exist under specific grants of authority from the state. In such situations, multiple expressions of the common good can often come in conflict with one another, thereby pitting the authority of local and state governments against the discretion of officials at institutions of higher learning as they make decisions about how their colleges and universities are to operate.

Colleges and universities can be dynamic, vibrant organizations, thereby necessitating changing uses for buildings and properties. In addition, postsecondary organizations can be assigned varying societal roles, including, in recent years, acting as initiators of regional economic development. These changing uses can precipitate conflicts between institutional officials and local zoning boards.

Insofar as colleges and universities provide an important state function, they have enjoyed considerable freedom from oversight or control by the municipalities in which they exist or by zoning boards and commissions representing those municipalities. The general rule seems to be that because institutions of higher learning provide an important state function, they should be permitted to operate with limited interference from local municipalities. In light of the potential town and gown tensions that can arise when the rights and needs of institutions and neighboring communities conflict, this entry examines legal issues associated with the means of addressing many of these concerns in the form of zoning.

Statutory Uses

Over the past 20 years, the legal tool that the courts used most often to determine whether postsecondary institutions enjoyed immunity from local zoning control is interpretation of statutory language about "uses" for which immunity is granted. Supplemental to this legal test is the interpretation of local municipal ordinances created under powers delegated to local governments by state statutes.

In interpreting statutory language, what state law describes as protected uses is critical. For example, while Wisconsin protects all "governmental uses," from local zoning, New York limits that protection to "educational uses." Even more narrowly, California restricts protection from local zoning laws to "classroom uses."

An example of interpretation of the very broad language under the Wisconsin statute, "governmental uses," can be found in *Board of Regents of University of Wisconsin System v. Dane County Board of Adjustment* (2000). When university officials chose to erect a radio tower for a student-run radio station, the county board of adjustment denied their request to do so. On further review of an order in favor of the university, an appellate

537

court affirmed that the institution could proceed as its officials had planned, because the radio tower was a governmental use under the statute.

As described above, New York protects "educational uses" from local zoning laws. When Dowling College in Islip, New York, chose to provide its students with catering services and to provide driver's education for nonmatriculated students, the town of Islip attempted to intervene. The town unsuccessfully argued that because both activities were outside of the scope of the statutory language, they were not educational uses. In affirming an order in favor of the college, an appellate court expansively included a range of activities for educational institutions, including "social, recreational, athletic, and other accessory uses (that) are reasonably associated with their educational purposes" (*Town of Islip v. Dowling College*, 2000, p. 161).

California's more narrow language relating to "classroom use" became the measure in *People v. Rancho Santiago College* (1990). Reversing an earlier order that had been entered in favor of the college, an appellate court was of the opinion that because the conversion of a parking lot on campus to a swap meet on weekends was not a "classroom use," the court had to enjoin use of the parking lot for the planned event.

Interpretation of Ordinances

In addition to interpreting statutory language, courts often examine zoning ordinances to distinguish immunity from zoning laws. For example, in the issue addressed in *Capricorn Equity v. Town of Chapel Hill* (1993), investors proposed to build duplexes to house graduate students. However, a local building inspector refused to provide a building permit on the ground that the duplexes were "boarding houses" subject to zoning control. Ruling in favor of the investors, the Supreme Court of North Carolina explained that references in the ordinance to "boarding houses" denoted housing for transient persons and that graduate students were not transient.

Interpretation of a local ordinance was also determinative in *Borough of Glassboro v. Vallorosi* (1990), where borough officials adopted an ordinance allowing only family units or the functional equivalent of family units to reside in residential areas. The officials enacted the ordinance in an attempt to confine students to living in dormitories or in areas where townhomes and apartments were permitted. Thwarting this attempt, the Supreme Court of New Jersey affirmed an order of a lower court that insofar as the 10 unrelated students living in a rental house were a "family unit" within the meaning of the ordinance, they could remain in the residential areas.

When officials at Oregon State University wanted to build a hotel and conference facility, the local zoning board was charged with deciding whether the hotel and conference facility was for a civic or commercial use. After the board decided that it was both, a petitioner attempted to block the board's decision by forcing it to choose one of the two uses on the basis that the uses were mutually exclusive. On direct appeal, the appellate court affirmed an order of the land use board of appeals that because the local zoning board's action was not "clearly wrong," it would uphold the board's action (*Schwerdt v. City of Corvallis*, 1999).

Exemptions and Variances

Zoning regulations sometimes place height, location, or bulk constraints on building programs for colleges and universities and other owners. Institutional officials may then respond to these constraints by seeking exemptions or variances to the local regulation. Exemptions thus grant institutions freedom from general duties imposed by zoning rules. Variances afford institutions permission to step outside the literal requirements of zoning rules due to unique hardship arising from special circumstances regarding their property. Further, exemptions can be identified as extensions of the concept of immunity. On the other hand, variances are waivers from the strict interpretation of zoning laws, arguably without sacrificing their statutory spirit and intent.

At issue in *Draude v. Board of Zoning Adjustment* (1990) were requests by officials at George Washington University for both exemptions and variances when its board attempted to build an addition to a building at its medical school. Owners of condominiums in neighboring buildings sued the local Board of Zoning Adjustment (BZA) when the latter granted the university three exemptions and two variances. The exemptions allowed the university to change its campus plan, to exceed an established limit on the bulk of the building, and to build a nonconforming roof structure. The variances allowed the university to extend a nonconforming bulk limit into the building addition and to have an open court area buffering the building addition with the adjacent condominiums that was eight feet narrower than required.

In the District of Columbia, exemptions by local zoning boards are subject to judicial review to evaluate whether they are consistent with the zoning regulations and supported by substantial evidence. At the same time, variances require a demonstration that strict interpretation of zoning regulations would have created extraordinary practical difficulties, would have been detrimental to the public good, or would have substantially impaired the purpose, intent, or integrity of existing zoning regulations. Under these standards, the District of Columbia Court of Appeals sustained the BZA's grant of all exemptions and variances. The court was satisfied that all of the BZA's actions were supported by sufficient evidence that led to the rational conclusion that they were consistent with the applicable statutes and regulations.

Spot Zoning

Spot zoning occurs when specific building lots are or a small property is singled out for different treatment than that given to similar surrounding land, indistinguishable in its character, for the economic benefit or detriment of the lots' or property's owner (*Milac Appeal,* 1965). In a case from Pennsylvania, neighboring property owners unsuccessfully protested the rezoning of university property from residential property to an institutional zoning designation, arguing that doing so was improper spot zoning. The record revealed that the property in question was across the street from the main campus and was adjoined by 14 acres of university land designated as institutional property containing dormitories. In light of the proximity of other university property, all designated as institutional in nature, an appellate court affirmed that impermissible spot zoning had not occurred (*Sharp v. Zoning Hearing Board of Township of Radnor and Villanova University,* 1993).

David L. Dagley

See also Tax Exemptions for Colleges and Universities

Further Readings

Dagley, D. (2005). Town and gown issues. In J. Beckham & D. Dagley (Eds.), *Contemporary issues in higher education law* (pp. 449–478). Dayton, OH: Education Law Association.

Legal Citations

Board of Regents of University of Wisconsin System v. Dane County Board of Adjustment, 618 N.W.2d 537 (Wis. Ct. App. 2000).

Borough of Glassboro v. Vallorosi, 568 A.2d 888 (N.J. 1990).

Capricorn Equity v. Town of Chapel Hill, 431 S.E.2d 183 (N.C. 1993).

Draude v. Board of Zoning Adjustment, 582 A.2d 949 (D.C. 1990).

Milac Appeal, 210 A.2d 275 (Pa. 1965).

People v. Rancho Santiago College, 277 Cal. Rptr. 69 (Cal. Ct. App. 1990).

Schwerdt v. City of Corvallis, 987 P.2d 1243 (Ore. Ct. App. 1999).

Sharp v. Zoning Hearing Board of Township of Radnor and Villanova University, 628 A.2d 1223 (Pa. Commw. Ct. 1993).

Town of Islip v. Dowling College, 712 N.Y.S.2d 160 (N.Y. App. Div. 2000).

Index

Entry titles and their page numbers are in **bold.**